PSYCHOLOGY

AN INTRODUCTION

SIXTH EDITION

BENJAMIN B.
LAHEY
UNIVERSITY OF CHICAGO

Boston, Massachusetts   Burr Ridge, Illinios   Dubuque, Iowa
Madison, Wisconsin   New York, New York   San Francisco, California   St. Louis, Missouri

McGraw-Hill

A Division of The ***McGraw-Hill*** *Companies*

PSYCHOLOGY: AN INTRODUCTION

This book is printed on recycled, acid-free paper containing 10% postconsumer waste.

3 4 5 6 7 8 9 0 QPD QPD 9 0 9

Library of Congress Catalog Card Number: 96-78737

ISBN 0-697-25310-4

Editorial director: *Jane Vaicunas*
Senior developmental editor: *Meera Dash*
Senior marketing manager: *Jim Rozsa*
Project manager: *Terry Routley*
Production supervisor: *Sandy Hahn*
Cover and interior design: *Lesiak/Crampton Design, Inc.*
Cover image: *"River Dream", 1992 © Christian Pierre/SUPERSTOCK*
Photo research coordinator: *Carrie Burger*
Compositor: *Shepard Poorman Communications Corporation*
Typeface: *10/12 Times Roman*
Printer: *Quebecor Printing Book Group/Dubuque*

When ordering this title, use ISBN 0-07-115357-8.

http://www.mhhe.com

For Megan, Ted, Erin, Clare, and Kate

BRIEF CONTENTS

CONTENTS

PART 2 AWARENESS 87

PART 4 THE LIFE SPAN 283

PART 5 THE SELF 325

PART 6 HEALTH AND ADJUSTMENT 431

PART 7 THE SOCIAL CONTEXT 523

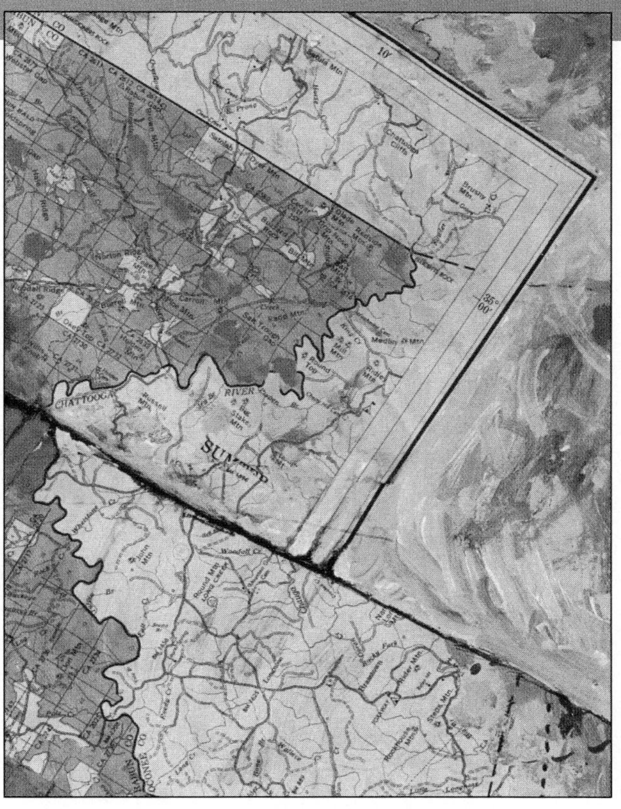

PREFACE

Although the preface is the first part of the book that you read, it is the last part that I wrote. It is my opportunity to reflect on the completed project in the hope that these reflections will help introduce you to the text. Over six editions, the unchanging goal for *Psychology: An Introduction* has been to *teach.* We (referring to the large group of talented psychologists, editors, consultants, and reviewers who have worked with me) have centered our efforts on giving you a text that fully captures the immense importance and fascination of the scientific study of ourselves. I am genuinely passionate about teaching psychology, and I have done all that I can to share that passion with you. You have my pledge that I have done my best to teach the concepts and facts of psychology in the clearest and most exciting manner possible. The gratifying responses of both instructors and students to the first five editions of this textbook have been a wonderful source of encouragement for these efforts.

We made three kinds of changes in this edition: (1) improved the written and visual presentation of information, (2) added new and timely information, and (3) revised the most important pedagogical feature in the book.

1. ***Improvements in the presentation of information.*** We have worked very hard to provide you with a textbook that sets a standard for the field through the *clarity* of both the written language and the visual illustrations. Students cannot learn what they do not understand, and this book goes to great lengths to make the science of psychology understandable. Every sentence in the textbook was reconsidered, and many were rewritten to make them clearer to the student. Similarly, several new illustrations were added and several were redrawn for greater clarity.

   As in previous editions, a concerted effort has been made to estimate realistically the memory required to process the meaning of complex passages. Most textbooks are based on the assumption that all information from previous sentences has been encoded in memory, when this is obviously not always the case. In this book, sentences have been written to avoid unrealistic reliance on previous sentences and to build repetition of key terms and concepts into the prose. These features are subtle, but they enhance readability.

   One of the most visible changes to the presentation of information is in chapter 1. The material has been reorganized considerably from the previous edition. This is true in two ways. First, the many founders of psychology are organized in a way that should make better sense to first-time readers. Even if they fought like cats and dogs at the time, historic figures whose ideas were very similar are grouped together to make better conceptual sense to students.

   Second, this edition marks a major milestone in portraying the role of women and ethnic minorities in the history of psychology. Two editions ago, I added a boxed feature saying that white males were not the only important figures in the history of psychology—women and minorities played important roles, too. In the last edition, I moved this section into the text discussion, but I kept it separate from the "main" history of psychology—the section describing what the white males did. But since I wrote the fifth edition I have spent some time reading the scientific contributions of these early psychologists. I concluded that several women and minorities have been excluded from the "official" history of psychology simply because of their gender or race. I have, therefore, done my best to tell the history of the beginnings of psychology as it happened. I have done my best not to "revise" history to fit modern conceptions of fairness, but have simply tried to set the record straight in a fair manner.
2. ***New information.*** New information has been included in this edition in several other ways. First, as always, one of the pleasures of revising a textbook is seeing how much the field advances in three short years. Although coverage of the fundamental principles in this edition has not changed greatly, much new information has been integrated. The book is filled with important new information on genetics, sleep and dreaming, memory, cultural differences, gender differences and similarities, aging, emotion, intelligence and occupational success, psychotherapy, stress and the immune system, the application of psychology to business, and many other topics. Psychology is clearly a discipline that is still in an age of rapid accumulation of information, even if radical changes to most basic concepts have not occurred in a long time. Happily, the responsibility of revising a basic textbook pushes me to read very broadly in the psychological literature. It is a fascinating field!
3. ***Improved Pedagogical Device.*** From the conception of the first edition almost 20 years ago and through every stage of its development, *Psychology: An Introduction* has been constructed with a single purpose in mind: to create a teaching tool from which

students will learn a great deal of basic information about psychology. The accent is on *meaningful* and *efficient* learning by students. Although psychologists devote a great deal of time to studying human learning, we have rarely put the information we have acquired to use in writing textbooks. Because I enjoy teaching psychology and have an interest in human learning, I based the pedagogical features of this textbook on what current research has told us about the way people learn.

Before each new edition is revised, the pedagogical plan of the text is evaluated according to the latest research on learning from textbooks. It is gratifying to see that the basic structure of each chapter continues to be supported by research on human learning and memory. As was true two decades ago, it is still true that the strongest learning aid that a book can offer is an *advance organizer.* Students learn and retain information better when they are told in advance what they are going to read. Having an advance understanding of the nature and structure of the new material facilitates learning and improves memory. In the last five editions, the student has been given three kinds of advance organizers before reading the main body of a chapter. First, the student was given a bare-bones **outline** of the chapter. That clearly shows the hierarchical organization of the material. Second, a **prologue** composed of high-interest material on the topic of the upcoming chapter was presented to pique the student's interest. Third, a **preview** described the major concepts covered in the chapter and how they are related to one another before the chapter opened. Thus, the student was provided with three forward looks at the chapter to create a cognitive organization upon which to "hang" new facts and concepts.

I have always felt that all three kinds of advance organizers were necessary, but I have been concerned that having to process three sections before starting the chapter may have tempted students to skip them all. I realized in preparing for this edition that the solution was to combine the high-interest material in the prologue with the prose preview. I was delighted to see that I could do so very easily, and still keep the new combined prologue shorter than the total of the two previous parts. Perhaps most importantly, the new advance organizers are more interesting to read. I don't know why it took me so long to think of this clearly better solution!

ACKNOWLEDGMENTS

The enormous job of revising this textbook did not fall on my shoulders alone. The revision process was helped tremendously by the input of numerous reviewers with a knowledge of both psychology and the art and science of teaching. Master teacher Laura Freberg wrote the first draft of the chapters on biological foundations, learning, memory, social psychology, and applied psychology. Her work has been of tremendous help to me and her efforts can be seen in the quality of these chapters. I confess, however, to a compelling urge to rewrite everyone's drafts to put them into my own language. Therefore, if these chapters are not perfect, the blame rests with me.

Reviewers

The following individuals have helped tremendously by reviewing this or previous editions of *Psychology: An Introduction;* their helpful guidance has been carried forward into the current edition.

Henry E. Adams, *University of Georgia*
Vincent J. Adesso, *University of Wisconsin, Milwaukee*
Robin A. Anderson, *St. Ambrose University*
Stuart Appelle, *SUNY, Brockport*
Brian C. Babbitt, *Missouri Southern State College*
Gladys J. Baez-Dickreiter, *St. Philip's College*
Roger Baumgarte, *Winthrop University*
Alan Bensley, *Texas Wesleyan University*
John B. Benson, *Texarkana College*
Michael Bergmire, *Jefferson College*
Thomas E. Billemek, *San Antonio College*
Tom Bourbon, *Stephen F. Austin State University*
Edward N. Brady, *Belleville Area College*
John P. Broida, *University of Southern Maine*
Thomas Brothen, *University of Minnesota*
Hazel J. Brown, *Harrisburg Area Community College*
Steven H. Brown, *DeVry Institute of Technology*
John J. Burke, *East Central University*
William Calhoun, *University of Tennessee*
Francis B. Colavita, *University of Pittsburgh*
Bridget Coughlin, *Hocking Technical College*
Kathleen Crowley-Long, *College of St. Rose*
Patrick T. DeBoli, *Nassau Community College*
Peter Derks, *College of William & Mary*
George M. Diekhoff, *Midwestern State University*
Peter H. Ditto, *Kent State University*
Ed Donnerstein, *University of Wisconsin, Madison*
George J. Downing, *Gloucester County College*
William O. Dwyer, *Memphis State University*
David C. Edwards, *Iowa State University*
Henry C. Ellis, *University of New Mexico*
Martha M. Ellis, *Collin County Community College*
Nolen U. Embry, *Lexington Community College*
Linda J. Enloe, *Idaho State University*
Joseph D. Eubanks, *San Antonio College*
Donald L. Fischer, *Southwest Missouri State University*

Laura Freberg, *California Polytechnic State University, San Luis Obispo*
Lawrence L. Galant, *Gaston College*
Grace Galliano, *Kennesaw State College*
David A. Gershaw, *Arizona Western College*
Gail S. Gibson, *Alabama A & M University*
Ajaipal S. Gill, *Anne Arundel Community College*
Randall D. Gold, *Cuesta College*
Peter Clark Gram, *Pensacola Junior College*
James E. Gruber, *University of Michigan, Dearborn*
Megan Gunnar, *University of Minnesota*
Mykol C. Hamilton, *Centre College*
Cheryl-Ann Hardy, *Columbia College*
James Hart, *Edison State Community College*
Janice L. Hartgrove-Friele, *North Harris County College*
Morton A. Heller, *Winston-Salem State University*
John Hensley, *Midwestern State University*
A. Herschberger, *Greater Hartford Community College*
Lyllian B. Hix, *Houston Community College*
Roger H. Hodgens, *Florence-Darlington Technical College*
Thomas Holland, Jr., *Houston Baptist University*
Neil B. Holliman, *Midwestern State University*
Paul W. Horn, *Indiana State University*
Sharon C. Hott, *Allegheny Community College*
R. Reed Hunt, *University of North Carolina*
Carl Johnson, *Central Michigan University*
Adrienne Joyce, *East Los Angeles College*
Seth C. Kalichman, *Medical College of Wisconsin*
Chester Karwoski, *University of Georgia*
Wilma Kirk-Lee, *Shorter College*
Daniel S. Kirschenbaum, *University of Wisconsin, Madison*
Richard A. Kribs, *Motlow State Community College*
Velton Lacefield, *Prairie State College*
Kathryn Ann Lambers, *Beal College*
James T. Lamiell, *Georgetown University*
Daniel K. Lapsley, *Brandon University*
Joseph T. Lawton, *University of Wisconsin, Madison*
Bernard H. Levin, *Blue Ridge Community College*
Susan D. Lima, *University of Wisconsin, Milwaukee*
Jonathan S. Lynton, *DeVry Institute of Technology*
Richard E. Mayer, *University of California, Santa Barbara*
Donald H. McBurney, *University of Pittsburgh*
Lynn E. McCutcheon, *Northern Virginia Community College*
Richard McKnight, *Nicholls State University*
Caven S. McLoughlin, *Kent State University*
Jodi A. Mindell, *St. Joseph's University*
Daniel D. Moriarity, *University of San Diego*
Paul Muhs, *University of Wisconsin, Green Bay*
David E. Neufeldt, *Hutchinson Community College*
Benjamin H. Newberry, *Kent State University*
James L. Nielson, *Evergreen Valley College*
James E. Oliver, *Henry Ford Community College*
Holly A. Pennock, *Hudson Valley Community College*
Carrol S. Perrino, *Morgan State University*
Thomas P. Petzel, *Loyola University of Chicago*
William Pfohl, *Western Kentucky University*
Bobby J. Poe, *Belleville Area College*
Sharon Presley, *California State University, Fullerton*
Robert R. Rainey, *Florida Community College*
Lillian M. Range, *University of Southern Mississippi*
Gail Reisman, *California State University, Fullerton*
Daniel W. Richards, *Houston Community College*
Deborah Richardson, *University of Georgia*
Matt L. Riggs, *California State University*
Ronald W. Rogers, *University of Alabama*
Anita Rosenfield, *Chaffey Community College*
Alan O. Ross, *State University of New York at Stony Brook*
David L. Salmond, *Vincennes University*
James F. Sanford, *George Mason University*
Gary Schaumberg, *Cerritos College*
Steven A. Schneider, *Pima Community College*
Michael T. Scoles, *University of Central Arkansas*
Laura S. Sidorowicz, *Nassau Community College*
Carolyn H. Simmons, *University of North Carolina at Wilmington*
Grant W. Smart, *Utah Technical College*
Leo Spindel, *Centennial College*
Donald M. Stanley, *North Harris College*
Michael R. Stevenson, *Ball State University*
Pamela E. Stewart, *Northern Virginia Community College*
Lawrence L. Stofan, *University of Maine*
A. Melton Strozier, Jr., *Houston Baptist University*
Roger L. Terry, *Hanover College*
W. Scott Terry, *University of North Carolina*
Roger K. Thomas, *University of Georgia*
Edward A. Thompson, *Southern Connecticut State University*
M. E. Thrasher, *San Bernardino Valley College*
J. David Tipton, *Gadsden State Community College*
John R. Tisdale, *Cedar Crest College*
William H. Van Hoose, *University of Virginia*
Benjamin Wallace, *Cleveland State University*
George Wang, *Cooke County College*
C. M. Whissell, *Laurentian University*
Lisa Whitten, *Arizona State University West*
Kenneth N. Wildman, *Ohio Northern University*
Maureen Rousset Worth, *Southern Seminary Junior College*

Many talented editors and illustrators also played essential roles. The results of that combined effort are before you, and I hope that it will serve the needs of students and instructors even better than did the previous edition.

In the two sections that follow, the mechanics of *Psychology: An Introduction* are explained in detail. "To the Instructor" describes the pedagogical strategy used in the textbook and my reasons for selecting the elements that are included. The next section, titled "To the Student: How the Book Works," explains in a step-by-step manner each teaching device I have used. It's essential that the student understand the purpose of each teaching device to derive maximum benefit from this book.

TO THE INSTRUCTOR

Psychology: An Introduction offers thorough topic coverage and standard organization designed to fit courses as they are most commonly taught. But it differs significantly from other textbooks in two main ways. First, every effort has been made to create a writing style that is—as one former student kindly described it—"friendly." This book is not a pompous attempt to impress students with the complexities of the science of psychology. It was written to provide a clear, informative, challenging, exciting, and personal introduction to psychology.

Second, *Psychology: An Introduction* differs from other textbooks in its emphasis on meaningful learning. This book contains many elements designed to enhance learning and remembering based on an organizational model of semantic memory. The content of the first course in psychology can be thought of as a *hierarchical organization* of concepts and facts. Quite simply, this means that information about psychology is not a disorganized jumble of new facts. Some information "goes with" other information, some concepts are detailed elaborations of more general concepts, and so on. To improve learning and memory, it is as important for students to understand the overall organization of new information as it is for them to understand the individual concepts and facts themselves.

Based on what is now known about learning from textbooks, this book helps the student understand how new information about psychology is organized and to process that information more deeply in five primary ways:

1. *Advance organizers.* Considerable research indicates that students learn and retain information better when they have an advance understanding of the hierarchical organization of the information being learned. To accomplish this, the student is given two kinds of advance organizers before reading the main body of the text. The student is first presented with an **outline** of the major topics covered within the chapter, a device common to many textbooks. But to add to the effectiveness of this bare-bones overview, a prose organizer, called the **prologue,** both piques the student's interest with exciting information and highlights the major concepts in the forthcoming chapter. Thus, the student is provided with two forward looks at the chapter to create a cognitive organization upon which to "hang" new facts and concepts. The prologues in this edition combine the best features of both the "prologue" and "preview" sections of previous editions by fusing high-interest material with an advance organizer.
2. *Questions to stimulate critical thinking.* An important feature of the sixth edition is the set of questions designed to stimulate critical thinking (Baron & Sternberg, 1987). These **critical thinking questions** appear at the end of each section. They are designed to catch the student's attention and stimulate thought for two reasons. First, it is important that students not passively absorb new information but, rather, critically evaluate and ponder what they are learning. Moreover, as suggested by Perkins (1987), it may well be more effective to teach critical thinking skills through the content of a specific course than in the abstract. And what course is more appropriate than psychology—in which human beings ponder themselves. Second, current research suggests that thinking about what you have just learned leads to deeper semantic processing and better retention (Ellis & Hunt, 1989). Thus, both as an aid to student reading and as a stimulus for classroom discussion, these high-interest questions at the end of each section should prove to be highly important pedagogical tools. To help students prepare to use these critical thinking questions, a section called "Critical Thinking" appears in the preliminary pages. In addition, the Instructor's Course Planner includes pertinent information to help the instructor.
3. *Nested hierarchical reviews.* The interrelationship of the new information is further strengthened in the **review** and **summary** sections. Following each major section within each chapter, the content of that section is briefly reviewed in prose. In addition, the student can test his or her knowledge of each section in the **check your learning** sections. At the end of each chapter, the main content of the chapter is again summarized, but this time in a hierarchical outline that visually highlights the organization of the material.
4. *Visual organizational cues.* Using hierarchical outlines in the end-of-chapter summaries is only one way in which the student is actually shown the organization of the new material. Close attention has been paid to the use of visual cues—such as typeface, type size, color of type, and indentations—to indicate the organization of the text. The difference between this book and others is intentionally subtle in this respect, but students should have little trouble distinguishing the superordinate-subordinate structure of A, B, and C levels of headings. In diagrams and figures, colors were chosen not to be decorative, but to show students which elements are related and which are different. In addition, lists—like the one you are reading

now—have been frequently (but not excessively) used to show that each element in the list is at the same level of organization and subordinate to the title of the list ("five ways to help students understand organizational structure" in the case of the list you are reading now).

5. *Verbal cues to organization.* Another important way to help readers see how concepts and facts are related is to simply tell them in words. Therefore, the textbook makes many references to the organization of the new information. This is done in two main ways. First, when a newly introduced concept is related to another concept that was discussed in an earlier section, this fact is specifically pointed out. Second, information that is subordinate to a concept is frequently introduced in a way that makes that relationship very clear (i.e., "The two factors that cause forgetting in short-term memory are . . ."). Although these cues are subtle so as not to interrupt the flow of the discussion, they have been added to help improve the student's comprehension and memory.

The use of these pedagogical devices was chosen over two other pedagogical approaches after much consideration. I chose not to use the SQ3R (survey, question, read, recite, review) method of organizing the text because the author, not the student, must ask the questions, which reduces student involvement and discourages the student from critically evaluating and deeply processing the new information. However, the SQ3R approach is useful as a general study method and can be used with any text, including this one. Therefore, I have included its application in the **study skills** section that follows the preface. For those instructors who wish to use instructional objectives, we have included them in the Student Study Guide and the Instructor's Course Planner that accompany this book. In addition, an appendix on measurement, research design, and statistics appears at the end of the book for those professors who wish to teach a more research-oriented course.

SUPPLEMENTARY MATERIALS

Psychology: An Introduction is accompanied by an integrated ancillary package designed to meet the unique needs of instructors and students. The goal has been to create a teaching package that is as enjoyable to teach with as it is to study from. Each element of the ancillary package has been created by talented individuals with many years of experience in teaching psychology.

The ***Instructor's Course Planner*** was prepared by Steven A. Schneider of Pima Community College. This flexible planner provides many useful tools to enhance your teaching. For each chapter, learning objectives, an extended chapter outline, suggestions for teaching, lecture/discussion suggestions, video and film suggestions, classroom activities, and handout forms are provided. The *Instructor's Course Planner* is also available on disk for IBM and Macintosh computers.

The ***Introductory Psychology Activities Handbook*** offers additional activities, in-class and out-of-class projects, and discussion questions. The activities handbook will help you get your students actively engaged and thinking critically.

A ***Test Item File*** with questions for all sixteen chapters will be available to instructors who adopt *Psychology: An Introduction* sixth edition. The questions in the Test Item File are also available on ***MicroTest III,*** a powerful but easy-to-use test-generating program by Chariot Software Group. MicroTest is available for your use in DOS (3.5" disks), Windows, and Macintosh versions. With MicroTest, instructors can easily select questions from the Test Item File and print tests and answer keys. Instructors can also customize questions, headings, and instructions; add or import their own questions; and print tests in a choice of printer-supported fonts.

The ***Student Study Guide*** was also created by Instructor's Manual author Steven A. Schneider. For each chapter of the text, the student is provided with learning objectives, a detailed chapter outline, a guided review of terms and concepts, and two multiple choice practice tests.

Transparencies of sixty key images drawn directly from this textbook are available for the instructor upon adoption. In addition, the ***Introductory Psychology Transparency Set*** provides over 100 additional transparencies illustrating key concepts in general psychology. It also includes an accompanying handbook with specific suggestions for classroom use by Susan J. Shapiro of Indiana University East. ***The Electronic Image Bank*** provides you with the same outstanding graphics on a CD-ROM for presentation from your PC or Macintosh. We provide our own generic viewer, but the contents can be downloaded into your own favorite presentation program, for instance, PowerPoint.

The Critical Thinker, Second Edition, by Richard Mayer and Fiona Goodchild, both of the University of California–Santa Barbara, explicitly teaches strategies for understanding and evaluating material in any introductory psychology textbook. This seventy-page booklet is available free to adopters.

The AIDS Booklet, Third Edition, by Frank D. Cox of Santa Barbara City College, is a brief but comprehensive introduction to the Acquired Immune Deficiency Syndrome, HIV, and related viruses.

The Encyclopedic Dictionary of Psychology provides easy reference access to the key figures, concepts, movements, and practices of the field of psychology.

Psychology: The Active Learner CD-ROM by Jane Halonen, Marilyn Reedy, and Paul Smith is an innovative interactive product that will help students learn key concepts taught in introductory psychology in a fun and dynamic way. Focusing on the concepts that tend to be most difficult for the beginning psychology student, this program contains fifteen modules containing tutorial review and critical thinking exercises for biological foundations, sensation and perception, states of consciousness, learning, memory, development, social psychology, and more.

The CD-ROM ***Explorations in Health and Psychology*** by George B. Johnson of Washington University in St. Louis helps students actively investigate processes vital to their understanding of psychology as they should be explored—with movement, color, sound, and interaction. This set of ten interactive animations on CD-ROM allows students to set and re-set variables in each (including modules on Life Span and Lifestyle, Drug Addiction,

Nerve Conduction, AIDS, Immune Response and more) and then evaluate those results. In addition to the colorful and precisely labeled graphics and animated illustrations, the CD-ROM also offers **narration in English and Spanish,** a glossary with written and oral pronunciations, and lists of additional recommended readings. Contact your sales representative for more information. A large selection of **videotapes** is also available to adopters based on the number of textbooks ordered. Consult your sales representative for ordering policies.

The Brain Modules on Videodisc, created by WNET in New York, Antenne 2 TV/France, the Annenberg/CPB Foundation, and Professor Frank J. Vattano of Colorado State University, is based on the Peabody-award-winning series *The Brain.* Thirty segments, averaging six minutes each, illustrate an array of topics in psychology. Consult your sales representative for details.

The ***Human Development Interactive Videodisc Set,*** produced by Roger Ray of Rollins College, vividly introduces life-span development with instant access to over thirty brief video segments from the highly acclaimed *Seasons of Life* series. Consult your sales representative for details.

The ***Reference Disk Set*** is available free to adopters. The disks include over 15,000 journal and book references arranged in files by topic. The complete set of five disks is available on IBM (3.5") or Macintosh disks.

Annual Editions®

Magazines, newspapers, and journals can provide current, first-rate, relevant educational information. *Annual Editions* provides convenient, inexpensive access to a wide range of current, carefully selected articles from magazines, newspapers, and journals. Written by psychologists, researchers, and educators, *Annual Editions: Psychology* provides useful perspectives on important and timely topics. *Annual Editions* is updated yearly, and contains a number of features designed to make it particularly useful, including a topic guide, annotated table of contents, and unit overviews. For the professor using *Annual Editions* in the classroom, an Instructor's Resource Guide with test questions is available.

Taking Sides®

Are you interested in generating classroom discussion? In finding a tool to fully involve your students in their experience of your course? Would you like to encourage your students to become more active learners and critical thinkers? *Taking Sides: Clashing Views on Psychological Issues* is a debate-style reader designed to introduce students to controversies in psychology. By requiring students to analyze opposing viewpoints and reach considered judgments, *Taking Sides* actively develops students' critical thinking skills.

Sources: Notable Selections in Psychology, Second Edition, brings together over forty selections including classic articles, book excerpts, and research studies that have shaped the study of psychology. New to the second edition are twenty-one selections from some of the most distinguished researchers, theorists, writers, and practitioners of psychology. If you want your students to gain greater background knowledge in reading and interpreting first-hand from source material, *Sources* collects a diverse array of accessible but significant readings in one place.

TO THE STUDENT

HOW THE BOOK WORKS

This book contains several learning devices, each of which is designed to accomplish five goals:

1. To focus your attention on the subject of the chapter.
2. To give you an advance overall view of what you are about to learn.
3. To show you how each fact and concept is related to the overall subject matter of the chapter.
4. To help you review what you have just learned to be sure that you have gotten it all and to strengthen the newly formed memories.
5. To help you think critically about the new information that you have learned and relate it to your own life.

These five goals must be reached if you are going to learn about psychology in a meaningful way, rather than just blindly memorizing facts and definitions. Let me show you how each feature of the book contributes to these five goals.

1 Chapter Outline Each chapter begins with an outline that organizes the key ideas of the chapter. Examine the outline carefully to see which topics will be studied, but notice also how the topics are arranged. Headings that show the major topics are called A heads (printed in capital letters); they define the breadth of coverage in each chapter. Under each A head are B heads; (indented) they reveal the depth and detail of coverage. Studying the outline for a few minutes will give you an advance look at the content of the chapter and show you how topics relate to one another. When you read a chapter, you may wish to refer to the outline from time to time. It will reinforce the relationships among topics and help you understand the structure of the chapter.

2 Prologue Each chapter begins with a short section designed to focus your attention on the theme of the chapter. It is a high-interest essay that introduces a bit of research or history to prepare you for the content of the chapter. The prologue highlights the most important concepts that will be covered in the chapter. Along with the chapter outline, it allows you to see what the chapter is going to be about before you read and start to grasp the details. A great deal of research suggests that having a general understanding of what is going to be learned will improve learning

CHAPTER 8

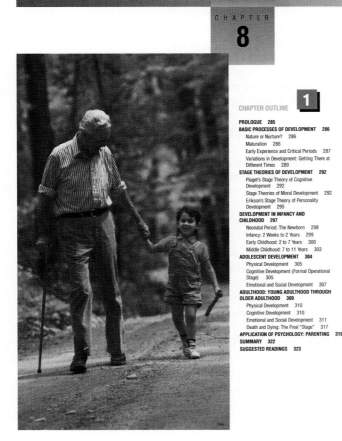

Developmental Psychology

1 CHAPTER OUTLINE

2 PROLOGUE

Jean Piaget was a notable Swiss scientist who studied the development of cognition in children until his death in 1980. His most important contribution was to show us that children of different ages understand the world in ways that are often very different from the way adults understand it. Indeed, young children understand their worlds in ways that are so different from adults that it is sometimes like trying to communicate with a creature from another galaxy!

Imagine that you drop by your instructor's office for a visit and sit down on the opposite side of her desk. Would the objects on top of the desk look exactly the same to you and your instructor? Of course not. The paper clip that you see in front of her coffee cup is hidden from her view, and you can't see the wad of bubble gum that is stuck to her side of the pencil sharpener. We adults have so little trouble understanding that our perception of things depends on our perspective that we take this ability for granted. However, we are not born with the ability to take another person's perspective—it develops over time.

A classic experiment by Piaget and his frequent collaborator Barbel Inhelder (1963) makes this point very well. Children of different ages were shown three small three-dimensional replicas of "mountains" arranged on a table top. On the other side of the table, a doll was seated. The children were asked to look at the mountains and then were asked to indicate which picture from several showed the mountains as the doll would see them. Six-year-olds could not do it at all, some 7- and 8-year-olds could, and children 9 to 11 years of age had no more trouble with the task than an adult would.

Life doesn't stand still. We are in a state of constant change throughout our lives. When we ask ourselves who we are, we think of ourselves in terms of who we are *now.* But we have been and will be many different people in our lifetime: an infant, a child, a teenager, a young adult, a mature person, and an aged person. The thread of continuity that runs through our lives

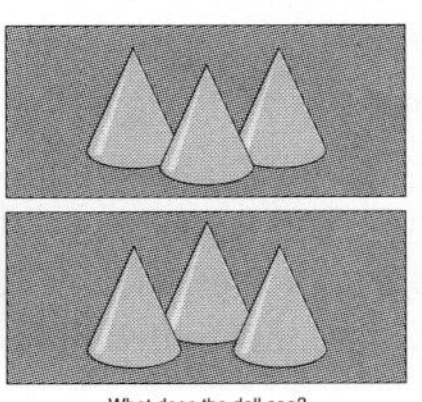

What does the doll see?

285

3 KEY TERMS

development 286
maturation 286
imprinting 288
critical period 288
early experiences 288
stage 292
neonatal period 298
sensorimotor stage 299
object permanence 299
attachments 300
separation anxiety 300
preoperational stage 301
egocentric 301
animism 301
transductive reasoning 302
concrete operational stage 303
conservation 303
adolescence 304
puberty 304
formal operational stage 305
adolescent egocentrism 306

Washoe and *Washoe tickle Roger* interchangeably as a request to be tickled. In contrast, a human speaker of ASL would recognize those statements as having different meanings.

At present, it appears that apes may have learned to use language at the level of a 2-year-old human, but they have not progressed beyond that point (Reynolds & Flagg, 1983). Still, their elementary use of language is more evidence of "humanity" than was once thought possible for apes. And the apes' progress has done much to "talk" at least some scientists out of their belief that only humans can learn human languages.

6

Thinking Critically About Psychology

1. Does it make sense to you to say that apes are not capable of using language in a human way?

2. The Greek language has three different words for love. Would that influence the way Greeks think about and understand love?

Review

Language is the efficient symbolic code used in human communication. It utilizes a finite set of sounds, units of meaning, and rules for combining them to convey a limitless set of meanings. The question of whether our language influences our cognition has not been satisfactorily answered, but current evidence suggests that it does in some ways. Although no animals have learned to use human language in the same ways as humans, surprisingly complex two-way conversations can occur between humans and apes who have been taught sign language—we can talk to some of the animals. 5

7

Check Your Learning

To be sure that you have learned the key points from the preceding section, cover the answers below and try to answer each question. If you give an incorrect answer to any question, return to the page given next to the correct answer to see why your answer was not correct.

1. While language is the term used to describe the symbolic code used in communication, the meaning of the code is termed ________.

   a. surface structure   c. semantics
   b. heuristics   d. syntax

2. Human language can be referred to as ________ in that an infinite set of utterances can be made using a finite set of elements and rules.

   a. divergent   c. semantic
   b. conceptual   d. generative

3. ________ refers to the rules of a language, such as the rules for the ways in which morphemes can be combined, that allow an infinite number of understandable utterances to be generated.

   a. Semantics   c. Phonemics
   b. Syntax   d. Morphemics

4. According to the ________ hypothesis, the vocabulary and structure of a language can influence the way speakers of that language think.

Correct Answers
1. c (p. 256), 2. d (p. 257), 3. b (p. 257), 4. linguistic relativity (or Whorfian) (p. 258).

INTELLIGENCE: THE SUM TOTAL OF COGNITION

4

intelligence
(in-tel´i-jens) The cognitive ability of an individual to learn from experience, to reason well, and to cope with the demands of daily living.

In the sense used in this book, **intelligence** refers to the cognitive abilities of an individual to learn from experience, to reason well, and to cope effectively with the demands of daily living. In short, intelligence has to do with how well a person is able to use cognition in coping with the world.

262   Part 3: Learning and Cognition

HUMAN DIVERSITY 8

Understanding Intelligence from the Cree Perspective

Each culture defines intelligence differently, and children in each culture are encouraged to be intelligent in those ways. It is difficult for us to understand that different cultures have different definitions of intelligence, however, because our own view seems to be the only correct one. By definition, any view of intelligence that is different from our own seems to be "unintelligent." But, in the multicultural world in which we live, it is essential that we develop a greater understanding of different views of intelligence.

An ingenious study of differing definitions of intelligence by John Berry and his colleagues (Berry & Bennett, 1992) creatively combined research techniques from anthropology and psychology to examine the definitions of intelligence among the Cree, a tribe of Native Americans and Native Canadians in Ontario. Berry and Bennett first asked Cree adults who spoke both English and Cree to give them Cree words that had to do with intelligence, thinking, being smart, or being wise.

Twenty words obtained through this technique were written in Cree script on cards. The cards were given in random order to 60 Cree people. The individuals were asked to sort the words into piles of words with similar meaning. In this way, they were able to see which words tended to be placed in the same piles because they had similar meaning to the Cree.

The first group of similar words included the Cree words for wisdom, thinking hard, and thinking carefully. These terms were often the first Cree words given as the translation of the English words *smart* or *intelligent*.

A second group included the Cree words for respect and respectfulness. To the Cree, respect refers to an appreciation for people, animals, the Creator, and the land. Respectfulness involves an active and positive involvement with these things and is seen as the opposite of laziness. Respect and respectfulness from the Cree point of view involve caretaking—looking after something that is highly valued.

A third group of Cree words referred to paying attention, self-discipline, and self-control. It involved thinking before taking action, and listening to what others say. Other concepts that are extremely important to Cree conceptions of intelligence include patience and perseverance, being able to look after yourself and survive without being a drain on others, and being open to new experiences. Thus, the Cree view of intelligence is much broader than that of the European-American view, including an emphasis on independence, self-reliance, self-discipline, respect for others, and respect for nature.

To instill these values in their children and raise intelligent adults, Cree parents and elders use child-rearing techniques that are sometimes quite different from those seen in many homes in the United States. For example, Cree children are encouraged to act independently without interference from adults. Adults rarely interfere with what an older child is doing, even if it is potentially dangerous, feeling that direct experience is the best teacher. In Cree culture, a high value is placed on not interfering in other peoples' affairs—and this courtesy is extended to children. Berry and Bennett note that some label this parenting style as neglectful, but they point out that Cree parents are often quite anxious when, for example, a child is playing with a sharp object, and they are noticeably relieved when the child puts the object down. Using such parenting methods, the Cree socialize children to be self-sufficient and independent. They learn that "one's destiny need rest in no hands but one's own" (p. 80).

How do these notions of intelligence and competence compare with those in your own culture? Give some thought to the ways in which the values that were taught in your neighborhood as you were growing up differ from those on the college campus you are attending. Keep in mind as you consider these things that the varying notions of intelligence and competence in different cultures are not superior or inferior to one another, simply different.

IQs that are over 100 indicate that the person is more intelligent than average (the MA is greater than the CA). For example, if a child obtains an MA of 10 years, but her CA is only 8 years, then her IQ would be 10/8 x 100 = 125. Conversely, IQs less than 100 indicate that the individual is less intelligent than average. A child who is 10 years in CA but obtains an MA of only 7 years would have an IQ of 7/10 x 100 = 70.

ratio IQ
Intelligence quotient based on the ratio between the person's mental age and chronological age.

Actually, Binet's approach to calculating the intelligence quotient from the ratio between the child's mental age and chronological age—called the **ratio IQ**—is no longer used in contemporary intelligence tests. There are several technical reasons that the ratio

268   Part 3: Learning and Cognition

and memory of the new material. The prologue will help you understand what you are learning, which is better than rote memorization of details.

3 Key Terms A list of the key terms you will encounter in the chapter is presented at the beginning of each chapter. You can use these terms to focus and check your learning. Because learning new vocabulary is half the battle in psychology, be sure you understand the meaning of each of these terms by the time you have finished studying a chapter. They will help you make sure that you have learned the most important terms when you are reviewing for a test. Page references help you locate definitions while studying.

4 Margin Glossary A running glossary with pronunciation guidelines defines new terms and shows you how to pronounce those that may be difficult. You will find these definitions and pronunciations in the outside margin of the text near the new terms that appear in boldface type within the text. These entries provide a convenient way of learning definitions without disrupting your reading.

5 Section Reviews Within each chapter are three to seven major sections. These are self-contained in the sense that they can be understood without an extensive understanding of the sections that precede or follow them. This flexibility will allow your instructor to assign sections to be read when the need arises instead of an entire chapter.

Following each major section is a brief review that summarizes the main ideas introduced in that section. This device will help you keep the overall organization of the new material in mind as you study and master the details.

6 Critical Thinking Questions Questions designed to stimulate critical thinking appear in the margin at the end of each section. These questions will further your critical thinking if you let them involve you actively in the process of learning. The few minutes of thought that each question provokes should help you to personalize your new knowledge of psychology, making it "your own" to keep and use over your lifetime. Directly following "How the Book Works" is a short section titled "Critical Thinking." Taking the time to read it now can help you get more out of the critical thinking questions in the rest of the book.

7 Check Your Learning Questions At the end of each section, you will also find "*Check Your Learning*" questions. These multiple-choice questions give you a chance to see if you have mastered the material in that section before moving on. The answers are provided to give you immediate feedback on the correctness of your own answers. If you give an incorrect answer, use the page number provided with each answer to guide you to the page or pages you should review.

8 Human Diversity Features Human diversity sections give special emphasis to major themes of this book, the importance of recognizing and respecting the differences among people and learning about the sociocultural factors that can contribute to the exciting variety among individuals. You'll find a human diversity section in most chapters.

9 Applications of Psychology An application of psychology is discussed near the end of every chapter. This section ties together the information in the chapter and helps you understand how your new knowledge of psychology can be used in your own life.

9

APPLICATION OF PSYCHOLOGY

PARENTING

During the important early stages of development—infancy, childhood, and most of adolescence—we typically live with our parents. They give us food and shelter, protect us from danger, and provide many of our early learning experiences. Parents play a key role in giving children a healthy start in life. But, although parenting is important, we as a society provide parents with no training in how to raise their children. Our schools teach reading, writing, and arithmetic, but not parenting. For this reason, we will look carefully at the topic of parenting, with an emphasis on the styles of parenting that are best for children.

Parenting and Infant Attachment

Let's begin with a look at the parents' role in helping their infant develop a secure relationship—or attachment—with the parents. The newborn in the hospital nursery seems equally happy to be rocked by anyone who has free arms, but sometime during the first year of life (usually by about 6 to 9 months) infants typically become closely attached to one or more of their caretakers. At this point in development, most infants develop a normal "stranger anxiety" and react fearfully and tearfully when strangers are present and cling to the safe fortress of the adult to whom they are attached (Ainsworth, 1979). By 18 to 24 months, however, most toddlers are better able to deal with stranger anxiety. They prefer to be near their primary caretaker when strangers are first encountered, but they are able to move out to explore the world and play, knowing that the safe caretaker is nearby. Infants who are able to deal with stranger anxiety in this way are said to be "securely attached."

Some infants and toddlers, however, are less securely attached to their parent. When separated from their caretaker, some "insecurely attached" toddlers cling excessively to the caretaker and become extremely upset when separated from the parent. Seemingly, the attachment is not secure enough to allow the toddler to turn her or his back on the parent for a moment. Other toddlers who are not securely attached rarely use the parent as a safe haven, but rather seem to ignore or even avoid the parent. It is as if the attachment to the parent is too weak to be helpful to the toddler.

What leads to secure attachment? Part of the answer is the child's inborn temperament. Some children are simply calmer and more receptive to the parent from birth. But parents play an important role as well. Parents can help their infants form secure attachments by taking care of the infant's needs in a consistent way and by being warm, affectionate, and accepting. In this case, being an accepting parent means staying calm and loving (most of the time, at least) when the baby "acts like an infant"—crying in the middle of the night, wetting diaper after diaper, and spitting every bite of cereal back into your hand (Goldsmith & Alansky, 1987)!

By age 18 to 24 months, "securely attached" toddlers are able to explore the world and play if they know a safe caregiver is nearby.

Our parents care for us from infancy through adolescence and provide us with many of our most important learning experiences.

It is important for parents to help their infants develop the firm foundation of a secure attachment, but how worried should the parent of an insecurely attached infant be? The best answer is that the parent should be concerned enough to look at his or her parenting to see whether healthy changes can be made, but not overly concerned. It is not uncommon for an extremely clingy 2-year-old who receives consistent and loving parenting to grow into a happy and secure 5-year-old—I've personally seen it happen more than once.

Parenting and Discipline Style

Discipline style is one of the most important parts of parenting. As soon as the infant can move, the adult must attempt to

Chapter 8: Developmental Psychology 319

10

Summary

Chapter 3 recognizes that we live in a physical world that we experience through our sense organs and interpret (perceive) by means of our nervous systems.

I. External stimuli are received through specialized sensory receptor cells.
   A. Sense organs receive stimuli, transduce sensory energy into neural impulses, and send neural messages to the brain for interpretation.
   B. Psychophysics is the field of psychology that studies the relationships between physical stimuli and psychological sensations and perceptions.

II. The sense organs of sight transduce light energy.
   A. The intensity of light waves largely determines brightness, while the wavelength (frequency) largely determines color.
   B. The eye, working much like a camera, is the primary sense organ for seeing.
      1. Light enters the eye through the cornea (with the iris regulating the size of the pupil) and the lens into the retina.
      2. Rods and cones transduce light waves into neural impulses for transportation to the brain.
      3. The 125 million rods, located throughout the retina except for the fovea, are active in peripheral vision and vision in dim light, but they do not play a role in color vision.
      4. The 6 million cones clustered mostly near the fovea code information for color.
      5. Both trichromatic theory and opponent-process theory are helpful in understanding color vision.

III. The sense of hearing detects sound waves.
   A. The frequency of sound waves determines pitch, while the intensity determines loudness.
   B. The ear is the primary sense organ for hearing.
      1. The outer ear functions as a sound wave collector.
      2. Sound waves vibrate the eardrum, which is connected to a series of three movable bones (hammer, anvil, stirrup) in the middle ear.
      3. The inner ear, containing the cochlea and the organ of Corti, transduces the sound wave energy into neural impulses for transportation to the brain.

IV. Chemical senses respond to chemicals rather than to energy in the environment.
   A. In the sense of taste, chemicals produce the perception of qualities of sweet, sour, bitter, and salty.
   B. In the sense of smell, chemicals produce the perception of odors.

V. Internal stimuli are also received by the sensory system.
   A. The vestibular organ provides information about body orientation, while the kinesthetic sense reports bodily position and movement.
   B. The various skin senses can detect pressure, temperature, and pain.
      1. Two sensations of pain reach the brain at slightly different times because they travel on different neural pathways.
         a. The first sensation reaches the somatosensory area quickly on myelinated neurons.
         b. The more emotional type of pain reaches the limbic system more slowly on unmyelinated neurons.
      2. Many factors can block the "pain gates" for the emotional aspect of pain.

VI. Sensory neural impulses, when transmitted to the brain, are interpreted in a process called perception; examining visual perception demonstrates the general nature of the process.
   A. Perception is an active mental process. Gestalt principles explain many of the ways in which humans tend to organize sensory information.
   B. Individual factors, such as emotion, motivation, and previous learning, also affect our perceptions.

11

Suggested Readings

1. If you think of yourself as a sensual person, and something of an intellectual, then treat yourself to the most wonderful book ever written about the senses: Ackerman, D. (1991). *A natural history of the senses*. New York: Vintage Books.
2. A readable but sophisticated examination of classical principles of perception and illusions is supplied by: Held, R., & Richards, W. (Eds.). (1972). *Perception: Mechanisms and models*. San Francisco: W. H. Freeman.
3. If you are a serious student of visual perception or of the visual arts, you may wish to tackle an excellent in-depth analysis of this subject: Hochberg, J. (1988). Visual perception. In R. C. Atkinson, R. J. Hernstein, G. Lindzey, & R. D. Luce (Eds.), *Stevens' handbook of experimental psychology: Vol. 1. Perception and motivation*. New York: Wiley-Interscience.
4. Perhaps the ultimate sensory illusion is experienced by persons who have lost an arm or leg. If you would like to learn about "phantom limbs," read: Melzack, R. (1992). Phantom limbs. *Scientific American*, April 120–126.

132 Part 2: Awareness

12

Special Review of the Sense Organs

A great deal of new information was covered in chapter 3 on the structure of the sense organs. A set of unlabeled illustrations have been prepared to help you check your learning of these structures. These reviews will be most helpful if you glance at the first one and then refer back to the illustration or illustrations on which they are based to memorize the names of the structures. Then, return to the illustration in this review section and try to write in the names of the key structures of the sense organs. Then check your labels by looking at the original figures once again. When you can label all the structures in one of the illustrations, move on to the next one.

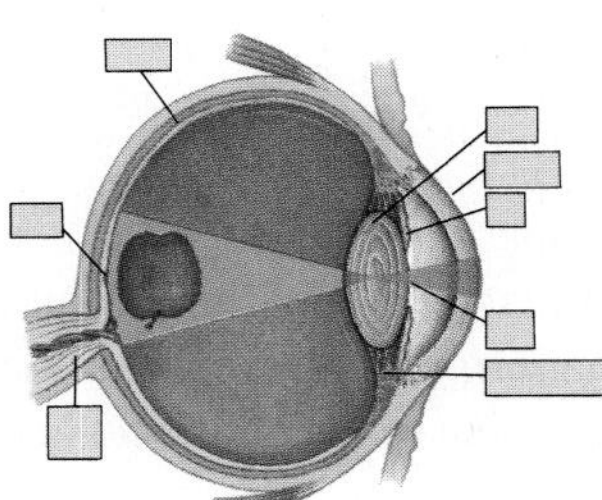

FIGURE 3.48
Key structures of the eye (based on fig. 3.3, p. 95).

Chapter 3: Sensation and Perception 133

10 Chapter Summaries At the end of each chapter, the content of the chapter is summarized in sentence outline form. This outline format is designed to give you one last look at the content of the chapter to see how all the pieces of new information fit together.

11 Suggested Readings A list of suggested readings is presented at the end of each chapter. This information will help you to learn more about a specific topic covered in the chapter.

12 Special Reviews In some chapters you'll find key illustrations from the chapter reprinted at the end of the chapter, only this time *without* the labels. Fill in the labels yourself to test your learning of the information. The original figure number, title, and page reference are given. Return to the original figure and description to check your answers and review if necessary.

SUPPLEMENTS TO THE BOOK

McGraw-Hill has prepared additional materials that may be helpful to you in this class. If you are interested in using any of the following items, ask your instructor to order them through your bookstore.

The **Student Study Guide** to accompany *Psychology: An Introduction* was written by Steven A. Schneider of Pima Community College specifically to help students master the material in this textbook. The study guide follows the same table of contents as each chapter of the book. For each chapter of the text, you are provided with a chapter overview, learning objectives, matching exercises for key terms, guided review exercises, a concept check exercise, and multiple-choice practice test items with instructional feedback.

MicroGuide is a computerized interactive version of the study guide, designed to help you in studying, reviewing and testing your comprehension of the textbook material. *MicroGuide* consists of four sections for each chapter of the book: Learning Objectives, Chapter Review, Key Terms, and Quiz Questions. *MicroGuide* is available in either DOS or Macintosh versions (3.5 inch disk size only).

CRITICAL THINKING

Like most college courses, the goal of this course is to teach you a great deal of new information. But, there is a second goal even more important than the first—to teach you to *think critically about human beings.* You are enrolled in a college or university to become well educated. That means, of course, that you want to learn more information, but it also means that you want to be better prepared to make decisions, plan for the future, and realize your goals. If we human beings are to be able to continue to inhabit this fragile planet, and if we are to make the most of our time here, we must all try to hone our intellectual skills.

Psychology provides an excellent vehicle for teaching critical thinking skills. By its very nature—as a *science* of human behavior—we will be looking critically at ourselves. As we discuss the many new facts and concepts that make up this course, we will describe many of the experiments that have helped psychologists reach tentative conclusions about the nature of our behavior and experience. *Psychological research is critical thinking in practice.* As you read about each experiment, take a moment to consider the logic that went into its design. Think for a moment about the thinking that helped the researcher decide between rival explanations for that facet of human life.

But, more important than seeing how scientists use their critical thinking skills, a major goal of this course is to encourage *you* to improve your own critical thinking skills. Success in every walk of life and meaningful participation in democratic society require more than the simple knowledge of facts—they require using facts intelligently.

What, then, is critical thinking? There are many aspects of critical thinking, but the steps that I will describe are a good start. As you read this textbook or approach any other source of new information—from political speeches to newspaper articles—try the following steps:

1. *What is the evidence?* I will present you with many statements in this textbook, and I expect you to demand that I back up my statements with evidence. When I tell you that, unlike 20 years ago, women and men place the same importance on love in marriage, you should look to see if I present evidence to support that conclusion. If I make a statement without supporting evidence, you should strongly question my statement.
2. *How good is the evidence?* Suppose I tell you that the reason that I believe that women and men place the same value on romance today is because my wife and my daughters say so. My wife and daughters happen to be very smart people, but would you believe the opinions of just three people? Would you be more convinced if I cite a study of 20,000 men and women? Not only should we demand evidence to support statements of fact, but we also should examine the quality of that evidence. In this book, I can tell you that I have thought carefully about the quality of evidence that supports every statement. But, you should completely disregard my reassurances and think critically about the evidence yourself. You might very well decide that I am wrong on some key issues, but at the very least, you will sharpen your critical thinking skills.
3. *What are the alternative interpretations of the evidence?* Even if I do provide you with solid evidence to support every conclusion, critical thinking cannot stop there. Facts are meaningless until they are *interpreted,* and there is almost always more than one interpretation of every set of facts in psychology.

   Let's think about an example. There is strong evidence that, other things being equal, most women are more attracted to men as marriage partners if they are more intelligent, hardworking, and successful. Those are the "facts," but what do they mean? One group of scholars believes that women have an *innate* need (part of every female in the human species) to guarantee the well-being of their children that leads them to prefer successful husbands who can help them provide for their children. Do you agree? Even if you agree, are there alternative explanations of these facts that would make just as much sense? Take a moment now to think about alternative explanations for these facts (really—I hope you will stop reading and try to think of alternative interpretations of these facts for a moment).

   Did you come up with any alternative explanations? It doesn't matter if you didn't come up with a brilliant explanation, but it is important that you see that alternative explanations of almost any set of facts are possible.

   So, what do we do with facts that can be interpreted in several different ways? Critical thinking requires two approaches to this situation. The first and most important step is to look for more facts that will help you choose between the alternative explanations. For example, do women in *all* cultures find successful men to be attractive? Do highly successful women in our culture find the man's success to be unimportant? Do women who do not want to have children still find successful men to be attractive? If the answers to these questions are not all yes, you might be less likely to believe that the preference for successful men reflects an innate need shared by all women. There are many ways in which new facts can be sought that might allow you to decide between alternative explanations for facts. Indeed, that is what science is all about.

The other way in which the critical thinker deals with alternative explanations of facts, however, is to *learn to live with alternative explanations!* At this point in the history of the science of psychology, there are many alternative explanations of facts that we cannot yet choose between. Indeed, one of the things that makes psychology exciting is that there is so much yet to learn. Many of the current disagreements among psychologists will be resolved ultimately through better experiments—the use of critical thinking to plan the logic of scientific studies. But, in other cases, the different ways of viewing the same phenomena will prove to be equally valid conceptions. Therefore, the ability to consider more than one perspective on issues in psychology—as in all walks of life—is important. Moreover, the discussion of these differing views will help refine your critical thinking about yourself and the human race in general.

4. *Go beyond the book.* This book only scratches the surface of psychology, and it provides only a few examples of how the facts and concepts of psychology might apply to your life. The final step in critical thinking is to ask questions about the information given in the textbook to expand its application to your experience. Each section of a chapter ends with critical thinking questions. These questions have no right or wrong answers, but are designed to stimulate and challenge you as you read the book. (The *Student Study Guide* contains more of these kinds of questions in the sections titled "Encouraging Critical Thinking: Beyond the Text.") But these questions are just a start. The most important "critical thinking" questions that you ask will be your own.

   Critical thinking is not only an academic exercise—it is a part of living. The thinking and evaluative skills that you develop in this and other courses will also serve you well as you solve problems and confront the challenges of daily life.

   If you are concerned that critical thinking takes time and might detract from your ability to memorize information that will be on tests, I have good news for you. Thinking critically about the information that you have just read will improve your memory for that information. In chapter 6, we will discuss the "deep processing" of information and present evidence that the more you think about information the more information you will remember. So, although you will still need to use the strategies for study skills presented at the end of chapter 1, critical thinking will improve your memory for information presented in this book. But, don't take my word for it! Read the section on levels of processing in chapter 6 and think about it critically. Better yet, try your own experiment to see if thinking critically about the information presented in this book makes this course a better learning experience.

PART 1

Introduction

CHAPTER 1

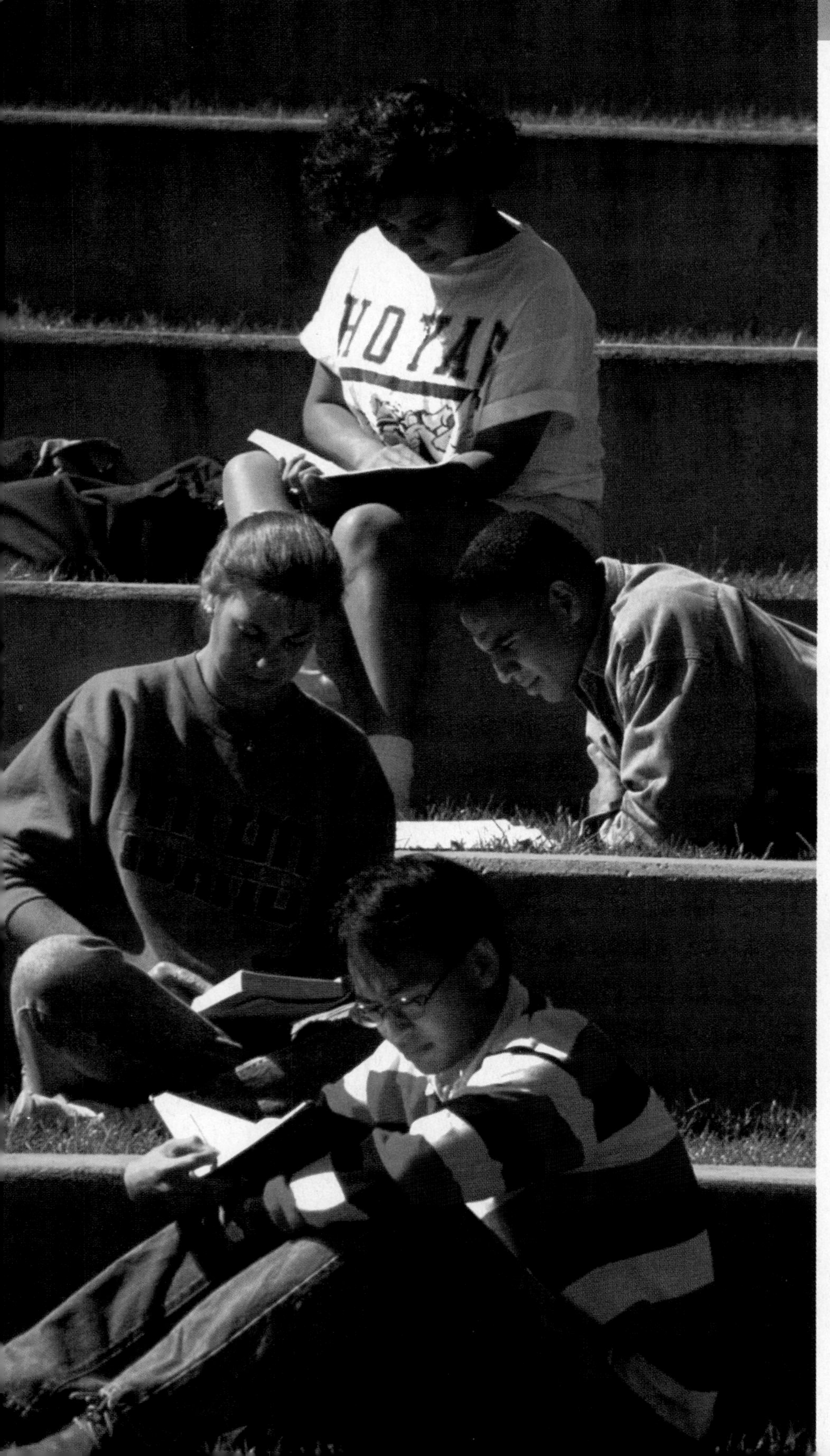

CHAPTER OUTLINE

What Is Psychology?

PROLOGUE

What will this course in psychology be about? You may have already glanced through the book and noticed the illustrations of nerve cells, the discussion of color vision, and the story of the dogs that were taught to salivate to the sound of a bell. This is psychology?! Are you getting worried that you signed up for the wrong course? If you're like me when I opened my first psychology textbook, you were surprised to see such topics in a book about psychology. I had expected to read tales of madness, love, and social ills, but instead I saw illustrations of brain structures, salivating dogs, and odor receptors.

I hope you looked through the book long enough to see that love, violence, mental disorders, and sexuality are in here, too. Almost everything that you expected is in this course, but a lot of topics that you probably didn't expect also will be covered. If I hadn't had an instructor who explained how all of these topics related to people, I think I would have changed majors. Why on earth would I want to know how to teach dogs to salivate on command? Why did I need to know how a taste bud works? Because I remembered very clearly what it was like to take my first psychology course, I wrote this book to help your instructor explain to you how all of these topics fit together to make up the field of psychology.

This text surveys the basic principles of psychology and shows you how these principles can be applied to solve some significant human problems. Because this is a first course in psychology, we cover more basic facts and principles than applications. But to help you make better sense of the fundamental concepts, this book describes applications throughout the course to illustrate the abstract principles in a concrete way.

All of the material in this book, even the most basic material, is relevant to human lives in some way. And many topics relate directly to everyone's personal efforts to make sense out of life. In this text we discuss emotions, ways of improving memory, relationships between employers and employees, and other important topics. Topics such as the meaning of dreams, out-of-body experiences, compulsive gambling, and hypnosis are also covered. We discuss such topics partly because they are fun to learn about—and fun is one of the legitimate goals of education. But we also study such topics because they can teach us about more basic psychological principles. Ultimately, a firm understanding of the basic concepts will be most useful to you later in life because they can be applied to any issue or situation you might encounter.

A huge amount of basic information must be surveyed in a brief span of time in an introductory psychology course, but we will try not to let you miss the forest for the trees. As we study the way nerve cells influence one another, for instance, you will be reminded that knowledge of this mechanism led to the development of modern tranquilizing drugs. When we study the way the eyes sense color, it will be pointed out that such knowledge led to the invention of color television. In psychology you are never far from an application to a human problem, no matter how technical the subject matter.

In this first chapter, we begin our study of psychology by telling you what things psychologists study and how they study them. You will be struck by the fact that psychology is a very broad field. Psychologists use the methods of science to study these things. They learn

KEY TERMS

about behavior, thoughts, and feelings by systematically *observing* them. Certainly psychologists think about human behavior, but as scientists, we believe that we always learn more by actually seeing how people behave than from speculating about it.

Observation is the heart of the scientific method of all the sciences, including psychology. Psychologists use a variety of methods of scientific observation, ranging from surveys to laboratory experiments. Each method of observation is valuable in helping us fit new pieces into the puzzle of human behavior and mental processes. The goal of all of this scientific observation is to describe behavior with enough precision that we can predict it better, understand it more fully, and learn how to influence human behavior in positive ways.

Although the first systematic writings about human behavior date back to the time of Aristotle, psychology did not become an independent science until 1879 when Wilhelm Wundt founded the first laboratory of psychology in Germany. Psychology actually had many other "beginnings" in the late 1800s, led by a number of scientists who were interested in very different aspects of human behavior and mental processes. These were exciting times for the early psychologists, filled with intense disagreements, sharp remarks, and occasional scandals. As you will soon see, psychology is still a very broad field today in which different theories abound and many facets of the human condition are studied. But we are making good progress toward our goal of using observation to describe, predict, and understand human behavior.

PSYCHE AND SCIENCE = PSYCHOLOGY

Welcome to psychology! You are invited to learn about one of life's most interesting subjects—yourself. You were enrolled in this course knowing that it had something to do with people. But what exactly is psychology?

The philosopher and early scientist, Aristotle

The earliest origins of psychology are in the writings of the ancient Greek philosophers about the nature of *life,* particularly the writings of Aristotle. Aristotle, who was born in 384 B.C., was interested in learning everything he could about the nature of life itself. He collected and dissected plants and animals in an attempt to see how their organs sustained life. He studied reproduction to see how life was re-created in each generation, and he studied the everyday actions of living people as they reasoned, remembered, and learned.

It was Aristotle's habit in his later years to discuss philosophy with his students as they strolled the covered walks of his school, the Lyceum. Imagine what he might have said to them about the nature of life:

> You'll understand what life is if you think about the act of dying. When I die, how will I be different from the way I am right now? In the first moments after death, my body will be scarcely different in physical terms than it was in the last seconds of life, but I will no longer move, no longer sense, nor speak, nor feel, nor care. It's these things that are life. At that moment the psyche takes flight in the last breath.

Aristotle used the term *psyche* to refer to the essence of life. This term is translated from Greek to mean "mind," but it is closely linked in meaning to the word *breath.* Aristotle believed that psyche escaped in the last dying breath that was exhaled. Modern psychologists are interested in the same actions, thoughts, and feelings of human beings as Aristotle. Indeed, the term *psychology* comes from Aristotle's word *psyche* plus the Greek word *logos,* which means "the study of."

Aristotle received his training in philosophical methods from the famous philosopher Plato, but he disagreed with Plato's belief that one could achieve a full understanding of anything simply by *thinking* about it. Aristotle felt that one must also *observe* the thing being studied—look at it, listen to it, touch it. Although he was not a scientist in the modern sense of the word, Aristotle's emphasis on observation is the basis for the methods of contemporary science. Progress in scientific methods from Aristotle to the present has involved no basic changes in this idea; scientists have only developed more precise and efficient ways of observing. Thus, Aristotle launched the study of life that evolved later into the modern science of psychology.

Definition of Psychology

In some ways it would be correct to say that psychologists still define psychology as the "study of life." The only thing that would be incorrect about this definition is that it is not specific enough to distinguish the modern discipline of psychology from other sciences such as biology that also study life. Today, therefore, **psychology** is defined as the *science of behavior and mental processes.*

Notice that this definition contains three key terms—science, behavior, and mental processes. Let's look at each of these terms separately. Psychology is considered to be a **science** because psychologists attempt to understand people through careful, controlled observation. This reliance on rigorous scientific methods of observation is the basis of all sciences, including psychology. The term **behavior** refers to all of a person's overt actions that others can directly observe. When you walk, speak, throw a Frisbee, or show a facial expression, you are behaving in this sense. The term **mental processes** refers to the private thoughts, emotions, feelings, and motives that others cannot directly observe. Your private thoughts and feelings about your dog catching a Frisbee in midair are examples of mental processes.

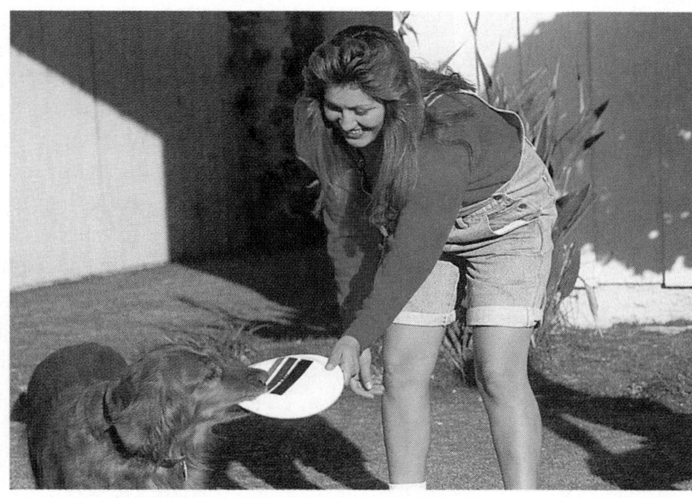

The term *behavior* refers to all of a person's overt actions that others can directly observe. When you walk, speak, throw a Frisbee, or show facial expression, you are behaving in this sense.

Goals of Psychology

What are the goals of the science of psychology? What are psychologists trying to accomplish? Psychologists study people by using scientific methods. The goals of this scientific enterprise are to describe, predict, understand, and influence behavior and mental processes. More on these four goals:

The goals of psychology are to describe, predict, understand, and influence human behavior.

1. *Describe.* The information gathered through scientific research helps us describe psychological phenomena more accurately and completely. For example, information gathered in a survey on the frequency of sexual behavior among college students without the protection of a condom would tell us whether they are at high risk for the spread of sexually transmitted diseases such as AIDS.
2. *Predict.* In some cases, psychologists are able to predict future behavior. For example, psychologists have developed tests that enable employers to improve their prediction of which job applicants will perform well.
3. *Understand.* We understand behavior and mental processes when we can explain them. Because there is still much more to learn, our current explanations are always tentative. In other words, our explanations are **theories,** not truths. Theories are tentative explanations of facts and relationships in sciences. It's essential that you understand this basic fact about science as you read this or any other textbook. The knowledge that we can offer you is always tentative. As the science of psychology progresses through research, our theories are always subject to revision.
4. *Influence.* Finally, psychologists hope to go beyond description, understanding, and prediction to influence behavior in beneficial ways. What can we do to help a teenage boy climb out of a period of severe depression? How can we help parents raise their rambunctious children better? What is the best way to help college students select a career? It's not until we can intentionally influence behavior that psychology completely fulfills its promise.

psychology
The science of behavior and mental processes.

science
Approach to knowledge based on systematic observation.

behavior
Directly observable and measurable human actions.

mental processes
Private psychological activities that include thinking, perceiving, and feeling.

theory
Tentative explanation of facts and relationships in sciences.

Thinking Critically About Psychology

1. What do you personally want to learn in this course?

2. How do your personal goals as a student of psychology relate to the four goals of the science of psychology?

Review

We have defined psychology as the science of behavior and mental processes. Behavior refers to all of your actions that other people can directly observe. Mental processes, in contrast, are private events, like thinking and feeling. The goals of psychology are to describe, predict, understand, and influence behavior and mental processes. Using the methods of science, we gather information through systematic observation that enables us to accurately describe psychological facts and relationships. When adequate descriptive information has been acquired, reasonably accurate predictions can be made and explanations proposed to help us understand these facts and relationships. Finally, when enough understanding and ability to predict has been acquired, we can sometimes intentionally influence people in ways that improve and enrich their lives.

Check Your Learning

One efficient way to learn information from textbooks is to be sure that you have mastered the keypoints in each major section before moving on to the next one. You can do this by asking yourself questions about the material that you have just read. If you cannot answer some of the questions, you can easily go back to that part of the section and reread it. Then, when you can answer all of your questions, it will be time to move on to the next part of the chapter. This step of asking and answering questions will take a little time, but you will learn and remember much more information.

To make it easier for you to check your learning in this way, I have written some questions at the end of each section. If you give an incorrect answer to any question, return to the page number given next to the correct answer to see why your answer was not correct. When you have mastered the information in this section, you will be ready to move on to the next section.

It is important for you to also ask *your own* questions, however, for two reasons. First, asking your own question will help you personalize the course and make it a more worthwhile learning experience for you. Second, I have asked you questions only about some of the key points in each section. If you learn only what I have emphasized in these few questions, you will miss a great deal of information. Therefore, it is best to use these questions only as a starting point in checking your learning.

1. The ancient Greek philosopher who wrote about "psyche" and first broadly defined the subject matter was

a. Plato. **b.** Aristotle. **c.** Hippocrates. **d.** Epicurus.

2. The modern definition of psychology is "the science of ________________ and ________________."

3. Mental processes are

a. directly observable. **b.** private.

4. The four goals of the science of psychology are to ________ behavior.

1. ____

2. ____

3. ____

4. ____

Correct Answers

1. b (p. 4), **2.** behavior and mental processes (p. 5), **3.** b (p. 5), **4.** 1. describe, 2. predict, 3. understand, 4. influence (p. 5).

THE MANY VIEWPOINTS IN PSYCHOLOGY AND THEIR ORIGINS

A psychologist could spend an entire career studying the causes of emotional disorders, or the way we recall facts, or methods of improving job satisfaction among employees, or the role of the brain in emotions, or the nature of racial prejudice, or any of a variety of topics within psychology. When we consider the range of possibilities, it's not surprising that the science of psychology is a very broad field with many divisions, each focusing on a different facet of human behavior. To better understand this diversity in the field of psychology, we need to look back again through the history of its development.

There was no formal discipline of psychology during the time of Aristotle and for 2,200 years after he lived. Like the other sciences, psychology was a part of philosophy. It wasn't until modern times that the sciences emerged from the general field of philosophy. In the seventeenth and eighteenth centuries, physics, biology, medicine, and other disciplines began to accumulate knowledge that set each somewhat apart from the others. Also, each science developed distinct ways of viewing nature. Eventually, psychology also developed its own distinct subject matter and scientific methods.

The launching of the separate field of psychology is usually credited to Wilhelm Wundt for establishing the first Laboratory of Psychology in Leipzig, Germany, in 1879. Some historians feel that William James deserves the honor for a less-publicized laboratory at Harvard University, however, which opened in 1875. Actually, many people "founded" psychology. Their varied interests and talents laid the foundations for the diverse field surveyed in this text. As you read about some of the most influential early psychologists, imagine how different their answers would be if you asked each of them, "What is the most important question for psychology?"

Wilhelm Wundt (1832–1920)

The Nature of Conscious Experience

The first topic studied by psychologists was private conscious experience. What are you thinking and feeling right now? Everything that you are aware of right now is part of your conscious experience. The first psychologists wanted to understand the basic elements of consciousness and how they worked together to create the experience of being alive.

Wundt, Titchener, and the Structuralists

Wilhelm Wundt was a professor of biology in Germany who was fascinated by human consciousness. His work was expanded by his student Edward Titchener, who later taught in the United States at Cornell University. Just as chemists sought to discover the basic elements that make up physical substances, Wundt and Titchener wanted to identify the basic elements of conscious experience. Indeed, sometimes their work is referred to as "mental chemistry." Wundt and Titchener studied the elements of consciousness using a method of looking inward at one's own conscious experiences, called **introspection.** Wundt and Titchener trained themselves to observe the contents of their own minds as accurately and unemotionally as possible in an attempt to isolate the basic elements of the mind. What does that mean exactly?

Edward Titchener (1867–1927)

introspection
(in´´tro-spek´shun) The process of looking inward at one's own consciousness.

Suppose that I visit your school some day and your instructor asks me to give a guest lecture on the history of psychology. Suppose also that I am in a particularly dramatic mood and decide to give the lecture playing the role of Edward Titchener. I arrive wearing a fake beard and the flowing black academic robes that he always wore and I choose you to be the subject of a demonstration of introspection. I ask you to close your eyes and I place a bit of apple in your mouth that you had not seen. Then I ask you to describe to me the raw *sensations* that this physical stimulus creates in your mind.

You hesitate a moment, then announce with a smile, "It's an apple!"

"Nein! Nein! Nein!" I shout, using the only word I can remember from German 101. "I asked you to tell me what you *sense,* not what the stimulus is. Don't tell me what the thing is on your tongue. Describe the sensations that you experience!"

You hesitate again, regain your composure, and hesitatingly say, "Sweet?"

"Yes! Yes!" I cry. "What else do you sense?"

"A little bit of sourness, and a grainy texture, and a wetness."

structuralism
(struk´tūr-al-izm) The nineteenth-century school of psychology that sought to determine the structure of the mind through controlled introspection.

J. Henry Alston

FIGURE 1.1
When you grasp a coil made up of two twisted pipes, one carrying cold water and the other carrying moderately warm water, the sensation is one of extreme heat because the receptors for both cold and warmth are stimulated.

Gestalt psychology
The school of thought based on the belief that human consciousness cannot be broken down into its elements.

gestalt
(ges-tawlt´) An organized or unified whole.

phi phenomenon
(fī fe-nom´ĕ-non) The perception of apparent movement between two stationary stimuli.

"Wonderful!" I shout, leading you to break into a grin. "Now, you're introspecting. Now, you're describing the elemental contents of your mind. Sweet, sour, grainy . . . those are a few of the building blocks from which consciousness is structured. Everything that you experience in life is based on a small number of these basic elements."

Because Wundt and Titchener were interested in the basic elements of the conscious experience and how those elements are organized, their viewpoint is known as **structuralism.** That is, they sought to determine the *structure* of the mind through controlled introspection.

J. Henry Alston

Although Wundt and Titchener were the first psychologists to study conscious experience, other scientists soon joined the effort. One notable early structuralist was J. Henry Alston. Alston is best known for his studies of the sensations of heat and cold. Alston discovered that we feel cold when one kind of nerve ending in the skin is stimulated, and we feel warm when a different kind of nerve ending is stimulated. Most interestingly, he found that we only feel intense heat when *both* the warmth and cold receptors in the skin are stimulated at the same time. Very hot objects—such as a hot iron—not only stimulate the warmth receptors, they stimulate the nerve endings that ordinarily only respond when it is cold.

Alston demonstrated this fact in a simple but elegant experiment in 1920. He constructed the apparatus shown in figure 1.1 by wrapping two water pipes together, one carrying moderately warm water and the other carrying cold water. When people grasped these pipes, they felt the sensation of intense heat! Because both the warmth and the cold receptors in the skin were stimulated by the twisted pipes, the individual in the experiment felt the sensation of intense heat.

J. Henry Alston is a notable figure in the history of psychology for another reason as well. The first research article published by an African-American psychologist in a journal of the American Psychological Association was written by J. Henry Alston.

Max Wertheimer and the Gestalt Psychologists

Max Wertheimer, a professor of psychology at the University of Frankfurt in the early 1900s, also was interested in the nature of conscious experience. His ideas about consciousness were quite different from those structuralists, however. Wertheimer led a group of psychologists known as **Gestalt psychologists.** Their approach to psychology was founded on the concept of the **gestalt,** or *whole*. The Gestalt psychologists felt that human consciousness could not be meaningfully broken down into raw elements as the structuralists tried to do. As they were fond of saying, "the whole is different from the sum of its parts." To illustrate, the two examples in figure 1.2 are drawn from exactly the same angled lines, but their organization greatly changes our perception of them. Although the parts are the same in each example, the whole is seen as a triangle in one example and arrows in the other. Similarly, the second element in the two rows in figure 1.2 is exactly the same each time, but it is perceived as a "13" in the first row and as a "B" in the second.

Gestalt psychologists also used the **phi phenomenon** to demonstrate that the whole is different from the sum of its parts (see fig. 1.3). When two lights are presented in rapid sequence, the viewer sees an apparent movement in the stimuli. That is, rather than perceiving two stationary lights, the viewer sees one light moving from one position to another. This is a highly important phenomenon to Gestalt psychologists, since what is seen—a moving light—is not present in the two parts of the stimulus at all. Movement is a property of the whole perception—the gestalt—but movement is not part of the stimulus. Motion pictures are based on the phi phenomenon. A series of still images that change slightly in each frame are projected on the screen so quickly that the image appears to be moving. The Gestalt psychologists used such examples to make their point that perception has meaning only when it's seen as a whole, rather than as a simple collection of elements as the structuralists implied.

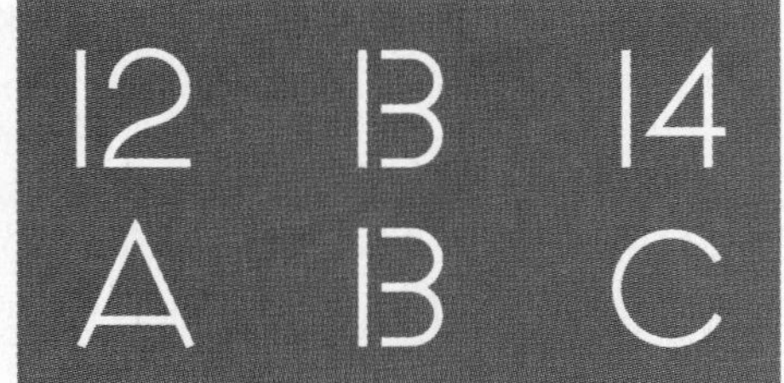

FIGURE 1.2
The organization of the lines in these two illustrations shows that only "whole" perceptions have meaning. The lines do not change but their meaning does.

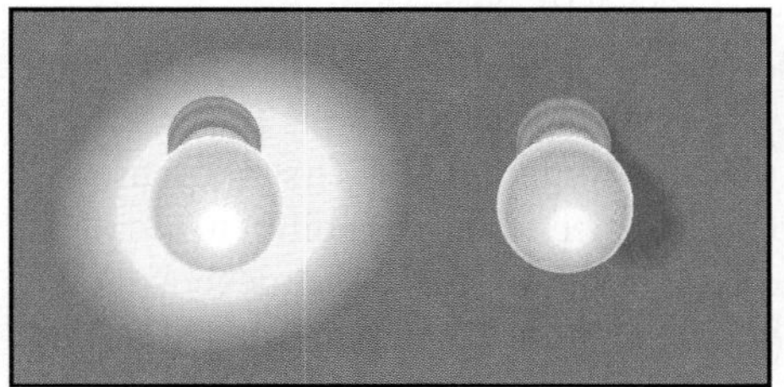
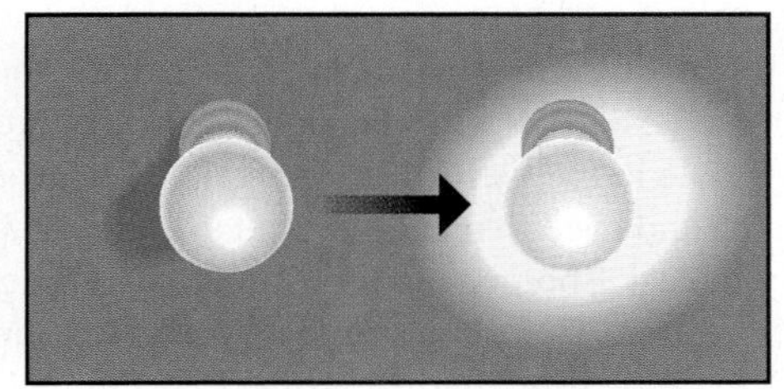

FIGURE 1.3
Though these lights are stationary, the rapid consecutive lighting of them creates an illusion of motion.

The Functions of the Conscious Mind

While many of the early psychologists were studying the nature of conscious experience, another group was trying to understand the *value* of consciousness to us as a species. What useful *functions* does consciousness serve?

William James and the Functionalists

In 1875 a young professor of biology and philosophy at Harvard University named William James taught the first course on "psychology," and in 1890 he published an influential early textbook of psychology. James was impressed with the work of biologist Charles Darwin, who suggested in his theory of evolution that every physical characteristic evolved in a species because it serves some purpose. James suspected that the same thing could be said about the human mind. He speculated that thinking, feeling, learning, remembering, and other processes of human consciousness exist only because they help us survive as a species. Because we can think, for example, we are better able to find food, avoid danger, and care for our children—all of which help the human species to survive. Because of its emphasis on the *functions* of consciousness, the school of thought known as **functionalism** emerged from the work of William James.

James was particularly interested in topics he considered to be evolutionarily important: conscious awareness, voluntary action (free will), habits, and emotions. Because James was concerned with what the mind could do rather than its structure, James criticized the structuralists for creating a barren approach to psychology. He compared human consciousness to a flowing stream: We could study that stream by isolating single molecules of water like the structuralists, but by doing so we would miss the nature and beauty of the whole stream. Moreover, studying the water molecules in a stream would tell us nothing about what the stream *does*—that it erodes riverbanks, provides a home for fish, carries barges, and so on. Similarly, studying the elements of the mind tells us nothing about how it functions to help us adapt to the demands of life. The functions of the mind, not its raw elements, were the subject matter of psychology to the functionalists.

Functionalism continues to have a strong influence on contemporary psychology, but the terminology has changed. Rather than speaking about the functions of human consciousness, psychologists now use the term "cognitive processes." **Cognition** is a broad term that refers to all intellectual processes—perceiving, believing, thinking, remembering, knowing, deciding, and so on. The modern cognitive perspective in psychology can be thought of as a modern version of functionalism, but with some key ideas from Gestalt psychology and structuralism thrown in for good measure.

Max Wertheimer

William James (1842–1910)

functionalism
(funk´shun-al-izm) The nineteenth-century school of psychology that emphasized the useful functions of consciousness.

cognition
(kog-nish´un) Mental processes of perceiving, believing, thinking, remembering, knowing, deciding, and so on.

Hermann Ebbinghaus (1850–1909)

Mary Whiton Calkins

Studies of Memory: Hermann Ebbinghaus and Mary Whiton Calkins

One of the most useful functions of our mental processes is memory. Because of memory, the lessons that we learn today can be remembered tomorrow. In 1885 Germany's Hermann Ebbinghaus published a book titled *On Memory*. This remarkable book described the first extensive set of experiments on a useful function of the mind. Ebbinghaus gave a detailed account of a series of studies spanning 6 years in which he served both as the scientist and the only subject. He memorized lists of information and measured his memory for them after different intervals of time. To be sure that the material he was learning was not affected by his prior experience with it, Ebbinghaus invented an entirely new set of meaningless items for his experiments called *nonsense syllables,* such as KEB and MUZ.

In a typical experiment, Ebbinghaus sat alone in his study listening to a metronome that clicked every few seconds. At the first click, he tried to say aloud the first nonsense syllable in the list. At the next click, he turned the card containing the first nonsense syllable and tried to recall the next syllable, and so on. He then tested his ability to recall the syllables. Ebbinghaus found that forgetting is very rapid at first but proceeds slowly thereafter. Almost half of his original learning was lost within 20 minutes, and almost all of the forgetting that was going to occur had occurred within about 9 hours (see fig. 1.4). We now know that memories for more meaningful information are not always forgotten in the same way as nonsense syllables, but Ebbinghaus's careful and detailed studies set an important example for how rigorous experimental methods could be used to study functions of human consciousness.

Mary Whiton Calkins was another early pioneer in the study of memory. Calkins was a student of William James at Harvard University in the late 1800s. Calkins was a prominent teacher and researcher who was a leader in research on memory. She developed a method to study memory that differed from the one used by Ebbinghaus. Calkins presented her subjects with a series of numbers, each paired with a different color. Later she would show the subjects the colors alone to see how many of the numbers they could recall. When physicians memorize the best medicines to prescribe for different illness, they are using the same kind of memorization. Variations on this method, called the *paired associates* method, dominated research on memory in the United States for more than 50 years (Madigan & O'Hara, 1992). As we will see in chapter 4, Calkins also pioneered the scientific study of dreams. In 1905 Calkins was honored for her contributions by becoming the first woman to be elected president of the American Psychological Association.

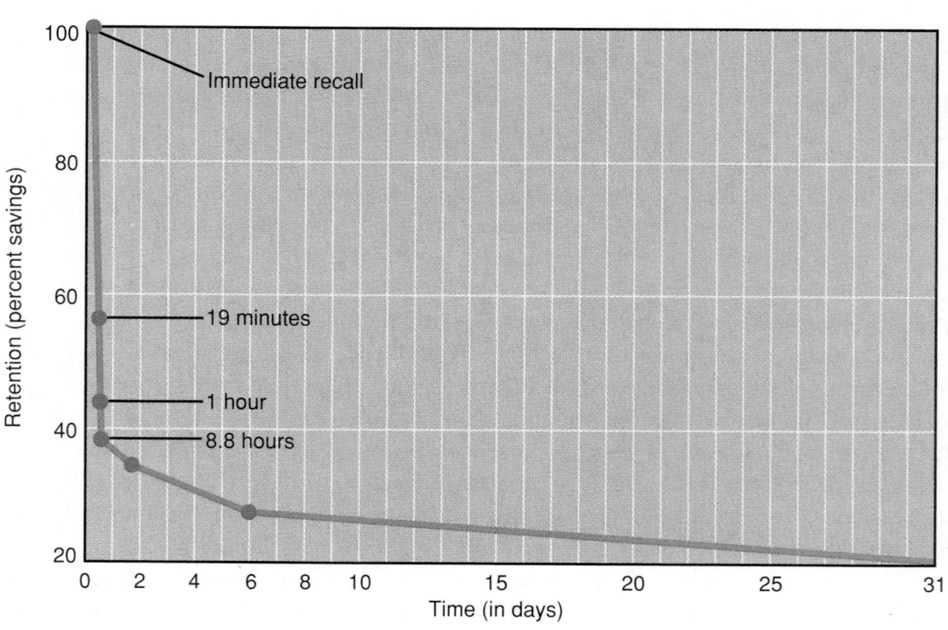

FIGURE 1.4

Hermann Ebbinghaus published these findings in 1885 showing that most forgetting occurs rapidly, with almost half of the original learning being lost within 20 minutes.

Source: Data from R. M. Tarpy and R. E. Mayer, *Foundations of Learning and Memory,* 1978, Scott, Foresman and Company.

Intelligence: Alfred Binet

In France a notable early psychologist by the name of Alfred Binet took the study of the useful functions of conscious mental processes in a very different, but very practical direction—he developed a way to measure intelligence. In the 1890s the Paris Ministry of Education was faced with a problem. They wanted to provide extensive education for all "intelligent" children and more practical, less academic kinds of schooling for less intelligent children. They wanted to be fair about choosing the children who would be given advanced academic training, but they also wanted to make the decision when the children were still young. How could they measure something so intangible as a child's intelligence?

They turned for advice to a professor at the University of the Sorbonne who had just founded the first psychology laboratory in France. By experimenting with a large number of test items, Binet and his collaborators were able to find a set of questions (e.g., arithmetic problems, word definitions, memory tasks) that could be answered by most children of a given age, but not by children who were younger or who had low intelligence. These questions were used to create an intelligence test that was later revised and translated in the United States to become the still widely used Stanford-Binet Intelligence Scale. Binet's work led to the modern branch of psychology that specializes in the measurement of intelligence, personality, job aptitude, and so on.

Behaviorism and Social Learning Theory

While Wundt and his followers studied the nature of conscious experience and James and others examined the usefulness of the conscious mental processes, a third group of founders of the science of psychology was getting started in Russia. Like James, this group was influenced by Darwin to study psychological processes that were useful in the struggle to survive. In this case, their emphasis was on *learning* from experience.

Ivan Pavlov

In the 1890s Russian psychologist Ivan Pavlov was conducting research on digestion in dogs when he noticed a curious thing. He had surgically implanted tubes in the cheeks of the dogs to study the reflexive secretion of saliva during eating. He noticed that after several feedings the dogs started salivating when they heard the *sounds* of food being brought to them rather than when the food was placed in their mouths. Pavlov recognized that the dogs had learned to associate the sound of the food being brought with the food itself. Because the sound had immediately preceded the food on many occasions, the dogs came to respond to the sound by salivating. He demonstrated that this interpretation was correct by conducting careful experiments using a clicking metronome instead of the sound of food being brought and small quantities of powdered meat. When the metronome and the meat powder were presented together, the dogs quickly learned to salivate to the metronome alone.

Ivan Pavlov (1849–1936)

Although teaching dogs to salivate to the sound of the metronome certainly is not important in its own right, Pavlov's accidental discovery was of tremendous importance to the new field of psychology. He had identified a simple form of learning—or *conditioning* to use his term—in which an inherited reflex (salivating) comes to be triggered by a stimulus that has nothing to do with that reflex (the metronome). Pavlov had shown that even inherited reflexes can be influenced dramatically by learning experiences.

Pavlov also developed a precise scientific way to study learning. By measuring the number of drops of saliva produced by a dog hearing the metronome, Pavlov was able to study many aspects of the learning process, such as the time interval between the sound and the food that produced the most rapid conditioning (one-half second in his studies). Pavlov felt that the study of conditioning was such an important breakthrough that he abandoned his research on digestion, for which he had already won the Nobel Prize, and spent the rest of his career studying his new discovery.

John B. Watson and Margaret Floy Washburn

Pavlov's research and theories were not immediately accepted in the United States, but in the 1920s the concepts were taken up in the writings of John B. Watson. He was deeply impressed by Pavlov's work on conditioning because of its scientific precision. Watson agreed with Pavlov that the importance of conditioning went far beyond salivating dogs, and that most human behavior was learned through classical conditioning. But Watson felt that it was impossible to study private mental processes because only outward behavior could be measured and scientifically understood. Because he felt that psychologists should study only overt behavior, Watson called the school of thought that was founded on Pavlov's work, **behaviorism.**

Margaret Floy Washburn was another influential early behaviorist. She was the first woman to actually receive a Ph.D. in psychology, obtaining her degree in 1908 from Cornell University (Furomoto, 1992). During her many years of teaching at Vassar College, Washburn published 90 scientific articles and books on learning and perception in animals.

Margaret Floy Washburn

Contemporary Behaviorism and Social Learning Theory

To some extent, behaviorism has survived as a distinct school of thought in contemporary psychology. Some psychologists are strict adherents of behaviorism and rule out the study of mental processes as did John B. Watson. Until his death in 1990, B. F. Skinner of Harvard University was the leading exponent of this strict form of behaviorism. Most psychologists who are influenced by behaviorism, however, endorse a broader version of behaviorism than Skinner's. Although contemporary behaviorism continues to emphasize the process of learning, it departs from the position of Watson and Skinner by stating that mental processes, particularly cognition, can be scientifically studied. Albert Bandura from Stanford University is the leading spokesperson for this broader viewpoint, which is referred to as **social learning theory.** This viewpoint states that the most important aspects of our behavior are learned from other persons in society; we learn to be who we are from our family, friends, and culture.

B. F. Skinner (1904–1990)

The Nature of the "Unconscious Mind"

While most of the founders of psychology were focusing on human consciousness, others were moving in a very different direction. These early pioneers believed that we humans are completely unaware of important parts of our mental processes—the so-called unconscious mind.

Sigmund Freud and Psychoanalysis

Sigmund Freud was an Austrian physician who practiced neurology, the treatment of diseases of the nervous system. Unlike the other founders of psychology, he was responsible for the day-to-day care of a large number of patients, many of whom had serious psychological problems. This fact, perhaps more than anything else, explains the enormous differences between his view of psychology and those of the other founders.

Freud believed conscious mental processes were of trivial importance compared with the workings of the **unconscious mind.** Sensation, learning, memory, and other cognitive processes so important to the other founding psychologists were of little interest to Freud. Freud felt that the roots of the psychological problems that he tried to treat were innate **motives,** particularly sexual and aggressive ones, that reside in an unconscious part of the mind. He believed that these unconscious motives and the conflicts that surround them influence our behavior even though we do not know they exist.

Psychoanalysis remains a significant force in modern psychology, even though Freud's theory has been subjected to a number of revisions since his death. Modern psychoanalysts still adhere to Freud's view that conflicts in the unconscious mind are the chief source of psychological problems. However, there are few "orthodox" psychoanalysts today. Most feel that Freud made an important contribution in calling our attention to the role often played by unconscious sexual and aggressive motives in our emotional conflicts but feel that other motives, such as the need to feel adequate in social relationships, are of

behaviorism
(be-hāv´yor-izm) The school of psychology that emphasizes the process of learning and the measurement of overt behavior.

social learning theory
The viewpoint that the most important aspects of our behavior are learned from other persons in society—family, friends, and culture.

unconscious mind
All mental activity of which we are unaware.

motives
Internal states or conditions that activate behavior and give it direction.

psychoanalysis
(si´´ko-ah-nal´ī-sis) The technique of helping persons with emotional problems based on Sigmund Freud's theory of the unconscious mind.

even greater importance. In addition, contemporary psychoanalysts place more significance on conscious cognition than did Freud. We will have more to say on the topic of psychoanalysis in the chapters on personality theory and therapies.

Sigmund Freud (1856–1939)

Humanistic Psychology and the Unconscious Mind

During the 1950s, another movement that focused on the role of the unconscious in psychological problems emerged, known as **humanistic psychology.** Leading humanists such as Abraham Maslow, Carl Rogers, and Viktor Frankl did not agree with Freud that conscious processes were unimportant. Indeed, the humanists believe that human beings determine their own fates through the conscious decisions they make. Like Freud, however, the humanists believe that the unconscious mind often defeats our efforts to make good decisions.

The humanists see society as being the cause of our self-defeating unconscious minds. To the humanists, the most important aspect of people is our view of what we are like—our *self-concept.* If you think that you are intelligent, you may sign up for a difficult college course. If you think that you are caring and helpful, you might volunteer to work on a telephone crisis line. These are examples of aspects of a person's self-concept that can influence important decisions.

The humanists believe, however, that society often makes it difficult to have an *accurate* self-concept. For example, we are constantly bombarded with information that says that only witty, athletic, and attractive people are worth loving. So what if you are like most of us and see yourself as someone who is a little dull, slightly clumsy, and not so attractive? The humanists believe that we often push such upsetting information about ourselves into the unconscious. This causes two kinds of problems. First, it means that most of us have an inaccurate self-concept—because we push out of consciousness information about ourselves that doesn't match what society values. Second, the negative unconscious information sometimes threatens our self-concept and makes us anxious. Thus, although the psychoanalysts and humanists view the unconscious mind in very different ways, they both see it as the most important cause of human problems.

Carl Rogers (1902–1987)

humanistic psychology
The psychological view that human beings possess an innate tendency to improve and determine their lives by the decisions they make.

Review

There was no formal science of psychology for 2,200 years after the time of Aristotle. Then in the late nineteenth century, a number of events led to the emergence of an independent discipline. Wilhelm Wundt founded his psychology laboratory in 1879. Wundt and his followers Edward Titchener and J. Henry Alston engaged in controlled introspective studies of human consciousness. Max Wertheimer and his associates in Germany developed Gestalt psychology, which emphasized the need to study consciousness in whole, meaningful units rather than the artificial elements studied by the structuralists. William James taught the first psychology course and published an influential early textbook stressing the evolutionary significance of consciousness. Hermann Ebbinghaus and Mary Calkins published influential studies of memory that showed how experimental methods could be used to study the functions of consciousness. Alfred Binet developed a useful intelligence test for selecting children for advanced education in Paris. John B. Watson and Margaret Floy Washburn introduced the United States to the research on classical conditioning conducted by Russian biologist Ivan Pavlov. Based on Pavlov's work, Watson advocated a science of psychology that included only overt behavior and made no attempt to study mental processes. Physician Sigmund Freud published his observations on psychoanalysis and the unconscious, which were followed half a century later by the different perspective on the unconscious of the humanists. Together these many founders of psychology launched a diverse science amidst a storm of energetic controversy.

Thinking Critically About Psychology

1. The founders of psychology each focused on different aspects of behavior and mental processes. If you had been one of the founders, on what topic do you think you would have focused?

2. Can you think of barriers that exist today to the success of women and minorities in scientific and professional fields that psychologists could study and help to eliminate?

Check Your Learning

To be sure that you have learned the key points from the preceding section, cover the answers below and try to answer each question. If you give an incorrect answer to any question, return to the page given next to the correct answer to see why your answer was not correct.

1. The early psychologist who first pioneered the introspective study of human consciousness and who is generally credited with founding the first laboratory of psychology in 1879 was

a. Ivan Pavlov.
b. William James.
c. Hermann Ebbinghaus.
d. Wilhelm Wundt.

2. The early American psychologist who founded the school of "functionalism," which emphasized the evolutionary importance of human consciousness, and who taught the first psychology course in a college was

a. Sigmund Freud.
b. William James.
c. Alfred Binet.
d. Wilhelm Wundt.

3. The functionalist who developed the paired associates method to study memory was

a. Alfred Binet.
b. Max Wertheimer.
c. Mary Whiton Calkins.
d. Margaret Floy Washburn.

4. The physician who founded psychoanalysis and its study of the unconscious mind and abnormal behavior was

a. Sigmund Freud.
b. William James.
c. Alfred Binet.
d. Max Wertheimer.

Correct Answers
1. d (p. 7), **2.** b (p. 9), **3.** c (p. 10), **4.** a (p. 12).

CONTEMPORARY PERSPECTIVES IN PSYCHOLOGY

We have just looked at several different viewpoints in psychology that emerged in the work of a number of turn-of-the-century scientists. Each had different interests and assumptions about human nature, so each defined the methods and subject matter of psychology in a different way. As you can imagine, the debates between adherents of these different points of view were often very heated in the early days of psychology.

Where are we today in psychology? No single point of view from the early days has emerged as the correct way of viewing human behavior and mental processes. Although there are some strict adherents of some of the traditional schools of thought—such as behaviorism and psychoanalysis—contemporary psychology could be said to combine the best ideas from all of its founders. In some ways the impact of their intermingled ideas is even more important than the original schools of thought.

Before we begin studying the methods and findings of psychology, it is important for us to look at two other perspectives that strongly influence contemporary psychology. These are the biological and sociocultural perspectives.

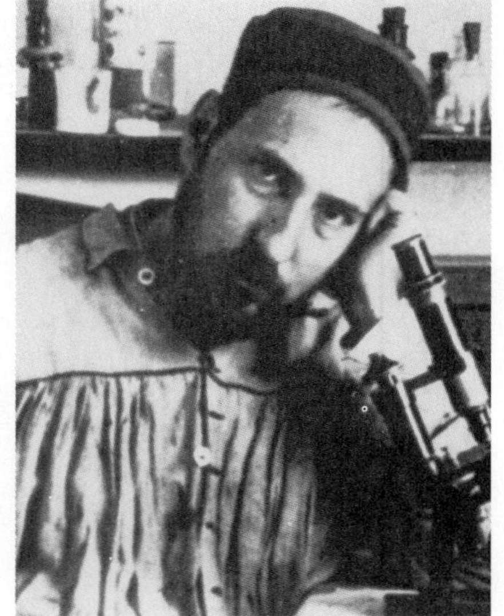

Santiago Ramón y Cajal

Biological Perspective

Psychologists have long been interested in the relationship between our psychological nature and our biological nature, particularly our brains. Spanish scientist Ramón y Cajal first identified *neurons*—the cells that make up the brain and nervous system—in the early 1900s. His view that the brain was made up of a network of interacting neural cells laid the foundation for our modern understanding of the role of the brain in psychology.

HUMAN DIVERSITY

Different, Yet the Same

It could be said that the theme of this book involves two opposite concepts. As I will say often throughout this book, all people are the same in some fundamentally important ways and yet different in other equally important ways. We are the sa me in the sense that a few basic principles of psychology apply equally to all of us. Your brain has the same working parts whether you are a woman of African-American descent who was raised in Costa Rica or a man of Swedish descent raised in Minneapolis. In the same sense, the principles of perception, motivation, learning, and personality also apply to all human beings. But people are also different from one another. Their gender, cultural heritage, age, sexual orientation, and unique experiences all contribute to these differences. What is your age, gender, and ethnic heritage? How well educated are the members of your family? What is your political philosophy and your sexual orientation? If all of these things about you were different, would you be a different person in any important ways? I am not asking if you would be a better or a worse person, because we are not talking of value judgments here. I am only asking if you would be psychologically different? Let's look at one aspect of the broader issue of human diversity as an example—being a parent. Do you think that, in general, men and women have the same feelings about becoming a parent? Do people of different cultures have different feelings about children?

The answer, of course, is that men and women of different cultures are similar in many ways in their feelings about being a parent, and different in other ways. Understanding the ways in which people differ is an essential part of psychology. Why, then, is most of the content of this psychology textbook about the ways in which people are the same? If you look ahead over the chapters in this book, you will see that they are about the basic principles that apply equally to all of us. Almost all textbooks of basic psychology are set up in the same way, because the goal of this course is to teach you basic principles of psychology that will broaden your perspective on the human experience in a general way.

Recently, however, many psychologists—myself included—have come to believe that the basic course in psychology overemphasizes the ways in which people are the same and neglects the important message that the human race comes in a rainbow of varieties. In every edition of this book, I have discussed the differences among human beings, especially in the chapters on learning, development, personality, and social psychology. But, in this edition, a new boxed feature termed ***Human Diversity*** will appear in every chapter to further counteract the false impression that all human beings are the same in the eyes of psychology. These boxed statements will explore differences related to gender, ethnicity, age, physical disability, and other factors.

Therefore, it would be fair to say that this text takes a "sociocultural" approach, as described in this chapter. As you read this text, please keep in mind that human diversity is discussed in every chapter to help us understand the broad natural range of differences in human beings. Those differences are never discussed in evaluative terms, but simply as elements of the human condition. While it will be said, for example, that males and females are different in some ways, those differences will never be taken to mean that one gender is superior to the other. The same holds for differences associated with ethnic groups and all other sociocultural factors.

Psychologists who approach the science from a *biological perspective* are interested in the areas of the brain that play roles in emotion, reasoning, speaking, and other psychological processes. They are seeking to determine the extent to which our psychological characteristics such as intelligence and emotional stability are influenced by heredity. Biological psychologists study the chemical substances that carry messages in the nervous system from one neuron to another, and they examine how some drugs, such as cocaine and marijuana, alter the action of these important brain chemicals. Similarly, biological psychologists conduct experiments on the role of hormones in the regulation of behavior.

Enormous progress has been made in unraveling the functions of the nervous system, heredity, and the hormonal systems, but understanding the connection between the brain and behavior is a problem that dwarfs any other problem facing science in its scale. The complexity of the brain alone is almost too staggering to comprehend. Its 100 billion neurons form more than 100 *trillion* connections with other neurons. Since each of these connections can be either active or inactive at any moment in time, that means there are

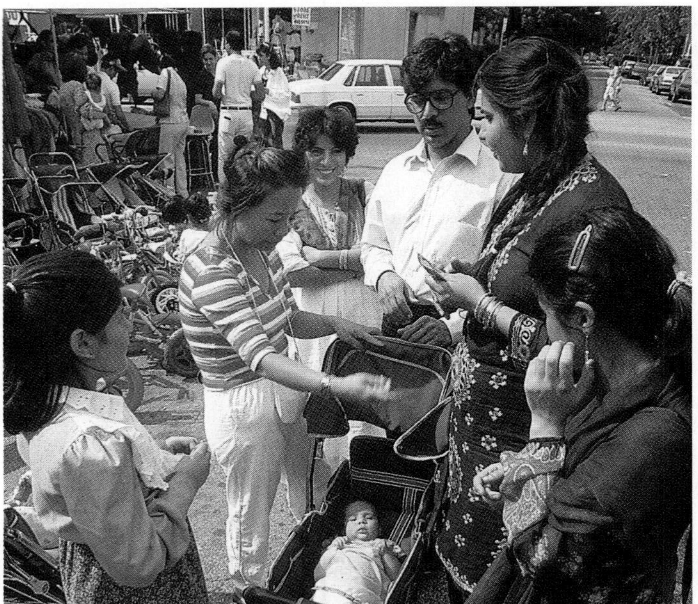

Ethnic identity refers to each person's sense of belonging to a particular ethnic group and sharing that group's beliefs, attitudes, skills, music, ceremonies, and the like.

far more possible states of a single human brain than the estimated total number of all of the electrons and protons in all of the atoms in the universe (Sagan, 1979)! We have just scratched the surface of this fascinatingly complex subject.

Sociocultural Perspective

An important perspective on psychology that has emerged in psychology in recent years is termed the **sociocultural perspective.** Like social learning theory, the sociocultural approach is based on the assumption that our personalities, beliefs, attitudes, and skills are learned from others. The sociocultural approach goes further, however, in stating that it is impossible to fully understand a person without understanding her or his culture, ethnic identity, gender identity, and other important sociocultural factors (Phinney, 1996).

For example, we are all shaped by our culture and must be understood in that context. **Culture** is defined as the patterns of behavior, beliefs, and values that are shared by a group of people. Culture includes everything—from language and superstitions to moral beliefs and food preferences—that we learn from the people with whom we live. When I worked in Miami for three years, I met many persons who were born in Cuba and had moved to the United States. They brought with them all of the beliefs, attitudes, and ways of Cuban culture, but they are now part of the culture of the United States. To fully understand my Miami friends, you would need to understand the ways in which Cuban and U.S. cultures are similar and different and how each has influenced their lives.

sociocultural perspective
The theory of psychology that states that it is necessary to understand one's culture, ethnic identity, and other sociocultural factors to fully understand a person.

culture
The patterns of behavior, beliefs, and values shared by a group of people.

ethnic group
A group of persons who are descendants from a common group of ancestors.

ethnic identity
Each person's sense of belonging to a particular ethnic group.

In addition, we must all be understood in terms of our ethnic group and ethnic identity. An **ethnic group** is a group of persons who are descendants from a common group of ancestors, usually from a particular country or area. **Ethnic identity** refers to each person's sense of belonging to a particular ethnic group and sharing that group's beliefs, attitudes, skills, music, ceremonies, and the like. Members of less powerful ethnic groups in any given country also often share a history of discrimination and repression by more powerful ethnic groups.

Members of a given ethnic group often share similar racial characteristics. Knowing a person's race is often less informative than knowing his or her ethnic identity, however. For example, my friend Maria is an immigrant to the United States from San Salvador. She grew up speaking Spanish and learned English only after moving to the United States as a teenager. She sees herself as a Hispanic, but she is of African descent and also identifies strongly with her fellow African Americans. Her racial heritage, then, reveals only part of her sense of ethnic identity. To take another example, my friend Barbara says that three of her grandparents are white, and one is African American. In racial terms, she is not mostly of African descent, but she was raised by her parents in a mostly African-American neighborhood in Los Angeles and proudly considers herself to be an African American. In the case of both of these women, understanding their ethnic identity will lead to more understanding of them as persons than just knowing their race.

gender identity
One's view of oneself as male or female.

A third term that is important to the sociocultural perspective is **gender identity.** This term refers to one's view of oneself as male or female. As boys and girls interact with their parents, siblings, teachers, and friends, they learn what it means to be a male or female in their society. In the United States, for example, males traditionally have been taught to be strong and assertive, whereas females have been taught to be nurturing and gentle. And although strides have been made in recent years to reduce the shaping of the two genders into narrow sex roles, the impact of socialization of this sort has had an impact on each of our gender identities.

According to the sociocultural perspective, all of us can be fully understood only if our culture, ethnic identity, and gender identity are taken into consideration. Other sociocultural factors must be considered as well. For example, gay men and lesbian women have identities as homosexuals that shape their lives. Similarly, women and men who have integrated a feminist perspective into their lives must be understood partly in that context. Any social or cultural force that influences human lives is important to the sociocultural perspective.

The sociocultural perspective not only encourages us to consider cultural and social factors when attempting to understand a neighbor or coworker but also requires that we not *misuse* that information. Two aspects of this perspective are particularly relevant to our discussion. First, the sociocultural perspective promotes **cultural relativity.** Although virtually every culture in the world views other cultures as inferior to themselves (Triandis, 1991), the sociocultural perspective encourages us to think of different cultures in *relative* terms rather than judgmental terms. That is, the sociocultural perspective promotes the view that different cultures, ethnic groups, genders, and sexual orientations are simply *different* rather than one being inferior to another. Indeed, the sociocultural perspective encourages us to view differences among persons in our diverse world as rich sources of new ideas and ways of coping with the demands of human life.

cultural relativity
The perspective that promotes thinking of different cultures in relative terms rather than judgmental terms.

Second, the sociocultural perspective reminds us that not all members of a given culture, ethnic group, or gender are *alike*. Some Asian men, for example, are tall and some are short; some are good at mathematics and some are as poor in math as I am. The same is true of any sociocultural group. On most characteristics (moral beliefs, interest in music, willingness to work hard in school, sports ability, etc.), there are usually more differences among persons within the same groups than between different groups.

The sociocultural perspective has become important in psychology in recent years, partly because psychologists who advise companies that conduct international business have been in great demand. This is because even small gestures and ways of speaking that would be perfectly acceptable in the United States can be insulting to members of another culture. For example, in the United States, we would expect an inventor who is presenting a new product to potential investors to make the new product seem very desirable (and to make the inventor seem brilliant). That approach might offend potential investors from Japan who are more used to hearing a presenter modestly play down the importance of the new product and even apologize for the inadequacies of the inventor (Kitayama & Markus, 1992).

But, although international business has given the sociocultural perspective its strongest push in psychology, the changing nature of Western world countries will continue to demand attention to this important new perspective. The United States is rapidly becoming a multicultural and multiethnic country. In 1989, 20 percent of all youth (up to 17 years of age) were members of minority ethnic groups. By the year 2000, that proportion will have grown to over 33 percent (Buenker & Ratner, 1992). If the United States is to continue to succeed and prosper, we must all learn to understand one another better and to extend more opportunity to groups that have been held at the bottom of the ladder by the kind of prejudice and discrimination that comes from lack of understanding.

Sociocultural Factors in the History of Psychology

Did you notice that most of the founders of psychology discussed earlier were white males? Key roles were played by women, African Americans, Hispanics, and others, but for many years the field of psychology was dominated by white males. Indeed, until recently the contributions of women and ethnic minorities were largely ignored when the founding of psychology was discussed in textbooks.

Laurel Furomoto and Elizabeth Scarborough (1986), Leonard Krasner (1988), and Ellen Kimmel (1992) have helped change our view of the role of women in the history of psychology by reminding us of some key facts. For example, although men greatly outnumbered women during the first 75 years of the profession, Christine Ladd-Franklin completed the doctoral program in psychology at Johns Hopkins in 1882 and was one of 10 women in the still new science to do so before 1900. However, women participated less in the development of psychology than men because sexual discrimination actively interfered with their ability to contribute. For example, although Christine Ladd-Franklin completed the doctoral program at Johns Hopkins, she was never given a degree because Johns Hopkins was an all-male institution at that time and would not grant her a degree.

Inez Prosser

Mamie and Kenneth Clark were among the first researchers to study African-American children.

George Sanchez

In the early days of psychology, it was extremely difficult for even the most qualified females to obtain admission to graduate programs, and when they did receive training, they were rarely offered teaching positions at the male-dominated institutions that had the best-equipped laboratories.

Furthermore, around the turn of the century a woman's decision to marry often meant the end of her career due to the then dominant stereotypes concerning a woman's role in the family. All of the early female psychologists who attained the rank of assistant professor or higher were unmarried. In describing the career of Dr. Ethel Puffer, Furomoto and Scarborough (1986) wrote, "In August 1908 she married an engineer, Benjamin Howes, at which point her career in psychology halted" (p. 41).

One unmarried woman who is recognized for her important contributions during the pioneering days of psychology is Mary Whiton Calkins. When I described the history of Mary Whiton Calkins earlier, I said that she was "a student of William James at Harvard University in the late 1800s." She completed the requirements for the Ph.D. at Harvard, but like Christine Ladd-Franklin, she was never awarded the degree. Like other all-male institutions, Harvard did not confer degrees on women at that time. Are you shocked and surprised that there was ever a time that universities felt that women should not receive Ph.D.s? You probably are well aware of the prejudice against women that still exists today and are not surprised by Calkins' experience—but I hope you care enough to be shocked nonetheless.

Similar prejudicial roadblocks slowed the entry of African Americans, Latins, and other ethnic minorities into psychology. Nevertheless, surprising numbers of dedicated individuals overcame the odds and became pioneers of the science of psychology. The first African American to be a professor of psychology in the United States was Gilbert Jones. Dr. Jones studied in Germany, where he obtained his Ph.D. in 1901 at the University of Jena. Inez Prosser was the first African-American woman to receive a Ph.D. in psychology in the United States. Prosser obtained her master's degree and taught for many years before receiving her Ph.D. in 1933 from the University of Cincinnati. Tragically, she was killed in an automobile accident shortly after receiving her degree. The landmark research by Mamie Phipps Clark and Kenneth Clark (1939) on the self-concept of African-American children provided the scientific basis for the *Brown v. Board of Education* decision by the U.S. Supreme Court that ruled that segregated school systems could no longer be considered to be "separate but equal." The research by the Clarks showed that legally barring minority group children from all-white schools implied to the segregated children that they were inferior. Thus, any segregated school system would be inherently unequal for the segregated ethnic group. In recognition of such research, Kenneth Clark was the first African American to be elected president of the American Psychological Association in 1971.

Similar important roles in psychology have also been played by Hispanics from the beginning. For example, more recently, George Sanchez's research discouraged the use of culturally biased tests for minority schoolchildren.

Although the number of women and ethnic minorities in psychology has grown dramatically in recent years, and all formal barriers against their entry into the field have long been dropped, prejudice still plays a negative role in psychology as in all scientific and professional fields (Howard et al., 1986). It is still the case that men greatly outnumber women at advanced academic ranks and in positions of authority, and it is still necessary to monitor the salaries of female psychologists to be sure that they receive equal pay for equal work. Furthermore, much remains to be done to provide child care and childbirth leave to facilitate the careers of women in psychology.

SPECIALTY AREAS OF MODERN PSYCHOLOGY

Psychology is, as we have seen, an unusually broad and diverse field. From the very beginnings of psychology, different founders studied different aspects of human behavior and declared their own theories and methods to be the correct way to look at psychology. Theoretical divisions still exist today, but the greatest diversity in modern psychology is in terms of subject-matter specialties. Even though a basic core of knowledge is shared by all psychologists, the interests and expertise of a psychologist who studies the sense of taste, for example, are quite distinct from one who evaluates employees in a large company for

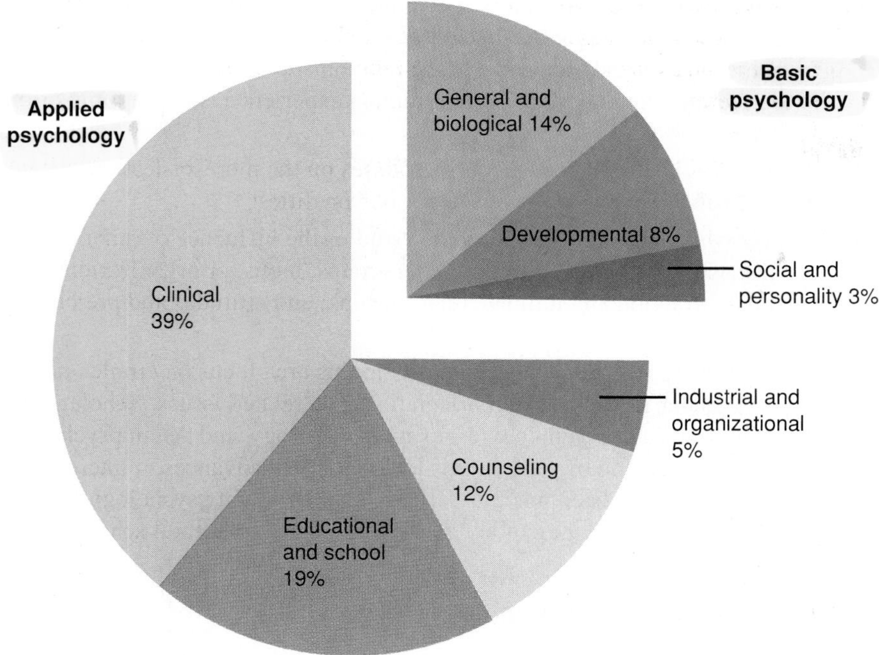

FIGURE 1.5

The percentage of psychologists engaged in each of the major basic and applied fields within psychology.

Source: Based on data from J. Stapp, et al., "Census of Psychological Personnel: 1983," in *American Psychologist,* 12:1317–1351. Copyright © 1985 by the American Psychological Association.

possible promotion to management positions, or one who works in a mental institution. Contemporary psychologists can be roughly divided into two groups: those who work in basic areas and those who work in applied areas of psychology (see fig. 1.5). Psychologists in the basic areas conduct research on psychological processes such as emotion, thinking, learning, prejudice, and gender identity by using the scientific methods described in the next section of this chapter. **Applied psychologists** use knowledge acquired by psychologists in the basic areas, and by their own applied research studies, to solve and prevent significant human problems such as emotional instability, marital difficulties, underachievement in school, and job dissatisfaction.

applied psychologist
A psychologist who uses knowledge of psychology to solve and prevent human problems.

Basic Areas of Modern Psychology

About one-fourth of all psychologists work in basic experimental areas of psychology (Stapp, Tucker, & VandenBos, 1985). They are broadly trained, but they tend to specialize in the study of a single psychological process. Most psychologists in the basic areas work in colleges and universities where they teach and conduct research, but some work in research institutions, government agencies, or other settings. Their domain is the basic knowledge of psychology on which all applications are built. The largest specialties within the basic experimental areas of psychology are as follows:

1. *Biological psychology.* Psychologists in this specialty field study the ways in which the nervous system and other organs provide the basis for behavior. Biological psychologists also study animal behavior, both to compare it to human behavior and to gain a better understanding of other species of animals.
2. *Sensation and perception.* This specialty is concerned with how the sense organs operate and how we interpret incoming sensory information in the process of perception.
3. *Learning and memory.* The ways in which we learn and remember new information, new skills, new habits, and new ways of relating to other people are studied in this specialty.
4. *Cognition.* Psychologists in this area are concerned with intelligent action: thinking, perceiving, planning, imagining, creating, dreaming, speaking, listening, and problem solving.
5. *Developmental psychology.* This field of psychology is concerned with changes that take place in people during their life span, as they grow from birth to old age.

6. *Motivation and emotion.* In this specialty, psychologists study the needs and states that activate and guide behavior, such as hunger, thirst, sex, the need for achievement, and the need to have relationships with others. The nature of the feelings and moods that color human experience is also a topic of this specialty.
7. *Personality.* The field of personality focuses on the more-or-less consistent ways of behaving that characterize our personalities.
8. *Social psychology.* This specialty area studies the influence of other people on our behavior: the behavior of people in groups, mobs, or organizations; interpersonal attraction and intimate relationships; and attitudes and prejudice toward others.
9. *Sociocultural psychology.* Psychologists in this area focus on ethnic and cultural factors, gender identity, sexual orientation, and related issues. Scholars in African-American psychology, Hispanic psychology, and Asian psychology have a long tradition of work in this area, but great advances in interest in other ethnic groups have been made in recent years. Feminist psychology and gay and lesbian psychology are other active areas of sociocultural scholarship.

Applied Areas of Modern Psychology

The other three-fourths of psychologists use basic psychological knowledge to solve human problems (see fig. 1.5). Some applied psychologists teach and do research, but most work in mental health centers, industries, school systems, medical centers, and other applied settings. The following are the major specialties within applied psychology:

1. *Clinical psychology.* Clinical psychologists try to understand and treat personal problems and correct abnormal behavior.
2. *Counseling psychology.* Specialists in this field help people with personal or school problems and with career choices.
3. *Industrial-organizational psychology.* This field focuses on ways to match employees to jobs, to train and motivate workers, and to promote job satisfaction and good relationships among workers.
4. *Educational and school psychology.* Educational psychology is concerned with the ways children learn in the classroom and with the construction of psychological and educational tests. School psychologists consult with teachers and about children who are experiencing learning or behavior problems, and they test children to see whether they could benefit from special educational programs.
5. *Health psychology.* Specialists in this field focus on the ways in which pressures, conflicts, hardships, and other factors may contribute to poor health. They seek to prevent health problems such as heart disease by teaching people to relax, exercise, control their diets, and stop high-risk behaviors such as smoking, for example.

The distinction between the basic and applied fields is not hard and fast. Often psychologists in the experimental fields work on important applied topics. For example, developmental psychologists work closely with the producers of the television program "Sesame Street" to be sure that the educational material is appropriate for young children. Social psychologists similarly work on applied topics such as helping businesses overcome prejudice based on gender or ethnicity in the workplace. There is something in psychology to interest or help just about everyone. If you glance ahead, you will see that the chapters of this book are organized to cover these experimental and applied facets of psychology.

Relationship Between Psychology and Psychiatry

Perhaps the question most often asked of a psychology instructor is, "What is the difference between a psychologist and a psychiatrist?" Although there are many similarities, there are numerous differences as well. A psychiatrist has completed medical school and has obtained the M.D. (doctor of medicine) degree, usually has done an internship in general medicine, and has completed residency training in psychiatry. Although some psychiatrists work as researchers, most are practitioners in clinics who see patients with emotional or behavioral problems. Because of their medical training, psychiatrists are licensed to prescribe drugs and use other medical treatments.

A psychologist has been trained in psychology but did not attend medical school. Psychology is a much broader field than psychiatry and contains many different specialty areas. The specialty within psychology that is most similar to psychiatry is clinical psychology. Clinical psychologists have attended graduate school in psychology and have obtained the degree of Ph.D. (doctor of philosophy) or Psy.D. (doctor of psychology) and have completed an internship in clinical psychology. Because they do not have medical training, they do not prescribe drugs or other medical treatments. On the other hand, a debate is currently going on among psychologists on a proposal to provide psychologists with enough additional training to allow them to prescribe psychiatric medications. It is too early to predict how this debate will turn out, but the topic is under intense discussion.

In addition to these professions, people with psychological problems often also seek help from clinical social workers, counselors, and other individuals. It is worth noting, however, that although nearly every state regulates the practice of clinical psychology, psychiatry, and clinical social work, most states do not regulate other helping professions. That means that persons with no training in psychology or any related field can advertise themselves as a "counselor" or "therapist" in many states. It's good advice, then, to ask about the training and professional background of anyone who is not licensed in her or his profession by the state.

Review

The sociocultural perspective emphasizes the need to understand persons in the context of the cultural, ethnic, and gender identities that shape their lives. In recent years a growth in the importance of the biological perspective has helped us better understand the relationship between the biological functioning of the brain and other parts of the body and our behavior and mental processes.

Generally, contemporary psychologists do not align themselves with a single theoretical position. Rather, they integrate the best contributions of each perspective into their own eclectic view. Although it is useful to study the different theoretical perspectives within psychology, it is also important to look at how psychologists divide the subject matter of psychology. Psychology can be divided into its basic areas, which use a variety of scientific methods to study psychological processes, and applied areas, which apply psychological knowledge to the solution of human problems. Each of these two major divisions of psychology can be further subdivided in terms of the specific subject matter studied or the kind of human problems to which the application is addressed.

Thinking Critically About Psychology

1. Which of the contemporary perspectives in psychology makes the most sense to you? Do any of these perspectives seem to have no value whatsoever?

2. Do you think that the ethnic identity or gender identity of a psychologist would influence the way in which she or he does research or counsels others? Should it?

3. In terms of helping solve an important social problem such as crime, which basic or applied area of psychology do you think is of the most importance?

Check Your Learning

To be sure that you have learned the key points from the preceding section, cover the answers below and try to answer each question. If you give an incorrect answer to any question, return to the page given next to the correct answer to see why your answer was not correct.

1. The approach that states that a person can be understood only in terms of her or his experiences related to culture, ethnicity, and gender that shape human lives is termed the

a. social learning theory.
b. cognitive perspective.
c. humanistic perspective.
d. sociocultural perspective.

2. The scientist who first discovered the neuron (individual nerve cell) in the brain was

a. B. F. Skinner.
b. Ivan Pavlov.
c. Santiago Ramón y Cajal.
d. Margaret Floy Washburn.

Check Your Learning—continued

3. The basic area of psychology that studies intimate relationships and prejudice is

   a. biological psychology.
   b. health psychology.
   c. counseling psychology.
   d. social psychology.

Correct Answers
1. d (p. 16), 2. c (p. 14), 3. d (p. 20).

SCIENTIFIC METHODS: HOW WE LEARN ABOUT BEHAVIOR AND MENTAL PROCESSES

As we discussed earlier, psychologists use scientific methods to describe, predict, understand, and influence behavior. But although it is easy to see how we might use the methods of science to study chemicals in a test tube, it is sometimes difficult to see how something as varied, complex, and apparently unpredictable as human behavior can be the subject matter of science. How can this be?

First, all scientists must believe that their subject matter is orderly and lawful before they begin their research. For example, if astronomers felt that the planets wandered aimlessly and randomly through space, they would have little reason to study their paths. The same is true of people. To have a science of psychology, we must believe that human behavior is at least somewhat predictable. Often, though, we see ourselves as capable of doing whatever we choose without being subject to the laws of nature. Although there may be some truth to that, psychologists believe that our behavior is much more orderly and predictable than most of us think.

I regularly begin teaching my own course in psychology with a disguised demonstration that human behavior is actually fairly predictable under some circumstances. It's a little corny, but it makes the point. After telling the students that I'm a very democratic fellow, I ask the class to decide how they want to be evaluated in the course. I tell them that I have to require a cumulative final examination, but that everything else is open to a vote! I give them the option of doing a term paper (to give them a way of being evaluated that is free from the pressure of classroom testing), and I also give them the options of having one, two, or three tests plus the final, or no tests plus the final. Then I take a vote.

In every class, a couple of students vote for the term paper (one student who writes well and one who thinks I'm too lazy to read the papers), but that option is always soundly defeated. A few students vote for no test or one test, and about 20 percent vote for two tests, but about three-quarters always choose three tests plus the final.

When the voting is over, I thank the students for their judicious decision and hand out the course syllabus. Then I point out that I correctly predicted their behavior—that 250 copies of the syllabus have already been printed that include no requirement of a term paper and give the dates of three tests plus the final examination. After the laughing, booing, and hissing have subsided, I say something like, "The science of psychology rests on the assumption that your behavior is a good deal more predictable than you might think. That's not to take anything away from the mysteries and complexities of human existence; it's just to say that we aren't immune to the laws of nature. We're predictable enough to study scientifically."

scientific methods
Methods of gathering information based on systematic observation.

In the sections that follow, we will briefly examine three general types of **scientific methods** used by psychologists—descriptive methods, correlational methods, and formal experiments. We will also examine some of the more specific strategies that psychologists employ in attempting to reach the goals of the science of psychology.

Descriptive Methods

As mentioned earlier, a number of rather different scientific methods are used in psychology, each with its own advantages and disadvantages. The different methods are best suited for answering different kinds of questions, so they tend to be relied upon to varying extent by individual specialties within psychology. The simplest methods of scientific inquiry involve description. Three descriptive methods are used in psychology: surveys, naturalistic observation, and the clinical method.

Survey Method

One of the most direct ways to answer a question about people is simply to ask the question of many people, called the **survey method.** Surveys are perhaps most widely used today by psychologists interested in consumer opinions about television programs, soft drinks, political candidates, and similar subjects. Surveys are frequently used for other purposes as well. For example, the myth-shattering surveys of sex researcher Alfred Kinsey (Kinsey, Pomeroy, & Martin, 1948) revealed that the number of people who engage in masturbation and extramarital intercourse was much higher in the general population than expected at the time.

survey method
A research method that utilizes interviews and questionnaires with individuals in the community.

A survey conducted by a group of researchers at the National Institute of Mental Health (Kasper, Wehr, Bartko, Gaist, & Rosenthal, 1989) provides another excellent example of the use of the survey method in psychology. Are you more likely to have bad moods during certain times of the year? Do they occur during the winter? A lot has been written in the popular press about "winter blahs" and "cabin fever"—periods of depression experienced during the short, cold days of the winter—but, until recently, there was little hard evidence to support this idea. These researchers conducted a random telephone survey of 416 persons living in Maryland and Virginia. They asked an adult in each household to name the month during which they "felt worst" during the past year. As shown in the top section of figure 1.6, there was a strong tendency for the winter months, particularly January and February, to be the times people reported that they felt worst. The bottom sections show that moods tend to be worse when the temperature is the lowest and the number of minutes of sunlight each day is the shortest. Keep in mind as you read about this study that it does not imply that everyone feels depressed during the winter. It simply suggests that more people feel lousy during the winter than during the summer.

The primary advantage of the survey method is that you can gather a great deal of information in a relatively short period of time. The main disadvantage is that the accuracy of

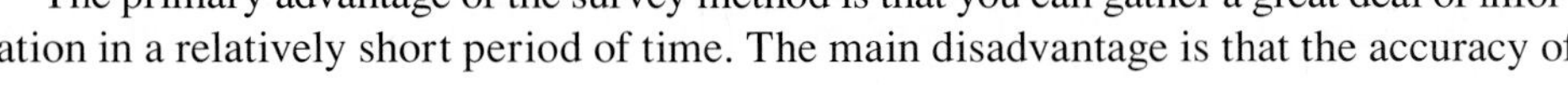

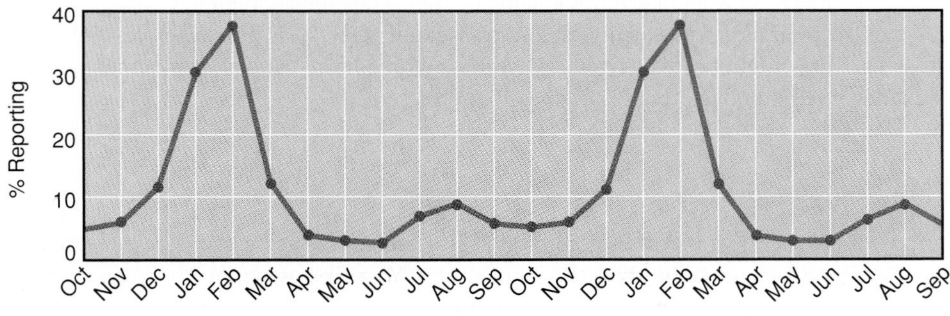

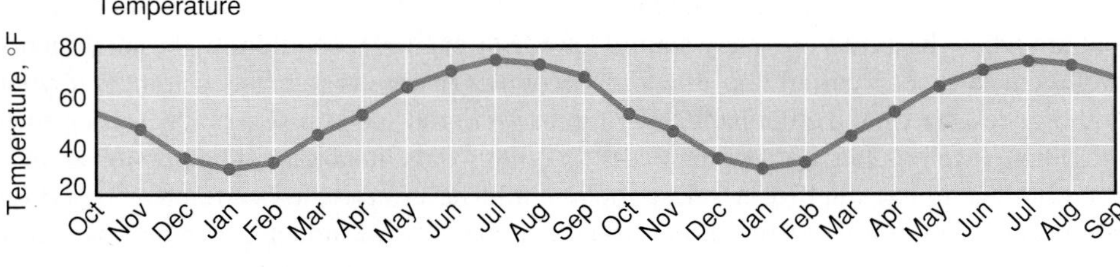

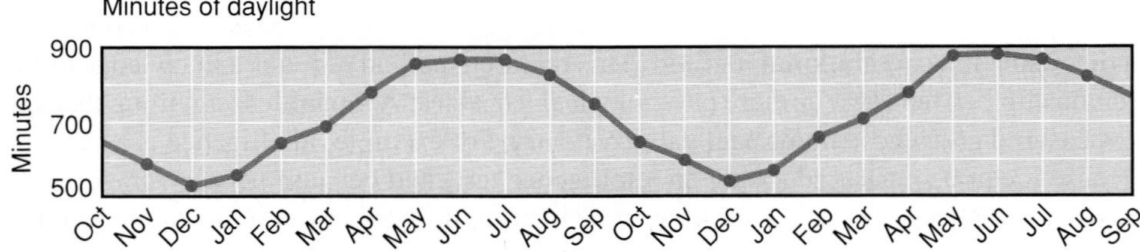

FIGURE 1.6

Results of a telephone survey of 416 adults living in Virginia and Maryland who were asked the month during which they "felt worst" during the previous year. The authors plotted the 12 months twice to show more clearly the seasonal patterns of depressed feeling.

Source: Data from S. Kasper, et al., "Epidemiological Findings of Seasonal Changes in Mood and Behavior" in *Archives of General Psychiatry,* 46–833.

Jane Goodall

information obtained in surveys may be questionable. We cannot always be sure that the answers are honest, especially to questions about such sensitive topics as sex and drug use.

Naturalistic Observation

Another straightforward way to learn about behavior is simply to watch and describe it as it naturally occurs. The careful observation and recording of behavior in real-life settings is called **naturalistic observation.** When internationally known scientist Jane Goodall goes to Africa, sits down in the jungle, and watches a troop of apes, she is using the method of naturalistic observation. She watches the apes in their natural habitat over long periods of time, taking careful notes of what she sees until specific patterns of behavior become evident. Using this method, she and her coworkers have learned that the social behavior and use of some tools by apes is often strikingly similar to that of humans. Sadly, she has discovered that apes are also capable of murder—ambushing and killing other apes over relatively minor incidents in a way that looks "intentional."

The method of naturalistic observation is not restricted to the study of animal behavior. It's a method also used to study such topics as the play and friendship patterns of young children, the leadership tactics of effective business managers, and the ways in which juvenile delinquents encourage antisocial behavior in one another.

"Don't shush me—and I don't care if she IS writing in her little notebook; just tell me where you were last night!"

Clinical Method

An important variation on naturalistic observation is the **clinical method,** which simply involves observing people while they receive help from a psychologist for their psychological problems. Although clinical observation is not as useful as observing people in the natural situations where they encounter problems—at home, school, or work—it does provide useful information. Sigmund Freud, for example, developed his theories of abnormal behavior from years of intensive work with patients in his "consulting room." He was able to observe their behavior in this one situation over long periods of time until he felt he saw consistent patterns in what they did, thought, and felt. The clinical method is also often used today for the preliminary evaluation of clinical treatment methods. For example, daily measures of anxiety might be taken on an individual before, during, and after treatment to evaluate a new method of treating excessive anxiety.

Correlational Methods

Suppose that a few years after graduation, you are asked to be the vice-president in charge of sales for a major toothbrush manufacturer. Your first assignment is to hire a group of new sales representatives to do something that has never been tried—to sell toothbrushes in little booths in shopping malls. You want to choose the best sales personnel, but you are not sure what characteristics they should have. For example, should they be intelligent? Intelligent salespeople might be able to think of clever ways to interest customers in your toothbrushes, but on the other hand, they might get bored spending every day selling such a commonplace product in shopping malls. In other words, it would not be possible to predict whether highly intelligent salespeople would be effective or ineffective based on commonsense reasoning. What should you do? You need to conduct a correlational study to see whether you can predict good sales performance on the basis of high intelligence.

Being able to predict behavior and mental processes is the goal of psychological studies using the **correlational method.** This research method requires a knowledge of the relationship between two or more psychological variables. A **variable** is anything that can be measured and whose numerical value can vary. For example, intelligence is a variable because it can be measured (using an intelligence test) and because people vary in intelligence. Similarly, sales effectiveness can be measured, in this case, in terms of the number of toothbrushes sold. You would conduct your correlational study simply by measuring

naturalistic observation
A research method based on recording behavior as it occurs in natural life settings.

clinical method
The method of studying people while they are receiving psychological help from a psychologist.

correlational method
(kor´´ĕlā´shun-al)
A research method that measures the strength of the relation between variables.

variable
A factor whose numerical value can change.

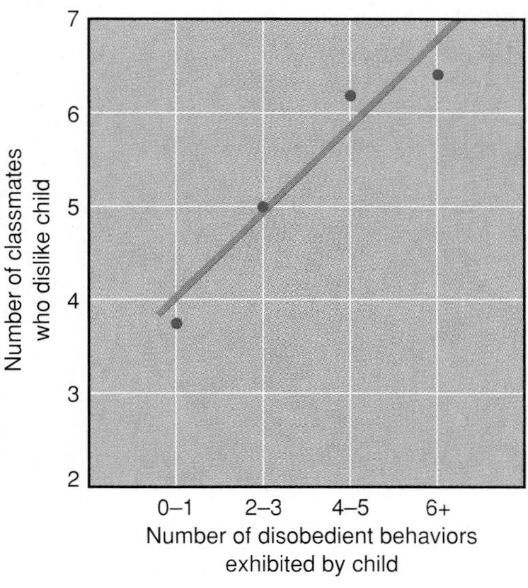

FIGURE 1.7

Example of a correlational study. Children who engage in more disobedient behaviors (fighting, lying, stealing, etc.) tend to be disliked by more of their classmates.

the intelligence of a number of salespeople and by measuring the number of toothbrushes each sold. You might find that salespeople with higher intelligence scores would be found to sell more toothbrushes. Because many other factors probably also influence sales performance (e.g., attractiveness, sense of humor, and emotional stability), its relationship to intelligence would not be a perfect one, but it might be strong enough to be useful. If so, you would want to hire mostly highly intelligent salespeople. But how strong does the correlation need to be to be useful? Mathematicians have developed a quantified way of expressing the strength of the relationship called the **coefficient of correlation** that is useful in evaluating correlations (see the appendix on statistics beginning on p. 593).

coefficient of correlation
The numerical expression of the strength of a relationship between two variables.

Let's look at an actual example of the use of the correlational method from my own research. As part of a larger study of the origins of juvenile delinquency, we wanted to test the commonsense notion that elementary schoolchildren who are disobedient are disliked by their classmates. The correlation between these two variables is shown in figure 1.7. As you can see, children who have more serious behavior problems (fighting, lying, stealing, etc.) tend to be disliked by more of their classmates. So, not surprisingly, having behavior problems is correlated to a considerable extent with being disliked by your peers.

When interpreting correlational data, we must remember that a relationship between two variables does not mean that one causes the other. The correlation between behavior problems and unpopularity may mean that having behavior problems leads other children to dislike the disobedient child, but it could also mean that being unpopular is so upsetting to some children that it leads them to develop behavior problems. Correlations tell us very little about which variable is the cause in cause-and-effect relationships. In fact, correlations often exist between two variables that are not causally related at all. For example, it could be that having abusive parents causes children to be both disobedient and unpopular, but that disobedience and unpopularity are not causally related to each other. We must be very careful about drawing conclusions from correlational evidence.

Formal Experiments

The most useful scientific method of observation is the **formal experiment.** Experiments are particularly helpful in reaching the goals of understanding and influencing behavior. Like the correlational method, experiments are designed to tell us about the relationship between two or more variables. Unlike other methods, however, the experiment involves deliberate arrangement of the variables involved. And unlike correlational methods, a carefully conducted experiment allows the researcher to draw conclusions about cause-and-effect relationships with more confidence.

formal experiment
Research method that allows the researcher to manipulate the independent variable to study its effect on the dependent variable.

FIGURE 1.8

Example of a formal experiment. The percentage of pedestrians who stopped to help a man with an arm cast who had dropped his books is compared under conditions of low and high noise.

Source: Data for graph from K. E. Mathews and L. K. Cannon, in *Journal of Personality and Social Psychology,* 32:571–577, 1975.

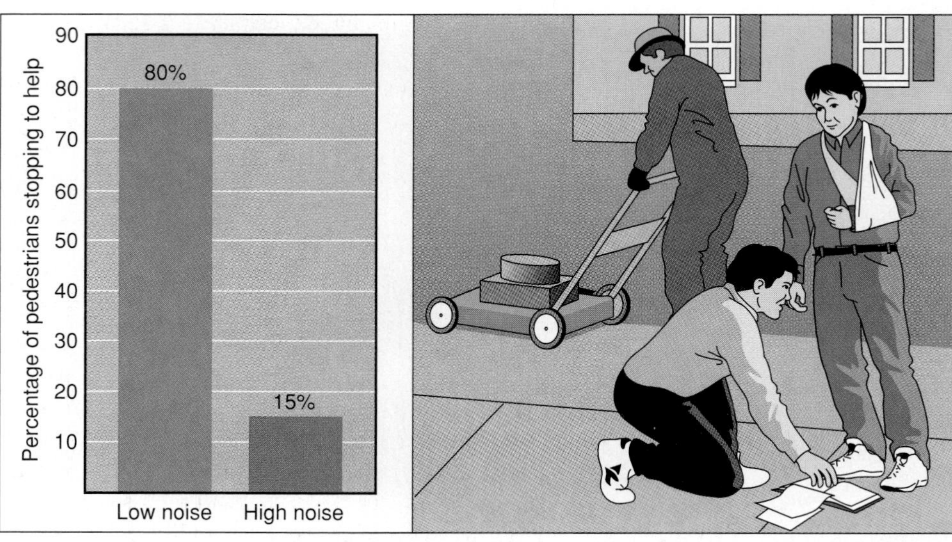

quantitative measures
(kwon´ti-tā-tiv) Capable of being measured in numerical terms.

The heart of an experiment is the comparison of **quantitative measures** of behavior under different conditions. For example, we have all heard about the supposedly damaging effects of "noise pollution." Do high levels of noise have a negative effect on our behavior and mental processes? Two psychologists (Mathews & Canon, 1975) conducted a simple, but very informative, study to shed experimental light on this question. They examined the effects of high levels of noise on one of the more admirable aspects of human behavior—our tendency to help others when they are in need. In this experiment, a person wearing a cast on his arm emerged from a car and dropped a large pile of books in front of a pedestrian. If you were the pedestrian, would you have stopped to help him pick up his books? You might not have if there had been a lot of noise in the background. Remember, the purpose of an experiment is to compare measures of helping behavior under different levels of noise. In this case, the number of people who stopped to help was compared under conditions of high noise (when a lawn mower without a muffler was running) or low noise (when no lawn mower was running). Figure 1.8 illustrates the results of this study. When there was little noise in the background, over five times as many pedestrians stopped to help the fellow with the broken arm than when there was a high noise level.

Another good example of formal experiments comes from researchers at the National Institute of Mental Health. Do you remember the survey study discussed previously that shows that more people become depressed during the short, cold days of the winter than during other seasons? The same group of researchers conducted a formal experiment to confirm the results of their survey. They identified individuals who experienced severe depression during the winter and divided them into two groups. Both groups were asked to go about their normal daily activities in the presence of bright light from bulbs (placed about three feet away) that duplicated the full spectrum of natural daylight. One group stayed in the light for two hours per day while the other group received five hours of light per day. The improvements in mood were significantly greater for the group receiving five hours of bright artificial sunlight, suggesting that winter blahs may result from the short period of daylight during the winter and the tendency for people to stay indoors (Kasper et al., 1989). Some persons can apparently avoid being depressed each winter with such therapy.

An important advantage of formal experiments is that they allow us to control the influence of variables other than those on which the experiment focuses. The goal is to eliminate all explanations for differences between the groups except the relevant one. This was accomplished in the study of noise levels by not changing anything in the two conditions except the amount of noise and in the winter depression study by varying only the amount of light that the two groups received.

dependent variable
The variable whose quantitative value depends on the effects of the independent variable.

independent variable
The variable whose quantitative value can be independently controlled by the researcher.

The number of people who stopped to help in the experiment on noise is termed the **dependent variable** because its value depends on the effects of the noise. The amount of noise is the **independent variable,** because the experimenter can independently control it. In the study of the effects of light on winter depression, the independent variable was the amount of light given to each group, and the dependent variable was the ratings of their mood provided by the participants in the two groups. All formal experiments have at least one independent and one dependent variable.

In the simplest experiments, one group receives none of the independent variable and is called the **control group.** The group that receives the independent variable is called the **experimental group.** Often there is more than one experimental group (the researchers at the National Institute of Mental Health could have given three experimental groups 2, 4, or 6 hours of bright light), and sometimes there is more than one control group designed to rule out different alternative explanations for the results of the study.

control group
The group in simple experiments that receives none of the independent variable and is used for comparisons with the treatment group.

experimental group
The group in an experiment that receives some value of the independent variable.

Through the logic and control of experiments, it's possible to test hypotheses about causal relationships. That is the primary advantage of formal experiments over other scientific methods. For all their utility, however, experiments also have their drawbacks. First and foremost, all experiments require some degree of artificiality. Remember that experiments allow the researcher to create and control conditions. In doing so, scientists risk creating experiments that are so artificial that the findings are difficult to apply to the real world, or they may even be entirely inapplicable. For example, the results of studies of crowding due to overpopulation in which college students are crowded into small rooms for an hour may not have much relevance to the long-term effects of crowded urban living conditions.

Second, experiments can also lead us to believe that because a scientist conducted them, the conclusions are necessarily valid. Experiments are complicated affairs and even the best experimenters make errors. We should be careful when evaluating experimental conclusions to question the logic, control, and relevance of the experiment. Finally, the power of formal experiments often leads us to reject the other scientific methods. Each method is valid within its restrictions and weaknesses. Psychology, like all sciences, depends on a blend of scientific methods and a healthy skepticism about their results.

Ethical Principles of Research

Psychological research is conducted to advance knowledge and improve the lives of all living things. It is a noble goal, but not so noble that any method of conducting research would be justifiable. To be considered ethical, research conduct on humans and animals must follow the ethical principles described in the next two sections.

Ethics of Research with Human Participants

Psychology depends heavily on research conducted with human participants for its database. But while researchers have an obligation to collect meaningful information through research, they also have an ethical responsibility to protect the welfare of their participants. Often the ethics of research with humans pose complicated issues for the researcher—issues that do not have simple solutions. As a human being, and especially as one who may be asked to serve as a participant in psychological research, you may wish to review some of the key ethical issues involved in psychological research with humans. A more complete discussion of these issues can be found in the American Psychological Association's Ethical Principles in the Conduct of Research with Human Participants (1982).

1. *Freedom from Coercion.* It's not ethical to coerce or pressure an individual into participating in an experiment. Students in college courses, for example, cannot be required to participate. They must be given an alternative way to meet any course requirement. Similarly, it would be considered unethical to offer strong special consideration in parole hearings to prisoners who volunteer to participate in psychological studies, since the promise of special considerations might constitute undue coercion.
2. *Informed Consent.* The experimenter must, under most circumstances, give potential participants a full description of the experiment in language they can understand before they are asked to participate. It's not ethical to allow individuals to participate in an experiment without knowing what they are getting into. Furthermore, once the experiment has begun, it must be made clear to participants that they are fully free to change their minds and withdraw from the

experiment without penalty, such as embarrassment, loss of course credit, and so on.

3. *Limited Deception.* Sometimes it's necessary to conduct experiments without the participant's knowing the true purpose of the study. For example, chapter 15 discusses a study in which individuals were asked to make judgments about the relative lengths of three lines after other individuals (actually employees of the experimenter who were acting out parts of the experiment) had given an obviously wrong answer. The question was, would the real participants give the wrong answer, too, under these conditions? Obviously, it was necessary to deceive the participants into thinking that the other individuals really believed their erroneous judgments about the lines. Is it ethical to deceive participants in this manner? The current guidelines suggest that deceptions can be used only if two conditions are met. First, the potential participants must be told everything they could reasonably be expected to need to know to make an informed decision about participation. That is, the deception can only involve aspects of the study that do not influence the decision to participate. Second, the nature of the deception must be fully revealed to individuals immediately after their participation in the experiment. Only under these conditions is it considered ethical to deceive research participants.
4. *Adequate Debriefing.* Research participants have a right to know the results of the study. Current practice dictates that all persons be provided with a summary of the study in language they can understand. If the results are not immediately available, the participants have a right to receive it when it is available.
5. *Confidentiality.* Researchers have an obligation to keep everything that they learn about the research participant absolutely confidential. This means that data from the study must be published in a way that protects the anonymity of the participants (no names or detailed descriptions of individuals). In addition, data must be stored without names attached in most cases to protect against future abuses of the information.

These are not all of the ethical issues raised by psychological research with humans, but they are some of the major ones. All institutions where research is conducted now require that proposals for human experimentation be approved by a board of other scientists to protect individuals from potential abuses.

Ethics of Research with Animal Subjects

The use of animals in research has received a great deal of public attention in recent years due to the activities of animal rights groups.

A great deal of research is also carried out using nonhuman animals as subjects. Why would some psychologists study animals when they could be studying people? There are a number of important reasons why psychologists study animal behavior.

Some kinds of studies are conducted using animals because it would be unethical to do the research to humans. Studies of the brain, for example, sometimes require surgically removing a part of the brain to discover its precise role in behavior. For similar reasons, studies in which infants are isolated from all social contact to study the absence of parental and peer relationships on development must be conducted with animals rather than humans. Although we must be very careful not to assume automatically that what is learned about animal behavior will apply to human behavior, much useful information has been learned from animal research.

In addition, it's possible to conduct experiments that are far more precisely controlled if we use animals rather than humans. A researcher can know and control almost every detail of a laboratory animal's life from birth: its environment, diet, and social experiences. This makes it possible to control a multiplicity of factors that must be left uncontrolled when using humans.

A great deal can be learned also by comparing the behavior of animals of different species. For example, a number of insights about human aggression have come from studies of aggression in other animal species. Similarly, much has been learned about the brain structures involved in sleep by identifying animals who have differing sleep patterns and comparing the evolutionary development of the sleep centers in these different species.

Furthermore, many psychologists study animal behavior not to learn about humans but to learn more about other animal species. If we are going to protect endangered species, we must understand their patterns of behavior. We must know, for example, how an endangered species hunts, mates, and raises its young before we can protect its ability to survive.

As with human participants, a number of principles govern the ethical conduct of research with animal subjects in psychology. Research with animals is considered ethical by the American Psychological Association only when all of the following conditions are met:

1. *Necessity.* Studies of animals are considered to be ethical only when they are necessary to significantly advance the understanding of human or animal behavior and mental processes.
2. *Health.* All animal subjects must be cared for in a manner that ensures good health.
3. *Humane treatment.* Every effort must be made to minimize the discomfort of the animal subject. Necessary surgery must be performed under anesthesia, and the animal's death must be as painless as possible. Studies that inflict pain or stress are considered ethical only when they are considered essential to worthwhile scientific aims.

The use of animals in research has received a great deal of public attention in recent years due to the activities of animal rights groups. Humans have long been concerned with the protection of their fellow animals, however. The Society for the Prevention of Cruelty to Animals was founded in 1824 in London, for example, and the American Psychological Association formed its Committee on Precautions in Animal Experimentation in 1925 (Dewsbury, 1990). Today, oversight committees at all research universities closely monitor all uses of laboratory animals. For more on this subject, see the American Psychological Association's Behavioral Research with Animals (1993).

Review

Psychology is a science, which means that it uses scientific methods to gather information and test ideas. Psychologists acquire new information through carefully controlled methods of observation. Although they are many and varied, scientific methods are all based on the assumption that behavior is lawful and orderly and capable of being understood in scientific terms. Each scientific method has different advantages and disadvantages and is best suited to answering different types of questions. The simplest scientific methods are descriptive methods. Information that allows us to describe a psychological phenomenon can be gathered by asking questions about it in surveys, by observing it in natural settings, or through extensive experience with it in clinical cases. When the scientific question concerns the relationship between two variables, correlational methods are often used. Both variables are measured quantitatively and the relationship between the two is noted; however, it's not possible to determine from such information whether one variable causes the other to change. To determine whether cause-and-effect relationships exist, formal experiments must be conducted.

In formal experiments, scientists rigorously control the conditions of the experiment so that only one explanation for the results is likely. In the simplest experiments, one factor—the independent variable—is artificially manipulated by the experimenter to see what effect it has on another variable—the dependent variable. Often one group of participants—the control group—receives none of the independent variable, whereas the independent variable is present in another group—the experimental group. In a study of the effects of alcohol on the memory of a list of words, for example, the alcohol is the independent variable. Alcohol is given to participants in the experimental group and not given to those in the control group, so its effects on the dependent variable, memory of the list, can be determined.

While it's important to conduct psychological research using humans, it's essential that we protect the rights of participants. Individuals must not be coerced in any way into participating and must be informed about the nature of the study before they are asked for their consent to participate. Research participants may be deceived about a study only if (1) the

Thinking Critically About Psychology

1. In what ways is conducting research in psychology similar to conducting research in other scientific fields, such as biology and chemistry? How is it different?

2. Even though research using animals has produced many beneficial results, not everyone agrees that it should be allowed. How do you think we should balance the rights of animals against the benefits to human society?

Review—continued

information withheld is not relevant to their decision to participate, and (2) they are informed about the true nature of the study immediately after it's over. Furthermore, the experimenter has an obligation to keep all information learned about the participant in an experiment confidential. Research with animal subjects is similarly considered to be ethical only when (1) the research is necessary, (2) the health of the animal is protected, and (3) pain and suffering are minimized.

Check Your Learning

To be sure that you have learned the key points from the preceding section, cover the answers below and try to answer each question. If you give an incorrect answer to any question, return to the page given next to the correct answer to see why your answer was not correct.

1. The basis of all scientific methods is systematic ____________________ .

2. A study of the relationship between intelligence scores and the number of illegal acts committed by teenagers would use which method?

a. naturalistic
b. clinical
c. correlational
d. formal experimental

3. The scientific method that allows the researcher to reach the strongest conclusions about cause and effect is

a. naturalistic.
b. clinical.
c. correlational.
d. formal experimental.

4. Research on humans is considered to be ethical only when the following five conditions are met:

1. ____________________
2. ____________________
3. ____________________
4. ____________________
5. ____________________

Correct Answers

1. observation (p. 22), **2.** c (p. 25), **3.** d (p. 25), **4.** absence of coercion, informed consent, limited deception, adequate debriefing, and confidentiality (p. 27).

WHAT WE KNOW ABOUT HUMAN BEHAVIOR: SOME STARTING PLACES

Now that we have looked at the origins of psychology, discussed the different beginnings of modern psychology around the turn of the century, reviewed psychology's basic assumptions and scientific methods, and surveyed its different theories and areas of specialization, we are ready to begin talking about the substance of psychology. The diversity in this large field is striking. Nevertheless, psychology is a unified science with many shared assumptions and beliefs. Lest we overemphasize the diversity within the field, let's identify some ideas that all psychologists have in common besides their history and scientific methods.

I have prepared a list of the most important things that contemporary psychologists "know" about human lives. This is not a list of universally accepted "truths." Since psychologists are known for their tendency to disagree with one another, there are sure to be differences of opinion about this or any other similar list. My intent, though, is to come as close as possible to a summary of the most important concepts that all psychologists share. These are educated guesses as to the "true nature" of human beings as seen from the perspective of the science of psychology. There are no questions to check your learning at the end of this section. It is designed to organize your thinking about this course rather than to give you facts to memorize. Because it forms the foundation for the rest of the course, however, it is an important section that should be read carefully and thought about.

1. *Human beings are biological creatures.* We take our biological nature so much for granted that we often do not realize how much it influences our behavior. We experience emotional highs and lows because of the way part of our nervous system is constructed. We spend much of our time preparing and eating food to satisfy the needs of our cells for energy. But even though our biology determines our behavior to a great extent, the limits it places on us are elastic; that is, we can stretch them. The muscles given to us by heredity can be strengthened through exercise. Our native intelligence can be stretched by a stimulating home environment. We can build airplanes to fly and aqualungs for breathing underwater to overcome physical limitations. Although creatures of our biological nature, we are not rigidly programmed by it.

2. *Every person is different, yet much the same.* Every human being is truly unique. With the exception of identical twins, each person's heredity is unique, even compared with one's own family members. And each person's experiences are different from anyone else's. It's inevitable that we should differ from one another in significant ways, and perhaps almost as inevitable that psychologists would devote much of their time to studying the ways in which our personalities, intellects, and interests differ. Differences are a normal part of life that greatly interest psychologists.

   Yet as members of the human race, we are similar in our capacities to think, feel, remember, and so on. Thus it's possible to have a single science of human psychology. If we were not alike in human qualities, we would have to develop a different psychology for each person. Fortunately, we are enough alike to be understood using one science of psychology, yet different enough to be interesting.

3. *People can be understood fully only in the context of their culture, ethnic identity, and gender identity.* We are shaped by our learning experiences with other members of our culture. Our beliefs about right and wrong, our food preferences, our language, religious beliefs, and many other facets of our lives come from cultural learning experiences. Among the most important things that we learn from others is our understanding of what it means to be male or female and a member of our own ethnic group. It is impossible to understand a person fully without understanding the sociocultural forces (such as culture, ethnicity, and gender) that influence them.
4. *Human lives are a continuous process of change.* From birth to death, humans are changing, developing organisms. We grow from helpless infancy through the time of playing with toys, through the time of adult work and rearing children, to the age of retirement. Change is almost

continuous; standing still is rare in human lives. Much of this developmental change is inevitably the result of our biological nature: Unless the process is disturbed, all creatures must grow from infancy to old age. Other aspects of change come from our experiences in life. Every time we learn a new concept from a college course, make a new friend, or adjust to a tragedy in our life, we change in some way.

These changes are usually so gradual that they slip by unnoticed. But the next time you ask yourself the question "Who am I?" remember that the answer you give today will be different from the answer you will give tomorrow. This is not to say that nothing stays constant in our personalities over time—I feel as strongly about prejudice as an adult as I did as a teenager—but change is an enormously important aspect of human life.

5. *Behavior is motivated.* Human behavior is not aimless. Rather, most of our actions can be viewed as attempts to meet our needs. We work to earn money for food, shelter, and clothing. We go on dates for companionship and perhaps to satisfy our sexual needs. We tell a joke at a party because of the sweet feeling of approval that laughter brings. However, all of our motives are not simple and selfish. Some of us are willing to spend long hours tutoring children with physical challenges just to see the joy of accomplishment in the children's faces. Others are internally motivated to express themselves in a painting or poem.

   Most basic motives (i.e., for food, warmth, companionship, sex) are shared by all people and seem to be part of our biological makeup. Other motives vary among different cultures and seem to be learned from others. For example, in some cultures most people want to be rich, famous, and important, whereas in other cultures most people try to avoid anything that will make them stand out from others in the community. Regardless of their origins, motives are important forces that guide our lives.

6. *Behavior has multiple causes.* The question "Why did I do that?" rarely has a single answer. Behavior can be influenced by many factors, and it is usually influenced by many of them at once. Think about the factors that went into your decision to go to the restaurant up the street for something to eat at 10:30 P.M. last night. You went because you were hungry; you had finished studying; you wanted to have some companionship; you had just heard the place advertised on the radio; you remembered the good time you had there last week; and so on. Behavior is influenced simultaneously by many "causes."

7. *Humans are social animals.* Like hives of bees or flocks of geese, people gather in social groups. The progress of modern civilization, and indeed the very survival of the human species, has been possible only because people work together in groups for the mutual benefit of all. From hunting large animals in the jungle to operating an assembly line, social groups are able to accomplish things that single individuals cannot.

   The social nature of human lives extends beyond mutual benefit, however. People need to have contact and relationships with one another. Imprisonment in solitary confinement is a harsh punishment because it deprives a person of human interactions. People seek out social support, friendships, and romantic relationships. When deprived of these social relationships for even short periods of time, we know the pain that loneliness brings. Social relationships are a significant part of our lives.

8. *People play an active part in creating their experiences.* Aristotle compared the mind of an infant to a blank clay tablet on which experiences leave their mark. In his view, we passively let experiences teach us about the world and become the person that they lead us to become. This is one of the few ideas of Aristotle that almost all contemporary psychologists have rejected. It seems to us today that people play a more active role in creating their experiences. The phi phenomenon discussed earlier was used by Gestalt psychologists to make this point: Often what we see—motion in this case—is not in the outside world at all; the human nervous system creates it.

   At a different level, it's clear that people play an active role in determining what kinds of experiences they will have by seeking out particular kinds of situations. Some people regularly choose relaxed, low-pressure situations; others get themselves into frenetic, exciting circumstances. We are shaped by these experiences, to be sure, but we play a role in choosing the experiences to which we will be exposed. We are active participants in the flow of life, not passive blank tablets.

9. *Behavior can be adaptive or maladaptive.* Humans have an amazing ability to adapt to the demands of life. We are flexible, capable creatures who generally use our wits to successfully adjust to whatever life dishes out in the way of challenges or pressures. Sometimes, however, we deal with life in ways that are harmful to us or to others. For example, some of us are excessively aggressive or much too timid, whereas others use a clinging dependency to get their way. These maladaptive ways of living can result from a combination of biological influences, excessive stress, or improper learning experiences. They are correctable, however, under the right conditions—such as good advice from friends, a change in life circumstances that encourages more adaptive ways to behave, or professional help.

These ideas serve as starting places for our study of psychology. As you read the following chapters, you may find it useful to glance back to these ideas to see how what you are studying relates to them.

APPLICATION OF PSYCHOLOGY

STUDY SKILLS

Psychology is a science that includes a great many topics, most of which have some direct relevance to our lives. One topic that has long been of interest to psychologists is human learning—the ways in which we learn and remember new information, such as the new information that you are learning about the field of psychology. Much has been discovered about learning and memory that can be translated into suggestions for more efficient learning. We do not absorb information like a sponge absorbs water; we have to work at learning course material. Human beings are highly effective learners, but we learn better in some ways than we do in others. If we understand the characteristics and quirks of the human learner, we can make better use of our study time. These characteristics will be discussed in some detail in chapters 5 and 6 on learning and memory, but before you begin to study the science of psychology, it may be useful to summarize some of the more helpful hints provided by psychologists for more effective learning and recall.

I have kept this section brief because I know how busy the beginning of the term can be, but the information contained in this section is worth your attention. From my own personal experience as a student, and from working with many students since that time, I know that learning better ways to study can make the learning process more enjoyable, can increase the amount of information that you learn and retain, and can improve your grades. I hope that the following suggestions will help you.

The SQ3R Method

The late Francis Robinson of Ohio State University suggested a method for studying textbooks known as the SQ3R method. These initials stand for the five steps in effective textbook study outlined by Robinson.

S: Survey. Look ahead at the content of the text before you begin to read.

Q: Question. Ask yourself questions about the material you are reading before and as you read.

R: Read. Read through the material in the normal way.

R: Recite. Recite the new information that you are learning out loud or silently.

R: Review. Go over the material that you have learned several times before you are tested on it.

Let's go through these steps in more detail to better understand them.

Human beings are highly effective learners, but we learn better in some ways than we do in others. If we understand the characteristics and quirks of the human learner, we can make better use of our study time.

SURVEY

Most of us think there is just one way to read—you start at the beginning and read to the end. That is the best way to read a novel because you don't want to know about the next plot twist or the surprise ending until you get there. But a very different strategy is needed when reading a textbook. It's important to survey, or look ahead, at what you are going to read. In fact, you should try to find out as much as possible about the text material you are going to read before you read it.

The reason behind this strategy of surveying before reading is based on the way humans learn and store new information in memory. Speaking loosely, we "hang" new information on what we already know. If we learn a new fact about marijuana, we hang that information on what we already know about mind-altering drugs; and the more organized knowledge we have of a topic, the better we are able to learn and remember new information about it. In particular, the more general information we possess about a topic, the easier it is to learn and remember new specific information about the topic (Ausubel, 1960; Deese & Deese, 1979).

There are several effective ways to survey this textbook. As in studying any text, you should look at the general content of each chapter by reading the headings within it. For your convenience, the headings within each chapter of this text are placed in an outline on the chapter opening page. Novels do not have headings because there is no reason to survey their content in advance; textbooks have them because they greatly aid surveying and reviewing. For example, did you look ahead at the headings in this section before beginning to read it? If you did, you developed an overall view of its content.

Next look at the prologue section at the beginning of each chapter. It gives you an advance look at the main points of the content you will be reading. Study this section carefully before going on, and it will increase the amount of information you learn as you read. When surveying some textbooks, you may need to add to what you learn from the headings by briefly skimming sections and looking at illustrations, but in this text, the chapter outlines and prologues provide the best sources of advance information. Is it really worth the time and effort to read the prologue section of each chapter to get an overview of what is ahead? Actually, I spent a considerable amount of time researching this question before I started writing this book. I didn't want to waste my time in writing the prologues—and your time in reading them—unless they would

Where is the thyroid gland located? What role does the thyroid gland play in Metabolism? What are the effects of thyroxin?

The **thyroid gland,** located just below the larynx, or voice box, plays an important role in the regulation of **metabolism.** It does so by secreting a hormone called **thyroxin.** The level of thyroxin in a person's bloodstream and the resulting metabolic rate are important in many ways. In children, proper functioning of the thyroid is necessary for proper mental development. A serious thyroid deficiency in childhood will produce sluggishness, poor muscle tone, and a type of mental retardation called **cretinism.**

actually increase what you learn. The value of prologues was tested by David Ausubel (1960) in a classic experiment conducted at the University of Illinois. One hundred and twenty students were divided into two groups that read a long passage with and without a prologue section preceding it. The passage covered the properties of carbon steel and contained many facts that were new to the students. After both groups had read the passage on carbon steel, they took a brief multiple-choice test covering the facts presented in the passage. As predicted, the group that read the prologue first correctly answered approximately 20 percent more of the questions (the difference between an F and a B in most courses). That is why a prologue was written to precede each chapter in this text—and that is why giving them your close attention is worth the effort.

Question

After you have surveyed the material you will be reading by reading the prologue and looking over the headings, Robinson suggests that you ask questions. Do this before and as you are reading. These questions should be those raised during your survey and first reading. They should reflect your own personal struggle to understand and digest the contents of this book. For example, included here are sample questions that you might ask while studying the thyroid gland in chapter 2, page 68. Asking such questions will help you become actively involved in the learning process and will focus your attention on relevant information. As you locate the information that answers your questions, you may find it helpful to underline or highlight such information with a felt-tip pen.

Read

After the S and Q steps, you are ready to begin reading in the usual way. Although you have put in a lot of time preparing for this step, your reading probably will be so much more efficient that it's worth the extra time. In fact, if you have the time to invest, you could improve the efficiency of your reading even more by skimming the material quickly before reading it more closely.

Recite

When studying, is it more beneficial to spend your time reading the material over and over again, or to read it and then practice reciting it (repeating it to yourself)? Reciting is definitely the most useful part of the study process. If nothing else, it alerts you to those things you do not really know yet (the things you cannot recite), and it may actually make learning more efficient. Regardless of how recitation works, it works. A. I. Gates (1917) found that individuals who spent 80 percent of their time reciting lists and only 20 percent reading them recalled twice as much as those who spent all of their time reading. This seems to be especially true of students who take the time to understand the meaning of what they are learning rather than memorizing it in rote fashion (Honeck, 1973). The "Check Your Learning" questions at the end of each section will help you "recite" what you have learned. In addition, the list of key terms at the beginning of each chapter and the marginal glossary can help you with this recitation. If you can recite the basic definitions of these terms, you will have learned the most important material.

Review

After you have learned the new information in the text by reading and reciting, you will need to add one final step that most students neglect: Review what you have learned several times before you are tested on it. The goal of the review process is to overlearn the material, which means to continue studying material after you have first mastered it. The learning process is not over when you can first recite the new information to yourself without error. Your ability to recall this information can be significantly strengthened later by reciting it several more times before you are tested (Krueger, 1929). To aid you with the review step, this text provides you with a review section following each major heading within the chapter and a sentence outline summary at the end of each chapter.

Strategies for Studying

The SQ3R method can improve your ability to learn information from textbooks. Several other study strategies may help you make even more efficient use of your study time.

Be Sure That You Are Actually Learning

The most common reason students "forget" information when taking tests is that they did not actually learn it in the first place. Since studying is not much fun, even when you are efficient at it, it's far too easy to act as if you are studying when in fact you are really listening to the radio, thinking about your sweetheart, or clipping your nails. If you are good at acting as if you are studying—I was a master of it during my first two years of college—you can easily fool your roommate, your best friend, or even yourself. Fooling yourself is the most dangerous possibility; do not fool yourself into thinking that you are studying when you are not really exerting the effort to become absorbed in the material. When you study, really study.

Find a Good Place to Study, and Only Study There

One way to help you really study during your study periods is to find a good place to study, and only study in that place. The goal is to associate that place only with effective studying. Begin by choosing a spot that is free from distractions. Some places in libraries are ideal for studying, but other places in libraries are great for talking and making new friends. Avoid the latter when you are studying, but feel free to visit these places when you are taking breaks. After you find a good place to study, never do anything there except study. If a friend comes over for conversation, get up and move to another area to talk. Return only when you are ready to study. Similarly, if you are in your study place and find that your mind is wandering, leave it until you are ready to study again. If you do this consistently—if you only study when you are in your study place—this spot will "feel" like a place to study, and you will be more apt to study efficiently while you are there. This doesn't mean that you cannot also study in other places—like on the bus when you have a 20-minute ride—but having a good place to study that becomes associated only with studying will help you study efficiently when you are there.

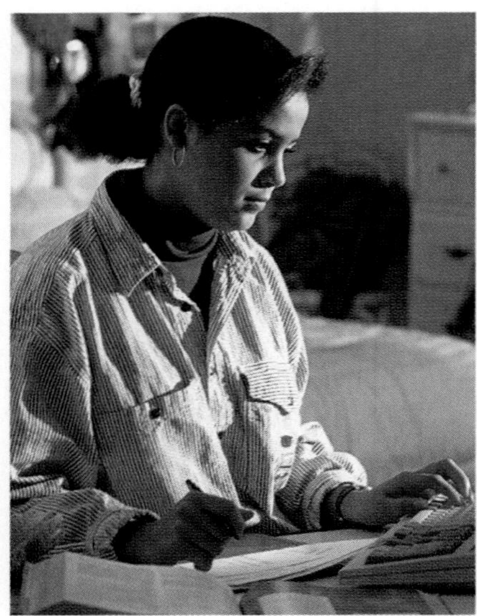

Choose a good spot to study, one that is free of distractions.

Space Out Your Study Time

As long ago as 1885, Hermann Ebbinghaus found that studying a list of new information once a day for several days resulted in better recall of that information than studying the list several times in one day. Since his time a great deal of research has shown that spaced practice often results in better learning and memory than massed practice (Bahrick, Bahrick, Bahrick, & Bahrick, 1993). This is especially true in learning motor skills (such as learning to play a musical instrument or learning large amounts of unfamiliar verbal material such as studying for a psychology test). This is why cramming (massing all your study time into one long session) is terribly inefficient. You can get better grades by spacing the same amount of study time over a longer period.

Use Mnemonic Devices

The suggestions given thus far concern how to study. The following suggestions are about how to memorize information when you are studying. Mnemonic devices are methods for storing memories so that they will be easier to recall. In each mnemonic device, an additional indexing cue is memorized along with the material to be learned. More is less with mnemonics; memorizing something more will improve retrieval and result in less forgetting.

1. *Method of Loci.* Loci is the Latin word for "places." In this method, the items in a list are mentally placed in a series of logically connected places. For example, if you are trying to remember a grocery list, you might think of a bag of sugar hanging on your garage door, a gallon of milk sitting in the front seat of your car, a carton of eggs perched on your steering wheel, and a box of donuts sitting in front of the grocery store door. Stanford University psychologist Gordon Bower (1973) found that persons who used the method of loci were able to recall almost three times as many words from lists as those who did not.

Spaced practice or study is much more efficient than massed practice (cramming).

2. *Acronym Method.* My favorite mnemonic device is the method of acronyms. Nearly every list of facts in psychology that I successfully memorized in college was memorized in terms of acronyms. In this simple method, the first letters of each word in a list are combined to form an acronym. For example, the four stages of alcoholism, which are Prealcoholic, Prodromal, Crucial, and Chronic, can be memorized using the acronym PPCC. Acronyms are even more useful if they form a real word. For most people, the word ape means an animal in a zoo, but the acronym APE helps me remember the names of the three subscales of the psychological test called the Semantic Differential Scale: Activity, Potency, and Evaluation.

   A system closely related to acronyms takes the first letter of each word in an ordered series but uses them in a new sentence. My high school biology teacher taught me to remember the hierarchy of biological classification using the sentence "Kathy Pulls Candy On Friday, Good Stuff." Notice that the first letter in each word of this sentence is the same as in Kingdom, Phylum, Class, Order, Family,

Genus, Species. As with acronyms, memory of a phrase or sentence is likely to spark recall of an entire list.

3. *Keyword Method.* We will see later in chapter 6 when we look at the psychology of memory that it is easier to memorize information that you understand than information that you do not. Some of the things that you need to memorize for college courses will be meaningful to you if you take the time to think about it before you try to memorize it, but sometimes you will have to give additional meaning to the things you are memorizing. Raugh and Atkinson (1975) demonstrated the value of teaching students to do this in memorizing Spanish vocabulary words, using what they called the *keyword* method. They asked one group of students to memorize English translations in the standard way of rotely associating the English word with the unknown Spanish word. Another group was taught to increase the meaningfulness of the association between the English and Spanish word pairs. As shown in figure 1.9 below, they were told to think of an English word that sounded like the Spanish word (like *charcoal* for the Spanish word for puddle, *charco*) and form a mental image of the English sound-alike word and the actual English translation (charcoal grill sitting in a puddle).

Students who learned the Spanish vocabulary in this more meaningful fashion were able to recall an average of 88 percent of the words, whereas the students who used rote memorization were able to recall an average of only 28 percent when tested later. By actively enhancing the meaningfulness of what was learned using the keyword method, the students were able to greatly improve its storage in memory.

Try some of these prescriptions for better learning and memory; they could make a big difference.

Additional Information on Study Skills

If you are interested in learning more about study skills, you might want to consult four books that deal with the topic in more depth.

Ellis, D. B. (1994). *Becoming a master student* (7th ed.). Rapid City, SD: College Survival, Inc.

Hettich, P. I. (1992). *Learning skills for college and career*. Pacific Grove, CA: Brooks/Cole.

Higgins, R. D. (Ed.). (1993). *The black student's guide to college success.* Westport, CT: Greenwood Press.

Parrott, L. (1994). *How to write psychology papers.* New York: HarperCollins.

FIGURE 1.9

In the "keyword" method of learning Spanish vocabulary, the student visualizes the Spanish noun with a noun that sounds like it in English. For example, the Spanish words for *puddle, lizard,* and *clown* sound similar to the English words for *charcoal, log,* and *pie.*

Summary

Chapter 1 defines psychology, discusses the history of psychology, describes the scientific methods that psychologists use, and reviews what psychologists have learned about human behavior.

- **I.** Psychology is defined as "the science of behavior and mental processes."
  - **A.** Psychology is considered to be a science because—like all sciences—knowledge is acquired through systematic observation.
  - **B.** The goals of psychology are to:
    1. describe
    2. predict
    3. understand
    4. influence behavior and mental processes
- **II.** Modern psychology has developed from the pioneering work of many different individuals during the late nineteenth and early twentieth centuries.
  - **A.** Early psychologists who studied the nature of conscious experience included:
    1. Wilhelm Wundt (structuralism)
    2. Edward Titchener (structuralism)
    3. J. Henry Alston (structuralism)
    4. Max Wertheimer (Gestalt psychology)
  - **B.** Founders of psychology who focused on the useful functions of conscious mental processes (functionalism) included:
    1. William James
    2. Hermann Ebbinghaus
    3. Mary Whiton Calkins
    4. Alfred Binet
  - **C.** Early psychologists who focused on observable behavior and the importance of learning (behaviorism) were:
    1. Ivan Pavlov
    2. John B. Watson
    3. Margaret Floy Washburn
  - **D.** Pioneers of psychology who examined the "unconscious mind" were:
    1. Sigmund Freud (psychoanalysis)
    2. Carl Rogers (humanistic psychology)
  - **E.** Two modern perspectives that strongly influence contemporary psychology are:
    1. The sociocultural perspective states that people can only be understood in terms of their culture, gender, and other sociocultural factors.
    2. The biological perspective states that we must understand the nature of the nervous system and other biological systems to understand our psychological nature.
  - **F.** Modern psychology can be divided into basic and applied areas.
    1. Psychologists working in the basic areas teach and conduct research on the biological basis of behavior, the processes of sensation and perception, learning and memory, cognition, human development, emotion, personality, social behavior, ethnic and gender identity, and sexual orientation.
    2. Applied psychologists put the basic knowledge of psychology to work in helping people. Then they specialize in applied fields such as clinical treatment, personal or marital counseling, industrial or educational applications, or health psychology.
- **III.** The general scientific method involves careful observation, forming hypotheses, and testing hypotheses against empirical facts.
  - **A.** Psychologists use three major scientific methods: descriptive methods, correlational methods, and formal experiments.
    1. Descriptive methods include the use of surveys, naturalistic observation, and clinical methods to describe behavior and mental processes; these help us reach the goal of description.
    2. Correlational methods are used to study the relationships between variables; these help us reach the goal of prediction.
    3. Formal experiments can be used to reach conclusions about cause-and-effect relationships between variables; these help us to reach the goals of understanding and influencing behavior.
  - **B.** Experiments usually involve at least one experimental group, which receives the independent variable, and a control group. Differences between the groups in the dependent variable can be said to be caused by the independent variable.
  - **C.** Ethical research carefully protects the rights of participants. Research using humans is considered to be ethical when the following conditions are met.
    1. Individuals are asked to participate without coercion.
    2. Individuals are informed about the nature of the experiment before giving consent to participate.
    3. Unnecessary deception of participants is avoided and carefully regulated when required.
    4. The nature of the study is fully explained to the participant after the study is over.
    5. All information learned about the participant is kept confidential.
  - **D.** Research involving animals is considered ethical when the following conditions are met.
    1. The study is necessary to understand an important issue concerning behavior and mental processes.
    2. The health of the animal subjects is protected.
    3. The animal subjects are treated humanely.
- **IV.** Most psychologists would agree that the following statements accurately describe human behavior and mental processes.
  - **A.** Human beings are biological creatures whose structure and physiology influence and limit behavior.
  - **B.** Each person is unique, yet enough similarities exist between individuals to allow a true science of behavior.
  - **C.** People can be fully understood only in the context of their culture, ethnic identity, and gender identity.
  - **D.** Human lives are a continuous process of change, evolving from birth to death.
  - **E.** Behavior is motivated, not random or aimless.
  - **F.** Behavior has multiple causes.
  - **G.** Humans are social animals who prefer to interact with others.
  - **H.** People play an active part in choosing their experiences and constructing perceptions.
  - **I.** Behavior can be either adaptive or maladaptive.

Suggested Readings

1. For more on the men and women who played key roles in the early history of psychology: Kimble, G. A., Wertheimer, M., & White, C. L. (Eds.). (1991). *Portraits of pioneers in psychology.* Washington, DC: American Psychological Association.
2. For a firsthand look at the writings of some of the most important psychologists throughout the history of science: Marks, R. W. (Ed.). (1966). *Great ideas in psychology.* New York: Bantam.
3. For an excellent discussion of the psychology of women, along with brief biographies of many women who are prominent in contemporary psychology: Paludi, M. (1992). *The psychology of women.* Dubuque, IA: Brown & Benchmark.
4. A thought-provoking brief article on the psychological forces that influence men in U.S. Culture (which may help men better understand the forces that affect women): Graham, S. R. (1992). What does a man want? *American Psychologist, 47,* 837–841.
5. For more on international aspects of the sociocultural perspective: Segall, M. H., Dasen, P. R., Berry, J. W., & Poortinga, Y. H. (1990). *Human behavior in global perspective.* New York: Pergamon Press. The topics of culture, ethnicity, and race in psychology are also addressed by Betancourt, H., & Lopez, S. R. (1993). The study of culture, ethnicity, and race in American psychology, *American Psychologist, 48,* 629–637.
6. For information on career opportunities in psychology: American Psychological Association. *A career in psychology.* Can be obtained free from the American Psychological Association, 750 First Street, N.E., Washington, DC 20002–4242.
7. An extremely readable introduction to scientific methods for the life sciences (although written over 30 years ago, it's entirely up-to-date): Dethier, V. G. (1962). *To know a fly.* San Francisco: Holden-Day.
8. For more on the protection of animal subjects in research: Dewsbury, D. A. (1990). Early interactions between animal psychologists and animal activists and the founding of the APA Committee on Precautions in Animal Experimentation. *American Psychologist, 45,* 315–327. Also see Thomas, G. V., & Blackman, D. (1992). The future of animal studies in psychology. *American Psychologist, 47,* 16–79. The position of medical researchers is described in *Science, medicine, and animals* by the National Academy of Sciences in 1991, published by National Academy Press in Washington, DC.

CHAPTER

2

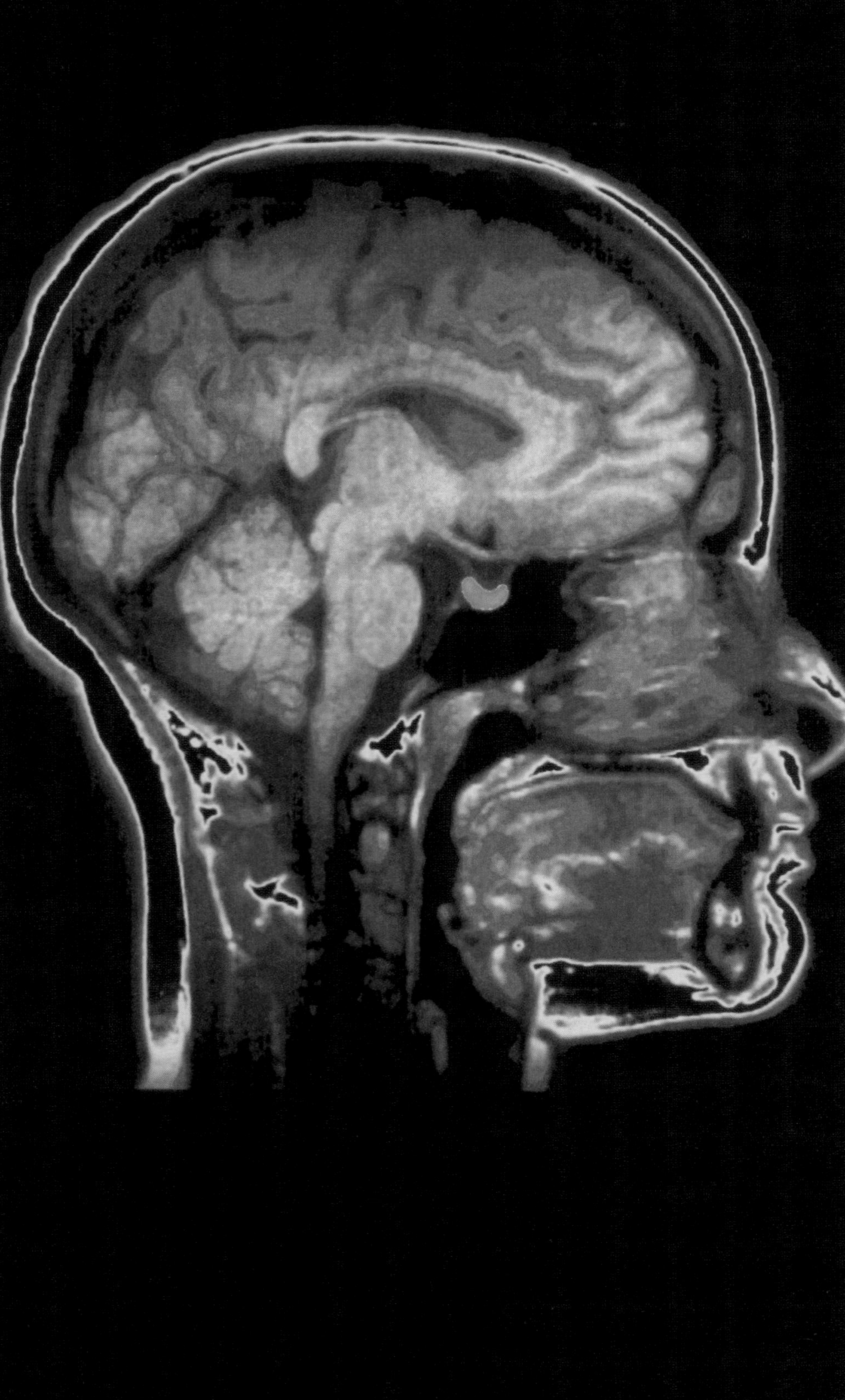

CHAPTER OUTLINE

Biological Foundations of Behavior

PROLOGUE

Where do you live? We don't think about it much, but the thinking, feeling, and acting part of you has to have a body to live in. Psychological life depends on biological life for its very existence. This means that the way we behave will be influenced to a great extent by the nature of the body. If humans did not have hands that grasp, we would never have learned to write, paint, or play racquetball. If we did not have eyes that could see color, we would see a world that existed only in shades of black and white. But the brain is the part of the body that is most intimately linked to psychological life.

A simple experiment conducted by Canadian brain surgeon Wilder Penfield in the 1930s dramatically revealed the role played by the brain. Dr. Penfield was conducting surgery on the surface layer of the brain known as the cerebral cortex while the patient was awake during local anesthesia. When Penfield placed a small rod that carried a mild electric current against the brain, there were astonishing results. The patient began to recall in vivid detail an incident from years before. She was in her kitchen, listening to the voice of her little boy playing in the yard. In the background, she could hear the noises of the neighborhood, the cars passing in the street. Penfield was amazed to discover that stimulation of particular spots on the brain could produce memories recalled by the patient in cinematic detail. Another patient recalled a small-town baseball game that included a boy trying to crawl under a fence. Another woman recalled a melody each time a certain point on the cortex was stimulated. The lesson of Penfield's experiments is clear—the brain and our psychological lives are intimately connected.

The importance of the brain to behavior is also dramatized by the concept of "brain death." When is a person considered legally dead? There is no doubt that a person is dead when the heart stops beating and breathing stops permanently. But many states now allow a physician to declare a patient dead even though the heart and lungs are still working if all of the parts of the brain involved in thinking, feeling, and acting are no longer alive. When these parts of the brain are dead, psychological life is gone and the person is considered to be dead.

This chapter is about topics that you would expect to find in a biology course. But it was written to help you understand psychology better. We discuss only those aspects of human biology that are directly relevant to understanding behavior: the brain and nervous system, endocrine glands, and genetic mechanisms. Without these biological systems, psychological life could not exist.

When we look at ourselves in this way, we see that we are psychological beings living in biological "machines." Just as electronic machines are built from wires, transistors, and other components, the nervous system is built from specialized cells called neurons. Billions of neurons in your nervous system transmit messages to one another in complex ways that make the nervous system both the computer and communication system of the body. The biological control center of the nervous system is the brain. It has many parts that carry out different functions, but the many parts of the brain operate together in an integrated way.

Surprisingly, we actually have two largely separate nervous systems instead of one. The somatic nervous system is the basis of our conscious awareness and thinking. The autonomic nervous system, on the other hand, regulates the internal body organs and activates motivation and emotion. It does most of its work automatically and unconsciously. It is partly

KEY TERMS

brain 42
neuron 42
dendrites 43
axons 43
nerve 43
myelin sheath 45
nodes of Ranvier 45
synapse 45
neurotransmitters 45
central nervous system 47
peripheral nervous system 47
afferent neurons 47
efferent neurons 47
interneuron 47
somatic nervous system 48
autonomic nervous system 49
sympathetic division 49
parasympathetic division 49
hindbrain 53
medulla 53
pons 53
cerebellum 53
midbrain 53
forebrain 53
thalamus 53
hypothalamus 55
limbic system 55
cerebral cortex 56
frontal lobes 56
parietal lobes 58
temporal lobes 58
occipital lobes 59
endocrine system 66
hormones 66
pituitary gland 66
adrenal glands 67
islets of Langerhans 68
gonads 68
thyroid gland 68
parathyroid glands 68
pineal gland 69
gene 70
chromosome 70

because thinking and emotion operate in largely separate nervous systems that we often have difficulty logically controlling our feelings. The brain is so important to our lives that the U.S. Congress has declared the 1990s to be the "Decade of the Brain" to encourage research on the brain and behavior.

The brain communicates with the body through an intricate network of neurons that fan out to every part of the body. But the brain also uses the endocrine glands to communicate with the body. These glands secrete chemical messengers called hormones that travel to the body through the bloodstream. Hormones regulate the functions of many parts of the body and influence our behavior and experience. Hormones are powerful tools of the brain, but they influence us in diffuse rather than precise ways. At times, therefore, it feels like they carry out their jobs in rather clumsy ways.

The fact that the nature of the nervous and endocrine systems influences our psychological functioning means that heredity can influence our behavior by shaping our biological makeup. Heredity operates through genes in the nucleus of the body's cells. These genes contain codes that allow heredity to influence the development of our bodies. We do not inherit specific behaviors in the same way that we inherit eye color, though. Instead, the genes influence the development of the brain, endocrine glands, and other body structures in ways that influence our behavior in very *broad* ways. For example, we do not inherit the ability to read, but it appears that heredity is one of the factors that influences how quickly a child learns to read. This is because heredity seems to be one of the factors that determines our intelligence. Similarly, it appears that heredity influences how much we react to psychological stress and other broad aspects of personality.

NERVOUS SYSTEM: THE BIOLOGICAL CONTROL CENTER

brain
The complex mass of neural cells and related cells encased in the skull.

spinal cord
The nerve fibers in the spinal column.

neuron
(nu´ron) An individual nerve cell.

The nervous system is both a powerful computer and a complex communication system. But unlike any computer, the complex mass of nerve cells called the **brain** not only thinks and calculates but also feels and controls actions. The brain is connected to a thick bundle of long nerves running through the spine, called the **spinal cord.** Individual nerves exit or enter the spinal cord and brain, linking every part of the body to the brain. Some of these nerves carry messages from the body to the brain to keep the brain informed about what is going on in the body. Other nerves carry messages from the brain to the body to regulate the body's functions and the person's behavior. Without the nervous system, the body would be no more than a mass of uncoordinated parts that could not act, reason, or experience emotions. In other words, without a nervous system, there would be no psychological life.

Neurons: The Units of the Nervous System

The basic units of which computers, telephone systems, and other electronic systems are made consist of individual wires, transistors, microchips, and other components that transmit and regulate electricity. These components are arranged in complex patterns to create functioning systems. The nervous system is similarly made up of components. The most important unit of the nervous system is the individual nerve cell, or **neuron.** We begin our discussion of the nervous system with the neuron and then progress to a discussion of the larger parts of the nervous system. As we discuss the neuron in technical, biological terms, try not to forget its importance to consciousness and behavior.

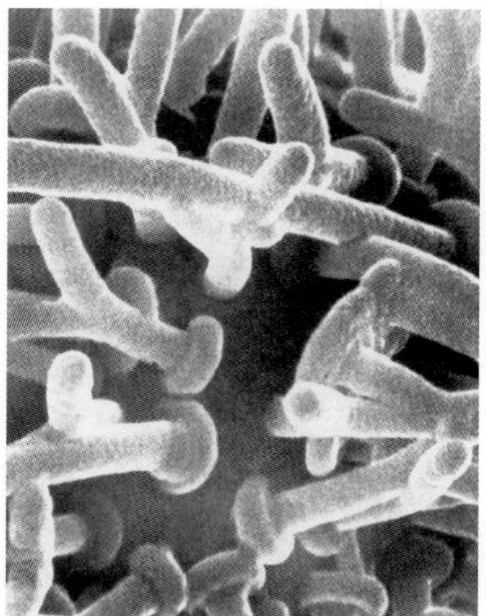

The knoblike tips of the axons are the small branches of the neuron that transmit messages to the next nerve cell.

In the early 1900s, Santiago Ramón y Cajal, the scientist who first discovered neurons, described them as "the mysterious butterflies of the soul, the beating of whose wings may some day—who knows?—clarify the secret of mental life." Since his time much has been learned about these building blocks of the brain. Much remains to be learned about neurons, but some current research is so advanced that it sounds more like science fiction than reality. For example, Masuo Aizawa (1994) has used specially treated living nerve cells to construct a simple "living computer" that processes information much like the nervous system does. In time, research like Aizawa's may lead to the ability to repair damaged nerves, like those of actor Christopher Reeve who was paralyzed by a fall from a horse.

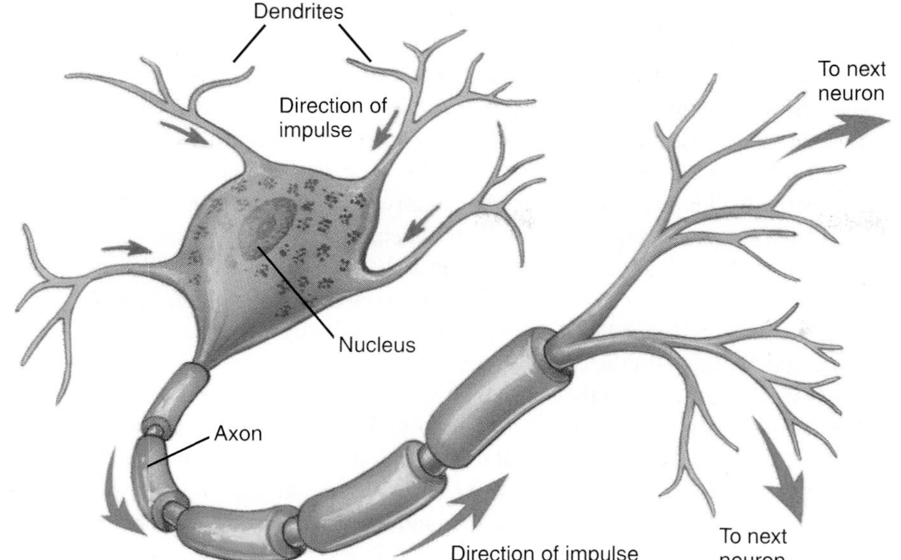

FIGURE 2.1

Neurons are typically composed of a cell body, which contains the nucleus of the cell, dendrites that receive impulses from other neurons, and an axon that passes the neural impulse on to the next neuron.

Parts of Neurons

Neurons range in length from less than a millimeter to more than a meter in length. Yet all neurons are made up of essentially the same parts (see fig. 2.1). The **cell body** is the central part of the nerve cell. It contains the cell's control center, or *nucleus*, and other components of the cell necessary for the cell's preservation and nourishment. **Dendrites** are small branches that extend out from the cell body and receive messages from other neurons.

The **axons** are small branches at the other end of the neuron that perform a function opposite that of the dendrites. They carry messages away from the cell body and transmit these messages to the next neuron. (It's easy to remember the difference between the functions of the dendrites and axons by remembering that the axon "acts on" the next cell.) The message transmitted along the axon may be picked up by the dendrites of one or more other neurons. Neurons, then, have a cell body, dendrites, and an axon. The shape and size of these parts can vary greatly, depending on what function the neuron serves.

cell body
The central part of the neuron that includes the nucleus.

dendrites
(den´drīts) Small extensions on the cell body that receive messages from other neurons.

axons
(ak´sonz) Neuron endings that transmit messages to other neurons.

nerve
A bundle of long neurons outside the brain and spinal cord.

Neurons are grouped together in complex networks that make the largest computer seem like a child's toy. The nervous system is composed of something on the order of 100 billion neurons (Kandel, Schwartz, & Jessel, 1995), about as many as the number of stars in our galaxy. Each neuron can receive messages from or transmit messages to a total of 1,000 to 10,000 other neural cells. All told, your body contains trillions of neural connections, most of them in the brain. These numbers are not important in their own right, but they may help us understand the incredibly rich network of neural interconnections that makes us humans (Iverson, 1979). Incidentally, be careful not to confuse the term *neuron* with the term **nerve;** they are not synonyms. A nerve is a bundle of many long neurons—sometimes thousands of them—outside the brain and spinal cord.

As described in the next two sections, neurons transmit messages in the nervous system in two steps: the transmission of the message from one end of the neuron to the other end (neural transmission), and from one neuron to the next neuron (synaptic transmission).

Neural Transmission

Neurons are the "wires" of the nervous system—messages are transmitted over the neuron much like your voice is transmitted over a telephone line. But neurons are very special living wires with their own built-in supplies of electrical power—they are the "batteries" of the nervous system, too.

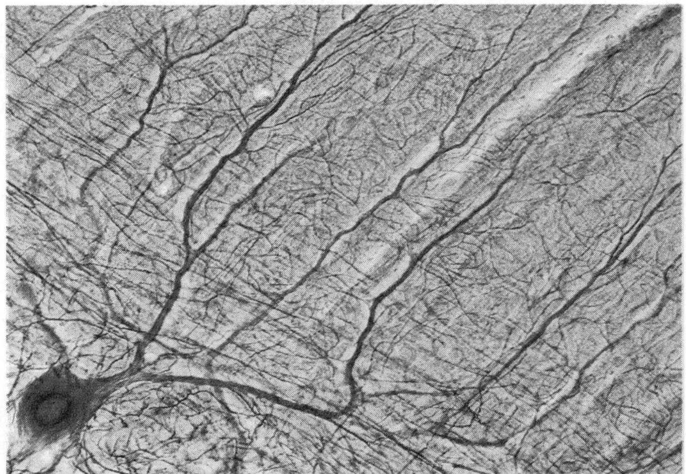

A neuron in the human brain showing the cell body and dendrites.

ions
(i´ons) Electrically charged particles.

cell membrane
The covering of a neuron or other cell.

semipermeable
(sem´´e-per´mē-ah-b´l) A surface that allows some, but not all, particles to pass through.

polarized state
(pō´lar-īz´d) The resting state of a neuron, when mostly negative ions are inside and mostly positive ions are outside the cell membrane.

depolarization
The process during which positively charged ions flow into the axon, making it less negatively charged inside.

all-or-none principle
The law that states that once an action potential is produced, its shape and size are always the same.

action potential
A brief electrical signal that travels the length of the axon.

Neurons can take on the functions of wires and batteries because, like all living cells, they are wet. Neurons are sacs filled with one type of fluid on the inside and bathed in a different type of fluid on the outside. This is an important fact. Both types of fluid are thick "soups" of dissolved chemicals including **ions,** which are particles that carry either a positive or negative electrical charge. More of the ions inside neurons are negatively than positively charged, making the overall charge of the cell a negative one. This negative charge attracts positively charged ions, just as the negative pole of a magnet attracts the positive pole of another magnet. Thus, the outside of the cell membrane becomes cloaked in positive ions, particularly sodium (Na^+). In the resting state, there are ten times as many positively charged sodium ions outside the membrane of the neuron than inside. This is the source of the neuron's electrical energy—it is electrically positive on one side of the membrane and negative on the other.

If you have trouble remembering which side of the membrane has most of the positive sodium ions, keep in mind that there is a lot of sodium in salty seawater. The fluid on the *outside* of neurons is almost identical to seawater in its chemical contents, including the high amounts of sodium. Why is this so? According to the theory of evolution, as animals evolved and moved from the oceans onto the land, they brought some of the seawater with them *in their bodies.* This seawater-like liquid fills the space between the body's cells. Therefore, it makes sense that the fluid bathing the neural cells is rich in sodium ions.

Many ions are able to move freely through the **cell membrane** of the neuron, but other ions cannot, including the sodium ions. For this reason, the membrane is said to be **semipermeable**—only some chemicals can permeate or pass through "holes" in the membrane. When the neuron is in its normal resting state, the membrane is semipermeable and does not let positive ions into the cell. Therefore, a balance exists between the mostly negative ions on the inside and the mostly positive ions on the outside. In this condition, the neuron is said to be electrically **polarized** (see fig. 2.2).

When the membrane is stimulated by an adjacent neuron, however, the semipermeability of the membrane is changed. Positively charged ions, including the important sodium ions, are then allowed to enter the neuron, making the inside less negative. This process is called **depolarization.**

Neural transmission operates according to the **all-or-none principle.** This means that a small amount of depolarization will not affect the neuron. A larger depolarization, however, will trigger a dramatic chain of events known as the **action potential.** It is the action potential that transmits the neural message. The depolarization must be strong enough to trigger an action potential, but the strength of the action potential does not depend on the strength of the depolarization. They are all the same once they get started.

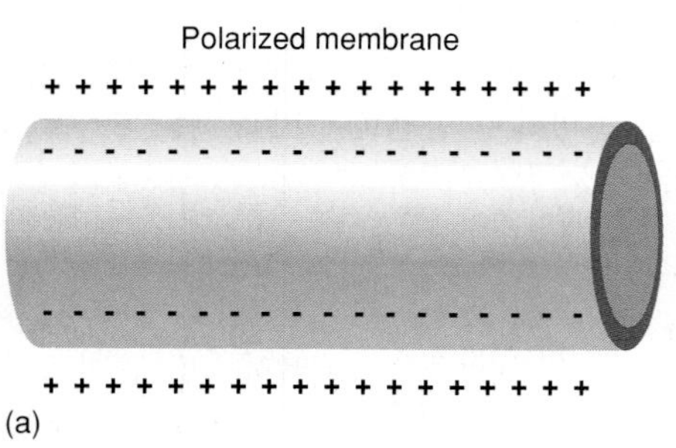

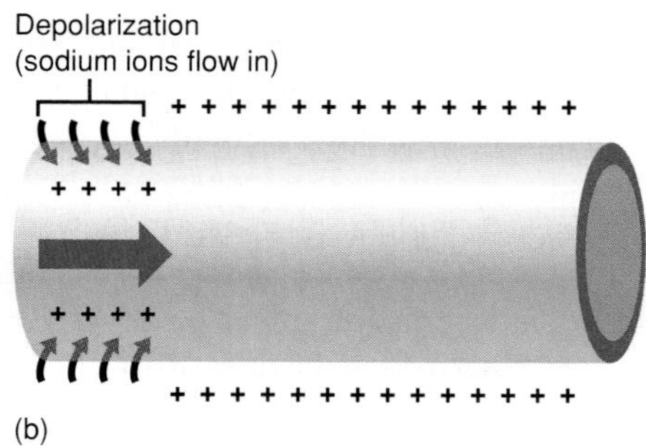

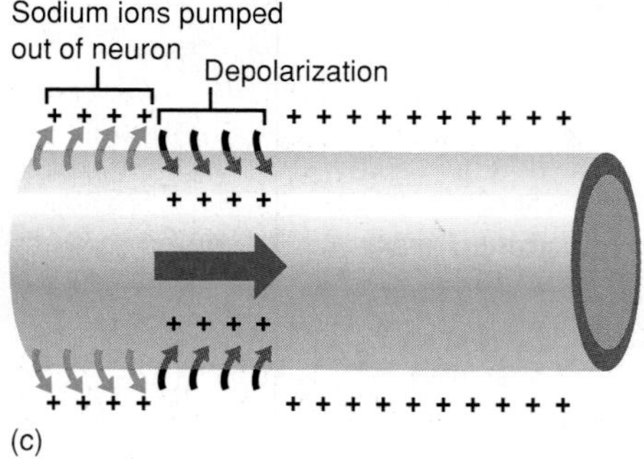

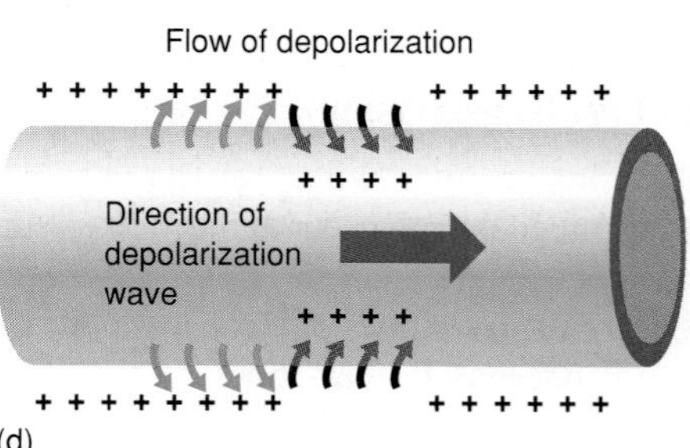

FIGURE 2.2
Short sections of an axon illustrating neural transmission. (a) When an axon is in its resting state, there is a balance between the number of positively and negatively charged ions along the membrane. (b) When the axon is sufficiently stimulated, the membrane allows positively charged sodium ions to pass into the cell, depolarizing that spot on the membrane. (c) This depolarization disturbs the adjacent section of membrane, allowing sodium ions to flow in again, while sodium ions are being pumped back out of the first section. (d) This process continues as the swirling storm of depolarization continues to the end of the axon.

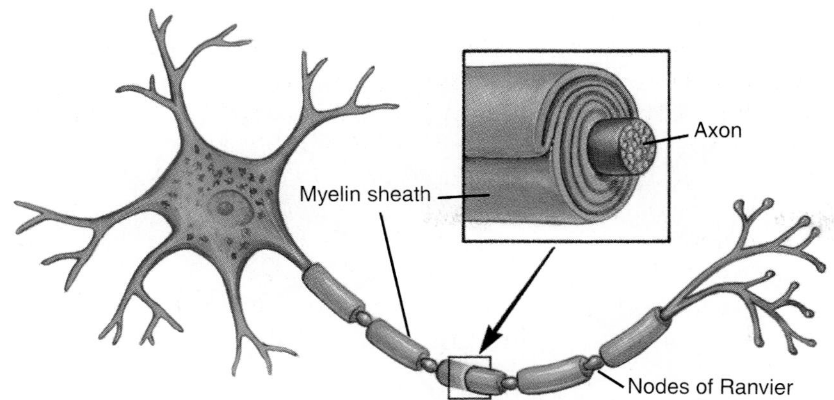

FIGURE 2.3

Many neurons are wrapped like a jelly roll in a white fatty substance called myelin. The myelin sheath speeds neural transmission by allowing the electrical disturbance to jump between widely spaced gaps in the myelin sheath, which are called the nodes of Ranvier.

During an action potential, a small section of the axon adjacent to the cell body becomes more permeable to the positive sodium ions. The sodium ions rush in, producing a dramatic depolarization in that part of the axon. Very quickly, however, the membrane regains its semipermeability and "pumps" the positive sodium ions back out, reestablishing the neuron's polarization. This tiny electrical storm of sodium ions flowing in and out of the neuron—which lasts approximately one-thousandth of a second—does not stop there, however. It disturbs the adjacent section of the membrane of the axon so that it depolarizes, which in turn disturbs the next section of the membrane, and so on. Thus, the action potential—the flowing storm of ions rushing in and out—travels the length of the axon.

Local anesthetics, such as the Novocain that your dentist injects, stop pain by chemically interrupting this flowing process of depolarization in the axons of nerves that carry pain messages to the brain.

Many axons are encased in a white fatty coating called the **myelin sheath.** This sheath, which is wrapped around the axon like the layers of a jelly roll, provides insulation to the axon and greatly improves its capacity to conduct neural impulses. In simplified terms, the myelin sheath speeds neural conduction by allowing the action potential to skip between its widely spaced gaps—known as the **nodes of Ranvier**—rather than flow the entire length of the neuron (see fig. 2.3). Sadly, the importance of the myelin sheath in neural transmission can be seen in victims of multiple sclerosis. This disease destroys the myelin sheath of many neurons, leaving them unable to operate at normal efficiency. As a result, individuals with multiple sclerosis have severe difficulties controlling their muscles and suffer serious vision problems (Morell & Norton, 1980).

myelin sheath
(mī′e-lin) The protective fatty covering wrapped around part of the neuron.

nodes of Ranvier
(rahn′-vé-á) Gaps in the myelin sheath covering the nerves.

synapse
(sin-aps′) The space between the axon of one neuron and the dendrite of another.

synaptic gap
The small space between two neurons at a synapse.

neurotransmitters
(nu′′rō-tranz′-mit-erz) Chemical substances produced by axons that transmit messages across the synapse.

synaptic vesicles
Tiny vessels containing stored quantities of the neurotransmitter substance held in the synaptic knobs of the axon.

synaptic knob
(si-nap′tik) The knoblike top of the axon.

receptor sites
Sites on the dendrite that are sensitive to the neurotransmitter substance.

Synaptic Transmission

Neurons are linked together in complex chains, but they are not directly connected to each other. The junction between one neuron and another is called the **synapse.** The small space between two neurons is known as the **synaptic gap.** The electrical action potential cannot jump across this gap, however. Instead, the neural message is carried across the gap by chemical substances called **neurotransmitters.** Neurotransmitters are stored in tiny packets called **synaptic vesicles** located in the knoblike ends of the axons—called **synaptic knobs.** When an action potential reaches the axon knob, it stimulates the vesicles to release the neurotransmitter into the gap. The neurotransmitter floats across the gap and fits into **receptor sites** on the adjacent dendrite membrane like keys fitting into locks. This depolarizes the receiving neuron, causing an action potential that continues the neural message on its way (see fig. 2.4).

Many different neurotransmitter substances operate in different parts of the brain that carry out different functions—probably as many as 50 different neurotransmitters (Kandel et al., 1995). Because of this fact, the process of synaptic transmission in a particular portion of the brain can be altered through the use of drugs that chemically alter the function of one of these neurotransmitters. Thus, our emerging knowledge about neurotransmitters has made the use of psychiatric drugs possible for helping to control anxiety, depression, and other psychological problems. Many of these drugs operate by increasing or decreasing the effectiveness of a specific neurotransmitter. For example, the drug *Thorazine* is

FIGURE 2.4

Neural messages are transmitted chemically from the axon of the sending neuron to the dendrite of the receiving neuron. The neurotransmitter substance contained in the synaptic vesicles is secreted across the synaptic gap. The neurotransmitter is able to stimulate the receiving neuron because its chemical "shape" matches that of receptor sites on the dendrite of the receiving neuron.

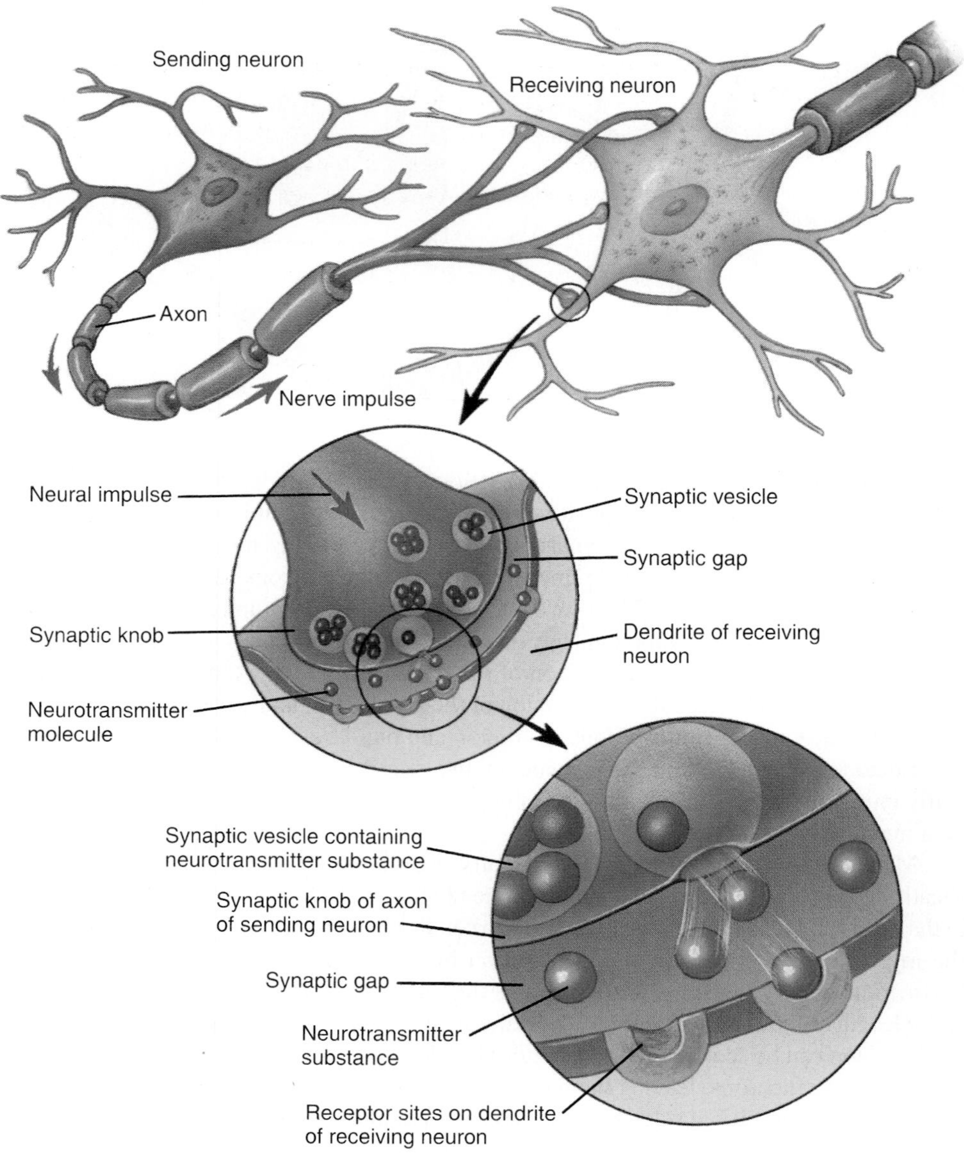

apparently effective in partially alleviating the psychological disorder known as schizophrenia because it blocks the actions of the neurotransmitter in the part of the brain responsible for emotional arousal (Sachar, 1985). Drugs like marijuana and LSD also influence conscious experience by affecting other neurotransmitters.

The capacity of the brain to process information is multiplied many times by the fact that not all neurotransmitters are *excitatory*. Some axons transmit *inhibitory* substances across synapses, which makes it more difficult for the next neuron to fire. Thus, the brain is composed of a staggering network of "yes" and "no" circuits that process and create our experiences (Kandel et al., 1995).

Review

The nervous system is a highly effective living computer and communication system built of neurons. These specialized cells transmit neural messages from their dendrites to their axons in a flowing swirl of electrically charged molecules produced by the changing semipermeability of their membranes. When the neural message reaches the tip of the axon, it is transmitted across the synaptic gap to the next neuron by a neurotransmitter substance. Many of the longer neurons are wrapped in an insulating layer called the myelin sheath, which increases the rate of transmission of neural messages.

Check Your Learning

To be sure that you have learned the key points from the preceding section, cover the answers below and try to answer each question. If you give an incorrect answer to any question, return to the page given next to the correct answer to see why your answer was not correct. Remember that these questions cover only some of the important information in this section; it is important that you make up your own questions to check your learning of other facts and concepts.

1. The part of the neuron that receives messages from other neurons is called the

   a. axon. **c.** dendrite.
   b. cell body. **d.** myelin sheath.

2. The part of the neuron that transmits the neural message to the next neuron by releasing a neurotransmitter across the synaptic gap is called the

   a. axon. **c.** dendrite.
   b. cell body. **d.** myelin sheath.

3. During the process of neural transmission, the balance of positive ions on the outside of the neuron and negative ions on the inside is disturbed for a moment (called "depolarization") when the ________________ are allowed to rush into the neuron through the semipermeable membrane of the cell.

   a. sodium ions **c.** LSD
   b. neurotransmitter **d.** negative ions

4. The fatty covering of some long neurons that insulates them and allows them to carry messages more rapidly is called the ________________.

Correct Answers

1. c (p. 43), **2.** a (p. 43), **3.** a (p. 44), **4.** myelin sheath (p. 45).

Thinking Critically About Psychology

1. The neurons in the nervous system are not directly connected to one another and messages must be transmitted across the synaptic gap using neurotransmitters. How would we be different if the neurons were simply connected like wires?

2. Some drugs that affect the nervous system are thought of as useful medications, whereas others are illegal because they are thought to be harmful. Why do such drugs have the potential to harm or help?

DIVISIONS OF THE NERVOUS SYSTEM

Neurons are the building blocks of the nervous system. But they do not fit together to create a single, simple nervous system that serves only one function. Ours is a nervous system with many different parts or divisions. The major divisions of the nervous system are the central nervous system and the peripheral nervous system. The **central nervous system** consists of the brain and the spinal cord. The **peripheral nervous system** is composed of those nerves that branch from the brain and the spinal cord to all parts of the body (see fig. 2.5). Nerves of the peripheral nervous system transmit messages from the body to the central nervous system. They also transmit messages from the central nervous system to the muscles, glands, and organs that put the messages into action.

Messages can travel across the synapse in only one direction. So messages coming from the body into the central nervous system are carried by one set of neurons, the **afferent neurons.** Messages going out from the central nervous system to the organs and muscles are carried by another set, the **efferent neurons.**

The spinal cord's primary function is to relay messages between the brain and the body, but it also does some rudimentary processing of information on its own. A simple reflex, such as the reflexive withdrawal from a hot object, is a good example. The impulse caused by the hot object travels up an afferent nerve to the spinal cord. Here a neuron, called an **interneuron,** transmits the message to an efferent neuron that, in turn, stimulates the muscles of the limb to contract (see fig. 2.6). Any behavior more complicated than a simple reflex, however, usually requires processing within the mass of interneurons that make up the brain.

central nervous system
The brain and the nerve fibers that make up the spinal cord.

peripheral nervous system
(pĕ-rif´er-al) The network of nerves that branch from the brain and spinal cord to all parts of the body.

afferent neurons
(af´er-ent) Neurons that transmit messages from sense organs to the central nervous system.

efferent neurons
(ef´er-ent) Neurons that transmit messages from the central nervous system to organs and muscles.

interneurons
Neurons that are not sensory or motor neurons.

FIGURE 2.5
Organization of the human nervous system.

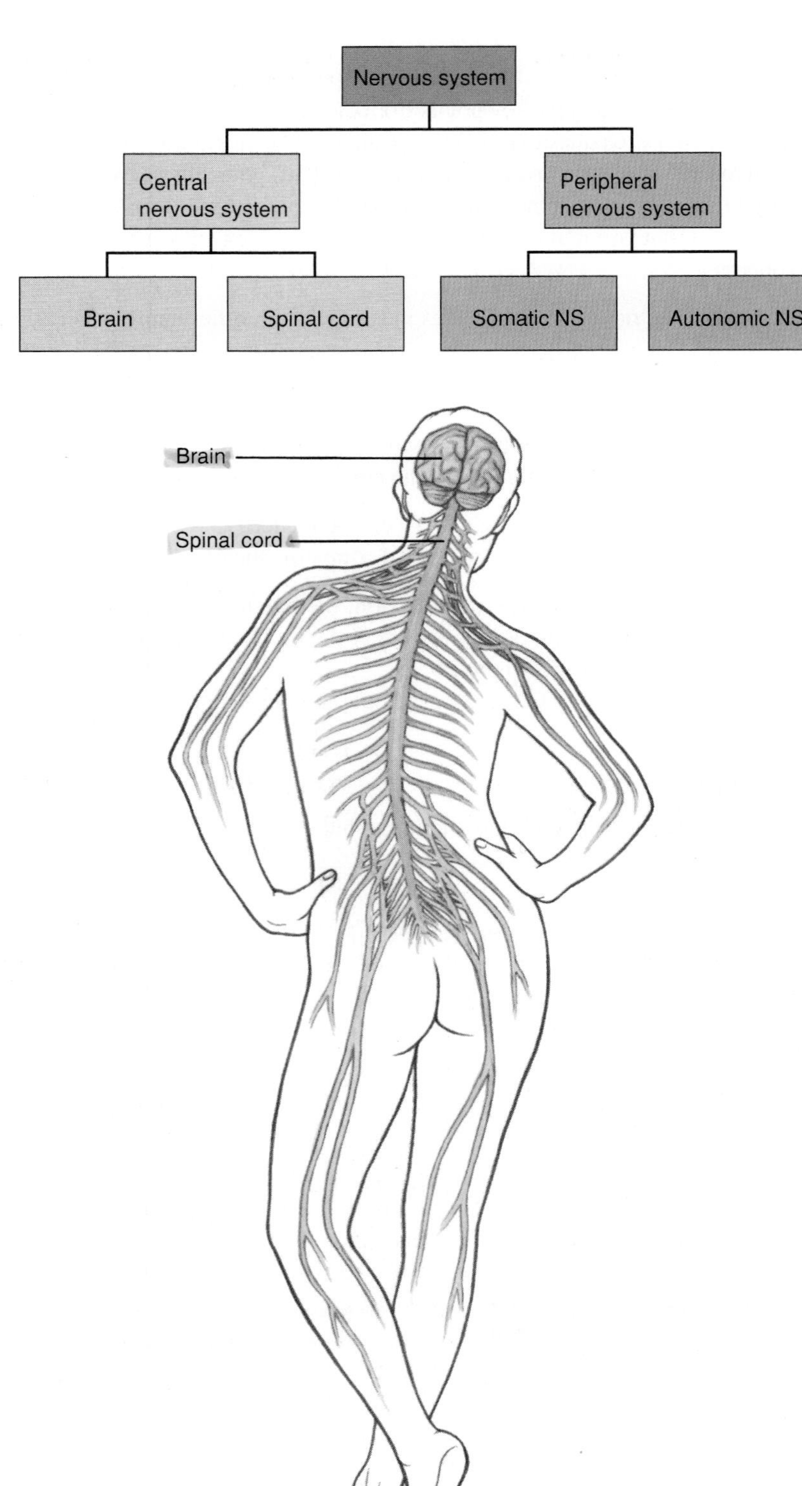

Divisions of the Peripheral Nervous System

somatic nervous system
(sō-mat´ik) Division of the peripheral nervous system that carries messages from the sense organs, muscles, joints, and skin to the central nervous system, and from the central nervous system to the skeletal muscles.

The peripheral nervous system is further divided into the somatic and autonomic nervous systems. The **somatic nervous system** carries messages from the central nervous system to the muscles of the skeleton that control movements of the body. These include voluntary movements, as when I type the words on a manuscript page, and involuntary movements, as when my eyes maintain fixation on the screen of my word processor in spite of small but frequent changes in the position of my head as I type. The somatic nervous sys-

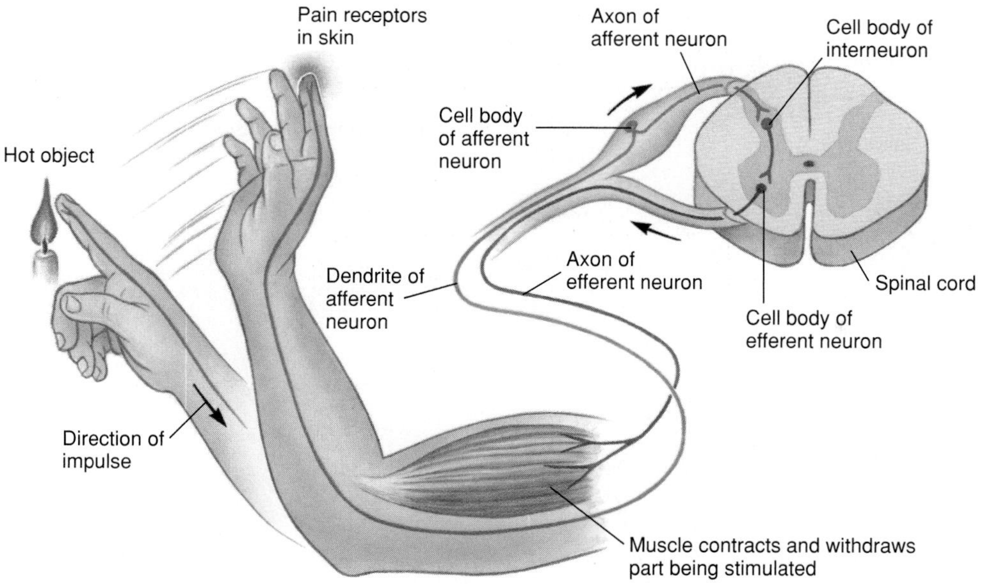

FIGURE 2.6
Some simple reflexes, such as the reflexive withdrawal of the hand from a hot object, are a result of a message traveling along an afferent neuron from the hot spot on the hand to the spinal cord. In the spinal cord, the message travels across a short interneuron to an efferent neuron, which causes the muscles in the limb to contract.

tem also receives and interprets incoming messages from the sense organs, muscles, joints, and skin.

The **autonomic nervous system** is composed of nerves that carry messages to and from the glands and visceral organs (heart, stomach, intestines, etc.). The autonomic nervous system only affects the skeletal muscles by influencing general muscle tension during stress. The autonomic nervous system has three primary functions:

autonomic nervous system
(aw´´to-nom´ik) The division of the peripheral nervous system that controls the involuntary actions of internal body organs, such as heartbeat and breathing, and is important in the experience of emotion.

1. *Essential body functions.* The autonomic nervous system automatically controls many essential functions of the body. Heartbeat, breathing, digestion, sweating, and sexual arousal operate through the autonomic nervous system.
2. *Emotion.* The autonomic nervous system also regulates emotion. Have you ever wondered why you sometimes get a stomachache, diarrhea, a pounding heart, or a headache when you feel anxious? It's because the autonomic nervous system regulates both the internal organs and the emotions. When a person becomes very emotional, the autonomic system often overdoes its job and throws our internal organs out of balance in minor, but uncomfortable, ways. As we will see in chapter 12, however, prolonged emotional arousal can sometimes adversely affect the true health of the organs controlled by the autonomic nervous system.
3. *Motivation.* Finally, the autonomic nervous system also plays an important role in the control of our motivations, *such as hunger and thirst.* That is why we tend to overeat or experience other changes in our motives when we are anxious or depressed.

Divisions of the Autonomic Nervous System

The autonomic nervous system can itself be divided into two parts. In general, the **sympathetic division** of the autonomic nervous system tends to activate the visceral organs during emotional arousal or when physical demands are made on the body. The **parasympathetic division** tends to "calm" the visceral organs after arousal (see fig. 2.7). For example, the sympathetic division increases the rate of heartbeat while the parasympathetic division decreases heartbeat. In tandem, therefore, these two divisions of the autonomic nervous system operate to control and balance the functioning of the visceral organs. Not all of the functions of the two autonomic divisions are in opposition to one another, however. For example, the parasympathetic division is responsible for vaginal lubrication and erection of the penis during sexual arousal, while the sympathetic division controls sexual orgasm.

sympathetic division
(sim´´pah-thet´ik) The division of the autonomic nervous system that generally activates internal organs during emotional arousal or when physical demands are placed on the body.

parasympathetic division
(par´´ah-sim´´pah-thet´ik) The division of the autonomic nervous system that generally "calms" internal organs.

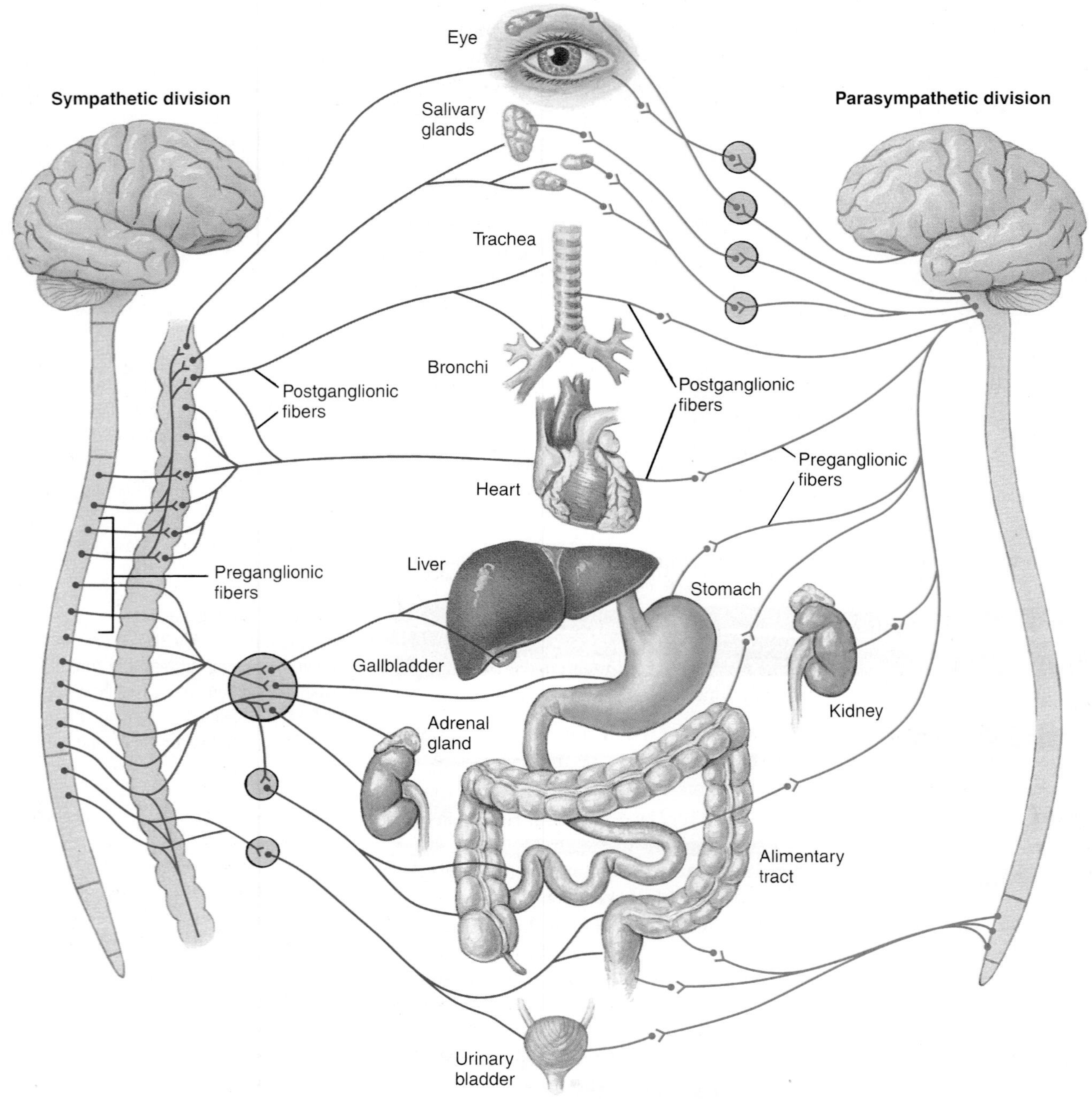

FIGURE 2.7
The sympathetic and parasympathetic divisions of the autonomic nervous system regulate many of the body's organs and play key roles in emotion and motivation.

ganglia
(gang´glē-ah) Clusters of cell bodies of neurons outside of the central nervous system.

The structure and the functions of these two divisions of the autonomic nervous system can be seen more clearly by referring to figure 2.7. Essentially all organs that are served by the sympathetic division are also served by the parasympathetic division. Note also that the clusters of cell bodies of neurons—called **ganglia**—are organized in different ways in the two divisions of the autonomic nervous system. The ganglia of the sympathetic division are all connected together in a chain near the spinal column. This arrangement results in the sympathetic division's operating in a diffuse manner. That is, when the sympathetic division is aroused, it tends to stimulate all of the organs served by it to some extent—because all of its parts are chained together. The ganglia of the parasympathetic division, in contrast, are separate and located near the individual organs. This allows the parasympathetic division to operate more selectively, which is particularly fortunate in some instances. For example, the parasympathetic division stimulates the flow of saliva and the flow of urine. If the parasympathetic ganglia that control the salivary glands and the urinary system were not separate, we would wet our pants every time we salivated!

We generally are not conscious of the actions of the autonomic nervous system. It carries out its regulation of the heart, lungs, intestines, sweat glands, and so on in an automatic way that does not require our awareness or intentional control. It plays its role in motivation and emotion in an equally automatic way.

Review

The nervous system can be divided into a central nervous system composed of the brain and spinal cord, and a peripheral nervous system composed of nerves that carry messages to and from the body. The peripheral nervous system is further divided into the somatic and autonomic nervous systems. The somatic nervous system carries messages from the sense organs, muscles, and joints to the central nervous system, and from the central nervous system to the skeletal muscles. The autonomic nervous system is responsible for the regulation of the internal organs, emotion, and motivation. Even the autonomic nervous system can be divided into two working parts: the sympathetic division, which primarily activates visceral organs, and the parasympathetic division, which primarily calms these organs.

Thinking Critically About Psychology

1. What are the advantages and disadvantages to human beings of an autonomic nervous system that largely operates automatically (that we do not voluntarily control)?

2. Why do you think the autonomic nervous system controls such different functions as fear, heart rate, and hunger?

Check Your Learning

To be sure that you have learned the key points from the preceding section, cover the answers and try to answer each question. If you give an incorrect answer to any question, return to the page given next to the correct answer to see why your answer was not correct.

1. The nervous system can be divided into two major parts, the peripheral and the ________ nervous system.

a. autonomic **c.** somatic
b. afferent **d.** central

2. The neurons in the somatic division of the peripheral nervous system that transmit messages from the sense organs to the central nervous system are called the ________ nervous system.

a. efferent **c.** sympathetic
b. afferent **d.** parasympathetic

3. The division of the peripheral nervous system that controls essential bodily functions, emotion, and motivations is called the ________ nervous system.

a. autonomic **c.** parasympathetic
b. sympathetic **d.** central

4. During stress, the division of the autonomic nervous system that arouses the heart, tenses the muscles, and prepares the body for exertion or danger is called the ________ nervous system.

a. visceral **c.** parasympathetic
b. sympathetic **d.** central

Correct Answers
1. d (p. 47), 2. b (p. 47), 3. a (p. 49), 4. b (p. 49).

STRUCTURES AND FUNCTIONS OF THE BRAIN

The brain is the fundamental basis for psychological life. We begin our discussion of the brain with a brief description of the new brain-imaging techniques that have revolutionized the study of the brain. We then turn to the structures of the brain and their functions.

Images of the Brain at Work

Scientists have long studied the brain, but during the past 15 years, a number of exciting new scientific tools have made the study of brain functions much easier. These techniques create images of the activities of the *living* brain by using computers to compile and interpret huge amounts of information from electrical activity, magnetic waves, radio waves, and other forms of radiation. These computer-enhanced images of the brain are far more accurate and revealing than conventional X rays. In a very real sense, the advent of modern brain-imaging techniques is as important to the development of psychology and medicine's understanding of the brain as the invention of the telescope was to astronomy.

electroencephalogram (EEG)
A recording of the electrical activity of the brain obtained through electrodes placed on the scalp.

A traditional method of studying the brain's activity is the **electroencephalogram,** or **EEG.** Electrodes are placed on the surface of the person's scalp, and electrical activity from the brain is recorded. The EEG is commonly used to study the sleep cycle and to diagnose medical conditions, such as seizure disorder.

One of the new brain-imaging techniques converts EEG recordings into computer-generated "maps" of brain activity. The head is covered with closely spaced electrodes to record brain activity. The computer converts these recordings into color images of the brain. The image in figure 2.8 shows the pattern of activity in the brain of psychiatric researcher Monte Buchsbaum moments after he administered a mild electrical shock to his own arm. The area of greatest neural activity (red and orange) is at the top of the brain. We will see later in this section that this is the area of the brain that receives skin sensations and controls movements of the arm (Buchsbaum, 1983).

positron emission tomography (PET)
A brain-imaging technique that produces an X-ray-like image.

A different kind of image is shown in figure 2.9. These images were created by computer interpretation of X-ray-like images obtained by **positron emission tomography,** or **PET** scanning. We see reduced activity in the outer portions of the brain beginning in image H and moving through image K as the powerful drug morphine (related to heroin) takes effect (London et al., 1990). In many similar experiments, the PET scan has given brain researchers "photographs" of the living brain at work. These pictures make their jobs far easier and more exciting.

magnetic resonance imaging (MRI)
A safe imaging technique utilizing magnetic resonance to obtain detailed views of brain structure and function.

Perhaps the most amazing of the new imaging techniques is called **magnetic resonance imaging,** or **MRI.** This painless technique detects magnetic activity from the nuclei of atoms in living cells and interprets that activity using computers to create visual images of the living brain. Figure 2.10 shows an MRI of a living brain. Notice the amazingly accurate picture

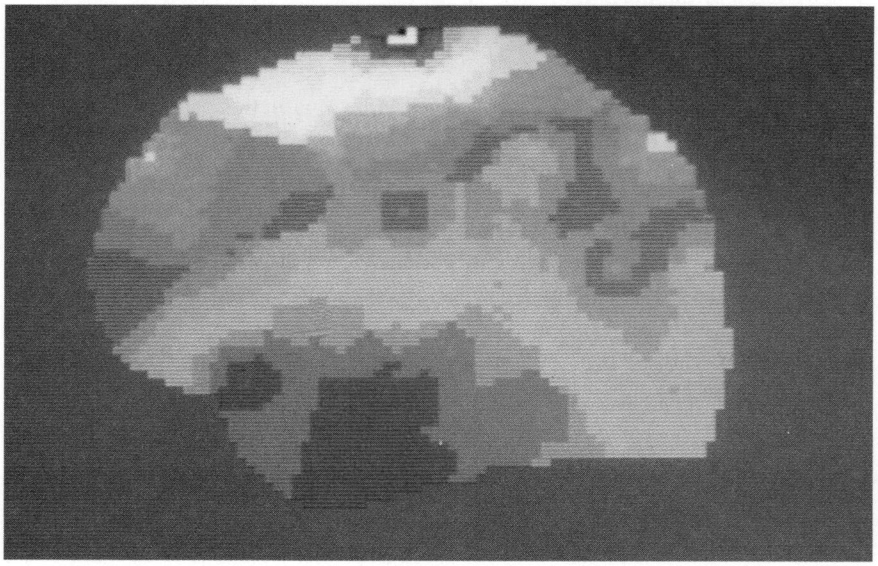

FIGURE 2.8
Image of the brain at work created by a computer from electrical recordings of the activity of the brain. The image shows the activation of areas of the cerebral cortex of Dr. Monte Buchsbaum immediately after he administered a mild electric shock to his own arm.

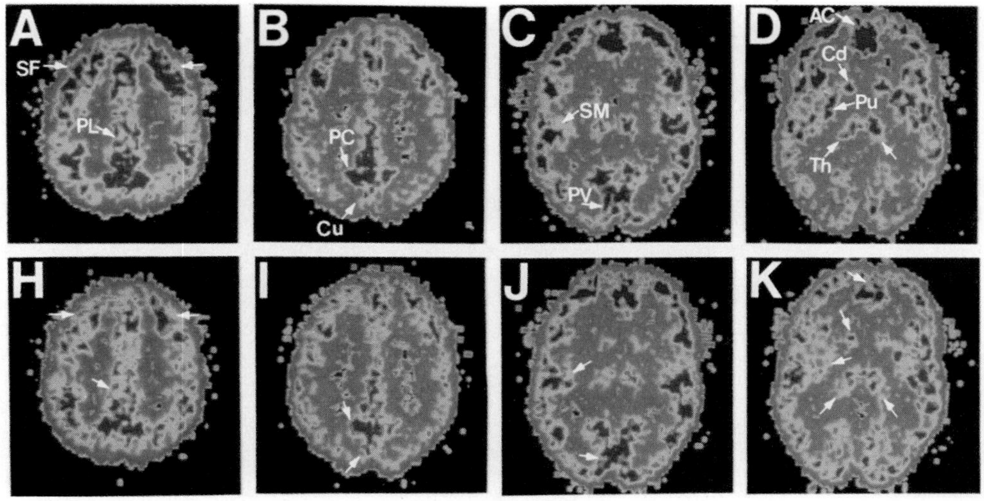

FIGURE 2.9

Color-coded PET scans showing rates of glucose use, a measure of brain activity, in a human volunteer who received placebo (A–D) and morphine, a drug related to heroin (H–K). These images are displayed in sequence from upper to lower levels of the brain (left to right). The lower images (H–K) show a reduction in brain activity when the subject received the drug.

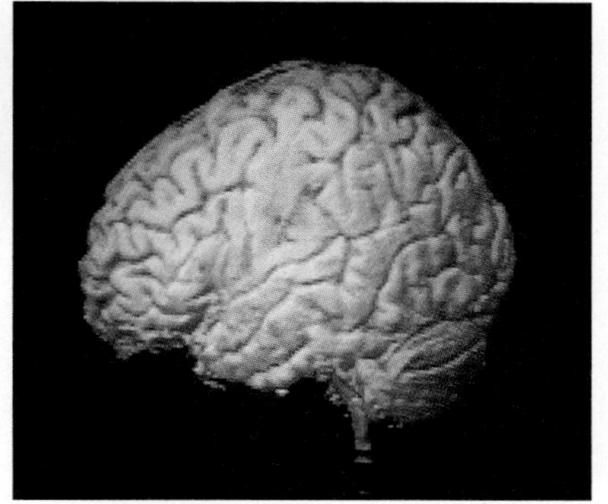

FIGURE 2.10

Three-dimensional image of the living brain based on computer-enhanced MRI.

of the brain tissue provided by the MRI. This new imaging technique has already found very important applications in understanding the role of the brain in neurological and psychological disorders and in the study of basic psychological processes.

Hindbrain and Midbrain: Housekeeping Chores and Reflexes

All mental functions require the integrated functioning of many parts of the brain; no function of the brain is carried out solely in one part. Still, the brain does have many specialized parts, each bearing primary responsibility for certain activities. The brain's many and complex structures can be classified in various ways. The most convenient classification divides the brain into three major parts: the hindbrain, the midbrain, and the forebrain. The major structures and functions of each part are described on the following pages. As we look at the brain, we start at the bottom and work our way up.

The **hindbrain** is the lowest part of the brain, located at the rear base of the skull. Its primary responsibility is to perform routine "housekeeping" functions that keep the body working properly. The hindbrain has three principal parts: the medulla, the pons, and the cerebellum (see fig. 2.11). The **medulla** is a swelling at the top of the spinal cord, where the cord enters the brain. It controls breathing and a variety of reflexes, including those that enable you to maintain an upright posture. The **pons** is concerned with balance, hearing, and some parasympathetic functions. It is located just above the medulla. The **cerebellum** consists of two rounded structures located to the rear of the pons. It is chiefly responsible for maintaining muscle tone and coordinating muscular movements.

The **midbrain** is a small area at the top of the hindbrain that serves primarily as a center for several postural reflexes, particularly those associated with the senses. For example, the automatic movement of the eyes to keep them fixed on an object as the head moves and the reflexive movement of the head to better orient the ears to a sound are both controlled in the midbrain.

hindbrain
The lowest part of the brain, located at the base of the skull.

medulla
(mĕ-dul´ah) The swelling at the top of the spinal cord responsible for controlling breathing and a variety of reflexes.

pons
(ponz) Part of the hindbrain that is involved in balance, hearing, and some parasympathetic functions.

cerebellum
(ser´´e-bel´um) Two rounded lumps behind the medulla responsible for maintaining muscle tone and muscular coordination.

midbrain
The small area at the top of the hindbrain that serves primarily as a reflex center for orienting the eyes and ears.

Forebrain: Cognition, Motivation, Emotion, and Action

By far the most interesting part of the brain to psychologists is the **forebrain.** Structurally, the forebrain consists of two distinct areas. One area, which contains the thalamus, hypothalamus, and most of the limbic system rests at the top of the hindbrain and midbrain (see fig. 2.12). The other area, made up primarily of the cerebral cortex, sits over the lower parts of the brain like the fat cap of an acorn covering its kernel. Not only are these two areas distinctly different in terms of structure, but they control very different functions as well.

Thalamus, Hypothalamus, and Limbic System

The **thalamus** is a switching station for messages going to and from the brain. It routes incoming stimuli from the sense organs to the appropriate parts of the brain and links the

forebrain
The parts of the brain, including the thalamus, hypothalamus, and cerebral cortex, that cover the hindbrain and midbrain and fill much of the skull.

thalamus
(thal´-ah-mus) That part of the forebrain that primarily routes sensory messages to appropriate parts of the brain.

FIGURE 2.11
Important structures of the hindbrain and midbrain.

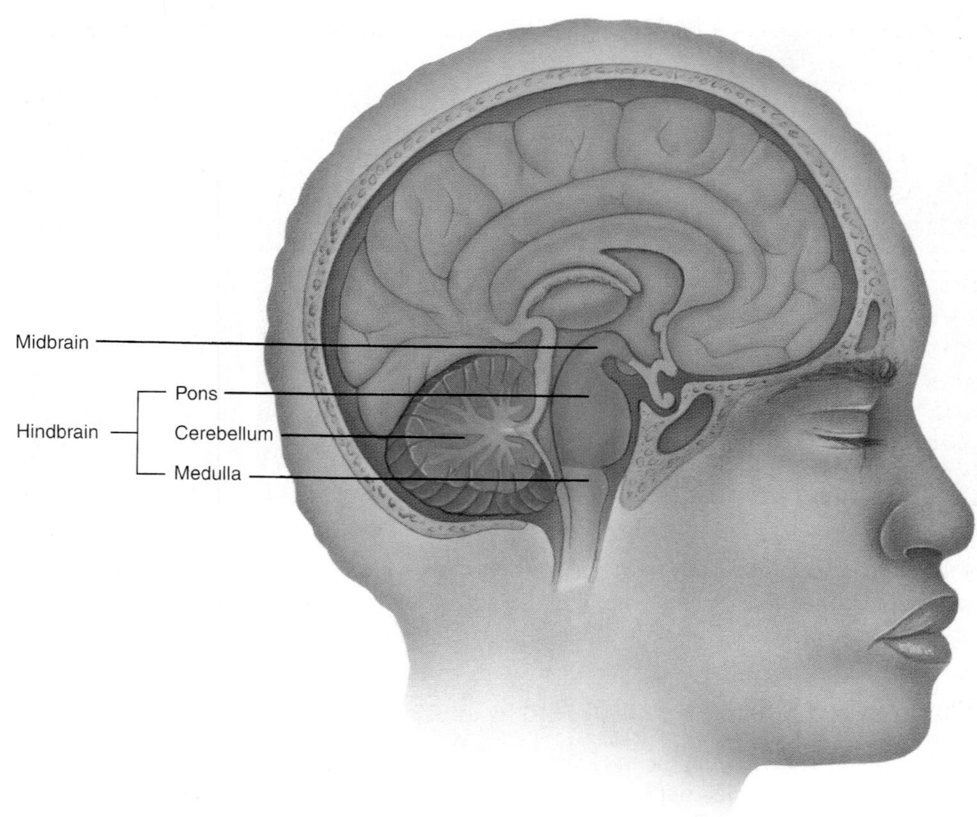

FIGURE 2.12
Key structures of the forebrain.

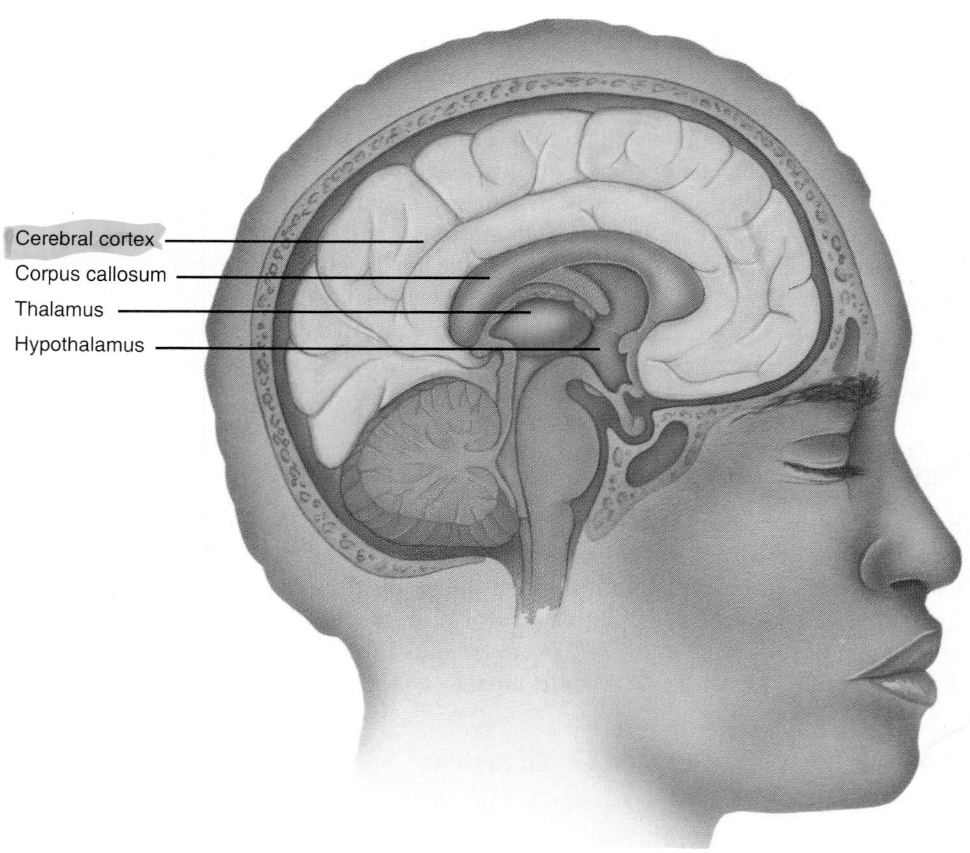

upper and lower centers of the brain. It also plays an important role in the filtering and preliminary processing of sensory information.

The **hypothalamus** is a small, but vitally important, part of the brain. It lies underneath the thalamus, just in front of the midbrain. The hypothalamus is intimately involved in our motives and emotions: eating, drinking, sexual motivation, pleasure, anger, and fear. It also plays a key role in regulating body temperature, sleep, endocrine gland activity, and resistance to disease; controlling glandular secretions of the stomach and intestines; and maintaining the normal pace and rhythm of such body functions as blood pressure and heartbeat (Brooks, 1988). Thus, the hypothalamus is the brain center most directly linked to the functions of the autonomic nervous system.

hypothalamus
(hī´´po-thal´ah-mus) The small part of the forebrain involved with motives, emotions, and the functions of the autonomic nervous system.

The hypothalamus is also involved in aggression. Laboratory studies have found that the degree of aggression in rats can be altered by chemically controlling the hypothalamus. Rats that normally kill mice on sight will stop this behavior when a drug that inhibits the actions of the hypothalamus is injected directly into it. In contrast, rats that normally do not attack mice will kill them when a stimulating drug is injected into the hypothalamus (Smith, King, & Hoebel, 1970).

The hypothalamus also appears to contain specific pleasure centers. Rats will repeatedly press a lever for hours to receive electrical stimulation in certain parts of the hypothalamus (Olds & Milner, 1954). Jose Delgado (1969), working with humans, appears to have identified particular parts of the hypothalamus where electrical stimulation produces intense generalized sensations of pleasure, and other parts where electrical stimulation produces strong specific sensations of sexual pleasure. Apparently, these parts of the hypothalamus are active when we experience pleasure in our daily lives.

The hypothalamus plays its role in emotional arousal by working in close harmony with the **limbic system.** This complex neural system is composed of the several parts shown in figure 2.13. The **amygdala,** a close neighbor to the hypothalamus, appears to play a strong part in activating the emotions of fear and rage. Damage to the amygdala typically results in a complete absence of anger and rage, but sometimes results in uncontrollable rage. Electrical stimulation of the amygdala similarly results in either intense fearfulness or the opposite, apparently fearless rage.

limbic system
Complex brain system composed of the amygdala, hippocampus, septal area, and the cingulate cortex that works with the hypothalamus in emotional arousal.

amygdala
(ah-mig´dah-lah) Part of the limbic system that plays a role in emotional arousal.

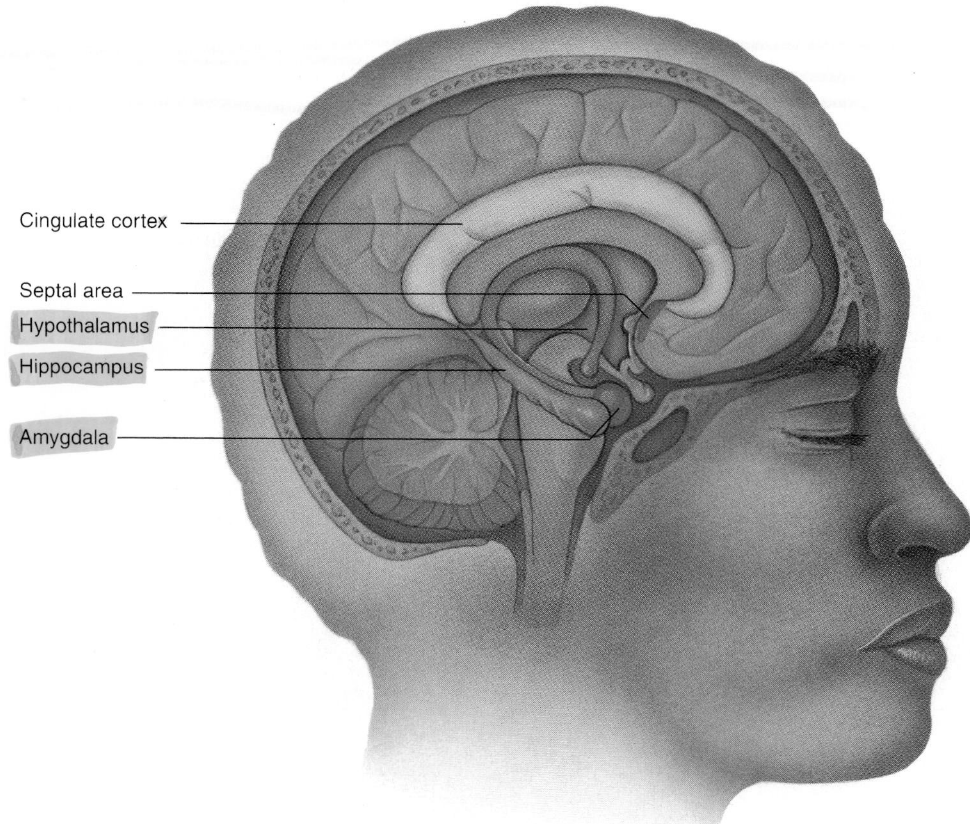

FIGURE 2.13
The structures of the limbic system, which play an important role in emotional arousal.

hippocampus
(hip´´o-kam´pus) Part of the limbic system that plays a role in emotional arousal and memory.

septal area
Part of the limbic system that processes cognitive information in emotion.

cingulate cortex
Part of the limbic system that processes cognitive information in emotion.

cerebral cortex
(ser´ĕ-bral) The largest structure in the forebrain, controlling conscious experience and intelligence and involved with the somatic nervous system.

Other structures of the limbic system play different but equally important roles. The **hippocampus** is not only important in the regulation of emotion, but it also is involved in the formation of new memories. The memory loss experienced by patients suffering from Alzheimer's disease (see p. 80) results in part from damage to the hippocampus. Along with the **septal area** and the cingulate gyrus, the hippocampus brings important cognitive elements into emotion. In comparison to the amygdala, which could be thought of as the "raging bull" of emotion, the hippocampus, septal area, and **cingulate cortex** are the "accountants" of emotion. They carefully watch for signs of possible danger and compare current information with information stored in memory.

Cerebral Cortex: Sensory, Cognitive, and Motor Functions

The largest structure in the forebrain is called the **cerebral cortex.** It is involved in conscious experience, voluntary actions, language, and intelligence—many of the things that make us human. As such, it is the primary brain structure related to the somatic nervous system. The word *cortex* means "bark," referring to the fact that the thin outer surface of the cerebrum is a densely packed mass of billions of neurons. The cortex has a gray appearance due to the presence of the cell bodies of the neurons and is often called the gray matter of the brain. The area of the cerebrum beneath the quarter inch of cortex is often referred to as the white matter, as it is composed primarily of the axons of the cortical neurons. The fatty myelin coating of these neurons gives them their white appearance. The gray and white areas of the cerebrum work together, but because of its rich interconnections, it is often said that the "business" of the cerebrum is mostly conducted in the cortex. Hence we often say that an intelligent person "has a lot of gray matter." The gray and white matter of the cerebral cortex can be seen clearly in the MRI image in figure 2.14.

Lobes of the Cerebral Cortex

Because of the importance of the cerebral cortex to our psychological functioning, let's look at it in more detail. The cerebral cortex can be thought of as being composed of four sections, or *lobes* (see fig. 2.15). Learning the names and locations of these lobes will help us discuss the major functions of the cerebral cortex.

frontal lobes
Part of the cerebral cortex in the front of the skull involved in planning, organization, voluntary motor movements, and speaking.

1. **Frontal lobes.** The frontal lobes occupy the part of the skull behind your forehead and extend back to the middle of the top of your head. The frontal cortex has a wide variety of functions, not all of which are understood. The frontal

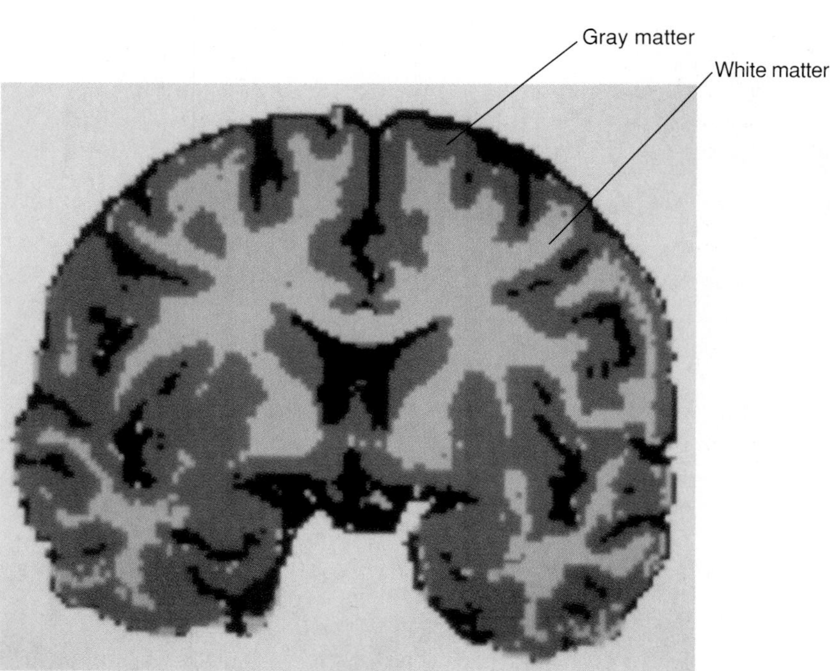

FIGURE 2.14
The gray matter and white matter of the cerebral cortex.

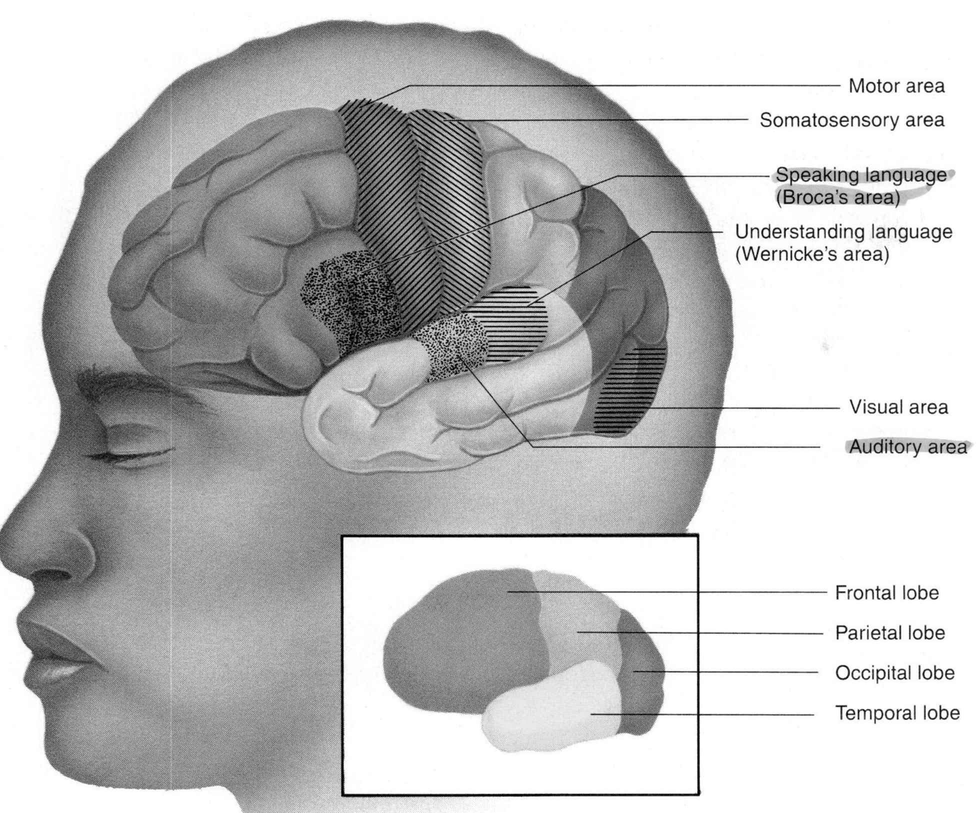

FIGURE 2.15

The four lobes of the cerebral cortex and the functions of key areas of the cerebral cortex.

lobes appear to play an important role in organizing our actions and in predicting the consequences of our behavior. Persons with damage to the frontal lobes often appear to be disorganized and to get into trouble because they act impulsively.

The frontal lobe of the left cerebral hemisphere also contains **Broca's area,** which plays a very specific role in our ability to speak language. This area is named for French neurologist Paul Broca who discovered its function in the late 1800s. He performed autopsies on persons who had earlier had nonfatal **strokes** that left them with a form of the language disorder termed **aphasia** in which affected persons are unable to understand language or to speak. He found that the strokes these patients suffered had occurred in what is now known as Broca's area. He concluded from his early studies that Broca's area was involved only in speaking language and that another area of the brain must be involved in understanding language.

Broca's area
An area of the frontal lobe of the left cerebral hemisphere that plays a role in the ability to speak language.

stroke
A rupture of a blood vessel in the brain that results in the destruction of a part of the brain.

aphasia
(ah-fā'ze-ah) An impairment of the ability to understand or use language.

The frontal lobes also are the major center for the control of voluntary movements of the limbs and body. Near the middle of the top of the head, a strip runs across the back portion of the frontal lobes called the motor area. Damage to this area of the cortex from strokes and other causes can result in paralysis and loss of motor control. Not surprisingly, the part of the motor area that serves the mouth, throat, and tongue are located near Broca's area and control the motor movements that are required by speech.

The effects of damage to the frontal lobes of the cerebral cortex on both intellectual and emotional functioning can be seen in the dramatic case of Phineas Gage. In 1848 Gage was excavating rock to make way for a new section of track for the Rutland and Burlington Railroad in Vermont. Gage, known as a reasonable, polite, and hardworking man, had been made a foreman by the railroad. On one particular afternoon in the fall, he was hard at work preparing to blast a section of rock when an accident happened. Gage was packing blasting powder into a hole with a long tamping rod when a spark ignited the powder. The explosion shot the rod up through his upper left jaw

FIGURE 2.16

A drawing of Phineas Gage's skull and the tamping rod that passed through his brain.

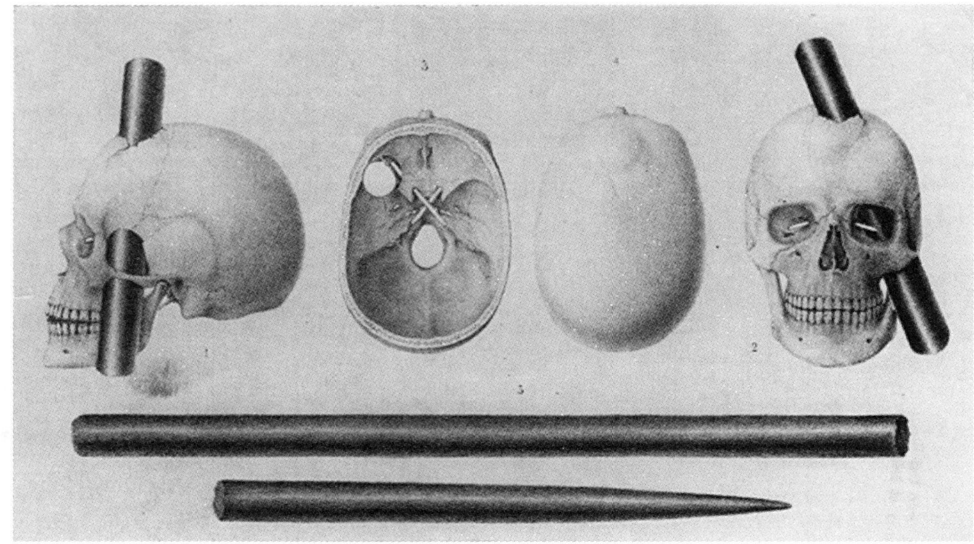

and completely through his skull. As you can see in figure 2.16, the damage from the rod was to the frontal lobes on his left side (close enough to the front to miss Broca's language area).

When Gage's coworkers reached him, he was conscious and able to tell them what had happened. He was rushed to a physician who was able to stop the bleeding and save his life, but the destruction of such a large amount of his left frontal lobe took a terrific toll on him. Gage became irritable, publicly profane, and impossible to reason with. He also seemed to lose much of his ability to think rationally and plan. As a result, he had trouble holding a job and was regarded as a "totally changed" man by his former friends (Bigelow, 1850).

The dramatic alteration in Gage's personality is impressive in what it reveals about the brain. Even though his wounds healed, Gage's left frontal lobe was destroyed. Because brain and behavior are inseparably linked, destruction of a part of his brain that plays an important part in cognition and emotion led to the destruction of important parts of his personality and intellect as well.

parietal lobes
(pah-rī´e-tal) The part of the cerebral cortex located behind the frontal lobes at the top of the skull containing the body sense area.

somatosensory area
The strip of parietal cortex running parallel to the motor area of the frontal lobes.

2. **Parietal lobes.** The parietal lobes are located just behind the frontal lobes at the top of the skull. The strip of parietal cortex running parallel to the motor area of the frontal lobes is termed the **somatosensory area.** This area is important in the sense of touch and the other body senses that tell us, among other things, where our hands and feet are and what they are doing. It is not surprising, then, that the somatosensory area is located next to the motor area, as their functions clearly go hand in hand. As noted earlier when we discussed brain imaging, the areas that were activated when Monte Buchsbaum (fig. 2.8) received a mild shock to his arm were the somatosensory areas of the cerebral cortex.

   Different areas of the somatosensory and motor areas serve different parts of the body. The amount of area of the cortex devoted to a particular part of the body is not in proportion to the size of that body part, however. Rather, it is proportional to the number of sensory and motor neurons going to and from that part of the body. Brain scientists have drawn amusing, yet informative, drawings of people with body features proportional to the space allocated to them in the somatosensory and motor areas (see fig. 2.17).

temporal lobes
The part of the cerebral cortex extending back from the area of the temples beneath the frontal and parietal lobes containing areas involved in the sense of hearing and understanding language.

3. **Temporal lobes.** As suggested by their name, the temporal lobes extend backward from the area of the temples, occupying the middle area at the base of the brain beneath the frontal and parietal lobes. In both hemispheres, the temporal lobes contain the auditory areas. These areas are located just inside the skull

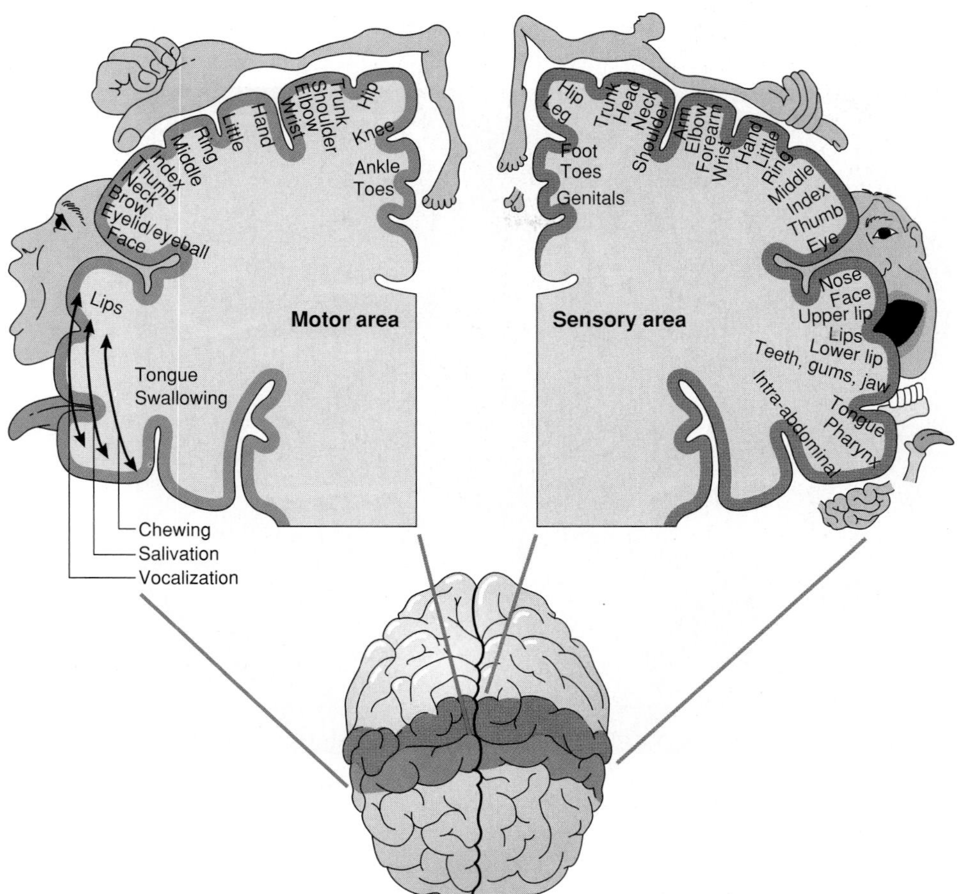

FIGURE 2.17

A cross section of the cerebral cortex in the motor control area and the skin sense area showing the areas in the cortex serving each part of the body. The size of the body feature in the drawing is proportional to the size of the related brain area.

Source: Data from W. Penfield and T. Rasmussen, *The Cerebral Cortex of Man.* Copyright © 1950 Macmillan Publishing Co., New York.

near the ears, immediately below the somatosensory area of the parietal lobes, and are involved in the sense of hearing.

Wernicke's area is located just behind the auditory area in the left hemisphere. This is the other language area of the cortex, the one that plays an essential role in the understanding of spoken language. In this sense, Wernicke's area further processes the messages arriving from the ears that are first processed in its next door neighbor, the auditory area. Damage from strokes and other sources of injury to this area of the cortex result in **Wernicke's aphasia.** Although persons with this form of aphasia can speak normally, they cannot make sense out of language that is spoken to them by others.

Wernicke's area
The language area of the cortex that plays an essential role in understanding spoken language.

Wernicke's aphasia
A form of aphasia in which persons can speak normally but cannot make sense out of language spoken to them by others.

4. **Occipital lobes.** The occipital lobes are located in the area at the base of the back of the head. Although it is the part of the brain that is located farthest from the eyes, the most important part of the occipital lobes is the visual area. The visual area plays an essential role in the processing of sensory information from the eyes. Damage to the visual area of the occipital lobes can result in partial or complete blindness, even though the eyes are able to function normally.

occipital lobes
(ok-sip´ĭ-tal) The part of the cerebral cortex located at the base of the back of the head that plays an essential role in the processing of sensory information from the eyes.

Notice in figure 2.15 that the specific functions of some areas of each of the four lobes of the cerebral hemispheres have been labeled, but many areas of each lobe have been left unlabeled. These unlabeled parts of the cerebral cortex are known as the **association areas.** The association areas play more general roles in cerebral activities, but they often work in close coordination with one of the nearby specific ability areas. This can be seen in the series of PET scan images presented in figure 2.18. The areas of the cerebral cortex that are yellow and red have the greatest amount of neural activity. Notice that when the person is hearing

association areas
Areas within each lobe of the cerebral cortex believed to play general rather than specific roles.

FIGURE 2.18
PET images of the brain at work on four different tasks.

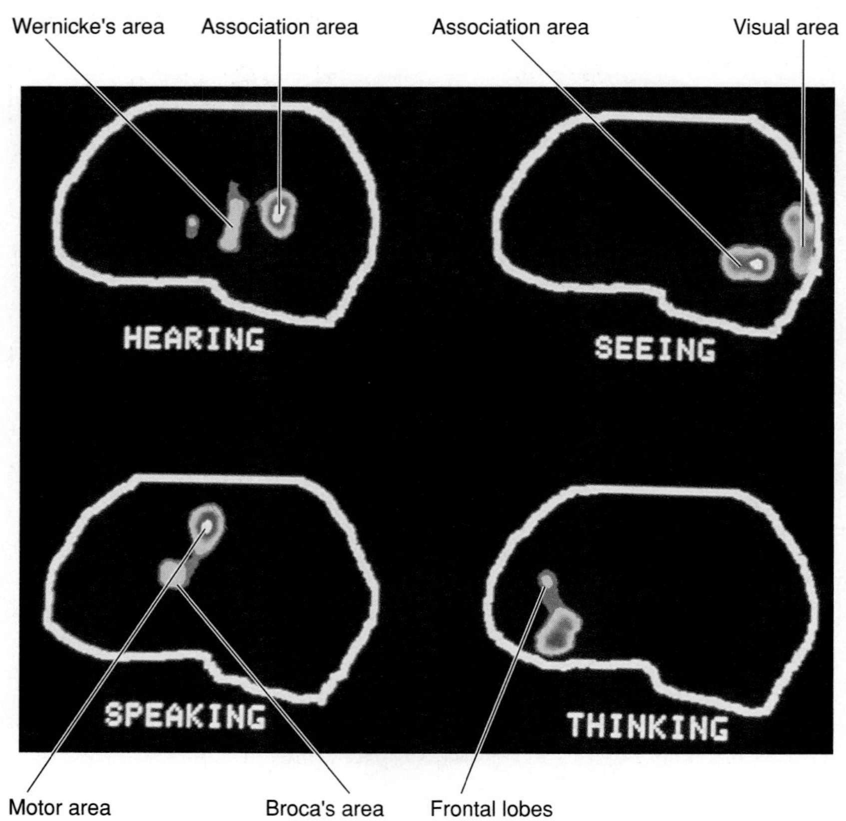

words, there is activity in and around Wernicke's area and in the association areas just behind it. When the person is seeing words, the visual area in the occipital lobe is activated along with part of the nearby association area. In contrast, when the person is speaking words, activation is found only in Broca's area and the motor area of the frontal lobes that controls speech movements, and when the person is thinking, the frontal lobes are active.

Neurologists sometimes call the association areas the "silent areas" of the cortex because strokes and other damage to them produce no permanent loss of motor control, language, or other specific abilities. They apparently serve the areas of the cortex that control specific abilities, but we can function quite well after the loss of considerable amounts of the association areas.

Hemispheres of the Cerebral Cortex

We just saw that the cerebral cortex is composed of four lobes—each of which is involved in different psychological functions. If we look down at the cerebral cortex from the top, however, we can see that it also is made up of two halves called the **cerebral hemispheres.** These two separate hemispheres are linked by the **corpus callosum,** allowing communication between the two halves of the cortex. Many of the functions of the cerebral cortex are shared by both hemispheres. However, the two hemispheres work together in a way that is different from what we might think. Input from the senses of vision and touch, for example, goes to the opposite hemisphere. Stimulation of the skin on the left hand goes to the right cerebral hemisphere, visual stimulation falling on the right visual field of each eye goes to the left hemisphere, and wiggling the toes on your left foot is controlled by the right hemisphere. To accomplish this, the major sensory and motor nerves entering and leaving the brain twist and cross over each other.

cerebral hemispheres
The two main parts of the cerebral cortex.

corpus callosum
(kor´pus kah-lo´-sum) The link between the cerebral hemispheres.

The left and right cerebral hemispheres also play different roles in processing information. For example, strong evidence suggests that the areas that exercise the greatest control over language are located in the left cerebral hemisphere in over 90 percent of the population (Milner, 1974). The right cerebral hemisphere, in contrast, appears to play a greater role in processing information about the location and relationships of things in space

and artistic abilities. As we will see in the following discussion, there is also mounting information that the two cerebral hemispheres play different roles in processing emotional information.

"Split Brains"

The complicated shared functions of the two cerebral hemispheres are possible, in large part, because they communicate through the corpus callosum. It is sometimes necessary to control the neurological disease of epilepsy by surgically cutting the corpus callosum to prevent seizures from spreading from one cerebral hemisphere to the other. When this is done, the right and left hemispheres have no way of exchanging information; the left brain literally does not know what the right brain is doing and vice versa. A number of experiments performed on these patients (referred to as "split-brain" patients) provide a major source of our knowledge about the different functions of the two cerebral hemispheres.

What would be the result of cutting the only line of communication between the two cerebral hemispheres? Surprisingly, a patient with a severed corpus callosum changes very little at first glance. But, although it would be difficult for you—or even for the patient—to notice any difference in daily living, clever psychological experiments have revealed the effects of cutting the connection between the two cerebral hemispheres. In one experiment, the split-brain patient was seated in front of a screen and asked to stare at a spot in the middle. A slide projector briefly flashed a word on one side of the screen so that it was seen by only the left or only the right visual field of the eye. This was done because the left visual field sends information only to the right cerebral hemisphere, and the right visual field sends information only to the left cerebral hemisphere. The nerves from the eye cross at the optic chiasm (see fig. 2.19), which is left uncut.

If the word *pencil* is presented in the right visual field of each eye, the information travels to the language control areas in the left hemisphere. In this situation, the patient has no difficulty reading aloud the word *pencil*. But if the same word is presented to the left visual field of each eye, the split-brain patient would typically not be able to respond when asked what word had been presented. This does not mean that the right side of the brain did not receive or understand the word *pencil*. Rather, it means that the patient cannot verbalize what she saw. Using the sense of touch, the split-brain patient can easily pick out a pencil as the object that matched the word from among a number of unseen objects—but only if she uses her left hand, which has received the message from the right cerebral cortex.

However, if the split-brain patient holds an unseen pencil in her left hand, she cannot tell you what she is holding. It's not that the right cortex does not know, but because it has

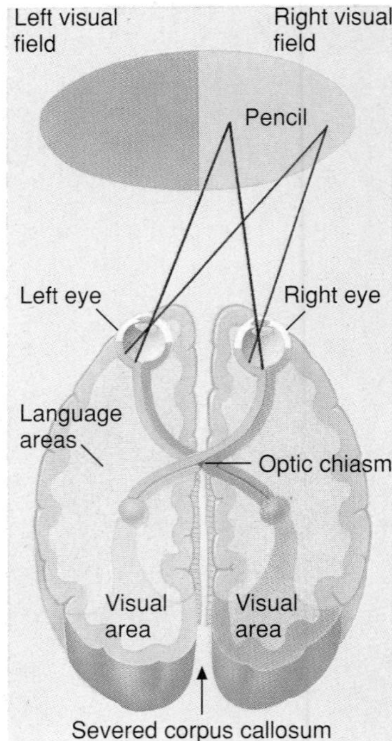

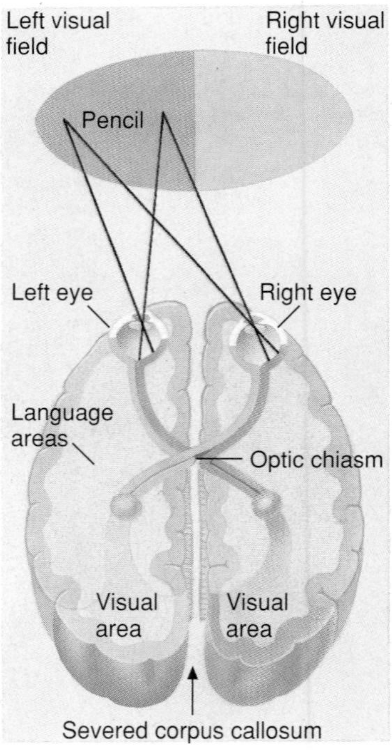

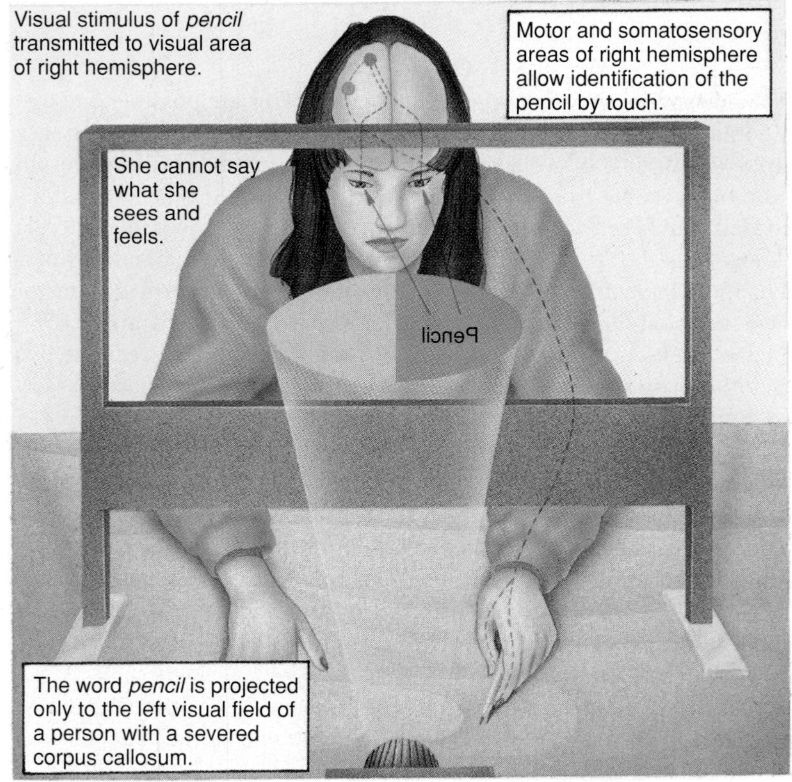

FIGURE 2.19

Studies of persons whose corpus callosum has been surgically cut to treat the disease of epilepsy tell us much about the different functions of the two cerebral hemispheres and the important role that the corpus callosum normally plays in allowing communication between the two hemispheres. When the word ***pencil*** is shown only to the right visual field, the information is sent only to the left cerebral hemisphere. The language areas in the left hemisphere allow the person to say that the word ***pencil*** has been seen. But, when the stimulus is shown only to the left visual field, the information is sent only to the right hemisphere, which does not have language areas. In this case, the person cannot confirm verbally that the word has been seen but can identify the pencil as the correct stimulus by the sense of touch.

no area controlling verbal expression, it cannot tell you what it knows. The left cortex that is "talking" to you cannot tell you either, because information in the right cortex cannot reach it in the split-brain patient. Such studies with split-brain patients clearly reveal the localization of language expression abilities in the left cerebral hemisphere (Gazzaniga, 1967; 1983).

Leonardo da Vinci (1452–1519)

Hemispheres of the Cerebral Cortex and Emotion

Although the cerebral cortex is primarily involved in sensory, motor, and cognitive processes, it also plays a key role in the processing of emotional information. As we have seen, there are marked differences in the cognitive functions of the two cerebral hemispheres. It is of great interest to psychologists, therefore, that the two cerebral hemispheres also appear to play different roles in emotion (Davidson, 1992).

Many researchers have concluded that the right hemisphere plays a dominant role in both the expression and perception of emotions. The left side of the face, which is primarily controlled by the right cerebral hemisphere, makes stronger expressions of emotion (Moscovitch & Olds, 1982). In other words, the left side of our mouth "smiles" and "frowns" more dramatically than the right side. One possible reason for our fascination with Da Vinci's painting of "Mona Lisa" is that she smiles more on her right side. We're not used to seeing people smile that way, and it catches our attention. Art historians tell us that Da Vinci finished some features of this painting while studying his own expressions in a mirror. Perhaps the "left-sided" smile that he saw in the mirror became the Mona Lisa's intriguing "right-sided" smile.

In addition to its role in the expression of emotion, the right hemisphere is also essential for understanding the emotions expressed by others (Blonder, Bowers, & Heilman, 1991). Beatty (1995) described how patients with right hemisphere damage failed to match emotional tones of voice to pictures of people expressing anger, happiness, sadness, and indifference. Patients with left hemisphere damage, although they had difficulty understanding the meaning of what was said, had no problems identifying the emotions.

Does this mean that there is no role whatsoever for the left hemisphere in emotion? Not at all. Think about the implications of the following observation. As long ago as 1861, physician Paul Broca noticed that patients who had suffered strokes in the left cerebral hemisphere often became depressed, while patients with right hemisphere strokes were much less likely to do so. Since Broca's time, his observation has been repeated many times (Kinsbourne, 1988; Robinson & Starkstein, 1990; Starkstein, Robinson, & Price, 1988). For example, the images of the brains shown in figure 2.20 (obtained using **computerized tomography [CT]** scans) of persons who developed depression following strokes show clearly that the damage to their brains was primarily on the left side of the cortex (Starkstein et al., 1988).

Mona Lisa by Leonardo da Vinci

In striking contrast, patients with right hemisphere damage are often cheerful, happy, and not at all depressed by their disability (Kinsbourne, 1988). It appears that the reason why left-hemisphere strokes cause depression has to do with the way in which the two hemispheres process emotional information. The right hemisphere appears to be more involved with the processing of negative emotions, whereas the left hemisphere plays a greater role in the processing of positive emotions. Some theorists believe that when the left hemisphere is damaged by a stroke, the negative emotions processed in the right hemisphere become dominant and cause depression (Starkstein & Robinson, 1988). This theory is strongly supported by studies in which a sedative injected directly into the artery supplying only the left side of the brain results in a sudden and

computerized tomography (CT)
An imaging technique utilizing X-rays to provide two-dimensional images of brain structure.

FIGURE 2.20

Drawings from computed tomographic (CT) scans of the brains of individuals who became depressed following a stroke. The shaded areas show the damaged cerebral tissue.

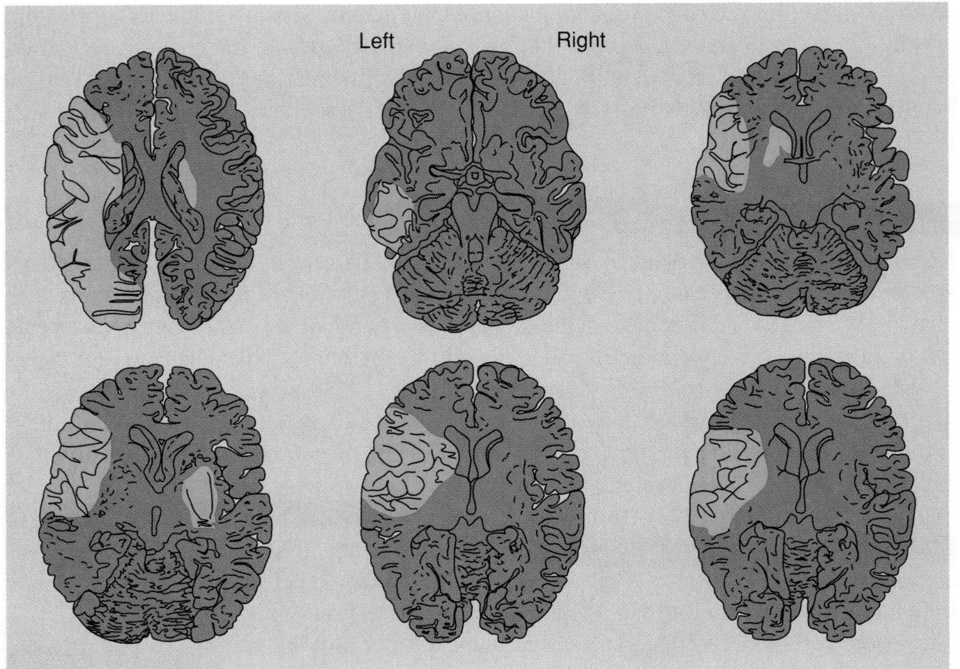

unexplained sadness. The left side of the brain is sedated, but the "gloomy" right side still functions (Kinsbourne, 1988).

The theory that the left cerebral hemisphere plays a greater role in processing positive emotions while the right cerebral hemisphere is more involved with negative emotions has been strengthened by dramatic findings reported by Richard Davidson of the University of Wisconsin (Davidson, Ekman, Saron, Senulis, & Friesen, 1990). In this study, several short films were shown to college students—some entertaining films of playful animals and some "quite gruesome" films of amputations and burn victims. As the students watched the films, their facial expressions were monitored. When they were smiling, EEG recordings indicated more activity in the left cerebral hemisphere, but when they showed disgust, their right hemisphere was more active. Apparently, positive emotions are processed more in the left hemisphere and negative emotions in the right hemisphere.

The Brain Is an Interacting System

Even though we find it convenient to think of the brain as being divided into many separate parts, you should know that the parts commonly work together in intellectual and emotional functioning. Consider, for example, your reaction in the following situation. You are waiting at a bus stop late at night. A poorly dressed man approaches, smelling of alcohol. He asks if you can spare five dollars. In his pocket, you see the outline of what might be a gun. Your reaction to this scene would involve many parts of your brain working together. Your cerebral hemispheres evaluate the possible threat to you and the alternative courses of action open to you. Your hypothalamus and limbic system are involved in a process of emotional arousal. If you fight, run, or even reach into your pocket to hand over the money, the motor areas of your cortex will work with your hindbrain and midbrain to coordinate the muscular movements involved. The many parts of the brain work together.

Sometimes the many parts of the brain interact because one part of the brain sends a message to another part, which then sends it on to a third part of the brain, and so on. More often, however, several parts of the brain process different kinds of related information at the same time. To use computer language, the brain often uses "parallel" processing (handling different information at the same time) rather than "serial" processing (handling one kind of information at a time (Rumelhart & McClelland, 1986). The brain's amazing capacity for parallel processing magnifies its ability to use its 100 billion neurons and their trillions of connections to produce our complex actions, emotions, and thoughts.

Review

The brain is a complex system composed of many parts that carry out different functions but work together in an integrated fashion. The hindbrain and midbrain mostly handle the housekeeping responsibilities of the body such as breathing, posture, reflexes, and other basic processes. The larger forebrain area carries out the more "psychological" functions of the brain: The thalamus integrates sensory input and the hypothalamus controls motivation, emotion, sleep, and other basic bodily processes. Both the thalamus and the hypothalamus lie beneath the cap of the cerebral cortex. Most of the limbic system, which plays an important role in emotional arousal, is located below the cortex, but lower cortical structures are involved as well. The cerebral cortex provides the neural basis for thinking, language, control of motor movements, perception, and other cognitive processes, but also processes emotional information. The cortex is composed of two halves, the cerebral hemispheres, which are connected to each other by the corpus callosum. Except for areas of the cortex that serve language, those that provide the basis for the other cognitive processes are found in both hemispheres. The two cerebral hemispheres are involved in different aspects of these cognitive processes, however. The right hemisphere serves spatial and artistic cognitive processes, while the left hemisphere is involved in logical, mathematical, and language-based processes. The two cerebral hemispheres also appear to process different aspects of emotion, with the left hemisphere being more involved in positive emotion and the right hemisphere playing a greater role in negative emotion.

Thinking Critically About Psychology

1. Imagine that you have put down this book and are taking a huge bite of your favorite kind of pizza. Think of the role that each part of the brain plays in this simple act.

2. Does what you have learned about the two cerebral hemispheres suggest that we should think of ourselves as having "two brains" or one? How about the autonomic nervous system—is that "another brain with a mind of its own?"

Check Your Learning

To be sure that you have learned the key points from the preceding section, cover the answers below and try to answer each question. If you give an incorrect answer to any question, return to the page given next to the correct answer to see why your answer was not correct.

1. The midbrain and hindbrain play the greatest role in which functions?

- **a.** motivation and emotion
- **b.** learning and thinking
- **c.** planning for the future
- **d.** bodily housekeeping and reflexes

2. The small but vitally important part of the forebrain that plays a key role in the control of motivation, emotion, endocrine gland activity, resistance to disease, blood pressure, and heartbeat (because it is the brain center most linked to the autonomic nervous system) is the

- **a.** cerebrum.
- **b.** cerebellum.
- **c.** hypothalamus.
- **d.** thalamus.

3. Broca's area, which controls speaking, is located in the ________ lobe of the left cerebral hemisphere.

- **a.** frontal
- **b.** temporal
- **c.** parietal
- **d.** occipital

4. Vision is controlled primarily by areas in the ________ lobe.

- **a.** frontal
- **b.** temporal
- **c.** parietal
- **d.** occipital

5. Positive emotions are processed more by the ________ cerebral hemisphere.

Correct Answers

1. d (p. 53), **2.** c (p. 55), **3.** a (p. 57), **4.** d (p.59), **5.** left (p. 63).

ENDOCRINE SYSTEM: CHEMICAL MESSENGERS OF THE BODY

endocrine system
(en´dō-krin) The system of glands that secretes hormones.

glands
Structures in the body that secrete substances.

hormones
(hor´mōnz) Chemical substances, produced by endocrine glands, that influence internal organs.

The nervous system, as we have just seen, is the vital computer and communication system that forms the biological basis for behavior and conscious experience. Another biological system also plays an important role in communication and the regulation of bodily processes—the **endocrine system.** This system consists of a number of **glands** that secrete chemical messengers called **hormones** into the bloodstream. The action of hormones is closely related to that of the nervous system in three ways. First, the hormones are directly regulated by the brain, particularly the hypothalamus. Second, some of the hormones are chemically identical to some of the neurotransmitters. Third, the hormones aid the nervous system's ability to control the body by activating many organs during physical stress or emotional arousal, and by influencing such things as metabolism, the level of blood sugar, and sexual functioning. Let's look briefly at the seven endocrine glands that are most important to our psychological lives (see fig. 2.21).

Pituitary Gland

pituitary gland
(pĭ-tu´ĭ-tār´´e) The body's master gland, located near the bottom of the brain, whose hormones help regulate the activity of the other glands in the endocrine system.

The **pituitary gland** is located near the bottom of the brain, connected to and largely controlled by the hypothalamus. It is sometimes thought of as the body's master gland because its hormones help to regulate the activity of the other glands in the endocrine system. Perhaps its most important function is regulating the body's reactions to stress and resistance to disease (Muller & Nistico, 1989). The pituitary gland secretes hormones that have other important effects on the body, notably in controlling blood pressure, thirst, and body growth. Too little or too much of the pituitary's growth hormone will make a person develop into a dwarf or giant. One special function of the pituitary gland is of particular importance to newborn infants. When the infant sucks the mother's nipples, a neural message is sent to the mother's hypothalamus, which sends a message to the pituitary gland. This causes the pituitary to secrete a hormone that releases breast milk for the baby.

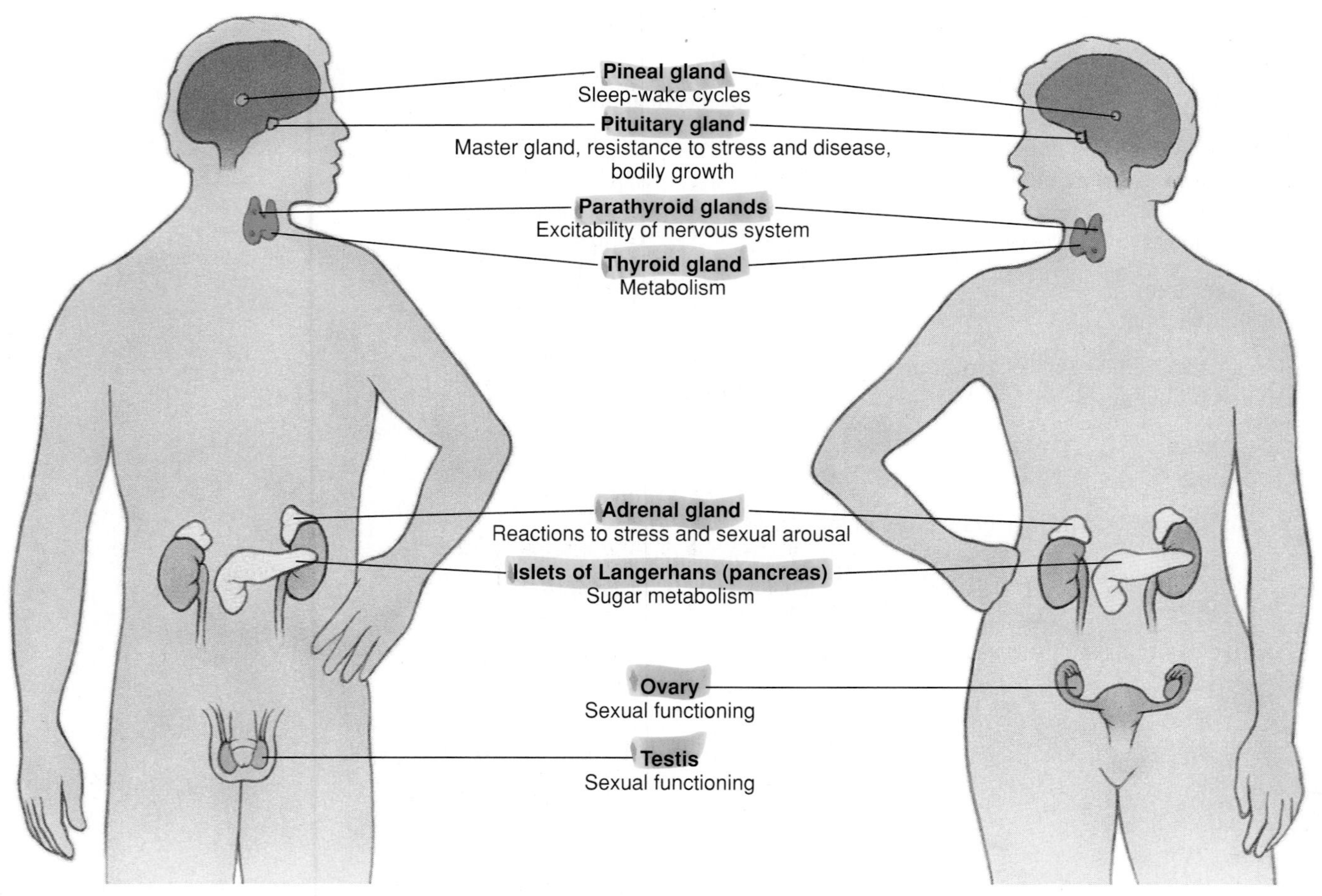

FIGURE 2.21
Locations of major endocrine glands and their principal functions

Adrenal Glands

The **adrenal glands** are a pair of glands that sit atop the two kidneys. They play an important role in emotional arousal and secrete a variety of hormones important to metabolism and sexual arousal. When stimulated either by a hormone from the pituitary gland or by the sympathetic division of the autonomic nervous system, the adrenal glands secrete three hormones, among others, that are particularly important in reactions to stress. **Epinephrine** and **norepinephrine** (which are also neurotransmitters) stimulate changes to prepare the body to deal with physical demands that require intense bodily activity, including psychological threats or danger (even when the danger cannot be dealt with physically). The effects of these two adrenal hormones are quite similar, but they can be distinguished in terms of their most potent effects. Epinephrine increases blood pressure by increasing heart rate and blood flow; causes the liver to convert and release some of its supply of stored sugar into the bloodstream; and increases the rate at which the body uses energy (i.e., metabolism), sometimes by as much as 100 percent over normal. Norepinephrine also increases blood pressure, but it does this by constricting the diameter of blood vessels in the body's muscles and by reducing the activity of the digestive system (Groves & Rebec, 1988; Hole, 1990). The adrenal glands also secrete the hormone **cortisol,** which also activates the body in terms of stress and plays a particularly important role in the regulation of immunity to disease.

adrenal glands
(ah-drē´nal) Two glands on the kidneys that secrete epinephrine and norepinephrine and that are involved in emotional arousal.

epinephrine
(ep´´i-nef´rin) A hormone produced by the adrenal glands.

norepinephrine
(nor´´ep-i-nef´rin) A hormone produced by the adrenal glands.

cortisol
A hormone produced by the adrenal glands.

Let's look at an example of the action of the adrenal glands during stress. Does giving a speech in public make you tense? Most people find public speaking to be at least mildly stressful. German scientist Ulrich Bolm-Andorff collected blood and urine from 10 physicians and psychologists at two different times: (a) just after they gave an important public speech to their colleagues, and (b) at the same time on another day when they were not speaking (Bolm-Andorff, Schwämmle, Ehlenz, Koop, & Kaffarnik, 1986). Three adrenal hormones (epinephrine, norepinephrine, and cortisol) were measured in these fluids. Look at figure 2.22 to see the dramatic increase in the secretion of adrenal hormones during the speech. Notice, too, the corresponding increase in heart rate and blood pressure.

The changes in heart rate and blood pressure were caused by the action of epinephrine and norepinephrine on the heart and blood vessels, but also by the direct action of the autonomic nervous system on these organs. Thus, the autonomic nervous system has two ways of activating the internal bodily organs: by directly affecting the organs and by

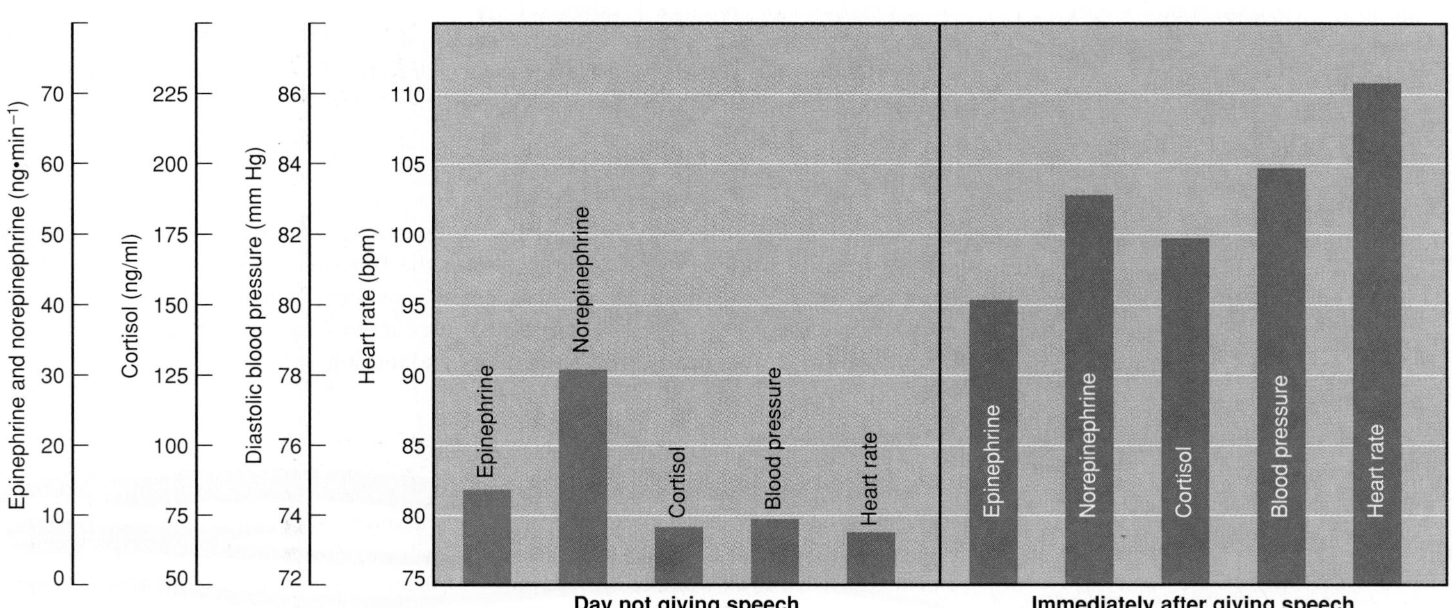

FIGURE 2.22

The effects of the stress of giving a public speech on hormones secreted by the adrenal glands and on heart rate and blood pressure.

Source: Data from V. Bolm-Andorff, et al., "Hormonal and Cardiovascular Variations During a Public Lecture" in *European Journal of Applied Physiology,* 54:669–674. Copyright 1986 Springer-Verlag, New York, NY.

islets of Langerhans
(i′lets of lahng′er-hanz) Endocrine cells in the pancreas that regulate the level of sugar in the blood.

pancreas
(pan′krē-as) The organ near the stomach that contains the islets of Langerhans.

glucagon
(gloo′kah-gon) A hormone produced by the islets of Langerhans that causes the liver to release sugar into the bloodstream.

insulin
(in′su-lin) A hormone produced by the islets of Langerhans that reduces the amount of sugar in the bloodstream.

ovaries
(o′vah-rēz) Female endocrine glands that secrete sex-related hormones and produce ova, or eggs.

testes
(tes′tēz) Male endocrine glands that secrete sex-related hormones and produce sperm cells.

gonads
(gō′nadz) The glands that produce sex cells and hormones important in sexual arousal and that contribute to the development of secondary sex characteristics.

estrogen
(es′tro-jen) A female sex hormone.

testosterone
(tes-tos′tĕr-ōn) A male sex hormone.

thyroid gland
(thī′roid) The gland below the voice box that regulates metabolism.

metabolism
(mĕ-tab′o-lizm) The process through which the body burns energy.

thyroxin
(thī-rok′sin) A hormone produced by the thyroid that is necessary for proper mental development in children and helps determine weight and level of activity in adults.

cretinism
(kre′tin-izm) A type of mental retardation in children caused by a deficiency of thyroxin.

parathyroid glands
(par′′ah-thī′roid) Four glands embedded in the thyroid that produce parathormone.

parathormone
(par′′ah-thor′mōn) A hormone that regulates ion levels in neurons and controls excitability of the nervous system.

stimulating the adrenals and other endocrine glands that affect the organs with their hormones. Incidentally, one reason it takes so long to feel calm after a stressful event has passed is because of this second route to activating the body. It takes quite a while for the hormones to leave the bloodstream, so their effects are rather long lasting.

Islets of Langerhans

The **islets of Langerhans,** which are embedded in the **pancreas,** regulate the level of sugar in the blood by secreting two hormones that have opposing actions. **Glucagon** causes the liver to convert its stored sugar into blood sugar and to dump it into the bloodstream. **Insulin,** in contrast, reduces the amount of blood sugar by helping the body's cells absorb it more easily from the bloodstream. Blood sugar level is important psychologically because it's one of the factors in the hunger motive and helps determine how energetic a person feels.

Gonads

There are two sex glands—the **ovaries** in females, the **testes** in males. The **gonads** produce the sex cells—ova in females, sperm in males. They also secrete hormones that are important in sexual arousal and contribute to the development of so-called secondary sex characteristics (e.g., breast development in women, growth of chest hair in men, deepening of the voice in males at adolescence, and growth of pubic hair in both sexes). The most important sex hormones are **estrogen** in females and **testosterone** in males.

Thyroid Gland

The **thyroid gland,** located just below the larynx, or voice box, plays an important role in the regulation of **metabolism.** It does so by secreting a hormone called **thyroxin.** The level of thyroxin in a person's bloodstream, and the resulting metabolic rate, are important in many ways. In children, proper functioning of the thyroid is necessary for proper mental development. A serious thyroid deficiency in childhood will produce sluggishness, poor muscle tone, and a type of mental retardation called **cretinism.**

In adults, the thyroxin level helps determine one's weight and level of activity. People whose thyroid glands secrete unusually large amounts of thyroxin are typically very active. They may eat large amounts of food but still not gain weight because their rapid metabolic rate burns off calories so quickly. Conversely, people with low thyroxin levels tend to be inactive and overweight. A "thyroid problem" is rarely the main cause of a weight problem, however. Thyroid disturbances can also lead to depression in adults. But, as with weight problems, most depression is not caused by a malfunctioning thyroid.

Parathyroid Glands

The four small glands imbedded in the thyroid gland are the **parathyroid glands.** They secrete **parathormone,** which is important in the functioning of the nervous system. Parathormone controls the excitability of the nervous system by regulating ion levels in the neurons. Too much parathormone inhibits nervous activity and leads to lethargy; too little of it may lead to excessive nervous activity and tension.

Pineal Gland

The **pineal gland** is located between the cerebral hemispheres, attached to the top of the thalamus. Its primary secretion is the hormone *melatonin.* Melatonin is important in the regulation of biological rhythms, including the daily regulation of sleep and wakefulness, and menstrual cycles in females. Melatonin levels seem to be affected by the amount of exposure to sunlight and, hence, "clock" the time of day partly in that fashion. Melatonin also appears to play a role in regulating moods. Seasonal affective disorder, a type of depression that occurs most frequently in the winter months, can be treated using bright light, which is thought to be effective because of the influence of light on melatonin.

Recently, many scientists have become concerned about the widespread use of melatonin in pill form to treat sleep disturbances and other problems (Haimov & Lavie, 1996). There is little evidence on possible harmful side effects of melatonin supplements.

Review

The hormones of the endocrine glands supplement the brain's ability to coordinate the body's reactions and activities. These chemical messengers are involved in the regulation of metabolism, blood sugar level, sexual functioning, and other body functions. Most important from the viewpoint of psychology is the role of epinephrine and norepinephrine in emotional arousal. These hormones, secreted by the adrenal glands, activate the bodily organs in a diffuse and long-lasting way that is partially responsible for the length of time necessary for us to feel calm following a stressful event.

Thinking Critically About Psychology

1. In what ways does epinephrine resemble a drug like alcohol?

2. When doing something stressful, like speaking in public, how do the effects of hormones secreted by our adrenal glands help us—how are they adaptive?

Check Your Learning

To be sure that you have learned the key points from the preceding section, cover the answers below and try to answer each question. If you give an incorrect answer to any question, return to the page given next to the correct answer to see why your answer was not correct.

1. The ____________________ secretes epinephrine, norepinephrine, and cortisol, which activate the body during stress (such as by increasing heart rate and blood pressure).

- **a.** adrenal gland
- **b.** parathyroid gland
- **c.** thyroid gland
- **d.** pituitary gland

2. Sugar metabolism and hunger are influenced by the ____________________ .

3. The ____________________ gland is called the "master gland" because its secretions influence many other glands.

- **a.** adrenal gland
- **b.** parathyroid gland
- **c.** thyroid gland
- **d.** pituitary gland

4. The excitability of the nervous system is regulated by parathormone which is secreted by the

- **a.** adrenal gland.
- **b.** parathyroid gland.
- **c.** thyroid gland.
- **d.** pituitary gland.

Correct Answers
1. a (p. 67), **2.** islets of Langerhans (p. 68), **3.** d (p. 66), **4.** b (p. 68).

pineal gland
(pin´e-al) The endocrine gland that is largely responsible for the regulation of biological rhythms.

GENETIC INFLUENCES ON BEHAVIOR: BIOLOGICAL BLUEPRINTS?

If you speak loudly like your father, is it because you inherited a loud voice from him or because you learned to talk that way by living with him? If you are good in math like your mother, was that inherited or learned? In general, what is the role of heredity in human behavior?

What Is Inherited?

It's obvious that children inherit many of their physical characteristics from their parents. Light or dark skin, blue or brown eyes, tall or short stature—these are all traits we routinely expect to be passed from parents to children. Many aspects of behavior are also influenced by inheritance, but it's more difficult to distinguish the influence of heredity from that of our experiences in psychology—to separate nature from nurture, as the saying goes.

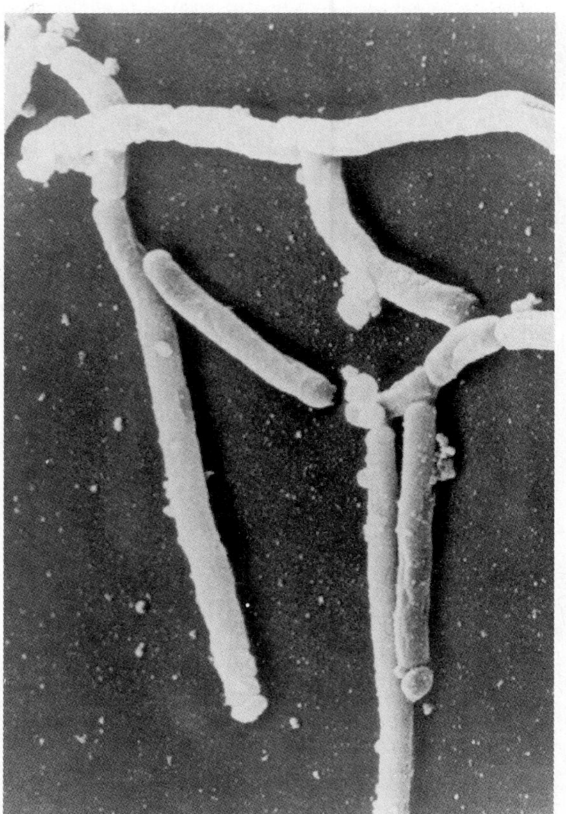

Individual human genes.

Research on the inheritance of behavior in animals has provided some valuable insights. For example, considerable research has been done on the nest-building behavior of a seabird called the tern. The question is: How does every female tern know how to build a nest? Is it a learned skill, or are the instructions for this behavior biologically programmed into the bird from birth? Experiments have made it clear that the latter is the case. If you raise a female tern in a laboratory, depriving it of the opportunity to see any tern nests from the time it hatches, it will still build precisely the same kind of nest its mother built. Obviously, "knowledge" of nest building is part of the tern's genetic inheritance.

Inheritance does not play such a direct and complete role in governing the behavior of humans, however. Humans do not inherit specific patterns of behavior like nest building in terns; rather, inheritance seems to influence broad dimensions of our behavior such as sociability, anxiousness, and intelligence (Plomin, 1989). Psychologists are not yet sure *how much* heredity influences these dimensions of behavior. It's probably never the sole cause but operates in conjunction with the effects of the environment.

Biological Mechanisms of Inheritance: Genetic Codes

People long wondered how inherited characteristics are passed on. For many years it was thought that they were transmitted through the blood—hence, old sayings like, "He has his family's bad blood." We now know that inheritance operates through genetic material called **genes** found in the nuclei of all human cells. The existence of genes was guessed more than a century ago by Gregor Mendel, the Austrian monk who helped found the science of genetics. It has been only during the last half of this century, however, that genes have actually been seen with the aid of electron microscopes.

gene
(jēn) The hereditary unit made up of deoxyribonucleic acid.

Mendel's theory that there are genes for a wide variety of traits, or characteristics, was based on a study of pea plants. If a pea was wrinkled, it was because it had a gene for wrinkled skin. If a pea plant (or by extension a person) was tall, it was because it (or he or she) had a gene for tallness. The genes, Mendel reasoned, were passed on from parents to children. If both parents passed on a gene for a particular trait, clearly that trait would be perpetuated. If the parents passed on conflicting genes, however, only one of the genes would dominate, and the child would show the trait reflecting the dominant gene. Although Mendel's theory attracted little notice in the nineteenth century, it gained a widespread following in the twentieth century and research has largely borne it out.

Genes and Chromosomes

deoxyribonucleic acid (DNA)
(de-ok′′sē-rī′′bō-nu-klā′ik) The complex molecule containing the genetic code.

chromosome
(krōmo-sōm) The strip in the cell nucleus that contains genes.

gamete
(gam′ēt) A sex cell, which contains 23 chromosomes instead of the normal 46.

fertilization
(fer′tĭ-li-zā′shun) The uniting of sperm and ovum, which produces a zygote.

zygote
(zī′gōt) The stable cell resulting from fertilization; it has 46 chromosomes—23 from the sperm and 23 from the ovum.

Genes provide their instructions to the organism through a complex substance called **DNA,** short for **deoxyribonucleic acid.** Not until the early 1950s did scientists begin to unravel the structure of DNA and begin to understand the way in which strands of DNA form a code that, in effect, instructs an organism how to develop and function. Research on DNA and its role in the genetic process is still continuing at an intense pace today.

The genes are arrayed on strips called **chromosomes,** which are found within the nucleus of each body cell (see fig. 2.23). Each of the 46 chromosomes of a normal cell contains thousands of genes. The chromosomes are arranged in 23 pairs. When cells divide in the normal process of tissue growth and repair, they create exact copies of themselves. However, when sex cells (sperm or ova) are formed, the chromosome pairs split so that the resulting sex cell has only 23 unpaired chromosomes. These sex cells, or **gametes,** are short-lived, but when a sperm unites successfully with an ovum in the act of **fertilization,** a stable cell, capable of life, is formed. The new cell, called a **zygote,** has a full complement of 23 pairs of chromosomes, 23 from the mother (ovum) and 23 from the father (sperm). If conditions are right, the zygote becomes implanted in the lining of the mother's uterus, and the embryo develops.

The chromosomes you receive from a particular parent are a matter of chance. That is why sisters and brothers can have substantially different genes and substantially different inherited traits. Think of each of your parents' 23 pairs of chromosomes for a moment as

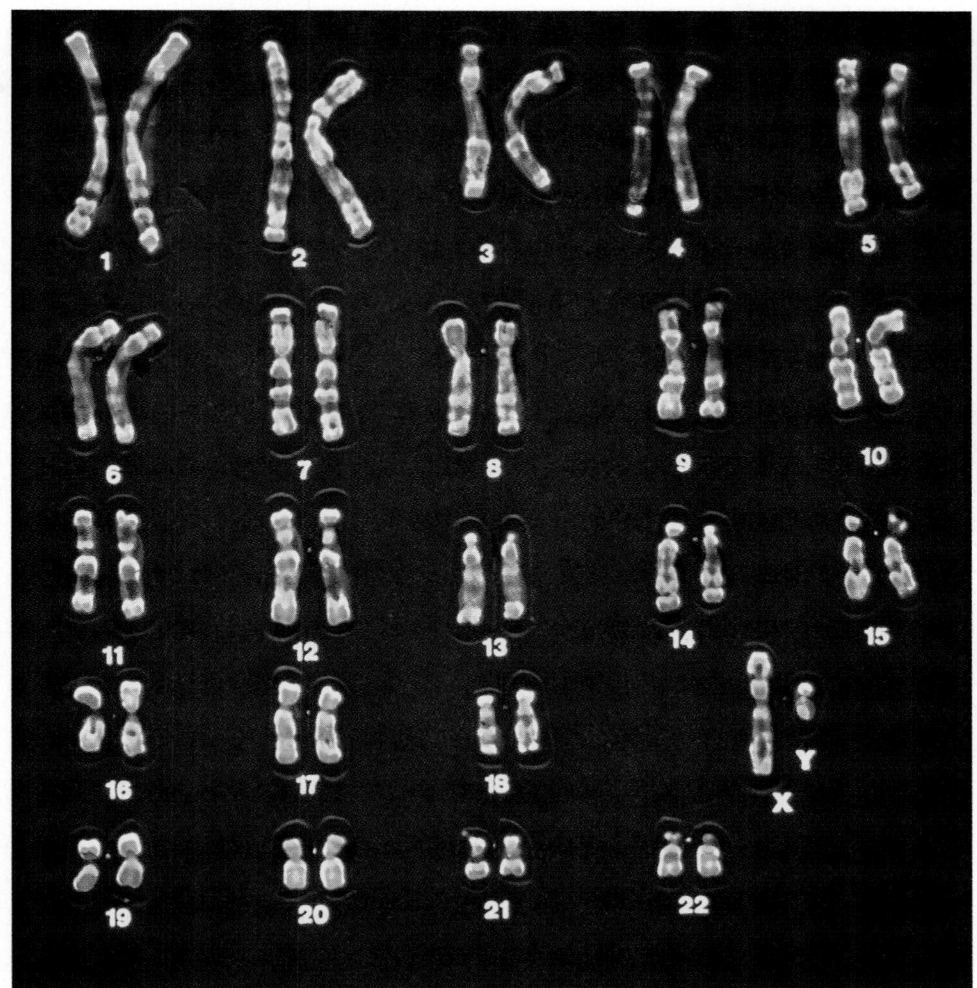

FIGURE 2.23

The nucleus of each human cell contains 46 chromosomes united in pairs, 23 from the sperm and 23 from the ovum. In this photograph, the 23rd pair is labeled X and Y.

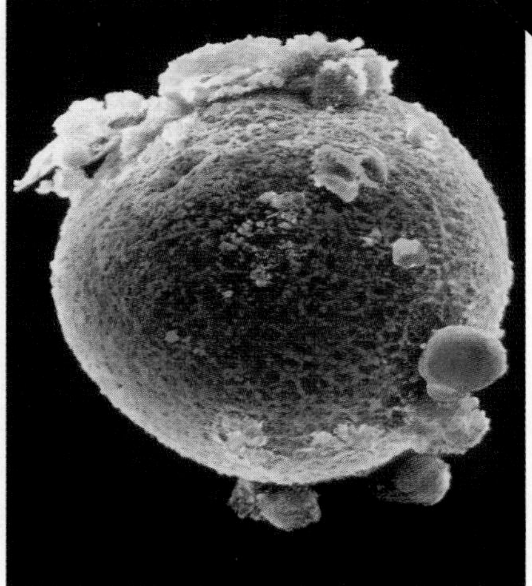

A human egg cell.

dominant gene
The gene that produces a trait in the individual even when paired with a recessive gene.

recessive gene
The gene that produces a trait in the individual only when the same recessive gene has been inherited from both parents.

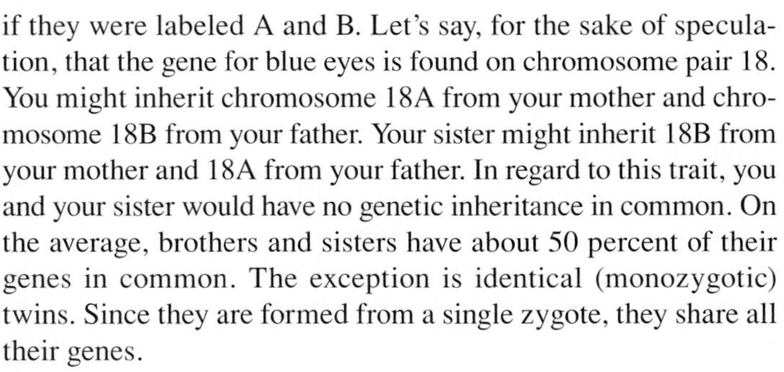

if they were labeled A and B. Let's say, for the sake of speculation, that the gene for blue eyes is found on chromosome pair 18. You might inherit chromosome 18A from your mother and chromosome 18B from your father. Your sister might inherit 18B from your mother and 18A from your father. In regard to this trait, you and your sister would have no genetic inheritance in common. On the average, brothers and sisters have about 50 percent of their genes in common. The exception is identical (monozygotic) twins. Since they are formed from a single zygote, they share all their genes.

Dominant and Recessive Traits

As we have just seen, the 23 chromosomes you get from your mother are matched to the 23 you get from your father. Each pair of chromosomes carries a gene from each of the two parents for the same characteristic. But what if they conflict? What if the gene from father says "blue eyes" and the gene from mother says "brown eyes"? The answer depends on which is the **dominant gene.** In the case of eye color, a gene for brown eyes is typically dominant over one for blue eyes. The gene for blue eyes is said to be **recessive.** A dominant gene will normally reveal its trait

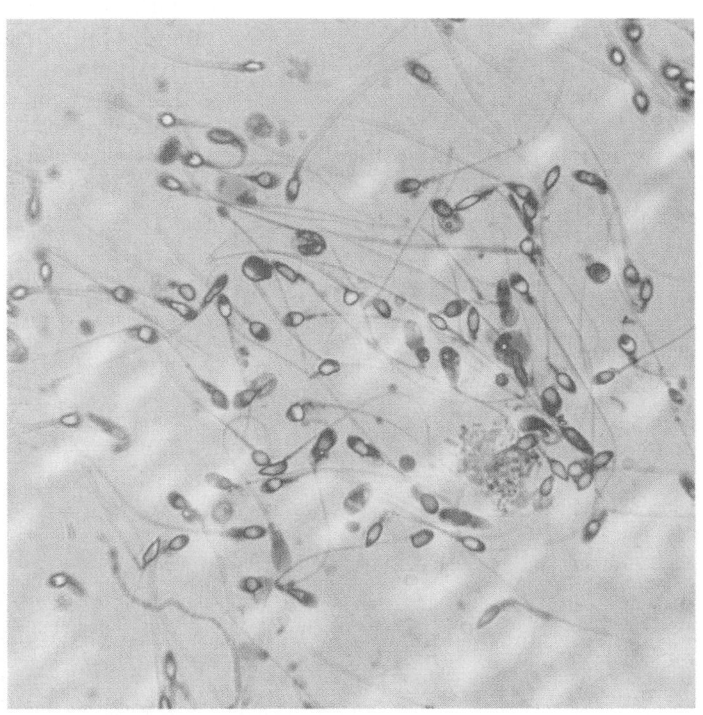

Human sperm, the tiny cells with the long tails.

whenever the gene is present. A recessive gene will reveal a trait only when the same recessive gene has been inherited from both parents and there is no dominant gene giving instructions to the contrary. Brown eyes, dark hair, curly hair, farsightedness, and dimples are common examples of dominant traits. On the other hand, blue eyes, light hair, normal vision, and freckles are recessive traits.

Although this description of genetic inheritance is a simplified one, you should understand that many physical and behavioral traits appear to be controlled not simply by one gene but by the interaction of several genes. A person's height is controlled by four genes, for example. Still, the basic principles described here are the same in all aspects of genetic inheritance.

Chromosome Abnormalities

Down syndrome
An abnormality caused by the presence of an additional 21st chromosome.

Unfortunately, the genetic mechanism does not always work properly. When chromosomes are damaged or malformed, abnormalities of body and behavior often result. A common example is **Down syndrome,** formerly called mongolism, which is caused by the presence of an additional 21st chromosome. Children with Down syndrome have obvious physical irregularities, including a thickened tongue and a skinfold at the corner of the eye. The most serious aspect of Down syndrome, as with many chromosomal abnormalities, is mental retardation.

Research on Inheritance in Humans

When Mendel wanted to study genetic influences on the physical characteristics of pea plants, he was able to breed selectively those plants with a particular characteristic, such as smooth skins, to see what that characteristic would be like in the next generation. That research strategy has been successfully used with animals, showing, for example, that aggressiveness and learning ability in rats and emotionality in monkeys are partially determined by heredity (Cooper & Zubek, 1958; Ebert & Hyde, 1976; Suomi, 1988). Selective breeding experiments cannot be carried out with humans for ethical reasons, of course, so it's much harder to untangle the strands of nature and nurture in human behavior.

monozygotic twins
(mon´´ō-zī-got´ik) Twins formed from a single ovum; they are identical in appearance because they have the same genetic structure.

dizygotic twins
(dī´´zī-got´ik) Twins formed from the fertilization of two ova by two sperm.

Instead, researchers interested in hereditary influences have had to use two descriptive methods of research. These are based on unusual situations that are not contrived by the experimenter, but nevertheless allow some conclusions to be reached about the role of the variable being studied. Because these studies do not allow for the same degree of experimental control as do formal experiments, conclusions drawn from them must be viewed cautiously. Still, they are of great importance in research on heredity. The two most common types of naturally occurring experiments in this area involve the study of twins and the study of adopted children (Plomin, 1989).

Identical or monozygotic twins are formed when a single fertilized egg breaks apart into two clusters of cells, each growing into a separate fetus.

Studies of Twins

There are two kinds of twins formed in two very different ways. In the case of *identical,* or **monozygotic twins,** a single fertilized egg begins to grow in the normal way through cell division in the mother's womb. Ordinarily, this cluster of cells will grow over the course of about nine months until it emerges as a baby. Monozygotic twins are formed, however, when that cluster of cells breaks apart into two clusters early in the growth process. If conditions are right, each of these clusters will grow into a baby. These infants will be "identical" not only in appearance but also in genetic structure, since they came from the same fertilized egg.

Dizygotic twins, in contrast, are formed when the female produces two separate eggs that are fertilized by two different sperm cells. These two fertilized eggs each grow into babies that are born at about the same time, but they are not genetically identical. Dizygotic twins are no more alike genetically than siblings born at different times. Like other siblings, dizygotic twins share only about 50 percent of their genes.

A number of studies have also looked at the role of inheritance in influencing normal aspects of personality. These studies used twin and adoption strategies to look at the role of genetics (Cattell, 1982; Loehlin, 1985) and, in the most conclusive study, to look at the similarity of monozygotic and dizygotic twins who had been adopted by different parents soon after birth (Bouchard, 1984). Since the twins were raised in different households, the usual argument against twin studies, that monozygotic twins might be treated more similarly than dizygotic twins because of their greater physical similarity, could not be valid. The results of these studies rather convincingly showed that about half of the variation in a wide range of personality characteristics is due to inheritance. In determining why some individuals are more dominant in social interactions than others, heredity was estimated to account for 48 percent of the influence in one study (Loehlin, 1985) and 61 percent in another (Bouchard, 1984). These studies similarly found that our genes explain 40 to 60 percent of the differences between people in a number of other personality characteristics, including the initiative to work hard to succeed, aggressiveness, the tendency to be nervous, the need for novelty and excitement, and the tendency to obey social rules and laws.

One of the more controversial questions regarding the role of inheritance in human behavior centers around a person's sexual orientation. Is a person's heterosexual or homosexual orientation a result of learning or heredity or both? Recent evidence points toward a significant contribution for heredity in sexual orientation. Bailey and Pillard (1991) found that 52 percent of the monozygotic twins of homosexual males were also homosexual, while only 22 percent of the dizygotic twin brothers and 11 percent of adopted brothers were also homosexual. Similar results were found for women. Forty-eight percent of the monozygotic twins of homosexual females were also homosexual, while 16 percent of the dizygotic twin sisters and 6 percent of the adopted sisters were homosexual. But the rates of homosexuality in monozygotic twins fell far short of 100 percent, indicating that heredity is, at most, only one of many reasons that a person is heterosexual or homosexual.

The search for a hereditary influence on sexual orientation has led some researchers on a search for a "sexual preference" gene. Hamer, Hu, Magnuson, Hu, and Pattatucci (1993) investigated the family histories of 76 gay men and discovered that homosexuality was most common among their mothers' male relatives. This led Hamer et al. to investigate the possibility of a gene for homosexuality located on the X chromosome inherited from the mother. In a study of 40 pairs of gay brothers, these researchers found that 33 pairs shared a set of genetic "markers" in a specific area of the X chromosome. Once again, that not all of the brothers fit the genetic pattern means that significant environmental influences must also be present.

When considered all together, these studies force us to take seriously the hypothesis that at least some aspects of human personality are partly determined by our genes before our unique experiences have had a chance to influence us (Plomin, 1989, 1995). But the fact that some aspect of our physical or psychological selves is influenced by heredity does not mean that it is etched in stone. Many highly heritable characteristics can be changed. William Angoff (1988) reminds us that even though height is strongly influenced by heredity, the average height in some countries has increased by over 3 inches since World War II. He believes that the characteristic of intelligence, in the right circumstances, has the same potential for change over time. Notice, too, that even the strongest estimate of the role of genetics in the formation of our personalities leaves a major role to be played by our childrearing, the stresses and strains of our lives, the decisions we make, our social relationships, and other psychological factors.

Review

Specific patterns of behavior are not inherited by humans, but heredity does influence broad dimensions of behavior. Among the characteristics that appear to be influenced to some degree by inheritance are intelligence, some aspects of personality, and some aspects of abnormal behavior. The hereditary blueprints that exert this influence are coded in thousands of genes arranged on pairs of chromosome strips in the nuclei of cells. One member

Thinking Critically About Psychology

1. What are the social implications of research suggesting that intelligence and some personality traits are, to a considerable extent, inherited?

2. What are the advantages of studying twins who have been raised apart? Can such studies give us a complete answer about the influence of heredity on human behavior?

Review—continued

of each chromosome pair comes from each parent, giving each individual two sets of genes. Sometimes these genes are in conflict, as when a person inherits a gene for blue eyes from her mother and brown eyes from her father. When this happens, some genes are dominant because they suppress the influence of the other conflicting gene for the same trait; other genes are recessive and will have an effect only when the same recessive gene is inherited from both parents.

The effects of heredity on human behavior have been examined in studies using twins and adopted children. For example, the fact that monozygotic (identical) twins have exactly the same genes while dizygotic twins share only about 50 percent of their genes can be used to study the role of heredity. Even though both kinds of twins grow up in comparably similar environments, monozygotic twins are more similar than dizygotic twins on several dimensions of behavior, suggesting that genetics plays some role in behavior. In addition, studies showing that adopted children resemble their biological parents in some ways more than they resemble adoptive parents who reared them indicate the role of inheritance. Although the influence of heredity on behavior is significant, many other factors influence behavior as well. We are far from being as rigidly programmed by our inheritance as some species of animals are.

Check Your Learning

To be sure that you have learned the key points from the preceding section, cover the answers below and try to answer each question. If you give an incorrect answer to any question, return to the page given next to the correct answer to see why your answer was not correct.

1. The genetic code is contained in structures called genes that are arranged on ____________________.

a. chromosomes
b. DNA
c. zygotes
d. sperm cells

2. A trait that will be found in the child only when the child receives the same gene for the same trait from both parents is a ____________________ trait.

a. recessive
b. dominant
c. Mendelian
d. dizygotic

3. To study inheritance in humans, scientists often study twins because one type of twins is genetically identical while the other type shares only about 50 percent of the same genes; the type of twin that is genetically identical is called

a. Mendelian.
b. adopted.
c. monozygotic.
d. dizygotic.

4. The results of a study of adopted children would indicate that a characteristic was influenced by inheritance if the children resembled more their ____________________ parents.

a. adoptive
b. biological
c. nonparous
d. dizygotic

Correct Answers
1. a (p. 70), **2.** a (p. 72), **3.** c (p. 72), **4.** b (p. 73).

MADNESS AND THE BRAIN

We began this chapter by stating the obvious fact that the brain is the most important biological organ to psychology. We will end the chapter by looking at two striking and sad examples in which the psychological lives of some people are seriously disturbed because the brain does not function normally—schizophrenia and Alzheimer's disease.

Schizophrenia and the Brain

Schizophrenia is an uncommon disorder that affects a little less than 1 percent of the general population. However, it's a severe psychological disorder that, unless successfully treated, renders normal patterns of living impossible. The central feature of schizophrenia is a marked abnormality in thought processes that leaves the schizophrenic "out of touch with reality." Persons with schizophrenia often hold strange and disturbing beliefs (such as believing that they receive telepathic messages from devils in another universe). They also often have strangely distorted perceptual experiences (such as hearing voices that are not really there that tell them to do dangerous things) and think in fragmented and illogical ways. At the same time, the emotions and social relationships of the person with schizophrenia are often severely disturbed.

Because schizophrenia is such a serious disorder, it has been the major focus of federal research funding from the National Institute of Mental Health for the past 20 years. As a result, great strides have been made recently in understanding the link between schizophrenia and the brain. Although this evidence is strong and impressive, a few words of caution might be wise before we look at this topic. First, researchers tend to study very severe cases of any disorder, including schizophrenia, to make the difficult task of finding the cause of the disorder a little easier. Therefore, when we look at the striking images in this section of the very abnormal brains of persons with schizophrenia, keep in mind that these are the brains of severe cases. Individuals with milder schizophrenia may have more normal brains or may not have any abnormalities of the structure of the brain at all. Second, although schizophrenia is uncommon, most of us know a relative, neighbor, or loved one who has been diagnosed as having schizophrenia. I hope that you will not think that you are looking at photographs of the brain of that person when you look at the images in this section. Not only might that person have a very mild form of the disorder and not have the kind of brain abnormalities described in this section, the person you know may not have been diagnosed correctly as having schizophrenia in the first place. Schizophrenia is a difficult diagnosis that should be made by an experienced specialist, but the term is often used loosely by less-trained physicians. Therefore, the discussion of the brain in this section may not apply to that person at all. The same can be said about our discussion of Alzheimer's disease later in this section.

With that caution in mind, let's look at what is known about schizophrenia and the brain. First, I need to remind you that there is strong evidence that a predisposition to schizophrenia is inherited. As discussed earlier in this chapter (p. 74), the role of genetics can be examined in studies comparing identical twins (who have identical genes) with fraternal twins (who share only about half of their genes). The fact that about 50 percent of identical twins both have schizophrenia if one has schizophrenia, compared with only about 10 percent of fraternal twins, is strong evidence for a genetic factor in the disorder. However, the fact that not *all* of the identical twins of persons with schizophrenia also have the disorder clearly shows that more than just heredity is involved. Some other factor or factors must play key roles in the cause of schizophrenia (Fowles, 1992).

Images of the Brains of Persons with Schizophrenia

Whatever those factors are that work along with heredity to cause schizophrenia, they produce marked changes in the brains of severe schizophrenics. An impressive number of studies using magnetic resonance imaging (MRI), PET, and other brain-imaging techniques show that the cerebral cortex and key structures of the limbic system are literally "shrunken" in persons with schizophrenia (Andreason et al., 1990; Berman, Illowsky, & Weinberger, 1988; Kelsoe, Cadet, Pickar, & Weinberger, 1988; McCarley et al., 1989; Nopoulos et al., 1995; Pearlson, Kim, et al., 1989). The easiest way to see the reduced size of the brain in schizophrenics using MRI imaging is to measure the size of structures called the *ventricles*. The ventricles are hollow pathways inside the cortex and midbrain that bathe the brain in fluid. If the underside of the cortex and nearby structures are shrunken, the ventricles will be enlarged.

The enlargement of the ventricles in schizophrenics is shown clearly in the two striking brain images in figure 2.25. These are MRI images of the brains of two identical twins, only one of whom has schizophrenia (Horgan, 1993). These images were made looking at the *back* of the head. The two lobes of the cerebral cortex can be seen at the top of the head, with the slightly darker cerebellum clearly visible at the base of the skull. The ventricles are two dark spots toward the bottom of the two hemispheres of the cerebral cortex. Which identical twin has schizophrenia—can you tell? The brain of the twin with schizophrenia is shown on the right. Notice that the ventricles are greatly enlarged because the interior portions of the cerebral cortex and limbic system are reduced in size.

An even more dramatic set of images is shown in figure 2.26 on page 79. These three-dimensional color photographs were constructed from computer-enhanced MRI images in the laboratory of Nancy Andreason at the University of Iowa School of Medicine (from Gershon & Rieder, 1992). In these images, the brain is seen from an angle, looking at the head from the front on the left side. In these images, the computer program has colored the ventricle closer to us in silver and the ventricle in the cerebral hemisphere that is farther away from us in white. Both the cerebral

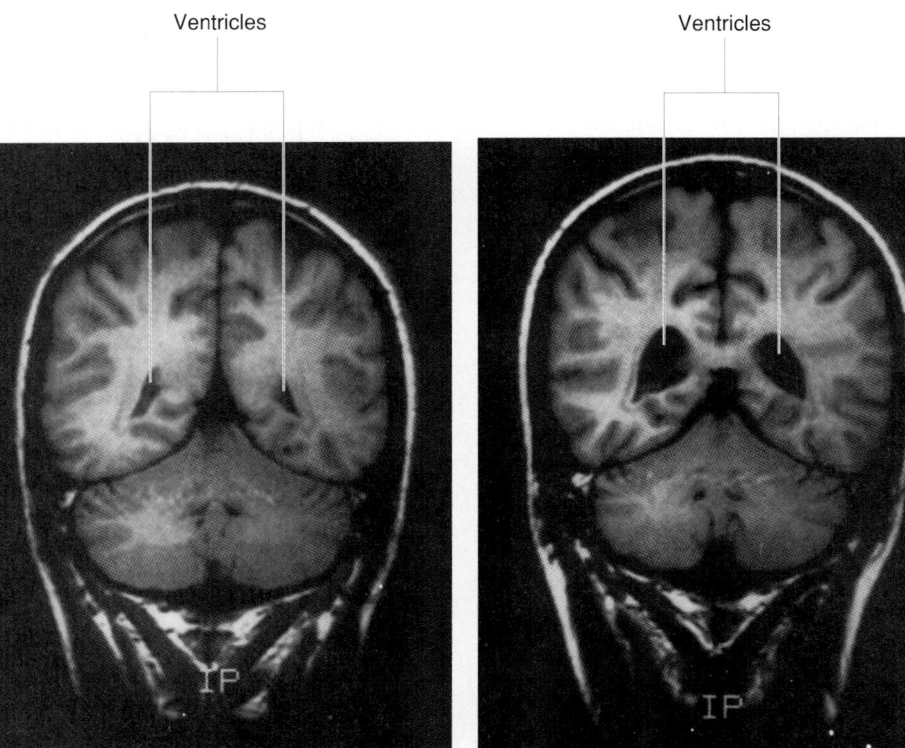

FIGURE 2.25

These are MRI images of the brains of two identical twins. The twin on the right has schizophrenia, but the twin on the left does not. Notice that the open spaces inside the brain, called the ventricles, are enlarged in the schizophrenic because the interior regions of the brain are reduced in size.

cortex and the cerebellum are outlined in red. The image at the right is of a person with schizophrenia, while the image at the left is of a normal person. Notice that the ventricles of the schizophrenic are enlarged in the middle and rear portions of the brain, showing reductions in size of the interior portions of the brain in these areas. Perhaps more interestingly, these color images also allow us to directly measure a key structure in the limbic system, the hippocampus, which is color coded in yellow. Recall that the hippocampus plays a key role in the regulation of both emotion and memory (see p. 56). In this image, the person with schizophrenia has a markedly smaller hippocampus.

The limbic system and the parts of the cerebral cortex surrounding the ventricles are important in their own right, but they also are the source of neurons that activate the frontal lobes of the cerebral cortex (p. 55). The frontal lobes play important roles in emotional control and logical planning—two qualities that are quite disturbed in schizophrenia. Look at the two PET images of the cerebral cortex shown in figure 2.27 that reveal more about the level of brain activity than the size of the structures. We are looking at the brain from the top, with the frontal lobes shown at the top of these images. High levels of activity in an area of the brain are shown in yellow and red, while cool greens indicate low levels of brain activity. Notice that the level of activity in the frontal lobes of the normal person (the top image) is high during a task that requires close attention. In contrast, the person with schizophrenia in the bottom image shows little activity in the frontal lobes—they appear to be "turned off."

More recent findings indicate that the thalamus may not function normally in individuals with schizophrenia (Buchsbaum et al., 1996). This is important because, as mentioned earlier in this chapter, the thalamus filters incoming sensory information. Perhaps the hallucinations experienced by schizophrenics result in part because the thalamus does not function normally.

Neurotransmitters and Schizophrenia

These images, and many similar ones from other studies using brain imaging and autopsy studies of schizophrenics who have died, strongly suggest that persons with schizophrenia experience life in abnormal ways partly because they have abnormalities in the hippocampus, the cerebral cortex, and other key brain structures. Interestingly, evidence shows that these abnormalities in brain structure are also reflected in abnormal levels of the neurotransmitter *dopamine* (Berman et al., 1988). This neurotransmitter is involved in the activities of many parts of the brain, including the frontal lobe of the cerebral cortex. For a variety of reasons, researchers have long suspected that dopamine was involved in schizophrenia. For example, great strides were made in the treatment of schizophrenia in the 1950s with the introduction of the *phenothiazine* drugs. The first clue to the specific effects of these drugs on the body was that phenothiazines often produce the serious side effect of muscular control problems like those found in Parkinson's disease. Since Parkinson's disease is caused by a deterioration of the parts of the brain that use the neurotransmitter dopamine to transmit neural messages, it was hypothesized that the phenothiazine drugs operate by interfering in some way with dopamine. Thus, if drugs that produce improvements alter dopamine transmission, it makes sense to theorize that schizophrenia is caused by abnormal dopamine transmission.

Another sort of evidence that supports the dopamine hypothesis comes from experience with the side effects of the stimulant drugs called *amphetamines.* These drugs are widely abused because of the intense high and feelings of energy they produce. Excessive use of amphetamines, however, can lead to a condition called *amphetamine psychosis* that closely resembles paranoid schizophrenia. The fact that this condition resembles schizophrenia is important since amphetamines produce this psychotic reaction by altering dopamine transmission (Snyder, 1974). Furthermore, the best treatment for amphetamine psychosis is phenothiazine medication, which is also the best treatment for schizophrenia.

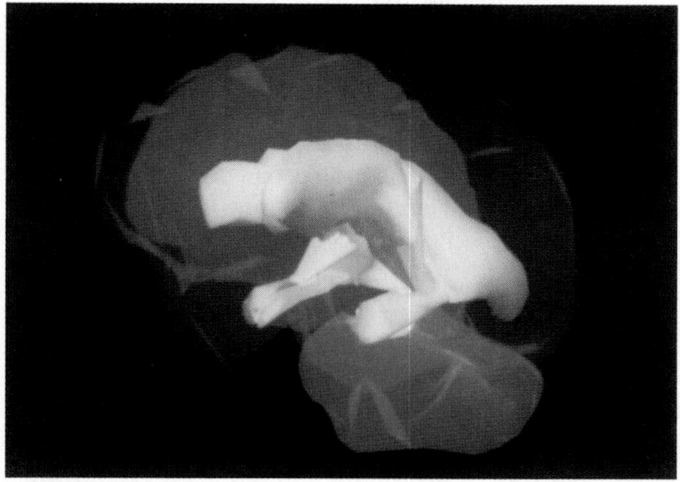

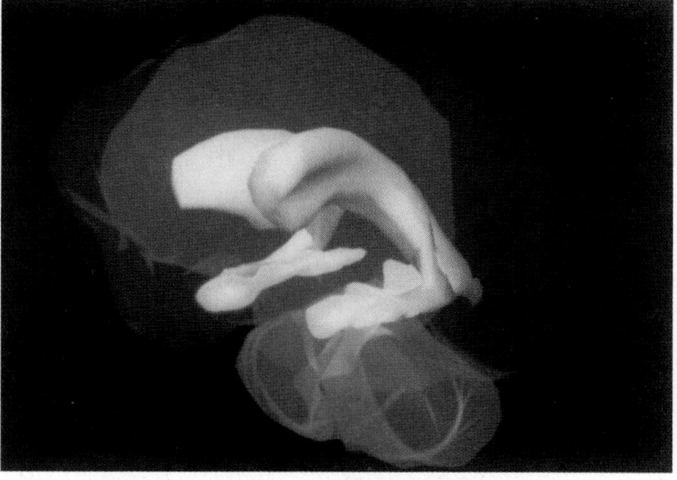

FIGURE 2.26
The brain of a person with schizophrenia (left) shows a shrunken hippocampus (in yellow) and enlarged fluid-filled ventricles (gray) in comparison to the brain of a person without schizophrenia (right).

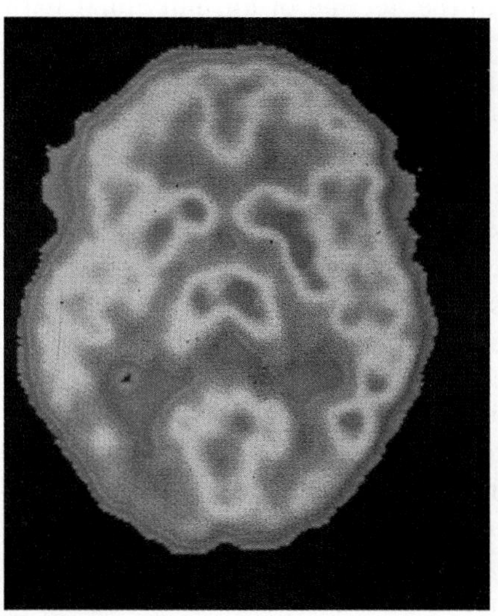

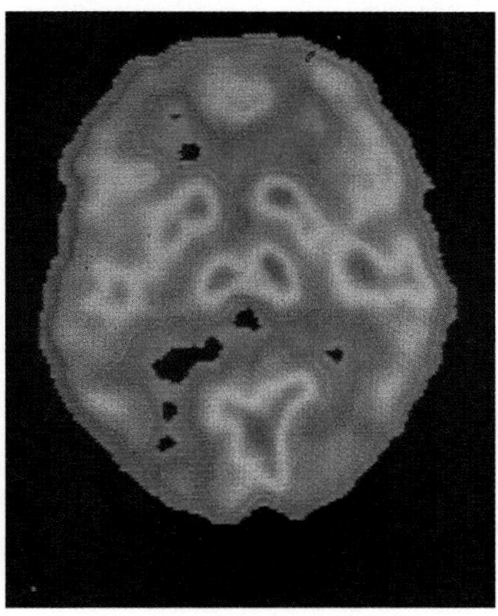

FIGURE 2.27
These PET scans demonstrate how functioning of the cerebral cortex can be affected in schizophrenia. The level of activity in the brain is indicated by the colors on the scan. Yellow and red indicate high levels, while green signifies a low activity level. During a task that requires close attention, the frontal lobes of the cerebral cortex (at the top of each scan) are highly active in a person without schizophrenia (left). In contrast, a person with schizophrenia, shown on the right, has little activity in the same area during the same task.

Causes of Schizophrenia

A great deal of evidence suggests that the brains of persons with schizophrenia are abnormal in structure and function, particularly in the action of the neurotransmitter dopamine. There is also evidence that a predisposition to schizophrenia is inherited, but it is also clear that some other factor or factors must play a role in causing schizophrenia because not even all identical twins both exhibit schizophrenia. What might the other factor or factors be that can cause schizophrenia in genetically predisposed persons? For one thing, there is evidence that *stress* causes persons who are genetically predisposed to have episodes of schizophrenia (Ventura, Neuchterlein, Lukoff, & Hardesty, 1989). However, because this is the chapter on the biological foundations of behavior, we focus on evidence that the genetic predisposition is most likely to lead to schizophrenia if the predisposed person suffered some disturbance of the development of the *brain* before birth or during birth (Mednick, Machon, Huttunen, & Bonett, 1988; Silverton, Mednick, Schulsinger, Parnas, & Harrington, 1988; Wyatt, 1996).

Studies by Sarnoff Mednick and his associates at the University of Southern California and the Institute of Psychiatric Demography in Denmark (Barr, Mednick, & Munk-Jorgensen, 1990; Cannon, Mednick et al., 1993; Mednick et al., 1988) support the so-called double strike theory of schizophrenia. Mednick hypothesizes that schizophrenia is most likely in persons with (a) a genetic predisposition to schizophrenia, and (b) some form of complication during pregnancy that alters the brains of individuals who are genetically predisposed to schizophrenia. According to this theory, a genetically predisposed individual who has no complications during pregnancy or birth would be unlikely to develop schizophrenia. Similarly, pregnancy complications would be unlikely to cause schizophrenia in individuals who are not genetically predisposed to it.

Emerging evidence suggests that brain development in genetically predisposed infants can be damaged by dehydration when the mother contracts influenza during pregnancy, severe malnutrition of the mother during pregnancy, an uncommon Rh incompatibility between the blood of the mother and the fetus, and birth complications that deprive the newborn of oxygen during birth (Kunugi et al., 1996; Susser et al., 1996; Wyatt, 1996).

For example, studies of large samples suggest that schizophrenia is more

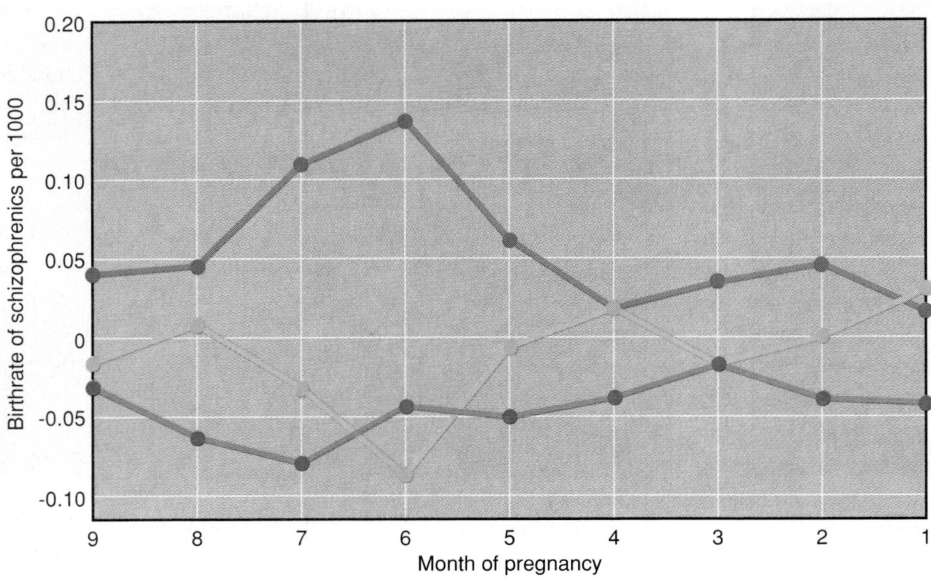

FIGURE 2.28

The average birthrate of persons who later develop schizophrenia when mothers were exposed to low, medium, or high levels of influenza during each month of their pregnancy. Negative birthrates are lower than average; positive birthrates are higher than average.

Source: Data from C. E. Barr, S. A. Mednick, and P. Munk-Jorgensen, "Exposure to Influenza Epidemics During Gestation and Adult Schizophrenia" in *Archives of General Psychiatry,* 47:869–874, 1990.

common in children whose mothers were pregnant during periods of epidemics of influenza. Figure 2.28 shows the rates of schizophrenia in persons whose pregnancies occurred during periods of low, medium, or high rates of influenza. Notice that the highest rates of schizophrenia are for the children of women who were exposed to influenza during the fifth through the seventh months of pregnancy, which is during the period of the most rapid development of the nervous system in the fetus. Other studies show that severe malnutrition of the mother during pregnancy and other pregnancy complications can also cause the same damage to the developing brain as influenza (Bracha, Torrey, Gottesman, Bigelow, & Cunniff, 1992; Susser & Lin, 1992).

But the clearest evidence in support of Mednick's double strike theory of schizophrenia comes from a recent long-term study (Cannon, Mednick, et al., 1993). Mednick's research team has been following a group of children of schizophrenic parents in Denmark for many years and has detailed information on them from birth to an average of 29 years of age. Some of the children had two schizophrenic parents (and are considered to have a very high genetic predisposition to schizophrenia), while others had only one schizophrenic parent (and are considered to be at high risk for schizophrenia). In contrast, a third group of children has been studied who have no schizophrenic parents (and, therefore, are thought to be at low risk for schizophrenia).

Mednick's research team obtained brain images at age 29 years using CT scans and looked to see whether the persons with the highest genetic predisposition were most likely to have the kind of brain abnormality associated with schizophrenia (enlarged ventricles). But because Mednick believes that a person with a genetic predisposition to schizophrenia will develop the disorder only if some form of pregnancy or birth complication occurred, the researchers looked at birth complications as well.

Mednick found that the size of the ventricles in the children of one schizophrenic parent was significantly larger than in the children of no schizophrenic parents, and the ventricles of the children with two schizophrenic parents were significantly larger than in the children in either of the other two groups, but *only* when a birth complication had occurred. Thus, this study provides strong support for the idea that both genetic predisposition and pregnancy and birth complications operate together to cause schizophrenia. These findings in support of Mednick's double strike theory may lead to new ways to understand and prevent schizophrenia.

Alzheimer's Disease and the Brain

Few facts portray the intimate relationship between the brain and our psychological selves more vividly or more sadly than the decline of an individual with Alzheimer's disease. Fully functioning individuals who develop this disorder fade rapidly in emotional and intellectual functioning, until they are "no longer themselves." Like schizophrenia, Alzheimer's disease results from the deterioration of the cerebral cortex, hippocampus, and other structures. In the case of Alzheimer's disease, this deterioration is due to the death of neurons, the accumulation of protein deposits, and the development of tangles of neuronal fibers. In most cases, this deterioration can be seen clearly using modern brain-imaging techniques. Alzheimer's disease is the principal cause of what we commonly refer to as senility.

The loss of brain functioning results in loss of memory for recent and past events, confusion, and errors in judgment. The individual may no longer recognize close relatives, forget to turn off the stove, become lost in a familiar supermarket, and often lose objects such as keys. Changes in personality are also common. A person who was formerly thought of as polite and socially inhibited may make coarse remarks, lewd jokes, and insulting sexual advances. A formerly shrewd businessperson may make extremely unwise investments. And a happy and loving parent may become apathetic, withdrawn, and unaffectionate.

Alzheimer's disease is uncommon before age 75, but it can develop as early as middle age. The cause of this massive deterioration of the brain is not presently

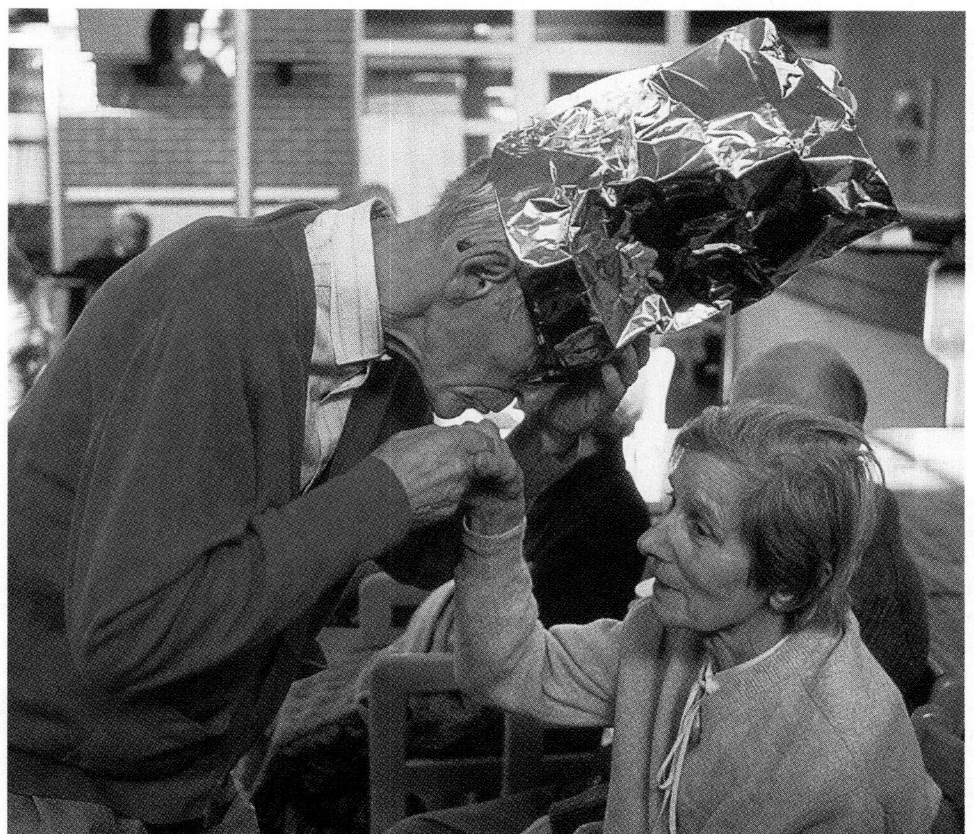

Individuals who develop Alzheimer's disease rapidly fade, particularly in intellectual capacity, until they are "no longer themselves."

known, but apparently there is an inherited predisposition to develop it. Close relatives of persons with Alzheimer's disease are four times as likely to develop the disorder by age 86 than individuals without a relative with the disorder (Mohs, Breitner, Silverman, & Davis, 1987). Recent advances in brain-imaging technology using magnetic resonance imaging (MRI scans) make it possible to see the deterioration of portions of the cerebral cortex that results in Alzheimer's disease. The image on the left in figure 2.29 is of an older adult with few symptoms; the image on the right shows the dramatic deterioration in both hemispheres of the cortex that accompanies severe symptoms of Alzheimer's disease (Bondareff, Raval, Woo, Hauser, & Colletti, 1990).

I hope this detailed discussion of two ways in which disorders of the brain can alter psychological lives will help give you a better understanding of why we must understand the brain to understand psychology. Also, this discussion hopefully will give you a more informed perspective on these two conditions.

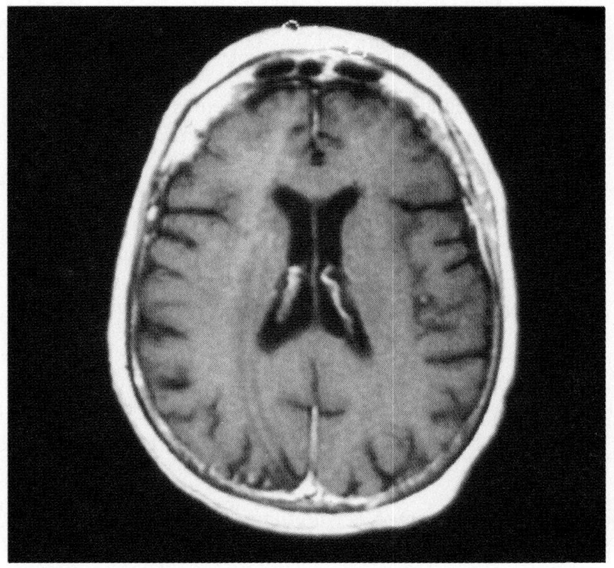

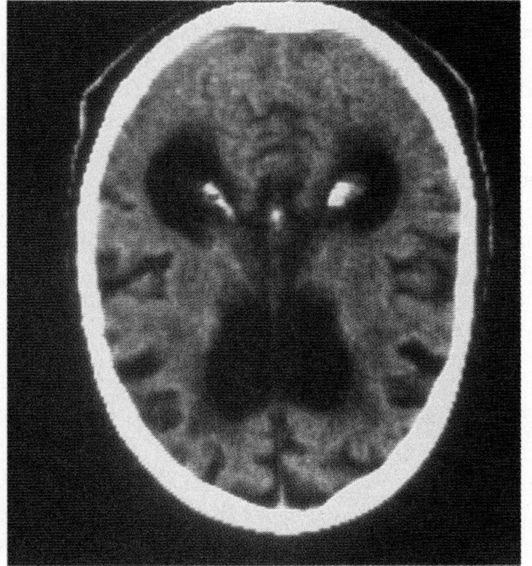

FIGURE 2.29

(Left): MRI scan of a normal older adult. (Right): MRI scan showing the deterioration of the two hemispheres of the cortex (viewed from the top) in a patient with severe Alzheimer's disease.

Summary

Chapter 2 describes people as psychological beings who live in "biological machines"; it looks at the role played by the nervous system, the endocrine system, and genetic mechanisms in our behavior and mental processes.

I. The nervous system is a complex network of neural cells that carry messages and regulate bodily functions and personal behavior.
- **A.** The individual cells of the nervous system (neurons) transmit electrical signals along the length of the neuron.
- **B.** Chemical substances called neurotransmitters transmit neural messages across the gap (synapse) between the axon of one neuron and the dendrite of the next.
- **C.** The central nervous system is composed of the brain and spinal cord. The peripheral nervous system carries messages to and from the rest of the body. It consists of the somatic and autonomic nervous systems:
  - **1.** The somatic nervous system carries messages from the sense organs, skeletal muscles, and joints to the central nervous system, and carries messages from the central nervous system to the skeletal muscles.
  - **2.** The autonomic nervous system regulates the visceral organs and other body functions, motivation, and emotional activity.

II. The brain has three basic parts: the hindbrain, the midbrain, and the forebrain.
- **A.** The hindbrain consists of the medulla, the pons, and the cerebellum.
  - **1.** The medulla controls breathing and a variety of reflexes.
  - **2.** The pons is concerned with balance, hearing, and several parasympathetic functions.
  - **3.** The cerebellum is chiefly responsible for maintaining muscle tone and coordination of muscular movements.
- **B.** The midbrain is a center for reflexes related to vision and hearing.
- **C.** Most cognitive, motivational, and emotional activity is controlled by the forebrain, which includes the thalamus, hypothalamus, limbic system, and cerebral cortex.
  - **1.** The thalamus is a switching station for routing sensory information to appropriate areas of the brain.
  - **2.** The hypothalamus and limbic system are involved with our motives and emotions.
  - **3.** The largest part of the brain is the cerebral cortex, made up of two cerebral hemispheres connected by the corpus callosum. The cortex controls conscious experience, intellectual activities, the senses, and voluntary functions.
- **D.** Each part of the brain interacts with the entire nervous system, and the parts work together in intellectual, physical, and emotional functions.

III. While the nervous system forms the primary biological basis for behavior and mental processes, the endocrine system of hormone-secreting glands influences emotional arousal, metabolism, sexual functioning, and other bodily processes.
- **A.** Adrenal glands secrete epinephrine and norepinephrine, which are involved in emotional arousal, increase heart rate and metabolism, and stimulate sexual arousal.
- **B.** Islets of Langerhans secrete glucagon and insulin, which control blood sugar and energy levels.
- **C.** Gonads produce sex cells (ova and sperm) for human reproduction, and estrogen and testosterone, which are hormones important to sexual functioning and the development of secondary sex characteristics.
- **D.** The thyroid gland secretes thyroxin, which controls the rate of metabolism.
- **E.** Parathyroid glands secrete parathormone, which controls the level of nervous activity.
- **F.** The pituitary gland secretes various hormones that control the activities of other endocrine glands and have important effects on general body processes.

IV. Some human characteristics and behaviors are influenced by genetic inheritance.
- **A.** Inherited characteristics are passed on through genes (containing DNA found in chromosome strips).
- **B.** Most normal human cells contain 46 chromosomes (23 pairs).
- **C.** The sex cells contain only 23 chromosomes each and are capable of combining into a new zygote with a unique set of chromosomes.
- **D.** Research has shown that inheritance plays a significant role in influencing behavior—including intelligence, some aspects of personality, and some aspects of abnormal behavior—but environmental and other personal factors are very important as well.

Suggested Readings

1. Perhaps the best summary of current knowledge of the brain written for educated laypersons is the Special Issue of the *Scientific American* on the "Mind and Brain," published in September 1992 (Volume 267, Number 3). If you are interested in knowing more about the brain, this issue, which is available in most college and public libraries, is an excellent place to begin.
2. The classic studies of patients with "split brains" are described in readable detail in: Gazzaniga, M. S. (1970). *The bisected brain.* New York: Appleton-Century-Crofts.
3. A fascinating look at the possible role played by neural factors in mental disorders is provided by Andreason, N. C. (1983). *The broken brain: The biological revolution in psychiatry.* New York: Harper & Row. She has also published an updated report of such research in Andreason, N. C. et al. (1992). Image processing for the study of brain function: Problems and programs. *Journal of Neuropsychiatry and Clinical Neurosciences, 4,* 125–133.
4. For more on the genetic basis of behavior: Plomin, P. (1989). Environment and genes: Determinants of behavior. *American Psychologist, 43,* 713–720.
5. For a more in-depth look at the biological foundations of behavior: Beatty, J. (1995). *Principles of behavioral neuroscience.* Dubuque, IA: Wm. C. Brown & Benchmark.

Special Review of the Brain Structures

Because so much information was covered in chapter 2 on the structures of the brain, a set of unlabeled illustrations have been prepared to help you check your learning of these structures. These reviews will be most helpful if you glance at the first one and then refer back to the illustration or illustrations on which they are based to memorize the names of the structures. Then, return to the illustration in this review section and try to write in the names of the brain structures. Check your labels by looking at the original figures once again. When you can label all of the structures in one of the illustrations, you can move on to the next one.

This special review section should help you learn the names of the structures of the many parts of the brain. Don't forget, however, to learn what the structures *do* (their functions). After you have gotten the names and locations of the structures straight, it should be easier for you to remember their functions, but it may take some additional reviewing.

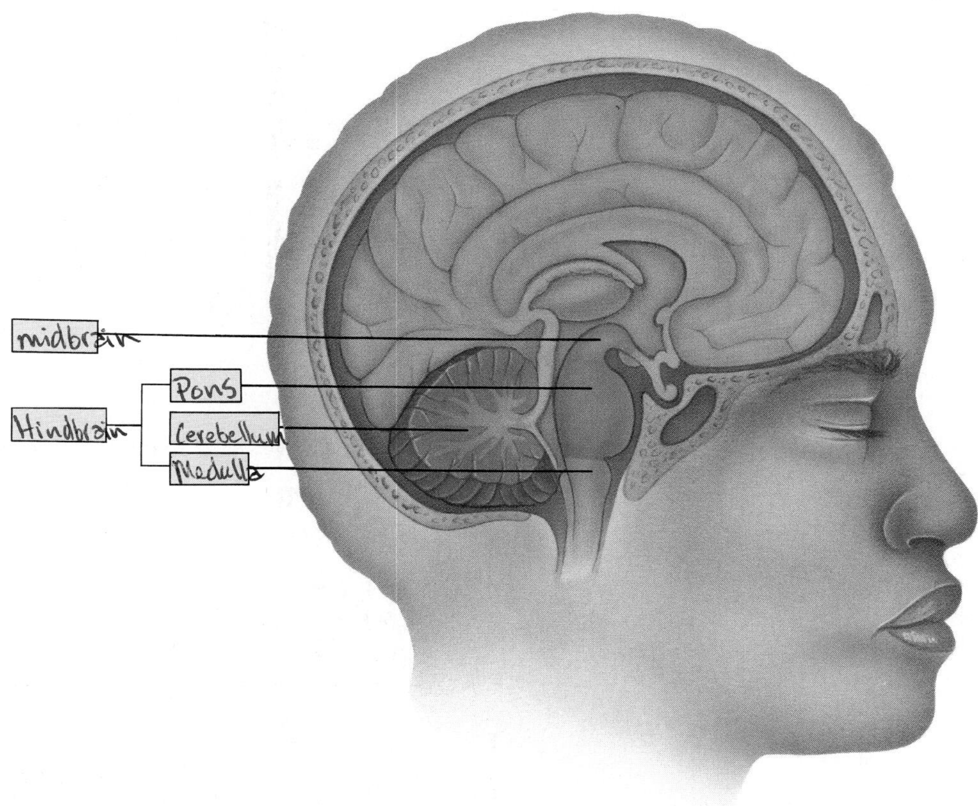

FIGURE 2.30
Key structures of the hindbrain and midbrain (based on fig. 2.11, p. 54).

FIGURE 2.31
Key structures of the forebrain (based on fig. 2.12, p. 54).

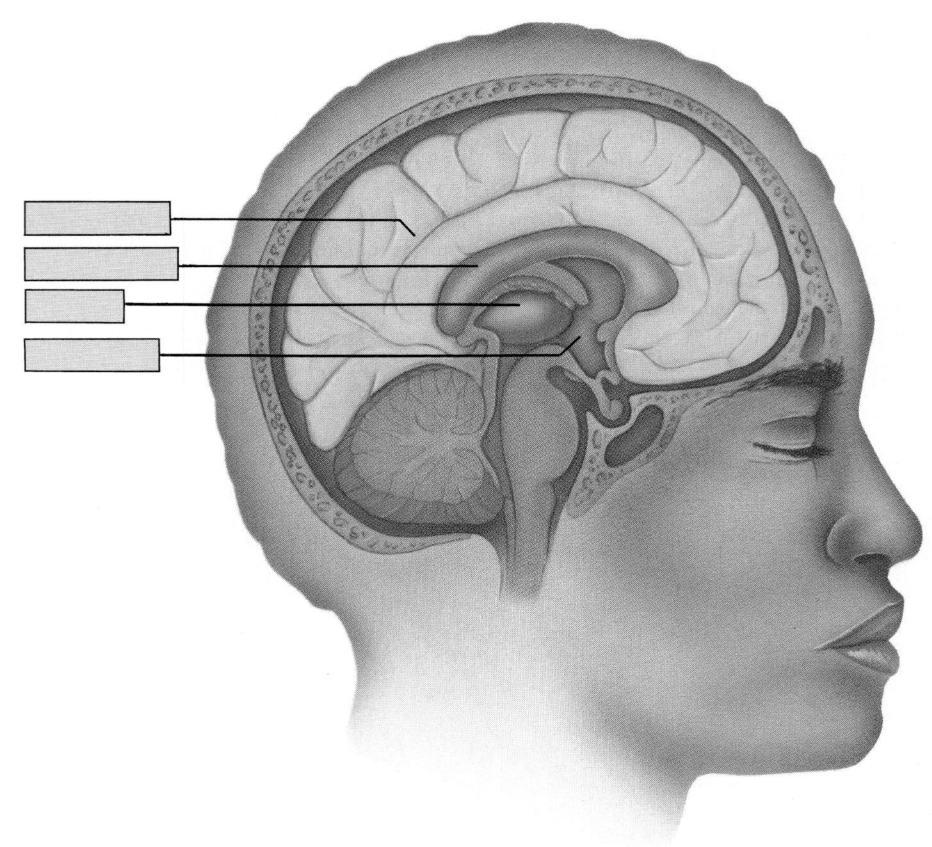

FIGURE 2.32
Key structures of the limbic system (based on fig. 2.13, p. 55).

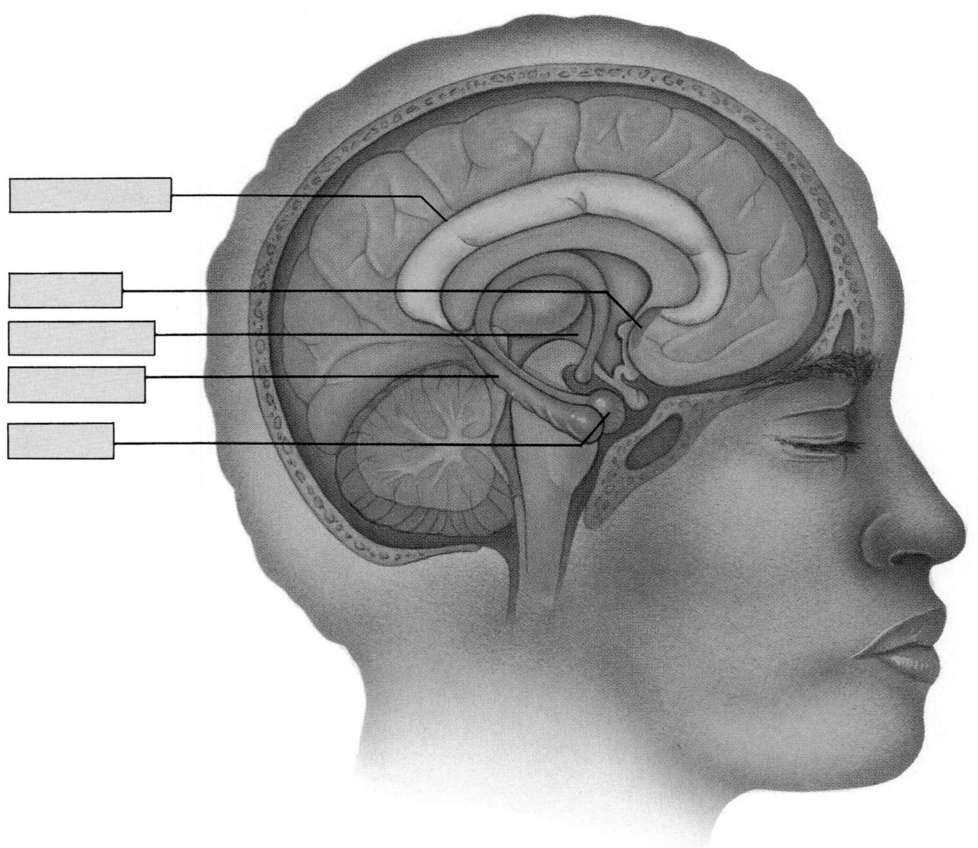

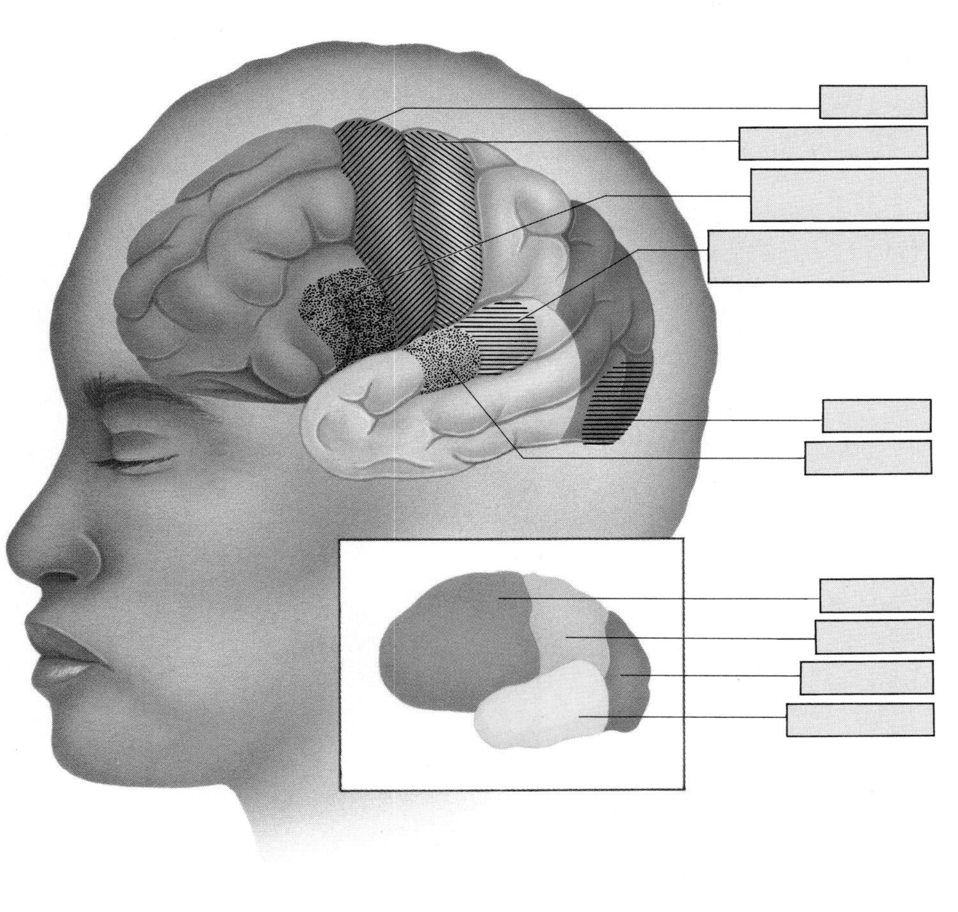

FIGURE 2.33

The four lobes of the cerebral cortex and areas with specific functions in the cerebral cortex (based on fig. 2.15, p. 57).

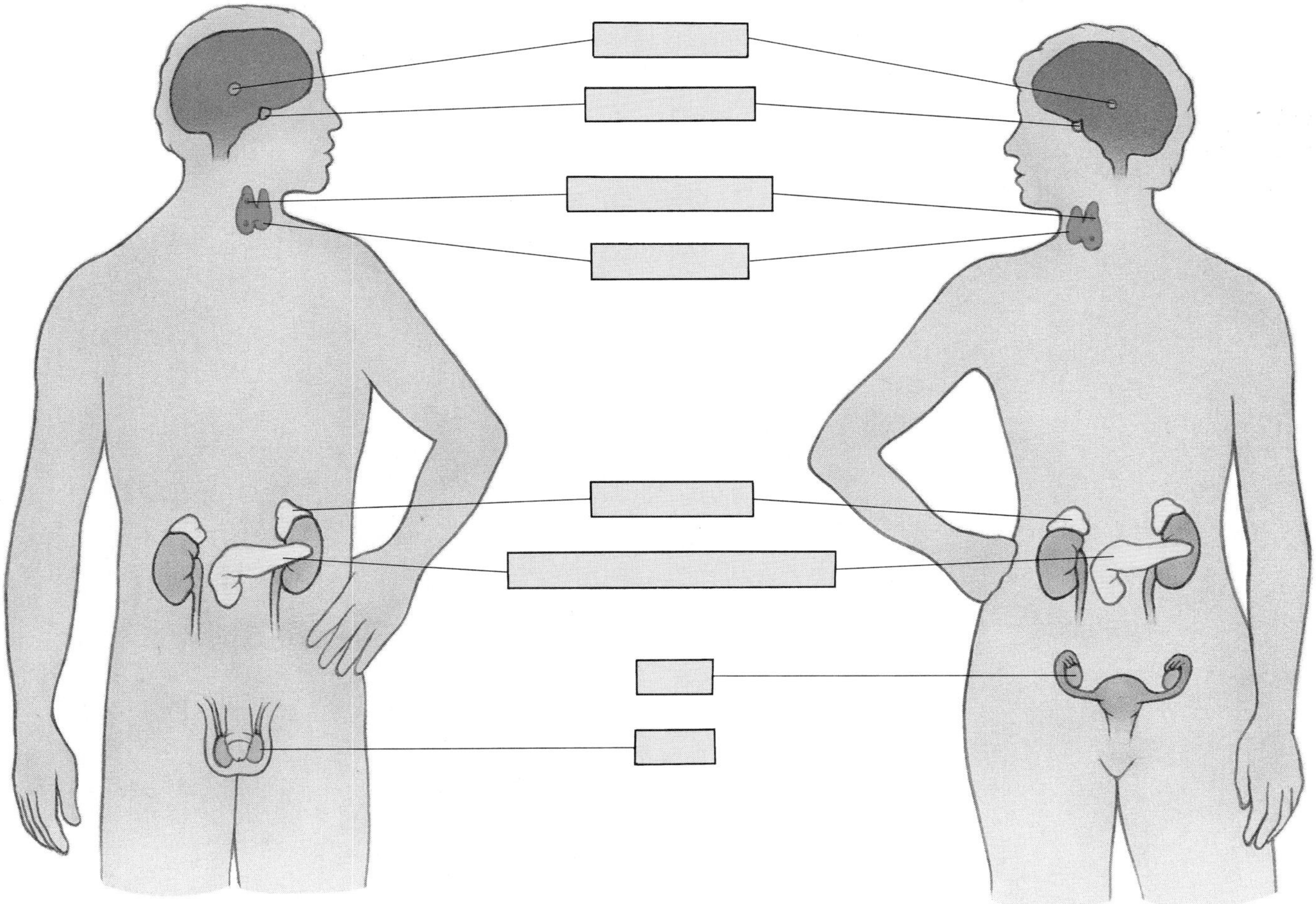

FIGURE 2.34

The endocrine glands (based on fig. 2.21, p. 66).

PART 2

Awareness

CHAPTER

3

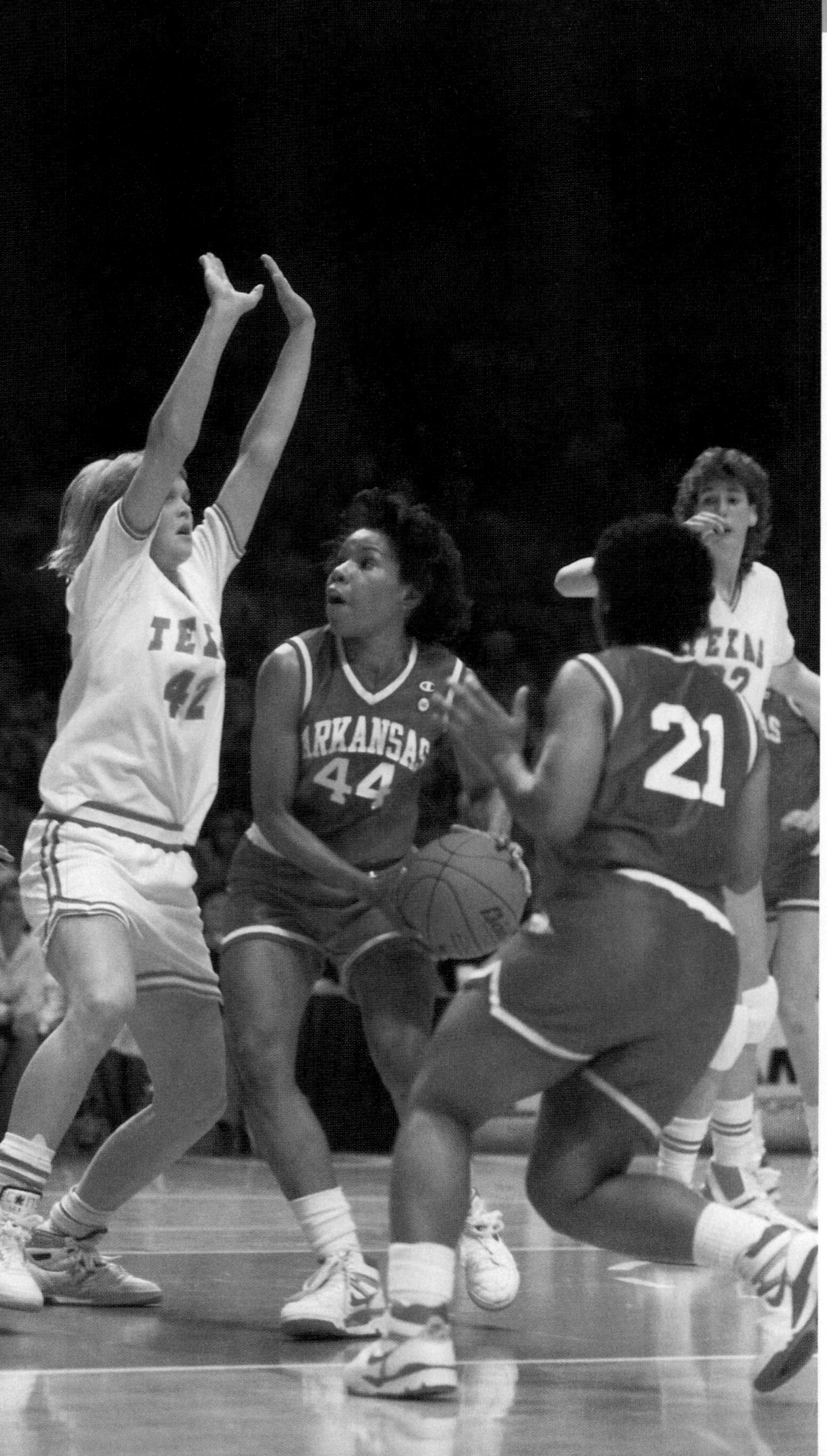

CHAPTER OUTLINE

Sensation and Perception

PROLOGUE

Last night I "saw" the University of North Carolina play Notre Dame in basketball—by listening to the radio. The play-by-play announcer watched the game, and he translated what he saw into a kind of information (words) that could be transmitted over the radio. Then I used that information to form a mental picture of the game. I did not see with my eyes, yet I was able to "watch" the game in my head.

I realized this morning that my way of seeing the game last night was not very different from how I see games in person. We never really "see" with our eyes alone. We use our eyes to gather information and translate it into a form that can be transmitted to the brain. It's in the brain that visual perception is created out of the incoming sensory information. The sensory information is the most important ingredient in a perception, but our moods and memories are part of the process, too.

Not surprisingly, though, we usually assume that we simply "see" what is "out there." The processes of seeing or smelling or touching seem so straightforward. In reality, however, perception is based on a complex chain of receiving, transmitting, and interpreting sensory information. Each step of this process actively changes the information in significant ways. Since we know "reality" only through our perceptions, we must understand the sense organs and the ways in which the processes of sensation and perception change sensory information.

In this chapter, we will study the four major senses: vision, hearing, the body senses, and the chemical senses. In vision, the eye collects, translates, and transmits energy from light to the brain. The ear—the sense organ for hearing—accomplishes the same for the energy in vibrating molecules of air. The body senses provide the brain with information from the skin about temperature, touch, and pain; and information from receptors in the inner ear, joints, and muscles tells us about the position and movement of the body—where we are and where we are going. The chemical senses use receptor cells in the nose and on the tongue to provide information to the brain about the chemicals in the air we breathe and in the things we drink and eat.

Raw sensations have little meaning until they are organized and interpreted in the process of perception. Perception is an active process that changes sensory information. As we discussed in the last chapter, we perceive actors as moving when we watch a motion picture. In reality, however, the sensory information is just a series of rapidly changing *still photographs.* The people on the movie screen don't actually move at all. We perceive them as moving only because the process of perception often goes well beyond the immediate sensory information. The brain creates the perception of motion in a movie that the sensory information only hints at.

In most cases, the ways in which the brain interprets information in the process of perception appear to be inborn. Our perceptions of reality are also colored by individual expectations, cultural learning experiences, or needs, however. As a result, different people sometimes have rather different views of the same world.

Human life would be very different without our ability to sense and perceive. Take friendships as an example. How could we have friends if we could not distinguish one person from another by sensing their differences? How could we communicate with our friends

KEY TERMS

sense organs 90
sensory receptor cells 90
sensation 90
perception 90
stimulus 90
transduction 90
absolute threshold 91
difference threshold 91
sensory adaptation 91
psychophysics 91
Weber's law 93
retina 95
rods 95
cones 95
fovea 95
optic nerve 96
blind spot 96
dark and light adaptation 98
trichromatic theory 99
opponent-process theory 100
audition 103
eardrum 104
hammer, anvil, and stirrup 105
cochlea 105
basilar membrane 105
organ of Corti 105
vestibular organ 108
kinesthetic receptors 108
semicircular canals 108
gustation 116
olfaction 116
stereochemical theory 117
perceptual constancy 120
monocular and binocular cues 121

if we could not hear their words properly or read their notes accurately or notice the expressions on their faces? How could we let them know that we cared if they could not feel the difference between a pat on the back and a push?

Without the processes of sensation and perception, life would be so different that we might not call it life. Without the ability to sense and perceive, we could not move (we would have no sense of balance or ability to avoid dangerous objects) or even safely eat (edible and spoiled food would smell and taste the same). No friends, no racquetball, and no food. Would that be living?

SENSATION: RECEIVING MESSAGES ABOUT THE WORLD

sense organs
Organs that receive stimuli.

sensory receptor cells
Cells in sense organs that translate messages into neural impulses that are sent to the brain.

sensation
(sen-sā´-shun) The process of receiving, translating, and transmitting messages from the outside world to the brain.

perception
(per-sep´-shun) The process of organizing and interpreting information received from the outside world.

We are aware of an outside world and the internal world of our own bodies only because we have a number of **sense organs** able to receive messages. These organs enable us to see, hear, taste, smell, touch, balance, and experience such feelings as body stiffness, soreness, fullness, warmth, pleasure, pain, and movement. Sense organs operate through **sensory receptor cells** that *receive* outside forms of energy (light, vibrations, heat) and *translate* them into *neural impulses* that can be *transmitted* to the brain for interpretation. Sense organs do the job of the basketball announcer who translates what he or she sees into words that can be transmitted on the radio. The process of receiving information from the outside world, translating it, and transmitting it to the brain is called **sensation.** The process of interpreting that information and forming images of the world is called **perception.**

Stimuli: What Messages Can Be Received?

stimulus
(stim´ ū-lus) Any aspect of the outside world that directly influences our behavior or conscious experience.

A key concept that you run into frequently throughout this text is **stimulus,** which refers to any aspect of the outside world that directly influences our behavior or conscious experience. The term *stimulus* comes from the action of *stimulating* sensory receptor cells.

Virtually anything that can excite receptor cells can be a stimulus. When you take a seat at a dinner party, the chair is a stimulus through your senses of sight and touch. When you begin to eat, the food becomes a stimulus through your senses of taste, smell, and sight. If the room is too hot, the temperature acts as a stimulus through the sensory receptors in your skin. The compliments you lavish on your hosts are also stimuli that increase your chances of being invited for dinner again. Whenever a person is aware of, or in some other way responds to, a part of the outside world, she or he receives a stimulus.

When I say that any part of the outside world can be a stimulus, I am using the term *outside* broadly. Even parts of the internal world of the body can be stimuli. If you eat too much at the dinner party, the bloated stretching of your stomach is a very noticeable stimulus.

Transduction: Translating Messages for the Brain

transduction
(trans-duk´shun) The translation of energy from one form to another.

Energy from stimuli cannot go directly to the brain. Light, sound, and other kinds of energy from the outside world are not able to travel through the nerves, and the brain cannot "understand" what they mean. To be useful to the brain, sensory messages must be translated into neural impulses that the neurons carry and the brain understands. The translation of one form of energy into another is called **transduction.**

Sense organs transduce sensory energy into neural energy. This is accomplished in the sense organ by the sensory receptor cells, which are specialized neurons that are excited by specific kinds of sensory energy and give off neural impulses from their axons. Some sensory receptor cells are sensitive to sound, some to light, some to chemicals, and so on. But in every case, the receptor cells give off coded neural impulses that carry the transduced sensory message to one of the sensory areas of the brain. The sense organs themselves (such as the ear, eye, and nose) are constructed in special ways that expose the receptor cells to sensory energy and help them translate it into coded neural impulses. At the center of every sense organ are receptor cells that do the transducing.

Note that we can be aware of a stimulus only if the receptor cells can transduce it. For example, we cannot see radio waves or hear some high-frequency tones, and we find some chemicals to be "tasteless" and "odorless" because we do not have receptors that can transduce these kinds of stimuli. Although a radio wave is just as real as the light reflected to our eyes from an apple, we cannot transduce the radio wave. We know that radio waves exist only because radios physically transduce them into sound waves that are in turn transduced by our ears into neural messages to the brain. There are many forms of energy in the world that we are not aware of because we do not have receptor cells that can transduce them (see fig. 3.1). If our planet were visited by aliens who had sensory receptors that were sensitive *only* to forms of energy different from our own, they would experience a world entirely different from the one we experience.

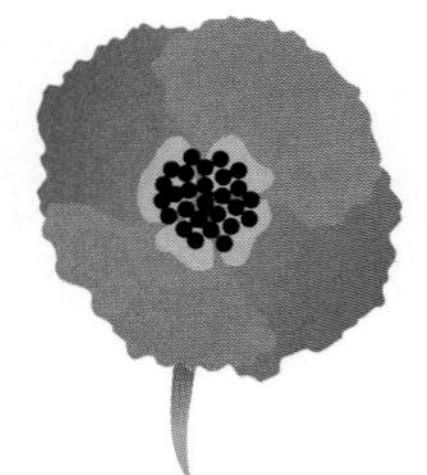

What humans see.

What bees "see."

FIGURE 3.1

The visual receptor cells of bees allow them to transduce ultraviolet light better than we can with our normal visual receptor cells. Therefore, bees "see" more of this form of energy. The flower on the left is as the human would see it; the bee, however, is able to see a "landing strip" on the flower that we do not see.

Sensory Limits: How Strong Must Messages Be?

Even when we have receptor cells that can transduce a kind of sensory message, not every message will be strong enough to be detected. The term *threshold* refers to the lower limits of sensory experience. The two primary kinds of thresholds are: (a) the smallest *magnitude* of a stimulus that can be detected and (b) the smallest *difference* between two stimuli that can be detected.

The **absolute threshold** is the smallest magnitude of a stimulus that can be detected. Look at the absolute thresholds for a number of common stimuli shown in figure 3.2 to gain a fuller appreciation of your remarkably sensitive receptor cells. Measuring such thresholds is no simple matter. People differ considerably in their sensitivity to weak stimuli, and the sensitivity of each of us differs from time to time. For this reason, absolute thresholds are defined as the magnitude of a stimulus that subjects can detect half the time. The smallest difference between two stimuli that can be detected *half the time* is called the **difference threshold.** For example, the smallest change in intensity of your stereo that you can distinguish as "louder" 50 percent of the time would be your difference threshold for that stimulus. Detailed knowledge of absolute and difference thresholds has, in fact, been used by the electronics industry to design better stereo systems.

absolute threshold
The smallest magnitude of a stimulus that can be detected half the time.

difference threshold
The smallest difference between two stimuli that can be detected half the time.

Sensory Adaptation

I just mentioned that an individual's sensitivity to a given stimulus differs from time to time. There are many reasons why this happens, such as fatigue or inattention, but **sensory adaptation** is one of the major causes. When a stimulus is continuously present or repeated at short intervals, the sensation that the same amount of sensory energy causes becomes gradually weaker, probably because the receptor cells become fatigued. When I was a teenager, I frequently went skin diving in an extremely cold spring in central Florida. At first the water was almost unbearably cold; when I jumped in from the dock, the intensity of the cold grabbed my attention so totally that for a moment I felt like only a cold skin of a person rather than a whole person. But after a few minutes the water felt comfortably cool. The water did not change in temperature, of course, but the sensation changed considerably because the temperature receptors in the skin adapted to the temperature of the water. This is sensory adaptation. It happens to some extent in all the senses; loud sounds and offensive odors, fortunately, also seem less intense as time goes by.

After being in cold water for a while, receptors in the skin adapt to changes in temperature and lessen the sensation of coldness.

Psychophysics

The specialty area within the field of psychology that studies sensory limits, sensory adaptation, and related topics is called **psychophysics.** The subject matter of this field is the relationship between the *physical* properties of stimuli and the *psychological* sensations they produce. Psychophysics is an important field because frequently there is *not* a direct or simple relationship between stimuli and sensations. Since our knowledge of the outside world is limited to what our sensations tell us, we need to understand under what conditions our sensations do not directly reflect the physical nature of the stimulus. Sensory adaptation is a process that alters the relationship between stimuli and sensations, but numerous other circumstances provide examples of this lack of a one-to-one relationship. The concept of the difference threshold provides another good example.

sensory adaptation
Weakened magnitude of a sensation resulting from prolonged presentation of the stimulus.

psychophysics
(sī´´kō-fiz´iks) A specialty area of psychology that studies sensory limits, sensory adaptation, and related topics.

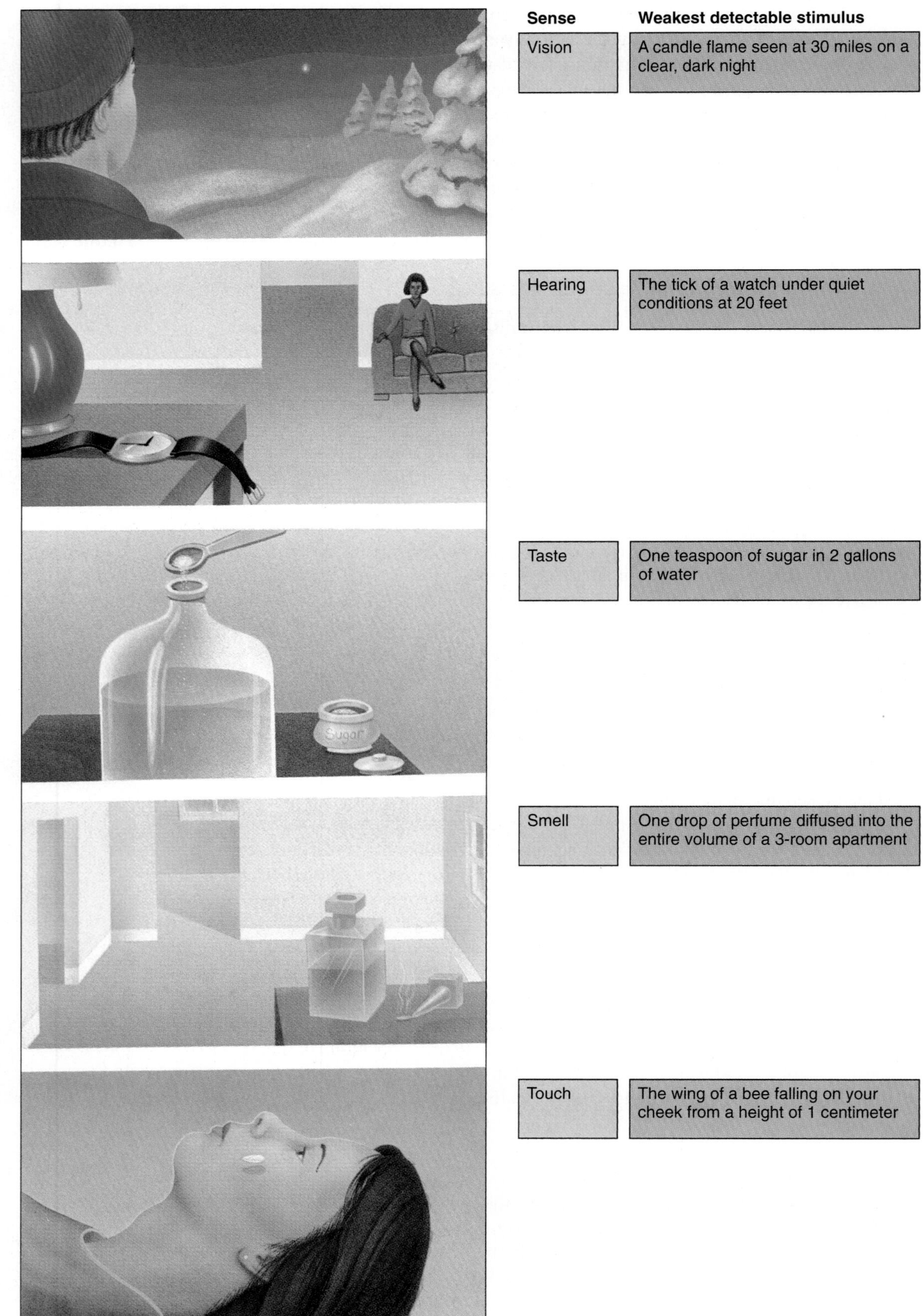

Sense
Weakest detectable stimulus
Vision
A candle flame seen at 30 miles on a clear, dark night
Hearing
The tick of a watch under quiet conditions at 20 feet
Taste
One teaspoon of sugar in 2 gallons of water
Smell
One drop of perfume diffused into the entire volume of a 3-room apartment
Touch
The wing of a bee falling on your cheek from a height of 1 centimeter
Sugar

FIGURE 3.2

The human senses are remarkably sensitive systems. Psychologist Eugene Galanter (1962) has offered these illustrative estimates of the weakest stimuli that we are capable of sensing.

A fact about difference thresholds that has captured the attention of psychophysicists since the nineteenth century is that the size of the difference threshold increases as the strength of the stimulus increases. When a stimulus is strong, changes in it must be bigger to be noticed than when the stimulus is weak. You can see this for yourself the next time you turn on a three-way light in a dark room. Most three-way bulbs provide light energy in three approximately equal steps (such as a 50-, 100-, and 150-watt bulb), but the greatest difference in brightness in the room is noticeable after the first click of the switch—the sofa that you just tripped over in the darkness is now plainly visible. Turning up the light to the next level adds a less noticeable increase in perceived brightness, and the third level adds even less in apparent brightness. At each level of increasing illumination, the difference threshold is greater, so the perceived increase in brightness is less. If you were to turn on another 50-watt bulb at this point—with the three-way bulb at its highest illumination—you might not see any increase in apparent brightness because your difference threshold is so high.

The ability to detect small changes in the intensity of weak stimuli, but only large changes in the intensity of strong stimuli, was first formally noted by German psychophysicist Ernst Weber. Today this phenomenon is known as **Weber's law.** Interestingly, the amount of the change needed to be detected half the time (the difference threshold) is almost always in direct proportion to the intensity of the original stimulus. Thus, if a waiter holding a tray on which four glasses had been placed is just able to detect the added weight of one glass, he would just be able to feel the added weight from *two* more glasses if the tray were already holding eight glasses. The amount of detectable added weight would always be in the same proportion, in this case 1/4.

Weber's law
A law stating that the amount of change in a stimulus needed to detect a difference is in direct proportion to the intensity of the original stimulus.

What is the relevance of this bit of information? Weber's law tells us that what we sense is not always the same as the energy that enters the sense organ. The same magnitude of physical change in intensity can be obvious one time, yet go undetected under different circumstances. This fact has important practical implications. Suppose, for example, that you are chosen to help design the instruments for a new airplane. The pilot wants an easier way to monitor the altitude of the plane, so you put in a light that increases in intensity as the plane nears the earth—the lower the altitude the more intense the light. That way, you assume, the pilot can easily monitor changes in altitude by seeing changes in brightness. Right?

According to Weber's law, this would be a dangerous way to monitor altitude. At high altitudes, the intensity of the light would be low, so small changes could be easily detected; but at low altitudes, the intensity would be so great that large changes in altitude—even fatal ones—might not be noticed. That is why the people who design instruments for airplanes, cars, and the like need to know about psychophysics.

Review

The world is known to us only indirectly because our brains are not in direct contact with the outside world. But sensory receptor cells have the ability to transduce physical energy into coded neural messages that are sent to the brain (sensation) where they are interpreted (perception). Not all forms of physical energy can become part of our perception of the world: We must have sensory receptor cells that can transduce that form of energy; the stimulation must be strong enough to exceed the sensory threshold. Our perception of external reality is complicated because there is no simple and direct relationship between the properties of physical stimuli and our conscious sensations. For example, a small change in the intensity of a stereo is noticeable when the stereo is being played softly, but the same size change would go unnoticed if the stereo were at high volume. The complicated relationship between physical stimuli and conscious sensations is the subject matter of psychophysics.

Thinking Critically About Psychology

1. How would life be different if human beings had a lower absolute threshold for the sense of sound? How about a higher absolute threshold for taste?

2. What is the difference between sensation and perception? Can you have a perception without a sensation?

Check Your Learning

To be sure that you have learned the key points from the preceding section, cover the answers below and try to answer each question. If you give an incorrect answer to any question, return to the page given next to the correct answer to see why your answer was not correct. Remember that these questions cover only some of the important information in this section; it is important that you make up your own questions to check your learning of other facts and concepts.

1. The ________________ is the smallest magnitude of a stimulus that can be detected half the time.

a. absolute threshold
b. visual threshold
c. difference threshold
d. relative threshold

2. When a stimulus is continuously present or repeated at short intervals, the sensation gradually becomes weaker. This is termed

a. sensory adaptation.
b. psychophysics.
c. desensitization.

3. According to ________________, the amount of the change in a stimulus needed to be detected half the time is almost always in direct proportion to the intensity of the original stimulus.

a. psychophysical dualism
b. McGurty's law
c. Weber's law
d. threshold variation

4. The specialty area within the field of psychology that studies sensory limits, sensory adaptation, and related topics is called ________________.

Correct Answers

1. a (p. 91), **2.** a (p. 91), **3.** c (p. 93), **4.** psychophysics (p. 91).

VISION: YOUR HUMAN CAMERA

In 1950 psychologist George Wald wrote an important paper comparing the eye to a camera. This is still a good analogy today. Both the eye and a camera are instruments that use a lens to focus light onto a light-sensitive surface on which the visual image is registered. The gross anatomy of the human eye shown in figure 3.3 makes the resemblance to a camera very apparent. This intricate and efficient instrument transduces the physical properties of light into elaborately coded neural messages.

Light: What Is It?

electromagnetic radiation
(e-lek´´trō-mag-net´ik) A form of energy including electricity, radio waves, and X rays, of which visible light is a part.

We need to have some knowledge of the nature of light to understand vision. Light is one small part of the form of energy known as **electromagnetic radiation** that also includes radio waves and X rays. Only a small portion of this radiation is visible—that is, our senses can transduce only a small part of it. We can best think of light as being composed of *waves* that have *frequency* and *intensity.* These two properties of light waves provide us with most of our information about vision.

wavelength
Frequency of light waves; determines the color we see.

The *intensity* of the light wave largely determines the *brightness* of the visual sensation. The light reflected by an apple that is lighted by a single candle would be low in intensity, so we would see the red of the apple as a dim rather than a bright sensation. The **wavelength** of the light largely determines the *color,* or *hue,* that we see—that is, light waves of different wavelengths are seen as different colors. But most light waves are not made up of a single wavelength and are therefore not seen as a pure color. Rather, they are made up of light waves of more than one wavelength. The more a color is composed of multiple wavelengths, the less *saturated* (or pure) the color is said to be. The relationship between the physical properties of light and what is seen is not always simple and direct, however.

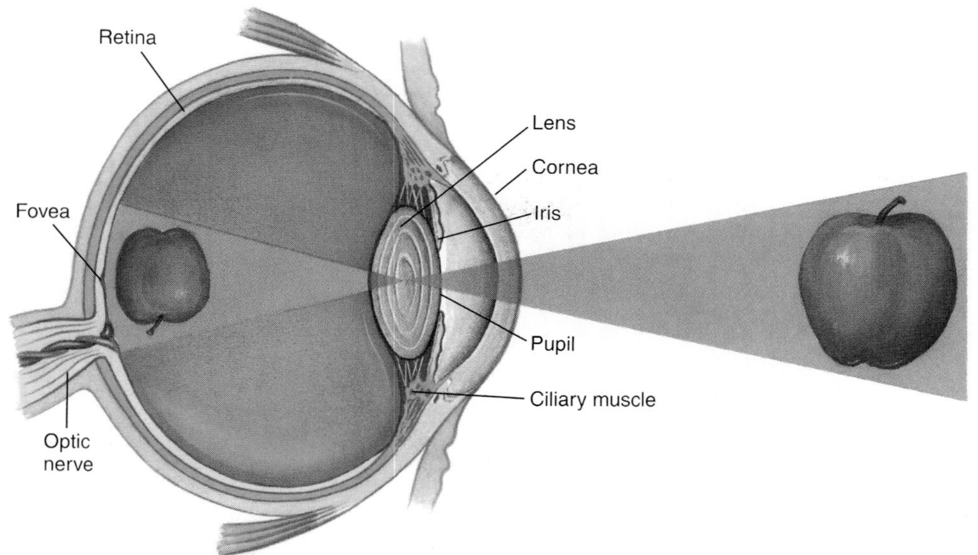

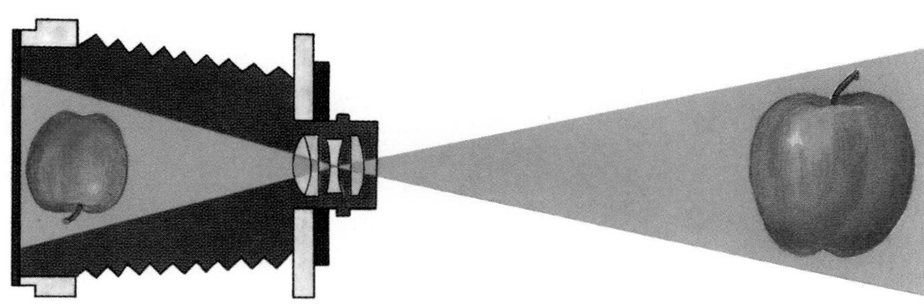

FIGURE 3.3

Optical similarities of eye and camera are apparent in their cross sections. Both utilize a lens to focus an inverted image on a light-sensitive surface. Both possess an iris to adjust to various intensities of light. The single lens of the eye, however, cannot bring light of all colors to a focus at the same point. The compound lens of the camera is better corrected for color because it is composed of two kinds of glass.

The Eye: How Does It Work?

The eye is an almost perfect sphere composed of two fluid-filled chambers. Light passes through the clear **cornea** into the first chamber. At the back of this chamber, the colored **iris** opens and closes to regulate how much light will pass through the **pupil** into the **lens.** The lens is held in place by ligaments that are attached to the **ciliary muscle.** This muscle focuses images by controlling the thickness of the lens so that a clear image falls on the light-sensitive **retina** at the back of the second chamber (see fig. 3.3). When the ciliary muscle is uncontracted, the tension of the ligaments stretches the lens relatively flat. When the ciliary muscle contracts, it lessens the tension of the ligaments and the lens thickens. The lens must be thickened to focus on close objects; that is why reading for long periods—which involves prolonged contraction of the ciliary muscle—makes your eyes feel tired.

The real business of transducing light waves is carried out in the retina by two types of receptor cells named the **rods** and the **cones** because of their shapes (see fig. 3.4). The cones are far less numerous than the rods—about 6 million cones compared with 125 million rods in each eye (Pugh, 1988). Cones are concentrated in the center of the retina, with the greatest concentration at a central spot called the **fovea.** In good light, **visual acuity** (the clearness and sharpness of vision) is best for images that are focused directly on the fovea, largely because of the high concentration of cones.

The rods are located throughout the retina except in the center (the fovea). Their role in vision differs from that of the cones in four main ways. First, because of their location, they are largely responsible for peripheral vision—vision at the top, bottom, and sides of the visual field—while the cones play little role in this aspect of seeing. Second, the rods are hundreds of times more sensitive to light than the cones. This means that they play a far more important role in vision in dim light than the cones. Third, the rods produce images that are perceived with less visual acuity than cones. This is largely because neurons leading from several rods often converge so that their impulses are sent to the brain on a single nerve fiber (shown in fig. 3.4). In contrast, cones more commonly send their messages

cornea
(kor´nē-ah) The protective coating on the surface of the eye through which light passes.

iris
(ī´ris) The colored part of the eye behind the cornea that regulates the amount of light that enters.

pupil
(pyoo´pil) The opening of the iris.

lens
Transparent portion of the eye that focuses light on the retina.

ciliary muscle
(sil´ē-ar´´e) The muscle in the eye that controls the shape of the lens.

retina
(ret´i-nah) The area at the back of the eye on which images are formed and that contains the rods and cones.

rods
The 125 million cells located outside the center of the retina that transduce light waves into neural impulses, thereby coding information about light and dark.

cones
The 6 million receptor cells located mostly in the center of the retina that transduce light waves into neural impulses, thereby coding information about light, dark, and color.

fovea
(fō´vē-ah) The central spot of the retina containing the greatest concentration of cones.

visual acuity
(vizh´-u-al ah-ku´i-te) Clearness and sharpness of vision.

FIGURE 3.4

Diagram of the microscopic structure of a section of the retina showing the rods and cones and their principal neural interconnections. Blowup shows individual rod and cone cells.

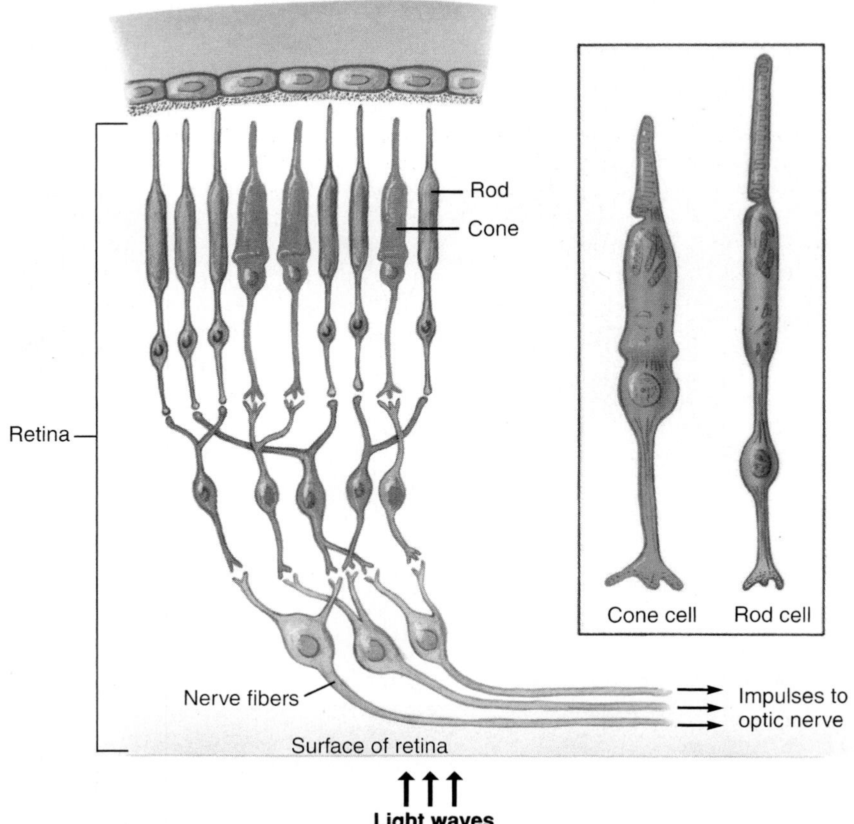

to the brain along separate nerve fibers, giving the brain more precise information about the location of the stimulation on the retina.

The fourth difference between the rods and cones concerns color vision. Both types of receptors respond to variations in light and dark (in terms of the number of receptors that fire and the frequency with which they fire), but only the cones can code information about color. Because the rods do not detect color, and because the cones can respond only in bright light, we can see only indistinct forms of black and gray in an almost dark room. Although light of different wavelengths is still present in the room during near darkness, the rods have no way of sending messages about them to the brain, so colors "disappear" from view.

Would you be surprised to learn that you are partially blind in each eye? The spot near the center of the retina where the **optic nerve** is attached contains no rods or cones. Because there is no visual reception at this point, it is known as the **blind spot.** We are not normally aware of this blind spot because we "fill in" the missing information during the process of seeing by using information coming in from the other parts of the retina. However, look at figure 3.5 for a demonstration of its existence.

optic nerve
The nerve that carries neural messages about vision to the brain.

blind spot
The spot where the optic nerve attaches to the retina, containing no rods or cones.

Coded messages from the rods and cones are processed in a preliminary way in the neurons of the retina and then sent to the visual areas of the left and right occipital lobe of the cerebral cortex for interpretation. Recall from chapter 2 that the information from the eyes is transmitted to the visual areas in a complicated fashion. As shown in figure 3.6, stimuli that are on your right fall on the left side of each eye. Information from the right visual field of both eyes is sent to the visual area in the occipital lobe of the left visual hemisphere after the optic nerves cross over at the **optic chiasm** in the brain. Information from stimuli on your left falls on the right side of each eye and is sent to the visual area in the right cerebral hemisphere. It's a bit confusing when you read about it for the first time, but the brain manages to keep it all straight.

optic chiasm
The area in the brain where the optic nerves cross.

Over the past 20 years, a great deal of information has been learned about the ways in which the nervous system processes and interprets visual information. For example, imagine that a friend were to walk into the room where you are sitting right now and toss an apple to you. You may be surprised to learn that different parts of the visual areas process the

Blind Spot

FIGURE 3.5

Demonstration of the blind spot. You can demonstrate to yourself the existence of the "blind spot" in the following way. Hold your book at about arm's length with the word *spot* in front of your eyes. Close your right eye and stare at the word *spot*. Move the book in slowly until the word *blind* disappears. At this point, its image is falling on the spot in the retina where the optic nerve is attached and there are no receptors. We are not normally aware of the existence of this blind spot because we "fill in" a perception to compensate for the missing information. In this case, we see the dotted line as continuous after the word *blind* disappears.

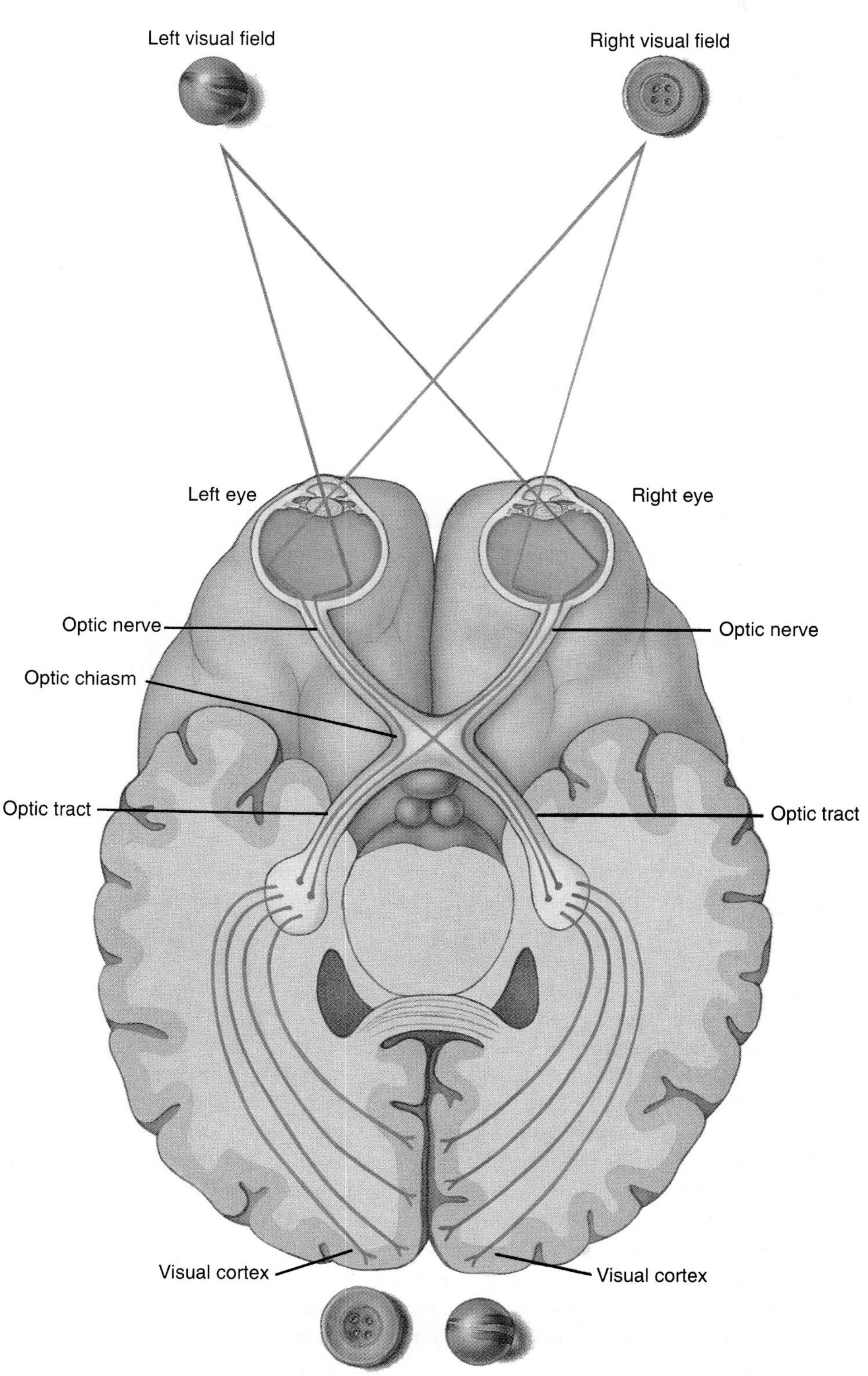

FIGURE 3.6

Images of objects in the right visual field are focused on the left side of each retina, and images of objects in the left visual field are focused on the right side of each retina. This information is conveyed along the optic nerves to the optic chiasm and the thalamus. The thalamus then relays the information to the visual cortex of the occipital lobes. Note that images of objects in the right visual field are processed by the left occipital lobe and images of objects in the left visual field are processed by the right occipital lobe.

shape, the color, and the movement of the apple. Different neural systems in the retina respond to these different qualities and the information is interpreted in different parts of the occipital lobes (Zeki, 1992). When you consider that information from the left and right visual fields is being processed in different cerebral hemispheres, you can see that the brain's strategy is to first keep many different aspects of the incoming visual information separate and then to integrate it into a visual perception. Depending on the nature of the visual information, neural messages are then sent to yet other parts of the brain. For example, your eyes are now processing language—the words on this page—so the visual messages are being sent on to Wernicke's language area in the temporal lobe for further interpretation.

Dark and Light Adaptation

When you walk into a dark movie theater from the daylight, you are "blind" at first; your eyes can pick up very little visual information. Within about 5 minutes, however, your vision in the darkened room has improved considerably, and very slowly it improves over the next 25 minutes until you can see fairly well. When you exit the theater from the matinee performance, you have the opposite experience. At first the intense light "blinds" you. You squint and block out the painful light, but in a little while you can see normally again. What is going on? How can you be sighted one moment and blind the next just because the intensity of light has suddenly changed?

The phenomena are called *dark adaptation* and *light adaptation.* Here is what happens in the retina during **dark adaptation.** In a lighted room, the rods and cones are being used frequently, so they are not very sensitive. When we enter darkness, the rods and cones are not sensitive enough to be stimulated by the low-intensity light and they stop firing almost completely. This gives the receptors a "rest," so they begin to regain their sensitivity by making a fresh supply of the chemicals used in light reception that have been literally "bleached out" by the intense light.

dark adaptation
Increased sensitivity of the eye in semidarkness following an abrupt reduction in overall illumination.

At first, both the rods and the cones are recovering their sensitivity, so improvement is fairly rapid. But the cones become fully sensitive (remember they are not very sensitive in weak light) within about 5 minutes, so the rate of improvement slows after that. The rods continue to improve in sensitivity slowly, reaching a level of sensitivity to light that is an amazing *100,000 times greater* than in bright illumination after about 30 minutes in the dark!

In **light adaptation,** eyes that have been in the dark for a while have built up a full supply of the chemicals used in light reception and are very responsive to light. When we are suddenly exposed to intense light, a barrage of rods and cones fires almost at once and, in essence, "overloads" the visual circuits. It's not until the intense light has had a chance to bleach out some of the receptor chemicals and reduce the sensitivity of the receptors to a normal level that we can see comfortably again. Fortunately, this process takes place in about a minute.

light adaptation
Regaining sensitivity of the eye to bright light following an abrupt increase in overall illumination.

By the way, your parents were right about carrots and good vision. The chemical involved in light reception in the rods is largely made up of vitamin A. This is why a deficiency of vitamin A can lead to "night blindness." And yes, there is a lot of vitamin A in carrots.

Color Vision

Energy of any wavelength within the spectrum of visible light will evoke a sensation of color when it stimulates the human visual system. But light energy is just that—energy; it has no color of its own. Color is the conscious experience that results from the processing of light energy by the eye and nervous system.

It's obviously useful to be able to discriminate among lights of different wavelengths: "blue" berries are ready to be eaten; "green" berries are not. But how does the human visual system produce the sensation of color? It has taken psychologists and other scientists more than a hundred years to reach our current understanding of the complex mechanisms of color vision.

In the early 1800s Thomas Young and Hermann von Helmholz made the observation that any color can be created by shining different combinations of the wavelengths of light

The color of this red apple hasn't changed, but in a dim light its color appears to fade. Cones in the eye pick up color but they work well only in bright light.

FIGURE 3.7
The trichromatic theory of color vision was based on the observation that all colors can be produced by combinations of red, blue, and green lights (and that all three lights together create white).

for red, blue, and green on a single spot. For example, as illustrated in figure 3.7, the combination of red and green light produces yellow. Based on this observation, Young and Helmholz guessed that there are three kinds of cones in the retina that respond mostly to light in either the red, green, or blue range of wavelengths. Their theory is referred to as the **trichromatic theory** of color vision. According to this theory, all sensations of colors result from different levels of stimulation of the red, green, and blue receptors.

trichromatic theory
(trī´´krō-mat´ik) The theory of color vision contending that the eye has three different kinds of cones, each of which responds to light of one range of wavelength.

Over the years, many types of studies have confirmed that there are indeed three kinds of cones. As shown in figure 3.8, each kind of cone contains pigments that mostly absorb light of the wavelengths that correspond to red, green, and blue. Does that mean that the trichromatic theory of Young and Helmholz was correct? Yes and no. Color vision is fascinatingly complex.

Soon after Young and Helmholz stated the trichromatic theory, other scientists pointed out that it could not explain three intriguing phenomena:

1. *Complementary colors.* Artists know that yellow and blue as well as red and green are complementary colors. You cannot mix lights of these colors to produce a yellowish-blue or a reddish-green. If color vision is simply a matter of combinations of impulses from cones that are mostly sensitive to red, green, and blue, how could some colors be complementary in this sense?
2. *Color afterimages.* If a patch of color is stared at for a while, and then the eyes are shifted to a white surface, you will see a ghostly "afterimage" of the patch in the color that is *complementary* to that of the original patch. For example, stare intensely for about 30 seconds at the white dot in the center of the word *red* that is printed in the color red in figure 3.9. Then stare at the blank white space above it. You will see an afterimage of the word *red,* but it will be *green!* The same thing occurs for all four of the complementary colors.

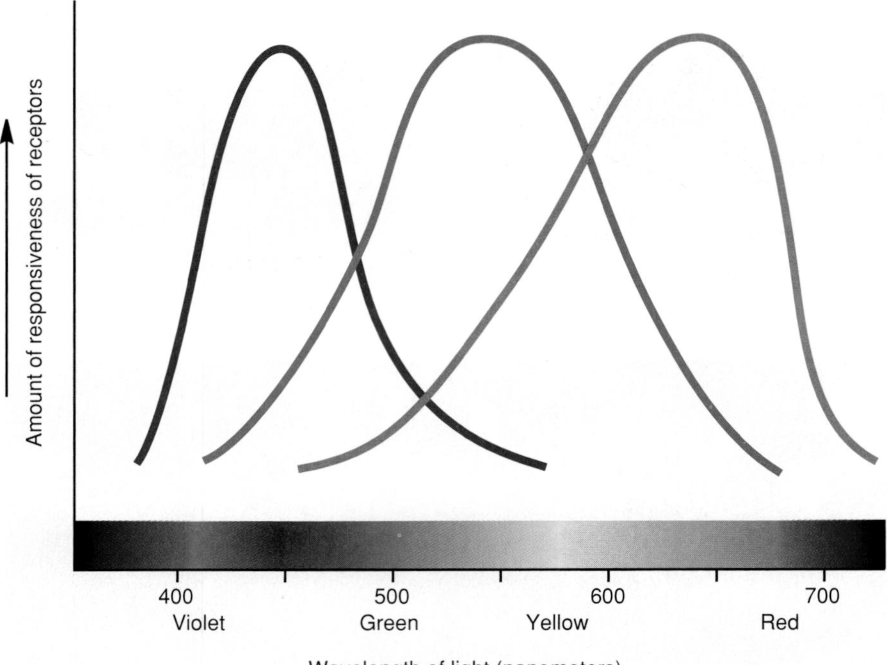

FIGURE 3.8

Our ability to see color is partly based on the fact that three kinds of cones contain pigments that respond mostly to light in the wavelengths for blue, green, and red. Note, however, that each type of cone also responds to other nearby wavelengths of light. This means, for example, that light in the yellow range stimulates both the red and the green cone receptors, but not as strongly as light in the red or green ranges, respectively.

RED

FIGURE 3.9

Stimulus used in the demonstration of afterimages.

3. *Color blindness.* Partial color blindness affects about 8 percent of males and 1 percent of females. Most people with partial color blindness seem to see the world *almost* normally, but in extreme cases the individual is completely unable to distinguish between two colors. Usually, color-blind individuals cannot tell the difference between red and green, but they see yellow and blue normally (in fewer cases, they cannot distinguish yellow from blue, but can see red and green normally). Note that the colors that look the same to a color-blind person are always complementary colors.

Color blindness does not make sense in the trichromatic theory. You could explain why a person could not distinguish between red and green by hypothesizing that something was wrong with either the red or the green receptors or both. But, according to the trichromatic theory, a person sees yellow because light of this wavelength stimulates both the red and the green receptors. If a person was color blind to red and green because there was something wrong with the red and green receptors, how could that person still see yellow? Psychologists soon realized that something more than three kinds of cones was involved in color vision.

opponent-process theory

The theory of color vision contending that the visual system has two kinds of color processors that respond to light in either the red-green or yellow-blue ranges of wavelength.

The **opponent-process theory** was developed to explain the three phenomena listed above that could not be explained just by the existence of three kinds of cones. The opponent-process theory states that there are also two kinds of *color-processing mechanisms* that receive messages from the three kinds of cones (see fig. 3.10). These two color-processing mechanisms respond in *opposite* ways that correspond to the two pairs of complementary colors. For example, suppose you look at a lemon (and light in the yellow range of wavelength reflects from the lemon onto your retinas). Light of this wavelength stimulates both the red and green receptors, but not the blue receptors (see figure 3.8). The *yellow-blue (Y-B) processing mechanism* is *activated* by signals from the red and green receptors but is *slowed down* by inhibitory signals from the blue receptors. Therefore, light in the yellow wavelengths leads the Y-B mechanism to send a rapid message along the visual system to the brain. This signal is the primary information used by the brain to produce the sensation of yellow on the peel of the lemon.

On the other hand, the *red-green (R-G) processing mechanism* is activated by signals from the red receptors but is slowed by signals from the green receptors. When light in the green wavelengths stimulates the green receptors, they send a strong inhibitory message to the red-green (R-G) opponent mechanism, which causes it to send slow neural signals

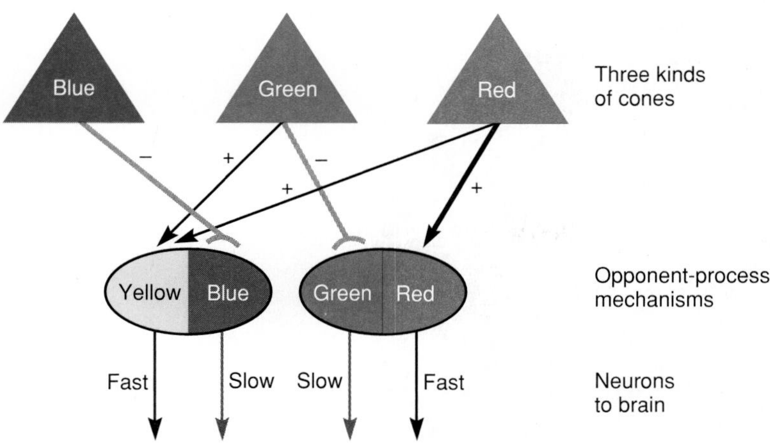

FIGURE 3.10

The modern theory of color vision combines the three kinds of cone color receptors of trichromatic theory with the two processing mechanisms of opponent-process theory. When light in the red wavelengths stimulates the red receptors, they send a strong excitatory message to the red-green (R-G) opponent mechanism, which stimulates rapid firing of neural signals to the brain. Light in the yellow wavelengths stimulates both the red and the green receptors somewhat. They both send weak excitatory messages to the yellow-blue (Y-B) opponent mechanism, but they are strong enough together to stimulate it to send fast signals to the brain. When light is in the blue wavelengths, it stimulates the blue receptors, which send strong inhibitory messages to the Y-B opponent mechanism, leading it to fire slowly. Light in the green wavelengths leads to slow firing of the R-G opponent mechanism in a similar fashion.

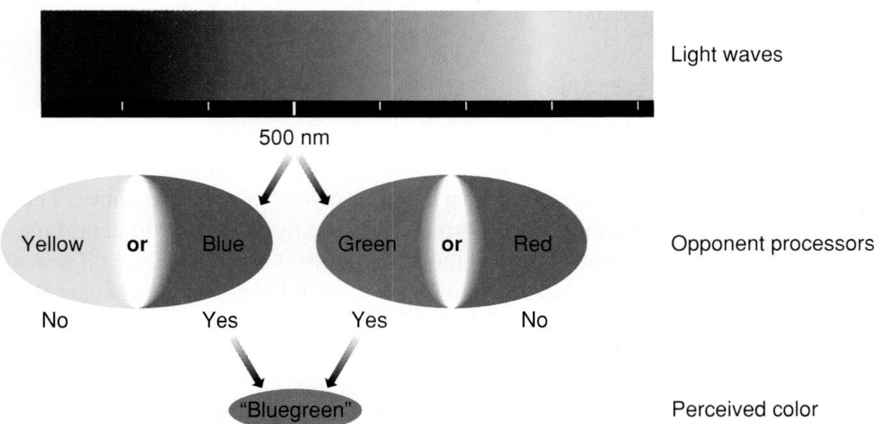

FIGURE 3.11

According to opponent-process theory, specialized cells in the brain transduce light into combinations of yellow or blue, and green or red in the process of color perception.

to the brain. In similar ways, combinations of signals from the opponent-processing mechanisms supply the brain with the information necessary for all color sensations (see fig. 3.11).

Notice that opponent-process theory explains the phenomenon of complementary colors because the R-G and Y-B mechanisms cannot signal both of their opponent colors at the same time. It also explains why afterimages are always in the opposite complementary color to the original stimulus. Staring at the red stimulus reduces the sensitivity of the red receptors (through sensory adaptation), leading the R-G system to send a signal to the brain that is interpreted as the sensation of green. The opponent-process theory also explains color blindness as an abnormality in one of the opponent-process mechanisms. Perhaps the strongest evidence for the opponent-process theory, however, is that neurons throughout the visual system respond to light in an opponent-process fashion. For example, if a specific neuron in the retina is excited by green light, then it is inhibited from firing by red light.

Thus, the trichromatic theory accurately describes events very well at the first level of neurons in the visual system—the cones within the retina—but the opponent-process theory best describes the activities of neurons in the rest of the visual system. They are both correct, in other words, when combined together (Pugh, 1988).

Individuals with normal color vision can see the number as 8. Red-green color-blind individuals see a 3 here.

This has been reproduced from Ishihara's Tests for Colour Blindness published by KANEHARA & CO., LTD., Tokyo, Japan, but tests for color blindness cannot be conducted with this material. For accurate testing, the original plates should be used.

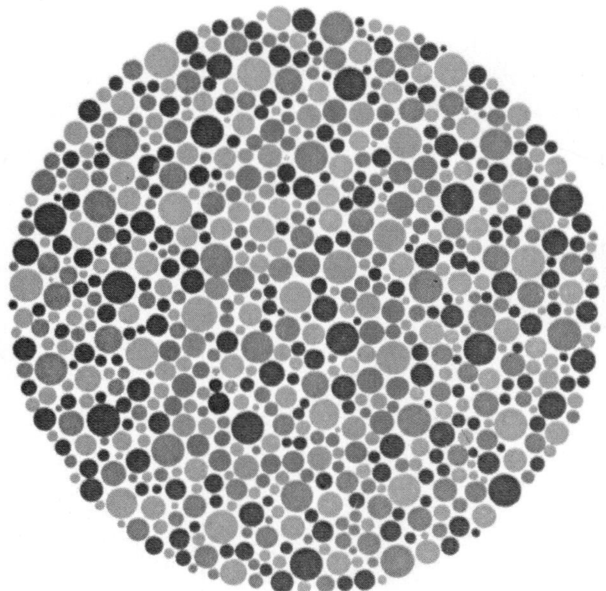

Thinking Critically About Psychology

1. If cones give us the best visual acuity, what is the advantage of having rods as well?
2. Which theory of color vision do you think would make the most sense to an artist? Why?

Review

The eye operates much like a human camera. The lens focuses a visual image on the retina of the eye, which contains two kinds of sensory receptor cells, the rods and cones. These transduce the wavelength, amplitude, and complexity of the light waves into neural messages. The two kinds of receptor cells perform their jobs somewhat differently. Cones work best in intense light, provide good visual acuity, and transduce information about color. Rods work well in weak light, do not provide good acuity, and do not transduce color. The eye does not function well when the intensity of light suddenly changes, but quickly regains its sensitivity through the processes of light and dark adaptation. There are two major theoretical explanations of how the visual system transduces color. One states that three different kinds of cones are most sensitive to light of different wavelengths. The other suggests that two kinds of color-processing mechanisms in the visual system process complementary colors. Each theory is "correct" at different stages of the information processing about the wavelength of light.

Check Your Learning

To be sure that you have learned the key points from the preceding section, cover the answers below and try to answer each question. If you give an incorrect answer to any question, return to the page given next to the correct answer to see why your answer was not correct.

1. The ________________ of the light largely determines the color that we see.

a. intensity
b. amplitude
c. saturation
d. wavelength

2. Light waves are transduced into neural messages by two types of receptor cells named rods and cones in the ________________ of the eye.

a. ciliary structure
b. pupil
c. retina
d. iris

3. Cones are concentrated in the ________________ .

a. periphery of the eye
b. fovea
c. iris
d. blind spot

Check Your Learning—continued

4. The theory of color vision that there are three kinds of cones in the retina that respond primarily to light in either the red, green, or blue range of wavelengths is the ________________ theory.

   a. opponent-process **c.** psychophysical
   b. trichromatic **d.** sensory adaptation

Correct Answers
1. d (p. 94), 2. c (p. 95), 3. b (p. 95), 4. b (p. 99).

HEARING: SENSING SOUND WAVES

Without hearing and vision, there probably would be no spoken or written languages, and without language most of the cultural and scientific accomplishments of human beings probably would have been impossible. The sense of hearing depends on the ear, a complex sensory instrument that transduces the physical properties of sound waves into neural messages that can be sent to the brain. Neural messages from the ears are first interpreted in the temporal lobes auditory area and then forwarded to other parts of the brain for additional interpretation.

Sound: What Is It?

Hearing, or **audition,** is the sense that detects the vibratory changes in the air known as **sound waves.** When an object such as a tuning fork vibrates back and forth, it sets in motion successive waves of *compression* and *rarefaction* (expansion) of the molecules of the air (see fig. 3.12). When the waves reach the ear, the reception of sound begins. As we shall see in a moment, the sound waves in the air cause a chain of small structures in the ear to vibrate in a way that is eventually translated into a neural message to the brain.

Not all sound waves are alike, however, and the nature of a sound wave determines to a great extent how we will sense it. For one thing, sound waves differ in the **frequency of cycles** of compression and rarefaction of the air (see fig. 3.12). Objects that vibrate slowly create low-frequency sound waves, while rapidly vibrating objects produce high-frequency sound waves. The frequency of sound waves is measured in **hertz (Hz)** units,

audition
(aw-dish´un) The sense of hearing.

sound waves
Vibratory changes in the air that carry sound.

frequency of cycles
Rate of vibration of sound waves; determines pitch.

hertz (Hz)
Measurement of the frequency of sound waves in cycles per second.

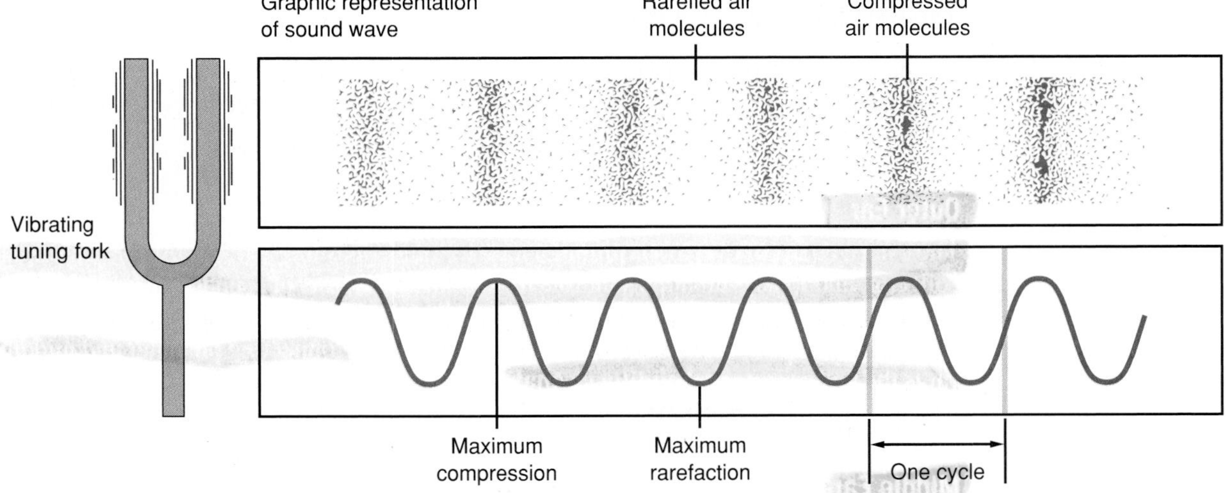

FIGURE 3.12
Vibrating objects such as a tuning fork create a sound wave of successive compression and rarefaction (expansion) in the air, which can be represented graphically as shown.

FIGURE 3.13

The loudness of common sounds as measured in decibel units.

Note: Prolonged exposure to sounds over 85 decibels can lead to permanent hearing loss. Even brief exposure to loudness of 150 decibels (being close to an explosion or the speakers at some rock concerts) can permanently damage hearing.

Decibels	Sounds
120	Loud thunder or rock concert
110	
100	Subway
90	City bus
85	Maximum level of industrial noise considered safe
80	Noisy automobile
70	
60	Normal conversation
50	
40	Quiet office
30	
20	Whisper
10	
0	Absolute threshold of human hearing

the number of vibratory cycles per second. The human ear is sensitive to sound waves in the range of 20 to 20,000 Hz. Sound waves also differ in terms of **intensity,** or how densely compacted the air molecules are in the sound wave.

intensity
Density of vibrating air molecules; determines the loudness of sound.

pitch
The experience of sound vibrations sensed as high or low.

decibel (db)
(des´i-bel) Measurement of the intensity of perceived sound.

timbre
(tim´ber, tam´br) The characteristic quality of a sound as determined by the complexity of the sound wave.

The frequency of a sound wave largely determines its **pitch,** or how high or low it sounds to us. For example, striking a glass with a spoon causes a higher frequency sound wave—which we hear as a higher pitch—than striking a bass drum. The loudness of a sound is largely determined by its intensity. Gently tapping a bass drum produces less dense compression and rarefaction, and a quieter sound, than striking it hard. Intensity is measured in **decibel (db)** units. This scale begins at zero at the absolute threshold for detecting a 1,000-Hz tone (and increases by 20 db as the intensity of the stimulus is multiplied by 10). Normal conversation averages about 60 db, while sounds of 120 db or more are quite painful (see fig. 3.13). The **timbre** of a sound (its characteristic quality) is determined by the complexity of the sound wave—that is, the extent to which it is composed of many waves of different frequency and intensity. The voices of different people sound different to us largely because of their unique timbres.

The relationship between the physical properties of sound waves and the sensation of sound is not as simple as I have just made it seem, however. Take loudness, for example. Two tones of equal intensity may not be heard as equally loud if they are not equal in frequency. Loudness seems greatest for tones of about 3,000 to 4,000 Hz; higher- or lower-frequency sounds of the same intensity seem less loud to us.

The Ear: How Does It Work?

The ear is a sensitive sensory instrument that transduces sound waves into neural impulses to the brain. It is composed of three major sections: the outer ear, middle ear, and the inner ear (see fig. 3.14).

Outer Ear

pinna
(pin´nah) The external part of the ear.

external auditory canal
The tube connecting the pinna to the middle ear.

The external part of the ear, or **pinna,** which we think of as the "ear," is useful as a sound collector, and it plays an important role in locating the origins of sounds. The shape of the pinna is especially important in sound localization, as shown by the fact that temporarily smoothing it over with putty impairs sound localization. Connecting the outer and middle ear is the hollow **external auditory canal.** It's the part that gets waxy and the part through which sound waves reach the *eardrum,* the first structure of the middle ear.

Middle Ear

eardrum
Thin membrane that sound waves cause to vibrate; the first structure of the middle ear.

The sound wave is transduced into mechanical energy in the middle ear. Sound waves set the thin **eardrum,** which resembles the skin on a drum, into vibratory movement. The eardrum is connected to a series of three movable, interconnected bones: the **hammer,** the

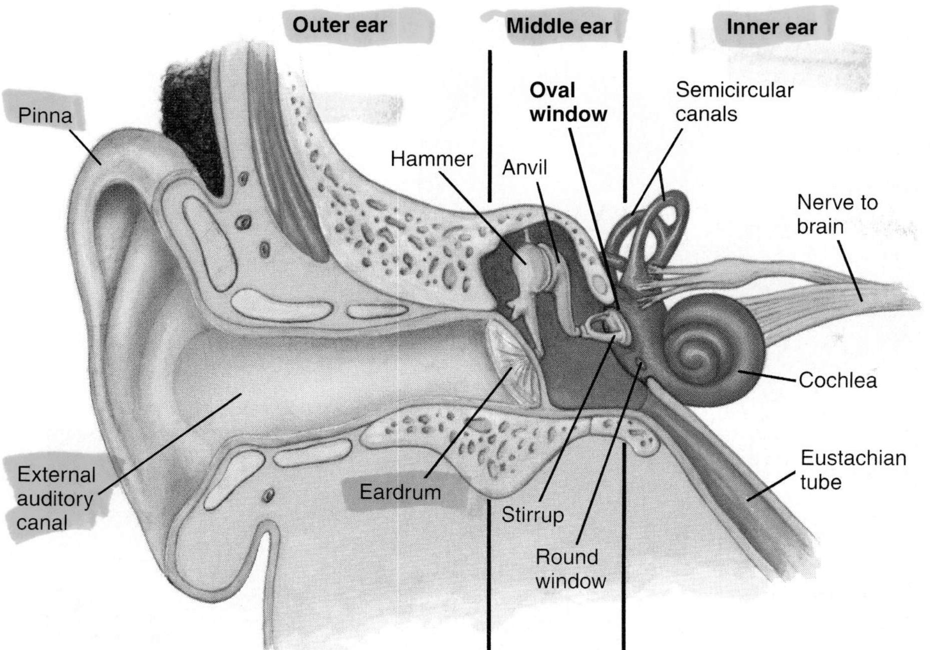

FIGURE 3.14
Diagram of the major structures of the ear.

anvil, and the **stirrup,** so named because of their shapes. The vibrating eardrum sets these bones into movement, passing the energy on to the inner ear.

hammer, anvil, and stirrup
Three linked bones of the middle ear that help pass sound waves to the inner ear.

Inner Ear

The vibrating stirrup shakes another eardrumlike structure called the **oval window** into motion. This membrane is at the end of a long, curled structure called the **cochlea,** which is filled with fluid. The vibrating oval window creates waves in the fluid of the cochlea (see fig. 3.15). The cochlea contains two long tubes that double back on themselves and are connected only at the tip end of the spiral. The pressure of the vibrating waves is relieved by a third eardrumlike membrane at the other end of the cochlea called the **round window.** Running almost the entire length of the cochlea are several layers of membranes that separate the two tubes. The lower membrane, called the **basilar membrane,** forms a floor on which the ear's sensory receptors sit. Hairlike receptor cells are contained in the **organ of Corti.** Vibrations in the cochlear fluid set the basilar membrane in motion. This movement, in turn, moves the organ of Corti and stimulates the receptor cells that it contains. These receptors transduce the sound waves in the cochlear fluid into coded neural impulses that are sent to the brain.

oval window
The membrane of the inner ear that vibrates, creating sound waves in the fluid of the cochlea.

cochlea
(cok´lē-ah) A curved structure of the inner ear that is filled with fluid.

round window
The membrane that relieves pressure from the vibrating waves in the cochlear fluid.

basilar membrane
(bas´ĭ-lar) One of the membranes that separates the two tubes of the cochlea and upon which the organ of Corti rests.

organ of Corti
(kor´tē) Sensory receptor in the cochlea that transduces sound waves into coded neural impulses.

How does the organ of Corti code neural messages for the brain? The *intensity* of a sound wave is coded by the number of receptors in the organ of Corti that fire. Low-intensity sounds stimulate only a few receptors; high-intensity sounds stimulate many receptors.

The *frequency* of the sound wave is apparently coded in at least two ways. First, sound waves of different frequencies stimulate firings of receptor cells at different *places* along the organ of Corti. Higher-frequency waves stimulate the organ of Corti close to the oval window; lower-frequency waves stimulate it farther along the cochlea (except for very low frequencies). Second, the frequency of the sound waves is duplicated to some extent in the *frequency* of the firings of the auditory receptors. Only at lower frequencies is each individual neuron able to fire at the same frequency as the sound wave. At higher frequencies, the coding of frequency is achieved by the firing of *volleys* of neural impulses by different groups of neurons that fire in turns at the same frequency as the sound wave.

Not all sounds travel this complete route from outer ear to cochlea. Some sounds are transmitted through the bones of the head directly to the cochlear fluid. We hear ourselves speak (and eat) largely through **bone conduction hearing.** This is an important consideration in diagnosing hearing problems. People who have suffered damage to the hearing apparatus of the middle ear can hear bone-conducted sounds fairly well, but not airborne sounds. People with damage to the auditory nerve—nerve deafness—cannot hear either type of sound.

bone conduction hearing
Sounds transmitted through the bones of the head directly to the cochlear fluid.

FIGURE 3.15

Vibrations from sound waves enter the cochlea through the oval window and travel the length of the cochlea where they are transduced into neural messages by receptors in the organ of Corti.

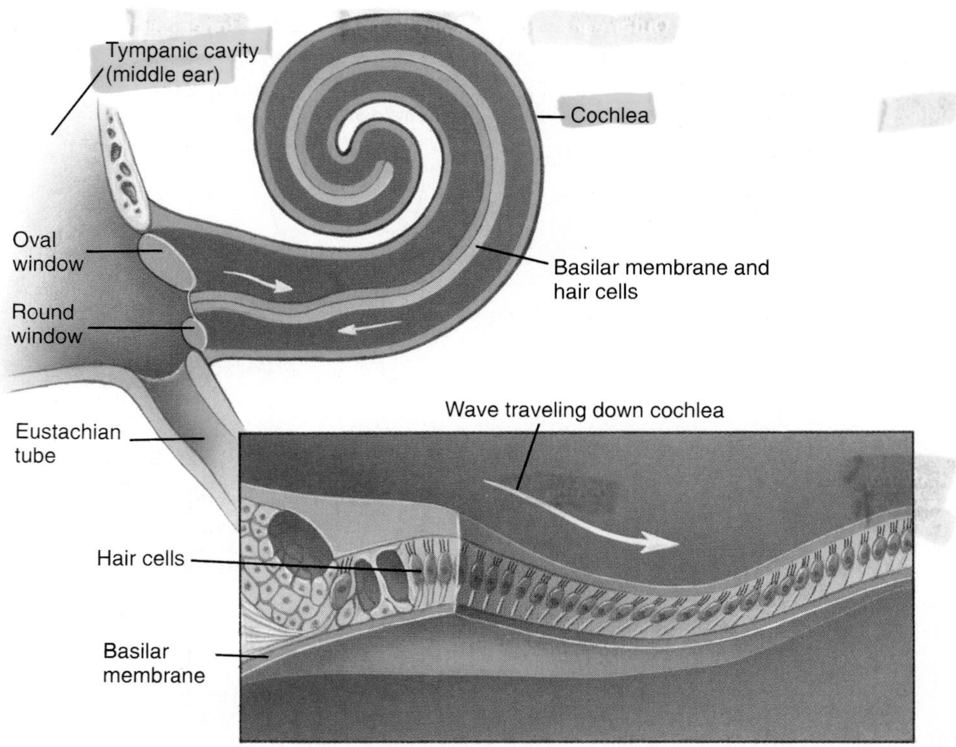

Two factors tell the listener the location of sounds. First, a sound wave that originates from the side reaches the closer ear slightly sooner than it reaches the farther ear. Second, the head blocks some of the sound wave that reaches the farther ear, reducing the intensity of stimulation.

One more thing about ears deserves mentioning. Ever wonder why people have two of them? For one thing, a pair of ears gives us a spare in case something goes wrong with one, but the fact that we have two ears also serves an important function in *locating* the origin of sounds. The ears locate sounds in two ways.

First, when a sound wave is coming from straight ahead or from straight behind us, the sound reaches both ears simultaneously. But when a sound is coming from the sides or from an angle, it reaches each ear at a slightly different time. The ears are sensitive enough to this difference that they allow us to locate the direction of sounds, especially high-frequency sounds. The reason you know that the person to the left of you is blowing her nose again is because your left ear heard it before your right ear did. Second, cues for the location of high-frequency sounds are also produced by the fact that your head dampens some of the sound reaching the more distant ear, creating a difference in the intensity of the sound waves that reach each of the ears.

The barn owl hunts at night, often inside dark barns and other structures that block the light. It uses its extraordinary sense of hearing to locate its prey in the darkness. The same cues used by humans to localize the source of sounds (differences in sounds reaching the two ears) enable the barn owl to find its scampering prey.

Review

Sound is a physical stimulus made up of successive waves of densely and sparsely compressed air. The ear is composed of a series of structures that transmit the sound wave from the outer ear to the inner ear where it produces vibrations in the fluid of the cochlea. The vibrations of the cochlear fluid are transduced by the ear's receptor cells that are located in the organ of Corti. Coded neural messages are sent to the auditory sensory areas of the brain where frequency, intensity, and complexity are interpreted as pitch, loudness, and timbre. Differences in the timing and intensity of sound waves reaching the two ears allow us to determine the location of the source of the sound.

Check Your Learning

To be sure that you have learned the key points from the preceding section, cover the answers below and try to answer each question. If you give an incorrect answer to any question, return to the page given next to the correct answer to see why your answer was not correct.

1. Objects that vibrate slowly create low-frequency sound waves that we hear as having ________________.

- **a.** low pitch
- **b.** high pitch
- **c.** simple timbre
- **d.** complex timbre

2. The sound wave is transduced into mechanical energy (the motion of the hammer, anvil, and stirrup) in the ________________ ear.

- **a.** outer ear
- **b.** middle ear
- **c.** inner ear
- **d.** pinna

3. The sound wave is transduced into neural impulses in the ________________, which is located in the cochlea in the inner ear.

- **a.** auditory nerve
- **b.** cochlear fluid
- **c.** organ of Corti
- **d.** pinna

4. You know that the person speaking to you is on your left because

- **a.** the sound reached your left ear slightly before it reached your right ear.
- **b.** the sound that reached your left ear was slightly louder than the sound that reached your right ear.
- **c.** both of the above.
- **d.** neither of the above.

Correct Answers

1. a (p. 103), **2.** b (p. 104), **3.** c (p. 105), **4.** c (p. 106–107).

Thinking Critically About Psychology

1. In terms of human adaptation and survival, what are the advantages and disadvantages of having our ears located on the sides of our heads rather than somewhere else on the body?

2. Juan and Patrick are close friends. Juan hears normally, but Patrick is totally deaf. How might this difference in the way they experience life influence their friendship?

BODY SENSES: MESSAGES FROM MYSELF

The body senses tell us how the body is oriented, where it moves, what it touches, and so on. Information about orientation and movement comes from a sense organ located in the inner ear and from individual receptors spread throughout the body. Information about touch and temperature is provided by a variety of receptors located below the surface of the skin. Information about pain comes from receptors in the skin and inside the body. Although we usually are not aware that we are using this information, the body senses play an important role in keeping us upright, moving straight ahead, and literally out of hot water. Information from all of the body senses is sent to the somatosensory area of the parietal lobe of the cerebral cortex.

Orientation and Movement

vestibular organ
(ves-tib´ū-lar) The sensory structures in the inner ear that provide the brain with information about movement.

kinesthetic receptors
(kin´´es-thet´ik) Receptors in the muscles, joints, and skin that provide information about movement, posture, and orientation.

saccule and utricle
(sak´ūl *and* ū´tre-k´l) Fluid-filled sacs of the vestibular organ that inform the brain about the body's orientation.

semicircular canals
(sem´´ē-ser´kū-lar) Three nearly circular tubes in the vestibular organ that inform the brain about tilts of the head and body.

Messages about the orientation, balance, and movement of the body come to us from two kinds of sense organs. A complicated set of sensory structures called the **vestibular organ** is located in the inner section of the ear where it provides the cerebral cortex with information about movement. Individual sensory receptors called **kinesthetic receptors** located in the muscles, joints, and skin provide additional messages about movement, posture, and orientation.

Vestibular Organ

The vestibular organ is composed of two smaller sensory structures: the *semicircular canals* and the linked *saccule* and *utricle* structures (see fig. 3.16). The **saccule** and **utricle** are fluid-filled sacs in the inner ear that contain sensory receptors that keep the brain informed about the body's orientation. The part of the vestibular organ that provides the most sensitive messages to the brain about orientation is the **semicircular canals.** This organ constitutes a marvelous bit of natural engineering perfectly suited to its purpose. The semicircular canals are composed of three nearly circular tubes (canals) that lie at right angles to one another, providing information on orientation of the body in three planes—left and

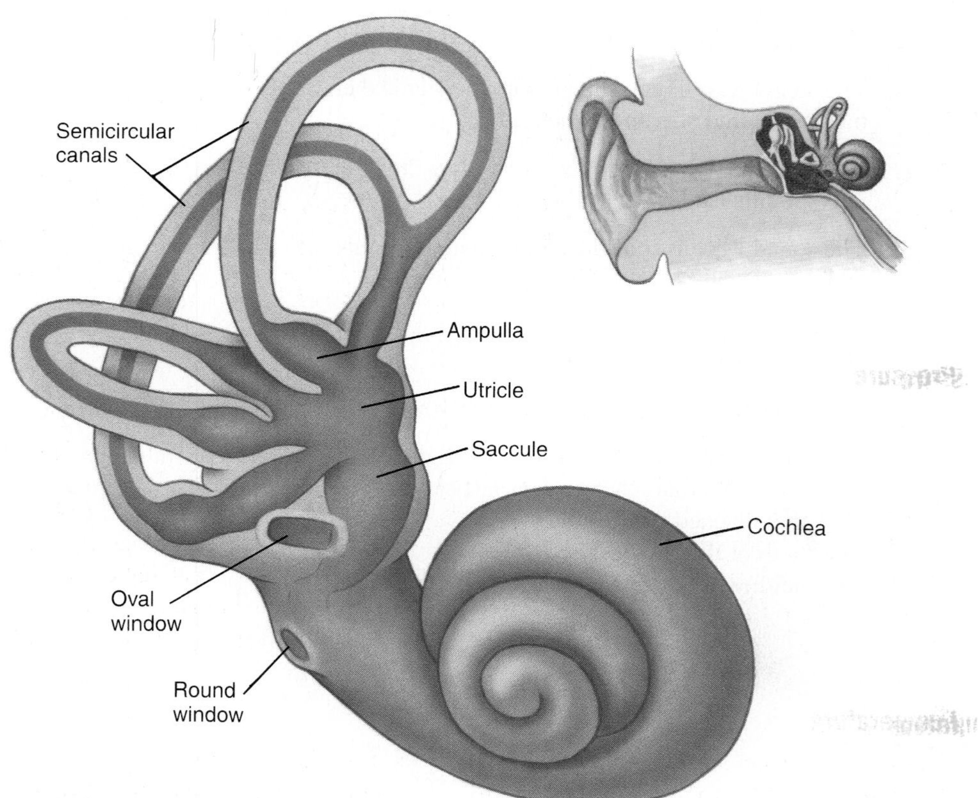

FIGURE 3.16
The major structures of the vestibular organ.

right, up and down, and front to back. Think of the semicircular canals as the corner of a room with one in the plane of the floor and the other two in the planes of the walls. At the base of each canal is an enlargement that holds the sensory receptors. A tuft of these hairlike cells is formed in a gelatinlike structure called the **cupula** that sticks out into the enlargement of the canal. As the head is tilted, the fluid flows through the canal in the opposite direction. This bends the cupula and causes its receptors to fire, sending a message of "tilt" to the brain. While the vestibular organ provides the brain with vital information about orientation and movement, it can turn from a friend to an enemy at times. When confused by rocking boats, bumping airplanes, or twisting circus rides, it can produce nausea. But why does that happen? Why would tilting the vestibular organ cause nausea and vomiting—as in "seasickness"? Experts think it is because the disorientation and dizziness of seasickness resemble the effects of poisoning. The body apparently vomits in response to dizziness regardless of the cause, just in case it is due to poisoning (Stern & Koch, 1996).

The vestibular organ and kinesthetic receptors help orient us even in unusual situations.

Kinesthetic Sense

Throughout the skin, muscles, joints, and tendons are kinesthetic receptors that signal when they are moved. As the body walks, bends, writes, and so on, these receptors provide information about the location and movement of each part of the body. Close your eyes, take off your shoes, and wiggle your toes. You can tell they are wiggling because of your kinesthetic sense. Unlike the vestibular organ, the kinesthetic receptors are individual receptors that are not clumped together into sense organs. But as reflected in the skilled movements of a musician, painter, or discus thrower, they are remarkably sensitive, allowing fine and complicated patterns of movement.

cupula
(ku´-pu-lah) A gelatinlike structure containing a tuft of hairlike sensory receptor cells in the semicircular canals.

free nerve endings
Sensory receptor cells in the skin that detect pressure, temperature, and pain.

basket cells
Sensory receptor cells at the bases of hairs that detect pressure.

tactile discs
(tak´til) Sensory receptor cells that detect pressure.

specialized end bulbs
Sensory receptor cells that detect pressure and skin pleasure.

Skin Senses

We usually do not think of the skin as a sense organ, yet it's capable of picking up a number of different kinds of sensory information. The skin can detect *pressure, temperature,* and *pain.* Feeling a kiss on the cheek, cold in the winter, pain from getting hit by a rock, and all other sensations involving the skin are made up of combinations of these three skin sensations.

Although the skin can detect only three kinds of sensory information, there are at least four different general types of receptors in the skin: the **free nerve endings,** the **basket cells** wound around the base of hairs, the **tactile discs,** and the **specialized end bulbs.** These are shown in figure 3.17. It appears that all four play a role in the sense of touch (pressure), with the specialized end bulbs being important in sexual pleasure. The free nerve endings are the primary receptors for temperature and pain (Groves & Rebec, 1988; Hole, 1990).

Pressure

The skin is amazingly sensitive to pressure, but sensitivity differs considerably from one region of the skin to another depending on how many skin receptors are present. In the most sensitive regions—the fingertips, the lips, and the genitals—a pressure that pushes in the skin less than 0.001 mm can be felt, but sensitivity in other areas is considerably less (Schiffman, 1976). Perhaps the most striking example of the sensitivity of the skin is its ability to "read." Many blind people can read books using the Braille alphabet, patterns of small raised dots that stand for the letters of the alphabet. An experienced Braille user can read up to 300 words per minute using the sensitive skin of the fingertips (see fig. 3.18).

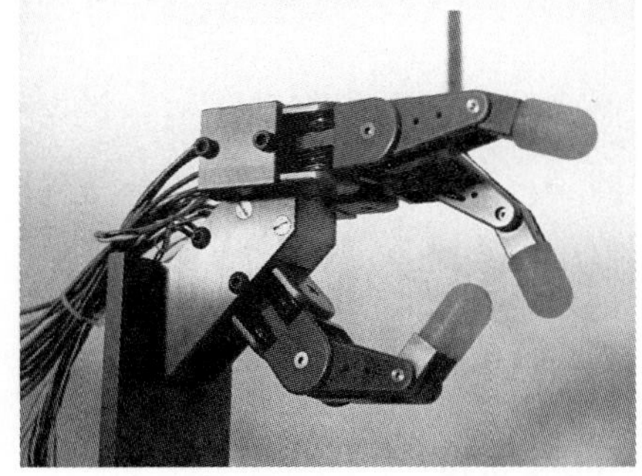

Robots are important to the safe handling of hazardous materials. Using what is known about the sense of touch, the inventors of the "Salisbury Hand" have given it sensors that simulate tension on the tendons of the hand and stimulation of the fingertips.

(Photo of Salisbury Hand at MIT AI lab courtesy of David Lampe, MIT)

Temperature

When the air outside is hot or cold, how do you sense this fact? It seems to most of us that the entire surface of the skin is able to detect temperature, but we actually sense skin

FIGURE 3.17

Diagram of the skin showing the major skin receptor cells.

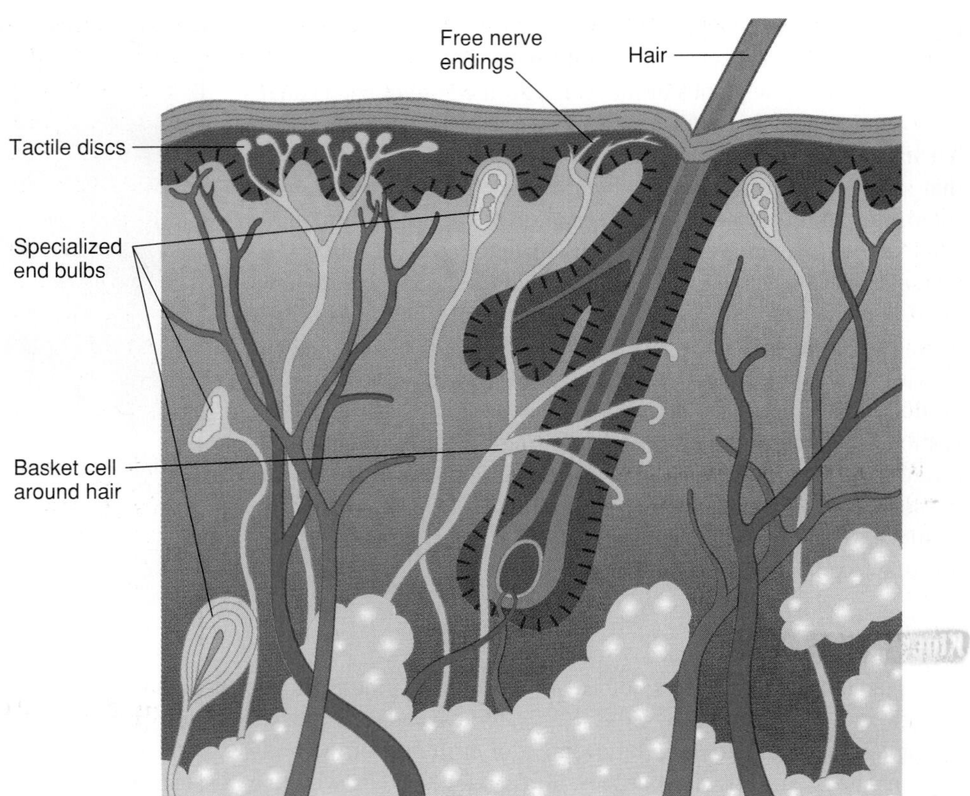

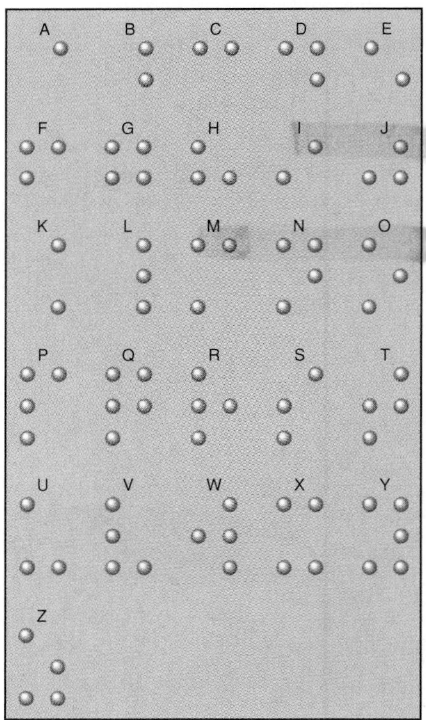

FIGURE 3.18

Raised dots are used in the Braille alphabet and are "read" with the fingertips.

temperature only through sensory receptors (free nerve endings) located in rather widely spaced "spots" on the skin. One set of spots detects warmth and one detects coldness. The information sent to the brain by these spots creates the feeling of temperature across the entire skin surface.

When the skin is warmed (for example, by air, sunlight, or water), the receptors in the warm spots send messages about warmness to the brain; when the skin is cooled, the cold spots send messages about coldness. Recall from chapter 1 (p. 8) that the sensation of intense heat is created by stimulation of *both* the warm and cold spots. Although the cold receptors are generally responsive only to cold temperatures, extreme heat will also make them fire. Therefore, high temperatures stimulate the receptors in both sets of spots to send messages simultaneously to the brain that are interpreted as hotness.

Pain

How do you know you have been hurt? Psychologists have only recently learned enough to begin answering this question. We know that free nerve endings in the skin and body are involved, but whether other kinds of skin receptors can also detect pain or how they operate is not known. A little more is known about the neural pathways that pain messages travel on their way to the brain. For instance, we know that the sensation of pain is transmitted along two different nerve pathways in the spinal cord—*rapid* and *slow* neural pathways. This is why we often experience "first and second pain" (Melzack & Wall, 1983; Sternbach, 1978).

The first pain sensation is a clear, localized feeling that does not "hurt" much, but it tells us what part of the body has been hurt and what kind of injury has occurred. The second pain is a more diffuse, long-lasting pain that hurts in the emotional sense. When you cut your finger with a knife, an initial sensation tells you that you have been cut and where the cut occurred, followed a second later by a more diffuse and painful sensation. The first sensation makes you drop the knife and grab your finger; the second makes you jump up and down and scream!

There are two reasons that we experience these two somewhat separate pain sensations in sequence. First, the two sensations travel on different neural pathways that have different speeds of transmission. The rapid pathway neurons are thicker and sheathed in myelin (see p. 45), which speeds transmission. The slow pathway neurons, in contrast, are smaller and slower unmyelinated neurons. The second reason that we experience first and second pain is that the two neural pathways travel to different parts of the brain. The rapid pathway travels through the thalamus to the somatosensory area. If you recall from chapter 2 (p. 58), this is the part of the parietal lobe of the cerebral cortex that receives and interprets sensory information from the skin and body. When the information transmitted to this area on the rapid pathway is interpreted, we know what has happened and where it has happened, but the somatosensory area does not process the emotional aspects of the experience of "pain." Information that travels on the slower second pathway is routed through the thalamus to the limbic system (p.55). It is here, in the brain system that mediates emotion, that the "ouch" part of the experience of pain is processed.

Pain involves more than the transmission of pain messages to the brain, however. There is not a direct relationship between the pain stimulus and the amount of pain experienced. Under certain circumstances, pain messages can even be blocked out of the brain. For example, a football player whose attention is focused on a big game may not notice a painful cut until after the game is over. The pain receptors transmit the pain message during the game, but the message is not fully processed by the brain until the player is no longer concentrating on the game.

Canadian psychologist Ronald Melzack of McGill University has proposed the *gate control theory of pain* to explain such phenomena (Melzack & Wall, 1983). Melzack believes that pain signals are allowed in or blocked from the brain by neural "gates" in the spinal cord and brain stem. For example, placing a sore foot in warm water helps to close the gate on pain from the toe. The warm sensations block some of the pain sensations by closing the neural gates. Apparently the rapid pain pathways do not pass through the pain gates and cannot be blocked. However, the slow pain pathways that carry the most distressing pain messages can be blocked in the pain gates under some circumstances (Melzack & Wall, 1983).

The pain gates appear to be operated by specialized neurons that block transmission in the neurons that carry "second pain" messages to the brain. The *gate neurons* inhibit the pain neurons using one of a number of substances called *endorphins.* The endorphins are similar to neurotransmitters, but as shown in figure 3.19, endorphins *inhibit* the firing of axons rather than stimulate the dendrites of other neurons. When signaled by other sensory neurons or by neural fibers from the cortex to close the pain gate, the gate neuron inhibits the pain neuron and stops the pain message from reaching the brain. Interestingly, recent evidence suggests that women have a second pain-gate mechanism, based on the hormone estrogen, that males do not have (Mogil, Sternberg, Kest, Marek, & Liebeskind, 1993). This second kind of pain gate in women was only recently discovered because, as in many other areas of research, the great preponderance of research on pain was on males (even when the subjects were rats and other animals). This additional pain gate may help women deal with the pain experienced in childbirth, and its discovery may explain differences between males and females in their experience of pain and lead to more effective pain-controlling medications for women.

The discovery of a second pain-gate mechanism does not reduce the importance of the endorphins in both men and women, however. The discovery of the endorphins in 1973 by Candace Pert and Solomon Snyder has helped to explain several mysteries about pain. First, a number of pain-killing drugs, such as the opiate morphine, clearly operate by duplicating the effects of the endorphins in inhibiting pain neurons. Indeed, the term *endorphin* means *endogenous* (produced inside the body) *morphine.* Second, the "high" that many runners feel during and right after endurance runs appears to be the result of the release

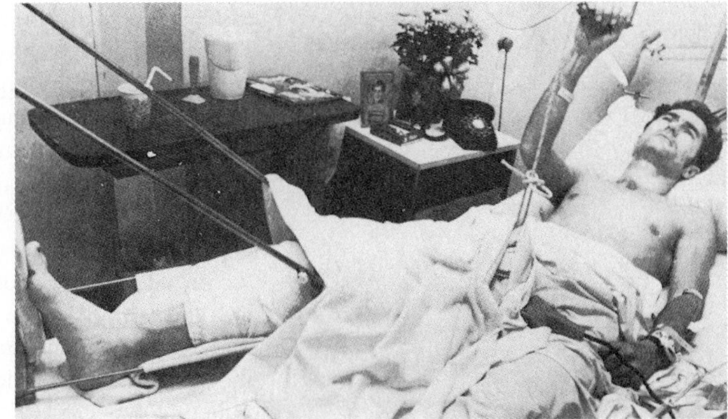

Guy Gertsch, who finished the 1982 Boston Marathon in a respectable 2 hours and 47 minutes, discovered at the finish line that he had run the last 19 miles with a broken thigh bone.

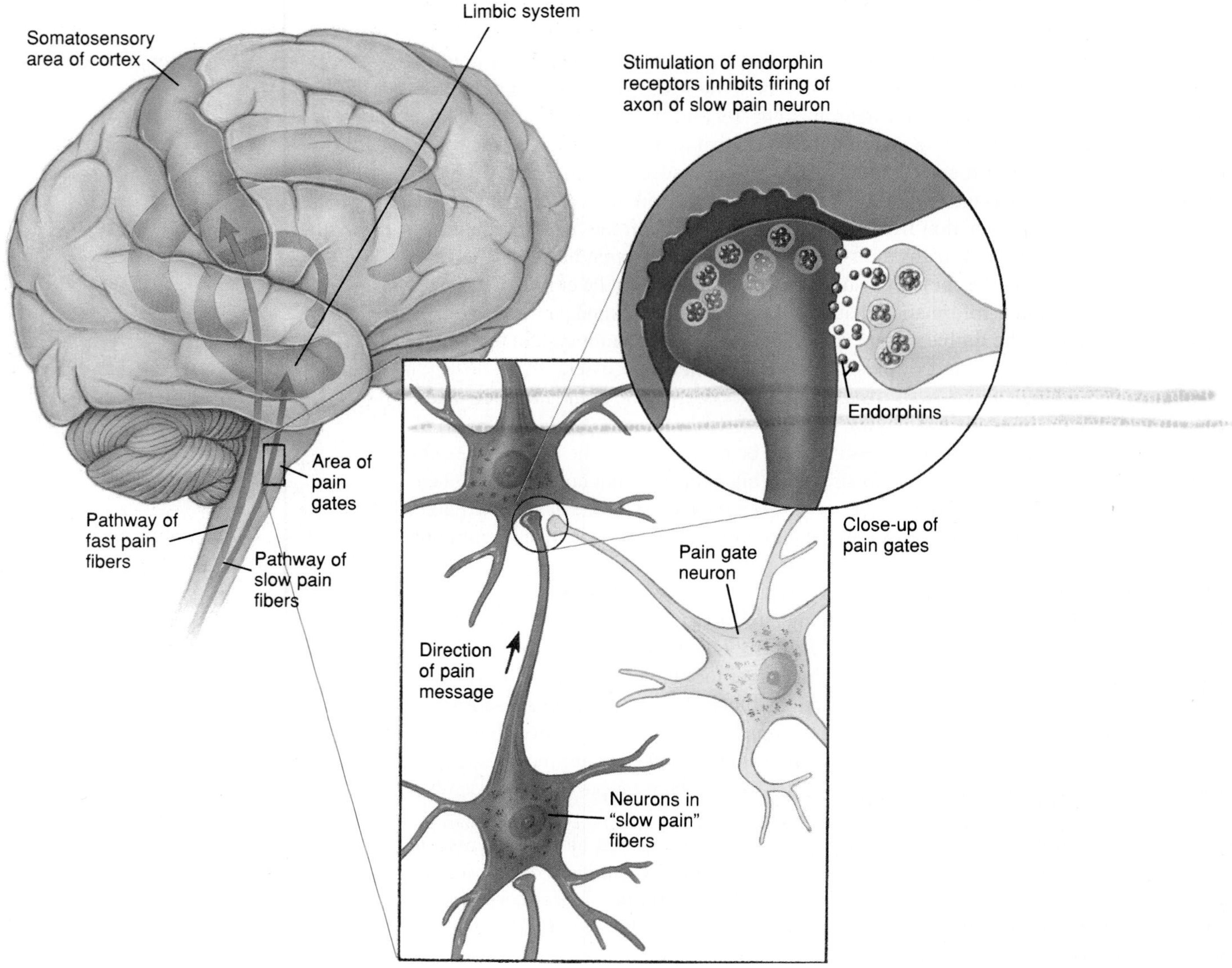

FIGURE 3.19

The operation of pain gates. Secretion of endorphins by gate neurons inhibits the firing of the axon of the neuron that transmits the pain message. Pain gates block only the transmission of "slow pain" fibers and are located primarily in the brain stem and spinal cord.

of high levels of endorphins. Endorphins are released not only by specialized neurons in the spinal cord and brain stem but also by the hypothalamus and pituitary gland under times of physical or psychological stress, including the stress of endurance running. Apparently runners are slightly high on the body's own supply of morphine.

In addition, two medical mysteries apparently can be explained by the endorphins—the effects of acupuncture and placebo medications. Pain can often be reduced by the Asian procedure of *acupuncture*. In this procedure, needles are inserted in the skin at special points and then twirled or heated. There is little doubt that some persons receiving acupuncture experience less pain, but the question is why? One possibility is that the needles stimulate the production of endorphins that block the pain in the pain gates. To test this hypothesis, a drug that blocks the action of the endorphins (naloxone) was administered to persons undergoing acupuncture. While the endorphin-blocking drug was active the person receiving acupuncture experienced the normal level of pain (Price, 1988). This suggests that acupuncture may close the pain gates by stimulating the endorphins.

Placebo medications are inactive substances, such as sugar pills or injections of saline solution, that are given during studies of new medications. The effects of the actual medication are compared with those of the placebo to see whether it is truly effective. Physicians have long been puzzled by the fact that placebos often make patients with a wide range of discomforts feel better. It now appears that endorphins also mediate the effects of placebos. As with the acupuncture studies, giving the endorphin-blocking drug naloxone eliminates the pain-killing effects of placebos (Levine, Gordon, & Fields, 1979). Apparently, being told that you have been given a medication that will help you stimulates the release of endorphins and you really do feel better. This raises the possibility that acupuncture is effective not because of the placement of the needles, but because of the placebo effect of believing that it will work.

In one sense, endorphins are wonderful things. They block pain, give runners a sense of euphoria, and make you feel better even when the doctor gives you a sugar pill. Endorphins undoubtedly play a positive role in lessening the aches and pains of everyday life. But there is a downside of endorphins, too. Endorphins probably have a negative effect on the immune system of the body (Calabrese, Kling, & Gold, 1987). This may be one reason why long-distance runners often experience the paradox of being in very good physical condition, yet being prone to catching colds and the flu.

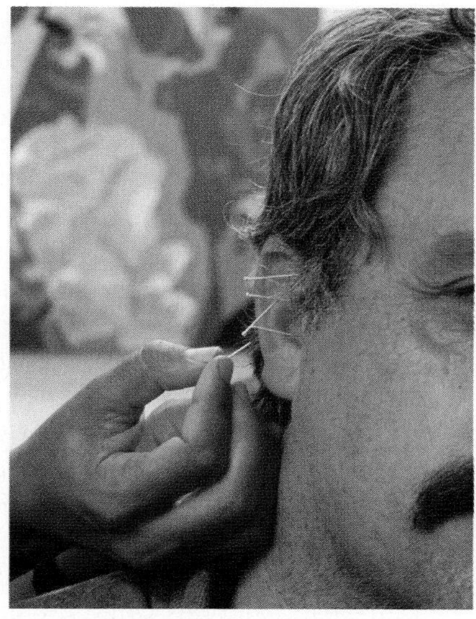

A man is being treated for pain by an acupuncturist. One theory for the effectiveness of acupuncture is that the needles stimulate production of pain-blocking endorphins.

Phantom Limbs

Suzanne Vega recorded a striking song in 1990 about lingering feelings for a lost love by drawing an analogy to a sad and curious phenomenon that often occurs to persons who have lost a limb:

> Men in a war
> If they've lost a limb
> Still feel that limb
> As they did before

Amazingly, most amputees experience the missing arm or leg as if it is still there. They feel a missing arm, for example, as if it is hanging by their side when they sit still, and swinging in coordination with their other arm and legs when they walk. This "phantom limb" is experienced not as a memory of the lost limb but as a clear and realistic sensation that the missing limb is actually there. Ronald Melzack (1992) wrote about a man who experienced his missing arm as sticking straight out to the side, so he turned sideways when he walked through doorways to avoid bumping his arm, even though he knew perfectly well that the arm was not really there.

The sadder part is that as many as 70 percent of amputees experience a disturbing pain in the phantom limb. The pain is often a burning sensation, with many persons with amputated legs reporting that their nonexistent toes feel like they are being seared by a hot fireplace poker. Similarly, persons with amputated arms often say that they feel their phantom hand is tightly clenched, with the fingernails digging painfully into their palms. A friend of mine recently wrote to say that, "My mother, who lost her left leg to polio in her early 20s, is now 73, and sometimes when I ask how her arthritis is, she often responds, 'The foot I don't have aches as much as my good one.' " Amputees are not the only persons who experience such sensations. Persons with spinal cord injuries can experience no true sensations from the parts of their body below the break in the neural pathways in the spinal cord, but they sometimes experience phantom sensations in their limbs or genitals. Similarly, persons born without arms or legs often experience phantom sensations in the missing limb (Melzack, 1992).

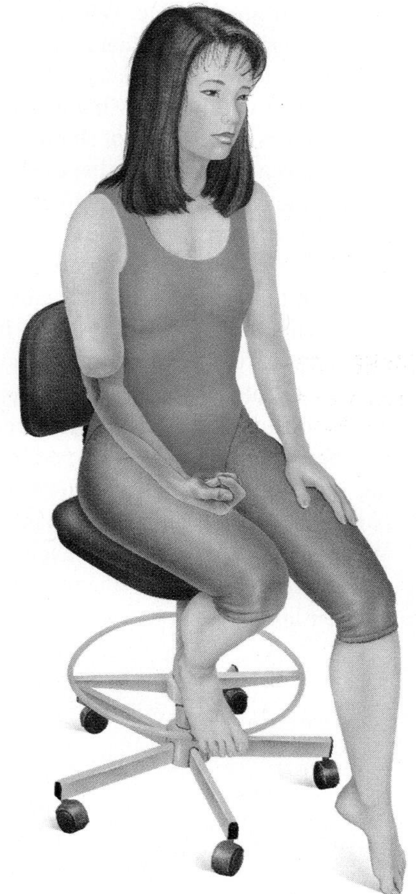

Some persons who have had limbs amputated still feel "phantom limbs" in place of the missing limbs. Often they feel pain in the phantom limbs.

How is it possible to "feel" sensations from a limb that does not exist and, therefore, cannot be transmitting sensations to the brain? A team of researchers from Germany and the United States appears to have provided the answer recently (Flor et al., 1995). Using sophisticated brain-imaging techniques, they found that when sensory and pain neurons from one part of the body have been cut, the area of the somatosensory cortex that served that part of the body becomes sensitive to input from parts of the body that activate *nearby* portions of the somatosensory cortex. For example, in the case of a woman who lost her left arm through amputation, the portion of somatosensory cortex that formerly served her left arm will often begin to receive input from her face (look back to figure 2.17, p. 59 to see that the area of the somatosensory cortex that serves the face is next to the area that receives input from the arm). In addition, cutting sensory neurons from one part of the body tends to reduce the efficiency of the "pain gates." This suggests that phantom pain that is

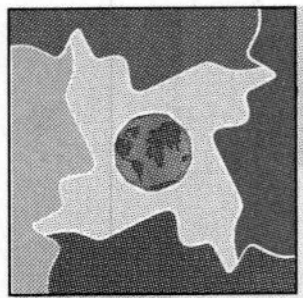

HUMAN DIVERSITY

Culture and Pain

In this chapter, we examine the ways in which neural impulses from the sense organs are experienced as sensations and perceptions. Although much of this process is determined by the biological nature of the sense organs and neurons, learning experiences in our cultures apparently can influence even basic sensations such as pain.

Let's consider an example of the impact of culture on the perception of pain. Members of the Bariba society in Benin, West Africa, appear to be able to tolerate pain more easily than members of most cultures. Bariba folklore includes many examples of honored people who showed strength in the face of pain, and this calm response to pain is seen as an integral part of Bariba pride (Sargent, 1984). For example, pregnant women are expected not to let the fact that they are experiencing labor pains show to others. When labor becomes advanced, they leave the company of others to go through labor and childbirth alone, only calling for help with cutting the umbilical cord.

To the Bariba, letting other people see that they are in pain is cause for great shame. When discussing pain, many Bariba quote a Bariba proverb that translates to, "Between death and shame, death has the greater beauty." According to a Bariba physician, an individual who displays pain lacks courage, and cowardice is the essence of shame. Rather than live in shame, a Bariba would literally rather die (Sargent, 1984). In this cultural context, one would do everything possible to avoid displaying signs of pain.

Do Bariba women who are in labor actually experience less pain than women in other cultures, or have they simply learned not to let the pain show? It is difficult to answer such questions, partly because of the difficulties involved in describing pain to another person. Because pain is a more private experience, language must be used to communicate the experience to others, and language is shaped by culture. It is not surprising that there is a more limited vocabulary for describing pain in the Bariba language than in most other languages. When the Bariba discuss the experience of pain, therefore, it is difficult to know how much their description is influenced by their language.

But there is some reason to believe that the cultural emphasis on not showing reactions to pain might actually reduce the amount of pain that the Bariba experience. As noted on page 345 of chapter 9, there is evidence that facial expressions are an important part of the experience of pain (Izard, 1977). Apparently, sensory feedback to the brain from facial muscles supplies part of the neural input for the perception of pain (along with input from the part of the body that is cramped or injured). Indeed, persons given electrical shocks report less pain when they were told to make no facial reactions than when they let their emotions show in their faces (Colby, Lanzetta, & Kleck, 1977). Maybe the calm face of a Bariba woman in labor results in the experience of less pain than the agonized grimace of women in other cultures.

According to Linda Garro (1990), it is important for medical professionals who work with persons in pain to understand the impact of culture on the expression of pain. If culture is not taken into account, the physician may overestimate or underestimate the amount of pain experienced by the patient. On the other hand, it is important to remember that all members of a culture are not the same. As in all other aspects of human diversity, it is important to be aware of variation within cultures.

What did you learn about pain in your own culture? Were you taught to minimize pain because it is important to be tough? Did you learn that no one will pay attention to your pain unless you exaggerate it? How do you respond when your parent or friends are in pain? Such questions will help you think about cultural influences on perception.

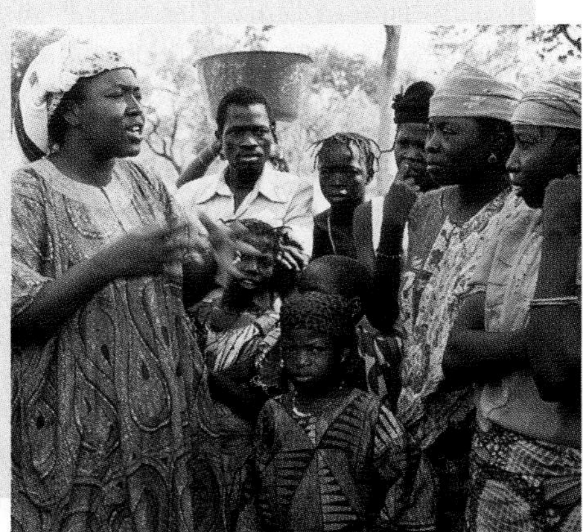

People in different cultures appear to have different thresholds for pain.

perceived as being in a missing arm may come from minor irritations to the face that are allowed through the pain gate and are perceived to be pain in the missing limb because the neural message stimulates the part of the cortex that used to serve input from the arm.

The phantom limb experience is another excellent illustration of the fact that our conscious experience is not always a direct and simple representation of the sensory information that reaches the brain. Sometimes, the brain "invents" sensations and pains in limbs that do not exist. As I said at the start of this section, Suzanne Vega's song used the phenomenon of phantom limbs as an analogy for lost love. Sometimes we experience a lost friend or love as if they are still there, somewhat like the experience of a phantom limb. One difference is that we usually get over the lost love, especially if we are lucky enough to move on to a better relationship. In contrast, even with treatment, many persons with phantom limb pain never stop experiencing pain in the missing limb.

Review

The body contains a number of sense organs that provide vital information about the body's movement and orientation in space and about the world as it contacts our skin. Information about posture, movement, and orientation is coded and sent to the somatic sensory area of the cortex by the vestibular organ in the inner ear and by kinesthetic receptors spread throughout the body. Skin receptors send information about temperature, pressure, and pain to the same area of the brain. We experience the pain from cuts in other injuries in two steps (a first pain that tells us what has happened and where it has happened, followed by a second more emotional pain) because these two aspects of the pain experience travel on different neural pathways to different parts of the brain. The phenomenon of pain provides a good example of the lack of direct relationship between physical stimuli and conscious sensations in that a number of psychological factors serve to increase or decrease the experience of pain. The phantom limb experience also provides compelling evidence that conscious experiences are constructed in the brain and do not always have a direct relationship to incoming sensations.

Thinking Critically About Psychology

1. In what ways is the experience of pain both a psychological and physical event?

2. Have you had experiences in your own life that would support the gate control theory of pain?

Check Your Learning

To be sure that you have learned the key points from the preceding section, cover the answers below and try to answer each question. If you give an incorrect answer to any question, return to the page given next to the correct answer to see why your answer was not correct.

1. Sensory receptors called ____________ receptors located in the muscles, joints, and skin provide the brain with messages about movement, posture, and orientation of the body.

- **a.** vestibular
- **b.** semicircular
- **c.** ciliary
- **d.** kinesthetic

2. Which is *not* one of the four different types of receptors in the skin?

- **a.** vestibular cells
- **b.** basket cells
- **c.** tactile discs
- **d.** specialized end bulbs

3. The sensation of intense heat is created by stimulation of ______ on the skin.

- **a.** warm spots
- **b.** cold spots
- **c.** both the warm and cold spots
- **d.** the vestibular cells

4. According to the ____________ theory of pain, placing a sore foot in warm water blocks pain signals on the slow pain pathway by closing neural "gates" in the spinal cord and brain stem.

Correct Answers

1. d (p. 109), 2. a (p. 109), 3. c (p. 110), 4. gate control (p. 111).

CHEMICAL SENSES: THE FLAVORS AND AROMAS OF LIFE

gustation
(gus-tā´-shun) The sense of taste.

olfaction
(ōl-fak´-shun) The sense of smell.

The sense of **gustation** (taste) or **olfaction** (smell) differ from the other senses in that they respond to chemicals rather than to energy in the environment. The chemical senses tell us about the things we eat, drink, and breathe.

Taste

taste cells
The sensory receptor cells for gustation located in the taste buds.

papillae
(pah-pil´e) Clusters of taste buds on the tongue.

We are able to taste food and other things because of the 10,000 *taste buds* on the tongue. Each taste bud contains approximately a dozen sensory receptors called **taste cells** that are grouped together much like the segments of an orange. It is the taste cells that are sensitive to chemicals in our food and drink (Bartoshuk, 1988) (fig. 3.20). The taste buds are further bunched together in bumps on the tongue called **papillae** that can be easily seen on the tongue.

The taste buds are responsive to thousands of chemicals but, interestingly, all of our sensations of taste appear to result from *four basic sensations of taste: sweetness* (mostly to sugars), *sourness* (mostly to acids), *saltiness* (mostly to salts), and *bitterness* (to a variety of other chemicals, most of which either have no food value or are toxic) (Bartoshuk, 1988). Every flavor that we experience, from lobster thermidor to peanut butter is made up of combinations of these four basic qualities. However, our perception of food also includes sensations from the skin surfaces of the tongue and mouth: touch (food texture), temperature (cold coffee tastes very different from hot coffee), and pain (as in Jalapeño peppers!). The sight and aroma of food also greatly affect our perception of food.

Although each taste bud seems to be primarily responsive to one of the four primary qualities, each responds to some extent to some or all of the other qualities as well (Arvidson & Friberg, 1980). Interestingly, the taste buds that are most sensitive to the four primary tastes are not evenly distributed over the tongue. They are bunched in different areas as shown in figure 3.21. This means that different parts of the tongue are sensitive to different tastes. We do not usually notice this because the differences in sensitivity are not great and because our food usually reaches all parts of the tongue during the chewing process anyway. But if you ever have to swallow a truly bitter pill, try placing it in the exact middle of the tongue where there are no taste receptors at all.

We lose taste buds as we age, especially over 45. Babies have the most taste buds and are the most sensitive to tastes. Older adults sometimes find that they develop a taste for hotter spices and find other ways to add to the zest of flavors.

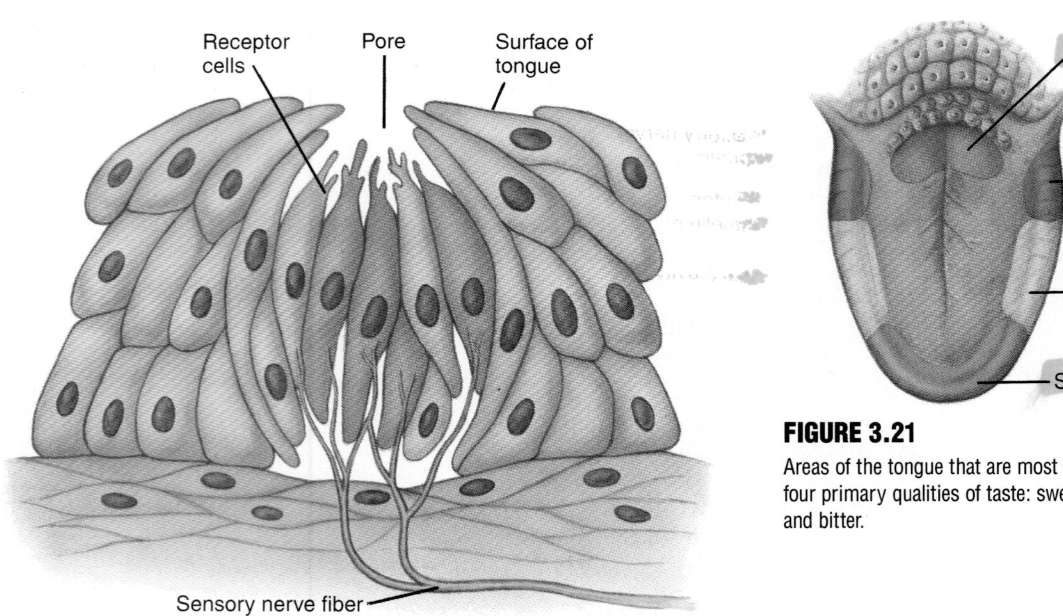

FIGURE 3.21
Areas of the tongue that are most sensitive to the four primary qualities of taste: sweet, salty, sour, and bitter.

FIGURE 3.20
Taste buds contain clusters of taste (gustatory) receptor cells.

Smell

Chemicals in the air we breathe pass by the olfactory receptors on their way to the lungs. These receptor cells are located in a dime-sized, mucous-coated sheet at the top of the nasal cavity called the **olfactory epithelium** (see fig. 3.22). As with taste, we seem to be able to smell only a limited number of primary odors. There is less agreement among psychologists about primary odors than about primary tastes, but one widely used system of classifying odors divides all of the complex aromas and odors of life into combinations of seven primary qualities: *resinous* (camphor), *floral* (roses), *minty* (peppermint), *ethereal* (pears), *musky* (musk oil), *acrid* (vinegar), and *putrid* (rotten eggs) (Ackerman, 1991; Amoore, Johnston, & Rubin, 1964). However professionals who create perfumes and other aromas distinguish 146 distinct odors (Dravnieks, 1983).

olfactory epithelium
(ōl-fak´to-rē ep´i-thē´lē-um) The sheet of receptor cells at the top of the nasal cavity.

Interestingly, nearly all of the chemicals that humans can detect as odors are organic compounds, meaning they come from living things. In contrast, we can smell very few inorganic compounds—the stuff that rocks and sand are made of. Thus, our noses are useful tools for sensing the qualities of plants and animals—necessary, among other things, to distinguish between poisonous and edible things (Cain, 1988).

Although we can only smell compounds derived from living things, chemists have long known how to create these organic compounds in test tubes. This means that any aroma can be custom created to order and no longer has to be painstakingly extracted from flower petal and spices. One of the first perfumes created entirely in a laboratory was also one of the most successful fragrances ever made, Chanel No. 5. Once Marilyn Monroe boasted that she wore only Chanel No. 5 to bed, cloaking herself in a romantic blend of organic compounds created in a chemistry laboratory in 1922 (Ackerman, 1991).

How do we smell these organic molecules? According to the **stereochemical theory,** the complex molecules responsible for each of these primary odors have a specific shape that will "fit" into only one type of receptor cell, like a key into a lock. Only when molecules of a particular shape are present will the corresponding olfactory receptor send its distinctive message to the brain (Cain, 1988).

stereochemical theory
The theory that different odor receptors can be stimulated only by molecules of a specific size and shape that fit them like a "key" in a lock.

The sense of smell is important in and of itself, of course, sometimes bringing joyous messages of sweet perfumes to the brain and other times warning us of dangerous and foul odors. But the sense of smell contributes to the sense of taste as well. Not only do we smell foods as they pass beneath our noses on the way to our mouths, odors rise into the nasal passage as we chew. We are usually unaware of the grand impact of smell on the sense of

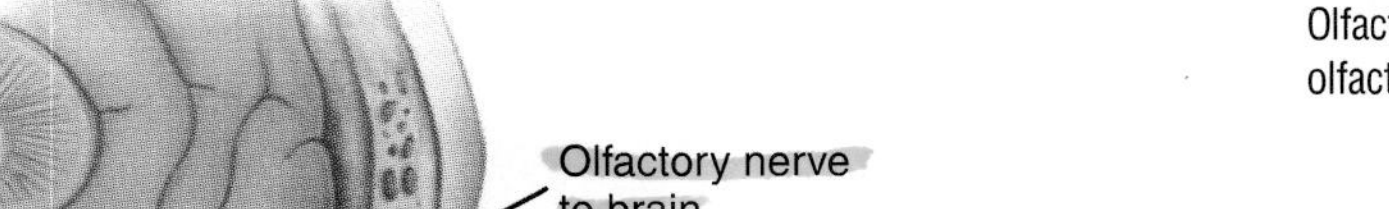

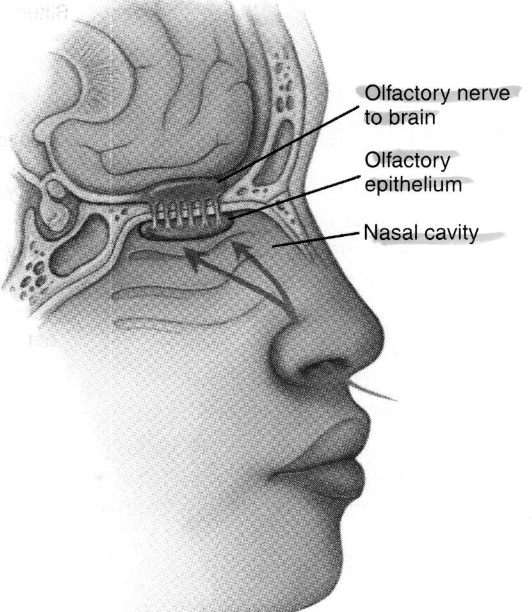

FIGURE 3.22
Olfactory receptor cells are located in the olfactory epithelium at the top of the nasal cavity.

taste, until a head cold makes everything taste like paste. The contribution of smell to taste is important partly because of the greater sensitivity of the sense of smell. The nose can detect the smell of cherry pie in the air that is 1/25,000th of the amount that is required for the taste buds to identify (Ackerman, 1991).

Thinking Critically About Psychology

1. Why do you think some people love the smell of coffee, but other people dislike it?

2. Why do you think there is an uneven distribution of taste buds on the tongue?

Review

Chemicals in the air we breathe and the things we eat and drink are sensed by the gustatory receptors (taste buds) on the tongue and the olfactory receptors in the nose. For both chemical senses, combinations of a relatively small number of primary sensations apparently make up the entire variety of our experiences of taste and smell.

Check Your Learning

To be sure that you have learned the key points from the preceding section, cover the answers below and try to answer each question. If you give an incorrect answer to any question, return to the page given next to the correct answer to see why your answer was not correct.

1. Each of the 10,000 ________________ on the tongue contains approximately a dozen sensory receptors called taste cells.

2. All of our sensations of taste appear to result from four basic sensations of taste: sweetness, sourness, saltiness, and ________________ .

3. The olfactory receptors are located in a dime-sized, mucous-coated sheet at the top of the nasal cavity called the ________________ .

a. gustatory center **c.** olfactory cortex
b. olfactory epithelium **d.** thalamus

4. According to the ________________ theory, the molecules responsible for each of these primary odors have a specific shape that will fit into only one type of olfactory receptor cell.

a. opponent-process **c.** stereochemical
b. trichromatic **d.** camphoraceous

Correct Answers

1. taste buds (p. 116), **2.** bitterness (p. 116), **3.** b (p. 117), **4.** c (p. 117).

PERCEPTION: INTERPRETING SENSORY MESSAGES

Sensations that are transmitted to the brain have little "meaning" of their own. They are in the form of raw neural energy that must be organized and interpreted in the process we call *perception.* The process is pretty much the same in all of us. If this were not the case—if we each interpreted sensory input in different ways—there would be no common "reality" in the sense of a perceived world that we all share. However, some aspects of perception are unique to a particular individual or members of a particular culture. The specific learning experiences, memories, motives, and emotions of the individual can influence perception. For example, we all perceive the visual stimuli of a knife in pretty much the same way because of the inborn ways we organize visual information. But a knife also has unique perceptual meaning to each individual depending on whether the person has been cut by a similar knife, has a similar favorite hunting knife, or has just been asked to carve a turkey for dinner.

In this section, we describe the inborn organizational properties that all humans share and briefly discuss some of the ways in which each individual's perceptions are unique. Keep in mind as we discuss perception that while it's easy to distinguish between sensation and perception in theory, it's very difficult to do so in practice. Visual perception, for example, begins in the complex neural structures of the eye before sensory messages are transmitted to the brain (Hochberg, 1988). The distinction between sensation and perception, then, is largely an arbitrary one to make our discussion of information processing by the sense organs and brain easier to understand.

Visual Perception

In the discussion that follows, we describe the major ways in which sensory information is interpreted into meaningful perceptions, including both those that are common to us all and those that are unique to each individual. This discussion focuses on visual perception rather than on all of the perceptual systems for several reasons: visual perception is a highly important sensing system; scientists better understand how it works than they do other systems; and it is representative enough of other systems to tell us something about the process of perception in general.

FIGURE 3.23
The distinction between figure and ground in visual perception is clearly illustrated by this vase prepared for Queen Elizabeth of England. Do you see a vase, or do you see the profiles of Queen Elizabeth and Prince Philip looking at one another? It depends on whether the dark space is the figure or the ground in your perceptual organization of the stimuli.

Perceptual Organization

Raw visual sensations are like the unassembled parts of a washing machine: they must be put together in an organized way before they are useful to us. Some of the fundamental ways in which the eye and brain organize visual sensations were described about 75 years ago by Gestalt psychologists in their pioneering writings on perception (see chapter 1). These principles of perceptual organization are still worthy of our attention today (Matlin, 1988; Prinzmetal, 1995). Five of the so-called "Gestalt principles" of perception are described and illustrated:

1. *Figure-ground.* When we perceive a visual stimulus, part of what we see is the center of our attention, the *figure,* and the rest is indistinct background, the *ground.* All perceptions have this quality, but the vase in figure 3.23 shows that this way of seeing does not simply reflect the nature of reality. The fact that the figure and ground of this photo can be reversed to perceive either a vase or two opposing faces shows that sensations can be organized by the brain in different ways.

   In the same way, the woman in figure 3.24 could be viewed as a young woman facing away or as a weathered older woman facing forward and downward depending on which parts you perceive as the figure and which parts you perceive as ground. This single principle is very useful in showing us that what we perceive often is based more on what goes on in our brains than what is in front of our eyes. The remaining Gestalt principles amplify this point.
2. *Continuity.* We tend to perceive lines or patterns that follow a smooth contour as being part of a single unit. In figure 3.25, at which point did child B start bouncing her pogo stick? We tend to organize our perceptions of the tracks so that it appears that girl B started at point 1, but both girls could have made sharp turns in the center and headed off at right angles. We do not naturally organize sensations in this way; however, we tend to perceive continuity in lines and patterns.
3. *Proximity.* Things that are proximal (close together) are usually perceived as belonging together. In figure 3.26, we see three vertical columns of blocks on the left side and three horizontal rows on the right side due to proximity.
4. *Similarity.* On the left side of figure 3.27, we perceive two vertical columns of apples and two vertical columns of pears, even though they are evenly spaced. On the right side, in contrast, a different arrangement results in the perception of two horizontal rows of each fruit. Similar things are perceived as being related.
5. *Closure.* Incomplete figures, such as in figure 3.28, tend to be perceived as complete wholes. Again, we fill in missing sensory information to create complete and whole perceptions.

FIGURE 3.24
This classic drawing—unflatteringly called "the wife or mother-in-law"—can be viewed as a younger or older woman depending on the viewer's figure-ground organization.

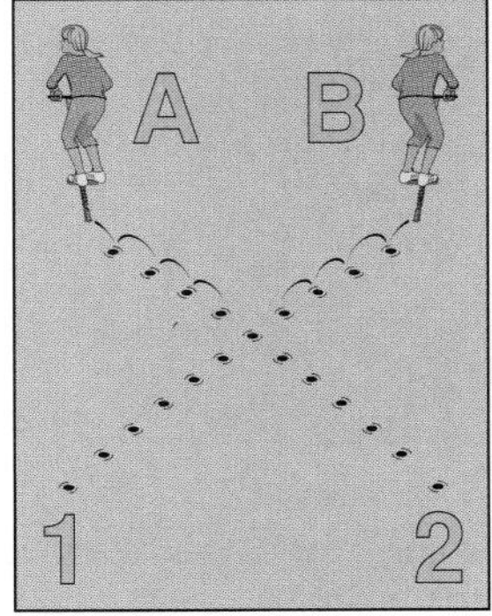

FIGURE 3.25
At which point did girl B start jumping on her pogo stick? According to the principle of continuity, we would tend to perceive point 1 as her starting point, although either 1 or 2 would be equally possible.

FIGURE 3.26
Do you see vertical or horizontal rows? The principle of proximity determines how these stimuli are organized perceptually.

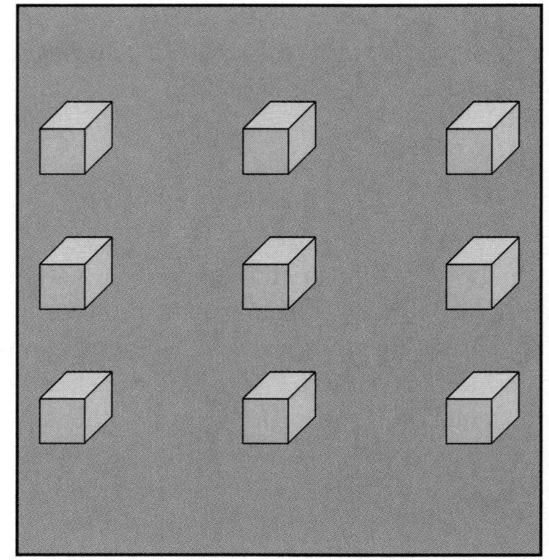

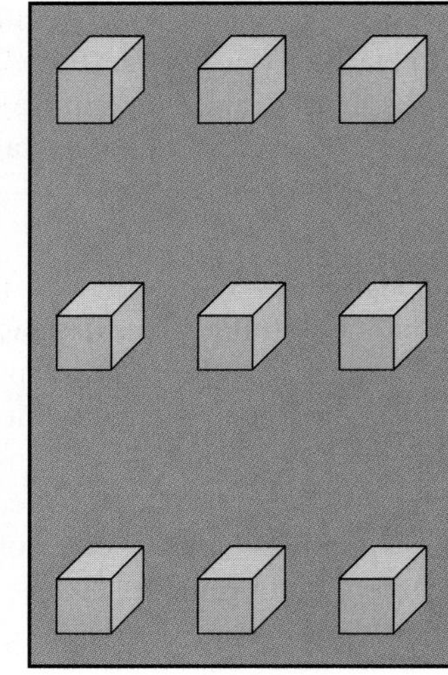

FIGURE 3.27
Do you see horizontal or vertical rows? The principle of similarity suggests that we would organize the figure on the left into vertical rows and the one on the right into horizontal rows, even though the objects are equally spaced.

FIGURE 3.28
We see a face rather than unrelated lines because of the perceptual principle of closure.

perceptual constancy
The tendency for perceptions of objects to remain relatively unchanged in spite of changes in raw sensations.

Our perceptions are actively organized according to these and other similar inborn principles.

Perceptual Constancy

We perceive the world as a fairly constant and unchanging place. Tables, lamps, and people do not change in size, shape, or color from moment to moment. Yet, the sensations that tell us about these things do change considerably from moment to moment. The size of the image that falls on the retina changes as a person walks away from us, but we do not perceive the person as shrinking in size. The shape of a pot seen from different angles is different on the retina, but we do not believe that the pot is changing shape. This characteristic of perception is called **perceptual constancy.** There are several types of perceptual constancy:

1. *Brightness constancy.* A piece of white paper does not change in perceived brightness when it moves from a weakly lit room to a brightly lit room even though the intensity of the light reaching the eye changes considerably. Fortunately for our ability to cope with the world, our perception corresponds to the unchanging physical properties of the paper rather than to the changing sensory information about its brightness. When you stop to think about it, this is a remarkable accomplishment, but one that we take so much for granted that you may not have been aware that it was happening until you read this paragraph.

2. *Color constancy.* Colors do not appear to change much in spite of different conditions of light and surroundings that change incoming visual information.
3. *Size constancy.* A dollar bill seen from distances of 1 foot and 10 feet casts different-sized images on the retina, but we do not perceive it as changing in size. Familiar objects do not change in perceived size at different distances.
4. *Shape constancy.* A penny seen from straight ahead casts a circular image on the retina. When seen from a slight angle, however, the image it casts is oval shaped, yet we continue to perceive it as circular.

Through the process of perceptual constancy, we automatically adjust our interpretations to correspond with what we have learned about the physical world rather than relying solely on changing stimulus input.

Perceptual constancy helps us to recognize this vase as unchanging, even though we are viewing it from different angles and from different distances.

Depth Perception

The retina is a two-dimensional surface. It has an up and down, and a left and right, but no depth. How is it then that we are able to perceive a three-dimensional world using a two-dimensional retina? The eye and brain accomplish this remarkable feat by using a number of two-dimensional cues to create a perceptual distance.

The ten major cues used in depth perception are listed here. The first eight are known as **monocular cues** because they can be seen by one eye (see fig. 3.29); the last two are known as **binocular cues** because they can only be perceived using both eyes. The monocular cues are as follows:

1. *Texture gradient.* The texture of objects is larger and more visible up close and smaller when far away. On curved surfaces, the elements of texture are also more slanted when they are farther away.
2. *Linear perspective.* Objects cast smaller images on the retina when they are more distant. As a result, parallel lines, such as railroad tracks, appear to grow closer together the farther away they are from us.
3. *Superposition.* Closer objects tend to be partially in front of, or partially cover up, more distant objects.
4. S*hadowing.* The shadows cast by objects suggest their depth.
5. *Speed of movement.* Objects farther away appear to move across the field of vision more slowly than do closer objects.
6. *Aerial perspective.* Water vapor and pollution in the air scatter light waves, giving distant objects a bluish, hazy appearance compared with nearby objects.
7. *Accommodation.* As discussed earlier in the chapter, the shape of the lens of the eye must change to focus the visual image on the retina from stimuli that are different distances from the eye. This process is called accommodation. Kinesthetic receptors in the ciliary muscle, therefore, provide a source of information about the distance of different objects. This information is useful, however, only for short distances up to about 4 feet.
8. *Vertical position.* When objects are on the ground, the farther they appear to be below the horizon, the closer they appear to be to us. For objects in the air, however, the farther they appear to be above the horizon, the closer they appear to be to us.

The binocular cues are as follows:

9. *Convergence.* When both eyes are looking at an object in the center of the visual field, they must angle inward more sharply for a near object than for a distant object (see fig. 3.30). Information from the muscles that move the eyes thus provide a clue as to the distance of an object from the viewer.
10. *Retinal disparity.* Because our two eyes are a couple of inches apart, they do not see the same view of three-dimensional objects, especially when the object is close. This disparity, or difference, between the images on the two retinas is a key factor in depth perception. Retinal disparity is the principle behind the

monocular cues
(mon-ok´ū-lar) Eight visual cues that can be seen with one eye that allow us to perceive depth.

binocular cues
(bīn-ok´ū-lar) Visual cues that require both eyes to allow us to perceive depth.

Texture gradient

Linear perspective

Shadowing

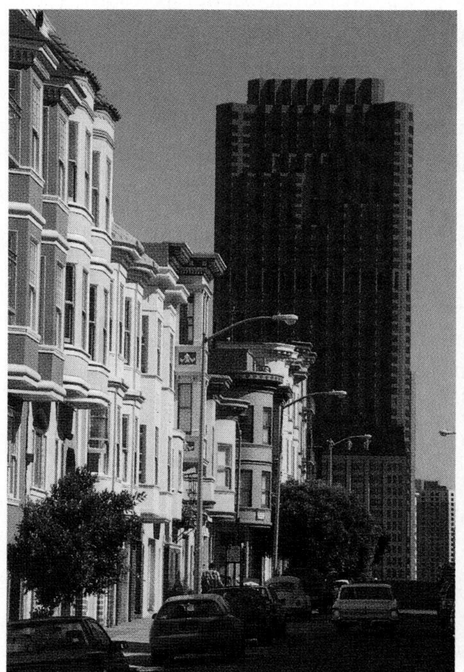
Superposition

Aerial perspective

FIGURE 3.29
Texture gradient, linear perspective, shadowing, superposition, and aerial perspective are all monocular cues used in depth perception.

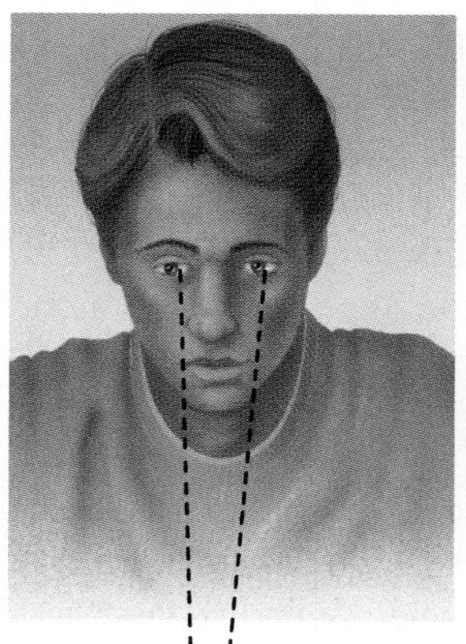
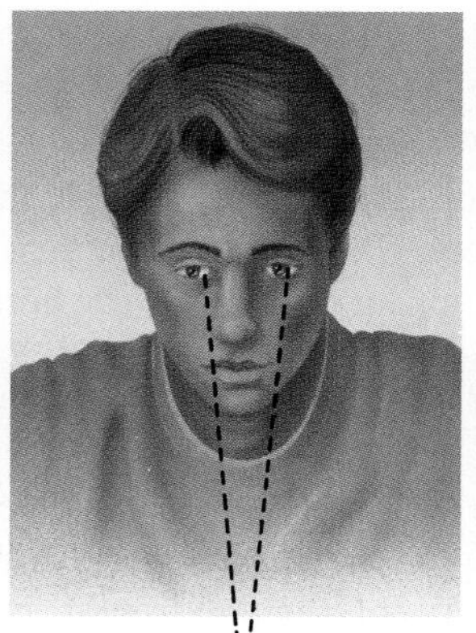
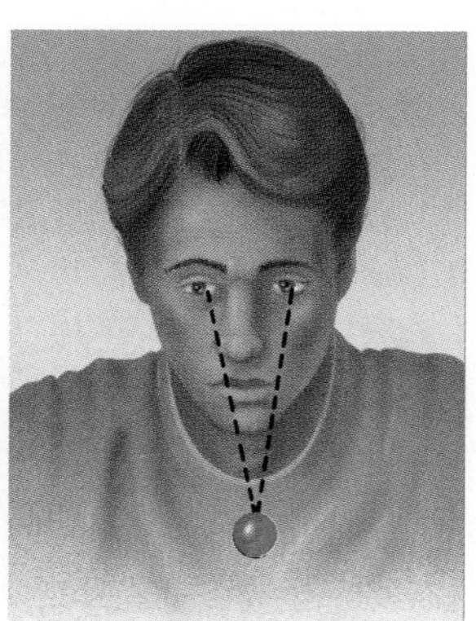

FIGURE 3.30
The degree to which the eyes must look inward (convergence) to focus on objects at different distances provides information on the distance of that object. It's a binocular cue in depth perception because it requires the use of both eyes.

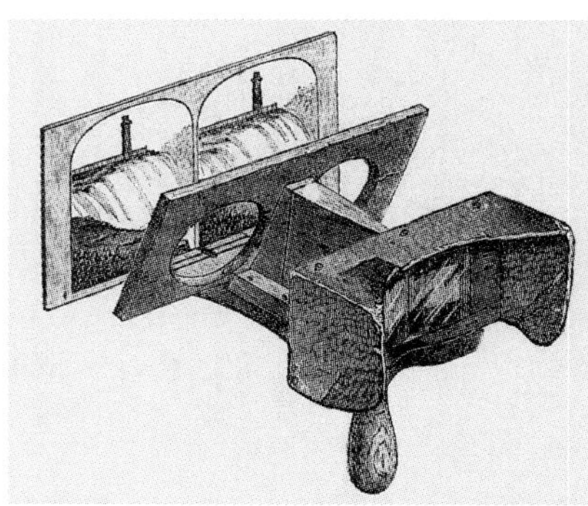

FIGURE 3.31

Two photos taken from slightly different angles are used in a stereopticon to create an illusion of depth through retinal disparity.

old-fashioned *stereopticon*. As shown in figure 3.31, the individual looks at two pictures of the same scene in a special viewer that lets each eye see only one of the two images. The images were photographed from two slightly different spots to duplicate the disparity between two retinal images. When seen in the stereopticon, the two images fuse into a single scene perceived in startlingly good three dimension. Try placing your hand edgewise between the two pictures and the bridge of your nose to allow each eye to see only one of the pictures. Look at them for a while to see if they fuse into a single three-dimensional scene.

Through a combination of these monocular and binocular cues we are able to perceive our three-dimensional world using only two-dimensional information.

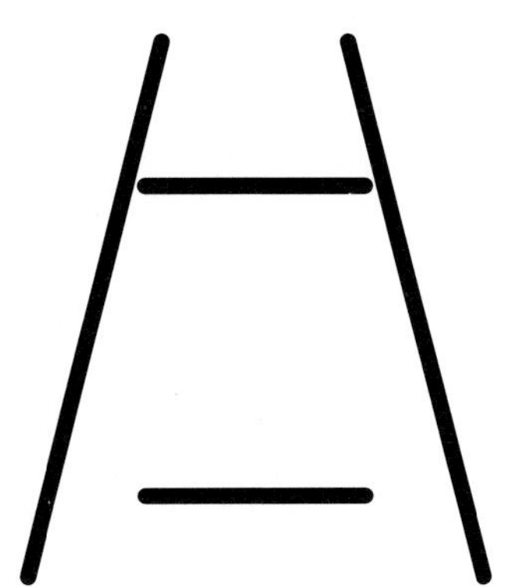

FIGURE 3.32

The Ponzo illusion. Are the horizontal lines the same length?

Visual Illusions

Instructors of introductory psychology have long enjoyed amusing their classes with visual illusions. These illusions intentionally manipulate the cues that we use in visual perception to create an illusory perception. They are instructive, therefore, in showing us more about the process of perception, and for showing us in yet *another* way that what we see is not always the same as the visual information that enters the eyes. For example, are the two horizontal lines in figure 3.32 (the Ponzo illusion) the same size (they are even though the upper line looks longer)? How about the two lines in figure 3.33 (the vertical-horizontal illusion)—most people see the vertical line as longer, even though they are the same length. My personal favorite is the Zoliner illusion shown in figure 3.34. Believe it or not, the diagonal lines are parallel! Even after you cover all but two lines or measure the distance between the diagonal lines for yourself, this illusion is amazing.

How do these illusions fool us? They do so by using monocular depth cues to create an illusion. Consider the Müller-Lyer illusion: The two vertical lines on the left of figure 3.35 are of different lengths—or are they? Actually, they just look different because of the context they are in. Ordinarily, the short lines at the end of the longer lines would be cues to depth, as in the two booklets shown on the right side of figure 3.35. We see the vertical line as longer when the cues suggest that it is farther away. In the Ponzo illusion, the two vertical lines appear to be converging in the distance, like railroad tracks, suggesting that the horizontal line at the top is farther away, so we see it as longer. The other visual illusions work in similar ways.

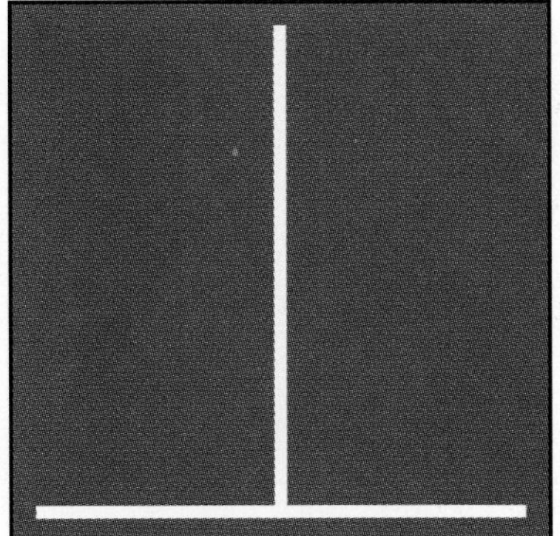

FIGURE 3.33

The horizontal figure often produces an illusory judgment of length. Which line is longer, the horizontal or the vertical line? Actually, they are both the same length.

FIGURE 3.34
The Zoliner illusion. Are the diagonal lines parallel?

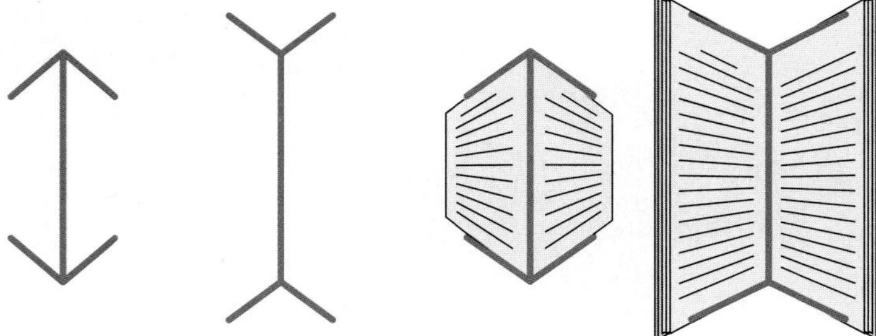

FIGURE 3.35
The Müller-Lyer illusion. Most people see the vertical line on the right as being longer, even though they are the same length. The shorter lines give an illusion of depth, as in the two books on the right.

Perhaps the most impressive visual illusion ever created in a psychology laboratory is the *Ames room.* When this room is viewed through a peephole made in one wall (used to restrict the availability of binocular cues), the room appears to be a normal square. Actually, however, the room is much deeper on one side than the other, but many cues of depth perception have been altered to give the illusion of equal depth for all sides of the back wall. The effect this room has on perception is startling when people are in the room (see figs. 3.36 and 3.37).

Not all visual illusions are laboratory demonstrations, however. They are common in everyday life. Few sights are more beautiful than a huge full moon on the horizon. Have you ever stopped to wonder why it always looks *bigger* on the horizon than overhead? It doesn't really grow, you know; it's an illusion. In fact, it's an illusion that still puzzles scientists. There is no widely accepted theory of the moon illusion (Reed, 1984; Rock & Kaufman, 1972), but it is partly based on the misperception of depth.

As shown in figure 3.38 an object that our senses tell us is *farther away* is perceived as being *larger* than an object that casts the same size image on the retina but appears to be closer. The two triangles in this figure are the same size, but the one at the top is perceived as larger because it appears to be farther away. Ordinarily the top triangle *would* be larger if it were farther away but could still cast as large a retinal image as a closer object.

The moon illusion is based partly on the same principle. When the moon is overhead, not only does it appear closer due to its vertical position, we have no distance cues, so depth cues do not accurately influence our perception of the moon's size. When it's near the horizon, however, it appears to be farther away because of its vertical position. In addition, we can see the moon is farther away than objects such as distant trees and buildings, which we know to be large but which cast a small image on the retina. When the size of the moon is perceived in comparison to these objects, it looks much bigger.

And then there is the dreaded Poggendorf illusion! Look at the diagonal line that appears to pass behind the green bar in figure 3.39. Which line on the right is the continuation of the diagonal line? Most persons choose the middle line. Now place the edge of a piece of white paper along the line. Which line on the right do you think is the continuation of the line on the left now? In the Poggendorf illusion, lines that appear to pass behind solid objects at an angle appear to be "moved over" when they emerge. You can demonstrate this phenomenon again by drawing a straight line with a ruler on a piece of paper and then covering it with a quarter (25-cent piece). The line now emerges from the quarter in the wrong place!

FIGURE 3.36

The Ames Room, which was constructed to illustrate how the monocular cues used in depth perception can be used to create illusions.

FIGURE 3.37

Although not apparent to the viewer, the right side of the room is one-half as deep as the left, the floor is higher and the ceiling is lower on the right, and the window on the right is smaller. All of these cues create the impression that the person on the right is much larger than the person on the left in the Ames room.

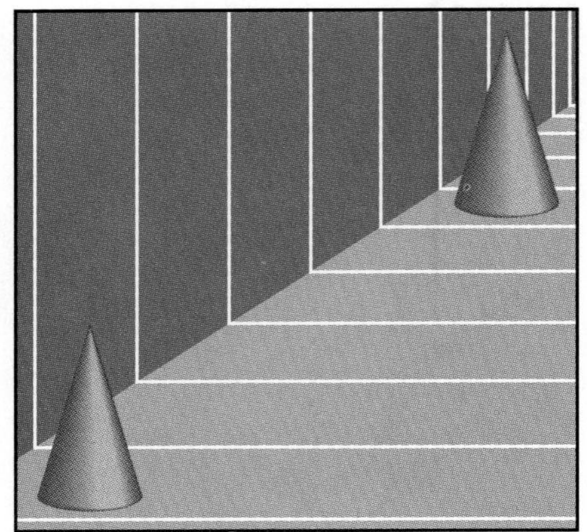

FIGURE 3.38

When two objects of the same size are perceived as being at different distances, the one farthest away is perceived as being larger.

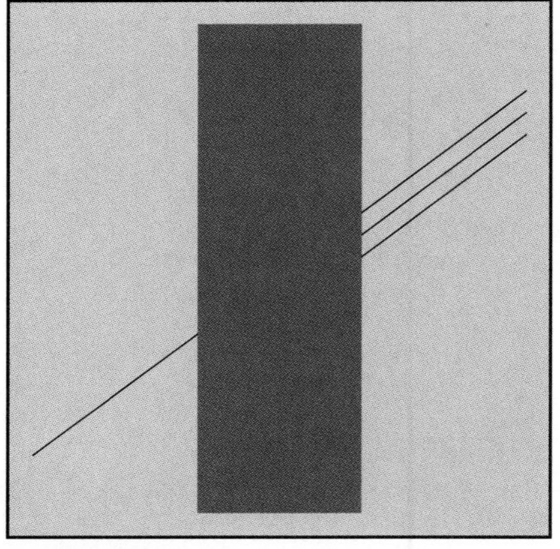

FIGURE 3.39

A demonstration of the Poggendorf illusion. Which line on the right is the continuation of the diagonal line on the left?

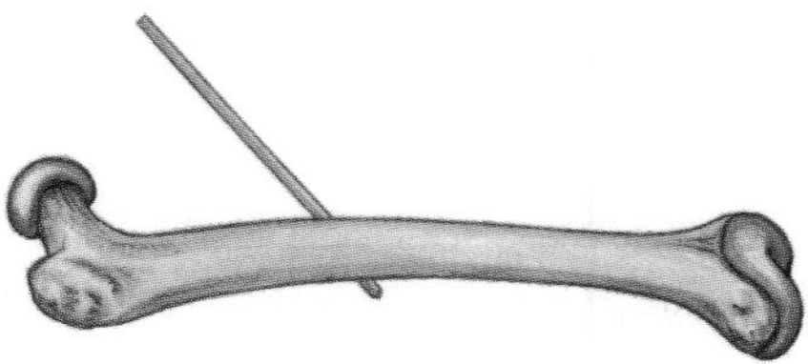

FIGURE 3.40

A dangerous example of the Poggendorf illusion. Will the surgeon's probe touch the top of the bullet?

The Poggendorf illusion is not only interesting, it can be downright *dangerous* (Coren & Girgus, 1978)! Consider the dilemma that might be faced by a surgeon illustrated in figure 3.40. Suppose the surgeon views a bullet that lies next to a bone on an X ray and lines up a probe to remove it. Will the probe touch the top of the bullet? Is it lined up correctly? If you place the edge of a piece of paper along the line of the probe, you will see that it will *miss* the bullet.

The Poggendorf illusion may even be involved in some air accidents. In 1965, two airplanes heading for a landing field near New York City passed on opposite sides of a cloud. Apparently because of the Poggendorf illusion, their paths seemed to be on line for a collision as they were estimated to emerge from the cloud. Tragically, the pilots changed course and collided, killing 4 persons and injuring 49 more (Coren & Girgus, 1978; Matlin, 1988).

Individual and Cultural Influences on Perception

Up to this point, we have discussed factors that determine perception in the same way for all of us—characteristics of the inborn "wiring" of the human brain and sensory systems. But perception is strongly influenced by other factors as well. For example, a number of studies tell us that *motivation* influences perception: Hungry college students are more likely to interpret ambiguous pictures as being of food; sexually aroused males perceive females as being more attractive physically; anxious persons are more likely to interpret ambiguous sentences as being threatening; and poor children estimate the size of coins as larger than children from higher incomes (Bruner & Goodman, 1947; Eysenck, Mogg, May, Richards, & Matthews, 1991; McClelland & Atkinson, 1948; Stephan, Berscheid, & Walster, 1971).

Perception is also influenced by the different *learning* experiences of persons living in different cultures. For example, the Zulus of southern Africa who live in their traditional settlements grow up in a culture that, by tradition, avoids building structures with straight lines and right angles—they prefer circular buildings. Thus, they have little experience with right angles. When they look at the Müller-Lyer figure (see fig. 3.35), therefore, they do not see the two vertical lines as being different in length—like you probably do. However, Zulus who have been living in the larger African cities long enough to become accustomed to rectangular structures are fooled by the Müller-Lyer illusion like most Americans (Segall, Campbell, & Herskovits, 1963).

Similarly, pygmies who live in the dense rain forests of the African Congo rarely see objects at long distances. In their world thick vegetation blocks the sight of distant objects. It is interesting, then, that if they travel to the African plains, distant buffalo are at first seen as tiny "insects" (Turnbull, 1962). When they draw pictures, they are flat, two-dimensional renderings without depth cues. Furthermore, when they are shown pictures like figure 3.41 and asked who the man is trying to spear, they answer "the tiny rhinoceros" because they do not perceive the rhinoceros as being in the distance. Even more striking evidence for the role of cultural learning experience in perception comes from studies of *pain* in different cultures. To take an example from anthropology that will be shocking to most members of western cultures, consider the *hook-swinging ceremony* practiced in some remote villages

FIGURE 3.41

One of the drawings used to study depth perception in different cultures. Which animal is the man about to spear?

The Zulus of southern Africa are not fooled by the Müller-Lyer illusion. Their culture prefers circular buildings, and they have little experience with straight lines and right angles. This different learning experience influences their perception, causing their interpretation of the Müller-Lyer illusion to differ from other cultures.

in India (Melzack, 1973). Each year a faithful celebrant is decked with flowers as two metal hooks are pushed through the skin and muscles of his back. He is hoisted on a primitive crane by ropes attached to the hooks and is taken from village to village where he blesses each child and farm. The celebrant apparently experiences a sense of "exaltation"—probably due in part to the morphinelike endorphins released by the damage to the skin (see pp. 111–113)—rather than the excruciating pain that most of us would experience (Melzack, 1973). Such evidence certainly suggests that emotional, motivational, and cultural factors are important in perception.

Thinking Critically About Psychology

1. What is the point of studying perceptual illusions? What can we learn from them?

2. What is the value of knowing that our perception is influenced by our emotions?

Review

Perception is the interpretation of meaningless sensations. It's an active process in which impressions are created that often go beyond the minimal information provided by the senses. Many of the ways in which we organize and interpret sensations are inborn and common to all humans. The Gestalt principles of perceptual organization, perceptual constancies, depth perception, and visual illusions provide examples of the active, creative nature of perception. Other factors that enter into the process of perception are more unique to the individual, such as motivational states and cultural learning experiences. These factors ensure that we will perceive the world in a way that is largely universal and common to all humans, but with a great deal of individuality due to differences in motivation, emotion, learning, and other factors.

Check Your Learning

To be sure that you have learned the key points from the preceding section, cover the answers below and try to answer each question. If you give an incorrect answer to any question, return to the page given next to the correct answer to see why your answer was not correct.

1. When we perceive a visual stimulus, the center of our attention is termed the "figure," and the indistinct background is called the "ground." Is it possible to change our perception of the same stimulus so that the figure becomes the ground and the ground becomes the figure?

a. yes
b. no

2. The cues used in depth perception that require both eyes are called

a. constant.
b. monocular.
c. binocular.
d. dichromatics.

3. The shape of the lens of the eye must change to focus the visual image on the retina from stimuli that are different distances from the eye, providing a cue used in depth perception. This process is called

a. superposition.
b. aerial perspective.
c. convergence.
d. accommodation.

4. Visual perception can be influenced by

a. motivation and emotion.
b. learning.
c. both a and b.
d. neither a or b.

Correct Answers
1. a (p. 119), **2.** c (p. 121), **3.** d (p. 121), **4.** c (p. 126–127).

APPLICATION OF PSYCHOLOGY

VISUAL PERCEPTION, ILLUSION, AND ART

During the Winter of 1993, I went to New York with my best friend to see an amazing collection of paintings, drawings, and sculpture by Henri Matisse at the Museum of Modern Art. The works were arranged in chronological order, showing the progression in his art from his first paintings to the collages that he assembled on his death bed. The sheer beauty and emotional impact of these works was amazing! But, ever being the psychologist, I sometimes found myself thinking about his paintings in terms of the monocular cues to depth perception.

Now, I have never said, nor will I ever say, that the study of depth perception for its own sake is more than just barely interesting. I know that depth perception is important to understand, but it is just not very interesting. On the other hand, the paintings of Matisse and other great artists are extremely interesting! And, as I thought about it, I found that the way that Matisse used monocular cues of depth perception in his art was pretty interesting, too. Maybe looking at some paintings from this perspective will add to our appreciation of the visual arts and teach us something about depth perception at the same time.

Painting and Depth Cues: Art Appreciation

When you think about it, the artist who paints a landscape, a still life, or a portrait of a person is creating a visual illusion. He or she uses what is known about the monocular cues of depth perception to create the *illusion* of a three-dimensional object (one with height, width, and depth) on a two-dimensional canvas (one with height and width only). No part of the flat canvas is farther away from the viewer than any other part, but the artist creates the illusion of depth—the impression that some parts of the painting are farther away than others—mostly using the cues of texture gradient, linear perspective, superposition, shadowing, and aerial perspective. Cues based on the way in which the eyes focus on objects that are different distances from the eye and the binocular cues that are based on differences in the alignment of the two eyes cannot be used by the artist, but artists often achieve striking illusions of depth with the few cues at their disposal.

FIGURE 3.42
Las Meninas (1656) by Diego Velazquez.
Erich Lessing/Art Resource, NY

Look at the striking illusions of depth created in two paintings. The painting in figure 3.42 by the Spanish painter Diego Velazquez (*Las Meninas,* 1656) uses four depth perception cues to suggest depth very effectively. Notice that the man standing in the doorway is smaller than the man standing on the left (a self-portrait of the artist) and even smaller than the young blonde child who appears to be standing in the front of the painting. Note also that the wall on the right is painted on the canvas as if it is shorter at the rear of the room than in the front of the room. These are uses of the monocular cue of *linear perspective,* and they give a powerful illusion of depth to the room. Notice also that the persons that Velazquez wishes us to perceive as being in the front of the room partially cover the persons portrayed as being at the rear of the room (the cue of *superposition*). The detailed texture of the clothing of the persons in the front of the room is also clearer than that of persons at the rear of the room (the cue of *texture gradient*). Velazquez also uses shadowing effectively to create an illusion of depth, but let's study this cue in the even more effective example by Artemisia Gentileschi (fig. 3.43).

A more subtle, but wonderfully effective illusion of depth has been created in this extraordinary self-portrait. She gives us an amazingly three-dimensional view of herself partly by using linear perspective (notice, for example, that her right hand appears to be farther away from us partly because it is smaller on the canvas than her left hand, which seems to be very close to us. In addition, her face partially hides the right shoulder that seems farther away from us (superposition). But, it is Gentileschi's exceptional mastery of shadowing that brings the illusion of subtle depth to life. Her face is painted on a flat canvas, but it seems as rounded as an apple. As a result, her left cheek seems inches closer to us than her nose.

Sometimes, Matisse was interested in creating a sense of depth, but sometimes he intentionally ignored depth. The reclining nude in figure 3.44 (*L'Atelier du Quai Saint-Michel*), for example, is positioned in a scene painted with powerful depth cues. Notice that the building seen outside the window is shorter on the canvas than the delicate table standing in front of the window. Compare that painting with a later painting in which he has portrayed exactly

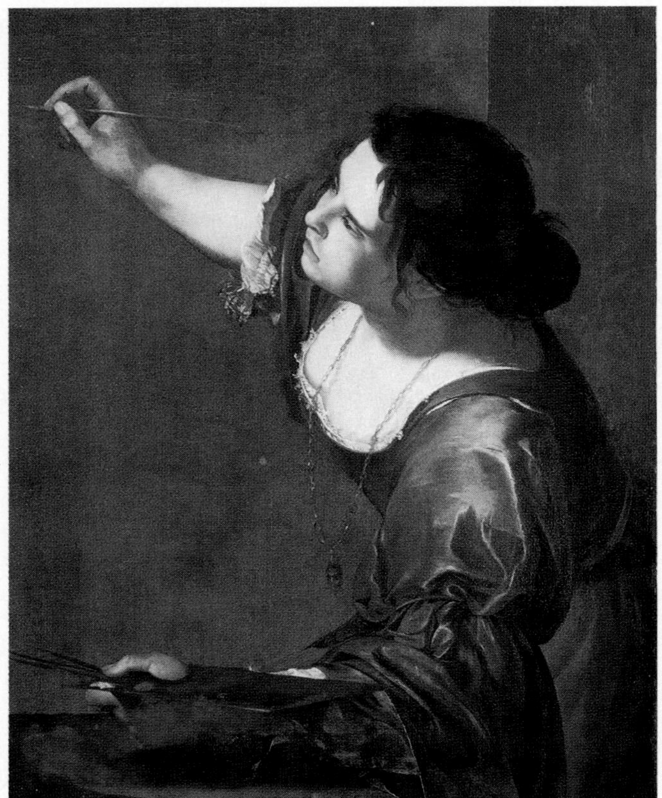

FIGURE 3.43
Self-portrait by Artemisia Gentileschi.
The Royal Collection © 1994 Her Majesty Queen Elizabeth II

FIGURE 3.44
L'Atelier du Quai Saint-Michel by Henri Matisse.
Art Resource, NY © 1995 Succession H. Matisse, Paris/Artists Rights Society (ARS), New York.

the same subject in a very different way. In *Grand Nu Couche* (fig. 3.45), Matisse has eliminated virtually all cues of depth from the painting, including depth through shadowing. The woman has become a flat surface in a flat room. Matisse eliminated the depth cues intentionally to force us to see only color and form! If he were a great chef, he might have asked us to focus on the flavors of his creations by wearing a blindfold during the meal to avoid distractions. By taking depth out of this painting, he leaves us with nothing to perceive but form and color. In Matisse's last work before his death (see fig. 3.46, for example) he has not only completely removed depth cues, but he has stopped using easily recognized forms to focus us even more strongly on the colors and shapes.

Painting and Depth Cues: Doing It Yourself

A few years ago, I came across some good advice on learning to paint realistic three-dimensional scenes with a good sense of depth on a two-dimensional canvas (Hochberg, 1988). As an enthusiastic, but untalented Sunday painter, who has a hard time rendering depth in believable ways, I was immediately interested.

The helpful advice is based on a solid understanding of the cues that we use to create the perception of depth using our own two-dimensional retinas. I would like to be able to attribute this advice to the research of a contemporary psychologist to show you how useful the science of psychology is even to your more artistic side, but the advice comes from the artist Leonardo da Vinci writing in the early sixteenth century. His keen observations will not only help your drawing and your appreciation of the work of other artists but will also help you understand depth perception better.

Leonardo suggests that we place a pane of clear glass the size of our canvas in front of the objects that we want to draw, as in figure 3.47. As we look at the objects, we should trace them exactly as they appear *on the flat surface of the glass* (which is how they appear on the surface of the retina and how we should draw them on the flat surface of the canvas). For example, child 1 and child 2 are actually the same height and are both smaller than adult 3 (see fig. 3.47a). However, as shown in 3.47b, child 1 appears much larger on the surface of the glass than child 2 because child 1 is much closer than child 2. In fact, when traced on the flat glass, child 1 is the same size as the much taller adult 3. By drawing these figures as they appear on the glass rather than as they are in reality, an illusion of depth is created on the canvas. Notice that object 5 looks farther away than object 4, partly because of linear perspective (5 is smaller than 4 on the glass) and partly because of superposition (4 is partially blocking the view of 5).

Now, if I can just improve my use of shadowing . . .

FIGURE 3.45

Grand Nu Couche by Henri Matisse.

The Baltimore Museum of Art: The Cone Collection, formed by Dr. Claribel Cone and Miss Etta Cone of Baltimore, Maryland BMA 1950.258. © 1995 Succession H. Matisse, Paris/Artists Rights Society (ARS), New York.

FIGURE 3.46

Thousand and One Nights by Henri Matisse.

The Carnegie Museum of Art, Acquired through the generosity of the Sarah Mellon Scaife family, 71.23. © 1995 Succession H. Matisse, Paris/Artists Rights Society (ARS), New York.

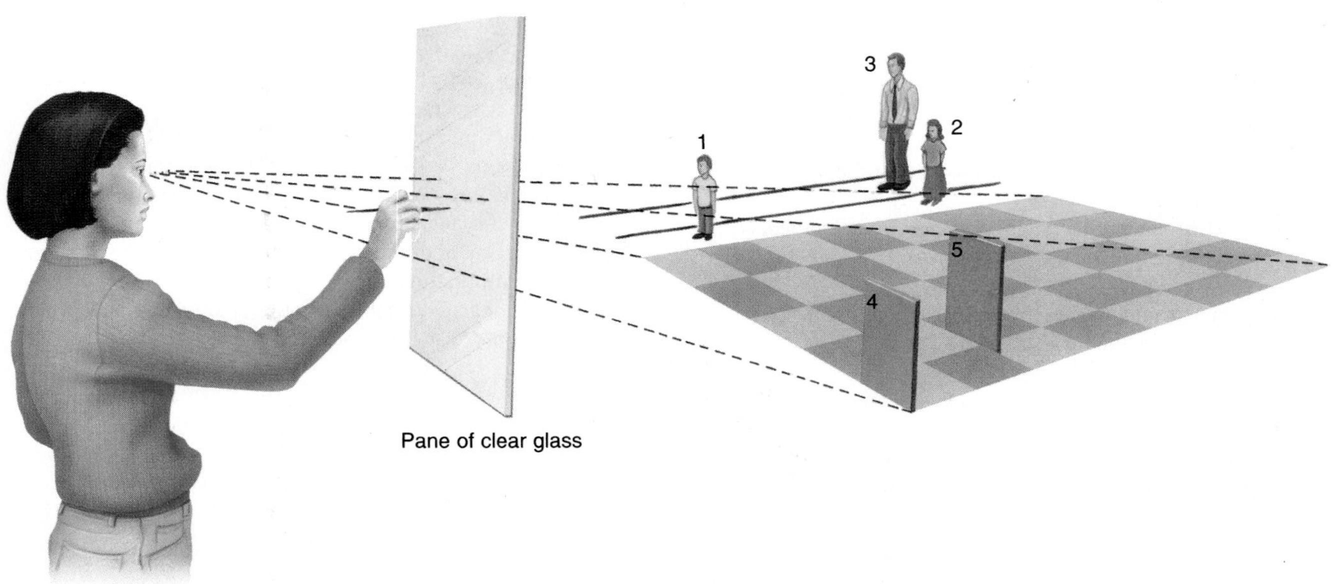

a.

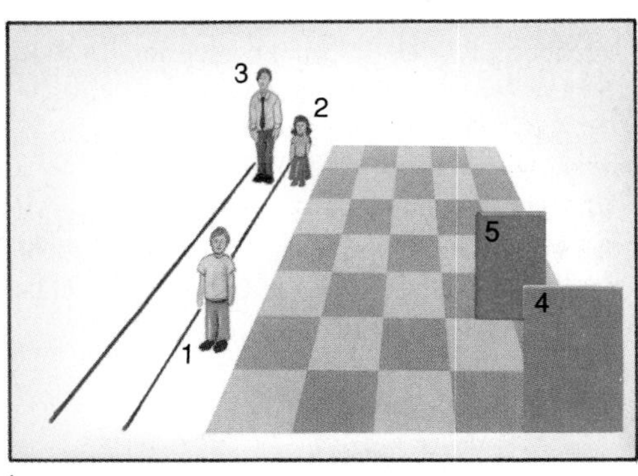

b.

FIGURE 3.47

Leonardo da Vinci suggested that we can learn to use the principles of linear perspective and superposition to give depth to our drawings by placing a pane of glass in front of the scene to be drawn. Trace the objects on the flat glass and you will see how to draw them on the flat canvas.

Summary

Chapter 3 recognizes that we live in a physical world that we experience through our sense organs and interpret (perceive) by means of our nervous systems.

I. External stimuli are received through specialized sensory receptor cells.
- **A.** Sense organs receive stimuli, transduce sensory energy into neural impulses, and send neural messages to the brain for interpretation.
- **B.** Psychophysics is the field of psychology that studies the relationships between physical stimuli and psychological sensations and perceptions.

II. The sense organs of sight transduce light energy.
- **A.** The intensity of light waves largely determines brightness, while the wavelength (frequency) largely determines color.
- **B.** The eye, working much like a camera, is the primary sense organ for seeing.
    1. Light enters the eye through the cornea (with the iris regulating the size of the pupil) and the lens into the retina.
    2. Rods and cones transduce light waves into neural impulses for transportation to the brain.
    3. The 125 million rods, located throughout the retina except for the fovea, are active in peripheral vision and vision in dim light, but they do not play a role in color vision.
    4. The 6 million cones clustered mostly near the fovea code information for color.
    5. Both trichromatic theory and opponent-process theory are helpful in understanding color vision.

III. The sense of hearing detects sound waves.
- **A.** The frequency of sound waves determines pitch, while the intensity determines loudness.
- **B.** The ear is the primary sense organ for hearing.
    1. The outer ear functions as a sound wave collector.
    2. Sound waves vibrate the eardrum, which is connected to a series of three movable bones (hammer, anvil, stirrup) in the middle ear.
    3. The inner ear, containing the cochlea and the organ of Corti, transduces the sound wave energy into neural impulses for transportation to the brain.

IV. Chemical senses respond to chemicals rather than to energy in the environment.
- **A.** In the sense of taste, chemicals produce the perception of qualities of sweet, sour, bitter, and salty.
- **B.** In the sense of smell, chemicals produce the perception of odors.

V. Internal stimuli are also received by the sensory system.
- **A.** The vestibular organ provides information about body orientation, while the kinesthetic sense reports bodily position and movement.
- **B.** The various skin senses can detect pressure, temperature, and pain.
    1. Two sensations of pain reach the brain at slightly different times because they travel on different neural pathways.
        - **a.** The first sensation reaches the somatosensory area quickly on myelinated neurons.
        - **b.** The more emotional type of pain reaches the limbic system more slowly on unmyelinated neurons.
    2. Many factors can block the "pain gates" for the emotional aspect of pain.

VI. Sensory neural impulses, when transmitted to the brain, are interpreted in a process called perception; examining visual perception demonstrates the general nature of the process.
- **A.** Perception is an active mental process. Gestalt principles explain many of the ways in which humans tend to organize sensory information.
- **B.** Individual factors, such as emotion, motivation, and previous learning, also affect our perceptions.

Suggested Readings

1. If you think of yourself as a sensual person, and something of an intellectual, then treat yourself to the most wonderful book ever written about the senses: Ackerman, D. (1991). *A natural history of the senses.* New York: Vintage Books.
2. A readable but sophisticated examination of classical principles of perception and illusions is supplied by: Held, R., & Richards, W. (Eds.). (1972). *Perception: Mechanisms and models.* San Francisco: W. H. Freeman.
3. If you are a serious student of visual perception or of the visual arts, you may wish to tackle an excellent in-depth analysis of this subject: Hochberg, J. (1988). Visual perception. In R. C. Atkinson, R. J. Hernstein, G. Lindzey, & R. D. Luce (Eds.), *Stevens' handbook of experimental psychology: Vol. 1. Perception and motivation.* New York: Wiley-Interscience.
4. Perhaps the ultimate sensory illusion is experienced by persons who have lost an arm or leg. If you would like to learn about "phantom limbs," read: Melzack, R. (1992). Phantom limbs. *Scientific American,* April 120–126.

Special Review of the Sense Organs

A great deal of new information was covered in chapter 3 on the structure of the sense organs. A set of unlabeled illustrations have been prepared to help you check your learning of these structures. These reviews will be most helpful if you glance at the first one and then refer back to the illustration or illustrations on which they are based to memorize the names of the structures. Then, return to the illustration in this review section and try to write in the names of the key structures of the sense organs. Then check your labels by looking at the original figures once again. When you can label all the structures in one of the illustrations, move on to the next one.

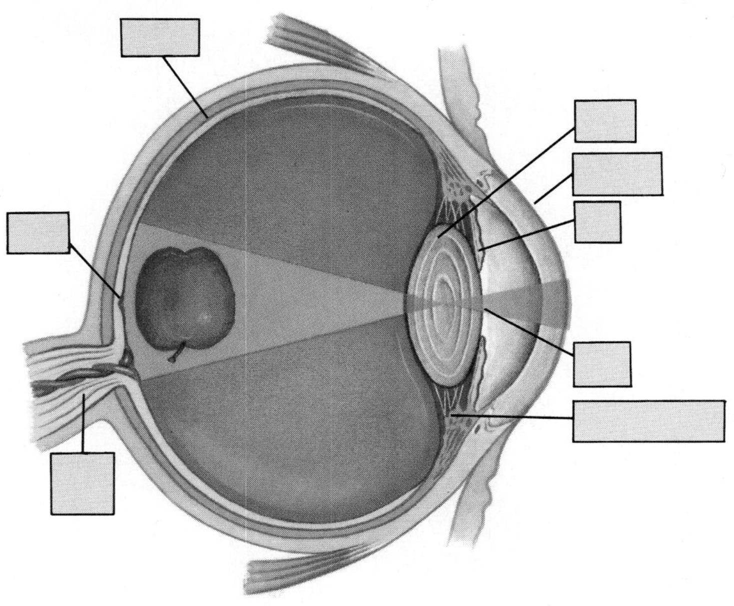

FIGURE 3.48
Key structures of the eye (based on fig. 3.3, p. 95).

FIGURE 3.49

Key structures of the ear (based on fig. 3.14, p. 105).

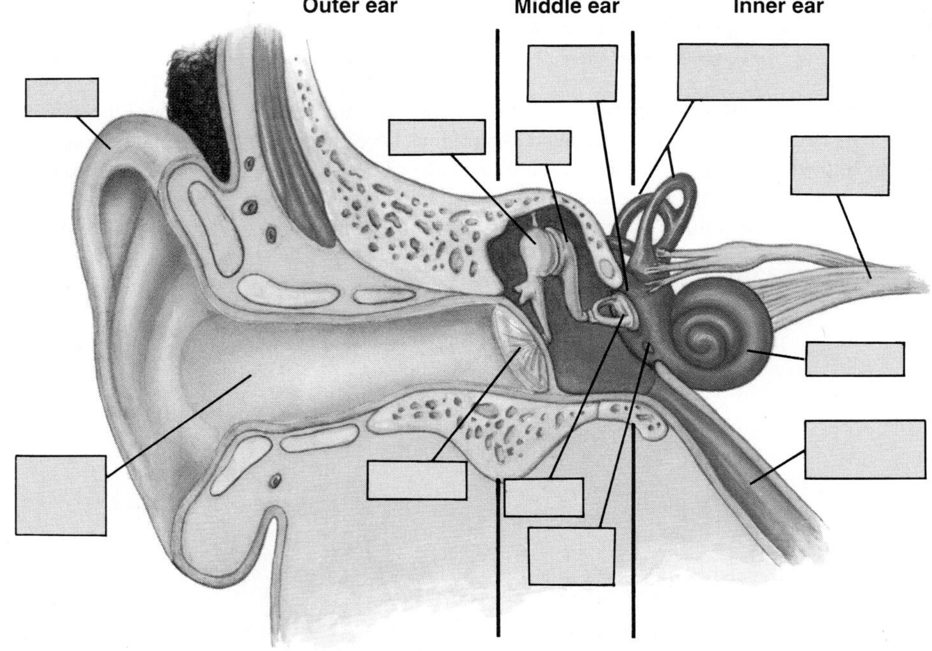

FIGURE 3.50

Key structures of the cochlea (based on fig. 3.15, p. 106).

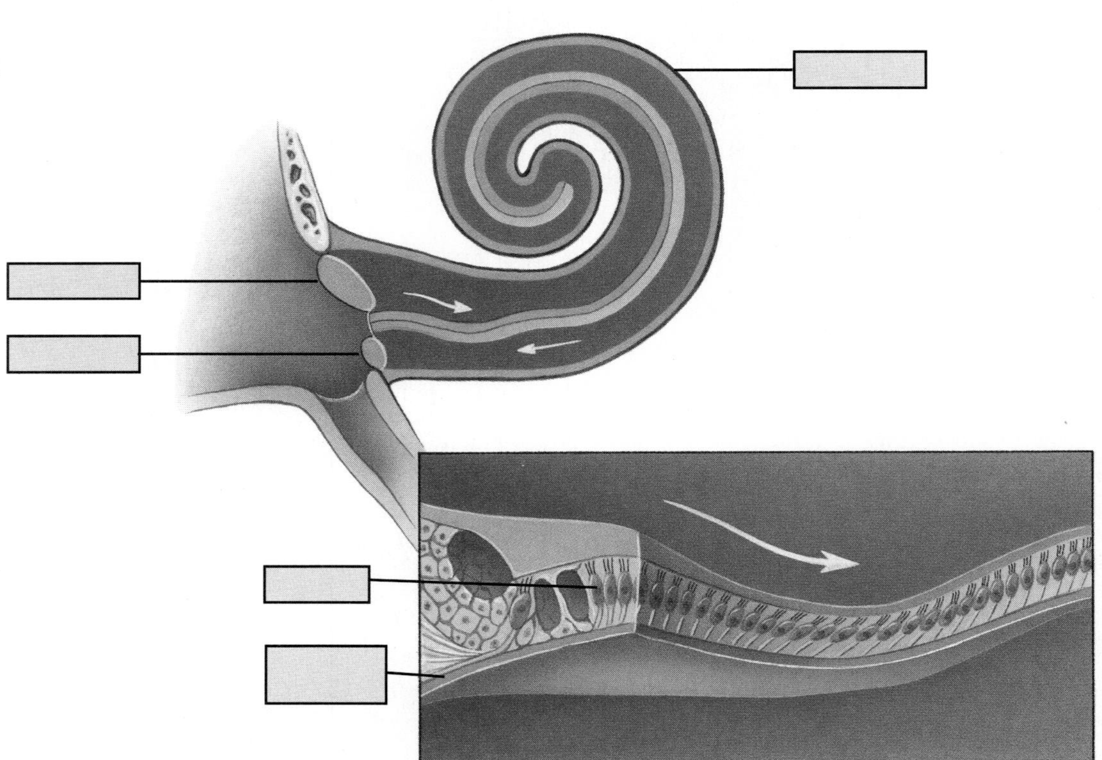

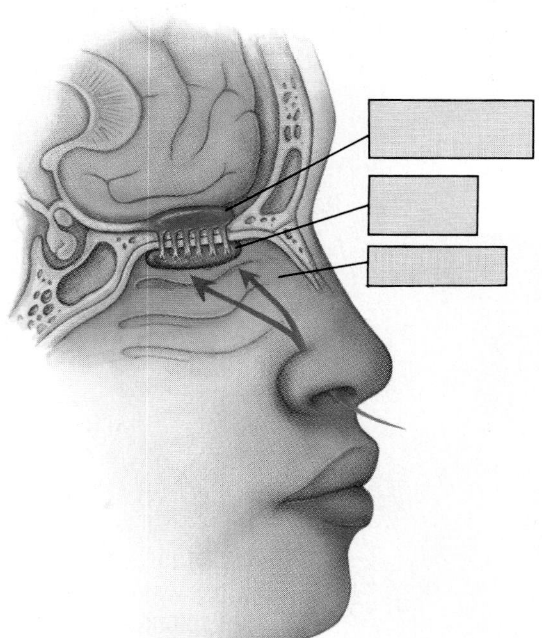

FIGURE 3.51

Key structures of the olfactory receptors (based on fig. 3.22, p. 117).

CHAPTER

4

CHAPTER OUTLINE

States of Consciousness

PROLOGUE

It will come as no surprise for me to tell you that you are presently awake, conscious, and focusing your attention on the words of this textbook. But stop for a moment at the end of this sentence and, with your eyes closed, imagine that your book rises slowly from your lap, drifts to your face, and closes, lightly pinching your nose. Try it—seriously.

Could you see the book rise in your imagination? Did you feel a little pinch on your nose? How about when you are daydreaming, do you sometimes get lost in your thoughts and have conversations with people who are not there but who speak clearly to you anyway?

My point is this: Life is made of many kinds of conscious awareness. Sometimes they are based on what is "out there," like when you are aware of the words in this textbook. But often we create our conscious experiences entirely in our brains—like the floating textbook that rose up and pinched your nose. We create realities in our consciousness that never were and often never will be. We do so every time we imagine, daydream, or dream.

Nancy Kerr of the Georgia Mental Health Institute conducted a fascinating study that illustrates my point beautifully (Foulkes, 1989). Kerr studied the dreams of adult men and women who had lost their eyesight as young children. She found that when they dreamed about friends, their dreams were very much like those of sighted adults. Indeed, when they dreamed about people they had met as blind adults—friends they had never seen—they dreamed about them in visual images. They could "see" what their friends looked like in their dreams, even though they had never seen them with their eyes. They created these visual images entirely in their brains.

In this chapter, we will define consciousness as a state of awareness—awareness of the outside world, of our own thoughts and feelings, and sometimes even of our own consciousness. Consciousness is not a single state, however. Rather, there are many different states of conscious awareness. Even during the course of a typical day our wakefulness is composed of a variety of states of consciousness: focused consciousness, loosely drifting consciousness, and daydreams.

When the waking day ends, moreover, we do not cease to be aware; rather, we experience other kinds of consciousness. As we drift off to sleep, we pass through a dreamlike "twilight" phase, and even amid the shifting stages of sleep itself, we experience the strange reality of dreams. Apparently, these dreams are important to our well-being. Indeed, it is believed that sleep does not rest and restore us for the next day if we do not dream sufficiently.

Other states of consciousness are experienced much less often. Some states of altered awareness occur spontaneously, such as hallucinations and other distorted perceptual experiences. Other altered states of consciousness are achieved in part through deep concentration and relaxation, such as during meditation and hypnosis. Still other altered states are induced by taking certain kinds of drugs. As you read about each form of consciousness, ask how much of the awareness comes through the sense organs that you just studied in the last chapter, and how much comes from within.

KEY TERMS

WIDE AWAKE: NORMAL WAKING CONSCIOUSNESS

consciousness
(kon´shus-nes) A state of awareness.

What does it mean to be conscious? Clearly, it has something to do with awareness. When conscious, we are aware of the sights and sounds of the outside world, of our feelings, our thoughts, and sometimes even of our own consciousness. When unconscious, we are not aware of any of these things. **Consciousness,** simply defined, is *a state of awareness.*

Yet, there is more than one kind of conscious state; it comes in more than the wide-awake-and-thinking variety. The qualities of conscious awareness that people experience when daydreaming, when hypnotized, when high on drugs, or when dreaming are so different from one another that we clearly need to think of consciousness as being many different states of awareness. To understand consciousness fully, we need to explore its many varieties and the conditions under which they occur. In this chapter we speak of dreams, trances, highs, and the like, both to understand the nature of these states and to help us better understand the conscious experience of being awake.

We spend our lives passing from one state of consciousness to another. We read a book, we daydream, we drift off to sleep, we dream, and so on. Each of these states of conscious awareness is so different from the next that the very sense of reality they impart differs. What is logical and possible in a dream may seem absurd when considered the next day. We seldom wonder which state contains the ultimate reality, however. We assume without questioning that the waking state in which we spend most of our lives is the "real" consciousness. It's the standard by which we judge other states and find them to be "distorted" or "unreal."

Waking consciousness is so much a part of us, in fact, that it's difficult to step back and look at it objectively. When we do, we see that it is not a single state of consciousness; instead it includes at least three varieties: directed consciousness, flowing consciousness, and daydreaming.

Directed Consciousness

directed consciousness
Focused and orderly awareness.

flowing consciousness
Drifting, unfocused awareness.

Sometimes our conscious awareness is directed toward a single focus. When we are reading a book, our awareness is mostly absorbed by the words and phrases on the page. During such an experience, our conscious awareness is focused, ordered, and one-tracked. The same is true during any intellectual activity that absorbs awareness, such as during intense emotions or intense sensations. This state is known as **directed consciousness.**

The next time you drink a cola, notice how easy it is to focus directed awareness to intensify the experience. Pay close attention to how wet the cola feels, how cold it is in your mouth. Feel the tingle of the bubbles and the cold pieces of ice against your lips. Taste the sweet flavor and try to imagine which taste receptors the flavor is stimulating. You will taste that cola like you never tasted one before—you will be aware of it in an intense, absorbing way. Try to focus your consciousness in the same way the next time you stop to look at a flower, kiss someone you care about, or shake your father's hand. You may even find that you can direct your awareness just as intensely the next time you study for a test!

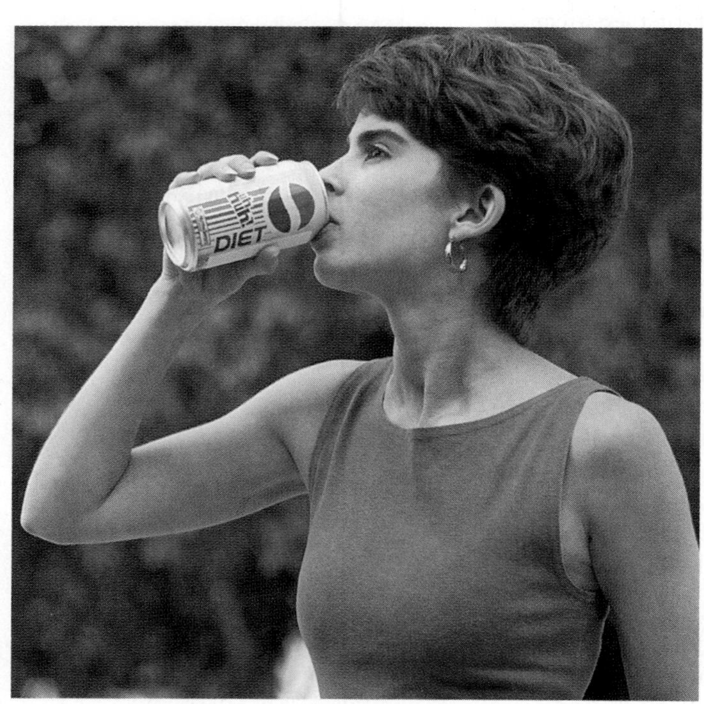

The next time you drink a cola, try directing your awareness to intensify the experience.

Flowing Consciousness

Most of our waking days are spent in a kind of consciousness that is less directed and single-purposed. In **flowing consciousness,** our awareness drifts from one thought to another, from an emotion to an irritating itch, and back to a reminiscence. The changing pattern of this kind of consciousness was compared to the flow of water in a stream by founding American psychologist William James (1890). He used this analogy to convey to students of psychology the idea that conscious experience is a process of images following images that flow so smoothly from one to another that there is never a gap in between. Stop yourself sometime in the midst of your flowing consciousness, and try to remember what you were aware of during the previous 2 minutes. You may be surprised by the flowing, swirling mixture of consciousness that you experienced. In one experiment, university students were asked to "think aloud"—describe the contents of their conscious awareness—when they were not performing any other task. Note the "flowing" nature of awareness in the following excerpt:

> I keep listening to the sound upstairs. Somebody said "hail!" She ought to go to a class this morning. (Name)'s probably given me her cough. She should have gone to the doctor. I had a dream that I had a two-room double. I might have swore that I have one now. I'll probably have a good time next year. (Name) and I get along very well. The room feels like it's shaking. People don't seem to give this girl a rest. It sorta kind of sounds like someone's swinging on a swing. Jungle Jim. I remember the time I fell off the swing at home. It was the time I broke my ankle. I had a pain behind my left eye. It feels like I have something in it. (Pope & Singer, 1980, p. 173)

Daydreams

Many features of directed and flowing consciousness and dreams are combined in the state of waking consciousness called **daydreams.** They are a period of thinking and feeling that is not bound by what is logical or likely to happen. Daydreams are not a sometime thing; most of us daydream many times each day. Why do we spend time in these dreamlike reveries instead of focusing all of our awareness productively on the concerns of the day?

daydreams
Relatively focused thinking about fantasies.

Sigmund Freud, the Austrian founder of psychoanalysis, believed that daydreams reduce the tension left by our unfulfilled needs and wishes. What we cannot do in reality, we accomplish in the fantasy world of daydreams. While daydreaming we win the race, see our lost love return, and build a rustic home in the country with our own hands.

Was Freud right? Are daydreams a way of reducing the tension of unmet needs and unfulfilled wishes? To answer this question, researchers have asked college students to jot down a summary of each of their daydreams for several days (Pope & Singer, 1978). As predicted by Freud, many daydreams involved the fulfilling of a wish. Also consistent with Freud's theory is the fact that most people feel quite relaxed during this type of daydreaming. Contrary to Freud's predictions, however, many daydreams are filled with regret, sorrow, and guilt. Other daydreams are highly sexual, such as those focusing on that gorgeous person you would love to know better. These daydreams *create* rather than release tension, casting doubt on Freud's theory of daydreaming. Instead of reducing tension, daydreams may be merely a slightly distorted reflection of our current concerns and emotions (Pope & Singer, 1978).

When do we do all of this daydreaming? You will not be surprised to learn that a series of studies has shown that we are most likely to daydream when we are in boring or routine situations and when we are sitting or lying down instead of moving about (Pope & Singer, 1980). Daydreams are turned on when our active behavior and directed awareness are turned off. To repeat yet another observation made by William James (1890), when we are awake, something is always going on in our consciousness—there are no gaps. If it's not productive behavior or thinking, it's flowing awareness or daydreaming.

"I'm sorry dear, I must have lost consciousness. What were you saying?"

Drawing by Chon Day; © 1982 The New Yorker Magazine, Inc.

Divided Consciousness: Being Two Places (Mentally) at the Same Time

Last Saturday I was asked to watch a friend record a demonstration tape of a song he had written. It was my first time in a studio and I was fascinated—they even let me record a few bars using my friend's guitar (I was less than excellent). Driving home, my thoughts raced about my own long-forgotten fantasies of making hit records. When I got home, I realized I had no recollection whatsoever of the 5-mile drive. I obviously had negotiated several stoplights and made a couple of turns, but I was lost in my thoughts and have no recollection of the drive. Stanford University psychologist Ernest Hilgard (1975) describes such phenomena as moments of **divided consciousness.** He believes that our conscious awareness becomes "split" and we simultaneously perform two activities requiring conscious awareness (in my case, driving and thinking about recording songs). This concept not only explains some strange moments in our everyday lives but also helps us understand the phenomenon of hypnosis.

divided consciousness
The splitting off of two conscious activities that occur simultaneously.

The Concept of the Unconscious Mind

unconscious mind
Mental processes that occur without conscious awareness.

In discussing conscious experience, it's important to compare the term *conscious* with the term *unconscious.* Most people beginning to study psychology expect to learn about the **unconscious mind.** It may surprise you to know, then, that until recently the term was not even mentioned in most modern introductory psychology textbooks. Psychology is taught in most American colleges and universities from a scientific viewpoint. The term *unconscious,* in contrast, is used primarily by psychologists who take a more philosophical approach to understanding people and their problems. It would be wrong to dismiss the unconscious simply as "unscientific" and not discuss it at all.

Today, most scientists agree that it's time to apply scientific thinking to the study of the unconscious (e.g., Hilgard, 1980). For example, when a person is in a room where more than one person is talking, most of the time we can pay attention to one voice and "tune out" the other voice. This has been called the *cocktail party phenomenon* because it happens so often at parties.

But what becomes of the other voice—the one we do not listen to? There is evidence that it reaches the brain, but the person is never *consciously* aware of it. In that sense, the voice is processed *unconsciously* by the brain. Andrew Mathews and Colin MacLeod (1986) have studied this phenomenon experimentally. Participants in the study were asked to listen to two messages presented simultaneously over different earphones. They were instructed to ignore one of the messages but to repeat the other message aloud. Some of the time, the words presented to the ignored earphone were nonthreatening words like *friend* or *concert,* while threatening words like *assault* and *emergency* were presented at other times. As they repeated the message, they also kept their eye on a computer screen and pressed a key as quickly as they could after the word *press* appeared on the screen (see fig. 4.1).

To be sure that the threatening words would have a great deal of emotional impact on the research participants, they were all highly anxious persons who were receiving treat-

FIGURE 4.1
Participants in Mathews and MacLeod's study of unconscious information processing listened to two different messages that were presented simultaneously through different earphones. The participants were able to completely ignore one message and repeat the other one. At the same time, they pressed a key as quickly as they could when the word *press* appeared on the computer screen. Although not consciously heard, threatening words disrupted the reaction time of highly anxious individuals. This suggests that these persons had unconsciously processed the emotional meaning of the threatening words.

ment for their problems. The participants reported that they were not consciously aware of any of the ignored words, because they focused all of their attention on the message they had to repeat. Yet, when threatening words were being presented, the anxious individuals pressed the key significantly less quickly than when nonthreatening words were presented. Apparently, the ignored words were being processed without conscious awareness, and the emotional impact of the threatening words disrupted their performance on the reaction time task. Careful experiments of this sort may well lead to a better understanding of mental processes that affect us without our being consciously aware of them.

Review

Consciousness is composed of many different states of awareness. Even normal waking consciousness can be seen to be three different states. During each day, we shift many times among directed consciousness, a less-organized flowing consciousness, and daydreaming. Each carries with it a somewhat different sense of conscious reality. At times, our consciousness appears to "do two things at once" in what Hilgard refers to as divided consciousness. At other times we appear to process information in an entirely unconscious way, opening the door to the possibility of scientific studies of unconscious mental processes.

Thinking Critically About Psychology

1. What is the value of daydreaming? Does it help humans survive as a species or hinder our survival?

2. Can you think of any instances when you've experienced divided consciousness?

Check Your Learning

To be sure that you have learned the key points from the preceding section, cover the answers below and try to answer each question. If you give an incorrect answer to any question, return to the page given next to the correct answer to see why your answer was not correct. Remember that these questions cover only some of the important information in this section; it is important that you make up your own questions to check your learning of other facts and concepts.

Match each definition with one of the following correct terms:

a. unconscious **c.** flowing consciousness
b. divided consciousness **d.** directed consciousness

________ **1.** Conscious awareness that has a single focus.

________ **2.** Mental processes that occur without conscious awareness.

________ **3.** Awareness that drifts from one thought to another; or drifting, unfocused awareness.

________ **4.** The splitting off of two conscious activities that occur simultaneously.

Correct Answers
1. d (p. 138), **2.** a (p. 140), **3.** c (p. 138), **4.** b (p. 139).

SLEEPING AND DREAMING: CONSCIOUS WHILE ASLEEP

Most nights, we slip gently from wakefulness into sleep, only to return from our nocturnal vacation the next morning. Is this all there is to sleeping? Is it a mere gap in awareness that consumes one-third of our lives? Sleep is not a single state; instead, it's a complex combination of states, some involving conscious awareness. We do not leave mental activity consciousness for the entire night when we sleep; rather, we enter worlds of awareness with properties that are very different from those of the wide-awake world.

Stages of Sleep

Several states of conscious awareness are a part of the sleep process. As we fall asleep, we pass from waking consciousness into a semiwakeful state, into four states of progressively deeper sleep (all of which contain little or no conscious awareness), then into dream sleep, which brings a kind of conscious awareness with a reality all its own. We need to look carefully at each of these steps in the sleep cycle.

Hypnagogic State

hypnagogic state
(hip´´nah-goj´ik) A relaxed state of dream-like awareness between wakefulness and sleep.

myoclonia
(mi´´o-klo´ne-ah) An abrupt movement that sometimes occurs during the hypnagogic state in which the sleeper often experiences a sense of falling.

We do not always go directly from wakefulness to sleep. Often, we daydream for a while, then pass into a "twilight" state that is neither daydreaming nor dreaming. This is the **hypnagogic state** (Mavromatis, 1987). We begin to lose voluntary control over our body movements; our sensitivity to outside stimuli diminishes; and our thoughts become more fanciful, less bound by reality. For most people, it's a highly relaxed, enjoyable state. On some occasions, however, we are rudely snapped out of the peaceful hypnagogic state; we suddenly feel like we are falling and our body experiences a sudden jerk called a **myoclonia.**

Stages of Light and Deep Sleep

electroencephalogram (EEG)
(e-lek´´trō-en-sef´ah-lō-gram) Measure of electrical brain activity.

After making the transition from the hypnagogic state to sleep, we pass through four stages of progressively deeper sleep. Most sleep researchers distinguish between four different levels of sleep defined on the basis of **electroencephalogram (EEG)** measures of electrical brain activity (Webb, 1968). The depth of sleep alternates upward and downward many times during the night. Indeed, young adults show an average of 34 shifts in the depth of sleep during the first 6 hours (Webb, 1968). Sleep, then, is not a single, continuous state; it is an almost constantly changing one (see fig. 4.2).

REM Sleep and Dreams

The year was 1952. University of Chicago graduate student Eugene Aserinsky was spending a sleepless night watching a child sleep in Dr. Nathaniel Kleitman's laboratory. Kleitman, Aserinsky's professor, was interested in the slow, rolling eye movements that occur during sleep in infants. The child was connected to a complicated network of wires that led from instruments to monitor many aspects of the body's functioning (such as brain waves, heartbeat, breathing) and a special instrument to measure eye movements.

As Aserinsky dutifully watched the instruments, he was startled to see an unexpected pattern of rapid eye movements. Half a dozen times during the night, the child's eyes

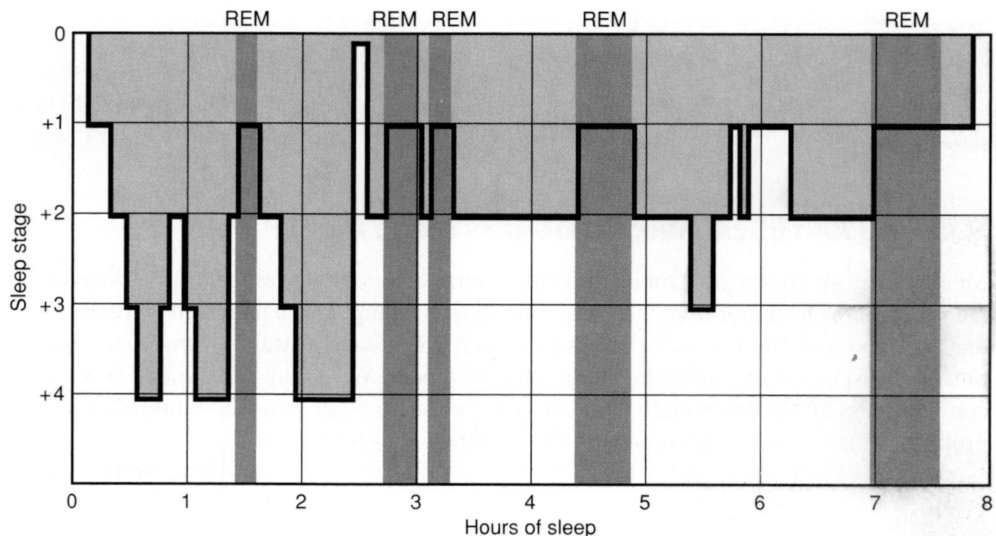

FIGURE 4.2
Each night we pass through a complicated and irregular pattern of shifts from one stage to another.

darted back and forth rapidly and irregularly under his closed eyelids. At first Aserinsky thought his instruments were not working properly, but he could easily see the eye movements of the child. When Aserinsky looked again at his instruments, he saw something even more startling: The brain waves of the subject looked more like he was awake than asleep. Each time the rapid eye movements returned, the same brain pattern resembling wakefulness returned.

When Aserinsky showed his professor the unexpected findings, the conclusion was almost inescapable—the child must have been dreaming. During the next several years, Aserinsky and Kleitman awakened many sleeping adult and child participants when they entered this peculiar stage of sleep characterized by rapid eye movements. If awakened and asked if they were dreaming, over 80 percent said yes.

The era of the scientific study of this elusive state of consciousness was ushered in by Aserinsky and Kleitman's surprising discovery of the relationship between dreaming and movements of the eyeballs (Kleitman, 1960). Their discovery that dreams are very common during a period of sleep that is marked by rapid eye movements and brain-wave activity suggesting the presence of conscious awareness provided a convenient way for scientists to know when dreams were occurring so that they could study them. Because of the characteristic eye movements, this phase of sleep is referred to as *rapid-eye-movement sleep*, or **REM sleep**.

REM sleep
Rapid-eye-movement sleep, characterized by movement of the eyes under the lids; often accompanies dreams.

"Autonomic Storms"

After three decades of study, it's now known that the eyeballs are not the only parts of the body that are busy during dreams. Sleep researcher Wilse Webb (1968) has likened dream sleep to an "autonomic storm." The autonomic nervous system and other parts of the peripheral nervous system (see chapter 2) are very active during dreams, causing noticeable changes in many parts of the body: Blood flow to the brain increases; the heartbeat becomes irregular; the muscles of the face and fingers twitch; and breathing becomes irregular. Interestingly, voluntary control of the large body muscles is largely lost during REM sleep, serving perhaps to keep us from acting out our dreams. Anyone who has watched a sleeping beagle twitch, make miniature running movements, and rasp muffled barks (at dream rabbits?) knows about these autonomic storms and knows that REM sleep is not limited to humans. This fact has been confirmed in many laboratory studies of sleeping mammals.

In addition, there is vaginal lubrication and erection of the clitoris in females and erection of the penis in males during REM sleep. Because of erections that begin during REM sleep, the penis of adult males is erect during one-fourth to one-half of an average night's sleep. This fact has led to advances in the diagnosis of conditions in which some males are unable to have an erection (known as *erectile dysfunction*, or *impotence*). By having the patient spend a night in a sleep laboratory to see if he has erections during REM sleep, it is possible to determine if the cause of the problem is psychological (he would have erections during REM sleep) or physical (he would not have REM erections).

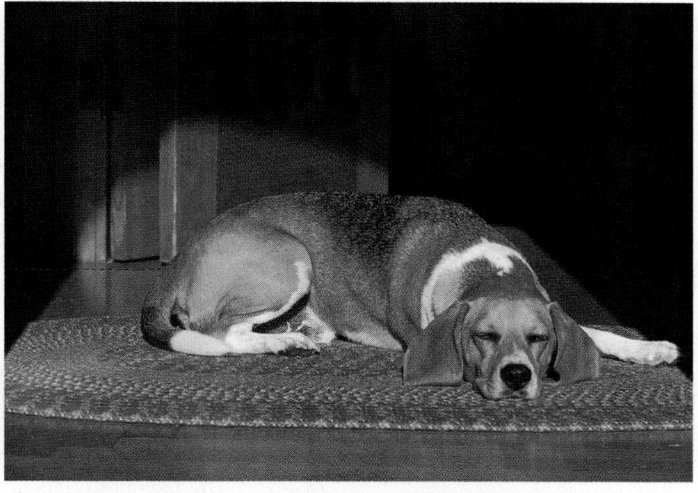

REM sleep is like an "autonomic storm," causing noticeable changes in many parts of the body—human or animal.

The Time Spent Dreaming

How often do you dream? In a survey of college-aged adults, about 15 percent said that they dream every night, and another 25 percent said that they dream on most nights. On the other hand, almost a third of young adults said that they rarely or never dream (Strauch & Meier, 1996). How often do you dream? Even if you recall a dream every night, you probably greatly underestimate the frequency of your dreams. We spend much more time in the world of dream consciousness than most of us realize!

Studies of dreaming conducted during the past 20 years show that the average college student spends about 2 hours a night in REM sleep, divided into about four to six separate

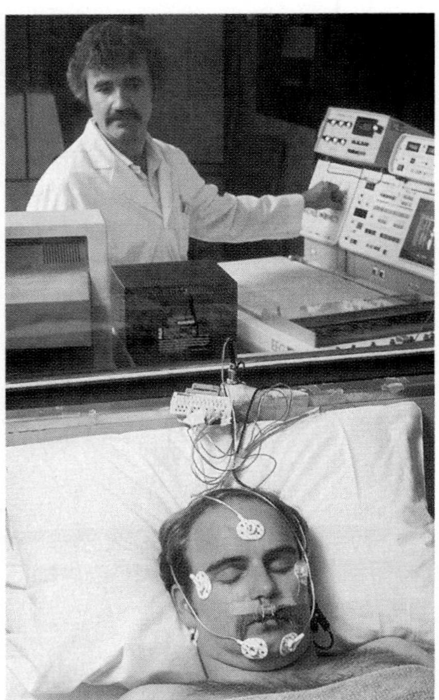

Electroencephalograms and eye muscle monitors allow psychologists to study dreams scientifically.

episodes. It is clear that we dream during at least 90 percent of these episodes of REM sleep (Strauch & Meier, 1996). The length of our REM dreams vary, but the longest REM dream, generally about an hour in duration, usually occurs during the last part of the sleep cycle (Hobson, 1989; Webb, 1982).

Therefore, young adults have 30 to 40 REM dreams per week! We do not remember dreaming nearly this often when we are awake because dreams are quickly forgotten unless the dreamer awakens during or soon after the dream. But you spend about 2 hours each night in the conscious state of REM dreams. There is much more to the story of consciousness while sleeping, however. REM sleep is not the only part of the sleep cycle that is filled with dreams.

Non-REM Sleep and Dreams

Initially, sleep researchers believed that dreams were uncommon during the non-REM parts of the sleep cycle (Kleitman, 1960). Subsequent studies soon showed, however, that the number of dreams that occur during non-REM sleep is much higher than suspected (Foulkes, 1962). Many studies have consistently shown that when participants are awakened during non-REM phases of sleep, they report dreaming about half of the time (Horne, 1988; Strauch & Meier, 1996).

The nature of non-REM dreams is quite different from REM dreams, however. Non-REM dreams are more likely to consist of brief, fragmentary impressions that are less emotional and less likely to involve visual images than REM sleep dreams. Whereas REM dreams are like watching or participating in a play, non-REM dreams resemble the ordinary process of thinking briefly about something during the daytime. In fact, non-REM dreams so resemble fleeting daytime thoughts that individuals awakened during a non-REM dream often deny that they had been asleep at all. Similarly, persons awakened during the non-REM phases of sleep report far more dreams if they are asked "what was going through your head before you were awakened?" instead of "were you dreaming?" (Foulkes, 1989). Non-REM dreams are so different from REM dreams that they are often not thought of as dreams at all by participants in sleep studies. Perhaps for similar reasons, it appears that non-REM dreams are less likely to be spontaneously recalled after waking than REM dreams (Foulkes, 1989; Hobson, 1989; Horne, 1988; Strauch & Meier, 1996).

When both REM and non-REM dreams are considered, we spend a surprising amount of time in states of consciousness during sleep. In addition to the 2 hours of REM dreaming per night, non-REM dream activity is occurring during half of the other 4 to 6 hours that you sleep each night! Unlike waking consciousness, most of the hours that we are conscious during sleep do not become part of the permanent records of our lives by being stored in memory, but modern sleep research has revealed that we are consciously aware during sleep much more than we would have ever suspected.

The Content of Dreams

Dreams are one of the most fascinating aspects of human consciousness. Since at least the time of the Egyptian pharaohs people have attempted to decipher the meaning of dreams—and psychologists are still trying. Let's begin our discussion of dreams by looking at psychological studies of what people dream about. Since dreams are private, it is interesting to compare our own dreams with those of others.

The first systematic study of dreams was conducted by Mary Whiton Calkins. You first learned Calkins's name in chapter 1, when we discussed the founders of psychology. Calkins was a pioneer in the study of memory, but she was also the founder of scientific dream research. Over a hundred years ago, Calkins and her partner wrote down a verbatim description of every dream they recalled over several months—often writing by candlelight in the middle of the night (Calkins, 1893). Since the time of Calkins, many researchers have studied thousands of dreams, both spontaneously recalled dreams and dreams that are recalled when research participants are awakened in sleep labs. Therefore, we can now confidently describe the content of human dreams.

The Images and Characters of Dreams

What do we experience in our dreams? Most of the conscious experience in dreams is visual. If you dream about washing dishes, you will almost always experience a visual image of dishwashing but will be less likely to "hear" the clatter of the dishes or to "feel" the hot, wet dishwater. Only about one-fourth of dream images include auditory sensations, and about 20 percent include bodily sensations. About half of the dreams that involve bodily sensations are sexual in nature—10 percent of all dreams. Less than 1 percent of dreams include tastes or smells (Hall, 1951; Strauch & Meier, 1996).

Do you dream in black and white or color? Most people dream in something that is in between. The visual images in dreams are usually as bright and clear as waking images, but they are murky and drab in color. Dreams usually include few intense colors and mostly have blurry backgrounds (Rechtschaffen & Buchignami, 1983). Who are the characters in your dreams? Your friends and family? Are there strangers in your dreams? Are you a character in your own dreams? Because we are always the "author" of our dreams, it is not surprising that we often play a leading role. The dreamer has an active role in nearly three-fourths of dreams, and we are absent from our own dreams only 10 percent of the time (Strauch & Meier, 1996). About half of the other characters in our dreams are friends, acquaintances, or family members, but the other half are people we do not know or cannot recognize—or are animals 4 percent of the time. The characters in dreams are about an even mixture of men and women, with men being slightly more likely to dream about men than women are (Hall, 1951; Strauch & Meier, 1996).

The Emotions of Dreams

About three-fourths of all dreams have some positive or negative emotional content. Of our emotionally tinged dreams, about 60 percent of dreams have a negative tone or a mixture of negative and positive emotions (Strauch & Meier, 1996). The emotional content of dreams that recur is particularly likely to be negative. In a survey of more than a thousand readers of the magazine *Psychology Today,* the most frequently reported recurrent dreams were of being chased or falling. Flying, appearing naked or scantily clothed in public, and taking exams when unprepared were also common themes of recurrent dreams (Stark, 1984).

There are sex differences in the emotional qualities of dreams, however. Overall, men are a little more likely to have positive dreams than are women. Similarly, the actions of the characters in men's dreams are somewhat more socially restrained than the characters in women's dreams. The people in men's dreams are both less likely to act in friendly ways toward other characters in the dream and less likely to act aggressively toward other dream players. When verbal or physical aggression occurs in dreams, both men and women are more likely to dream that they are the victim than the perpetrator of that aggression, but this tendency is somewhat stronger for women than men (Strauch & Meier, 1996).

Creative and Bizarre Aspects of Dreams

Dreams fascinate us largely because they can be amazingly creative and bizarre. Most of our dreams actually resemble normal everyday life, but even our more realistic dreams often contain creative and usual elements. About three-fourths of our dreams contain at least one bizarre and unrealistic element, usually mixed into an otherwise realistic dream. On the other hand, 10 percent of our dreams involve mostly nonsensical story lines and another 10 percent of dreams are almost completely fantastic and bizarre. Our dreams are twice as likely to be about fictional people and events than real ones, and the settings for our dreams also are more likely to be fictional than real, with sudden and unrealistic changes from one setting to another occurring in one out of four dreams (Hall, 1951; Strauch & Meier, 1996).

The Meaning of Dreams

Why do we dream about the things that fill our heads during sleep? What is the meaning of dreams? A century of research suggests that some of the content of dreams is easy to understand, but the rest is still a mystery.

Day Residue and Stimulus Incorporation

day residue
Content in dreams that is similar to events in the person's waking life.

A large part of the content of dreams is directly related to things that are going on in our lives during the day—which Sigmund Freud called **day residue.** The majority of dreams contain at least one character or event from the preceding day—or less often, from the preceding week, month, or even earlier in the dreamer's life. The most important characters and events are more likely to reflect day residue than less central parts. One clear demonstration of the importance of day residue in the content of dreams is that half of all dreams reported by research participants in sleep laboratories include the sleep researchers or parts of the laboratory in the dream (Strauch & Meier, 1996).

The role of day-to-day events and people in our dreams also has been demonstrated in a well-designed study conducted at the Max Planck Institute of Psychiatry in Munich, Germany (Lauer, Riemann, Lund & Berger, 1987). Participants slept in the sleep laboratory after being shown either a neutral film or an upsetting film depicting violence, humiliation, and despair. They were awakened during their first REM stage and asked if they were dreaming. After viewing the upsetting film, the participants' REM dreams were rated as containing considerably more aggressive and anxious content than on the night following the neutral film. Furthermore, about one-third of the dreams contained images or themes directly related to the content of the upsetting film.

A more naturalistic study of the impact of daytime events on the content of dreams was conducted by Wood, Bootzin, Rosenhan, Nolen-Hoeksema, & Jourdon (1992). On October 17, 1989, a major earthquake hit the San Francisco area that caused more than 5 billion dollars in damage and killed 62 people, including 42 who were killed when a freeway collapsed on them. The researchers asked students at two universities in the San Francisco area to keep track of the number of upsetting dreams that they had during a three-week period immediately following the earthquake. As a control group, students at the University of Arizona who had not been near the earthquake did the same thing. Not surprisingly, the students in the area of the earthquake reported more vivid, upsetting dreams than the students in Arizona. In addition, 40 percent of the students in the San Francisco area reported at least one dream about earthquakes, compared with 5 percent of the students in Arizona (Wood et al., 1992). Clearly, events and concerns in our daily lives are among the most common things that we dream about.

Our current concerns are reflected in our dreams. After the 1989 earthquake, students in the San Francisco area reported more upsetting dreams than did students in other locations.

stimulus incorporation
Stimuli that occur during sleep that are incorporated into dreams either directly or in altered form.

Sometimes the real-world event that is included in the dream is something that is going on while we are asleep. Have you ever had a dream that somehow included the telephone or alarm clock that was ringing in your ear at the time? This phenomenon is called **stimulus incorporation.** Sometimes the stimulus in the real environment is directly incorporated into the dream, but more often it is "transformed" somewhat. In a Swiss study, sleep participants were presented with the recorded sound of a jet plane while asleep. About one-third later reported dreaming about flying or reported hearing something that sounded like a jet plane (such as a sputtering gas stove) in their dream, but the sound was usually not heard in the dream exactly as it actually sounded (Strauch & Meier, 1996).

Dream Interpretation

So, we know that some of the content of dreams simply reflects the events and concerns of daily life, but what about the rest? And what is the meaning of the bizarre and fictional images in dreams? Different psychologists have very different views of the meaning of dreams, ranging from the opinion that they mean virtually nothing, to the belief that they provide a rich source of information about hidden aspects of our personalities that cannot be gotten easily in other ways.

To followers of Sigmund Freud, dreams are the "royal road to the unconscious." They allow us to travel deep into the unconscious mind and view hidden conflicts and motives cloaked only by the symbols of dreams. To Freud, there are two levels of the content of dreams: manifest and latent. The events that we experience in dreams are their **manifest content.** This level held little interest for Freud; he felt that it was necessary to get beyond the surface and find out what the manifest content of the dream symbolized to discover its true meaning, or **latent content.** For example, the manifest content of a young woman's dream might involve riding on a train and becoming frightened as it enters a tunnel. On the surface the dream was about trains and tunnels. But what does the manifest content of the dream symbolize? Freud might see the train as symbolizing a penis and the tunnel as symbolizing a vagina. Hence, the hidden, or latent, content of the dream might concern the young woman's conflicts about having sex.

manifest content
According to Freud, the obvious, but superficial, meaning of dreams.

latent content
According to Freud, the true meaning of dreams that is found in the symbols in their manifest content.

Such interpretations are provocative and fascinating, but are they accurate? Psychologists simply do not agree on this issue. Since symbols can be interpreted in an infinite number of ways, we can never be sure that our interpretations are correct. Perhaps as a result, most contemporary psychologists place much less emphasis on dream interpretation than did Freud.

Why Do We Sleep and Dream?

Why do we sleep and dream? Do we need to sleep? What effects does a lack of sleep have on us? It is clear that we need sleep in the sense that we apparently create a "sleep debt" that needs to be made up if we miss sleep. College students at the University of Florida who participated in a sleep experiment were limited to 2 hours of sleep for one night. The next day they were somewhat irritable, fatigued, and inefficient, and the next night they fell asleep more quickly and slept longer than usual (Webb & Bonnet, 1979).

Longer periods of sleep deprivation produce more pronounced inefficiency and fatigue, but people are remarkably able to do without a lot of sleep. For example, teenager Randy Gardner set a new world record by staying awake for 264 hours as a science project with no serious ill effects, but he felt more fatigue, sleepiness, and irritability. However, when a group of volunteers gradually reduced their sleep from 8 to 4 hours a night for a period of 2 months, there were no detectable effects at all (Webb & Bonnet, 1979). It's when we abruptly reduce the amount of sleep, or reduce it to less than 4 hours, that we are most likely to feel ill effects and an intense need for sleep.

Sleep researchers have not yet reached an agreement as to why we sleep. There is some evidence that sleep plays a role in the restoration of the body. Long-distance runners, for example, sleep longer and show more deep sleep than usual after a race (Shapiro, Boortz, Mitchell, Bartel, & Jooste, 1982). In addition, the rate of protein synthesis is high during REM sleep (Drucker-Colin & Spanis, 1976). Harvard University researcher J. Allan Hobson (1989) has proposed a specific theory in which sleep plays a restorative role. His theory is based on the existence of a center in the brain stem that is active when we are awake (called the **sleep-inhibiting system**) and two other centers in the brain stem that are activated when we are sleeping—especially when we are dreaming (called the **sleep-promoting systems**) (see fig. 4.3). Hobson suggests that we need to sleep and dream to give the sleep-inhibiting system a chance to rest and replenish itself.

sleep-inhibiting system
An area of the brain stem that inhibits sleep.

sleep-promoting systems
Two areas of the brain that lead to sleep.

Sleep researcher Wilse Webb (1975) has proposed a very different theory of why we sleep that suggests that sleep serves a protective rather than a restorative role. Webb has not been convinced that humans have much of a physiological need for sleep. Because the eyes of animals that sleep at night are not very efficient in low light, however, he hypothesizes that we fall asleep to keep us from moving around in the dark of night! In his view, sleep serves to keep us from wasting energy, falling off cliffs, and being eaten by animals with better night vision that hunt at night.

From a psychological viewpoint, it's interesting that we may have a "need" to dream. In a number of experiments, sleeping individuals were awakened whenever they entered REM sleep. They were otherwise allowed to get a normal amount of sleep each night.

FIGURE 4.3

Sleep is controlled by the balance of sleep-promoting and sleep-inhibiting systems in the brain.

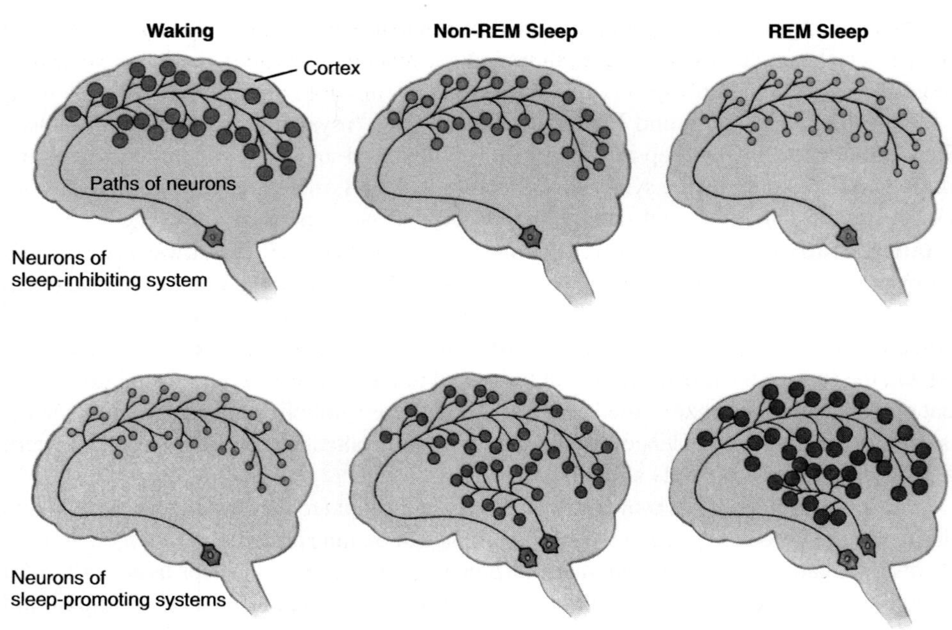

Depriving participants of approximately 2 hours of REM sleep each night had the same effects as much longer deprivations of sleep in general. The participants were irritable, inefficient, and fatigued. On subsequent nights, they showed an increase in the amount of REM sleep, suggesting that they had a need to catch up on REM sleep—and perhaps on their vivid dreaming. Other studies have also shown that deprivation of the deepest part of non-REM sleep has much the same effects (Hobson, 1989; Webb & Bonnet, 1979).

Research has shown the importance of REM sleep in another way. When volunteers gradually reduced their nightly sleep by 4 hours, they were able to get by on reduced amounts of sleep because they packed their 2 hours of REM sleep tightly into their shortened sleeping time (Webb & Bonnett, 1979). The amount of non-REM sleep that occurs between REM periods was greatly reduced when total sleep time was cut, but the amount of dream sleep stayed fairly constant.

Nightmares and Other Sleep Phenomena

nightmare
A dream that occurs during REM sleep whose content is exceptionally frightening, sad, angry, or in some other way uncomfortable.

We have all had the terrifying kind of dreams known as **nightmares.** These are dreams that occur during REM sleep whose content is exceptionally frightening, saddening, provoking, or in some other way uncomfortable. They are upsetting enough to wake us up during the dream, so we can vividly remember our nightmares, even though they account for only a small proportion of the dreams most of us have (Hartmann, Russ, Oldfield, Sivian, & Cooper, 1987).

night terror
An upsetting nocturnal experience that occurs most often in preschool-age children during deep non-REM sleep.

Night terrors are a less common, but perhaps even more upsetting nocturnal experience. The individual awakens suddenly in a state of panic, sometimes screaming, and usually with no clear recollection of an accompanying dream. A sense of calm usually returns within a few minutes, but these are terrifying experiences. Unlike nightmares, they do not occur during REM sleep but occur during the deepest phases of non-REM sleep. Night terrors are most common in preschool-age children, but sometimes adults experience them (Hartmann et al., 1987).

sleepwalking
Waking and carrying on complicated activities during the deepest part of non-REM sleep.

Sleepwalking is another interesting phenomenon that occurs primarily during the deepest parts of non-REM sleep. Sleepwalkers rise from the bed and carry on complicated activities, such as walking from one room to another, even though they are sound asleep. Sleepwalking is most common in children before the age of puberty but is not particularly unusual in adults. Sleepwalking usually reappears in adults only during periods of stress, but except for the danger of accidents while wandering around in the dark, it's not an abnormal behavior.

Sleeptalking is a fairly common phenomenon that can occur during any phase of the sleep cycle. In this, the soundly sleeping person says words, sometimes making fairly coherent statements for a brief period of time. It's most common in young adults but occurs at all ages.

sleeptalking
Talking during any phase of the sleep cycle.

Sleep Disorders

Although we all sleep, some people sleep more or less than they would prefer or experience other serious difficulties with the sleep process. The term **sleep disorders** is often used to refer to these troublesome but highly treatable disorders.

Insomnia refers to a variety of difficulties in which the individuals report that they sleep less than they wish. There are two major varieties of insomnia. In *sleep-onset insomnia* the individual has difficulty falling asleep at the hour at which they would like, but sleep is normal after it begins. In contrast, *early-awakening insomnia* is characterized by waking up earlier than desired, either several times in the middle of the night or early in the morning. Both are found in individuals experiencing no other psychological problems but are more common in individuals undergoing periods of stress, anxiety, or depression.

People with sleep-onset insomnia have difficulty falling asleep.

Narcolepsy is a rare sleep disorder, occurring in less than one-half of 1 percent of the general population, but its impact can be quite serious. The narcoleptic often falls unexpectedly into a deep slumber in the middle of work or even conversations with others, especially when upset or stressed. Often the individual experiences loss of muscle tone and shows a lack of body movement as if she or he has suddenly fallen into dream sleep, but laboratory studies show that narcoleptic sleep is not REM sleep. Often these sudden bouts of sleep cause serious difficulties with the use of dangerous machines and other job-related activities (Groves & Rebec, 1988).

Sleep apnea is the sudden temporary interruption of breathing during sleep. This phenomenon is common, particularly in older adults who snore. It is caused either by too much relaxation of the muscles of the throat, or by a cessation of brain signals for breathing. Generally the individual experiences a few apneas each night that are not problematic. But some individuals experience so many apneas, with the resulting loss of oxygen to the brain, that medical conditions are aggravated or the individual is exhausted the next day and may develop a condition like narcolepsy (Ancoli-Israel, Kripke, & Mason, 1987).

sleep disorders
Any of a variety of disturbances of sleep.

insomnia
Disorder in which the person sleeps less than desired.

narcolepsy
Sleep disorder in which the person suddenly falls asleep during activities usually performed when fully awake.

sleep apnea
Sudden interruption of breathing during sleep.

Circadian and Other Rhythms

When is it time to go to sleep? For some of us, drowsiness takes over not long after sundown. Others are "night owls" who find that they are wide awake until the wee hours of the night. But all of us—even those who do not sleep well—are on a cycle of waking and sleeping that regulates our pattern of sleep, called the **circadian rhythm** (*circa* = about; *dia* = day). Much remains to be learned about circadian rhythms, but the pineal gland seems to be its primary internal "clock" and the hormone *melatonin* a key factor in regulating sleepfulness.

circadian rhythm
A cycle of waking and sleeping that regulates our pattern of sleep.

The body has many other circadian rhythms, most of which follow the pattern of the sleep-wake cycle. For example, an important hormone of the pituitary that plays a key role in body growth and repair, *growth hormone,* is secreted mostly during the first 2 hours of sleep, with little secreted during the waking hours of the day. Apparently this reflects the role that sleep plays in normal growth and the maintenance of health.

Body temperature also follows a circadian rhythm that is linked to the sleep cycle. As you can see in figure 4.4, our temperature falls just as we are beginning to feel sleepy and continues to fall until the middle of the sleep period. This is why you sometimes want to pull on more covers in the middle of the night, even when the temperature in your room is controlled by a thermostat.

Figure 4.4 also shows that *cortisol,* the hormone of the adrenal glands that reflects stress levels, follows a circadian rhythm that is tied to the sleep period in yet another pattern. Cortisol secretion begins to rise shortly after you fall asleep and continues to rise through the night. This is another indication that REM sleep is not a calm period for the body. The peak of cortisol secretion is just before awakening, the time of the longest period of REM

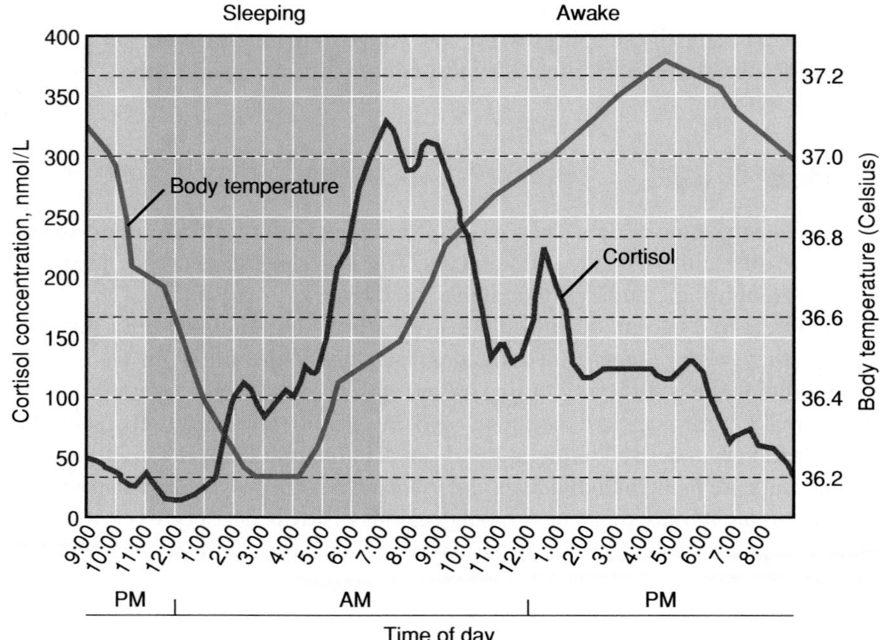

FIGURE 4.4

The concentration of the adrenal hormone cortisol in the blood follows a circadian rhythm, reaching its peak just before waking from sleep, while the circadian rhythm for body temperature follows an almost opposite pattern.

Source: Data based in part on J. Puig-Antich, et al., "Cortisol Secretion in Prepubertal Children with Major Depressive Disorder," *Archives of General Psychiatry,* Vol. 46:801–812, 1989.

sleep. The "autonomic storm" (p. 143) that takes place during REM dreams results in the same activation of the adrenal glands that occurs during physical or emotional stress. Ironically, a good night's sleep may be good for us, but in many ways, it is not a "restful" time for the body or—as we have seen when we spoke of dreams—for our consciousness.

The circadian sleep-wake cycle is obviously influenced to some extent by differences in illumination during the day and night. Although many cultures take "siestas" during the day and cultures living near the poles have long periods without "days and nights" as we know them, people throughout the world generally are awake when it is light and sleep when it is dark. Some clever experiments have shown us that the circadian sleep rhythm continues even when individuals are isolated in chambers that are always kept lighted, but surprisingly, the rhythm quickly changes to a *25-hour cycle* (Aschoff, 1981; Horne, 1988). Much the same thing happens to me during vacations when I do not use an alarm clock. I find that I go to sleep and wake up about an hour later each day and then pay the price for it the first day I have to go back to work. Has the same thing ever happened to you?

The most dramatic way that most of us will become aware of circadian rhythms is by disrupting them with long airline flights. If you fly west from Atlanta to Hawaii, for example, you will experience a much longer period of daylight and will generally stay awake longer than usual on the first day. If you fly to Paris, however, you will have a very short first night. Both trips will disrupt your circadian rhythms and make you inefficient and feel "out-of-sorts"—a phenomenon known as "jet lag." People differ in how much they are affected by jet lag, but interestingly, the time required to readjust to local time is generally longer when we travel from west to east (Moore-Ede, Sulzman, & Fuller, 1982) (see fig. 4.5). So you shouldn't expect to tour the entire Louvre museum the morning after arriving in Paris. You'll be lucky to have the energy to break your French bread.

The same phenomenon is seen when workers rotate the times of their work shifts (Wilkinson, Allison, Feeney, & Kaminska, 1989). It is less disruptive to rotate from the night shift (midnight to 8 A.M.) to the day shift (8 A.M.) or from the day shift to the swing shift (4 P.M. to midnight) than to rotate in the opposite direction. This is because you stay awake longer on the first day of each rotation. It is apparently better to move from night to day shift and to travel from east to west because these changes are consistent with our natural tendency to lengthen our circadian rhythms (Moore-Ede et al., 1982). The topics of jet lag and work-shift rotations are the subject of considerable study as it is important to the scheduling of airline pilots, nurses, and other key employees, and to the timing of travel for diplomatic, business, and military purposes.

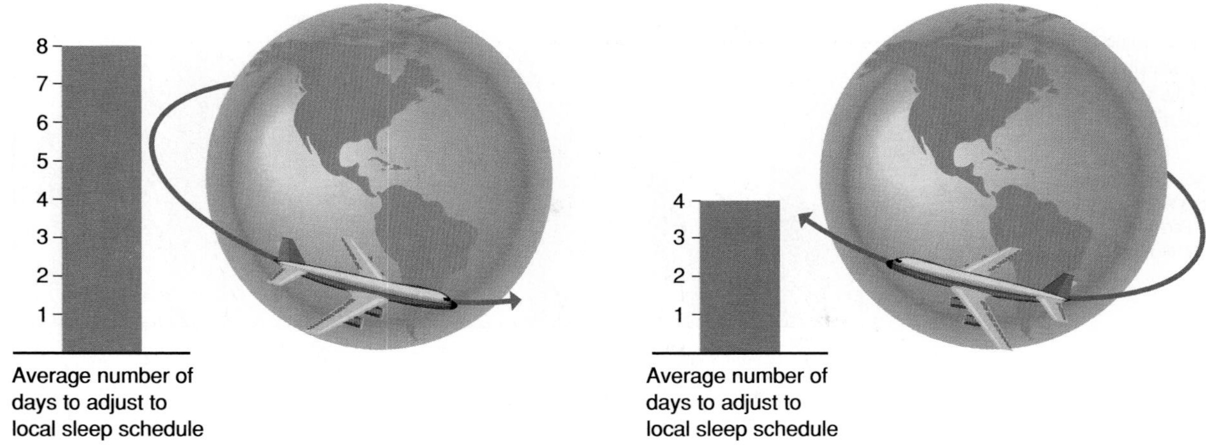

FIGURE 4.5

It generally takes longer to adjust to local sleep schedules and get over "jet lag" when traveling west to east.

Source: Data from M. C. Moore-Ede, F. M. Sulzman, and C. A. Fuller, *The Clocks That Time Us.* Copyright 1982 Harvard University Press.

Not all of the natural rhythms of life are daily rhythms, however. Obviously the menstrual cycle follows a 28-day rhythm, and, as we saw in chapter 1 (p. xx), there is an annual cycle in which many individuals are in better moods during the long days of the summer than the short days of the winter. It has been suggested that this yearly cycle of mood is regulated by the effect of light on melatonin, the same hormone thought to play a key role in the control of the sleep cycle.

A recent study also suggests that there may even be a 7-day mood cycle for many people. You have heard the phrase "blue Monday" and you have probably heard gleeful disk jockeys bellowing "T.G.I.F." on the radio as the weekend begins. Are Mondays blue, and do we feel best on weekends? Randy Larsen and Margaret Kasimatis (1990) of the University of Michigan and Purdue University did a study to find out. Larsen and Kasimatis tested the common belief that Mondays are blue days by asking 74 female and male college students to rate their mood every day for three months. On the average, the students rated their moods as least pleasant on Mondays and most pleasant on Fridays and Saturdays. As shown in figure 4.6, the weekly rhythm of mood was found both for students who are relatively shy and tense (introverted) and for more relaxed and outgoing students (extroverted), but the weekly pattern was a little stronger for the introverted students who were less happy overall. So, are Mondays blue? Apparently for many people they are less happy than weekends, although for most people, they don't dip into the "unpleasant" range. Perhaps knowing this fact will help us all take Mondays a little less seriously.

Review

Each night, we depart the world of waking consciousness and enter another world that we scarcely remember the next morning. Alternating among periods of sleep that contain no conscious experience, we live a life of dreams that are accompanied by a flurry of activity in the body. When studied systematically, much of the content of dreams is found to reflect daily events and concerns. Still, the meaning of dreams has long fascinated us and played a major role in Freud's attempts to understand the hidden workings of the mind. Sleep eludes some of us for part of the night, or is troubled in some other way—the sleep disorders. The daily rhythm of sleep and wakefulness is only one of numerous natural rhythms that tend to follow daily, weekly, or annual patterns.

Thinking Critically About Psychology

1. Why do you think we dream?

2. What does research on sleep-wake cycles suggest about being at your best when taking a test?

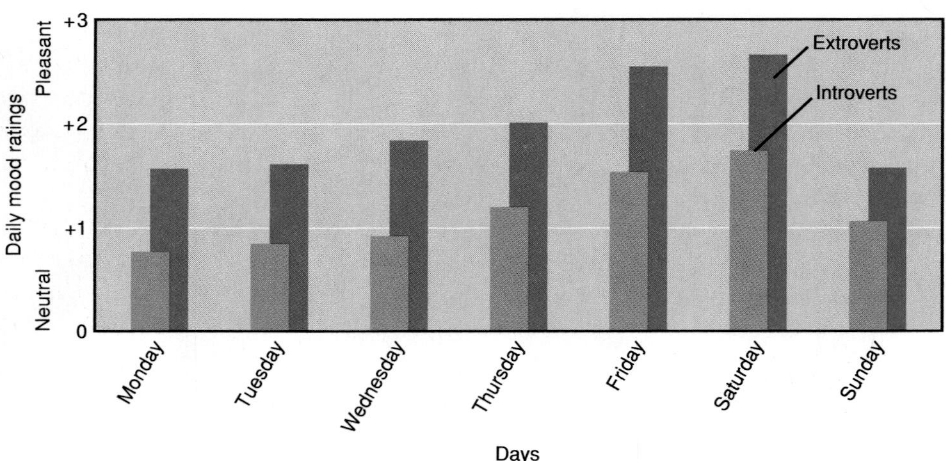

FIGURE 4.6

Average mood ratings of college students on different days of the week. A weekly rhythm of mood can be seen for both shy, tense, students (introverts) and outgoing, relaxed students (extroverts).

Source: Data from R. J. Larsen and M. Kasimatis, "Individual Differences in Entrainment of Mood to the Weekly Calendar" in *Journal of Personality and Social Psychology,* 58:168, © 1990 by the American Psychological Association.

Check Your Learning

To be sure that you have learned the key points from the preceding section, cover the answers below and try to answer each question. If you give an incorrect answer to any question, return to the page given next to the correct answer to see why your answer was not correct.

1. Research suggests that ________________ may be the most important components of sleep because subjects deprived of this type of sleep were irritable, inefficient, and fatigued.

a. hypnagogic sleep
b. myoclonia and REM sleep
c. REM sleep and deep sleep
d. naps

2. According to Freud, the ________________, or true meaning of dreams, reveal(s) hidden conflicts and motives in the unconscious mind.

a. latent content
b. manifest content
c. events
d. colors

3. ________________ is a rare sleep disorder in which the person suddenly falls asleep during activities usually performed when fully awake, such as during conversations with others.

a. Sleep apnea
b. Insomnia
c. Epilepsy
d. Narcolepsy

4. Body temperature and hormones such as cortisol follow a ________________, or daily cycle linked to the sleep cycle.

Correct Answers

1. c (p. 147), **2.** a (p. 147), **3.** d (p. 149), **4.** circadian rhythm (p. 149).

ALTERED STATES OF CONSCIOUSNESS

Thus far, we have talked about states of consciousness with which we are all familiar. We all know what it feels like to think about a problem, to dream, to let our minds wander. Next we turn to more unusual and less familiar realms of conscious experience, the so-called altered states of consciousness. We begin by looking at some general characteristics of altered states of consciousness.

There are many kinds of altered states of consciousness that differ from one another in important ways. Yet these altered states—whether they occur during meditation, when taking drugs, during an unusually intense sexual orgasm, or during a moment of religious conversion—have been described as having a number of characteristics in common (Deikman, 1980; Pahnke, 1980; Tart, 1975):

1. *Distortions of perception.* In altered states of consciousness, distortions often occur in what is seen, heard, and felt. Time passes differently, and the body may seem distorted—indeed, the body may even seem to have been left behind and observed from the outside.
2. *Intense positive emotions.* People who have experienced altered states of consciousness frequently describe them as joyful, ecstatic, loving, and tranquil experiences.
3. *Sense of unity.* Individuals often experience a sense of being unified with nature, blended with the universe, or "one" with a spiritual force.
4. *Illogical.* Many of the experiences and "revelations" of the altered states of consciousness do not make sense by the standards of everyday logic. For example, the experience that "I exist as a separate person, yet I am one with the universe" is typical of altered states.
5. *Indescribable.* Individuals who have experienced altered states of consciousness usually feel that words cannot adequately express the nature of their experience. Our languages may not have words for many of the qualities of the experience, but the difficulty also may come from trying to describe illogical experiences with language.
6. *Transcendent.* The altered states are experienced as transcending—going beyond—what is normally experienced. In particular, the individual may experience a new perspective that goes beyond ordinary conceptions of space and time limitations.
7. *Self-evident reality.* New revelations and insights are experienced that concern "ultimate reality" and are felt to be "real" in a way that requires no proof. The insight is intuitively and immediately understood as the truth; it requires no explanation or justification.

Given these qualities—particularly the euphoric emotionality of experiencing self-evident revelations—it may be wise to state the obvious here. Our evaluation of the insights obtained through altered states of consciousness clearly depends on the perspective we take. From the standpoint of a logical science, we can only say that altered states of consciousness are different from everyday waking consciousness. No claims can be made that one "reality" is more "real" than another. From the perspective of those who have experienced the "self-evident reality" of altered states, however, our everyday reality is often seen as false. Who is right? It depends on which perspective you believe is correct; it is a question for philosophy, not science.

Meditation

Although most of us think of waking consciousness as the normal state, others seek a different, more "perfect" state. One method of searching for an alternative to waking consciousness is **meditation.** This was a popular exercise in the United States during the 1960s and 1970s and continues to be somewhat popular today. Its popularity in the Western world is dwarfed, however, because meditation is an important part of Zen Buddhism and other religions for many tens of millions of Asians.

meditation
(med´´i-tā-shun) Several methods of focusing concentration away from thoughts and feelings and generating a sense of relaxation.

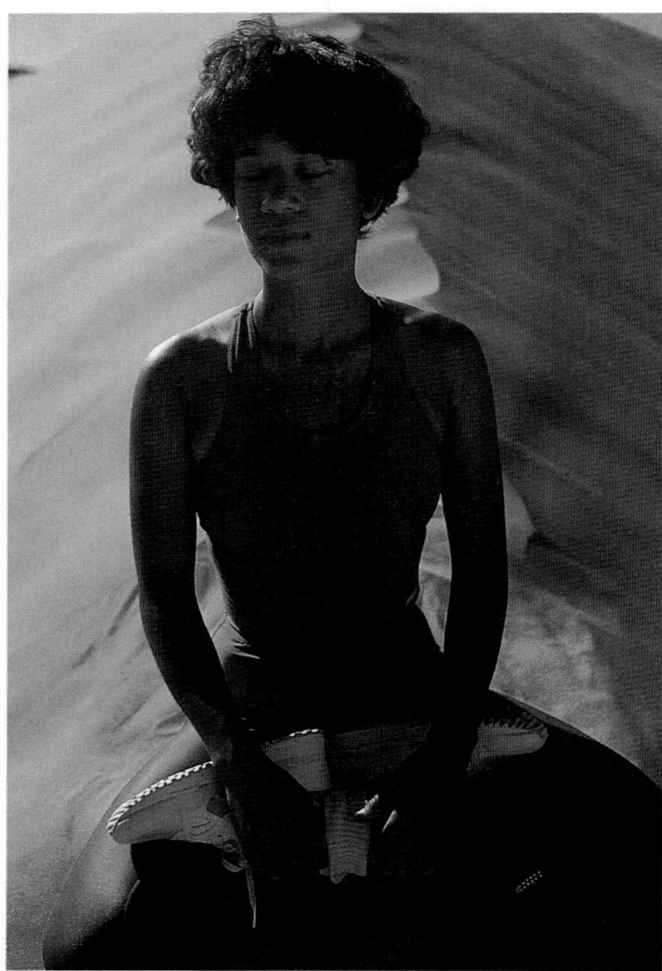

Many persons achieve altered states of consciousness and deep relaxation through meditation.

There are many varieties of meditation, some very difficult to master and others much simpler. In its simplest form, meditation involves assuming a relaxed sitting or lying position and breathing deeply, slowly, and rhythmically. Attention is directed only at the breathing movements of the diaphragm, and all other thoughts and feelings are gently blocked from consciousness. Although this feat is very difficult to accomplish at first, if you do not pressure yourself, it becomes easier with practice. In some forms of meditation, the individual also repeats a sound or word silently to himself or herself. These words often have special religious meaning **(mantra),** but researchers have found that any pleasant sound or word (such as calm or one) has the same effect of further focusing attention away from thoughts and feelings (Benson, 1975).

Once mastered, the practice of meditation can produce what many describe as a desirable altered state of consciousness. If nothing else, meditation generally produces a relaxed state (Beiman, Majestic, Johnson, Puente, & Graham, 1976). Some experienced meditators also report achieving an altered state of consciousness—the so-called **transcendental state**—that is very different from normal consciousness.

Because the state of meditation often involves a reduction in sympathetic autonomic arousal (Wallace & Benson, 1972) meditation has been prescribed for more than 20 years as a "natural remedy" for stress-related medical problems ranging from high blood pressure to insomnia. As a result, many thousands of individuals practice meditation in the belief that it counteracts the physiological effects of stress. Is this assumption correct? Does meditation beneficially dampen sympathetic autonomic arousal?

In a cogent review of research on this topic, psychologist David Holmes (1984) argues that teaching individuals to meditate does not lead to greater reductions in blood pressure, heart rate, oxygen consumption, general muscle tension, skin sweat, or any other measure of sympathetic arousal than that produced by simple relaxation. Other researchers, however, suggest that the form of meditation called transcendental meditation produces greater reductions in anxiety and stress-related medical illness than other forms of meditation or relaxation (Eppley, Abrams, & Spear, 1989; Orme-Johnson, 1987). As a result, there is not a consensus in the scientific community regarding the benefits of meditation at this time.

mantra
(man´trah) A word or sound containing religious meaning used during meditation.

transcendental state
An altered state of consciousness, sometimes achieved during meditation, that is said to transcend normal human experience.

Hypnosis

A person who has been hypnotized can sometimes be so convinced that she is standing in a snowstorm without a coat that she shivers. Similarly, a hypnotist can tell a hypnotized person he is going back to his fourth birthday party and watch him act like he is playing with other 4-year-olds. People who have been hypnotized like this often tell us that they actually felt the cold wind and believed that they had reexperienced the birthday party. What is it about this state of **hypnosis** that makes it so fascinatingly different from waking consciousness?

hypnosis
(hip-nō´sis) An altered state of consciousness in which the individual is highly relaxed and susceptible to suggestions.

The person becoming hypnotized focuses his or her attention firmly on the hypnotist's voice and is talked and lulled into an altered state of consciousness. This hypnotic state differs from individual to individual but typically has the following characteristics:

1. *Relaxation.* A sense of deep relaxation and peacefulness exists, often accompanied by changes in the way the body feels, such as floating, sinking, and shrinking.
2. *Hypnotic hallucinations.* When told to do so, the person may see, feel, or hear things in distorted ways, or may even experience things that are not there, such as smelling a flower that does not exist.

3. *Hypnotic analgesia.* When told to do so, the person may lose the sense of touch or pain in some region of the body. This is one of the best validated aspects of hypnosis and has led to the use of hypnosis in surgery, dentistry, and childbirth (Harmon, Hyan, & Tyre, 1990; Hilgard, 1978; Miller & Bowers, 1993; Price & Barber, 1987).
4. *Hypnotic age regression.* The person can sometimes be made to feel that he or she is passing back in time to an earlier stage of life, but most experts do not believe that hypnosis improves the recall of childhood events (Kirsch & Lynn, 1995).
5. *Hypnotic control.* The actions of hypnotized individuals sometimes seem as if they are out of their own control. When told that her arm can float, a hypnotized person's arm may seem to float up as if it were lifted by invisible balloons rather than by her own muscles (Bowers, 1976).

What is the nature of this altered state of consciousness? To understand it best, we should look briefly at the fascinating history of hypnosis.

A person being hypnotized focuses attention firmly on the hypnotist's voice and is lulled into an altered state of consciousness.

Mesmer and Mesmerism

Franz Anton Mesmer was a practicing physician in Paris in the late 1700s. Although he was trained in classical medicine, his medical practice was decidedly unusual—so unusual that he had earlier been driven from his native Austria by the medical establishment for alleged "quackery." He treated patients with medical or psychological problems in what he called *magnetic seances.* Mesmer believed that all living bodies were filled with magnetic energy and that diseases resulted when these magnetic forces were out of balance. His treatment, therefore, consisted of passing his hands, which he believed had become magnetized, over the afflicted part of the patient's body and having the patient touch metal rods that protruded from a large tub. The tub was filled with water, chemicals, ground glass, and iron filings—a mixture that Mesmer thought created magnetism.

What Mesmer actually created, however, was something quite different—an atmosphere that induced a mysterious and powerful hypnotic trance. He entered the darkened and silent room wearing flowing lilac-colored robes. He lulled his patients into a deep state of relaxation and made them believe deeply in his healing powers; that is, he *hypnotized* them. He told them that their problems would go away, and some of them did. The process of putting people into hypnotic trances came to be known for many years as *mesmerism.* Only much later was it referred to as hypnosis.

In recent years, hypnotism has been intensively studied, and understood to some extent. It took psychologists a long time to decide that it was respectable to study a phenomenon with such a shady and controversial past, but in the past 20 years, hypnosis has finally seen the hard light of scientific inquiry (Barber, 1969; Bowers, 1976; Crasilneck & Hall, 1985; Miller & Bowers, 1993; Allen, Iacono, Laravuso, & Dunn, 1995). Psychologists are still not in agreement on how to characterize hypnosis, however. Theodore Barber (Barber & Wilson, 1977; Kirsch & Lynn, 1995) suggests that hypnosis should not be thought of as a "trance" but as a highly relaxed state in which the person's conscious awareness is highly focused, imagination is intensified, and the person is highly susceptible to the instructions of the hypnotist. Ernest Hilgard (1975), in contrast, believes that hypnosis is based on divided consciousness (see p. 139). According to Hilgard, individuals can, for example, experience a loss of pain through hypnosis because that part of consciousness can be separated from waking consciousness.

In recent years hypnosis has gained limited acceptance by the medical and dental professions for the relief of pain through hypnotic analgesia (Price & Barber, 1987). For example, patients who could not use analgesic medications for a variety of reasons have been able to have extensive operations or undergo childbirth under hypnosis with little or no pain (Harmon et al., 1990; Hilgard & Hilgard, 1975).

Depersonalization

depersonalization
(dē-per´sun-al-i-zā´-shun) The perceptual experience of one's body or surroundings becoming distorted or unreal in some way.

Not all altered states of consciousness occur when we are striving to attain them; some occur quite spontaneously. This section describes one of the more common of these experiences. The term **depersonalization** refers to the perceptual experience of one's body becoming "distorted" or "unreal" in some way, or the sense of strange distortions in one's surroundings. Although very bizarre, such experiences are not necessarily abnormal or even uncommon among young adults. British researchers interviewed 891 university students and found 76 who had experienced depersonalization. Excerpts from the accounts of a number of different students help to portray these experiences (Myers & Grant, 1972):

> I felt slightly unreal and as though I wasn't part of my surroundings, but watching from a distance; my voice sounded strange to me and did not seem to be part of me.
>
> The feeling of not belonging to my body but being outside it.
>
> I do not feel the sensation of it being my hand; it is something else which is there but nothing to do with me.
>
> I suddenly felt that I was really behind myself, not watching myself but detached from everything including my body to some extent.
>
> My mother and I were walking towards each other from opposite ends of a street, and I suddenly felt an odd sense of estrangement, as if I had never seen her face in my life before.
>
> I felt disembodied . . . only my mind seemed to exist . . . I would have to pinch myself to reassure myself that I did exist. (p. 60)

Suppose that this afternoon you feel as if your mind is leaving your body and floating up to the ceiling where it watches you. Does this mean you have gone crazy? Have you had a psychic or religious experience? Depersonalization experiences sometimes include the illusion that the mind has left the body and traveled about in a so-called out-of-body experience, or **astral projection.** When such experiences are recurrent, they may be an indication of psychological problems, but isolated experiences seem to be quite normal, even if somewhat unnerving.

astral projection
(as´tral) Depersonalization that includes the illusion that the mind has left the body.

Near-Death Experiences

In the past few decades, information has become available on the experience of nearly dying. Not surprisingly, many of these reports describe such experiences in religious terms. Our purpose in describing near-death experiences is to see how they relate to the other altered states of consciousness that we have just examined. Recent developments in medicine have made it possible in some instances to bring people who are "clinically dead" back to life. Stopped hearts can sometimes be started again. Interviews have been conducted with these individuals by psychiatrist Raymond Moody (1976) to gain an understanding of what the moment of death feels like. His findings are impressive because these individuals, even though they had no contact with one another and had never heard of another person's experience with death, reported similar experiences. It must be kept in mind, however, that they were not "dead" at all in the sense that their brains ceased to function, and it is difficult to know how much they were affected by drugs given to them during their medical crises. But even if these interviews only give us tentative information about the moment just *before* death—and can therefore shed no light on the existence of an afterlife—they are still fascinating.

The individuals who had "died" typically reported the following sequence of events. First, their heads were filled with a pleasant, sometimes musical ringing or buzzing sound. Next, they sensed their minds or "spirits" separated from their bodies. Sometimes they were able to watch the physician trying to revive them, but more often they felt that they were being transported quickly away from their bodies. This was experienced as moving through what felt like a long tunnel. At first, the experience of dying was an unpleasant one as the individual fearfully fought death. But a sense of peace soon settled over them. Many individuals reported seeing the spirits of dead loved ones while passing through the tunnel and in time, the tunnel brightened and a shining God-like spirit of love was felt at the end of the tunnel. But at this point all of the interviewed individuals returned to normal "living" as their hearts were restarted.

More recently, nationally known pollster George Gallup reported the results of a survey of individuals who had nearly died but had been revived following sudden accidents (Gallup & Proctor, 1982). The near-death experiences reported by these individuals were considerably less similar to one another than the ones described by Moody (1976), but quite a number of Gallup's interviewees did report experiences like the ones just described. What do you think? Did these individuals experience death, or did they just have a depersonalization experience when their hearts stopped pumping oxygen to their brains?

Review

Sometimes a kind of consciousness is experienced that is greatly different from normal waking consciousness. These altered states of consciousness may be unwelcome and upsetting occurrences (as with depersonalization), but others are intentionally induced through meditation and hypnosis. Meditation produces a transcendent sense of relaxation that is helpful in combating stress; and hypnosis has been found to be useful in relieving pain under some circumstances. Near-death experiences are fascinating events that are similar in form to depersonalization experiences.

Thinking Critically About Psychology

1. Why do you think hypnosis is not more widely used in our society as a substitute for anesthesia in surgery?

2. What has been your experience with altered states of consciousness? How would you describe them in terms of current scientific explanations?

Check Your Learning

To be sure that you have learned the key points from the preceding section, cover the answers below and try to answer each question. If you give an incorrect answer to any question, return to the page given next to the correct answer to see why your answer was not correct.

1. ____________________ is the focusing of conscious awareness away from thoughts and feelings and generating a sense of deep relaxation.

- **a.** Sleep
- **b.** Depersonalization
- **c.** Hallucination
- **d.** Meditation

2. One of the first persons to use what is now called hypnosis was ____________, who used it while treating patients in so-called "magnetic seances."

- **a.** Ernest Hilgard
- **b.** Franz Anton Mesmer
- **c.** Sigmund Freud
- **d.** David Holmes

3. ____________________ refers to the perceptual experience of one's body becoming "distorted" or "unreal" in some way, or the sense of strange distortions in one's surroundings.

- **a.** Meditation
- **b.** Psychosis
- **c.** Depersonalization
- **d.** Hypnosis

Correct Answers

1. d (p. 153), **2.** b (p. 155), **3.** c (p. 156).

ALTERING CONSCIOUSNESS WITH DRUGS

Up to this point we have been discussing altered states of consciousness that are "natural" in the sense that they can be experienced by anyone without artificial inducements. Perhaps the most distinctly different types of altered consciousness, however, involve taking chemicals into the body—using drugs. Specifically, we are talking about **psychotropic drugs,** a class of drugs that alters conscious experience. These drugs exert their effects by

psychotropic drugs
(sī´´-ko-trop´pik) The class of drugs that alters conscious experience.

influencing specific neurotransmitters in the brain, or by chemically altering the action of neurons in other ways. The range of effects of psychotropic drugs is enormous, from mild relaxation to vivid hallucinations. Perhaps even more enormous than the range of their effects, however, is the frequency of their use in contemporary society.

Psychotropic drugs can be divided into four major categories. *Stimulants* are drugs that increase the activity of motivational centers of the central nervous system, providing a sense of energy and well-being. *Depressants* reduce the activity of inhibitory centers of the central nervous system, leading to a sense of relaxation and lowered inhibitions. *Hallucinogens* produce dreamlike alterations in perceptual experience. *Inhalants* are common household chemicals that are put to dangerous use by being inhaled, which produces feelings of intoxication. Not fitting easily into this classification is the drug marijuana, which induces a relaxed sense of well-being in most persons. Common members of these classes of drugs are summarized in table 4.1. Their patterns of use will be discussed in the section that follows. We will begin with a section that focuses on illegal drugs and frequently abused prescription drugs. The Application of Psychology section at the end of this chapter will cover the most commonly used legal consciousness-altering drugs: alcohol, caffeine, and nicotine.

Drug Use: Some Basic Considerations

Although the effects of psychotropic drugs are quite varied, we need to consider a number of issues that are relevant to all of them. These issues include the wide variation in responses to drugs and the problems that are associated with their use.

Variable Response to Drugs

In the sections that follow, we look at the psychological effects of a number of widely used drugs. In discussing these effects, we must keep in mind that the effects drugs have on us

TABLE 4.1 Major psychotropic drugs.

Depressants	Stimulants	Hallucinogens
Tranquilizers Equanil (meprobamate) Librium (chlordiazepoxide) Miltown (meprobamate) Valium (diazepam) Xanax (alprazolam) Narcotics Opiates (opium and its derivatives) Codeine Heroin Morphine Opium Synthetic narcotics Demerol Methadone Percodan Sedatives Alcohol (ethanol) Barbiturates Nembutal (pentobarbital) Quaalude (methaqualone) Seconal (secobarbital) Tuinal (secobarbital and amobarbital) Veronal (barbital)	Amphetamines Benzedrine (amphetamine) Dexedrine (dextroamphetamine) Methedrine (methamphetamine) Cocaine Caffeine (in coffee, tea, and colas) Nicotine (in tobacco)	LSD (lysergic acid diethylamide–25) Mescaline (peyote) PCP (phencyclidine hydrochloride) Psilocybin (psychotogenic mushrooms)
	Inhalants (volatile hydrocarbons)	**Marijuana Family**
	Cleaning fluids Gasoline Glue Nail-polish remover (acetone) Paint thinner	Marijuana Hashish

are far from perfectly reliable and predictable. Many factors influence the individual's response to a drug; most important among them are:

1. *Dose and purity.* Obviously the amount of the drug taken will influence its effect. Less obvious is the fact that drugs purchased on the street are often cut (mixed) with other substances that can alter the effects of the drug.
2. *Personal characteristics.* The weight, health, age, and even the personality of the person taking a drug can influence the drug's effect.
3. *Expectations.* The effect that we expect a drug to have, based on our own past experiences and what we have heard from others, will partly determine the effect of the drug.
4. *Social situation.* Other people influence our response to the drug; we may respond differently if the drug is taken alone versus in the midst of an upbeat party.
5. *Moods.* The mood that the person is in at the time of taking the drug can dramatically alter its effects. Alcohol, for example, can make a happy person happier, a sad person more depressed, and can unleash violence in an angry individual.

When you consider the interplay of these factors, it's easy to see how their effects are at least partly unpredictable.

Problems Associated with Drug Use

The use of drugs to alter conscious experience carries with it certain risks. These risks differ considerably from drug to drug, but the risks associated with all drugs involve the same basic issues.

1. *Drug abuse.* A drug is being abused if taking it causes some kind of physical damage (as in liver damage caused by alcohol) or impairment of psychological or social functioning (as in frequent drinking of alcohol leading to marital conflicts).
2. *Psychological dependence.* A psychological dependence has been developed when the individual needs to use the drug regularly to maintain a comfortable psychological state, as when a person gets edgy if she or he does not smoke marijuana daily.
3. *Physiological addiction, tolerance, and withdrawal.* Many drugs quickly become involved in the chemical functioning of the individual's body. The body chemistry adjusts to accept the drug into it to such a degree that when the drug is not present, the body cannot function properly and the person experiences painful *withdrawal* symptoms. Addictive drugs produce progressively stronger addiction because over time the body learns to adapt more easily to the drug in its system. As *tolerance* for the drug increases, larger doses are needed to produce the same effect on consciousness. Therefore, the addicted person's body chemistry becomes progressively more tied to the drug.
4. *Direct side effects.* The direct dangers of drugs that we have just described are not the only risks associated with their use. Psychotropic drugs rarely have effects that are limited to a single neurotransmitter or organ system. They often have powerful and potentially serious *side effects.* Some of these are merely annoyances, such as the temporary numbness in the throat caused by inhaling cocaine, while others are far more serious. Brain damage, heart attacks, loss of control of automobiles, violence, and suicide are only some of the common side effects of psychotropic drugs.
5. *Indirect side effects.* It has recently become clear that drugs are not only dangerous due to their direct psychological and medical side effects but because of their indirect effects as well. The obvious example is the greatly increased risk of infection with hepatitis or human immunodeficiency virus (HIV), which causes acquired immune deficiency syndrome (AIDS), as a result of sharing

needles used for drug injection. Many drugs, however, result in slower and less immediately obvious impairment of immune system functioning that increases the risk of serious disease.

Psychotropic Drugs

Many consciousness-altering drugs are used and abused today. The drugs described in the following paragraphs are powerful in their effects, are often powerfully addictive, and are used illegally in most circumstances.

Stimulants

stimulants
Drugs that increase the activity of the central nervous system, providing a sense of energy and well-being.

amphetamines
(am-fet´ah-minz) Powerful stimulants that produce a conscious sense of increased energy and a euphoric high.

Stimulants, often called *uppers,* are drugs that activate the central nervous system. *Caffeine,* which is found in coffee, tea, soft drinks, and some nonprescription medicines, and *nicotine,* which is found in cigarettes and other tobacco products, are by far the most widely used stimulants. As described later, these relatively mild stimulants are, nonetheless, extremely addictive and pose major health risks.

Amphetamines (trade names Dexedrine, Benzedrine, and Methedrine) are stimulant drugs that generally produce a conscious sense of increased energy, alertness, enthusiasm, and a euphoric high. They are not physically addictive but produce rapid and intense psychological dependence. Hence, the possibility for abuse is very high. The amphetamines are dangerous physically, particularly in their effects on the heart. Psychologically, the greatest risk is known as **amphetamine psychosis**—a prolonged reaction to excessive use of stimulants characterized by distorted thinking, confused and rapidly changing emotions, and intense suspiciousness.

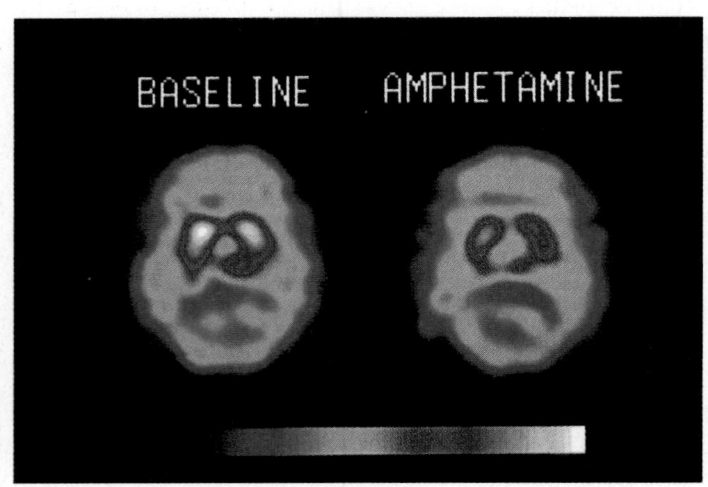

This is an image of a human brain (baseline, on left). On the right is a human brain on amphetamine. The change in color shows a profound change in the limbic system.

Source: Tamminga, C. A. (1996). Images in neuroscience: Neuroimaging, XIII. *American Journal of Psychiatry, 153,* 1249.

The use of amphetamines in the United States was on the decline until the late 1980s, particularly use of the dangerous form of amphetamine known as *methamphetamine,* or *speed.* Apparently word had gotten around the street that "speed kills." But, unfortunately, when the street name for methamphetamine changed to "crystal" and "crystal meth," the bad reputation that speed had earned for serious psychological and medical side effects was lost. Today this white powder—which is usually sniffed but is also swallowed or injected—is used in virtually epidemic proportions in some areas of the country.

Cocaine is one of the more widely abused drugs in the United States. Cocaine, a stimulant much like amphetamine, is made from the leaves of the coca plant. It is taken in many forms but is most commonly inhaled as a powder, injected, or smoked in the dangerously powerful form known as crack. Cocaine produces alertness, high energy, optimism, self-confidence, happiness, exhilaration, and talkativeness. It raises body temperature, breathing, and heart rate and reduces the desire for food and sleep.

amphetamine psychosis
(sī-kō´sis) A prolonged reaction to the excessive use of stimulants, characterized by disordered thinking, confused and rapidly changing emotions, and intense suspiciousness.

Because the cocaine high only lasts a matter of minutes, its use is often repeated each time the effect wears off. These binges of repeated cocaine use sometimes last for hours or even days, until a state of exhaustion is reached. At this point, the cocaine user *crashes,* feeling immensely tired, hungry, and in need of long periods of sleep. In the first few days following a cocaine binge, the user is absolutely miserable. Depression, agitation, confusion, paranoia, anger, and exhaustion are all part of the cocaine crash (Weddington et al., 1990).

Repeated cocaine use rapidly leads to addiction because of the way in which it exerts its effect on the brain. Like most consciousness-altering drugs, cocaine passes into the brain in the fluids that bathe the neurons. Here, they alter the functioning of the brain by influencing neurotransmission at the synapse. Cocaine does not chemically interact with the neurotransmitters themselves but interferes with one part of a synaptic transmission for a class of neurotransmitters called *catecholamines* (Pearlson et al., 1993). After the neurotrans-

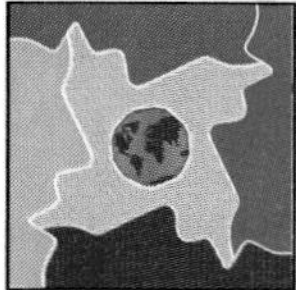

HUMAN DIVERSITY

Substance Abuse and Human Diversity

Without doubt, drug and alcohol abuse is a major problem in the United States. A recent large-scale study of the U.S. population (Kessler et al., 1993) found that 25 percent of adolescents and adults have had a substance abuse problem at some time in their lifetime—that's one person out of every four! Alcohol abuse alone cost the country an estimated $10 billion in 1991 in terms of lost work time, accidents, increased medical costs, and other economic costs (Heien & Pittman, 1993), but the human cost of drug and alcohol abuse is much greater.

Who abuses drugs and alcohol in our society? Gender, ethnicity, and income level are important factors that influence the likelihood of substance abuse. Men consistently have been found to be twice as likely to abuse substances as women. The problem is very serious among women, but substance abuse is much more widespread among men.

In terms of ethnicity, African American have been found to be 35 percent less likely to abuse drugs and alcohol than both whites and Hispanics, but the rates of substance abuse of whites and Hispanics do not differ (Kessler et al., 1993). Apparently, there are cultural traditions in the African-American community that protect against substance abuse. The lower rates of substance abuse among African Americans—which has been found in several U.S. surveys—are even more striking when findings for education and income level are considered. Persons with less education who earn less money in the United States are more likely to abuse substances than persons with more money. Thus, even though African Americans tend to earn less money, on the average, than white Americans in the United States at this time in history, their rates of substance abuse are much lower. The protective influence of ethnicity is so strong that it counters the trends associated with income and education.

It is important to understand the ways in which human diversity—gender, ethnicity, and education and income level—are linked to substance abuse. We will not fully understand the causes of substance abuse until we understand why women, African Americans, and the affluent are so much less likely to abuse drugs and alcohol.

It is equally important to remember to treat everyone as an *individual,* however. Although African-American women from high-income families are at the lowest risk for substance abuse, some members of this select group have serious substance abuse problems. Similarly, most low-income white males have no difficulties with drugs and alcohol whatsoever.

Why do you think persons with low income and little education are more likely to abuse substances? What makes men more likely to abuse drugs and alcohol than women? In your opinion, why are African Americans at less risk for the abuse of these substances? Could the answers to those questions be used to reduce everyone's risk for substance abuse? Many hundreds of researchers in psychology and psychiatry are actively at work today trying to answer these important questions.

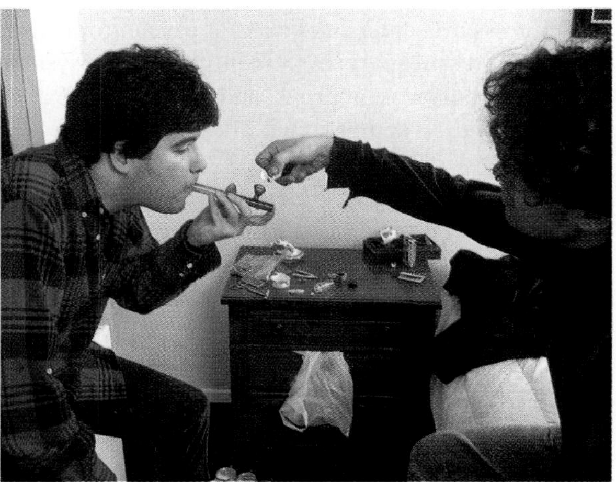

Cocaine was originally an ingredient of Coca-Cola at a time when use of the drug was legal. It is now an illicit stimulant, which can lead to dependence on the drug whether snorted or smoked in the form of crack.

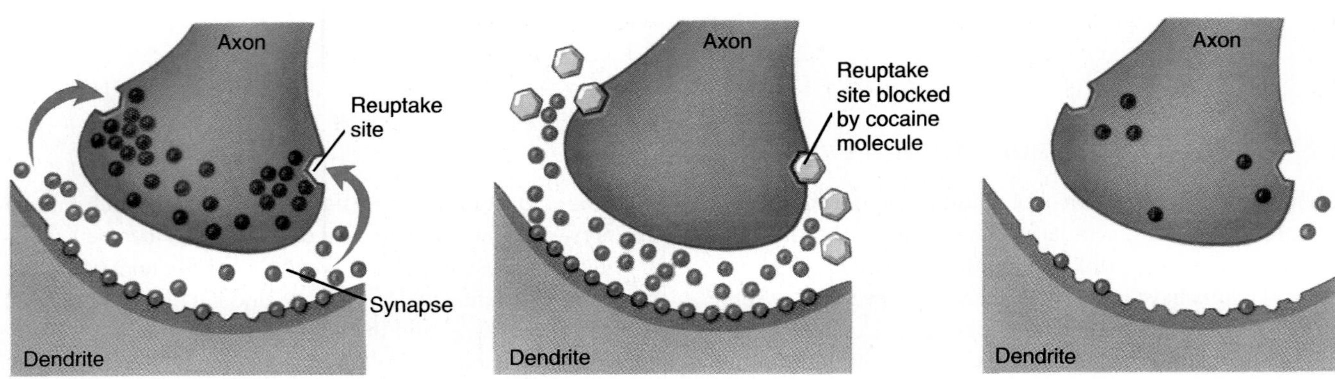

FIGURE 4.7
The steps in cocaine dependence looked at from the point of view of changes in the transmission of neural messages across the synapse.

mitter is secreted from the axon, a large part of it is absorbed back into the axon to be used again—a process called *reuptake* (see fig. 4.7). However, cocaine blocks the reuptake openings and prevents the reabsorption of the neurotransmitter by the axon. This means that the neurotransmitter stays in the synapse longer than normal and continues to stimulate the dendrite of the next neuron. This is how cocaine has its stimulating effect. However, after a while, the inability of the axon to reabsorb the neurotransmitter means that it "runs low" on it and the individual crashes into a postcocaine depression. This state, unfortunately, increases the craving for cocaine, and the relief that is felt when cocaine is next used results in a rapid addiction to the substance (Cooper, Bloom, & Roth, 1986).

Withdrawal from cocaine addiction differs considerably from withdrawal from heroin or nicotine addiction, especially in the absence of changes in heart rate and blood pressure, the absence of chills and sweats, and the absence of physical pain. The intense depression, agitation, and craving for cocaine during withdrawal is a mean and miserable monkey on the back of the cocaine addict, however. Although the craving diminishes as the crash wears off, it returns when the person is exposed to cocaine again, or to the people and places that are associated with cocaine use. Going straight after becoming dependent on cocaine is an enormous challenge, although it is one that can be met by genuinely motivated persons given proper treatment (Weddington et al., 1990).

Cocaine is dangerous even to the occasional user. Even small doses can lead to fatal heart attacks, and because tolerance for cocaine varies considerably, it is dangerously easy for experienced occasional users to accidentally overdose. Ironically, cocaine was once a legal drug in the United States. Coca-Cola, originally marketed as a "nerve tonic," initially contained cocaine as part of its "secret formula." In 1906 the cocaine was replaced by the milder stimulant caffeine.

Depressants

depressants
Drugs that reduce the activity of the central nervous system, leading to a sense of relaxation, drowsiness, and lowered inhibitions.

sedatives
Depressants that in mild doses produce a state of calm relaxation.

The **depressants** are a large class of psychotropic drugs that influence conscious experience by depressing parts of the central nervous system. Tranquilizers, sedatives, and narcotics are all depressant drugs, and as we will see at the end of this chapter, alcohol is the most widely used depressant of all.

Sedatives and tranquilizers. **Sedatives,** often called **downers,** are depressants that in mild doses generally produce a state of calm relaxation. They are prescribed in the United States as drugs to aid sleep and sometimes to combat anxiety. Common trade names for these drugs are Seconal, Tuinal, Nembutal, and Quaaludes (which are no longer sold in the United States but are still abused). Because they are highly addictive and dangerous to withdraw from without medical supervision and because overdoses are highly dangerous (and even small doses are dangerous when taken with alcohol), they are prescribed by physicians less frequently now than in the past. They are still widely abused through illegal drug markets.

Tranquilizers are milder drugs that are similar to sedatives in that they typically produce a sense of calm relaxation for a brief period of time. As such, they are often prescribed to reduce anxiety. Common trade names are Xanax, Valium, Librium, Ativan, Miltown, and Equanil. Like sedatives, most are dangerously addictive, often difficult to withdraw from, and are very dangerous when mixed with alcohol; they must be taken with great care. Also like sedatives, these types of downers are widely sold illegally.

Narcotics. **Narcotics** are powerful and highly addictive depressants. The use of the narcotic drug opium derived from the opium poppy dates back at least 7,000 years in the Middle East. Derivatives of opium, including morphine, heroin, and codeine, are powerful narcotic drugs that dramatically alter consciousness. They generally relieve pain and induce a sudden, rushing high, followed by a relaxed, lethargic drowsiness. Narcotics create a powerful physiological addiction very rapidly. With prolonged addiction, the physical effects on the body are profoundly damaging. Compared with other drugs, narcotic use in the United States is not high, but the drastic effects of opiates, including the crimes that many addicts commit to maintain their increasingly expensive habits, make it an extremely significant drug abuse problem. It became an especially difficult problem during the Vietnam War. Perhaps due to a combination of its availability and the stress of war, it was estimated that 20 percent of all Vietnam veterans tried heroin at least once (Harris, 1973).

narcotics
Powerful and highly addictive depressants.

Opium and its derivatives (the **opiates**) are not the only kinds of narcotic drugs. In recent years, synthetic narcotics have been artificially produced in drug laboratories. These synthetic narcotics include widely used painkilling drugs with trade names such as Demerol, Percodan, and Methadone.

opiates
(ō´pē-ats) Narcotic drugs derived from the opium poppy.

Inhalants

Substances that when inhaled produce a sense of intoxication are called **inhalants.** To produce a "high," toxic (poisonous) substances such as glue, cleaning fluid, paint, and so on are typically placed in paper bags and inhaled ("sniffed"). This type of intoxication is common among children because the materials are relatively easy to obtain. This is particularly sad, because inhalants are highly addictive and extremely dangerous. These toxic fumes often cause permanent brain damage and other serious complications.

inhalants
(in-hā´lants) Toxic substances that produce a sense of intoxication when inhaled.

Hallucinogens

The drugs that most powerfully alter consciousness are **hallucinogens** such as lysergic acid diethylamide (LSD), mescaline (derived from the peyote cactus), and psilocybin (derived from a kind of mushroom). These drugs typically alter perceptual experiences, but only large doses cause vivid hallucinations. In these unusual states, the drugged individual experiences imaginary visions and realities that, ironically, sometimes seem more "real" to the drug user than waking consciousness. This latter fact, however, may be more attributable to the drug taker's dissatisfaction with everyday life than to the powers of the drug itself.

hallucinogens
(hah-lū´si´´no-jenz) Drugs that alter perceptual experiences.

The hallucinogens are generally not physiologically addictive, but individuals can quickly become psychologically dependent on them. In addition, while many of the drug-induced states (trips) produced by hallucinogens are experienced as pleasant, "bad trips"—frightening and dangerous drug responses—are not uncommon (McWilliams & Tuttle, 1973). Individuals who are frightened about taking the drug but do so because of peer pressure are more likely to experience bad trips. These trips, both good and bad, can sometimes recur in flashbacks without the individual taking the drug again. About 65 percent of flashbacks are bad trips, apparently being triggered by stress or anxiety. About 25 percent of all regular LSD users experience flashbacks, sometimes several months after the original trip (Matefy & Kroll, 1974).

One other hallucinogenic drug needs to be discussed because of its dangers. The drug phencyclidine or PCP (angel dust), which was originally developed as an animal tranquilizer, has come into common use in recent years, especially among adolescents. The effects of PCP typically last from 4 to 6 hours. In some cases, the individual experiences auditory or visual hallucinations, but more likely the experience includes feelings of numbness, lack of muscular coordination, anxiety, and a sense of detachment from the environment. Euphoria, a sense of strength, and "dreaminess" may also be present. The individual on PCP may also engage in unconventional behavior such as going into public places nude. Violent behavior toward others, suicide, and psychotic episodes are other possible reactions to this drug. It's generally considered one of the most dangerous drugs now on the street (Petersen & Stillman, 1978).

Marijuana

Marijuana is a popular consciousness-altering drug that generally produces a sense of relaxation and well-being. In some cases, the drug alters sensory experiences and the perception of time. Not since Prohibition has any drug been so hotly debated or so widely used in spite of being illegal. It's not physically addictive, and in fact many users experience a reverse tolerance, in which smaller amounts of the drug eventually come to produce the same high. However, some psychological dependence is possible. Although the evidence as to possible physical or psychological harm is not conclusive, there is some evidence that prolonged marijuana use decreases the efficiency of cognitive processing, weakens the body's immune response, and decreases the action of male sex hormones (Wallace & Fisher, 1983). Moreover, like smoking any type of cigarette, marijuana increases the risk of lung cancer over time. Driving an automobile or using any other form of machinery when intoxicated by marijuana (or any other substance) is also obviously dangerous.

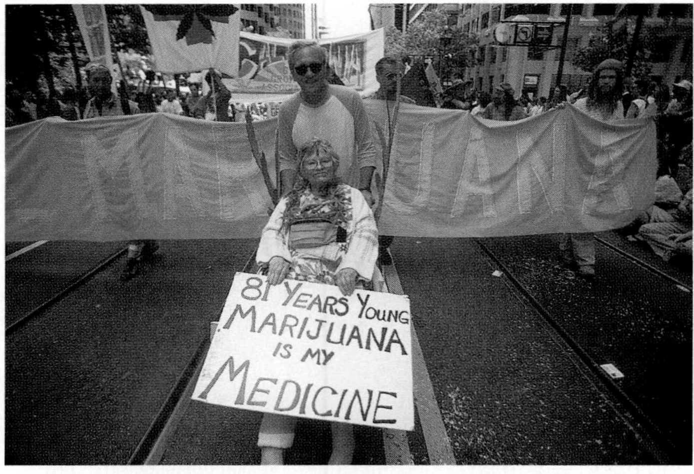

Not since Prohibition has any drug been as hotly debated as marijuana.

Act-Alike and Designer Drugs

Until the 1980s, it was legal in most states to manufacture and sell drugs that looked and acted like illegal substances such as amphetamines but contained only substances that were legal to sell openly. For example, combinations of high doses of powdered caffeine and some over-the-counter decongestants produce some of the effects of amphetamines. Hence, these drugs are sometimes called *act-alike* drugs.

States have had to scramble to find ways to block the sale of act-alike drugs. These drugs are considered dangerous because of their own serious adverse effects; in addition, because the strength of drugs that act like amphetamines varies considerably, the risk of accidental overdose is very high.

Amateur chemists try to stay ahead of the law by designing new drugs that have not yet been classified as illegal—the so-called *designer drugs.* For example, the designer drugs MDA and MDMA (*ecstasy*) are derivatives of amphetamines that produce a dreamlike high lasting for up to 8 hours. Because these substances were legal until identified by law enforcement agencies as narcotics, they could be sold without penalty for a while. But the constant push to design new mind-altering drugs to stay ahead of the law means that new drugs are widely sold and used before anyone has a chance to evaluate their potential side effects. This is a very real concern since any substance powerful enough to change the functioning of the brain generally carries with it serious medical and psychological risks (Carroll, 1989).

Polydrug Abuse

In many ways, the most difficult problem that consciousness-altering drugs present is that there are so many of them. Unfortunately, it's not uncommon for the same individual to abuse many of these drugs at the same time—so-called *polydrug* abuse. This greatly increases the possibilities of addiction and dependence; the chances that the use of drugs will interfere with an individual's adjustment to school, work, or family; and the chances that the drugs will interact chemically to produce toxic effects. The use of any drug carries dangers with it, but polydrug abuse is especially dangerous. Perhaps it is not surprising, therefore, that polydrug abusers have a particularly high rate of previous emotional problems (Halikas & Rimmer, 1974). Polydrug abuse is not a very "sane" thing to do.

Review

Altered states can be induced by taking psychotropic drugs that alter conscious experience by influencing the action of neurons in the brain. These drugs produce changes in consciousness, ranging from mild alterations of mood to vivid hallucinations, but they also carry with them the danger of abuse, dependence, addiction, and direct physical damage in some cases. The effect of drugs on consciousness depends on a variety of factors, including dose and purity; the weight, health, age, and personality of the person taking a drug; expectations about the effects of the drug; the social situation; and the mood that the person is in at the time of taking the drug.

Thinking Critically About Psychology

1. What social and personal factors induce millions of people to abuse drugs despite the publicity regarding the negative effects of drug abuse?

2. Our society makes a distinction between drugs like alcohol or caffeine, which are legal to use, and others such as marijuana or cocaine, which are not. Does this make sense?

Check Your Learning

To be sure that you have learned the key points from the preceding section, cover the answers below and try to answer each question. If you give an incorrect answer to any question, return to the page given next to the correct answer to see why your answer was not correct.

1. Many factors influence an individual's response to a drug, such as the dose and purity of the drug, expectations about the drug, and one's mood, making the response somewhat unpredictable.

- **a.** True
- **b.** False

2. Psychologically, the greatest risk of amphetamine abuse is known as ____________________, which is a prolonged reaction to excessive use of stimulants characterized by distorted thinking, confused and rapidly changing emotions, and intense suspiciousness.

- **a.** schizophrenia
- **b.** amphetamine psychosis
- **c.** overdose
- **d.** withdrawal

3. A long-lasting drug originally developed as an animal tranquilizer that typically produces numbness, lack of muscular coordination, a sense of detachment from the environment, euphoria, a sense of strength, and sometimes results in unconventional, psychotic, or violent behavior is

- **a.** phencyclidine (PCP).
- **b.** amphetamine.
- **c.** cocaine.
- **d.** ecstasy (MDMA).

4. The drugs that most powerfully alter consciousness are __________ such as lysergic acid diethylamide (LSD), mescaline (derived from the peyote cactus), and psilocybin (derived from a kind of mushroom).

- **a.** inhalants
- **b.** stimulants
- **c.** hallucinogens
- **d.** depressants

Correct Answers

1. a (p. 159), **2.** b (p. 160), **3.** a (p. 163), **4.** c (p. 163).

THE LEGAL CONSCIOUSNESS-ALTERING DRUGS

Each day, many of us use consciousness-altering drugs, usually without even being aware that we are taking "drugs." Your coffee contains the stimulant drug, caffeine, cigarettes contain the stimulant drug of nicotine, and alcohol is a powerful depressant drug. Millions of individuals who would never consider using "drugs" use, abuse, or are addicted to these drugs. What are their consciousness-altering effects (and side effects)?

The average American drinks 36 gallons of coffee each year.

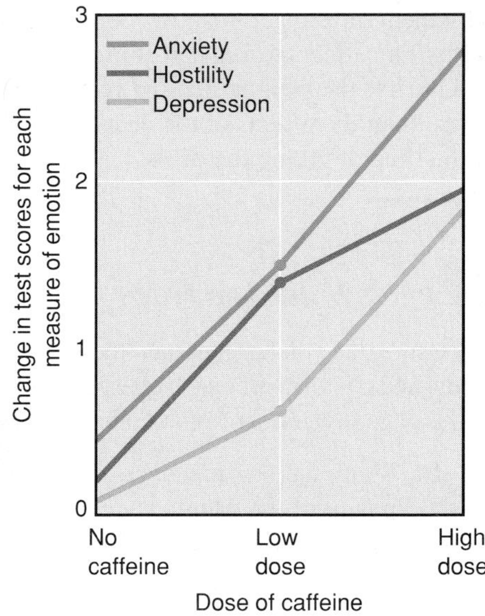

FIGURE 4.8

Change in measures of emotion after drinking either decaffeinated coffee or coffee containing small or large amounts of caffeine.

Source: Data from D. M. Veleber and D. T. Templer, "Effects of Caffeine on Anxiety and Depression," *Journal of Abnormal Psychology,* 93, 120–122, 1984. © 1984 by the American Psychological Association.

Caffeine

Eighty-five percent of Americans ingest caffeine daily (Hughes, Oliveto, Helzer, Higgins, & Bickel, 1992). Indeed, each year the average person in the United States drinks 36 gallons of coffee, 7 gallons of tea, and 30 gallons of cola and uses untold amounts of over-the-counter drugs containing caffeine (Ray, 1974). At approximately 125 milligrams (mg) per cup of coffee, that is an enormous consumption of caffeine.

You've seen the ads on television: The attractive woman, frazzled by the day's hassles, is restored to peaceful balance with a cup of coffee. Is that a good way to cope with our emotions when they have been bent and abused by life? Is caffeine good medicine for our nerves? Because caffeine is a stimulant, it does produce an increase in alertness that helps explain the popularity of coffee, tea, colas, and other beverages that contain caffeine in the morning. But does it make you feel *better?*

Physicians and psychologists have long suspected that caffeine actually produces negative changes in emotions in many persons. David Veleber and Donald Templer (1984) conducted a study of the effects of caffeine on emotions using volunteer college students and businesspeople in the San Joaquin Valley of California. The participants completed a psychological test that measures the degree of depression, anxiety, and hostility that the individual is experiencing at the time of the test. They took the test before and one hour after drinking a cup of coffee. Some of the participants drank decaffeinated coffee, whereas others received a low or high dose of caffeine in their coffee (the individuals did not know how much caffeine they were drinking, if any). The amount of caffeine was adjusted for the individual's body weight, with a 100-pound person receiving the equivalent of either one (low dose) or two cups (high dose) of strong brewed coffee.

As shown in figure 4.8, the caffeine produced small but significant changes in all three emotions. Most of us feel no ill effects from small amounts of coffee, but a large amount of caffeine is an invitation to lousy moods for all of us and even small amounts may cause distress for sensitive individuals.

Unfortunately, serious health risks are associated with the use of caffeine. Although caffeine produces relatively small changes in consciousness, it has powerful effects on the body. It has long been known that consumption of eight or more cups of caffeinated coffee per day (1,000 mg) constitutes a dangerously high level of intake (Greden, 1974). Common effects of such consumption for a prolonged period of time include excessive stomach acid and ulcers, abnormal heart rhythms and accelerated heart rate, increased kidney activity, anxiety, irritability, insomnia, sensory disturbances, and definite physiological addiction with intense withdrawal symptoms when caffeine is not consumed (Greden, 1974; Hughes et al., 1992). Prolonged use of caffeine at even moderate levels can also result in a physiological addiction to the substance.

Caffeine also produces marked increases in blood pressure, particularly during times of stress (Pincomb, Lovallo, Passey, Brackett, & Wilson, 1987). Moreover, drinking large amounts of coffee (five or more cups per day) over a period of years is associated with a two to three times greater risk of coronary heart disease, at least in men (LaCroix, Mead, Liang, Thomas, & Pearson, 1986). Drinking excessive amounts of coffee is a behavior that produces serious health risks, but even moderate amounts appear to pose some risk.

Nicotine

Nicotine found in tobacco is another widely used drug. Although it's technically a stimulant like caffeine, it can also have relax-

A person who never smokes has a life expectancy of 8 years longer than a person who smokes two packs of cigarettes a day. Consequently, the cost of the smoker's life insurance averages 25% higher.

ing effects under some circumstances. Its effects on consciousness are so mild, however, that they are often not noticed by experienced smokers.

The wonder, in fact, is that so many people (about 40 percent of all adults) use this relatively ineffective drug. Not only are its pleasant effects minimal, but nicotine is a highly dangerous drug. The life expectancy of regular smokers is reduced because smoking *greatly* increases the chances of lung and mouth cancer, heart attacks, pneumonia, emphysema, and other life-threatening diseases (Jenkins, 1988). In addition, cigarette smoking during pregnancy greatly increases the risk of lower birth weight, premature delivery, and death of the infant. Each year, approximately 135,000 people die of lung cancer in the United States; of those deaths 101,000 are directly attributable to smoking (Jeffrey, 1988). A person aged 25 who never smokes has a life expectancy that is more than *8 years longer* than a person who smokes two packs a day. Why, then, do people smoke?

The answer to that question seems to have several parts. First, it appears that most people start smoking because they see others do it. Adolescents see adults smoking in both advertisements and everyday life and perhaps imitate it because of its association with adult status. They also see their friends smoking and are thus subjected to peer pressure to smoke. In addition, virtually all smokers begin during their teenage years when a normal part of adolescent development involves defying the wishes and expectations of adults. Thus, some teenagers begin to smoke as an act of rebellion.

But for whatever reason smokers begin smoking, other factors soon begin to take over. Smokers quickly develop a psychological dependence on cigarettes and soon become physically addicted to the nicotine. At this point, smokers smoke primarily to avoid the discomfort of not smoking rather than for any positive effects the drug might have. As a result of this two-stage process, 95 percent or more of smokers become addicted in a relatively short time (Russell, 1971). As their tolerance for nicotine increases, their need for higher daily doses increases. As a result, it's very difficult to stop smoking cigarettes once the habit becomes regular. Only about 20 percent of all smokers are able to stop completely without help (Russell, 1971).

Alcohol

Are beer, wine, and liquor drugs? Although we do not generally think of alcohol as a "drug," it's a powerful and widely abused psychotropic drug that happens to come in liquid form. Alcohol works principally as a depressant, but it is experienced as a drug that "stimulates" sociability and exuberant activity ("partying"). This is because alcohol depresses inhibitory mechanisms in the brain. Thus, alcohol seems to stimulate the person because it makes the drinker less inhibited.

Alcohol also reduces tension and anxiety and increases self-confidence and self-esteem by erasing doubts about ourselves (Steele & Josephs, 1990). Alcohol has other effects as well. It impairs visual judgment and motor control and induces sleepiness (Matthews, Best, White, Vandergriff, & Simpson, 1996). In addition, alcohol can worsen negative moods, particularly deepening depression and making it more likely that anger will result in verbal or physical aggression (Steele & Josephs, 1990).

Most states consider an individual legally intoxicated when .10 percent (one-tenth of 1 percent) of the volume of her or his circulating blood is alcohol. At this level, sensory and motor performance are noticeably impaired. Unfortunately, even blood alcohol levels of .03 percent are sufficient to make driving an automobile or operating other machinery dangerous.

It is not easy to translate blood alcohol levels into amounts of alcohol consumed because many factors influence blood alcohol levels. Drinking on an empty stomach, drinking carbonated alcoholic beverages, drinking quickly rather than sipping, and drinking higher-proof beverages all lead to higher levels of blood alcohol even when the same amount of alcohol is consumed under other circumstances (Chruschel, 1982). The principal complicating factor, however, is the amount of fluid in the body, which differs according to body size and sex. The liver can remove from the bloodstream the alcohol in one 12-ounce can of beer (or one glass of wine or 1 ounce of 100-proof liquor) in about 1 hour; the remainder stays in the blood. Figure 4.9 shows the average blood levels that can be expected for males and females of different sizes, but keep in mind that these are merely averages.

Except for nicotine, alcohol is the most widely abused addictive drug in the United States. Assessing the exact extent of alcohol abuse is difficult for two main reasons. First, the amount of alcohol consumption that can lead to harmful effects varies markedly from person to person and from situation to situation. An individual who has only four drinks every New Year's Eve is an alcohol abuser if he drives himself home when intoxicated; a surgeon who has two drinks a day may be an alcohol abuser if she drinks them right before performing surgery. Second, the potential harmful effects of alcohol abuse are so varied. Heavy drinking can affect job performance, disrupt marriages, and harm one's health. It is involved in about half of all fatal fire and automobile accidents, one-third of all suicides, and two-thirds of all murders (Marlatt & Rose, 1980). Alcohol abuse frequently leads to highly stressful consequences such as divorce and loss of employment; these stressful consequences then take a toll on health. In addition, alcohol has directly harmful effects on the liver, brain, and circulatory system.

As a result, the life span of the addicted alcoholic is 12 years shorter than average (National Institute on Alcohol Abuse and Alcoholism, 1987). Even moderately high levels of alcohol consumption create a health risk (Hennekens, Rosner, & Cole, 1978; Jenkins, 1988).

Males — Alcohol consumed in one hour

Weight	(100 proof liquor)	Blood alcohol level
150 lbs	2 oz	.05
150 lbs	4 oz	.10*

Females — Alcohol consumed in one hour

Weight	(100 proof liquor)	Blood alcohol level
100 lbs	2 oz	.09
100 lbs	4 oz	.18

*Note: Blood alcohol concentration of .03 can impair automobile driving; concentrations of .10 constitute intoxication according to most state laws.

FIGURE 4.9
Average blood alcohol levels as a result of drinking.

In addition, drinking during pregnancy has been linked to a form of combined physical defects and mental retardation in the infant known as *fetal alcohol syndrome* (Briggs, Freeman & Yaffee, 1986). Although heavy drinking is most likely to lead to birth defects, no "safe" level of alcohol consumption during pregnancy has been established—and there may not be one.

In spite of the difficulties involved in defining alcohol abuse, surveys have been taken with eye-opening results. Using a broad definition of alcohol abuse, it has been found that while about two-thirds of all adults drink at least occasionally, nearly one-third of the individuals surveyed reported at least one serious alcohol-related problem (for 21 percent of females and 41 percent of males) (Cahalan, 1970; Cahalan & Room, 1974).

Because of its powerful mood-altering qualities, alcohol can rapidly result in psychological dependence and physiological addiction (**alcoholism).** In about one-third of all addicted individuals, this addiction results in a progressively deteriorating series of changes known as *classic alcoholism.* The four stages of classic alcoholism are well known:

1. *Prealcoholic stage.* During this stage drinking begins to serve the important function of releasing tension. As drinking continues, the tolerance for alcohol increases, so the amount that must be consumed to provide the same release of tension increases.
2. *Prodromal stage.* The drinking level is excessive during this stage. Blackouts or memory losses begin to occur, and drinking behavior shifts from sipping to gulping. Guilt, anxiety, and promises to stop drinking are also common during this period.
3. *Crucial stage.* During the crucial stage, deterioration occurs in self-esteem and in general social functioning, including loss of friends. Once the individual begins to drink, the drinking is uncontrollable ("binges"), but the individual can still avoid taking the first drink for relatively long periods of time. He or she begins to rationalize drinking as acceptable. Excessive drinking generally leads to neglect of nutrition.
4. *Chronic stage.* The alcoholic has reached a stage of almost constant drinking, with little or no control over either starting or continuing to drink. Impairment of thinking and loss of social standards are very common. Fears, hallucinations, and tremors often develop along with serious medical complications.

This is not to say that alcohol is always harmful. In the survey cited above (Cahalan & Room, 1974), more than half of all drinkers reported no harmful side effects. Indeed, under some conditions, small amounts of alcohol may be beneficial to the health of some individuals. Individuals who drink an average of about one drink per day appear to be slightly less likely to die of heart attacks than individuals who drink less alcohol or do not drink at all (Hennekens et al., 1978; Jenkins, 1988).

Kicking Legal Drug Habits

What about people who want to stop using these legal consciousness-altering drugs? How can they stop? Some people just stop, of course. But, for those who find stopping difficult, psychologists have designed a number of programs to help individuals stop smoking and reduce caffeine consumption. Because most heavy smokers are physically addicted to the nicotine in cigarettes, one of the best, time-tested methods is to gradually reduce the individual's dependence on nicotine before asking him or her to stop smoking altogether (Foxx & Brown, 1979). In an experimental evaluation of this method, smokers were given a list of cigarettes that stated the nicotine content of each brand. During the first week, the smokers were allowed to smoke their accustomed number per day of their own high-nicotine brand. During the second week, they were asked to smoke the same number of a brand of cigarettes that contained 30 percent less nicotine. During the third week, they were instructed to smoke the same number of a brand containing 60 percent less nicotine, and the fourth week brought a change to a brand containing 90 percent less nicotine. At that time 40 percent of the smokers were able to stop smoking permanently and another 30 percent were able to smoke at reduced rates of nicotine and tar intake. Similar methods have also been developed to help people reduce caffeine consumption by gradually switching to decaffeinated coffee (Foxx & Rubinoff, 1981). A computer program has even been written to allow individuals to enter information about their progress in quitting smoking. The individuals receive feedback from the computer telling them when it is time either to switch to the next lower level of nicotine cigarette or to quit altogether (Burling et al., 1989).

Because dependence on alcohol is a more complicated issue, the individual who cannot reduce drinking to a controlled and healthy level or quit altogether should, by all means, seek professional assistance. The same advice holds for any consciousness-altering drug from which anyone cannot walk away.

Summary

Chapter 4 explores human awareness, normal waking consciousness, sleeping and dreaming, and altered states of consciousness.

I. Consciousness is defined as "a state of awareness" and is experienced in a variety of states.
   - **A.** Directed consciousness occurs when our awareness is directed toward a single focus.
   - **B.** In the state of flowing consciousness, awareness drifts from one thought to another.
   - **C.** Daydreams combine the features of directed consciousness and dreamlike fantasies.
   - **D.** At times, consciousness appears to become divided, with different conscious activities occurring simultaneously.
   - **E.** Recently, psychologists have conducted studies to determine whether it makes sense to say that unconscious mental processes operate in our lives.

II. Approximately one-third of our lives is spent in sleep, but not all of sleep is unconscious.
   - **A.** Sleep begins with a semiwakeful hypnagogic state and moves through stages of progressively deeper sleep.
   - **B.** Dreams mostly occur during the phase of sleep known as REM sleep, but a different type of dream is common in non-REM sleep as well.
   - **C.** Sleeping and dreaming seem important to health, but even extended periods of sleep deprivation have been shown to cause only fatigue, inefficiency, and irritability.
   - **D.** Nightmares, night terrors, sleepwalking, and sleeptalking are fairly common sleep phenomena.
   - **E.** Some persons suffer from the sleep disorders of insomnia (inability to get sufficient sleep), narcolepsy (falling asleep during daily activities), and sleep apnea (breathing stops briefly during sleep).

III. We sometimes experience more unusual altered states of consciousness.
   - **A.** Many individuals practice meditation to achieve a highly relaxed state.
   - **B.** Hypnosis is sometimes used to alter consciousness and to relieve pain.
   - **C.** Altered consciousness is sometimes experienced in the form of depersonalization.

IV. Consciousness can also be altered through the use of various psychotropic drugs.
   - **A.** Psychotropic drugs may be classified as stimulants, depressants, hallucinogens, and inhalants; the drug marijuana does not fit easily into this classification.
   - **B.** Though risks differ from drug to drug, all drug use can lead to abuse, dependence, or addiction.
   - **C.** Even the more common legal drugs (caffeine, nicotine, alcohol) produce definite physical and psychological effects and can be quite harmful if used in excess.
   - **D.** The more powerful drugs cause radical changes in consciousness, can lead to serious physical and psychological problems, and are often illegal.
     1. Stimulants are not physically addictive but produce psychological dependence; they can be dangerous, particularly in their effects on the heart.
     2. Sedatives and tranquilizers are highly addictive and can be highly dangerous, particularly when taken in large doses or with alcohol.
     3. Narcotics are powerful and dangerous depressants; physiological addiction occurs rapidly, and prolonged use has profoundly damaging effects on the body.
     4. Inhalants are usually toxic and often cause permanent brain damage.
     5. Hallucinogens radically alter perception, cause hallucinations, and are often associated with bizarre or even violent behavior; though not physiologically addictive, psychological dependence is common.
     6. Marijuana is a drug that produces a sense of well-being in most persons and sometimes alters perception.

Suggested Readings

1. For a readable discussion of meditation without its metaphysical or religious trimmings, read: Benson, H. (1975). *The relaxation response.* New York: Morrow.
2. For a fascinating and sensible look at hypnosis: Bowers, K. S. (1976). *Hypnosis for the seriously curious.* Monterey, CA: Brooks/Cole.
3. For more on the contents of dreams, written by Freudian psychologist: Hall, C. S. (1951). What people dream about. *Scientific American,* 84: 60–63. For additional information on the study of sleeping and dreaming: Webb, W. B., & Agnew, H. W. (1973). *Sleep and dreams.* Dubuque, IA: Wm. C. Brown; Horne, J. (1988). *Why we sleep.* New York: Oxford University Press; Hobson, J. A. (1989). *Sleep.* New York: Scientific American Library; and Stauch, I., & Meier, B. (1996). *In search of dreams: Experimental dream research.* Albany, NY: State Univesity of New York Press.
4. A fascinating and in-depth analysis of the hypnogogic state: Mavromatis, A. (1987). *Hypnogogia.* London: Routledge.
5. For thorough summaries of mind-altering drugs: Carroll, C. R. (1989). *Drugs in modern society* (2nd ed.). Dubuque, IA: Wm. C. Brown; and Julien, R. M. (1992). *A primer of drug addiction* (6th edition). San Francisco: Freeman.
6. Broad overviews of the topic of consciousness are provided by: Wallace, B., & Fisher, L. E. (1991). *Consciousness and behavior,* (3rd ed.). Boston: Allyn & Bacon; and by Ornstein, R. (1991). *The evolution of consciousness.* New York: Prentice-Hall.

PART 3

Learning and Cognition

CHAPTER

5

CHAPTER OUTLINE

Basic Principles of Learning

PROLOGUE

You behave the way you do largely because you *learned* to act that way. Take a moment and think about who you are. Now imagine that you had been adopted as an infant by a family in a distant part of the world. You would now speak a different language, eat different foods, and act in ways that are characteristic of a different culture. You would be a different person in all of these ways simply because your learning experiences were different.

In 1934 a young scientist named Ruth Benedict (pictured p. 172) published a book about remote cultures that were very different from one another. Her book tells a remarkable story about the power of learning experiences in shaping human lives. In the 1930s the Dobu were a competitive people who generally did everything they could to acquire more possessions than anyone else. Theirs was a very violent culture, with high rates of assault and murder. In a way, they were very much like Americans—only more so. But the Zuñi people, who are native Americans who once flourished in the Southwest, were very different. The Zuñi people found greed and ambition to be repugnant. Instead they valued generosity and modesty. They shared all wealth equally with one another and actively avoided doing anything that would bring them individual fame. Perhaps as a result, violence among the Zuñi was rare. Benedict argued that if there were some cultures in which greed, ambition, and violence are rare, then it cannot be true that these are inborn traits of all humans—they are learned traits that could be changed.

Are you still not convinced of the power of learning in shaping personalities? Benedict used courtship and marriage as another example of the great differences among cultures due to learning. In Zuñi society, male and female children were strictly separated until adolescence, allowing almost no contact before marriage. If a female and a male interacted in any way, their parents quickly arranged their marriage. Courtship often consisted of no more than the male's asking a young woman whom he had never met for a drink of water as she returned from the stream with a water jug. If she gave him a drink, they were soon married.

Courtship among the Dobu was dramatically different than among the Zuñi. In Dobu society, male and female children were not only allowed to play with each other, sex play among children was common and approved by adults. When children reached puberty, frequent sex was common among the unmarried males and females, with the lovemaking generally occurring openly in the one-room home of the girl's parents.

By showing scholars in the Western world that not all people are like us, Benedict helped convince many scholars that learning experiences are far more important in shaping human behavior than realized until that point. In this chapter, you will learn about three different kinds of learning. In one of these types of learning, parts of the environment that you hardly noticed before become stimuli that influence your behavior. If your water pipes made a groaning sound one morning while you were in the shower, you probably wouldn't pay much attention to it. But if the groaning always immediately preceded a sudden change in the temperature of your shower—from warm to icy cold—you would soon learn to jump at the sound of the groan. The groan would become a powerful stimulus for you.

Another kind of learning results from the *consequences* of your behavior. If you behave in a way that leads to something positive, you will probably behave that way more often in the future. If your behavior leads to something negative, on the other hand, you will be less likely

KEY TERMS

learning 174
classical conditioning 179
operant conditioning 181
positive reinforcement 182
fixed ratio schedule 184
variable ratio schedule 184
fixed interval schedule 185
variable interval schedule 185
shaping 185
negative reinforcement 187
punishment 188
extinction 194
response prevention 194
spontaneous recovery 195
disinhibition 195
cognitive map 197
learning set 199
modeling 201
superstitious behavior 206

Learning is any relatively permanent change in behavior brought about through experience.

to behave that way again. For example, let's say you stay up all night studying for a test. The next day, you can hardly stay awake and you can't remember half of what you learned the night before. Those are negative consequences that will lead to learning not to try that again. In contrast, if studying for a few hours each night for five nights before the test resulted in your first "A," you would be more likely to use that strategy again. The consequences of our behavior are a powerful source of learning.

The third type of learning comes from watching those around us. When you are in a new situation, such as your first day in a college class, you tend to notice how other students are behaving. Everybody else is taking notes—I guess I should, too. Instead of always having to learn from the consequences of our own actions, we can benefit from the experience of others.

As you learn about the details of the process of learning, try not to lose sight of the overall importance of the topic. Learning is one of the most important forces that made you the person you are today.

DEFINITION OF LEARNING

learning
Any relatively permanent change in behavior brought about through experience.

Life is a process of continual change. From infancy to adolescence to adulthood to death, we are changing. Many factors produce those changes, but one of the most important is the process of **learning.** Through our experiences, we learn new information, new attitudes, new fears, and new skills. We also learn to understand new concepts, to solve problems in new ways, and even to develop a personality over a lifetime. And in the course of reading textbooks, we learn new definitions for words like *learning:* In psychology the term *learning* refers to any relatively permanent change in behavior brought about through experience—that is, through interactions with the environment.

As the definition states, not *all* changes in behavior are the result of learning. The term is restricted to the relatively permanent, as opposed to temporary, changes that are the result of experience, rather than changes due to biological causes such as drugs, fatigue, maturation, injury, or the like. If a baseball pitcher throws the ball differently this season because his pitching coach demonstrated a new way to pitch, we would say that learning has occurred—a relatively permanent change in pitching due to the experience of the coach's demonstration. But if the pitcher's changed style was due to an injury, fatigue from throwing too much before each game, an arm strengthened by weight lifting, or biological maturation (if he was a 7-year-old Little League pitcher), we would not refer to the change in pitching as learning.

The *change in behavior* will not always be immediately obvious, however. If you watch a film on the proper way to hit backhands in tennis this winter, the change will not be evident until you are on the tennis court again next spring. Notice also that the definition of learning does not restrict its usage to intentionally produced changes in behavior or even to desirable changes in behavior. For instance, if you begin to loathe fish sandwiches because you get sick after eating one, learning has occurred. The new disgust for fish sandwiches is undesirable and certainly unintentional, but it's still the result of learning.

Over the years, psychologists have isolated and studied a number of ways that learning takes place. As a result, we now understand a number of different principles of learning. In the following sections we describe these principles of learning and indicate some of the ways that they can influence us in our daily lives.

CLASSICAL CONDITIONING: LEARNING BY ASSOCIATION

We begin our study of specific types of learning with a simple form called *classical conditioning*. The scientific study of classical conditioning began around the turn of the century with an accidental discovery made in the Leningrad laboratory of Ivan Pavlov. Pavlov was a Russian physiologist who had been awarded the Nobel Prize for his work on the role of saliva in digestion. To study salivation, Pavlov surgically implanted tubes in the cheeks

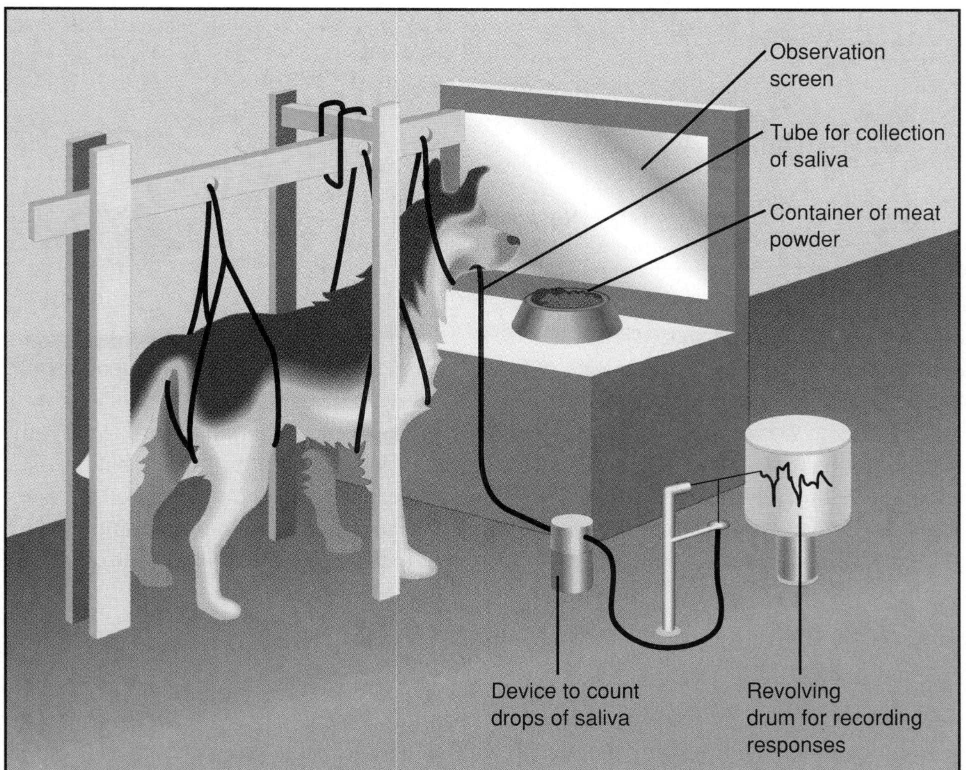

FIGURE 5.1

Apparatus originally used by Pavlov to study the role of salivation in digestion, and later in his studies of classical conditioning.

Ivan Pavlov accidentally discovered that dogs learn to associate the sounds of food being prepared with the food itself.

of his dogs. This allowed him to measure the amount of saliva produced when food was placed in their mouths (see fig. 5.1). Pavlov noticed, however, that dogs that had been in the experiment a few days started salivating when the attendant entered the room with the food dish *before* food was placed in their mouths. The sights (and probably sounds) of the attendant had come to *elicit* (evoke or produce) a reflexive response that only the food had originally elicited. This fact would have gone quite unnoticed had the tubes not been placed in the dogs' cheeks—that is the accidental part of the discovery. Noticing that a dog salivates whenever he or she sees the laboratory attendant who brings food may not seem like a great step forward for science at first glance. But Pavlov recognized that a reflexive response to food, which was biologically "wired into" the nervous system, had come under the control of an *arbitrary* stimulus—the sight of the attendant.

Stated in a different way, Pavlov knew he had witnessed a form of learning that was based on nothing more than the repeated association of two stimuli. Remember from

chapter 3 that a *stimulus* is anything that can directly influence behavior or conscious experience. Because the dog's experience of food was linked to the sight of the attendant, the behavior of the dog was changed—the dog now salivated to the stimuli of the approaching attendant. That is, the stimuli elicited a *response*. When you were born, you could respond to the outside world with only a limited repertoire of inborn reflexes, but now you are a marvelously complex product of your learning experiences. Pavlov wanted to understand this process of learning, so over his colleagues' objections, he hastily completed his studies of digestion and devoted the rest of his career to the study of learning (Watson, 1971).

Association: The Key Element in Classical Conditioning

More than 2,000 years before Pavlov, Aristotle noted that two sensations repeatedly experienced together will become *associated*. For example, if you have frequently visited the seashore with a friend, visiting the seashore alone will probably trigger memories of that friend. If you got sick the last time you ate a hot dog, you will likely feel nauseous the next time you see one. Learning through association is a common part of our lives.

Pavlov considered classical conditioning to be a form of learning through association—the association in time of a neutral stimulus (one that originally does not elicit the response) and a stimulus that does elicit the response. Pavlov used the apparatus that was already constructed in his laboratory to measure the progress of learning, and he used food as the stimulus to elicit the response (of salivation).

Specifically, Pavlov presented (as the neutral stimulus) a clicking metronome that the dog could easily hear. After a precisely measured interval of time, he would blow a small quantity of meat powder into the dog's mouth to elicit salivation. Every 15 minutes the same procedure was repeated, and soon the dog began salivating to the metronome when it was presented alone. By continuously measuring the amount of saliva drained through the tube in the dog's cheek, the strength of the new learning was accurately monitored throughout the process of classical conditioning.

Keep in mind that the key phrase in classical conditioning is the "association" of the two stimuli. The more *frequently* the metronome and the food are associated, the more often the metronome will come to elicit salivation (see fig. 5.2). The *timing* of the association of the two stimuli is also highly important. Pavlov found, for example, that he obtained the best results when the metronome preceded the food powder by about a half a second. Longer time intervals were less effective, and almost no learning occurred when the metronome was presented at the same time as the food or when the food was presented slightly before the metronome.

Thus, Pavlov took advantage of a chance observation and began a systematic study of one aspect of the learning process. Although learning had been studied before Pavlov's time, his experiments were highly influential because of their extensiveness and precision. But perhaps his true genius lay in seeing that this simple form of learning had important implications far beyond clicking metronomes and salivating dogs. Pavlov's writings became an important part of American psychology when they came to the attention of John B. Watson, who expanded upon and popularized Pavlov's views in English.

Terminology of Classical Conditioning

Before we can proceed much further in our understanding of classical conditioning, we need to learn some new terminology. Although these terms are a bit awkward at first, they will

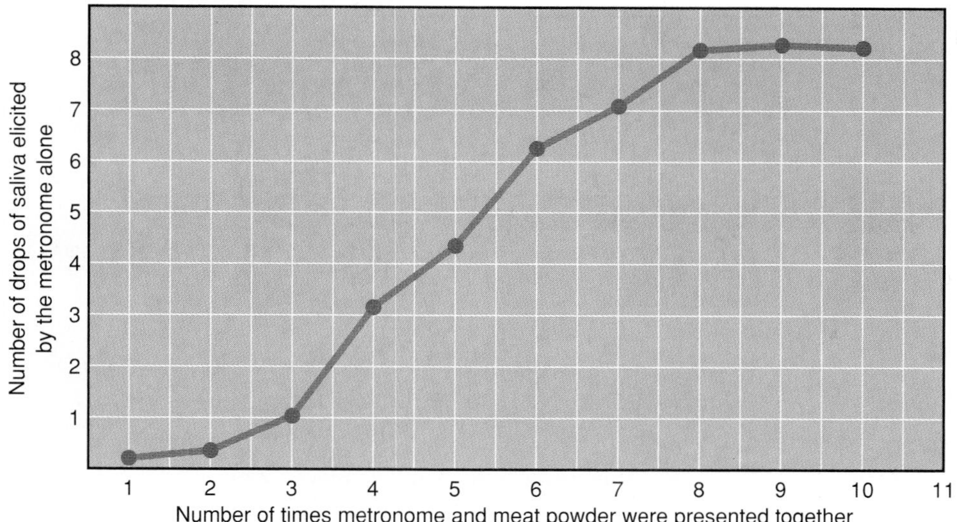

FIGURE 5.2
In Pavlov's studies, the more often the metronome was associated in time with meat powder, the more effective it was in eliciting salivation.

help us expand our discussion of classical conditioning to topics more relevant to your life than salivating dogs. First we use each of these four new terms to refer to the specific stimuli and responses in Pavlov's experiments; then we use them with new examples. The new terms are as follows:

1. *Unconditioned stimulus.* The meat powder was the **unconditioned stimulus (UCS)** in Pavlov's experiment. This is a stimulus that can elicit the response without any learning. In other words, the response to an unconditioned stimulus is essentially inborn.
2. *Unconditioned response.* Salivation was the **unconditioned response (UCR).** It's an unlearned, inborn reaction to the unconditioned stimulus.
3. *Conditioned stimulus.* The metronome was originally unable to elicit the response of salivation, but it acquired the ability to elicit the response through the process of classical conditioning. It was the **conditioned stimulus (CS)** in Pavlov's studies.
4. *Conditioned response.* When the dog began salivating to the conditioned stimulus, salivation became the **conditioned response (CR).** When a learned response is elicited by the conditioned stimulus, it's referred to as the conditioned response.

unconditioned stimulus (UCS)
A stimulus that can elicit a response without any learning.

unconditioned response (UCR)
An unlearned, inborn reaction to an unconditioned stimulus.

conditioned stimulus (CS)
A stimulus that comes to elicit responses as a result of being paired with an unconditioned stimulus.

conditioned response (CR)
A response that is similar or identical to the unconditioned response that comes to be elicited by a conditioned stimulus.

To summarize: The meat powder was the unconditioned stimulus (UCS); the metronome was the neutral stimulus that became the conditioned stimulus (CS); salivation was the unconditioned response (UCR); and when the salivation was elicited by the conditioned stimulus, it became the conditioned response (CR). These are difficult terms to keep straight at first; it may help to read through the diagram in figure 5.3 to review the meaning of these terms.

As a further example of classical conditioning, here's another dog story. One of my all-time best friends was a beagle named Lester. Lester had a number of fine qualities that are not always found in humans; he was affectionate, warm, and genuinely loyal. But, in all candor, Lester was also a profound coward. I will never forget the time I took him to the veterinarian for the first of a weekly series of shots. He stood perfectly still with a friendly beagle smile on his face until the needle was stuck into his hindquarter. At that point, he produced a flinching, lurching, terrified yelp. After a few injections, Lester began yelping before the injection when he saw the vet with the needle in her hand.

Now, to be completely honest, I cannot criticize Lester too much for his cowardly behavior, because I also yelp when I see a needle coming my way. Why do you suppose that is so? Why should both of us, a grown man and a grown dog, react so strongly to the sight of a needle? After all, the sight of the needle cannot hurt you; only its stab can do that. The answer, of course, is that we have been classically conditioned to yelp at needles.

FIGURE 5.3
Diagram of classical conditioning.

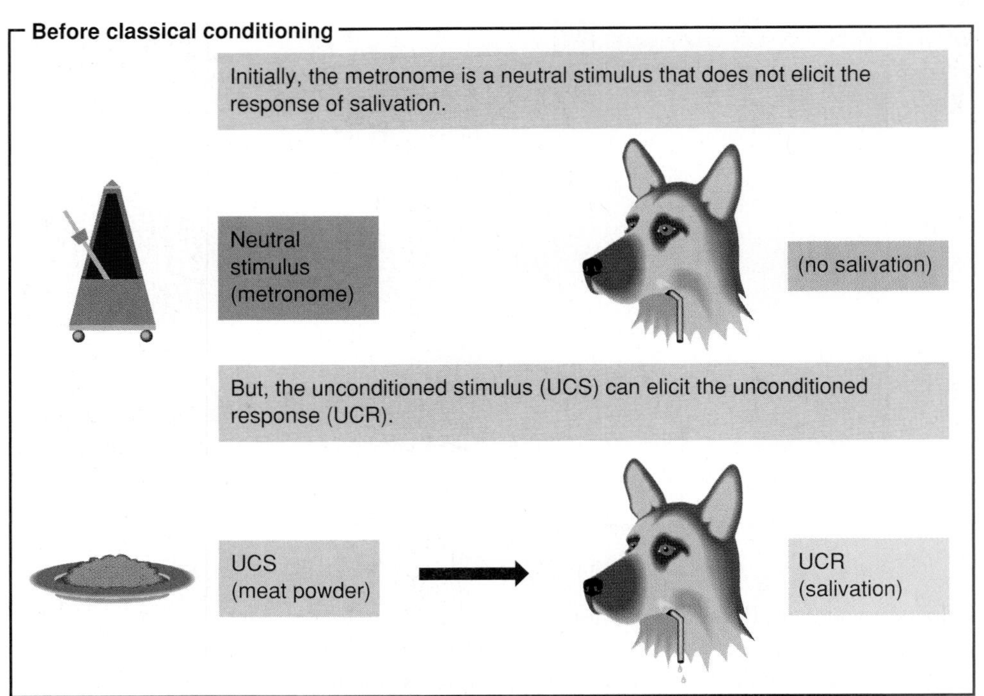
Before classical conditioning
Initially, the metronome is a neutral stimulus that does not elicit the response of salivation.
Neutral stimulus (metronome)
(no salivation)
But, the unconditioned stimulus (UCS) can elicit the unconditioned response (UCR).
UCS (meat powder)
UCR (salivation)

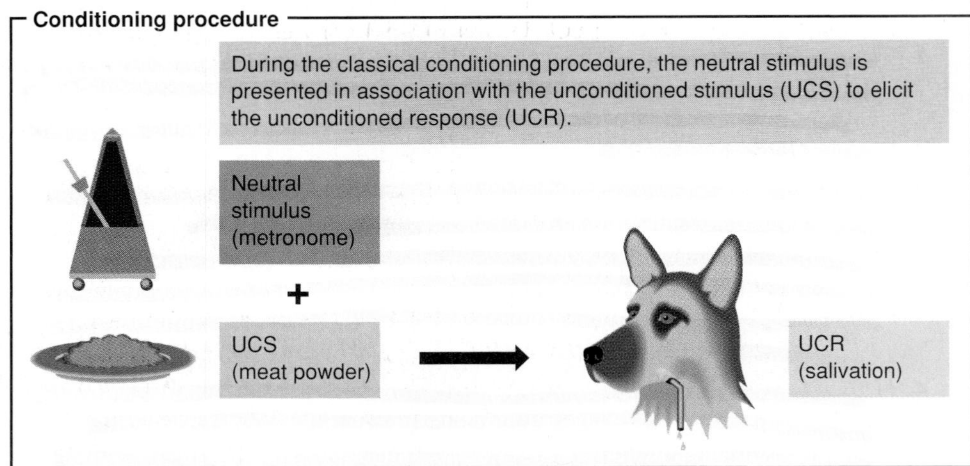
Conditioning procedure
During the classical conditioning procedure, the neutral stimulus is presented in association with the unconditioned stimulus (UCS) to elicit the unconditioned response (UCR).
Neutral stimulus (metronome)
+
UCS (meat powder)
UCR (salivation)

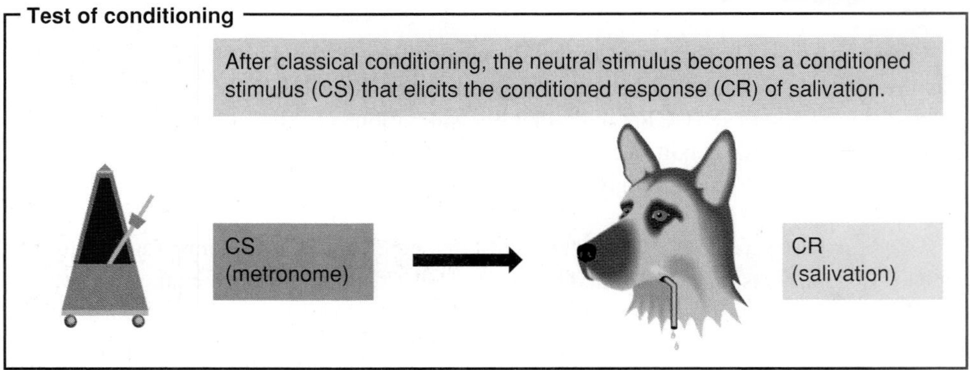
Test of conditioning
After classical conditioning, the neutral stimulus becomes a conditioned stimulus (CS) that elicits the conditioned response (CR) of salivation.
CS (metronome)
CR (salivation)

Stop for a minute and read back through the example of Lester's fear of needles and see if you can identify the CS, UCS, UCR, and CR.

The sight of the needle is the CS because it originally did not elicit the yelp; the painful stab of the needle is the UCS because it biologically elicited the yelp; the yelp after the stab is UCR; and when the CS comes to elicit yelping, the yelp is the CR. I feel a little better knowing that my yelping at needles is simply a CR to a CS, but not a whole lot better; I still hate the things.

Definition of Classical Conditioning

We have finally covered enough terminology to be able to give a precise definition of classical conditioning. **Classical conditioning** is a form of learning in which a previously neutral stimulus (CS) is followed by a stimulus (UCS) that elicits an unlearned response (UCR). As a result of these pairings of the CS and UCS, the CS comes to elicit a response (CR) that in most cases is identical or very similar to the UCR.

classical conditioning
A form of learning in which a previously neutral stimulus (CS) is paired with an unconditioned stimulus (UCS) to elicit a conditioned response (CR) that is identical to or very similar to the unconditioned response (UCR).

For classical conditioning to take place, a CS must also serve as a reliable signal for the occurrence of the UCS (Rescorla, 1967, 1988). An emergency siren that goes off only in a real emergency (no routine tests or false alarms) will generate more fear responses than sirens routinely tested once a month. Similarly, if the sound of a metronome is always followed by food, salivation will be stronger than if the metronome is followed by food only some of the time.

Note that we consider classical conditioning to be a form of learning not because a new behavior has been acquired but because old behavior can be elicited by a new stimulus; behavior is "changed" only in that sense. It's important to notice also (for reasons that will be clear to you later in the chapter) that the process of classical conditioning *does not depend on the behavior of the individual* being conditioned. The metronome and the meat powder were paired whether the dog salivated or not, and the sight of the needle was followed by the stab whether Lester yelped or not. The critical elements in classical conditioning are that the CS and UCS be closely associated in time and that the CS be a reliable predictor of the UCS. Our behavior simply provides evidence that conditioning has taken place. As we will see later, if the behavior of the individual can determine whether the stimulus is presented or not, the process is not called classical conditioning.

By the way, are you curious as to why it's called *classical* conditioning? This term simply refers to the fact that Pavlov performed the *classic* laboratory studies of learning. For the same reason, classical conditioning is also referred to as *Pavlovian* conditioning.

Importance of Classical Conditioning

The concept of classical conditioning would not be so widely studied by psychologists if it applied only to salivating dogs. On the contrary, classical conditioning is helpful in understanding a number of important and puzzling issues concerning our behavior.

In 1920 behaviorist John B. Watson and his associate Rosalie Rayner published what must be the most widely cited example of classical conditioning in psychology. Watson was convinced that many of our fears are acquired through classical conditioning and sought to test this idea by teaching a fear to an 11-month-old child, the now famous "Little Albert." Albert was first allowed to play with a white laboratory rat to find out whether he was afraid of rats: He was not at that time. Then as he played with the white rat, an iron bar was struck loudly with a hammer behind Albert's head. As might be expected, the noise caused Albert to cry fearfully. After seven such pairings, Albert showed a strong fear response when the rat was placed near him. He had learned to fear the rat through classical conditioning.

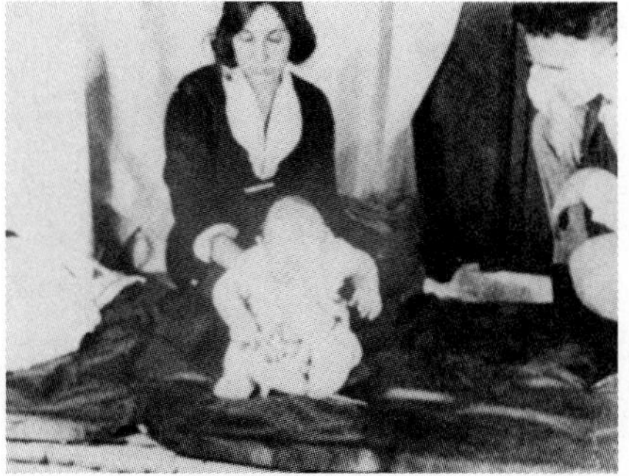

This photo shows behaviorist John Watson and his graduate student assistant Rosalie Rayner with Watson's most famous subject—Little Albert. In this early study on the classical conditioning of fear reactions, Watson was able to demonstrate the importance of the environment in the development of human emotions

Courtesy of Prof. Benjamin Harris, Ph.D. Univ. of Wisconsin, Parkside.

Watson's own words provide the best description of the experiment's outcome: "The instant the rat was shown the baby began to cry. Almost instantly he turned sharply to the left, fell over on his left side, raised himself on all fours, and began to crawl away so rapidly that he was caught with difficulty before reaching the edge of the table" (Watson & Rayner, 1920, p. 3).

For understandable reasons, this experiment would not be considered ethical by today's standards. By today's standards, it is particularly distressing that Watson and Rayner chose not to reverse the conditioning of Albert's fear (Watson & Rayner, 1920). In a subsequent study (Jones, 1924), however, Mary Cover Jones and Watson successfully reduced fear of rabbits in another small child by gradually pairing the rabbit (CS) with cookies (UCS). This method of reversing a classically conditioned response by pairing the CS (the rabbit, in this case) with a UCS (cookies, in this case) for a response (eating the cookies) that cannot occur at the same time as the undesirable CR (crying fearfully) is called **counterconditioning.** As in the present example, the UCS for the incompatible response is typically presented first (Mary Cover Jones initially let the child start eating the cookie),

counterconditioning
The process of eliminating a classically conditioned response by pairing the conditioned stimulus (CS) with an unconditioned stimulus (UCS) for a response that is stronger than the conditioned response (CR) and that cannot occur at the same time as the CR.

then the CS (the rabbit) for the undesirable CR (fearful crying) is introduced only briefly. Over time the CS for the undesirable response can be presented for longer periods of time until it no longer elicits the undesirable CR.

Recently, classical conditioning has proved useful in explaining several questions about our health (Ader & Cohen, 1993). When the body is exposed to threats to health, such as viruses, a number of blood cells that attack the invading germs are produced. The immune system is an amazingly effective defense against disease, but it does not always operate at full capacity. Not only can fatigue and psychological stress adversely affect the functioning of the immune system (Ader, 1981), but it is now clear that immune system responses can be classically conditioned. Robert Ader (Ader & Cohen, 1981) administered a drug (the UCS) to rats that suppressed the activation of their immune system cells (the UCR). The drug was given at the same time that the rats drank saccharin-sweetened water (the CS). After several pairings of the drug and the sweetened water, the rats showed a suppression in immune cell production (the CR) just from drinking the sweetened water.

One particularly important type of cell in the immune system's arsenal is called the *natural killer,* or *NK,* cell. These cells are essential to health because they play a key role in resistance to viruses and tumors. Dennis Dyck and associates at the University of Manitoba (Dyck, Greenberg, & Osachuk, 1986) have shown that suppression of the activity of NK cells can be classically conditioned. The full implications of these studies have not been worked out, but it appears that classical conditioning could play a role in our resistance to disease.

Sexual arousal has also been shown to be influenced by classical conditioning (Zamble, Mitchell, & Findlay, 1986). Male rats were placed in a distinctive cage with a sexually receptive female rat. A screen prevented sexual intercourse, but the presence of the sexually receptive female (UCS) led to sexual arousal (UCR) in the male. The question was, would the pairing of the receptive female with the distinctive cage (CS) lead to classical conditioning of sexual arousal to the cage? This was shown by placing the male rats in the same cage later with another receptive female—but this time without the dividing screen. Compared with male rats who had not had the classical conditioning experience, males for whom the cage was a CS for sexual arousal became aroused and engaged in intercourse considerably more quickly.

The fact that sexual arousal can be classically conditioned has been used to explain the origins of unusual *sexual fetishes.* Humans sometimes find that they have become classically conditioned to be sexually aroused by nonsexual objects such as shoes, leather gloves, and other objects (Rachman, 1966).

Later in this chapter we will look at the role of classical conditioning in aversions to specific kinds of food, and in chapter 13 we will examine its possible role in the origins of the intense fears that we call *phobias.* Classical conditioning is a simple concept, but it helps us understand some of the complex puzzles of human life.

Thinking Critically About Psychology

1. How might a student develop a classically conditioned fear response to a specific college classroom?

2. Is our ability to learn through classical conditioning generally an advantage or a disadvantage? How would Little Albert answer that question?

Review

Your behavior is not static; it will change from day to day and from year to year as a result of your experiences. This process of behavior change is called learning. Learning is defined as any relatively permanent change in behavior or in the potential for behavior brought about by experience (rather than by biological causes). The prominence of the study of learning in American psychology can be traced in part to studies of a simple, but important, form of learning launched around the turn of the century by Russian medical researcher Ivan Pavlov. Pavlov was studying salivary reflexes when he noticed that, after a few days in the study, his dogs began salivating before the food was placed in their mouths. He reasoned that they had learned to salivate at the sight of the attendant bringing the food because this stimulus was always associated with (immediately preceded by) the food. Pavlov tested this explanation in a series of studies in which a clicking metronome was repeatedly paired with the presentation of meat powder. As a result, the metronome soon came to elicit the response of salivation. In general, when a neutral stimulus is repeatedly paired with another stimulus that elicits an unlearned response, the previously neutral stimulus will begin to elicit the same or a very similar response. We call this form of learning *classical conditioning.*

Check Your Learning

To be sure that you have learned the key points from the preceding section, cover the answers below and try to answer each question. If you give an incorrect answer to any question, return to the page given next to the correct answer to see why your answer was not correct. Remember that these questions cover only some of the important information in this section; it is important that you make up your own questions to check your learning of other facts and concepts.

1. The term learning refers to ____________________ .

2. The critical element in classical conditioning is that the UCS and the ________ be closely associated in time.

   a. CS　　　c. UCR
   b. CR　　　d. REM

3. A(n) ____________________ is a response that is similar or identical to the unconditioned response that comes to be elicited by a conditioned stimulus.

   a. unconditioned stimulus　　　c. conditioned stimulus
   b. unconditioned response　　　d. conditioned response

4. Ivan Pavlov first studied classical conditioning, but ____________________ popularized the idea that classical conditioning and other forms of learning were important to the development of our personalities and abilities.

   a. B. F. Skinner　　　c. Albert Bandura
   b. John B. Watson　　　d. Karen Horney

Correct Answers

1. any relatively permanent change in behavior brought about through experience (p. 174), 2. a (p. 179), 3. d (p. 177), 4. b (p. 179).

OPERANT CONDITIONING: LEARNING FROM THE CONSEQUENCES OF YOUR BEHAVIOR

If you started parking your car in a new parking space marked "For the President Only" and your car was towed away every day as a consequence, you would probably stop parking there after a while. Similarly, if you moved to a new seat in class and suddenly an interesting, attractive person started talking to you, you would probably choose to sit in that seat for the remaining classes of the semester. To a great extent, people increase or decrease the frequency with which they do things depending on the *consequences* of their actions. We call learning from the consequences of our behavior *operant conditioning*. The term is derived from the word *operate*. When our behavior "operates" on the outside world, it produces consequences for us, and those consequences determine whether we will continue to engage in that behavior. We can define **operant conditioning,** then, as that form of learning in which the consequences of behavior lead to changes in the probability of its occurrence.

operant conditioning
(op´e-rant) Learning in which the consequences of behavior lead to changes in the probability of its occurrence.

Operant conditioning was first described by American psychologist Edward Thorndike (1911). Thorndike was interested in the question of animal intelligence, which he investigated using an apparatus he called a "puzzle box." A hungry cat was placed inside the box, food was placed outside, and the cat's efforts to escape were observed. With each trial, the cat became more efficient at getting out of the box. Based on these observations, Thorndike formulated the "law of effect," which states that the consequences of a response determines whether the response will be performed in the future. Thorndike's law of effect formed the basis for subsequent study of what is now referred to as *operant conditioning* in contemporary psychology. In the sections that follow, we examine three ways in which desirable and undesirable consequences influence our behavior: positive reinforcement, negative reinforcement, and punishment.

Positive Reinforcement

positive reinforcement
(rē´´in-fors´ment) Any consequence of behavior that leads to an increase in the probability of its occurrence.

In *positive reinforcement,* the consequences of a behavior are *positive,* so the behavior is engaged in *more frequently.* Simply stated, we say that **positive reinforcement** has occurred whenever a consequence of behavior leads to an increase in the probability of its occurrence.

In the early 1960s, a team of preschool teachers conducted a classic study in which they helped a young girl overcome her shyness in what has become a widely cited example of the principle of positive reinforcement (Allen, Hart, Buell, Harris, & Wolf, 1964). The teachers were worried because the girl spent little time playing with the other children and too much time with her adult teachers. They decided to encourage peer play through positive reinforcement. They knew that she enjoyed receiving praise from the teachers, so they decided to praise her *only* when she was playing with another child. The results of this use of positive reinforcement are shown in figure 5.4. To be able to evaluate the results of their positive reinforcement program, the teachers first counted the frequency with which the little girl interacted with other children and with adults before anything was done to help her. Then they started to positively reinforce (praise) her for playing with other children, but otherwise they paid very little attention to her (so that she would get positive reinforcement from her teachers only for playing with peers). As can be seen in the second segment of figure 5.4, the little girl's frequency of playing with peers increased markedly when the teachers reinforced her. To be sure that the positive reinforcement was responsible for the changes and not some other factor, the teachers stopped reinforcing her for playing with peers in the third segment (the *reversal* phase) of figure 5.4, and then reinforced her again during the fourth phase. As can be seen, the frequency of peer play dropped when the positive reinforcement was discontinued but increased again when it was resumed in the fourth phase. Thus, the teachers were able to intentionally teach a more adaptive pattern of playing to this child by using positive reinforcement.

Many other applications have been made of this principle, ranging from teaching hospitalized schizophrenic adults more normal patterns of behavior to teaching employees to reduce the amount of damage sustained when sorting boxes for airfreight delivery. In each case, the behavior that becomes more frequent is termed the *operant response* and the positive consequence of that response is called the *positive reinforcer.*

Three important issues in the use of positive reinforcement should be noted:

1. *Timing.* The positive reinforcer must be given within a short amount of time following the response, or learning will progress very slowly, if at all. There are

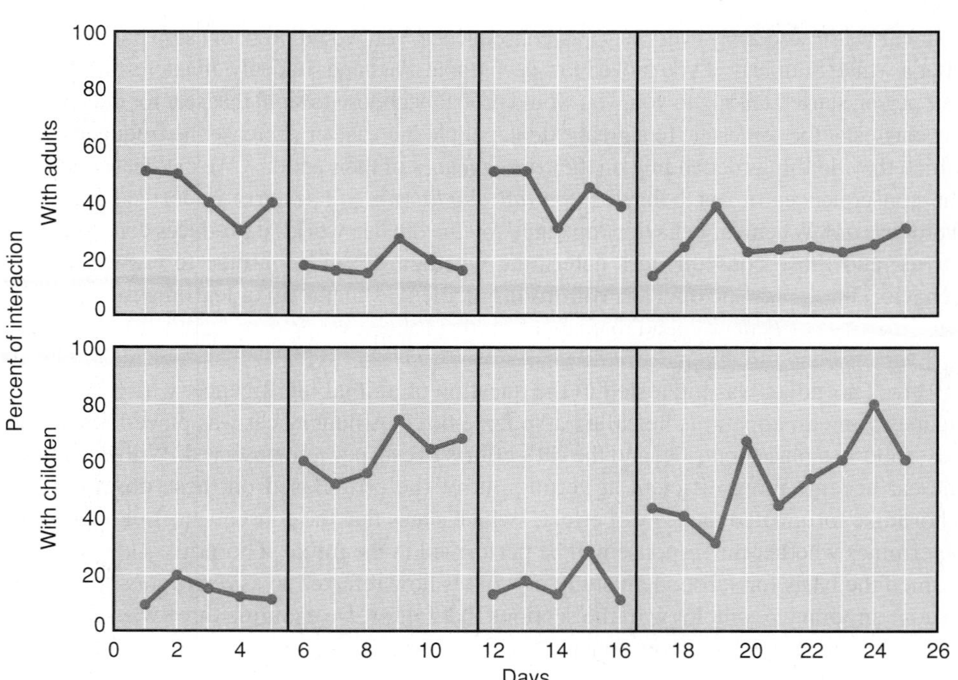

FIGURE 5.4
Increasing the amount of time that a child spends playing with other children through the use of positive reinforcement.

Source: Data from K. Eileen Allen, et al., "Effects of Social Reinforcement Isolate Behavior of a Nursery School Child" in *Child Development,* 35:511–518, 1974. Copyright © 1964 The Society for Research in Child Development.

some ways to get around this issue of timing (such as immediately telling an employee that she will get a bonus for making an important sale, even though the bonus will not come until the end of the month), but in general the greater the delay between the response and the reinforcer, the slower the learning. This phenomenon has been referred to as the principle of **delay of reinforcement.**

Drawing by M. Stevens; © 1987 The New Yorker Magazine, Inc.

2. *Consistency in the delivery of reinforcement.* For learning to take place, the individual providing positive reinforcement must consistently give it after every (or nearly every) response. After some learning has taken place, it's not always necessary, or even desirable, to reinforce every response (as we shall see later in the section "Schedules of Positive Reinforcement"), but consistency of reinforcement is essential in the beginning of the learning process.
3. *What we use as a positive reinforcer must, in fact, be reinforcing.* I remember very well making a mistake of this sort. I was working in a child psychology clinic with a child who had a number of problems, among them the fact that at 6 years of age he still did not speak or even make spontaneous speech sounds. To begin a language-training program with this child, I decided to use positive reinforcement to increase the rate of spontaneous speech sounds. I spent a number of fruitless days, however, trying to reinforce his vocalizations with M&Ms. When no increases occurred at all, I asked his mother, who had watched every session without making any comment, what she thought the problem might be. She responded that she thought the candy might have something to do with it—her son hated candy! Indeed, the candy did seem to have something to do with it, because when I switched to a positive reinforcer that he liked, raw carrots, his rate of vocalizations rose rapidly. In any intentional use of positive reinforcement, we must be sure that we are actually using a consequence that is reinforcing. Heaping praise on your college roommate for finally cleaning the bathroom may embarrass and annoy your roommate rather than reinforce the cleaning up. The only way we can be sure that something is a reinforcer is to try it out and see if it increases the likelihood of the behavior.

delay of reinforcement
The passage of time between the response and the positive reinforcement that leads to reduced efficiency of learning.

I do not want to give the impression through this discussion that positive reinforcement is something that occurs only when it's intentionally arranged. The natural consequences of our behavior can be reinforcing as well. For example, we learn that some ways of interacting with our friends or supervisors just naturally lead to happier relationships, and that is positively reinforcing. We are *always* affected by the consequences of our behavior and hence are always in the process of learning to adjust to our world through positive reinforcement.

Primary and Secondary Reinforcement

Where do positive reinforcers come from? Are they inborn or do we have to acquire them through learning? Actually, it turns out that some are inborn and some are learned. There are two types of positive reinforcement, primary and secondary reinforcement. **Primary reinforcers** are ones that are innately reinforcing and do not have to be acquired through learning. Food, water, warmth, novel stimulation, physical activity, and sexual gratification are all examples of primary reinforcers.

primary reinforcement
Reinforcement from innate positive reinforcers that do not have to be acquired through learning.

secondary reinforcement
Reinforcement from learned positive reinforcers.

Secondary reinforcers (which play an important part in operant conditioning) are learned through classical conditioning. Remember that classical conditioning involves the association of two stimuli: A neutral stimulus can be turned into a secondary reinforcer by pairing it repeatedly with a primary reinforcer. Consider an example from dog training. In teaching dogs to perform complex acts, such as those required of Seeing Eye dogs, primary reinforcers such as pieces of food are used extensively. It's much more convenient, however, to reinforce the dog for good behavior simply by saying "good dog!" than

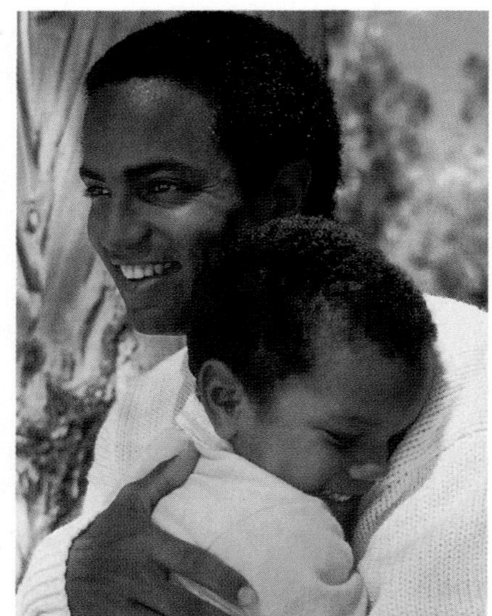

Secondary reinforcers like praise are learned from primary reinforcers such as gentle physical contact.

Gold medals are powerful secondary reinforcers.

fixed ratio schedule
A reinforcement schedule in which the reinforcer is given only after a specified number of responses.

variable ratio schedule
A reinforcement schedule in which the reinforcer is given after a varying number of responses have been made.

always lugging around a pocketful of dog biscuits. Unfortunately, dogs do not know what you are saying when you praise them and would not care much if they did—that is, not until you *teach* them to care. So, how would you go about making praise into a secondary reinforcer? Actually, it's quite simple. You would only need to say "good dog" to the dog every time you give the dog a biscuit. After enough pairings of these two stimuli, the praise will become a secondary reinforcer and will be effective in reinforcing the dog's behavior.

Dogs are not the only creatures that learn secondary reinforcers, however. People do it, too. How many of the things that motivate us—such as school grades, prize ribbons, money, applause—were acquired through pairing with primary reinforcers? Learning undoubtedly plays a key role in turning these things into powerful reinforcers for some people.

Schedules of Positive Reinforcement

Up to this point, we have talked about positive reinforcement as if every response were always followed by a reinforcer, a situation known as continuous reinforcement. The world is not constructed in such a regular and simple way, however. So what happens when reinforcement follows behavior on some other schedule? In addition to continuous reinforcement, psychologists have described four different schedules of reinforcement and have shown us the effects of each on behavior (Ferster & Skinner, 1957).

1. *Fixed ratio.* On a **fixed ratio schedule** of reinforcement, the reinforcer is given only after a specified number of responses. If sewing machine operators were given a pay slip (to be exchanged for money later) for every six dresses that were sewn, the schedule of reinforcement would be called a fixed ratio schedule. This schedule produces a fairly high rate of response because many responses need to be made to get the reinforcer, but there is typically a pause after each reinforcer is obtained (see fig. 5.5).
2. *Variable ratio.* On a **variable ratio schedule** of reinforcement, the reinforcer is obtained only after a varying number of responses have been made (see fig. 5.6). These schedules produce very high rates of responding and the learning is quite permanent. For example, why do even successful sales representatives hustle so? They know from past experience that on the average they will make a sale, for example, after every sixth presentation. But the fact that they cannot predict which presentation will make the sale—this one? the next one?—keeps them hopping. Another good example of reinforcement on a variable ratio is gambling. Slot machine players are reinforced for putting money into the machine and pulling the lever just often enough in an unpredictable fashion to addict many individuals to gambling.

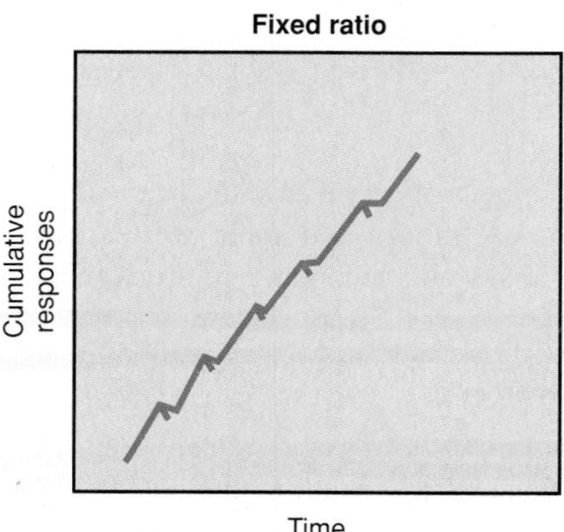

FIGURE 5.5
Pattern of behavior typically produced by a fixed ratio schedule of reinforcement. The hash marks show the delivery of reinforcement. In figures 5.5 to 5.8, steeper slopes indicate higher rates of responding.

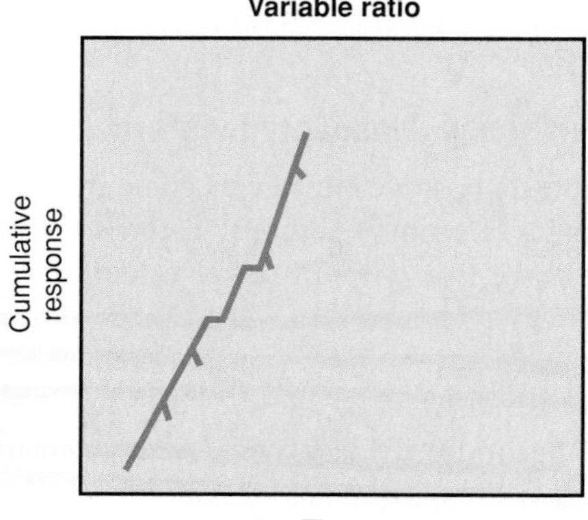

FIGURE 5.6
Pattern of behavior typically produced by a variable ratio schedule of reinforcement.

3. *Fixed interval.* In other cases, the schedule of reinforcement is not based on the *number* of responses but on the passage of *time*. The term **fixed interval schedule** is used when the first response that occurs after a predetermined period of time is reinforced. This produces a pattern of behavior in which very few responses are made until the fixed interval of time approaches and then the rate of responding increases rapidly (see fig. 5.7). A fellow professor of psychology provided this great example of a fixed interval schedule: While in graduate school he worked as a guard at night in a steel mill. He was paid for walking around the mill each hour and punching in the time clock each time as he passed it on his rounds. He confessed that this schedule of reinforcement led to 40 minutes of sitting around each hour, followed by a brisk 20-minute walk around the mill to the time clock! Members of Congress also are on a fixed interval schedule for the response of visiting with the voters in their districts. Making a visit back home to talk to the people is of little value to the politicians until the fixed two-year interval between elections starts to elapse. Then visits back home are reinforced by votes, so the rate of visits rises dramatically.
4. *Variable interval.* Finally, there is the schedule of reinforcement in which the first response made after a variable amount of time is reinforced. Like the variable ratio schedule, this **variable interval schedule** produces high rates of steady responding (see fig. 5.8), and although it's not a good schedule for initial learning, it produces highly stable performance when the response has already been partially learned through continuous reinforcement. Where I grew up in Florida, you saw lots of people sitting on docks and bridges with fishing poles in their hands because of variable reinforcement. You can't tell when fish are going to bite—they're unpredictable. But, for some people, catching a fish every now and then is a strong enough variable interval reinforcement to keep their lines in the water as much as they can.

Casino operators may not claim to use variable ratio schedules of reinforcement, but they know that an occasional jackpot will keep players at the slot machines.

fixed interval schedule
A reinforcement schedule in which the reinforcer is given following the first response occurring after a predetermined period of time.

variable interval schedule
A reinforcement schedule in which the reinforcer is given following the first response occurring after a variable amount of time.

Thus, we have seen that different schedules of positive reinforcement result in distinct patterns of behavior. It is very important for anyone responsible for managing another person's behavior, such as teachers, parents, or supervisors, to make informed choices regarding the type of reinforcement schedule to be used.

Shaping

In many situations, the response that we want to reinforce never occurs. For example, let's say you want to positively reinforce your child for cleaning her or his room. You might have to wait a long time for that behavior to occur! If left to their own devices, most children would spend little if any time cleaning their rooms. What we need to do in this case is to reinforce responses that are progressively more similar to the response that you finally want to reinforce (the "target response"). In doing so, you will gradually increase the probability of the target response and can then reinforce it when it occurs. This is called **shaping,**

shaping
A strategy of positively reinforcing behaviors that are successively more similar to desired behaviors.

Fixed interval

Cumulative response

Time

FIGURE 5.7
Pattern of behavior typically produced by a fixed interval schedule of reinforcement.

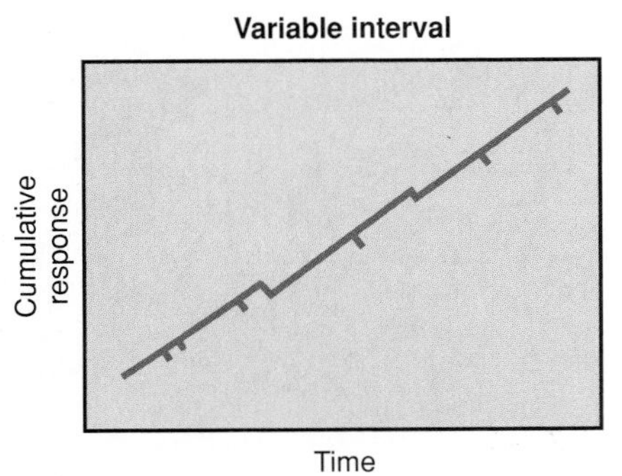

FIGURE 5.8
Pattern of behavior typically produced by a variable interval pattern of reinforcement.

Reinforcement of successive approximations by a violin teacher who understands shaping will help this girl become a better violinist.

or the *method of successive approximations,* because we "shape" the target response out of behaviors that successively approximate it.

Before considering the practical applications of the concept of shaping, let's go back to the animal learning laboratory where so many of the principles of learning that are useful to humans were first carefully researched. Suppose you wanted to teach a rat to press a lever in the special kind of learning apparatus called the **Skinner box,** named after its creator B. F. Skinner of Harvard University (see fig. 5.9). If you continue to take psychology courses, you may in fact be given this assignment in a lab course: "Here's a rat and here's a Skinner box; do not come back until you have taught him to press the lever!" What do you do? If you have not read the section on shaping in your textbook, you might program the Skinner box to drop a little pellet of rat food into the food tray every time the lever is pressed and then wait—and wait and wait—for the rat to press the bar. This strategy might work in time—the rat *might* accidentally press the lever enough times to get reinforced by the food pellets enough to make this a frequent response—but I wouldn't bet on it. Rats generally do not go around pressing levers. When placed in a Skinner box they groom themselves, bite the Plexiglas walls, urinate, defecate, and sniff a lot, but they do not press levers. How then do you teach the uncooperative rodent to press the lever?

Skinner box
A cage for animals equipped with a response lever and a food tray dispenser used in research on operant conditioning.

You use shaping! First, whenever the rat (we'll call him "B. F." in honor of B. F. Skinner) gets up and *moves toward the lever,* give him a food pellet. After you do that a few times, the rat ought to be moving toward the lever quite a bit. Then you can wait until B. F. *touches* the lever in some way to reinforce him. Do that a few times and then wait until he *touches it with a downward pushing movement* (if at any time you have failed to reinforce him enough, you can go back a step). Then, after he is reliably touching the bar in a downward motion, B. F. should have quite a high probability of *pushing it down enough* to activate the automatic feeder, which will reinforce him for the complete response of lever pressing.

The principle of shaping has great importance outside of the rat lab. For example, most beginning skiers cannot be reinforced for making perfect post turns because they just are not able to do them yet. But they can be reinforced for successive approximations to good turns and thereby shaped into good skiing. In programs for children with developmental handicaps, shaping is used to teach basic skills such as brushing teeth, performing useful jobs, and using public transportation. And how about shaping 3-year-olds to clean their rooms? At first you have to reinforce them for putting one toy away—even though the rest

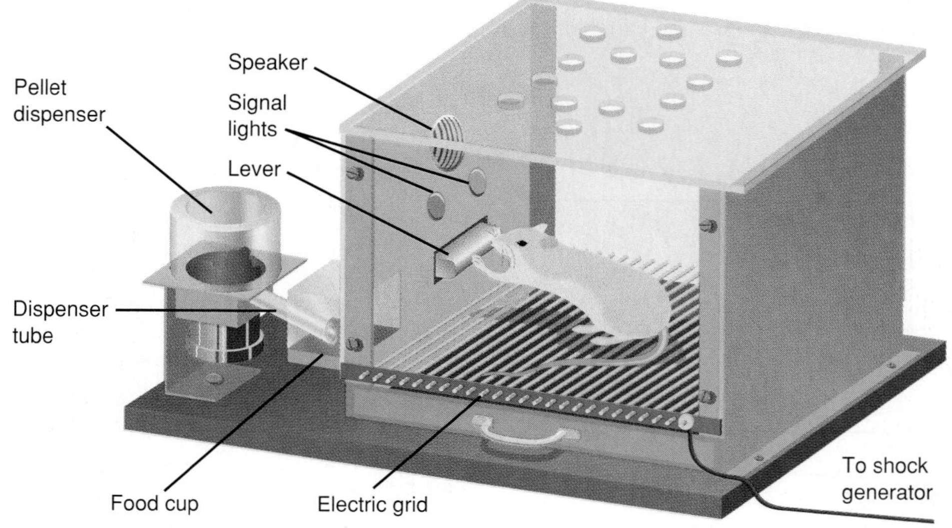

FIGURE 5.9
In this Skinner box designed for rats, the response under study is lever pressing. Food pellets, which serve as reinforcers, are delivered into the food cup on the left. The speaker and light permit manipulations of visual and auditory stimuli, and the electric grid gives the experimenter control over negative consequences (mild shock) in the box.

of the room is littered with junk. After doing that a couple of times, reinforce them for putting several toys away, and then for an "approximately" clean room, and so on until the target response occurs.

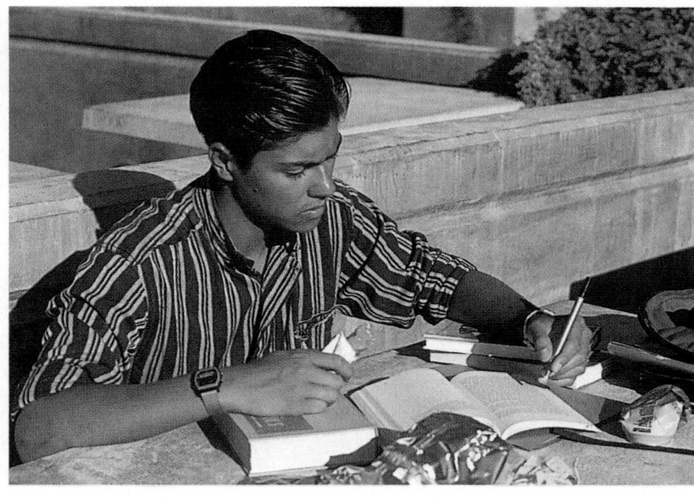

We all learn that eating removes the negative feeling of hunger.

Negative Reinforcement

Reinforcers are not always positive events; sometimes the reinforcing consequence is the *removal or avoidance of a negative event.* Suppose the fellow in the apartment next door plays his stereo so loud that it has kept you awake every night this week. If you assertively ask him to turn it down and the loud music stops, that consequence will reinforce your assertive behavior. Two types of operant learning based on negative reinforcement, escape conditioning and avoidance conditioning, play an important, but often unnoticed, role in influencing our behavior.

The concept of negative reinforcement is one that students frequently find confusing for two reasons. First, to many students, the name implies that a negative or undesirable behavior—like a bad habit—is being reinforced. That actually is not implied in the name at all—the behavior that is negatively reinforced may be either desirable or undesirable. Second, even more students find the term *negative reinforcement* confusing because it sounds like a new term for punishment, which it is not! When we look at the concept of punishment later in this chapter, you will see that it is a quite different phenomenon.

What the term **negative reinforcement** *does* mean is this: A behavior is reinforced (and, therefore, is strengthened) because something negative (or unpleasant or aversive) *is removed* by the behavior or does not happen at all because of the behavior. In the previous example, the loud music was the negative thing that your assertive behavior got rid of. Your asking him to turn down the volume was reinforced through negative reinforcement (stopping the loud music) and you probably would be more likely to be assertive in the future as a result.

negative reinforcement
Reinforcement that comes about from the removal or avoidance of a negative event as the consequence of behavior.

Two types of learning are based on negative reinforcement: escape conditioning and avoidance conditioning. As we discuss these in detail in the next two sections, the concept of negative reinforcement will become more clear.

Escape Conditioning

In **escape conditioning,** the behavior causes the negative event to *stop*. For example, if a young boy has been confined to his room for an hour, that is probably a pretty negative situation to him. If he starts to cry softly and pitifully murmur that no one loves him, and if this causes his parent to relent in a few minutes and let him out of his room, then negative reinforcement has occurred. Which behavior has been strengthened? Probably he will be much more likely to act pitifully the next time he is sent to his room because it made something negative—the confinement—stop. Escape conditioning, therefore, is a form of negative reinforcement because something negative is removed. It's called escape conditioning because the individual *escapes* from something negative (in the sense of causing it to stop).

escape conditioning
Operant conditioning in which the behavior is reinforced because it causes a negative event to cease (a form of negative reinforcement).

Avoidance Conditioning

In the other form of negative reinforcement, called **avoidance conditioning,** the behavior has the consequence of causing something negative *not to happen* when it otherwise would have happened. Suppose you are terrified of pit bulldogs, but the route that you walk to campus takes you past a yard where a particularly vicious pit bull is loosely penned up. If you find a new route to school that does not take you past a single pit bull, you will probably continue to take this route because it causes the negative event of passing the pit bull not to occur. Even if it does make you feel a bit like a coward, finding a new route is a highly

avoidance conditioning
Operant conditioning in which the behavior is reinforced because it prevents something negative from happening (a form of negative reinforcement).

reinforcing consequence. This is an example of avoidance conditioning, because the behavior of taking a new route was reinforced by avoiding something negative (the pitbull).

Negative reinforcement is a very powerful method of reinforcement, so we learn patterns of behavior quickly and easily from it. Unfortunately, what we learn are often immature ways of dealing with unpleasant situations rather than mature ways of facing them directly. The child in our first example would have been better off taking his punishment and learning how not to get into trouble next time, and the college student would have been better off getting over the fear of the penned pit bull. It's often too easy to learn a quick and easy, though inappropriate, solution through negative reinforcement.

Incidentally, when the parent let the child who was acting pitifully out of his room, the parent was probably reinforced for that lapse in discipline, too. Through what principle of operant conditioning was the parent reinforced? Since the act of letting the child out of his room caused the child's unpleasant whining to stop, the parent was reinforced through escape conditioning. Negative reinforcement of inappropriate behavior is a frequent occurrence that we need to avoid.

Punishment

punishment
A negative consequence of a behavior that leads to a decrease in the frequency of the behavior.

Sometimes the consequence of behavior is negative, and as a result, the frequency of that behavior will decrease. In other words, the behavior has been *punished.* For example, if you buy a new set of pots and pans with metal handles and pick up a hot pan without a pot holder, a negative consequence will surely occur! And you will probably not try to pick up your new pans in that way again. **Punishment** is a negative consequence that leads to a reduction in the frequency of the behavior that produced it (Church, 1969; Tarpy & Mayer, 1978). When appropriately used, punishment can be an ethical and valuable tool for discouraging inappropriate behavior. In our society, however, painful forms of punishment are commonly used with children by parents, teachers, and others in authority. Spankings, for example, are a common feature of child rearing in the United States. But in addition to the obvious ethical issues, there are serious dangers inherent in the use of punishment that must be weighed against its potential benefits.

Dangers of Punishment

The dangers inherent in punishment are as follows:

1. The use of punishment is often *reinforcing to the punisher.* For example, if a parent spanks a child who has been whining and the spanking stops the child from whining, the parent will be reinforced for spanking through negative reinforcement. This, unfortunately, may mean that the frequency of spankings, and perhaps their intensity, will increase, thereby increasing not only the amount of physical pain the child endures but also the dangers of child abuse.
2. Punishment often has a *generalized inhibiting effect* on the individual. Repeatedly spanking a child for "talking back" to you may lead the child to quit talking to you altogether. Similarly, criticizing your bridge partner for mistakes may lead him or her to give up playing the game altogether, or at least stop playing with you.
3. We commonly react to painful punishment by *learning to dislike* the person who inflicts the pain, and perhaps by *reacting aggressively* toward that person. Sometimes an individual takes out his or her resentment on someone else if it's not possible to react directly against the person who gave the pain. Thus, punishment may solve one problem but only lead to a worse problem, namely, aggression.
4. What we think is punishment is not always effective in punishing the behavior. In particular, most teachers and parents (and many supervisors, roommates, etc.) think that *criticism* will punish the behavior at which it's aimed. However, in many settings, especially homes and classrooms filled with young children, it has been demonstrated that criticism is often a *positive reinforcer* that increases the rate of whatever behavior the criticism follows. This has been called the

criticism trap (Becker, Engelmann, & Thomas, 1975). For example, some teachers or parents see a behavior they do not like and criticize to get rid of it. But children are sometimes reinforced by the attention they receive when criticized. In this way the criticism reinforces rather than punishes the behavior, and the criticized behavior increases in frequency. The adult then uses more criticism in an effort to quell this misbehavior. This reinforces the behavior even more and increases its rate in an upwardly spiraling course.

criticism trap
An increase in the frequency of a negative behavior that often follows the use of criticism, reinforcing the behavior it is intended to punish.

5. Even when punishment is effective in suppressing an inappropriate behavior, it does not teach the individual how to act more appropriately instead. Punishment used by itself may be self-defeating; it may suppress one inappropriate behavior only to be replaced by another one. It's not until appropriate behaviors are taught to the individual to replace the inappropriate ones that any progress can be made.

Guidelines for the Use of Punishment

The preceding list is an indictment of punishment as a method of changing behavior in child-rearing, industry, education, or any other setting. It should not be considered to be a total condemnation of punishment, however. In some instances, punishment may be a morally justifiable method of changing behavior. For example, in teaching a young child not to run out into a busy street, punishment may be the only method that makes sense. In these instances, however, every effort should be made to minimize the negative side effects of punishment by following some guidelines for its use.

1. Use the least painful punishment possible to avoid negative reactions to the pain by the punished person. Taking away TV time from a 10-year-old or placing a 4-year-old in a chair in the corner for 3 minutes is at least as effective as spankings, and certainly more humane.
2. Make sure that you positively reinforce appropriate behavior to take the place of the inappropriate behavior you are trying to eliminate. Punishment will not be effective in the long run unless you are also reinforcing appropriate behavior.
3. Make it clear to the individual what behavior you are punishing, and remove all threat of punishment as soon as that behavior stops. In other words, it might be okay to punish a certain behavior, but it does more harm than good to become generally angry at the other person for doing something inappropriate. *Do not punish people; punish specific behaviors.* And stop punishing when the inappropriate behavior ceases.
4. Do not mix punishment with rewards for the *same* behavior. For example, do not punish a child for fighting and then apologetically hug and kiss the child you have just punished. Mixtures of this sort are confusing and lead to inefficient learning.
5. Once you have begun to punish, do not back out. In other words, do not reinforce begging, pleading, or other inappropriate behavior by letting the individual out of the punishment. It both nullifies the punishment and reinforces the begging and pleading through negative reinforcement.

Contrasting Classical and Operant Conditioning

We have just talked about a number of different forms of "conditioning." This blitz of new concepts can be confusing. However, if you can understand the distinction between classical and operant conditioning, the rest will be easy.

Classical and operant conditioning differ from each other in three primary ways:

1. Classical conditioning involves an association between two stimuli, such as a tone and food. Operant conditioning involves an association between a response and the resulting consequence, such as studying hard and getting an "A."

Comparison of the types of operant conditioning: positive reinforcement, negative reinforcement, and punishment. The two types of reinforcement, positive and negative, are called *reinforcement* because the response is strengthened by the consequence.

Notice that the terms *positive* and *negative reinforcement* and *punishment* have nothing to do with the nature of the response that is strengthened or weakened. This example uses a very "negative" response; however, a "positive" response could have been used to illustrate the same results in each case.

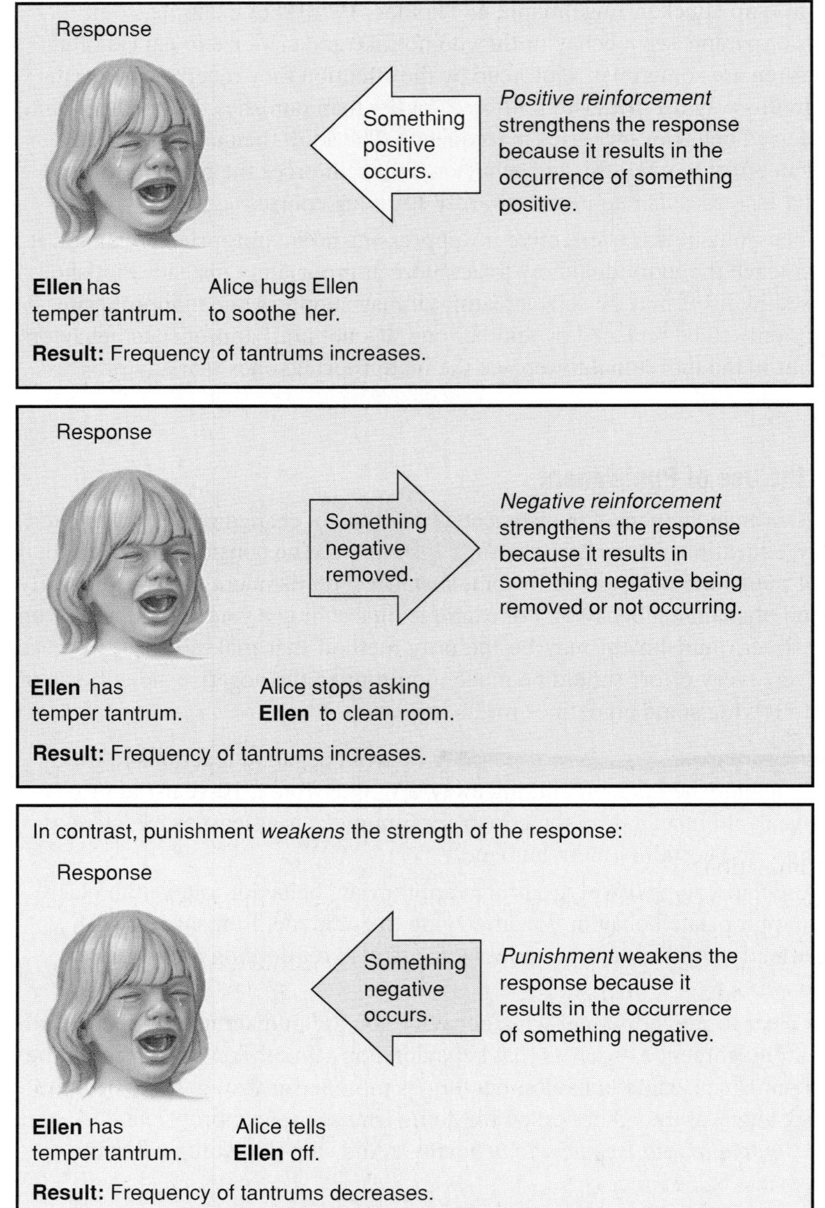

Response
Something positive occurs.
Positive reinforcement strengthens the response because it results in the occurrence of something positive.
Ellen has temper tantrum.
Alice hugs Ellen to soothe her.
Result: Frequency of tantrums increases.
Response
Something negative removed.
Negative reinforcement strengthens the response because it results in something negative being removed or not occurring.
Ellen has temper tantrum.
Alice stops asking **Ellen** to clean room.
Result: Frequency of tantrums increases.
In contrast, punishment *weakens* the strength of the response:
Response
Something negative occurs.
Punishment weakens the response because it results in the occurrence of something negative.
Ellen has temper tantrum.
Alice tells **Ellen** off.
Result: Frequency of tantrums decreases.

2. Classical conditioning usually involves reflexive, involuntary behaviors that are controlled by the spinal cord or autonomic nervous system. These include fear responses, salivation, and other involuntary behaviors. Operant conditioning, on the other hand, usually involves more complicated voluntary behaviors that are mediated by the somatic nervous system.
3. The most important difference, however, concerns the way in which the stimulus that makes conditioning "happen" is presented (the unconditioned stimulus, or UCS, in classical conditioning and the reinforcing stimulus in operant conditioning). In classical conditioning, the UCS is paired with the conditioned stimulus (CS) *independent of* the individual's behavior. The individual does not have to *do* anything for either the CS or UCS to be presented. In operant conditioning, however, the reinforcing consequence occurs *only if* the response being conditioned has just been emitted; that is, the reinforcing consequence is *contingent on* the occurrence of the response.

Stimulus Discrimination

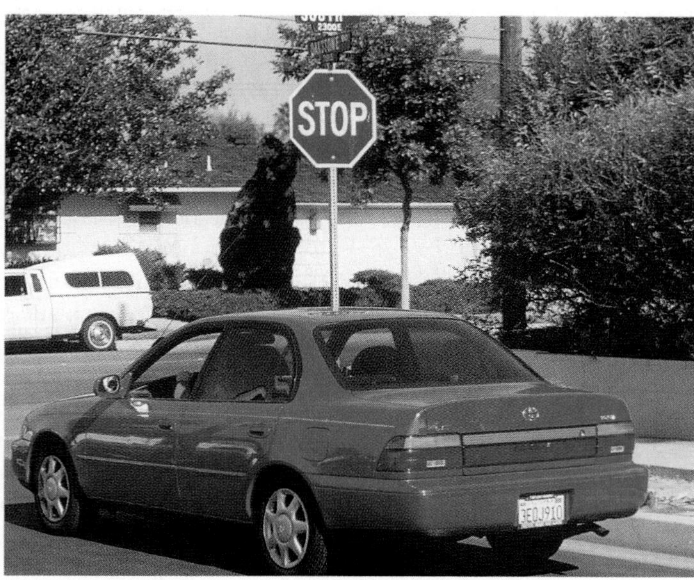

Stopping for a stop sign is one stimulus discrimination drivers must learn.

Most responses do not have an equal probability of occurring in any situation. They are more likely to occur in some circumstances than in others. For example, schoolchildren are more likely to behave well when the teacher is in the room than when the teacher is not. Similarly, you are more likely to clean up your apartment when your new girlfriend or boyfriend says "I'll be over after class" than when no one is coming. Most responses are more likely to occur in the presence of some stimuli than in the presence of others. We call this phenomenon **stimulus discrimination,** meaning that we discriminate between appropriate and inappropriate occasions for a response.

Let's go back to the rat lab and see one way in which stimulus discrimination might be learned. The last time you were in the lab, you taught your rat B. F. to press the lever through shaping and positive reinforcement for lever pressing. Let's suppose that you want him to press the bar only in the presence of a specific stimulus such as a light; that is, you want B. F. to learn a stimulus discrimination. We would start by turning on a light over the lever, letting B. F. press the lever and receive the reinforcer several times. Then we turn off the light for a little while and we do *not* reinforce lever presses when the light is out. Then we turn the light back on and reinforce responses, turn it off and do not reinforce responses, and so on many times. The stimulus in which the response is reinforced is called S^{d} (short for *discriminative stimulus*) and the stimulus in which the response is never reinforced is called S^{delta}. Soon, if we followed the teaching program just outlined, B. F. would begin pressing the lever almost every time the light came on, and almost never press it when the light is off. He would have learned a stimulus discrimination.

stimulus discrimination
The tendency for responses to occur more often in the presence of one stimulus than others.

Humans have to learn stimulus discriminations, too—lots of them. We have to learn to say "car" only to the stimulus of a car and not to a toy wagon; we have to learn to say "dog" to the stimulus of the printed letters *D-O-G* and not to other letters; and so on. Many of the stimulus discriminations that we learn are much more subtle than that, however. For example, we must learn to introduce ourselves to others at a party when they are showing interest in us (rather than no interest). We have to learn to express sympathy when a sad thing has been told to us. Responses made during the presence of an S^{d} for that behavior will lead to favorable consequences, whereas the same behavior made during S^{delta} will often lead to unfavorable consequences. Introducing yourself to a person showing interest in you will lead to a pleasant conversation; introducing yourself to a person showing no interest can make you both feel extremely uncomfortable.

Stimulus discrimination does not occur only in operant conditioning, however. Let's say that your lab instructor wants you to use classical conditioning to teach B. F. to stop moving and crouch in the presence of a slow-ringing bell but not a fast-ringing bell. First you need to know that rats explore freely in dim light but crouch defensively in bright light. You would start classical conditioning in the normal way, by pairing the slow ring with the UCS (bright light) for the response of crouching. After several pairings, B. F. should be crouching whenever the slow-ringing bell is sounded. If we now begin presenting the fast ring sometimes, B. F. will respond to that with the crouch response, too. But if we continue to present both the slow and fast rings, *but only pair the bright light with the slow ring,* B. F. would soon respond with the fear response only to the slow ring and not the fast one; he will have learned a stimulus discrimination through classical conditioning.

Stimulus Generalization

The opposite of stimulus discrimination is **stimulus generalization.** This term indicates that people (as well as rats and other creatures) do not always discriminate between stimuli that are similar to one another. Stated another way, the more similar two stimuli are, the more likely the individual is to respond to them as if they were the same stimulus. We call a

stimulus generalization
The tendency for similar stimuli to elicit the same response.

1994 Buick and a 1995 Buick by the same name, "Buick," because they are very similar in appearance. Similarly, we call beagles and basset hounds "dogs" because they look, act, sound, and smell a lot alike. And the person who is deathly afraid of cats is usually afraid of Siamese, tabby, and alley cats alike.

As with everything else, let's go back to the lab to demonstrate stimulus generalization based on similarity in the color of the stimulus. This time, however, we will use a pigeon as our laboratory animal instead of a rat, because rats are color blind and pigeons are not. For example, we could reinforce the pigeon only for responding in the presence of a *yellow-green* light whose wavelength is 550 nanometers (a unit used to measure the wavelength of light). In a while, the pigeon will emit lever presses only when the S^d of the light is present. In this part of our study of his learning, however, the fact that he presses the lever only in the presence of the light is important to us only because it gives us a tool for carefully studying stimulus generalization. If we begin changing the wavelength of the light stimulus, we will be able to see that the more we change the wavelength, the less likely the pigeon will be to respond to it. If we carefully change the wavelength many times in small gradations, we will be able to make a graph that shows us this fact about stimulus generalization. We have drawn the results of such a study in figure 5.10. Notice that the more similar two stimuli are, the more likely the pigeon is to respond to them as if they are the same; and the less similar they are, the less likely they are to be responded to as the same.

Before we leave this concept, let's look at one more example of stimulus generalization, in this case generalization involving classical conditioning. Recall the famous experiment with Little Albert, in which Albert was classically conditioned to fear a white laboratory rat by pairing a loud noise with the rat. In addition, the fear generalized to other similar objects. Five days later, Albert reacted fearfully to a white rabbit, a white dog, and a white coat. He also showed mildly fearful reactions to balls of cotton and a Santa Claus mask.

Thinking Critically About Psychology

1. Do your friends ever reinforce you for behaving in ways that are not good for you? In what ways?

2. What kinds of behaviors does our culture encourage? Is this done more through positive reinforcement, negative reinforcement, or punishment?

Review

We learn from the consequences of our behavior. If our behavior leads to a positive consequence, we will be more likely to engage in that behavior again, with the specific pattern of behavior depending in part on the schedule with which reinforcement is delivered. The events that serve as positive reinforcers are both inborn (primary reinforcers) and learned (secondary reinforcers). Positive reinforcement can even increase the probability of behaviors that initially never occur by reinforcing successive approximations to that behavior (shaping).

Behavior can be reinforced not only when the consequence is positive but also when the behavior removes or avoids a negative consequence (negative reinforcement). Actually, two slightly different forms of learning are based on negative reinforcement: (a) escape conditioning in which the behavior removes a negative event, and (b) avoidance conditioning in which behavior causes the negative event not to occur. Punishment, which is different from negative reinforcement, is a negative consequence of behavior that reduces the probability of its future occurrence.

Behavior that is reinforced only in the presence of a specific stimulus will tend to occur only in the presence of that stimulus (stimulus discrimination). On the other hand, there is a strong tendency to respond to similar stimuli as if they were the same (stimulus generalization). The phenomena of stimulus generalization and discrimination also occur in classical conditioning.

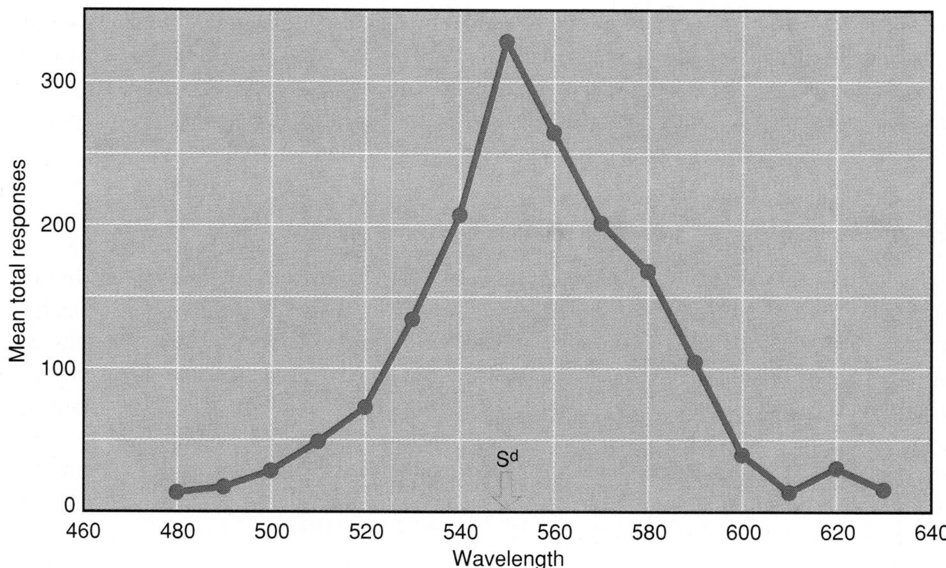

FIGURE 5.10

Stimulus generalization means that the more similar stimuli are, the more likely they will be responded to as if they are the same. In this case, the more similar the wavelength of light is to the original stimulus, the more frequent the response of a pigeon who had been reinforced for pecking when a light measuring 550 nanometers (a measure of wavelength) was present.

Check Your Learning

To be sure that you have learned the key points from the preceding section, cover the answers below and try to answer each question. If you give an incorrect answer to any question, return to the page given next to the correct answer to see why your answer was not correct.

1. Learning from the consequences of our behavior is called ________________ .
   - **a.** operant conditioning
   - **b.** classical conditioning
   - **c.** environmental learning
   - **d.** cognitive learning
2. Slot machine players are on a ________________ of reinforcement.
   - **a.** variable interval schedule
   - **b.** variable ratio schedule
   - **c.** fixed ratio schedule
   - **d.** fixed interval schedule
3. Negative reinforcement is another term for punishment.
   - **a.** True
   - **b.** False
4. The more similar two stimuli are, the more likely the individual is to respond to them as if they were the same stimulus. This is termed ________________ .
   - **a.** stimulus discrimination
   - **b.** generalized responding
   - **c.** stimulus generalization
   - **d.** stimulus conditioning

Correct Answers
1. a (p. 181), **2.** b (p. 185), **3.** b (p. 187), **4.** c (p. 191).

EXTINCTION: LEARNING WHEN TO QUIT

The process of learning is essential to human life. Through it we learn to cope with the demands of the environment. But the world is apt to change at any time, so people have to change, too. If we were able to learn only once and never change, we would not be able to survive changes in the environment. For example, if we were Stone Age people who learned to get oranges from the tops of orange trees by shaking the trees, that learned behavior would be very useful—that is, it would be positively reinforced. But the learned behavior of shaking orange trees would no longer be useful after all the oranges had been shaken out of the tree. At that point, we would need to quit shaking orange trees! If changes in the environment did not lead to changes in our learned behavior, we would be in big trouble.

If a learned response stops occurring because the aspect of the environment that originally caused the learning changes, we say **extinction** has occurred. The process of extinction is similar in many respects for both classical and operant conditioning.

extinction
(eks-ting´shun) The process of unlearning a learned response because of the removal of the original source of learning.

Removing the Source of Learning

Extinction occurs because the original source of the learning has been removed. In classical conditioning, learning takes place because two stimuli are repeatedly paired together. If Pavlov's dog stopped receiving meat powder with the sound of the metronome, the dog would eventually stop salivating to the metronome. Or if you are hurt a couple of times when you are in the dentist's chair, the dentist's chair will come to elicit the autonomic response of fear (from the pairing of pain with the previously neutral chair). Let's suppose, however, that the clumsy dentist sells his practice to a new, truly painless dentist and you no longer get hurt in that chair. In this case, the cause of learning to fear the dentist's chair is removed. Eventually (classically conditioned fears are difficult to extinguish), the fact that the conditioned stimulus is presented alone (the dentist's chair is never again paired with pain) will lead to the extinction of the response of fear to the dentist's chair. In essence, you will have learned that the chair no longer predicts pain. So, using the terminology of classical conditioning, a CR will be extinguished if the CS for that response is presented repeatedly but the UCS for that stimulus is no longer paired with it.

In the case of operant conditioning, extinction results from a change in the consequences of behavior. If a response is no longer reinforced, then that response will eventually decline in frequency. If Skinner's rat no longer was given food pellets for bar presses, the bar pressing would eventually stop. Similarly, when there are no longer any oranges in the tree, the response of shaking it will no longer be reinforced and shaking will eventually stop.

There is one notable difference between extinction in classical and operant conditioning. During the early stages of the operant extinction process, "frustration" often occurs. This may lead to a brief, rapid burst of responding before the response finally begins to disappear. When you first discover that no more oranges fall out of the tree, you might shake the tree angrily for a while.

The schedule of reinforcement and the type of reinforcement greatly influence the speed with which the extinction of operant conditioning takes place. This phenomenon is known as the **partial reinforcement effect.** Responses that have been continuously reinforced are extinguished more quickly than responses that have been reinforced on variable ratio or variable interval schedules. Perhaps this is so because it's easier to see that the reinforcement is not going to come again if it used to come after every response. It may not be a bad thing that parents, employers, teachers, and others are often too busy to reinforce every good response; a variable pattern of reinforcement makes the good response more resistant to extinction.

The most difficult responses of all to extinguish, however, are responses learned through avoidance learning. Extinction of an avoidance response should result from the removal of the negative consequence. However, if you continue to perform avoidance responses, you will never see that the situation has changed. For example, if you continue to avoid the pit bull by taking the longer route to school, you will never learn that the owner and his dog have moved to another neighborhood.

Avoidance responses can be extinguished rapidly, however, using a technique called **response prevention.** This technique does exactly what its name implies. Avoidance responses are simply *prevented* to be sure that the individual sees that the negative consequence does not occur. The technique of response prevention has useful applications in treating disorders such as obsessive-compulsive disorder (see chapter 13). When compulsive behaviors, such as frequent hand washing, are physically prevented, the individual has an opportunity to discover that the feared consequences, such as terrible illness, are not really going to happen (Steketee & Cleere, 1990).

response prevention
The prevention of avoidance responses to ensure that the individual sees that the negative consequence will not occur to speed up the extinction of avoidance responses.

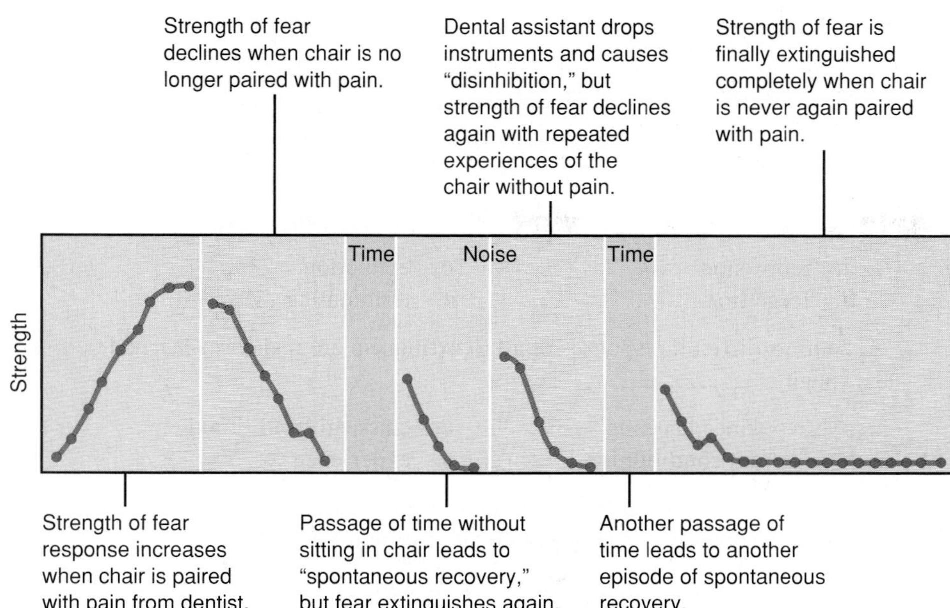
Strength of fear
declines when chair is no
longer paired with pain.
Dental assistant drops
instruments and causes
"disinhibition," but
strength of fear declines
again with repeated
experiences of the
chair without pain.
Strength of fear is
finally extinguished
completely when chair
is never again paired
with pain.
Time
Noise
Time
Strength
Strength of fear
response increases
when chair is paired
with pain from dentist.
Passage of time without
sitting in chair leads to
"spontaneous recovery,"
but fear extinguishes again.
Another passage of
time leads to another
episode of spontaneous
recovery.

FIGURE 5.11
The course of extinction of a classically conditioned fear of dental chairs.

Spontaneous Recovery and Disinhibition

The course of extinction is not always smooth. Normally, the learned response occurs many times before extinction is complete. Consider again the fear of the dental chair: The strength of the response gradually decreases because the CS (chair) is never again paired with the UCS (pain). If, however, there is a long period of time between presentations of the CS (such as a year between visits to the dentist), the fear can reappear the next time the CS is presented (see fig. 5.11). This is termed **spontaneous recovery.** It may occur several times during the course of extinction, but as long as the stimulus continues to be presented alone, the recovered response will be extinguished more quickly each time until the response no longer recovers.

spontaneous recovery
A temporary increase in the strength of a conditioned response that is likely to occur during extinction after the passage of time.

In some cases, the strength of the extinguished response returns for a reason other than spontaneous recovery. If some intense but unrelated stimulus event occurs, it may cause the strength of the extinguished response to return temporarily. For example, if the dentist's assistant dropped a tray of dental instruments while you were sitting in the chair, your fear response might come back for a while. This phenomenon is called **disinhibition.** That term will not seem to fit the phenomenon unless you understand that Pavlov, for theoretical reasons, believed that no response was ever really unlearned, just "inhibited" by another part of the brain. He termed this temporary increase in the strength of the response "disinhibition" because he felt that noise temporarily reduced the inhibition of the response. Both spontaneous recovery and disinhibition occur during the course of operant as well as classical extinction.

disinhibition
(dis´´in-hi-bish´un) A temporary increase in the strength of an extinguished response caused by an unrelated stimulus event.

Review

To adapt fully to a changing world, we must be able to unlearn as well as learn. The process of extinction begins as soon as the source of the original learning is removed. In classical conditioning, this means that no longer pairing the UCS with the CS will produce extinction of the CR. In operant learning, no longer reinforcing the response will extinguish the response. The course of extinction is often irregular, with the strength of the response often spontaneously recovering after long periods of time or when a strong disinhibiting stimulus occurs.

Thinking Critically About Psychology

1. What makes some behaviors more difficult to extinguish than others?

2. What kinds of behaviors do people commonly try to unlearn? How have you personally tried to eliminate unwanted behaviors?

Check Your Learning

To be sure that you have learned the key points from the preceding section, cover the answers below and try to answer each question. If you give an incorrect answer to any question, return to the page given next to the correct answer to see why your answer was not correct.

1. The process of unlearning a learned response because of a change in the aspect of the environment that originally caused the learning is termed __________ .

   a. repression **c.** extinction
   b. forgetting **d.** terminating

2. The most difficult responses of all to extinguish are responses learned through ______________ .

   a. avoidance learning **c.** classical conditioning
   b. operant conditioning **d.** experience

3. ______________ refers to a temporary increase in the strength of an extinguished response caused by an unrelated stimulus event.

   a. Spontaneous recovery **c.** Revival
   b. Disinhibition **d.** Learning

Correct Answers
1. c (p. 194), 2. a (p. 194), 3. b (p. 195).

THEORETICAL INTERPRETATIONS OF LEARNING

What is learned? When an individual's behavior changes as the result of classical or operant conditioning, what exactly has happened to the individual? One view dating back at least to the time of Pavlov is that neural *connections* between brain regions associated with specific stimuli and specific responses are acquired during the learning process. For example, when a rat is reinforced for pressing a lever in the presence of a light, a connection is believed to be automatically created between brain regions associated with the light and the specific pattern of muscle movements of the lever press. The next time the light is turned on, the neural connections to the muscles will cause the lever press to occur. Research based on the connection approach emphasized readily observable changes in behavior and basically ignored internal mental processes.

Some psychologists continued to argue that internal mental processes played a central role in the learning process and were therefore deserving of study. For these psychologists, learning involves changes in cognitions rather than specific neural connections. As noted earlier in the text, the term *cognition* refers to the intellectual processes of thinking, expecting, believing, perceiving, and so on. Adherents to this view consider that the individual (rat or human) changes his or her cognitions about a given situation during the learning process. For example, you flinch when a light comes on that has previously been paired with an electric shock, because you *expect* it to be followed by a shock. A rat turns left in a maze because he *knows* that the food was down that way the last 10 times she ran through the maze.

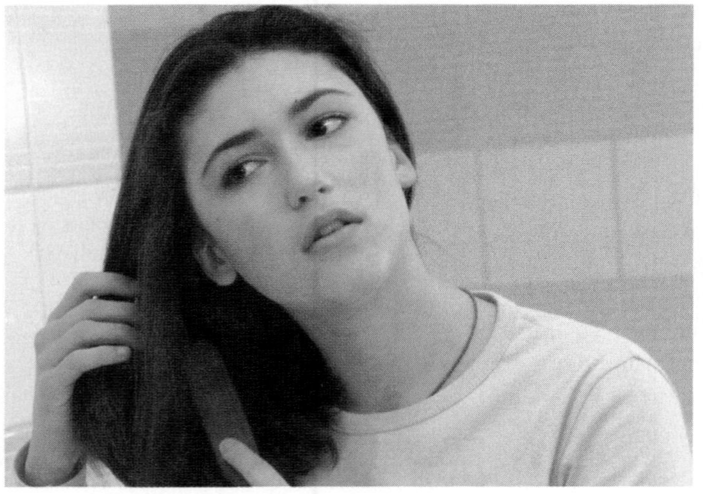

This young woman has learned that good grooming usually elicits compliments from her dates. Is this best thought of as learned behavior involving a stimulus-response connection or is it a behavior based on expectations?

Cognition or Connection?

A considerable amount of research has been conducted through the years to evaluate the connection and cognition theories of learning. Although most of it has been carried out using animals as subjects, what has been learned about the nature of learning is relevant to us human animals, too.

Place Learning

An ingenious experiment to test the cognitive view of learning was designed by the late Edward C. Tolman of the University of California at Berkeley (Tolman, Ritchie, & Kalish, 1946). Rats were initially trained to run down the elevated path shown in figure 5.12. They started at point A, made a series of turns (left, right, right), and ran to point B where food was provided. In the connection view of learning, the rats learned to do this by learning connections between the stimuli of the alley and the particular muscle movements of running and turning. Tolman took a cognitive view, however. He believed that the rats had learned a **cognitive map** of where the food was located relative to the starting place. They did not acquire a fixed pattern of muscle movements; they acquired knowledge of the location of the food.

cognitive map
(kog´ni-tiv) An inferred mental awareness of the structure of a physical space or related elements.

How can we distinguish between the cognitive and connectionist interpretations? Tolman's experimental test was ingenious. Suppose we give the rats a chance to take a shortcut directly to the food, will they take it? Or will they be unable to recognize it as a better path, since all they had learned was connections between maze stimuli and patterns of muscle movements? Tolman and his colleagues answered this question by blocking the old path (as shown in fig. 5.13) and providing a variety of new choices. Interestingly, the greatest number of rats chose the path that led directly to where the food had been. Tolman interpreted this as meaning that they had learned a new cognition, knowledge of the location of the food.

Latent Learning

Tolman conducted another informative experiment that evaluated the cognitive interpretation of learning in a rather different way (Tolman & Honzik, 1930). Suppose we allowed a rat to run around in a complex maze of alleys like the one shown in figure 5.14. Would the rat learn anything? The connectionist view would say no: Learning would occur only if reinforcement were delivered at the end of the maze to "stamp in" a connection between the stimuli of the maze and a specific series of movements leading from the starting box to the box containing the food. Tolman, on the other hand, felt that the rat would learn a cognitive map of the maze, but we would not be able to see that he had learned it until the rat was given a good reason (like food) to run to the food box.

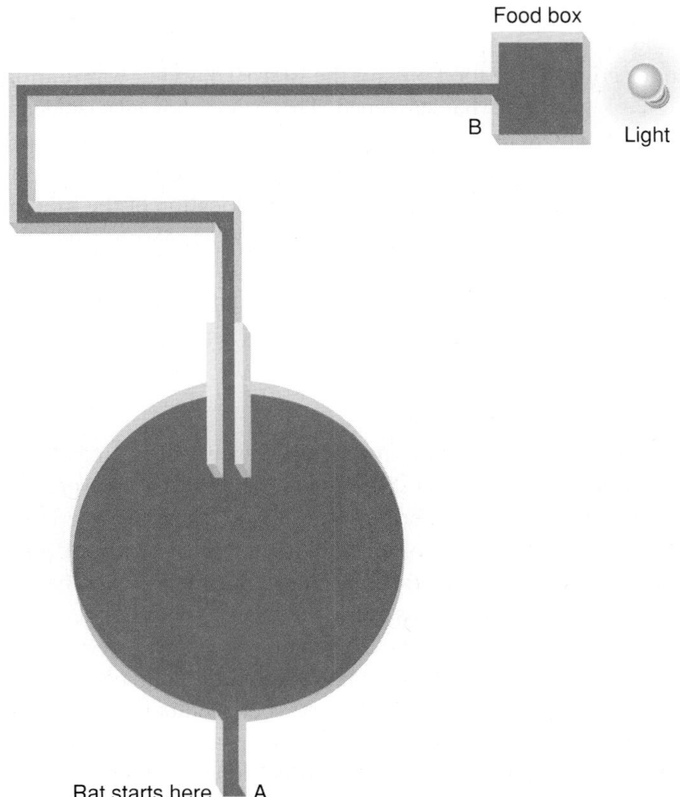

FIGURE 5.12

The initial part of the apparatus used in Tolman's study of cognitive aspects of learning in rats. The rat begins at point A and receives food when point B is reached.

Source: E. C. Tolman, B. F. Ritchie, and D. Kalish, "Studies in Spatial Learning I: Orientation and the Short-Cut" in *Journal of Experimental Psychology,* 36:13–25, 1946.

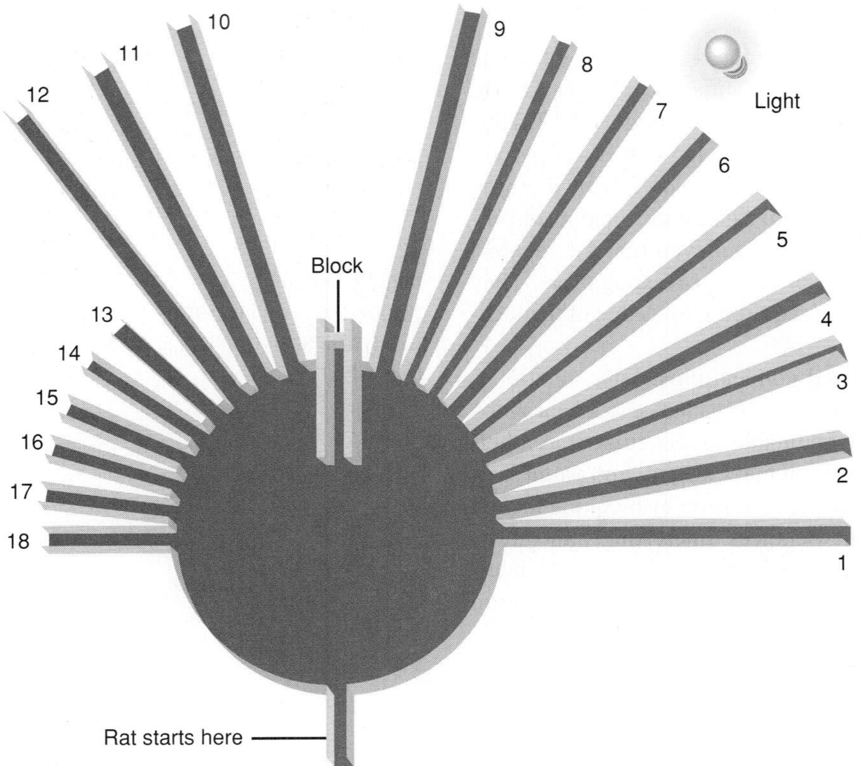

FIGURE 5.13

The modified apparatus used in the second part of Tolman's study of cognitive aspects of learning in rats.

Source: E. C. Tolman, B. F. Ritchie, and D. Kalish, "Studies in Spatial Learning I: Orientation and the Short-Cut" in *Journal of Experimental Psychology,* 36:13–25, 1946.

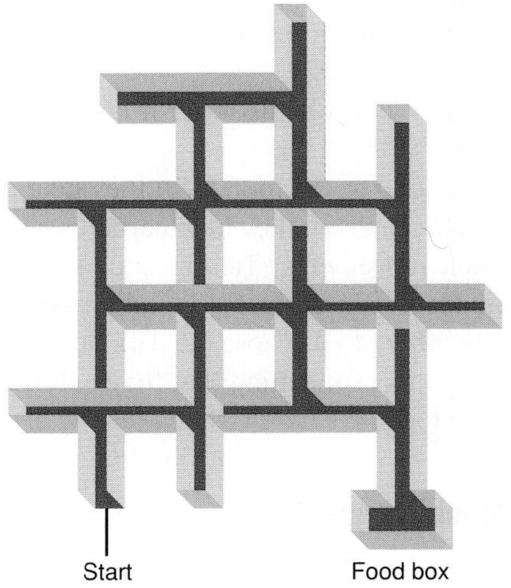

FIGURE 5.14

The maze used in Tolman's study of latent learning in rats.

E. C. Tolman and C. H. Honzik, "Introduction and Removal of the Reward, and Maze Performance in Rats," *University of California Publications in Psychology,* 4:257–275, 1930.

In Tolman's experiment, three groups of hungry rats were placed in the maze and timed to see how long it took them to reach the food box. One group was reinforced each time they reached the food box, so they learned to run to it quickly. A second group was never reinforced, so they wandered aimlessly in the maze (never decreasing the time it took to reach the food box). The third group of rats was the interesting one, though. This group was not reinforced for going to the food box for the first 10 days but was reinforced from then on. Look at figure 5.15 to see what happened. This group showed a sudden decrease in the amount of time it took them to reach the goal, catching up almost immediately to the group that had been reinforced every time. Tolman interpreted these results as showing that the unreinforced rats had learned just as much about the location of the food box as the reinforced group, but they showed their learning only when given a reason to do so (the food). If learning were a matter of reinforcement strengthening connections between stimuli and responses, no learning would have been expected prior to the introduction of reinforcement.

Insight Learning and Learning Sets

Perhaps the most striking evidence for the cognitive view of learning comes from a series of experiments conducted by a German Gestalt psychologist during World War I. Wolfgang Köhler was visiting the island of Tenerife (in the Canary Islands) when the war broke out and he found himself interned there for the duration of the war. He took good advantage of a poor situation, however, by conducting learning experiments with apes that were native to the island. His best-known study was carried out using an ape named *Sultan.* Köhler put Sultan in a cage where a bunch of bananas and two bamboo sticks (which could be fitted together) were hanging from the ceiling. Sultan originally spent a great deal of time trying to knock down the bananas with one of the sticks, but eventually gave up. Then as he was fiddling idly with the two sticks, he joined the sticks together into one long pole. Sultan immediately got up and knocked the bananas down with the long pole. And every subsequent time

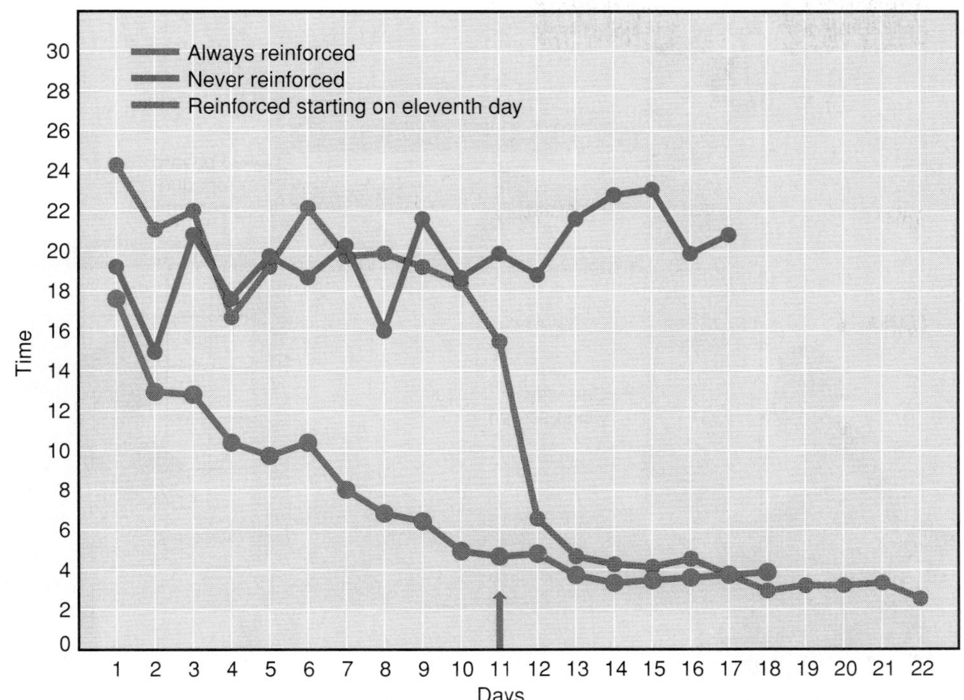

FIGURE 5.15

The results of Tolman's study of latent learning in rats. A group of rats that was never reinforced for reaching the food box did not improve in the amount of time required to reach it. But a group of rats that was reinforced each time gradually improved. A third group of rats was not reinforced for the first 10 days but was reinforced from then on. Their rapid improvement indicated that they had "latently" learned about the maze before they were reinforced.

Source: E. C. Tolman and C. H. Honzik, "Introduction and Removal of the Reward, and Maze Performance in Rats," *University of California Publications in Psychology,* 4:257–275, 1930.

he was presented with the same problem, he immediately solved it the same way.

Köhler repeated this basic experiment many times with other problems, such as providing several boxes that had to be stacked to reach the bananas. Each time, the ape would fail to make any progress and then suddenly learn how to reach the bananas. Köhler said that Sultan learned because of a *cognitive change*—a new **insight** that he had developed about the problem. As soon as he figured out the solution, the learning process was over.

Connection theorists have great difficulty explaining this type of insightful learning, but a series of studies conducted by Harry Harlow of the University of Wisconsin (1949) took some of the mystery out of the insightful behavior of the apes. Harlow showed that the ability to solve problems insightfully is itself at least partially learned.

This ape can be said to have experienced a cognitive change when it discovered that the stick can be used to pry open the box. Köhler described the phenomenon as insight learning.

The apparatus shown in figure 5.16 was used in the study. A tray was presented to the monkey with two objects on it. Although the objects differed from problem to problem, food was always located under one of the objects. The monkeys had six chances to solve each problem. The monkeys in Harlow's experiments solved a total of 312 different problems because Harlow's interest was in whether the ability of the monkeys to solve the problems improved with experience. As can be seen in figure 5.17, their problem-solving ability improved dramatically. Look first at their performance on the first group of problems (problems 1 through 8). While their percentage of correct performance improved gradually over the six trials, they were still choosing the correct object only about 75 percent of the time by the sixth trial. In contrast, look at their performance on problems 257 through 312. On the first trial, they had to guess which object the food was under, so they were correct only 50 percent of the time. But note that if they did not get it right the first time, they "insightfully knew" that it must be under the other object and made the correct choice from the second trial on.

In Harlow's terms, the monkeys had acquired a **learning set;** that is, they had learned to learn insightfully. Harlow's point was that the insightful performance of Köhler's apes is not characteristic of all learning; rather, one must *learn* how to solve a particular class of problems insightfully. Further supporting Harlow's contention is a follow-up study

insight
(in´sīt) A form of cognitive change that involves recognition of previously unseen relationships.

learning set
Improvement in the rate of learning to solve new problems through practice solving similar problems.

FIGURE 5.16

The apparatus used by Harlow to study learning sets (learning to learn insightfully) in monkeys.

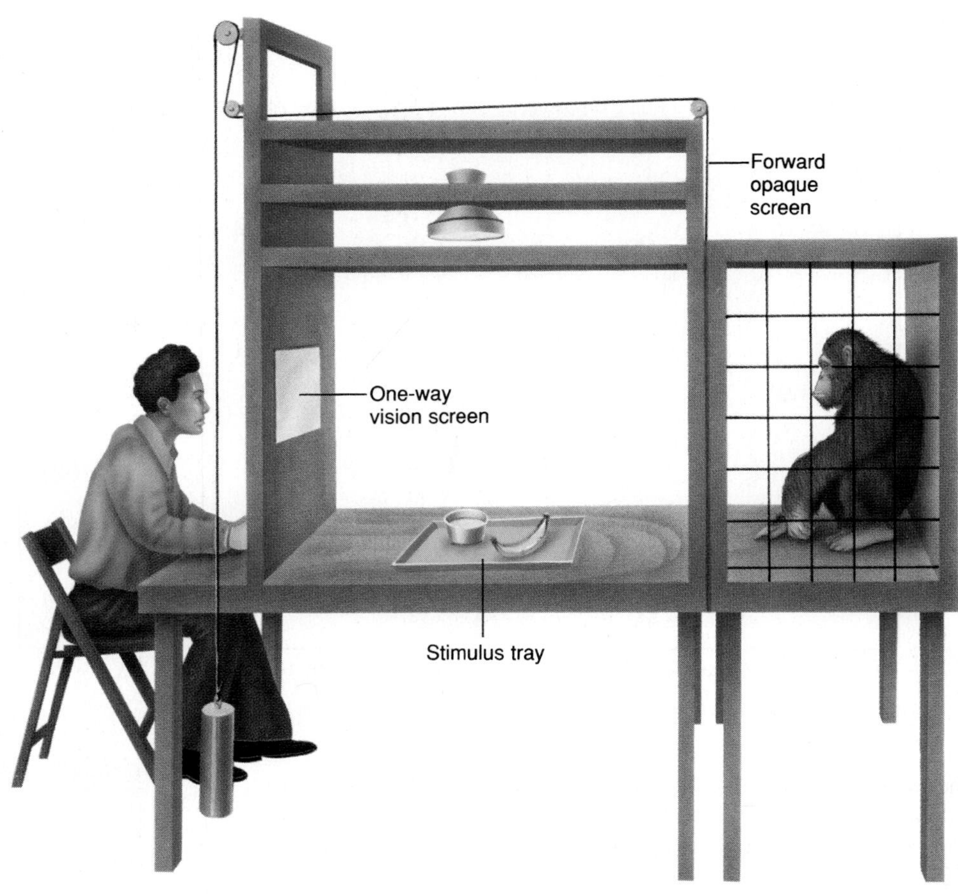

FIGURE 5.17

Monkeys learn which object is hiding food very slowly the first few times they are given this type of problem (problems 1–8). But they learn quickly (insightfully) after they have had a great deal of experience with such problems (problems 257–312).

Source: H. F. Harlow, "The Formation of Learning Sets" in *Psychological Review,* 56:51–56, 1949.

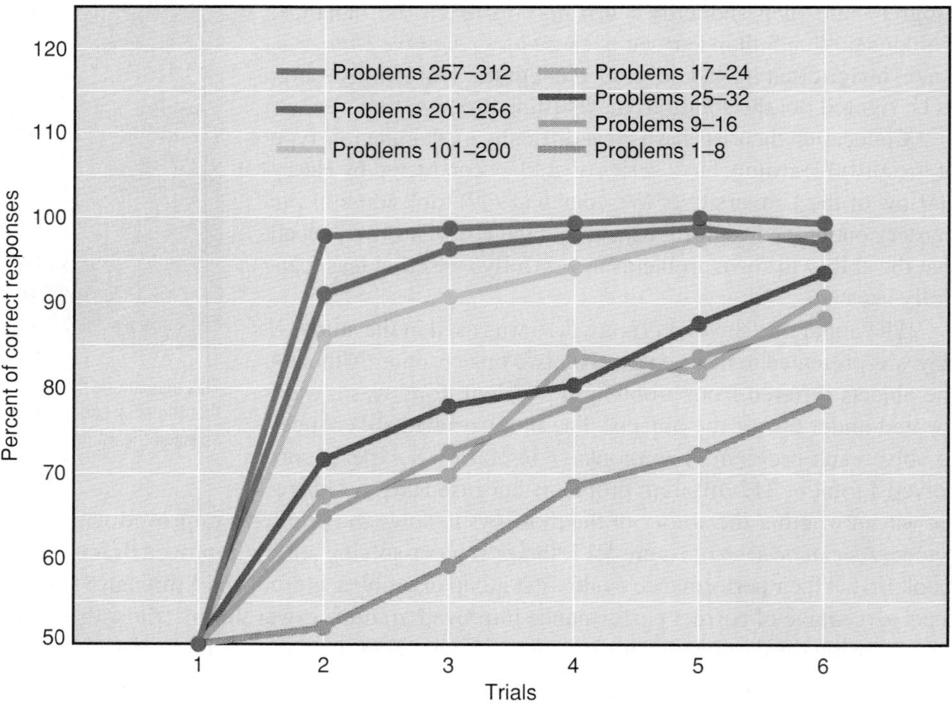

of Köhler's banana-and-stick problem (Birch, 1945). Chimpanzees who had no previous experience playing with sticks could not solve the problem. However, after these chimps had been allowed to play with the sticks for only three days, they were able to solve the banana-and-stick problem easily. Evidently, they had learned something in their play that enabled them to learn insightfully.

Modeling: Learning by Watching Others

Albert Bandura's views about modeling predict that this toddler will learn about carpentry from watching his father work on home projects.

Stanford University psychologist Albert Bandura is one of the most influential contemporary proponents of the cognitive view of learning. Perhaps his most important contribution has been to emphasize that people learn not only through classical and operant conditioning but also by observing the behavior of others. Bandura calls this **modeling.** In Egypt, for example, where grasshoppers are considered to be a delicacy, people learn to eat them partly by watching other people enjoy themselves while eating grasshoppers. In the United States, in contrast, we learn to think of grasshoppers as disgusting creatures largely by seeing other people's negative reactions to them ("Get the sprayer, Mabel, there's a grasshopper in the kitchen!"). There is nothing inherently good or bad about grasshoppers, but we learn that they are either a delicacy or disgusting by seeing how others feel about them. Similarly, patterns of speech, styles of dress, patterns of energy consumption, methods of rearing children, and myriad other patterns of behavior are taught to us through modeling.

Bandura considers modeling to be an important demonstration of the role of cognition in learning. A child who watches his older sister play baseball for several years will be able to come pretty close to playing the game properly (that is, know how to hold the bat, how to swing, where to run if he hits the ball) the very first time he is allowed to play. In Bandura's view, a great deal of cognitive learning takes place through watching, *before* there is any chance for the behavior to occur and be reinforced. But we can learn more than skills through modeling. Bandura has suggested that modeling can also remind us of appropriate behavior in a given situation, reduce our inhibitions concerning certain behaviors that we see others engaging in, or suggest to us what behaviors will lead to reinforcement.

modeling
Learning based on observation of the behavior of another.

In Bandura's ground-breaking laboratory studies of modeling, children learned to be more aggressive or less fearful as a result of simply observing the behavior of models in films. In one study (Bandura, Ross, & Ross, 1963), one group of children saw an adult kick, hit, and sit on a blow-up Bobo doll. When these children were placed in a playroom (then frustrated by having all toys except the Bobo doll taken away), they were significantly more aggressive toward the Bobo doll than a group of children who had not seen the film—they learned to act more aggressively through modeling. In a similar study with a more uplifting conclusion, research participants who were initially strongly afraid of snakes gradually learned to be less fearful by imitating a series of actions of the model, ranging from looking at a caged snake to holding it (Bandura, Blanchard, & Ritter, 1969). Modeling can be an important and powerful form of learning.

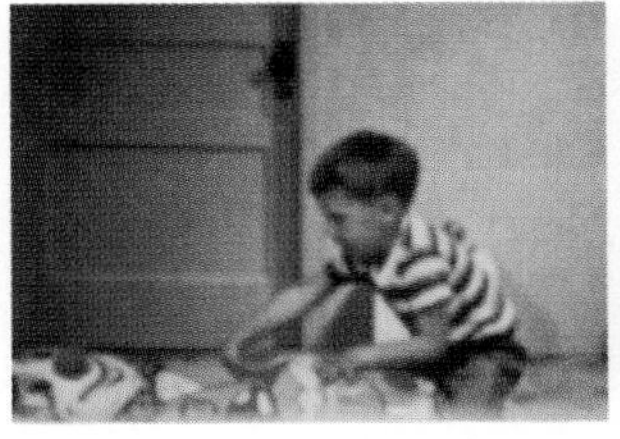

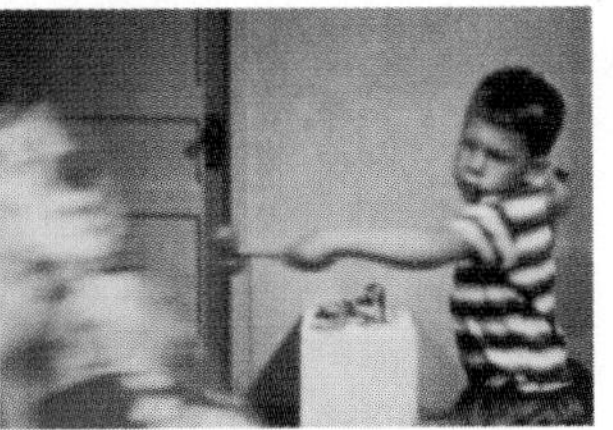
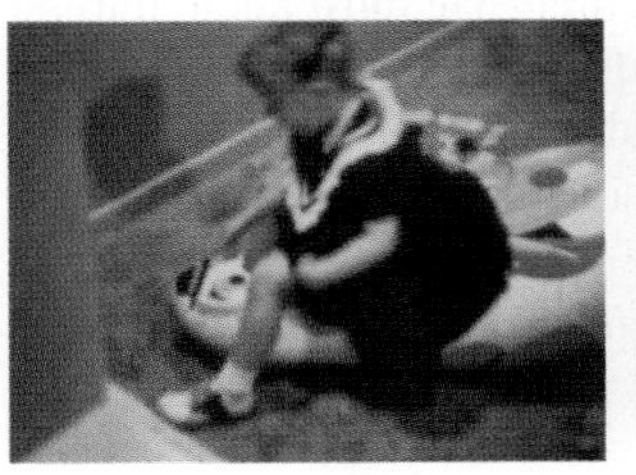

Bandura found that children who observed adult models play aggressively with a Bobo doll played more aggressively themselves.

Children who were initially afraid of snakes were less fearful after imitating adult models' approaches to and handling of a harmless snake.

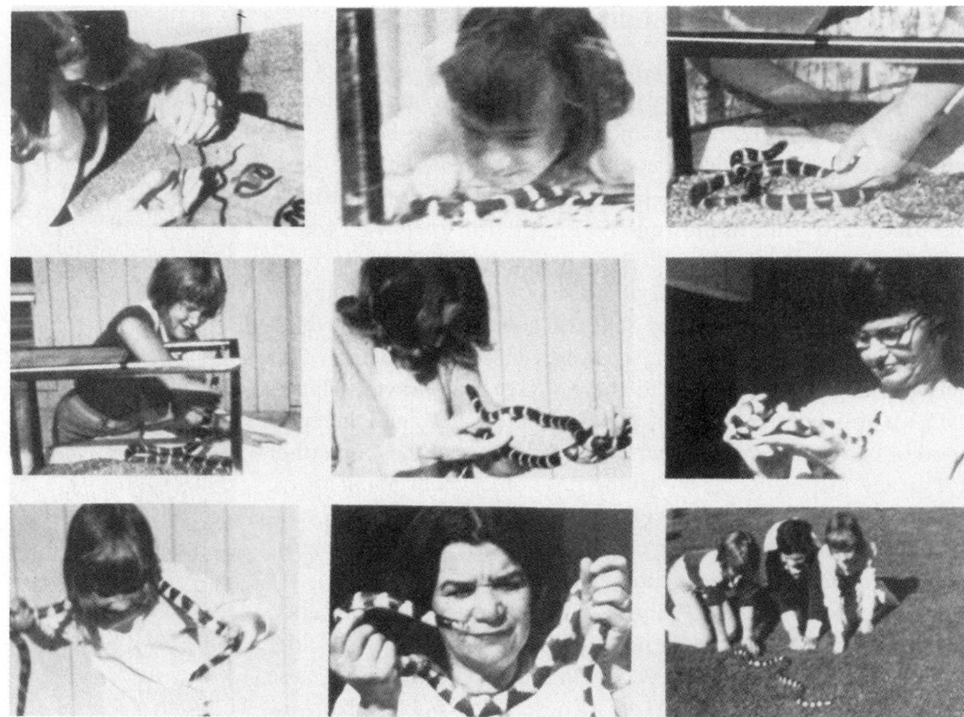

vicarious reinforcement
(vī-kar´ē-us) Observed reinforcement of the behavior of a model that also increases the probability of the same behavior in the observer.

vicarious punishment
Observed punishment of the behavior of a model that also decreases the probability of the same behavior in the observer.

We are not equally likely to imitate all behavior of all models, however. We are considerably more likely to imitate a model whose behavior we see reinforced **(vicarious reinforcement)** than when we see that behavior punished in the model **(vicarious punishment).** In the absence of direct knowledge of vicarious reinforcement and punishment, we are more likely to imitate the behavior of models that are high in status, attractive, likable, and successful, perhaps because we assume that their behavior often leads to reinforcement (Bandura, 1977).

In recent years, a great deal of debate has centered on the types of models that are presented to our children through the medium of television. Unfortunately, there is solid experimental evidence that seems to confirm these fears. It appears that television does teach children to prefer sugary foods, encourage sex-stereotyped roles, and, perhaps most disturbingly, teach violence. Although not all psychologists accept their conclusions (e.g., Freedman, 1984), a number of studies have found that the high rate of violent behavior shown on television, from cartoons to westerns, does encourage aggressive behavior in children and adolescents (Berkowitz, 1984; Caprara et al., 1987; Eron & Huesmann, 1984; Liebert, Neale, & Davidson, 1983; Rubenstein, 1983). In recent years, the television networks have made some strides in improving the amount of prosocial and healthful behavior and attitudes that are modeled on television, but there is still much room for improvement. Moreover, it sometimes appears that accurately reported news events provide more dangerous models than fictitious programs—as when one terrorist act that successfully draws media attention leads to many "copycat" acts of terrorism.

Biological Factors in Learning

Learning is a powerful process that quite literally shapes our lives. But we must not overstate the importance of any psychological process, even learning. We must keep in mind that our ability to learn from experience is not limitless; it's influenced in a number of ways by biological factors. We know that it's impossible to teach goldfish to fly and owls to swim, but has it ever occurred to you that our biological nature influences what people can learn?

For example, it appears that people are biologically prepared to learn some kinds of fears more readily than others (Mineka & Sutton, 1992). It's far easier to classically condition a fear of things that have some intrinsic association with danger (snakes, heights, blood, etc.) using electric shock as the UCS than it is to condition a fear of truly neutral things (such as lunch boxes and skate keys) (Cook, Hodes, & Lang, 1986; Mercklebach, van den Hout, Jansen, & van der Molen, 1988; Ohman, Erixon, & Löfberg, 1975). Interestingly, we are prepared to learn to fear only those things that would have been frightening to our evolutionary ancestors. Fears cannot be easily conditioned to modern dangerous stimuli such as electric outlets (Hugdahl & Karker, 1981). A quick look at a textbook of abnormal psychology will tell you, too, that people do have phobias of the things that have always posed danger to humans (heights, snakes, blood, etc.), but that almost no one is afraid of lunch boxes or newspapers.

Apparently the process of evolution has prepared us to learn potentially useful fears through classical conditioning more readily than useless ones. The research of Susan Mineka of Northwestern University and her colleagues has shown that the biological preparedness to learn to fear some things more readily than others is true of learning fears through modeling as well. In a particularly clever study, Cook and Mineka (1990) showed laboratory-raised monkeys who had never seen a snake videotapes of wild monkeys behaving fearfully in the presence of artificial snakes and behaving nonfearfully in the presence of artificial flowers. As would be expected, the laboratory-raised monkeys showed large increases in their fear of the artificial snakes. Another group of laboratory-raised monkeys, however, was shown edited videotapes that made it appear that the wild monkeys were fearful of the flowers and not of the snakes. As would be expected, exposure to this videotape did not lead to fear of the artificial flowers. We are biologically prepared to learn some fears and not others.

John Garcia and his associates have discussed another form of learning that exemplifies the role of biological factors in learning (Garcia, Hankins, & Rusiniak, 1974). An example of their experiments can be shown through one of my own experiences as a child. On one fateful evening I ate eight hot dogs. Two hours later I became more than just a little nauseous. As a result, it was many years until I ate another hot dog.

This experience of learning to dislike hot dogs is an example of a **learned taste aversion.** Learned taste aversions have been the subject of much study by psychologists because they provide another good example of the role of biological factors in learning. Note that I learned to dislike the hot dogs through classical conditioning: The hot dogs were the CS and the nausea was the UCS. But think about two facts: The two stimuli were paired only *once,* but I learned a dislike that lasted for years. Moreover, there was a time interval of 2 hours between the conditioned and unconditioned stimuli. Normally a gap of more than a couple of seconds is enough to make classical conditioning impossible. For learning to take place under these conditions, we must be highly "prepared" for such learning. Indeed, this makes good sense from an evolutionary perspective; animal species that quickly learn to avoid foods that make them sick (and hence may be poisonous) are species that are more likely to survive. A species that does not quickly learn to avoid poisonous foods is likely to perish (Kehoe & Bass, 1986).

learned taste aversion
(ah-ver´shun) Negative reaction to a particular taste that has been associated with nausea or other illness.

A particularly sad outcome of our readiness to acquire classically conditioned taste aversions can be seen in the treatment of cancer. Some effective forms of chemotherapy and abdominal radiation therapy have the side effect of causing the patient to be nauseous for a while after treatment. Individuals undergoing these types of treatment not only are quite uncomfortable but also tend to lose their appetite, causing weight loss that complicates their health problems. Ilene Bernstein (1978, 1985) of the University of Washington reasoned that the loss of appetite may be caused in part by learned taste aversions produced by the frequent nausea. To test her hypothesis, a group of children with cancer were given an unusual flavor of ice cream (mapletoff—a mixture of maple and black walnut flavorings) immediately before their regular chemotherapy treatment. Later they were offered the ice cream again. Compared with a group of children who were given the ice cream just before a different kind of treatment that does not produce nausea, far fewer of the children who had become nauseous after eating the ice cream wanted the ice cream again. Similarly a group of children who underwent the same nausea-inducing chemotherapy, but had not been given the ice cream just before the treatment, showed no aversion to it.

Apparently nausea from the chemotherapy can create learned taste aversions for foods that are eaten prior to therapy and, over a period of time, can lead cancer patients to avoid many foods. Fortunately, Bernstein and her colleagues (Bernstein, Webster, & Bernstein, 1982) have developed some strategies to avoid this problem. First, fasting before the chemotherapy reduces the chances of developing any taste aversions. Second, eating a novel and distinctive tasting food (such as the mapletoff ice cream) with the meal preceding chemotherapy often results in a conditioned aversion *only* to the distinctive food. Nutritionally unimportant food, therefore, can be used as shields against aversions to more important foods. In addition, Redd et al. (1987) have found that allowing youths to play videogames is distracting enough to disrupt the conditioning of the nausea.

On a more positive note, a creative and useful application of our knowledge of learned taste aversions has been made by John Garcia and his colleagues in the area of wildlife preservation (Gustavson, Garcia, Hankins, & Rusiniak, 1974). A serious conflict exists in some western states between the interests of sheep ranchers and wildlife preservationists. Because coyotes kill many of the ranchers' sheep, the ranchers kill so many coyotes every year that they endanger their survival as a species. Garcia's research group has developed an alternative plan that keeps the coyotes from killing sheep without being killed themselves. These researchers have demonstrated that if the sheep ranchers place on the range sheep meat containing a chemical that will make the coyotes nauseous, the coyotes will develop an aversion to the taste of sheep and no longer hunt them. Through this method, sheep and coyotes can peacefully coexist.

Many other biological limits on the learning process have been identified by psychologists. Keller and Marian Breland (1961), a husband-and-wife team of psychologists, tell a revealing story about their experiences in training animals to do tricks for circus sideshows. In one case, they taught a raccoon to deposit tokens in a metal box in order to obtain food. They had no trouble when they gave the raccoon just one token, but when they gave her two, a strange thing happened. She started rubbing the tokens together and "dipped" them into the slot repeatedly, only to pull them out and rub them again. Apparently, the raccoon was engaging in the kind of "food-washing" behavior that is natural for the species. Moreover, this tendency to wash food was so strong that it overrode her hunger. The raccoon washed her "food" so long that she hardly ever deposited it in the slot to get the real food.

These stories about raccoons, phobias, and learned taste aversions are not terribly important in themselves, but they make an important point about the biological limits on learning. We are not able to learn everything equally well. Learning is a powerful process, and humans are good learners, but even people have biological limits on their learning.

Thinking Critically About Psychology

1. Why are place learning, latent learning, and insight learning all considered to support cognitive theories of learning?

2. Who do you model your behavior after? What events or personal qualities have made them your models?

Review

Some psychologists believe that learning is based on the strengthening of neural connections between stimuli and specific patterns of muscle movements. Others suggest that learning involves changes in cognition (knowing what to do, where food is located, what to expect next, and so on). Research on place learning, latent learning, and insight learning provides strong support for the cognitive view of learning. Perhaps the most important learning phenomenon thought to be based on cognitive change is modeling; a great deal of our behavior is learned simply by observing the behavior of others. Regardless of the true nature of learning, our biological characteristics place limits on it, making us better prepared to learn some things more than others.

Check Your Learning

To be sure that you have learned the key points from the preceding section, cover the answers below and try to answer each question. If you give an incorrect answer to any question, return to the page given next to the correct answer to see why your answer was not correct.

1. ________________ refers to a sudden change in behavior that results from a recognition of previously unseen relationships.

- **a.** Insight
- **b.** Modeling
- **c.** Operant learning
- **d.** Conditioning

2. Harry Harlow's work on learning sets shows that insightful learning is

________________________ .

- **a.** learned
- **b.** innate
- **c.** only possible in humans
- **d.** all of the above

3. Learning by observing the behavior of others is termed ________________ by Albert Bandura.

- **a.** stimulus discrimination
- **b.** classical conditioning
- **c.** operant conditioning
- **d.** modeling

4. The process of learned taste aversions in which humans and nonhuman animals learn to avoid foods that make them sick is interesting because the time interval between the CS (the taste of the food) and the UCS is much ____________ than in most instances of classical conditioning.

- **a.** longer
- **b.** shorter

Correct Answers

1. a (p. 199), **2.** a (p. 199), **3.** d (p. 201), **4.** a (p. 203).

APPLICATION OF PSYCHOLOGY

LEARNING THE WRONG THINGS

In this chapter, we saw that one of the good things about operant conditioning is that it helps us adapt to the realities of life. If our behavior is effective in bringing us good things, it will be positively reinforced and we will be more likely to engage in these behaviors than in those that bring us bad things. On the other hand, ways of behaving that do not bring good things will be extinguished, and behaviors that bring negative consequences will be punished. We are always in the process of learning to adjust to our world through operant conditioning. But, *sometimes,* unfortunately, we learn the wrong things.

Are you superstitious? Did you ever wonder where your superstitions come from? There are probably many ways in which they are learned, but B. F. Skinner made the interesting suggestion that some of our superstitions are *learned through flukes in positive reinforcement.*

Skinner was working with pigeons who were being reinforced for pecking at a small disk when he noticed that some of them had learned superstitions. Sometimes a pigeon would engage in some unrelated behavior, such as turning around just before pecking the disk. The consequent reinforcer would reinforce the pigeon both for pecking and for the irrelevant response of turning. If the pigeon then happened to turn around again before another reinforced response, he would probably begin turning before every peck, even though turning had nothing to do with the delivery of the food. The food would have come after the peck whether the pigeon turned or not. In Skinner's terms, the pigeon had learned a **superstitious behavior,** a behavior that is reinforced when the reinforcing stimulus accidentally follows the response. Like all superstitions, the pigeon stubbornly keeps engaging in this act even though it served no real purpose.

You can also see superstitious behavior acquired in this way by carefully watching a discus thrower just before he or she starts to throw. Many of them go through odd little rituals. Each time the discus thrower steps in the ring, he or she engages in an identical pattern of superstitious behavior. As odd as it looks, it's probably just another form of superstitious behavior. This is how it might have been acquired: When the discus thrower is first learning to throw, the behaviors that occur before starting to throw are pretty much random. But when the thrower uncorks a really good throw (a big reinforcer for a discus thrower), any of the random behaviors that were occurring just before the throw will be reinforced through superstitious reinforcement. This is called superstitious because the reinforcement of the good throw had nothing to do with some behavior like touching the shoulder before beginning to throw. In this way, a whole series of irrelevant behaviors may become the superstitions of the discus thrower without his or her ever actually noticing what has happened. Baseball players develop similar superstitious behaviors before batting or pitching. Many other everyday superstitions are probably learned in much the same way. Do you have any superstitions like this?

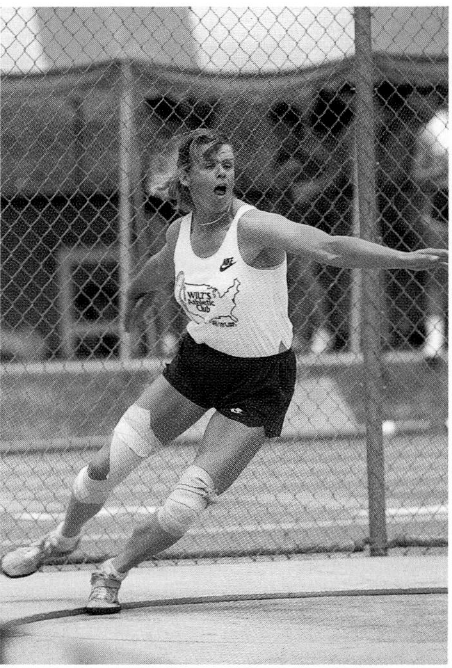

Athletes often learn superstitions from reinforcing stimuli that accidentally follow a response.

Sometimes the unintended and maladaptive effects of reinforcement are more serious. Consider the case of the serious psychological disorder called **schizophrenia** (which we will study in detail in chapter 13). The causes of schizophrenia are not currently known. I say that because I do not want to give you the impression that I am saying that positive reinforcement is the cause of schizophrenia (it is not). However, one of the most impressive demonstrations of the power of positive reinforcement in shaping human behavior in maladaptive ways comes from a series of classic studies of persons with schizophrenia conducted at Anna State Hospital in Illinois by Teodoro Ayllon. In these studies, Ayllon showed that the abnormal behavior of hospitalized individuals with schizophrenia could be rather easily modified using positive reinforcement and extinction. For example, these patients frequently made delusional statements such as, "I'm the queen; the queen wants a smoke; How's King George, have you seen him?" (Ayllon & Haughton, 1964). Ayllon noticed that these statements frequently got the attention of the attendants on the ward who would try to explain to the patient that she was not the queen. When the patients spoke normally, however, the attendants often ignored them and went on with their duties.

Ayllon suspected that the attention the patients got for their delusional statements was reinforcing them and he decided to test this hypothesis in a clinical experiment (Ayllon & Haughton, 1964). Three schizophrenic women who frequently made delusional statements were used as the study's participants. The first step of the study was simply to measure the total frequency of delusional statements in the three women (labeled as baseline in fig. 5.18). Next, an attempt was made to increase the frequency of delusional statements by reinforcing them more systematically. That is, the attendants were told to pay attention to the women every time they made a delusional statement but to ignore them totally whenever they made normal statements. As can be seen, this more systematic reinforcement of the delusional statements produced a dramatic increase in their frequency. In the third and therapeutic phase of the study, the attendants were asked to

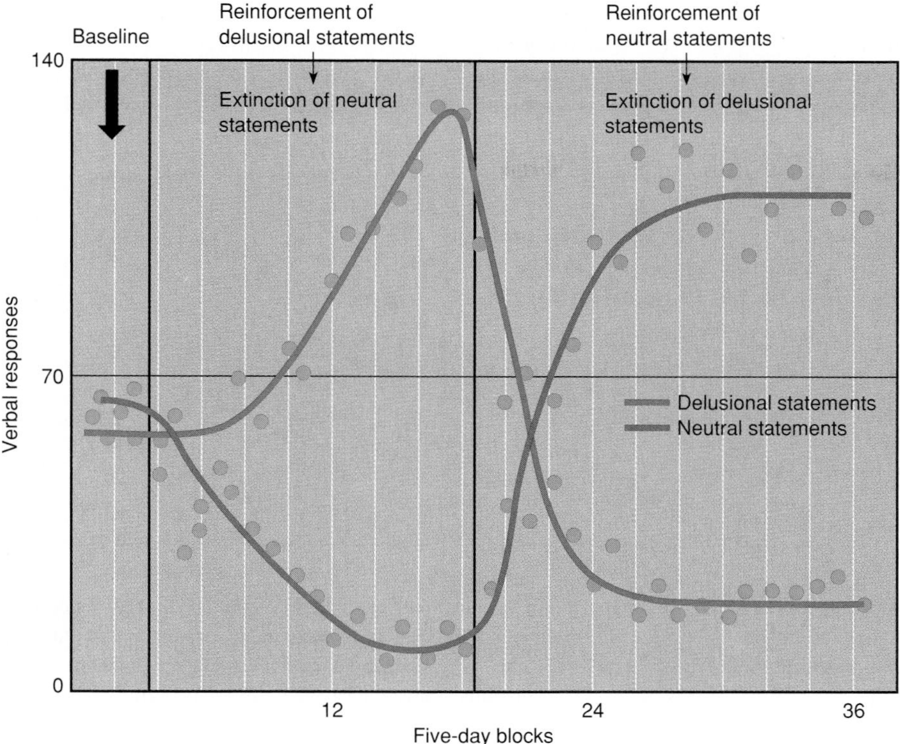

FIGURE 5.18

The results of Ayllon and Haughton's study of the role of reinforcement from ward attendants in maintaining the delusional statements of schizophrenic women. The rate of delusional statements rises when the women are reinforced only for making them, and decreases when they are reinforced for making normal statements and no longer reinforced (placed on extinction) for making delusional statements.

reverse the manner in which they paid attention to the women. They were to pay attention to every normal statement but completely ignore every delusional statement. That is, the delusional statements were placed on extinction in the third phase of the study. This produced a drop in the frequency of delusional statements to well below the level in baseline and a corresponding increase in the frequency of normal statements.

These findings were an important breakthrough in the treatment of schizophrenia. It's clear that schizophrenic individuals will act more or less normally depending on the reinforcement that the people around them provide. Schizophrenia cannot be eliminated using only positive reinforcement for normal behavior, but appropriately arranged consequences can sometimes make a dramatic difference.

The implications are no less important for those of us who are not schizophrenic, however. Ayllon's findings make it obvious that our behavior can be influenced to a rather astounding degree by subtle reinforcers, like the amount of attention we receive. Have you learned to be polite (rowdy, funny, shy) because of the attention you receive for it?

Another way in which operant conditioning can go wrong sheds light on another psychological disorder, that of **depression.** Depressed individuals experience an extreme sadness, lack of energy, negative self-evaluation, and a pervasive sense of hopelessness and helplessness that lasts for weeks or even months on end. Life is miserable for individuals who are depressed, the future looks bleak, and they feel helpless to do anything to improve their lives. Psychologist Martin Seligman (1975) believes that the depressed individual's helplessness (a pattern of no longer trying to avoid negative events) is a primary cause of depression and is itself a *learned* pattern of behavior. He calls this pattern of operant conditioning gone wrong **learned helplessness.**

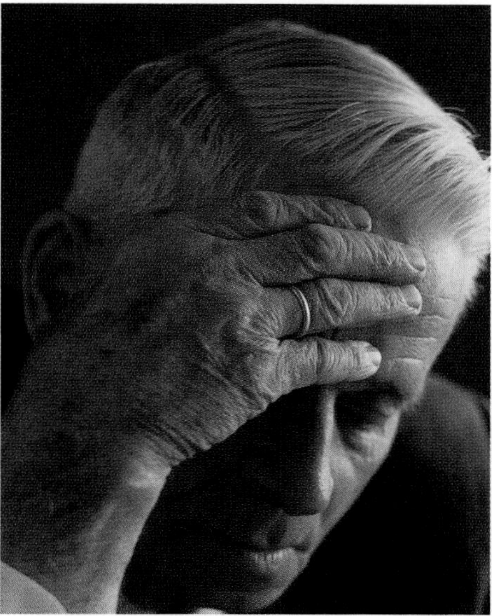

Psychologist Martin Seligman believes that learned helplessness is a factor in depression.

Seligman and his colleagues have conducted a number of studies designed to show that a helpless pattern of behavior can be learned. The original experiment involved placing dogs in a box where they received a series of random electric shocks. Seligman felt that these shocks were analogous to stressful events that humans sometimes experience over which they have no control.

In the next part of the experiment, the dogs were placed in an apparatus called a shuttle box, a box divided into two compartments by a low hurdle over which the dogs could easily jump. The dogs were again shocked in the shuttle box, but this time the shock was *escapable;* the dogs could easily jump to the safe side of the shuttle box and escape the shock. Normally, dogs learn to escape the shock very easily (they are reinforced through negative reinforcement), but Seligman's dogs who had been exposed to the previous random shocks seemed helpless in this situation. They crouched, whined, and endured the shocks, but they did not learn to escape them. Outside of the shuttle box, the helpless dogs showed many signs of "depression." They moved listlessly, ate poorly, lost weight, interacted little with other dogs, and showed diminished interest in sex.

How did operant learning go wrong in this case? Because the dogs experienced shocks that they initially could not escape, they never attempted to escape the shocks when escape was possible during the shuttle box experience. It is the fact that the dogs *failed to respond* by jumping that prevented them from learning the relationship between jumping and escape from shock. In operant conditioning situations, no learning can take place until a response occurs. There is reason to believe that random negative events may also make humans depressed and helpless to control their lives. For example, battered spouses who never try to leave their abusers cannot learn to escape from their situation; the result too often is depression and continued abuse.

Thus, although operant conditioning usually makes our behavior adaptive by increasing the likelihood of effective behaviors and decreasing the likelihood of ineffective behaviors, it can sometimes go far astray. As a result, people sometimes need a little help from others in changing the patterns of reinforcement in their lives.

Summary

Chapter 5 is about the psychological study of learning. Emphasis is on classical conditioning, operant conditioning, and extinction. The last section of the chapter explores theoretical interpretations of learning.

I. Learning refers to any relatively permanent change in behavior or in the potential for behavior brought about through experience.

II. Classical conditioning is a form of learning in which a previously neutral stimulus (conditioned stimulus, CS) is paired with an unconditioned stimulus (UCS) that elicits an unlearned or unconditioned response (UCR). As a result, the CS comes to elicit a conditioned response (CR) that is identical or very similar to the UCR.

- **A.** Classical conditioning occurs because of the association in time of a neutral stimulus that already elicits the response. The CS becomes a signal that predicts the occurrence of the UCS.

III. Operant conditioning is a form of learning in which the consequences of behavior lead to changes in the probability of its occurrence.

- **A.** In positive reinforcement, a positive consequence of behavior leads to an increase in the probability of the occurrence of the response.
  1. Primary reinforcers are innately reinforcing.
  2. Secondary reinforcers are learned through classical conditioning.
  3. Four different schedules of reinforcement that result in different patterns of behavior are fixed ratio, variable ratio, fixed interval, and variable interval.
  4. Shaping is the process of positively reinforcing responses that are progressively more similar to the response that is wanted.
- **B.** Negative reinforcement occurs when the reinforcing consequence is the removal or avoidance of a negative event.
  1. The type of negative reinforcement in which the response ends a negative stimulus is called escape conditioning.
  2. The type of negative reinforcement in which the response prevents the occurrence of the negative stimulus is called avoidance conditioning.
- **C.** Punishment is the process through which an aversive consequence of behavior reduces the frequency of a behavior.

IV. New stimuli come to influence behavior through the process of learning.

- **A.** We say that a stimulus discrimination has been learned when a response is more likely to occur in the presence of a specific stimulus than in its absence.
- **B.** Stimulus generalization has occurred when an individual responds in the same way to a stimulus that is similar to the original stimulus.

V. The process of unlearning a learned response because of the removal of the aspect of the environment that originally caused the learning is termed extinction.

- **A.** Extinction is sometimes slowed because of spontaneous recovery and external disinhibition.

VI. Psychologists disagree about whether learning results from neural connections between specific stimuli and specific responses or whether learning is a change in cognition.

- **A.** Research that supports the cognitive view includes Tolman's studies of place learning and latent learning, Köhler's studies of insight learning, and Bandura's work on modeling.
- **B.** The ability of humans to learn from experience is not limitless; it is influenced in a number of ways by biological factors.

Suggested Readings

1. Excellent summaries for the serious student of learning: Hearst, E. (1988). Fundamentals of learning and conditioning. In R. C. Atkinson, R. J. Herrnstein, G. Lindzey, & R. D. Luce (Eds.), *Stevens' handbook of experimental psychology: Vol. 2, Learning and cognition.* New York: Wiley-Interscience. Domjan, M. (1996). *Essentials of conditioning and learning.* Monterey: Brooks-Cole.
2. For more on modeling: Bandura, A. (1977). *Social learning theory.* Englewood Cliffs, NJ: Prentice-Hall.
3. For B. F. Skinner's views of operant conditioning and on the science of psychology in general: Skinner, B. F. (1974). *About behaviorism.* New York: Knopf; and Skinner, B. F. (1971). *Beyond freedom and dignity.* New York: Knopf.
4. For a firsthand account of early research on classical conditioning: Pavlov, I. P. (1927). *Conditioned reflexes.* Gloucester, MA: Peter Smith.
5. A still cogent and controversial novel describing the utopia that one psychologist believes could result from our using the principles of learning to design society is: Skinner, B. F. (1948). *Walden two.* New York: Macmillan.

CHAPTER

6

CHAPTER OUTLINE

Memory

PROLOGUE

If we are to benefit from our experiences, we must be able to remember them. If you couldn't remember anything tomorrow that you read in this chapter today, there would be no point in reading it. Remembering what you learn is as important as learning it in the first place.

Alexander Luria, a prominent Russian physician, was widely known for his research on the brain. One day, a young man (referred to as S) came to his hospital office complaining that his memory was *too good.* He often recalled experiences in such vivid detail that he could not shake them from his consciousness. They lingered in a distracting, haunting way that impaired his ability to concentrate on his current circumstances. Because the man was clearly distraught, Luria agreed to study his problem.

Over many years, Luria tested S's memory in a number of different ways. The best known of these tests involved showing S a sheet of paper containing four columns of a dozen numbers each. After viewing the numbers for a few minutes, S was able to write them out from memory without error. Moreover, without looking at the numbers again, he was able to refer to a mental image of them and tell Luria the numbers in any sequence requested. He could "read" a mental image of the numbers across the rows, down the columns, and across diagonals with apparent ease. Months later, S could still reproduce the table of numbers with few errors. In one series of experiments he was even able to recall complex verbal material in detail after more than 15 years had elapsed.

Luria was never able to help S, but S himself found a way to make his life more comfortable. After losing many other kinds of jobs, he decided to go on stage as a "memory expert." He was able to astound audiences with his ability to recall information and was able to earn a comfortable living.

Most of us are not troubled by remembering too much. Quite the opposite—most college students would like to be able to remember a lot more every time they take a test. Learning about S might help us feel a little better about our own memories, but most of us would still like to be able to remember more.

This chapter describes the ways in which the human memory works and discusses the reasons that we forget. New information that we learn can be thought of as passing through three stages in the human memory. The first stage holds information for very brief intervals—often less than a second. The next stage retains information longer, but only a little longer—up to about half a minute. But the third stage seems to hold information indefinitely. These three stages of memory operate according to different rules and mostly serve different functions. But because information must pass through each stage to reach the most permanent memory store, they work together as three linked stages in the memory process.

Forgetting appears to occur for different reasons in the three stages of memory. In the first stage, information is lost because it decays quickly over time unless it moves to the next stage. Forgetting in the second stage also occurs because of the simple passage of time unless something is done to protect the information. But memory traces are frequently lost in the second stage because of interference from other memories. For example, if you look up a number in the telephone book, you may forget it if you try to remember what you planned to say.

KEY TERMS

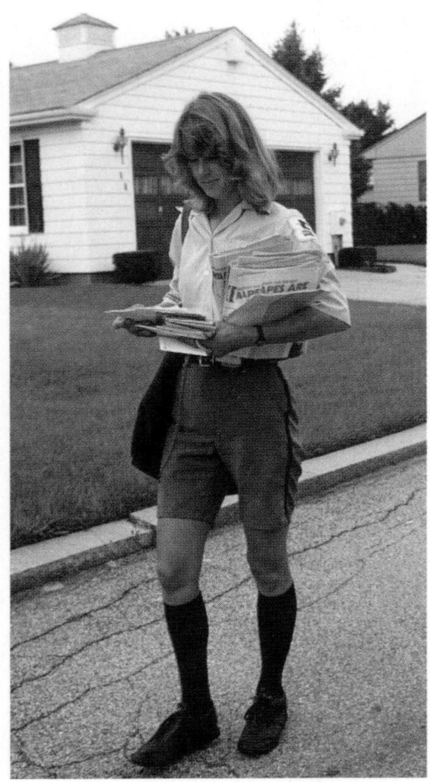

A postal worker needs a good memory. According to the information-processing model, memory is a process involving attention, encoding, and transfer to storage from which information can be retrieved.

The third stage of memory is called long-term memory. Information that reaches this stage seems to stay there permanently. Nonetheless, we are often unable to recall information from long-term memory for several reasons. Interference from similar memories is a common reason for being unable to recall long-term memories. In addition, long-term memories tend to change over time, sometimes to the extent that the information is no longer accurate. Finally, we are sometimes unable to recall some very unpleasant or threatening memories.

It's not known yet how the memory trace is stored in the brain, but several theories have been proposed. It seems likely that learning causes some kind of lasting change in the synapses of neurons that forms the basis of long-term memories. As you will see, our best clues about the biological basis of memory have come from the study of persons with a severe form of memory loss called amnesia.

THREE STAGES OF MEMORY: AN INFORMATION-PROCESSING VIEW

In recent years, psychologists have attempted to develop theories of memory using the computer as a model. These *information-processing* theories of memory are based on the apparent similarities between the operation of the human brain and the computer. This is not to say that psychologists believe that brains and computers operate in exactly the same way. Clearly they do not, but enough general similarity exists to make the information-processing model useful. Before looking at specific theories, let's look briefly at the general information-processing model and its terminology.

In the information-processing model, information can be followed as it moves through the following operations: input, storage, and retrieval. At each point in the process, a variety of *control mechanisms* (such as attention, storage, or retrieval) operate. Information enters the memory system through the sensory receptors. This is like your entering a term paper into your computer by typing on the keyboard. Attention operates at this level to select information for further processing. The raw sensory information that is selected is then represented—or **encoded**—in a form (sound, visual image, meaning) that can be used in the next stages of memory.

encode
(en´cōd) To represent information in some form in the memory system.

Other control mechanisms might then transfer selected information into a more permanent memory storage, like saving the term paper you typed into your computer on a disk. When the stored information is needed, it is *retrieved* from memory. Before printing out your paper, you must first locate your file on the disk and retrieve it. Unfortunately, with both computers and human memory, some information may be lost or become irretrievable.

Some information needs to be stored in memory for only brief periods of time, whereas other information must be tucked away permanently. When we look at a cookbook to see how much wine to add to the chicken cacciatore, we need to remember that bit of information for only a few seconds. However, you must remember your social security number or your sister's name for your entire lifetime. The influential **stage theory of memory** (Atkinson & Shiffrin, 1968) assumes that we humans have a three-stage memory that meets our need to store information for different lengths of time. We seem to have one memory store that holds information for exceedingly brief intervals, a second memory store that holds information for no more than 30 seconds unless it's "renewed," and a third, more permanent memory store. Each of these memories operates according to different rules and serves somewhat different purposes. Because information must pass through each stage of memory to get to the next more permanent one, these memory stores are best thought of as three closely linked "stages" of memory, rather than three separate memories. The three stages are known as the sensory register, short-term memory, and long-term memory (see fig. 6.1).

stage theory of memory
A model of memory based on the idea that we store information in three separate but linked memories.

Sensory Register

The first stage in memory—the **sensory register**—is a very brief one, designed to hold an exact image of each sensory experience until it can be fully processed. We apparently retain a copy of each sensory experience in the sensory register long enough to locate and focus on relevant bits of information and transfer them into the next stage of memory. For visual information, this "snapshot" fades very quickly, probably lasting about one-quarter of a second in most cases. You can observe this phenomenon by waving your fingers back

sensory register
The first stage of memory, in which an exact image of each sensory experience is held briefly until it can be processed.

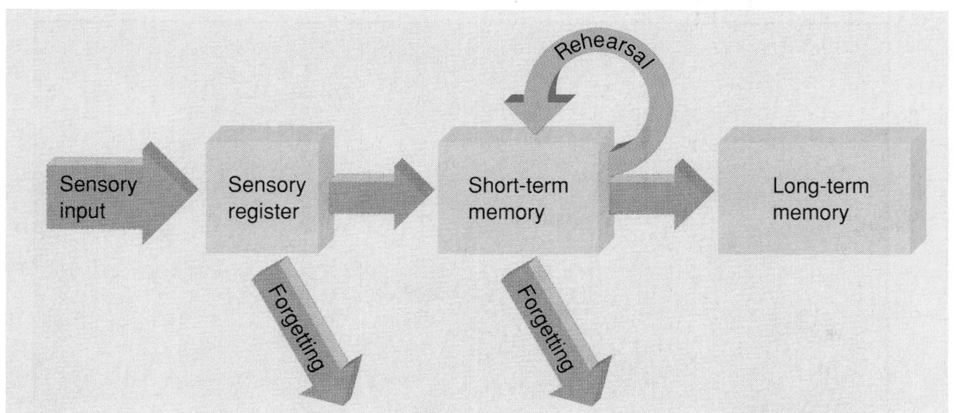

FIGURE 6.1
Stage model of memory.

and forth in front of your eyes, causing you to "see" many fingers for a brief time. For auditory information, a vivid image of what we heard is retained for about the same length of time, one-quarter of a second (Cowan, 1987), but a weaker "echo" is retained for up to 4 seconds (Tarpy & Mayer, 1978).

The information stored in the sensory register does not last long, but it's apparently a complete replica of the sensory experience. This fact has been demonstrated in an important experiment by George Sperling (1960). Sperling presented research participants with an array of 12 letters arranged in three horizontal rows of four letters each (see fig. 6.2). He showed the participants these letters for 1/20 of a second and then asked them to recall all of the letters in one of the three rows. He did not tell them ahead of time which row he would ask them to recall. Instead, he signaled to them using a tone. A high-pitched tone indicated the first row, a medium tone indicated the second row, and a low tone indicated the third row. If the tone was presented very soon after the presentation of the array of letters, the participants could recall most of the letters in the indicated row. But if the delay was more than one-quarter of a second, the participants recalled an average of just over one letter per row, indicating how quickly information is lost in the sensory register.

Visual information in the sensory register is lost and replaced so rapidly with new information that we seldom are aware we even have such a memory store. Sometimes the longer-lasting echolike traces of auditory information can be noticed, though. Most of us have had the experience of being absorbed in reading when a friend speaks. If we divert our attention from the book quickly enough, we can "hear again" what was said to us by referring to the echo of the auditory sensation stored in the sensory register.

FIGURE 6.2
Array of letters like those used in the sensory register experiments conducted by Sperling (1960).

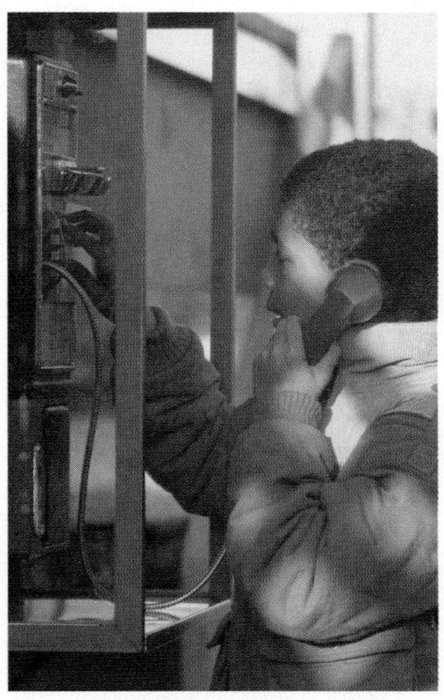

When we dial a number that we have just looked up in the telephone book, we are generally using information that has been stored only in short-term memory.

Short-Term Memory

When a bit of information is selected for further processing, it's transferred into **short-term memory,** or **STM.** It's not necessary to intentionally transfer information to STM; generally, just paying attention to the information is enough to transfer it. You might not intentionally try to memorize the price of your dinner, but you will be able to recognize that you were given the wrong amount of change. Once information has been transferred to short-term memory, a variety of control processes may be applied. Rehearsal and chunking are two important examples of these control processes.

Rehearsal in Short-Term Memory: Overcoming STM's Limited Life Span

As the name implies, short-term memory (STM) is good for only temporary storage of information. In general, information is lost from STM in less than half a minute unless it's "renewed," and it is often lost in only a few seconds (Ellis & Hunt, 1993). Fortunately, information can be renewed in STM by mental repetition, or **rehearsal,** of the information. When a grocery list is rehearsed regularly in this way, it can be held in STM for relatively long periods of time. If the list is not rehearsed, however, it's soon lost. Rehearsing the information stored in STM has been compared to juggling eggs: The eggs stay in perfect condition as long as you keep juggling them, but as soon as you stop juggling, they are lost.

short-term memory (STM)
The second stage of memory, in which five to nine bits of information can be stored for brief periods of time.

rehearsal
Mental repetition of information for retention in short-term memory.

FIGURE 6.3

The accuracy of recall for a single group of three consonants declines rapidly when subjects are prevented from rehearsing by being asked to count backward.

Source: R. L. Peterson and M. J. Peterson, "Short Term Retention of Individual Items" in *Journal of Experimental Psychology* 58:193–198, 1959.

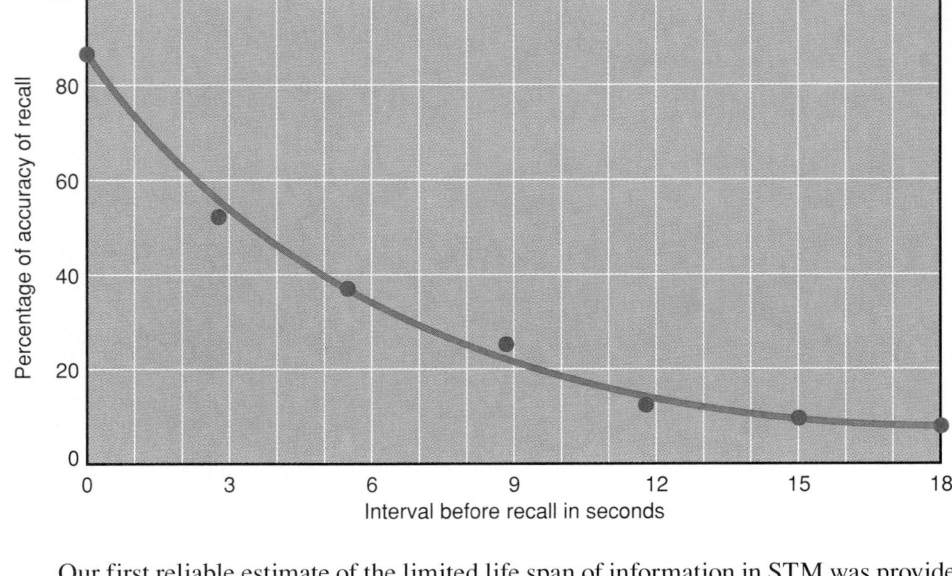

Our first reliable estimate of the limited life span of information in STM was provided by an experiment conducted by Lloyd and Margaret Peterson (1959). The participants were shown a single combination of three consonants (such as LRP) and asked to remember it as they counted backward by threes to keep them from rehearsing the letters. The individuals counted backward for brief intervals (0 through 18 seconds) and then were asked to recall the letters. As shown in figure 6.3, the participants were able to remember the three consonants less than 20 percent of the time after only 12 seconds had passed. These findings make it clear that memories are quite impermanent in STM unless kept alive by rehearsal.

The information stored in STM can be of many different types of memories: the smell of a perfume, the notes of a melody, the taste of a fruit, the shape of a nose, the finger positions in a guitar chord, or a list of names. But we humans have a preference for transforming information into sounds, or *acoustic codes,* whenever possible for storage in STM. If I asked you to memorize a list of letters (*B, P, V, R, M, L*), you would most likely memorize them by their "names" (bee, pee, vee, etc.) rather than by the shape of the letters. We know this because most people say they do it this way, and because the errors people make are most likely to be confusions of similar sounds (recalling *zee* instead of *bee*) rather than confusions of similar shapes (recalling *O* instead of *Q,* or *R* instead of *P*) (Reynolds & Flagg, 1983). We probably use acoustic codes in STM as much as possible because it's easier to rehearse by mentally talking to ourselves than by mentally repeating the images of sights, smells, and movements. Nonetheless, STM can store any form of information that can enter the brain through the senses.

George Miller says that STM will hold 7 ± 2 bits of information. This shopper probably needs a written list.

Chunking in Short-Term Memory: Overcoming STM's Limited Capacity

Perhaps the most important thing to know about STM is that its storage capacity is quite limited. The exact capacity differs slightly for different kinds of information, but as psychologist George Miller (1956) put it, it's constant enough to call it the *magic number 7 plus or minus (±) 2.* Estimates of the span of STM are obtained by asking research participants to memorize simple lists (of randomly ordered numbers, letters, and unrelated words) of different lengths. The length of the list that the participants can recall half the time is considered to represent the capacity of STM (Miller, 1956). Rarely are we able to hold more than five to nine bits of information in STM, regardless of the nature of that information. This is a very limited capacity, indeed.

In addition to temporarily storing information, STM serves another important function that further limits its already small capacity—it serves as our "*working memory*" (Baddeley, 1992). This means that space in STM is used when old memories are temporarily brought out of long-term memory to be used or updated. Space in STM is also used when we think about this information (Morris, 1986). This is why you cannot remember the telephone number of the hardware store that you just looked up if you begin thinking about your purchase before you dial—thinking takes up space in STM and forces out the numbers. The fact that thinking utilizes STM also explains why it's difficult to think about problems that involve more than 7 ± 2 issues. We keep forgetting some of the aspects of the problem because they exceed the limited capacity of STM. In such situations, writing out all the issues on paper helps to keep them straight while you are thinking.

One advantage of the small storage capacity of STM is that it's easy to "search" through it. When we try to remember something in STM, we apparently examine every item that is stored there. Experiments conducted by Saul Sternberg (1969) confirm that we exhaustively search STM every time we try to recall something. Sternberg's experiments even give us an estimate of how long it takes us to examine each bit of stored information. Participants were asked to memorize lists of numbers of different lengths. They were then shown a number and asked if it was in the list they had just memorized. When individuals had just memorized a long list of numbers, it took them longer to respond than when they had memorized a short list. In fact, the amount of time required to respond increased by a rather constant .04 of a second for each item in STM. Apparently that's how long it takes to examine each item in STM.

Fortunately, there are some effective ways to get around the limited capacity of STM. One way is to learn the information well enough to transfer it into long-term memory, which as we shall see shortly has no real space limitation. Another way is to put more information into the 7 ± 2 units of STM.

George Miller (1956) calls the units of memory **chunks.** Although it's true that we can hold only five to nine chunks in STM, we can often put more than one bit of information into each chunk. If you were to quickly read this list of 12 words once,

chunks
Units of memory.

east
spring
fall
dorsal
west
medial
winter
lateral
north
ventral
summer
south

you probably would not be able to recall it perfectly 10 seconds later since 12 chunks normally exceed the capacity of STM. But if you reorganized the words into *three* chunks (points of a compass, seasons, and anatomical directions) and memorized those, the list could be remembered quite easily. This strategy would work for you only if you could regroup the list into meaningful chunks, however. If you did not know the four anatomical directions, it would do you no good to memorize these terms because you could not generate the four directions when you recalled them.

Other chunking strategies can also be used to expand the amount of information that can be stored in STM. It's no accident that social security numbers (as well as bank account numbers and telephone numbers) are broken up by hyphens. Most people find it easier to remember numbers in chunks (319–588–1451) than as a string of single digits.

To sum up what we have just said: STM is a stage of memory with limited capacity in which information—often stored in acoustic codes—is lost rapidly unless it's rehearsed. The capacity of STM can be expanded by increasing the amount of information in each chunk to be learned. But no matter how good a job we do of chunking and rehearsing, STM is not a good place to store important information for long periods of time. Such information must be transferred to long-term memory for more permanent storage.

Long-Term Memory

Long-term memory, or **LTM,** is the storehouse for information that must be kept for long periods of time. But LTM is not just a more durable version of STM; the stage model of memory suggests it's a different kind of memory altogether.

long-term memory (LTM)
The third stage of memory, involving the storage of information that is kept for long periods of time.

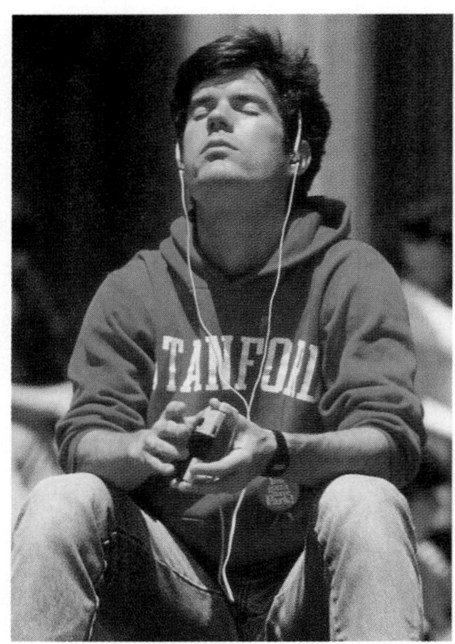

Hearing an old favorite song can bring back memories of the earliest times you heard the song. We can use cues like old songs either intentionally or unintentionally to retrieve long-term memories.

LTM differs from STM in four major ways: (1) how information is recalled, (2) the form in which information is stored in memory, (3) the reasons that forgetting occurs, and (4) the physical location of these functions in the human brain. Let's look at each of these four differences between STM and LTM separately:

1. Because the amount of information stored in LTM is so vast, we cannot scan the entire contents of LTM when we are looking for a bit of information like we do in STM. Instead, LTM has to be *indexed.* We retrieve information from LTM using *cues,* much like we use a call number to locate a book in the library. This retrieval can be an intentional act (such as, "What was the name of the secretary in Accounts Receivable?") or an unintentional one, as when hearing a particular song brings back memories of a lost love. In either case, only information relevant to the cue is retrieved rather than the entire contents of LTM.
2. LTM differs from STM in the kind of information that is most easily stored. You will recall that information is usually stored in STM in terms of the physical qualities of the experience (what we saw, did, tasted, touched, or heard), with a special emphasis on acoustic codes. Although sensory memories can be stored in LTM, information is primarily stored in LTM in terms of its meaning, or *semantic codes* (Cowan, 1988).
3. LTM also differs from STM in the way forgetting occurs. Unlike STM, where information that is not rehearsed or processed appears to drop out of the system, information stored in LTM is not just durable but actually appears to be permanent. In a dramatic demonstration of LTM, Bahrick (1984) tested memory for Spanish using individuals who had studied the language in high school 50 years ago! Bahrick's participants retained much of their knowledge of Spanish even after a period of 50 years. Not all psychologists agree that memories in LTM are permanent (Loftus & Loftus, 1980), but there is a great deal of evidence supporting this view. If memories in LTM are indeed permanent, this means that "forgetting" occurs in LTM not because the memory is erased but because we are unable to retrieve it for some reason (Matlin, 1983; Reynolds & Flagg, 1983).
4. The different stages of memory are handled by different parts of the brain. STM is primarily a function of the frontal lobes of the cerebral cortex (Fuster, 1995; Goldman-Rakic, 1992; Williams & Goldman-Rakic, 1995), while information that is stored in LTM is first held in the hippocampus and then transferred to the areas of the cerebral cortex involved in language and perception for permanent storage.

I have illustrated the brain structures involved in the different stages of memory in figure 6.4. I have used a visual stimulus as the example because last week I saw the Rocky Mountains for the first time in my life and I have a clear memory of them that I hope will be permanent. When I saw the mountain that the Shoshoni people named "Going to the Sun," the visual stimulus traveled to the thalamus where it was routed to the visual area of the occipital lobe of the cerebral cortex where I perceived the wonderful visual image (part 1 of fig. 6.4). This neural activity leaves the brief trace that we call the *sensory register.*

If I had immediately turned around and closed my eyes, I would have been able to recall the visual image of the mountain and hold it for a while in STM in the frontal lobes of the cerebral cortex (shown in part 2 of fig. 6.4) (Goldman-Rakic, 1992). For the memory to be stored permanently, however, it would need to be stored temporarily (for up to several weeks or months) in the hippocampus. This key structure holds information as it is being transferred from STM to LTM (Kandel & Hawkins, 1992). Eventually, my visual image of the mountain will be stored permanently in the occipital lobe, near where it was first processed.

I have simplified this description of how my brain processed the memory of the visual image of the mountain to show how many brain structures are involved in just one aspect of memory, but the process is usually more complex. For example, I made a conscious effort to memorize the name of the mountain, "Going to the Sun." A team of researchers at the University of Michigan has recently shown using PET brain imaging that

FIGURE 6.4

Stages of memory and the brain.

1. Visual information is first routed through the thalamus to the visual area of the cerebral cortex. This neural activity is the basis for the sensory register.

2. The information is then relayed to the frontal lobes where it can be held in short-term memory.

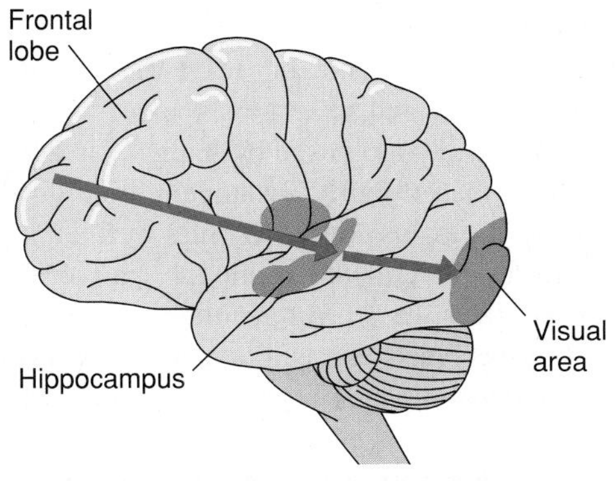

3. Information that is stored in long-term memory is then held in the hippocampus for weeks or months, and then transferred to the area of the cerebral cortex near where it was originally processed for long-term storage.

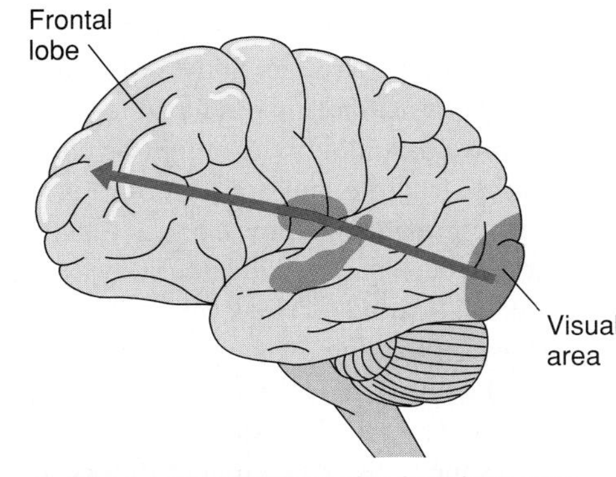

4. When we recall information from long-term memory, it is routed again to the frontal lobes where it is held in short-term (or "working") memory.

the verbal areas of the left cerebral hemisphere are actively involved in the rehearsal of verbal information in STM prior to transfer to LTM. Like the other psychological processes that make us human, memory is marvelously complex.

Types of Long-Term Memory: Procedural, Episodic, and Semantic

Tulving (1972, 1985, 1987) has proposed the existence of three kinds of long-term memory storage, each with distinctly different properties, and each probably based on different brain mechanisms. I think I can best explain the differences among these kinds of LTM by telling you another one of my stories. Last week, I came across a photograph taken of me on my 14th birthday in my home in St. Petersburg, Florida. I was holding my birthday present—my first guitar. I took guitar lessons for a while and played in several mediocre rock bands until my junior year in college. Then, I sold my guitar and concentrated on my studies. About 10 years ago, however, I bought another guitar, and playing guitar in mediocre rock bands was once again a fun part of my life for a few years.

That's the story; now for the three types of LTM:

1. When I picked up my new guitar in the music store, I found that I could still play the basic chords even though I had not played them in years. That is a long-term **procedural memory**—memory for skills and other procedures. Our memories of how to ride a bicycle, to cook, or to kiss are procedural memories.

procedural memory
Memory for motor movements and skills.

2. Although I did not stop to think about it, I also obviously remembered what a guitar is. I knew what it was when I saw it, knew what it is used for, and so on.

semantic memory
(se-man´tik) Memory for meaning without reference to the time and place of learning.

episodic memory
(epĭ-sod-ik) Memory for specific experiences that can be defined in terms of time and space.

In other words, I had not forgotten the semantic memory of the meaning of "guitar." **Semantic memory** is memory for meaning. When you remember what a father is, what pudding is, and what the phrase "peace of mind" means, you are recalling meaning from long-term semantic memory.

3. Until my memory was jogged by finding the old photograph, however, it had been years since I had remembered when and where I had gotten my first guitar. **Episodic memory** is the kind of LTM that stores information about specific experiences that took place at specific times and in specific places.

The LTM mechanisms are apparently able to store procedural and semantic memories quite effectively, but LTM handles episodic information much less well. I immediately knew what a guitar was (semantic) and how to play it (procedural), but it took a photograph to recall the time and place of getting my first guitar (episodic). A great deal of research has been done to show that greater ability of LTM to store semantic than episodic memories. A clever study of the memorization of sentences by J. D. S. Sachs (1967) clearly illustrates this point. The experimenter had research participants listen to passages containing a number of different sentences. After intervals of different lengths, she asked the individuals to listen to more sentences and tell her whether they were exactly the same as one of the sentences in the passage. Some of the test sentences were the same, but some were changed either in physical form or in meaning. For example, an original sentence in the passage such as "Jenny chased Melissa" might be changed to "Melissa was chased by Jenny" (change in physical structure, but not meaning) or to "Melissa chased Jenny" (change in both physical structure and meaning). Sachs found that the participants could tell quite well if a sentence had been changed in either way as long as the test interval was within the span of STM (about 30 seconds). However, at longer intervals they were only accurate in detecting changes in meaning. Apparently, the meaning of the sentences (semantic memory) was held in LTM while details about their physical structure (episodic memory) were forgotten when they were lost from STM.

declarative memory
Semantic and episodic memory.

In spite of these apparent differences, some psychologists group semantic memory and episodic memory together under the heading **declarative memory** (see fig. 6.5). Semantic and episodic memories are quite different, but they are alike in an important way as well: They are easily described (declared) in words. For example, I would have no difficulty telling you what a guitar is. This is in contrast to *procedural memory,* which can be accessed only through performance—as in when I play a song on my guitar (Squire, 1987). It is difficult, if not impossible, to verbally describe how to play a song on the guitar without playing it. This distinction between procedural and declarative memories will be important to our discussion of amnesia later in the chapter.

Organization in Long-Term Memory

We noted earlier that it's possible to make more efficient use of the limited capacity of STM by organizing information into larger chunks (Miller, 1956). Organization of information is also important for LTM, but it's probably not related to a need to save capacity, since LTM presumably has unlimited capacity. Rather, organization helps to facilitate the retrieval of information from the vast amount stored in LTM. The retrieval task in LTM is vastly different from STM: Instead of 7 ± 2 items that can be easily searched, LTM stores such an extensive amount of information that it almost certainly must be *organized* in some fash-

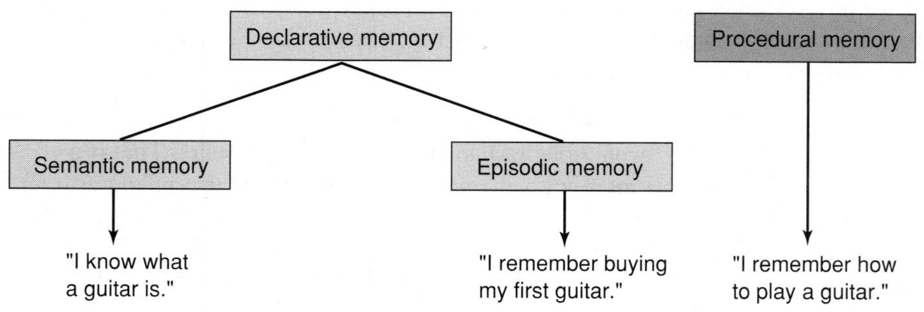

FIGURE 6.5
Semantic and episodic memory are sometimes grouped together under the term *declarative memory* because both kinds of memory can be easily described (declared) in words. In contrast, procedural memories are difficult to describe in words because they involve skills like playing the guitar that can be seen only when the task is performed.

ion. It's sometimes inconvenient that the 60-odd books in my office are not organized on my bookshelves, but I can still find what I am looking for by searching long enough. It would be impossible, on the other hand, to find the same book in the university library if the books were as unorganized and randomly placed on the shelves as mine. Like LTM, the library needs an organized way of storing and retrieving a huge amount of information.

LTM does not use the Dewey decimal system, but like a library, LTM organizes information to facilitate retrieval.

Evidence for the organization of LTM has been available for some time. When research participants are asked to recall items from categories (such as makes of automobiles or animals) that they learned, they recall them in bursts of related items, pause briefly, and then recall another group of items, and so on (Bousfield & Sedgewick, 1944). Seemingly, the bursts of items that are recalled reflect the way they are organized in LTM. Furthermore, when participants memorize new lists of items that could be categorized, they tend to recall them in related groups. For example, Weston Bousfield (1953) asked individuals to memorize a list of 60 words that could be conceptually grouped into four categories: animals, vegetables, names, and professions (muskrat, blacksmith, panther, baker, wildcat, Howard, Jason, printer, and so on). Even though the words were presented in random order, participants recalled them in categorical groupings significantly more often than would be expected by chance. Apparently, the words were stored in LTM according to organized categories.

In addition, there is clear evidence that recall from LTM is better when we impose more organization on the information that is stored there. Gordon Bower's Stanford University research group (Bower & Clark, 1969) asked participants to memorize 12 lists of 10 words like the following:

boy
boat
dog
wagon
ghost
rag
wheel
hat
house
milk

Half of the individuals were given the usual instructions to memorize the lists of words in any order, but the others were asked to "make up stories" containing all of the words in the list—to organize them into a single story. For example, the previous list could be memorized as "The boy with the hat pulled his dog and his boat in his wagon with the crooked wheel. He saw a rag hanging on a house that he thought was a ghost. It scared him so much that he spilled his milk." The group that organized the words into stories recalled an amazing 90 percent of the 12 lists of words, whereas the other group recalled only 15 percent!

The organization of memory in LTM has been characterized as an *associative network* by some theorists (Ellis & Hunt, 1993; Raaijmakers & Shiffrin, 1992). According to this view, memories are associated, or linked together, through experience. Your experience forms links between that special song and memories of your summer vacation, or between algebra and that unbearable teacher. Researchers have studied the operation of associative networks by asking research participants to answer general knowledge questions. For instance, suppose you were asked to answer the question, "Is a canary a bird?" How do you access your store of information to answer correctly? An influential network model known as the *spreading activation model* (Collins & Loftus, 1975) attempts to explain this process. According to Collins and Loftus, we form links between various concepts and their characteristics based on our experience. When we are asked a question, representations of the concepts or characteristics are activated. As shown in figure 6.6, the question would activate separate memory representations of "canary" and "bird." The model then assumes that this activation spreads out along previously formed links to other representations. In the case of "canary" and "bird," which are very closely associated for many people, the lines of activation spreading from these representations meet quickly, and a decision can be made.

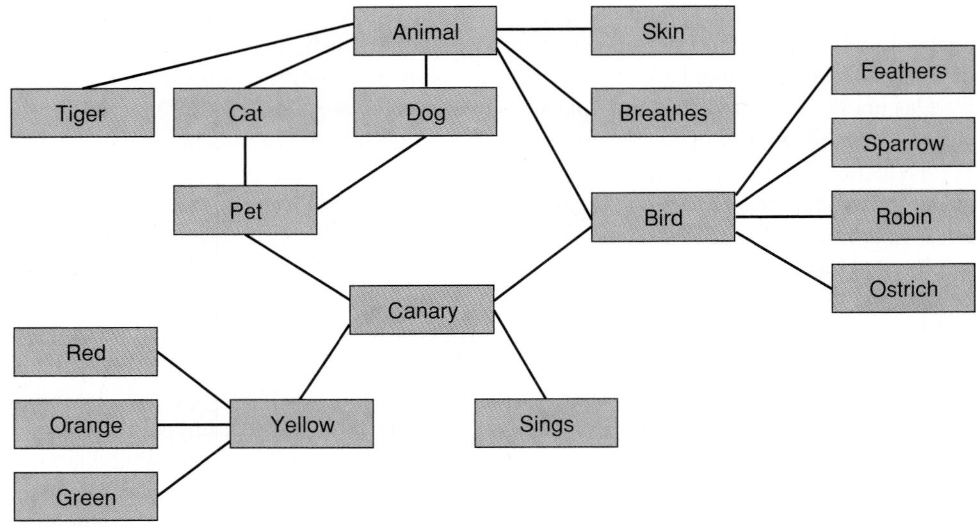

FIGURE 6.6
An example of the associative links that are hypothesized to exist among bits of information stored in long-term memory in the spreading activation theory.

If representations are not as closely associated, it takes a longer time to respond. If you were asked whether or not a penguin is a bird, your answer would probably be slower than in the canary example.

Experimental support for the spreading activation model can be seen in a clever study (Meyer & Schvaneveldt, 1971). Research participants watched while groups of letters were flashed on a computer screen. Some of the letter groups spelled out real words, but others (like *plame* or *blop*) just *looked* like words. The participants were asked to respond by hitting a "yes" button when a real word was shown and a "no" button when a made-up "word" was shown. The important part of this study is the time it took them to hit the button each time a real word was shown. The researchers found that the participants' reaction times were much faster for words that had been shown immediately preceded by a related word (bread-butter) than by an unrelated word (nurse-butter).

What does this mean for the spreading activation model of long-term memory? According to this theory, activation of "bread" would spread along the network to related items, including "butter." Therefore, "butter" would be partially activated even before the word appeared on the screen, producing a very fast reaction time. Thus, these results support the spreading activation model.

Retrieval of Long-Term Memories

Students are very familiar with the frustration that comes from knowing that you know something but being totally incapable of retrieving it (until, of course, you step outside the exam room!). Research on types of retrieval, serial learning, and the "tip-of-the-tongue" phenomenon provide us with important insights into the retrieval process in long-term memory.

Three Ways of Testing Retrieval: Recall, Recognition, and Relearning

recall method
A measure of memory based on the ability to retrieve information from long-term memory with few cues.

recognition method
A measure of memory based on the ability to select correct information from among the options provided.

Psychologists have distinguished three different ways of measuring memory retrieval that differ from one another in important ways. In the **recall method,** you are asked to recall information with few, if any cues: Who did Bill Clinton defeat for the presidency of the United States in 1992? This is a recall method of assessing your memory for that fact.

In the **recognition method,** you are asked to recognize the correct information from among alternatives. The same question could be asked as a recognition question.

In 1992, Bill Clinton defeated ____________________ for the presidency of the United States.

a. Bob Dole
b. George Bush
c. Pat Buchanan
d. Jimmy Carter

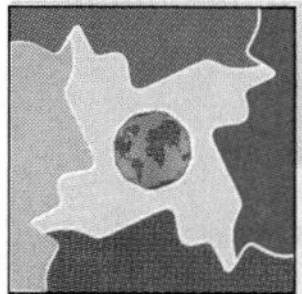

HUMAN DIVERSITY

Cultural Circumstances and Memory Skills

Does culture influence even basic intellectual skills such as memory? Some psychologists believe that our cultural circumstances have a powerful impact on many fundamental aspects of intelligence. For example, psychologist Judith Kearins (1986) hypothesized that Australian aboriginal peoples possess better visual memory skills for objects than white Australian children. She reasoned that excellent visual memory skills have allowed the aboriginal people to thrive in the different physical desert environments in which many of them live.

In Kearins's experiments, aboriginal and white adolescents were given 30 seconds to memorize the location of objects arranged on a rectangular grid. The experimenter then mixed the objects up and the adolescent was asked to replace them in their original positions. Two of the tasks involved manufactured objects (matchbox, ring, eraser) and two involved natural objects (twig, seed pod, feather, bone, etc.). The aboriginal adolescents performed significantly better than white Australians on all of the tasks. While adolescents performed better when the task material was manufactured objects than they did when the objects were natural, but this distinction did not affect the performance of the aboriginal children.

Kearins found that aboriginal and white Australian adolescents used different memory strategies to approach the task. The aboriginal adolescents sat very still, were silent, and appeared to concentrate deeply. They were slow and methodical in replacing the objects. Most of the white adolescents, on the other hand, tended to fidget and mutter and replaced the first few objects hurriedly. Kearins speculated that the white children were muttering the verbal labels of the objects in an effort to remember them, whereas the aboriginal children were more likely to memorize the arrangement of the objects in visual terms. Perhaps the different cultures emphasize verbal or visual approaches to memorization because of the importance of those skills in each culture.

Think about your own approach to memorization. How would you have approached the memory task in Kearins's experiment? Would you have memorized the placements of the objects in visual terms, or would you have memorized verbal labels for the objects ("The feather in the top-left, then moving clockwise, the stick, the weird-looking bone . . .")? What type of information is most important for you to remember to survive in your ethnic group? What cultural differences have you noticed between your community and other ethnic communities in terms of their approach to intellectual skills? Finally, has your ethnic community influenced your approach to memorization and other intellectual skills—and, if so, how has it done so?

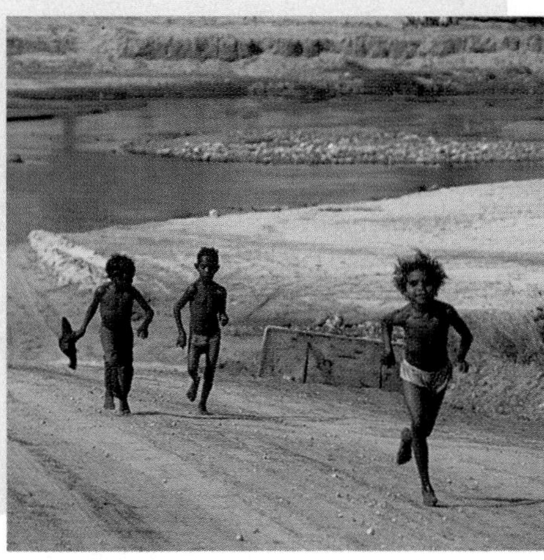

Generally, we can "remember" more when tested by the recognition rather than the recall method, because recognition tasks provide more cues for retrieving information from long-term memory. Our greater ability to recognize rather than to recall remembered information was demonstrated vividly in an experiment on everyday memory to which we can all relate (Bahrick, Bahrick, & Wittlinger, 1975). Two years after graduation from high school, college students were found to be able to *recall* an average of 60 percent of the names of students in their class when looking at their photographs. However, when they were shown their yearbook pictures and asked to *recognize* the corresponding name from a list, they could match names correctly 90 percent of the time.

relearning method
A measure of memory based on the length of time it takes to relearn forgotten material.

The **relearning** (or *savings*) **method** is the most sensitive of all three of the methods of evaluating memory. Even when you can neither recall nor recognize information, it may be possible to measure some memory of it using the relearning method. In this method, you relearn previously memorized information. If the relearning takes less time than the original learning, then the information has been "remembered" in this sense. For instance, at some point in your life, you probably learned how to find the area of a right triangle. You might be unable to remember how to do that now, but you could "relearn" the method much faster than it took you to learn it the first time. Your ability to relearn the technique rapidly shows that the memory was never truly "lost."

It is easier to retrieve long-term memories using recognition than to try to recall the information.

Serial Learning

In some special types of retrieval tasks, the order in which we memorize a list is as important as the items in the list. It would be useless to memorize the steps in defusing a bomb if you did not remember them in the right order! When psychologists have studied memory for serial lists (lists of words, numbers, and the like that must be recalled in a certain order), a surprisingly consistent finding has emerged. The recall of items in the serial lists is often better for items at the *beginning* and *end* of the list than in the middle. This is called the **serial position effect.** Many explanations have been suggested for this effect over the years, but it's perhaps best explained in terms of the differences between short-term and long-term memory. The last items in a list are remembered well because they are still in STM, whereas the first items in a list are remembered well because they can be rehearsed enough times to transfer them firmly into LTM.

serial position effect
The finding that immediate recall of items listed in a fixed order is often better for items at the beginning and end of the list than for those in the middle.

Two experiments provide strong support for this explanation. First, Vito Modigliani and Donald Hedges of Simon Fraser University (1987) have shown that better recall for items at the beginning of lists is indeed related to greater opportunities for rehearsal. In a second experiment on the serial position effect (Glanzer & Cunitz, 1966), research participants attempted to memorize a list of 15 items. As shown in figure 6.7, the serial position effect was clearly found when the individuals were asked to recall the list immediately after learning it. Recall was better for items at both the beginning and the end of the list. But when the participants were asked to recall the list after a delay of 30 seconds—just beyond the limits of STM—the serial position effect was only half there. Recall was better at the beginning of the list—presumably because those items were rehearsed more and stored in LTM—but not at the end of the list, probably because the participants could not hold the last items in STM that long. The serial position effect shows that we are simultaneously using both STM and LTM in an attempt to soak up and retain as much of what's going on as possible.

The "Tip-of-the-Tongue" Phenomenon

We have all had the maddening experience of trying to recall a fact that we can *almost* remember—it's on the "tip of my tongue." Fortunately, there is a lesson in this on the nature

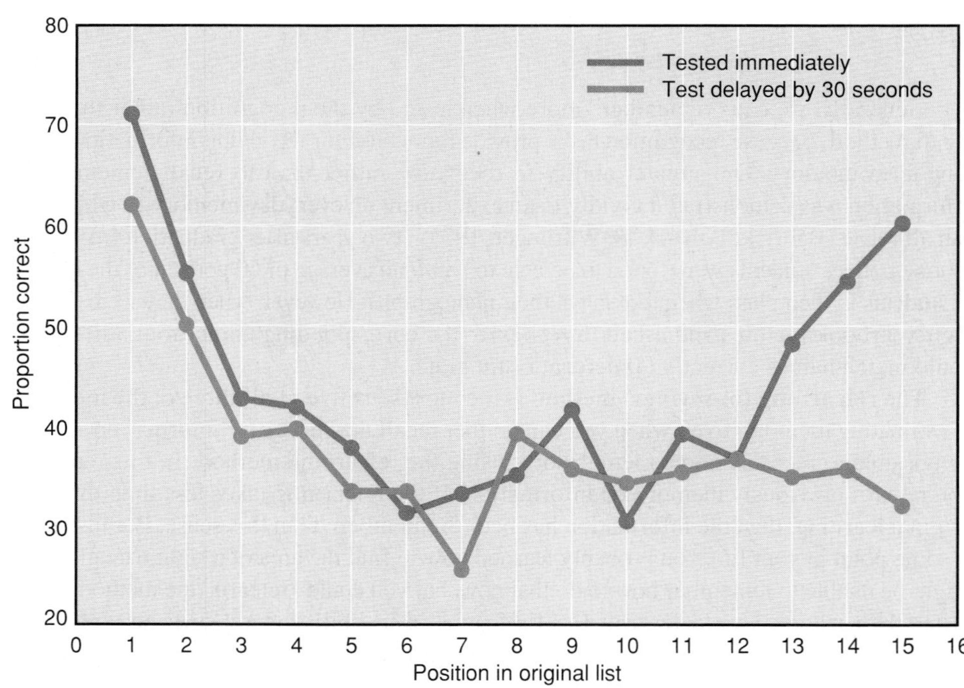

FIGURE 6.7
When recall of a serial list of 15 items is tested immediately after the presentation of the last item, participants recall the first and last items better than the middle items. But when the test is delayed by 30 seconds, fewer of the last items are recalled, suggesting that at least some of the last items in the list were stored only in short-term memory.

Sources: Data from M. Glanzer and A. R. Cunitz, "Two Storage Mechanisms in Free Recall," *Journal of Verbal Learning and Verbal Behavior,* 5:351–360, 1966 Academic Press; and R. M. Tarpy and R. F. Mayer, *Foundations of Learning & Memory,* © 1978 Scott, Foresman.

of retrieval from LTM. The "tip-of-the-tongue" phenomenon was investigated by Harvard University psychologists Roger Brown and David McNeill (1966) by giving definitions of uncommon words to college students and asking them to recall the word. For example, they might be read the definition of *sampan* ("a small boat used in shallow water in the Orient that is rowed from behind using a single oar"). Often the students could recall the word *sampan.* Sometimes, though, they could not quite recall the word, and the researchers were able to create the tip-of-the-tongue sensation in these students. When this happened, the students found that they were able to recall some information about the word ("It starts with *s.*" or "It sounds like *Siam*"), or recall something about the thing the word referred to ("It looks a little like a junk"), even when they could not retrieve the word. And then moments later, the word would pop into memory for some students, proving that it was there all the time but just could not be retrieved for the moment.

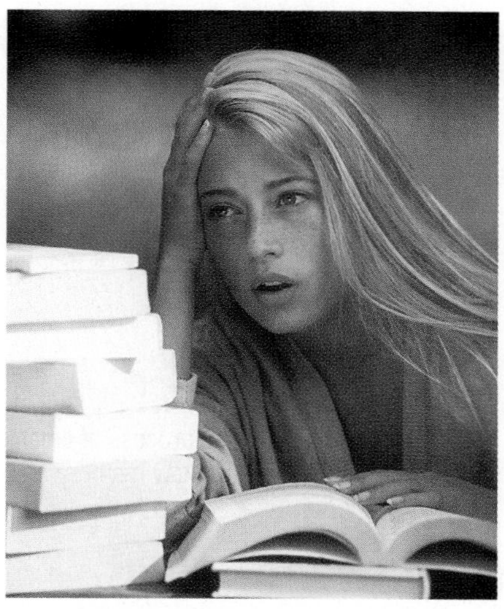
It is possible that all information stored in long-term memory is still there but cannot always be retrieved.

The tip-of-the-tongue phenomenon is important because it is consistent with the notion that long-term memory is permanent. That is, it seems that *all* information that was ever stored in your long-term memory is still there, but it just cannot always be retrieved. Let me give you a case in point: Have you ever had the experience of being reminded of a past event that you thought was long forgotten? Maybe you run into a friend in your hometown who asks, "Do you remember the time in second grade when . . .", and you suddenly remember a rich set of details that you had not thought about in years. Perhaps these long-term memories were irretrievable until the right cue (your friend's question) was used to call them out of storage.

The tip-of-the-tongue phenomenon also tells us that retrieval is not an "all or none" process. Instead, we appear to recall bits of information related to the target, such as its starting letter or number of syllables, during our search process. These cues might actually help us locate the target information, but we're not aware of them unless the search is slow or unsuccessful.

Levels of Processing: An Alternative to the Stage Model

The model suggesting that there are three separate stages of memory (sensory register, STM, and LTM) has been enormously helpful in making sense of the complex phenomenon of memory. However, this view may be too simplistic. Fergus Craik and Robert Lockhart (1972) have proposed an alternative **levels of processing model,** suggesting that the distinction between short-term and long-term memory is a matter of *degree* rather than separate stages. In brief, Craik and Lockhart believe that there is only one memory store beyond the sensory register. The durability of stored information depends on how well it is processed as it is being encoded for memory. Information will be kept only briefly if it's processed at a *shallow* level, but it will be kept much longer if it's processed at a *deeper* level. Thus, the differences that we have just described between STM and LTM are not, in this view, differences between two different memory systems operating according to different principles. Rather, these differences are the results of different levels of processing during the encoding process. Furthermore, according to Craik and Lockhart, there is a continuum of levels of processing ranging from very shallow to very deep, rather than just two types of storage (short and long).

levels of processing model
An alternative to the stage theory of memory stating that the distinction between short-term and long-term memory is a matter of degree rather than different kinds of memory and is based on how incoming information is processed.

What is the difference between deep and shallow processing? One way of putting it is to say that shallow processing involves the encoding of superficial perceptual information, whereas deep processing encodes meaning (Ellis, 1987). Consider the following list of adjectives:

soft
swift
warm
sharp
witty
bright
clean
beautiful

If you asked 10 acquaintances to process this list in a superficial way ("Look at each word for 5 seconds; then circle the adjectives containing the letter *i*") and asked 10 other acquaintances to process it in a deep way ("Look at each word for 5 seconds; then circle the adjectives that describe you"), which group do you think would remember more of the words if, without warning, you asked them to recall the list 10 minutes later? Craik and Lockhart's levels of processing view correctly predict that the individuals who processed the words deeply by thinking about their meanings (the second group) recall more of the words—not because they had stored the words in a different memory (LTM vs. STM) but because information processed more deeply is stored more permanently.

elaboration
(e-lab´´ or-rā´ shun) The process of creating associations between a new memory and existing memories.

Deep processing also involves greater *elaboration* of memories during the encoding phase than shallow processing. **Elaboration,** in this sense, means creating more associations between the new memory and existing memories (Ellis, 1987; Ellis & Hunt, 1993). For example, if you read a paragraph in a textbook and spend a few minutes relating its contents to what you had learned in the previous chapters or to your own life, you will be elaborating the memory—linking it to existing memories. We have already seen how the associative network model assumes that these links are vital to your ability to use stored information. Therefore, deeply processing the new information in this way will improve your memory of the paragraph and your ability to use the information later. In contrast, simply going through the motions of rereading a paragraph several times without really thinking about it is a much less successful study technique. What is also interesting about this newer view of deep processing is that even superficial perceptual information can be richly elaborated, such as by relating a new telephone number to existing memories about the person you are calling.

The levels of processing view probably will not replace the STM/LTM stage model. This is particularly true because new evidence on the biology of memory in the brain that we will look at later in this chapter indicates that STM and LTM are based on different biological mechanisms. This is not to say that the levels of processing view of memory is unimportant, however. It is a useful reminder to us that information that is learned in a shallow, rote manner will not be around in our memories very long. If you want to retain information for a long time and have the ability to retrieve it easily, you need to take the time and effort to understand and elaborate the information as you learn it.

Thinking Critically About Psychology

1. Semantic memories are more durable than episodic memories in long-term memory. This is sometimes inconvenient, but is it also advantageous in some ways?

2. Can you think of some episodic memories that have stayed especially clear through the years? What is it about those events that has caused them to be so durable?

Review

We can think of human memory as being composed of three different, but related, stages of memory. The sensory register holds a replica of the visual, auditory, or other sensory input for a very brief interval while relevant information is selected for further processing. Short-term memory holds information, generally as acoustic codes, for about a half minute unless it's renewed through rehearsal. The capacity of short-term memory is quite limited unless information is organized into larger chunks. Long-term memory stores information primarily in terms of its meaning, or semantic codes. Its capacity is very large and memories stored there seem to be permanent. The store of information in LTM is so vast that it must be organized in some way to facilitate retrieval of information. Current theories suggest that the organization is primarily in terms of categories of meaning or in associative networks. Forgetting occurs because information is distorted or can no longer be retrieved rather than because it's lost from the long-term memory store.

The division of memory into a distinct STM and LTM has been questioned by some theorists, however. They suggest, instead, that the duration that information can be held in memory depends on the *depth* at which it's processed, not the *stage* of memory in which it's held. Information that is processed deeply during the encoding process—more richly elaborated—is stored more permanently than information that is processed in a shallow way. If this distinction is kept in mind, however, it still may be useful to think of memory in terms of the STM/LTM stage model.

Check Your Learning

To be sure that you have learned the key points from the preceding section, cover the answers below and try to answer each question. If you give an incorrect answer to any question, return to the page given next to the correct answer to see why your answer was not correct. Remember that these questions cover only some of the important information in this section; it is important that you make up your own questions to check your learning of other facts and concepts.

1. The ________________ assumes that we humans have a three-stage memory that meets our need to store information for different lengths of time.
   - **a.** lateral processing theory of memory
   - **b.** stage theory of memory
   - **c.** psychoanalytic theory of memory
   - **d.** progression theory of memory
2. The first stage in memory is the ________________, which is designed to hold an exact image of each sensory experience for a very brief time until it can be fully processed.
   - **a.** short-term memory
   - **b.** primary store
   - **c.** sensory register
   - **d.** initial memory store
3. The ________________ is used to temporarily store information and to think while holding information in "working memory."
   - **a.** short-term memory
   - **b.** long-term memory
   - **c.** sensory register
   - **d.** primary store
4. Long-term memory is similar to short-term memory in terms of how information is recalled, why forgetting occurs, and the form in which information is usually stored.
   - **a.** True
   - **b.** False
5. The ________________ is a memory model suggesting that the distinction between short-term and long-term memory is a matter of degree rather than separate stages.

Correct Answers
1. b (p. 212), **2.** c (p. 212), **3.** a (pp. 213–215), **4.** b (p. 216), **5.** levels of processing model (p. 223).

FORGETTING AND WHY IT OCCURS

So far we have talked about remembering and forgetting in terms of the three stages of memory. We have noted that forgetting is different in STM and LTM, but we have skirted the issue of the causes of forgetting. Why do some memories become lost or irretrievable? What causes forgetting to occur? There are four major theories of forgetting that should be discussed in some detail: *decay theory,* which states that time alone causes memory traces to fade; *interference theory,* which suggests that other memories interfere with remembering; *reconstruction theory,* which proposes that memory traces become distorted with time, sometimes to the point of becoming unrecognizable; and the *theory of motivated forgetting,* which suggests that we forget information that is unpleasant or threatening.

Decay Theory

According to **decay theory,** memories that are not used fade gradually over time. This theory has been around for a long time and fits our commonsense understanding of forgetting. It had been discarded by psychologists as being wholly incorrect until recent years, however. As we shall see in a moment, forgetting is more complicated than the mere fading of

decay theory
The theory that forgetting occurs as the memory trace fades over time.

Forget the combination? According to the decay theory, forgetting occurs because time passes.

memory traces and involves factors other than time. The acceptance by most psychologists of some version of the three-stage conception of memory has brought the decay theory back at least into limited favor. It appears that the simple passage of time is a cause of forgetting both in the sensory register and in STM. It does not appear that decay due to the passage of time is a cause of forgetting in LTM, however. Memory "traces" appear to be "permanent" once they make it into LTM. Forgetting does not seem to happen in LTM because of disuse over time, but because other factors, *particularly interference,* make memories irretrievable.

Interference Theory

interference theory
The theory that forgetting occurs because similar memories interfere with the storage or retrieval of information.

Interference theory is based on considerable evidence that forgetting in LTM does not occur because of the passage of time, but because other memories interfere with the retrieval of what you are trying to recall, particularly if the other memories are similar to the one you are trying to remember. Suppose you take an interest in French impressionist painters and you read a book about the painting techniques of Degas, Monet, and Matisse. It would be no great feat to memorize each painter's techniques and keep them straight, but suppose you then learn about the techniques of three more French impressionists, and then three more. Pretty soon, recall becomes difficult, partly because the similar memories interfere with the retrieval of one another. This also happens when you try to remember a lot of telephone numbers, grocery-list items, or math formulas.

The fact that the other memories must be similar to the one you are trying to recall in order to interfere with its retrieval has been shown in a simple experiment by Delos Wickens and his associates (Wickens, Born, & Allen, 1963). Wickens asked one group of research participants to memorize six lists of three-digit combinations (632, 785, 877). As can be seen in figure 6.8, these individuals became progressively worse at recall as they memorized more and more lists. The previously memorized lists interfered with the recall of each new list. By the sixth list, their performance was quite poor. A second group of individuals was asked to memorize five lists of combinations of three letters, and then to memorize a list of three-digit combinations like that used in the first group. As can also be seen in figure 6.8, these participants became progressively less successful at recalling the letter combinations due to the buildup of interference. But when they memorized the list of digit combinations instead of a sixth list of letters, their memory performance shot up, showing that the letters were too dissimilar to the digits to interfere with their recall. Interference primarily comes from *similar* memories.

In the experiment by Wickens, the interference came from memories that were formed *before* learning the last list; the prior memorization of similar material caused interference

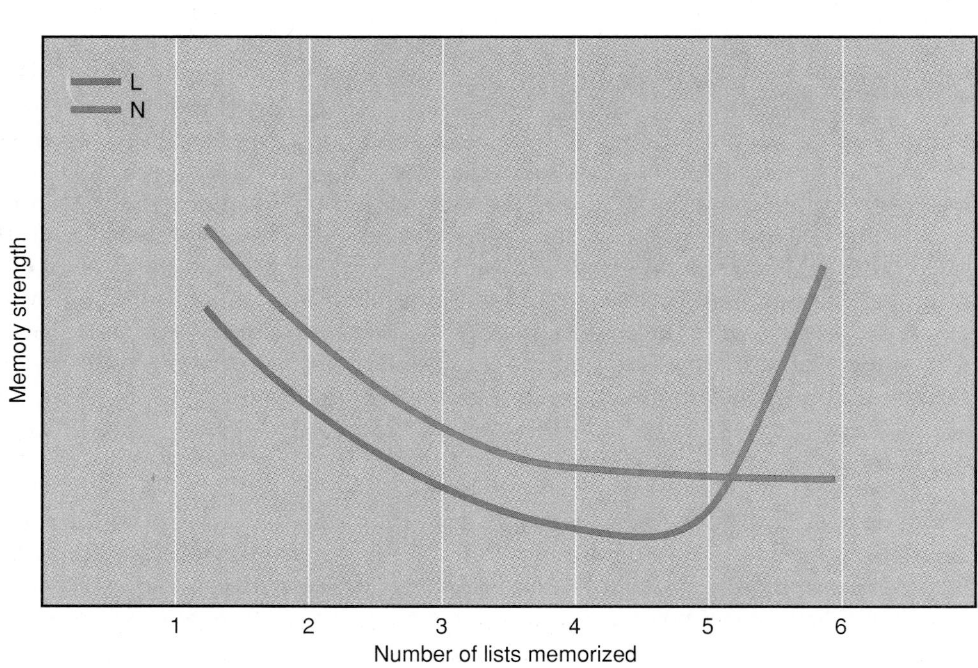

FIGURE 6.8
As two groups of participants memorized additional lists of letter combinations (L) or number combinations (N), proactive inhibition built up from the earlier lists, and memory declined. When one group shifted from memorizing letters to memorizing numbers, their recall improved dramatically. The proactive inhibition affects only memory for very similar material; the previously learned letters do not affect memory for numbers.

Source: Data from D. D. Wickens, D. G. Born, and C. K. Allen, "Proactive Inhibition Item Similarity in Short Term Memory," in *Journal of Verbal Learning and Verbal Behavior,* 2:440–445, 1963. © 1963 Academic Press.

with the recall of newly learned material. Interference can also come from memories that are formed *after* memorizing the material in question. If the individuals in the Wickens study had tried to recall the first digits they had learned after memorizing five additional lists, they would have found that a great deal of interference had been created. Psychologists refer to the interference built up by *prior* learning as **proactive interference** and to interference created by *later* learning as **retroactive interference.**

proactive interference
(prō-ak´ tiv in´´ter-fēr´ ens) Interference created by memories from prior learning.

retroactive interference
(ret´´ rō-ak´ tiv) Interference created by memories from later learning.

Suppose you meet two interesting people, Rolf and Kate, on your first day of vacation at the beach. First, Rolf tells you his room number, as you listen carefully and commit it to memory. Later, Kate tells you her room number and you memorize it. Later, you try to go to Kate's room and, oops, you can't remember the number. You are the victim of *proactive interference*. The recall of Kate's number was blocked by interference from the memorization of the number that *preceded* it.

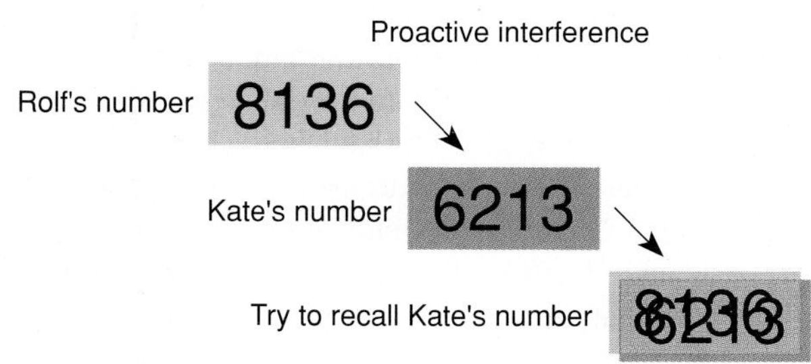

On the other hand, if you had tried to recall Rolf's number rather than Kate's, you might not have been able to remember it due to *retroactive interference*. The prefix *retro* means "going back." Hence, in retroactive interference, the second memorization interferes with recall of what was memorized before it.

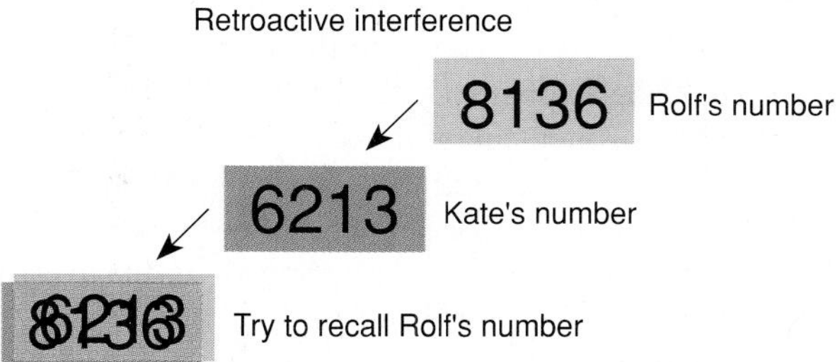

Up to this point, we have talked about interference as a cause of forgetting, or retrieval failure, in LTM. Interference is also a cause of forgetting in STM, but it may operate in a different way to disrupt memory. Whereas interference appears to confuse the process of retrieval in LTM, interfering memories seem to disrupt STM either by overloading its capacity or by weakening or completely knocking an item out of storage (Klatzky, 1980). If you look up the telephone number 689-2354 and someone says "Maybe it's 698-5423" before you can dial, you may experience interference in STM.

Although much evidence supports the interference theory of forgetting in both STM and LTM, we should not be too quick in deciding that it's the only factor involved in forgetting. For one thing, nearly all of the research evidence we have on interference in LTM concerns memory for isolated facts, even though LTM is better suited for storing meaning. Tulving (1972) reminds us that it is a very different matter to forget in a memory experiment that the list we were supposed to memorize included the word *frog* than to forget what a frog is.

Reconstruction Theory

First stated in 1932 by Sir Frederic Bartlett, **reconstruction theory** suggests that some memory traces become so distorted over time that they are unrecognizable. Memories change with time in such a way as to become less complex, more consistent, and more congruent with

reconstruction theory
The theory that forgetting is due to changes in the structure of a memory that make it inaccurate when retrieved.

"Hey, good buddy! how you doin'?"

"Can't kick, big fella. What's shakin'?"

what the individual already knows and believes. For example, if you hear a long story about Max (whom you dislike) that is favorable to him on some points and slightly negative on other points, your recollection of that story might be somewhat different a week later when you retell it to a friend. In general, the story would tend to become shorter and less detailed. But because your preconceived view of Max was negative, the most obvious changes would be a forgetting of positive facts, an exaggeration of negative facts, and maybe even the addition of a few fictional facts more in line with your feelings about him. Am I right? Have you ever passed on a slightly distorted tale? Would you trust someone who does not like you to recall accurately a story about you?

The distortion of memories has been demonstrated in a classic experiment (Carmichael, Hogan, & Walter, 1932). Researchers showed the participants ambiguous line drawings as shown in the middle column of figure 6.9 (labeled "stimulus figures"). The participants were given verbal labels telling them what each figure represented, but two different groups of individuals were given different labels for each figure (shown in the figure as "word list I" and "word list II"). For example, half of the participants were told that the second figure in figure 6.9 was a "bottle" while the other half were told that it was a "stirrup." Later the participants were asked to draw figures that they had seen from memory. As predicted by reconstruction theory, the drawings were distorted to fit the labels that they had been given for the ambiguous figures.

Several experiments make it clear that the distortions of memories hypothesized by Bartlett do not occur gradually over time but occur during the process of retrieval itself (Reynolds & Flagg, 1983). First, when the Carmichael, Hogan, and Walter (1932) study was repeated by Prentice (1954), no differences were found among the three groups when the participants were asked to *recognize* the original visual stimuli (instead of drawing them). The verbal labels apparently did not alter what was stored in memory or how well it was retained. More convincing is the fact that the distorting effect of the visual labels is even more dramatic when the individuals were given the labels (*bottle, stirrup,* etc.) *just before* they were asked to draw the shapes (Hanawalt & Demarest, 1939; Ranken, 1963). It seems likely that reconstructive forgetting mostly is due to errors created during the process of remembering (retrieval).

Reconstruction theory provides an interesting view of forgetting in LTM that is intuitively appealing. But until recent years, this theory has had little impact on the research on memory, perhaps because Bartlett (1932) stated it in rather vague terms in the first place. Recent versions of reconstruction theory use the distinction made by Tulving (1972) between episodic and semantic memory. For example, John Bransford and Jeffrey Franks (1971) have suggested that we tend to distort, or reconstruct, memories because in LTM we store the meaning of events better than the episodic details. If we try to recall an event later, we will be more likely to remember its meaning than the details. Thus, without being aware that we are doing so, we make up details that are consistent with the meaning we have remembered.

Bransford and his associates tested this version of reconstruction theory in the following experiment (Johnson, Bransford, & Solomon, 1973). Research participants listened to passages such as the following.

> It was late at night when the phone rang and a voice gave a frantic cry. The spy threw the secret document into the fireplace just 30 seconds before it would have been too late.

Later, the participants were asked if they had heard the following sentence.

> The spy burned the secret document 30 seconds before it would have been too late.

Notice that this is not a sentence that they had previously heard; the original sentence said nothing about actually burning the document (there might not have been a fire in the

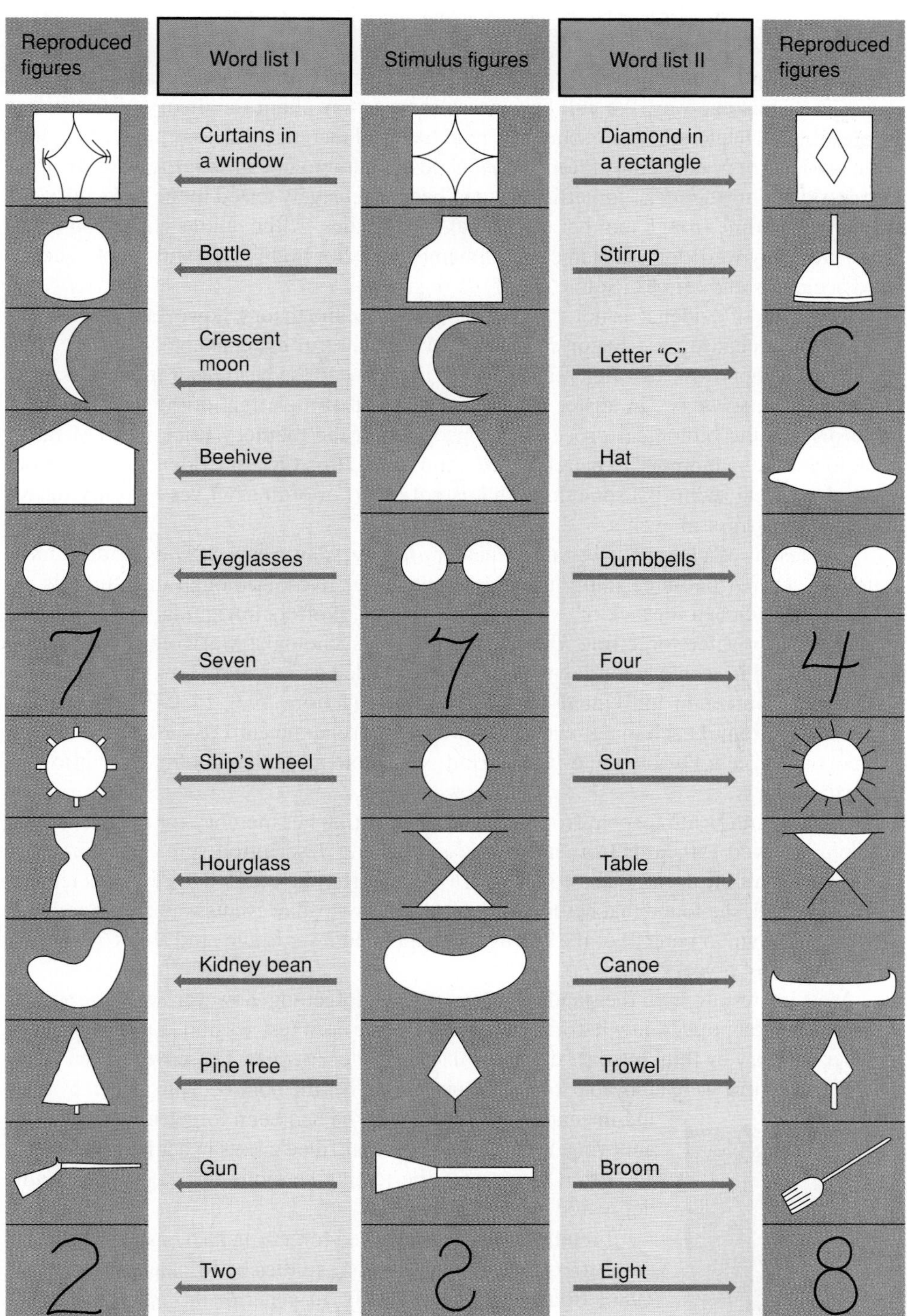

FIGURE 6.9

Individuals were shown the list of stimulus figures presented in the middle column along with one of the two word lists. As can be seen in the left and right columns, the figures they drew later were reconstructed to fit the labels they had learned for them.

Source: Redrawn from L. Carmichael, H. P. Hogan, and A. A. Walter, "An Experimental Study of the Effect of Language on the Reproduction of Visually Perceived Form" in *Journal of Experimental Psychology,* 15:78–86, 1932.

fireplace). Most participants, however, said that they had heard the second sentence. According to Bransford and colleagues, the meaning of the sentence, which strongly implies the document was burned, was retrieved from LTM, but the details were reconstructed to fit this meaning rather than directly remembered. As Bartlett (1932) said, memory is partly an "imaginative reconstruction" of experience.

We saw in chapter 3 that the human brain must construct full perceptions out of the often inadequate sensory information given to it, such as filling in the blind spot in our visual perception. The reconstruction theory and its supporting evidence suggest that at times we also construct our memories from minimal information. Unfortunately, this reconstructed memory is then stored in LTM as a highly believable "fact."

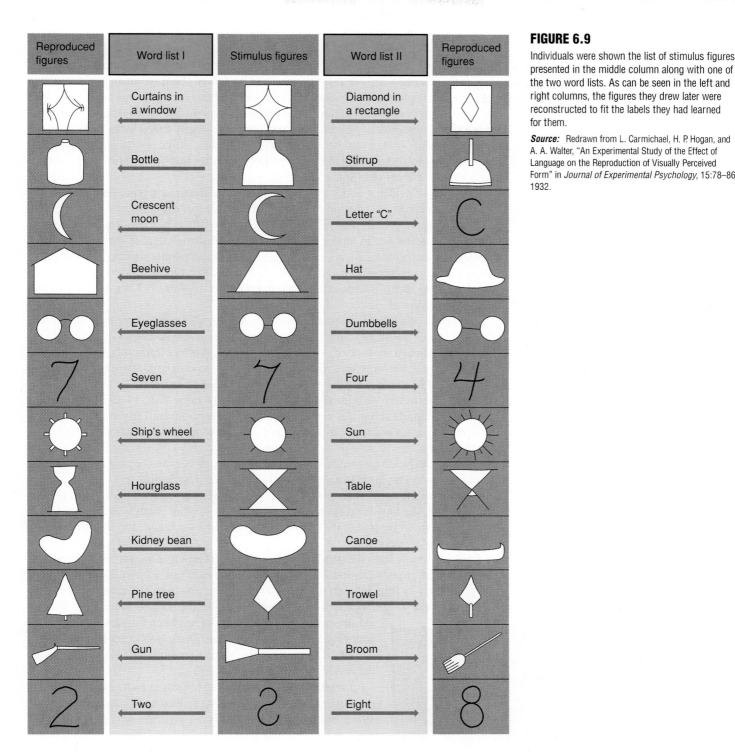

Motivated Forgetting

motivated forgetting
Forgetting that is believed to be based on the upsetting or threatening nature of the information that is forgotten.

repression
Sigmund Freud's theory that forgetting occurs because the conscious mind often deals with unpleasant information by pushing it into unconsciousness.

Many years ago, Sigmund Freud suggested that we forget information because it's threatening to us in some way. We will have much more to say about the theory of **motivated forgetting** in chapter 11 on personality. Freud believed that the conscious mind often deals with unpleasant or dangerous information by pushing it into unconsciousness, by an act of **repression.** This theory of forgetting has not been extensively tested in the laboratory, but support has come from a number of clinical case studies. Although it's a rare condition, there are many well-documented cases of memory loss for highly stressful events, such as auto accidents and crimes (Squire, 1987).

This type of evidence is not strongly supportive of the theory, however, for three reasons. First, because case histories do not involve careful experimental control, other causes of memory loss are often possible, such as a blow to the head in an automobile accident. Second, as we see in a later section, it may be that the effect of the stressful event is to disrupt the biological process of consolidating the memory trace in LTM rather than to cause the memory to be repressed. And, third, this type of evidence makes motivated forgetting seem like something that is not a part of ordinary lives but only related to unusually stressful events.

The results of a fascinating study of memory for everyday events show us a side of motivated forgetting that is certainly more relevant to our lives. Although this study is not immune to criticism for lack of experimental control, it offers intriguing support for the concept of motivated forgetting. University of Utah psychologist Marigold Linton (1979) was interested in memory for day-to-day events and decided to study it extensively using one highly motivated individual—herself. Every day from 1972 to 1977 she wrote a brief description of each major event in her day on a separate card (e.g., "landed at Orly Airport in Paris"). During the 6-year period, she wrote more than 5,000 descriptions of everyday events.

Each month, Linton spent from 8 to 12 hours testing her memory for the events; she randomly pulled 150 cards from her file, read the brief description, and tried to recall a mental image of the event. If she could form a clear image, she counted the event as remembered. Overall, she found that her memory for these day-to-day events was quite good. She could remember 95 percent of the events that happened 2 years ago, and about 70 percent of the events of 5 years ago.

Most interesting from the standpoint of motivated forgetting, however, was a systematic bias that Linton noticed in what was forgotten. Before each test session, Linton "warmed up" her memory by thinking over the major events of the past year. These were often pleasant memories that were enjoyable to think about. But as her memory became jogged by reading the cards, she found that she had been forgetting many of the annoying, upsetting, and tension-filled events in her life. As a result, she often found that the testing sessions left her feeling quite depressed about her life.

According to Freud, motivated forgetting can occur as a result of repressing details of stressful events.

Freud's theory of motivated forgetting also has been tested in two better-controlled laboratory studies by Michael Bock (Bock, 1986; Bock & Klinger, 1986). In general, the results were the same as those of Marigold Linton's study. When individuals were shown a list of words and asked to recall them later, they were better able to recall words with positive emotional impact (such as *kiss* or *prize*) than words with negative emotional impact (such as *disease* or *loss*). However, words with neutral emotional impact were recalled least well of all in Bock's studies. This suggests that although Freud may be right in saying that experiences with positive emotional impact are recalled more easily than negative ones, any kind of emotional impact appears to improve recall.

Do you agree with that statement? Have you had any experiences in your own life that lead you to believe that emotional experiences are easy to recall? Most of us have experienced some kind of event that can be recalled in vivid detail—so-called *flashbulb memories* (Brown & Kulik, 1977). I can recall with disturbing clarity the first television reports of the assassination of President John Kennedy, and one particularly disturbing newscast describing atrocities committed during the Vietnam War still sticks with me. Both still seem like flash photos printed on my brain.

Michael McCloskey and colleagues (McCloskey, Wible, & Cohen, 1988) of Johns Hopkins University studied flashbulb memories of the tragic explosion of the space shuttle *Challenger* that occurred in late January of 1986. Do you remember first hearing about the explosion? Students, faculty, and staff of McCloskey's psychology department wrote down what they remembered of the explosion three days later, and then again 90 days later. Although their memories of first hearing about the disaster remained vivid after 90 days, many details were forgotten or distorted through reconstruction. Thus, although intense emotional experience may enhance the amount and vividness of recall, even so-called flashbulb memories are subject to the normal processes of forgetting.

Review

There are four major causes of forgetting, each with different relevance to the three stages of memory. Forgetting in the sensory register seems to occur primarily because of simple decay of the memory over time. Forgetting in short-term memory can be attributed to decay over time but also to interference from other similar information stored in memory. Interference from other memories explains some forgetting in long-term memory, but much forgetting also seems to be caused by the reconstruction of memories to the point that they are inaccurate or irretrievable. Memories may also be lost from LTM because they are unpleasant or threatening to us in some way (motivated forgetting), but both positive and negative emotions appear to facilitate memory.

Thinking Critically About Psychology

1. Suppose you have started a company that manufactures cameras. Design an experiment to see if teaching the same employees to do two different assembly tasks produces proactive interference.

2. Based on your understanding of the four major causes of forgetting, what improvements could you make in your general study habits to improve your test performance?

Check Your Learning

To be sure that you have learned the key points from the preceding section, cover the answers below and try to answer each question. If you give an incorrect answer to any question, return to the page given next to the correct answer to see why your answer was not correct.

1. According to ________________ theory, forgetting occurs simply because the memory trace fades as time passes.

- **a.** decay
- **b.** disintegration
- **c.** diminishing
- **d.** decline

2. ________________ theory states that forgetting occurs because similar memories block the storage or retrieval of information.

- **a.** Disruption
- **b.** Interference
- **c.** Disturbance
- **d.** Freudian

3. ________________ theory suggests that some memories become so distorted over time that they are unrecognizable.

- **a.** Reconstruction
- **b.** Destruction
- **c.** Retrieval
- **d.** Distortion

4. Forgetting that occurs because the memory is upsetting or threatening is termed ________________.

Correct Answers

1. a (p. 225), **2.** b (p. 226), **3.** a (p. 227), **4.** motivated forgetting (p. 230).

BIOLOGICAL BASIS OF MEMORY: THE SEARCH FOR THE ENGRAM

engram
(en´ gram) The as yet unidentified memory trace in the brain that is the biological basis of memory.

It's obvious that some physical change must take place in the nervous system when we learn something new (McGaugh, 1983; Rosenzweig, 1984). If some physical change did not occur, how would we be able to recall the new learning at a later time? The "something" that remains after learning—the "memory trace," or **engram** as early memory researcher Karl Lashley called it—is the biological basis of memory. Although neuroscientists have searched for the engram for a long time, there is not yet a full consensus as to what or where it is. However, this is one of the most active areas in psychological research, and much is already known.

Synaptic Theories of Memory

synaptic facilitation
Process by which neural activity causes structural changes in the synapses that facilitate more efficient learning and memory.

A theory stated many years ago by the late Canadian researcher Donald Hebb (1949) may turn out to be an accurate model of the physiological processes responsible for learning and memory. According to Hebb, **synaptic facilitation** is the biological basis of learning and memory. Individual experiences result in unique patterns of neural activity, which "reverberate" through neural loops. This causes structural changes in the synapses to occur. These changes make firing in the loop more likely in the future. In other words, synapses become more efficient, or facilitated. Thus, for Hebb, changes in the synapses are the biological basis of memory.

In a series of clever experiments conducted on sea snails (*Aplysia*), Eric Kandel and his associates (Dale & Kandel, 1990; Dash, Hochner, & Kandel, 1990; Kandel & Schwartz, 1982) have provided evidence that strongly supports Hebb's synaptic theory. Sea snails were chosen for study because they have very simple nervous systems in which it is easy to study individual neurons.

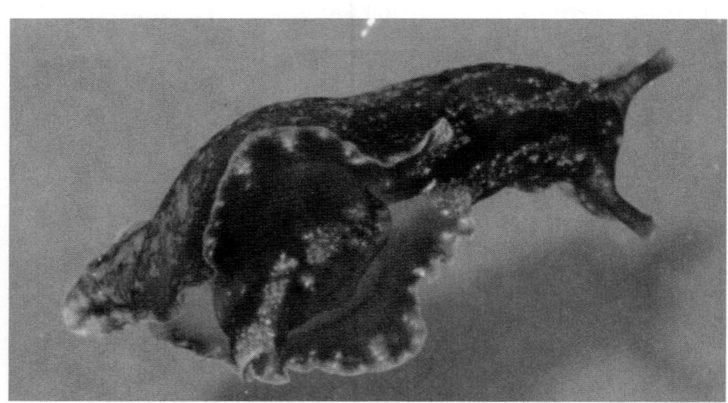

Aplysia, the sea slug that opened new vistas to understanding the cellular basis of learning and memory.

In one key study (Castelluci & Kandel, 1976), the snails were classically conditioned to withdraw their gill and water siphon. First, the snails were prepared for the study by gently touching the siphon many times. Ordinarily, sea snails retract their gill and siphon at the slightest stimulation, but they soon habituate to being touched and stop withdrawing their gill and siphon. Then, the classical conditioning began: The snail's siphon was touched (CS); then the snail was given a mild electric shock (UCS), which caused the withdrawal of the gill and siphon (UCR). Later, when the snail was touched (CS), the gill and siphon were withdrawn (CR). (See p. 177 if you don't remember what the terms CS, UCS, UCR, and CR mean.)

The change in the synapses was studied by measuring the amount of neurotransmitter in the neuronal connections involved in the withdrawal of the gill and siphon. In the first part of the study, as the sea snail stopped withdrawing its gill and siphon when touched, the amount of neurotransmitter present at the synapse *declined;* but after classical conditioning, the amount of neurotransmitter *increased.* Thus, Hebb appears to be correct—at least for some forms of simple learning, the learning is "remembered" at the synapse. Recently, several groups of scientists have published evidence that suggests that the changes in the synapses are based on changes in their proteins for LTM, but not for STM (Ezzell, 1994). This finding is important not only for understanding the biological basis of memory but also for indicating that STM and LTM are based on different processes in the brain.

Amnesia: Disorders of Memory

Major disorders of memory deserve our attention, both because they are important conditions in their own right and because of what they tell us about the biological basis of memory. We begin with a clinical case history describing an individual who suffers from severe memory loss, known as *anterograde amnesia,* as a result of brain surgery. His tragic case tells us much about memory disorders and vividly shows us how important an intact memory is for the normal experience of life.

Anterograde Amnesia

Anterograde amnesia, a disorder of memory characterized by an inability to consciously retrieve new information in LTM, is well exemplified in the case history of H. M. (Milner, Corkin, & Teuber, 1968). H. M. began suffering major epileptic seizures at the age of 10. The *seizures* increased in frequency to about once a week by age 27 despite the use of antiseizure medications, leading his neurosurgeon to conclude that surgery must be performed to stop them. The surgery destroyed several brain structures important in memory. The procedure dramatically reduced the incidence of the seizures but left H. M. with severe anterograde amnesia. He retained his above-average intelligence and had nearly normal memory for anything that had been stored in LTM *prior* to the surgery, but he had severe memory deficits for events that occurred *after* the surgery.

anterograde amnesia
(an´ ter-o-grād) Disorder of memory characterized by an inability to store and/or retrieve new information in long-term memory.

H. M.'s short-term memory was generally normal after the surgery. Like most people, he could retain verbal information in STM for about 15 seconds without rehearsal and could retain it for longer intervals if he was allowed to rehearse it. However, H. M. had serious problems in *storing new information in LTM* and then retrieving it. He had almost no knowledge of current events because he forgot the news as soon as it slipped out of STM; he could read the same magazine over and over because they were "new" to him each time; he had no idea what time of day it was unless he had just looked at a clock; and generally he could not remember that his father had died since H. M.'s operation.

The most dramatic disruption caused by his memory problems, however, was to his social life. Although he could recognize friends, tell you their names, and relate stories about them, he could only do so if he had met them before the surgery. People that H. M. met after the surgery remained, in effect, permanent strangers to him. Each time a person came to his house, he had to learn the person's name again, but he could remember it for no more than 15 seconds or so unless he continued to rehearse it. This effectively meant that H. M. was incapable of forming new social relationships—a poignant but dramatic lesson in how important a basic cognitive function like memory is to our lives.

H. M.'s inability to make new use of LTM was not total, however. His ability to learn and retain perceptual and motor skills in LTM (procedural memory) remained good, allowing him to learn to perform employable skills under supervision. However, he had to be reminded each day what skill it was that he knew how to perform; if he left his job for a short while, he could not remember what kind of work it was that he did. Similarly, when other individuals with anterograde amnesia have been taught to play a simple tune on the piano, they have been able to play it the next day but are surprised by their ability to do so because they have no recollection of being taught to play the tune on the day before (Hirst, 1982). These cases illustrate again the differences between *procedural memory,* on the one hand, and the two kinds of *declarative memory* (episodic and semantic), on the other hand. Anterograde amnesia usually does not affect the ability to acquire procedural memories but seems to destroy some declarative memories. Thus, the difficulties experienced by the anterograde amnesia patient in using LTM are highly selective; some kinds of long-term memories are affected while others are not.

What caused H. M. to have this peculiar and sadly debilitating form of memory disorder? What happened to him during the surgery that damaged his ability to make new use of LTM? The key biological structure that was damaged in H. M.'s surgery, and is often damaged in anterograde amnesia, is the **hippocampus** (Kandel & Hawkins, 1992; Scoville & Milner, 1957). As noted earlier in the chapter, this brain structure is believed to govern the transfer of memories from STM to LTM. The case of H. M. also suggests that the hippocampus plays an important role in declarative memory, but not procedural memory (Squire, 1987; Squire, Knowlton, & Musen, 1993). Persons with anterograde amnesia like H. M. perform very badly on long-term declarative memory tasks but perform as well as normal individuals on procedural memory tasks (Graf, Squire, & Mandler, 1984; Squire et al., 1993). Damage to the hippocampus spares both new and old procedural memories but prevents the formation of new long-term declarative memories.

hippocampus
(hip´ po-kampus) Forebrain structure believed to play a key role in long-term memory.

Sadly, anterograde amnesia also can be caused by brain tumors, lack of oxygen to the brain, damage to blood vessels in the brain, senility, and severe nutritional deficiencies. In addition, hard blows to the head can cause anterograde amnesia, although it's quite often only a temporary condition (Hirst, 1982).

Retrograde Amnesia

retrograde amnesia
(ret´ ro-grād) Disorder of memory characterized by an inability to retrieve old long-term memories, generally for a specific period of time extending back from the beginning of the disorder.

Some individuals are unable to recall old information from the past; that is, they cannot retrieve old long-term memories. **Retrograde amnesia** is just the opposite of anterograde amnesia, then, in that old rather than new long-term memories cannot be recalled. As in anterograde amnesia, however, there is typically little or no disruption of STM. Generally, the period of memory loss is not for the individual's entire lifetime. Rather, it extends back in time from the beginning of the disorder. Memory might be lost for a period of minutes, days, or even years.

Retrograde amnesia can be caused by seizures, brain damage of various sorts, a blow to the head, or by highly stressful events. When retrograde amnesia has been caused by seizures or by stress, it generally occurs alone. When it has been caused by brain damage or a blow to the head, however, it generally occurs along with anterograde amnesia. Indeed, most brain-damaged individuals with anterograde amnesia also experience retrograde amnesia for the period of a few days or weeks prior to the onset of their amnesia (Hirst, 1982).

Korsakoff's syndrome
(Kor-sak´ ofs) A disorder involving both anterograde and retrograde amnesia caused by excessive use of alcohol.

Both anterograde and retrograde amnesia are experienced by individuals with **Korsakoff's syndrome,** a disorder caused by prolonged loss of the vitamin thiamine from the diet of chronic alcoholics. Because of their extreme degree of memory loss, individuals with Korsakoff's syndrome often engage in *confabulation*—when they cannot remember something that is needed to complete a statement, they make it up. Generally, they are not being knowingly dishonest but are engaging in an exaggerated version of normal reconstructive distortion.

Retrograde amnesia has also been cited as further evidence for the stage theory of memory. Electroconvulsive shock (ECS) reliably produces retrograde amnesia. If rats are given ECS following a learning experience, their retention of the learning will be greater as the interval between the learning and the shock increases. The ECS appears to interfere with the transfer or consolidation of learning from short-term to long-term memory.

Enhancing Memory: Do Smart Drugs Really Work?

Psychologists have searched for a long time for chemicals capable of enhancing memory. Such discoveries could greatly benefit patients who have disorders of memory such as amnesia and Alzheimer's disease. It's also possible that the normal population (students included) might benefit.

Animal research tells us that central nervous system stimulants such as caffeine improve retention of learning if injected shortly after learning (McGaugh & Dawson, 1971). How do stimulant drugs enhance memory? When an animal is excited, either by a stimulant drug or by a stressful event, epinephrine is released into the bloodstream (see chapter 2). The epinephrine itself does not affect memory, but it causes an increase in blood sugar. The sugar nourishes the brain and enhances consolidation of memories (McGaugh, 1990). Human research also shows that the accuracy of college students' memories is better when their level of blood is higher (Benton & Sargent, 1992). So don't starve yourself when you are studying.

Recent research into the causes of Alzheimer's disease has led to the identification of other chemicals that have the potential for enhancing memory. Alzheimer's disease systematically destroys neurons containing the neurotransmitter *acetylcholine.* As a result, neuroscientists have assumed that acetylcholine plays an important role in memory. Studies have shown that drugs that block the action of acetylcholine disrupt the formation of memory. Drugs that facilitate acetylcholine also appear to act as memory enhancers, at least in laboratory animals (Meck, Smith, & Williams, 1989).

Recently it has also been shown that drugs that interfere with protein synthesis block the formation of long-term memories (Kandel et al., 1995). As our understanding of the biochemistry of memory develops, effective medications may be developed to help people with very serious memory disorders. However, until additional research is completed, memory enhancement drugs are still controversial and should be viewed with caution (Thal, 1989). It is even more clear that we should be highly suspicious of so-called smart drugs marketed on the street and in "health food" stores as there is no evidence whatsoever to support their effectiveness. Students wishing to improve their memory performance will get much safer and more reliable results from using the study skills section in chapter 1.

Review

The memory trace, or engram, must be stored in the brain in some form after learning; otherwise, recall at a later time would not be possible. Theories have been proposed about the specific nature of the engram, suggesting that it's most likely a change at the level of the neural synapse. However, conclusive evidence has not been provided yet to support these theories.

A group of disorders involving memory loss, known as amnesia, are instructive to study. Anterograde amnesia is characterized by a normal STM, normal memory for information that was in LTM prior to the onset of the amnesia, but an inability to consciously retrieve new information from LTM. This condition is almost always caused by brain damage, generally involving the hippocampus. The memory disorder known as retrograde amnesia involves a loss of memory for old long-term memories, usually for a specific period of time extending back from the cause of the amnesia, such as a blow to the head, a stressful event, or a seizure. Chronic alcoholics sometimes experience such extensive brain damage due to nutritional deficiencies that they develop Korsakoff's syndrome, which is marked by both anterograde and retrograde amnesia.

Study of the neurochemical basis for Alzheimer's disease, which also involves profound memory loss, suggests that drugs that stimulate production of acetylcholine might serve as memory enhancers, or so-called smart drugs. This possibility will require further research before conclusions can be reached.

Thinking Critically About Psychology

1. What would life be like without your long-term memory? What role do memories play in your life?

2. Could the molecular theory and the synaptic theory of memory both be correct?

Check Your Learning

To be sure that you have learned the key points from the preceding section, cover the answers below and try to answer each question. If you give an incorrect answer to any question, return to the page given next to the correct answer to see why your answer was not correct.

1. Scientists study the brain in hopes of discovering the ________________ , which is the change in the brain that occurs when a "memory trace" is stored.

2. The process of ________________ , which can produce long-lasting changes in synapses, may be the neural basis of memory formation.

a. electroconvulsive shock
b. anterograde amnesia
c. synaptic facilitation
d. operant conditioning

3. ________________ is a disorder of memory characterized by an inability to store and/or retrieve *new* information in LTM.

4. ________________ is a memory disorder characterized by an inability to retrieve *old* long-term memories.

Correct Answers

1. engram (p. 232), **2.** c (p. 232), **3.** Anterograde amnesia (p. 233), **4.** Retrograde amnesia (p. 234).

APPLICATION OF PSYCHOLOGY

EYEWITNESS TESTIMONY AND MEMORY

No evidence is more convincing to a jury than the testimony of an eyewitness to the crime. If you were a juror and you heard an intelligent, credible witness say that she *saw* Professor Plum murder the victim in the conservatory with the candlestick, wouldn't you be convinced? But eyewitness testimony is based on *memories* of the crime, and as we have seen already in this chapter, what "comes out" of memory is not always the same as what "goes in."

Consider the following case: The three men pictured in figure 6.10 were involved in an actual case of double mistaken identity by eyewitnesses to a crime. Lawrence Benson (left) was mistakenly arrested for rape, and George Morales (right) was erroneously arrested for robbery. Both men were arrested because they had been identified in police lineups by eyewitnesses to the crimes. Benson was cleared of the charges, however, when Richard Carbone (center) was arrested and more convincingly implicated in the rapes. After his conviction for rape, he cleared Morales by confessing to the robbery as well (Buckhout, 1974). Although it's easy to see how eyewitnesses could have confused these three similar-looking individuals, it's frightening to think that two such nightmarish instances of mistaken identity could happen in the same case. But our scary story about eyewitness testimony is just beginning. The following discussion will hopefully give you a better understanding of the role of basic psychological processes such as memory in important everyday events such as courtroom testimony.

FIGURE 6.10
Mistakes in eyewitness testimony led to the arrest of the man on the left and the man on the right for separate crimes. Both were cleared following the conviction of the man in the middle for both crimes.

Inaccurate Recall Due to Biased Questioning

Several researchers have looked at factors that lead to inaccurate recall of information by eyewitnesses to crimes (Zaragoza & Mitchell, 1996). A number of studies suggest that information contained in questions asked of the eyewitness can be a potent source of distortion. When a lawyer or a police investigator asks questions about the crime, the questions contain cues that may influence retrieval to a great extent. Elizabeth Loftus has conducted several important studies that look at the effect of the questions asked of eyewitnesses. In one study (Loftus & Palmer, 1974), individuals were shown a film of an automobile accident. Later, half of the research participants were asked the first question and half were asked the second question:

> "About how fast were the cars going when they smashed into each other?"
>
> "About how fast were the cars going when they hit each other?"

The speed was estimated to be considerably faster by individuals who were asked the first version of the question ("smashed") than by those asked the second question ("hit"). One week later, all of the participants were asked the same question,

> "Did you see any broken glass?"

Although the film showed no broken glass, 32 percent of the participants who had been asked how fast the cars were going when they "smashed" into each other "remembered" seeing broken glass, compared with only 14 percent of the participants who were asked the more neutral version of the question. The reconstruction theory of forgetting that we studied in this chapter would suggest that they incorrectly remembered seeing broken glass when it was not there because broken glass would be consistent with two cars "smashing" together. Apparently the memory was reconstructed to include broken glass to make it more consistent.

Vicki Smith and Phoebe Ellsworth (1987) of Stanford University conducted a similar experiment in which college students watched a videotape of a bank robbery in which the robber was not wearing gloves and did not carry a gun. Later, some of the students were asked neutral questions such as:

> "Were they wearing gloves?"
>
> "Did the other guy have a gun?"

The other students were asked misleading questions such as:

> "What kind of gloves were they wearing?"
>
> "What did the other guy's gun look like?"

As in Loftus's original studies, the misleading questions cued inaccurate recall of nonexistent gloves and guns. Interestingly, this happened only when the questioner was thought to be knowledgeable about the crime. Apparently, the memory was reconstructed to include gloves and guns only when the implication that gloves and guns were present was believable. Thus, the way in which an eyewitness is questioned can greatly affect the accuracy of the information recalled. This means that we must be extremely careful to allow only neutral questions in legal proceed-

"What did the other guy's gun look like?"

ings, particularly if the witness believes the questioner has actual knowledge of the crime—as is often the case with attorneys in trials.

Are you losing your confidence in eyewitness testimony? Consider one more experimental finding. A simulated crime was staged in the early 1970s at California State University at Hayward in which a student "attacked" a faculty member (Buckhout, 1974). The staged crime was videotaped to have a record of what happened and then compared with the eyewitness accounts of 141 students who saw the attack. Overall, the witnesses were accurate on an average of only about 25 percent of the facts that they recalled. By now you know that eyewitness testimony is frequently inaccurate. But the more interesting part of this experiment is that the eyewitnesses were later asked to pick out the "attacker" from a set of six photos of similar-looking college men. Half of the eyewitnesses were shown the photos under unbiased conditions: All of the photos were head shots facing front and the witnesses were asked *if* the attacker was pictured. The other half of the eyewitnesses were shown the photos in a biased fashion: The photo of the actual attacker was different in head angle and was tilted slightly in the presentation. In addition, the eyewitnesses were told that one of the photos *was* the attacker and were asked to pick him out. Under these biased conditions, 50 percent more of the eyewitnesses chose the attacker. In this case, the presentation was biased against the actual attacker, but the same kind of subtle bias could be unintentionally introduced when an investigator was questioning a witness about a suspect that the investigator falsely believed was guilty. Unfortunately, a number of subtle factors in the questioning of eyewitnesses have been shown to influence their testimony (Haney, 1980; Kassin, Ellsworth, & Kassin, 1989).

Inaccurate Recall Due to Characteristics of the Eyewitness

The eyewitness may have been tired, upset, or intoxicated at the time that the crime was observed—what effect, if any, would that have on the accuracy of recall? One study showed that intoxication can reduce the accuracy of recall under some circumstances, but not others (Yuille & Tollestrup, 1990). In this study, some research participants were given enough alcohol to bring their blood alcohol level up to .10, the level of legal intoxication for operating an automobile. The other participants were given no alcohol. Both sets of individuals watched a brief videotape of staged theft and were shown photos of possible thieves a week later for identification.

When a photograph of the person who played the role of the thief in the videotape was one of the photographs shown to the participants, there was no difference in the accuracy of the recall of the drunk and sober eyewitnesses. However, when none of the photos were of the actual thief, the intoxicated eyewitnesses falsely identified persons who had not been in the videotape as the thief more often than the sober eyewitnesses.

Gordon Allport of Harvard University conducted a classic experiment some years ago that demonstrated the extent to which our perceptions and memories can be distorted by our beliefs and prejudices (cited in Buckhout, 1974). Allport had individuals look briefly at the picture shown in figure 6.11. Look carefully to see who is holding the straight razor. Now be prepared for a shock when you learn that an amazing 50 percent of Allport's subjects later recalled that the African-American man was holding the razor! Prejudice can obviously play a significant role in determining what eyewitnesses "see." This study also suggests that the recollections of eyewitnesses tend to become distorted and "filled in" with details over time to make the recollection more consistent with their beliefs. If eyewitness testimony is not given immediately—and it rarely is—time will have a chance to work its distortions on the "facts."

Improving the Accuracy of Eyewitness Testimony

A common investigative tactic used by police investigators that increases the risk of inaccurate identifications by eyewitnesses is the "police lineup." The witness is typically asked whether she or he can identify the perpetrator of the crime from among a group of five or six persons. It is well known that a number of factors can influence the accuracy of such identifications (Wells, 1993). If, for example, the eyewitness saw a blond man steal a purse, a lineup that includes only one blond man will be biased toward the identification of that man. In contrast, if all blond men were presented in the lineup, greater confidence could be placed in the identification.

Recent research using simulated crimes indicates that lineup identifications can be made more accurate in a number of ways. For example, if a "blank lineup" is presented first (one that does not contain

FIGURE 6.11

Psychologist Gordon Allport showed individuals this picture for a very brief period of time to test the accuracy of their "eyewitness" testimony in a situation in which racial prejudice might influence their perception.

A common tactic used by police investigators that can increase the risk of inaccurate identifications by eyewitnesses if it is handled improperly is the "police lineup."

the perpetrator), the perpetrator is identified more accurately in a second lineup. Similarly, eyewitness identification is more accurate if the persons in the lineup are presented one at a time rather than in a group (Wells, 1993). Research on a variety of similar strategies is being conducted to improve the accuracy of eyewitness identification (Fisher & Geiselman, 1988).

Recall of "Repressed Memories" of Sexual and Physical Abuse

The most compelling eyewitness testimony is from victims themselves. Court cases often have been in the news lately in which adult women and men recall that they had been abused as children but that they had not been able to remember the abuse for many years. Some psychologists believe that memories of sexual and physical abuse are often suppressed. Other psychologists who specialize in the study of memory believe that it is difficult to know when so-called repressed memories of abuse are accurate. This issue poses a serious dilemma for psychologists (Frankel, 1995). On the one hand, no psychologist wants to discourage anyone from reporting sexual abuse. The sexual abuse of children is a sadly common occurrence and any victim with the courage to report it should be supported in every way. On the other hand, there is reason to believe that not every adult who recalls that sexual abuse occurred in childhood is recalling something that actually occurred (Pope, 1996; Spanos, 1996).

What is the evidence on the repression of upsetting memories like sexual abuse? One study of 590 persons who had been in automobile accidents found that 14 percent of the accident victims did not remember being in the accident one year earlier (Loftus, 1993). Similarly, in a study of adult women who reported that they had been sexually abused as children, 18 percent reported that they had gone through a period in which they had lost their memory of the sexual abuse and then recovered it later (Loftus, Polonsky, & Fullilove, 1993). These data suggest that it is possible that some persons who experienced sexual abuse as a child may not remember it during parts of their adulthood.

On the other hand, it is well known that information that adults recall from childhood can be very inaccurate. The most famous example is that of Jean Piaget's "kidnapping." As you will see in chapter 8, Piaget was a well-known Swiss child psychologist. For a large part of his adult life, he remembered in some detail an incident in which someone attempted to kidnap him when he was a young child. His nanny, however, was able to chase off the would-be kidnapper and save young Jean. Many years later, however, the nanny confessed that she had made up the entire incident to gain attention. She confessed because she felt guilty about the watch she had received as a reward. Piaget concluded that he must have heard a description during early childhood of the kidnapping attempt that never occurred and formed a memory from his visual images of what he imagined had taken place when he heard about it as a child. Later those visual images seemed like a memory of a real event to Piaget.

Similar false memories have been documented in other cases, suggesting that it is possible that some memories that seem to be recovered in childhood may be erroneous (Loftus, 1993; Roediger & McDermott, 1995). For example, Elizabeth Loftus (1993) reported that she successfully implanted a false memory for a childhood event that never happened. A 14-year-old boy volunteered to be the subject in the study, but he was not told until later that it was about false memories. During the course of an interview with the boy, the experimenter said that she had learned that the boy had been lost in a mall at the age of five. Although he initially had no memory of the event—which is not surprising since it never really occurred—

The way questions about a past event are phrased can affect people's memory of the event. For example, after seeing a football player collapse with heart trouble, over a fourth of spectators recalled seeing blood on his jersey when questioned in a way that suggested he had been bloody.

Controversy surrounds the use of hypnosis to aid the recall of eyewitnesses.

the boy gradually "recovered" more details every day about being lost and the way that he felt. After a number of days, he had a very complete, but completely false, "memory" of the entire fictional experience, which he believed completely.

Has anything like this ever happened to you? Has a friend ever said something like, "Remember when we rode that Ferris wheel together in the sixth grade?" You struggle to remember, and begin to have a faint picture of it, but you really aren't sure of the details. Then he says, "Oh, no, that was Maritza that I was with." Many psychologists believe that people who are struggling to understand their emotional problems could be unintentionally influenced to recall ambiguous moments in their childhood (a bath, an accidental encounter with a relative who is bathing, etc.) as sexual abuse after reading about repressed memories of sexual abuse. Or perhaps a well-meaning therapist might say something like: "There is a lot of evidence that people with problems like yours have been sexually abused as children, but have repressed the memory. Do you have any trace of a memory from childhood that might indicate that you were abused?" (Loftus, 1993). Could being asked such a question lead a person to unknowingly construct a memory of an event that never happened?

The discussion of the unintentional but powerful influences that can lead to errors in the recall of eyewitnesses to events that happened recently suggests that this could be the case. Let me provide another relevant example: A psychologist interviewed a large number of persons who had witnessed a real-life drama. A high school football player went into cardiac arrest and apparently died (but, fortunately, was revived after he was taken from the field). Later errors in recalling what had happened were common among the spectators. When some of them were intentionally questioned in a way that suggested that there might have been blood on his jersey, more than 25 percent of the spectators "remembered" seeing it there (Abhold, 1992). In summarizing many similar research studies, memory researcher Elizabeth Loftus put it this way:

> . . . there are hundreds of studies to support a high degree of memory distortion. People have recalled nonexistent broken glass and tape recorders, a cleanshaven man as having a mustache, straight hair as curly, and even something as large and conspicuous as a barn in a bucolic scene that contained no buildings at all. Clearly, then, inaccurate memories of traumatic childhood events are possible as well. Perhaps as psychologists learn more about memory we will be able to play a more effective role in helping others distinguish between real and imagined memories (Loftus, 1992, p. 530).

Hypnosis and Eyewitness Testimony

Some psychologists believe that hypnosis can be used to help individuals recall the past. Witnesses to crimes are sometimes hypnotized to help them remember details, and individuals who cannot recall traumatic events may be hypnotized to improve their recall during psychotherapy. The popular belief that hypnosis improves memory is reinforced frequently by dramatic cases in the news. For instance, in 1976, a school bus driver was able to recall the license plate of the children's kidnappers while under hypnosis (Kroger & Douce, 1979). This type of hypnosis involves what is termed *hypnotic age regression.* In this procedure, hypnotized individuals are told that they are no longer in the present but are in the past—at the scene of a crime that occurred a month ago, or even 20 years ago in their childhood. The purpose of the procedure is to allow individuals to "relive" parts of their earlier life and recall important but forgotten experiences.

Can repressed memories of traumatic childhood experiences such as physical or sexual abuse be recalled in this way? Does hypnotic age regression really work? In some ways it does appear to work. For example, when individuals are regressed to 3 years of age, they clearly act like 3-year-olds (Nash, Drake, Wiley, Khalsa, & Lynn, 1986). But are they actually reliving their third year of life and recalling those forgotten memories? Michael Nash of North Texas State University and his colleagues (1986) conducted a clever experimental test of age regression. Nash hypnotized a group of undergraduate volunteers and told them that they had regressed to 3 years of age. As in previous studies, most of the participants vividly experienced a sense of being a young child. Nash then asked the students to tell him about any objects they clung to for security as a 3-year-old—like blankets and teddy bears. Their reports were later compared with those of their parents. Interestingly, the reports of hypnotically age-regressed research participants were accurate about 20 percent of the time, whereas the recall of participants who were not hypnotized was accurate 70 percent of the time! Nash (1987) and others interpret these findings as meaning that the experience of hypnotic age regression is in the heightened *imagination* of the hypnotized individual and that "memories" dredged up during age regression are more erroneous than factual.

Similar controversy surrounds the use of hypnosis to aid the recall of eyewitnesses to more recent crimes. Some studies suggest that hypnotized individuals may actually recall more accurate information (Dywan & Bowers, 1983; Nogrady, McConkey, & Perry, 1985). But this advantage is greatly outweighed for most legal purposes because hypnotized individuals also recall more erroneous information as well, but they are more confident in their belief in its accuracy. For this and other reasons, a great deal of controversy surrounds testimony obtained under hypnosis, even though it is admissible as evidence in some courts.

Summary

Chapter 6 examines how we process information and how we remember or forget that information.

- **I.** Human memory is composed of three stages of memory.
  - **A.** The sensory register holds an exact image of each sensory experience for a very brief interval until it can be fully processed.
  - **B.** Short-term memory holds information for about half a minute.
    - **1.** Information fades from short-term memory unless it is renewed by rehearsal.
    - **2.** Short-term memory has a limited capacity of 7 ± 2 items.
    - **3.** The capacity of STM can be increased by organizing information into larger chunks.
  - **C.** Long-term memory stores information primarily in terms of its meaning. Information is organized in LTM primarily in categories of related meanings and according to how frequently events have been associated in our experience.
    - **1.** Procedural memory refers to memory for skills and other procedures.
    - **2.** Episodic memory refers to memory for specific experiences that can be defined in terms of time and space.
    - **3.** Semantic memory refers to memory for meaning.
    - **4.** Declarative memory, which includes both episodic and semantic memory, refers to memory that is described easily in words.
  - **D.** The levels of processing model views the distinction between short-term and long-term memory in terms of degree rather than separate stages.
- **II.** There are four major causes of forgetting, each with different relevance to the three stages of memory.
  - **A.** Decay theory states that forgetting occurs simply because time passes. This occurs in the sensory register and STM, but probably does not occur in LTM.
  - **B.** Interference theory states that forgetting occurs when other memories interfere with retrieval. Interference can occur from memories that were formed by prior learning (proactive interference) or from memories that were formed by later learning (retroactive interference).
  - **C.** Reconstruction theory states that memories retrieved from LTM become partially distorted or totally unrecognizable during the process.
  - **D.** Memories may be lost from long-term memory through repression because they are unpleasant or threatening.
- **III.** The biological basis of memory is the memory trace or engram.
  - **A.** Synaptic theories view the engram as a change in the pattern or strength of synaptic linkages between neurons.
  - **B.** Amnesia is a major disorder of memory.
    - **1.** An inability to consciously retrieve new information in LTM is anterograde amnesia. Damage causing anterograde amnesia occurs in the hippocampus and other brain structures.
    - **2.** The inability to retrieve old, rather than new, long-term memories is known as retrograde amnesia.
  - **C.** Research on Alzheimer's disease has led to the identification of chemicals that have been shown to enhance memory in laboratory animals.

Suggested Readings

1. A scholarly yet very readable analysis of cognition and memory: Ellis, H. C., & Hunt, R. R. (1996). *Fundamentals of cognitive psychology* (6th ed.). Madison, WI: Brown & Benchmark.
2. A fascinating discussion of memory that is solidly based on research evidence: Loftus, E. (1980). *Memory: Surprising new insights into how we remember and why we forget.* Reading, MA: Addison-Wesley.
3. For a detailed look at the relationship between mood and memory: Bower, G. H. (1981). Mood and memory. *American Psychologist, 36,* 129–148.
4. For more information on the biological basis of memory: Squire, L. R. (1987). *Memory and the brain.* New York: Oxford University Press.

CHAPTER 7

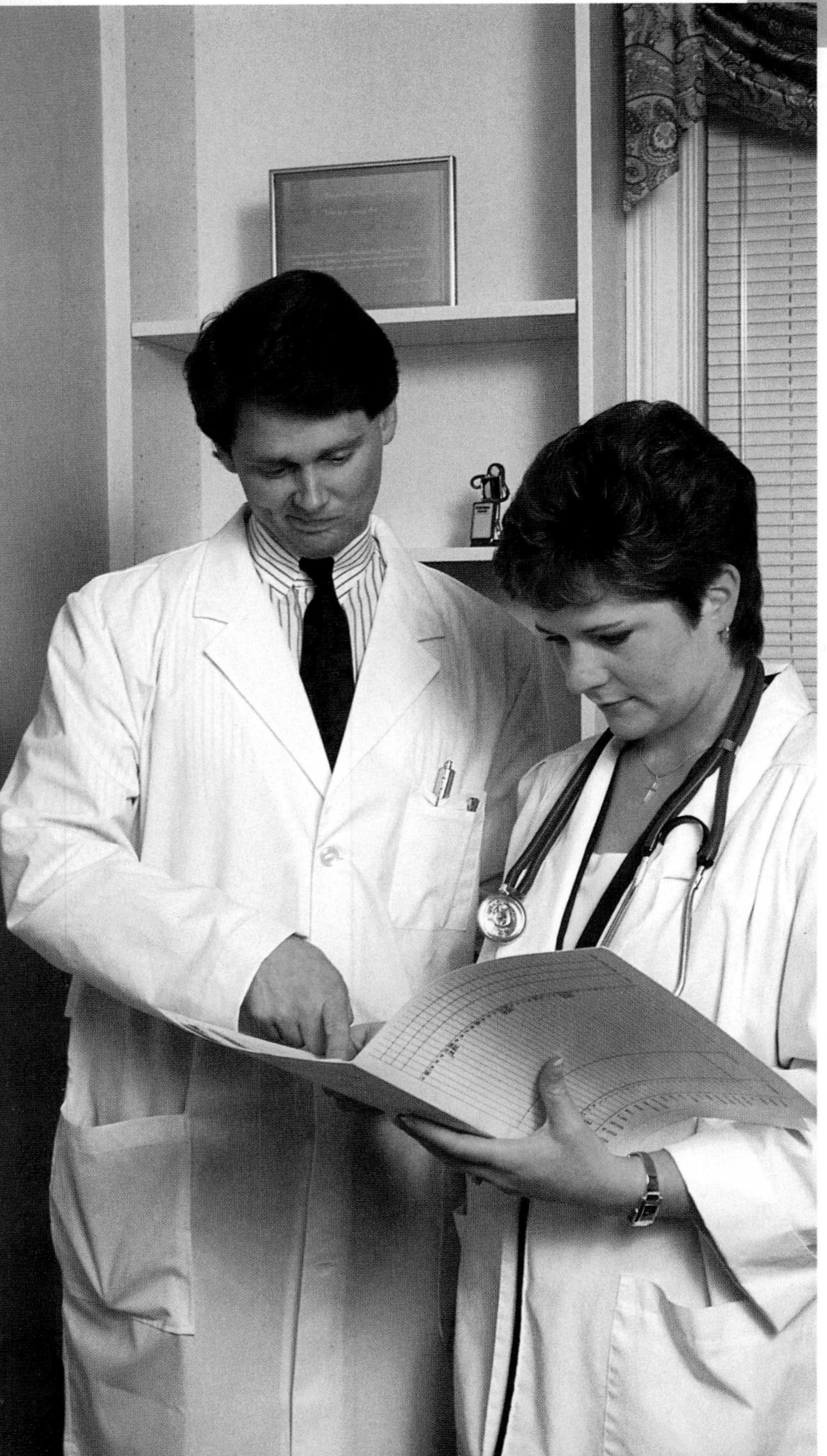

CHAPTER OUTLINE

Cognition, Language, and Intelligence

PROLOGUE

Perhaps the most important reason that the human race has survived for more than 1.5 million years is that we are intelligent. We aren't the strongest, the fastest, or the most ferocious. But compared with other animal species, we are extremely good at solving problems. We survive cold weather by building shelters and making warm clothing; we invent wheels to move heavy objects; and we develop antibiotics when threatened by disease.

But we speak of human intelligence here not to praise it, but to marvel at its quirks, foibles, and flaws! If human intelligence is a miracle of evolution, it's an amazingly flawed miracle. When our intellectual processes are examined carefully, it's sometimes amazing that we soft-skinned and slow-moving humans have been able to survive by our wits.

To help us understand the sometimes peculiar properties of human reasoning, Daniel Kahneman and Amos Tversky conducted a fascinating series of experiments. In one study, a group of physicians were presented with the following problem.

> Imagine that the United States is preparing for the outbreak of a rare Asian disease, which is expected to kill 600 people. Two alternative programs to combat the disease have been proposed. Assume that the exact scientific estimates of the consequences of the programs are as follows: If Program A is adopted, 200 people will be saved. If Program B is adopted, there is a 1/3 probability that 600 people will be saved and a 2/3 probability that no people will be saved. Which of the two programs would you favor? (Kahneman & Tversky, 1982, p. 163)

What decision would you have made? The majority of physicians polled by Kahneman and Tversky chose Program A. The guarantee of saving 200 lives made it a better alternative than a long shot of saving all of the lives. But a fascinating thing happened when the researchers presented exactly the same problem in a different way. A second group of physicians was presented the following version of the same problem.

> If Program A is adopted, 400 people will die. If Program B is adopted, there is a 1/3 probability that nobody will die and a 2/3 probability that 600 people will die. (pp. 163–164)

Would framing the problem in this different manner have influenced your decision? It did influence the physicians. When presented in the latter way, the majority chose B. The sure death of 400 people was too difficult to accept when stated this way. There is actually no logical difference between the two ways of asking the question. Stated either way, 200 people would live and 400 people would die if Program A were adopted. But the physicians' decision making was strongly influenced by the way the question was framed. Cold logic is sometimes less important than the way in which the problem is framed.

Perhaps the best way to view human intelligence is to recognize its amazing capacity and great importance to our survival, yet to use our intelligence to understand its shortcomings and compensate for them. In this chapter we examine both the capacity and the limits of human reasoning.

We will use the term *cognition* in this chapter to refer to all of the intellectual process through which we obtain information from the world, change it to meet our needs, store it for later use, and use it to solve our problems. Clearly it's a very broad concept. Cognition is an important

KEY TERMS

topic in nearly every chapter in this book. We first discussed the term in the first chapter and have discussed important aspects of cognition when we studied perception, learning, and memory. In later chapters we will discuss cognition again in other contexts. But in this chapter we discuss several fundamental aspects of cognition—thinking, language, and intelligence.

We will begin our discussion of thinking by looking at concepts. Concepts are basic units of thinking because they allow us to reason in general ways that make the most of what we know. Perhaps the most important use of concepts is in problem solving. This kind of thinking is successful only when we formulate problems correctly, flexibly evaluate the information and tools available to us, and generate and evaluate alternative solutions effectively. In this chapter we will discuss all the steps in problem solving, and the many ways in which they can be derailed.

Fortunately we humans have developed ways to help each other deal with life's problems. The key to our ability to do so is language. Language is the symbolic code that we use to communicate information from one person to another. Humans are not the only animal species that uses language, but our languages are more flexible than animal languages. We can communicate an unlimited amount of information using a small set of sounds and rules for combining them into communications. In contrast, animal languages are much less flexible.

Intelligence can be thought of as the sum total of all of our useful cognitive abilities. The concept of intelligence is important in psychology today partly because we have tests that can measure intelligence. These are useful in predicting with fair accuracy an individual's performance in many school and job situations. Like most human characteristics, we will find that intelligence seems to be influenced both by heredity and experience.

DEFINITION OF COGNITION

cognition
The intellectual processes through which information is obtained, transformed, stored, retrieved, and otherwise used.

Cognition can be defined as those intellectual processes (such as perception, memory, thinking, and language) through which information is obtained, transformed, stored, retrieved, and used. Let's analyze this complicated definition and its three primary facets:

Cognition involves intellectual processes through which information is obtained, transformed, stored and retrieved, and put to use.

1. *Cognition processes information.* Information is the stuff of cognition: the stuff that is obtained, transformed, kept, and used. Much of this information is dealt with in the form of categories or concepts, the subject of the next section.
2. *Cognition is active.* The information that the world gives us is actively changed, kept, and used in the process of cognition. In cognition, information is:
   - **a.** *Obtained* through the senses.
   - **b.** *Transformed* through the interpretive processes of perception and thinking.
   - **c.** *Stored and retrieved* through the processes of memory.
   - **d.** *Used* in the processes of problem solving and language.
3. *Cognition is useful.* It serves a purpose. We think because there is something we do not understand. We use language when we need to communicate something to others. We create when we need something that does not exist. Humans use cognition to survive physically and to live in a social world.

Much has been learned about cognition in the past 50 years. In this chapter we survey those findings for problem solving, concept formation, language, and general intelligence. Other important aspects of cognition have already been discussed in the chapters on perception, consciousness, learning, and memory. And more aspects of cognition will be mentioned in later chapters on development, emotion, personality, stress, abnormal behavior, and social psychology. Cognition is more than a topic in the science of psychology; it's a theme that cuts across many diverse topics.

CONCEPTS: THE BASIC UNITS OF THINKING

Concepts are the basic units of thinking. Concepts are general categories of things, events, or qualities that are linked by some common feature or features in spite of their differences. About an hour ago, I went for a ride on my new bicycle. My bicycle is a specific object, but *bicycle* in general is a concept. I passed several people on bicycles as I rode—each bicycle was different in some ways from every other one, but I knew that they were all bicycles because they shared a list of characteristics (two wheels, pedals, handlebars, etc.) that all bicycles share. I also passed a lot of things that were not bicycles (cars, trucks, barbecue grills, etc.), but being a clever fellow, I knew in a flash that they were not bicycles because they did not have the features shared by all bicycles. Keep in mind that concepts are categories of more than just concrete things—the terms *vacation, romance,* and *generosity* refer to concepts as well.

concepts
(kon´septs) Categories of things, events, or qualities that are linked together by some common feature or features in spite of their differences.

Adults take for granted that all these objects belong to the concept *bicycle.*

Nearly all productive thinking would be impossible were it not for concepts. Consider the following syllogism.

> All human beings are mortal.
> I am a human being.
> Therefore, I am mortal.

When I reason in that way, I am using the general concepts of *human beings* and *mortality.* Without concepts we would be able to think only in terms of specific things and acts. Concepts allow us to process information in more general, efficient ways. In this way, concepts are the basic units of logical thinking.

Simple and Complex Concepts

Some concepts are based on a single common feature, such as the concept *red.* If a thing is red, it belongs to the concept *red* regardless of its other characteristics. Red apples, red balls, and red T-shirts are all examples of the concept *red,* in spite of the other ways in which these objects differ. Other concepts are more complex. **Conjunctive concepts** are defined by the simultaneous presence of two or more common characteristics. The concept of *aunt* is an example of a conjunctive concept because it has two simultaneous defining characteristics (female and sister of one of your parents). To be considered an aunt, a person must have both characteristics. **Disjunctive concepts** are defined by the presence of one common characteristic or another one, *or both.* For example, a person might be considered to be schizophrenic if he persistently has distorted perceptual experiences (such as hearing strange voices that are not there) *or* persistently holds distorted false beliefs (such as believing he is a king or a CIA agent), *or both.* The concept *schizophrenic person* is a disjunctive concept because it is defined by the presence of either of two characteristics or both of them.

conjunctive concepts
(kon´´junk-tiv´) Concepts defined by the simultaneous presence of two or more common characteristics.

disjunctive concepts
(dis´´-junk-tiv´) Concepts defined by the presence of one of two common characteristics or both.

Concept Formation: Learning New Concepts

As interesting as concepts are, how they are learned is perhaps even more interesting to study. For both the child learning basic concepts (each child must learn from scratch all of the concepts like *bigger, dogs,* and *red* that we adults take for granted) and for adults learning more complex concepts, concept formation is a fascinating process.

Suppose you are a psychiatrist working for the U.S. Army and are trying to determine the best way to treat "combat fatigue," a psychological reaction to the stress of combat that sometimes renders soldiers unfit for further combat. Note that you are trying to learn a new concept. The "best way to treat combat fatigue" is a category of ways of handling soldiers that would differ somewhat from case to case but would have one or more common characteristics.

How would you go about learning this new concept? How would you identify the common feature or features that distinguish effective from ineffective treatment? You might start by looking at the records of 100 cases of combat fatigue victims and dividing them into piles of those who responded well to treatment and those who did not. Then you would look for features that distinguished the two groups. Being a psychiatrist, your first hypothesis might be that those soldiers suffering from combat fatigue who were given medications responded better than those who were not. If you tested this hypothesis by looking to see if most of the soldiers who were given drugs improved, while those who were not given drugs did not improve, however, you would see that this was not the key to effective treatment. Soldiers given medications were not more likely to improve than soldiers who were not given drugs.

You might also test, and then reject, hypotheses about the type of professional giving the treatment (psychiatrist, nurse, or medical assistant) or the diet given the soldier, and so on. Eventually, you would discover, as did Dr. T. W. Salmon who actually went through this exercise, the following conjunctive concept. The effective treatment of combat fatigue: (a) consists of simple rest and talking about combat, (b) is given immediately, and (c) is provided near the front lines. When treatment is handled this way, combat fatigue tends to pass quickly.

Let's not miss the forest for the trees. The purpose of this story was not to teach you about combat fatigue but to give you an example of concept formation in practice. Concept formation is a special kind of thinking in which hypotheses about the defining characteristics of the concept are tested by examining positive and negative instances of the concept. In the example just discussed, those cases that were successfully treated were positive instances and those cases that were unsuccessfully treated were negative instances.

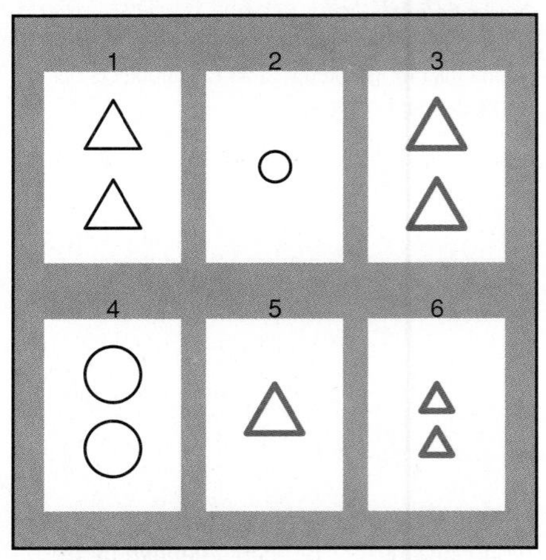

FIGURE 7.1
Cards like those used in laboratory studies of concept formation.

The formation of concepts has been extensively studied in the psychology laboratory using arbitrary concepts. For example, a person was shown cards that each contained a geometric figure. As shown in figure 7.1, the figures can be either a circle or a triangle, can be colored either black or red, can be presented singly or in pairs, and can be either large or small. The cards were shown to the research participant with the information that some of the cards belonged to the concept and the others did not. The individual then had to learn what the concept was. Each time the person saw a card, she guessed whether it was a member or nonmember of the concept, and the experimenter told her whether she was right or wrong. Suppose the six cards in figure 7.1 were presented to you in the order shown (left to right). The odd-numbered cards are members of the concept and the even-numbered cards are not. What is the concept?[1] Research on concept formation using such a procedure has revealed much about this aspect of cognition. For example, concepts with more irrelevant dimensions (number and color are irrelevant in the example in figure 7.1) are more difficult to learn (Bourne, 1966).

Natural Concepts

Eleanor Rosch (1973) has suggested that some concepts are easier for humans to learn than others; some are more *natural* than others. This idea is an important extension of the notion discussed in chapter 5 that we are biologically prepared to learn some things more readily than others. Rosch suggests that, by virtue of being born human beings, we are prepared to learn some concepts more easily than others. According to Rosch, natural concepts have two primary characteristics; they are *basic* and *prototypical*. Let's define these terms.

Natural Concepts Are Basic

A *basic concept* is one that has a medium degree of *inclusiveness*. Inclusiveness simply refers to the number of members that are included in a concept. Three levels of inclusiveness have been distinguished by Rosch:

1. *Superordinate concepts are very inclusive*. Therefore, they contain a great many members. For example, *vehicles* is a superordinate concept that contains all of the many cars, boats, planes, wagons, and so on that carry loads (see fig. 7.2).
2. *Basic concepts are of a medium degree of inclusiveness*. *Cars* is an example of a basic concept because it is less inclusive than the superordinate concept *vehicles,* yet this category still includes many members.

1. The concept illustrated in this example is large triangles.

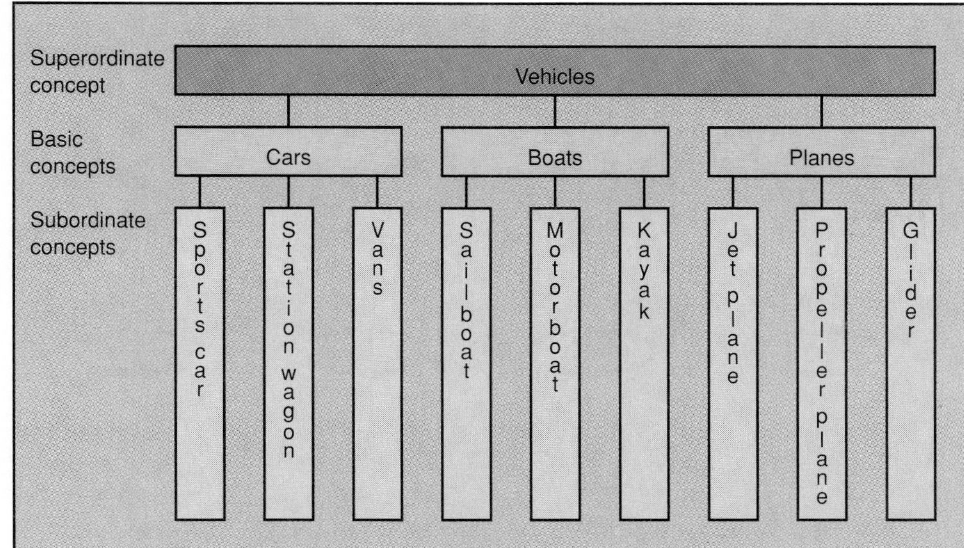

FIGURE 7.2

Basic concepts, which neither include the most nor the least other concepts under them, are easier to learn than superordinate or subordinate concepts.

3. *Subordinate concepts are the least inclusive level of concepts.* For example, the subordinate concept *sports car* includes far fewer members than the basic concept *cars* or the superordinate concept *vehicles.*

Medium-degree inclusive concepts such as *cars* are called basic concepts; the broader concept of *vehicle* is a superordinate concept; and the narrower concept of *luxury sedan* is a subordinate concept.

Rosch suggests that basic concepts are more natural and, hence, easier to learn and use. She offers an observation on the way in which young children learn concepts as evidence. Children generally learn basic concepts, such as *cars,* before they learn superordinate or subordinate concepts, such as *vehicles* or *sports cars.* Why is this so? Why are basic concepts easier to learn than either superordinate or subordinate concepts? Rosch suggests that the explanation lies in several characteristics of basic concepts that "fit" the human intellect very well (Matlin, 1983; Rosch, Mervis, Gray, Johnson, & Boyes-Braem, 1976).

1. *Basic concepts share many common attributes.* For example, the members of the basic concept *screwdriver* are all used to turn screws, have a metal protrusion, have a handle, are usually 4 to 10 inches long, and so on. Members of the superordinate category of *tools* have far fewer characteristics in common. Although the members of the subordinate category of chrome-plated screwdrivers have many common characteristics, only a few of them are not also common to the basic concept of screwdrivers (Jones, 1983).
2. *Members of basic concepts share similar shapes.* All screwdrivers (a basic concept) are shaped about the same, but the same cannot be said about all tools (a superordinate concept). The shapes of all chrome-plated screwdrivers (a subordinate concept) are also similar, but they are distinguishable from other screwdrivers on the basis of only one difference—the chrome plating—that has nothing to do with shape.
3. *Members of basic concepts often share motor movements.* The motor movements associated with members of basic level concepts are similar (turning screwdrivers), but the same cannot be said for superordinate concepts (the motor movements for using different kinds of tools are very different). Members of subordinate concepts like chrome-plated screwdrivers also share motor movements, but they are generally the same or similar to the basic concept to which they belong (see fig. 7.3).

FIGURE 7.3
Members of the basic concepts like *screwdrivers* often share the same motor movements in spite of other differences.

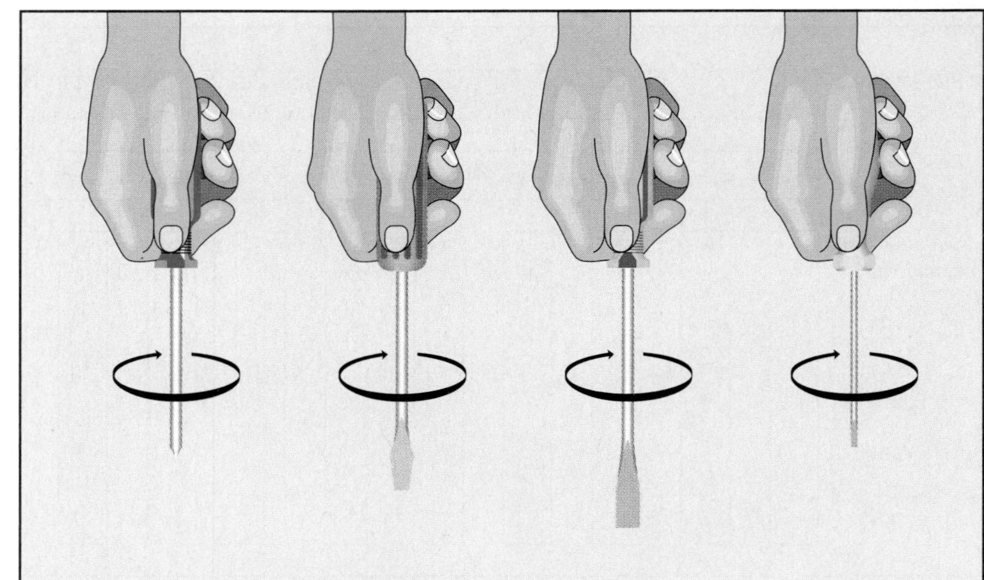

4. *Basic concepts are easily named.* If you were asked to name a half-dozen objects in your classroom, most of the words that you would use would probably refer to the basic concepts to which the objects belong. When referring to a chrome-plated screwdriver, we tend to say *screwdriver* instead of *tool* or *chrome-plated screwdriver.*

Rosch believes that these four characteristics of basic concepts make them more "natural"—easier to learn and use in the human information-processing system.

Natural Concepts Are Good Prototypes

The second defining characteristic of natural concepts is that they are good examples, or *prototypes* (Rosch, 1975). If you were asked to give the best example, or the prototype, of the superordinate concept *toy,* you might say *doll* or *toy fire truck,* but you would be unlikely to say *sandbox.* Similarly, you might think of *chair* or *sofa* as prototypes of the superordinate concept of *furniture,* but not *carpet.* Rosch suggests that natural concepts tend to be both basic and good prototypes.

Rosch (1973) has provided intriguing evidence to support her notion that natural concepts are good prototypes in her research with the Dani tribe of New Guinea. This tribe, which possesses a very limited technology, has only two color concepts in its vocabulary: *mola* for light colors and *mili* for dark colors. Hence, these people are ideal individuals for research on learning new color concepts.

Rosch's Dani research participants were taught to give a label to members of a color category that corresponded to both "pure" primary colors (wavelengths that are near the middle of the range described as red or blue, for example) and intermediate colors (such as bluish-green). Both kinds of color names are basic concepts (with the superordinate concept being *color*), but the Dani learned the names of the primary colors more easily. Perhaps because of the nature of the color transducers in the eye (the cones), some color concepts are more prototypical—and hence more natural—than others. This conclusion is supported by the fact that the relatively pure hues of red, blue, green, and yellow are the most universally named in the world's languages (Berlin & Kay, 1969).

Review

Concepts are the basic units of thinking. They allow us to reason because they permit us to think in general categories. Concepts are categories that have one or more features in common in spite of differences among members of that concept. All red things belong to the concept of *red* even though apples, fire trucks, and red balls differ from one another in many ways. Some concepts are defined by a single characteristic whereas others are defined by multiple characteristics in complex ways. The learning of new concepts has been compared to the testing of hypotheses: The individual examines members and nonmembers of the concept until the common feature or features have been identified. However, all concepts are not equally easy to learn; apparently some concepts are more "natural" than others. These natural concepts are easy to learn because they are of a medium degree of inclusiveness and are good prototypes.

Thinking Critically About Psychology

1. What are the limitations of studying concept formation in a laboratory setting? How might your findings not apply to concept formation in the "real world"?

2. What is your favorite kind of thing (think of a concept, not a specific thing)? Try to describe in words the prototype of that thing.

Check Your Learning

To be sure that you have learned the key points from the preceding section, cover the answers below and try to answer each question. If you give an incorrect answer to any question, return to the page given next to the correct answer to see why your answer was not correct. Remember that these questions cover only some of the important information in this section; it is important that you make up your own questions to check your learning of other facts and concepts.

1. ____________________ are categories of things, events, or qualities that are linked by some common feature or features in spite of their differences.

2. The concept of *aunt* is an example of a ____________________ because it has two simultaneous defining characteristics (female and sister of one of your parents).

- **a.** disjunctive concept
- **b.** conjunctive concept
- **c.** simple concept
- **d.** natural concept

3. By virtue of being born human beings, we are prepared to learn some concepts more easily than others. These concepts are termed ________________.

- **a.** simple concepts
- **b.** disjunctive concepts
- **c.** natural concepts
- **d.** conjunctive concepts

4. Which of the following statements is *not* true?

- **a.** Basic concepts share many common attributes.
- **b.** Basic concepts share similar shapes.
- **c.** Basic concepts often share motor movements.
- **d.** Basic concepts are difficult to describe in words.

Correct Answers

1. Concepts (p. 245), **2.** b (p. 245), **3.** c (p. 246), **4.** d (p. 248).

PROBLEM SOLVING: USING INFORMATION TO REACH GOALS

Without concepts, sophisticated thinking would be impossible. Understanding concepts gives us insight into the *content* of thinking. Let's look now at an important example of the *process* of thinking—the question of how we use concepts to solve specific problems.

What should you do when you think you have upset your boss with the hotly political statement that you made at last night's cocktail party? Do you tell her you were just joking? Do you talk to her again tomorrow in the hope that you can agree to disagree without animosity? Do you forget about it on the assumption that she will not let politics interfere with her evaluation of your job performance? Do you wait and see if she acts as if you really did offend her—remember you only *think* you upset her—before you do anything further? What do you do?

problem solving
The cognitive process through which information is used to reach a goal that is blocked by some obstacle.

Fortunately, no one really expects textbook writers to answer such knotty questions but merely to discuss the general process through which we solve such problems. **Problem solving** can be defined as the cognitive process through which information is used to reach a goal that is blocked by some kind of obstacle. Let's examine that process.

Cognitive Operations in Problem Solving

The focus of much current research is on the cognitive *operations* of problem solving. Operations remove obstacles to goals. What cognitive operations do we follow in trying to solve problems and reach our goals?

There are three major types of cognitive operations involved in problem solving that apparently must be performed in sequence. First, we have to perceive and formulate the problem to decide what kind of problem we face. Second, we need to evaluate the elements of the problem to decide what information and tools we have to work with. Finally, we often need to generate a list of solutions and evaluate them.

Formulating the Problem

Before we begin to solve a problem, we must be able to define it. Sometimes the problem we face is obvious. For example, I want to drive to Key West, but I don't have enough cash to buy gas; what do I do? At other times, the nature of the problem is not at all clear. For example, you may know that the goal of being promoted in your job is not being reached, but you may not know what is preventing you from being promoted. Do I need to perform my job better? Do I need to get along with my superiors better? Do I need to be more assertive in requesting a promotion? To solve a problem, *you have to know what the problem is.*

As Michael Posner (1973) has pointed out, the key to effective problem solving is often our initial formulation of the problem. Take the problem illustrated in figure 7.4, for example. If you know the radius of the circle, what is the length of line *l*? See if you can figure it out.

The trick is in *not* thinking of it as a problem involving the triangle *l, d, x*. Formulating the problem in *that* way blocks our being able to see what solution is called for. As can be seen in figure 7.5, the problem can be easily solved by thinking of *l* as the diagonal of the rectangle with sides *x* and *d*. The radius of the circle, then, is the other diagonal of the rectangle (dashed line in fig. 7.5), and since our geometry teachers taught us that the two diagonals of a rectangle are equal, it's easy to determine that line *l* is the same length as the radius.

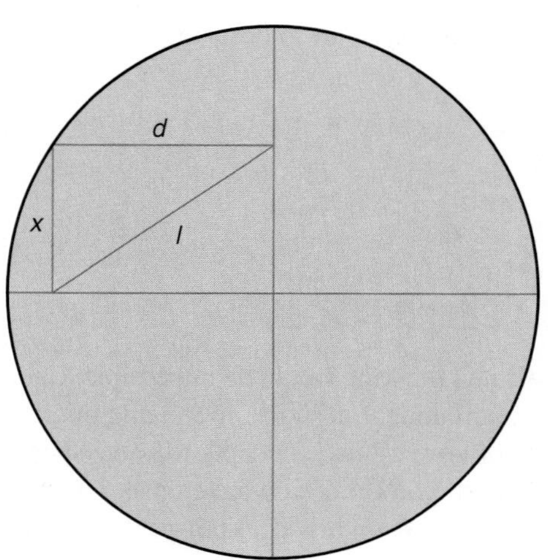

FIGURE 7.4
If you know the length of the radius of the circle, what is the length of line *l*? This problem shows the importance of formulating a problem in the correct way.

Source: After W. Kohler, *The Task of Gestalt Psychology.* Copyright © 1969 by Princeton University Press.

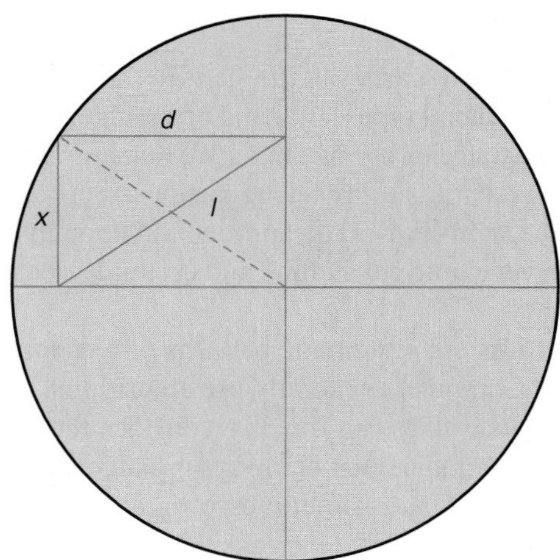

FIGURE 7.5

The problem given in figure 7.4 can be easily solved if it's viewed in the right way. Its solution requires you to think of line *l* as one of two diagonals of a rectangle rather than as part of a triangle. Line *l* is equal to the other diagonal (dotted line), which is the radius of the circle.

Source: After W. Kohler, *The Task of Gestalt Psychology.* Copyright © 1969 by Princeton University Press.

If you take the Quantitative Abilities section of the Scholastic Aptitude Test (SAT) or the Graduate Record Examination (GRE), you'll face a number of problems whose mathematical solutions are probably well known to you, but they are difficult because they require you to formulate the problem in a way that is not immediately obvious. The trick is in being able to shift from one formulation to another until the correct one is found, but your *first* formulation is often difficult to leave behind even when it's incorrect (Posner, 1973).

FIGURE 7.6

A Duncker candle problem. How can you mount the candle on the wall so that it will not drip wax on the table or floor when it's burning? See figure 7.7 for a good solution.

Understanding and Organizing the Elements of the Problem

After formulating the problem, we must make an inventory of the elements of the problem—the information and other resources available to us. Often, effective problem solving requires that we *flexibly* interpret the meaning and utility of these elements. Many of life's problems require an insightful reorganization of the elements of the problem: When you lock your keys in your car, a bent coat hanger becomes a door opener. One of the ways in which human problem solving is rather predictably fallible, however, is that we are often *not* flexible enough in evaluating the elements in problems. Consider the following situation. Karl Duncker (1945) has provided a problem for you to solve. See in figure 7.6 that you are given three candles, some thumbtacks, and a box of matches. Your problem is to find a way to put one of the candles on the wall in such a way that it will not drip wax on the floor or table when burning. Look at figure 7.7 when you have come up with an answer and check it out.

The limitations most of us experience in evaluating the elements of problems is that we get stuck in "mental ruts," or in psychological terms, we get stuck in mental sets. The term **mental set** refers to a habitual way of approaching or perceiving a problem. Because problems often require a novel or flexible use of their elements, a habitual way of looking at the elements of a problem can interfere with finding a solution. If you had trouble with the Duncker candle problem, it was probably because you—like most people—thought of the box in the habitual way; the box is not immediately thought of as part of the solution because it is merely seen as an incidental item that holds the matches. For more on the issue of mental sets in problem solving, see the Application of Psychology section, "Improving Everyday Problem Solving," at the end of this chapter.

mental set
A habitual way of approaching or perceiving a problem.

Generating and Evaluating Alternative Solutions

Very often a problem has more than one solution. Our task then is to generate a list of possible solutions, evaluate each one by attempting to foresee what effects or consequences it would produce, choose the best solution, and then develop an effective way of implementing it.

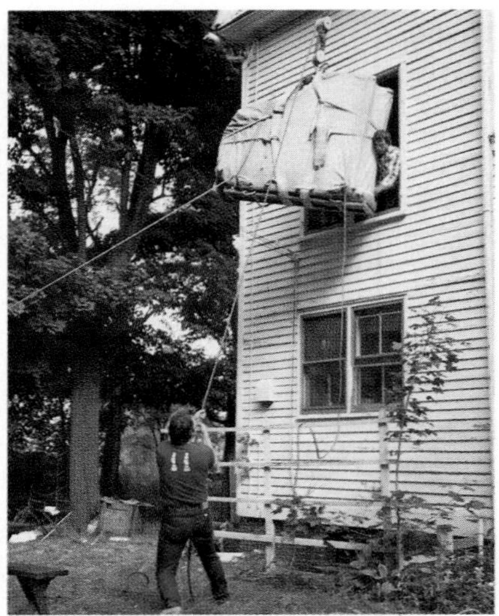

In solving a problem, we perceive and formulate the problem; we evaluate the elements; and we generate a list of possible solutions.

FIGURE 7.7

The solution to the Duncker candle problem. The candle problem requires a new perception of the function of the box in which the matches came. Tacked to the wall, the box becomes a candle holder.

Problem-Solving Strategies

The cognitive strategies used to carry out the steps in the problem-solving operations just described can be of three general types: trial and error, algorithmic, or heuristic. Let's look at each of these cognitive strategies one at a time. We humans often approach problems without any cognitive strategy at all, simply trying one possible solution after another. This is usually referred to as the **trial-and-error** approach. Although common, this approach to problem solving can be very time consuming and certainly does not guarantee that a solution will be discovered.

In contrast, **algorithms** are systematic patterns of reasoning that (if followed) guarantee a correct solution. Computers generally use algorithms. Indeed computers are especially suited for them, since they can quickly consider the many alternatives required by complex algorithms. Computers do not always use algorithms, however. For extremely complex problems, computers are sometimes programmed to use shortcuts known as **heuristics.** Heuristics are strategies that increase the probabilities of finding a correct solution. But since they do not systematically evaluate every possible solution, heuristics do not guarantee finding the correct one. Indeed, they often lead to poor solutions.

The concept of heuristic reasoning is derived partially from research that attempts to simulate human intelligence using computers. Efforts to program computers to play the game of chess, for example, were originally frustrated by the enormous number of possible solutions that would have to be considered before making each move. To avoid such extensive algorithmic programs, heuristic programs were written. For example, the program is written to maximize protection of the queen or to control the center of the board. Moves that meet these goals are executed, but the long-range consequences of each move are not considered by the artificial intelligence program. That is why excellent chess players can generally beat computers at chess.

The concept of heuristic reasoning is an important one because there is reason to believe that humans operate using heuristics more than algorithms. This is so either because algorithms require so much cognitive capacity and effort or because we simply do not possess algorithms for most of the problems we face in life.

Suppose you are presented with the following problem: What occupation should Steve pursue in college? You are told that Steve is shy, helpful, good with figures, and has a passion for detail. You are also told that you can ask and receive additional information to use in solving the problem. How would you solve this problem?

Amos Tversky (Tversky & Kahneman, 1973) has identified two heuristics that are frequently used in human problem solving: representativeness and availability. The *representativeness* heuristic makes predictions based on the similarity between the information you have and the outcome you want to predict. For example, we might use this heuristic to predict Steve's best choice of an occupation on the basis of which occupation we believe his personality is most representative (accountant, pharmacist, etc.). This might be a good strategy, but it leads us not to seek and evaluate other information that might be helpful (such as Steve's preferences, his previous school grades, or the employment opportunities in different occupations).

The *availability* heuristic bases decisions on the availability of relevant information in memory. Rather than seeking additional information, we take another shortcut and use whatever information we can remember. In the case of predicting Steve's best occupation, we might recommend that he become an attorney based on our recollection of an attorney to whom Steve bears a striking resemblance in ability and temperament. These cognitive shortcuts are obviously efficient in terms of effort but certainly do not always lead to effective problem solving. However, humans frequently think heuristically.

trial and error
The random application of one possible solution after another.

algorithms
(al´go-rith´m) Systematic patterns of reasoning that guarantee finding a correct solution to a problem.

heuristics
(hu-ris´tik) Patterns of reasoning that increase the probability of finding a correct solution to a problem.

artificial intelligence
Computers that are programmed to think like human brains.

Artificial Intelligence

In 1956, John McCarthy first used the term **artificial intelligence** to describe computers that were programmed to think like human brains. Computers and human brains share many processes. They encode, store, and retrieve data. They perform logical functions, and they frequently use heuristics. However, there are significant differences. Computers perform some functions, such as rapid computation, much better than human brains but perform others much worse. For example, computers have a hard time reading handwritten messages (such as addresses on letters). Psychologists study artificial intelligence to gain additional insight into human cognition through the use of the computer as a model. Conversely, computer scientists can program their computers to perform more complex functions by using the human brain as a model. This relationship between psychology and computer science has been highly productive for both fields.

A recent interest in the area of artificial intelligence is the design of **expert systems,** or problem-solving computer programs that operate in a very narrow area. MYCIN is an experimental program that helps physicians diagnose and treat blood diseases and meningitis (Shortliffe, Axline, Buchanan, Merigan, & Cohen, 1973). The program not only recommends a medication based on the patient's age and medical history, but it can also provide a statistical probability of success and a rationale for its decision. MYCIN agrees with human medical experts 72 percent of the time but obviously is not a substitute for expert judgment.

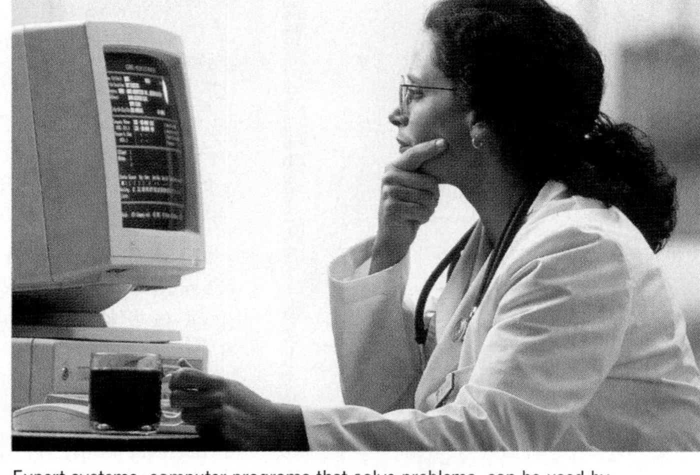

Expert systems, computer programs that solve problems, can be used by physicians to help diagnose and treat illnesses.

expert systems
Problem-solving computer programs that operate in specific areas such as diagnosis and treatment of medical disorders.

In general, the use of computers in problem solving is most effective when the problem area is *well defined.* In other words, computers succeed in situations where there is clearly a correct solution and an agreed-upon means of reaching the solution. Playing chess or developing an algebraic proof fall into this category. Unfortunately, most human problems do not. In the previous example of a student choosing an occupation, the question becomes *ill defined,* and there is no consensus regarding a correct solution. These types of questions do not lend themselves to computer solution. In addition, ill-defined questions require careful definition and formulation. As we discussed earlier, the successful solution often depends on our ability to frame the problem correctly. To date, computers can be used to solve the problems that humans define, but computers do not have the capability to define problems on their own. The science fiction computer that surpasses human intelligence is still a dream, not a reality.

Experts and Expertise

While attempting to program expert computer programs, researchers realized that it would be very helpful to understand how humans who are experts in some area behave. Studying the development of expertise is important for more reasons than learning how to program expert computer systems, however. For instance, if we know how a beginner becomes an expert, we should be able to refine educational techniques and improve our own performances. After reviewing many studies on different types of expertise, Glaser and Chi (1988) summarized the major characteristics of human experts:

1. *Experts excel in a limited number of areas.* Expert chess players, for instance, should not be expected to excel equally at medical diagnosis or music. Expertise is usually limited to a few specific areas.
2. *Experts are fast.* Expert typists, mathematicians, and computer programmers work on their specialty with much greater speed than do beginners.
3. *Experts spend enough time analyzing a problem.* Even though chess masters can play with dazzling speed, they do not make moves until they are ready. A master chess player may take hours before making a critical move in a complicated game. Problems are reviewed from many angles, not just one. Beginners, on the other hand, tend to make impulsive moves.
4. *Experts recognize more "patterns" than novices.* To a beginner in chess, every situation is a new challenge. A master chess player quickly recognizes many common situations and knows how to respond to them.
5. *Experts use their memory more effectively.* Master chess players may not have better memories than beginners, but they store information in memory about the chess board more efficiently. Beginners try to remember their opponents'

Architects need to use divergent thinking when creating the design and convergent thinking to be sure the building is structurally sound.

moves one at a time. Master chess players remember patterns of moves that are more efficiently stored in memory as single "chunks."

6. *Experts use a deeper level of analysis.* A beginning chess player focuses on one move at a time, whereas the master is pursuing a strategy.
7. *Experts use self-monitoring.* Experts have a high level of awareness of their errors and are able to make corrections promptly. Expert typists know when they have hit the wrong key even before they see the results on the screen.

How does a person become an expert—hours and hours and hours of practice (Ericsson, Krampe, & Teschmer, 1993). Any professional athlete or musician can tell you that regardless of natural talent, you can't achieve success without putting in the time.

Creative Problem Solving: Convergent and Divergent Thinking

Creativity is highly valued in our culture but is a difficult concept to define. No specific scientific definition has been widely accepted among researchers, and a wide gulf exists between the ways in which scientists define creativity and the way it's thought of by those in the arts. We can define **creativity** in general terms, however, as the ability to produce "products" (such as plays, solutions to social problems, poems, sources of energy, symphonies) that are both novel and socially valued (useful, aesthetically beautiful, informative, and so on).

creativity
The ability to make human products and ideas (such as symphonies or solutions to social problems) that are both novel and valued by others.

convergent thinking
Thinking that is logical, conventional, and that focuses on a problem.

divergent thinking
Thinking that is loosely organized, only partially directed, and unconventional.

We typically view creativity as an individual ability or attribute, similar to intelligence. What, then, determines whether a particular individual is creative? Guilford (1950, 1967) has used the concepts of convergent and divergent thinking to evaluate creative ability. **Convergent thinking** is logical, factual, conventional, and focused on a problem until a solution is found. When you are asked to solve an algebra problem, you would use your convergent thinking skills to provide the answer. If this type of thinking sounds familiar, it should. Most formal education emphasizes the teaching and assessment of convergent thinking. Students are encouraged to discover the "right" answers. In contrast, **divergent thinking** is loosely organized, only partially directed, and unconventional. Unlike convergent thinking, divergent thinking produces answers that must be evaluated subjectively. If we were asked to list many possible uses for a brick, it is likely that some of our answers would be unique, and the "correctness" of our answers would be less clear. Guilford suggests that individuals who list the most novel uses for common objects, whether they are "sensible" uses or not, are considered to be the most divergent thinkers. Divergent thinkers in other words, more easily break out of mental sets that limit our thinking. In our culture, people who are good divergent thinkers tend to be thought of as creative (Butcher, 1968).

An individual's creativity might also be a result of intelligence. Most of the individuals that we think of as being highly creative are also highly intelligent (Butcher, 1968). However, most researchers in the area of creativity believe that creative thinking is to some extent separate from general intelligence. Raaheim and Kaufmann (1972) provide evidence that people who successfully solve novel problems are different from unsuccessful problem solvers in the amount of effort they make, rather than their basic intelligence. Successful problem solvers attempted more solutions to the problem before giving up. Anne Roe (1946, 1953) found that a group of creative scientists and artists shared only one common characteristic—the willingness to work really hard. It is possible to be highly creative without being highly intelligent, and vice versa.

Regardless of individual ability, how does the creative process occur? Many years ago, Wallas (1926) suggested that creative problem solving typically proceeds in four steps. The first step, *preparation,* includes initial attempts to formulate the problem, recall relevant facts, and think about possible solutions. The second step, *incubation,* is a period of rest. Wallas used the term *incubation* to compare the creative solution to an egg that needed to be incubated for a while before it is "hatched." People trying to solve difficult problems that require creative solutions generally feel the need to set the problem aside for a while after the initial preparation period. Wallas believes that the creative solution needs this time to "incubate." The third step, called *illumination,* refers to a sudden insight pertaining to the solution. The final step, *verification,* involves the necessary but somewhat anticlimactic step of testing the correctness of the solution.

Unfortunately a creative solution to important human problems does not always emerge in this way, but many anecdotes in history show how difficult problems have been creatively solved in a burst of insight following periods of preparation and incubation. For example, the creative problem-solving abilities of the Greek scientist Archimedes were challenged by his king. The king was suspicious that his beautiful new crown was not truly made of solid gold but was actually made of a thin layer of gold plate over wood or some other inexpensive substance. Archimedes was asked by the king to determine if the crown was solid gold. This would not ordinarily be a difficult problem, as Archimedes could easily cut through the crown or melt it and examine its contents, but the king loved the crown and instructed Archimedes not to harm it. After much initial thought (preparation), Archimedes gave up on the problem for a while (incubation) and took a bath. While floating in the bath he achieved illumination. He realized that he could solve his problem by placing the crown in water and measuring the amount of water it displaced (how much water rose in the container). Because he knew how much water was displaced by gold and less dense substances such as wood, he easily could determine the gold content of the crown without scratching it (only giving it a nice bath). Archimedes was so thrilled by the moment of insight that he ran naked through the town shouting "Eureka! I have found it!"

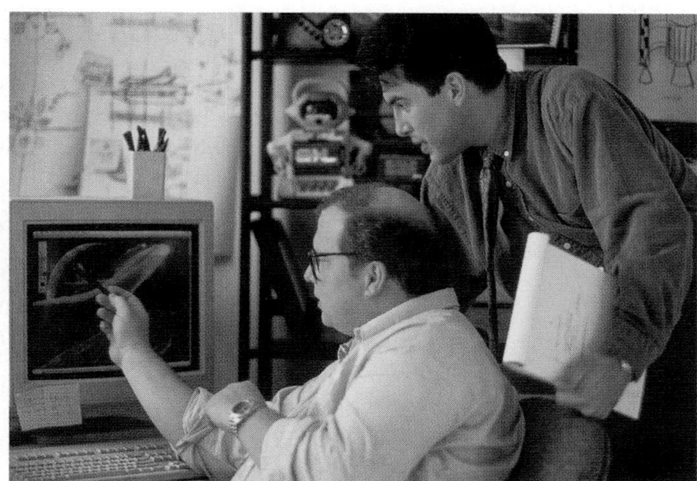

People do their best creative work in an uninhibiting atmosphere.

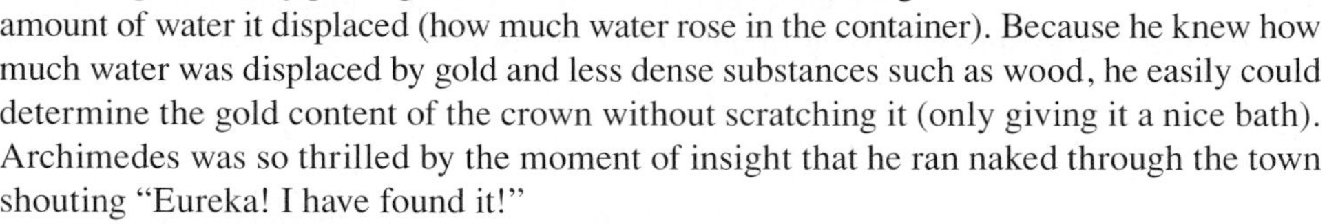

Hayes (1978) proposes three ways of making creative thinking more likely. First, individuals must have a *knowledge base*. Most creative geniuses appear to build their best work on a firm foundation of knowledge of their field. Learning as much as you can about your problem will increase your chances of solving it creatively. Second, we require the right *atmosphere* for creativity. People do their best creative work when they are given time to let their ideas incubate and are not inhibited by criticism for novel ideas. Often, working with a group of people (brainstorming), provides an effective atmosphere for developing creative solutions. Finally, people can develop creative solutions to problems by considering *analogies*, or similarities with other problems that have been solved in the past. A fourth hint, implied by the earlier discussion regarding individual differences in creativity, suggests that you can improve your own creative problem solving by being persistent.

Recently, Robert Sternberg of Yale University has likened creativity to a good investment strategy in the stock market (Sternberg & Lubart, 1992, 1993). Sternberg believes that many creative problem solvers succeed in spite of not being provided with an atmosphere that promotes creativity. He points out that creative people, like successful inventors, "buy low and sell high." In other words, creative solutions are often not valued by others at first—they seem odd and unlikely. The creative thinker frequently has to put up with being ignored, or even scorned, at first. Creative problem solvers must have a high tolerance for this initial skepticism. Indeed, Sternberg suggests that many creative problem solvers enjoy breaking new ground even if their ideas are not valued at first. When a creative new idea does achieve acceptance, creative people often move on to something new.

Review

Problem solving is the process of using information to reach a goal that has been blocked by some obstacle. We use cognitive operations to solve problems. Key steps in this process are the initial formulation of the problem, the understanding of the elements of the problem (the information and resources available for problem solving), and the generation and evaluation of alternative strategies. Problem solving can fail at any of these levels. We can be unsuccessful because we define the problem incorrectly, because we get stuck in mental sets in perceiving the elements of the problem, or because we fail to fully evaluate the consequences of alternative solutions. Creative problem solving requires the ability to think in flexible and unusual ways (divergent thinking), but the most useful creative solutions are ones that have also been thought out logically (convergent thinking). Fortunately, some intelligent people excel in both divergent and convergent thinking.

Thinking Critically About Psychology

1. Could a computer be programmed to conduct psychological research? What kinds of programs would be needed?

2. In solving problems, do you consider yourself to be more a convergent thinker or a divergent thinker? How does this affect the way you formulate and solve problems?

Check Your Learning

To be sure that you have learned the key points from the preceding section, cover the answers below and try to answer each question. If you give an incorrect answer to any question, return to the page given next to the correct answer to see why your answer was not correct.

1. ___________________ can be defined as the cognitive process through which information is used to reach a goal that is blocked by some kind of obstacle.

- **a.** Concept formation
- **b.** Problem solving
- **c.** Inductive reasoning
- **d.** Natural logic

2. The limitation most of us experience in evaluating the elements of problems is that we get stuck in "mental ruts," or ___________________ , which refers to a habitual way of approaching or perceiving a problem.

- **a.** sets
- **b.** gemutlichheits
- **c.** algorithms
- **d.** divergent thinking patterns

3. ___________________ are cognitive strategies that do not guarantee but do increase the probability of finding a correct solution.

- **a.** Algorithms
- **b.** Problem-solving strategies
- **c.** Concepts
- **d.** Heuristics

4. ___________________ thinking is unconventional, loosely organized, and only partially directed.

- **a.** Algorithmic
- **b.** Semantic
- **c.** Divergent
- **d.** Convergent

Correct Answers
1. b (p. 250), **2.** a (p. 251), **3.** d (p. 252), **4.** c (p. 254).

LANGUAGE: SYMBOLIC COMMUNICATION

language
A symbolic code used in communication.

Language is one of the most significant cognitive achievements of the human species. Without language, human beings and human civilization would be a pale shadow of what they are. **Language** is a symbolic code used in communication. Without an efficient means of communication, it would not be possible to coordinate the efforts of many people in a division of labor, to regulate their behavior for the common good through laws, or to amass the wisdom learned through experience by previous generations and pass it on through education. And perhaps the most keenly felt loss of all is that psychology textbooks could neither be written nor read!

"Matthews . . . we're getting another one of those strange 'aw blah es span yol' sounds."
THE FAR SIDE cartoon by Gary Larson is reprinted by permission of Chronicle Features, San Francisco, CA.

Semantics: The Meaning of What Is Said

The function of language is to say something to someone. The "something" is the meaning (the **semantic content**) that is communicated through language. Suppose you want to communicate to your child that *the peanut butter is on the top shelf.* That idea must be translated into the language code and expressed to your child who must receive and comprehend it by translating it back into the same idea. Thus, meaningful ideas are sent from person to person via the system of symbols that we call language.

The fact that *semantic content* and language codes are not the same thing can easily be seen in a number of ways. For example, it is possible to express the same meaning in more than one way. *The peanut butter is on the top shelf* and *it's on the top shelf that the peanut butter is located* are physically very different patterns of sounds, but they express exactly the same meaning. Furthermore, it would be possible to express the same proposition in Chinese, Latin, French, or sign language. This distinction was made by linguist Noam Chomsky (1957), who called the superficial spoken or written structure of a statement its **surface structure** and the underlying structure that holds the statement's meaning its **deep structure.**

semantic content
(se-man´tik) The meaning in symbols, such as language.

surface structure
The superficial spoken or written structure of a statement.

deep structure
The underlying structure of a statement that holds its meaning.

generative property of language
(jen´e-ra´´tiv) The ability to create an infinite set of utterances using a finite set of elements and rules.

Generative Property of Language: Elements and Rules

Human language is a highly *efficient* system. It's particularly efficient in accomplishing so much while putting so little demand on our memories. Stop for a second and think about the sheer magnitude of language. Consider how many different things you have said in your lifetime. If we could accurately estimate the number, it would be staggering. Now let's imagine that human language were not an efficient system. Imagine that we had to learn and remember a different utterance for everything we wanted to say. Although it would be theoretically possible to store that many utterances in long-term memory, we would have to spend every waking hour of our lives doing nothing but memorizing utterances. Obviously we do not spend anywhere near that amount of time learning language. More importantly, humans do not speak using a fixed stock of utterances. We could get by in a crude and uninteresting way if we talked like that, but fortunately we do not. Every day you say utterances that no one has ever said before.

If we do not memorize our utterances, where do they come from? We make them up as we go along. In more precise terms, we "generate" language from a set of elements and a set of rules for combining them into speech. When we say that language is **generative,** we mean that an infinite set of utterances can be made using a finite set of elements and rules (Chomsky, 1957). What are these elements and rules?

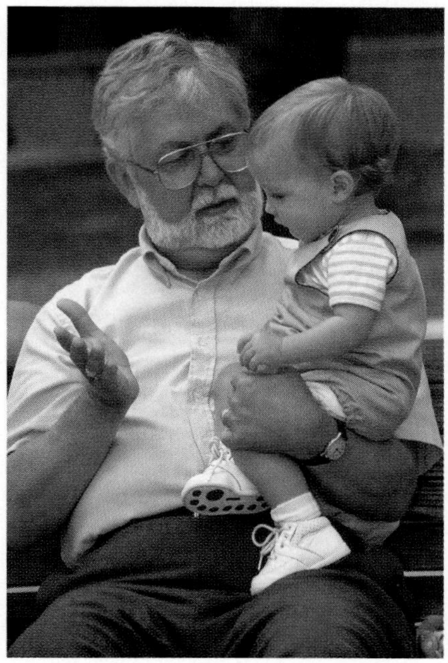

We learn language by first learning phonemes, then morphemes, followed by syntax.

Phonemes

One way of looking at the elements of language is to consider its individual sounds. The **phoneme** is the smallest unit of sound in a language. In English, everything we say, and everything that we will ever say, is made up of only 44 phonemes (there are more phonemes than letters of the alphabet in English, because some letter combinations such as *ch* and *th* stand for separate phonemes). Different languages have different numbers of phonemes, but the principle is the same in every language: Every utterance is generated from a surprisingly small number of sounds.

Morphemes

When most people think about the individual building blocks of language, they have in mind something like morphemes. The **morpheme** is the smallest unit of meaning in a language. Morphemes are closely related to but are not the same as words. Some morphemes stand alone as words. *Word, stand,* and *fast* are each single freestanding morphemes. Other morphemes can exist only if they are bound to other morphemes. Examples are the morpheme for past tense in push*ed,* the plural morpheme in car*s,* and the prefix morpheme *anti* meaning "against" in the word *antibiotic.* The average person knows thousands of morphemes but can speak an infinite number of utterances using a finite set of morphemes and rules for combining them.

phoneme
(fō´nēm) The smallest unit of sound in a language.

morpheme
(mor´fēm) The smallest unit of meaning in a language.

syntax
(sin´-taks) The grammatical rules of a language.

Syntax

The rules of a language that allow an infinite number of understandable utterances to be generated are called **syntax.** There are rules for the ways in which phonemic sounds can be combined in morphemes and rules for how morphemes can be combined in utterances. For instance, in English, we learn that the suffix *-ed* communicates past tense and that the *-s* suffix denotes a plural. We learn the importance of word order. For example, we wouldn't say "this an interesting class is." These rules of syntax are the heart of generative language, for without them, only a finite number of things could be said with the finite set of morphemes. These rules allow us to make new sentences that will immediately and effortlessly be understood by all speakers who speak normally in the same language.

It is interesting to consider, however, the differences between rules of syntax and the *prescriptive rules* of grammar that are usually taught by authorities, such as parents and teachers. Everyone who speaks a language in a way that can be understood by others knows the syntax of that language, but not everyone uses "proper" grammar. Winston Churchill, an undisputed master of the English language, provides a humorous example of the artificiality of prescriptive rules when he wrote the awkward but grammatically correct "this is the kind of language up with which I will not put." It is also interesting to note that few cultures emphasize prescriptive rules of syntax other than cultures that originated in Western Europe. Other cultures feel that speaking in an understandable way is all that matters.

We discuss the way that language develops in the next chapter on child development, but it's interesting to note that children develop language by learning phonemes first, then morphemes, and then syntax. Children first learn to babble in the speech sounds of their language, then they use some freestanding morphemes by themselves (*mamma, milk, bye-bye*), and then they begin to acquire syntactic rules for combining morphemes into longer and more complex utterances.

Language and Thought: The Whorfian Hypothesis

Language and thinking are closely related phenomena. Although we often think in visual images, sounds, and images of movements—and some thought may involve no conscious images at all—much of our thinking takes place in the form of silent conversations with ourselves. If this is true, does language exert any influence on our thinking? If so, it is possible that people who speak different languages might think somewhat differently.

linguistic relativity hypothesis
The idea that the structure of a language may influence the way individuals think.

This hypothesis was stated by Benjamin Whorf (1956) and is known as the *Whorfian* hypothesis, or **linguistic relativity hypothesis.** Although Whorf was most concerned with the impact of different languages on the thinking of people from different cultures, his concrete examples of how this might happen generally concerned the relationship between language and perception. For example, Eskimos have several different words for *snow* and can discriminate among different kinds of snow better than, say, residents of Florida. Does the fact that Eskimos have more words to describe different kinds of snow—and can notice small differences among different kinds of snow—mean that their additional words improve their perception of snow? Whorf proposed that the presence of these words in the Eskimo vocabulary improves visual perception. It seems at least as plausible to assume that the Eskimos first learned to perceive slight differences among different kinds of snow and *then* invented a vocabulary for talking about them to others.

A strong test of the Whorfian, or linguistic relativity hypothesis has been performed by researchers at the University of Alberta (Hoffman, Lau, & Johnson, 1986). Their experiment was based on the fact that each language contains terms referring to "personality types" that are important in each culture. For example, most of us understand that the "artistic type" is a person who is interested in the arts, imaginative, intense, moody, and unconventional. Each language contains such terms, but not every language has terms to describe the same personality types. For example, the Chinese language does not have a term for the artistic type, but it contains labels for other personality types that are not found in the English language. For example, the "shēn cáng bū lòu" type is recognized by speakers of Chinese to be a very knowledgeable person but one so shy that he or she is reluctant to reveal knowledge and skills unless it is absolutely necessary.

The Whorfian hypothesis suggests that these labels for personality types influence how we think about people. Do they? Fluent speakers of English were compared in their memory for, and reasoning about, hypothetical persons whose personality types were described by the experimenters. Individuals whose language contained a label for the particular personality type described by the experimenter were able to recall the hypothetical person more easily and thought about them in ways that were more consistent with the personality type. For example, English-speaking research participants recalled the characteristics of the hypothetical person described as artistic more often and reasoned about the artistic type in ways that reflected the description of his or her personality more accurately than Chinese-speaking participants. The opposite was true of the shēn cáng bū lòu type. In this sense, the words in our language do seem to influence our cognition.

However, another test of the Whorfian hypothesis that reached a different conclusion was conducted by Eleanor Rosch with the same Dani tribe from New Guinea used in her research on learning natural color concepts (Heider & Oliver, 1972). She compared the mem-

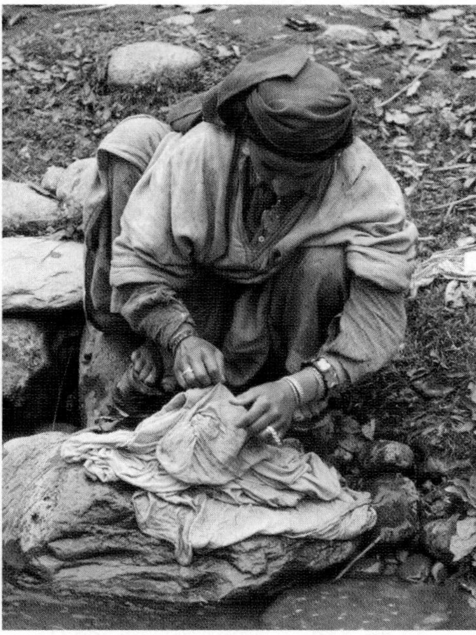

These people from different cultures have different words to describe water. According to Benjamin Whorf, the vocabulary of a language can influence the way speakers of that language think.

ory of the Dani for colors, whose language uses only two color names, with that of American college students whose language contains many color names. The participants were briefly shown single color chips and asked to find the same color 30 seconds later among 40 color chips. According to the Whorfian hypothesis, a person's language should influence memory for colors. Specifically, colors with the same name should be confused in memory more easily than colors with different names; so the Dani were expected to remember less than the English speakers. The results did not support Whorf's theory. Neither Dani nor American individuals confused colors equally different in wavelength any more often when they had the same color names than different color names, in spite of the large differences in the number of color names in the two languages. Perhaps the Whorfian hypothesis is correct only for some aspects of cognition.

Linguistic relativity has led us to reexamine some of our common language usage. Persons concerned about gender equity have lobbied for the substitution of gender-neutral terms for unnecessarily masculine terms, as in the case of changing *chairman* to *chairperson.* If Whorf is correct, using *chairman* might subtly affect the way we think about the capabilities of females to serve in leadership roles. Although some of the changes seem initially odd to some people (*server* instead of *waiter* or *waitress*), they seem to be rapidly taking over common usage. Producers of "Star Trek, the Next Generation" took this trend one step further when the original "where no *man* has gone before" changed to "where no *one* has gone before." Neither females nor nonhumans are now excluded.

Animal Languages: Can We Talk to the Animals?

Although humans have the most flexible and symbolic language for communicating propositions, we are not the only species that can communicate. Bees, for example, use a simple but elegant system to communicate messages such as *flowers containing a nectar supply are about 200 meters away on a line that is 20 degrees south of the angle of the sun.* The bee who discovers the nectar tells the other bees about it not through speech or written memos but through a symbolic dance.

If the nectar is within 100 meters of the hive, the bee does a *round dance* (see fig. 7.8), first turning a tight circle in one direction, and then reversing and circling in the opposite direction. This dance does not communicate the direction of the nectar find, so it sends swarms of bees flying out in all directions within 100 meters of the hive looking for the nectar. If the nectar is 200 to 300 meters from the hive, the "speaker" bee gives better directions to his attentive audience. The bee does a *tail-wagging dance.* This dance is in the form of a tight figure eight. The direction of the nectar is communicated through the angle of the middle part of the dance relative to the sun. The distance is communicated by

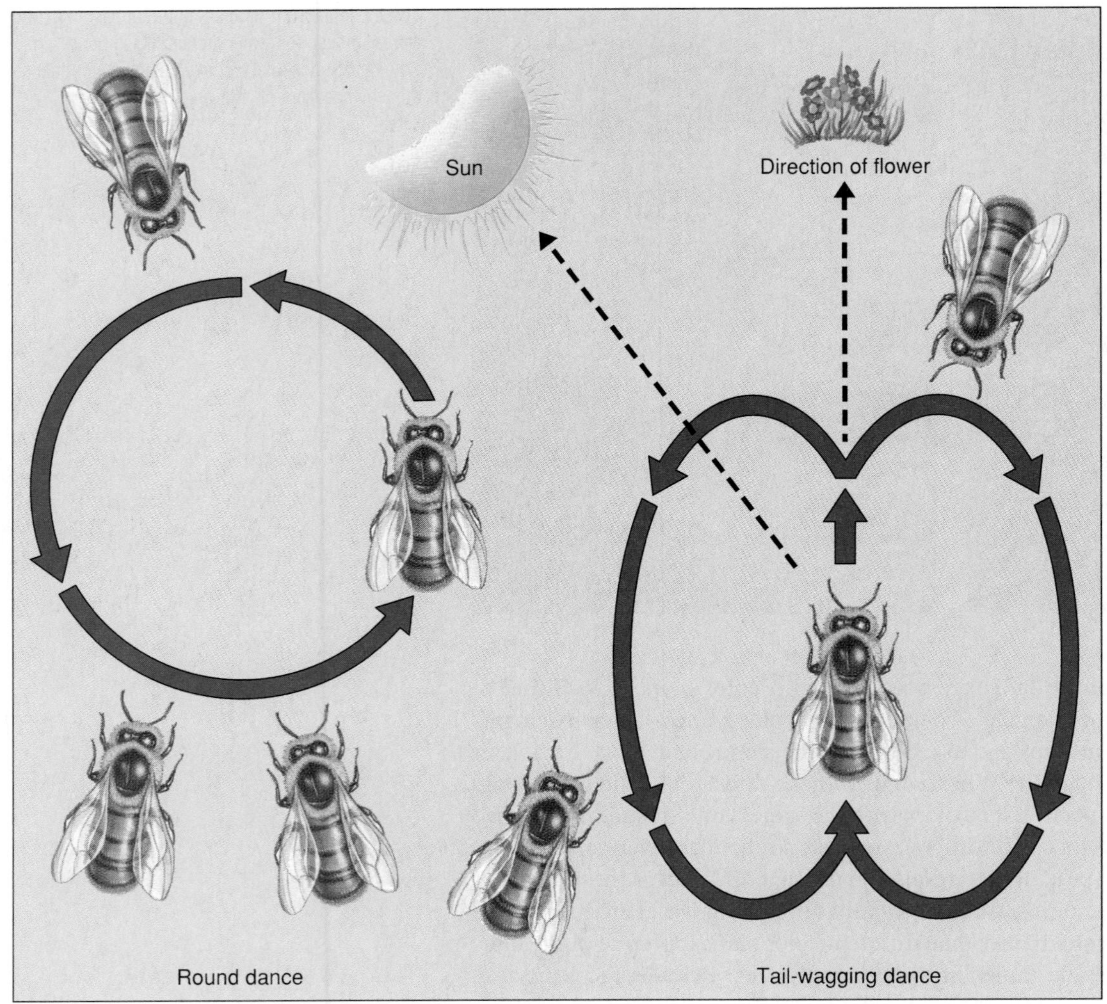

FIGURE 7.8

The language dances of honeybees. The round dance indicates that nectar is within 100 meters of the hive. The tail-wagging dance points in the direction of the nectar when it's over 200 meters away. Distances between 100 and 200 meters are signaled by a third dance.

the rate of turning, the rate of tail wagging, and the sound made by the vibration of the wings. Distances between 100 and 200 meters are communicated through much looser figure-eight patterns in the tail-wagging dance (von Frisch, 1953).

Using these dances, bees are able to communicate rather complex messages very efficiently. Unlike humans, however, they have a limited vocabulary and can only communicate in a way that is firmly limited by inheritance. Human language, in contrast, must be learned through interactions with fluent speakers. In addition, human languages are more flexible. Animal communication can be varied little, whereas humans can generate an infinite number of unique and novel utterances.

These differences between human and animal languages have led some psychologists to assume that only humans can ever acquire a human language because we alone have the mental abilities needed for a generative language (Lenneberg, 1967). Until recently, this was an assumption that was difficult to challenge. A few attempts had been made to teach human language to animals, but they had failed. Two husband-and-wife teams of psychologists had even taken infant chimpanzees into their homes and raised them like their own children, tutoring them intensively in language. However, the better of the two chimps learned to say only four words crudely (Hayes & Hayes, 1951; Kellogg & Kellogg, 1933).

If humankind's nearest cousins, the apes, could not learn human language, then it seemed a safe bet to assume that human abilities were required to learn a human language.

However, another wife-and-husband team of psychologists, Beatrix and Allen Gardner (1971), dramatically reopened the question. They reasoned that chimpanzees have not been able to learn to speak English simply because they possess a mouth and throat that is not well suited for spoken language rather than because they lack adequate mental abilities. To prove their point, the Gardners raised a young chimp, Washoe, to whom they taught American Sign Language (ASL), a language made up of hand signals used by the deaf. Washoe has acquired a limited but real command of the ASL version of English. She uses more than 150 signs and uses them in combinations like *gimme sweet drink.*

Perhaps the most engaging story about Washoe's language is her teaching it to another chimp. After Washoe had reached her full level of proficiency, she was given a young male chimpanzee to "adopt." In less than two weeks, the young adopted chimp began to imitate Washoe's signs. In many cases, the learning appeared to be incidental, as with much of human language learning, but it appeared that Washoe intentionally taught several signs to her young protégé. For example, when food was brought, Washoe repeatedly made the sign for *food* in front of the young chimp. She even took his hand and molded it into the same sign and touched his hand to his mouth several times. She taught him the sign for *come* by first making the sign and then approaching and pulling him. Then she signed *come* and approached him. Later she made the sign and waited for him to come.

Washoe uses more than 150 ASL signs, many in combinations. Here Washoe signs *sweet* in response to the lollipop.

Washoe is not the only ape to learn a human language. Penny Patterson (1977) has taught more than 600 signs to Koko, a gorilla who may be showing even more spontaneous and generative use of language than Washoe. Koko signs "That Koko" when she sees herself in the mirror; she once called a ring, a sign she had not been taught, a *finger bracelet;* and she once replied to the question "How are you feeling?" by signing "I was sad and cried this morning." Perhaps most impressively, Koko knows enough sign language to have taken an intelligence test and she scored only slightly below the average for humans of her age. If that does not impress you, try this: A few years ago, a reporter for *Food and Wine* asked Koko (with Penny Patterson serving as the interpreter) what food she most liked to eat (for an article on food fantasies of the rich and famous). Koko's answer: "Champagne, because it's like candy and coke on my lips" (Wyler, 1985).

The fact that we can now have two-way conversations with apes is an unsettling reality that will rightly force many of us to rethink our views of "dumb animals." These findings should be kept in proper perspective, however. The linguistic accomplishments of even the most-advanced adult apes are very limited compared with those of human children. So far, apes use language almost exclusively as a tool to get food, to ask the trainer to play tickling games, and the like. They rarely just comment on their world or ask questions to gain information (Rumbaugh & Gill, 1976; Slobin, 1979). At this point we cannot carry on more than superficial conversations with them.

Although there is no question that apes can learn the basics of sign language, debates continue concerning a theoretical issue: Are apes capable of learning true human language? Columbia University psychologist Herbert Terrace (1980) has also taught ASL to a chimp named Nim Chimpsky ("named" after famous linguist Noam Chomsky, whom we mentioned earlier). Nim Chimpsky mastered ASL about as well as Washoe did. However, Terrace concluded that Nim was unable to master true human language. At issue are two primary questions: (a) Do the chimps use language spontaneously? and (b) Do they exhibit an understanding of syntax; that is, can they generate novel, meaningful sentences in which the order of the signs conveys the intended meaning?

Terrace suggests that the answer to both questions is no. None of the chimps trained to date uses language spontaneously very often. For example, only about 10 percent of Nim's statements were spontaneous; the rest were in response to a statement by a human and were generally direct imitations. More importantly, it is not clear that the order in which signs are made is regular and used to convey meaning. Washoe's utterances do not seem to show a syntactic use of the order of signs. For example, Washoe apparently used *Roger tickle*

Washoe and *Washoe tickle Roger* interchangeably as a request to be tickled. In contrast, a human speaker of ASL would recognize those statements as having different meanings.

At present, it appears that apes may have learned to use language at the level of a 2-year-old human, but they have not progressed beyond that point (Reynolds & Flagg, 1983). Still, their elementary use of language is more evidence of "humanity" than was once thought possible for apes. And the apes' progress has done much to "talk" at least some scientists out of their belief that only humans can learn human languages.

Thinking Critically About Psychology

1. Does it make sense to you to say that apes are not capable of using language in a human way?

2. The Greek language has three different words for love. Would that influence the way Greeks think about and understand love?

Review

Language is the efficient symbolic code used in human communication. It utilizes a finite set of sounds, units of meaning, and rules for combining them to convey a limitless set of meanings. The question of whether our language influences our cognition has not been satisfactorily answered, but current evidence suggests that it does in some ways. Although no animals have learned to use human language in the same ways as humans, surprisingly complex two-way conversations can occur between humans and apes who have been taught sign language—we can talk to some of the animals.

Check Your Learning

To be sure that you have learned the key points from the preceding section, cover the answers below and try to answer each question. If you give an incorrect answer to any question, return to the page given next to the correct answer to see why your answer was not correct.

1. While language is the term used to describe the symbolic code used in communication, the meaning of the code is termed ________________.

- **a.** surface structure
- **b.** heuristics
- **c.** semantics
- **d.** syntax

2. Human language can be referred to as ________________ in that an infinite set of utterances can be made using a finite set of elements and rules.

- **a.** divergent
- **b.** conceptual
- **c.** semantic
- **d.** generative

3. ________________ refers to the rules of a language, such as the rules for the ways in which morphemes can be combined, that allow an infinite number of understandable utterances to be generated.

- **a.** Semantics
- **b.** Syntax
- **c.** Phonemics
- **d.** Morphemics

4. According to the ________________ hypothesis, the vocabulary and structure of a language can influence the way speakers of that language think.

Correct Answers

1. c (p. 256), **2.** d (p. 257), **3.** b (p. 257), **4.** linguistic relativity (or Whorfian) (p. 258).

INTELLIGENCE: THE SUM TOTAL OF COGNITION

intelligence
(in-tel´i-jens) The cognitive ability of an individual to learn from experience, to reason well, and to cope with the demands of daily living.

In the sense used in this book, **intelligence** refers to the cognitive abilities of an individual to learn from experience, to reason well, and to cope effectively with the demands of daily living. In short, intelligence has to do with how well a person is able to use cognition in coping with the world.

The term *intelligence* was not in widespread use until it was popularized in the late 1800s by the writings of Sir Francis Galton. Galton was a cousin of Charles Darwin, the scientist credited for developing the theory of evolution based on natural selection of inherited characteristics. Galton believed that intellectual ability was inherited, and he tried unsuccessfully to develop an intelligence test to use in his research. Although he was unsuccessful in his own research, Galton gave psychology the concept of intelligence.

Sir Francis Galton (1822–1911)

Differing Views of Intelligence

Since Galton's time, intelligence has been the subject of intensive research, theoretical pronouncements, and often heated debate. After nearly 100 years of scrutiny, however, psychologists still cannot agree on several basic issues. Opinions differ on how many kinds or dimensions of intellectual ability exist, but a promising new approach suggests that instead of trying to answer that question, we should work to identify the basic cognitive components of intelligence.

Intelligence: General or Specific Abilities?

In Galton's view, intelligence is a single *general factor* that provides the basis for the more specific abilities that each of us possesses. According to this conception, if we are generally intelligent, we will be more likely to develop strong mechanical, musical, artistic, and other kinds of abilities. This view that a general factor of intelligence underlies each of our more specific abilities has been advocated in more modern times by psychologist Charles Spearman (Spearman & Wynn-Jones, 1950), who uses the term **g** to refer to the general factor of intelligence. Spearman based his opinion on complex mathematical analyses of intelligence test scores that support, but do not prove, his theory of general intelligence. The concept of a *g* factor of intelligence is also held by David Wechsler, who is the author of the most widely used intelligence tests for children and adults in the United States today (Wechsler, 1955).

g
A broad general factor of intelligence, a concept endorsed by some investigators of intelligence.

Other psychologists have argued that intelligence is not a single general factor but a collection of many separate specific abilities. These psychologists make a great deal of the fact that most of us are much better in some cognitive skills than others, rather than being generally good at everything. Louis Thurstone (1938), for example, developed an alternative to tests of general intelligence, called the *Primary Mental Abilities Test,* that measures seven different intellectual abilities. J. P. Guilford (1982), taking an even more extreme position than Thurstone, suggested that some 150 different abilities make up what we call intelligence.

Howard Gardner (1983) also has argued that there are multiple types of intelligence. Gardner became convinced that there are many separate kinds of intelligence partly by studying patients who had suffered brain damage to only some parts of the cerebral cortex. He found that these individuals lost some kinds of intellectual abilities while other kinds of intelligence were left intact. This suggested to him that different types of intelligence are mediated by different parts of the brain. Gardner also studied the fascinating abilities of rare individuals with *savant syndromes.* These individuals have low general intelligence, but show extraordinary splinter skills in art, music, or arithmetic computation. As a result of his investigations, Gardner suggests that there are *seven independent types of intelligence:*

1. linguistic (verbal)
2. logical-mathematical
3. musical
4. spatial (artistic)
5. kinesthetic (athletic)
6. interpersonal (social skills)
7. intrapersonal (personal adjustment)

Gardner's definition of intelligence is much broader than the traditional one, as Gardner believes that great skill in music or basketball should be said to reflect special

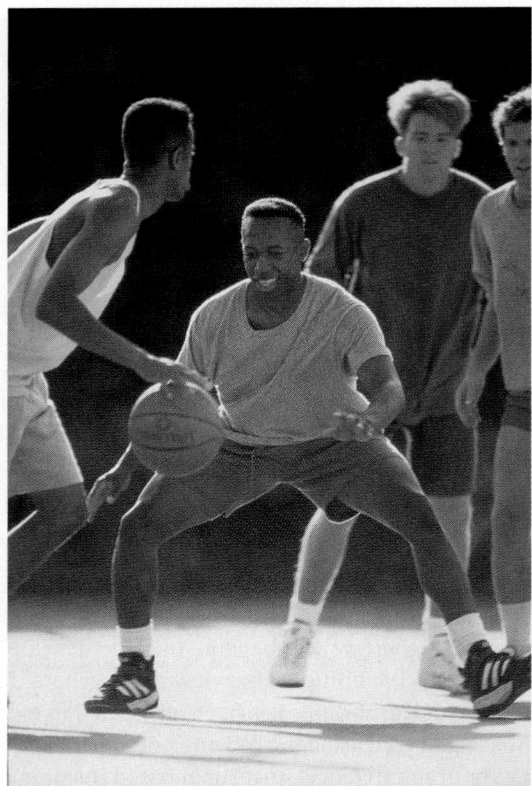

Howard Gardner's definition of intelligence is much broader than the traditional one. He believes great skill in music or basketball reflects intelligence as much as great skill in mathematics.

intelligence just as much as great skill in mathematics. Most tests of intelligence focus on just verbal and logical-mathematical areas of intelligence.

The issue of one versus many types of intelligence remains unsettled today, but most authorities believe that there is truth to both approaches. That is, it is probably correct that a general factor underlies all intelligence, but people can be strong in one specific area of intelligence and weak in another. Interestingly, people with higher than average intelligence show more peaks and valleys in specific facets of their intelligence than people with below average intelligence (Hunt, 1995). Because both overall intelligence and specific strengths and weaknesses are important, it's common practice when measuring the intelligence of individuals to provide estimates of both general and more specific facets of intelligence.

Cognitive Components of Intelligence

A promising new way of conceptualizing and studying intelligence has been proposed by psychologist Robert Sternberg (Sternberg, 1979, 1981; Sternberg & Gardner, 1982) and others. This approach suggests that the basic nature of intelligence can be illuminated by applying what we have learned in research on cognition, particularly research carried out using an information-processing model of cognition.

Sternberg has proposed a tentative theory of intelligence that specifies the cognitive steps that a person must use in reasoning and solving some kinds of problems—or in simple terms, the cognitive components of intelligence. For example, consider the following analogy problem (Sternberg, 1979).

LAWYER is to CLIENT as DOCTOR is to?

a. MEDICINE

b. PATIENT

To solve this problem, Sternberg believes that we must go through a number of cognitive steps. Among these steps, the person must:

1. *Encode* (mentally represent in the memory system in some usable form) all relevant information about the problem. In this case, the person might encode information related to the term *lawyer* that includes: knows the law, represents others before the courts, is paid fees for providing services, and so on. For the term *client,* the information that this is an individual who obtains professional assistance and pays a fee for those services would need to be encoded, and so on for all of the attributes of all of the terms in the problem.
2. *Infer* the nature of the relationships between the terms in the problem. In this case, it is essential to see that *lawyer* and *client* are related because a lawyer provides a service for a fee and a client obtains a service by paying a fee.
3. *Map* or identify common characteristics in relevant pairs of elements. In this case, the person must see that both lawyers and doctors provide services for fees and that both clients and patients obtain services by paying fees.
4. *Apply* the relationship identified between lawyer and client to the relationship between doctor and patient.
5. *Compare* the alternative answers.
6. *Respond* with an answer; in this case, "patient."

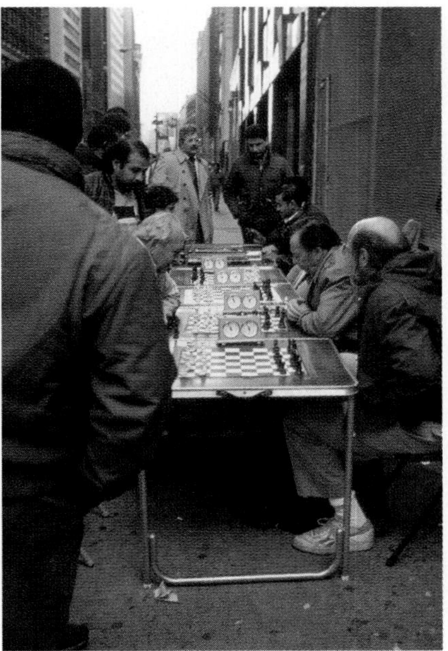

Robert Sternberg proposes five steps in reasoning. Expert chess players seem to perform the first step, encoding information about the positions of the pieces, more effectively than beginners.

Sternberg suggests that this way of looking at intelligence does more than provide us with a convenient way of describing the steps in intelligent reasoning. It gives us a framework for discovering which components are most important in determining whether one person is "more intelligent" than another. For example, several initial studies have provided a finding that is, at least at first glance, rather surprising (Sternberg, 1979). Better reasoners take more time to complete the encoding component than poor reasoners, but they are *faster* at all of the other stages. Sternberg explains this finding by drawing a parallel to a lending library. A library that invests more time in carefully cataloging books (like the encoding component) will be more than repaid for this investment of time in terms of more rapid access to the books. As we have seen earlier, one of the critical differences between expert and beginning chess players is that experts encode the board positions more effectively (Chase & Simon, 1973). Such findings hold promise in identifying the key cognitive elements in effective intelligence and may even allow us to improve intelligence in the future by training people to carry out those key components more effectively (Sternberg, 1981).

Sternberg (1985a) suggests that there are three general components of intelligence. Because he distinguishes three kinds of components, he refers to his view as a **triarchic theory of intelligence.** He distinguishes between three components of intelligence:

triarchic theory of intelligence (trī-ar´-kik) Sternberg's theory distinguishing three aspects of intelligence: learning new information, solving specific problems, and solving problems in general.

1. *Knowledge-acquisition components.* One part of intelligence is the ability to learn new information.
2. *Performance components.* A second aspect of intelligence is knowing how to solve specific problems.
3. *Metacomponents.* A third part of intelligence is knowing general ways to approach problem solving.

For example, physicians prescribe different doses of some medicines for children depending on the weight of the child. If a medicine is supposed to be prescribed at a dosage of 0.3 milligram for every kilogram that the child weighs, an accurate prescription depends on all three of Sternberg's components of intelligence. The physician must use metacomponents to see that the problem involves ratios and to see that the child's weight in pounds is divided by the ratio of kilograms to pounds and the result multiplied by 0.3. Using knowledge-acquisition components, the physician must have memorized the dosage formula and the ratio of kilograms to pounds. Finally, performance components are used to accurately carry out the mathematical steps of division and multiplication. Sternberg (1985a) argues that a full conception of intelligence must take into account all of these components, but he believes that the most important differences between more and less intelligent individuals lie in the metacomponents of intelligence.

Fluid and Crystallized Intelligence

fluid intelligence
The ability to learn or invent new strategies to deal with new problems.

crystallized intelligence
The ability to use previously learned skills to solve familiar problems.

In almost the same way that Sternberg distinguished between three components of intelligence, other psychologists tell us that it is important to distinguish between **fluid intelligence** and **crystallized intelligence** (Hunt, 1995). *Fluid intelligence* is the ability to learn or invent new strategies for dealing with new kinds of problems. In Sternberg's terminology, the knowledge-acquisition components and the metacomponents of intelligence are the chief components of fluid intelligence. *Crystallized intelligence* is the ability to use previously learned skills to solve familiar problems. In Sternberg's terms, these are the performance components of intelligence. We began with Sternberg's way of looking at the components of intelligence, because it is helpful to see the link between intelligence and specific cognitive skills. We will use the more widely used distinction between fluid and crystallized intelligence in the rest of the book, however.

It is important to note that the distinction between fluid and crystallized intelligence is not just a logical one. It is well supported by research and is essential for our understanding of the role of intelligence in human lives. The strongest evidence that fluid and crystallized intelligence are different comes from four kinds of studies. First, fluid and crystallized intelligence change differently with age. Crystallized intelligence—the ability to use familiar skills—improves throughout the years that adults work. That is one reason that most leadership jobs are held by persons over 40 (Hunt, 1995). In contrast, fluid intelligence—the ability to learn new skills for new problems—declines from middle age on. To some extent, it really is harder to teach an old dog new tricks, but we old dogs do okay with our still-growing crystallized intelligence!

Second, since World War II, average test scores on tests of fluid intelligence have increased in North America and Europe, but average scores on tests of crystallized intelligence have declined (Hunt, 1995). The reason for these changes are not known, but the fact that they have been in opposite directions supports the distinction between fluid and crystallized intelligence. Third, as Sternberg would suggest, the two kinds of intelligence are based on different cognitive skills. For example, persons who are high in fluid intelligence have better short-term memory capacity. Fourth, some things that harm parts of the brain, such as alcoholism, harm fluid intelligence much more than crystallized intelligence. These facts suggest that fluid and crystallized intelligence may be based on different brain functions (Hunt, 1995).

Measures of Intelligence: The IQ Test

Intelligence would be too vague a concept to be of much use to psychologists if it were not for the reasonably accurate and meaningful tests that have been developed to measure it. A measure of intelligence makes it possible to use the concept of intelligence in both research and clinical practice. As noted in chapter 1, the first person to develop a useful measure of intelligence was Alfred Binet. In 1903 he began working on developing a test that he hoped would distinguish intellectually normal from subnormal Parisian schoolchildren. In the United States, Binet's test was refined by Lewis Terman of Stanford University, as the still widely used *Stanford-Binet Intelligence Scale.* Similar tests were also developed by David Wechsler, known as the *Wechsler Intelligence Scale for Children* (3rd ed.), or *WISC-R,* and the *Wechsler Adult Intelligence Scale, Revised,* or *WAIS-R.* Items similar to those on the WISC-R are as follows:

Subject	***Examples of Items***
Information	"Which president signed the Emancipation Proclamation?"
Similarities	"How are a bell and a violin alike?"
Arithmetic	"If you buy five pieces of gum for 18 cents each, how much change would you get back from a dollar?"
Vocabulary	"What does *dissipate* mean?"
Comprehension	"What should you do if you see another child bitten by a dog?"

Picture completion	"Show me the part that is missing in this picture." (wheel of a car)
Picture arrangement	"Arrange the pictures on these cards so they tell a story that makes sense."
Block design	"Arrange these blocks so they look like the design in this picture."
Object assembly	"Put this puzzle together as quickly as you can." (jigsaw puzzle of a dog)
Coding	"Use this key that matches numbers with geometric shapes to write the shape that goes with each number in the block below it."

How is it possible to develop a test that measures intelligence when psychologists cannot decide what intelligence is? Intelligence tests are no more than a small sample of *some* of the cognitive abilities that constitute intelligence. These tests are considered useful not because we are sure they measure the right things, but because they do a fairly good job of *predicting* how people will perform in situations that seem to require intelligence, such as in school or on the job. This state of affairs has led some psychologists to say—only slightly in jest—that intelligence should be defined as whatever intelligence tests measure. We cannot be very confident that intelligence tests are very good at measuring "intelligence," whatever that turns out to be. But intelligence tests are fairly good at picking out those individuals who perform well on tasks that seem to require intelligence.

Construction of Intelligence Tests

We can perhaps better understand the nature of intelligence tests and the meaning of the related term *IQ* by taking a brief look at how intelligence tests were originally constructed. Binet constructed his test by looking for a large number of items related to cognitive efficiency that differentiated children of different ages. That is, he looked for items that he thought about half the children of one age could answer, but that nearly all older children could answer and very few younger children could answer. He did this based on the assumption that intellectual abilities improve with age during childhood.

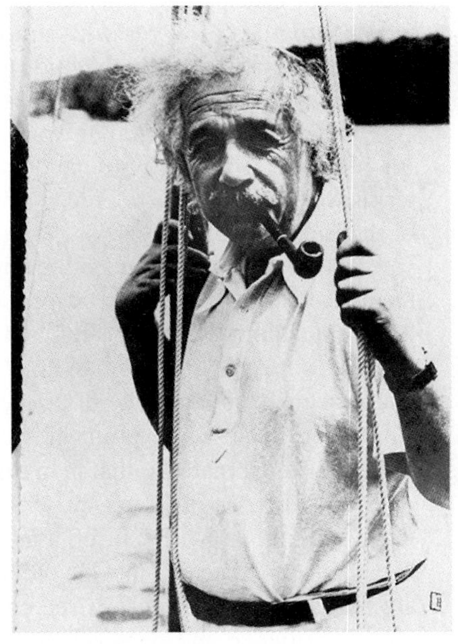

Albert Einstein had uncommon intelligence. Only about 2 percent of the general population have IQs above 130.

Once Binet had compiled a list of items, he gave them to a large number of children of different ages to determine exactly how many children at each age level could answer each question. Then he arranged the order of the questions in the test from the least to the most difficult.

In simplified terms, the score obtained on Binet's intelligence test is equal to the number of questions answered correctly, but it's expressed in terms of the age of the children for which that score is the *average*. For example, if a child correctly answers 18 items, and the average number of items answered by children 8 years and 6 months in age was 18, then the score on the test would be expressed as "8 years 6 months." Binet called this score the *mental age (MA)*. If your mental age is higher than your actual age *(chronological age, CA),* then you would be considered bright because you answered the average number of items for older children. If your mental age is lower than your chronological age, then you would be considered below average in intelligence because you could answer only the average number of questions answered by younger children. This is all that an intelligence test is: a measure that compares your performance with the performance of individuals of different ages on items believed to reflect intelligence.

Is a child with a mental age of 9 years 4 months and a chronological age of 7 years 2 months brighter than a child with a chronological age of 8 years 5 months and a mental age of 10 years 3 months? Because it's difficult to compare the mental ages of children of different chronological ages, a more easily used score than the mental age was later developed for intelligence tests called the **intelligence quotient,** or **IQ.** The intelligence quotient is obtained by dividing the mental age (MA) by the chronological age (CA) so that children of different chronological ages can be directly compared. To remove the decimal point, the result is multiplied by 100. Thus, IQ = MA/CA x 100. For example, if a child's MA is 6 years 6 months and his chronological age is also 6 years 6 months, then his IQ would be 100.

intelligence quotient (IQ)
A numerical value of intelligence derived from the results of an intelligence test.

HUMAN DIVERSITY

Understanding Intelligence from the Cree Perspective

Each culture defines intelligence differently, and children in each culture are encouraged to be intelligent in those ways. It is difficult for us to understand that different cultures have different definitions of intelligence, however, because our own view seems to be the only correct one. By definition, any view of intelligence that is different from our own seems to be "unintelligent." But, in the multicultural world in which we live, it is essential that we develop a greater understanding of different views of intelligence.

An ingenious study of differing definitions of intelligence by John Berry and his colleagues (Berry & Bennett, 1992) creatively combined research techniques from anthropology and psychology to examine the definitions of intelligence among the Cree, a tribe of Native Americans and Native Canadians in Ontario. Berry and Bennett first asked Cree adults who spoke both English and Cree to give them Cree words that had to do with intelligence, thinking, being smart, or being wise.

Twenty words obtained through this technique were written in Cree script on cards. The cards were given in random order to 60 Cree people. The individuals were asked to sort the words into piles of words with similar meaning. In this way, they were able to see which words tended to be placed in the same piles because they had similar meaning to the Cree.

The first group of similar words included the Cree words for wisdom, thinking hard, and thinking carefully. These terms were often the first Cree words given as the translation of the English words *smart* or *intelligent.*

A second group included the Cree words for respect and respectfulness. To the Cree, respect refers to an appreciation for people, animals, the Creator, and the land. Respectfulness involves an active and positive involvement with these things and is seen as the opposite of laziness. Respect and respectfulness from the Cree point of view involve caretaking—looking after something that is highly valued.

A third group of Cree words referred to paying attention, self-discipline, and self-control. It involved thinking before taking action, and listening to what others say. Other concepts that are extremely important to Cree conceptions of intelligence include patience and perseverance, being able to look after yourself and survive without being a drain on others, and being open to new experiences. Thus, the Cree view of intelligence is much broader than that of the European-American view, including an emphasis on independence, self-reliance, self-discipline, respect for others, and respect for nature.

To instill these values in their children and raise intelligent adults, Cree parents and elders use child-rearing techniques that are sometimes quite different from those seen in many homes in the United States. For example, Cree children are encouraged to act independently without interference from adults. Adults rarely interfere with what an older child is doing, even if it is potentially dangerous, feeling that direct experience is the best teacher. In Cree culture, a high value is placed on not interfering in other peoples' affairs—and this courtesy is extended to children. Berry and Bennett note that some label this parenting style as neglectful, but they point out that Cree parents are often quite anxious when, for example, a child is playing with a sharp object, and they are noticeably relieved when the child puts the object down. Using such parenting methods, the Cree socialize children to be self-sufficient and independent. They learn that "one's destiny need rest in no hands but one's own" (p. 80).

How do these notions of intelligence and competence compare with those in your own culture? Give some thought to the ways in which the values that were taught in your neighborhood as you were growing up differ from those on the college campus you are attending. Keep in mind as you consider these things that the varying notions of intelligence and competence in different cultures are not superior or inferior to one another, simply different.

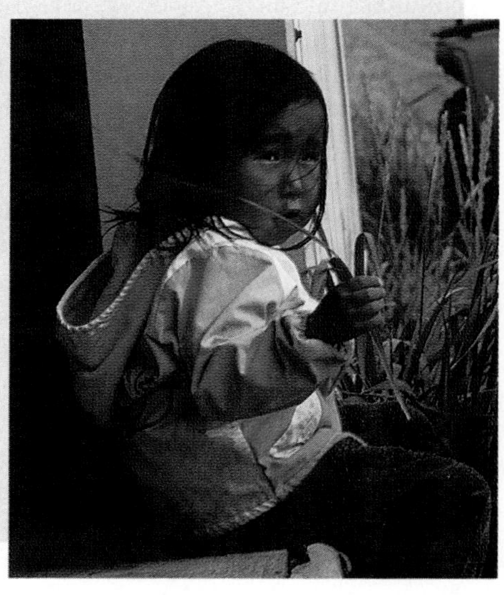

IQs that are over 100 indicate that the person is more intelligent than average (the MA is greater than the CA). For example, if a child obtains an MA of 10 years, but her CA is only 8 years, then her IQ would be 10/8 x 100 = 125. Conversely, IQs less than 100 indicate that the individual is less intelligent than average. A child who is 10 years in CA but obtains an MA of only 7 years would have an IQ of 7/10 x 100 = 70.

ratio IQ
Intelligence quotient based on the ratio between the person's mental age and chronological age.

Actually, Binet's approach to calculating the intelligence quotient from the ratio between the child's mental age and chronological age—called the **ratio IQ**—is no longer used in contemporary intelligence tests. There are several technical reasons that the ratio

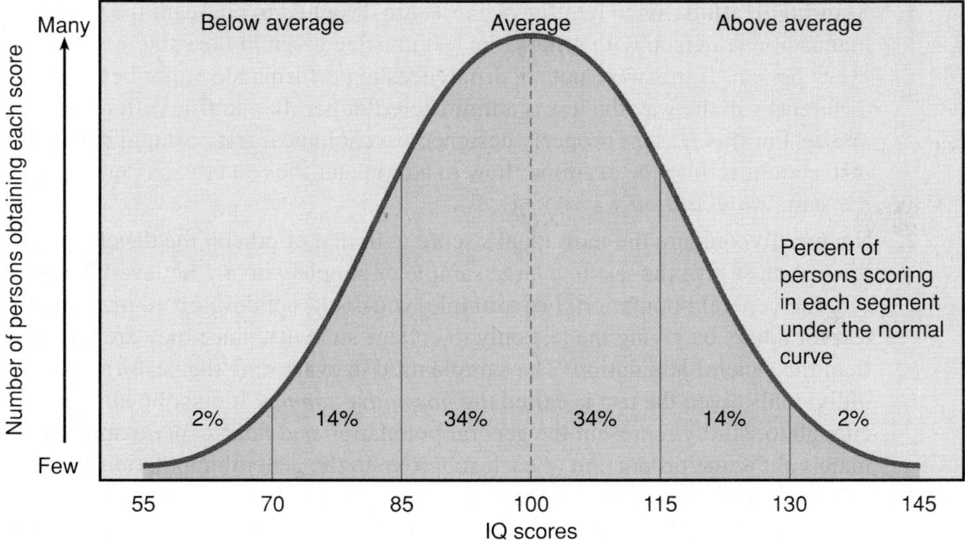

FIGURE 7.9

The normal distribution of scores on a test of intellectual ability.

IQ is no longer used, but the most important reason to understand is that there are some significant limitations to the concept of mental age. For example, a very bright 4-year-old with an IQ of 150 has the mental age of the average 6-year-old but would not handle many situations demanding intellectual ability as well as the older 6-year-old. Conversely, a child with low intelligence will often seem less competent than an average younger child with the same mental age.

For these reasons, a new approach to the measurement of intellectual ability, termed the **deviation IQ,** was developed. The deviation IQ is based on an intriguing mathematical property of measurements of many phenomena, including intellectual ability. As shown in figure 7.9, the scores of large numbers of persons on tests of intelligence fall in a **normal distribution.** This means that most people will obtain the *average* score, or scores that are close to the average, on the test. As scores *deviate* from the average in either direction (either higher or lower than average), the scores become progressively less common. Thus, scores a few points above or below average are common, but scores that are many points above or below average are very uncommon.

deviation IQ
Intelligence quotient based on the degree of deviation from average of the person's score on an intelligence test.

normal distribution
The symmetrical pattern of scores on a scale in which a majority of the scores are clustered near the center and a minority are at either extreme.

Instead of defining an average IQ as one in which the mental age and chronological age are the same (IQ of 100), the average score on the intelligence test (the midpoint of the normal distribution) is assigned an IQ score of 100 and, based on the shape of the curve, scores above the average are assigned IQ scores above 100 and below average scores are assigned IQ scores below 100. The exact IQ score is based on how much the score deviates from the average. Look carefully again at figure 7.9 to see how this works.

Deviation IQ scores work very well for adults. They also work well for children, but children's scores have to be compared with different normal distributions for each age group since their scores increase as children grow older. The same concept of deviation from the midpoint of the normal distribution is also used in many other tests of human characteristics. Scores on the tests of academic achievement that you took in school, some of the tests of specific job skills that you will take when you apply for employment, and some tests of personality are based on the same concept as the deviation IQ.

Characteristics of Good Intelligence Tests

When you measure the size of a window with a yardstick before buying drapes, you don't have to ask how good yardsticks are for measuring length. For the purpose you are using it, yardsticks are good measuring instruments. However for something as important, yet difficult to define, as intelligence, it makes sense for us to ask how accurate the measuring instrument is. The following is a list of criteria that an intelligence test must meet before we accept it as an adequate measuring instrument. In chapter 11, in the section on personality tests, you will see how these criteria apply equally to all psychological tests.

standardization
Administering a test in the same way to all individuals.

1. **Standardization.** Since intelligence tests are designed to compare the performance of one person with others, the test must be given in the same way to every person. If this were not so, differences in performance might be due to differences in the way the test is administered rather than to true differences in ability. For this reason, properly designed psychological tests contain detailed instructions telling the examiner how to administer the test to each person in the same *standardized* way.

norms
Standards (created by the scores of a large group of individuals) used as the basis of comparison for scores on a test.

2. **Norms.** To compare the individual's score with that of others, the developer of the test must give the test to a large sample of people who are believed to represent the general population. For example, you could not develop an intelligence test for adults by giving the test only to college students, since they are brighter than the general population. The sample used in evaluating the performance of individuals given the test is called the *normative sample.* It must be large enough to validly represent the general population and must contain approximately the same proportion of each subgroup in the general population to be a valid standard of comparison for anyone taking the test. For example, a normative sample that contained no Hispanic children would not have the same validity when used to evaluate young Hispanics.

objectivity
Lack of subjectivity in a test question so that the same score is produced regardless of who does the scoring.

3. **Objectivity.** An intelligence test must be constructed so that there is little or no ambiguity as to what constitutes a correct answer to each item. If there is ambiguity, and the scoring is subjective rather than *objective,* then factors other than the individual's performance might influence the scoring, such as the examiner's mood or prejudices.

reliability
A test's ability to produce similar scores if the test is administered on different occasions or by different examiners.

4. **Reliability.** To be useful, an intelligence test must be *reliable.* This means that the scores obtained would be approximately the same if administered on two different occasions or by two different examiners. If the scores change a great deal from one testing to the next, no faith can be put in the scores.

validity
The extent to which a test measures what it's supposed to measure.

5. **Validity.** Most importantly, an intelligence scale must be *valid;* that is, it must measure what it's supposed to measure. Validity can be evaluated in a number of different ways, but for intelligence tests, the most important issue is the degree to which the test *predicts* performance on other tasks that most people agree require intelligence. This is referred to as *predictive validity.* For example, the Wechsler and Stanford-Binet intelligence tests are considered valid in part because they are fairly good predictors of performance in school. About 25 percent of the differences in school performance among a group of students can be predicted from IQ scores. This is not a high level of predictability. As you are well aware, many factors besides intelligence, such as motivation and personality, contribute to school performance. But intelligence test scores are better predictors of school performance than any other measure that psychologists or educators now possess. So, in this sense, intelligence tests are valid.

Importance of Intelligence in Modern Society

Psychologist Richard Herrnstein and sociologist Charles Murray (1994) recently published a book on intelligence, called *The Bell Curve,* that made IQ the focus of a heated national debate. The book angered many because of its conclusions regarding race and genetics, which we discuss later in this chapter, but that anger stimulated some of the best minds in psychology to reexamine the role played by intelligence in the success or failure of individuals in technological societies.

Herrnstein and Wilson (1994) argued that the increasing technological complexity of jobs in modern society will widen the split between the group of intelligent and affluent persons at the top and the less intelligent and less affluent at the bottom of the economic ladder. They believe that this is because more and more of the well-paid jobs in our society—especially jobs that are most important to the nation's economic prosperity—require high levels of intelligence. They argue that little can be done to solve this problem, moreover, as intelligence cannot be modified. Are Herrnstein and Wilson correct?

There is no doubt that the most complex and highly paid jobs in our society usually go to the most intelligent individuals. The average IQ of truck drivers is a little under 100, whereas the average IQ of doctors and lawyers is 125 or higher (Hunt, 1995). At the other end of the IQ spectrum, persons with IQs below 85 (about 15 percent of the population) are very likely to have dropped out of high school, to live below the poverty line, to be unemployed for long periods, to be divorced, to receive aid for dependent children, to have health problems, and to have a criminal record. Indeed, the correlation between IQ and success in education and occupations is about as high as the correlation between people's heights and weights (Hunt, 1995)!

Thus, Herrnstein and Murray (1994) are correct in stating that intelligence is important to a person's occupational success. Earl Hunt's (1995) and Robert Sternberg's (1995) powerful critiques of *The Bell Curve,* however, suggest that the problem lies more in society's *response* to differences in intelligence than in differences in intelligence per se. If Hunt and Sternberg are right, we may be able to reduce the economic segregation between the more and less intelligent members of society and improve the overall economic success of society as a whole at the same time.

Part of the reason that people in the highest-paying jobs have higher IQ scores is that society uses IQ as one of the criteria for entering the educational programs needed to enter those professions. You cannot become an attorney without going to college and law school, and tests that require higher intelligence are used to admit students to these schools. But is high intelligence *necessary* to learn and perform complex jobs well? There is evidence that many complex jobs require a minimum level of fluid intelligence, but variations in fluid intelligence above that minimum level are unrelated to success on the job (Hunt, 1995). It also is true that higher fluid intelligence leads to the *faster* learning of skills needed to be successful in complex jobs.

On the other hand, once a less intelligent individual has learned all of the necessary skills for many complex and important jobs, her or his performance will be almost as good as that of a more intelligent person. Many studies have shown that fluid intelligence is an important predictor of performance for new employees, but much less so for experienced employees (Hunt, 1995). The exception is that some professions—such as medicine—require frequent coping with new challenges, and persons with higher fluid intelligence tend to be better able to do so.

Therefore, within broad ranges of intelligence, society could open the door to many complex occupations for many additional persons if the quality of educational and job training programs were improved. An important part of improving educational programs is simply understanding that some persons may take longer to learn their jobs well than other people. In most educational programs today, however, all students are given the same amount of time to master the material, and those who cannot do so are flunked. If we were to invest in educational programs that allowed students to reach a high level of expertise at their own rates, the investment might be a very wise one. It is probably not true that any person of any level of intelligence could become a computer programmer if he or she studied long enough, but it may be true that the occupational opportunities for every citizen could be improved through improved education.

Intelligence is less important than *The Bell Curve* asserts in another way as well. Many studies tell us that motivation, health, emotional well-being, and other factors are key factors in the performance of even complex and sophisticated jobs. Among persons who have the minimum level of intelligence needed for the job, these factors can be more important to good job performance than intelligence (Hunt, 1995). Thus, investment by employers in programs that improve employee well-being, such as adequate health plans and child care, are essential as well. So, maybe it would be correct to say that the pessimistic future warned about in *The Bell Curve* will only come true if we continue to misunderstand the role of intelligence in occupational success.

Scores on intelligence tests are not strongly related to a person's everyday intelligence, for example, the ability to choose winning horses at the racetrack.

Evaluating "Everyday Intelligence"

We have said that intelligence tests are considered to be useful because they allow psychologists to predict how well individuals will perform in situations that require intelligence. The predictions are not very precise, but they are accurate in extreme cases. That is, children with an IQ of 120 will almost always perform better in school than children with an IQ of 80, but we could not predict with much confidence that children with an IQ of 105 will perform better than children with an IQ of 95. Still, in spite of their lack of precision, intelligence tests are useful predictors.

It is also important to understand that intelligence tests are *limited in what they can predict.* They are most useful in predicting school achievement. This should not be surprising since, from the time of Binet's pioneering work (p. 267), intelligence tests have been designed specifically to predict school performance. However, because we generally think of the term *intelligence* as referring to much more than the kind of abilities needed in the classroom, it is important to point out this limitation of intelligence tests—they primarily measure "school intelligence."

everyday intelligence
The intellectual abilities needed to deal with everyday problems, rather than perform well in school.

Recently, a number of writers have proposed that intelligence tests do not accurately measure intelligence very well outside the classroom—**everyday intelligence.** Scores on intelligence tests are not strongly related, for example, to a person's ability to shop within a budget or make accurate change in a supermarket—or to the ability to choose winning horses at the racetrack (Galotti, 1990; Schmidt & Hunter, 1993). This does not mean that everyday intelligence cannot be measured, but it does mean that it is different enough from school intelligence to require different tests to measure it most accurately.

What do these tests of everyday intelligence measure that is not measured by formal intelligence tests? Kathleen Galotti (1990) of Carleton College suggests that everyday intelligence tests primarily assess practical knowledge and skills in getting things done. In an effort to assess this practical knowledge, Sternberg and Wagner (1993) presented scenarios describing work-related situations to their research participants. Participants were then instructed to rate the quality of a number of possible solutions. The resulting measure of persons' practical knowledge was found to predict job performance moderately well across a variety of jobs. Since each kind of everyday challenge, from handicapping horses at the racetrack to selling insurance, may require different practical knowledge and skills, it is not surprising that specialized tests of each facet of everyday intelligence might be the best predictors of success in that area.

Contributing Factors: Individual Differences in IQ

Why is one person highly intelligent while another person is less so? Is it heredity—do we inherit high or low IQs? Or is it the intellectually stimulating or impoverished environment in which we grow up that determines our IQ? Until recent years, most psychologists believed that only the learning environment in which the child was reared was important, but considerable evidence now exists showing that Sir Francis Galton was at least partially correct: Intelligence is partly determined by heredity.

In chapter 2 (pp. 72–73) we mentioned that the two main sources of information about heredity in humans are twin studies and adoption studies. Both have been conducted with intelligence test scores, and both clearly point to the influence of heredity. The IQ scores of genetically identical monozygotic (identical) twins are considerably more similar than the scores of dizygotic twins even though both kinds of twins are reared in essentially the same intellectual environment. Dizygotic twins, who are no more alike genetically than siblings born at different times, are no more similar in IQ than any other siblings. Furthermore, it makes little difference whether monozygotic twins grew up in the same home or were adopted and raised in *separate* homes. In both cases, their IQs are very similar (Erlenmeyer-Kimling & Jarvik, 1963; Hunt, 1995; Lewontin, 1982).

Adoption studies have similarly indicated that heredity is one of the more important factors determining IQ. A large number of studies have shown that the IQs of adopted children are more similar to the IQs of their biological parents with whom they never lived than their adoptive parents who raised them. Taken together, the twin and adoption studies make a strong case that heredity is one of the determinants of IQ. So, if you are as smart as you think you are, your parents are probably smarter than you thought they were!

The child's exposure to the world of adult intelligence through interaction with caregivers seems essential to normal intellectual development.

The intellectual environment in which a child is reared is also an important factor in intelligence, however. The exposure that children have to the world of adult intelligence through interactions with their caregivers seems essential to normal intellectual development. Children who have been so severely neglected by their parents as to be deprived of this stimulation show very slow intellectual development but usually develop more rapidly when placed in good foster homes (Clarke & Clarke, 1976). Schiff and Lewontin (1986) studied a group of children of poorly educated mothers who put one of their children up for adoption but raised their other children themselves. The children were adopted shortly after birth by much better educated families. Years later, the IQs of the adopted children averaged 109, whereas their nonadopted siblings averaged 95. It appears that access to a stimulating environment plays a role in reaching one's full intellectual potential.

But although the role of the environment in intellectual development is an important one, there appear to be broad limits on the nature of the needed environmental stimulation. This is perhaps best shown by the classic study of Skeels (1966). Skeels was a psychologist who worked with orphans who were reared in a state institution in Iowa in the 1930s. At that time, the amount and quality of the care provided by adult attendants was very poor; ratios of 10 infants to 1 caretaker were not unusual. Many of the children who grew up in this institution were tested and found to be mentally retarded. Yet Skeels noted that some orphan infants who, due to lack of space, were reared in a ward for adult women who were mentally retarded showed unexpected improvements in IQ. Skeels reasoned that the stimulation provided by the retarded women was sufficiently better than the almost nonexistent stimulation provided in the orphanage. To test this idea, he had 13 orphans with low IQs placed in the adult ward for 18 months. These children showed an average increase in IQ of more than 25 points, placing them in the normal range of intelligence! In sharp contrast, a group of orphans who were left in the orphanage showed an average *drop* in IQ of 25 points. Clearly, heredity and environment are both important in determining intelligence.

How might heredity and environment act together to produce an intelligent brain? Recent research by Richard Haier and his colleagues (Haier, Siegel, & MacLachlan, 1992; Haier, Siegel, & Tang, 1992) provides some fascinating insights into this process. Haier used PET scans to observe his volunteers' brain activity as they played the video game "Tetris." Tetris requires players to move and rotate shapes to form solid blocks. Using the PET scan, Haier was able to track changes in brain activity as his volunteers became more expert at playing the game. At first, the volunteers expended a huge amount of energy in the regions of the cerebral cortex involved in thinking. After several weeks of practice, however, the volunteers used much less energy, although their scores improved 700 percent. In addition, Haier observed that the drop in energy use for a particular volunteer was directly related to the volunteer's IQ. The higher the IQ, the greater the drop in energy use with practice.

Haier's findings suggest the possibility that what we call intelligence may be a matter of neural efficiency. Intelligent brains do less work than less intelligent brains. Greater neural efficiency (and hence higher intelligence) may result from greater success in a normal maturational process known as **neural pruning.** During the early years of development, the neurons in the brain have many dendrites that connect to many different brain circuits. In fact, it appears that we have too many connections in the beginning to use our brains most efficiently. Fascinatingly, many of these connections are actively destroyed between the ages of 5 years and the early teens—apparently resulting in greater efficiency (O'Leary, 1992). It has been suggested that more intelligent people actually experience more "pruning" of

neural pruning
The process in which inefficient neural connections are actively destroyed, or "pruned," between the ages of 5 and the early teens.

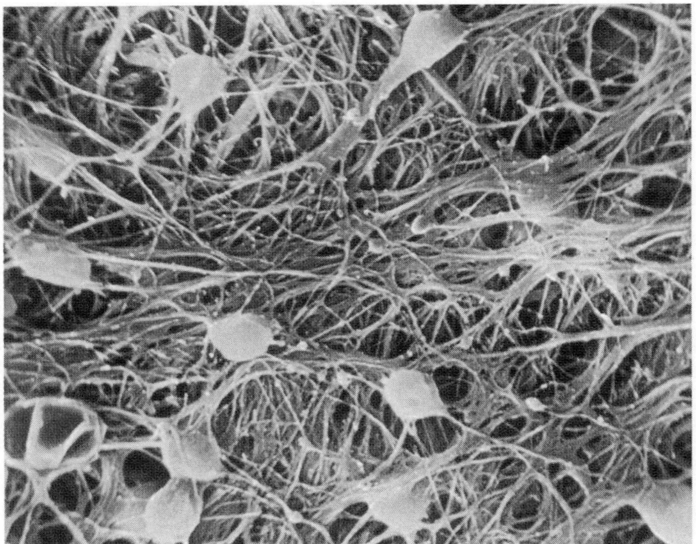

During early childhood the neurons of the brain have many dendrites that are connected to many different neurons. During childhood and early adolescence (ages 5–15 years), however, unnecessary connections are "pruned," leaving only necessary connections. Some researchers believe that persons with higher intelligence went through a process of more extensive pruning that left them with more efficient neural processing abilities.

excess neural circuits, leaving their remaining circuits much more efficient. The brains of persons with lower intelligence work much harder, perhaps due to inefficient circuits that have not been sufficiently pruned (O'Leary, 1992).

Ethnic Differences in Intelligence Scores: Heredity vs. Environment

It has long been known that African Americans and Hispanic Americans score an average of 10 to 15 points less than whites on IQ tests. This fact is accepted by most psychologists, but the interpretation of the finding has been the subject of heated debate. In 1973 Arthur Jensen of the University of California at Berkeley argued not only that the differences in IQ scores reflected actual differences in intellectual ability but also that these differences were genetically based. That is, Jensen stated that African Americans are innately inferior to whites. His most recent statement no longer explains these differences in genetic terms (Jensen, 1980), but Richard Herrnstein and Charles Murray (1994) have argued more recently in their controversial book *The Bell Curve* that ethnic differences in intelligence are mostly due to genetics.

Most psychologists, however (Hunt, 1995; Kamin, 1974), believe that these group differences mean very little about the real intellectual potential of individuals. Kamin (1974) points to three issues. First, most intelligence tests are based on items that are common to the white culture and are standardized mostly on non-Hispanic whites. Because many African Americans and Hispanics come from a somewhat different culture than whites, they are at a disadvantage compared with whites in answering IQ test items. Therefore, this group argues that intelligence tests may not be valid for use with African Americans and Hispanics and that the differences in test scores reflect cultural rather than intellectual differences. To bolster this point, psychologist Robert L. Williams (1972) has shown that when an intelligence test was constructed using items common to the African-American culture, whites scored lower than African Americans on the average.

Second, it is possible that doing well on tests of intelligence is more important to members of some American subcultures than others. Bradley-Johnson, McCarthy, and Jamie (1984) tested this hypothesis in a clever experiment. They rewarded each correct answer on an intelligence test by giving the child a token that could be exchanged for toys after the test. Low-income African-American children receiving tokens scored 13 points higher than a group of low-income African-American children who took the test without tokens. Tokens did not improve scores substantially for white children from middle-income families.

Third, Kamin (1974) points to the fact that, although some real improvement has been made in recent years, most living African Americans grew up in a distinctly prejudiced environment where economic and educational disadvantages may have influenced their intellectual development. The differences in IQ scores may be a measure of the discrimination African Americans have suffered rather than true differences in intellectual capacity.

Fourth, substantial evidence exists that refutes the notion that African Americans are genetically inferior. For example, Loehlin, Lindzey, and Spuhler (1975) studied German children born after World War II whose fathers had been American servicemen. Half of the children had African-American fathers and half had white fathers. All of the German mothers were white and were approximately equal in education and income. If having genes from two white parents were better than from one white parent, one would expect the children of white fathers to have higher IQs. When the children were tested, there was no difference in IQ between the two groups. This result supports the belief that environmental factors, rather than genetic factors, are responsible for observed ethnic differences in IQ in the United States.

The best news, however, is that American ethnic group differences in IQ appear to be dwindling as prejudice and economic barriers are weakening. Lyle Jones (1984) of the

University of North Carolina reported that differences between African Americans and white Americans on average scores on the Scholastic Aptitude Test narrowed considerably between 1976 and 1983. It has been widely reported that scores on this test, which measures a combination of intelligence and school achievement and is used for admission to many colleges and universities, have declined by an average of 8 points on the verbal section and 9 points on the mathematics section for white high school students. In contrast, during the same period the scores for African-American high school students *increased* by 7 points on the verbal section and by 15 points on the mathematics section. More recently, Mullis, Dossey, Foertsch, Jones, and Gentile (1991) reported substantial gains by African Americans on performance in reading, mathematics, and science as measured in the National Assessment of Educational Progress. These results strongly suggest that the dwindling differences between African Americans and whites are based on prejudice and economic disadvantages that are, hopefully, also fading.

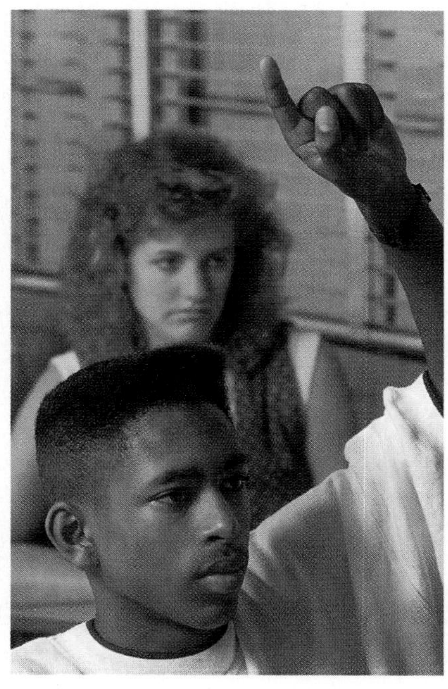

Group differences on intelligence tests, such as college entrance exams, between African Americans and white Americans appear to be dwindling as prejudice and economic barriers weaken.

Extremes in Intelligence: Mental Retardation and Giftedness

Intelligence testing provides one of the main criteria for diagnosing mental retardation. The usual line of demarcation is an IQ of 70 or below, which results in about 2 percent of the American population being diagnosed as retarded. In addition to IQ, an individual's ability in self-care activities and relating to others is considered in making a diagnosis. Degrees of retardation range from mild to profound: individuals with IQs from 50 to 70 are mildly retarded; 35 to 49, moderately retarded; 20 to 34, severely retarded; and under 20, profoundly retarded.

Retardation can result from a wide number of conditions. Genetic disorders, birth trauma, maternal infections, maternal use of alcohol or psychoactive drugs, or sensory or maternal deprivation early in life are only a few of the possible causes linked to retardation. Since the 1960s educational efforts for those who have mental retardation have improved greatly. Since approximately 90 percent of the people who have retardation fall in the mild range, the vast majority of people with retardation can lead satisfying and productive lives (Tyler, 1965). Recently, people who have mental retardation have played featured roles in popular television shows, which has educated the general population by highlighting their abilities, rather than disabilities.

At the other end of the scale, public school systems across the United States provide special educational programs for "gifted" children. "Gifted" is usually defined in terms of high IQ scores, but with some attention being paid to creativity. These programs are funded on two grounds: (a) that the nation needs to enrich the education of its brightest future leaders, and (b) that these children are so bright that they sometimes need help to avoid developing psychological problems. This latter argument—that being more intelligent than one's peers causes problems—is not universally accepted. Is it true that being intelligent is generally a handicap or is it an advantage like we have heretofore assumed?

The best answer to this question comes from the research of Lewis Terman (1925), creator of the Stanford-Binet Intelligence Scale and expert on high intelligence. In the early 1920s Terman identified more than 1,500 highly intelligent boys and girls living in California. They were mostly between the ages of 8 and 12 when identified and had IQs that averaged about 150. Terman studied these geniuses—affectionately nicknamed the "Termites"—both as children and later as adults. Follow-up evaluations of Terman's Termites when they reached their 60s and 70s were reported by Richard Herrnstein (1971) and Daniel Goleman (1980).

As children, the gifted Termite group was found to be functioning very well in every evaluated area of life. They made better grades in school, were considered more honest and trustworthy, and were taller and stronger than their peers of average IQ. In their middle 40s, the Termites were still found to be highly successful. About 70 percent had graduated from college (compared with about 8 percent of their generation), 40 percent of the male graduates had earned law degrees, medical degrees, or Ph.D. degrees, and 85 percent were working as professionals or as managers in business. Their total family incomes were more than double the average for families from the same ethnic group and socioeconomic status, but perhaps reflecting the era during which they grew up, the educational and occupational success of the women was well behind that of the men. Physically, the gifted Termite group was still considered superior to their peers, in that their death rate was one-third less than the national average. The Termites experience no fewer minor emotional problems than average but showed lower rates of alcoholism and criminal convictions. The highly intelligent Termites are still doing far better than average in many ways near the end of their working years. These results clearly suggest that high intelligence is generally a good quality to possess.

Recently, a similar follow-up study was published of a sample of 210 highly intelligent adults (mean IQ of 159) who had attended an elementary school for gifted children in New York City in the 1940s and 1950s (Subotnik, Kassan, Summers, & Wasser, 1993). Like the highly intelligent persons in the Terman study, this group was found to be highly successful and healthy during middle adulthood. Over 80 percent had obtained at least a master's degree, and their incomes were much higher than the national average. Perhaps because they were born 25 years later, however, when barriers to success for women were less restrictive, the highly intelligent women were much more successful than in the Terman study. Forty percent of the women had earned a Ph.D., law degree, or medical degree, and the same percentage of women were working in professional careers as men (53 percent of both). Only two of the gifted women identified themselves as primarily homemakers.

Not surprisingly, however, the men in this sample received significantly more income than the women, reflecting the large gender differences in earnings in the U.S. population as a whole. Even when women and men in this sample were matched on their occupations, the women made 40 percent less than the men on the average.

Do you have any children? If so, is one of your children gifted? Depending on the age of your child, it may be too early to tell. It is possible to test the IQ of young children, but intelligence scores can change quite a bit over time in young children. The Berkeley Growth Study followed a large number of individuals from birth to age 25. One major interest of the researchers was the stability of IQ scores at different ages (Bayley, 1965). The results of this study showed that there was virtually no relationship between IQ scores taken at age 2 and age 18. This means that it is not possible to predict an individual's adult IQ from an IQ test given at age 2 (Jensen, 1980). Prediction of adult IQ from scores obtained at age 6 is fairly good, but IQ scores don't become truly stable until about age 7 to 10. We must not be in too big a rush to measure a child's IQ—it might change considerably between early childhood and adulthood.

Review

The term *intelligence* refers to our ability to use cognitive processes to cope with the demands of daily life. This vague concept has found an important place in contemporary psychology because tests have been developed that predict with reasonable accuracy performance on tasks that require intelligence, particularly school performance. Scores on these intelligence (IQ) tests indicate whether an individual has correctly answered as many questions as the average person of his or her own age. Higher IQs indicate that the person has scored the same number of points as the average person of an older age; lower IQs indicate the opposite. Useful IQ tests must be standardized, evaluated against proper norms, objective, reliable, and valid.

Most psychologists think of intelligence both as a single general factor and as many independent facets of intellectual ability. Consequently, the most widely used IQ tests report both a general score and several more specific scores. Some facets of intelligence, however, particularly everyday intelligence, are not measured well by general tests of intelligence that focus more on school intelligence. It is probable that both heredity and environmental factors help determine all aspects of an individual's level of intelligence.

Thinking Critically About Psychology

1. If psychologists do not agree about the nature of intelligence, how is it possible for them to agree on a test of intelligence?

2. Having read this material about what intelligence may be and how it is tested, what relationship do you think exists between the different aspects of intelligence and success in life?

Check Your Learning

To be sure that you have learned the key points from the preceding section, cover the answers below and try to answer each question. If you give an incorrect answer to any question, return to the page given next to the correct answer to see why your answer was not correct.

1. The term ________________ refers to the cognitive abilities of an individual to learn from experience, to reason well, and to cope effectively with the demands of daily living.

2. Although the "deviation IQ" is now used in most modern intelligence tests, the original "ratio IQ" stated that IQ was equal to

- **a.** mental age divided by chronological age.
- **b.** chronological age divided by mental age.
- **c.** mental age divided by chronological age x 100.
- **d.** chronological age divided by mental age x 100.

3. Sternberg's ________________ theory of intelligence states that there are components of intelligence that allow us to (a) learn new information, (b) solve specific problems, and (c) approach problems in general.

4. Heredity is the only factor that determines a person's intelligence.

- **a.** True
- **b.** False

Correct Answers

1. intelligence (p. 262), **2.** c (p. 267), **3.** triarchic (p. 265), **4.** b (p. 273).

APPLICATION OF PSYCHOLOGY

IMPROVING EVERYDAY PROBLEM SOLVING

It could be said that a happy person is not a person who has no problems—for all of us have problems—but a person who is able to solve most of the problems that life tosses his or her way. But as I have stated in this chapter, we human beings are not particularly effective at problem solving. Our abilities to reason and deal with life—as impressive as they may be compared with every other creature on earth—are not always equal to the problems that face us.

Is that a difficult statement for you to accept? Are you still not convinced that we need to take a hard look at our problem-solving abilities to see where they can be improved? If so, let's look at some more typical difficulties in problem solving and then look for solutions. We begin by returning to the important topic of mental set.

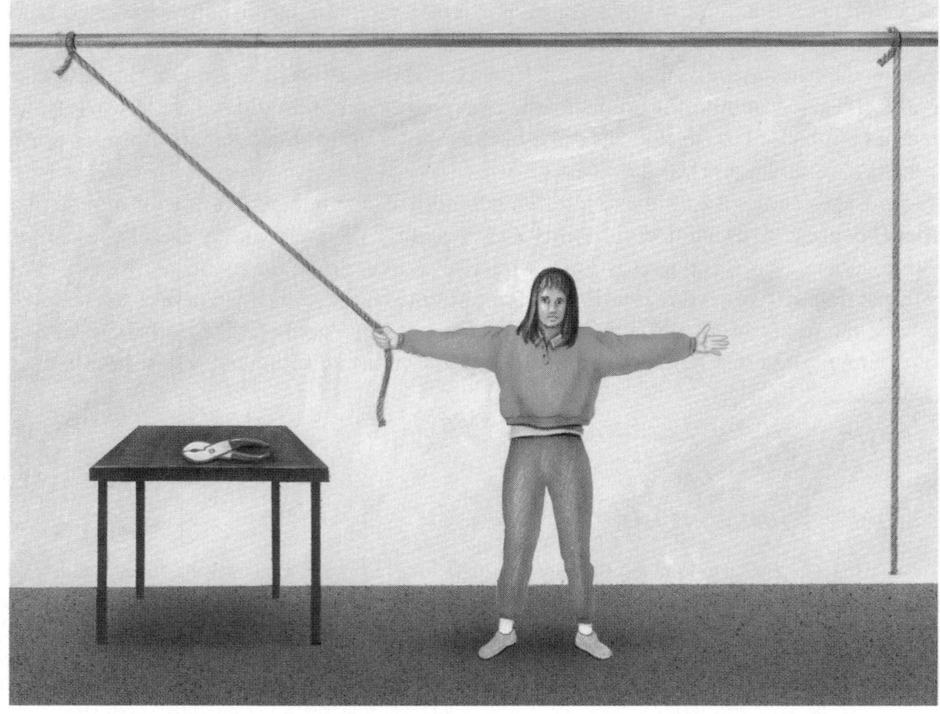

FIGURE 7.10

The Maier string problem. How do you tie the two strings together if you cannot reach them both at the same time? See figure 7.11 for the solution.

The Problem of Mental Set in Problem Solving

As discussed in this chapter, mental set is one of the most common barriers to effective problem solving. Sometimes we must break out of our habitual ways of viewing the elements of the problem to discover a solution. One of the most troublesome of these sets has been referred to as *functional fixedness*. Before we define this term, let's look at a problem where it's encountered. Consider the Maier (1931) string problem. Figure 7.10 shows that you are in a room where two strings are hanging from the ceiling. Your job is to tie the strings together. The problem is that when holding onto one string, you cannot reach the other. The only other thing in the room with you is a pair of pliers, but even holding onto one string with the pliers, you cannot reach the other string. What do you do? Look at figure 7.11 for the solution. The difficulty that most people have in solving this problem is similar to the one in Duncker's candle problem. We are simply not accustomed to using pliers as a pendulum to move a string, just as we wouldn't ordinarily use a matchbox as a candle holder. Karl Duncker (1945) referred to the difficulty we have in seeing new uses for objects as functional fixedness. It's a kind of set that interferes with problem solving by focusing our thinking about the elements in a problem on their habitual uses. Often the key to effective problem solving is being able to break out of functional fixedness and other interfering sets when appropriate.

Let's look at another famous problem that was developed to illustrate the interference of mental set. Psychologist Karl Luchins (1942) asked college students to imagine that they had three jars of different sizes; they then were asked how they would measure an amount of water that was different from that held by any single jar. For example, they might be asked to measure five quarts when the three jars held the quantities as shown here.

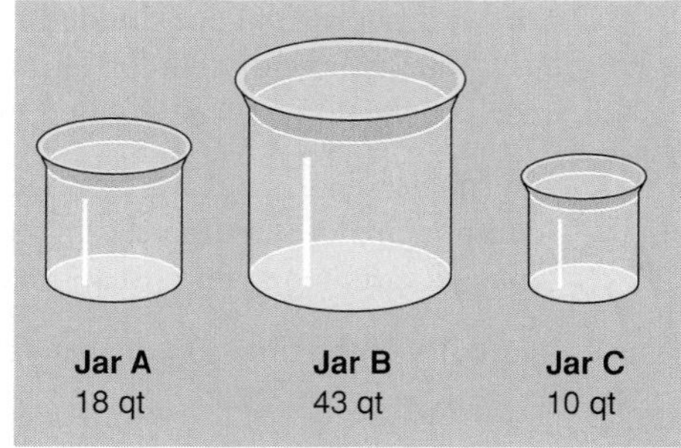

How would you solve this problem? Five quarts can be measured by filling jar B, then pouring water from it until jar A is filled, leaving 25 quarts in jar B. Then jar C is filled twice from jar B, leaving 5 quarts in jar B. It's simple when you catch on to the method. In algebraic terms, the solution can be expressed as B – A – 2C.

After solving five more problems using jars of different sizes, all of which could be solved using the equation B – A – 2C, the subjects were given a problem like this: Measure 20 quarts when jar A contains 24 quarts; jar B contains 52 quarts, and jar C contains 4 quarts. This

FIGURE 7.11

The solution to the Maier string problem is to use the pliers as a pendulum to bring the second string closer.

problem could also be solved using the equation B – A – 2C, but did you solve it that way? Or did you see that it could be solved more simply by subtracting one jar C from jar A (A – C)? In Luchins's study, more than three-fourths of his students solved the problem the long way.

Why did Luchins's students make a difficult problem out of a simple one? Do people just have a tendency to do everything the hard way? Luchins ruled out that unlikely possibility in his experiment by having another group of students skip the first six B – A – 2C problems and solve the seventh problem *first*. These students *all* used the simple A – C solution. The students who took the long solution to the seventh problem after solving six B – A – 2C problems simply had fallen into a "mental rut" or set.

Are you becoming convinced that human problem solving is rather predictably fallible? If not, try your intellect on one last example of the interfering effects of set:

> A small boy and his father were out together for a bicycle ride when a runaway truck hit them. They were both seriously injured and were rushed, unconscious, to the nearest hospital. While the more critically injured father was taken directly to an operating room, the boy was wheeled to an emergency ward for examination. A doctor on call was summoned; the doctor entered the emergency ward and exclaimed in surprise, "Oh heavens, that's my son!" (Reynolds & Flagg, 1983, p. 53)

Do you see how the doctor's statement could be correct? If not, let me give you a hint to break the effect of set. Are you being sexist? That's right—the doctor is the boy's mother. None of us should fall victim to that kind of prejudicial set in these enlightened times, but many of us still do.

As we look for ways to improve problem solving in everyday life, we must be careful to examine our way of understanding the elements of the problem to avoid functional fixedness, prejudice, or other forms of mental set that may be interfering with optimal problem solving. The problem may be solvable if you look at it the right way.

Heuristics and Difficulties Reasoning About Probabilities

Human problem solvers often have great difficulty reasoning about probabilities—the likelihood that something will happen. Unfortunately, many of the most important decisions that we face in life involve estimating probabilities. You have to choose a major in college that you think will give you the best chance of a satisfying career, choose a partner with whom you feel you can have a long and meaningful relationship, buy enough insurance to cover all likelihoods, and so on. Being able to reason well about probabilities is extremely important.

Let's look at a common problem in reasoning about probabilities called the *conjunction fallacy* by Amos Tversky and Daniel Kahneman (1983). In one of their studies, college students were asked to judge which of the following two occurrences was more probable during the coming year:

> **A.** A massive flood somewhere in North America, in which more than 1,000 people drown.
>
> **B.** An earthquake in California, causing a flood in which more than 1,000 people drown.

Which do you think is the more likely event? Logically, A is much more likely than B for two reasons. First, alternative B is limited to a specific part of North America, whereas the flood in alternative A could happen *anywhere* in North America, *including California*. More pertinent to our discussion is the fact that alternative B requires the *conjunction*—meaning the joint occurrence—of two events (the flood killing more than 1,000 people and the earthquake causing the flood must *both* occur). Mathematically, the probability of two independent events occurring together is calculated by multiplying the probability of one event times the probability of the other event. That is, if the probability of an earthquake is 1/1,000 and the probability of a major flood caused by an earthquake is

1/1,000, then the probability of both occurring together is 1/1,000 × 1/1,000 or one in a million!

Thus (using our hypothetical estimates as approximations), alternative A is at least a *thousand* times more likely to occur than B. In spite of this fact, the majority of the students in this study thought that B was more probable! Why is this so? Tversky and Kahneman suggest many people make this error because they reason in shortcut heuristics. Because we think of California as being a high-risk area for earthquakes, the presence of the terms *California* and *earthquake* makes alternative B seem intuitively (heuristically) more likely. Human logic is easily led astray by such heuristic thinking.

So how do we avoid such errors in reasoning? One strategy would be to avoid making snap judgments based on intuitive heuristics. If you did not choose the wrong alternative in the flood question, you have already learned to look carefully at questions of probability and reason logically about them. If you chose the wrong alternative, you may be in the habit of using your intuition more than your logic.

A General Strategy for Effective Problem Solving

A number of psychologists have frequently written about the need for all of us to learn to solve problems more effectively (Goldfried & Davison, 1976; Turkat & Calhoun, 1980). No one is going to solve all problems well, but we could all stand a little improvement. A simple flowchart that outlines effective problem solving may help.

You might try going through a hypothetical problem using this strategy just to see how it works. Suppose you run out of money for school—what would the best solution to this problem be for you? A loan? A part-time job? By trying this general outline for problem solving and the other ideas presented in this section, you may be better prepared to deal with the next curve ball that life throws at you.

1. What is the problem?
   a. Define the problem in clear, specific terms.
   b. Avoid mental sets and try to think about the problem in flexible ways.
2. Generate all possible solutions.
   a. At first, do not judge any solution—just keep thinking of alternative solutions.
   b. Wild ideas are welcome!
   c. See if some of your possible solutions can be combined to make a better possible solution.
3. Now, eliminate any possible solutions that are clearly poor choices.
   a. Alternatives with no chance of success should be dropped.
   b. Intuitive solutions based on heuristic reasoning should be eliminated in situations where logical (algorithmic) reasoning is possible.
4. Examine the likely consequences of the remaining possible solutions one at a time.
   a. List all possible negative consequences of this option.
   b. List all possible positive consequences of this option.
   c. Eliminate the option if it is more likely to produce negative than positive consequences.
   d. Go on to the next option (and repeat steps a–c).
   e. Compare all remaining options in terms of likely consequences.
   f. Select the solution with the greatest likelihood of more positive consequences than negative consequences.
5. Generate all possible ways to implement the solution you have chosen (how can I best do this?)
   a. Use steps 2–4 to select the best way to implement the solution.
6. Implement the solution.

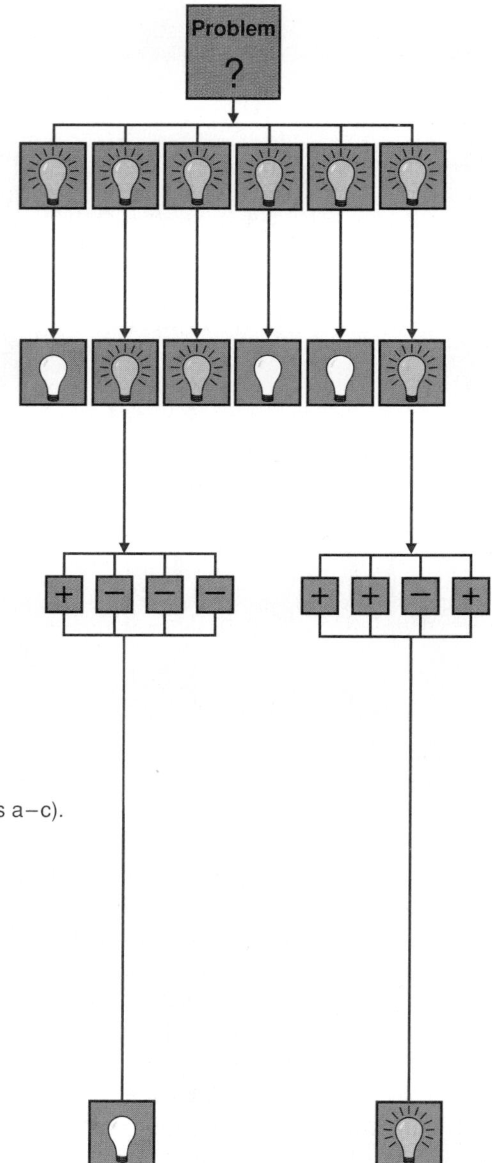

Summary

Chapter 7 discusses our intellectual processes, how we use language, and how human intelligence is measured.

I. In the process of cognition, information is obtained through the senses, transformed through the interpretive processes of perception and thinking, stored and retrieved through the processes of memory, and used in the processes of problem solving and language.

II. Concepts, the basic units of thinking, are categories of things, events, or qualities linked together by some common feature or features.
   - A. Some concepts are categories based on a single common feature; others are more complex.
      1. Members of categories defined by conjunctive concepts have two or more common characteristics.
      2. Members of disjunctive concepts have either one common characteristic or another one, or both.
   - B. Concept formation is a special kind of learning in which hypotheses about the defining characteristics of a concept are tested by examining positive and negative instances of the concept.
   - C. All concepts are not equally easy for us to learn; some are more natural than others.

III. In problem solving, information is used to reach a goal that is blocked by an obstacle.
   - A. Cognitive operations are used to solve problems. After we decide what kind of problem we face, we evaluate the elements of the problem and decide what information and tools we have to work with. Then we generate a list of solutions and evaluate them.
   - B. Algorithmic and heuristic operations are two types of cognitive strategies used in solving problems.
   - C. Creative problem solving requires the ability to think in flexible and unusual ways (divergent thinking); the most useful creative solutions are also thought out logically and realistically (convergent thinking).

IV. Language is a symbolic code used in human communication.
   - A. Semantic content is the meaning communicated through language.
   - B. We generate language from a set of elements and a set of rules for combining them into speech.
      1. The phoneme is the smallest unit of sound in a language. The English language has only 44 phonemes.
      2. Morphemes are the smallest units of meaning in a language.
      3. Syntax is the rules of a language through which an infinite number of understandable utterances are generated.
   - C. Much of our thinking is in the form of language.
      1. The Whorfian, or linguistic relativity, hypothesis states that the structure of language influences how people think.

V. Intelligence refers to the cognitive abilities of an individual to learn from experience, to reason well, and to cope effectively with the demands of daily living.
   - A. Intelligence is viewed as a single general factor by some psychologists and as many independent kinds of intellectual ability by others.
   - B. Intelligence tests measure a small sample of the cognitive abilities that constitute intelligence.
      1. Useful IQ tests must be standardized, objective, reliable, valid, and evaluated against proper norms.
   - C. Intelligence tests measure "school intelligence" better than "everyday intelligence," which may be assessed better with more specialized tests.
   - D. Both heredity and environmental factors help determine an individual's level of intelligence.

Suggested Readings

1. A classic statement on the psychology of language is provided by: Slobin, D. I. (1979). *Psycholinguistics.* Glenview, IL: Scott, Foresman.
2. A scholarly and readable overview of cognition: Ellis, H. C., & Hunt, R. R. (1996). *Fundamentals of human memory and cognition* (6th ed.). Madison: Brown & Benchmark.
3. For a firsthand account of Francine (Penny) Patterson's attempt to teach language to a gorilla and of Herbert Terrace's experiences with the chimpanzee Nim Chimpsky: Patterson, F., & Linden, E. (1981). *The education of Koko.* New York, NY: Henry Holt; and Terrace, H. S. (1980). *Nim.* New York: Knopf.
4. For differing views on the topic of ethnic differences in intelligence: Jensen, A. R. (1980). *Bias in mental testing.* New York: Free Press; Kamin, L. J. (1974). *The science and politics of IQ.* Potomac, MD: Lawrence Erlbaum; Mackenzie, B. (1984). Explaining race differences in IQ: The logic, the methodology, and the evidence. *American Psychologist, 39,* 1207–1213; Herrnstein, R. J., & Murray, C. (1994). *The bell curve: Intelligence and class structure in American life.* New York: Free Press; and Hunt, E. (1995). The role of intelligence in modern society. *American Scientist, 83,* 356–368.
5. For good statements on intelligence: Frederiksen, N. (1986). Toward a broader conception of human intelligence. *American Psychologist, 41,* 445–452; and Neisser, U. et al. (1996). Intelligence: Knowns and unknowns. *American Psychologist, 51,* 77–101.

PART 4 The Life Span

CHAPTER 8

CHAPTER OUTLINE

Developmental Psychology

PROLOGUE

Jean Piaget was a notable Swiss scientist who studied the development of cognition in children until his death in 1980. His most important contribution was to show us that children of different ages understand the world in ways that are often very different from the way adults understand it. Indeed, young children understand their worlds in ways that are so different from adults that it is sometimes like trying to communicate with a creature from another galaxy!

Imagine that you drop by your instructor's office for a visit and sit down on the opposite side of her desk. Would the objects on top of the desk look exactly the same to you and your instructor? Of course not. The paper clip that you see in front of her coffee cup is hidden from her view, and you can't see the wad of bubble gum that is stuck to her side of the pencil sharpener. We adults have so little trouble understanding that our perception of things depends on our perspective that we take this ability for granted. However, we are not born with the ability to take another person's perspective—it develops over time.

A classic experiment by Piaget and his frequent collaborator Barbel Inhelder (1963) makes this point very well. Children of different ages were shown three small three-dimensional replicas of "mountains" arranged on a table top. On the other side of the table, a doll was seated. The children were asked to look at the mountains and then were asked to indicate which picture from several showed the mountains as the doll would see them. Six-year-olds could not do it at all, some 7- and 8-year-olds could, and children 9 to 11 years of age had no more trouble with the task than an adult would.

Life doesn't stand still. We are in a state of constant change throughout our lives. When we ask ourselves who we are, we think of ourselves in terms of who we are *now.* But we have been and will be many different people in our lifetime: an infant, a child, a teenager, a young adult, a mature person, and an aged person. The thread of continuity that runs through our lives

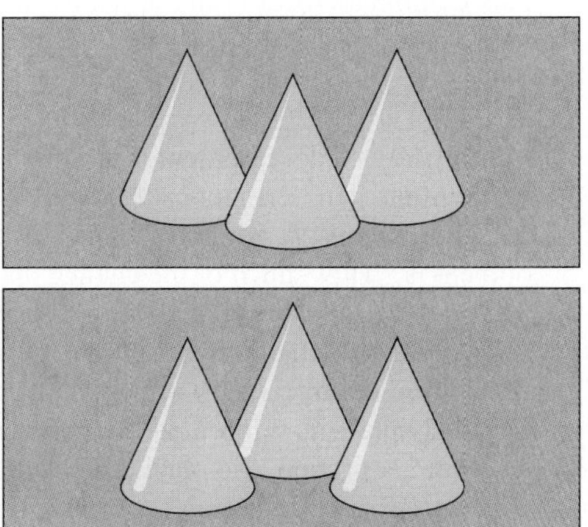

What does the doll see?

KEY TERMS

development
The more-or-less predictable changes in behavior associated with increasing age.

developmental psychology
Field of psychology that focuses on development across the life span.

is very real, but we change more than we realize. To understand ourselves fully, we must understand the process of **development,** the more-or-less predictable changes in behavior associated with age.

Why do we change as we grow older? Psychologists differ on the question of how much of our development is biologically determined or shaped by the learning environment, but most believe that development is the product of the combined forces of "nature" (biology) and "nurture" (environment). **Developmental psychology** is the field of psychology that focuses on development across the life span. This chapter on developmental psychology is about the person that you were yesterday, are today, and will become tomorrow. Just as we cannot understand butterflies without understanding their metamorphosis from caterpillars, we cannot understand human beings without understanding how they change across the life span.

BASIC PROCESSES OF DEVELOPMENT

What forces cause us to change as we pass through life? What factors determine whether we grow up to be baseball players or umpires, musicians or opticians? In this section we look at the factors that play key roles in the process of development. As you have probably already learned to expect, not all psychologists agree about these factors. So a variety of viewpoints are presented in this chapter.

Both nature and nurture work together in development. Without seeing others play (nurture) a child can't use a baseball glove correctly. But the child must be physically developed enough to use the glove (nature).

Nature or Nurture?

In the past, some psychological theorists asserted that nearly all important developmental changes are controlled by biological factors (nature): Our behavior "unfolds" over time, like a plant growing from seed to flower. Other theorists asserted that the psychological environment (nurture) is the master of our development: Our behavior is "molded" by experiences, like clay in the hands of a sculptor. Current thinking asserts that both nature and nurture combine to influence our actions, thoughts, and feelings (Santrock, 1995).

Language provides a good example of the rich interplay of nature and nurture in our lives. There can be no question that experience is important in language development. Children will learn to use language only if they are exposed to language, and will learn to speak the language to which they are exposed. For example, a French child adopted by a Chinese-speaking family will grow up speaking Chinese, not French. But neither goldfish nor marmosets will learn to speak a human language when given the same amount of experience required by a human child to learn language. One must have a human brain (or as discussed in chapter 7, an ape brain might be sufficient) to learn a human language. In the absence of the right nature, nurture can accomplish nothing.

Other examples of the blending of nature and nurture abound in child development. Children cannot use a baseball glove correctly unless they have seen others play ball (nurture). But you cannot effectively teach children to do much with a glove until age 4 or so when considerable physical development has taken place (nature). We are creatures of complex combinations of both our nature and nurture.

Maturation

maturation
(mach´´u-rā´shun) Systematic physical growth of the body, including the nervous system.

In the study of development, the most important aspect of nature (biological factors) is **maturation.** This term refers to systematic physical growth of the nervous system and other bodily structures. A primary question for the psychologist specializing in the study of development is, "How much of the change that we see occurring with age is the result of physical maturation rather than increased experience?"

Although both experience and maturation are important in most developmental changes, maturation is surprisingly important in many specific contexts. For example, experience obviously plays an important role in toilet training—children must be taught to use the toilet—but maturation also plays a key role. According to research, successful toilet training is difficult for most children before the age of 24 months. They are simply not *maturationally*

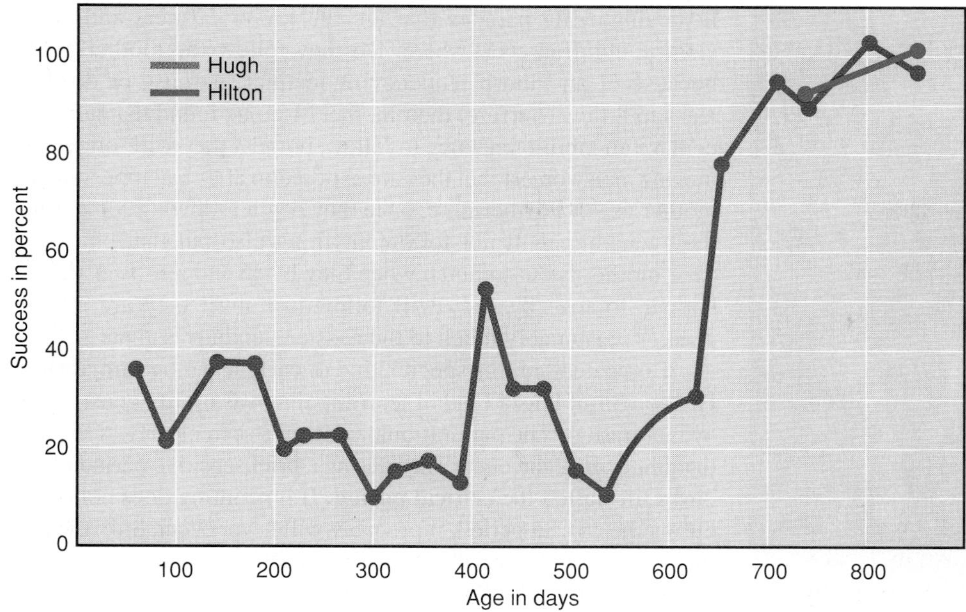

FIGURE 8.1

The importance of maturational readiness is shown in McGraw's (1940) study of toilet training twin boys named Hugh and Hilton. Although Hugh's training was begun at 50 days of age, no progress was achieved until he was about 650 days of age. In contrast, Hilton's progress was rapid because training was begun when he was maturationally ready.

Source: Data from M. B. McGraw, "Neural Maturation as Exemplified in Achievement of Bladder Control," *Journal of Pediatrics,* 16:580–590, 1940.

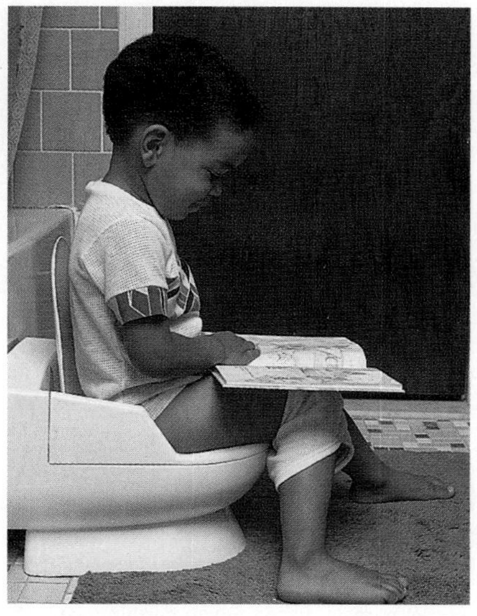

Toilet training, typical of many human behaviors, is learned more quickly when the child is maturationally ready.

ready to learn that task. After 24 months of age, however, most children learn to use the toilet rapidly.

An experiment using identical twin boys illustrates the idea of maturational readiness beautifully. Toilet training was begun for one boy, Hugh, when he was only 50 days old. Training for Hilton, the other twin, did not begin until 700 days of age (almost 2 years). As shown in figure 8.1, Hugh made no real progress until about 20 months of age, whereas Hilton's progress was rapid from the beginning. Both children learned, but only when they reached the proper level of maturation (McGraw, 1940).

Maturation seems to function in much the same way in intellectual, social, and other areas of development. For example, children perform cognitive tasks more quickly and accurately as they grow older largely because the myelin coating that speeds neural transmission in the cerebral cortex (see p. 45 to refresh your knowledge about myelin) continues to grow throughout childhood (Bjorklund & Green, 1992). Perhaps partly as a result, cognition changes dramatically with age. It's unlikely that we could teach an 18-month-old to play cooperatively with other children, teach a 4-year-old the concept of physical mass, or teach the concept of justice to a 6-year-old. These behaviors and concepts generally cannot be learned until later ages, suggesting that maturation of the brain is one of the factors involved in the development of cognition.

Early Experience and Critical Periods

When the Puritans came to America in the 1600s, they brought with them a belief about children that most of us still hold today—namely, that early childhood is the "formative period" for our personalities. We believe that the experiences that we have as a young child powerfully and permanently shape our adult behavior. This is not just a belief held by laypeople; many psychologists hold it, too. But is it true that early experiences irreversibly form our personalities?

Imprinting

Supporting this view that our early experiences are of prime importance is a large body of research on nonhuman animals. German biologist Konrad Lorenz (1937), for example, has extensively studied the behavior and development of the graylag goose. During one phase of his investigations, he wanted to know why young goslings followed their mothers in the

Konrad Lorenz followed by some of his goslings.

little single-file parades that are the joy of farmers and park-visiting children everywhere. Do they follow the mother goose because of an inborn tendency or instinct (nature), or do they learn to follow (nurture) their mother? Lorenz found that goslings do have an inborn tendency to follow, but that they will follow any moving, noisy object that they are exposed to after hatching, not just mother geese. Furthermore, once they begin following something, they generally will not follow anything else but that object. If their mother is out to lunch when they hatch and a rooster should happen to strut by, they will follow him until they are mature geese—presumably much to the rooster's embarrassment.

Lorenz called this special kind of early learning **imprinting.** He thought of it as a kind of learning that was highly constrained by maturation. The maturational control is seen clearly in the fact that imprinting can occur only during a brief sensitive period of the bird's life called the **critical period.** If imprinting does not occur during the critical period, it probably will never occur. Still, the fact that imprinting is a kind of learning—part of nurture—is obvious because the birds will learn to follow anything that meets the biological requirements. Goslings have been imprinted on quacking duck decoys and footballs pulled by squeaking pulleys. A famous *Life* magazine photo even shows Konrad Lorenz being followed by a flock of goslings who had imprinted on him. It's not clear, however, that anything comparable to imprinting occurs in humans, although we do form attachments to our caregivers through prolonged experience with them.

imprinting
(im´print-ing) A form of early learning that occurs in some animals during a critical period.

critical period
A biologically determined period in the life of some animals during which certain forms of learning can take place most easily.

early experiences
Experiences occurring very early in development, believed by some to have lasting effects.

Early Social Deprivation

Studies conducted with monkeys, who are closer to humans on the evolutionary ladder than geese, also show the long-lasting effects of early experience in a way that seems more relevant than imprinting to the human condition. Harry and Margaret Harlow (Harlow & Harlow, 1965; Harlow & Novak, 1973) carried out a number of studies of the role of early social experiences in development. Are our earliest social experiences especially important to the development of social behavior in childhood and adulthood? Sigmund Freud would have us believe that these **early experiences** are of the greatest significance, but until the Harlows, few researchers had experimentally tested Freud's claims.

The Harlows raised a group of infant monkeys in complete isolation for the first few months of life. Later they returned the monkeys, who had never lived with a mother, to regular group cages with other monkeys. When the monkeys reached adulthood (about 3 years of age), they were placed in breeding cages with another monkey of the other sex. It was then that the Harlows noticed that the social, sexual, and emotional behavior of these monkeys was distinctly abnormal. Females raised without early experience with a real mother appeared fearful and viciously attacked the male when a sexual advance was made. The males, on the other hand, alternated between fearfulness and overenthusiastic, clumsy sexual advances.

Although they had normal social experiences for 2 1/2 years, these monkeys' abnormal experiences during the first 6 months of life had a continuing detrimental effect on their social behavior. Moreover, when a few of the females finally became pregnant and had offspring, the lasting effects of the early social deprivation were made more clear. When the mother-deprived monkeys became mothers themselves, they rejected and even attacked their own infants. Some of the mother-deprived mothers even killed their own infants, and the rest had to be removed from the cage to prevent their deaths.

When imprinting studies go awry.

THE FAR SIDE cartoon by Gary Larson is reprinted by permission of Chronicle Features, San Francisco, CA.

These findings are consistent with other facts about the social development of animals. For example, lambs who are removed from the flock and bottle-fed by humans will never return to the flock, even as adults. They show an interest in other sheep, but vacillate between approaching and avoiding them. If artificially impregnated, they allow their young to nurse from them, but they are indifferent mothers.

These studies clearly suggest that abnormal experiences can have a dramatic effect on later social behavior in some kinds of animals, but much less is known about the effects on humans of abnormal early experiences. As a result, opinion is deeply divided among psychologists about this issue. Some believe that abnormal experiences produce irreversible damage (e.g., Bruner, 1974), while others believe that under favorable conditions, the early effects may not be permanent (Kagan, 1984; Parker, Barrett, & Hickie, 1992). Humans may be more open to the effects of experience throughout the life span. Still, this tentative conclusion is based on only a handful of studies of children with abnormal early experiences who were placed in good homes at an early age and showed marked improvement. Children with abnormal early experiences who live in marginally stable families might be less able to recover.

Harry Harlow (1905–1981)

Margaret Harlow (1918–1971)

The Harlow studies of early social deprivation in monkeys revealed that abnormal experiences during the first 6 months of life have a detrimental effect on the social behavior of adult monkeys.

Variations in Development: Getting There at Different Times

Anyone who deals with children as a parent, teacher, or other professional must understand that it's normal for development to be highly variable. This is true in two senses: (a) there are differences between children in their development; (b) and children vary in the rate of their own development from one period to the next.

Different children develop at different rates. It's normal for one child to walk or talk several months before another child. When we look at charts of the normal age at which children sit, walk, speak in sentences, and so on, we must remember that variations from those norms may mean nothing at all. Deviations from the average are not unusual. Variation is the rule, not the exception, in child development. Any large variation in development should be discussed with a pediatrician or child psychologist, but small variations should not be a cause for concern.

It's also normal for children to be variable in their own development. Children who are shorter than their age-mates often shoot up suddenly to become taller than most. A fussy baby can become a calm, happy child. And it's not unusual for a child who was above average on an IQ test at age 4 to be just average at age 9 or vice versa. Discontinuities in development, again, are the rule rather than the exception.

Studies suggest that the effects of abnormal early experiences can be reversed by positive, appropriate experiences at later ages. Sometimes these positive experiences are with adoptive parents.

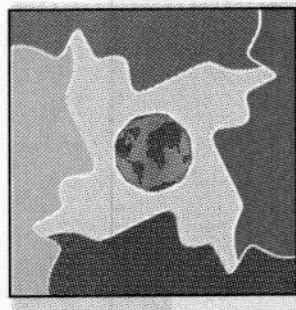

HUMAN DIVERSITY

Raising a Child Who Cannot Hear

All parents must make important decisions about raising children that can have a major impact on their child's emotional and intellectual development. The parents of children who are challenged by physical or sensory limitations, however, face a number of additional decisions. In the case of children with little or no hearing, for example, parents must first decide if the child will learn to speak orally (called "voice") or will learn sign language. The parents of Montreal Expos team member Curtis Pride felt that he would always be an outsider if he did not learn to voice (Gildea, 1993). Other parents disagree, however. They feel that the child will not be able to enter the *deaf culture* (Rutherford, 1988) if sign language is not learned. Many deaf people consider themselves as part of a distinct cultural group rather than having a physical disability. They feel that a deaf child who does not learn sign language will not fully join the only culture that will truly accept the child.

Another choice parents must make is whether to send their child to a residential school for deaf children or to send her or him to a neighborhood school with hearing children. Some parents of deaf children feel that it is best for them to learn to be part of the mainstream culture. Many deaf persons, however, feel that residential schools are better because they allow deaf children to be part of an accepting community, to communicate freely with others, and to develop more fully. Unlike some other groups who are different from the majority of the population, many deaf persons object to being "integrated" into the hearing world. No matter how hard they might try to be part of the mainstream culture, they feel that they will remain separate because few hearing people know sign language.

Jan Hafer and Ellen Richmond (1988) encourage hearing parents of deaf children to learn sign language, and to learn about deaf culture and history by interacting with successful deaf persons. But many deaf children live in families where no one has learned sign language. Sign language is a complex language, and it can take parents months or years to learn it. Often, financial and time constraints make it difficult for parents to attend sign language classes, but some experts believe that not doing so can lead to isolation of the child and slow his or her language development (Dolnich, 1993, p. 48).

Technology is progressing in ways that will soon create new options for parents—and new difficult decisions to make. Several years ago the television program "60 Minutes" ran a story about a deaf girl who had a device implanted in the cochlea of her ears that improved her hearing. The parents of the girl described the operation as "a miracle of biblical proportions" (Dolnick, 1993, p. 43). But some deaf persons wrote letters asserting that the surgery amounts to genocide or child abuse. For example, Roslyn Rosen, president of the National Association of the Deaf, stated that she would not prefer to be able to hear. "I'm happy with who I am, and I don't want to be 'fixed'. Would an Italian American rather be a WASP? In our society everyone agrees that whites have an easier time than blacks. But do you think a black person would undergo operations to become white?" (Dolnick, 1993, p. 38).

Do you have any characteristic that sets you apart from other persons or has created barriers for you? Are you in the minority because of your height, weight, ethnicity, sexual orientation, religion, intelligence, attractiveness, or any other feature? Some of the ways in which human beings differ from one another are more challenging or lead to greater discrimination than others, but most of us are in the minority in some way. How has this influenced you? How do you think you would be different if you had a more challenging physical characteristic?

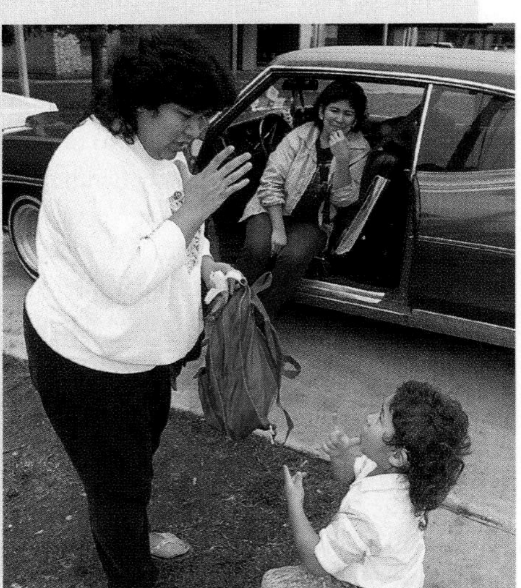

Parents of deaf children often decide to learn to use sign language along with their child, but not everyone thinks this is a good idea.

Review

Children change dramatically from birth to adulthood. This fact has led some theorists in the past to assert that developmental changes in behavior are biologically programmed to "unfold" with increasing age. Other theorists have argued that changes in behavior occur because the learning environment "molds" our development. Today it's generally believed, however, that development results from a blend of both biological and environmental influences. Maturation provides an important example of this interaction between biology and environment: Some forms of learning (that clearly depend on the environment) can occur efficiently only when the child has reached a certain level of readiness through physical maturation.

Experiences during critical periods of early development can have lifelong effects on animal behavior. The Harlows' experiments with social deprivation during the infancy of monkeys also show long-lasting effects of abnormal early experiences. Studies of human infants who have had abnormal early experiences, but who were adopted by normal families during childhood, however, suggest that humans may be less permanently influenced by early experience than other animals, and may be more open to environmental influences throughout the entire life span.

Thinking Critically About Psychology

1. Is there any practical difference in implications of the "molding" and "unfolding" views of development for parents?

2. Do you think there are critical periods in human development?

Check Your Learning

To be sure that you have learned the key points from the preceding section, cover the answers below and try to answer each question. If you give an incorrect answer to any question, return to the page given next to the correct answer to see why your answer was not correct. Remember that these questions cover only some of the important information in this section; it is important that you make up your own questions to check your learning of other facts and concepts.

1. In developmental psychology, the term nurture refers to ________________ factors that influence development.

a. biological
b. environmental
c. both of the above
d. none of the above

2. In the study of development, the most important biological factor is ________________, the systematic physical growth of the body, including the nervous system.

a. maturation
b. hormones
c. growth factors
d. environment

3. A biologically determined period in the life of some animals during which certain forms of learning can take place most easily is called a ______________.

a. stage
b. milestone
c. critical period
d. landmark

4. It is normal for the development of children to be ________________.

Correct Answers

1. b (p. 286), **2.** a (p. 286), **3.** c (p. 288), **4.** variable (p. 289).

STAGE THEORIES OF DEVELOPMENT

stage
One of several time periods in development that is qualitatively distinct from the periods that come before and after.

Although all psychologists agree that people change over time, they disagree considerably over how to conceptualize those changes. One group sees us as changing gradually with age; the other school of thought sees people as going through a series of abrupt changes from one stage to the next. To relate this difference in opinion to our previous discussion, those who see gradual changes generally lean more toward a "molding" view by which they interpret behavior as gradually changing, mostly due to increasing experience. Those who see **stages** in development typically lean toward a view in which behavior "unfolds" over time, largely due to biological maturation.

Stage theorists believe that the changes occurring from one stage to the next make children qualitatively different (different in "kind") rather than quantitatively different (different in amount) from what they were at a previous stage. When a child learns to use simple words to express herself, for example, she has changed qualitatively; that is, she has become different from the kind of child she was when she could not use language. This qualitative change opens up new experiences and possibilities. Although stage theorists believe that changes between stages are qualitative, they believe that children also change quantitatively during each stage. For example, once the child has mastered some simple words, she will progress for a while by learning more simple words before the next qualitative change takes place (combining words syntactically).

Stage theorists also believe that all children must pass through the same qualitatively different stages in the same order. Stages are believed to be biologically programmed to unfold in a fixed sequence in all normal persons. In addition, they believe that a child cannot progress to the next stage until the current one has been mastered.

One notable critic of stage theory has been British psychologist T. G. R. Bower (1971). He has pointed out in a variety of studies that the transition from one "stage" to another is often quite gradual and variable. A close examination of the writings of even the staunchest stage theorists, however, shows that they recognize that the transition from one stage to the next is a gradual blending. In other words, a child may master one part of a new stage while still struggling with part of a previous stage. One gifted professor of psychology suggested to me that the stages of child development are like a rainbow: We can see that there are different colors in a rainbow, but it's not possible to see exactly where one color stops and the next one begins. Stages of development, like the colors in a rainbow, blend together.

In the sections that follow, we discuss several major stage theories of cognitive development, moral development, and personality development. By taking a close look at each of these theories, we will better appreciate stage theories in general and learn a little about the development of children in each of these three important areas.

Piaget's Stage Theory of Cognitive Development

Jean Piaget (1896–1980)

Perhaps the best-known stage theory in psychology is that of Jean Piaget. Piaget was a Swiss scholar who wrote extensively about the development of cognition in children. Piaget distinguished four major stages of cognitive development. These four stages are summarized in table 8.1. Note that the child's cognitive capacities develop rapidly until about the time of puberty, but change little after that. Note, also, the magnitude of the changes in cognition that occur during the childhood stages. On the average, children progress from human beings who cannot reason in mental symbols to persons fully capable of adult reasoning in 11 short years, with many dramatic changes along the way.

We will look more closely at each of the stages of cognitive development as we follow the course of normal development in detail later in the chapter.

Stage Theories of Moral Development

Two theorists have provided us with stage theories that are related to Piaget's theory of cognitive development but that focus on the development of moral reasoning. Lawrence Kohlberg (1969) proposed the first complete theory of moral development, followed by an important alternative theory provided by Kohlberg's colleague at Harvard University,

TABLE 8.1 Piaget's Stages of Cognitive Development

Sensorimotor Stage (Birth to 2 Years)	Preoperational Stage (2 to 7 Years)	Concrete Operational Stage (7 to 11 Years)	Formal Operational Stage (11 Years On)
The child deals with reality in terms of sensations and motor movements. At this stage, children are unable to reason in mental symbols.	During the preoperational stage the child is capable of symbolic thought and rapidly acquires the ability to use language. Young children's thought is still quite different from that of adults, however. It is often "illogical" in numerous ways that reveal the unique nature of the preoperational child's cognition.	During middle childhood, the child has the ability to reason like an adult in every way except for reasoning about abstract concepts such as justice, infinity, or the meaning of life.	By the end of the stage of childhood, most individuals have progressed to full adult cognition, including the ability to reason using abstract concepts.

Carol Gilligan (1982). Gilligan's stage theory of moral development is also important to psychology for reasons that go beyond the issue of moral development. Her theory represents an effort to ensure that researchers do not unintentionally portray developmental changes in boys as being synonymous with developmental changes in humans in general. Gilligan persuasively argues that females sometimes deal with ethical problems differently than males do. For this reason, when judged by standards developed from research on moral development that primarily used boys as research participants, girls might be seen as being less advanced in their ethical reasoning than boys. As we will see, Gilligan provides an important alternative to this view.

Lawrence Kohlberg (1927–1987)

Kohlberg's Theory of Moral Development

Kohlberg collected the data on which to base his stage theory of moral development by presenting boys with moral dilemmas and asking for evaluations of the people and actions involved. The following is an example of the type of dilemma used by Kohlberg in his research:

> In Europe, a lady was dying because she was very sick. There was one drug that the doctors said might save her. This medicine was discovered by a man living in the same town. It cost him $200 to make it, but he charged $2,000 for just a little of it. The sick lady's husband, Heinz, tried to borrow enough money to buy the drug. He went to everyone he knew to borrow the money. He told the man who made the drug that his wife was dying and asked him to sell the medicine cheaper or let him pay later. But the man said, "No, I made the drug and I'm going to make money from it." So Heinz broke into the store and stole the drug.

Did Heinz do the right thing? Kohlberg was interested in the logical process through which people arrived at their answers to moral dilemmas. He concluded that we pass through the three major levels of the development of moral reasoning shown in table 8.2, although not everyone progresses through all stages of moral development. Nearly all children use only premoral reasoning at age 7, but conventional moral reasoning predominates after age 11. Thus, Kohlberg sees the first two major shifts in moral reasoning as occurring at the same times as the beginnings of the preoperational and concrete operational stages in Piaget's theory of cognitive development. According to Kohlberg, we engage in little principled moral reasoning until age 13, and very few of us ever make it to a stage in which we reason mostly in principled ways. He gives Mahatma Gandhi, Martin Luther King, and Eleanor Roosevelt as examples of persons at the principled stage of moral reasoning (Kohlberg, 1964).

"Not guilty, because puppies do these things."
Drawing by C. Barsotti; © 1987 The New Yorker Magazine, Inc.

Look carefully at the description of each of Kohlberg's stages of moral development and decide if Heinz did the right thing. At the premoral level, he did the wrong thing because it would get him into trouble. At the conventional stage of moral development, Heinz would

TABLE 8.2 Kohlberg's Levels of Moral Development

Premoral Level	Conventional Level	Principled Level
Yong children have no sense of morality as adults understand it. They make moral judgments to obtain rewards and avoid punishment.	At this stage, children make moral decisions on the basis of what they think others will think of them, particularly parents and other persons of authority. Because society's rules, or conventions, state what is expected of them, persons at the conventional level of moral development make moral decisions based on rules.	At this stage, we judge actions on the basis of ethical principles rather than the consequences to us (as in the first two stages). The most advanced moral reasoning within this stage, according to Kohlberg, is based on one's principles of morality, even if they differ from the rules of the larger community.

be judged to be wrong because he clearly broke the law (the conventions of right and wrong). However, from the perspective of principled reasoning, it could be argued that Heinz did the right thing. After trying to obtain the drug legally, he ignored the consequences of his action (imprisonment), disregarded the community's conventions (the laws against theft), and followed what he probably thought was the higher moral principle of saving his wife's life. Does that evaluation bother you? Not everyone would agree that this use of principled reasoning is correct because it tends to place the individual above the law. Indeed, an individual could also explain why Heinz was wrong in terms of the principled stage of moral development. For example, an individual's personal principles might say that it is better for society as a whole to always respect the property rights of others and allow Heinz's wife to die. It is not the particular decision that differs at the different levels of moral development, but the nature of moral reasoning involved.

Gilligan's Theory of Moral Development

Carol Gilligan

Because Kohlberg and others used mostly boys in the initial studies that led to Kohlberg's theory of moral development, Carol Gilligan (1982) has suggested that Kohlberg's theory does not always accurately describe moral development in girls. She argues that female children pass through somewhat different stages. Whereas male development begins with selfish self-interest and moves toward greater reliance on abstract principles of justice, females progress from self-interest toward a balanced concern for the welfare of self and others. Female moral reasoning, in other words, centers on the needs of people rather than on abstractions.

Specifically, Gilligan (1982) suggests that females progress through the three stages of moral development shown in table 8.3. How would the morality of Heinz's actions be judged at each of these stages of moral development? As in Kohlberg's premoral stage, the kind of immature moral reasoning that Gilligan terms the morality as individual survival stage would judge Heinz to be wrong simply because he would be punished. At the morality as self-sacrifice stage, Heinz might be judged to be correct in sacrificing his own welfare to save his wife. At the morality as equality stage, one would have to equally balance the benefits of his actions to Heinz, his wife, and all members of the community in making a moral judgment.

Gilligan's contribution to our understanding of moral development has been acknowledged by Kohlberg and others (Levine, Kohlberg, & Hewer, 1985). However, Kohlberg argues that Gilligan has overemphasized possible sex differences in moral reasoning. Indeed, a review of research on the subject (Walker, 1986) has shown that males and females are more similar in moral reasoning than they are different. This is especially true when men and women with equal levels of education and who hold similar jobs are compared to equate the factor of experience.

TABLE 8.3 Gilligan's Stage Theory of Moral Development

Morality as Individual Survival	Morality as Self-Sacrifice	Morality as Equality
The young child's first sense of what is "right" is what is good for him or her. Young children follow rules to obtain rewards for themselves and to avoid punishment.	The next stage of moral reasoning is attained after becoming aware of the needs of others. In this stage, the person believes that to be good and to be approved of by others, they must sacrifice their own needs and meet the needs of others.	In the most advanced stage of moral development, the person views his or her own needs as equal to those of others. Persons as this stage of moral development have progressed from believing that they must always please others at the expense of their own wishes, to a belief that everyone's needs should be met when possible, and that sacrifices should be shared equally when the needs of different persons cannot all be met. This is a stage of advocacy of nonviolence—it is not right for anyone to be intentionally hurt, including the person himself or herself.

Erikson's Stage Theory of Personality Development

Erik Erikson provides us with a very different example of a stage theory of development. His focus is on the relationships people develop with others in their social world. But, although Erikson, Piaget, Gilligan, and Kohlberg are interested in very different aspects of development, their theories share the common assumptions of stage theory: Each person will pass through a series of qualitatively different stages in a fixed order.

Erik H. Erikson (1902–1994)

Erikson's stages are conceived of somewhat differently than Piaget's or Kohlberg's. They are not periods in which a particular pattern of cognition or moral reason prevails; Erikson's stages are turning points, or *crises,* the outcome of which will partly determine the course of future personality development. In using the term crises, Erikson was not suggesting that these turning points are always experienced as emotionally difficult periods, although they certainly can be for some individuals. Rather, Erikson chose this term to emphasize they can be turning points with far-reaching implications.

The eight stages of Erikson's theory of personality development, which contain the crises, are presented in table 8.4. The name given to each stage by Erikson reflects the two possible outcomes of the stage. To a great extent, particularly in infancy and childhood, the outcome is influenced by the actions of children's parents and other significant people. For example, if infants' parents provide consistent, warm, and adequate care during their child's first year (stage of basic trust vs. mistrust), they will learn to trust the world as a basically safe place. If infants are cared for inconsistently or are physically or emotionally abused, they will consider the world an unsafe place that cannot be trusted. Erikson believed that this basic sense of trust or mistrust is usually carried with the individual throughout life.

To take another example, the challenge of the fourth stage (industry vs. inferiority) is learning to meet the demands placed on the child by parents (to clean his or her room in a way that pleases the parents), by teachers (to read, write, and calculate), and by peers (to ride a bike, to take turns). If the children master these demands, they develop a belief that effort (industry) leads to success. If they fail to meet the demands of this stage, Erikson believed that a lifelong feeling of inferiority develops.

At this point in our discussion of development, the content of these four stage theories is less important than the fact that each illustrates the concept of stages in child development very well. However, we discuss the first three of Piaget's stages more fully as we describe the normal course of human development in the next chapter.

TABLE 8.4 Erik Erikson's Stages of Personality Development

Age	Name of Stage	Developmental Accomplishments or Failures
0–1 year	Basic trust vs. mistrust	Learns to feel comfortable and trust parents' care; or develops a deep distrust of a world that is perceived to be unsafe.
1–3 years	Autonomy vs. shame and doubt	Learns sense of competence by learning to feed self, use toilet, play alone; or feels ashamed and doubts own abilities.
3–5 years	Initiative vs. guilt	Gains ability to use own initiative in planning and carrying out plans; or if cannot live within parents' limits, develops a sense of guilt over misbehavior.
5–11 years	Industry vs. inferiority	Learns to meet the demands imposed by school and home responsibilities; or comes to believe that he or she is inferior to others.
11–18 years	Identity vs. role confusion	Acquires sense of own identity; or is confused about role in life.
18–40 years	Intimacy vs. isolation	Develops couple relationship and joint identity with partner; or becomes isolated from meaningful relationships with others.
40–65 years	Generativity vs. stagnation	Develops a concern with helping others, leaving children, products, and ideas to future generations; or becomes self-centered and stagnant.
65–years on	Integrity vs. despair	Reaps benefits of earlier stages and understands and accepts meaning of a temporary life; or despairs over ever being able to find meaning in life.

Thinking Critically About Psychology

1. What are the similarities between the most advanced stages of moral reasoning described by Kohlberg and Gilligan?

2. What are the advantages of theories like Erikson's for understanding life-span development? What are its disadvantages?

Review

Psychologists who lean toward a view that developmental changes "unfold" largely through maturation also see those developmental changes as occurring in distinct steps or "stages," through which all children pass in the same order. Those psychologists who lean toward a view of developmental changes as being "molded" by learning experiences tend to perceive these changes as being more gradual in nature and not marked by clear-cut stages. It's useful to think of development as occurring in something like stages, but ones that are not clearly separable from one another. Stage theorists view many aspects of human existence as unfolding in stages: cognition (Piaget), moral reasoning (Kohlberg and Gilligan), and personality (Erikson). Although stage theories tend to give us the impression that all children develop at the same rate, variation in development is normal within broad limits.

Check Your Learning

To be sure that you have learned the key points from the preceding section, cover the answers below and try to answer each question. If you give an incorrect answer to any question, return to the page given next to the correct answer to see why your answer was not correct.

1. ____________________ distinguished four major stages of cognitive development, the sensorimotor stage, the preoperational stage, the concrete operational stage, and the formal operational stage.

a. Jean Piaget
b. John Bowlby
c. Sigmund Freud
d. Harry Harlow

2. Kohlberg's theory of moral development was criticized by Gilligan primarily because ____________________ .

a. the data did not support his conclusions
b. it was based on a study of boys only
c. it was done so long ago
d. his subjects consisted of urban children only

Check Your Learning—continued

3. Gilligan suggests that moral reasoning in ________________ centers on the needs of people rather than on abstractions.

   a. males
   b. females
   c. both males and females

4. In Erikson's stage theory of personality development, the stages are turning points, or ________________ , the outcome of which will partly determine the course of future personality development.

Correct Answers

1. a (p. 292–293), 2. b (p. 294), 3. b (p. 294), 4. crises (p. 295).

DEVELOPMENT IN INFANCY AND CHILDHOOD

Let's turn our attention to a description of the normal course of development across the life span. Our topic is the change that takes place from infancy to old age. Do you have any pictures of yourself that were taken when you were an infant? How about photos of you as a child or when you were in high school? I thought it might help me to write about the concept of the "life span" if I were to lay out snapshots of my own life from infancy to today. Six of my photos are on this page. It would have been far better if I could have laid out *your* pictures instead of mine. That way you would have been able to *feel* the point I am trying to make as well as understand it intellectually. You might want to try this later with your own pictures—it's an eye-opening experience.

Look at the changes! The person in all the photos is me—the thread of continuity in my life is very clear—but the changes are certainly obvious, too. Look at that bewildered infant! It's amazing to me that I was ever that small—as an infant I weighed less than 5 percent of what I weigh now—or that there was a time when I could neither walk nor talk. By the time I was 5 and was going off to kindergarten in that dashing sailor suit, I was walking, talking, and tying my shoes. But I could not yet read a book, let alone imagine that I would ever write one.

In high school, I played football and took the advice of my coach that the only proper way to cut hair was *off.* I learned to play guitar the same year that this photo was taken. Later, in the sixties, I grew a lot more hair and sang and played a lot of folk songs (very badly, but it was cool then to sound as bad as Bob Dylan). By the seventies, I was a young professor and clinical child psychologist, working hard to establish a career. I worked long hours and spent a great deal of time with my children. I was so busy that I did not even own a guitar for most of the seventies. Is that a bit of gray creeping into my shaggy head of hair?

In the eighties, my hair was still long, but no longer brown. During this decade, I found time to play the guitar again. In fact, a friend of mine owned a recording studio and he let me live out a childhood fantasy of recording a song! That's me in the studio listening intently to the advice of my bass player, who happens also to be my son. Many changes had taken place in my life by midlife, but when I listened to the recording I found that I still played the guitar badly and sang even worse! The last photo is me in the nineties—back to short hair and showing more than a few wrinkles—but life is still an excellent adventure. Once again, there is little time for the guitar now, but considering my lack of talent, that's for the best.

Now, consider this question: Which picture best represents me—the real me? The answer: all of them. And that is exactly the point of this section on the life span. We are all in a constant state of change—called development—throughout our lives. If you are going to understand human lives, you must understand that fundamental point.

We now begin to tell the story of development across the life span. We follow the child from infancy through the stages of childhood, through adolescence, and finally through the stages of adult life.

Neonatal Period: The Newborn

neonatal period
(ne´´ō-nā´tal) The first 2 weeks of life following birth.

rooting reflex
An automatic response in which an infant turns its head toward stimulation on the cheek.

The first two weeks of life are termed the **neonatal period** and mark the transition from the womb to independent life. What is the world of the neonate like?

Physically, the neonate is weak and dependent on adults. It cannot raise its head or roll over by itself. It does have a repertoire of a few useful reflexive behaviors, however. When stimulated on one side of the mouth, for example, the neonate turns its head toward the stimulation and begins searching and sucking until something is in its mouth. This **rooting reflex** enables the baby to take its mother's nipple in its mouth and nurse.

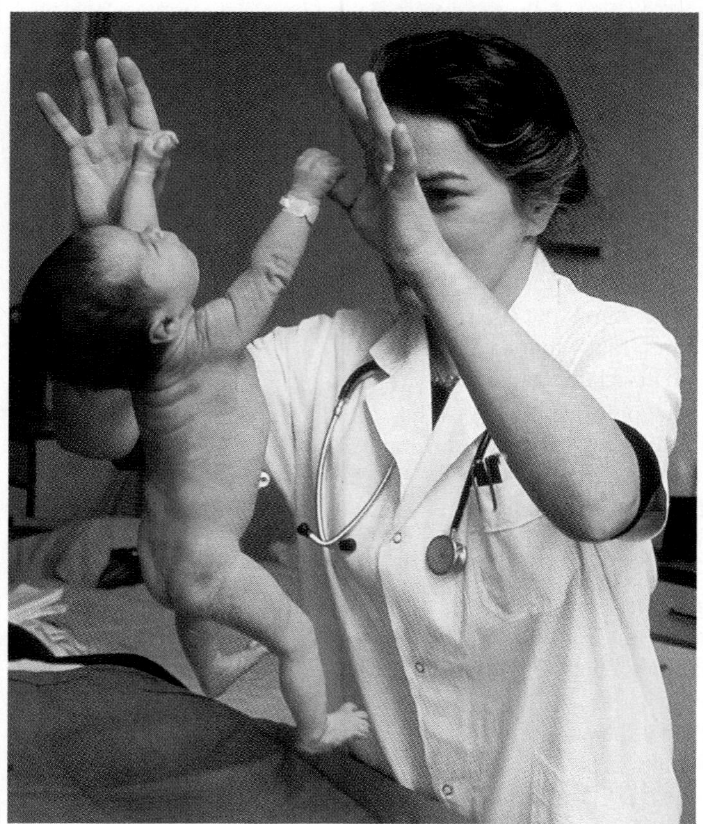

A neonate will reflexively grasp anything that is placed in its hand.

The sensory abilities of neonates are surprisingly well developed. Their hearing is fairly good, and they react differently to different odors and tastes (Santrock, 1995). However, they are distinctly nearsighted little people! They can see fairly well (but probably fuzzily) up to about 12 inches from their eyes, but the world farther away is probably a blur to them (Salapatek, 1977). It was previously believed that the skin senses of neonates were poorly developed, but it is now clear that they are quite sensitive to touch (Santrock, 1995) and that male neonates definitely react to circumcision of the penis without anesthesia as if it is painful (Gunnar, Malone, & Fisch, 1988).

Some cognitive abilities are already developed at birth. A 36-hour-old neonate can imitate some facial expressions of its mother, especially surprise (Field, Woodson, Greenberg, & Cohen, 1982). A 2-week-old neonate can also show some memory for a visual form and can react to different faces as if they are members of the same conceptual class (Cohen, 1979; Santrock, 1995). The process of cognitive development is just beginning, however, and will progress rapidly over the next few years.

The emotions of the neonate are quite diffuse. It's believed that only five basic emotional states can reliably be distinguished in the neonate: surprise, happiness, discomfort, distress, and interest (Izard, 1978). A sixth state, sleep, is very common at this stage, occupying about 16 hours a day (Roffwarg, Muzio, & Dement, 1966). The neonate engages in little of what could be called social behavior, except the intimate contact between neonate and parent in cuddling and nursing. At first, the neonate is a passive participant, but as we will see in a moment, it soon becomes an active partner in social interactions.

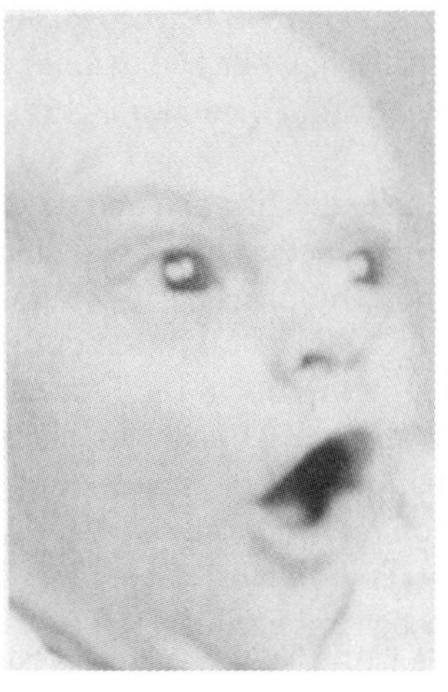

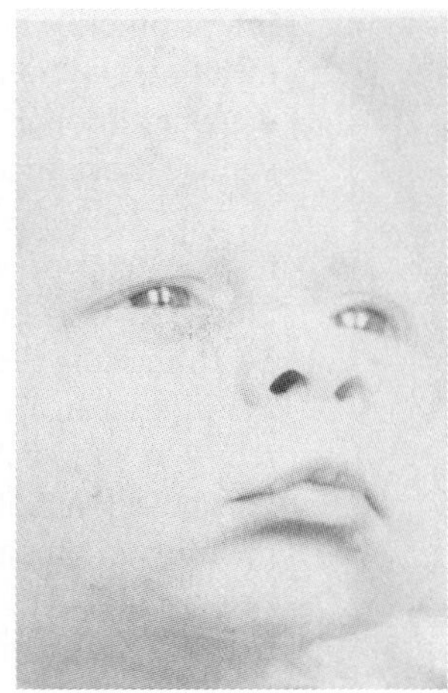
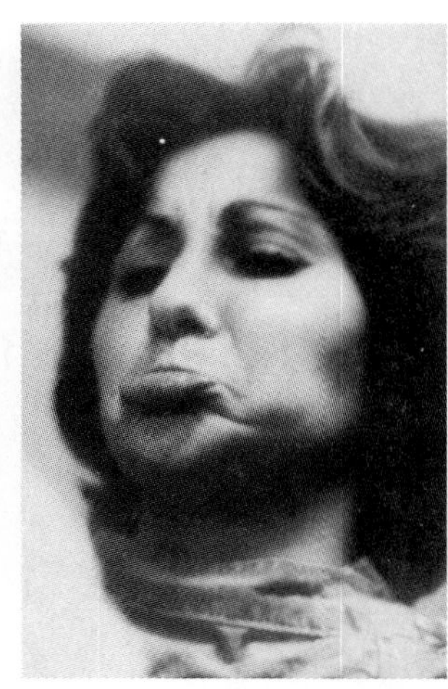

Infancy: 2 Weeks to 2 Years

Physical Development

At 2 weeks of age, the baby acquires the official title of infant. Much is going on developmentally during this period of rapid change. Physical development and growth are more rapid during the first year than at any other time in life. By 2 months, many infants can raise their head and chest on their arms and can grasp an object that is held directly in front of their head and shoulders. By 6 months, many can roll over from back to front, sit, and soon begin to crawl. By 1 year, many can walk alone and grasp small objects with their fingers and thumbs. By 2 years, they are "getting into everything" and walking well, but with the peculiar gait that earns them the nickname of "toddlers."

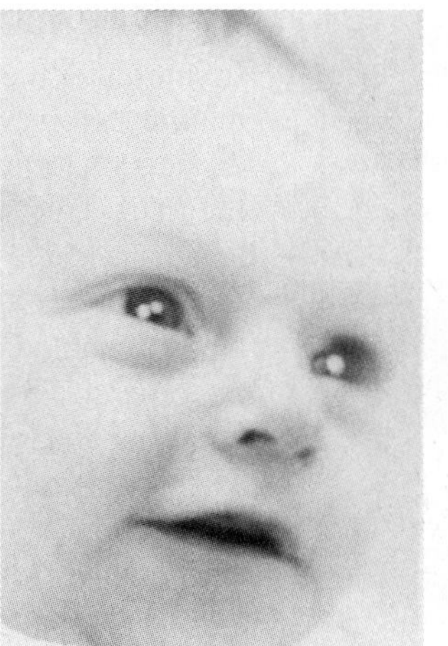

Neonates can imitate the facial expressions of adults to some extent.

From 2 weeks to 2 months, rapid change takes place in all senses. Clear vision increases to 12 feet during this period. By 6 months of age, their vision is 20/20 (normal). Young infants amuse themselves, and their families, by staring at interesting visual stimuli. They prefer to look at patterned stimuli with sharp contours (Banks & Salapatek, 1981). Fortunately for parents, human faces fall into this category.

Cognitive Development (Sensorimotor Stage)

Infancy is the **sensorimotor stage** according to Jean Piaget. During the early part of this stage the infant moves from pure reflexive actions to the ability to coordinate sensations and motor movements, such as voluntarily taking a nipple into the mouth and sucking. From about 2 months on, the infant begins to interact actively with its environment. It no longer passively stares at objects but takes great pleasure in pushing, pulling, and mouthing them. This kind of experience, in which the infant actively changes the sensations it receives by using its hands and feet to alter the environment (sensorimotor experience), is believed to be important in the development of motor behaviors such as crawling (Held & Hein, 1963). By 4 1/2 months most infants respond positively to the sound of their names (Mandel, Jusczyk, & Pisoni, 1995).

sensorimotor stage
In Piaget's theory, the period of cognitive development from birth to 2 years.

Later in this stage, children develop the ability to represent objects from the real world in their mind as an image. For example, by 6 to 9 months of age, the child begins to understand that objects exist even when they are out of sight. This is called **object permanence.** Before that time, if an object at which the infant is looking is hidden from sight by a card, the infant will not push the card aside to look for it. It's as if the infant does not know that the object is still there—a variation of "out of sight, out of mind." After 6 to 9 months of age, however, the infant will search for the object behind the cloth, suggesting that the infant knows that it's back there somewhere. This is both a happy and a sad development for parents. Now that the 9-month-old knows that spoons still exist when thrown on the floor, the

object permanence
The understanding that objects continue to exist when they are not in view.

infant quickly masters the game of "dropsies" (McCall, 1979). They joyously fill their mealtimes with the game of throwing their spoons on the floor while dad or mom picks them up. But although the child can represent parts of the world in mental images, she cannot yet use those images to reason.

By 9 months, too, infants begin to understand some nouns like *ball* and *cookie* and can respond to *bye-bye* and other gestures. These changes mark the beginning of a far more complex level of cognitive functioning. By 12 months, most infants can say some words, and by 18 months the infant has a speaking vocabulary of 20 words. By 18 months the average infant can also understand prohibitions ("No, no . . . don't touch") and can respond correctly to "Show me your nose (ear, toe, mouth, etc.)." By age 2, the infant has a speaking vocabulary of 250 words and speaks in word combinations that fascinate adults in accomplishing so much by saying so little. It has often been referred to as **telegraphic speech** because it leaves out the same words that would be left out of a brief telegram. Sentences like "milk all gone" and "Daddy silly" say all that needs to be said.

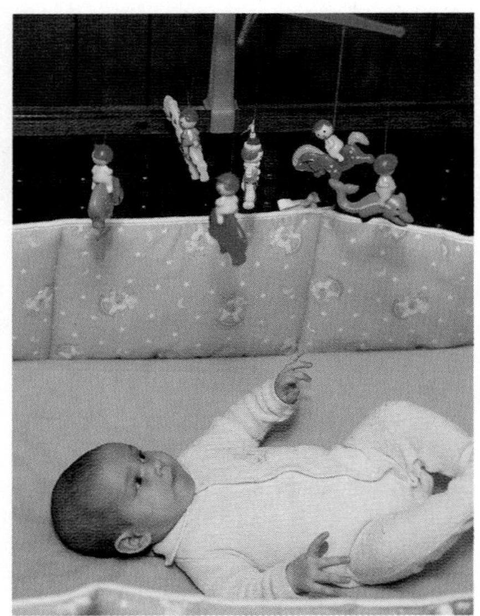

During the sensorimotor stage, infants will stare at interesting visual stimuli, including human faces.

Emotional and Social Development

Infants enter the world with a restricted range of emotions that grows more complex as they mature. Neonates are capable of only three emotional expressions: surprise, pleasure, and distress (National Advisory Mental Health Council, 1995). By about 2 months, they show their first true social behavior—they smile at the faces of their caregivers. By 4 months, they have added a fourth emotion to their repertoire—anger! The infant's repertoire of emotions expands again between 6 to 9 months, when shyness, fear of strangers, and fear of being separated from their caregivers emerge for the first time. Before 6 to 9 months, infants are generally comfortable with any adult who will take care of them, but after that time they are often fearful of anyone but their mother, father, or other caregiver (National Advisory Mental Health Council, 1995). Infants also first learn to fear the sight of a hypodermic needle at about 6 to 9 months (Izard, 1978; Sroufe, 1978). The emergence of social smiling at 2 months is a nice reward for parents who change diapers and walk the floor at night, but the appearance of anger and fear between 4 and 9 months is not always welcome. Both are signs of normal, healthy development of the infant's emotions, however.

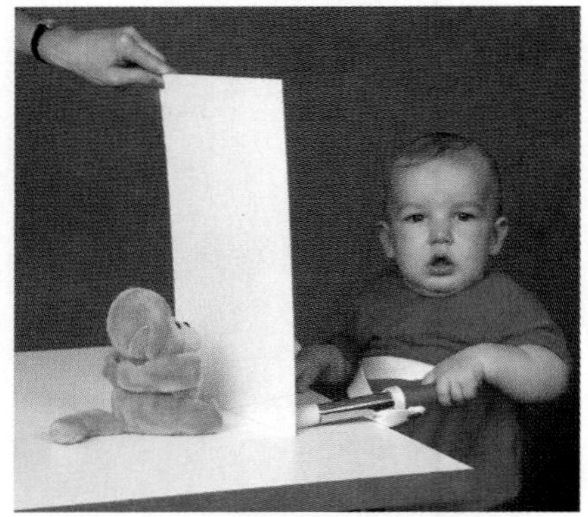

Awareness that objects still exist after they are removed from view (object permanence) occurs between the ages of 6 and 9 months.

Cornell University psychologist Eleanor Gibson has developed an interesting method of studying the development of the fear of heights (Gibson & Walk, 1960). When 6- to 9-month-old infants are placed on the "visual cliff" (see fig. 8.2), they show fear and avoidance of the "deep" side. The visual cliff is made using a clear sheet of Plexiglas. Under one side, a patterned floor is right under the glass. On the other side, the pattern is several feet below the glass. When lighted properly, it appears to be a cliff off of which the infant could fall. It's interesting to note that infants can *perceive* the depth of the visual cliff several months before they show any fear of it. They look puzzled when placed on the deep side of the visual cliff at 4 months but do not show fear until after they can crawl and have experienced stumbling and falling firsthand (Lewis & Rosenblum, 1978; Scarr & Salapatek, 1970).

By 2 years, emotions grow even more complex. By this time, many infants act guilty after misbehavior and seem to feel ashamed after failure. Two-year-old infants are richly social creatures, who have formed strong **attachments** to their parents or other caregivers (Lewis & Rosenblum, 1978). The strength of this attachment can be seen in three ways. First, infants often cling, grasp, grab, and do whatever else they can to stay close to their parents. Nothing short of the parent's physical closeness and undivided attention will suffice at times. Second, when infants 6 to 9 months or older are separated from their parents, they often show intense **separation anxiety**—the crying, fussing, and screaming that babysitters know so well. Third, infants of this age sometimes also exhibit fear of strangers; no one but the adults to whom they are attached (parents, day-care workers, grandparents) have the same soothing effect.

telegraphic speech
The abbreviated speech of 2-year-olds.

attachment
The psychological bond between infants and caregivers.

separation anxiety
The distress experienced by infants when they are separated from their caregivers.

Early Childhood: 2 to 7 Years

According to Piaget, a dramatic change occurs as the child reaches the preoperational stage at about 2 years of age. Notice as you read this section how different the young child is from the infant. Early childhood is still a period of rapid growth, but growth is far less explosive than in infancy and declines in rate annually. Great improvements in the coor-

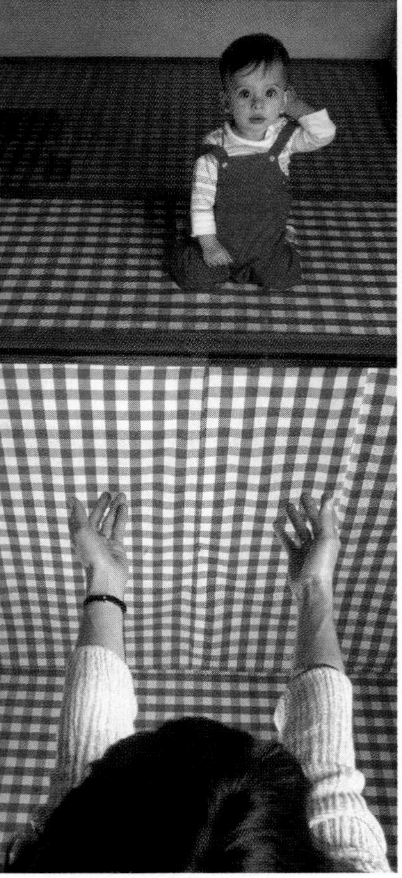

FIGURE 8.2
Eleanor Gibson and Richard Walk (1960) developed the visual cliff to test infant depth perception. The visual cliff consists of a thick sheet of glass placed on a table. The "shallow" end of the visual cliff has a checkerboard surface an inch or so below the glass. The "deep" end of the visual cliff has a checkerboard surface several feet below the glass. An infant who has reached the crawling stage will crawl from the center of the table across the shallow end, but not across the deep end, to reach his or her mother. This indicates that by at least the age of 6 months infants can perceive depth.

dination of small and large muscle groups take place during this period, which sees the emergence of hopping, skipping, throwing, and the other motor behaviors that are so much a part of early childhood.

Cognitive Development (Preoperational Stage)

The **preoperational stage** begins at 2 years of age and is a time of dramatic change in cognition. By about 2 years of age most children are first capable of thinking in mental images. The young child's ability to think is quite different from that of adults, however.

preoperational stage
In Piaget's theory, the period of cognitive development from ages 2 to 7.

The preoperational child's thinking is often quite illogical by adult standards. Indeed, the name of this stage comes from the fact that the child still cannot perform logical mental operations. There are a variety of other ways in which the cognition of the preoperational child is wonderfully distinct. For example, the young child's thought is **egocentric,** or self-centered. Piaget does not mean by this term that the child is selfish, but that the child is simply not able to understand that he or she is not the center of the universe. For example, egocentrism leads young children to believe that inanimate objects are alive, just as they are (known as **animism**). It's common for children of this age to believe that the moon is alive and actually follows them around when they are walking or riding in a car at night.

egocentrism
(e´´gō-sen´trizm) The self-oriented quality in the thinking of preoperational children.

animism
(an´ĭ-mizm) The egocentric belief of preoperational children that inanimate objects are alive like children are.

The child's imagination is often very active at this stage, and because of her egocentrism, it's difficult at times for the child to distinguish real from imaginary. That's why imaginary friends that seem very real to the child are relatively common during this stage. Other errors of logic are quite common, too, giving young children a special kind of logic demonstrated in comments such as "Grandma, he's not your son; he's my dad!"

The amusing beliefs of young children are another good source of information about their logic (Berger, 1986). Many children 3 to 4 years of age believe that babies are purchased, that their parents buy them at hospitals or stores. One child of this age approached his parents with all of his saved money and asked them to buy him a little brother or sister. Other children in this age range understand that children grow inside their mothers, but they have their own special understanding of this process. One 4-year-old thought that his

Strong attachments are formed between infants and caregivers during the first two years of life.

mother had eaten a rabbit or duck and that it had turned into a baby. Another preschooler asked her mother to grow her either a baby or a puppy, whichever she preferred. Another, after hearing a full explanation of sexual reproduction from his mother, responded, "That's the silliest story I ever heard."

Transductive reasoning—errors in inferring cause-and-effect relationships—is also common in the preoperational child. For example, a preoperational child might conclude that spiders cause the basement to be cold. Indeed, the basement *is* cold and there *are* spiders in it, but young children often confuse the cause-and-effect relationships among such facts.

By the end of this period, the preoperational child begins to grasp logical operations and makes fewer cause-and-effect errors. At age 5, the child may be able to pick out all the blue marbles from a jar or all the big marbles, but thinking about two concepts at one time is still difficult. Picking out all the big, blue marbles may still be too much.

Children in the preoperational stage show egocentric thought. They may believe, for example, that the moon is following them as they walk or ride in a car.

Perhaps the most impressive developmental change during the preoperational stage is the growth in language. From a speaking vocabulary of 250 words at age 2, the child reaches a vocabulary of more than 14,000 words by age 6, learning a phenomenal average of almost nine new words per day (Carey, 1977; Santrock, 1995)! From simple two- or three-word combinations at age 2, the child masters much of adult syntax during the same period. Seemingly, the child has finally achieved the maturational capacity to learn language and proceeds to do so without hesitation.

transductive reasoning
(trans-duk´tiv) Errors in understanding cause-and-effect relationships that are commonly made by preoperational children.

solitary play
Playing alone.

parallel play
Playing near but not with another child.

cooperative play
Play that involves cooperation between two or more children.

Emotional and Social Development

Both positive and negative emotions are fairly well developed by age 2, but they become considerably richer and more intricate during the preoperational stage. Most of this elaboration of emotion seems to be linked to cognitive development. For example, children do not develop fears of unexperienced things—such as fires, drowning, and traffic accidents—until well into the preoperational period when they are capable of understanding the concepts behind the fears.

The most notable social changes during this period occur in relationships with peers. At age 2, most children engage in **solitary play.** That is, they play by themselves, even if other children are present. This type of play rapidly decreases in frequency from ages 2 to 5. At first, solitary play is replaced by **parallel play,** in which children play *near* one another in similar activities, but not *with* one another. By the end of the preoperational stage, **cooperative play,** which involves a cooperative give-and-take, has become the predominant type of play (Barnes, 1971).

The shifting pattern of play seems to parallel cognitive development. In the early part of the preoperational stage when thinking is highly "egocentric," it's not surprising that "selfishness" and lack of cooperation should prevail. Young children may not be able to understand any other type of play. As they reach the end of the stage, however, egocentric thinking declines and cooperative play increases.

A similar shift occurs in emotional outbursts from the beginning to the end of the preoperational stage. Two- and 3-year-olds typically engage in temper tantrums that are directed at no one, while 4- to 7-year-olds direct their aggression at others (Sheppard & Willoughby, 1975). Although this kind of behavior is hardly "sociable," it's a more social, less egocentric form of emotion.

By age 2, most boys and girls have begun to act in sex-typed ways. Males tend to play with trucks, airplanes, and blocks; girls play mostly with dolls, stuffed animals, and dress-up clothes (Fagot, 1974). By this early age they seem to have a conscious awareness of their own sex (McConaghy, 1979) and understand the sex stereotypes of the culture concerning clothing, occupations, and recreation (Ruble & Ruble, 1980).

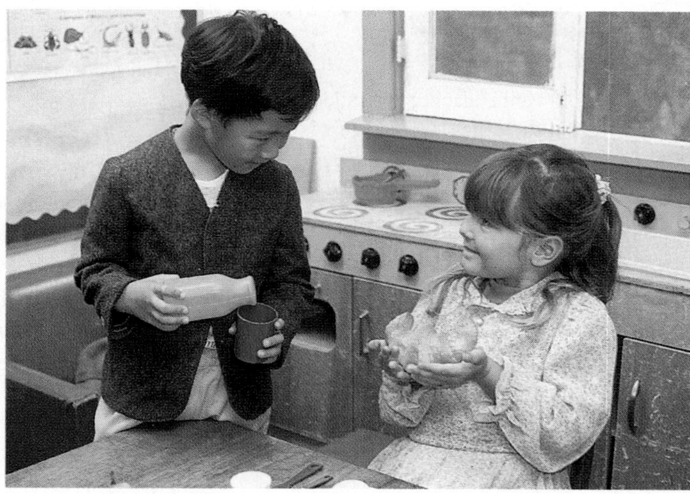

The most notable social changes in the preoperational period are in peer relationships. Between the ages of about 2 and about 7, children go from mostly solitary play, through parallel play, and finally on to cooperative play.

Middle Childhood: 7 to 11 Years

These are the elementary school years. It's no accident that formal education begins in earnest during this period, because most children are then intellectually and socially ready for the demands of school. Physical growth proceeds at a fairly slow pace in middle childhood, but it's a healthy period in which most children experience little illness. Continued improvements in strength and coordination are the only notable advances.

Cognitive Development (Concrete Operational Stage)

The opening of the **concrete operational stage** is marked by important cognitive changes. Children emerge as capable thinkers who use most adult concepts except those that are abstract. They can order objects (seriation) according to size, weight, and other dimensions. They understand the **reversibility** of logical operations; having added together 7 + 2 = 9, they have little trouble reversing the operation to see that 9 – 2 = 7.

One of the most fascinating acquisitions of the concrete operational child is the concept of **conservation.** When children younger than 7 are shown two wide beakers containing equal amounts of water, they have no trouble seeing that they contain the "same amount" of water. But when the water from one beaker is poured into a tall, narrow beaker right in front of their eyes, they usually think the tall beaker contains "more" water because it's higher. Children over the age of 7 who are in the concrete operational period are not fooled by appearances in this way. According to Piaget, the concrete operational children are able to deal with conservation problems because their thought is more **decentered,** which means that they can think of more than one thing at a time. Consequently, the concrete operational child no longer has trouble picking out the big, blue marbles from a jar; he or she can deal with both concepts at the same time. The rapid growth in cognitive ability during middle childhood is based on rapid increases in children's speed of processing information and expansions in the capacity of short-term memory (Fry & Hale, 1996).

In the concrete operational stage, children learn to recognize that the volume of a liquid does not change when it is poured into a glass of a different shape.

Emotional and Social Development

Few changes of note occur in the expression of emotions during the concrete operational stage, but social relationships are markedly different than before. Children enter this period with close ties to their parents. Although these continue to be important, relationships with peers become increasingly significant during this period. Before age 7, children have friendships, but they generally are not enduring, and typically are not close. After 7, peer friendships become more important to children and tend to last longer. Friendship groups, or *cliques,* also emerge during the concrete operational stage. Most friendships are with members of the same sex, and those cross-sex friendships that do exist are generally "just friends." While the terms *boyfriend* and *girlfriend* are freely used, they have little meaning in the adult sense.

concrete operational stage
In Piaget's theory, the period of cognitive development from ages 7 to 11.

reversibility
(re-ver´sĭbil-ĭ-tē) The concept understood by concrete operational children that logical propositions can be reversed (if 2 + 3 = 5, then 5 – 3 = 2).

conservation
(kon-ser´vā-shun) The concept understood by concrete operational children that quantity (number, mass, etc.) does not change just because shape or other superficial features have changed.

decenter
(dē-sen´ter) To think about more than one characteristic of a thing at a time; a capacity of concrete operational children.

Thinking Critically About Psychology

1. If you were a teacher of kindergarten children, how would knowledge of the preoperational stage of cognitive development influence the way you would teach?

2. If you were forced to choose, would you describe development in infancy and childhood as a series of stages or a continuous process? How would you support your choice?

Review

When we look back over the explosive growth of the neonate into a child, it appears that there may be some utility in discussing development in terms of "stages." Interrelated changes in several behavioral systems do occur that may be dramatic enough to justify the phrase "qualitatively different stage." However, the entrance to a new stage is not marked by abrupt changes. Developmental changes are gradual, inconsistent, and take place both within and between stages. There is value, then, in thinking of human development in terms of stages, but there are limits on that value. The detailed picture of infant and child development presented in this section shows that human growth is both a series of landmark steps and a continuous, flowing process. There are no shortcuts to describing the marvelous complexities of human development.

Check Your Learning

To be sure that you have learned the key points from the preceding section, cover the answers below and try to answer each question. If you give an incorrect answer to any question, return to the page given next to the correct answer to see why your answer was not correct.

1. While an infant during the ________________ (first two weeks of life) is weak and dependent on adults, it does have useful reflexive behaviors and has already begun to learn.

a. trimester
b. neonatal period
c. toddler period
d. prenatal period

2. By 6 to 9 months of age, a child begins to understand that objects exist even when they are out of sight. This is called ________________ .

a. object permanence
b. continuation
c. constancy theory
d. conservation

3. According to Piaget, the ________________ stage (ages 2 to 7 years) is marked by a phenomenal growth in language.

a. operational
b. concrete operational
c. infancy
d. preoperational

4. ________________ describes the concept understood by concrete operational children (ages 7 to 11 years) that quantity does not change just because shape or other superficial features have changed.

a. Object permanance
b. Conservation
c. Quantity maintenance
d. Continuity

Correct Answers
1. b (p. 298), **2.** a (p. 299), **3.** d (p. 302), **4.** b (p. 303).

ADOLESCENT DEVELOPMENT

adolescence
The period from the onset of puberty until the beginning of adulthood.

puberty
(pu´ber-tē) The point in development at which the individual is first physically capable of sexual reproduction.

Adolescence is ushered in by the monumental physical changes of **puberty** through which the person who was a child only yesterday becomes sexually capable of being the parent of a child. The adolescent period is marked by rapid physical growth and change and by a heightening of sexual and romantic interest in others. And it's a time in which peers are often more important than parents in terms of attachment and influence. The adolescent is capable of reasoning in abstractions for the first time. Partly for this reason he or she may spend a great deal of time contemplating abstract issues such as justice and equality. There is no clear-cut demarcation of the end of adolescence in our society. Rather than at any specific age, individuals pass from adolescence to adulthood when they establish adult social relationships and adult patterns of work.

Neither scientists nor poets are quite sure how to conceptualize adolescence. It's frequently portrayed as a time of storm and stress, but it's just as frequently portrayed as the happy days of carefree youth. This confusion probably stems from the fact that adolescence, like life itself, can be either very happy or exceedingly tormented (or both for the same adolescents at different times). In any case, one thing is certain: Adolescence is a period of dramatic change.

Activation of sexual desire occurs during adolescence.

Physical Development

A number of psychologically important physical changes occur during adolescence, particularly during puberty, which signals the onset of adolescence. These changes alter physical appearance so much that—in what seems like a moment—girls come to look like women and boys like men. Height and weight increase sharply, pushing adolescents suddenly to adult size. A look in the mirror changes forever the adolescent's image of himself or herself.

Puberty begins with the production of sex hormones by the ovaries in females and the testes in males. These hormones trigger a series of physiological changes that lead to ovulation and menstruation in females and the production of sperm cells in males. These are the **primary sex characteristics** that indicate that the adolescent has the ability to reproduce. These physical changes are accompanied by activation of sexual desire and corresponding increases in dating, kissing, petting, masturbation, and other sexual activities.

primary sex characteristics
Ovulation and menstruation in females and production of sperm in males.

menarche
(mĕ-nar´ke) The first menstrual period.

Menarche, or the first menstrual period, occurs on the average at about 12 years, 6 months in American females, and the production of sperm begins about two years later in males (Tanner, 1970). The age of menarche is younger today than in the past and younger here than in many foreign countries. In 1900 the average age of menarche in the United States was about 14 years, and even today, the average age in one New Zealand tribe is over 17 years (Tanner, 1970). Researchers believe that these differences are due to improved nutrition and health care in the United States over the years and that menarche will not begin much younger in the future as the natural limit appears to have been about reached (Petersen, 1979).

The more obvious changes occurring during puberty are the development of the **secondary sex characteristics.** In females, the first change is an accumulation of fat in the breasts that results in a slight "budding," followed by a gradual enlargement of the breasts over a period of several years. There is also a growing accumulation of fat around the hips resulting in a broadening that further gives the appearance of the adult female body shape. Finally, about the time of menarche, pubic hair begins to grow.

secondary sex characteristics
Development of the breasts and hips in females; growth of the testes, broadening of the shoulders, lowered voice, and growth of the penis and facial hair in males; and growth of pubic and other body hair in both sexes.

In males, the first secondary sexual change is the growth of the testes, followed by a broadening of the shoulders, lowering of the voice, and growth of the penis. Soon, pubic and facial hair grow, thus creating the physical image of an adult male.

Another outwardly obvious sign of puberty is the rapid increase in weight and height known as the **adolescent growth spurt.** Just before puberty, rapid weight gain is common, mostly in the form of fat. This can be a source of concern to both the adolescent and her or his parents, but soon most of this weight is redistributed or shed. At about the onset of puberty, the adolescent suddenly shoots up in height. As shown in figure 8.3, the rate of growth in height steadily declines after infancy, but it rises sharply for a little over a year in early adolescence. During the year of most rapid growth, many boys gain as much as 4 inches and 26 pounds, and many girls add as much as 3 1/2 inches and 20 pounds.

adolescent growth spurt
The rapid increase in weight and height that occurs around the onset of puberty.

Cognitive Development (Formal Operational Stage)

At about age 11, the shift from the concrete operational to formal operational thought begins in some adolescents. Other individuals do not begin the shift as early or reach this advanced level of thinking until early adulthood, and some never reach it at all (Piaget, 1972; Santrock, 1995). The **formal operational stage** is characterized by an ability to use abstract concepts. The logic of formal operational thinking goes beyond the concrete details of each incident or problem to the underlying abstract principles involved.

formal operational stage
In Piaget's theory, the period of intellectual development usually reached by about age 11 and characterized by the ability to use abstract concepts.

FIGURE 8.3

The adolescent growth spurt can be seen by the rapid increase in height that occurs in males and females at the beginning of puberty.

Source: Data from J. M. Tanner, R. H. Whitehouse and M. Takaishi, "Standards from Birth to Maturity for Height, Weight, Height Velocity and Weight Velocity" in *Archives of Diseases in Childhood,* 41:555–571, 1966.

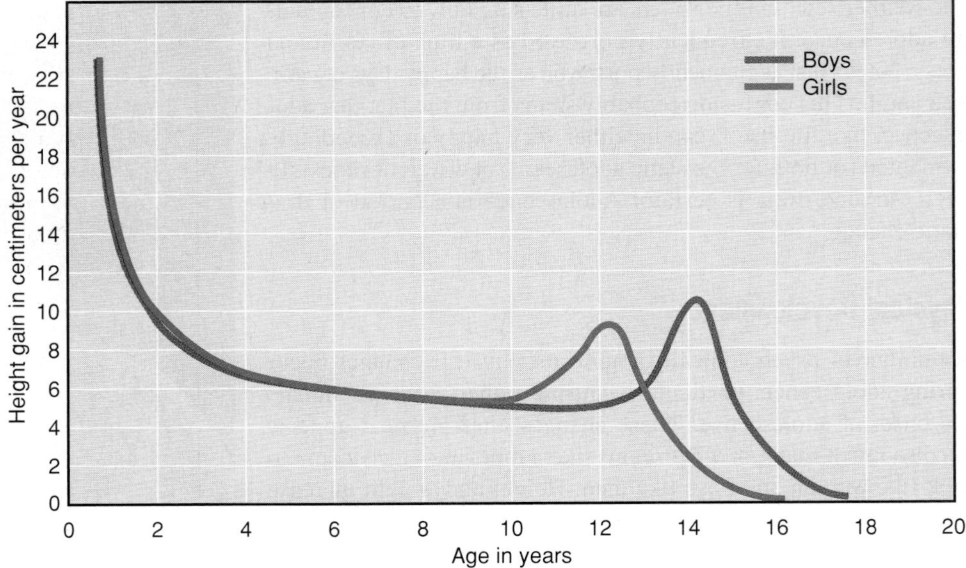

In a classic experiment conducted by Swiss developmental psychologists Barbel Inhelder and Jean Piaget (1958), children and adolescents of different ages were given two weights that could be hooked at different places on the arms of a scale; their job was to make the scale balance. Seven-year-olds—who were at the beginning of the concrete operational stage—were generally unable to balance the scale at all. They could understand that the two weights must be placed on opposite arms of the scale, but they did not seem to understand the importance of where the weights were hooked on the arms. By the end of the concrete operational stage, age 10, most children were able to balance the scale through trial and error, but they were not able to explain in words how it worked.

By about age 14, many of the subjects had reached the stage of formal operational thinking and were able to explain that the farther a weight is placed from the center (fulcrum) of the scale, the more downward force it exerts. These children were able, without trial and error, to place a 5-kilogram weight twice as far from the fulcrum as a 10-kilogram weight on the other side. They could also easily deduce from this principle that weights of 3 and 6 or 2 and 4 kilograms would balance on the same hooks used by the 5- and 10-kilogram weights. They understood, in other words, the *abstract* principle that it's the *ratio* of weights and distances that matters, not the specific weights involved in any one example. They were able to think in abstract logical terms.

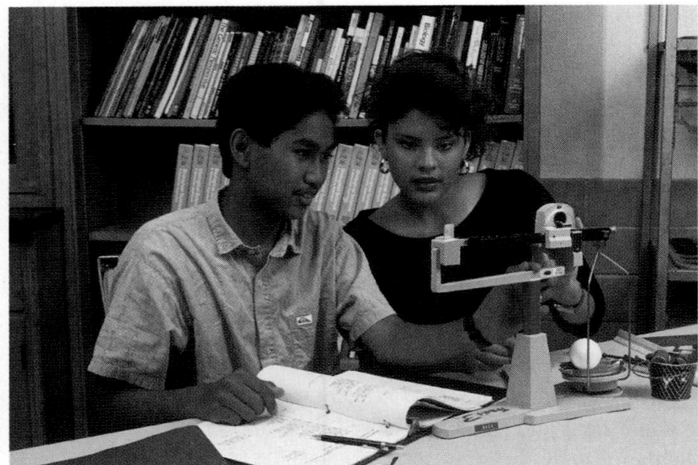

The ability to understand abstract concepts is a characteristic of formal operational thought.

Individuals who have achieved formal operational thinking are able to use it in many areas of their lives. Piaget suggests, for example, that adolescents often seem preoccupied by concepts such as truth, justice, and the meaning of life partly because the capacity to think in such abstract terms is so new to them.

Although most adolescents have reached the level of formal operational reasoning, their cognition at times often retains an immature quality. This is not really surprising; they have recently developed the ability to reason abstractly but have little experience on which to base their abstract thoughts. In particular, David Elkind (1967, 1981; Elkind & Bowen, 1979) has pointed out that adolescents often possess a form of egocentrism that, while different from the egocentrism of young children, similarly distorts their perception of reality. There are four primary features of **adolescent egocentrism.** As you will readily notice, the thinking of fully mature adults is not always free of these characteristics. However, the four reality-distorting qualities described by Elkind are more characteristic of the adolescent stage than any other, and they

adolescent egocentrism

The quality of thinking that leads some adolescents to believe that they are the focus of attention in social situations, to believe that their problems are unique, to be unusually hypocritical, and to be "pseudostupid."

help explain why conversations between adolescents and adults are sometimes so frustrating to both parties.

The primary characteristic of adolescent egocentrism has been termed the *imaginary audience*—an audience that adolescents believe is watching everything they do. If they stumble, stammer, or wear the wrong clothes, *everyone* will notice and talk about it. The adolescent also often lives what seems to be a *personal fable*—he or she believes that no one has similar problems or could possibly understand what they are going through. Adolescent egocentrism is also characterized by excessive *hypocrisy*—it's okay to copy someone else's homework, but a teacher who steps out of class to take a short personal telephone call is unforgivably irresponsible in the adolescent's eyes. Finally, adolescent egocentrism involves what Elkind (1981) calls *pseudostupidity*—oversimplified logic. For example, when adolescents say, "If alcoholics know they are going to die of cirrhosis of the liver, why don't they just stop?" they fail to consider the many factors that contribute to an addiction to alcohol. Thus, their thinking is sometimes distorted a bit by their egocentrism, making their relationships with each other and with adults more difficult at times.

Emotional and Social Development

The shift from childhood to adolescence and from adolescence to adulthood is marked by changes in the emotional and social spheres of our lives. Until relatively recently, however, these changes have been more the subject of speculation than of research.

Adolescent Social Development

Adolescents also show marked changes in their social relationships. Adolescence is a time of drifting and sometimes of breaking away from the family unit. While relationships with peers become increasingly important through late childhood, by adolescence peers have become the most important people in the individual's life. The onset of puberty particularly brings a distancing from parents (Galambos, 1992). The shift in orientation from parents to peers can be seen in the dramatic increase in conformity to the ideas and judgments of the peer group that occurs at the beginning of puberty (ages 11 to 13) but declines from age 15 on (Costanzo & Shaw, 1966).

By adolescence, peers have become very important. The onset of puberty usually signals a dramatic increase in conformity to the ideas and judgments of the adolescent's peer group.

At the same time that friendships and romantic relationships become more intense, the adolescent becomes less interested in family activities, may begin to reject some family values, and may rebel against parental authority. Although most adolescents do not go through a stormy period of rebelliousness (Adelson, 1979; Offer & Schonert-Reichl, 1992), nearly all distance themselves somewhat from their parents during this period. One study found that even on weekends, young adolescents spend more than twice as much time with peers as with parents (Condry, Simon, & Bronfenbrenner, 1968).

If we think of adolescence as a *transition* phase between childhood and adulthood, distancing and even a certain amount of rebelliousness can be thought of as positive steps toward developing an independent adult lifestyle. These changes are not always viewed in a positive light by the parents and teenagers involved, however. As peer influence becomes more powerful than parental influence, adolescents begin to adopt the values, attitudes, style of dress, and language of their peers. Sometimes peer influence is in direct opposition to the wishes of the parents, resulting in painful conflict—which reaches its height at about the ninth grade (Santrock, 1995)—as parents attempt to reassert their authority.

Adolescent Emotions

Since 1904 when the first American text on adolescent psychology was published by G. Stanley Hall, a debate has continued unabated about the nature of adolescent emotions. Is it a carefree period of happiness or, as Hall would have it, a time of "storm and stress"?

Contrary to popular views of adolescence, current research suggests that about 80 percent of adolescents experience a relatively happy youth. However, risky behavior is common and some adolescents do experience serious emotional and behavior problems.

Like many philosophical debates that are eventually settled by scientific evidence, the truth lies somewhere between the extreme viewpoints.

Contrary to popular views of adolescence, current research suggests that about 80 percent of adolescents experience a relatively happy youth, marked by mostly good relationships with both peers and parents (Offer & Schonert-Reichl, 1992). Another 20 percent of adolescents, however, experience a difficult adolescence marked by emotional or behavior problems (Offer & Schonert-Reichl, 1992). This may seem like a high percentage, but it is exactly the same as the percentage of both children and adults who are unhappy or distressed (Myers & Diener, 1995; Offer, Ostrov, & Howard, 1981; Offer & Schonert-Reichl, 1992).

Therefore, compared with when they were children and with when they will be adults, adolescents do not appear to be more likely to experience severe emotional turmoil. There are two important reasons, however, why it still may be fair to say that adolescence is a time of heightened emotional stress. First, the topics over which parents and normal teenagers have conflict are often more upsetting to both sides. It is common for adolescents to wish to be with peers instead of at home, and there is a marked increase during adolescence of risky behaviors, such as unsafe automobile driving, unprotected sex, and alcohol and drug use (Arnett, 1995; Buchanan, Eccles, & Becker, 1992). In addition, about half of all teenagers break the law (purchasing alcohol underage, minor theft, truancy, etc.) at least once, with the rate reaching a peak in middle to late adolescence before declining (Elliott, Huizinga, & Menard, 1989). These issues create grounds for arguments between parents and adolescents that are far more heated than the debates in childhood over Brownie Scout uniforms, Little League games, Nintendo, and dolls.

Second, although the overall rate of serious emotional difficulties does not change from childhood to adolescence (about 20% at all ages), there are changes in the kinds of difficulties that youths with serious difficulties experience. During childhood, boys are more likely to have problems than girls, mostly relatively minor behavior problems and hyperactivity. Both sexes have equal rates of problems with anxiety during childhood, but these tend to be relatively minor difficulties with general worry or anxiety about being separated from the parent. From the onset of puberty on, however, severe episodes of depression, the disorder known as schizophrenia, the eating disorder called anorexia nervosa, several kinds of anxiety (nervous) conditions, and suicide increase *tenfold* (Hawton & Osborn, 1984). The increased rates in depression, anxiety, and eating disorders are mostly in girls. The overall rate of serious difficulties does not increase during adolescence for boys, but when teenagers do experience behavior problems or depression, these problems tend to be more serious than in childhood. In addition, although the rates of most serious difficulties are lower in males than in females during adolescence, adolescent males are more likely to seriously injure another person or to commit suicide (Offer & Schonert-Reichl, 1992).

Sadly, there was an overall increase in the frequency of adolescent suicides in older adolescents from 1956 to 1978, but rates have leveled off or have declined slightly since then (Holinger & Offer, 1993). There is no widely accepted explanation for this increase in suicide rates. It is tempting to blame it on the pressures of contemporary life, but that explanation may not be correct. Long-term statistics suggest that suicide rates among older adolescents were high during the first 10 years of this century, then dropped dramatically, and have recently risen again to the older, higher level (Hawton & Osborn, 1984). Fortunately, the rate of suicide in teenagers is still extremely low compared with that of adults. Recent statistics indicate that approximately 18 males and 4 females aged 15 to 19 commit suicide for every 100,000 persons of that age (Holinger & Offer, 1993).

Thus, the popular view of adolescence as a period of universal turmoil does not hold up to scientific scrutiny. Not all adolescents are in a constant state of conflict with their parents or within themselves. But risky behavior (unprotected sex, drug use, dangerous driving) is common, and some adolescents do experience serious emotional and behavior problems. Overall, adolescence is a decade of transition: Many changes occur and many challenges are met between the ages of 11 and 21. For a sizable minority of adolescents, this transition is very difficult most of the time, but for the great majority of adolescents, it's only difficult some of the time.

Review

In the span of about a decade, each individual passes from childhood to adulthood. This adolescent period of transition begins with the adolescent growth spurt and the emergence of primary and secondary sex characteristics (puberty) and ends with the assumption of adult patterns of work, living, and relationships. It's a period of dramatic physical changes. Considerable gains are made in height, weight, and strength; body fat is redistributed; and boys and girls come to look like men and women. These physical changes are often of considerable concern to self-conscious adolescents, particularly when irregularities and sex differences in physical development are obvious. Cognitively, most adolescents develop formal operational thinking, which gives them the ability to reason abstractly, but they experience an adolescent form of egocentrism. Socially, they complete the shift from a focus on parents to a focus on peer relationships. Adolescence can be a period of stormy emotions for some adolescents, but most adolescents experience emotional difficulties only some of the time.

Thinking Critically About Psychology

1. Although adolescence is a time when peer influence often outweighs parental influence, most adolescents continue to hold values and attitudes that are similar to those of their parents. What factors might account for this?

2. What psychological changes mark the period called adolescence? Do they seem significant enough to be treated as a separate developmental period?

Check Your Learning

To be sure that you have learned the key points from the preceding section, cover the answers below and try to answer each question. If you give an incorrect answer to any question, return to the page given next to the correct answer to see why your answer was not correct.

1. ____________________ is the period from the onset of puberty until the beginning of adulthood and is marked by rapid physical growth and change, and by a heightening of sexual and romantic interest in others.

2. The rapid increase in weight and height that occurs around the onset of puberty is known as the ____________________ .

a. maturation stage
b. adolescent growth spurt
c. physical development stage
d. menarche

3. The ____________________ stage is characterized by an ability to use abstract concepts.

a. concrete operational
b. formal operational
c. preoperational
d. operational

4. About the same percentage of adolescents experience serious emotional and behavior problems as children or adults, but it is a time in which suicide and risky behavior decrease compared with childhood.

a. True
b. False

Correct Answers
1. Adolescence (p. 304), **2.** b (p. 305), **3.** b (p. 305), **4.** b (p. 308).

ADULTHOOD: YOUNG ADULTHOOD THROUGH OLDER ADULTHOOD

Adulthood is the time of taking on adult responsibilities in work and social relationships. Adulthood is not a single phase of life. The challenges of adult love, work, and play change considerably during adulthood. The demands of maintaining a marriage are very different for newlyweds, parents of infants, parents of teenagers, or a couple in their 70s.

Similar changes occur in the demands of work and play. In other words, adulthood is not the end of the process of development. Developmental changes *continue* throughout adulthood.

Physical Development

The life span is a continuous process of physical change. We continue to strengthen and grow well into early adulthood, but the body begins a slow process of physical decline after early adulthood. Physical speed and endurance decline gradually from early adulthood on. More and more of us need reading glasses for near vision with increasing age and have difficulty seeing in weak light and in the periphery of vision due to a loss of rod cells in the retina after middle age. Our ability to hear high-pitched tones declines after age 20, with loss of ability to hear low-pitched sounds beginning in the 60s. Our sense of taste remains pretty much intact into later life, but many older adults report that food tastes more bland. This is due to marked declines in the sense of smell with aging, which plays an important role in our appreciation of foods. Overall, men are likely to suffer these declines in hearing and smell earlier than women (Steinberg, 1995). A substantial number of older adults show marked declines due to cerebral arteriosclerosis (hardening of the arteries) that results in serious loss of intellectual ability. The rate and extent of these declines differ markedly from individual to individual, depending in part on the level of healthy exercise and activity that the individual maintains during adulthood.

Cognitive Development

It may surprise you to learn that cognitive development continues to take place during adulthood. Most of us think that cognition develops to its full potential in childhood and adolescence, then remains unchanged during adulthood. Actually, some cognitive abilities improve, some remain unchanged (at least into the 70s), and some decline during adulthood. Small but steady improvements occur from the 20s to the 70s in knowledge of facts and word meanings (Cornelius & Caspi, 1987). No declines occur before about age 75 in such fundamental aspects of intelligence as the ability to reason about everyday problems, to understand mathematical concepts, or to learn and remember meaningful information (Schaie & Parham, 1977; Schulz & Ewen, 1988). Indeed, there are small increases during the adult years in our ability to solve problems of life in ways that are judged to be "wise" (Baltes & Staudinger, 1993).

On the other hand, slight declines do occur in some aspects of cognitive performance during later adulthood. Older adults tend to perform slightly less well than younger adults in abstract problem solving, perceptual integration, divergent thinking, most cognitive tasks that must be performed quickly, and some aspects of short-term memory (Cornelius & Caspi, 1987; Grady et al., 1995; McCrae, Arenberg, & Costa, 1987; Shimamura, Berry, Mangels, Rusting, & Jurica, 1995). Older adults tend to perform less well on short-term memory tasks that require recall than on tasks that require recognition (see p. 220 to refresh your memory of the distinction between recall and recognition). For example, Fergus Craik and Joan McDowd (1987) of the University of Toronto compared the performance of two groups of individuals in their 20s and 70s on two memory tasks. In one task, the participants had to recall a list of words without cues, whereas in the other memory task they had to recognize the word from two similar alternatives. The younger participants did better recalling words without cues, but the older participants did as well as the younger persons on the recognition task.

Therefore, we can summarize research on the development of cognitive abilities through adulthood by concluding that older adults perform as well as younger adults on some tasks (learning and reasoning about everyday concepts), do better than younger adults on some tasks (e.g., word meaning and wise decision making), but perform less well than younger adults in other ways (abstract reasoning and divergent thinking). The cognitive performance of younger adults is also less quick than younger adults, and older adults sometimes need cues more to jog their retrieval of memories.

It is important to place the few cognitive declines that occur in older adulthood into perspective, however. First, the average differences between older and younger adults into their 70s are small and not significant in most real-life situations. Second, not all adults age at the same rate. There are large differences among older individuals in their cognitive abilities. In one study of adults, 50 percent of adults in their mideighties had scores on a verbal recall task that fell within the range of scores of 20-year-olds (Rapp & Amaral, 1992). Significant declines in cognitive abilities do occur in some older adults, especially ones who are seriously ill, but many healthy older adults show little evidence of intellectual decline through their seventies (Shimamura et al., 1995).

Emotional and Social Development

What about changes in our emotions and social relationships? Do we pass through developmental changes in these facets of human existence during adulthood, too? The answer is not a simple one: As we move through adulthood we mostly stay the same, but we experience a number of important changes as well.

Traits such as enjoyment of being with other people, enjoyment of excitement, high general level of activity, anxiousness, self-consciousness, and openness to feelings are quite stable throughout adulthood (Costa & McCrae, 1976; McCrae & Costa, 1994). Other traits such as desire for power, aggressiveness, and need for achievement seem to decline somewhat (Skolnick, 1966). There is also evidence of a few other positive personality changes that most adults can expect to go through in their middle and later adult years. Adults often become more insightful, dependable, comfortable, candid, and more accepting of life's hardships (Haan, 1976; Neugarten, 1964). Men also become more aware of their need for affection and their aesthetic needs, while women tend to become more confident, assertive, and independent in middle adulthood (Gutmann, 1977; Helson & Moane, 1987; Neugarten, 1968). These changes are typically relatively small, however, if they occur at all. Overall, it appears that fundamental aspects of personality are stable across the adult life span (Schulz & Ewen, 1988).

Although personality traits remain stable throughout adulthood, most adults can expect some personality changes in their middle and later years. Some of these are positive; for example, middle-age men often become more aware of their need for affection. Middle-age women often become more self-confident.

Moreover, it should be obvious to anyone who knows the life histories of even a few individuals that most human lives are not "stable" in the strictest sense. Most of us experience periods of happiness and stability in alternation with periods of discontent and change. The woman who grows unhappy with her career in retailing after 15 years and returns to college to become a minister and the man who happily remarries after an unhappy 14-year marriage are but two examples.

But, although few would deny that most adult lives are characterized by periods of calm and periods of change, there is much disagreement as to the way in which to think about such changes. Some psychologists believe that adulthood consists of a series of "stages of development," rather like the stages of child development proposed by Piaget and others. Erik Erikson (1963) and Daniel Levinson (1978, 1986) have each proposed a set of stages of adult life, although Levinson prefers to use the term *periods* to distinguish them from stages of childhood (Levinson, 1986). These stages are somewhat different from the stages of infant and child development in that (a) not every adult is believed to go through every stage; (b) the order of the stages can vary for some individuals; and (c) the timing of the stages is not controlled by biological maturation. Although Erikson proposes three stages of adulthood and Levinson proposes nine stages, Levinson's theory is based on Erikson's and can be thought of as an elaboration of Erikson's views. For this reason, we will discuss both stage theories together. Notice that both theorists see adulthood as a series of *alternating* periods of stability and transition.

Early Adulthood: Intimacy vs. Isolation (17 to 45 Years)

Erikson (1963) discussed his proposed stages of adult life in terms of the challenges, or crises, faced at each stage and the consequences of successfully or unsuccessfully meeting those challenges. If you refer again to table 8.4, page 296, you can see that these adult stages are the continuation of the stages of development Erikson believed begin in infancy. He referred to early adulthood as the stage of *intimacy versus isolation.* The challenge of this stage is to enter into committed, loving relationships with others that partially replace the bonds with parents. If we are successful in this task, we will have the intimacy needed to progress in adult life; if not, we will become isolated and less capable of full emotional development according to Erikson.

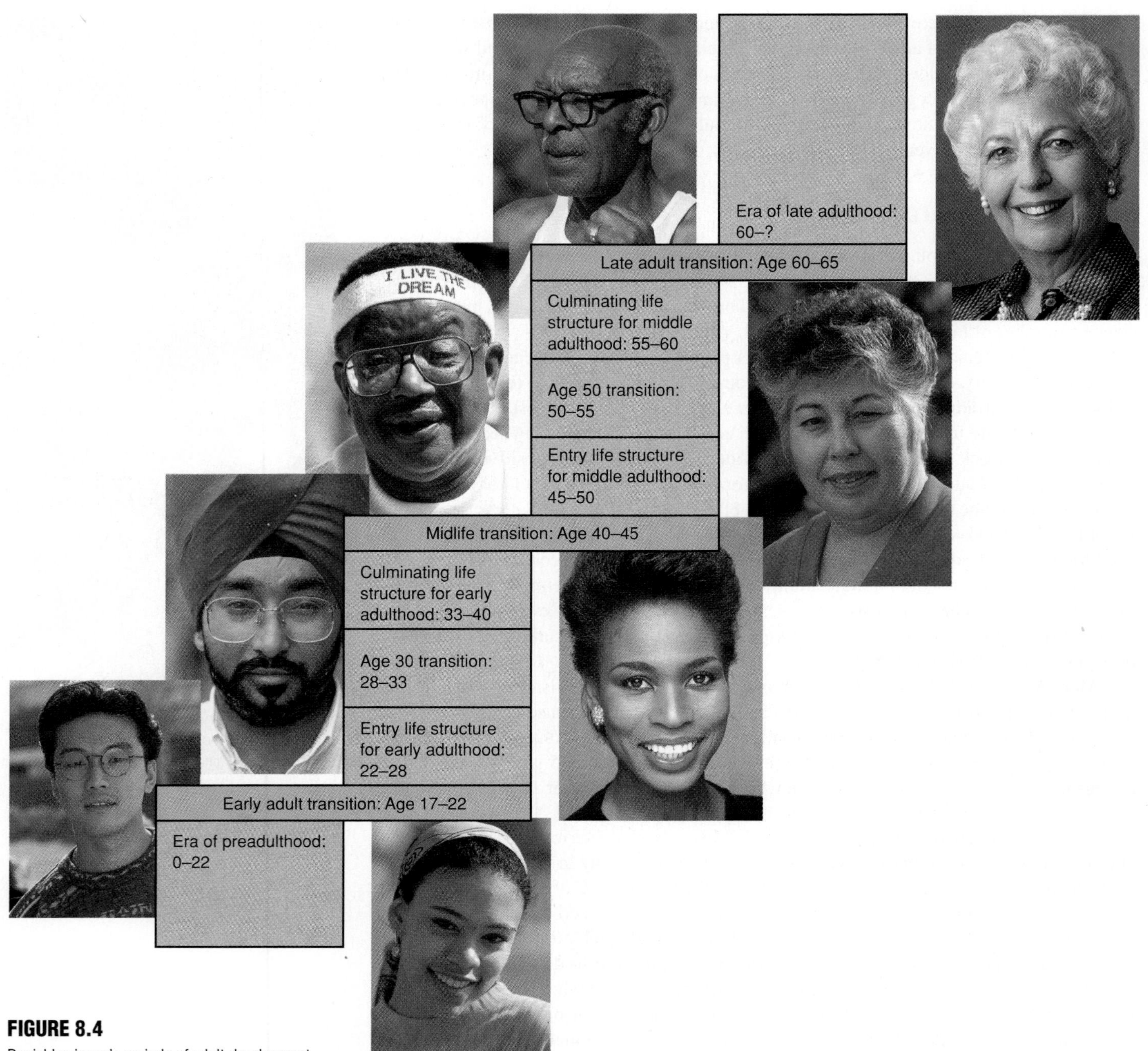

FIGURE 8.4
Daniel Levinson's periods of adult development.

Levinson (1986) sees the transition to early adulthood as beginning sometime between the ages of 17 and 22 for most individuals (see fig. 8.4). Early adulthood itself consists of three briefer stages. The *entry to early adulthood* lasts until approximately age 28. This is a time of creating an adult manner of working and living independently and often a time of marriage and young children. The *age 30 transition* (28 to 33) is a time of reevaluating one's start into adult life. Is this the right job for me? The right city? The right spouse? A sense of pressure often accompanies these decisions—they must be made "before it's too late." Sometimes major changes are made and sometimes the individual decides that his or her initial choices were the right ones, but either way the process of reevaluation can often be uncomfortable.

The *culmination of early adulthood* is a time of working hard toward one's goals. It extends roughly from the early 30s to about age 40. During this phase adults sometimes join the PTA Executive Board to improve the quality of their children's school, plant trees in the yard, and work long hours for promotion to a senior position at work. The individual is often aware of feeling like a full member of the adult generation at this time.

In general, the stage of early adulthood is a demanding one. The young adult usually takes on the challenges of a career, a marriage, and parenthood during the same period. Usually, too, large debts are incurred in buying homes and automobiles in anticipation of greater income, which has not yet arrived. As Levinson (1986) points out, crucially important decisions must be made concerning family and occupation before one has the maturity and life experience to make them comfortably. It is, at the same time, a period of vigorous health and sexuality, rich family rewards, and the potential of occupational advancement. For most of us, it is a time when the rewards exceed the costs.

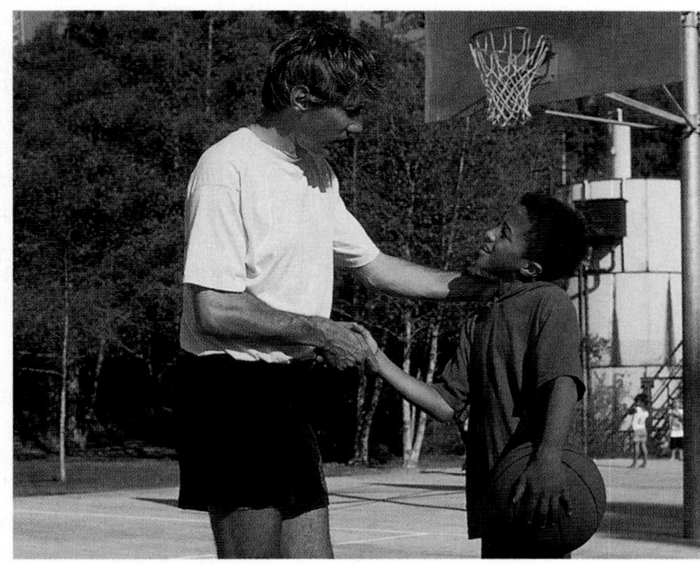

Erikson believed that to successfully navigate middle adulthood, people must develop a sense of generativity, or a devotion to endeavors that will last beyond their own life span.

Middle Adulthood: Generativity vs. Stagnation (40 to 65 Years)

During this stage, the individual must come to grips with what her or his life has become. By this time the adult usually realizes that the ambitious dreams of early adulthood cannot all be fulfilled. Few of us who dreamed of becoming famous scientists, wealthy business executives, community leaders, or the like are still able to cling to these dreams in middle adulthood. Too many promotions have been missed, too many investments have gone bad, and too many elections have been lost to believe that we can be the unqualified successes we once dreamed of being. The challenge of this stage then, which Erikson refers to as the stage of *generativity versus stagnation,* is to find meaning in the things that we can do in our work and family lives and continue to be productive *(generative).* If not, many individuals will compare what they are so unfavorably with what they wish they were that they will give up and stagnate.

The importance of being generative, or productive, during middle adulthood is not just a matter of mere work to Erikson. The person who successfully navigates middle adulthood develops a devotion to endeavors that live beyond their own life span. This might take the form of building a family business, guiding one's children or grandchildren, or taking younger coworkers under one's wing as a mentor. Generativity is a matter of "reaching out" rather than being self-centered. A person who merely works hard may only be meeting his or her own selfish needs. According to Erikson, this person is self-absorbed or stagnant and will find that life loses much of its meaning during middle adulthood.

For women who spent their earlier adult lives as homemakers rearing children, work may be a more important part of the challenge of remaining generative than for men. The woman who faces an "empty nest" during middle adulthood may feel suddenly useless. Having spent the last 25 years or so giving to others, she now finds that her role as the mother of grown children requires little from her. At this point, she may maximize her generativity by returning to the workforce, taking a job that she has previously put off to meet the needs of others. For some women, then, the move back into the workforce to maintain generativity can be seen as the opposite of the move of men, who have long been employed and shift toward doing more for others outside of work (Lowenthal, Thurnher, & Chiriboga, 1975). But this move may accomplish the same purpose in avoiding stagnation.

Levinson describes four brief stages of middle adulthood. Middle adulthood opens with the *midlife transition.* This transitional stage reaches a peak in the early 40s. For some individuals, this transition is quite easy, but for others it's a period of anguish and turmoil. The majority of a sample of 40 men studied by Levinson—10 executives, 10 biologists, 10 factory workers, and 10 novelists—experienced at least some turmoil during their early 40s. Erikson described this stage as the early peak of the struggle between generativity and stagnation—can I find meaning in my life the way it's turning out? It's also a time to face growing evidence of biological aging and to accept or agonize over one's wrinkles and gray hair.

The *entry to middle adulthood stage,* from about 45 to 50, is a period of calm and stability for most people who have emerged from the midlife transition. It's sometimes marked by career changes, new health fitness programs, geographical moves, or divorce. But more often, this stage is a continuation of the life that preceded it. Individuals who are

"Nothing serious, Bob—just a case of the forties."
Drawing by Mankoff; © 1988 The New Yorker Magazine, Inc.

happy with themselves following the midlife transition often find this period to be one of the most productive and creative times of their lives. The illusory ambitions that were shattered during the midlife transition have often been replaced with more attainable goals that are pursued with vigor. Individuals often feel that the painful process of reassessment during their early 40s led to changes that left them a better person.

The *age 50 transition is* a stage that is similar to the age 30 transition. For most adults this is a time to reassess the goals and lifestyle chosen during midlife and the entering middle adulthood stages. Another stable period from about age 55 to 65 follows the age 50 transition. Levinson refers to this stage as the *culmination of middle adulthood.*

Climacteric

climacteric
(klī-mak´ter-ik) The period between about ages 45 and 60 in which there is a loss of capacity to sexually reproduce in women and a decline in the reproductive capacity of men.

menopause
(men´o-pawz) The cessation of menstruation and the capacity to reproduce in women.

Although most psychologists believe that the changes that characterize adult development are timed more by the "social clock" rather than biological aging, one biological event that has an impact for many persons is the **climacteric.** The climacteric is a period beginning at about age 45 when a loss of the capacity to sexually reproduce in women and a decline in the reproductive capacity of men occurs.

In women, the decrease in the level of sex hormones during this period eventually leads to the end of menstruation, or **menopause.** This event, which takes place at 46 to 48 years of age on the average (but can normally take place between the ages of 36 and 60) is sometimes an uncomfortable time for women. It's sometimes accompanied by "hot flashes," anxiety, and depression, although most women do not find it as difficult as they were led to expect (Hultsch & Deutsch, 1981). Although 50 percent of women experience some discomfort during menopause, only 10 percent go through severe distress (McKinlay & Jeffreys, 1974).

Many women expect that menopause and the loss of the ability to reproduce as well as the accelerated aging of physical appearance that can occur with menopause will be accompanied by a loss of sexual interest. But this is definitely not a necessary outcome. Women who enjoy and regularly engage in intercourse before menopause experience no sexual difficulties or loss of sexual interest after menopause (Masters & Johnson, 1966). Many women, in fact, report increased sexual interest because the risk of pregnancy has passed. These findings suggest that the difficulties experienced by some women after menopause may be caused, in part at least, by the *expectation* that it will be difficult.

In the stage of integrity versus despair, older adults who see meaning in their lives when considered as a whole will continue to find life satisfying.

The changes that accompany the male climacteric are generally less notable than in women. There is a decline in the number of sperm cells produced, and slight changes in the pattern of sexual arousal, but the decrease in sex hormones that occurs during the climacteric appears to have few psychological or sexual effects.

Later Adulthood: Integrity vs. Despair (65 Years On)

Erikson refers to the late 60s and beyond as the stage of *integrity versus despair.* Levinson devotes little of his theory to the later adult years and adds little to Erikson's ideas. The older adult who sees meaning in her or his life when considered as a whole continues to live a satisfying existence instead of merely staying alive. The person who sees life as a collection of unmet goals and unanswered riddles may despair of ever achieving a meaningful life and will often withdraw and live out the remaining years like a prison sentence.

But far more older Americans find meaning rather than despair in their lives. This may come as a surprise to you. Just as most of us once thought that the process of development ended in childhood, most of us *still* think that there is little real life after age 65. Too often we think of older adults as leading colorless, joyless, passionless lives. It's surprising to some of us to learn that real *living* can continue until death (Baltes & Staudinger, 1993; Shneidman, 1989).

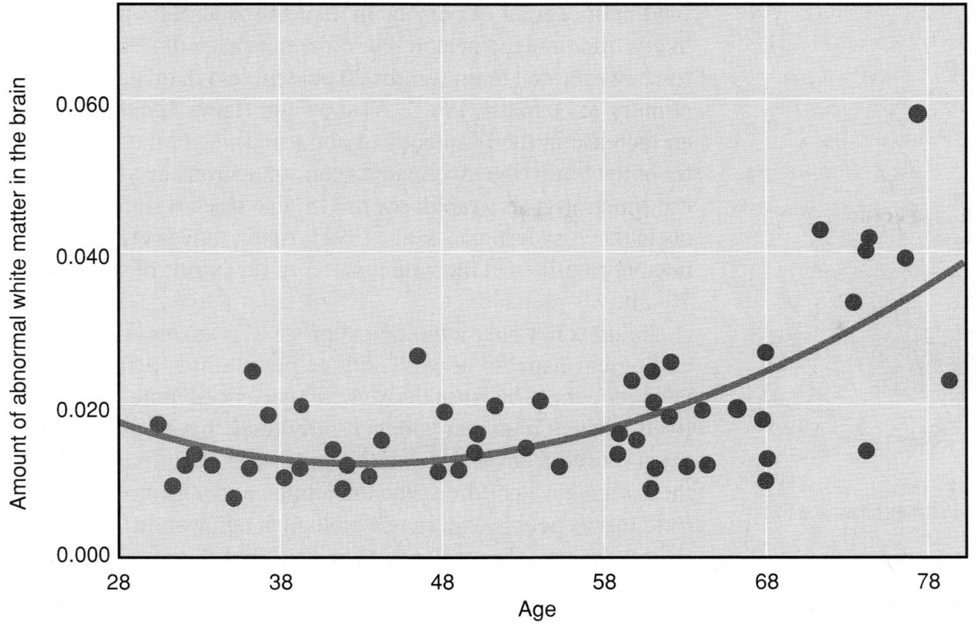

FIGURE 8.5

Images of the brain using MRI show that there is an increase in the number of persons with abnormalities (deposits, tangles, etc.) in the white matter of the brain (made up of the myelin sheaths of long axons) starting at about age 70 years. Each circle represents the amount of abnormal white matter in one person. Notice that some older adults have high numbers in their 70s, but other adults continue to have low numbers like younger adults. The effects of aging on the brain differ markedly from one person to another.

Source: Based on T. L. Jernigan, et al., "Cerebral Structure on MRI, Part I: Localization of Age-Related Changes," *Biological Psychiatry* 29:55–67, 1991.

Evaluation of Stage Theories of Adulthood

The theories of adult development offered by Erikson and Levinson clearly had men more in mind than women. Indeed, Levinson's studies included only male participants. It is not clear, therefore, that their theories are equally applicable to women. For example, we live in a society that tells males that they should establish an identity (particularly a career) before they marry, so that they can "provide for" their wives. Therefore, Erikson's model, which states that the development of identity normally precedes that development of intimacy, makes sense for men. Although changes have occurred in recent years, women are told that they do not really have an identity until after they marry. In the United States, heterosexual women are still expected to change their last names and take on a new identity when they marry! Thus, given the expectation that women will not form an identity until after they have developed a lasting intimate relationship, does this element of Erikson's model apply to women?

Priscilla Roberts and Peter Newton (1987) have reviewed four studies of adult development in women and found that Levinson's stages apply reasonably well in broad terms. Although women seem to experience and resolve the transitions between stages somewhat differently, the notion of alternating periods of stability and instability appears to hold for all of us. Hopefully, future research will lead to a clearer description of the similarities and differences in male and female adult development.

It is important to note that not all developmental psychologists believe that adulthood can be thought of as a series of stages, or at least believe that the idea of stages has been exaggerated in recent years. Rossi (1980), for example, argues that the inevitability and negative impact of the midlife transition have been dangerously exaggerated. Indeed, theorists who oppose the idea of "stages" of adulthood have conducted studies of their own suggesting that predictable changes do not take place at the times indicated by the stage theorists. For example, two studies found no evidence that "midlife crises" are common during the early 40s (Costa & McCrae, 1978, 1994; Farrell & Rosenberg, 1981). Rather, it appears that individuals who have true crises during their early 40s tend to be less emotionally stable individuals who have had crises at other times as well. Such studies have led some researchers to conclude: "Currently, few (if any) psychologists who study adult personality development accept the idea of universal, unidirectional stages" (Schulz & Ewen, 1988, p. 206).

Causes of Aging and Predictors of Longevity

Aging is partly a biological process. Over the years, the body deteriorates—skin sags and wrinkles, artery walls become less flexible, muscular strength is lost, cardiac and respiratory efficiency declines. And there are changes in the brain as well. On the average, the

"I was grinding out barnyards and farmhouses and cows in the meadow, and then, suddenly, I figured to hell with it."

Drawing by Stevenson; © 1971 The New Yorker Magazine, Inc.

total brain weight of persons in their 80s is about 8 percent less than a middle-aged person. For older persons with senile dementia, however, the brain weighs 20 percent less than in middle age (Emery & Oxmans, 1992). As shown in figure 8.5, there is also an increase in the frequency of abnormalities in the white matter of the brain (the myelinated axons of neurons in which neural transmission is very rapid; see p. 315) that reaches significant levels in the 70s (Jernigan et al., 1991). Again, however, there were no abnormalities in the white matter of the brains of some of the 70- and 80-year-olds.

Aging is not only a biological process; it involves many psychological aspects as well. Older people are different from younger people because they have experienced more. They have lived through eras that younger individuals have not, they have often retired from their jobs, they no longer have living parents, they often have children who are adults, and a host of other factors. Just as people experience biological aging at different rates, the psychological experience of aging also differs from person to person.

The key psychological variables that seem to be associated with happy aging are (a) whether one stays "engaged" in life's activities and (b) whether one believes myths about old age. Considerable research suggests that older individuals who continue to be actively engaged in meaningful activities are the happiest as older adults (Maddox, 1964; Neugarten & Hagestad, 1976). These activities can involve family, hobbies, volunteer service, or continued employment. All that matters is that they be activities that are meaningful to the individual.

One key to happy aging is not believing the myths about old age. Many people are quite productive in their later years. For instance, author Isaac Bashevis Singer wrote many books late in life and won the Nobel Prize for literature in 1978, before his death at age 87 in 1991.

The other key to a satisfactory older adulthood seems to be in ignoring the restrictive myths and stereotypes of old age so prevalent in our society. Many older adults are active in sports and creative in the arts and sciences. They sometimes attend college or throw exciting parties. In general, they do not behave like the passive, irritable "old people" of the stereotype. Philosopher Bertrand Russell, artists Marc Chagall and Pablo Picasso, political leaders Golda Meir and Mao Tse-tung, and psychologists Jean Piaget and B. F. Skinner continued to be creative and productive well into their 80s.

Not only has psychology learned much about the factors that predict a well-adjusted older adulthood, we have recently learned something about psychological factors that predict how long people will live. In 1921 Lewis Terman began a study of 1,528 highly intelligent schoolchildren who were studied frequently across their life spans. As of the early 1990s, about half of the subjects had died and half were still living. Psychologist Howard Friedman and his colleagues (1995) have looked back at the records of the Terman study to determine whether psychological factors predicted the subjects' longevity. Because the subjects in Terman's study were all well above average in intelligence, we cannot be sure that the conclusions apply to the U. S. population in general. On the other hand, because college students and professors tend to be above average in intelligence, the results may well be relevant to us.

Friedman found that subjects in the Terman study lived longer if they were rated as having a "conscientious, dependable, and truthful" personality during childhood—they were 30 percent less likely to die during each year of life. On the other hand, children who were rated as being "cheerful" tended to die earlier. This surprising finding is explained partly by the fact that cheerful children were more likely to take risks and were more likely to smoke and drink as adults, and early death was linked to risk taking, smoking, and drinking. In addition, conscientious and dependable children were less likely to be involved in dangerous accidents and were more likely either to have a stable marriage or to remain single—and going through a divorce was linked to early death. If the parents of the children were divorced, the risk of early death was increased even more (by an average of four years). It is not clear that divorce is still stressful enough to result in premature death today—now that it is more common—but it is clearly still a stressful event for everyone involved. When Terman's subjects reached their 30s, they were interviewed about their emotions and behavior. Those with the most emotional difficulties also were more likely to die early.

So if you were a cheerful child with divorced parents, should you take out extra life insurance? No, but if you smoke, drink, take risks, and were thinking about leaving a good marriage just for a change of scenery, you might consider changing your behavior. We will return to the relationship between psychological factors and health in chapter 12 where we will examine ways to change our behavior in ways that promote better health and longevity.

Death and Dying: The Final "Stage"

Everything has an end, including each of our lives. The life cycle begins with the life of a single cell and ends with the death of the person who unfolded from that cell. In recent years, the topic of death and dying has received some long overdue scientific attention and produced some interesting results.

Several variables affect how much we fear our own death. For example, highly religious people seem to have less fear of death than do nonreligious people.

Thoughts of death are an important part of the last stages of life for many individuals. Older adults spend more time thinking about death than do younger adults. Contemplating and planning for one's death is a normal part of old age (Kalish & Reynolds, 1976). Happily, older adults tend to be less frightened by death than are younger adults. Older adults usually come to accept its inevitability with little anguish.

One's fear of death is related to other variables besides age, however. One significant factor is religious belief. Highly religious individuals experience the least fear of death. Nonreligious individuals experience moderate levels of anxiety about death, while religious people who do not consistently practice their faith experience the greatest fear of dying (Nelson & Nelson, 1973).

Psychiatrist Elisabeth Kübler-Ross (1969; 1974) provided us with new and important insights on the process of dying through her interviews of hundreds of terminally ill patients at the University of Chicago teaching and research hospital. From these interviews, she developed a theory that people who learn of their impending death (and sometimes their loved ones) tend to pass through five rather distinct stages:

1. *Denial.* At first, the individual strongly resists the idea of death by denying the validity of the information about his or her terminal illness. It's common at this stage for the terminally ill person to accuse his or her doctor of being incompetent, to seek a more favorable diagnosis, or to look for a "miracle cure." Sometimes the denial is more subtle, however. The individual may simply act like the news of impending death had never been revealed and proceed as if nothing is wrong for a while.
2. *Anger.* After the initial denial, the terminally ill person reacts to the fact of her or his impending death with anger: Why me? It's not fair that this should be happening to me! There is much hostility, envy of others, and resentment during this stage. As a result, the terminally ill person is often highly irritable and frequently quarrels with nurses, doctors, and loved ones.
3. *Bargaining.* The anger and denial of the impending death are largely gone by this third stage, and the terminally ill person fully realizes that death is coming. But death still is not accepted as inevitable. Instead, the person tries to strike bargains to prolong his or her life. These bargains may be in the form of willingness to undergo painful treatments to extend life, but they are more often silent deals with God, such as "I'll leave most of my money to the church if I can have 6 more months." Interestingly, if the person does live past this bargaining stage, the bargain is usually broken—the church does not get the money.
4. *Depression.* Eventually, the reality of impending death leads to a loss of hope. Bargains no longer seem possible; death is coming no matter what. The person often begins to feel guilty about leaving loved ones behind, incapable of facing death with dignity, and quite depressed.
5. *Acceptance.* In time, the depression lifts and the person finally achieves an acceptance of death. This generally is not a happy feeling of acceptance, but a state of emotional exhaustion that leaves the individual peacefully free of negative emotions.

Kübler-Ross (1974) and others point out that not every terminally ill person passes through these same stages. Reactions to impending death are highly individual (Feifel, 1990). If we go through the process of dying with a loved one, we must be careful not to impose on him or her our views of how the process of accepting death should proceed.

Thinking Critically About Psychology

1. How might an understanding of Erikson's and Levinson's theories of development affect your own experience of adult developmental stages?

2. Do you think that your personality has changed in the past 10 years? Do you expect it to change in the future?

Review

Intelligence and personality remain relatively constant throughout the adult years in most healthy adults, but some change does take place. Some aspects of intellectual ability improve throughout adulthood, while other aspects do not change. Still, minor declines in some aspects of intelligence occur in most of us, particularly after age 70. Similarly, a few positive changes in personality seem to take place. Psychologists disagree as to whether the changes in adulthood can be thought of as a series of stages. Erikson and Levinson have outlined a series of stages of adult life, but we still have much to learn about adult development.

Although some older adults despair of ever achieving a meaningful pattern of living, many others achieve a sense of integrity and continue to find life meaningful and joyful until death. Aging is partly a biological process of physical deterioration, but aging is also a psychological process that can be slowed to some degree by staying engaged in meaningful activities and by not believing many of the negative myths about old age so prevalent in our society. Regardless of how the individual lives out the later adult years, the final "stage" of life is always death. Older adults tend to accept their impending deaths, especially religious adults, but individuals who must face the knowledge of their impending death earlier in the life span generally go through several stages of anguish before reaching a state of acceptance.

Check Your Learning

To be sure that you have learned the key points from the preceding section, cover the answers below and try to answer each question. If you give an incorrect answer to any question, return to the page given next to the correct answer to see why your answer was not correct.

1. The challenge of the ________________ stage is to enter into committed, loving relationships with others that partially replace bonds with parents.

a. early adulthood **c.** later adulthood
b. middle adulthood **d.** midlife

2. According to Erikson, a person in middle adulthood must be ____________ (or productive) to find meaning in life.

a. stagnant **c.** generative
b. creative **d.** flexible

3. One key to a satisfactory older adulthood seems to be in ignoring the restrictive myths and stereotypes of old age so prevalent in our society.

a. True
b. False

4. ________________ is one significant factor related to one's fear of death.

a. Marital status **c.** Success in life
b. Local climate **d.** Religious belief

Correct Answers

1. a (p. 311), 2. c (p. 313), 3. a (p. 316), 4. d (p. 317).

APPLICATION OF PSYCHOLOGY

PARENTING

During the important early stages of development—infancy, childhood, and most of adolescence—we typically live with our parents. They give us food and shelter, protect us from danger, and provide many of our early learning experiences. Parents play a key role in giving children a healthy start in life. But, although parenting is important, we as a society provide parents with no training in how to raise their children. Our schools teach reading, writing, and arithmetic, but not parenting. For this reason, we will look carefully at the topic of parenting, with an emphasis on the styles of parenting that are best for children.

Parenting and Infant Attachment

Let's begin with a look at the parents' role in helping their infant develop a secure relationship—or attachment—with the parents. The newborn in the hospital nursery seems equally happy to be rocked by anyone who has free arms, but sometime during the first year of life (usually by about 6 to 9 months) infants typically become closely attached to one or more of their caretakers. At this point in development, most infants develop a normal "stranger anxiety" and react fearfully and tearfully when strangers are present and cling to the safe fortress of the adult to whom they are attached (Ainsworth, 1979). By 18 to 24 months, however, most toddlers are better able to deal with stranger anxiety. They prefer to be near their primary caretaker when strangers are first encountered, but they are able to move out to explore the world and play, knowing that the safe caretaker is nearby. Infants who are able to deal with stranger anxiety in this way are said to be "securely attached."

Some infants and toddlers, however, are less securely attached to their parent. When separated from their caretaker, some "insecurely attached" toddlers cling excessively to the caretaker and become extremely upset when separated from the parent. Seemingly, the attachment is not secure enough to allow the toddler to turn her or his back on the parent for a moment. Other toddlers who are not securely attached rarely use the parent as a safe haven, but rather seem to ignore or even avoid the parent. It is as if the attachment to the parent is too weak to be helpful to the toddler.

What leads to secure attachment? Part of the answer is the child's inborn temperament. Some children are simply calmer and more receptive to the parent from birth. But parents play an important role as well. Parents can help their infants form secure attachments by taking care of the infant's needs in a consistent way and by being warm, affectionate, and accepting. In this case, being an accepting parent means staying calm and loving (most of the time, at least) when the baby "acts like an infant"—crying in the middle of the night, wetting diaper after diaper, and spitting every bite of cereal back into your hand (Goldsmith & Alansky, 1987)!

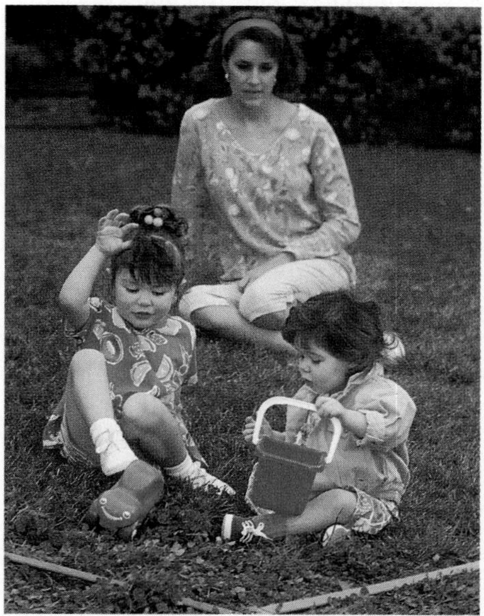
By age 18 to 24 months, "securely attached" toddlers are able to explore the world and play if they know a safe caregiver is nearby.

Our parents care for us from infancy through adolescence and provide us with many of our most important learning experiences.

It is important for parents to help their infants develop the firm foundation of a secure attachment, but how worried should the parent of an insecurely attached infant be? The best answer is that the parent should be concerned enough to look at his or her parenting to see whether healthy changes can be made, but not overly concerned. It is not uncommon for an extremely clingy 2-year-old who receives consistent and loving parenting to grow into a happy and secure 5-year-old—I've personally seen it happen more than once.

Parenting and Discipline Style

Discipline style is one of the most important parts of parenting. As soon as the infant can move, the adult must attempt to regulate the child's behavior to protect the child and point the child in healthy directions. In other words, the parent must provide guidance and discipline. What discipline style is the best for children? Psychologist Diana Baumrind (1983) has extensively studied the discipline styles used by parents and has divided them into three types: authoritarian, permissive, and authoritative.

The *authoritarian* parent gives strict rules to the child or adolescent with little discussion of the reasons for the rules. It is the "because I say so" approach to rules. Authoritarian parents are openly critical of their children and frequently give them instructions on how to behave. Rules are enforced by punishing a child who does not obey, sometimes quite harshly.

In contrast, the *permissive* parent gives the child or adolescent few rules and rarely punishes misbehavior. The child is given great respect and autonomy but often too much independence at too early an age.

The *authoritative* parent (notice the difference in spelling between *authoritative* and *authoritarian*) is an authority figure to the child but provides good explanations for all rules and freely discusses them with the child. In allowing their children to freely state their opinions about rules, and sometimes being persuaded to alter the rules by a logical argument from them, authoritative parents give children a greater sense of involvement in their own rules. Authoritative parents emphasize reinforcement of appropriate behavior and affectionate warmth over punishment, and often do not use any physical punishment at all. They encourage independence, but within clearly defined limits to take the child's level of development into consideration. In short, authoritative parents show their children that they are loved and respected but provide the amount of authority that the child needs.

Which of these approaches to discipline works best? Baumrind's research clearly indicates that children whose parents adopt an authoritative style are better behaved, more successful, and happier than the children of parents who use other styles of discipline, and their families are more harmonious (Baumrind, 1983, 1991). However, some evidence suggests that the authoritative style may not be the best discipline style in all American cultures. For example, use of an authoritative disciplinary style is strongly associated with greater success in school for white and Hispanic children, but not as strongly for African-American and Asian-American children (Darling & Steinberg, 1993). Indeed, some evidence shows that an authoritarian style might be better for African-American girls in terms of promoting greater assertiveness (Baumrind, 1972). We do not yet understand cultural differences in disciplinary style well enough to explain them. The increased interest of developmental psychologists in cultural differences in recent years is a healthy, if long overdue, change. Hopefully, it will not be long until the best child-rearing practices for all American cultures are understood.

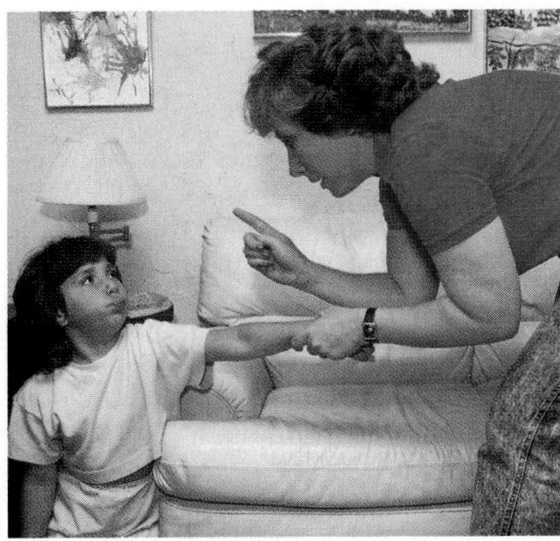

A child's temperament may have as much effect on disciplinary style as the parent's choice. Lytton found that parents who usually used the authoritative style tended to become more authoritarian when faced with an unruly child.

Direction of Effect in Child Rearing: The Two-Way Street

University of Virginia professor Richard Bell (1968) pointed out some time ago that we must be very careful in our interpretations of studies of parenting. We just learned that children whose parents are authoritative are better behaved and happier than children whose parents use other styles of discipline. Does this necessarily mean that authoritative parenting causes good behavior in children? Most developmental psychologists think so, but it is very likely that something else is going on as well. It is probable that children who are happy and easy to get along with make it easier for their parents to adopt an authoritative style of discipline. A happy, reasonable child can be given a great deal of independence and needs little strict discipline. But would the same parent adopt a different style of discipline if the child were irritable, defiant, and aggressive? Several studies suggest that this might be the case—that children affect their parents as much as parents affect their children.

Hugh Lytton of the University of Calgary (Anderson, Lytton, & Romney, 1986) has compared parents of normal, well-behaved children with parents to children who were so disobedient and aggressive that they had been referred to psychologists for help. He observed these two groups of parents interacting with their children in a playroom in his laboratory. As in previous studies, Lytton found that the parents of the badly behaved children were less affectionate, less likely to reward positive behavior, more critical, and gave many more instructions to their children on how to behave than the parents of the well-behaved children.

Generally, psychologists have concluded that it is exactly this pattern of authoritarian parenting that causes the children to behave badly (e.g., Baumrind, 1983). But Lytton provided a clever twist to his study. He exchanged parents and children—so that the parents of well-behaved children were matched with badly behaved children and vice versa—and observed their interactions again. When the parents of well-behaved children were faced with an aggressive, disobedient child, the formerly model parents behaved just like the parents of the badly behaved children. Quickly, they also resorted to the unpleasant, critical, authoritarian style of discipline.

So who influences whom in the family? Does the parent's discipline affect the child's behavior, or does the child's behavior influence the parent's discipline? Clearly a great deal of both is going on. This is a very important point. Effective parenting is a very important influence on the child, but even the best parents know that different children will evoke different parenting responses from them. The parents of temperamental, difficult children will have to resist the natural tendency to make authoritarian responses to their children's provocative behavior if they are going to help their children eliminate their misbehavior.

Myth of the Perfect Parent

Loving and effective parenting is the greatest gift that a parent can give a child. But, it is important to point out that *perfect* parenting is not as important as some of us seem to think. Many parents act as if their children are as delicate as spun glass. They are paralyzed in their attempts to be good parents by their fear that they will do the wrong thing and scar their children for life.

Actually, children are pretty resilient creatures. Within broad limits, they will grow up very well in spite of the fact that none of them have perfect parents. They will not be miserable forever if their parents sometimes lose their temper and speak in harsh tones; and they will learn to play with other children without being coached in every step.

That is not to say that parents cannot harm their children. Unfortunately, children are hurt badly every day by neglectful and abusive parents. But most of the minor imperfections of parenting that are characteristic of every child's upbringing are of relatively little consequence.

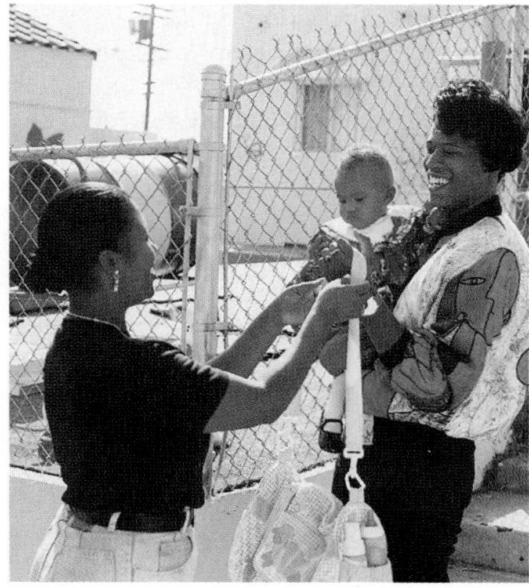

In the words of one researcher, "Child care is now as essential to family life as the automobile and the refrigerator." (Scarr, 1990). A key element in children's successful adaptation to day care is the quality of care provided.

Day Care, Divorce, and Parenting

Until relatively recently, most children in the United States were cared for by one of their parents—almost always the mother—who stayed at home full time to raise the children and care for the home while the other parent worked outside the home. And most of us felt that this way of raising children was the "natural" way of things. Indeed, the image of the "caretaker mother and breadwinner father" is so deeply embedded in our view of child rearing that most of us are shocked to learn that very few children are raised in that manner today. In actuality, only 7 percent of all children in the United States are raised by two married parents through their entire childhood, with the mother not working outside the home (Braverman, 1989; Silverstein, 1991)!

In many families, both married parents have chosen—or have felt compelled by economic necessity—to be employed full time outside the home. Indeed, the percentage of women with school-age children who work outside the home has risen from 40 percent in the 1970s to 75 percent in the 1990s (Silverstein, 1991). In many other cases, divorce results in the custodial parent (usually the mother) being more likely to work outside the home. About 50 percent of all marriages now end in divorce, and divorced women are 50 percent more likely to work outside the home than married women (Scarr, Phillips, & McCartney, 1990). In addition, more children are raised now by single parents who have never married than ever before (up over 350 percent since the 1970s) (Silverstein, 1991).

All of these changes in the nature of the American family over the past quarter century have resulted in mothers spending less time raising their children. Who cares for the children, then? It is distressing to learn that the increased entry of mothers into the labor force has not led fathers to spend more time with their children. On the average, fathers still spend 26 minutes a day with their children under age 6, with that time decreasing to 16 minutes a day as the children grow older! Some of the job of child rearing has fallen to other family members, but many children now spend a great deal of time in day care. As psychologist Sandra Scarr put it, "Child care is now as essential to family life as the automobile and the refrigerator" (Scarr et al., 1990, p. 26).

Have these changes in how our children are raised had a harmful effect on the children? In spite of the great anguish of parents and psychologists alike, extensive research suggests that, in general, children who are in day care do not differ from children who are raised by parents in their own homes in terms of physical health, emotional or intellectual development, or attachment (Hoffman, 1989). The key elements in the successful adaptation of children to day care appear to be the quality of the day-care environment and the quality and quantity of time spent with parents in the evenings and on weekends. The available research supports the common sense conclusion that a poor day-care environment is harmful to children, while a positive day-care environment is good for children (Hoffman, 1989; Scarr & Eisenberg, 1993).

The other common situation that reduces the amount of parenting is divorce. Is divorce harmful to children? There is little doubt that divorce is stressful and upsetting to all the adults and children involved. Few children make it through the time of divorce without some emotional turmoil that results in misbehavior and problems at school, but usually the disruption is for a relatively brief period of time (Hetherington, 1979). The children who are affected the longest by divorce are the ones whose parents were openly conflictual before the divorce and continue to have conflict in front of the children after the divorce (Atkeson, Forehand, & Rikard, 1982), or whose parents have serious psychological difficulties (Lahey et al., 1988). Children generally adapt well to divorce when their parents work out their differences after the divorce well enough to cease arguing in front of the children and cooperate in allowing each other to share in the duties and pleasures of parenting.

Summary

This chapter summarizes key concepts in developmental psychology and the major theories that explain the process of development. It describes the normal course of development from infancy and childhood, adolescence, adulthood, and later adulthood, to the time of death.

I. Some psychologists believe that developmental changes in behavior are biologically programmed to "unfold" with increasing age while others believe that changes in behavior are "molded" by the environment that we experience.
  - **A.** Maturation, the systematic physical growth of the nervous system and other parts of the body, is a key concept to "unfolding" theorists; learning is the key concept to "molding" theorists.
  - **B.** Today, most psychologists believe that both nature (biological factors) and nurture (environment) combine to influence our actions, thoughts, and feelings.

II. Some theorists believe that early childhood is the "formative period" for our personalities.
  - **A.** Research on imprinting in animals shows that experiences during critical periods of early development can have long-lasting effects on animal behavior, but there may not be such clear-cut critical periods in human development.
  - **B.** Margaret and Harry Harlow's experiments with social deprivation during the infancy of monkeys show long-lasting effects of abnormal early experiences, but human infants seem capable of recovering to a great extent from early abnormal experience.
  - **C.** Parents play a key role in fostering the development of their children, but the emotions and behavior of the child also influence the parents' choice of parenting styles.

III. Stage theorists believe all children must pass through the same qualitatively different stages in the same order.
  - **A.** Piaget identified four stages of cognitive development from infancy to adulthood.
    1. During the sensorimotor stage (birth to 2 years) an infant experiences the world in terms of sensory information and motor activities.
    2. In the preoperational stage (2 to 7 years), children can think in mental images, but they think in ways that are illogical by adult standards.
    3. The concrete operational stage (7 to 11 years) is marked by increased ability to reason logically, except for abstract reasoning.
    4. In the formal operational stage (11 years on), an individual uses full adult logic and understands abstract concepts.
  - **B.** Kohlberg's theory of moral development is concerned with the logical process of arriving at answers to moral dilemmas.
    1. At the premoral level, a child has no sense of morality as adults understand that term.
    2. A child's moral view is based on what others will think of him or her as stated in laws and rules at the conventional level.
    3. At the principled level, individuals judge right and wrong according to ethical principles rather than by rules or expected reward or punishment.
  - **C.** Carol Gilligan has provided a theory that she believes more accurately describes moral development in females than does Kohlberg's.
    1. The young girl follows rules to obtain rewards and avoid punishment in the earliest stage, "morality as individual survival."
    2. Later, in the "morality as self-sacrifice" stage, the girl believes that to be good she must sacrifice her needs at times to meet the needs of others.
    3. In the most mature stage of "morality as equality," she believes that everyone's needs should be met when possible and that sacrifices should be shared equally when they are necessary.
  - **D.** Erik Erikson's theory of development focuses on the person's developing relationships with others in the social world.

IV. Average ages at which changes in development take place are used to portray the pattern of age-related changes.
  - **A.** During the prenatal period, development is a process of rapid growth and differentiation of the major systems and organs of the body.
  - **B.** The neonatal period is the first 2 weeks of life and marks the transition from the womb to independent life.
  - **C.** Infancy (2 weeks to 2 years) is a time of rapid physical, perceptual, cognitive, linguistic, social, and emotional development.
  - **D.** During early childhood (2 to 7 years) growth is less explosive and rapid than during infancy.
  - **E.** Middle childhood (7 to 11 years) is characterized by slow physical growth, but important cognitive changes occur, such as the emergence of conservation.

V. Adolescence is the developmental period from the onset of puberty until the beginning of adulthood.
  - **A.** The production of sex hormones in puberty triggers biological changes known as the primary sex characteristics.
    1. Menarche, the first menstrual period, occurs at about 12 years and 6 months in American females.
    2. Production of sperm begins about two years later in males.
  - **B.** Secondary sex characteristics appear in both sexes during puberty.
  - **C.** The adolescent growth spurt lasts for a little over a year in early adolescence.
  - **D.** Girls tend to experience puberty about two years earlier than boys.
    1. For both sexes, different parts of the body grow at different rates, and weight and physique change in irregular ways.
    2. Within each sex, there is wide variation in the age at which puberty begins.
  - **E.** Piaget's formal operational stage—the ability to use abstract concepts—occurs in some individuals by about age 11.
  - **F.** Many adolescents go through what Erikson calls an identity crisis, but for most adolescents the period is not particularly stormy.
  - **G.** Peers replace the family as the most important influence on the adolescent. However, most adolescents remain relatively close to their parents in terms of values and attitudes.

VI. Adulthood is not a single phase of life. Some changes involving love, work, and play continue throughout adulthood.
   A. Intelligence appears relatively stable throughout adulthood in healthy adults, with small declines beginning between ages 50 and 60, especially in the speed of intellectual processing. Some larger declines occur after age 70 in some aspects of intelligence, particularly in individuals with arteriosclerosis and other brain impairment.
   B. Some relatively predictable personality changes that occur for many people during adulthood include becoming more insightful, dependable, and candid. Most aspects of personality remain relatively constant across adulthood, however.
   C. Some psychologists believe that we pass through "stages" of development during adulthood.
      1. Developmental stages of adulthood appear to differ from those of childhood in that not every adult goes through each stage, the order of the stages can vary, and the timing of the stages is not controlled by biological maturation.
      2. Erikson calls early adulthood the stage of intimacy versus isolation, during which many individuals enter committed, loving relationships.
      3. Erikson calls middle adulthood the stage of generativity versus stagnation, during which many individuals find meaning in work and family lives.
   D. Other psychologists dispute the concept of "stages" of adult development, however.

VII. Erikson calls the period from the late 60s on the stage of integrity versus despair; older adults who see meaning in their lives when considered as a whole continue to live a satisfying existence.
   A. Psychological variables associated with happy aging are whether one stays "engaged" in life's activities and whether one believes the myths about old age.
   B. Older adults tend to be less frightened by death than are younger adults. Studies by Kübler-Ross suggest that people who learn of their impending death tend to pass through five distinct stages: denial, anger, bargaining, depression, and acceptance.

Suggested Readings

1. To read Erikson's own words about his theory of personality development: Erikson, E. (1950). *Childhood and society*. New York: Norton.
2. To learn more about theories of moral development: Gilligan, C. (1982). *In a different voice*. Cambridge: Harvard University Press; and Kohlberg, L. (1981). *The philosophy of moral development: Moral stages and the idea of justice*. New York: Harper & Row.
3. For a view of adolescence by adolescents themselves: Offer, D., Ostrov, E., & Howard, K. I. (1981). *The adolescent: A psychological self-portrait*. New York: Basic Books.
4. For differing perspectives on stages of adult life: Levinson, D. J. (1978). *The seasons of a man's life*. New York: Knopf; Lowenthal, M. F., Thurnher, M., & Chiriboga, D. (1975). *Four stages of life: A comparative study of women and men facing transitions*. San Francisco: Jossey-Bass; Schulz, R., & Ewen, R. B. (1988). *Adult development and aging: Emerging realities*. New York: Macmillan; and McCrae, R. R., & Costa, P. T. (1994). The stability of personality: Observations and evaluations. *Current Directions in Psychological Science, 3*, 173–175.
5. Behaviorist B. F. Skinner and a colleague, writing in his early eighties, discuss ways to rearrange one's life circumstances to enjoy old age to its fullest. Skinner, B. F., & Vaughn, M. E. (1983). *Enjoy old age*. New York: Norton.
6. A call for new directions in psychological and medical research on aging that is fascinating and written in nontechnical language: Science Directorate, Vitality for Life: Psychological Research for Productive Aging. Washington, DC: American Psychological Association.
7. A terrific summary of normal and abnormal infant development can be found in: Zeanah, C. H., Boris, N. W., & Larrieu, J. A. (1977). Infant development and developmental risk: A review of the past 10 years. *Journal of the American Academy of Child and Adolescent Psychiatry, 36*, 165–178.

P A R T 5

The Self

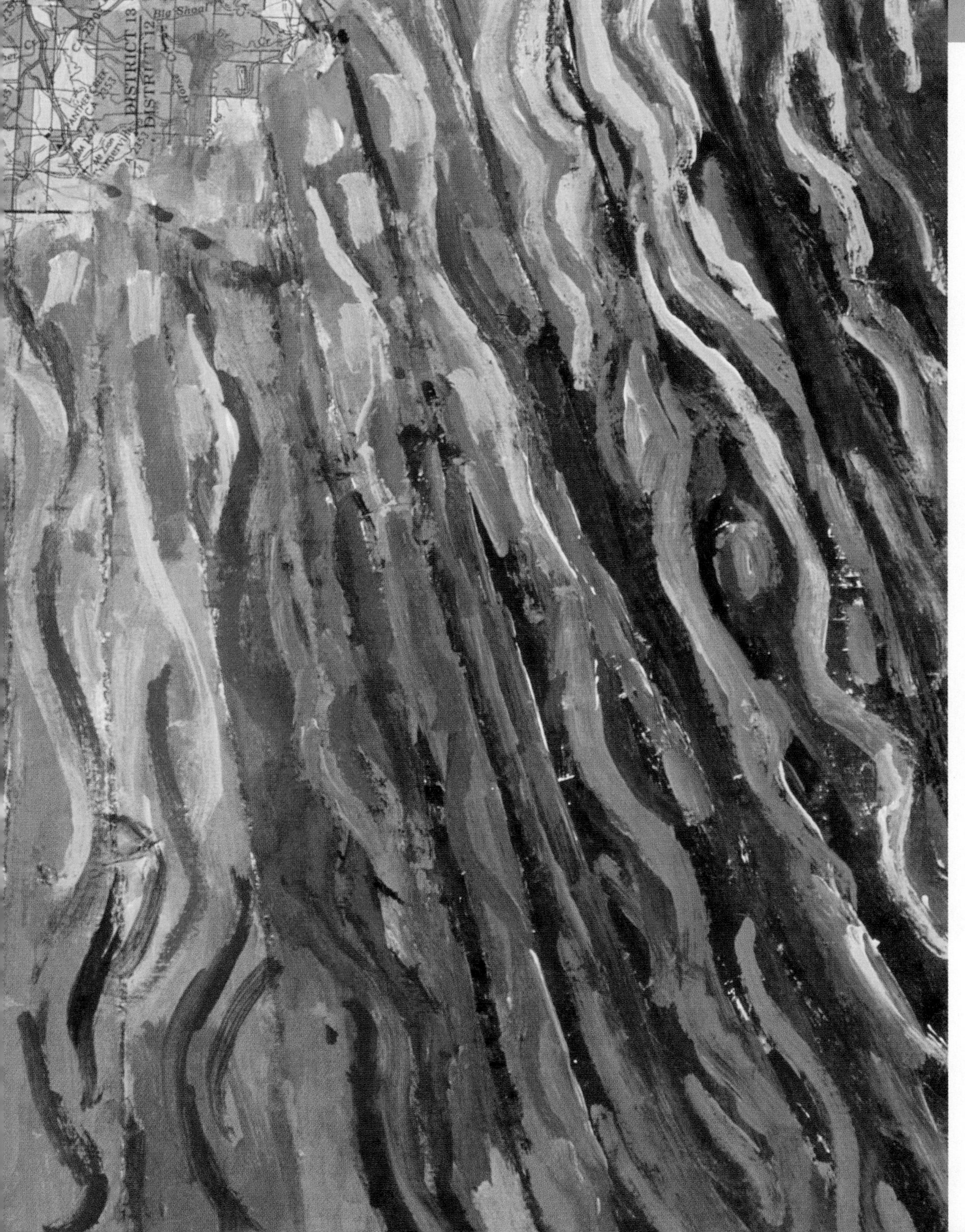

CHAPTER

9

CHAPTER OUTLINE

Motivation and Emotion

PROLOGUE

Conducting research is one of the most consistently enjoyable parts of my career. Even if I never contribute anything really important to psychology through research, each study is an intriguing puzzle and I love finding each clue to a mystery that puts any spy novel to shame. Still, for all my love of research, I wonder if the great researcher Walter Cannon could have talked me into doing for science what he persuaded his colleague A. L. Washburn to do to understand the motive of hunger.

Cannon and Washburn (1912) were trying to isolate the biological mechanism of hunger. They believed that the feeling of hunger was caused by contractions of the stomach wall. To determine whether this idea was correct, Cannon convinced Washburn to swallow a balloon that was attached to a long tube connected to an air pump. The balloon was then inflated to fill Washburn's stomach. In this way, stomach contractions could be mechanically detected because they squeezed the balloon and increased the air pressure in the tube (see fig. 9.1). While the intermittent contractions were being measured, Washburn, who could not talk because of the tube gagging his mouth and throat, indicated when he felt a conscious sensation of hunger by pressing a key connected to a recording instrument. (History does not tell us, however, whether Washburn used his other hand to signal more negative feelings to Cannon during this unpleasant experiment.)

As predicted, Washburn did feel hungry when his stomach contracted, leading them to conclude that hunger was no more than the rumbling contractions of an empty stomach. As we shall see later in the chapter, such contractions are still believed to be part of the feeling of hunger for many people, but sadly, considering Washburn's selfless contribution to science, stomach contractions are only one factor in hunger, and one of the least important factors at that.

This chapter is about our motives and our emotions. Motives are states that make us active rather than inactive and lead us to do one thing rather than another. If I have just eaten, I may take a nap or quietly read the newspaper; but if I am hungry, I will get up and fix food. The motive of hunger activates and directs my behavior. Some motives are based on the survival needs of the body for food, water, and warmth. These biological motives are regulated by intricate and sensitive mechanisms under the control of the hypothalamus that detect the body's needs.

Other motives—the so-called psychological motives—are not directly related to the survival needs of the body. The motive to maintain a moderate level of novel stimulation and activity, the motive to achieve and be successful, and the motive to have friendly relationships with others are examples of psychological motives. These motives are often strongly influenced by learning experiences and therefore differ from individual to individual and culture to culture.

Emotions are special states that often motivate us. Emotions are a complex mixture of three different but intimately related psychological processes. First, emotions involve a positive or negative conscious experience. That simply means that all emotions feel good or bad; if they were neutral, we wouldn't call them emotions. Second, emotions are accompanied by

KEY TERMS

FIGURE 9.1

Diagram of the device used in the experiment by Cannon and Washburn (1912) to find out if stomach contractions cause a conscious feeling of hunger. Note the balloon swallowed by Washburn to measure the contractions.

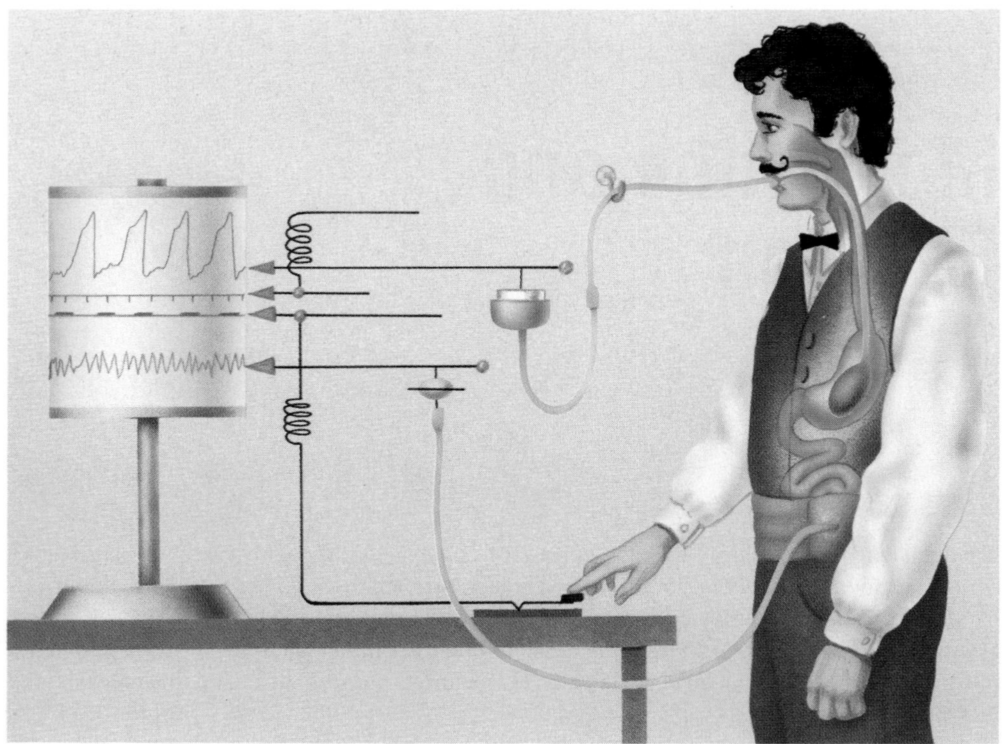

physiological arousal of the autonomic nervous system, some endocrine glands, and other physiological systems. And, third, they usually involve some kind of related behavior. When you see a car driving toward you, you feel a negative conscious experience, your autonomic nervous system churns you up, and you run. As we will see, some aspects of emotions appear to be inborn, while other aspects are shaped by our learning experiences.

Hungry grocery shoppers are motivated shoppers who are likely to buy more food than nonhungry shoppers.

DEFINITIONS OF MOTIVATION AND EMOTION

To people who are interested in human behavior, the key question is *why?* Carol wants to know why she continues to have sex with Michael when she knows she does not love him and is afraid of getting pregnant. The manager of the packing plant wants to know why two of her employees do not seem to care about doing a good job. A father wants to know why his son is not willing to work hard for good grades in school. Answers to questions like these often involve the concept of motivation—if they lead us to look *inside* the person.

The term **motivation** refers to an *internal* state that activates and gives direction to our thoughts. Meg was starting to feel a little hungry when an ad on television for tacos made her feel famished, reminded her that she had food in the refrigerator, and sent her scrambling to the kitchen. If her motive for hunger had not been activated, perhaps her motive to succeed in school might have led her in a different direction—maybe to read her psychology textbook. If no motives at all were activated, she would be doing nothing—just sitting around or maybe taking a nap. Motives are at the center of our lives—they arouse and direct what we think, feel, and do.

Some motives, such as hunger, are clearly based on internal physiological states. As we will see, several internal factors, such as the level of sugar in the blood, are important in regulating hunger. But other motives, such as the motive to succeed, are not based on simple internal physiological states. For all motives, however, *external cues* play an important role. Seeing the ad for tacos on television was an external cue that stimulated Meg's hunger motive; hearing her roommate worry aloud about passing her next psychology test would be an external cue that could have stimulated her motive to succeed.

Motivation is closely related to the topic of emotions. **Emotions** are positive or negative feelings—generally reactions to stimuli—that are accompanied by physiological arousal and characteristic behavior. When we are afraid, for example, we experience an

motivation

Internal state or condition that activates and gives direction to our thoughts, feelings, and actions.

emotions

Postive or negative feelings generally in reaction to stimuli that are accompanied by physiological arousal and related behavior.

acutely unpleasant feeling: The sympathetic division of our autonomic nervous system is aroused and the fear generally shows in our behavior. The emotion of passion, on the other hand, is a conglomeration of very different feelings, biological changes, and behavior.

Motivation and emotions are closely linked concepts for three reasons: (a) The arousal of emotions activates behavior as motives do; (b) motives are often accompanied by emotions, (for example, the motive to perform well on a test is often accompanied by anxiety; sexual motivation is generally blended with the emotions of passion and love); and (c) emotions typically have motivational properties of their own—because you are in love, you are motivated to be with your special person; because you are angry you want to strike out at the object of your anger. We begin this chapter with a discussion of basic motives necessary for biological survival, then move to a discussion of more "psychological" motives, and end with a discussion of human emotions.

PRIMARY MOTIVES: BIOLOGICAL NEEDS

Many human motives stem from the *need* for things that keep an organism alive: food, water, warmth, sleep, avoidance of pain, and so on. We consider these to be **primary motives** because we must meet these biological needs or die. The sexual motive is also considered to be a primary motive, not because we would die if it were not fulfilled, but because the species could not reproduce and survive if the sexual motive were not satisfied.

primary motives
Human motives for things that are necessary for survival, such as food, water, and warmth.

This chapter focuses on the biological motives of hunger and thirst, partly because they are the best understood of the primary motives. Elsewhere in the book, information is provided on the primary motives of avoidance of pain in chapter 3 and the need for sleep in chapter 4.

Homeostasis: Biological Thermostats

Most of the primary drives are based on the body's need to maintain a certain level of essential life elements: adequate sugar in the blood to nourish cells, sufficient water in the body, and so on. These critical levels are regulated by **homeostatic mechanisms.** These mechanisms sense imbalances in the body and stimulate actions that restore the proper balance. The homeostatic mechanisms of the body are often compared to the thermostats of home heating systems. When the temperature of the house falls below a preset level, the thermostat senses that fact and signals the heater to produce heat until the proper temperature has been restored; then it signals the heater to turn off. Bodily responses to imbalances can involve both internal reactions and overt behavior. For instance, when the water level in body cells falls below a safe level, a signal is sent to the kidneys to reabsorb additional water from the urine. At the same time, a signal is sent to the brain that leads the animal—human or otherwise—to seek out and drink liquids. Similar homeostatic mechanisms are involved in hunger and the maintenance of body temperature.

homeostatic mechanisms
(hō´´mē-ō-stak´ik) Internal bodily mechanism that senses biological imbalances and stimulates actions to restore the proper balance.

Hunger: The Regulation of Food Intake

It's 10:30 A.M. and I am not hungry, but sometime during the next 2 or 3 hours, I will feel hungry enough to leave my computer and eat lunch. How will my body know that I need to eat? What will happen inside to make me feel hungry? And how does this process regulate my food intake and body weight?

During the years since I wrote the first edition of this book, and first paid close attention to the physiological mechanisms regulating hunger, I have been watching my eating and activity level. The only thing that is consistent about my eating and exercising habits is my inconsistency. I usually stick carefully to a healthy low-fat diet that would bring tears to the eyes of mother nature, but at times I have been the best customer of the Häagen-Dazs Ice Cream people. I usually exercise regularly, but at other times I have been a real couch potato.

As my activity level and eating have fluctuated, my weight has changed—particularly after I stopped being thirtysomething. But the surprising fact is that my weight has not fluctuated nearly as much as my exercise and eating habits have, and the same is true for most people. How does the body manage to maintain its weight within relatively narrow limits

FIGURE 9.2

Three parts of the hypothalamus play a key role in the control of hunger: the lateral feeding center, the ventromedial satiety center, and the paraventricular nucleus. The lateral feeding center directly stimulates hunger and eating. The paraventricular nucleus controls hunger through the control of blood sugar. The ventromedial satiety center operates in a feedback loop with the body's adipose cells. Secretions of Ob lead to the ventromedial satiety center to directly inhibit eating, stimulate the paraventricular nucleus, and increase the metabolism of fat cells through activation of the sympathetic nervous system (Ezell, 1995).

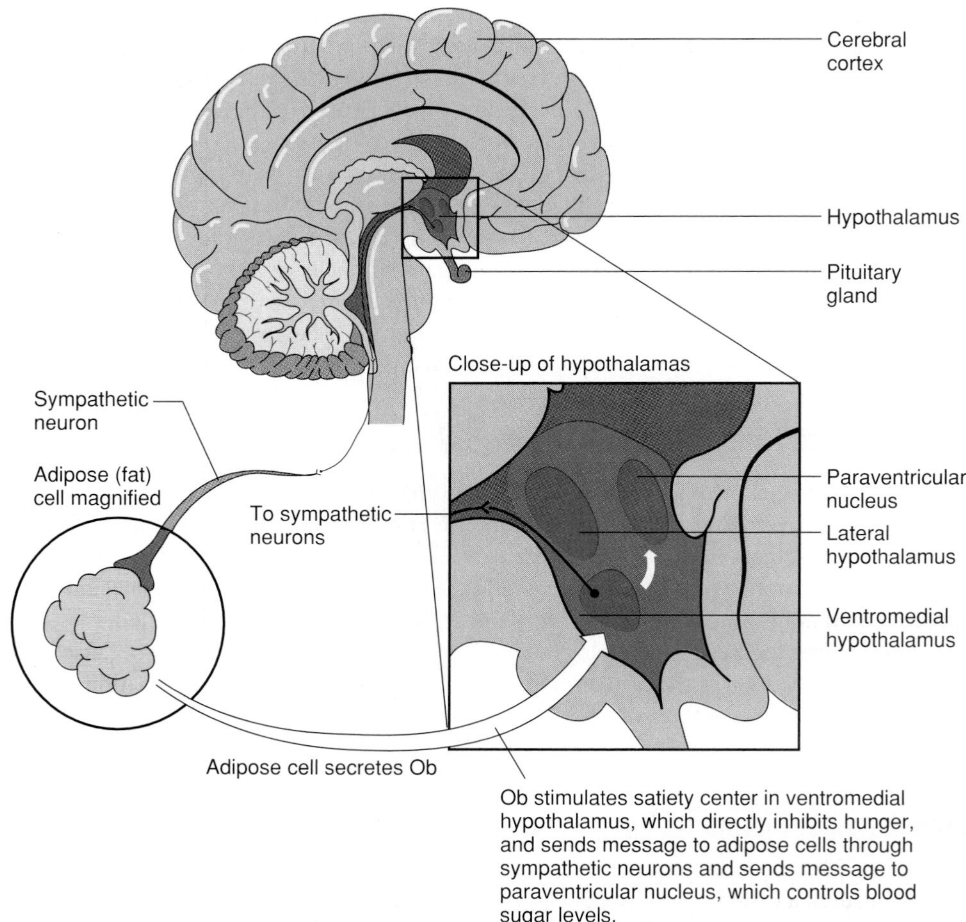

in spite of changes in diet and exercise? We give a tentative answer to this question by taking a close look at the biological and psychological factors that play a role in hunger.

Biological Regulation of Hunger

The biological control center of hunger is not the rumbling stomach. It does play a minor part in the control of hunger, but a much less important one than most of us think. Instead, the **hypothalamus** plays the controlling role in the motivation of hunger (Mook, 1986; Petri, 1986). This small but extremely important forebrain structure that we first discussed in chapter 2 is involved in the regulation of many motives and emotions (see fig. 9.2).

hypothalamus
(hī´´pō-thal´ah-mus) The part of the forebrain involved with motives, emotions, and the functions of the autonomic nervous system.

Recent advances in our understanding of the brain have revealed that hunger is regulated by three centers in the hypothalamus. Two of these hypothalamic control centers operate in opposing ways. A *feeding system* that initiates eating when food is needed is located in the **lateral hypothalamus,** and a *satiety system* that stops eating when enough food has been consumed is located in the **ventromedial hypothalamus.**

lateral hypothalamus
A portion of the hypothalamus involved in feeling hungry and starting to eat (the feeding center).

ventromedial hypothalamus
A part of the hypothalamus involved in inhibiting eating when sufficient food has been consumed (the satiety center).

hyperphagia
(hī´´per-fā´´jē-ah) Excessive overeating that results from the destruction of the satiety center of the hypothalamus.

Studies of laboratory rats have shown that when the lateral hypothalamus (the feeding system) is electrically stimulated, rats that are too satiated (full) to eat will begin eating again. If this part of the hypothalamus is destroyed, on the other hand, rats will stop eating altogether and will starve to death if not artificially fed. Conversely, if the ventromedial hypothalamus (the satiety system) is surgically destroyed, the rats will overeat into a startling state of obesity (excessive fat). Figure 9.3 shows a normal rat and a rat with **hyperphagia** whose body weight tripled after surgical destruction of the hypothalamic center associated with satiety. These rats do not eat more times each day than normal rats but continue eating much longer each time they eat. Apparently, the destruction of part of the satiety system eliminates the homeostatic signal to stop eating when enough food has been consumed.

Alexander Reeves and Fred Plumb (1969) reported a clinical case study of a woman with tragic damage to the satiety center in the hypothalamus that bears striking resemblance to hyperphagic laboratory animals. A 20-year-old bookkeeper sought medical help for her suddenly abnormal appetite and weight gain. X rays identified a tumor in the hypothalamus, but it could not be surgically removed. Prior to her death 3 years later, she regularly consumed 10,000 calories per day in an endless attempt to satisfy her hunger.

The third part of the hypothalamus that plays a role in the regulation of hunger is the **paraventricular nucleus.** This center both increases and decreases appetite by controlling the level of sugar in the blood (Martin, White, & Hulsey, 1991).

What information do the three centers of the hypothalamus use in regulating hunger? Apparently, two cues are used to regulate hunger on a daily basis, and a third cue is used to regulate body weight on a long-term basis.

1. *Stomach contractions.* Cannon and Washburn, whom we discussed at the beginning of the chapter, were partly right about the role of stomach contractions. The most immediate cue in the regulation of hunger really does come from the stomach. Contractions signal the lateral hypothalamic feeding system, whereas a full stomach activates the ventromedial satiety system.
2. *Blood sugar levels.* Eating is also regulated on a short-term basis by the amount of sugar (glucose) in the blood. The hypothalamus contains specialized neurons that can directly detect the level of glucose in the bloodstream, but two other organs provide most of the information to the hypothalamus. The liver, which is a storehouse for sugar, detects blood glucose levels, and the upper small intestine, or *duodenum,* detects sugar in food that has just been eaten. Both organs send chemical messages to the paraventricular nucleus of the hypothalamus that plays a role in initiating or stopping eating (Petri, 1986; Ezell, 1995).

   The role of blood glucose in the regulation of hunger has been experimentally demonstrated in three major ways. Two of the experimental methods involve the two hormones secreted by the islets of Langerhans (chapter 2, p. 68). When **insulin** is injected into the bloodstream of a satiated person, it causes a drop in the level of glucose, and the person feels hungry. Conversely, when the hormone **glucagon** is injected into the bloodstream of a hungry person, it produces an increase in blood glucose, and the individual no longer feels hungry.

   Blood glucose levels are a key mechanism in the short-term control of hunger, so it is important to understand a simple fact about blood glucose and hunger. When you eat, it takes a few minutes for food to be digested and enter the bloodstream in the form of glucose. If you eat slowly, therefore, your brain will have enough time to detect the increase in blood glucose and make you feel "full" before you eat more than you need. In other words, the faster you eat, the more you will eat before you feel full.
3. *Body fat levels.* The long-term maintenance of body weight is managed by the ability of the hypothalamus to detect the level of fat in the body (Mook, 1986; Petri, 1986). Recent research has revealed that the adipose (fat) cells that live on your waist, hips, and elsewhere secrete a protein nicknamed *Ob* (for obesity) into the bloodstream. The more full of fat that the adipose cells are, the more Ob they secrete. When the circulating Ob reaches the hypothalamus, structures in and around the ventromedial hypothalamus detect it. This causes the hypothalamus to react in three ways to control body weight. First, the ventromedial satiety center sends a direct message to inhibit eating. Second, it signals the paraventricular nucleus to control hunger by regulating the level of blood sugar.

   The third action taken by the ventromedial satiety center to control body weight in response to Ob has recently been discovered. It provides a new and absolutely fascinating chapter on the sublime complexity of the human body. When Ob levels are high, the ventromedial hypothalamus activates the sympathetic nervous system. Tiny branches of this nervous system actually end on the adipose cells. Stimulation of the adipose cells by the sympathetic neurons causes their metabolism to increase to burn off fat in the form of heat (Ezell, 1995)!

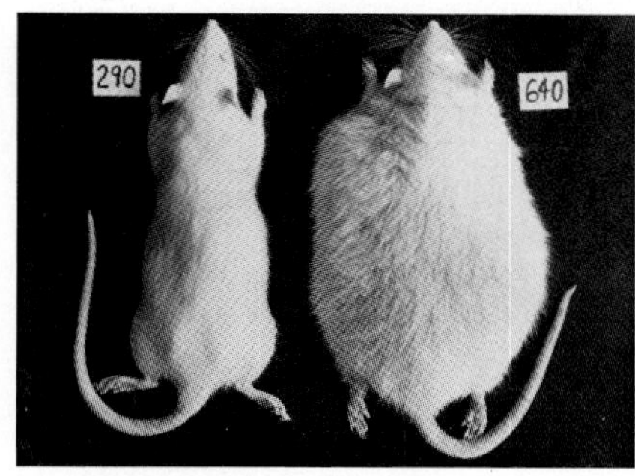

FIGURE 9.3

Destruction of the part of the hypothalamus that is involved in the satiety system causes rats to eat themselves into a state of extreme obesity called hyperphagia. A normal rat is shown on the left.

paraventricular nucleus
A part of the hypothalamus that plays a role in the motive of hunger by regulating the level of blood sugar.

insulin
(in´´su-lin) A hormone produced by the islets of Langerhans that reduces the amount of sugar in the bloodstream.

glucagon
(gloo´´kah-gon) A hormone produced by the islets of Langerhans that causes the liver to release sugar into the bloodstream.

Body Weight and the "Set Point"

As we have just seen, increases in body fat signal the body not only to eat less but also to increase the metabolism of the cells that store fat. This feedback system must work differently for different people, however. Otherwise, we would all have more or less the same amount of body fat. This has led scientists to hypothesize that each of us has a different *set point* for body fat that determines when the ventromedial hypothalamus will initiate actions to reduce eating and increase metabolism. It is like the point that you set on your home's thermostat to control the heater.

It appears to be very difficult to raise or lower body weight above or below this set point for very long (as we will see in the last section of this chapter in which losing weight is discussed). It is not known which step or steps in the feedback loop determine the set point, but medical researchers are very interested in understanding why the set point is so high for highly obese persons with medical complications. Therefore, the discovery of the feedback loop shown in figure 9.2 has stimulated medical research companies to invest hundreds of millions of dollars in research to find a cure for obesity.

Specific Hungers

Did you ever get a craving for a particular kind of food? Did you wonder if your body was trying to tell you something—that it needed a nutrient in that food? Animals who are experimentally deprived of protein, a vitamin, or fat will tend to eat greater quantities of foods containing that element when later given a choice (National Advisory Mental Health Council, 1995). For example, a rat whose adrenal glands have been surgically removed—producing a fatal deficiency in the body's supply of sodium unless sodium is consumed in the form of salt—shows a preference for salty water within 15 seconds of its being offered (Nachman, 1962). Since human eating is strongly influenced by learning and other psychological factors, it's not known whether we are as good as rats at listening to the nutritional needs of our bodies. But that craving might be telling you something important.

Learning plays a role in eating habits. Many families encourage and model overeating.

Psychological Factors in Hunger

Although hunger is clearly a motive that is tied to biological needs, psychological factors are also involved in the regulation of food intake. Through maturation and learning, we go from an infant who only drinks milk to an adult with distinct food preferences that play an important role in our lives (Rozin, 1996). If you grew up in the American South, you might adore chittlins (deep-fried pig intestines) and stewed okra. If you grew up in another part of the world, however, the very idea of these foods might be disgusting. A Catholic woman might enjoy beef, pork, and shellfish, but eating these foods might violate deeply held religious beliefs of some of her Hindu and Jewish neighbors. Learning plays a powerful role in determining *what* we eat, *when* we eat (we are often ready to eat at our customary times for eating, even if we have just had a snack), and even *how much* we eat (many families encourage and model overeating). Studies of nonhuman animals show that even rats and chimpanzees learn what to eat by watching older animals (National Advisory Mental Health Council, 1995).

Emotions also play a role in eating. People who are anxious often eat more than usual, and people who are depressed may lose their appetite for long periods of time. Ironically, though, individuals who get depressed after starting a new regime of healthy eating and exercise often lose the will to continue. If you are temporarily depressed enough to believe that nobody cares if you live or die—even you—why would you bother to eat healthfully?

incentives
External cues that activate motives.

Perhaps the most troublesome psychological factors to those who are trying to control their eating, however, are **incentives.** How many times have you finished dinner at a restaurant or family gathering, feeling a bit overstuffed, only to be tempted into eating more by a seductive dessert? Incentives are external cues that activate motives. The smell of fresh-baked bread makes you hungry; passing a fast-food joint on your way home from school creates a craving for french fries; and the sight of the dessert creates a desire to eat even when you are way past the point of biological hunger. Incentives have their effect through the same brain mechanisms that regulate the biological aspects of hunger. The sight of food causes neurons in your hypothalamus to fire, particularly if it's a favorite food, and the smell of food triggers the release of insulin, which stimulates hunger by causing your blood sugar to drop (Rolls, Burton, & Mora, 1976). Laboratory research with animals has shown that incentives can be powerful enough under some circumstances to push weight above the natural set point. All rats will overeat to the point of obesity if they have easy access to large quantities of a variety of high-calorie tasty foods (National Advisory Mental Health Council, 1995). Unless you are trying to gain weight, therefore, it is not a good idea to keep large quantities of a variety of high-calorie tasty foods in your kitchen.

External incentives, such as the look or smell of a food, can increase our motivation to eat.

Thirst: The Regulation of Water Intake

Just as we must control the intake of food to survive, we must also regulate the intake of water. What is the homeostatic mechanism involved in thirst? Actually, there are several mechanisms as in the case of hunger; like hunger also, the key regulatory centers are in the hypothalamus.

Biological Regulation of Thirst

A *drink system* and a *stop drinking system* are regulated by different sections of the hypothalamus. Surgical destruction of the drink system causes the animal to refuse water; destruction of the stop drinking system results in excessive drinking. Although the control centers for thirst occupy much of the same space as the centers for hunger, they operate separately by using different neurotransmitters (Grossman, 1960).

The hypothalamus uses three principal cues in regulating drinking: mouth dryness, loss of water by cells, and reductions in blood volume.

Learning influences which beverages we drink, as well as when we drink them. For example, drinking cola at breakfast is a fairly recent idea.

1. *Mouth dryness.* Dryness of the mouth is the thirst cue of which we are most consciously aware. In the 1920s, biologist Walter Cannon studied the role of mouth dryness in thirst, this time using himself as the subject. After drinking large amounts of water to be sure he was not thirsty, he injected himself with a drug that stops the flow of saliva. Very soon, he felt thirsty. Next, he injected his mouth with a local anesthetic that blocked all sensations from his mouth. This quickly eliminated the sensation of being thirsty. Cannon concluded that mouth dryness was the cue that led to the sensation of thirst, but he was only partially correct again. We know today that other factors play more important roles.
2. *Cell fluid levels.* When the total amount of water in the body decreases, the concentration of salts in the fluids of the body increases. Of particular importance to the regulation of thirst are *sodium salts* that exist primarily in the fluids outside the body's cells (because salts cannot pass through the semipermeable membranes of the cells). Decreases in the total body fluids of even 1 to 2 percent produce increases in the sodium concentration that are large enough to draw water out of the cells and *dehydrate* them (Hole, 1990; Petri, 1986). This happens to cells throughout the body, but when certain specialized cells in the drink center of the hypothalamus dehydrate and shrivel, they send two messages to correct the situation. They chemically signal the **pituitary gland,** which is located just below the hypothalamic drink center, to secrete the **antidiuretic hormone (ADH)** into the bloodstream. When ADH reaches the kidneys, it causes them to conserve water in the body by reabsorbing it from the urine. In addition, the hypothalamic center simultaneously sends a message of thirst to the cerebral cortex, which initiates searching for and drinking liquids.
3. *Total blood volume.* The third cue used by the hypothalamus to regulate thirst is total blood volume. As the volume of water in the body decreases, the volume of blood—which is composed mostly of water—decreases as well. A decreased volume of blood is first sensed by the kidneys. The kidneys react in two ways. First, they cause blood vessels to contract to compensate for the lowered amount of blood. Second, in a series of chemical steps, they cause the creation

pituitary gland
(pi-tu´i-tār´ē) The body's master gland, located near the bottom of the brain, whose hormones help regulate the activity of the other glands in the endocrine system.

antidiuretic hormone (ADH)
(an´´tī-di´´ū-ret´ik) A hormone produced by the pituitary that causes the kidneys to conserve water in the body by reabsorbing it from the urine.

angiotensin
(an´´jē-ō-ten´sin) A substance in the blood that signals the hypothalamus that the body needs water.

of the substance **angiotensin** in the blood. When angiotensin reaches the hypothalamus, the drink center sends a thirst message to the cerebral cortex, which eventually leads to drinking.

Psychological Factors in Thirst

Psychological factors also play a role in the regulation of drinking, although overall this role does not appear to be as large as in hunger. Learning influences *which* beverages we drink (the average citizen of Nepal prefers yak's milk to cow's milk) as well as *when* we drink them (an advertising campaign has been mounted in recent years to convince us to drink colas for breakfast). Incentives, such as the sight of a glass of beer, may activate thirst in a person who is otherwise not thirsty. Stress and emotions seem to have little effect on drinking compared with eating, except in the case of beverages that contain alcohol or stimulants (coffee, tea, colas, and so on) that alter our moods.

Thinking Critically About Psychology

1. If you were trying to help someone control her or his food intake, how would your advice be different after reading this section?

2. How have your personal experiences influenced the expression of your hunger and thirst motives?

Review

The term *primary motivation* refers to states based on biological needs that activate and guide behavior. Examples of primary motives include hunger, thirst, maintaining warmth, and avoiding pain. These motives must be satisfied if the organism is to survive. Primary motives are generally based on a complex number of biological factors. For example, the control centers for eating and drinking are located in the hypothalamus. The hypothalamus responds directly or indirectly to a number of bodily signals that food or water is needed. In the case of hunger, stomach contractions, levels of blood glucose, and levels of blood fat are all involved in the regulation of eating. Thirst is similarly regulated by a combination of mouth dryness, level of fluids in the body cells, and the total volume of blood in the body.

Although the primary motives are based on biological survival needs, psychological factors are involved in these motives as well. External stimuli, such as the sight of a highly preferred food or beverage, can act as an incentive that activates eating or drinking, even when the individual is satiated. Learning also influences what, when, and how much we eat and drink.

Check Your Learning

To be sure that you have learned the key points from the preceding section, cover the answers below and try to answer each question. If you give an incorrect answer to any question, return to the page given next to the correct answer to see why your answer was not correct. Remember that these questions cover only some of the important information in this section; it is important that you make up your own questions to check your learning of other facts and concepts.

1. The term ________________ refers to an internal state or condition that activates and gives direction to our thoughts, feelings, and actions.

a. cognition
b. incentive
c. motivation
d. physiology

2. A ________________ is an internal bodily mechanism that senses biological imbalances and stimulates actions to restore the proper balance.

3. The hunger and thirst motives are controlled by excitatory and inhibitory brain systems, with centers in the ________________ playing key roles.

a. cerebellum
b. hypothalamus
c. thalamus
d. hippocampus

Check Your Learning—continued

4. ________________ refers to an external cue that activates primarily hunger motivation.

   a. Incentive
   b. Efferent
   c. Catalyst
   d. Stimulus

Correct Answers

1. c (p. 328), 2. homeostatic mechanism (p. 329), 3. b (p. 330), 4. a (p. 332).

PSYCHOLOGICAL MOTIVES

Psychological motives are motives that are not directly related to the biological survival of the individual or the species. They are "needs" in the sense that the individual's happiness and well-being depend on these motives. Even more than primary motives, psychological motives vary considerably in the degree to which they are influenced by experience. Some psychological motives are found in every normal member of a species and seem to be innate, while others seem to be entirely learned. In this section, we look at three psychological motives: the need for novel stimulation, the need for affiliation with others, and the need for achievement.

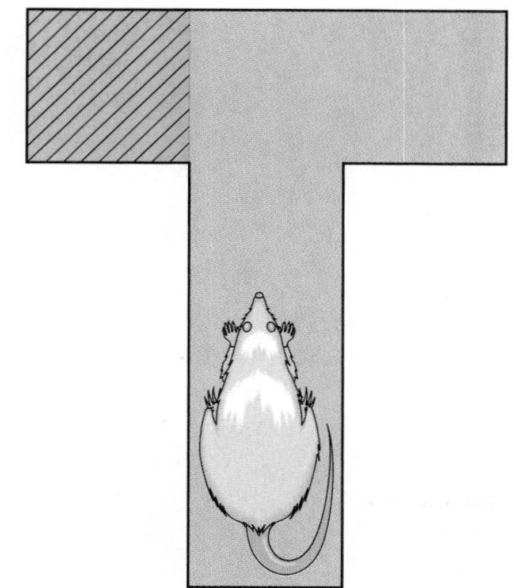

FIGURE 9.4

T-maze like those used to study stimulus motivation in rats.

psychological motives
Motives related to the individual's happiness and well-being, but not to survival.

novel stimulation
New or changed experiences.

Stimulus Motivation: Seeking Novel Stimulation

Did you ever come home to an empty house and flip on the radio or television just to kill the silence? Have you ever spent all day Saturday writing a term paper and then felt you *had* to get up and take a walk or talk to someone just for sheer diversion? Most people get bored easily if there is little overall stimulation or if the stimulation is unchanging. We, and other animals, have an apparently inborn motive to seek **novel stimulation.**

If you put a rat in a T-maze (see fig. 9.4) in which it must choose between turning right into an alley painted gray or turning left into one pointed with complex stripes, the rat will explore the more complex, more "interesting" alley first. But the next time it will be more likely to turn into the gray alley, which it has not seen yet, apparently because it is "curious" about it (Dember, 1965).

Monkeys that are kept in boring cages will similarly work hard pressing a lever to earn a chance to look at other monkeys or even to watch a model train run (Butler, 1953). Monkeys will also work manual puzzles for hours without any reward except finally getting them apart (Harlow, Harlow, & Meyer, 1950) (see fig. 9.5). Watch a human infant play with her crib toys for a few minutes and you will see that humans, too, are motivated to manipulate, investigate, and generally shake up their environments. If you go without physical activity for a while, you will see that you have a need for activity, too.

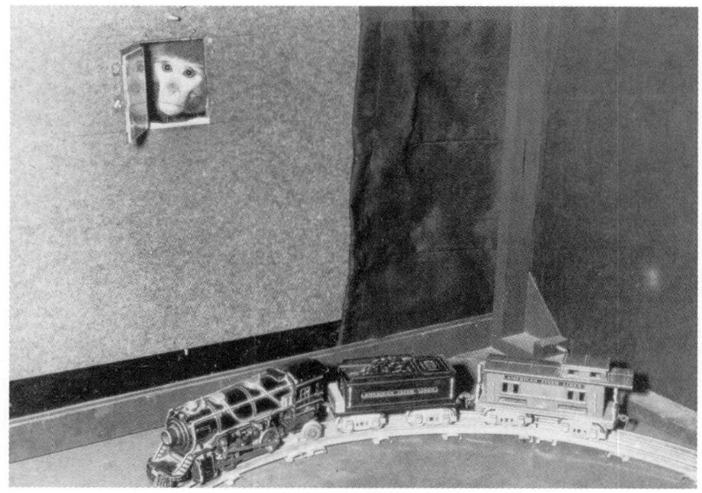

The need for novel stimulation motivated this monkey to learn to unlock the window that opens into the room with an electric train.

Optimal Arousal Theory

Although no known homeostatic mechanism accounts for our need for novel stimulation, we clearly must have a certain amount of it to feel comfortable. But just as too little stimulation is unpleasant and will motivate us to increase stimulation, *too much* stimulation is unpleasant and will motivate us to find ways to decrease it. Too many people talking at once, too much noise, or a room that contains too many clashing colors and patterns will send a person off in search of a few minutes of peace, quiet, and reduced stimulation. Apparently, a desirable level of stimulation does exist; and we feel uncomfortable going either above or below this level (Korman, 1974).

FIGURE 9.5

A monkey disassembling mechanical lock puzzles for no reward other than the activity and novel stimulation involved in the process.

Our apparent "need" for an optimal level of stimulation has led psychologists to suggest that each individual strives to maintain an **optimal level of arousal** in the nervous system. *Arousal,* as used in this way, is a rather vague term, but it refers to the overall state of alertness and activation of the person. The individual who is sleeping is at a very low level of arousal; the relaxed person is at a somewhat higher level; the active, alert person is functioning at a moderate level; the anxious person is experiencing a high level of arousal; and the person in a frenzied panic is at an extremely high level. Arousal is linked to the activity of the **reticular formation** described in chapter 2 and, at higher levels of arousal at least, to the activity of the sympathetic division of the autonomic nervous system. Optimal arousal theory does not suggest, however, that there is a biological need for a moderate or optimal level of arousal. The individual can survive at high or low levels of arousal, but he or she is motivated to achieve a comfortable, optimal level of arousal by acting in ways that increase or decrease stimulation.

Arousal and Performance: The Yerkes-Dodson Law

Not only is arousal an important motivational concept, it's also linked to the efficiency of our performance in various situations. If arousal is too low, performance will be inadequate; if it's too high, performance may become disrupted and disorganized. This simple notion is often referred to as the **Yerkes-Dodson law,** but it's somewhat more complicated than it looks at first. The ideal level of arousal for different kinds of performance varies considerably. Football players "warm up" and "psych up" physically and emotionally to reach high levels of arousal for the game. It would be difficult to exceed the ideal level of arousal needed for highly physical contact sports. On the other hand, the performance of a skilled artisan applying pottery glazes by hand would be most efficient at much lower levels of arousal (see fig. 9.6). Too much arousal, as in the form of high levels of anxiety, would tend to disrupt the delicate, skilled performance of the potter.

Some people always seem to need high levels of sensation. The optimal arousal theory would suggest that they are usually below their optimal level of arousal.

optimal level of arousal
The apparent human need for a comfortable level of stimulation, achieved by acting in ways that increase or decrease it.

reticular formation
(re-tik´ū-lar) The system of neural structures spanning parts of the hindbrain, midbrain, and forebrain that plays a role in cortical arousal and attention.

Yerkes-Dodson law
A law stating that effective performance is more likely if the level of arousal is suitable for the activity.

Affiliation Motivation

Do you usually enjoy being with friends? Do you feel lonely during periods when you do not have many friends? Human beings are social creatures. Given the opportunity, we generally prefer to be with other people. In this sense, it can be said that people have a **motive for affiliation** (Houston, 1985).

The need for affiliation is present in all normal humans, but most research on this topic concerns differences between individuals who have different levels of this motive. Individuals who are high in the need for affiliation, for example, tend to prefer being with others rather than satisfying other motives. When asked to perform a clerical task with a partner, individuals who are high in the need for affiliation, but low in the need for achievement, choose to work with a friend, regardless of how competent the friend is. In contrast, individuals who are low in the need for affiliation, but high in the need for achievement, choose the partner who they believe is most competent (French, 1956).

Two theories have been proposed to explain our apparent need for affiliation (Houston, 1985). Some believe that affiliation motivation is an inborn need that is based on natural selection. A stone age human who chose to hunt alone would have been less able to kill large animals for food and to avoid being the prey of other animals, and thus to survive, than a human who felt a need to live and hunt with others. Thus, the forces of nature may have selected those humans with a need for affiliation—because they were the ones who survived. Other psychologists, however, believe that each human learns the motive to affiliate through his or her own learning experiences. Because infants experience being fed, cleaned, tickled, kept warm, and other positive forms of nurturing in the presence of another human being, other human beings may become "positive stimuli" through classical conditioning. Similarly, because our actions that lead us to be in the presence of others—smiling,

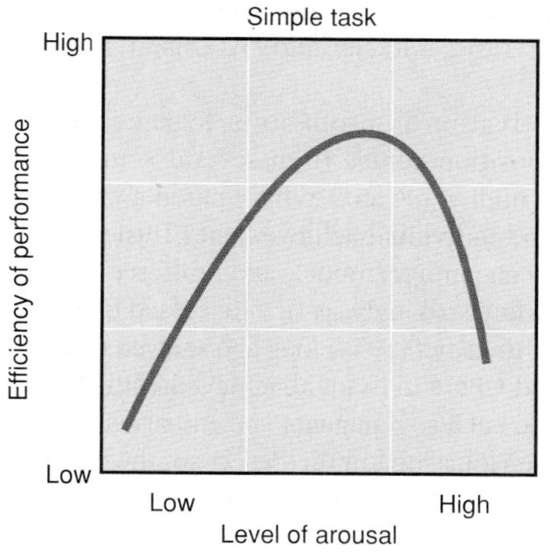

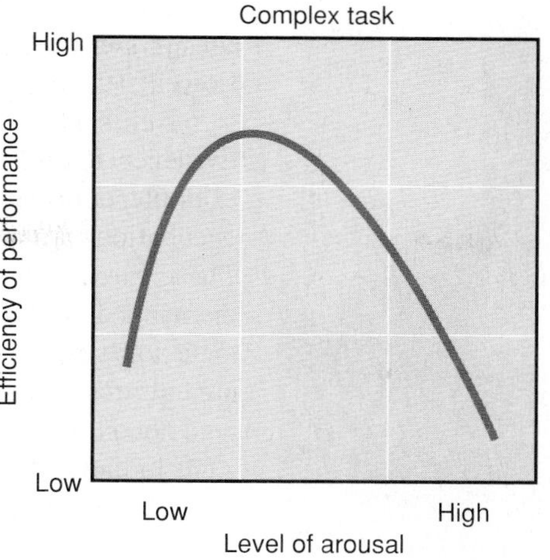

FIGURE 9.6

The Yerkes-Dodson law describes the relationship between the amount of arousal and the efficiency of performance. In general, either insufficient or excessive arousal results in insufficient performance, but the optimal level of arousal is higher for simple, physically active tasks than for complex, highly skilled tasks.

stretching out our baby arms for a hug, and the like—often lead to pleasant outcomes, then affiliative behaviors are likely to be positively reinforced (Houston, 1985).

That affiliation motivation may be related in some way to the greater chance that humans who affiliate—flock together—will survive, receives some support from the fact that affiliation motivation appears to be stronger when we are frightened about our well-being. Stanley Schachter (1959) has conducted a number of experiments on the relationship between anxiety and the need for affiliation. In a typical experiment, female university students were brought to the laboratory in small groups. There they met a man dressed in a white coat who introduced himself as Dr. Gregor Zilstein, a professor of neurology and psychiatry. He told half of the research participants that they would be participating in an experiment involving painful electric shocks—and they were shown the forbidding shock apparatus in the background. He told the other half of the participants that they would receive very mild shocks that they would experience as a mere tickle. Presumably, the first group was made far more anxious than the second group, as shown by the students' own ratings of their anxiety. Both groups were given the choice of waiting alone in individual waiting rooms or together in a group waiting room.

The need for affiliation is present in everyone to some extent, but people differ in the strength of their need to be with others.

As Schachter predicted, almost two-thirds of the subjects who were made to feel anxious chose to wait in groups, indicating a high level of need for affiliation. However, only one-third of the low anxiety group chose to wait together. Apparently, threats to our well-being increase our motive to affiliate—"misery loves company" as the saying goes, perhaps because "there is safety in numbers."

motive for affiliation
The need to be with other people and to have personal relationships.

Achievement Motivation

Who was voted "most likely to succeed" in your high school class? Was he or she a "go-getter" who was willing to work hard to gain success? Was it someone who was not afraid to accept responsibility and seemed to perform best in competitive situations? If so, your class probably voted for someone high in **achievement motivation,** abbreviated as **n Ach** (need to achieve). Achievement motivation is the psychological need for success in school, sports, occupation, and other competitive situations. Chances are good that this person went into an occupation that provides rewards for *individual* achievement, such as sales, engineering, architecture, or law, rather than one that does not single out successful individuals for rewards, such as a bureaucratic government job. Chances are, too, that your high school's most likely to succeed went into an occupation that was realistically matched to her or his abilities. Individuals who are high in *n Ach* generally experience little anxiety or fear of failure but tend to choose jobs and other challenges (such as college courses) in which they have a realistic chance for success. And when success is achieved, the high *n Ach*

achievement motivation (n Ach)
The psychological need in humans for success in competitive situations.

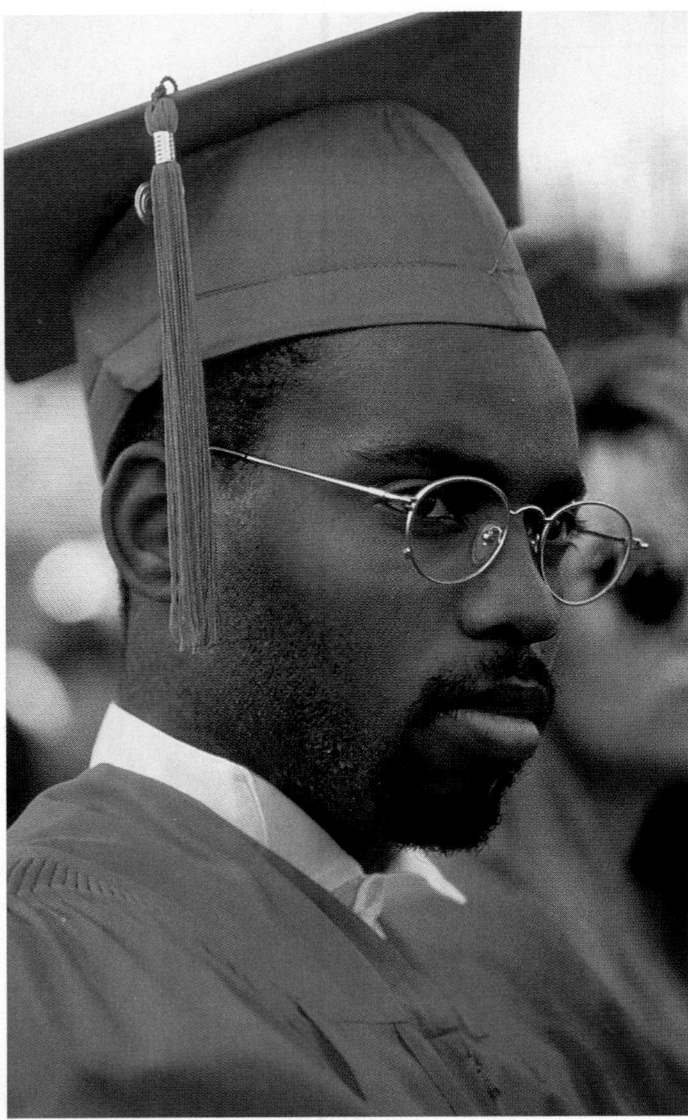

People who have high achievement motivation look for opportunities to use their abilities to excel.

individual enjoys the fruits of his or her labors more than the average person (Atkinson, 1964; McClelland, Atkinson, Clark & Lowell, 1953).

Achievement motivation is probably a learned motive. Evidence for this proposition comes from several sources. For example, children with high *n Ach* tend to have parents who are in occupations that demand individual achievement (Turner, 1970). These parents probably encourage, model, and reinforce achievement in their children. More strikingly, as first discussed in the prologue to chapter 5, Ruth Benedict (1934) long ago showed that there are cultures in the world where individual achievement is considered not only undesirable but also repugnant and embarrassing. The Zuñi Indians, who once flourished in the desert southwest of the United States, actively avoid personal achievement or recognition. An individual who found himself in the public spotlight—such as by heroically saving a child from stampeding horses—would be so embarrassed that he would banish himself from the tribe and physically punish himself for months before feeling ready to return quietly. Further evidence along these lines has been provided by David McClelland. He was able to show the influence of learning on *n Ach* by *teaching* it to business leaders from countries that were traditionally low in achievement motivation. The teaching not only raised scores on measures of *n Ach* but also increased their business productivity as well (McClelland & Winter, 1969).

Fear of Failure

High *n Ach* often leads to the fruits of success, but it also brings its share of problems. High achievers must learn to balance the demands of hard success-oriented work with the need for leisure, family, and friends. We will see in chapter 12, furthermore, that some individuals with excessive needs to succeed—Type A personalities—may suffer ill health because of it.

However, being low in *n Ach* does not guarantee a happy life either. Some low *n Ach* people are not interested in achieving status or material success and are happy to spend their time and energy in other ways. Many other individuals low in *n Ach,* however, are very anxious in competitive situations, such as tests and sales competitions, and greatly fear failure. These emotions may lead some individuals to avoid competitive occupations for which they are otherwise well suited or to experience considerable discomfort if they do enter such jobs (Atkinson, 1964).

Solomon's Opponent-Process Theory of Acquired Motives

Richard Solomon (1980) of the University of Pennsylvania has proposed a theory that has important implications for our learning of *new* motives, particularly ones that are difficult to understand in any other way. Why do some people love to jog, fight in karate matches, or parachute out of airplanes? How do some people become so "addicted" to their spouses, boyfriends, or girlfriends that they cannot leave them, even when they *do not enjoy* being with them anymore?

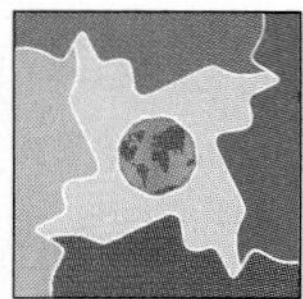

HUMAN DIVERSITY

Conflict and the First-Generation College Student

Are you the first member of your family to attend college? If so, this fact may lead to conflicting emotions in you. Let's look at the college experiences of a man named John who now works as a psychologist. He is from a poor white family and was the first of 4 siblings and 16 cousins to finish college. He knew that his family was proud of him, but he sometimes felt that he had left his family and old friends behind in his quest for higher education. Sometimes these feelings interfered with his motivation to complete school.

Many first-generation college students struggle with similar feelings (Piorkowski, 1983; Whitten, 1992). They often perceive themselves, and are perceived by their families, as moving into a new social class. This can be anxiety provoking for both the student and the family. Issues related to group loyalty arise as the student's interests, vocabulary, and worldview become different from those of his family and neighborhood friends. Family members sometimes accuse first-generation college students of "changing" or "thinking they are better" than the family. These issues are particularly challenging for members of groups that traditionally attended college infrequently. Not only do they face strained relationships with their family and friends, but they often do not fit into the college community if they attend a majority-culture institution.

Many first-generation college students handle these conflicts very successfully. They recognize that they are part of both their college and home communities and develop strategies for moving comfortably from one to the other. They speak standard English on the college campus and speak the language of their home community, which might be Spanish, Creole, or Black English, when they are among friends. They reassure their family members by word and deed that they still feel a part of their home even though they are changing in some ways. This is important because students who are able to integrate their old and new lifestyles more successfully make higher grades than students who experience a high degree of conflict (Whitten, 1993b).

But first-generation college students are not the only ones who experience conflicts based on their backgrounds at college. Consider Roslyn, a 38-year-old African-American woman who is a third-generation college graduate. Her grandparents were college-educated teachers and her parents both have graduate training. As a college student she usually hid this background from her African-American peers. She often had a sense of isolation because she was one of the few African-American students in her dormitory whose education was being paid for entirely by her parents. She also felt guilty about having more material goods than her peers and other African Americans in her neighborhood.

What is the climate like at your institution for first-generation college students and students who do not fit the mold in other ways? How effective is your college when it comes to addressing diversity issues? How do your family and friends feel about your decision to enter college? Thinking about these questions may help you identify sources of potential conflict in yourself or understand the experience of other students better.

opponent-process theory of motivation Solomon's theory of the learning of new motives based on changes over time in contrasting feelings.

Solomon provides an intriguing answer to these and other questions with his **opponent-process theory of motivation** (try not to confuse this with the opponent-process theory of color vision). Solomon explains craving such diverse things as parachute jumping, drugs, and lost lovers by means of two concepts: (a) every state of positive feeling is followed by a *contrasting* negative feeling, and vice versa, and (b) any feeling—either positive or negative—that is experienced many times in succession loses some of its intensity.

The classic example is parachute jumping. Solomon summarizes data (which no one doubts!) that show that parachute jumping is frightening at first. When the novice jumper lands, he or she is generally in a mild state of shock but soon begins smiling and talking excitedly about the jump. That is, the negative state of fear is followed by the contrasting positive state of euphoria. The shift from negative fear to positive euphoria that reinforces the act of jumping is shown graphically in the left part of figure 9.7. But, after many jumps, the fear becomes less intense. This change is shown in the right side of figure 9.7. There is a lessening in fear from the first experiences with jumping to later jumps. However, note that the amount of reinforcing *contrast* in the two parts of figure 9.7 stays the same. This means that as the fear is reduced, the amount of euphoria produced afterward becomes even stronger. This is Solomon's explanation of the learning of new motives like karate, motorcycle racing, and jogging—even using saunas. Not only does the initial negative state diminish due to repetition, but you get hooked by the contrasting shift to increasingly more intense levels of positive feeling.

The process of becoming addicted to things that feel good at first follows the opposite course. The wonderful, druglike feeling that comes from being with that new guy that you have a crush on, for example, is followed by a contrasting feeling of missing him when he is not with you. Not only is being with him positive, but getting him back is doubly reinforcing because it stops the negative feeling of missing him. Furthermore, as the positive feelings diminish, as shown in figure 9.8, the feeling of missing—even needing—the loved one becomes more intense. If you stop seeing him because the positive feeling is gone, it is this negative feeling of missing him that motivates you to go back. This is Solomon's explanation for why it's often so hard to end a loveless relationship. It's not the happiness that holds you—that is long since gone—it's the negative withdrawal symptoms that are so difficult to get through. If this sounds like a drug addiction, it's no accident. Solomon sees addictions to heroin and other drugs as forming in exactly the same way. First comes the pleasurable "rush," followed by the uncomfortable feeling of coming down. After frequent use, the pleasure of using the drug (cocaine, nicotine, etc.) in the same amount is greatly diminished, but the pain of withdrawal is much worse. It's the pain of withdrawal that powerfully motivates the addict to take more of the drug, not the diminished pleasure that the drug brings. Solomon's theory is not relevant to all motives, but it may help us understand the learning of some perplexing motives.

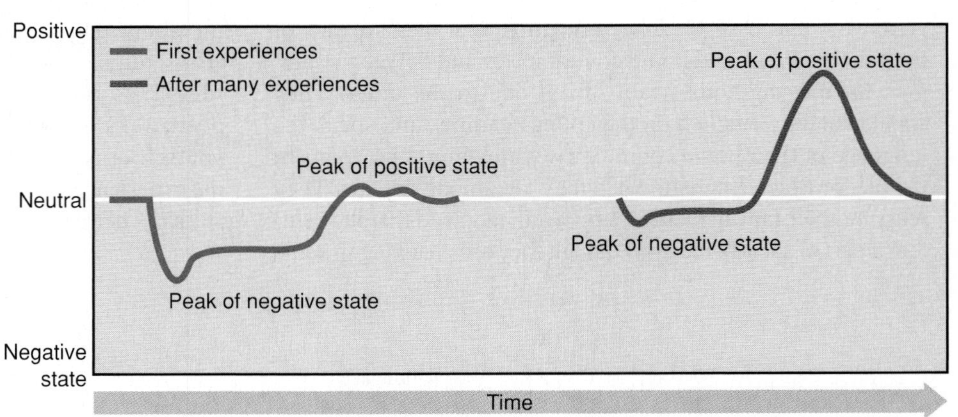

FIGURE 9.7

General illustration of Solomon's opponent-process theory of acquired motives as it applies to initially negative experiences, such as parachute jumping.

Source: Data from Richard L. Solomon, "The Opponent-Process Theory of Acquired Motivation," in *American Psychologist,* 35:691–712. Copyright © 1980 by the American Psychological Association.

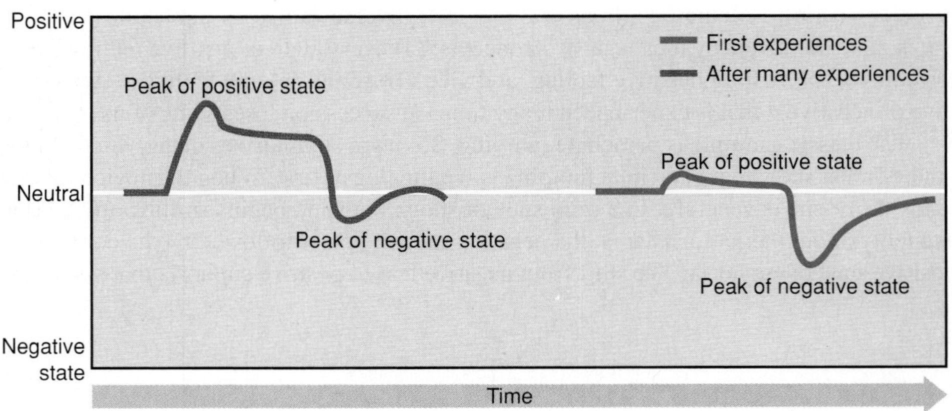

FIGURE 9.8

General illustration of Solomon's opponent-process theory of acquired motives as it applies to initially positive experiences, such as taking euphoric drugs.

Source: Data from Richard L. Solomon, "The Opponent-Process Theory of Acquired Motivation," in *American Psychologist,* 35:691–712. Copyright © 1980 by the American Psychological Association.

Intrinsic and Extrinsic Motivation

It is important to distinguish between intrinsic and extrinsic motivation. We speak of **intrinsic motivation** when people are motivated by the inherent nature of the activity, their pleasure of mastering something new, or the natural consequences of the activity. For example, the monkeys that we mentioned earlier who will take apart mechanical puzzles for no reward other than getting them apart are intrinsically motivated to solve puzzles. People who read nonfiction books that are unrelated to their work just because it is fun to learn new things are intrinsically motivated. Similarly, people who donate anonymously to charity because they wish to help people without being recognized are intrinsically motivated. **Extrinsic motivation,** on the other hand, is motivation that is external to the activity and not an inherent part of it. If a child who hates to do arithmetic homework is encouraged to do so by payment of a nickel for every correct answer, he is extrinsically motivated. That is, he works for the external payment rather than because of an intrinsic interest in math. Similarly, a person who works hard to be a good employee because he wants to be admired by others—rather than because of a genuine interest in the work—is extrinsically motivated. People who are intrinsically motivated tend to work harder, and respond to challenges by working even harder. They enjoy their work more and often perform more creatively and effectively than people who are extrinsically motivated (National Advisory Mental Health Council, 1995).

intrinsic motivation
(in-trin´sik) Human motives stimulated by the inherent nature of the activity or its natural consequences.

extrinsic motivation
(eks-trin´sik) Human motives stimulated by external rewards.

Perhaps the most interesting and significant issue concerning the distinction between intrinsic and extrinsic motivation is the question of when extrinsic rewards should be supplied by parents, teachers, and employers in an effort to increase motivation. When is it wise to use extrinsic motivation in the form of positive reinforcement to increase the frequency of some behavior (such as completing homework, delivering packages on time, and so on)? Considerable evidence suggests that if a behavior occurs infrequently—and its intrinsic motivation can be assumed low for that individual—then extrinsic motivation is successful in increasing the frequency of occurrence of the behavior. Children who hate to do their math homework often will do it diligently if rewarded with additional allowance money. And sometimes the success will help the child come to enjoy math intrinsically (Rimm & Masters, 1979). On the other hand, if the individual is already intrinsically motivated to perform an activity, adding extrinsic motivation will often detract from the intrinsic motivation. For example, when young children who like to draw pictures in school were given certificates for good drawing, they drew pictures less often than children who had not received certificates (Lepper, Greene, & Nisbett, 1973). We must be careful to avoid squelching intrinsic motivation by providing unnecessary extrinsic rewards.

Maslow's Hierarchy of Motives

We have touched on only a few of the human motives, but it's already obvious that we are creatures of many and varied needs. Abraham Maslow (1970) has put forward an interesting theory about our many motives. According to Maslow, we are not a crazy-quilt confusion of motives; rather, our motives are organized in a hierarchy arranged from the most basic to the personal and advanced.

Maslow's hierarchy of motives (needs) is shown in figure 9.9. If lower needs in the hierarchy are not met for the most part, then higher motives will not operate. Higher needs lie dormant until the individual has a chance to satisfy immediately pressing lower needs like hunger, thirst, and safety. When the lower needs have been met, then motives to develop relationships with others, to achieve a positive self-esteem, and to realize one's full potential ethically, artistically, and philosophically (**self-actualization**) become important to the individual.

Maslow's hierarchy of motives
The concept that more basic needs must be met before higher-level motives become active.

self-actualization
According to Maslow, the seldomly reached full result of the inner-directed drive of humans to grow, improve, and use their potential to the fullest.

Maslow's hierarchy of motives helps to explain such things as why starving peasant farmers are not particularly interested in the political philosophies of rival governments; or why, throughout history, science, art, and philosophy have mostly been produced when a nation could afford to have a privileged class who did not have to work to eat. The concept

FIGURE 9.9

Maslow's hierarchy of needs.

Source: Diagram based on data from *Hierarchy of Needs from Motivation and Personality,* Third Edition, by Abraham H. Maslow. Revised by Robert Frager, et al., Harper & Row, Publishers, Inc., 1954, 1987.

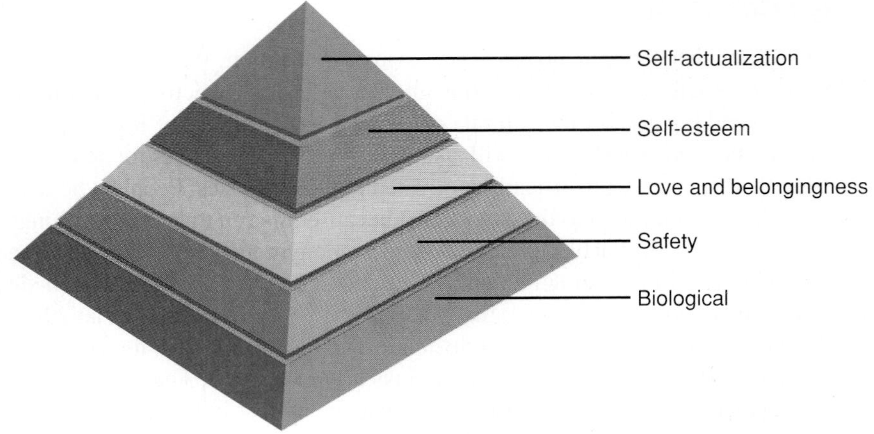

of the hierarchy of motives also helps us understand why a person would give up a prestigious, but time-consuming, career to try to save a marriage with a much-loved spouse. Higher motives become unimportant when lower motives are unmet.

But as helpful as Maslow's hierarchy of motives is, there are some obvious exceptions to it. The hierarchy does not explain why an individual would risk her or his life to rescue a friend from a burning building. Nor does it explain why imprisoned members of the Irish Republican Army intentionally starved themselves to death in 1981 to gain what might be seen by outsiders as minor changes in how political prisoners are treated. Similarly, the hierarchy fails to shed light on the common occurrence of an individual's ignoring spouse and children to pursue self-esteem in a career. Obviously, humans are sometimes willing to endure unmet lower motives to pursue higher ones. Still, Maslow's hierarchy appears to explain more facets of motivation than it fails to explain.

Thinking Critically About Psychology

1. Do you think our need for affiliation is an inborn need or a learned motive? Why?
2. Is our society's description of achievement motivation biased toward a particular definition of success? What other definitions are possible?

Review

Psychological motives are not directly linked to the biological survival of the individual or species. Some psychological motives are common to all normal members of a species and seem to be innate, while others appear to be primarily, if not entirely, learned. The stimulus motive—the need to maintain a moderate level of novel stimulation and activity—is an example of an apparently inborn psychological motive. The stimulus motive has led psychologists to speculate that individuals seek to maintain an optimal level of arousal in the nervous system by regulating stimulus input and activity levels.

Motives for achievement and affiliation seem to be influenced more by learning and differ from individual to individual or culture to culture. Competitive persons who seek occupations with a high probability of personal success and willingly accept responsibility tend to have parents with similar traits, suggesting that these individuals learn this achievement motive from their parents. Other individuals appear to avoid competitive occupations because they have learned either to fear failure or to fear success. Increased levels of anxiety also tend to increase the need to affiliate. Some motives are intrinsic; that is, individuals engage in the activity because of its inherent value. Other motives are extrinsic and will stimulate action only if there is an external incentive.

The many human motives do not appear to operate as a disorganized hodgepodge; rather they appear to be organized in a hierarchy. Lower-level motives, particularly the biological motives, must be satisfied before motives higher in the hierarchy become active and important.

Check Your Learning

To be sure that you have learned the key points from the preceding section, cover the answers below and try to answer each question. If you give an incorrect answer to any question, return to the page given next to the correct answer to see why your answer was not correct.

1. ________________ motives are related to the individual's happiness and well-being, but not to survival.

- **a.** Primary
- **b.** Hunger
- **c.** Psychological
- **d.** Tertiary

2. The ________________ law states that effective performance is more likely if the level of arousal is suitable for the activity (neither too high nor too low).

- **a.** tort
- **b.** opponent-process
- **c.** Weber-Fechner
- **d.** Yerkes-Dodson

3. Threats to our well-being generally increase our ________________ (or need to be with other people).

- **a.** achievement motivation
- **b.** power motivation
- **c.** affiliation motivation
- **d.** intimacy motivation

4. ________________ motivation is the psychological need for success in school, sports, occupation, and other competitive situations.

- **a.** Affiliation
- **b.** Aggression
- **c.** Acceptance
- **d.** Achievement

5. According to Maslow's ________________ an individual moves from one level of motivation to the next after fulfilling the basic needs on the lower level.

Correct Answers

1. c (p. 335), **2.** d (p. 336), **3.** c (p. 337), **4.** d (p. 337), **5.** hierarchy of motives (p. 341).

EMOTIONS

What do poets write about? Of all the facets of human existence, which do they choose for their themes? It's not depth perception, neural transmission, or cognitive development; it's not classical conditioning or intelligence. They write mostly about *emotions,* the experiences that give color, meaning, and intensity to our lives. One obvious reason poets focus on emotions is that emotions are interesting. People love to mull over their feelings and passions and to learn about the real or imagined emotions of others. If we did not enjoy our emotions so much, poems, plays, novels, and soap operas probably would not exist. But there is another reason why poets write about emotions: Trying to capture emotions in words is such a *challenge*. Psychologists, too, find it difficult to write about emotions. There is probably more disagreement on how to define the word *emotion* than any other term in psychology.

In their textbooks on emotion, Robert Plutchik (1980) and K. T. Strongman (1987) quoted more than 30 different definitions. Still, there is some agreement among psychologists as to what emotions are. Most definitions distinguish the same four elements to define emotion: (a) there is a *stimulus situation* that provokes the reaction; (b) there is a positively or negatively toned *conscious experience*—the "emotion" that we feel; (c) there is a bodily state of *physiological arousal* produced by the autonomic nervous system and endocrine glands; and (d) there is related *behavior* that generally accompanies emotions—the animal that is afraid cringes, trembles, then runs (Lang, 1995).

How many different emotions are there? In one sense, the list is almost endless. A truly complete listing of emotions would have to deal with many subtle distinctions. How is *liking*

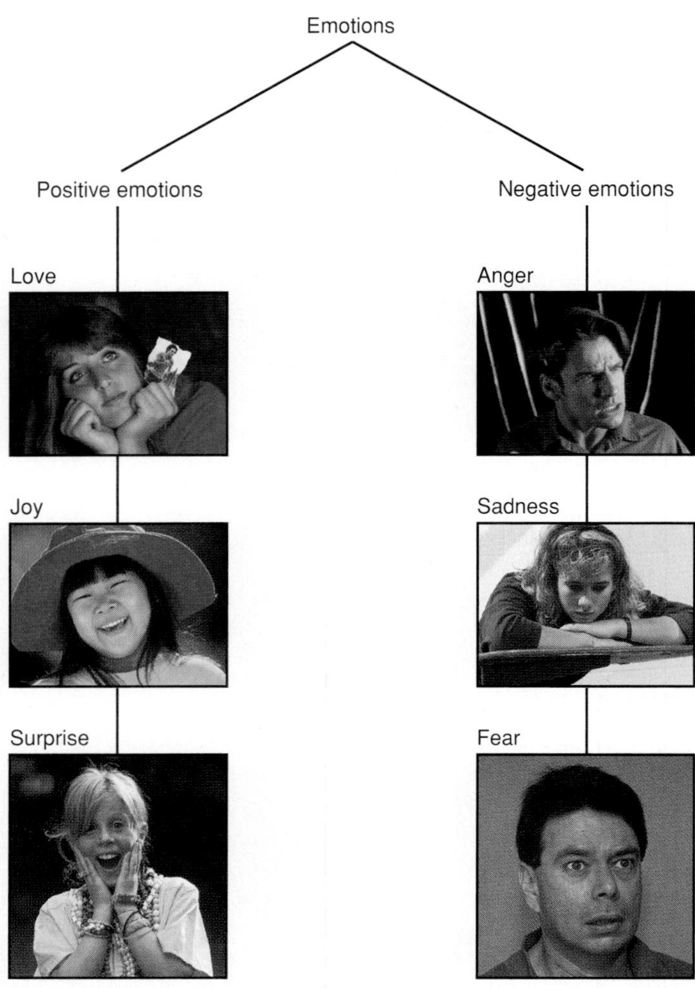

FIGURE 9.10

All of the varied emotions of human experience are thought to be combinations of three basic positive emotions and three basic negative emotions.

a person different from *respecting* a person? How does *love* differ for a spouse, a child, a parent, or a lover? But, recently, many psychologists who study emotion have come to agree on a list of six basic emotions (National Advisory Mental Health Council, 1995). Other emotions are considered to be variations on these basic emotions or combinations of the basic emotions. Using a clever statistical analysis of the terms that researchers use to describe emotions, Shaver, Schwartz, Kirson, and O'Connor (1987) showed that the six basic emotions are love, joy, surprise, anger, sadness and fear.

As illustrated in figure 9.10, all of the varied emotions that we experience are believed to be combinations of these six basic emotions (National Advisory Mental Health Council, 1995a). Just as all of the flavors that we taste are combinations of salty, sweet, bitter, and sour, all of life's emotional experiences are combinations of love, joy, surprise, anger, sadness, and fear. The six basic emotions are believed to be universal among humans. That is, cross-cultural research has found these six basic emotions in all of the many cultures studied to date. This suggests that they develop from our basic biological inheritance as humans. As discussed in chapter 2 (pp. 69–76), there is strong evidence that positive and negative emotions are processed in different parts of the brain, explaining how it is possible to experience combinations of both positive emotions at the same time (National Advisory Mental Health Council, 1995a). Have you ever felt both joyful and frightened at the same time? Or felt both love and anger at someone?

Three Theories of Emotion

Perhaps the most important differences among psychologists, however, concern the order in which the four elements of emotions (stimulus, conscious experience, physiological arousal, and behavior) are related to one another. Three main theories have been proposed to explain the workings of emotions. (It may help if you refer to fig. 9.11 as you read the following theories.)

James-Lange Theory

The commonsense view of emotions is that the stimulus of seeing a mugger makes us consciously feel afraid and that the conscious fear leads us to tremble and run. William James (1890) suggested that this view is just backward, however. He believed that the emotional stimulus is routed (by the sensory relay center known as the thalamus) directly to the limbic system, which produces the bodily reactions of fear through the hypothalamus and sympathetic division of the autonomic nervous system. The sensations from this bodily reaction are then sent back to the cortex and produce what we feel in the conscious experience of emotion. According to James, "we feel sorry because we cry, angry because we strike, afraid because we tremble." A number of years later, Danish physiologist Carl Lange (1922) independently proposed the same theory, so it's known today as the **James-Lange theory of emotion.**

James-Lange theory of emotion
The theory that conscious emotional experiences are caused by feedback to the cerebral cortex from physiological reactions and behavior.

Because we tend to "feel" emotions throughout our bodies rather than just in our heads, the James-Lange theory makes sense. But several years after the death of William James, Harvard University biologist Walter Cannon (1927) published a set of strong criticisms of the James-Lange theory. His four major points were as follows:

1. Animals whose nerves have been surgically cut to deprive them of feedback from the organs aroused by the autonomic nervous system still seem to experience normal emotional reactions.

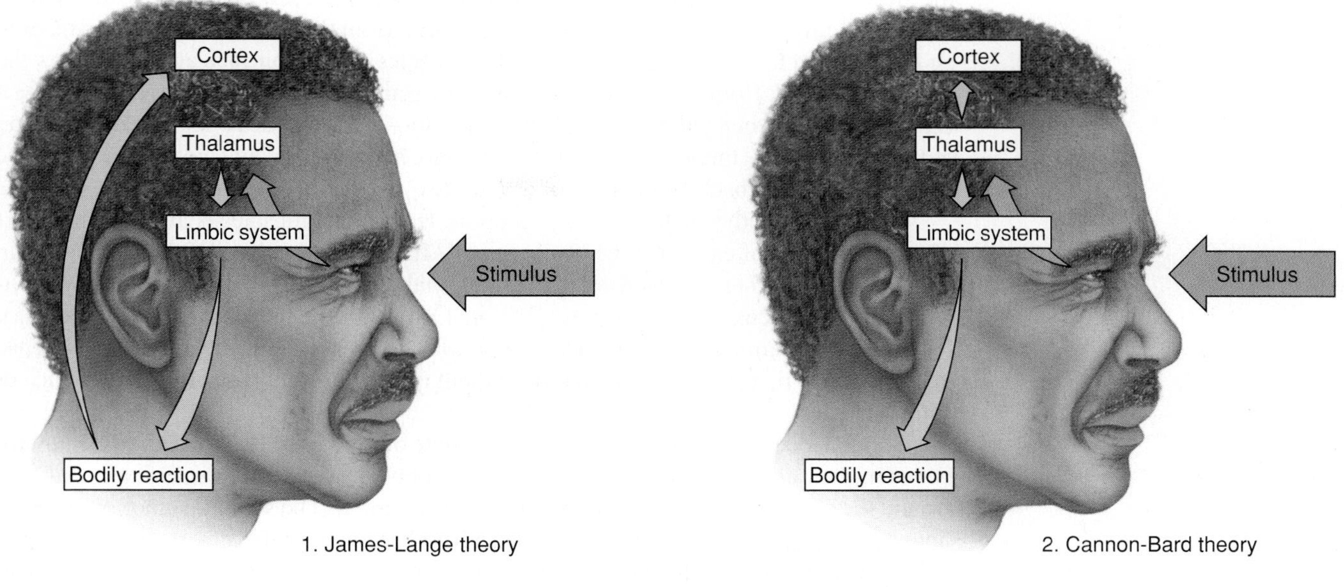

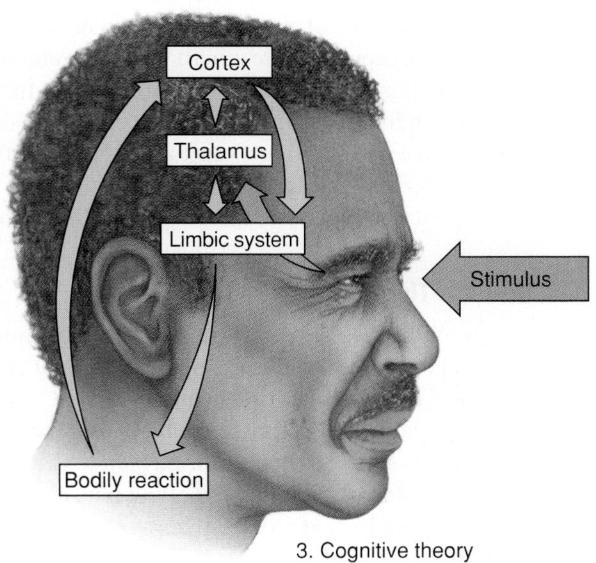

FIGURE 9.11
Illustration of three major theories of emotion: (1) the James-Lange theory, (2) the Cannon-Bard theory, and (3) the cognitive theory.

2. The physiological reactions that accompany different emotions are so similar that it's hard to see how a person could feel distinctly different emotions like fear and rage simply from the first sensory feedback provided by autonomic arousal.
3. The internal organs respond relatively slowly to the autonomic nervous system—too slowly, according to Cannon, to provide the nearly instantaneous emotional experience involved, for example, in seeing a mugger.
4. Artificially inducing physiological arousal by injecting human subjects with the hormone epinephrine (adrenaline) produces a sensation of arousal, but not a feeling of emotion.

Cannon's criticisms did not disprove the James-Lange theory, but they certainly made it seem less plausible.

Contemporary psychologist Carroll Izard (1972, 1977, 1991) has modified the James-Lange theory to get around Cannon's criticisms by hypothesizing that the most important sensory feedback in producing the conscious experience of emotion does not come from the slow-reacting organs that are activated diffusely by the autonomic nervous system. Rather, the most important sensory feedback comes from the *facial muscles.* Stop reading and smile for a few seconds. Did you fee the muscles move your face around? That's the sensory feedback from your facial muscles. Now smile a big, happy smile. Did you feel a little bit happier when you smiled? Most people do—that's the idea behind Izard's version of the James-Lange theory. Part of what you feel when you have an emotional experience is just sensory feedback from your facial muscles.

Does the hypothesis that sensory feedback from facial muscles is an important part of the experience of emotions seem silly to you? If so, consider this: Of the 44 muscles in the human face, 40 are devoted solely to emotional expression—the other 4 are for opening the mouth, speaking, and chewing (National Advisory Mental Health Council, 1995a). If so many facial muscles are devoted to emotional expression, maybe it does make sense to hypothesize that sensory feedback from them is an important part of the experience of emotions.

Solid evidence exists that favors Izard's update of the James-Lange theory of emotion. For example, the facial expression of emotions in both Western and non-Western cultures around the world has been found to be surprisingly similar. The six basic emotions expressions are associated with facial expressions that have been found to be almost universal: anger, disgust, happiness, sadness, surprise, and fear. Even people who have been blind from birth and cannot see facial expressions of emotions in others show the six basic emotional facial expressions themselves (Ekman, 1992; Ekman & Oster, 1979). This suggests that these patterns of emotional expression are inborn in humans and supports Izard's contention that facial expressions are important in emotions. Furthermore, there is some experimental support for Izard's theory. Individuals who were given electrical shocks reported less pain when they were told to make no facial reactions to the shock than when they let their emotions show in their faces. Perhaps the sensory feedback from their facial expressions made the difference in the amount of pain they experienced (Colby, Lanzetta, & Kleck, 1977).

Cannon-Bard Theory

Cannon-Bard theory of emotion
The theory that conscious emotional experiences and physiological reactions and behavior are relatively independent events.

Walter Cannon (1927) did not just criticize the James-Lange theory; he proposed an alternative theory of his own. This theory was later revised by Philip Bard (1934) and is known as the **Cannon-Bard theory of emotion.** Cannon believed that information from the emotional stimulus goes first to the brain relay center, called the thalamus. From there, the information is simultaneously relayed *both* to the cerebral cortex, where it produces the emotional experience, and to the hypothalamus and autonomic nervous system, where it produces the physiological arousal that prepares the animal to fight, run away, or react in some other way. To Cannon and Bard, the conscious emotional experience and physiological arousal are two simultaneous and largely independent events.

Cognitive Theory

cognitive theory of emotion
The theory that the cognitive interpretation of events in the outside world and stimuli from our own bodies is the key factor in emotions.

A third, more contemporary theory of emotion views the *cognitive interpretation* of emotional stimuli—from both outside and inside the body—to be the key event in emotions. Although it is fair today to characterize the **cognitive theory of emotion** as a single theory (Frijda, 1988; Lazarus, 1991; Leventhal & Tomarken, 1986), a number of different individuals contributed different facets of the theory over many years. The key theorists in the development of the cognitive theory of emotion are Magda Arnold (1960), Albert Ellis (1962), and Stanley Schachter and Jerome Singer (1962). According to these theorists, the process of cognitive interpretation in emotions has two steps: (a) the interpretation of stimuli from the environment, and (b) the interpretation of stimuli from the body resulting from autonomic arousal. We will look at each of these steps individually.

Interpretation of Incoming Stimuli. The cognitive perspective on the interpretation of stimuli relevant to emotions from the external world harkens back to the ancient Greek philosopher Epictetus who said, "People are not affected by events, but by their interpretations of them." For example, if you receive a box in the mail that makes a ticking sound, will you be happy or afraid? If the return address says the box is from Violet, and Violet is your deadly enemy, you might think it contains a time bomb and feel afraid. If Violet is a loving friend, however, you would open the box feeling happy, expecting to find a clock. In this case, the interpretation of the stimulus, not the stimulus itself, causes the emotional reaction. Thus, in the cognitive theory of emotion, information from the stimulus travels first to the cerebral cortex where it is both interpreted and experienced. Then a message is sent down to the limbic system and autonomic nervous system that results in physiological arousal.

Evidence supporting this aspect of the cognitive theory has been provided by an experiment in which four groups of college students were shown an upsetting film showing a number of crude circumcisionlike operations conducted without anesthesia as part of the puberty ceremony of an Australian aborigine tribe (Speisman, Lazarus, Mordokoff, & Davison, 1964). One group of students saw the film without a soundtrack. A second group heard a soundtrack that emphasized the agony experienced by the boys. A third group heard a soundtrack that described the operations in a detached intellectual way. And a fourth group heard a soundtrack that ignored the painful operation by talking about irrelevant details.

Although all of the students saw the same film, the soundtracks apparently had a big effect on their cognitive interpretation of what they saw. The group who heard the soundtrack emphasizing the agony of the operations showed much greater autonomic arousal than the group with no soundtrack. The soundtrack that emphasized the agony led to an interpretation of the film as a more upsetting stimulus. The groups who heard soundtracks that de-emphasized the emotional nature of the events, either by intellectualizing or ignoring it, showed less autonomic arousal. The cognitive interpretation (provided by the soundtrack) altered the emotional meaning of the film considerably.

Interpretation of Bodily Stimuli. The second step in the cognitive theory of emotion is the interpretation of stimuli from within the body that results from autonomic arousal. Cognitive theory resembles the James-Lange theory in emphasizing the importance of internal bodily stimuli in the experience of emotion, but it goes further in suggesting that cognitive *interpretation* of these stimuli is more important than the internal stimuli themselves.

"David, you're denying your feelings again, aren't you?"

Drawing by Koren; © 1981 The New Yorker Magazine, Inc.

This aspect of the cognitive theory of emotion was suggested by Stanley Schachter and Jerome Singer (1962). They believe that emotional arousal is diffuse and not specific to the different emotions. That is, the autonomic nervous system and endocrine glands are activated in the same global way regardless of which emotion is being experienced. The internal stimuli from the emotional arousal of the body play an important role in the experience of the emotion, but only through a cognitive interpretation of the *source* of the arousal. For example, if you are all churned up inside after hearing gunshots in your neighborhood, you will interpret the feelings from your body as fear. But if you feel all churned up after a kiss, you will interpret the feelings as love.

Schachter and Singer's addition to cognitive theory helps explain such things as why sexual attraction is often mistaken for love and why frightened hostages often develop friendly feelings toward their captors if they are treated with even a slight amount of respect. Because the autonomic sensations produced in emotional situations are not distinctive, it's easy to misinterpret their meaning. Sexual arousal can be mistaken for love, and fear for friendship, if we interpret the arousal incorrectly.

Schachter and Singer (1962) tested this facet of cognitive theory in an important experiment. People were brought to a laboratory for what they thought would be a study of the effects of a vitamin on vision. They were given an injection of the supposed vitamin and asked to wait with another research participant for the experiment to begin. The other person was actually an actor who worked for the experimenters. The injection contained the hormone epinephrine, a substance that causes arousal of the cardiac system and other organs. Schachter and Singer were interested in how the subjects would cognitively *interpret* this arousal under a number of different circumstances.

The actor behaved in a happy, silly manner with half of the participants; with the other half, he acted angry and walked out of the experiment. As predicted by Schachter and Singer, the behavior of the actor influenced the participants' cognitive interpretations of their own arousal. When they were with a happy actor, they rated themselves as happy; when they were with an angry actor, they interpreted their arousal as anger. Importantly, this effect was found only when the participants were not accurately informed about the true effects

The swaying bridge at Capilano Canyon

The solid bridge at Capilano Canyon

of the injection. When they were informed, the behavior of the actor did not influence their emotions—they simply attributed the arousal to the drug.

A much more interesting test of Schachter and Singer's hypothesis about the interpretation of internal arousal in emotions was conducted by Donald Dutton and Arthur Aron (1974). The research participants were unsuspecting males between the ages of 18 and 35 who were visiting the Capilano Canyon in British Columbia, Canada, without a female companion. An attractive female experimenter approached the men and asked them to answer questions as part of a survey that she was supposedly conducting on reactions to scenic attractions. The key item in the study required them to make up a brief story about an ambiguous picture of a woman. Their stories were later scored for the amount of sexual content, which was considered a measure of the amount of sexual attraction that the male participants felt toward the attractive interviewer. To provide a second measure of interpersonal attraction, the interviewer tore off a piece of paper from the survey and gave her name and phone number to a participant, inviting him to call her if he wanted to talk further.

Have I mentioned where the interviews took place? Half of the interviews were conducted in such a way as to create a high level of arousal (fear) in the male, and the other half were conducted to create a low level of arousal. The high-fear interviews were conducted while the males were *on* a 450-foot-long cable and wood suspension bridge with low handrails that stretched across the Capilano Canyon some 230 feet above rocks and shallow rapids. The authors reported that the bridge had "a tendency to tilt, sway, and wobble, creating the impression that one is about to fall over the side" (p. 511). I visited Capilano Canyon a few years ago with one of my daughters and walked the suspension bridge, and I can personally attest to the fact that it wobbles, sways, and is generally fearsome! The low-fear interviews were conducted upstream on a solid wooden bridge that any coward could cross.

The results strongly supported Schachter and Singer's (1962) theory that the autonomic arousal that accompanies all emotions is similar and that it's our cognitive interpretation of the cause of that arousal that is important. The participants who were highly aroused (confirmed by their own later reports) while on the high-fear swaying suspension bridge made up stories that contained significantly more sexual imagery than the low-fear participants. The high-fear group was also more than four times as likely to call the female interviewer later. Apparently, the high-fear group interpreted their autonomic arousal as a greater degree of attraction to the interviewer.

Similar enhancement of attraction presumably occurs in other highly arousing situations, such as football games, emergency landings of airplanes, and the like. So, be careful to separate all the possible sources of arousal when you are trying to decide if you are in love. On the other hand, if you really want a blind date to be attracted to you, you might arrange to meet him or her on the Capilano Canyon suspension bridge. Of course, there's always the possibility that your date will interpret the arousal as anger toward you for getting him or her up there!

Rainer Reisenzein (1983) of the Free University of Berlin reviewed the experimental evidence relevant to Schachter and Singer's contribution to the cognitive theory of emotion that had been gathered in the 20 years since it was first stated. He concluded that the most convincing support for this theory has come from studies showing that *misinterpreted* arousal can intensify emotional experiences. Recent advances in our ability to measure autonomic arousal suggest that slightly different patterns of arousal may be associated with somewhat different emotions, but these differences are quite subtle (Ekman, Levenson, & Friesen, 1983; Lang, 1995). The basic premise of Schachter and Singer's hypothesis, that the physiological arousal associated with different emotions is pretty much the same, is probably still reasonable in spite of these subtle differences. The interpretation of the arousal is apparently the critical variable in emotions.

The Physiology of Emotion and Lie Detectors

Last night on television the lawyer of a senator who was accused of committing a crime recommended that she take a private *lie-detector test,* and that if she passed it, they should announce the results in a press conference. What is a lie-detector test and how valid is it for the investigation of crimes? In a lie-detector test, the individual is asked questions about the crime while physiological measurements are taken that indicate sympathetic arousal of the autonomic nervous system—such as sweating, blood pressure, heart rate, breathing rate, and muscle tension—using a device called a *polygraph.* This test is based on the assumption that people react emotionally—and therefore autonomically—when they tell lies.

The lie-detector examination uses a procedure known as the *guilty knowledge test.* In this procedure, the individual is asked questions about information that would be known only by the guilty party. For example, the examiner might ask if the person had stolen a long list of items (e.g., ring, watch, wallet). If the suspect answered "no" to most of the items but showed reaction in the sympathetic autonomic nervous system only to those items that were actually stolen, the results would suggest the guilt of the suspect. The guilty knowledge test is necessary because even innocent people often react emotionally to questions like "Did you rob the Smith's house?"

The idea behind lie-detector tests is a reasonable one, but there are some serious problems with it. First, as we have just seen, autonomic reactions are pretty much the same in all intense emotions, so there is the possibility that emotions other than guilt will lead either to a false indication of guilt or to confusing results (Bashore & Rapp, 1993). Second, some hardened criminals feel little or no guilt about their crimes, so they do not appear guilty in the examination. For these reasons, lie-detector tests are not completely accurate. They are estimated to be wrong *at least* 5 percent of the time even when conducted by highly trained persons under ideal conditions (Lykken, 1979), and they may be inaccurate far more often than that under everyday conditions (Saxe, Doughterty, & Cross, 1985). Five percent is not a large percentage, but it's significant when you consider that it could lead to the release of 5 out of 100 guilty individuals or the conviction of 5 innocent ones. In addition, lie-detector tests are often conducted by unqualified persons and their results are sometimes used in unscrupulous ways, raising serious questions about their use.

Since you are not likely to commit a crime, the shortcomings of lie-detector tests may seem like a pretty abstract issue. But it may be directly relevant to you some day. Although recent decisions by the Supreme Court have greatly restricted their use, some companies still use lie-detector tests to screen potential employees or to reevaluate their honesty each year. This means that you may have to take a lie-detector test, with a great deal riding on the accuracy of the results. This is particularly troubling when you realize that the chances of error are probably higher than 5 percent when broad questions are asked, such as "Have you ever stolen from your employer?" or "Have you ever used illegal drugs?" Fortunately or unfortunately a new generation of lie-detectors may be on their way soon, based on the analysis of brain activity rather than autonomic responses (Bashore & Rapp, 1993). Time will tell if they will provide a truly accurate method of detecting lying.

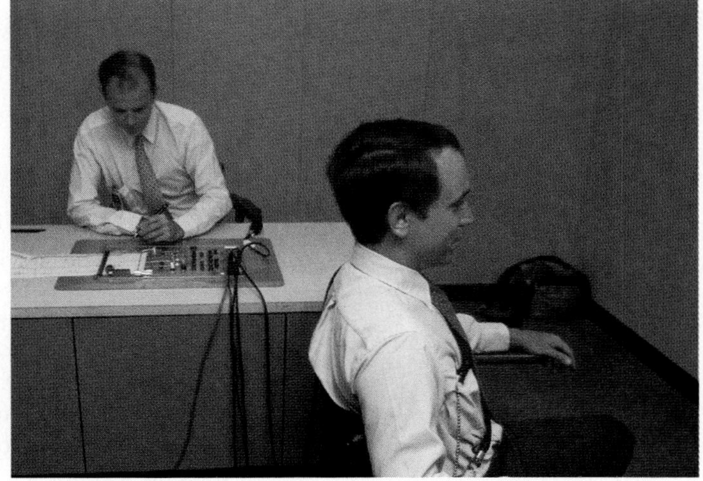

The polygraph, or lie-detector, test assumes that people react emotionally with autonomic arousal when they tell lies.

Role of Learning and Culture in Emotions

Most psychologists who specialize in the study of emotions believe that at least the most basic emotions are inborn and do not have to be learned. Cats do not have to be taught how to hiss and arch their backs in rage; dogs do not have to be trained to wag their tails; and people probably do not have to learn their basic emotions, either. Izard (1978) has studied

Culture influences the way we show emotions. For example, the Japanese culture tends to discourage the expression of negative emotions.

infants to support his view that emotional reactions appear at such young ages that it seems unlikely that parents have already taught them to their infants. More convincingly, even children who are deprived of most normal learning experiences because of being born both deaf and blind show normal emotional reactions (Eibl-Eibesfeldt, 1973).

Comparisons of different cultures, however, suggest that learning does play an important role in emotions in two ways. First, cultural learning influences the *expression* of emotions more than what is experienced. For example, some cultures encourage free emotional expression, whereas other cultures teach people, through modeling and reinforcement, to reveal little of their emotions in public (Bandura, 1969). Paul Ekman (1992) of the University of California at San Francisco and his colleague conducted a clever study of the influence of cultural learning on emotional expression. They showed Japanese and American participants films of unpleasant scenes involving pain and injury and videotaped their facial expressions. When the persons from the two cultures were alone, there were no differences in their facial expressions of emotion, but when an authority figure was also present in the room, the "Japanese more than the Americans masked negative expressions with the semblance of a smile" (Ekman, 1992, p. 34). It seems likely that the Japanese cultural prohibition against the expression of negative emotions made the difference.

A colleague recently drew my attention to an excellent and deeply moving example of a similar cultural prohibition against the expression of some emotions in men. In the summer of 1993, one television network covered the evacuation of a few Muslims from war-ravaged Bosnia. As a young boy was handed up to his father on the truck, the boy began to weep. When the father saw this, tears began to roll down his own face. The father immediately turned away from the boy and arranged and rearranged the boy so that he could not see the tears on his father's face. The father then appeared to be attempting to distract himself so that he would no longer cry. Much in our cultural learning experiences influences the expression of emotions.

Second, it's also clear that learning has a great deal to do with the stimuli that produce emotional reactions. As described more fully in chapter 5, there is evidence that many individuals with excessive fears (*phobias*) of elevators, water, automobiles, and the like learned their fears through modeling, classical conditioning, or avoidance conditioning (Marks, 1969).

Review

Emotions are fascinating psychological states that are difficult to describe and define. Most definitions of emotion, however, contain four elements: (a) the stimulus that provokes the emotion; (b) the positively or negatively toned conscious experience; (c) the state of arousal of the body produced by the autonomic nervous system and endocrine glands; and (d) the behavior that characteristically accompanies emotions. Psychologists cannot agree, however, on how these four elements work together during emotions. Three primary theories have been proposed to explain emotions: the James-Lange theory, the Cannon-Bard theory, and two versions of cognitive theory, each viewing a different relationship between stimulus, experience, arousal, and behavior. Many elements of emotions are apparently inborn in all humans, but learning seems to play a role in determining how much emotion will be displayed, how it will be displayed, and which stimuli will evoke emotional reactions.

Thinking Critically About Psychology

1. Think of an intense emotion you have recently experienced and explain the sequence of events according to each of the three theories discussed in the text.

2. Overall, which theory of emotion best explains your own experience? Why?

Check Your Learning

To be sure that you have learned the key points from the preceding section, cover the answers below and try to answer each question. If you give an incorrect answer to any question, return to the page given next to the correct answer to see why your answer was not correct.

1. ________________ are the experiences that give color, meaning, and intensity to our lives.

2. The ________________ theory of emotion is the theory that conscious emotional experiences are caused by feedback to the cerebral cortex from physiological reactions and behavior.

   a. Izard **c.** James-Lange
   b. Cannon-Bard **d.** Schachter

3. The ________________ theory of emotion is the theory that the interpretation of the incoming stimuli and the interpretation of bodily stimuli together cause the emotional experience.

   a. cognitive **c.** Cannon-Bard
   b. psychoanalytic **d.** social learning

4. Cultural learning plays a role in the expression of emotions.

   a. True **b.** False

Correct Answers
1. Emotions (p. 343), **2.** c (p. 344), **3.** a (p. 346), **4.** a (p. 350).

AGGRESSION: EMOTIONAL AND MOTIVATIONAL ASPECTS

Aggression is a topic of paramount importance to the human race. We pride ourselves on being humane creatures who have left the brutal jungle to establish "civilized" societies. But the sad reality is that no other animal species even comes remotely close to our record of violent and harmful acts against members of our own species. While fights to the death do sometimes occur over mates and territory in lower mammals, and apes do apparently "intentionally murder" other apes on rare occasions, no species rivals the frequency of human aggression. In my lifetime alone, hundreds of millions of humans have been killed by other humans in wars, revolutions, and acts of terrorism.

Human beings are the most aggressive species on the planet, and violence has increased in recent years. What can we do to curb violence in our society?

Violent crimes and murder have always been a part of human societies, but in recent years their frequency has reached unprecedented levels in many parts of the world. In the United States, violence has become the second-most common cause of death among 15- to 24-year-olds after accidents, and it is the leading cause of death among African-American males (Lore & Schultz, 1993). Perhaps most incomprehensible is the frequency of aggression toward members of one's own family. More than a third of the murders investigated by the FBI have been committed by one family member against another and some 3 percent involve the murder of a child by a parent. Each year in the United States, 4 million husbands and wives violently attack each other, resulting in severe injuries in a quarter million of the cases. Each year, too, 2 million children are kicked, beaten, or punched by their parents.

Why are human beings so aggressive? Can we do anything to curb violence in our society? Aggression is a complex phenomenon with both motivational and emotional aspects that we should carefully examine. Like most important topics in psychology, aggression has been the focus of a great deal of research and theoretical speculation. One view holds that aggression is a natural instinct; another suggests that it's a natural reaction to adverse events such as frustration and pain; and a third viewpoint considers aggression as learned behavior. We will look at these theoretical positions one at a time.

Freud's Instinct Theory: The Release of Aggressive Energy

Sigmund Freud suggested that all animals, humans included, are born with potent aggressive instincts. These instincts create a drive to commit aggressive acts that must be satisfied. In other words, they create an uncomfortable pressure that must be released in some way. Often the aggressive instinct is released in an overt act of aggression. But the key to curbing violence, according to **Freud's instinct theory,** lies in finding nonviolent ways to release aggressive energy, such as competing in business or sports, watching aggressive sports, or reading about violent crimes.

Freud's instinct theory
The theory that aggression is caused by an inborn aggressive instinct.

Freud's central point that aggression is instinctual has been echoed in modern times by a number of biologists who suggested that violence is necessary for the "survival of the fittest" (Lorenz, 1967). Author Robert Ardrey (1966) put it this way:

> Man is a predator whose natural instinct is to kill with a weapon. The sudden addition of the enlarged brain to the equipment of an armed, already successful, predatory animal created not only the human being but also the human predicament. (p. 332)

The most controversial aspect of Freud's theory is his belief that instinctual aggressive energy must be released in some way. He calls the process of releasing instinctual energy **catharsis.** Freud's suggestion that societies should encourage the nonviolent catharsis of aggressive energy has been much debated. In particular, some psychologists believe that the ways that Freud and his followers have suggested as safe means of catharsis actually have the effect of increasing aggressions. A bit later in this section we look at research bearing on this topic.

catharsis
The process of releasing instinctual energy.

Frustration-Aggression Theory

Other psychologists believe, like Freud, that aggression is an inborn part of human nature, but they do not agree that it stems from an ever-present instinctual need to aggress. Instead, they believe that aggression is a natural reaction to the frustration (blocking) of important motives. This **frustration-aggression theory** (Dollard, Doob, Miller, Mowrer, & Sears, 1939; Berkowitz, 1993) suggests, for example, that a child who takes a toy from another child may very well get a sock in the nose, or that a nation that frustrates another nation's desire for oil or for a seaport might become a target of war. People and nations who are frustrated react with anger and aggression. It is not surprising, therefore, that violence is more common among people who live in poverty, as they are chronically frustrated in their attempts to meet even the most basic human needs (Staub, 1996). But it is not only frustration that elicits violence—any aversive event can increase the likelihood of violence, including physical pain and sultry summer temperatures (Berkowitz, 1989).

frustration-aggression theory
Theory that aggression is a natural reaction to the frustration of important motives.

Social Learning Theory

To Freud, people have a need to aggress that must be relieved. According to the frustration-aggression hypothesis, people aggress only in response to frustrating or other adverse circumstances. In contrast, Albert Bandura (1973) and other social learning theorists believe that people are aggressive only if they have *learned* that it's to their benefit to be aggressive. Social learning theorists do not deny that frustration can make us more likely to be angry and aggressive, but they state that we will act aggressively in reaction to frustration only if we have learned to do so. We must see others be successful by being aggressive, or we must win victories of our own through aggression (make someone stop bothering us or take away someone else's possession) before we will become aggressive people.

Social learning theorists directly conflict with Freud on the topic of catharsis. Freudian psychologists believe that we must find cathartic outlets for our aggressive energy to keep it from emerging as actual aggression. They recommend such things as yelling when angry, hitting a punching bag, and vicariously experiencing aggression by reading violent books or watching violence on television. Social learning theorists argue that these activities will not decrease violence but instead will *increase* it by teaching violence to the person (Bandura, 1973). The evidence on the practice of yelling or hitting a punching bag instead of hitting the person with whom you are angry is inconsistent, but sometimes, at least, these activities increase violent behavior (Geen & Quanty, 1977).

The evidence against the idea of vicarious catharsis through watching violence on television is quite clear, however. Televised violence does not decrease violence in those who watch it; it *increases* it. The evidence is particularly clear for children. As discussed more completely in chapter 5, evidence indicates that watching televised violence increases violent play, increases actual violence, and makes children less likely to intervene in the violent acts of other children (Bandura, 1973; Liebert et al, 1983; Thomas & Drabman, 1975). Since 75 percent of the television programs in the United States contain violence (compared, for example, with 10 percent in Sweden), the issue of televised violence is understandably one of national concern (Wood, Wong, & Chachere, 1991).

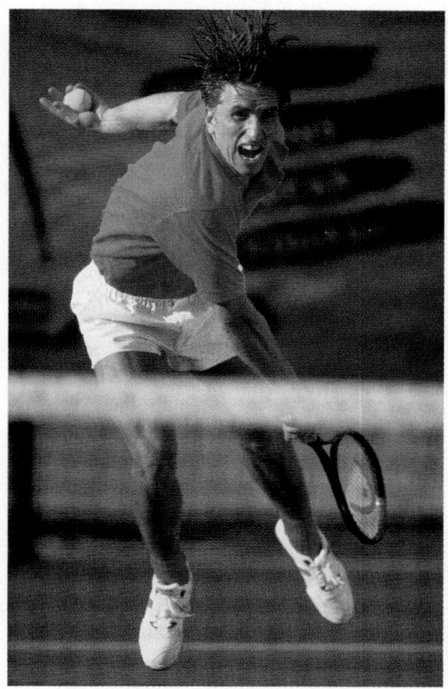

Freudian psychologists believe releasing aggressive feelings in a nonharmful way, like sports, reduces the chance of violent behavior. However, social learning theorists believe that watching or practicing aggressive behavior, even in nonharmful ways, can actually increase the chances for violence.

Culture and Aggression

One of the more obvious and puzzling facts of American life is that rates of violent aggression are quite different for different ethnic and cultural groups. Richard Nisbett (1993) has recently taken a look at this issue from a perspective that is consistent with the social learning theory of aggression and with the sociocultural perspective described in chapter 1 (p. 16). Nisbett (1993) suggests that some groups have higher violence rates than others because they have passed attitudes favorable to violence from one generation to the next through social learning. He has focused on the higher rates of violence among white males who live in some sections of the U.S. South and Southwest compared with the North. For example, the rates of homicide among white males in the South is three times higher than in New England in small cities and twice as high in large cities (Nisbett, 1993).

Nisbett argues that the first wave of settlers to the North were "sober Puritans, Quakers, and Dutch farmer-artisans" (p. 442) who lived side by side on established farms and banded together and cooperated for the common good. Violence was uncommon in this segment of society, partly because there was little temptation to steal the corn and potatoes of a neighbor and because the common good was promoted by harmony. Nisbett suggests that this attitude has been passed down through social learning to generations of Northern whites.

In contrast, large sections of the South and Southwest were settled by "swashbuckling Cavaliers . . . who took their values not from tilling the soil and the requirements of civic responsibility but from the knightly, medieval standards of manly honor and virtue" (p. 442). In addition, large segments of the South were settled by groups with long histories of animosity in Europe (e.g., the Irish, the Scottish, and the English). Most of these earned their living by herding pigs, sheep, or cattle. Thus, many settlers in the South and Southwest found themselves with potentially hostile neighbors who could wipe out a family's livelihood in a moment by stealing their herd. In this atmosphere, Nisbett suggests, men in particular felt that they had to be prepared to defend themselves with violence, and they have passed this attitude down through the generations.

Nisbett tested his model by conducting interviews of large numbers of Southern and Northern whites. Southerners do not approve of violence in general any more than Northerners, but Southerners believe that violence is an appropriate response to either a threat or an insult. Nisbett (1993) suggests that such socially learned attitudes are the basis of the differences in rates of violence among different ethnic groups in the United States. What do you think? Is Nisbett portraying Southern and Northern white Americans accurately? Is social learning a factor in violent behavior?

Violent Youth Gangs

The United States has long had a problem with crimes committed by urban adolescents who have joined together in gangs, but there has been a recent increase in both the number of youth in gangs and the violence that they commit. Psychologist Ervin Staub (1996) has provided a plausible theory to explain the increase in gang violence in America that incorporates elements of both the frustration-aggression and social learning theories of aggression. According to Staub (1996), the problem begins in the homes of young adolescents who later join gangs. When parents use harsh physical punishment to discipline their children, they are modeling aggression for the child to imitate. In addition, the child is likely to react to the pain of the harsh punishment with even more aggressive misbehavior. This often leads the parent to write off the aggressive child as "no good" and to cease to supervise his or her activities—giving the child the freedom to spend time with older gang members.

The harsh and inadequate parenting creates children who act in aggressive ways toward their classmates at school, leading to rejection by most of their peers—most kids fear and dislike aggressive bullies. But gangs composed of other aggressive youths offer a place for aggressive kids to belong who have been rejected by their families and peers. The person most likely to respect an aggressive adolescent is another aggressive adolescent who has been rejected by family and peers.

Unfortunately, the gangs provide a place to belong at the cost of encouraging strong feelings of "us" versus "them." Gangs encourage their members to hate and demean the members of other gangs and to think of them as an "opposing army." Conflicts between rival gangs are made more frequent and intense because the sale of drugs by gangs gives poor adolescents their first opportunity to rise above the grinding frustrations of poverty.

Like all of us, youth in gangs live in society that bombards them with the message that violence is an effective way to solve problems. They see it on television shows, at the movies, and just by observing violence in their homes and neighborhoods. If they watch the news on television, they see a nation that applauds violence when the "us" is the United States and the "them" is, for example, the army of Iraq. We give celebrations in honor of military leaders who organize the killing of hundreds of thousands of the enemy in wars, and we encourage our war heroes to run for president. All of this provides a clear social learning experience that killing your enemies not only is okay but also is a source of great pride. Finally, the widespread availability of highly lethal automatic weapons in our society makes it easy for the small armies that we call "gangs" to be well armed. And guns in the hands of aggressive youth who believe that they are at war with other gangs means death.

Research is desperately needed to test this and other theories of the rise of gang violence in the United States. This is a promising theory, but our society must be willing to invest in research on gangs, domestic violence, warfare, and other forms of violence if we are going to find ways to curb aggression.

Review

Aggression is a topic of fear and concern to everyone. Three major theories have been proposed to explain human aggression. Sigmund Freud proposed that aggression is the result of an inborn motive to aggress that needs to be released. The frustration-aggression theory suggests that aggression is an inborn reaction to frustration and pain. And social learning theory suggests that aggression is not an inborn behavior, but that people will aggress only if they have learned to do so. The most interesting conflict between these theories concerns Freud's prescription for reducing violence in society. Freudian psychologists suggest that an outlet—catharsis—must be found for the aggressive motive, but that this can be a nonviolent outlet such as hitting a punching bag or watching violence on television. Much research on this topic suggests that Freud was wrong and supports the social learning theory view that such supposed outlets merely teach people to be more violent.

Thinking Critically About Psychology

1. In your opinion, which theory of aggression offers the best ideas for reducing gang violence?

2. Does the link that has been established between aggression and violence in television prove that social learning theorists are correct? Why or why not?

Check Your Learning

To be sure that you have learned the key points from the preceding section, cover the answers below and try to answer each question. If you give an incorrect answer to any question, return to the page given next to the correct answer to see why your answer was not correct.

Match each definition with one of the following terms:

Terms:

a. social learning theory
b. Freud's instinct theory
c. frustration-aggression theory

1. According to ________________, aggression is caused by an inborn aggressive instinct.

2. According to ________________, aggression is a natural reaction to frustration and pain.

3. According to ________________, people act aggressively only if they have learned to do so.

Correct Answers

1. b (p. 352), **2.** c (p. 352), **3.** a (p. 352).

APPLICATION OF PSYCHOLOGY

SHOULD YOU TRY TO LOSE WEIGHT? IF SO, HOW?

We live in a society that values thinness. Women are told in countless subtle—and sometimes blatant—ways that you must be thin to find love, to be successful, and to be happy. And men are told that fat is the equivalent of softness, weakness, and unattractiveness. Watch television one evening this week: You will see sleek and slender women and men working as attorneys, physicians, and executives. The mechanics and secretaries are much more likely to be heavy (except for the secretary for whom the husband leaves his shrill and plump wife). Who falls in love on television or in the movies? With few exceptions, it is the slender men who fall in love with slender women, and vice versa. The chubbier ones are the humorous friends who rarely find romance and never receive the big promotion at work.

When these shows break for a commercial, we are offered countless ways to deal with the fact that we aren't the fortunate skinny ones. Advertisements for liquid diets, artificial sweeteners, and weight-loss plans are shown many times each day.

How many of us are actually "overweight" to the extent that it poses at least a minor health risk? In the United States, 31 percent of men and 24 percent of women are overweight (about half of whom are severely overweight in medical terms). Now, how many of us think we are overweight? In the United States, 37 percent of men and 52 percent of women feel that they are overweight (Brownell & Rodin, 1994). That means that a few more men think that they are overweight than actually are overweight, but more than *twice* as many women think they are overweight than is actually the case! As a result, 24 percent of men and a whopping 40 percent of women are on a diet at any one time. We Americans are very likely to decide we are too fat and try to do something about it through dieting—even if we are not actually overweight—especially American women.

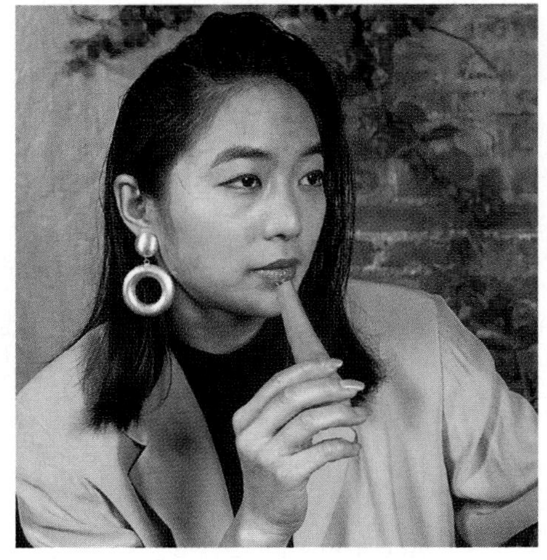

The pressure to be thin leads to unhealthy eating patterns for many people. If this carrot is not part of a balanced diet, this woman's desire to be thin may harm her health.

We are so bombarded by the message that thin is desirable that it seems to be an unquestionable truth. It is not; it is a belief that happens to have been part of American culture since the 1960s, but not all peoples during all times have considered thin to be beautiful. Take a trip to an art museum and look at the beautiful nude women painted by artists during the seventeenth and eighteenth centuries. By current U.S. standards, these women are overweight. Even looking back to the 1950s in the United States, the women that men found to be ideal sex symbols (Marilyn Monroe, Jane Russell, and Jayne Mansfield) probably would be on diets today. Furthermore, there are considerable differences among different ethnic groups in the United States today concerning ideal body weight, with whites having stricter standards than most other groups. In addition, in many contemporary non-Western cultures, much higher amounts of body fat are considered to be beautiful. For example, the Anay tribe of Nigeria encourage weight gain in women, with the ideal body weight in excess of 400 pounds.

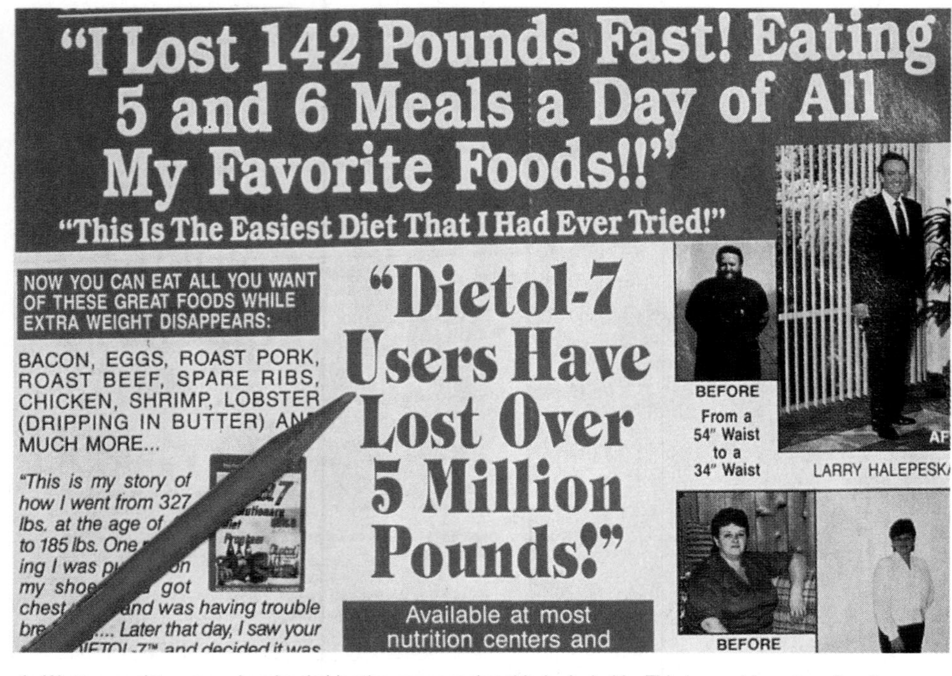

In Western society we are bombarded by the message that thin is desirable. This has not been true for all cultures at all times.

People in our society, however, are unquestionably prejudiced against persons who are overweight. If you are considerably heavier than is desirable in our culture, you may be less likely to land the job, get the promotion, or attract the person that you wish to attract. That is certainly not to say that you will necessarily be a less successful or happy person, but you may find that you have one strike against you.

Should you try to lose weight, then, to avoid the prejudice? It is important to keep in mind that our heredity and past history of eating and exercise determine how thin we can be to a great extent. Some people can eat whatever they wish and remain thin through long periods of their life.

Others will never be able to reach the cultural ideal no matter how much they diet and exercise and would not be able to stay there if they reached it (Brownell, 1991).

The most important issue to consider in thinking about dieting is that it can be dangerous. The constant pressure that women, in particular, receive to be thin leads many to dangerous patterns of eating. Some starve themselves until they reach an unhealthy body weight, sometimes to the point that they are considered to exhibit *anorexia nervosa.* Others find themselves purging (inducing vomiting) after eating large amounts of calories, sometimes to the extent of being considered to exhibit *bulimia.* Although the most serious cases of these disorders involve more than a simple desire to be thin (distorted body image, compulsively rigid eating patterns, etc.) (Ruderman & Besbeas, 1992), the pressure to be thin undoubtedly leads to unhealthy patterns of eating in many Americans.

The most common threat to health, however, is so-called *yo-yo dieting.* Many dieters lose quite a few pounds, gain it back, then diet again. At first, their weight goes down and up with their eating habits like a yo-yo, but soon dieting stops working. What has happened? The body's internal *set point* mechanism for regulating body fat does not like to allow the body to lose fat. The body seems to think that fat is necessary for survival in case a famine strikes. When you diet and lose weight once, the body thinks that a famine has struck, and it learns from the experience. The next time that you diet, the body rapidly compensates for the lost calories by slowing down the rate at which you use energy *(metabolism).* So, instead of losing weight on your next diet, your reduced intake of food causes your metabolism to slow down enough to offset the reduced calories (Steen, Oppliger, & Brownell, 1988; Thompson, Jarvie, Lahey, & Cureton, 1982).

Thus, yo-yo dieting is eventually self-defeating. More importantly, it is dangerous. Repeated yo-yo dieting has been found to be associated with increased heart disease in the Framingham health study, probably because it leads to fluctuations in fat levels in the bloodstream (Lissner et al., 1991). Thus, dieting is, in fact, dangerous to your health.

So, all things considered, should you diet? If you do not consider yourself to be overweight, you are probably convinced beyond a doubt that dieting is ridiculous. However, if you consider yourself to be overweight and were planning on losing a few pounds, you might be much less convinced. In fact, you may be quite confused and concerned at this point.

Fortunately, the alternatives are not simply to diet or not to diet. Instead of dieting, we have the alternative of making permanent lifestyle changes in eating and exercise. These changes will probably improve your health and will result in the loss of some weight. If you top off these changes in eating and exercise by giving up the wish to look like a star of "Friends," you will really be ahead of the game.

Consider the following suggestions:

1. *Don't "diet."* Do not try to regulate your weight by eating less for a brief period of time than is comfortable or healthy for you. In other words, do not go on diets. Weight that is lost in that way will almost always be regained when you return to a more natural pattern of eating (Brownell, 1991). You may recall the experience with dieting of television personality Oprah Winfrey in 1990. She dieted and her weight fell from 190 to 123, but when she stopped the diet, she regained all of the lost weight and some additional weight. Her story is not at all unusual, as the great majority of persons who lose weight through dieting regain the weight after stopping the diet, often leading to a pattern of yo-yo dieting. But seeing a respected celebrity regain lost weight helps us see the likely pitfalls of dieting. In 1993, Oprah lost 60 pounds again, but this time without dieting. She changed her lifestyle to include plenty of exercise and proper nutrition and has kept her weight down. If she can continue with this new lifestyle, she will have successfully broken the cycle of yo-yo dieting.
2. *Eat differently.* Instead of dieting, commit yourself to a lifelong pattern of eating *differently* that you can live with. You do not have to starve yourself; you just need to choose your calories carefully. Reducing the amount of saturated fat that you eat in the form of meat and dairy products makes terrific sense, and it also reduces your chance of cardiovascular disease and some forms of cancer.

   Second, reducing the amount of processed sugar makes sense because sugar gives you calories with very little nutrition and only briefly satisfies your hunger. When you eat sugar, you feel an immediate drop in hunger, but the sugar causes a sudden increase in insulin levels that typically purges the blood of more sugar than you ate, making you feel more hungry in an hour or two (Rodin, 1985). Most of us also think of candy and soft drinks as "high-energy food" that can work as a "pick-me-up" when we are tired. To test this idea, Robert Thayer (1987) and a group of his students conducted a study of the effects of eating a candy bar on feelings of energy and general tension. He compared the effects of eating a candy bar to taking a brisk 10-minute walk. Eating a candy bar in the morning when our energy levels tend to be low did produce an increase in feelings of energy that lasted for 2 hours. On the other hand, eating a candy bar in the afternoon when energy levels tend to be higher led to a brief increase in energy that dissipated in an hour and was followed by a *decrease* in energy level 2 hours after eating the candy bar. In contrast, the 10-minute walk always led to a greater increase in energy and a reduction in feelings of tension.

   Thus, eating differently means focusing on complex carbohydrates (fruits and vegetables) and reducing saturated fat and sugar intake.
3. *Emphasize exercise.* Increased exercise is beneficial in many ways. We are told that a pound of body fat is the equivalent of 3,500 calories, so if you cut down by 500 calories a day, you should lose a pound every

week (7 days × 500 calories = 3,500 calories in a week). Right? That arithmetic works only if your metabolism does not *slow down* by 500 calories a day to offset the loss of calories taken in.

As I said, *the body does not like to lose fat.* As a result, you must *increase* your metabolism by increasing your activity level (Thompson et al., 1982). If you burn calories through regular and moderate aerobic exercise, you stand a much better chance of losing weight than by restricting calories alone for two reasons. First, depending on your level of fitness and what is sensible for you, a good workout might burn 300 to 500 calories by itself. But, more importantly, *regular* moderate aerobic exercise keeps the metabolism from falling if you reduce your calorie intake. In addition, of course, exercise is beneficial to your cardiovascular health and helps promote a relaxed sense of well-being.

4. *Do not give in to lapses in your healthy lifestyle.* We're only human; it's easy to commit to a lifestyle change in eating, but many things can knock you off your healthy course. A week spent with your family, a vacation trip, taking exams, and other things can disrupt your plans to exercise and eat right. This is inevitable, but it need not mean that your plans to eat better and exercise more are impossible dreams. Just start exercising again!

It is very important to understand why lapses occur. First, they are caused by temptations (or incentives, see page 332). We are more likely to eat the things that we have decided not to eat if they are right there in front of us. For example, we had friends over last night, and although I know it is not smart, we served them chocolate cake for dessert. Unfortunately, the rest of it is still in the kitchen and it is singing to me—begging and pleading, in a lovely singing voice—for me to feast on it. I am resisting now because I know you are watching me and I have to set a good example, but what will happen when I turn off the word processor? Tempting foods are incentives that stimulate hunger—avoid them. (Excuse me for a moment while I take the cake to the neighbors; let them worry about it!)

Second, lapses in healthy lifestyles are caused by temporary losses in self-control. These losses in self-control can be caused by a variety of things, but high on the list are boredom and bad moods (Grilo, Shiffman, & Wing, 1989). If you sit around all day watching boring television, you may find yourself eating much more than usual. Similarly, a lousy mood caused by a bad day at work, the breakup of a relationship, or some other cause often leads to an attitude of "Who cares if I eat well or exercise? What good is it doing me?" Maybe understanding this fact will help you delay your decision about ending your fitness program until after a bad mood passes. Besides, exercise is a great natural antidote to a bad mood.

In addition to knowing what causes lapses, it is essential to understand that they are *inevitable.* Everyone has them, and that's okay. The secret to long-term fitness is understanding that one piece of cake won't wreck your improved lifestyle unless you stop your fitness program because of it. If you miss exercising for a few days or overeat on a trip, don't say, "See! I knew I couldn't stick to a healthy lifestyle! I'm a potato chips and ice cream person, and that's that!" Instead, just realize that you have suffered a minor setback and get right back on your plan. People who have lifelong patterns of healthy eating and exercise aren't people who never have lapses; they are people who never let a lapse become permanent.

I should hasten to add that there are exceptions to every rule. Some people *can* go on a diet, lose weight, and keep it off for long periods of time. In addition, there are people who should diet for health reasons (obesity, diabetes, etc.). For these persons, assistance from experts who have developed effective weight-control strategies would be wise (Grilo et al., 1989).

Lapses are inevitable when you change to a healthy eating style. It's important to remember that setbacks are only temporary and to get back to your plan as soon as you can.

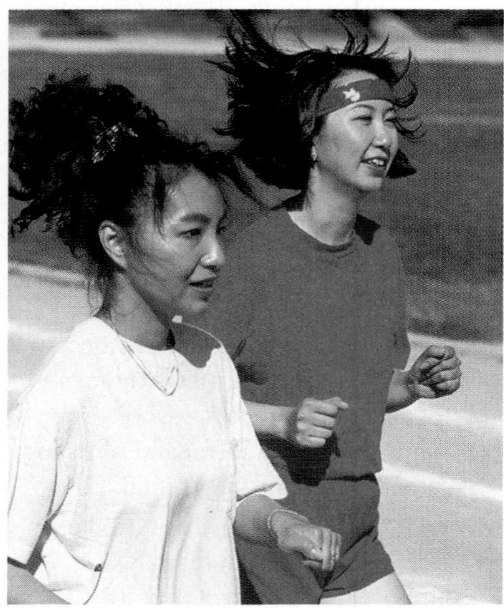

Regular moderate aerobic exercise keeps your metabolism up and provides important cardiovascular conditioning.

Summary

Chapter 9 defines motivation and emotion, discusses primary motives and psychological motives, and explores three theories of emotions. The topic of aggression is included in the chapter because of its close link to both emotion and motivation.

I. Motivation refers to those factors that activate behavior and give it direction. Emotions are positive or negative feelings usually accompanied by behavior and physiological arousal that are generally reactions to stimulus situations.

II. Primary motives are human motives that stem from the need for those things that keep a person alive.

- **A.** Homeostatic mechanisms in the body sense imbalances of essential life elements and stimulate actions that will restore the proper balance.
- **B.** Hunger is biologically regulated by three centers in the hypothalamus.
  - **1.** Rats become hyperphagic (obese because of overeating) if the satiety center is destroyed.
  - **2.** Cues for regulating hunger on a daily basis are stomach contractions and blood sugar levels; body fat is apparently involved in the long-term regulation of hunger.
- **C.** Learning influences when we eat, what we eat, and how much we eat. Hunger, as well as other motives, is affected by incentives—external cues that activate motives.
- **D.** The hypothalamus also controls thirst. Cues used to regulate drinking are mouth dryness, loss of water by cells, and reductions in blood volume.
- **E.** Learning influences drinking behavior and incentives can activate thirst.
- **F.** Sex centers in the hypothalamus function to initiate or inhibit sexual behavior. In many nonhuman mammals, hormones and odors affect sexual behavior.
- **G.** The sexual motive differs from the other primary motives in several ways, the most obvious of which is that we do not have to satisfy the sexual motive to survive.

III. Psychological motives are "needs" in the sense that the individual's happiness and well-being, but not survival, depend on these motives.

- **A.** Humans and other animals have an inborn motive to seek novel stimulation; humans seek an optimal level of arousal. The Yerkes-Dodson law states that if arousal is too low, performance will be inadequate; but if it is too high, performance may become disrupted and disorganized.
- **B.** Individuals high in affiliation motivation tend to prefer being with others rather than satisfying other motives.
- **C.** Achievement motivation (*n Ach*) is the psychological need for success.
- **D.** Intrinsic motivation refers to motives stimulated by the inherent nature of the activity. External motivation is motivation stimulated by external rewards.
- **E.** According to Maslow, motives are organized in a hierarchy arranged from the most basic to the most personal and advanced.

IV. Emotions are the experiences that give color, meaning, and intensity to our lives.

- **A.** Theories that attempt to explain emotions include the James-Lange theory, the Cannon-Bard theory, and the cognitive theory.
- **B.** Most psychologists believe that many basic emotions are primarily inborn, but that learning also plays an important role in emotions.

V. Aggression is a complex phenomenon.

- **A.** Freud suggested that all people are born with potent aggressive instincts that are released through catharsis.
- **B.** Other psychologists say aggression is a reaction to the frustration (blocking) of important motives (the frustration-aggression hypothesis).
- **C.** Social learning theorists explain aggression as learned behavior.

Suggested Readings

1. A scholarly review of the topic of motivation, but one that can be easily understood, is provided by: Petri, H. L. (1986). *Motivation: Theory and research* (2nd ed.). Belmont, CA: Wadsworth Publishing Co.
2. A scholarly work on emotion: Strongman, K. T. (1987). *The psychology of emotion* (3rd ed.). New York: John Wiley & Sons.
3. An interesting look at human emotion is given by: Plutchik, R. (1980). *Emotion: A psychoevolutionary synthesis.* New York: Harper & Row.
4. The relationship between cognition and abnormal emotions is discussed by: Ellis, A. (1962). *Reason and emotion in psychotherapy.* New York: Lyle Stuart; and Beck, A. T. (1976). *Cognitive therapy and the emotional disorders.* New York: International Universities Press.
5. For a psychological perspective on human aggression: Bandura, A. (1973). *Aggression: A social learning analysis.* Englewood Cliffs, NJ: Prentice-Hall. Also see an excellent article by Lore, R. K., & Schultz, L. A. (1993). Control of human aggression: A comparative perspective. *American Psychologist, 48,* 16–25.

CHAPTER

10

CHAPTER OUTLINE

Gender and Sexuality

PROLOGUE

What are women like? What are men like? Based on what you have observed, what psychological characteristics do you think distinguish women from men? In general, are women strong, caring, and wise? Are women less aggressive and independent than men? How about emotional and fearful—are those traits of women or men? Let me tell you how the great anthropologist Margaret Mead answered these questions about women and men—she said the answers depend on their culture.

Mead had studied many remote cultures during the 1920s to learn how cultures shape people through social learning. The topic of one of her most famous books was the differences between women and men in three cultures (Mead, 1935). She said that among the Arapesh people of New Guinea, neither men nor women are likely to be aggressive or hostile. They show very little competitiveness, but work together on joint projects such as farming that benefit everyone in the tribe equally. Mead described both men and women as maternal, gentle, and actively involved in raising their children. Jealousy, envy, and conflict, even between parents and adolescents, were almost nonexistent.

The Mundugamor people were quite different from the Arapesh, however. For example, both men and women were highly competitive and physically aggressive, and both found childrearing to be an unrewarding burden. Gentleness and caring were rare in dealing with children, who were required to be independent from an early age.

Among the Arapesh, therefore, both men and women displayed traits that would have been considered "feminine" in American culture, while both women and men displayed stereotypically "masculine" traits among the Mundugamor. Mead also described the Tchambuli people. Marked differences existed between men and women among these people, but they were the opposite of American culture. Women held the power in the village and were preoccupied with farming, fishing, and manufacturing, while the men played a passive, secondary role.

What are women and men like then? To a great extent it depends on the ways they have been shaped by their culture.

This chapter discusses two topics that are often referred to by same name—sex: (a) the gender of a person—male or female, and (b) sexual behavior. Much of who you are and what you do is related to your gender and sexuality. Your experiences as a young boy or girl, the expectations that you learned from society of what it means to be a woman or a man, and how you view the sexual aspects of your self are central to your total being.

We first discuss gender identity, gender roles, and sexual orientation. The ways in which we view our gender and our sexual orientation are a product of both biological and psychological factors. These factors result in some differences between men and women in Western cultures, but we will find that women and men are more similar in psychological terms than they are different.

Your sexuality is the product of both your biology and your social experiences during all periods of development. Starting with a brief history of the scientific study of sexuality, we will focus our attention on the biological and psychological aspects of sexual motivation and the sexual response cycle, describe some common problems of sexuality and their solutions, discuss

KEY TERMS

atypical and abnormal sexuality, and finally turn our attention to several social problems associated with human sexuality, including sexual violence and sexually transmitted diseases.

DEFINITIONS OF SEX, GENDER, SEXUALITY, AND SEXUAL ORIENTATION

sex
The distinction between male and female based on biological characteristics.

gender
The psychological experience of being male or female.

gender identity
One's view of oneself as male or female.

gender role
The behaviors consistent with being male or female in a given culture.

A person's **sex** is defined by their male or female genitals. **Gender,** in contrast, is the psychological experience of one's sex (Gentile, 1993). In most cases, a person's sex and gender are the same, but not always. As we will see later in this chapter, it is possible for persons with male genitals to feel that their gender is female and vice versa.

It will help advance our discussion to distinguish between two important aspects of gender, gender identity and gender roles. **Gender identity** is the subjective experience of being a male or a female. As is true for all aspects of personal identity, gender identity is a part of our personalities and a central component of our self-concept. **Gender role,** on the other hand, refers to all of the behaviors that communicate to others the degree to which we are "masculine" or "feminine" in the terms defined by our culture (Money, 1987b, 1988). Thus, your gender role is the outward behavioral expression of your gender identity. Gender roles vary from culture to culture and provide a set of expectations for persons on the basis of their sex.

sexual orientation
The tendency to prefer romantic and sexual partners of the same or different sex.

The term *sexuality* refers to the behaviors in which we engage to obtain sexual pleasure and to all of the feelings and beliefs that are interwoven with sexual behavior. One aspect of our psychological selves that is very much a part of both our sexuality and gender identity is **sexual orientation**—our tendency to prefer romantic and sexual partners of the same or different sex. This chapter will discuss all of these aspects of gender and sex.

GENDER AND SEXUAL ORIENTATION

We begin our discussion of gender and sex with a detailed look at the psychological aspects of being a male or female. We will look at the development of the identity and behaviors associated with gender and look at similarities and differences between women and men. We will also look at the related topic of sexual orientation—the gender to whom a person is drawn romantically and sexually.

Gender Identity and Gender Roles

Gender identity develops early in infancy. Immediately after the infant is born (and sometimes well before birth through ultrasound imaging) the newborn is identified as either male or female based on her or his genitals. The parents select a name appropriate to the baby's gender and greet the newborn infant with cultural expectations for the behavior of boys or girls. Children quickly learn the gender behaviors that are expected of them. Parents, other family members, peers, teachers, and others communicate their behavioral expectations for girls and boys in mostly subtle, but very effective, ways.

Gender roles are the behaviors and characteristics that a culture expects of males and females based on their biological sex. Members of a culture classify behaviors as to whether they are appropriate and expected of males and females. *Feminine* behaviors are expected of females, and *masculine* behaviors are expected of males. For better or for worse, traditionally masculine traits in North American cultures include things such as aggressiveness, strength, and independence. On the other hand, traditional feminine gender roles include nurturance, emotional expressiveness, and dependence.

Early in the study of gender roles, masculinity and femininity were thought of as discrete categories (you were either masculine or feminine) that matched exactly with a person's biological sex. More recent views, however, have conceived of gender roles as being a graded continuum, with people displaying varying degrees of *both* masculinity and femininity (Bem, 1974; Spence & Helmreich, 1978). There are two reasons for this change in thinking about gender roles. First, masculinity and femininity are not opposites of each other, but rather are two separate dimensions. And, second, both women and men can be both masculine and feminine. A person who has both masculine and feminine characteristics is referred to as **androgynous.** For example, in the United States today, a woman or man who is sensitive to others, nurturing, and emotionally expressive (traditional

androgynous
Having both feminine and masculine characteristics.

Androgynous men and women combine the best characteristics of the stereotypical masculine and feminine roles.

feminine traits) and strong, independent, and competitive (masculine traits) would be considered to be androgynous.

There is considerable evidence that people who are androgynous are more likely to adapt well to a variety of situations because they are more flexible in their approach to life's demands (Garcia, 1982; Taylor & Hall, 1982). Let's consider a simple example: A friend of mine named Kate was driving her 7-year-old friend, Kevin, to the library one afternoon when she had a sudden blowout in her car. The tire ruptured with a loud bang and the car skidded and wobbled for a few frightening moments until Kate brought it under control. Kate heaved a sigh of relief, then spent a few minutes calming her young friend (a traditionally feminine behavior). Soon they were both belly-laughing at their inelegant halt on the side of the road. Then, she efficiently changed the tire (a traditionally masculine behavior) and drove Kevin to the library. Kate's behavior was wonderfully androgynous in that it contained the most adaptive elements of both masculine and feminine genders. Today, a growing number of men and women easily cross traditional lines of gender roles.

Gender Similarities and Gender Differences

Gender roles are less distinct now than they used to be, but are there other psychological differences between women and men? This is a difficult question to answer for many reasons, some of which are scientific and some of which are not. Alice Eagly (1995) of Purdue University has written: "When psychologists publish research that compares the behavior of women and men, they face political as well as scientific issues" (p. 145). The political issue is that some people—women and men alike—welcome studies that indicate that women and men are different, whereas others believe that it encourages a sexist view of women. Moreover, from a purely scientific perspective, it may be premature to reach any firm questions about psychological differences between the sexes at this point. Research is progressing at such a rapid pace that opinions are still changing. Indeed, so much has been learned in the last three years that some of the statements in this edition of this book are different from statements made in the previous edition. Such rapid changes in knowledge are encouraging but make me feel tentative—perhaps new research conducted over the next three years will change views on sex differences again by the next edition. With that caution in mind, this is my best attempt at summarizing what research now says about psychological sex differences.

Psychology textbooks usually contain statements such as these: "Males are better in math and females are better in English." "Women master language skills better than men, while men are better at organizing objects in a spatial layout." "Women are more nurturing and less aggressive than men." "Men are less likely to be anxious or depressed than women." The results of hundreds of studies of potential psychological differences between women and men are summarized in table 10.1. Only the most consistently identified

TABLE 10.1 Consistently Identified Psychological Differences Between Women and Men

On the average, women score higher than men on tests of:	On the average, women are more likely than men to:	On the average, men score higher than women on tests of:	On the average, men are more likely than women to:
Language Spelling Reading comprehension Perceptual speed Associative memory	Smile Understand the emotions of others Be nurturing and concerned about others Be sociable (extroverted) Be trusting Be anxious Be depressed To emphasize character and career ambition when choosing a mate	Mathematics ability Science ability Social Studies ability Mechanical reasoning Electronics, automobile, and shop information	Interrupt others in mixed-sex conversations Commit most kinds of crimes (especially sex crimes) Be aggressive Be assertive Be comfortable with casual sex Have high self-esteem To emphasize physical attractiveness when choosing a mate

References: Dindia & Allen, 1992; Doyle & Paludi, 1991; Eagly, 1995; Feingold, 1994; Guisinger & Blatt, 1994; Hedges & Nowell, 1995; Hyde & Plant, 1995; Keenan, in press; Maccoby & Jacklin, 1974; Nolen-Hoeksema, 1987.

differences are listed in the table. Are these descriptions of psychological differences between women and men accurate?

Current evidence suggests that they are probably *accurate* but are nonetheless potentially *misleading* because: (1) the differences between women and men in averages scores are usually *small*, and (2) women and men are *far more similar than dissimilar*, even on psychological characteristics for which sex differences have been found (Eagly, 1995; Hedges & Nowell, 1995; Hyde & Plant, 1995). Look at figure 10.1 to see what I mean. This figure represents the scores—arranged from the lowest to the highest—of a large number of men and women on a test of mathematical ability. Although the average score of men is higher than the average score of women, the difference between the averages of women and men is extremely small *compared with the range of differences among members of the same sex*. The difference in mathematical ability between the highest scoring males and lowest scoring males is vastly greater than the difference between the "average" woman and "average" man. Notice also that the two distributions overlap so much that if you picked 10 of the highest scoring men in the United States, you would have no trouble finding 10 women in the country with the same scores.

If women and men are very similar, even on characteristics for which sex differences have been found, does this mean that psychological sex differences are completely meaningless? No, they may be quite meaningful in some situations. Let's look at figure 10.1 again to see why. A recent summary of research on sex differences by Larry Hedges and Amy Nowell (1995) suggests that women are slightly more likely to have scores that fall close to the average than men. This means that there are slightly more men with very high scores or very low scores than women.

For tests on which males score higher on the average than females, the tendency for males to have more extreme scores means that many more males will have extremely high scores than females. On one test that is used to identify high school students with talent for college training in mathematics, 50 percent more males than females scored in the top 5 percent, and seven times as many males as females fell in the top 1 percent of scores (Hedges & Lowell, 1995). If these findings are correct (and they seem to be), it helps to explain why males are more likely than females to be admitted to the top science and engineering schools, to receive the top scholarships, and to excel in such fields.

On the other hand, persons with very high mathematics scores represent only a small portion of the workforce, even in scientific and engineering fields. A more powerful reason for the greater success of men in scientific and technological fields may be prejudicial barriers erected against women, and barriers in the minds of women themselves. It

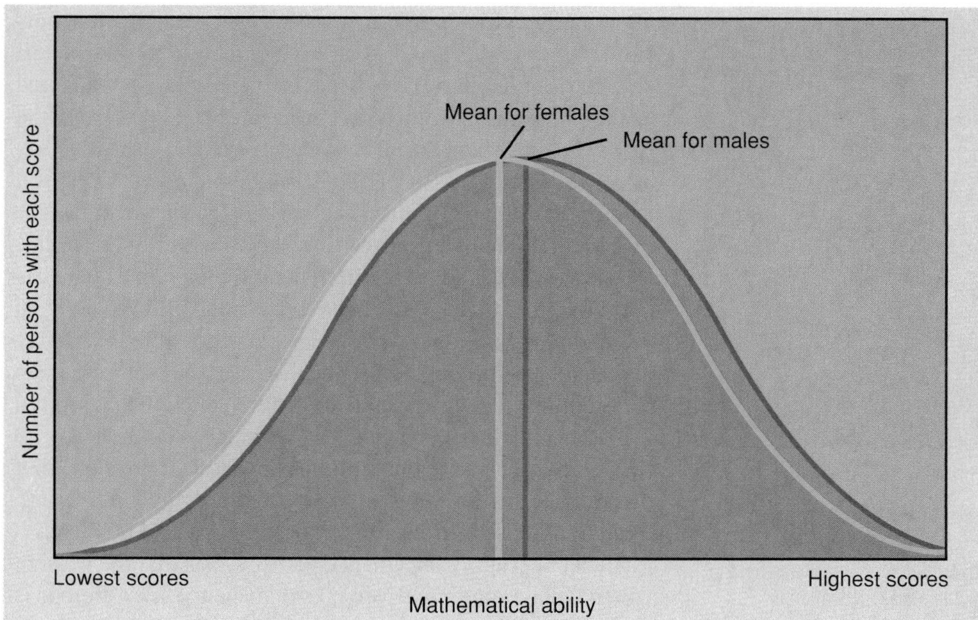

FIGURE 10.1

The number of persons receiving each score (from the highest to the lowest) on a test of mathematical ability. The mean is somewhat higher for males than females, but the vast majority of males receive scores in the same range as females. Because the mean is a little higher for males, and because the spread of scores around the mean is greater for males, a higher proportion of males than females receive the highest scores.

is important to note that, on the average, women receive *higher* grades than males in the mathematics courses at all educational levels. This would suggest that women are better prepared for careers in scientific and technological fields. Women, however, tend to attribute their success in mathematics courses to hard work, whereas men are more likely to attribute their success to their intellectual ability (Kimball, 1989). This difference in the way women and men think about their success in mathematics courses may play an important role in how they approach careers that involve mathematics.

Susan Chapman and her associates (Chapman, Krantz, & Silver, 1992) conducted a study of the career interests of women among freshmen entering Barnard College, a highly selective women's college of Columbia University. Chapman found that women's interest in careers involving mathematics was not related at all to their scores on tests of mathematics ability and achievement. On the other hand, women who reported more anxiety about their skills in mathematics were less interested in careers in science, regardless of their mathematical ability. This suggests that lack of confidence in mathematics may be a greater barrier for women than lack of ability in mathematics.

It would be a serious mistake to focus our discussion of sex differences only on areas in which males have an advantage. There are several areas in which males are at a serious disadvantage as well. For example, although men score only slightly lower on tests of reading and spelling on the average, men are twice as likely to fall in the lowest 10 percent of scores. These essentially illiterate males have enormous difficulty finding employment in our information-based economy (Hedges & Nowell, 1995).

Origins of Sex Differences

What is the cause of these likely sex differences in cognitive ability, personality, and behavior? Do they result from biological differences between the sexes, or are they the result of differences in the way females and males are raised? There is no answer to these questions yet, but there certainly is evidence that is interesting to think about.

On the biological side, there is evidence that the brains of women and men are different in some subtle ways (Hopkin, 1995). It has been known for some time that men's brains are about 15 percent larger than women's brains on the average (Hopkin, 1995). Scientists such as Sandra Witelson of McMaster University have found more specific differences. For example, Witelson (1991) has found greater numbers of neurons in the auditory cortex and corpus callosum of females than males. Other differences have been found in the hypothalamus, limbic system, and cerebellum. The clearest finding of a difference in brain functioning between men and women comes from a study by Bennett and Sally Shaywitz of Yale University. Figure 10.2 shows a composite image of the brain activity of 19 males and

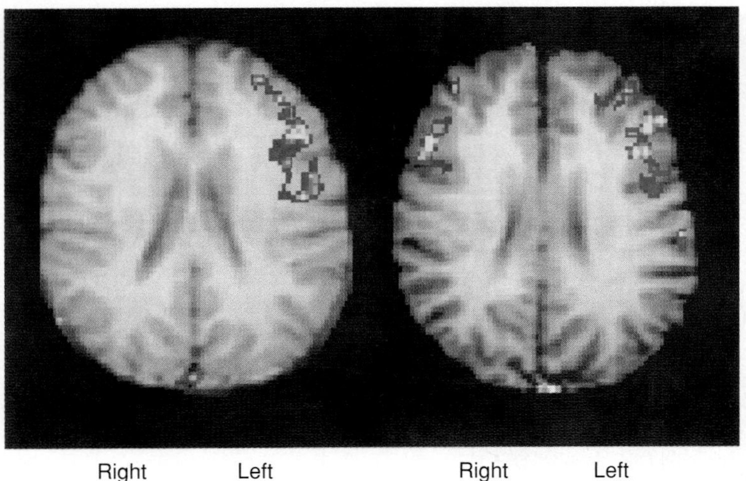

FIGURE 10.2

These composite magnetic resonance images show the distribution of active areas in the brains of males (left) and females during a "rhyming task." In males, activation is lateralized (confined) to the left interior frontal regions, but in females the same region is active bilaterally (on the right as well as on the left).

19 females while performing a rhyming task. Men performed this verbal task using only language areas in the left cerebral hemisphere (note that in these images right and left are reversed). Women, in contrast, also used areas in the right cerebral hemisphere. The differences in this study were not small. None of the 19 males showed increased activity in the right hemisphere during rhyming, whereas 11 of 19 females showed activation on both sides of the brain.

So, do these and other differences in the brain explain the psychological differences between women and men? They might and they might not. It is certainly possible that inherited biological differences between women and men give them different brains, which leads to differences in behavior. On the other hand, our experiences influence the growth and functioning of our brains, too. It is possible, therefore, that differences in the ways in which females and males are treated cause sex differences in both brains and behavior.

There certainly is evidence that suggests that the ways in which females and males are raised influence sex differences in their behavior. Recent studies suggest that differences in mathematical and science abilities between men and women are smaller today than in the past (Hedges & Nowell, 1995; Hyde, Fennema, & Lamon, 1990; Hyde & Linn, 1988; Linn & Peterson, 1986; Maccoby, 1987). Perhaps our current generation of young adult women and men were raised and educated in more similar ways that has reduced sex differences in these areas.

This possible explanation is supported by the fact that differences in cognitive abilities are more related to *gender* than to biological sex. For example, Kalichman (1989) studied the performance of men and women on a spatial reasoning task on which males tend to perform slightly better. In this study, however, masculine gender role was found to be more related to accurate performance than was male sex. That is, both women and men with stronger masculine gender roles outperformed men and women with more feminine gender roles. Other studies also have shown that both men and women who are characterized by androgynous gender roles (high in both masculinity and femininity) perform more accurately on a wide range of cognitive tasks (Halpern, 1992; Nash, 1975; Signorella & Jamison, 1986).

Thus, it seems possible that sociocultural factors that influence the person's gender identity are more important to the development of mental abilities than biological sex. That is, raising children to have the characteristics that are traditionally associated with masculinity or femininity may slant their cognitive abilities along traditional lines (females higher in verbal abilities, males higher in mathematical and spatial reasoning), whereas raising children to be androgynous may result in a more even distribution of specific cognitive skills. Researchers will undoubtedly continue to debate the degree to which biological factors (such as differences in hormones and brain structures) and sociocultural factors (such as social expectations and different rewards for gender behaviors in boys and girls) influence these differences between men and women (Halpern, 1992). It is likely, however, that both inherent biological differences between men and women and sociocultural influences work together in complex ways to shape human behavior.

Theories of Gender Identity

The process of gender development is complex and has captured the interest of many psychological theorists. By 2 or 3 years of age, children know that they are a boy or a girl and show differences in their play behavior. Children of this age already prefer to play with children of their same gender, and they play with sex-typed toys. Girls play more with "feminine" toys (tea sets and dolls) and boys play more with "masculine" toys (airplanes and guns). It is not until about age 7, however, when the concrete operational stage is reached, that children have a stable concept of what it means to be a boy or girl (Bem, 1981; Bussey & Bandura, 1992; Kohlberg, 1966). Before this stage, children recognize that boys and girls are different, but they see these differences only in terms of superficial physical features

By the age of 2 or 3, children begin playing with gender-stereotyped toys. Freud suggested children learn gender by identification with their same-sex parent. Social learning theorists believe gender is learned by observing and imitating other people.

such as hair style or clothing. As a result, young children often believe that boys and girls can change into each other by changing their hair style or by wearing different clothes (Tavris & Wade, 1984).

In the section that follows, we will look at the way that several schools of thought in psychology have tried to explain the development of gender identity. Each theory is a tentative and partial explanation at best and focuses on a somewhat different aspect of the formation of gender identity. As you read them, ask yourself if there are useful ideas in each of these theories.

Psychoanalytic Theory

Sigmund Freud suggested that young children usually take on the manners and ways of their parent of the same sex in a process called *identification*. Freud assumed that all children wish to win the approval of both parents and to avoid rejection. They adopt the gender role and act just like mom or dad for two reasons. First, as we will discuss more fully in later chapters, Freud believed that children are frightened by their powerful parents. One way to avoid getting into trouble with the same-sex parent is to adopt the behaviors of that parent. The second reason for adopting the gender identity of the same-sex parent, however, is to win the approval of the other-sex parent. The child sees that the intimate relationship between the parents gives the same-sex parent benefits that the child does not have. For example, the same-sex parent gets to sleep in the same bedroom with the other-sex parent. Freud believes that the child unconsciously identifies with the same-sex parent largely to be loved more by the other-sex parent. Freud's theory is interesting but does not easily explain why children develop normal gender identities when raised in single-parent families.

Social Learning Theory

Social learning theorist Albert Bandura (1969, 1977; Bussey & Bandura, 1992) proposed a theory of gender identity that is very different from Freud's. He suggested that children learn behavior appropriate to their gender through observations of adults and older siblings and through reinforcement and punishment of gender behaviors. According to this theory, children initially imitate the behaviors of both men and women, but parents and other members of their social world reward them for acting like a boy or girl and do not reward them (or punish them) for acting as the other sex does. For example, a little boy who dresses up like a girl will likely be told in emphatic terms that "boys don't wear those clothes!" Similarly, a little girl who cries may be given the message that it is okay to cry because girls are expected to express their emotions, while boys may be told that "big boys don't cry." A number of studies have suggested that parents spend a great deal of time encouraging their children to engage in gender role behavior that is consistent with their biological sex (Bell & Carver, 1980; Hyde, 1985).

Thus, social learning theory suggests that gender roles are not an inherent part of our biological makeup but are learned from society. One implication is that gender roles could be quite different than they are today. In the United States, for example, many people believe that we should teach boys and girls to be more androgynous by rewarding assertiveness, strength, and emotionally expressive behavior in both sexes. If the social learning theory is correct, encouraging both female and male children to have the best features of the traditional male and female gender roles should result in less different gender roles in the future.

Sexual Orientation

heterosexuals
Persons who are romantically and sexually attracted to those of the different sex.

homosexuals
Persons who are romantically and sexually attracted to those of the same sex, as distinguished from heterosexuals.

Close your eyes and imagine the perfect partner for you for a romantic and sexual relationship. The gender of the person that you imagine reveals a great deal about your sexual orientation. Persons who are sexually attracted to members of the other sex are termed **heterosexual.** In contrast, persons who are attracted to members of the same sex have a **homosexual** orientation. Most homosexual men use the term *gay,* while most homosexual women prefer the term *lesbian.* Other people are attracted to varying extents to both members of their same sex and members of the other sex. When this is the case, the sexual orientation is termed *bisexuality.*

A recent national survey of more than 3,000 adults conducted by the University of Chicago (Michael, Gagnon, Laumann, & Kolata, 1994) has provided the first reliable figures on sexual orientation and same-sex sexual behavior among Americans. As shown in figure 10.3, nearly 10 percent of adult males report that they have had sex with another male since puberty. About 60 percent of the males who have an early same-sex experience continue to have homosexual experiences after age 18 (4 percent of all adult males), and 2.8 percent of males identify themselves as either homosexual or bisexual.

Among women, 4 percent have had sex with another woman since puberty, with these experiences almost always occurring after age 18. About 1.4 percent of all adult women in the United States identify themselves as homosexual or bisexual. Thus, fewer women have same-sex experiences than men (and women tend to have these experiences at later ages), and fewer women than men identify themselves as homosexual or bisexual.

Homosexual experiences and gay and lesbian orientations were found in the recent University of Chicago survey to be somewhat less common than suggested by Kinsey (1948) and other early researchers who were not able to interview samples of persons that were representative of the United States. If you live in a large city, the percentages of homosexual and bisexual orientations reported by the University of Chicago study may seem low to you. That is because gays and lesbians tend to live in larger cities, rather than in suburban or rural areas. In the 12 largest U.S. cities, over 9 percent of males consider themselves to be homosexual or bisexual—over three times as many as in the U.S. population as a whole. Among women who live in large cities, nearly 3 percent identify themselves as homosexual or bisexual, more than twice as many as in the general population. In rural areas of the United

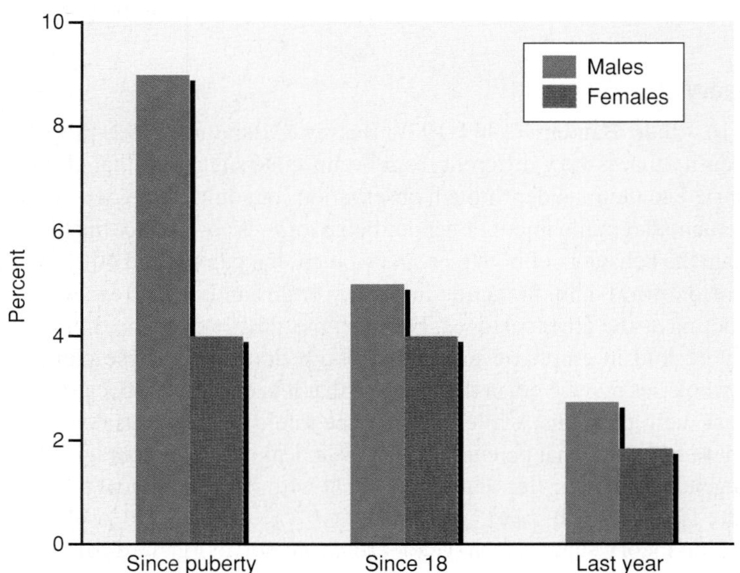

FIGURE 10.3
The percentage of males and females in the United States who have had a sexual experience with a person of the same sex since puberty, since age 18, or in the last 12 months. The percentage of persons who identify themselves as homosexual or bisexual is equal to the percentage who report having sex with a person of the same sex in the past 12 months. (Based on figure 13, page 175, Michael, Gagnon, Laumann, & Kolata, 1994.)

States, only 1.3 percent of males and virtually no females identify themselves as homosexual or bisexual, often making life a lonely experience for the gay and lesbian men and women who live in rural areas (Michael et al., 1994).

Origins of Sexual Orientation

It is not known why a person develops a particular sexual orientation. A good guess, however, is that it develops through a complex interaction of biological and sociocultural factors. John Money (1987a, 1988) has proposed a specific theory of sexual orientation that balances the roles of biological and sociocultural influences. He states that sexual orientation has its origins in the womb when the nervous system is still developing. Money believes that the brain is shaped during fetal development by a complex interplay of genetics and hormones. The factors organize the brain in a way that predisposes the person toward either heterosexuality or homosexuality. Later, during sensitive periods of development in childhood or adolescence, sexual orientation is shaped by social and interpersonal experiences, but persons are more likely to develop a sexual orientation that is consistent with their biological predisposition.

Other evidence is consistent with Money's theory of biological predisposition (Friedman & Downey, 1993). For example, Swaab and Hofman (1990) and LeVay (1991) have tentatively identified differences in the brain structures (part of the hypothalamus) of heterosexual and homosexual men. The area of the hypothalamus found to be different is known to be directly related to sexual behavior and to differ between heterosexual men and women. In addition, research has found that identical twins with the same genetic makeup who were adopted at birth and raised in different families have a higher probability of both being homosexual than do nontwin siblings raised in the same family (Eckert, Bouchard, Bohlen, & Heston, 1986). This suggests that heredity may predispose persons to homosexuality. These results support (but do not prove) the hypothesis that differences in the areas of the brain that control sexual behavior may be one cause of sexual orientation.

But Money believes that sexual orientation is not only determined by brain structures. He suggests that sexual orientation is like handedness. The brain may be preset to develop a right- or left-handed person, but a naturally left-handed person can be shaped through early childhood experience to develop right handedness. Similarly, some people may develop a lasting heterosexual or bisexual orientation even when they were biologically predisposed to be homosexual, and vice versa. A great deal of research will be needed in the future to fully understand the determinants of sexual orientation.

Many myths surround homosexuality and bisexuality. For example, it is commonly believed that homosexual persons take on the gender roles of the other sex. That is, that gay men act feminine and lesbian women are masculine. In fact, homosexual persons, like heterosexuals, exhibit a wide range of gender roles. Another myth is that gays and lesbians try to seduce heterosexuals into becoming homosexual. Again, no evidence supports this belief.

Heterosexual persons hold myths and stereotypes about gay men and lesbian women.

But as is true of myths and stereotypes about any group of people, they tend to be used to justify discrimination against members of the group. Persecution of gays and lesbians is common and has a long history. For example, homosexuals were one of the groups singled out for destruction in Nazi Germany. Still today, persecution of gays and lesbians often reaches extreme forms of violence. Acts of aggression perpetrated against gays and lesbians simply on the basis of their sexual orientation is referred to as *gay bashing*. Thousands of gays and lesbians are victimized in this way every year in the United States, making violence against homosexuals a major social problem.

The issue of whether to allow people who are openly homosexual to serve in the military has become controversial recently. What is your opinion?

Gays and Lesbians in the Military

Less than two weeks after his inauguration in 1993, President Bill Clinton announced that he had asked the Secretary of Defense to prepare a policy that would ban discrimination against homosexual men and women in the armed forces. The then-current policy prevented an admitted gay or lesbian from joining the armed services and required that openly homosexual soldiers be dismissed dishonorably if discovered while in military service. President Clinton's position was that the policy was based on unfounded prejudice against gays and lesbians and he opposed any official policy of discrimination. However, the harsh reaction from heterosexual military personnel and many people in all walks of life made this a hotly debated issue and led to only a partial change in policies regarding gays and lesbians in the military.

The opponents of the proposed changes in the policy banning openly homosexual men and women from military service first alleged that gays and lesbians perform their military jobs poorly, but these charges were quickly withdrawn when no evidence could be found to support them. Indeed, in testimony in congressional hearings, top military officers have stated that homosexual men and women perform their jobs as well as their heterosexual counterparts (Herek, 1993). However, the military leaders that oppose liberalization of the policy on gays and lesbians state that having admitted homosexuals in the military would be bad for the morale of heterosexuals. They argue that homosexuals have difficulties controlling their sexual urges and would sexually harass and attempt to seduce heterosexuals. They further argue that heterosexuals would not be able to adjust to having homosexuals in their units when they have to live in barracks and share showers and latrines with them (Herek, 1993).

Similarly, a less public debate has arisen about the government's policy to deny security clearances to many gays and lesbians on the basis of their sexual orientation. Gays and lesbians are routinely denied security clearances that are necessary for many jobs in government and private industry because they are considered to be bad security risks. Homosexual men and women are considered to be more likely to suffer from a psychological disorder, to be easier to blackmail, and to be less likely to be loyal to the United States and keep its secrets.

When you read this list of allegations against gays and lesbians, what do you think? If your sexual orientation is heterosexual, do you think that gays and lesbians are more unstable and untrustworthy? Are they more likely to sexually harass other soldiers or sailors? Would heterosexuals have great difficulties in accepting gays and lesbians in the military? Many Americans believe that the answer to all of these questions is yes. But are these allegations based on facts?

Psychologist Gregory Herek (1990, 1993) of the University of California at Davis has reviewed the large body of research on gays and lesbians to see whether there is evidence that they are poor security risks and unfit for military service. His review suggests that there is no evidence to support any of the allegations made against homosexuals. Herek cites studies that clearly show that homosexual men and women are not more likely to have psychological disorders or to be unstable or disloyal. He similarly cites evidence that gays and lesbians are not more likely to sexually harass others and attempt to seduce heterosexuals into homosexual behavior.

It would be difficult to deny, however, that the presence of openly gay men in the service would upset some heterosexual male soldiers and sailors. The distressing record of gay bashing by male soldiers has been tragically reinforced by recent events in which gays have been killed because of their sexual orientation. Does this mean that we could not have a military force with good morale if admitted gays and lesbians were allowed to join? Herek (1993) likens the prejudice against gays and lesbians to the prejudice against African Americans and women in the military. It has only been since 1948 that African Americans were allowed to serve in the same units as whites. Before that time, they served in segregated units commanded by white officers. Over the past 40 years, however, the military has conducted active training programs to reduce and control prejudice against ethnic minorities in the military. As a result, the American military is able to function effectively as an ethnically integrated unit. Similar strides have been made in integrating women more completely into the military. Although their roles were greatly restricted in the past, and they still face many barriers, women and men were able to function together effectively in the Persian Gulf War of 1991. Women served well, without serious problems, in battle zones where they shared latrines, shower facilities, and tents with their male counterparts.

Herek (1993) suggests that the same programs that effectively decreased and managed prejudice against ethnic minorities and women could be used to solve morale problems that would result from allowing admitted gays and lesbians to serve in the military. He reminds us of two things: First, heterosexual and homosexual men and women have been working together effectively and sharing showers and toilets in the military without problems for many years—the heterosexuals simply did not usually know who the homosexuals were most of the time. If homosexuals managed to coexist peacefully in the past, why could they not do so in the future? Second, extensive research on the psychology of prejudice makes it clear that when people who are prejudiced against each other get to know one another by working together, the prejudice diminishes markedly (Herek, 1993). If supported by active campaigns against prejudice and active campaigns to protect gays and lesbians against retaliation, Herek (1993) believes that this official form of prejudice on the basis of sexual orientation could be brought to an end without sacrificing the morale of the military. What do you think?

Review

The term *sex* refers to the biological characteristics of being male or female, while the term *gender* refers to the identity and behaviors associated with being a male or female in a given culture. Gender identity, the internalized sense of being either male or female, is a central aspect of the personality. It gives rise to behaviors that society expects of males and females, referred to as gender roles. The achievement of gender identity and the gender role one adopts are the product of a complex developmental process. Psychoanalytic theory emphasizes the child's identification with the same- and other-sex parents in the development of gender roles. Social learning theory suggests that children initially imitate the behavior of both same- and other-sex persons but learn which gender behavior is expected for their sex from the reactions of adults and other children. Gender roles are classified as masculine or feminine, but a person may express high levels of both masculinity and femininity, a pattern referred to as androgyny. Males and females are less different in terms of specific cognitive abilities than in the past, with females showing slightly higher scores on verbal skills and males having slightly higher scores on tests of mathematical and spatial reasoning. However, these differences are more associated with one's gender identity (masculine, feminine, or androgynous) than with one's biological sex. In addition to gender identity and gender roles, persons also differ in how they express their sexuality in intimate relationships. Sexual orientation directs a person's sexual arousal toward either other-sex (heterosexual) or same-sex (homosexual) partners, or both (bisexual). Researchers have not yet established what causes differences in sexual orientation, but both biological and social factors may be important.

Thinking Critically About Psychology

1. What do you think has been more important in your choice of a major and in your plans for a career—your sex or your gender identity?

2. Why do you think that crimes of violence are so common against gay males ("gay bashing")? What could be done to solve this social problem?

Check Your Learning

To be sure that you have learned the key points from the preceding section, cover the answers below and try to answer each question. If you give an incorrect answer to any question, return to the page given next to the correct answer to see why your answer was not correct. Remember that these questions cover only some of the important information in this section; it is important that you make up your own questions to check your learning of other facts and concepts.

1. The set of behaviors that communicate to others the degree to which we are masculine or feminine are referred to as our

a. sex. **c.** gender role.
b. sexual orientation. **d.** gender identity.

2. A person who has both feminine and masculine gender characteristics is referred to as

a. androgynous. **c.** bisexual.
b. polygamous. **d.** heterosexual.

3. Persons with a more masculine gender identity tend to score slightly higher on tests of spatial ability than persons with a more feminine gender identity.

a. True **b.** False

4. Gays and lesbians are not more likely to be unstable, disloyal, or to have a psychological disturbance than heterosexuals.

a. True **b.** False

Correct Answers
1. c (p. 362), **2.** a (p. 362), **3.** a (p. 366), **4.** a (p. 370).

BIOLOGICAL AND PSYCHOLOGICAL ASPECTS OF SEXUALITY

Sexuality is a topic that is full of emotion for most of us. It plays a pivotal role in many intimate relationships, is the subject of intense moral debates, and is plagued by misinformation more than perhaps any other natural aspect of human life. The emotional nature of sexuality may be evident to you now as you begin to read this chapter. Are you approaching the topic of sexuality in the same dispassionate manner that you read about thirst or memory? Consider this: In a society where the majority of college women and nearly all men masturbate, when was the last time you spoke to a friend as openly about your enjoyment of masturbation as about your enjoyment of music, jogging, or pizza? Very few of us are completely comfortable with the topic of sexuality.

In this section we will briefly discuss sexuality in scientific terms. In describing sexuality in this academic fashion, we will compare sexuality in human and nonhuman animals, and contrast the sexual motive to other motives. We will not begin to do justice to the importance of sexuality in human lives, but at least we may combat the misinformation to a degree.

Images and themes of sexuality appear in art and literature reaching as far back as the earliest civilizations, but the scientific study of sexuality has only recently emerged. Two European physicians working at the turn of the twentieth century were at the forefront of early studies of sexuality. Richard Von Krafft-Ebing (1840–1902), a Viennese neurologist, extensively studied variations and deviations in human sexual behavior. Sadly, Krafft-Ebing's view of sexuality was mostly negative and his work was filled with misconceptions. For example, Krafft-Ebing believed that masturbation caused all sexual deviations and was at the root of sexual problems. Today we know that this basic premise of Krafft-Ebing's views of sexuality is false.

A second major figure in the study of human sexuality was Henry Havelock Ellis (1859–1939). An English physician, Ellis was the first to extensively discuss the role of social and cultural influences in shaping human sexual behavior and one of the first scholars to study homosexuality. He also stated for the first time that men and women experience similar sexual desires and that psychological problems such as anxiety and depression can influence physical sexual functioning.

Subsequent to the many published volumes of research by Krafft-Ebing and by Ellis in the early part of the century, there was surprisingly little scientific study of human sexuality for many years. In many ways, the scientific world was not yet prepared to discuss human sexuality objectively. A major turning point in the study of sexuality occurred, however, in the 1950s with the work of Alfred C. Kinsey (1894–1956). Kinsey became interested in human sexual behavior when he was made aware of the extremely limited amount of scientific information available on this topic. He conducted large surveys that allowed him to describe many aspects of human sexuality, including the broad range of sexual activities (Kinsey et al., 1948, Kinsey, Pomeroy, & Martin, 1953).

The work of researcher Alfred C. Kinsey in the 1940s was a major turning point in the study of sexuality. He is now credited with beginning the modern era of the scientific study of sexuality.

Other modern pioneers in the study of sexual behavior include John Money of Johns Hopkins University. Money is best known for his studies in sexual development and his classic research of *gender roles,* a term that he first coined (Money, 1955). Also of great importance was the work of Virginia Masters and William Johnson. They conducted groundbreaking laboratory studies of volunteers who were observed during the sexual response cycle from the initial excitement to the moment of orgasm, while Masters and Johnson measured the physiological changes that accompany the sexual behavior. Masters and Johnson's two most important books, *Human Sexual Response* (1966) and *Human Sexual Inadequacy* (1970), helped to form the basis for our understanding of human sexual functioning and sexual problems, and stood as the foundation for sex therapy.

Sexual Anatomy and Functioning

The major structures of the sexual anatomy of females and males are presented in figures 10.4 and 10.5, respectively. The **uterus** is a pear-shaped muscular structure that carries the fetus during pregnancy. After conception, the fertilized egg implants itself in the wall of the uterus where it grows and develops during gestation. Except during pregnancy, it is this inner lining of the uterus that is shed during the menstrual cycle approximately every 28 days.

The **ovaries** are the pair of structures that produce estrogen and other hormones and produce *ova,* or eggs, for reproduction. The **fallopian tubes** branch off from the top of the uterus, extending near, although not quite touching, the ovaries. The fallopian tubes form a passage in which ova are transported from the ovaries to the uterus. At the bottom of the uterus is the **cervix,** which is the neck of the uterus that is connected to the vagina. It is through the cervix that menstrual flow is discharged and through which the newborn is passed into the birth canal during delivery.

The female external genitals (fig. 10.4) consist of a set of structures collectively referred to as the **vulva,** made up of the mons, labia majora, labia minora, and the clitoris. The **mons,** a fleshy mound of tissue that sits at the top of the vulva, is the upper area covered with pubic hair. The **labia majora,** or large lips of the vulva, are the outer set of vaginal lips that surround the inner lips, or **labia minora.** The two labia provide folds that cover the opening of the vagina and are a sensitive source of pleasure during sexual stimulation. The folds of the labia minora converge at the top of the vagina to form a hood for the **clitoris,** which is the structure at the upper part of the vagina that is most highly responsive to sexual stimulation. The labia and clitoris both play critical roles in female sexual response.

uterus
The muscular structure that carries the fetus during pregnancy.

ovaries
Female endocrine glands that secrete sex-related hormones and produce ova, or eggs.

fallopian tubes
Tube through which ova (eggs) reach the uterus.

cervix
The neck of the uterus that is connected to the vagina.

vulva
The external genital structures of the female.

mons
Fleshy mound that sits at the top of the vulva.

labia majora
The larger outer lips of the vulva.

labia minora
The smaller inner lips of the vulva.

clitoris
The structure at the upper part of the vagina that is most sensitive to sexual stimulation in females.

FIGURE 10.4
Major structures of the female sexual anatomy.

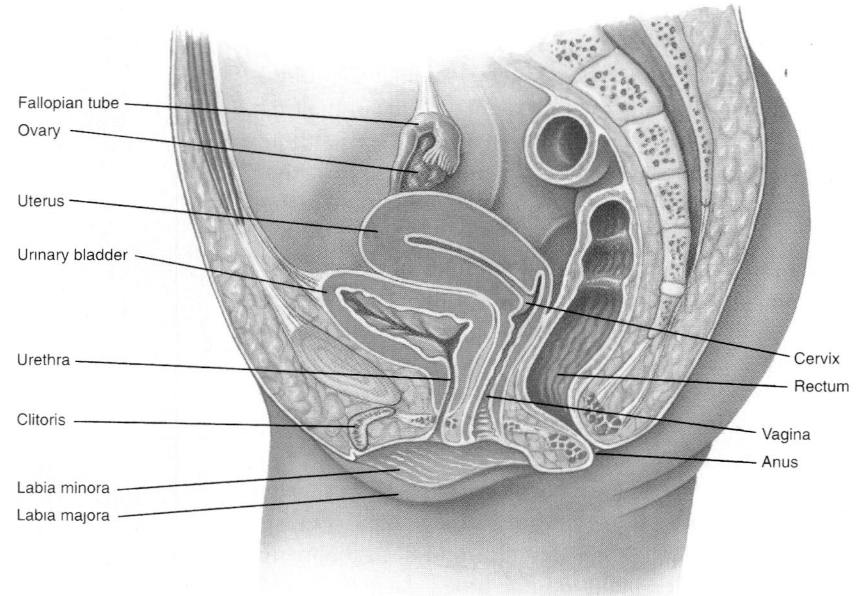

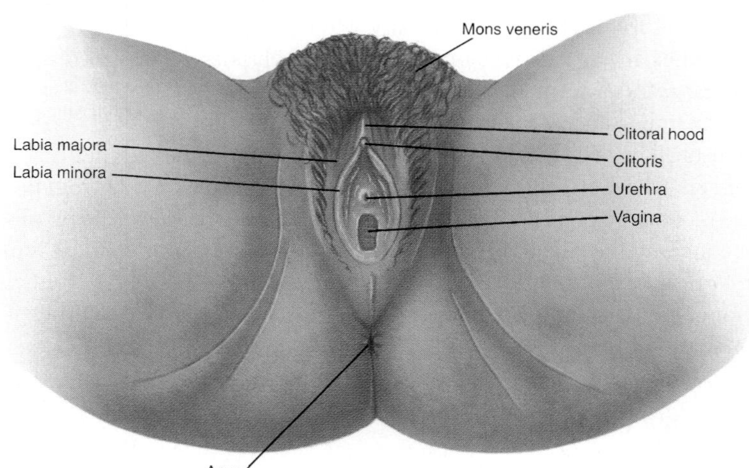

testes
Male endocrine glands that secrete sex-related hormones and produce sperm cells.

epididymis
Structure that holds sperm cells until ejaculation.

vas deferens
Structure that carries sperm from the epididymis toward the outside of the body during ejaculation.

semen
The fluid that contains sperm cells.

prostate gland
One of the structures that produces fluid for semen.

seminal vesicle
One of the structures that produces fluid for semen.

penis
The tubular structure that becomes erect during sexual arousal and through which sperm is ejaculated.

scrotum
The loose skin sac that encloses the testes.

The male reproductive system consists of the testes (testicles) and a related system of tubes and glands. Like the ovaries, the **testes** produce both hormones and reproductive cells. The male reproductive cells are the sperm, which carry the father's genetic information for conception. The testes are suspended below the abdomen away from the heat of the body because sperm are only produced at a temperature slightly lower than the 98.6° temperature of the rest of the body. Extending from each testicle is the **epididymis,** which holds mature sperm cells after they have been produced in the testes and connects with the tube vas deferens. The **vas deferens** is the tube that carries sperm from the epididymis toward the outside of the body. The sperm cells are carried in a fluid called **semen,** which is produced by the **prostate gland** and **seminal vesicle.**

The external genitals of the male and female are structured to allow sexual intercourse. The external male genitals, shown in figure 10.5, consist of the penis and scrotum. The **penis** is a tubular structure filled with three spongy tubes that fill with blood during sexual response. It is the filling of the penis with blood that causes it to become stiff and erect during sexual arousal. The **scrotum** is a loose skin structure that extends behind the penis and supports the testes. The scrotum responds to changes in temperature, contracting when cold and relaxing when warm, to ensure that the testes remain at a temperature optimal for sperm production.

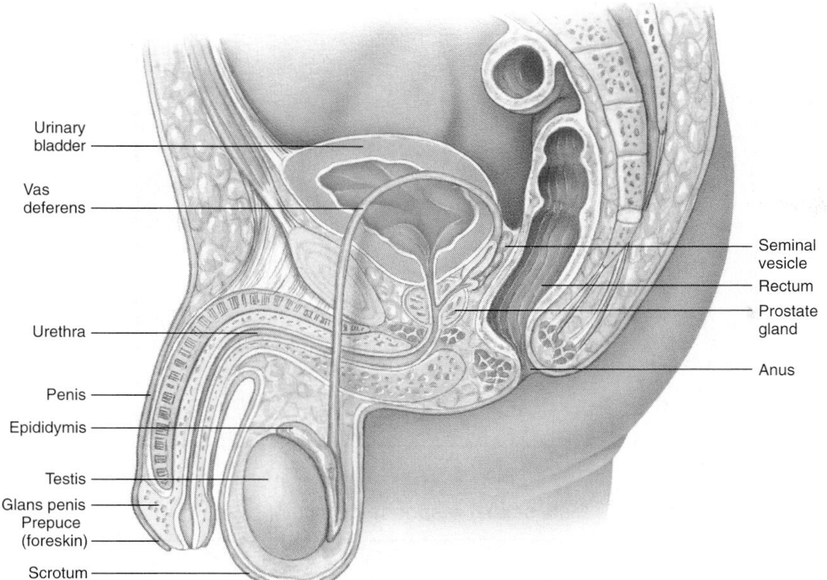

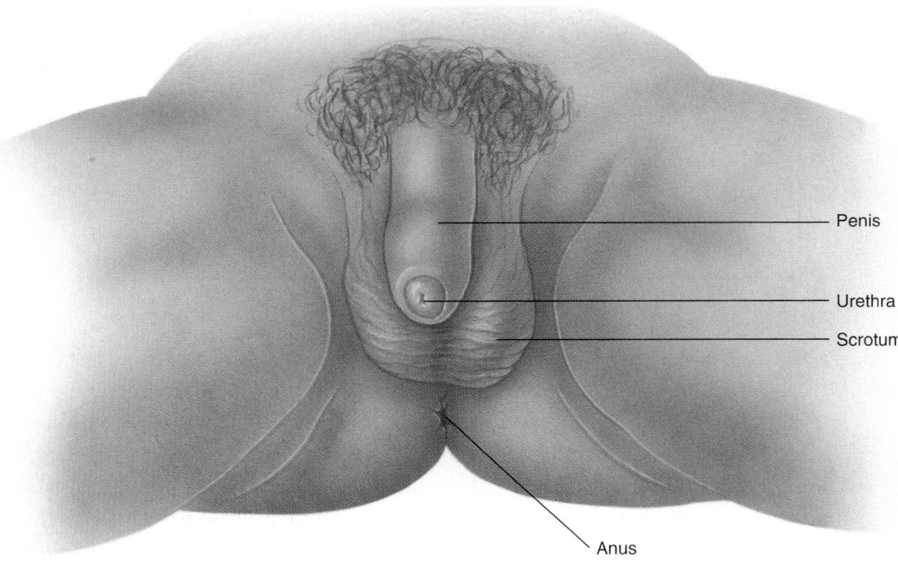

FIGURE 10.5
Major structures of the male sexual anatomy.

The Sexual Response Cycle

The response of humans to sexual stimuli involves a predictable biological response known as the *sexual response cycle*. Although there are substantial similarities between the sexual response cycles of women and men, there are some important differences. As shown in figure 10.6, Masters and Johnson (1966) describe four stages of the sexual response cycle:

1. *Excitement phase*. Both women and men show an initial increase in physiological arousal, called the **excitement phase.** This may begin from visual stimulation, physical contact, odors, fantasies, and the like. Blood flows to the penis and the vagina, erection and lubrication occur, the nipples become erect, the heart beats faster, blood pressure rises, and the body becomes aroused in other ways.
2. *Plateau phase*. If the sexual stimulation is intense enough, sexual arousal builds quickly to the **plateau phase,** which is characterized by high levels of arousal that are often sustained for many minutes. The degree of sexual pleasure is very high, but not yet at a maximum.

excitement phase
The first stage of the sexual response cycle during which the penis becomes erect and the vagina lubricates.

plateau phase
High levels of sexual arousal and pleasure that are maintained for variable periods of time.

FIGURE 10.6
The human sexual response cycle.

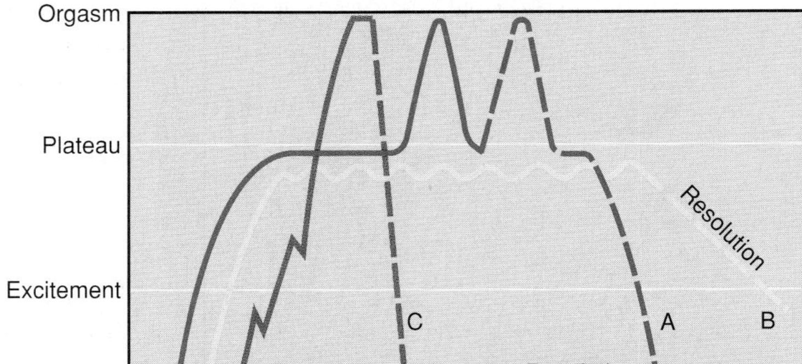

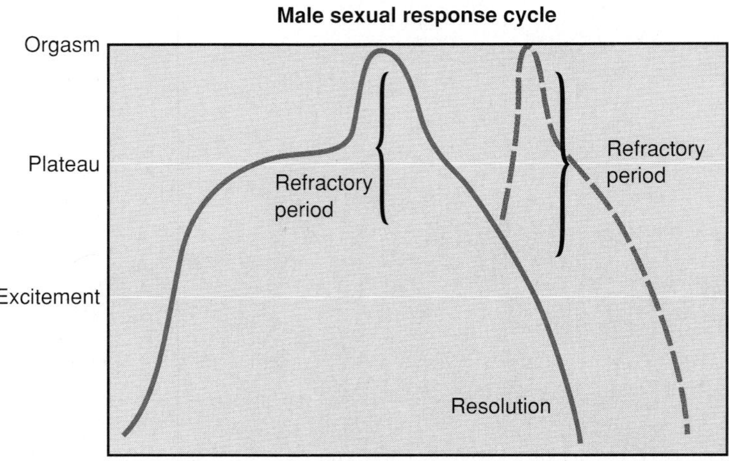

orgasm
The reflexive phase of the sexual response cycle accompanied by peak levels of arousal and pleasure and usually by ejaculation in males.

3. *Orgasmic phase.* With sufficient stimulation, and under the proper psychological circumstances, the individual usually progresses to the reflexive stage of **orgasm.** A peak of physical arousal and pleasure is reached. Breathing is rapid, blood pressure and heartbeat reach high levels, the skin flushes, and the individual partially loses muscular control for a brief time and experiences involuntary spasms of many muscle groups. There is little variability in the orgasmic phase of men, but much more variation in the orgasms of women. Three common patterns of female orgasmic response have been distinguished (Masters & Johnson, 1966). Some women reach a single brief and intense orgasm like that of men. Other women, depending on the circumstances, experience multiple intense orgasmic peaks. Other women experience a large number of smaller peaks of orgasm.
4. *Resolution phase.* Following orgasm, the body's level of physical arousal rapidly declines in the **resolution phase.** Within a few minutes the body returns to a condition much like its original state prior to the beginning of the response cycle, although heightened relaxation and tiredness are common. In males, the resolution phase is accompanied by a period of time when the male is unresponsive to further sexual stimulation, termed the **refractory period.** Although women briefly may be too sensitive to enjoy further sexual stimulation during the resolution phase, with individual preferences determining her interest in further stimulation, there is no refractory period in which women are physically incapable of resumed sexual arousal.

resolution phase
The stage in the sexual response cycle following orgasm when arousal and pleasure diminish.

refractory period
The period of time following orgasm during which males are incapable of sexual arousal.

Recent research has found that some basic assumptions about differences between men and women's sexual response are not completely true. For example, contrary to earlier writings, researchers have found that a small number of men, like many women, appear to experience repeated or multiple orgasms at times (Robins & Jensen, 1978; Zilbergeld, 1978). In addition, some females expel a clear fluid into the vagina during orgasm in a way that is similar to male ejaculation (Belzer, 1981; Perry & Whipple, 1981). It is important to understand the ways in which the sexuality of women and men differ, but the more we learn, the less different they seem.

Sexual Motivation

It will come as no surprise to you to learn that human beings have a sexual motive, much as we have motives for hunger or thirst. Without a sexual motive, humans and other animals that depend on sexual reproduction would soon be extinct. While hunger, thirst, and other primary motives are necessary for the survival of the individual, sexual motivation is a primary motive that is essential to the survival of the species. The same basic biological mechanisms are involved in sexual motivation in all mammals, but the biological controls that govern sexual behavior are less significant in humans than in most other animals.

Similarity to Other Primary Motives

We will understand sexual motivation better if we compare it with other primary motives (p. 328). The sexual motive resembles hunger, thirst, and other primary motives in a number of important respects:

1. *Hypothalamic control.* Like hunger and thirst, the sexual motive is controlled by our hardworking friend, the hypothalamus. One center in the hypothalamus and related brain structures activates motivation and sexual behavior. This system is the equivalent of the hypothalamic feeding and drinking systems. If the hypothalamus is surgically destroyed, sexual behavior will not be initiated even in the presence of sexually provocative stimuli. A second system of the hypothalamus inhibits sexual behavior. If this inhibitory system is destroyed in laboratory animals, the animals become hypersexual; that is, they engage in unusual and unrestrained amounts of sexual behavior. These two centers act in balance to regulate sexual motivation.
2. *Role of external stimuli.* Like hunger, which can be stimulated by external stimuli known as incentives such as the sights and aromas of dessert stimulating the hunger of a well-fed person, sexual motivation is highly sensitive to external stimuli. The person who initially is not sexually aroused, whether male or female, will often be aroused by erotic photos or romantic fantasies. Indeed, external stimuli play a very important role in arousing the sexual motive (Wilson, Kuehn, & Beach, 1963). One aspect of the role of external stimuli has been termed the *Coolidge effect.* Following intercourse, males of many animal species will have intercourse again with the same receptive female some time after the refractory period has elapsed. Bermant (1976), for example, found that a ram (male sheep) will have sex an average of five times with the same ewe (female sheep) before seeming to lose interest. However, if a *different* receptive ewe is introduced after each mating, the ram will mate more than three times as often before losing sexual interest, and it will reach orgasm much more quickly than with the same ewe. Apparently, variety is a powerful external factor in sexual motivation for many mammalian species.
3. *Role of learning.* We have already seen that learning can play a powerful role in shaping the primary motives. What, when, and how much we eat, for example, is greatly influenced by our learning experiences. Sexual motivation is influenced by learning, at least to the same degree and probably to an even greater extent. The enormous variety in the sexual behavior of the members of any society at any point in history strongly points to the role of learning in sexuality. In the United States today, for example, many individuals consider oral stimulation of the genitals to be a natural and loving part of a couple's sexual repertoire, while many others consider it to be a "crime against nature."

Comparing attitudes in the same culture at different times in history and in different cultures provides an even clearer picture of the role of learning. For example, the following statement from a "marriage manual" published in 1869 would be considered completely untrue by most Americans today:

> As a general rule, a modest woman seldom desires any sexual gratification for herself. She submits to her husband, but only to please him; and, but for the desire of maternity, would far rather be relieved from his attentions. The married woman has no wish to be treated on the footing of a mistress. (Hayes, 1869, p. 277)

Differences between cultures in sexuality also portray the influence of learning experiences on sexual motivation. Contrast our own sexual behavior to the Polynesian residents of the island of Mangaia. Sexual pleasure is a principal concern of the Mangaians, young and old alike. Sex play among Mangaian children is common, with sexual intercourse usually beginning between the ages of 12 and 14. Most young males begin intercourse with an older, experienced woman who teaches a variety of oral and genital sexual skills to him. Soon the frequency of masturbation drops and intercourse with age-mates becomes an every-night affair. This intense level of sexuality continues into married adulthood, with the average 20-year-old male reporting two to three orgasms per night, six nights per week. The quality of sexual intimacy is not overlooked in Mangaia, however, in spite of the quantity. There is a strong cultural emphasis on both partners experiencing intense pleasure in intercourse. One of the worst insults that can befall a Mangaian male, in fact, is to be accused of reaching orgasm too quickly and not being interested in the pleasure of his female partner.

4. *Role of emotions.* Like the other primary motives, especially eating, sexual motivation is influenced to a great extent by our emotions. Because stress, anxiety, and depression are accompanied by increased sympathetic autonomic arousal, and because sexual arousal is mediated by parasympathetic arousal, which is in opposition to sympathetic activity, these emotions generally result in a decrease in sexual motivation. Because the balance between the sympathetic and parasympathetic systems is complicated, however, anxiety and depression sometimes result in an increase in sexual motivation. Just pointing to the obvious influence of strong negative emotions on our sexuality, however, does not begin to do justice to the intricate interplay of emotions and sexuality. Far more than any other motive, sexual passion is powerfully linked to even the delicate nuances of romantic love and other subtle emotions.

Differences from Other Primary Motives

Although sexual motivation is similar to the other primary motives in the many ways just mentioned, there are important differences as well (Houston, 1985):

1. *Survival value.* We must satisfy the primary motives of hunger, thirst, need for warmth, and so on to survive as individuals and, collectively, to survive as a species. Although satisfaction of the sexual motive is essential to the survival of the species, it is not necessary for individual survival.
2. *Increases and decreases in arousal.* We are motivated to *decrease* the physiological arousal created by hunger and other primary motives. However, humans are obviously motivated to both *increase* and *decrease* their sexual arousal. The intimate behaviors that we engage in to initiate the arousal phase of the sexual response cycle ("foreplay") obviously increase arousal. Yet the fact that Americans spend many millions of dollars each year on erotic videos, erotic telephone "conversations," and topless bars is strong testimony to our motive to increase sexual arousal and then to decrease it through sexual activity.
3. *Role of deprivation.* Motives such as hunger and thirst rather predictably rise and fall according to the length of time since they were last satisfied. A person who has just eaten a large meal will not be hungry, but a person who has been

deprived of food for 8 hours will be ravenous. To an extent, the same is true for sex. If you are used to a regular sex life, the 2 weeks that your lover goes home to visit family may lead to a noticeable increase in sexual interest. But sexual motivation is far less linked to deprivation than the other primary motives. Except during the refractory period, humans are susceptible to sexually arousing stimuli and situations at almost all times. On the other hand, individuals without a sexual outlet report going long periods of time without the arousal of sexual longings. Indeed, it has often been observed that we don't really need sex until we have it—the more often we are sexually aroused and satisfied, the more sexual motivation we seem to have.

4. *Decreases in energy*. The other primary motives lead to behavior that increases the body's store of energy and other bodily needs. In contrast, sexual behavior results in a marked decrease in energy. But who needs all that much energy anyway?

Hormones and Sexual Behavior

In nonhuman animals, hormones from the endocrine system play a major role in regulating sexual motivation. Female dogs, cats, and rats are receptive to sexual intercourse only when they are ovulating—a time referred to as being "in heat." Males of these species are less influenced by hormones than females and are receptive to sexual stimulation at most times. In some species, however—mice, deer, and goats, for example—males will engage in sexual intercourse only during annual or biannual seasons ("ruts") when they are producing sperm. This means that sexual behavior in nonhuman animals is limited to those few times when fertilization and reproduction are highly likely.

The sexual motive is unlike other primary motives because we are motivated not just to decrease it, as we would hunger and thirst, but to increase sexual motivation as well.

The sexual motivation of humans is far less influenced by hormonal factors (Geer, Heiman, & Leitenberg, 1984), and intercourse is equally likely during periods in which impregnation is and is not possible. This lack of a strong connection between sexuality and reproduction in humans is a major difference between animal and human sexual behavior, and it opens the door to the many meanings that sexuality has in our lives. That is not to say, however, that sexual motivation in humans is unrelated to the endocrine system. Although sexual motivation is not governed by hormones in humans, sexuality and hormones are certainly related. For example, Brecher and Brecher (1976) found that when men were sexually aroused by viewing erotic films, their blood level of testosterone (p. 61) rose markedly. Since it is speculated that testosterone plays an important role in the health of males, sexual arousal stimulates the production of an important hormone.

The sexual behavior of many species is also regulated by odors, such as those produced by your dog when she's in heat that attract every male dog in the neighborhood. Monkeys, apes, and humans appear to be much less influenced by hormones and odors than lower animals.

Patterns of Sexual Behavior

The recent large-scale national survey of sexual behavior carried out by the University of Chicago (Michael et al., 1994) was conducted to learn who we have sex with, what we do, and how often we do it to allow experts to predict how rapidly and how far the AIDS epidemic will spread. What was learned also will help us understand our own sexuality better.

Who do we have sex with? Are we as sexually promiscuous as it seems on television and at the movies? As shown in the left side of figure 10.7, the great majority of female and male Americans over the age of 18 have either had no sex partner or only one sex partner in the last 12 months. Very few Americans of either sex have had more than one sex partner in a one-year span, and many of these individuals had more than one partner only because one relationship ended and another began during the past 12 months. Only 5 percent of males and 2 percent of females have had five or more sex partners in the last year. Among married individuals, 95 percent have had no sex partner other than their spouse in the last year. Indeed, about 85 percent of married women and 75 percent of married men never have sex with someone other than their spouse while they are married (Michael et al., 1994). Americans are much less promiscuous than we often think.

On the other hand, the average American does not have sex only with one partner in her or his lifetime. As shown in the right side of figure 10.7, less than one-fourth of adult males and less than one-third of adult females have had only one sex partner. Among females, a little more than 50 percent have had between 2 and 9 sex partners in her lifetime. Among males, one out of three men has had 10 or more sex partners in his lifetime. It is clear that we tend to be quite faithful when we are in a relationship, but that we have many sex partners as we move from one relationship to another (Michael et al., 1994). This pattern of sexual relationships is often called *serial monogamy*.

How often do Americans have sex with their partners? As shown in figure 10.8, most adult women and men have sex with their partners a little less than once a week. A little more than a fourth of us have sex two to three times a week, with fewer than 10 percent of Americans having sex four or more times a week. Most men and women say that they spend between 15 minutes and an hour making love each time. Some of you will be

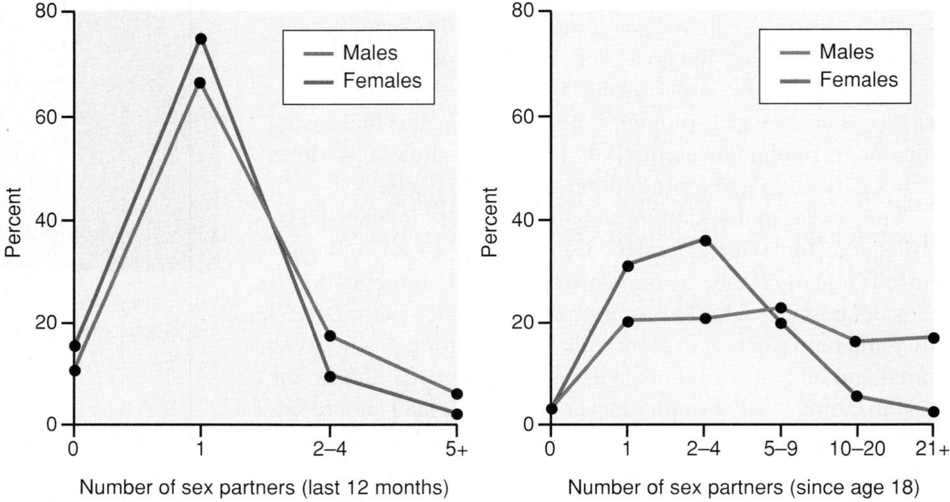

FIGURE 10.7

Number of sex partners in the last 12 months (left) and since age 18 (right) for males and females.

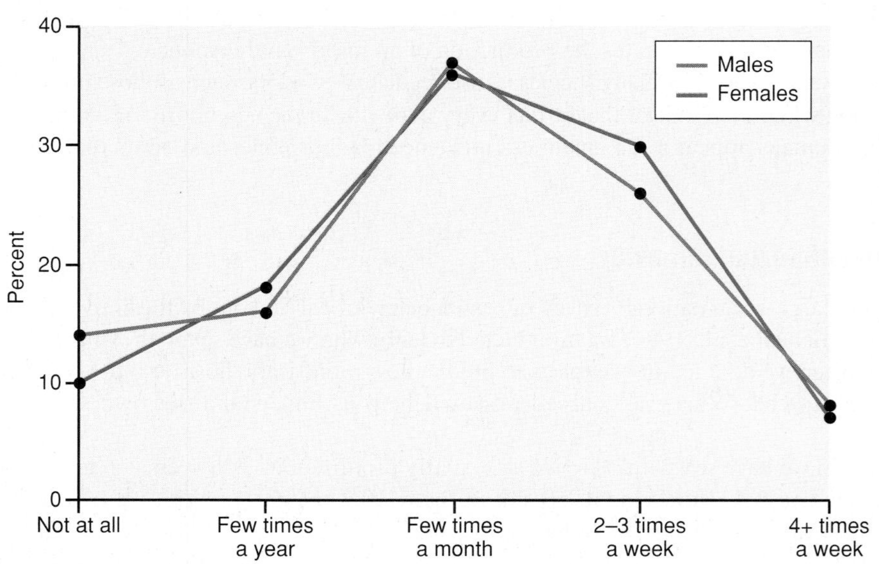

FIGURE 10.8

Frequency of having sex with a partner over the past year for females and males.

surprised (and some of you will not be surprised) to learn that people who are in committed relationships have sex more often than single persons (Michael et al., 1994). There are not many "swinging singles" who are having sex as often as their friends who are in committed relationships.

When Americans have sex with their partners, vaginal intercourse is by far the preferred practice, but certainly not the only sexual practice that is enjoyed. About 95 percent of both women and men report that vaginal intercourse is "appealing." Nearly two-thirds of 18- to 44-year-old women view receiving oral sex as appealing and over half enjoy performing oral sex. Both percentages were lower in women over 44, however. Over 75 percent of men 18 to 44 years old find both receiving and performing oral sex to be appealing. Again, both percentages were lower for middle-aged and older men, however. Relatively few men and fewer women (less than 5%) find anal sex appealing. By and large, our sexual practices match our preferences: The last time that they had sex, 95 percent of men and women said that they had vaginal intercourse, about 25 percent performed oral sex, and the same percentage received oral sex. Only 1 percent of women and 2 percent of males said that anal sex was part of their last sexual encounter.

It was fascinating that the University of Chicago sex survey found few differences in sexual behavior across levels of education, religion affiliation, or ethnic group. Hispanic men and women reported somewhat higher frequencies of sex, but the only large ethnic difference was in the age of first having sex. African-American males reported an average age of first having intercourse of about 15 1/2 years. In contrast, all other men and women reported first having intercourse at about age 17 (Michael et al., 1994). Otherwise, there are fewer sociocultural differences in sexual behavior than might have been expected.

The best news from the survey is that most people who are having sex in committed relationships are enjoying it a great deal. Among 18- to 59-year-old adults, 95 percent of men and 71 percent of women say that they usually or always have an orgasm when they have sex with a partner. About 90 percent of persons in committed relationships say that they receive "great physical pleasure" and about 85 percent say they receive "great emotional satisfaction" (Michael et al., 1994). Not surprisingly, a happy sex life is strongly related to general happiness. In the University of Chicago sex survey, nearly everyone who was generally happy was also happy with their sex life—and almost all of these happy people were in monogamous, committed relationships. Also not surprising is the finding that happy people have sex more often than unhappy people. In the University of Chicago sex survey, 72 percent of people who said they were extremely happy with their lives said that they had sex once a week or more. In contrast, only 27 percent of unhappy people had sex at least once a week. Does happiness lead to more frequent sex or is frequent sex the secret to happiness? What do you think?

As you read about the sexual behavior of Americans, I hope you will not fall into the trap of thinking that what is "average" is "normal." If you have sex less often or more often than average, and you and your partner are happy with your sex life, what could be more normal than that? The same is true for the average time spent making love, preferred sexual practices, and so on. Learning about norms and averages is useful, but the focus should be on what is happy and healthy for each of us as individuals.

Review

Sex and sexuality have been discussed throughout history in philosophy, literature, and the arts, but the scientific study of sex and gender is a relatively new field. The first scientific discussions of sexuality date back only to the early 1900s, and it was only in the 1940s that Kinsey conducted the first objective surveys of sexual behavior. The anatomy of both males and females is constructed to provide the most efficient means of copulation and reproduction. Sexual functioning, referred to as the sexual response cycle, is similar for males and females, with the primary differences being that men have a refractory period that requires a regeneration of energy between response cycles and women do not have such a refractory period, increasing the potential for repeated orgasms. The differences between men and women in terms of sexual response, however, are far less than once believed. The sexual motive is similar to other primary motives like hunger in that centers of the

Thinking Critically About Psychology

1. We will study the psychology of love in chapter 16—can learning about sexual anatomy and the sexual response cycle teach us anything that is relevant to romantic love?

2. How could an understanding of sexual motivation help a person maintain a committed relationship with a spouse?

Review—continued

hypothalamus play an important role, external sexual stimuli can stimulate the sexual motive, and the sexual motive can be influenced by learning experiences and emotions. The sexual motive is different from other primary motives, however, in that it is not necessary to the survival of the individual, it does not always lead to decreases in arousal, is not influenced by deprivation in the same way, and leads to a decrease rather than an increase in energy.

Check Your Learning

To be sure that you have learned the key points from the preceding section, cover the answers below and try to answer each question. If you give an incorrect answer to any question, return to the page given next to the correct answer to see why your answer was not correct.

1. The penis is the part of the male body that is most responsive to sexual stimulation. The part of the female body that is most responsive to sexual stimulation is the

- **a.** clitoris.
- **b.** mons.
- **c.** cervix.
- **d.** uterus.

2. The four stages of the sexual response cycle were described by

- **a.** Freud.
- **b.** Krafft-Ebing.
- **c.** Kinsey.
- **d.** Masters and Johnson.

3. Hormones have a greater influence on sexual motivation in humans than in other animals.

- **a.** True
- **b.** False

Correct Answers
1. a (p. 373), **2.** d (p. 375), **3.** b (p. 379).

ATYPICAL AND ABNORMAL SEXUAL BEHAVIOR

atypical sexual behavior
Sexual practice that differs considerably from the norm.

Human beings differ widely in their sexual preferences and practices. In the sections that follow, we look at the range of unusual or **atypical sexual behavior.** In the first section, atypical patterns of sexuality are described that are considered abnormal only if the individuals who engage in the sexual practices consider them abnormal for themselves. In the next sections, we will examine patterns of sexuality that are usually considered to be abnormal (fetishism, sexual sadism, and masochism) or always considered to be abnormal (voyeurism, exhibitionism, and forced sex).

Transvestism and Transsexualism

transvestism
(trans-ves´tizm) The practice of obtaining sexual pleasure by dressing in the clothes of the opposite sex.

transsexualism
(trans-seks´u-ah-lizm) A condition in which an individual feels trapped in the body of the wrong sex.

These two superficially similar patterns of sexuality are often confused because they both involve dressing in the clothing of the other sex. But they have little else in common except that they are rarely harmful to anyone. **Transvestism** refers to the practice of dressing in the clothes of the other sex. Transvestites often state that they cross-dress because it is sexually stimulating, but many transvestites say they cross-dress to free themselves from confining sexual stereotypes. Transvestites are almost always males who have relatively well-adjusted heterosexual lives.

Transsexualism, on the other hand, refers to a condition in which the individual feels trapped in a body of the wrong sex. For example, a person who is anatomically male feels that he is actually a woman who somehow was given the wrong body. Transsexuals may occasionally or permanently dress in clothes of the other anatomical sex, but this cross-sex dressing has nothing to do with sexual arousal. These individuals merely feel that they are dressing in the clothes of their true sex.

In some instances, these individuals will undergo hormone injections and plastic surgery to change their sex organs to those of the desired sex. For example, physician Richard Raskin had a sex-change operation because he felt like a female trapped in a male body. After the operation, he adopted the name Renee Richards and briefly played on the women's professional tennis circuit. Male-to-female sex change operations are much more common than the opposite, probably in part because surgically created penises are less satisfactory than surgically created vaginas (for example, there is less genital sexual pleasure).

The sex-change clinic at Johns Hopkins Medical Center stopped doing sex-change operations during the 1970s because follow-up studies showed that their patients were no happier with their lives after surgery than before. Follow-up studies of patients from other centers, however, have shown that the patients were generally happy with their new bodies if properly selected for surgery and counseled on what to expect from it (Baker, 1969; Pauly, 1968).

While many authorities consider the unusual patterns of sexual behavior just described to be normal under most circumstances, the following patterns range from ones that are *usually* considered to be abnormal to ones that are *always* considered to be abnormal because of the harm caused to the individual and/or others.

Richard Raskins (top) became Renee Richards (bottom) after having sex-change surgery. Raskins felt before the surgery that she was trapped in the wrong body.

Fetishism

Fetishism refers to the fact that some individuals are primarily or exclusively aroused by specific physical objects or types of material (such as leather or lace). In some cases, the fetish is only an exaggeration of normal interest in specific body parts. For example, some individuals are only or primarily aroused by breasts, buttocks, blue eyes, and so on. But the term *fetish* is usually reserved for cases involving inanimate objects, such as panties, shoes, or stockings. A fetish is considered to be abnormal if it interferes with the sexual adjustment of the person or his or her partner. Often, the fetishist (who is usually a male) is aroused only by "used" articles and is sexually aroused by the act of stealing them from an unknowing woman. Because this can be frightening to the victim and is dangerous and illegal, fetishism is considered abnormal when practiced in this manner.

Sexual Sadism and Masochism

Sexual sadism is the practice of receiving sexual pleasure from inflicting pain on others. **Sexual masochism** is the condition in which receiving pain is sexually exciting. Sometimes verbal abuse or "degradation" is substituted for physical pain. Approximately 5 to 10 percent of men and women find giving or receiving pain to be sexually exciting at times, but this is the preferred or only method of sexual arousal for very few individuals. Many individuals who practice sadism and masochism, or *S&M,* do so with a consenting partner who also enjoys the practice, and they do not inflict pain that is severe or medically dangerous—for example, mild spankings, pinching, and so on. In such cases, S&M may be considered normal if care is taken to avoid accidental harm and one's partner is *truly* willing. In some cases, however, the partner is unwillingly coerced into participation in S&M activities. In some cases, furthermore, S&M involves intense pain (such as whipping, burning, and kicking). S&M is always considered abnormal if there is any question about voluntary participation by both partners or if physical harm is inflicted. In rare cases, the sadist mutilates or even murders the victim to receive pleasure. Such practices are unquestionably abnormal.

Voyeurism and Exhibitionism

Voyeurism is the practice of obtaining sexual pleasure by watching others undressing or engaging in sexual activities. Voyeurs generally find this exciting only when the person they are watching is unaware of their presence and when there is an element of danger involved. They are no more aroused than the average person at a nudist camp or watching a stripper but become very excited peeping into windows (Tollison & Adams, 1979). Because they

fetishism
(fet´ish-izm) The practice of obtaining sexual arousal primarily or exclusively from specific objects.

sexual sadism
(sād´izm) The practice of obtaining sexual pleasure by inflicting pain on others.

sexual masochism
(mas´-o-kizm) A condition in which receiving pain is sexually exciting.

voyeurism
(voi´yer-izm) The practice of obtaining sexual pleasure by watching members of the opposite sex undressing or engaging in sexual activities.

often frighten the person they are watching, and because the activity is illegal, voyeurism is considered to be abnormal. The voyeur is generally a heterosexual male who has trouble establishing a normal sexual relationship; some voyeurs commit rape and other serious crimes, but most are not physically dangerous.

exhibitionism
(ek´´sĭ-bish´ŭ-nizm´´) The practice of obtaining sexual pleasure by exposing one's genitals to others.

Individuals who practice **exhibitionism** obtain sexual pleasure from exposing their genitals to others. Almost all exhibitionists are heterosexual males who typically are married but who are shy and have inhibited sex lives. Exhibitionists generally want to shock their victims but rarely are dangerous in other ways (Tollison & Adams, 1979). Because such behavior is illegal and frightening, however, exhibitionism is considered abnormal.

Forced Sexual Behavior

Several other forms of deviant sexual behavior are clearly abnormal because they involve actual, threatened, or implied force to the victim. These acts include rape, sexual abuse of children, incest, and sexual harassment.

Rape

rape
The act of forcing sexual activity on an unwilling person.

In **rape,** an individual forces another person to engage in a sexual act. In the vast majority of cases, the rapist is a male and the victim is a female—a woman is raped every 6 minutes in the United States (Federal Bureau of Investigation, 1990). In the United States, 22 percent of adult women and 2 percent of adult men have been forced to do something sexual at least once since age 13. The percentage of women who have been raped is strikingly similar across different ages, ethnic groups, places of residence (city, suburban, or rural), levels of education, and marital groups. In almost every instance, women were forced by men (or by two or more persons—at least one of whom was a male—almost a third of the time). Contrary to expectations, the person who forced the women to do something sexual was a stranger only 4 percent of the time and a casual acquaintance only 19 percent of the time. When women are raped, it is almost always by someone they know well (22%), are in love with (46%), or their husband (9%). In the much less common instances of men being forced into sex, they were forced by women two-thirds of the time.

rape trauma syndrome
Effects of rape on the emotions, behavior, and well-being of many victims long after the rape occurred.

The aftermath of rape is traumatic. Rape victims almost invariably feel that their entire life has been altered due to their assault (Nadelson, 1990). Many victims of rape experience mental anguish, often referred to as the **rape trauma syndrome,** characterized by intense feelings of anxiety and fear as well as disturbances in sleep, relationships, and daily functioning (Calhoun & Atkeson, 1989; Thornhill & Thornhill, 1990). Unfortunately, many myths in Western culture have become attached to rape victims. These myths tend to place the responsibility for the rape on the victim while absolving the offender of personal responsibility for the rape.

There is no specific psychological profile for sexual offenders. Indeed, if one thing characterizes rapists it is that they are highly heterogeneous and cannot be characterized by generalities (Kalichman, 1990). Theories of rape, however, have stated that most men who rape are driven by aggressive impulses or the need to feel powerful and dominating, rather than by sexual desire (Ellis, 1989; Groth, 1979). Many rapists will have raped numerous women before they are finally apprehended (Abel, Barlow, Blanchard, & Guild, 1977).

Victims often hesitate to report a rape because the process of testifying against the rapist is often made unpleasant by the investigating officers and the rapist's defense attorney. For this reason, many communities have established rape crisis centers that provide ongoing support for victims throughout the reporting, investigation, and prosecution processes. Rape crisis centers also provide counseling to rape victims to assist them in readjusting after their victimization. See table 10.2 for a summary of rape myths and facts.

Sexual Abuse of Children

Children are frequently sexually assaulted and exploited. In a large survey, Kohn (1987) found that 27 percent of women and 16 percent of men reported being sexually violated during childhood. Some statistics suggest that as many as 40 million persons in the United States have been sexually victimized as children. There are a variety of different types of child sexual abuse. When the sexual contact is perpetrated by a family member, the sexual

TABLE 10.2 Rape Myths and Rape Facts

Myth: A woman who goes to the home of a man on their first date implies she is willing to have sex. **Fact:** A person going anywhere does not imply they want to do anything. Rapists distort their perceptions to fit their beliefs.	**Myth:** One reason that women falsely report a rape is that they have a need to call attention to themselves. **Fact:** It is very rare for a woman to falsely report a rape. Reporting a rape is a traumatic event.	**Myth:** Any healthy woman can resist a rapist if she really wants to. **Fact:** Rapes are brutal and violent acts that may be worse with resistance.	**Myth:** Women who go around braless or wearing short skirts are asking for trouble. **Fact:** No victim has ever asked to be raped. Rapists are responsible for their actions.

abuse is termed **incest.** When there is force or threat of force used, the sexual assault is **child rape.** When there is no clear threat of force, the sexual abuse of children is referred to as **child molestation.** Even child molestation is considered to be a form of forced sexual behavior, however, because the child cannot consent in any meaningful way to the sexual behavior.

Children who have been sexually violated demonstrate a wide range of emotional and behavioral reactions. If the sexual contact is not threatening to the child, such as in sexual exploration by an older child, there are rarely serious psychological effects for the child if the parents calmly handle the occurrence with love and understanding. When the sexual abuse is upsetting to the child, as is almost invariably the case when the perpetrator is an adult or when threat of force is involved, the psychological effects on the victim can be quite serious.

Many of the effects of child sexual abuse are believed to be long term. Indeed, the aftermath of child sexual abuse may be similar to that of adult sexual assault, in that children tend to be traumatized and suffer serious traumatic reactions (Finkelhor, 1990). Children are likely to act out sexually in response to sexual victimization, experience a sense of personal betrayal by the person who violated them, feel that they are powerless and lack control, and feel stigmatized because they were assaulted (Finkelhor & Browne, 1985).

Adults who engage in **pedophilia** experience sexual pleasure primarily through sexual contact with children. They usually first gain the trust and acceptance of their victims before engaging in sexual behavior. This means that child molesters and rapists are usually known and trusted by the child victim. Indeed, the molester or rapist is a neighbor, family member, or someone who knows the child before the incident in 90 percent of cases (Mohr, Turner, & Jerry, 1964). The child molester is typically a male heterosexual and the victim is usually a young girl. In some cases, the molester is a male homosexual or a heterosexual female and the victim is a young boy. Tragically, many child molesters will have violated hundreds of children before they are caught. Like persons who rape adults, men who rape or molest children tend to be highly heterogeneous in their psychological makeup (Finkelhor & Browne, 1985).

incest
(in´sest) Sexual relations between relatives.

child rape
Sexual behavior with a child achieved by force or direct threat of force.

child molestation
Sexual behavior with a child without force or direct threat of force.

pedophilia
(pe´´do-fil´e-ah) The practice of obtaining pleasure from sexual contact with children.

sexual harassment
Unwanted sexual advances, comments, or any other form of coercive sexual behavior by others.

Sexual Harassment

Unwanted sexual advances; requests for sexual favors; unwanted touching of the legs, breasts, or buttocks; sexually suggestive comments; and any other form of coercive sexual behavior by others constitute **sexual harassment.** As many as 60 percent of women in the United States have been subjected to one or more of these forms of sexual harassment (Hotelling, 1991). But sexual harassment also includes the leering looks and inane remarks that men often foist on women on the street, which have made nearly every woman uncomfortable (angry, frightened, disgusted) at one time or another. Although it is less common, men are also the victims of sexual harassment in colleges and in the workplace.

Many Americans first developed a clear awareness of the issue of sexual harassment when attorney Anita Hill alleged that she previously had been sexually harassed by then Supreme Court nominee, Justice Clarence Thomas. One key component of sexual harassment is that it occurs between persons with different amounts of power, often in schools or the workplace. For example, a woman who is sexually harassed by her boss may think that she cannot report the situation without risking the loss of her job. But differences in power can exist even between two students or two employees with the same job if the person

Many people first developed a clear awareness of sexual harassment when attorney Anita Hill alleged that she previously had been sexually harassed by Clarence Thomas.

engaging in the harassment is physically stronger than the other (and even if no explicit threat of force is made). There are laws (such as the Civil Rights Act of 1964), regulations, and policies that guarantee every person's right to attend school and work in a nonthreatening environment. However, because of the imbalance in power inherent in sexual harassment, it is undoubtedly still true that most incidents of sexual harassment are not reported to authorities. Every victim of sexual harassment suffers in the sense of becoming less comfortable and relaxed at school or work. In some cases, however, sexual harassment can provoke serious levels of anxiety and depression.

Thinking Critically About Psychology

1. Have you ever experienced, engaged in, or witnessed sexual harassment? What do you think can be done to reduce the frequency of this problem?
2. Many people believe that those who practice transvestism or other atypical sexual behavior are not psychologically healthy. How do you feel?

Review

Atypical patterns of sexual behavior that involve no harm to the individual or others are considered to be normal even though they are unusual and perceived as immoral by some members of society. Other forms of deviant sexual behavior are considered abnormal if they result in harm to anyone. The transvestite obtains sexual pleasure from dressing in clothing of the other sex. Transsexualism is the condition in which individuals consider themselves to be trapped within bodies of the other sex. Unless the individual is troubled by the condition, transvestism and transsexualism are generally not harmful to anyone. Fetishism—obtaining sexual pleasure from specific objects—need not be harmful but can be if the objects are stolen or the preference causes trouble in some other way. Sadism—sexual arousal from inflicting pain—may be harmless if practiced in a mild way with a completely willing partner but is generally considered abnormal because of the pain and medical risk involved. Masochism—sexual arousal from receiving pain—is generally considered abnormal for the same reason. Voyeurism refers to the practice of obtaining sexual pleasure by peeping at nude or sexually involved individuals. Exhibitionism is the practice of obtaining sexual excitement by exposing one's genitals to an unwilling person. Because of the frightening nature and illegality of these activities, both exhibitionism and voyeurism are considered abnormal. Forced sexual behaviors—including rape, sexual abuse of children, incest, and sexual harassment—are always considered abnormal because of the inherent psychological and physical harm that may occur.

Check Your Learning

To be sure that you have learned the key points from the preceding section, cover the answers below and try to answer each question. If you give an incorrect answer to any question, return to the page given next to the correct answer to see why your answer was not correct.

1. Sexual behavior is considered to be abnormal if it is

a. atypical.
b. strange or bizarre.
c. harmful.
d. infrequent.

2. A person who obtains sexual pleasure from dressing in clothing of the other sex is said to be

a. a transvestite.
b. a transsexual.
c. a transylvanian.
d. all of the above.

3. A person who obtains sexual pleasure by watching others undressing or engaging in sexual activities is said to be

a. an exhibitionist.
b. a pedophile.
c. a masochist.
d. a voyeur.

4. Most persons who commit child molestation are

a. homosexual females.
b. heterosexual females.
c. homosexual males.
d. heterosexual males.

Correct Answers
1. c (p. 383), **2.** a (p. 382), **3.** d (p. 383), **4.** d (p. 385).

SEXUAL DYSFUNCTION AND SEXUAL HEALTH

Several types of problems can interfere with successful and pleasurable sexual intercourse. As mentioned earlier, these problems are common and considered abnormal only when they are prolonged. Even when prolonged, however, they do not mean that the individual has "psychological problems." Sexual problems can and usually do occur in perfectly normal individuals (Munjack & Staples, 1977).

Sexual dysfunctions are disturbances in any phase of the sexual response cycle. Different dysfunctions may have several different potential causes, both physical and psychological in origin. The most common physical causes of sexual dysfunction are drug or alcohol abuse, side effects of some medications, and some forms of illness. It is important, therefore, that all persons with problems with sexual functioning first be evaluated by a physician who specializes in the sexual-reproductive system, such as a gynecologist or urologist (Diokno & Hollander, 1991). Fortunately, solutions are available for sexual difficulties caused by medical problems. Many sexual dysfunctions are caused by psychological factors, however.

sexual dysfunction
An inability to engage successfully or comfortably in normal sexual activities.

Sexual dysfunctions are classified according to the phases of sexual response within which they occur: sexual desire, sexual arousal, and orgasm.

Dysfunctions of Sexual Desire

Among the most common sexual dysfunctions are those involving interest and desire in sexual relations (LoPiccolo & Friedman, 1988). It is important not to confuse sexual desire with sexual frequency, because a person can have frequent sexual encounters to please his or her partner but have very little desire for these sexual interactions. In contrast, a person may have strong sexual desire but not engage in sex for any number of reasons.

It is also important to note that everybody has a different natural level of sexual interest. A person is said to have a disorder of sexual desire only if he or she lacks almost any desire for sexual contact and is troubled by the lack of desire. Two specific types of dysfunctions involve sexual desire. First, **inhibited sexual desire** occurs when a person has sexual desire very infrequently or not at all. The second desire problem is called **sexual aversion disorder** and is characterized by a nearly complete fearful avoidance of sexual contact with others (American Psychiatric Association, 1994).

inhibited sexual desire
Condition in which a person desires sex rarely or not at all.

sexual aversion disorder
Condition in which a person fearfully avoids sexual behavior.

Both men and women experience disorders of sexual desire. There are numerous possible causes of these problems, including extreme anxiety about sexual intimacy or having had a sexually traumatic experience. In other cases, the person may not have a general lack of desire but may lack interest in their sexual partner because of problems in that relationship (Beck, 1995; Kaplan, 1983; LoPiccolo & Friedman, 1988).

Therapists who work with sexual desire problems first examine the person's overall relationship with their partner. If there are few such problems, therapy for sexual desire problems tends to focus on the anxiety that the person may experience in relation to sexual intimacy. Anxieties may block desires for sexual contact and interfere with sexual interest. Sexual inhibitions may result from experiences and characteristics of the person. These issues are examined in the context of sex therapy, where persons evaluate their anxieties and employ strategies to reduce them. Often therapy will involve both members of a couple to address specific aspects of their sexual interactions (Rosen & Leiblum, 1995).

Therapy can often help couples with sexual dysfunction.

Dysfunctions of Sexual Arousal

Sexual arousal disorders occur when there is a lack of sufficient sexual arousal—including erection of the penis for the male and lubrication of the vagina for the female—during the excitement phase of sexual response. Note, however, that a person is said to have a disorder of sexual arousal only if this failure to respond occurs consistently, occurs even with adequate levels of sexual stimulation, and interferes with sexual pleasure or causes discomfort. Thus, in sexual arousal dysfunctions, an interruption of the physical processes occurs in the excitement phase of sexual response, namely blood flow to the genital region and muscle tension. Women may develop **female sexual arousal disorder** (previously referred to unkindly as "frigidity"), which is characterized by a lack of vaginal lubrication and a minimal subjective experience of sexual excitement (American Psychiatric Association, 1994). Disruptions that occur during female sexual arousal disorder are specifically associated with the physical experiences of sexual excitement. Because most women experience transient forms of these difficulties when circumstances do not lend themselves to sexual arousal on occasion, the lack of arousal must be persistent under even favorable circumstances to be considered a sexual dysfunction.

female sexual arousal disorder
Condition in which sexual arousal does not occur in appropriate circumstances in a female.

Other less common female dysfunctions are vaginismus and dyspareunia. **Vaginismus** refers to involuntary contractions of the walls of the vagina that make it too narrow to allow the penis to enter for sexual intercourse. In **dyspareunia,** the woman experiences pain during intercourse. Often, but not always, these conditions are accompanied by orgasmic dysfunction and anxiety associated with sex. Like the male dysfunctions, the female dysfunctions can usually be eliminated with professional help.

vaginismus
(vaj´´i-niz´mus) A female sexual dysfunction in which the individual experiences involuntary contractions of the vaginal walls, making the vagina too narrow to allow the penis to enter comfortably.

dyspareunia
(dis´´pah-roo´ne-ah) A sexual dysfunction in which the individual experiences pain during intercourse.

Similar to sexual arousal disorder in women, **male sexual arousal disorders** directly reflect the physiological process of sexual excitement in the male sexual response cycle. In men, the most common sexual arousal disorder is **erectile dysfunction** (previously called "impotence"). Specifically, despite high levels of sexual stimulation, there is insufficient arousal to result in the penis gaining an erection suitable for sexual penetration. As is the case for women, to be considered a sexual dysfunction, these difficulties must be persistent even under ideal circumstances and must be accompanied by a lack of sexual pleasure.

male sexual arousal disorder
Condition in which sexual arousal does not occur in appropriate circumstances in a male.

erectile dysfunction
Condition in which the penis does not become erect enough for intercourse under sexually arousing circumstances.

There are many potential causes of dysfunctions of sexual arousal, most of which represent a complex interaction between physical and psychological processes (LoPiccolo, 1985). Anxiety, fear, distractions, fatigue, relationship problems, depression, and substance abuse can all cause sexual arousal disorders. Even just worrying about having an erection can sometimes lead to prolonged erectile failure. Sex therapy, therefore, usually addresses these issues in counseling. However, specific sex therapy techniques can be used to reduce sexual anxieties and increase subjective experiences of sexual sensation. For example, a couple may be instructed in how to pay maximum attention to their senses during sexual contact to increase their pleasure experience (Masters & Johnson, 1970).

Orgasm Dysfunctions

Orgasm dysfunctions involve the disruption of the climax phase of the sexual response cycle. Thus, while the person has a sufficient level of desire and arousal, the sexual response cycle does not progress to orgasm. In women, sexual dysfunctions of orgasm are referred to as **inhibited female orgasm.** This is defined as a persistent absence or prolonged delay of orgasm, despite sufficient sexual stimulation and arousal (American Psychiatric Association, 1994).

inhibited female orgasm
A female sexual dysfunction in which the individual is unable to experience orgasm.

Notice the important phrase at the end of this definition, "despite sufficient sexual stimulation and arousal." The term *inhibited female orgasm* should not be used if the sex partners do not fully understand what constitutes adequate stimulation for the woman or if the partner is not caring enough to provide sufficient stimulation. In addition, because women experience many different normal patterns of sexual response and orgasm, the delay or absence of orgasm must be dissatisfying to the individual woman before it is thought to be a sexual dysfunction. Still, inhibited orgasm is a common reason for women to seek sex therapy from psychologists (Heiman & LoPiccolo, 1983).

Inhibited orgasm has many potential causes, including performance anxiety, relationship difficulties, fear of abandonment, and depression. Like other sexual dysfunctions, inhibited orgasm may be the result of sexually traumatic experiences. On the other hand, failure to achieve orgasm is commonly the result of a lack of adequate clitoral stimulation (Goldsmith, 1988). Many of the sex therapy techniques used to reduce fears and anxieties discussed earlier may be used to treat female inhibited orgasm. In addition, inhibited orgasm may be caused by specific aspects of a relationship or situation that can become the focus of counseling.

In men, the most common orgasm dysfunction involves ejaculating as a result of minimal levels of sexual stimulation, usually just after or even before penetration occurs. When this problem persists over time and becomes distressful, it is considered a sexual dysfunction referred to as **premature ejaculation** (American Psychiatric Association, 1994). There are many causes of premature ejaculation, including inexperience, performance anxiety, fears, and unfortunate learning experiences early in one's sexual history (Annon, 1984). A variety of potential treatments for premature ejaculation can lengthen the period of time before ejaculation occurs. One method, called the *squeeze technique,* requires either the man or his partner to apply a comfortable but firm squeeze to the penis (either just below its head or at its base) to stop the impending orgasm. The pressure from the squeeze causes a delay of ejaculation when applied several times before ejaculation occurs. With repeated use, it can be an effective treatment for premature ejaculation, as the need for squeezing diminishes over time (Masters & Johnson, 1970).

premature ejaculation
A male sexual dysfunction in which the individual reaches orgasm and ejaculates sperm too early.

Some men, in contrast, have an orgasm dysfunction known as **retarded ejaculation.** In this case, the man is rarely able to have an orgasm in spite of adequate sexual stimulation or is able to reach orgasm only after very long periods of stimulation (American Psychiatric Association, 1994).

retarded ejaculation
Condition in which a male does not ejaculate despite adequate sexual stimulation.

All sexual dysfunctions share several things in common. First, because they involve sexual behavior, it is often difficult and embarrassing to seek help or discuss the problem. Society sometimes places unrealistic and demanding expectations on the sexual performance of women and men. Second, people with sexual problems may believe that they are the only persons who have such difficulties, leading them to believe that they are psychologically abnormal. Finally, because society places limitations on discussing sexual matters, people often believe that when they do have a sexual problem they have nowhere to turn for help. This too is incorrect—there are many sources of help for sexual dysfunctions.

Often the first place to seek help for a sex problem is a medical doctor who can evaluate the person for possible physical problems related to the sexual difficulty. A physician can also refer persons with sexual dysfunctions to a psychologist who specializes in sex therapy if needed. Sex therapists must be certified by the American Association of Sex Educators, Counselors, and Therapists or other similar professional organization. Before starting therapy, be sure to verify that a therapist has received the proper training and credentials for the practice of sex therapy.

Health Problems Related to Sexual Anatomy

Several health problems related to female and male sexual anatomy require our attention. These include forms of cancer and sexually transmitted diseases, including AIDS. Although these are medical problems, they have a psychological component—namely the behaviors that we engage in that increase or decrease our risk and opportunity for early detection.

Cancers of Sexual Anatomy

It is important for women to have regular gynecological examinations to check for possible cancers of the cervix, uterus, and ovaries. Any unusual changes in the menstrual cycle or atypical discharges should be reported to a physician. In addition, it is important for women to perform breast self-examinations each month. Breast self-examination should be performed at the end of each menstrual period when the breasts are least likely to be swollen or tender (in older women who have experienced menopause, self-examinations should be done on a monthly basis). Women should carefully feel and look for any changes in size, shape, or color of the breasts and nipples. Signs of breast cancer include puckering of the skin, dimples, lumps, bumps, soreness, or any unusual nipple discharge or bleeding. Any such indications should be immediately reported to a physician. Although many such bumps or changes are not dangerous, it requires a medical professional to determine this. Early detection of breast cancer offers the best hope for fighting this serious health threat. In addition to performing monthly breast self-examinations, it is also important for women to have their breasts examined by a physician after the age of 20. Further, women should also ask their doctors when they should receive a *mammogram,* a special low-dose X ray that is particularly accurate at detecting cancers before they can be felt in a self-examination.

There are also health problems related to male sexual anatomy. Men, particularly over 40, should have regular examinations by a physician that include checks for abnormalities of the prostate that may indicate prostate cancer. It is important for men to learn how to perform a self-examination of their testicles to detect early signs of testicular cancer. This is particularly crucial between the ages of 16 and 35, when testicular cancers are most common. The examination should be performed once a month. After showering, when the scrotum is likely to be relaxed and the testicles are loosely suspended, men should roll each testicle gently between their thumb and forefinger, feeling carefully for any lumps, bumps, or tenderness. Testicles are smooth when they are healthy, so bumps or indentations are possible signs of cancerous growths. It is, however, normal to feel the epididymis, which may seem like a bump, along the back of each testicle. Not all bumps are cancers, but it requires a medical professional to distinguish dangerous bumps from harmless ones. If detected early, testicular cancer has a very high rate of cure. However, when undetected, testicular cancer is among the most deadly forms of cancer.

Sexually Transmitted Diseases

sexually transmitted diseases (STD)
Physical diseases, such as syphilis and AIDS that are often transmitted through sexual contact.

Diseases that are caused by microorganisms spread through sexual contact were once called venereal diseases but today are referred to as **sexually transmitted diseases (STD).** Throughout the ages, countless occurrences of STD epidemics have ravaged people across continents. Today in the United States, several STDs threaten the health of millions of persons each year. Some are easily treated and cured if detected early in their course; others are incurable and may eventually lead to death. When untreated and unattended, all STDs can cause chronic illness, infertility, and pose serious threats to pregnant women and their offspring. All STDs are serious health problems that require immediate medical attention. Not surprisingly, the likelihood of contracting all sexually transmitted diseases increases sharply with the number of different sex partners a person has and with the frequency of unsafe sex (Michael et al., 1994). In this section, we discuss the four general types of infectious agents that cause STDs.

syphilis
A sexually transmitted disease caused by the spirochete bacteria.

Syphilis. Caused by a spiral, corkscrew-shaped bacteria called a spirochete, **syphilis** has been increasing in incidence in the United States in recent years, with more than 40,000 cases occurring each year. Syphilis progresses through a series of stages of infection. The first stage is referred to as *primary syphilis,* which may last between 2 weeks to a month after infection. Early symptoms of syphilis infection usually include the appearance of a painless sore in the area where the spirochete entered the body, most often the penis or vaginal area. This sore is called a *chancre* and may at first appear to be a pimple, but usually it will become open and appear infected. The chancre goes away, but the person still has syphilis, which then enters its secondary stage. *Secondary syphilis* is characterized by bumpy skin rashes that develop over various areas of the body (including the palms and soles) and are accompanied by several common symptoms of illness, including fever, headache, nausea, swollen glands, sore throat, loss of hair, and loss of appetite. During the primary and secondary stages, syphilis can be cured in most cases with antibiotics. However, if untreated, syphilis eventually develops into its *tertiary* stage which includes numerous serious health complications. The spirochetes may infect the tissues of the heart, brain, spinal cord, joints, and a number of other organ systems, and eventually can cause death.

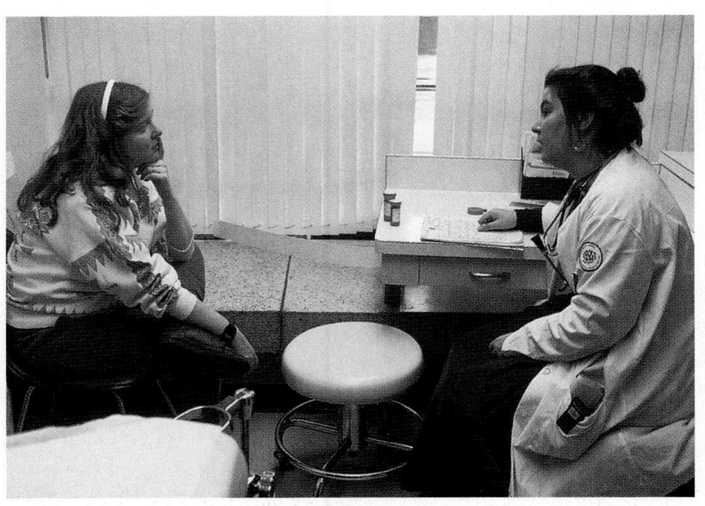

Taking steps to prevent sexually transmitted diseases is an important part of any sexual relationship.

Gonorrhea. More than 700,000 cases of gonorrhea in the United States are reported to the Centers for Disease Control each year, with actual rates of the disease estimated at over 2 million per year. Like syphilis, gonorrhea is a bacterial infection. However, the course of gonorrhea infection is quite different from syphilis. In men, gonorrhea's earliest symptoms involve the discharge of pus from the penis and painful burning and itching during urination. These symptoms usually occur within the first weeks of infection. In women, the early symptoms of gonorrhea infection usually involve a yellow-green vaginal discharge. Women may also experience vaginal itching when infected with gonorrhea, but most infected women do not detect the infection early in its course. In men and women, untreated gonorrhea can result in numerous serious health threats, including progression of the infection to the bladder, kidneys, heart, and brain. Fortunately, when detected, gonorrhea is usually cured easily with antibiotics. However, in recent years, strains of gonorrhea and syphilis that are very difficult to treat with antibiotics have become common, especially among ethnic minorities and the poor in large cities (Aral & Holmes, 1991).

Chlamydia. Chlamydia is the most common STD, with between 4 and 10 million cases occurring each year in the United States with as many as 10 percent of college students being infected (Schacter, 1989). Chlamydia is caused by a small organism that invades several different types of cells in the body and uses them to multiply itself. The symptoms of chlamydia are usually vague and difficult to define. Often, there are no immediate signs of infection, with infection becoming apparent after a long period of time. Men may experience burning sensations during urination and may have a pus discharge from the penis. Chlamydia may also move into the testes and cause infertility. In women, the symptoms may include burning and itching of the vagina and burning sensations during urination. Untreated infections in women may progress to the fallopian tubes, causing infertility, and may develop into pelvic inflammatory disease, resulting in fever and serious illness. If detected, chlamydia is treated with antibiotics and is usually curable. However, chlamydia may be recurrent.

Pubic Lice. This STD, commonly called "crabs," is caused by very small parasitic organisms that can just barely be seen that bite into the skin and feed on blood, causing skin itching. Pubic lice are treated with a variety of medicated shampoos and other applications.

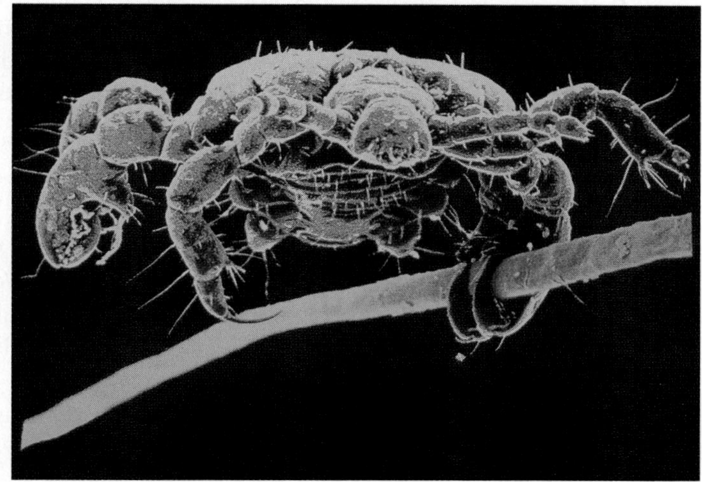

A magnified photograph of a pubic louse, or crab, which can cause itching when it bites into the skin.

Genital Herpes. Caused by the *herpes simplex virus (type-2),* genital herpes is treatable, but not curable. Similar to herpes simplex type-1, which causes cold sores, the symptoms of genital herpes are principally small painful lesions that appear in the genital area. These lesions appear to be like small blisters that open and become wet. When present, herpes lesions are highly contagious and allow for the transmission of the virus to others who come in contact with them. It is also important for the infected person to avoid touching the herpes lesions and to wash thoroughly after doing so. Exposure of the herpes virus to the eyes can be particularly dangerous, potentially causing damage to the cornea. After the initial outbreak, the lesions will eventually go away. However, in most cases, the lesions reoccur over a period of time because the virus lays dormant in the body. Although herpes cannot be cured, it can be treated with antiviral medication that slows its development and can help reduce the occurrence of further outbreaks. Herpes, as is true for all STDs, requires the attention of health care professionals for proper treatment.

Genital Warts. Caused by the *human papilloma virus,* genital warts usually appear months after infection. The warts vary in color, size, and texture, and may appear on the penis, vulva, anal area, or inside the urethra. Genital warts are not usually painful and are not considered dangerous themselves, although they are related to the development of other serious conditions, such as certain cancers of the reproductive organs. The treatment of genital warts involves their removal through freezing, surgical removal, or other methods.

Acquired Immunodeficiency Syndrome (AIDS)

Caused by the *human immunodeficiency virus (HIV),* AIDS is a fatal STD. In the United States alone, over two million people have been infected with HIV. HIV is transmitted through blood, semen, and vaginal fluids. Sexually, HIV is primarily transmitted from

acquired immune deficiency syndrome (AIDS)
A viral disease spread by blood and other bodily fluids that eventually destroys the body's immune system.

person to person through vaginal, anal intercourse, and oral sex. HIV destroys specific blood cells, called T-Helper cells, which are responsible for the body's immune response to infectious agents. When infected with HIV, a person does not become ill for a long period of time, usually years. However, the person can infect others during the years prior to becoming ill. In time, the number of T-Helper cells diminishes, leaving the body vulnerable to a wide range of potential infections. Usually 7 to 10 years after infection, a person may become ill with one of many infections, such as an intestinal flu, pneumonia, or some other ailment, and may not be able to recover from it. After the person experiences one of several specific infectious diseases or when a specific number of T-Helper cells have been depleted, the person is diagnosed with AIDS. It is not possible to tell if someone is infected with HIV by looking at him or her. The only definitive test for HIV is a specific blood test.

There is no cure for HIV infection or AIDS. However, several antiviral medications slow the progression of HIV, and numerous medications have been introduced that prevent the development of many infections that can be life threatening to persons infected with HIV. HIV infection and AIDS have been deemed the most serious global health threat of all time. Because HIV is transmitted from one person to another, and because we now live in a world where persons travel across vast areas in very short periods of time, AIDS threatens entire populations of people. HIV has been spread across all continents of the world and is rapidly spreading among numerous diverse populations (Mann, Tarantola, & Netter, 1992). In the United States, every state and major city has been affected by HIV and AIDS.

Studies continue to show that many people misperceive the realities of AIDS and hold inaccurate beliefs about HIV and AIDS (i.e., Kalichman, Hunter, & Kelly, 1992). These misperceptions exist despite massive efforts to educate the public. Several facts about AIDS that are not widely understood are important to know:

1. A person with the AIDS virus looks healthy for a long period of time.
2. There is no evidence that the AIDS virus can be spread through casual contact or kissing.
3. There is no cure for AIDS, but treatments can help people infected with HIV stay healthy.
4. A person cannot get the AIDS virus by sharing kitchens and bathrooms with someone who has AIDS.
5. You cannot get the AIDS virus by being around an infected person who sneezes near you.
6. You cannot get HIV from donating (giving) blood.
7. You cannot get AIDS by touching a person with AIDS.
8. A person *can* get the AIDS virus after having sex one time with a person who has the virus.
9. Women *can* give the AIDS virus to men, and men can give the virus to women.
10. A person who got the AIDS virus from using intravenous drugs *can* give the virus to someone by having sex.

Although AIDS has been more common in the United States among gay males and users of intravenous drugs, AIDS is not limited to these subgroups. Indeed, although the rate of spread has slowed among gays, it has increased in heterosexuals in the past ten years. The reality that AIDS is a disease that can affect all people, regardless of their lifestyle, was not understood by many Americans until November 7, 1991, when basketball star Earvin "Magic" Johnson announced to the world that he was infected with HIV. Magic Johnson's announcement led many people to look at their own risk for HIV for the first time (Kalichman & Hunter, 1992). Magic Johnson's message has been that HIV is a real danger for everyone who is sexually active, but that people can take steps to reduce their risk for getting HIV. Specifically, avoiding all forms of sexual intercourse or using latex condoms when engaging in any form of sexual intercourse can reduce or eliminate the risk for

The HIV/AIDS virus is found in blood, semen, and vaginal fluids.

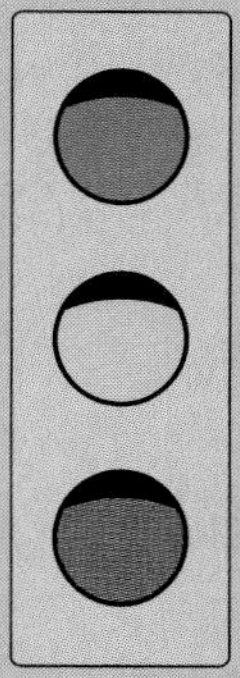

Red light: activities with very high risk
- Vaginal and anal intercourse without a condom
- Oral sex to orgasm
- Sharing sex toys and devices

Yellow light: activities with some risk
- Vaginal and anal intercourse, oral sex with a condom
- Oral sex without a condom, stopping before orgasm

Green light: little or no risk
- Hugging, holding hands
- Body rubbing, massage, touching
- Mutual masturbation, avoiding contact of fluids on cuts

FIGURE 10.9
HIV risk and reduced-risk behaviors.

HIV infection. Figure 10.9 shows that certain behaviors create a high risk for HIV, while others are of less risk, and still other behaviors create no risk for getting HIV. Thus, personal decisions about how much risk a person is willing to take determines their chances of becoming HIV infected.

The most effective means of not becoming infected with any STD is to not come in contact with the bacteria, chlamydia, lice, and viruses that cause the infection. For most STDs, this means not having direct contact with the partner's genital organs, semen, vaginal fluids, or blood. This is where the use of condoms can help. Condoms made of latex provide a reasonably effective barrier against the spread of AIDS and most other STDs. Indeed, condoms provide reasonably good protection against pregnancy as well. In fact, condoms are the only form of contraception that can reduce the chances of both pregnancy and STDs.

In addition, there are numerous sexual activities that reduce the risk for infection. These behaviors all share the common feature of not involving the exchange of semen, vaginal fluids, or exposure to blood. For more information about STDs, you can call the STD National Hotline 1-800-227-8922 and for more information about HIV/AIDS, call the National AIDS Hotline 1-800-342-2437 (1-800-344-7432 for information in Spanish).

Review

A number of sexual dysfunctions interfere with pleasurable and successful sexual intercourse. Problems in sexual desire, sexual arousal, and orgasm occur in both men and women. When their cause is not physical, lack of information, anxiety, and relationship difficulties are commonly at the root of sexual dysfunctions. For this reason, sex therapists specialize in addressing psychological issues that can lead to sexual difficulties. For both females and males, there are important health issues related to sexual anatomy, including breast, cervical, and testicular cancer, all of which can be effectively treated if detected early. Sexual behavior also increases the risk of a variety of sexually transmitted diseases. These include diseases caused by bacteria (such as syphilis and gonorrhea), lice (pubic lice), or viruses (such as genital herpes and genital warts), which may be treated for symptoms but are not curable. The most deadly and rapidly spreading sexually transmitted disease is HIV infection, the virus that causes AIDS.

Thinking Critically About Psychology

1. Other than through the loss of sexual pleasure, how would a sexual dysfunction interfere with the individual's quality of life?

2. How would a sexually transmitted disease such as genital herpes change a person's life?

3. What can you personally do to protect the persons that you love from contracting AIDS?

Check Your Learning

To be sure that you have learned the key points from the preceding section, cover the answers below and try to answer each question. If you give an incorrect answer to any question, return to the page given next to the correct answer to see why your answer was not correct.

1. Involuntary contractions of the walls of the vagina that make it too narrow to allow the penis to enter for sexual intercourse are called

   a. orgasm dysfunction.
   b. dyspareunia.
   c. vaginismus.
   d. chlamydia.

2. The squeeze technique can be an effective treatment for

   a. erectile dysfunction.
   b. dyspareunia.
   c. inhibited orgasm.
   d. premature ejaculation.

3. Genital warts and genital herpes can usually be cured with medication.

   a. True
   b. False

4. Which of the following is a way that a person *can* get the AIDS virus (HIV)?

   a. sharing a kitchen or bathroom with someone who has AIDS
   b. having an infected person sneeze around you
   c. touching a person with AIDS
   d. having vaginal intercourse one time with a person who has HIV

Correct Answers
1. c (p. 388), **2.** d (p. 389), **3.** b (p. 391), **4.** d (p. 392).

Summary

Chapter 10 describes the biological bases of sex, the psychological dimensions of gender and sexual orientation, and the psychological and social problems related to sex and gender.

I. The terms *sex, gender identity*, and *gender role* refer to important aspects of the human experience.
  A. A person's *sex* is defined by their male or female genitals. Gender identity is the personal experience of being a male or a female. Gender role refers to the patterns of behavior that communicate to others the degree to which we are masculine or feminine in the terms defined by our culture.
  B. Gender identity, gender roles, and sexual orientation are important aspects of our self-concepts and personalities.
    1. Gender roles are described based on how feminine or masculine the person's behavior is in terms of the expectations of their culture.
    2. Persons who show a healthy combination of many masculine and feminine characteristics (androgyny) may be better able to cope with the complex demands of life than persons who are exclusively feminine or masculine.
  C. Gender similarities and gender differences have been the subject of a great deal of study by psychologists.
    1. On the average, women are slightly better at tests of verbal cognitive abilities than men, and men are slightly better at tests of mathematical and spatial skills.
      a. The differences between women and men on these tests of specific cognitive abilities are smaller since the early 1970s than in previous eras.
      b. Performance on tests of specific cognitive abilities has been found to be more related to gender roles than to biological sex.
      c. These findings suggest that raising females and males in more similar ways in recent years has contributed to the decline in specific cognitive differences between men and women.
      d. In spite of the small differences in mathematical ability, however, women are less confident of their ability, and this lack of confidence influences choice of career.
  D. Two major theories of the development of gender identity have been proposed, both of which emphasize that gender identity develops from our interaction with others rather than being a simple reaction to our anatomical sex.
    1. Psychoanalytic theory states that children usually identify with their same-sex parent to gain parental approval and to avoid rejection.
    2. Social learning theory suggests that children imitate both females and males initially, but gender behavior that is consistent with their anatomical sex is usually learned because it is positively reinforced and other sex behavior is punished.

E. Sexual orientation is another key issue of our self-concept and sexuality.
   1. Persons are considered to be heterosexual, homosexual, or bisexual on the basis of the degree of romantic and sexual attraction to members of the same or other sex.
   2. It appears that both biological and social factors play a role in development of sexual orientation.

II. The scientific study of sexuality is a relatively recent event but has resulted in a good understanding of biological and psychological aspects of sexuality.
   A. The first scientific writings on sexuality were published in the early 1900s by Richard Von Krafft-Ebing and Henry Havelock Ellis.
   B. Serious scientific research on sexuality has increased since the 1950s, when Alfred Kinsey conducted groundbreaking surveys that provided the first accurate description of sexual behavior in American women and men.
   C. In the 1970s Virginia Johnson and William Masters conducted laboratory studies that provided the first detailed description of the human sexual response cycle from initial excitement to orgasm.

III. Although sexuality is far more than the activity of sex organs, an understanding of sexual anatomy and physiology is essential to understanding sexuality.
   A. Sexual motivation is similar to other primary motives in a variety of ways (including control by hypothalamic centers and the powerful role played by external stimuli, learning, and emotions), but it differs from other primary motives in a number of ways related to arousal and deprivation.
   B. Hormones play a less important role in the regulation of sexual behavior in humans than other animals.

IV. A number of uncommon patterns of sexual behavior are considered to be normal even though they are unusual, unless they cause distress in the person. Other uncommon patterns of sexuality are usually or always harmful to the person and his or her partner.
   A. Transvestism and transsexualism are atypical sexual patterns that deviate considerably from the norm but are not considered to be abnormal unless the individual is unhappy with his or her sexual pattern.
   B. Abnormal patterns of atypical sexual behavior include voyeurism, exhibitionism, fetishism, sadism, masochism, rape, incest, pedophilia, and sexual harassment.
   C. Sexual violence (including rape and the sexual assault and molestation of children) and sexual harassment are important social problems.
   D. Sexual dysfunctions are problems that can interfere with successful and pleasurable sexual intercourse. These include:
      1. Disorders of desire
      2. Disorders of arousal
      3. Orgasmic disorders
   E. A number of health problems are related to sexual anatomy. These include:
      1. Cancers of sexual anatomy.
      2. Sexually transmitted diseases caused by bacteria (syphilis, gonorrhea, and chlamydia).
      3. Sexually transmitted lice.
      4. Sexually transmitted diseases caused by viruses (genital warts, and the fatal Acquired Immunodeficiency Syndrome, or AIDS).

Suggested Readings

1. Craig, M. E. (1990). Coercive sexuality in dating relationships: A situational model. *Clinical Psychology Review, 10,* 395–423.
2. Groth, N. (1979). *Men who rape: The psychology of the offender.* New York: Plenum.
3. Halpern, D. (1992). *Sex differences in cognitive abilities* (2nd ed). Hillsdale, NJ: Erlbaum.
4. Money, J. (1972). *Man & woman, boy & girl.* Baltimore, MD: Johns Hopkins University Press.
5. Money, J. (1986). *Lovemaps.* New York: Irvington.
6. Money, J. (1988). *Gay, straight, and in-between.* New York: Oxford University Press.
7. Kalichman, S. (1996). *Answering your questions about AIDS.* Washington, DC: American Psychological Association.

APPLICATION OF PSYCHOLOGY

DATE RAPE

The topic of this section is a common form of rape—rape committed by a person who is on a date with the victim. Because the rapist is usually a male and the victim is usually a female, I will speak of the rapist and victim in those terms. It is important to acknowledge, however, that both men and women commit rape, both women and men are victims, and rapes occur among both heterosexuals and homosexuals. No one is completely free of the threat of rape.

Most of us think of rapists as a stranger lurking in the shadows with a knife, stalking his victim. Such rapists certainly do exist, but the truth is that more than 75 percent of rapists are acquaintances of the victim (National Victim Center, 1992). Indeed, many rapes are committed by a male who took the victim to a movie and drank a couple of beers with her afterward. Date rape is a common occurrence on college campuses across the United States. It is estimated that 33 percent of all college women have experienced unwanted sexual intercourse of this sort (Koss & Oros, 1982). Most often, the perpetrator is a trusted and well-liked male student who did not stop advancing sexual contact after protests from his date. In many cases, the date rapist became angry at the rejection and knowingly and brutally forced his date to have sex. In other cases, however, the date rapist had no intention of committing a rape and did not know that he was doing so. He didn't understand that she was saying "no," or thought that nice girls say "no" when they really mean "yes"!

Because our society has only recently awakened to the problem of date rape, there have been few criminal prosecutions of date rapists until recent years. These few cases, however, have spawned a national dialogue that may help everyone distinguish clearly between what constitutes acceptable behavior on a date and what constitutes the crime of rape. Some of the questions being asked today include the following: Does a person have to say "no" for the other person to stop sexual advancements, or is an expression of ambivalence or discomfort sufficient? How clearly must a woman communicate her feelings about sex to be sure that her desires are understood?

In many cases, date rapes begin with a miscommunication between the persons. Studies of dating have shown that it is common for men and women to miscommunicate their sexual interests to others. In a series of studies, Abbey and her colleagues (Abbey, 1982; Abbey & Melby, 1986) have shown that college men are quite likely to misinterpret college women's behavior. When women think they are only being friendly and not expressing any sexual interest at all, men often think the woman is making a sexual advance. This miscommunication occurs because males tend to misinterpret subtle aspects of friendly behavior, such as pleasant facial expressions, standing close to the male, and maintaining eye contact, as indications of sexual interest. In simple terms, many males engage in a lot of wishful thinking about sex and often see what they want to see in the woman's behavior.

One reason that men and women often miscommunicate about sex is that they differ in their beliefs and attitudes about sexuality. For example, if you were not in a relationship and you met someone that you really liked on Friday night, would it be okay to have sex with her or him on Sunday afternoon? When a large sample of college freshmen were asked about sex with someone that they had just met, 66 percent of the men said it would be okay, but only 38 percent of the women agreed (Astin, Korn, & Berz, 1991).

Another aspect of dating that is related to date rape is alcohol. Drinking plays a role in sexual aggression in a number of ways. First, some men use alcohol to reduce the resistance of a date who has not previously consented to sexual activity. Some men do this intentionally to trick the woman into agreeing to something that she would not agree to when sober. Most men, however, give the role of alcohol no thought and simply offer alcohol to their dates as part of the normal dating ritual. The problem is that these men believe that a woman who consents to sex when intoxicated is giving her consent (Koss, Leonard, Beezley, & Oros, 1985).

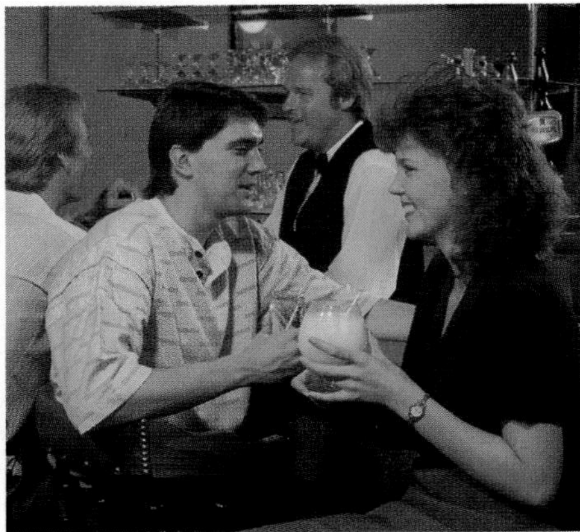

Date rape is a common occurrence on college campuses. Alcohol is often a factor in date rape.

Second, alcohol lowers inhibitions and often increases interest in sexual activity. And because it lowers inhibitions, alcohol makes it more likely that the male will do something—such as using force—that he would not do when he had not been drinking. Drinking may also lead the female to act in ways that are interpreted by her date as a sexual invitation. Finally, drinking allows people to attribute their behavior to the alcohol rather than their own choices. That is, alcohol can provide a means of evading responsibility for one's actions. It is easy for a person to say that he had been drinking and did not know what he was doing.

What are the implications of these findings? Is there anything that you can do to prevent date rape? The ongoing discussion of what constitutes date rape is an important positive step. Everyone understands that an intentional and forceful rape is wrong under any circumstance, but the boundaries need to be clarified for some cases of date rape. Here are some simple guidelines that may help.

Guidelines for Men

1. *It is always rape when she says "no."* Women do not mean "yes" when they say "no." Be clear about this—"no" means "no." The

research of psychologist Charlene Muehlenhard suggests that men often think that "no" means "yes" in sexual situations, especially if it is not stated emphatically (Muehlenhard & Hollabaugh, 1988). Men need to be aware of their tendency to think wishfully about women's sexual availability and to realize that even an unclear statement of "no" is a clear warning sign that he may be committing the felony of rape if he does not stop his sexual advances.

2. *If it is not clear that she has consented to sex, she has not consented.* Just learning to take "no" for an answer is not enough to avoid committing date rape. What should a male do if his date does not say "no" to a sexual advance, but says something like "I really don't know if this is a good idea?" Is it rape if he continues anyway? Sexual situations are filled with pressures that make it difficult to communicate clearly, and men tend to misinterpret subtle signals. This means that the only appropriate decision is to discontinue sexual advances when it is not perfectly clear that they are wanted. If she really wants you to continue, she will tell you more clearly later; but if she was saying "no," you will have avoided becoming a rapist.
3. *If she is drunk or high, she cannot give consent to sex.* Whether a male is intentionally trying to loosen his date's inhibitions or not, a drunken (or unconscious or stoned or high) date cannot give consent to sex. Decisions made while drunk can be tomorrow's tragedy—both to the woman who finds that she had sex with a man with whom she had no intention of having sex and to the man who is arrested for raping a woman who he thought had given consent. And remember, a male who has been drinking is more likely to do things that he would not otherwise have done. Like drinking and driving, drinking and dating is a dangerous combination.

Guidelines for Women

1. *Communicate your wishes about sex clearly and early.* As noted earlier, men have a tendency to hear women say "yes" about sex more often than women say it, especially if the communication from the woman is not crystal clear from the very start (Muehlenhard & Hollabaugh, 1988). This means that, to be safe, women who do not want sexual contact may need to communicate that fact in a way that leaves no room for doubt as soon as the first sexual advance is made. Our society teaches us to communicate about sexuality in subtle and indirect ways, but women who communicate their desires and limits clearly and assertively from the very beginning can reduce their chances of being the victim of a date rape.
2. *The combination of alcohol and sexual situations is dangerous.* Alcohol and other drugs bring out the worst in people. When a male has been drinking, he will be more likely to disregard a clear "no" or to become angry and violent when frustrated than when he has not been drinking. Similarly, when a female has been drinking, she may be less likely to say "no" to unwanted sex or may even be unable to make a rational decision about sex if she is intoxicated. Even moderate drinking can create serious problems, but heavy drinking is an invitation to date rape.
3. *Even "nice guys" can commit rape.* Because rapists are not characterized by any particular type of personality, it is not possible to predict who will commit rape. As stated earlier, most date rapists are men who seemed like nice guys to the victim before the rape. This is not to say that all men are potential rapists, but you should not assume that a male could not rape you under the wrong circumstances just because he seems nice. Try to avoid miscommunication and risky situations with all men.

Finally, if you or someone you know has been raped or if you are concerned that you might rape someone, help is available. Most college campuses have come to recognize date rape as a serious problem. The majority of counseling centers and student development centers have methods for addressing the date rape problem. Student organizations often assemble meetings to discuss issues of dating and dating violence. Off campus, community resources, such as mental health centers and crisis lines, offer services to persons concerned about being a victim of sexual assault or about the possibility that one could become sexually assaultive. There are many possibilities for improving the present problem of date rape, but all require open and honest communication and a willingness to evaluate one's own behavior.

CHAPTER

11

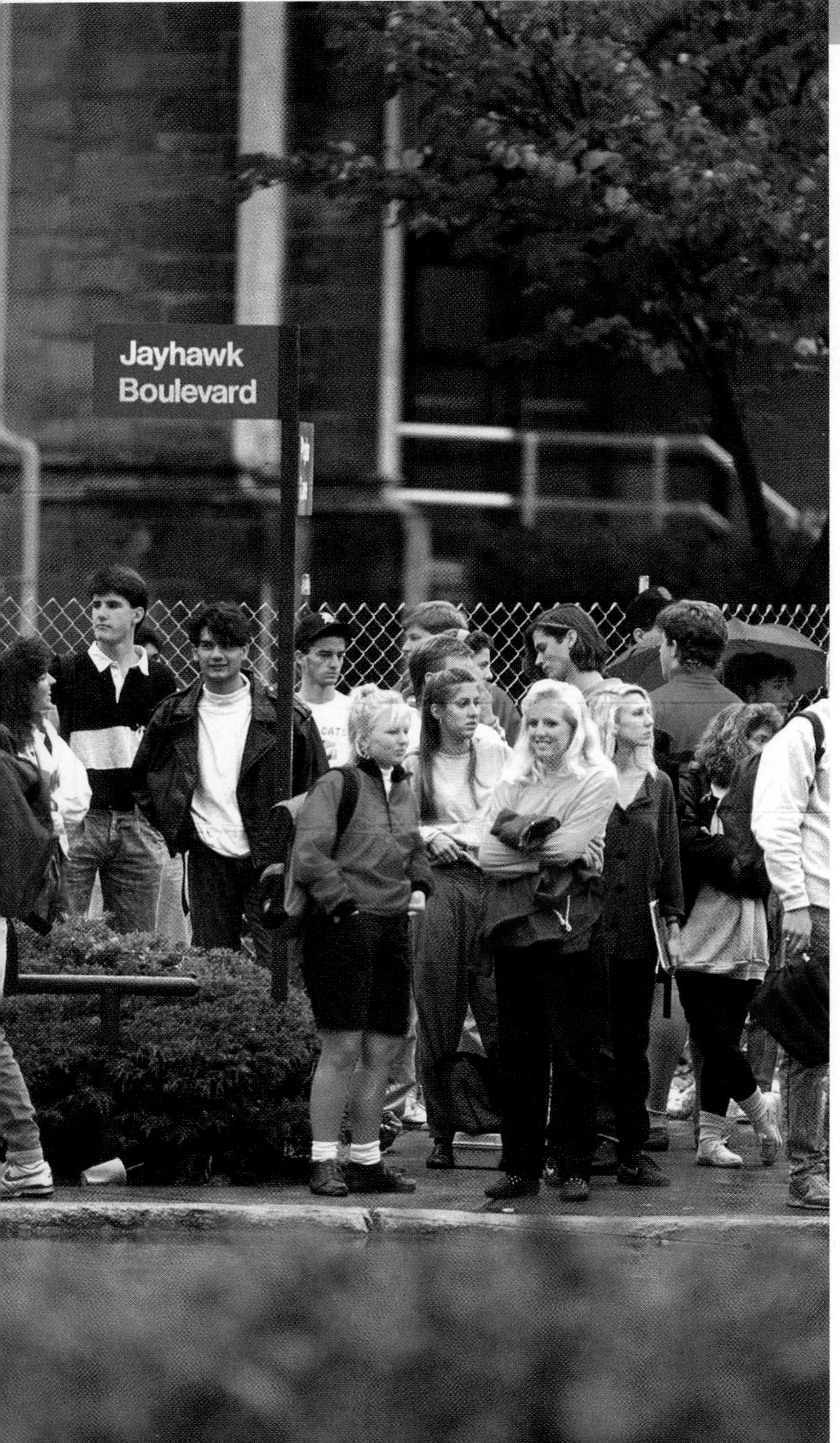

CHAPTER OUTLINE

Personality Theories and Assessment

PROLOGUE

It's obvious that not everyone thinks, feels, and acts in the same way. In psychology, we use the term *personality* to refer to the typical ways of acting, thinking, and feeling that make one person different from another. So, how would you describe your personality? What are you like?

There are thousands of words in the English language that we could use to describe our personalities, but many psychologists believe that an individual's personality can be summed up pretty well using just five basic concepts. How would you rate yourself on the five dimensions of personality below? On the first dimension, if you tend to be very relaxed and secure, give yourself a "1"—but if you tend to be very tense and insecure, give yourself a "3." If you are neither very tense nor very relaxed, give yourself a "2" on this dimension. You could even give yourself 1.5 if you think that you are somewhere between a 1 and a 2 on this dimension of personality. Now, rate yourself on the other four dimensions in the same way.

1	*2*	*3*
Relaxed and secure		Tense and insecure
Quiet and not social		Talkative and sociable
Down-to-earth and unadventurous		Imaginative and daring
Irritable and ruthless		Good-natured and kind
Careless and unreliable		Careful and reliable

Do these five dimensions of personality do a good job of describing you? If not, what aspects of your personality were left out?

This chapter begins with a definition of personality and with three psychological theories that try to explain *why* you have the personality that you have. These are the psychoanalytic theory, the humanistic theory, and the social learning theory.

The psychoanalytic view was first stated by Sigmund Freud. Psychoanalysts believe that your personality is the net result of a struggle between opposing forces within your mind. Roughly speaking, they believe that we are born with selfish instincts, such as sexual and aggressive instincts, and that our experiences with society lead us to develop a conscience and the ability to think realistically that holds those selfish instincts more or less in check. The particular ways in which each of us balances these three forces of the mind (instincts, realistic thinking, and conscience) give us our unique personality.

Humanistic psychologists view the development of personality in an almost completely opposite way. Rather than believing that we come into the world equipped with only selfish instincts, humanists believe that each person is born with a healthy, positive drive to realize his or her full potential. And rather than viewing society as a positive factor in the development of our personalities like the psychoanalysts, humanists believe that society often impedes our ability to grow positively. To humanists, the most important aspect of personality is the person's view of his or her self. An accurate view of oneself is essential to proper personality functioning, but humanists believe that society often sets unrealistically high standards for what is "good" that make it difficult to view ourselves truthfully.

KEY TERMS

The social learning theory of personality takes a simpler view of personality development. From this perspective, personality is simply something that is learned through our interactions with other members of society. People are not born with powerful negative or positive drives that collide with society. We simply learn our personalities from our interactions with others.

In this chapter, we also discuss the ways that psychologists attempt to measure personalities. Their methods are similar to the one that you have just used to describe yourself—only more complicated and sophisticated.

DEFINITION OF PERSONALITY

Who is Ben Lahey anyway? What am I like? You have read thousands of words that I have written by now, but you really don't know very much about me. What would I need to tell you so that you would feel that you knew me as a person? I would probably start out with a description of my physical appearance—height, weight, eye color, hair color. I would tell you what I like to eat and about my job, but that's pretty superficial stuff. If you saw me eating at the student union, you would pick up most of that information in the first few seconds. But to really get to know me as a person, you would need to know something about my thoughts, my feelings, my actions. In other words, I would need to describe my personality to you.

But what do we mean when we use the term *personality?* It's no accident that the word *person* is in the word *personality.* Your personality defines you as a person, rather than just a biological conglomeration of organs. One's **personality** is the sum total of all of the ways of acting, thinking, and feeling that are *typical* for that person and make that person *different* from all other individuals.

personality
The sum total of the typical ways of acting, thinking, and feeling that makes each person unique.

Notice that the two emphases in this definition are on the terms *typical* and *different.* An individual's personality is composed of all the relatively unchanging psychological characteristics that are *typical* for that person. Some people are typically generous; others are typically impulsive; others are typically shy. If people did not have at least some relatively unchanging qualities, we would never know what to expect from them. Each time we encountered a friend, it would be like dealing with a stranger. We know what to expect from our friends because of the relatively unchanging psychological characteristics that make up each person's personality.

Dennis Rodman's tendency to be flamboyant is a well-known aspect of his personality.

The second emphasis in the definition of personality is on the term *different.* Each person's unique pattern of typical ways of acting, thinking, and feeling sets him or her apart from each other person. Each of us is a unique person because no one else has exactly our combination of typical psychological qualities. Even if every person were exactly identical in every physical characteristic—eye color, height, weight, tone of voice—we would be able to distinguish one person from another because of their typical ways of acting, thinking, and feeling.

Psychologists who specialize in the study of personality want to know *why* each individual develops the unique personality that he or she does. Are personalities learned? Are they inherited? Or are they formed by critical events that occur during early childhood?

Psychologists also want to know how to *assess,* or measure, personalities. The first section of this chapter acquaints you with three major theories of personality development, and the second section explores some of the major methods used to measure personality.

PSYCHOANALYTIC THEORY: SIGMUND FREUD

Sigmund Freud was a young physician building a medical practice in Vienna in the late 1800s. He was particularly interested in treating patients with emotional problems but felt frustrated by the lack of knowledge that existed at that time. Although he had devoted many years of study in Austria and France to the disorders of the brain and nerves, Freud found that what he had learned was of little help to his patients. Thus, being a person of considerable confidence and intelligence, Sigmund Freud set out to develop his own methods of treatment. In the course of his development of treatment methods, Freud also developed a general theory of personality, an explanation for why people develop their unique patterns of typical behavior. His view is known today as **psychoanalytic theory.**

psychoanalytic theory
Freud's theory that the origin of personality lies in the balance between the id, the ego, and the superego.

Freud's theory of personality began with a very limited question. He wanted to understand the condition known today as *conversion disorder.* In this condition, the individual appears to have a serious medical problem such as paralysis or deafness for which there is no medical cause. To understand Freud's theory—which some of you will find quite shocking—we should begin with a description of one of Freud's first case studies. I think you will see the origins of his unusual ideas about what shapes our personalities in this amazing description. The young woman was not treated by Freud, but he helped her physician write up the case—one that had a lasting impact on his theories.

Bertha Pappenheim's unusual problems began at age 21. After 6 months of caring for her dying father each night, the formerly healthy young woman suddenly became paralyzed in her legs, arms, and neck, and lost the ability to talk except in a meaningless garble. Surprisingly, her physician could find nothing physically wrong with her. In time, her speech and muscular coordination returned, only to be followed by other strange symptoms. She was plagued by hallucinations of writhing snakes and grinning skulls; she was deaf for a time; experienced blurred vision; and had difficulty swallowing water for 6 weeks. But after 18 months of frequent therapy sessions with her physician, Joseph Breuer, she was free of these bizarre maladies.

Bertha Pappenheim (1861–1936)

Dr. Breuer terminated his relationship with Ms. Pappenheim partly because of her improvement, but partly because he had developed strong emotional feelings for her and he suspected that she had similar feelings for him. On the evening after his last session with Ms. Pappenheim, the young physician sat eating supper with his family when he was summoned back to Bertha's home by her maid. When Breuer arrived, he found Bertha writhing in bed, complaining of painful cramps in her lower abdomen. Suddenly, she shocked Breuer with the words, "Now Dr. Breuer's baby is coming! It is coming!" She was giving birth to a completely imaginary baby! Because of his complicated emotional feelings toward Ms. Pappenheim, Dr. Breuer transferred her to the care of another physician.

In 1895 Breuer and Freud jointly published an account of Bertha Pappenheim's problems, giving differing interpretations of her symptoms. To protect her identity, she was given the pseudonym of "Anna O." Freud's theory was shocking: Freud believed that 6 months of being alone with her father while he was sick in bed heightened unconscious sexual desires for her father to the point that they threatened to become conscious. The paralysis and other symptoms, according to Freud, served the purpose of making it impossible for her to express her sexual longings; they held in check her nearly uncontrollable and wholly unacceptable desires. Later, some of these sexual feelings were transferred to Dr. Breuer, by whom she unconsciously wished to become pregnant.

It was only after her father died and she left Dr. Breuer's care that her unusual problems cleared up. Bertha Pappenheim's poignant story after her treatment by Breuer, however, was one of torment, triumph, and tragedy. Her new physician attempted to treat her with morphine. She soon became addicted to the drug, however, and had to be placed in a mental institution. But by age 28, she had recovered and moved with her mother to Frankfurt. Although wealthy, Bertha began working in an orphanage for illegitimate children, first as a volunteer and then as its director. Gradually, the scope of her work grew to encompass educating unwed mothers, fighting anti-Semitism, and becoming an important activist for women's rights. In 1904 she founded the Federation of Jewish Women, which was successful in stopping the slave trade that exported impoverished Jewish girls to South America where they were forced into prostitution. She also went against the orthodox religious views of her time and founded a school for Jewish women, the Beth-Jakob Seminary. Bertha Pappenheim's death in 1936 spared her from the worst of the Nazi persecution of Jews and the ultimate rape of her efforts. In 1938 the Nazis announced that the seminary would become a brothel and its students prostitutes. Rather than suffer this indignity, the 93 young women dressed in their finest clothes and swallowed poison (Freeman, 1972).

Freud's Mind: Three Levels of Consciousness

Freud distinguished three levels of conscious awareness—the *conscious mind,* the *preconscious mind,* and the *unconscious mind.* We are presently aware of the contents of the first level of the mind, but temporarily unaware of the contents of the second level, and more permanently unaware of the contents of the third.

conscious mind
That portion of the mind of which one is presently aware.

preconscious mind
That portion of the mind containing information that is not presently conscious but can be easily brought into consciousness.

unconscious mind
The part of the mind of which we can never be directly aware; the storehouse of primitive instinctual motives and of memories and emotions that have been repressed.

repression
Sigmund Freud's theory that unpleasant information is often pushed into unconsciousness without our being aware of it.

To Freud, the mind is like an iceberg; the **conscious mind** is merely the tip visible above the surface, whereas the bulk of the important workings of the mind lurk mysteriously beneath the surface (see fig. 11.1). Just below the surface is what Freud called the **preconscious mind.** It consists of memories that are not presently conscious but can be easily brought into consciousness. You are not thinking right now about your last meal, the name of your psychology instructor, or the taste of your favorite drink, but you could quickly bring those items into conscious awareness if you wanted to. The preconscious mind is the vast storehouse of easily accessible memories. The contents of the preconscious were once conscious and can be returned to consciousness when needed.

Further down from consciousness lies the **unconscious mind.** It stores primitive instinctual motives plus memories and emotions that are so threatening to the conscious mind that they have been unconsciously pushed into the unconscious mind through the process of **repression.** The contents of the unconscious mind, unlike the preconscious mind, are not normally accessible to consciousness. They can rarely be made fully conscious, and then only with great difficulty.

Freud's Mind: Id, Ego, and Superego

Freud also divided the mind into three parts in a different, but related, way. The best-known aspect of Freud's theory of personality is his view that the mind is composed of three parts, each with a different function: the *id,* the *ego,* and the *superego* (see fig. 11.1).

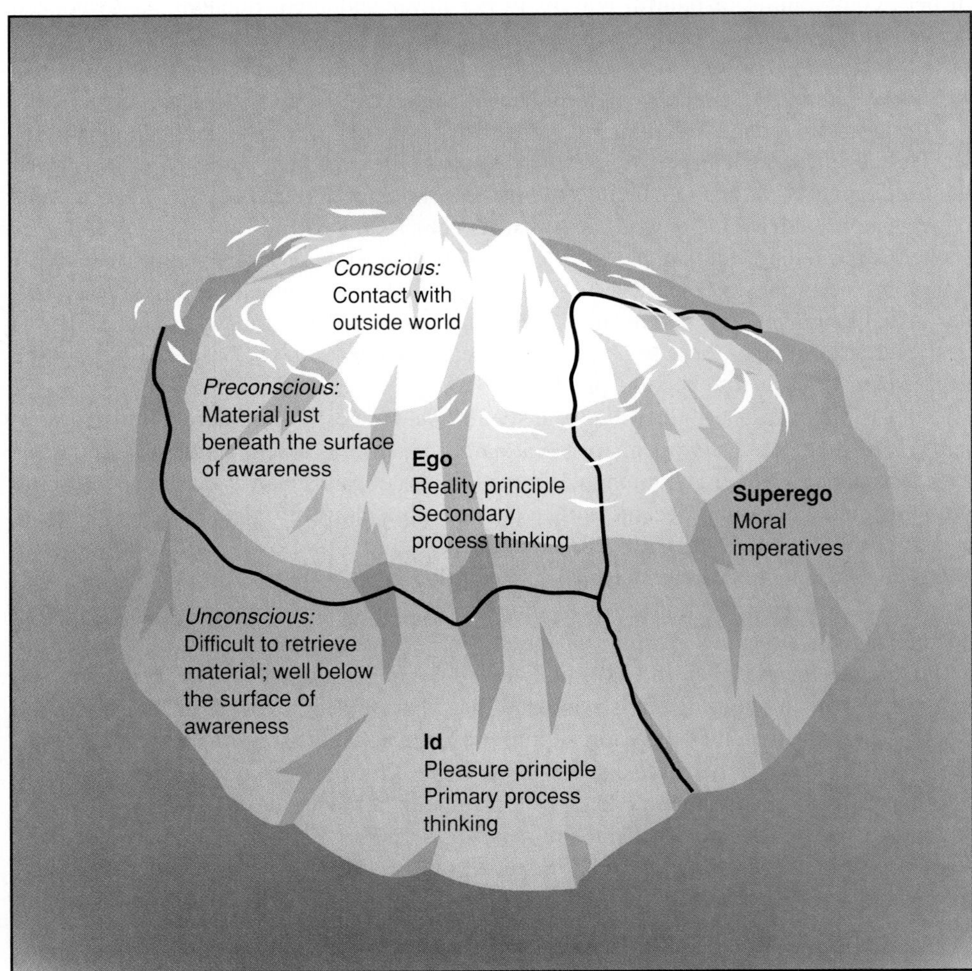

FIGURE 11.1
Freud's model of personality structure. Freud theorized that we have three levels of awareness—the conscious, the preconscious, and the unconscious. To dramatize the enormous size of the unconscious, he compared it to the portion of an iceberg that lies beneath the water's surface. Freud also divided personality structure into three components—id, ego, and superego—which operate according to different principles and exhibit different modes of thinking. In Freud's model, the id is entirely unconscious, but the ego and superego operate at all three levels of awareness.

Id: The Selfish Beast

When the infant is born, the mind has only one part, the **id.** The id is composed primarily of two sets of instincts, *life instincts* and *death instincts.* Freud wrote relatively little about the death instincts, but he believed that aggression and even suicidal urges arose from these instincts. The life instincts give rise to motives that sustain and promote life, such as hunger, self-protection, and sexual desire. To Freud, the sexual and aggressive urges are by far the most important of these motives. As strange as it may seem, sex and aggression are used by Freud to explain a vast range of personality characteristics, from kindness to shyness to cruelty. From birth on, Freud believed that every person's life is dominated by these two motives—the desire to experience sexual pleasure and the desire to harm others. Because the id operates entirely at the unconscious level of the mind, however, we are generally not aware of these motives. Only safe, watered-down versions of our true sexual and aggressive urges ever reach conscious awareness.

"Good morning, beheaded—uh, I mean beloved."

Freud's view of the dark side of the human mind is not an easy one for most of us to accept. Freud tells us that there lives within each of us a selfish, cruel beast. The beast—the id—operates according to the **pleasure principle.** The id wants to obtain immediate pleasure and avoid pain regardless of how harmful it might be to others. But the id's selfishness is not its most alien characteristic to most of us. According to Freud, the id seeks to satisfy its desires in ways that are totally out of touch with reality. The id, in fact, has no conception whatsoever of reality. The id attempts to satisfy its needs using what Freud calls **primary process thinking**—by simply forming a wish-fulfilling *mental image* of the desired object. We use the primary process when we daydream about having sex or think about eating chocolate fudge cake, or angrily plan how to get revenge on the person who embarrassed us yesterday. Dreams are also a primary process means of fulfilling motives. The primary process satisfies motives through imagination rather than in reality.

id
According to Freud, the inborn part of the unconscious mind that uses the primary process to satisfy its needs and that acts according to the pleasure principle.

pleasure principle
According to Freud, the attempt of the id to seek immediate pleasure and avoid pain regardless of how harmful it might be to others.

primary process thinking
According to Freud, the attempt by the id to satisfy its needs by forming a wish-fulfilling mental image of the desired object.

But a person could not actually survive for long living by the pleasure principle (eventually you would get hurt if you fulfilled every selfish desire without regard for the feelings of others) or using only the primary process of wish fulfillment (forming a mental image of food will not meet the biological needs of the body for nutrition). Fortunately, during infancy, the period of time when we have only an id, we have adults around who see to it that our needs are realistically and safely met. As we grow up, our interactions with our parents and other parts of the real world lead us to convert part of the id into two other parts of the mind—the ego and the superego—that help us cope more effectively with the world. To borrow a phrase told to me by one of your instructors, the ego and superego help us "keep a lid on the id."

Ego: The Executive of Personality

The **ego** is formed because the id has to find realistic ways of meeting its needs and avoiding trouble caused by selfish and aggressive behavior. The ego operates according to the **reality principle.** This means that it holds the id in check until a safe and realistic way has been found to satisfy its motives. The id would be happy to form a mental image of a sex object, and when that was not wholly satisfying, it would want to immediately rape the object. The ego, on the other hand, holds the id in check long enough to charm and seduce the sex object. The ego's goal is to help the id fulfill its needs. It only opposes the id's wishes long enough to find a realistic way to satisfy them. The ego can be thought of as the *executive of the personality* because it uses its cognitive abilities to manage and control the id and balance its desires against the restrictions of reality and the superego.

ego
(ē´go) According to Freud, that part of the mind that uses the reality principle to satisfy the id.

reality principle
According to Freud, the attempt by the ego to find safe, realistic ways of meeting the needs of the id.

Superego: The Conscience and Ego Ideal

The id and ego have no morals. They seek to satisfy the id's selfish motives without regard for the good of others. The ego tries to be realistic about how those motives are satisfied. But as long as the needs are *safely* met, it does not care if rules are broken, lies are told, or

"Fifty is plenty,"
"Hundred and fifty."

Drawing by Bill Woodman; © 1979 The New Yorker Magazine, Inc.

superego
According to Freud, that part of the mind that opposes the desires of the id by enforcing moral restrictions and by striving to attain perfection.

conscience
According to Freud, the moral inhibitions of the superego.

ego ideal
According to Freud, the standard of perfect conduct of the superego.

displacement
(dis-plās´ment) A defense mechanism in which the individual directs aggressive or sexual feelings away from the primary object to someone or something safe.

other people are wronged. While each of us wants our desires to be satisfied immediately, if everyone acted in this manner simultaneously, society would fall into chaos.

Restrictions are placed on the actions of the id and ego when the **superego** develops, the part of the mind that opposes the desires of the id by enforcing moral restrictions and by striving to attain a goal of "ideal" perfection. Parents are the main agents of society in creating the superego. They teach moral principles to their children by punishing transgressions and rewarding proper behavior. These experiences become incorporated into the child's mind as the two parts of the superego. According to Freud, parental punishment creates the set of moral inhibitions known as the **conscience,** while their rewards set up a standard of perfect conduct in the superego called the **ego ideal.** These two parts of the superego work together by punishing behavior that breaks the moral code through guilt and rewarding good behavior through pride. As the superego develops strength, children are able to control themselves and behave in ways that allow society to function smoothly. According to Freud's view, most of us do not steal, murder, and rape not because we do not want to or because our egos could not find relatively safe ways to do so but because our superegos hold these desires in check.

Displacement and Identification: Becoming a Member of Society

The ego is not always able to find ways to satisfy id motives that avoid trouble and stay within the moral boundaries of the superego. Sometimes the ego must settle for a *substitute* for the goal of the id. A child who would really like to kick his father may have to settle for slugging his little brother instead. Or if his superego prohibits hurting his brother, he may have to kick his teddy bear. The process of substituting a more acceptable goal is called **displacement.**

In terms of the interests of society, the best kind of displacement is called **sublimation.** In this form of displacement, a socially desirable goal is substituted for a socially harmful goal. Competing in school is a sublimation of aggressive motives; painting nude portraits is a sublimation of sexual motives, and so on. Indeed, Freud believed that all of the cultural and economic achievements of society were the result of sublimation. Thus, the individual who sublimates id energy is not only able to fit into society but contributes to its advancement as well.

Another process that allows individuals to learn to operate in society without friction is **identification.** This term refers to the fact that we tend to base the way we think, act, and feel on other individuals who are successful in gaining satisfaction from life. According to Freud, this is more than just a superficial act of imitation; we incorporate the other person's goals, actions, and values into our personalities. Thus, children come to behave more like the adults they identify with. In this way, identification serves an important role in socializing children. Indeed, according to Freud, identification is the key step in the development of the superego. We do not fully incorporate the morals and goals of society until we identify with the same-sex parent and internalize his or her values and ideals.

Competition in sports is one way of sublimating unacceptable aggressive impulses, according to Freud.

Growing Up: The Stages of Psychosexual Development

Freud's theory of personality is a *developmental* theory. He believes that our personalities are formed as we pass through a series of developmental stages from infancy to adulthood. Events that happen as the individual passes through these stages can be critical in the formation of personality. Excessive punishment or reward from parents or traumatically stressful events experienced during a period of development can leave the person's personality "stuck" or *fixated* at that stage. This fixation of personality development will, according to Freud, leave a lifelong mark on the personality.

To Freud, the developmental stages represent a shifting of the primary outlet of id energy, particularly sexual energy, from one part of the body to another. For this reason, they are called **psychosexual stages.** The five stages of psychosexual development are as follows.

Oral Stage (Birth to 1 Year)

The infant's earliest source of id gratification is the mouth. During the **oral stage,** the infant gets pleasure from sucking and swallowing. Later when he has teeth, the infant enjoys the aggressive pleasure of biting and chewing. If the infant enjoys swallowing too much, however, she may fixate on this stage and become an **oral receptive personality** who continues to seek pleasure through the mouth by overeating and smoking and by being a gullible person who "swallows" ideas too easily.

If the infant's oral pleasures are frustrated, on the other hand, such as by a mother who sticks rigidly to a feeding schedule regardless of the infant's desire to eat, he may grow up to be a fixated **oral aggressive personality** who seeks aggressive pleasure through the mouth, for instance, by being verbally hostile to others. Similar fixations are possible at every stage of development.

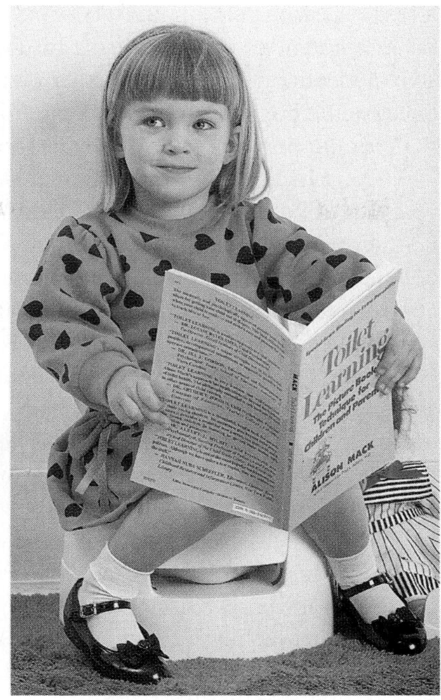

According to Freud, we pass through five developmental stages with the primary outlet of id energy or pleasure, moving from one part of the body to another. From ages 1 to 3, Freud believes we are in the anal stage.

Anal Stage (1 to 3 Years)

When parents decide to toilet-train their children during the **anal stage,** the children learn how much *control* they can exert over others with their anal sphincter muscles. Children can have the immediate pleasure of expelling feces, but that may cause their parents to punish them. If they delay gratification until they are on the toilet, children can gain the approval of their parents. According to Freud, excessive punishment of failures during toilet training may create a fixated personality that is either stingy, obstinate, stubborn, and compulsive (**anal retentive**) or cruel, pushy, messy, and disorderly (**anal expulsive**).

Phallic Stage (3 to 6 Years)

During the **phallic stage,** the genitals become the primary source of pleasure. According to Freud, the child begins to enjoy touching her or his own genitals and develops a sexual attraction to the parent of the opposite sex. Freud believed that the shift to genital pleasure goes on in the unconscious mind, so we are not consciously aware of the touching or the incestuous urges. Instead, the child merely feels an intense love for the opposite-sex parent: Daughters become "daddy's girl" and sons become "mommy's boy." These sexual attractions bring about the intense unconscious conflict that Freud calls the *Oedipus complex* for boys and the *Electra complex* for girls.

Freud borrowed the term **Oedipus complex** from the ancient Greek play *Oedipus Rex* by Sophocles. It tells the mythical story of an infant who was abandoned by the King and Queen of Thebes and grew up in a rival city. As a young man, not knowing who his parents are, Oedipus returns to Thebes, kills his father, and marries his mother. Freud believes that the play reveals a wish that is in all of us during the phallic stage of development.

According to Freud, all males unconsciously want to kill their fathers and sexually possess their mothers. Note that I said that this is an *unconscious* wish of which the boys are not consciously aware. Because such desires are unacceptable, they are blocked from consciousness. But the incestuous desires remain in the unconscious id where they cause considerable discomfort. The child unconsciously senses that if these hidden impulses ever become unleashed, he will enrage his father. A fear arises in the immature mind of the boy that his father will punish his sexual desires toward his mother by removing his genitals—

sublimation
(sub´´li-mā´shun) According to Freud, a form of displacement in which a socially desirable goal is substituted for a socially harmful goal; the best form of displacement for society as a whole.

identification
The tendency to base one's identity and actions on individuals who are successful in gaining satisfaction from life.

psychosexual stages
In the personality theory of Sigmund Freud, developmental periods during which the sexual energy of the id finds different sources of satisfaction.

oral stage
According to Freud, the first psychosexual stage (from birth to 1 year), in which id gratification is focused on the mouth.

oral receptive personality
A personality type in which the person seeks pleasure through overeating, smoking, and other oral means.

oral aggressive personality
A personality type in which the person seeks pleasure by being verbally hostile to others.

anal stage
According to Freud, the second psychosexual stage (from 1 to 3 years), in which gratification is focused on the anus.

anal retentive personality
A personality type based on anal fixation in which the person is stingy, obstinate, stubborn, and compulsive.

anal expulsive personality
A personality type based on anal fixation in which the person is cruel, pushy, messy, and disorderly.

phallic stage
(fal´ik) According to Freud, the third psychosexual stage (from 3 to 6 years), in which gratification is focused on the genitals.

Oedipus complex
(ed´i-pus) According to Freud, the unconscious wish of all male children to kill their fathers and sexually possess their mothers.

castration anxiety
(kas-trā´shun) According to Freud, the fear of a young boy that his father will punish his sexual desire for his mother by removing his genitals.

Electra complex
(e-lek´-trah) According to Freud, the transfer of a young girl's sexual desires from her mother to her father after she discovers she has no penis.

penis envy
According to Freud, the desire of a girl to possess a penis.

latency stage
According to Freud, the fourth psychosexual stage (from about 6 to 11 years), during which sexual energy is sublimated and converted into socially valued activities.

genital stage
(jen´i-tal) According to Freud, the psychosexual stage (from 11 years through adulthood), in which sexual and romantic interest is directed toward one's peers.

a fear called **castration anxiety.** This fear eventually leads the boy to repress desires for his mother and to avoid angering his father by identifying with him. As noted above, this step of identification with the father is crucial for the development of the superego to Freud, because the boy incorporates the moral values and ideals of the father when he identifies with him in the resolution that ends the Oedipal complex.

The **Electra complex** of female children is the counterpart of the male Oedipus complex in Freud's theory. In the Greek myth, Electra has an incestuous relationship with her father. When her mother finds out, she murders the father. The enraged daughter in turn convinces her brother to murder her mother. The Electra complex is one of Freud's most controversial doctrines, as contemporary readers find that it portrays women in an outrageously negative light (Chodorow, 1989).

In Freud's theory, the Electra complex begins with the girl's "upsetting" discovery that she does not have a penis, but has an empty space instead. According to Freud, the girl unconsciously concludes that she has been castrated and blames the mother for letting this happen. As a result she transfers her love and sexual desire from her mother to her father. In doing so, she hopes to share the father's valued penis because she has lost hers. The desire to possess a penis is termed **penis envy** by Freud.

However, the girl's sexual and emotional attachment to the father is too dangerous because of the prohibitions of society against her feelings. To resolve the Electra complex, therefore, her feelings for her father must be transformed into wholesome affection and she must accept that she is "inferior" like her mother and identify with her mother. In doing so, according to Freud, she will accept her role in society and develop her superego by incorporating the values of her mother.

Freud believes that females frequently fail to resolve the Electra complex because society allows her feelings toward her father to persist with less repression than in the male Oedipus complex. In addition, Freud felt that many women fail to identify fully with their mother because they resist the acceptance of their inherent "inferiority."

Latency Stage (6 to 11 Years)

The **latency stage** is that period of life from about age 6 to age 11 in which sexual interest is relatively inactive. Sexual desire has been strongly repressed through the resolution of the Oedipal or Electra complexes and is not a source of trouble at this time. Instead, sexual energy is being sublimated and converted into interest in schoolwork, riding bicycles, playing house, and sports. To pass successfully through this developmental period, the child must develop a certain degree of competence in these areas.

Genital Stage (11 Years On)

With the arrival of puberty and the **genital stage,** there is renewed interest in obtaining sexual pleasure through the genitals. Masturbation often becomes frequent and leads to orgasm for the first time. Sexual and romantic interest in others also becomes a central motive. But because the parents have been successfully ruled out as sex objects through the Oedipus and Electra complexes, the new sex objects are peers of about the same age.

Although some interpersonal relationships are entered into merely to obtain selfish genital pleasure, the individual who has reached the genital stage is able to care about the welfare of the loved one as much as or more than herself. This forms the basis for the more or less lasting relationships that characterize the genital stage and extend throughout adulthood. Sublimation continues to be important during this period as sexual and aggressive id motives become transformed into energy for marriage, occupations, and child rearing.

Theories Derived from Psychoanalysis

Psychoanalytic thinking continues to be important in some applied areas of contemporary psychology, especially clinical and counseling psychology, but mostly through revised versions of Freud's theory of personality. Some modern psychologists adhere to an orthodox version of psychoanalysis, but far more endorse somewhat newer versions that grew out of

Freudian thinking but differ on several major points. These revisions of psychoanalysis each differ from one another in some ways, but they share the common view that Freud placed too much emphasis on unconscious sexual motivation and aggression, gave too little importance to positive aspects of personality, underemphasized the importance of adequate social relationships, and was highly prejudicial toward women.

The revisions of Freud's thinking began in a storm that took place during his own lifetime. As Freud's fame spread throughout Europe, he developed a group of followers. But when two of these followers, Carl Jung and Alfred Adler, disagreed with Freud on the issue of sexual motivation, they were angrily dismissed from the loyal fold. Freud was an authoritarian individual who tolerated little disagreement from others.

Carl Jung (1875–1961)

Carl Jung

Carl Jung was a physician who had just begun his career working in a psychiatric hospital in Switzerland when he read Freud's most influential early work, *The Interpretation of Dreams*. He began to correspond with Freud and travel to Vienna for meetings. As Jung and Freud became friends, Jung joined the inner circle of Freud's followers as an influential member. Jung published a number of works that used Freud's ideas to explain aspects of severe mental illness, but gradually Jung came to question Freud's emphasis on sexual motivation. Within 7 years of their first meeting, these differences in opinion led to a severing of their personal and professional relationship.

Jung felt that Freud took a one-sided negative view of the human condition. Although Jung thought that the unconscious mind did contain selfish and hostile forces, he believed that it also contained positive, even spiritual, motives. In fact, a fundamental characteristic of the human mind to Jung was that all important elements came in the form of *opposites*. We possess the potential to be both good and evil, feminine and masculine, mother and father. The question is simply how much of each do we manifest in our personalities.

One of Jung's most original and lasting contributions to the understanding of personality is the pair of opposite personality traits known as *extroversion* and *introversion*. Each of us possesses a desire to be friendly, open to the things happening in the world, and concerned about others (**extroversion**); but each of us also possesses a tendency to focus our attention on ourselves, to be shy, and to meet our own needs (**introversion**). As with all of the polar opposites, Jung felt that it was important to allow a balance of these two opposing tendencies. We should not be too much of an introvert or too much of an extrovert.

Each of us, according to Jung, is a blend of extrovert and introvert. Jung felt that a balance of these two opposing tendencies is desirable.

Jung also modified Freud's view of the unconscious. He felt that we each possess both a *personal unconscious* and a *collective unconscious*. The **personal unconscious** contains those motives, conflicts, and information that we have repressed into unconsciousness because they are threatening to us. The **collective unconscious** is the unconscious mind with which all humans are born. He used the term *collective* to emphasize that its contents are the same for all humans. Much of his later career was devoted to blending his interest in psychology with his childhood interest in cultures from the past. He assembled a variety of evidence to suggest that every culture expresses the same sorts of unconscious motives in very much the same symbolic ways. For example, in Jung's view the sexual symbol of the phallus (the penis) has appeared in many cultures throughout history in the form of totem poles, scepters held by kings to symbolize authority, and structures such as the Washington Monument.

extroversion
(eks´´tro-ver´zhun) According to Jung, the tendency of some individuals to be friendly and open to the world.

introversion
(in-tro-ver´zhun) According to Jung, the tendency of some individuals to be shy and to focus their attention on themselves.

personal unconscious
According to Jung, the motives, conflicts, and information that are repressed by a person because they are threatening to that individual.

collective unconscious
According to Jung, the content of the unconscious mind with which all humans are born.

Alfred Adler

Alfred Adler was a young physician practicing medicine in Vienna when he was invited to join the Vienna Psychoanalytic Association. He soon became a favorite of Freud and was asked to be the second president of the society succeeding Freud himself. In time, however, the two argued over the publication policies of the association's journal and parted company. Differences between the psychological views of the two men had already become apparent, but they became increasingly obvious after the personal dispute.

Adler agreed with Freud that the struggle to come to grips with one's sexual and hostile impulses was important to the development of personality, but he did not feel it was

Alfred Adler (1870–1937)

Karen Horney (1885–1952)

feelings of inferiority
According to Adler, the feelings that result from children being less powerful than adults that must be overcome during the development of the healthy personality.

the most important factor. In his early career, Adler felt that the primary struggle in personality development was the effort to overcome **feelings of inferiority** in social relationships and to develop feelings of superiority. At first, he limited this view to individuals who were born with physical defects, as was Adler himself, but later he expanded this view to include physically normal individuals as well. Because we are all small and dependent on the protection of adults as children, we all begin life with feelings of inferiority. The task of personality development, according to Adler, is to outgrow the inferiority of childhood and to see ourselves as competent adults. Adler felt that the role of parents and other caretakers was so important in this crucial process that he devoted much of his time to the development of a preschool program that he thought fostered proper personality development. Even today, "Adlerian" preschools are popular in many parts of Europe and the United States.

Later in his career, Adler de-emphasized the importance of struggling to outgrow childhood feelings of inferiority. In fact, he felt that the effort to achieve feelings of superiority over other individuals was an essentially unhealthy motive. Instead, he focused on two other factors as the most important elements in personality development. First, Adler felt that all human beings are born with a positive motive, *social interest,* to establish loving, helpful relationships with other people. The full development of a healthy personality requires that the individual learn to express this motive fully in his or her relationships with others. This contrasted with Freud's belief that only selfish motives are inborn. Second, Adler felt that people's lives are governed by their *goals*. Often these goals are not realistic at all, but they regulate our actions anyway as we strive to achieve them. Adler's emphasis on goals, by giving such importance to a cognitive ego function, was also in sharp contrast to Freud's belief.

Karen Horney

German-born and educated physician Karen Horney became a leader in the revisions of psychoanalysis some 20 years after the first contributions of Jung and Adler. But, perhaps in part because she continued to write into the 1950s, she remains the most influential of the three. Readers today generally find her ideas more contemporary than those of Freud, Jung, or Adler. Horney considered herself to be a "Freudian" throughout her career because she agreed that unconscious conflicts were the source of most human misery and maladjustment. Like Jung and Adler, however, Horney felt that Freud placed too much importance on sexual conflicts. Moreover, she believed that conflict was not the inevitable result of inborn motives in the id. She believed instead that conflicts developed only as the result of inadequate child-rearing experiences. If the child feels loved and secure, no conflicts will develop and positive aspects of the personality will dominate. If, however, the child loses confidence in parental love—because of the parent's indifference, harshness, overprotection, or other reasons—the child becomes anxiously insecure. And this anxious insecurity is the source of all conflicts. For example, an insecure individual may develop a need to be "perfect" and feel tormented by all revelations that he is not. Another individual may aggressively push away the affection of others out of fear that they, too, will not consistently love her, but the need to push away others is in deep conflict with the underlying need to be loved.

Horney was also an important critic of Freud's view of women. She rejected Freud's notion that penis envy is the central feature of the feminine psychological makeup. She felt that the issue was not envy of the penis or of masculinity per se but of the power and privilege of the male role in society.

Most contemporary psychoanalytic psychologists have continued to revise the theories of Freud in much the same directions. Writers such as Erich Fromm, Harry Stack Sullivan, and Erik Erikson (the latter theorist's views were presented in chapters 8 and 9 because of their relevance to development across the life span) have continued to develop the neo-Freudian view of personality. They revise Freud's image of women, de-emphasize the importance of sexual and aggressive motives, emphasize positive aspects of personality, and assert the importance of adequate social relationships.

Review

Sigmund Freud's theory of personality grew out of his early interest in the cause of the unusual symptoms of some of his patients. He decided that, since they had no conscious reason to have such symptoms, the cause must be unconscious, specifically repressed sexual or aggressive desires. Through the course of many years of treating patients with a variety of psychological problems, Freud came to believe that unconscious motives, particularly sexual and aggressive ones, were the source of most aspects of our personalities. Freud divided the mind into three levels of consciousness (conscious, preconscious, and unconscious) and into three parts with different functions (id, ego, and superego). The id is the storehouse of the unconscious sexual and aggressive instincts, and the inborn, selfish part of the mind that operates according to the pleasure principle. The id seeks immediate satisfaction of its needs without concern for the welfare of others. The ego is the executive of the personality, which controls the id through adherence to the reality principle; it seeks to satisfy the needs of the id in ways that are both realistic and safe. The superego represents society's rules of right and wrong that often hold the id in check, not on the basis of what is realistic but on what is moral.

The process of becoming an acceptable member of society is aided by the psychological processes of displacement and identification. When it's too dangerous to directly satisfy an id motive, the motive is displaced on a safer, substitute goal. The most desirable form of displacement from society's perspective is sublimation, in which dangerous motives are transformed into socially desirable motives. The process of identification with social models further aids the individual's acceptance as a member of society by leading to the full development of the superego.

Sexual energy is transformed during the life span in yet another way. As the individual matures from infancy to adulthood, the principal means of obtaining sexual pleasure shifts from one part of the body to another. Pleasure shifts from the mouth to the anus and then to the genitals; it passes through a period when it lies more or less dormant and then reemerges as genital sexuality. Abnormal experiences at any of these stages can lead to fixations that hinder the full development of an effective personality.

Following the lead of Jung, Adler, and Horney, who broke away from orthodox psychoanalytic views during Freud's lifetime, contemporary psychoanalysts generally deemphasize the importance of sexual and aggressive motives. They have revised Freud's view of the inferiority of women, have emphasized the importance of social relationships in personality formation, and have stated that Freud overlooked important positive aspects of our personalities.

Thinking Critically About Psychology

1. Does Freud's theory describe human behavior only for Europeans and Americans of his era or does it apply to people of any generation or culture?
2. Why do you think Karen Horney and Sigmund Freud had such different views of women?

Check Your Learning

To be sure that you have learned the key points from the preceding section, cover the answers below and try to answer each question. If you give an incorrect answer to any question, return to the page given next to the correct answer to see why your answer was not correct. Remember that these questions cover only some of the important information in this section; it is important that you make up your own questions to check your learning of other facts and concepts.

1. One's ____________________ is the sum total of all of the ways of acting, thinking, and feeling that are *typical* for that person and make that person *different* from all other individuals.

2. The __________ mind is the part of the mind containing information that is not presently conscious but can be easily brought into consciousness.

   a. conscious
   b. preconscious
   c. unconscious
   d. suppressed

Check Your Learning—continued

3. According to Freud, the ________ is the inborn part of the unconscious mind that uses the primary process to satisfy its needs and that acts according to the pleasure principle.

   a. id **c.** superego
   b. ego **d.** reality principle

4. To Freud, the five developmental stages represent a shifting of the primary outlet of id energy, particularly sexual energy, from one part of the body to another. For this reason, they are called ________________ .

5. Carl Jung disagreed with Freud's one-sided negative view of the human condition and proposed that all important elements came in the form of ________ such as introversion and extroversion, good and evil.

   a. positive conditions **c.** opposites
   b. synonyms **d.** matches

Correct Answers
1. personality (p. 400), **2.** b (p. 402), **3.** a (p. 403), **4.** psychosexual stages (p. 404), **5.** c (p. 407).

SOCIAL LEARNING THEORY: ALBERT BANDURA

The social learning view of personality is vastly different from that of the psychoanalysts. Little or no attention is paid to topics such as instincts, the unconscious mind, or the developmental stages that are of primary importance to psychoanalysis. Instead, social learning theorists focus on a psychological process that is largely ignored by psychoanalysts, *learning.* To the social learning theorist, personality is simply something that is learned; it's the sum total of all the ways we have learned to act, think, and feel. Because personality is learned from other people in society, the term *social learning* is used.

social learning theory
The viewpoint that the most important parts of our behavior are learned from other persons in society—family, friends, and culture.

Social learning theory had its origins in the behavioral writings of Ivan Pavlov, John B. Watson, and B. F. Skinner. Each of these theorists argued that personality is no more than learned behavior and that the way to understand personality is simply to understand the processes of learning. To social learning theorists, the key concepts in the study of personality are not id, ego, and superego, but classical conditioning, operant conditioning, and modeling, which were discussed in chapter 5. We will not repeat our discussion of these principles here, but it may be helpful for you to glance back over this material.

Role of Learning in Personality

In the social learning theory view, a person will develop an adequate personality only if he or she is exposed to good models and is reinforced for appropriate behavior. An inadequate learning environment, on the other hand, will result in inadequate personality development.

A study by Susan Mineka of Northwestern University of the origins of fear provides a good example of the social learning position (Mineka, Davidson, Cook, & Keir, 1984). This study examined the learning of snake fears in rhesus monkeys (because researchers cannot ethically expose human children to social situations that may transmit fears), but the results may well apply to humans as well. Mineka and colleagues found that young monkeys who had been raised in a laboratory—and had never seen a snake—could learn to fear snakes through modeling. Although none of the monkeys showed fear of snakes when initially tested, they showed a strong and lasting fear after observing older monkeys (who had been raised in the wild and feared snakes) react fearfully to live or toy snakes. Simply seeing an adult react fearfully transmitted the fear to the younger monkeys and changed the monkey's "personality" in this specific way. To the social learning theorist, personality is formed through many such learning experiences.

Albert Bandura (1925–)

The leading figure in social learning theory today and the person who gave the theory its name is Stanford University psychologist Albert Bandura (1977, 1989). In one sense, Bandura is very much a behaviorist. He agrees with the view that personality is the sum total of learned behavior. But he broke with traditional behaviorism in two main ways: (a) he sees people as playing an active role in determining their own actions, rather than being passively acted upon by the learning environment, and (b) he emphasizes the importance of cognition in personality.

Bandura (1977) portrays us as playing an active role in our own lives by stating that social learning is an example of **reciprocal determination:** Not only is a person's behavior learned, but the social learning environment is altered by the person's behavior (see fig. 11.2). The environment that we learn from, after all, is made up of people. If we behave toward them in a timid way, or a friendly way, or a hostile way, those people will react in very different ways to us—and will hence be teaching us very different things about social relationships. The aggressive, overconfident person will learn that the world is a cold, rejecting place; the friendly person will learn that the world is warm and loving. Personality is learned behavior, but it is also behavior that influences future learning experiences.

reciprocal determination
(re-sip´´ro-kal) Bandura's observation that the individual's behavior and the social learning environment continually influence one another.

Role of Cognition in Personality

According to Bandura, our cognitions are also a prime determinant of our behavior. A person who believes that helping others makes them less self-reliant will be stingy; and a person who thinks that other people find her boring will act quiet and shy. Bandura (1982) places particular emphasis on our cognitions about our ability to handle the demands of life. In his terms, **self-efficacy** is the perception that one is capable of doing what is necessary to reach one's goals—both in the sense of knowing what to do and being emotionally able to do it. People who perceive themselves as self-efficacious accept greater challenges, expend more effort, and may be more successful in reaching their goals as a result. A person with a poor sense of self-efficacy about social poise may not accept a promotion at work because it would involve giving many speeches and having to negotiate with dignitaries.

self-efficacy
According to Bandura, the perception of being capable of achieving one's goals.

FIGURE 11.2
Social learning theorists believe in reciprocal determination; we learn our behavior from interactions with other persons, but our behavior influences how other persons interact with us.

Although our perceptions of self-efficacy are learned from what others say about us, our direct experiences of success and failure, and other sources, these cognitions continue to influence our behavior "from the inside out."

Bandura (1977, 1989) also emphasizes the learning of personal standards of reward and punishment by which we judge our own behavior. We learn our personal standards from observing the personal standards that other people model and from the standards that others use when rewarding or punishing us. But, although we are the passive recipients of these standards in a sense, we then actively use them to govern our own behavior in the process that Bandura calls **self-regulation.** When we behave in ways that meet our personal standards, we cognitively pat ourselves on the back—we reinforce ourselves. We generally do not actually say to ourselves, "Good going, fellow, you did okay!" Rather, we feel a self-reinforcing sense of pride or happiness when we have met our standards (like Freud's ego ideal). Conversely, we punish ourselves (feel guilty, disappointed) when we fail to meet our personal standards (like Freud's conscience). In these ways, self-regulation serves much the same purpose as Freud's superego.

self-regulation
According to Bandura, the process of cognitively reinforcing and punishing our own behavior, depending on whether it meets our personal standards.

Like the most recent neo-Freudian versions of psychoanalytic theory, social learning theorists view the primary challenge of personality development as the development of adequate social relationships. To do this, the person must *learn* both appropriate ways to relate to other people and appropriate *cognitions* (beliefs, expectations) about himself or herself and about relationships with others. Adequate social relationships are important not only because few people are happy without them but also because they influence the process of social learning.

Review

Albert Bandura is the leading proponent of social learning theory. Although this approach to personality theory grew out of the behaviorism of Pavlov, Watson, and Skinner, Bandura expanded behavioral thinking by emphasizing the importance of cognition in personality and the active role played by individuals in the social learning process. To the social learning theorist, the process of learning is of central importance to personality development. The relatively consistent pattern of acting, thinking, and feeling that we refer to as personality is the result of learning from our experiences with other members of society and the cognitions we learn in that process that influence future behavior.

Thinking Critically About Psychology

1. How might you use Bandura's theory of personality to help you better understand your own personality?

2. What methods might a social learning theorist suggest for increasing our own sense of self-efficacy?

Check Your Learning

To be sure that you have learned the key points from the preceding section, cover the answers below and try to answer each question. If you give an incorrect answer to any question, return to the page given next to the correct answer to see why your answer was not correct.

1. ________________ is the theory that our personalities are formed primarily through learning from other members of society where the key concepts are classical conditioning, operant conditioning, and modeling.

2. Albert Bandura suggests that social learning is __________: Not only is a person's behavior learned, but the social learning environment is altered by the person's behavior.

a. bilateral
b. reciprocally determined
c. bipolar
d. interactive

3. According to Bandura, __________ is the belief that one is capable of doing what is necessary to reach one's goals.

a. cognition
b. self-regulation
c. confidence
d. self-efficacy

Check Your Learning—continued

4. According to Bandura, our cognitions are also a prime determinant of our behavior. The concept of self-regulation illustrates this point.

   a. True   b. False

Correct Answers

1. Social learning theory (p. 410). 2. b (p. 411). 3. d (p. 411). 4. a (p. 412).

HUMANISTIC THEORY: MASLOW AND ROGERS

The **humanistic theory** of psychology is often referred to as the *third force* in psychology. Although it has deep historical roots in philosophy, it has only been since the 1950s that humanism has become an influential movement in psychology. As influential as this approach to personality is, however, it's the least unified and well defined of the three major viewpoints. This lack of unity is probably due less to the newness of humanistic psychology than to its origins. Each of the other two schools of thought began with the ideas of a single person. Although the views of the original leaders were subsequently revised by later followers, the original writings of Pavlov and Freud gave a certain unity to the theories that followed. Humanistic theory, on the other hand, emerged from the writings of a number of figures who shared a few basic concepts.

humanistic theory
The psychological view that human beings possess an innate tendency to improve and to determine their lives by the decisions they make.

The founders of humanistic psychology include Carl Rogers, Abraham Maslow, Victor Frankl, Virginia Satir, Fritz Perls, and Rollo May, to name only a few. It's impossible, therefore, to write a single statement that adequately summarizes the humanistic approach to personality. For this reason, we focus primarily on the views of Carl Rogers and secondarily on the views of Abraham Maslow, emphasizing the parts of their theories that are consistent with the views of humanists in general.

Inner-Directedness and Subjectivity

Humanists believe that humans possess an internal force, an **inner-directedness,** that pushes them to grow, to improve, and to become the best individuals they are capable of being. People have the freedom to make choices, and they are generally pretty good at making intelligent choices that further their personal growth. This inner-directedness is the primary force behind the development of personality.

inner-directedness
A force that humanists believe all people possess that internally leads them to grow and improve.

Obviously, humanists have a positive view of the human species, but they are not blind to the fact that life is a struggle for everyone at some point and that many people consistently make a mess of their lives. We lose our ability to grow and to make good choices when we live with critical, rejecting people or when society tries to force us to be something that we are not. And, as Maslow has pointed out, the transition to higher motives is stunted when more basic motives are unsatisfied.

The personality that develops through the positive push of inner-directedness can only be understood "from the inside out," that is, from the perspective of the individual. To the humanist, the only reality is **subjective.** Everyone views life in somewhat different, highly personal terms. What is real for you may not be real for me. You may see people as basically immoral, whereas I see them as basically moral. Each person's personality is a direct reflection of the individual's subjective view of reality. Our consistent ways of acting, thinking, and feeling reflect our unique perceptions of what life is all about. And, as we will see in the next section, no subjective view of reality is more important to humanistic theorists than our subjective view of ourselves.

subjective reality
Each person's unique perception of reality that, according to humanists, plays a key role in organizing our personalities.

The Self-Concept

The concept of the "self" is central to the personality theory of Carl Rogers and other humanists. Our **self-concept** is our subjective perception of who we are and what we are like. Of all of our subjective views of life, our view of ourself is most important to our personalities.

self-concept
Our subjective perceptions of who we are and what we are like.

Carl Rogers (1902–1987)

The concept of self is learned from our interactions with others: You might learn that you are a good athlete by seeing that you run faster than most other people or by your parents telling you that you are a good athlete.

Rogers distinguishes between two self-concepts. There is the **self**—the person I think I am—and the **ideal self**—the person I wish I were. For example, I am pretty sure I can never be better than a "C" class racquetball player (self), but I would *love* to win tournaments in the "A" class (ideal self). On a higher plane, I see myself as a fairly nice person, but I wish I could learn to be less selfish at times. Rogers' concept of the ideal self is very similar to Freud's ego ideal.

self
According to humanists, the person one thinks he or she is.

ideal self
According to humanists, the person one wishes he or she were.

Both self-concepts are so important that psychological problems can arise from either of two difficulties with the self and ideal self. First, excessive discrepancies between the self and the ideal self can be uncomfortable. It's okay for the ideal self to be slightly out of reach—that can stimulate us to improve ourselves. But if the ideal self is so unrealistically perfect that we know it can never be reached, then we feel like failures.

A study by Timothy Strauman (1992) at the University of Wisconsin confirmed this notion. Students in introductory psychology classes were interviewed and tested to determine whether there were discrepancies between the way they view themselves (their concept of self) and the way that they think they would like to be or ought to be (two aspects of the ideal self). Students who saw themselves as different from the way that they would like to be were more likely to experience sadness in their lives, and students who saw themselves as different from the way they ought to be were more likely to be anxious. Very similar results were found in an almost identical study conducted at the University of Iowa (Scott & O'Hara, 1993).

Second, an inaccurate self-concept can also cause problems. If our view of our "selves" is not reasonably *congruent* (similar to the way we actually act, think, and feel), then we will develop an obscured view of ourselves. For example, if I see myself as totally free from prejudice, but I feel a twinge of resentment when someone from a minority group gets preference over me in a job promotion, then my feelings of resentment would not "fit" my self-concept. According to Rogers, I might deny those feelings that are incongruent with my self-concept by not admitting them to awareness. In Rogers' terms, we are aware of feelings and information only when they are mentally **symbolized.** The failure to symbolize parts of our experience is harmful not only because it leads to inaccurate concepts of self, but also because feelings can continue to influence us, often in conflicting or anxiety-provoking ways, even when we are not aware of them.

symbolization
In Rogers' theory, the process of representing experience, thoughts, or feelings in mental symbols of which we are aware.

We also begin to deny awareness to some of our feelings and experiences as a result of our parents' reactions to our behavior. By reacting with warmth and praise to some of our actions (sharing a toy with little sister), but with coldness and punishment to others (hitting little sister with the toy), our parents create **conditions of worth.** They let us know that they find us "worthy" under some conditions and "unworthy" under other conditions. We internalize many of these and perceive ourselves as worthwhile only when we act and feel in accordance with those conditions. Furthermore, we often deny feelings that are inconsistent with the internalized conditions of worth. The child, for example, may not symbolize her hostile feelings toward her sister, robbing herself of a valuable bit of self-awareness.

conditions of worth
The standards used by others or ourselves in judging our worth.

Rogers' concept of unsymbolized feelings is similar in some ways to Freud's view of repressed feelings. Both can continue to influence the person, often in a harmful manner. But Freud views some repression as a necessary part of life, whereas Rogers believes that lack of awareness is always harmful. If we are to allow full expression to our inner-directed tendency to grow, we must be fully aware of (symbolize) all of our feelings and experiences. Only in this way can we accurately understand and accept ourselves for exactly what we are (while always striving to do better).

Self-Actualization

A major tenet of humanistic psychology is that humans possess an inner drive to grow, improve, and use their potential to the fullest. Abraham Maslow calls the ultimate in completed growth **self-actualization.** According to Maslow, the self-actualizing person is reaching the highest level of personal development and has fully realized her or his potential as a human being. What is a self-actualizing person like? Maslow (1967, 1970) gives the following description.

self-actualization
According to Maslow, the seldomly reached full result of the inner-directed drive of humans to grow, improve, and use their potential to the fullest.

1. The self-actualizing person has reached a high level of moral development and is more concerned about the welfare of friends, loved ones, and humanity than self.
2. The self-actualizing person is usually committed to some cause or task, rather than working for fame or money.
3. Life is experienced in intense, vivid, absorbing ways, often with a sense of unity with nature.
4. Self-actualizing people are open and honest and have the courage to act on their convictions even if it means being unpopular.
5. Self-actualizing individuals are not particularly interested in fads, fashion, and social customers, and often appear unorthodox.
6. Self-actualizing individuals enjoy friends but are not dependent on their company or approval; they enjoy privacy and independence. On the other hand, their feelings for their close friends are intensely positive and caring.
7. Life is always challenging and fresh to the self-actualizing person.
8. They have an accurate, rather than a romanticized, view of people and life, yet they are positive about life.
9. Self-actualizing individuals are spontaneous and natural in their actions and feelings.

Abraham Maslow (1908–1970)

Do not despair if you do not compare too well against Maslow's list. For one thing, self-actualization is at the end of a lifelong process of improvement according to Maslow. You just may not have gotten there yet! Remember, too, from the chapter on motivation that *all* lower-level motives must be satisfied before a person can proceed toward self-actualization. If you are like most of us, you still have an unmet motive or two that is blocking your full development. Maslow felt that there are really very few self-actualizing individuals in the world. He identified a few that he thought probably were and studied them. His list included Albert Einstein, Eleanor Roosevelt, and Ludwig van Beethoven.

Maslow believed that we partially actualized souls get an occasional glimpse of what it is like to be self-actualizing in what he calls **peak experiences.** These are intensely moving, pleasurable, beautiful experiences when a person is fully absorbed in the experience, forgets his or her selfish interests, and feels a sense of unity with the world. These experiences can occur when looking at the stars, watching the birth of a baby, making love with your beloved, or even during something mundane like taking a shower. Most of us will experience some peak experiences in our lifetime, but Maslow tells us that they are more common for self-actualizing individuals.

peak experience
An intensely moving experience in which the individual feels a sense of unity with the world.

Albert Einstein (1879–1955)

Eleanor Roosevelt (1884–1962)

Ludwig van Beethoven (1770–1827)

TABLE 11.1 Comparison of Psychoanalytic, Social Learning, and Humanistic Theories of Personality

	Psychoanalytic	Social Learning	Humanistic
An "unconscious" or "unsymbolized" mind exerts a powerful influence on us.	Yes	No	Yes
We learn what is "good" and "bad" from our families and cultures.	Yes	Yes	Yes
Our internalized knowledge of what is "good" and "bad" is an important part of our personalities.	Yes (superego and ego ideal)	Yes (self-regulation)	Yes (ideal self)
People are inherently . . .	Selfish and evil	Neither good nor bad	Good
Society . . .	Usually teaches us to convert our selfish nature into positive behavior	Can influence us in either positive or negative ways	Often harms or destroys our inherent tendency to be healthy and good

Humanism Compared with Psychoanalysis and Social Learning Theory

Humanism, psychoanalysis, and social learning theory differ from one another in their views of the basic nature of human beings and of society. In psychoanalytic theory, people are seen as selfish and hostile at birth; they are nothing but id. Society is seen as a good force that instills the ego and superego into children, thus enabling them to behave realistically and morally enough to live in the social world.

To the humanist, the psychoanalytic view is exactly wrong. People possess a positive inborn drive to grow and improve. Instead of being born evil, the human is born basically good. Society, on the other hand, is seen by the humanist as a frequently destructive force that leads people to deny their true feelings (of jealousy, insecurity, passion) and creates unattainable ideal self-concepts (for example, American society tells us that we should all be attractive, athletic, sexy, famous, and rich).

Social learning theorists differ from psychoanalytic and humanistic theorists in their evaluation of the basic nature of humans and society. Social learning theorists see humans as neutral at birth, having the potential to learn to be either good or bad. Similarly, society can be either destructive or constructive. A part of society that teaches inappropriate behavior to its children is destructive, while a part of society that teaches appropriate behavior is constructive.

All three theories, however, believe that we internalize society's standards of what is desirable and moral and guide our behavior accordingly. Freud spoke of the conscience and ego ideal of the superego, Bandura used the concept of self-regulation, and Rogers spoke in terms of the ideal self. Although they differ in important ways, these are highly similar ideas about why we tend to obey the rules and standards of society. For a comparison of all three theories, see table 11.1.

For the most part, however, the three major contemporary theories of personality differ in many fundamental ways. Psychology was born in a state of disagreement—remember, there were many different "founders"—and we may always have to live with disagreements. When you are dealing with a subject as complicated and emotionally compelling as human beings, disagreements are to be expected.

Thinking Critically About Psychology

1. If, as the humanistic perspective suggests, reality is subjective, how can individuals ever hope to agree on anything?

2. Why do you think that humanistic, psychoanalytic, and social learning theories disagree so fundamentally about human nature?

Review

Humanism is the least unified of the three movements; but several basic concepts about personality are shared by nearly all humanists. The most significant factor in the development of personality is the positive inner-directed drive to grow and improve. Unless our

Review—continued

experiences with society interfere with this drive, it can be counted on to direct personal growth in positive directions. The personality that develops from this growth can be understood only from the point of view of the individual. Personality is seen as reflecting each person's subjective view of reality. We act, think, and feel in accordance with how we view reality. And the most important aspect of that view of reality is our subjective concept of self. The ways I view both the self that I think I am and the self I would like to be are powerful determinants of my personality. If my ideal self is unattainably perfect, I will always fall painfully short of my standards. If my self-concept is inaccurate, I will not be able to deal with information about myself that is incongruent with my self-concept. Incongruent information is not admitted to consciousness, a state of affairs that humanists view as unhealthy for the personality.

Humanists, psychoanalysts, and social learning theorists take very different views of the basic nature of people and society. Psychoanalysts view humans as wholly selfish and hostile ids at birth. Society, in contrast, is seen as a positive force providing experiences that create the ego and superego that allow humans to function effectively in society. Humanists view people as essentially good but see society as a negative force that often interferes with the individual's inner-directed growth. Social learning theorists see people as having the potential to develop in either positive or negative ways depending on whether their personality was learned from positive or negative aspects of society.

Check Your Learning

To be sure that you have learned the key points from the preceding section, cover the answers below and try to answer each question. If you give an incorrect answer to any question, return to the page given next to the correct answer to see why your answer was not correct.

1. According to ________ theory, human beings possess an innate tendency to improve and to determine their lives by the decisions they make.

a. social learning
b. psychoanalytic
c. humanistic
d. conditioning

2. According to the humanists, the ________ is the person one wishes he or she were.

a. real self
b. ideal self
c. new self
d. self

3. Our ________ is our subjective perception of who we are and what we are like.

a. self-concept
b. ideal self
c. self efficacy
d. actualized self

4. Humanists believe that humans are born neither good or evil.

a. True
b. False

Correct Answers

1. c (p. 413), 2. b (p. 414), 3. a (p. 413), 4. b (p. 416).

TRAITS AND SITUATIONS: DESCRIBING THE CONSISTENCIES OF PERSONALITY

Psychologists of all three theoretical persuasions are often called upon to *describe* an individual's personality. What is the best way to do this? How can an individual's entire personality be reduced to a few words? Typically, we use terms like *friendly, aggressive, flirtatious,* and *fearful.* We are so fond of describing people in such terms, in fact, that there

traits
Relatively enduring and consistent ways of thinking, acting, and feeling that are believed by some theorists to be the basic units of personality.

are more than 17,000 words for them in the English language (Allport & Odbert, 1936). In psychological terms, these words refer to **traits.** Traits are defined as relatively enduring and consistent ways of behaving. When we say that a person has the trait of friendliness, for example, we mean that she is friendly to most people in most situations and that her friendliness does not change much as time goes by.

Trait Theories of Personality

Some psychologists have developed their ideas about traits to the extent that they are considered to be theories of personality, but they are not theories in the same sense as the psychoanalytic, social learning, and humanistic theories of personality just discussed. Trait theories are more concerned with *describing* the nature and operation of traits than *explaining* their origins. For example, Freud postulated that stinginess had its origins in the anal stage of psychosexual development (explanation). Trait theorists, in contrast, would be more concerned with whether stinginess actually was a trait, how it relates to other traits, and the like (description). Although there are many important trait theories of personality, the best known are those of Gordon Allport and Raymond B. Cattell.

Gordon Allport (1897–1967)

Allport's Trait Theory

Allport (1937, 1961) believed that the most important traits were those motivational traits related to our *values.* Allport tells us that the best way to understand people and predict how they will behave in the future is to find out what they value—the things that they will strive to attain. A person who values money more than family life, for example, can be expected to accept a promotion that would mean greater pay but would require spending more time away from home. A person who values family life over money, in contrast, could be predicted to make the opposite decision.

An important topic to all trait theorists is the ways that traits are related to one another and are organized. Because humans distinguish so many different traits in one another, each trait theorist has tried to reduce this confusing complexity by showing that some traits are more important than others. Allport (1961) believed that traits could be ranked in terms of their importance as *cardinal, central,* or *secondary*. Cardinal traits are those that dominate a person's life. The quest for knowledge could be said to be one of the cardinal traits that dominated Albert Einstein's life, while the desire for social justice dominated Mahatma Gandhi's behavior. Allport felt that relatively few people possess such cardinal traits. Much more common, however, are the central traits. These are important traits that influence and organize much of our behavior. For example, one person's behavior might mostly be aimed at obtaining intimacy and sexual gratification. Another person, on the other hand, may be relatively uninterested in intimacy or sex but may strongly desire power and prestige. Secondary traits are much more specific (such as being rude to door-to-door salespeople) and much less important to a comprehensive description of a person's personality.

Allport's distinction between cardinal, central, and secondary traits helps us sift through the many possible ways of describing and understanding an individual's personality. Unfortunately, there can be no fixed list of cardinal or central traits because they differ from person to person. One individual may have no cardinal traits at all, while another person does, and what is a central trait in me may be a secondary trait in you. Furthermore, Allport believes that although some traits can be found in all people (the *common traits*), other traits are found only in some individuals (the *personal dispositions*).

Cattell's Trait Theory

Another influential trait theory of personality is the more recent theory of Raymond B. Cattell (1950, 1966, 1982). Cattell has made extensive use of sophisticated statistical techniques to identify traits; as a result, his theory aspires to much greater mathematical precision than Allport's. Like Allport, he believes that motivational traits related to values (which Cattell calls *dynamic* traits) are important in understanding personality, but he also emphasizes two other types of traits. *Ability* traits relate to our effectiveness in satisfying motives, such as intelligence, social skills, and the like. *Temperament* traits describe largely inherited aspects of our behavior, such as energy level, speed of action, and emotional reactivity.

Like Allport, Cattell attempts to reduce the confusion inherent in the description of traits by specifying some as more important than others. *Surface* traits are relatively unimportant clusters of behaviors that appear to go together, whereas *source* traits are the more important underlying traits on which the surface traits are based. Cattell has identified 16 source traits and has developed a personality test to measure them (Cattell, Saunders, & Stice, 1950).

The Five-Factor Model of Personality Traits

Over the years, many trait models like those of Allport and Cattell have been proposed, each stating that a different set of traits best describes our personalities. None of these models of personality was widely accepted in psychology, however, until recent years. Thanks in part to improvements in statistical methods and experimental strategies used to study personality traits, there is now considerable consensus among trait theorists that five basic traits provide a complete description of our personalities (Goldberg, 1993; McCrae & Costa, 1987; Wiggins & Pincus, 1992).

The so-called "big five" personality traits are described in table 11.2. The most important adjectives that describe each trait are listed under the overall label of the trait. Notice that the adjectives are listed as opposites. Personality tests have been developed to measure these five traits. The goal is to use information that the person taking the test gives to determine whether the person is, for example, more "calm or worrying" or more "at ease or high-strung." Then an overall score would be generated from these items to yield a description of the person on that trait and the other traits. For example, a person who revealed himself or herself as worrying, nervous, high-strung, insecure, and self-conscious would be considered to be high on neuroticism. A person who answered questions on the

TABLE 11.2 Brief Description of the "Big Five" Personality Traits

1. Neuroticism			4. Agreeableness		
Calm	versus	Worrying	Irritable	versus	Good-natured
At-ease	versus	Nervous	Ruthless	versus	Soft-hearted
Relaxed	versus	High-strung	Selfish	versus	Selfless
Secure	versus	Insecure	Callous	versus	Sympathetic
Comfortable	versus	Self-conscious	Vengeful	versus	Forgiving
2. Extroversion			**5. Conscientiousness**		
Retiring	versus	Sociable	Negligent	versus	Conscientious
Sober	versus	Fun loving	Careless	versus	Careful
Reserved	versus	Affectionate	Undependable	versus	Reliable
Quiet	versus	Talkative	Lazy	versus	Hardworking
Loner	versus	Joiner	Disorganized	versus	Well organized
3. Openness					
Conventional	versus	Original			
Down-to-earth	versus	Imaginative			
Uncreative	versus	Creative			
Narrow interests	versus	Broad interests			
Unadventurous	versus	Daring			

personality test indicating that she or he was calm, at ease, relaxed, secure, and comfortable, would be considered to be very low in neuroticism. Most people, of course, would be somewhere in between.

These five basic traits are thought to be quite stable across the life span (McRae & Costa, 1994) and to be the result of both inheritance and life experiences (Zuckerman, 1995).

As I said, there is considerable agreement among trait theorists that these five traits are the basic units of personality, leading to renewed excitement in research on this topic in recent years (Goldberg, 1993). Be cautious as you look at table 11.2, however. Please resist the temptation to seriously evaluate your own personality using this brief description of the traits. It is difficult to evaluate ourselves accurately under any circumstance, but formal personality tests have the advantage of being able to compare your answers with those of many other persons who have taken the test to put your answers in context. Furthermore, as we will see in the remaining parts of this chapter, there are many reasons to be a bit skeptical about personality traits and the tests that measure them.

Situationism and Interactionism

Skinner (1953), Mischel (1968; Mischel & Shoda, 1995), and others have argued strongly against the concept of traits, however. They suggest that behavior is determined by the situations people find themselves in, not traits inside the person. This viewpoint, known as **situationism,** suggest that our behavior is consistent only as long as our situations remain consistent. These situations generally involve other people. A person might be friendly most of the time to her husband and nice neighbors, but cold and distant to her spiteful and gossipy coworkers and stiff and formal with her boss. A woman might be conventional and hardworking for years, but become carefree and eccentric after her divorce. According to the situational view, people behave in ways that suit their situations, and—since situations are apt to change—behavior cannot be consistent enough to be adequately described in terms of traits.

situationism
(sit´´ū-ā´shun-izm) The view that behavior is not consistent but is strongly influenced by different situations.

More recently, social learning theorists have suggested a compromise between the trait and situationism positions (Bandura, 1977; Mischel, 1984). Not only is it a logical compromise, but considerable evidence supports the validity of this view (Bowers, 1973; Buss, 1989). The compromise view, known as **person x situation interactionism,** suggests that our behavior is influenced by a combination of characteristics of the person's traits *and* the situation. You might know somebody who is friendly and even fairly dominant when alone with you, but painfully shy in a group. Or you might know somebody who is fairly quiet and dull in a one-to-one conversation but a witty, vibrant conversationalist at crowded parties. The important point about these two people is that although the situations changed them both (alone with you versus the crowded party), it changed them in *different* ways. People are influenced by situations, it's true, but different individuals are affected by situations in different ways. That is the point of interactionism. The only way to fully describe a person's personality is to describe both the person's personal characteristics and how the person behaves in different situations.

person × situation interactionism
(in´´ter-ak´shun-izm) The view that behavior is influenced by a combination of the characteristics of both the person and the situation.

The interaction between personal characteristics and situations is somewhat more complicated than it first appears for two reasons. First, people play a role in selecting and even creating the situations in which they live. For example, a very shy person may avoid social situations, whereas an aggressive person would tend to seek out challenging situations and may even provoke hostile encounters with others. If we select and create our own situations based on our personal characteristics, this means that situational factors tend to play less of a day-to-day role in influencing our behavior than they otherwise might (Emmons & Diener, 1986).

Second, Darryl Bem (Bem & Allen, 1974) has added another interesting and important footnote to the concept of interactionism. He reminds us that one of the important ways in which individuals differ from one another is that some people are influenced more by situations than others. Some people are grumpy with everybody all the time, whereas other people are friendly with some people, grumpy with others, and in-between with the rest. With this in mind, a complete description of personality must also indicate the degree to which the person is influenced by different situations.

Bem's footnote about interactionism also raises an interesting question: Is it better to be a person who is strongly or weakly influenced by situations? While it certainly would not be good to be wishy-washy and change your behavior every time the wind blows, Bem suggests that it's also not good to be too unchanging. Only individuals with serious psychological problems are rigidly insensitive to their surroundings. It's probably best to respond to changing situations to a moderate degree.

Review

Psychologists typically describe the consistencies in personality by using trait descriptions. A number of psychologists have developed their ideas about traits to the extent that they can be considered theories of personality, but they describe personality more than explain it. Situationists have suggested that trait descriptions are inadequate because people do not behave as consistently across different situations as the trait concept implies; they behave differently in different situations. Social learning theorists have recently suggested that the most adequate description of personality must include both a description of traitlike consistencies in behavior and a description of how the individual's behavior is influenced by different situations.

Thinking Critically About Psychology

1. How would the kinds of research conducted by trait theorists differ from that of situationists?

2. How might trait theorists and interactionists differ in their attempts to solve violent crime?

Check Your Learning

To be sure that you have learned the key points from the preceding section, cover the answers below and try to answer each question. If you give an incorrect answer to any question, return to the page given next to the correct answer to see why your answer was not correct.

1. __________ are defined as relatively enduring and consistent ways of behaving.

a. States **c.** Characteristics
b. Traits **d.** Conditions

2. Trait theories are more concerned with describing the nature and operation of traits than explaining their origins.

a. True **b.** False

3. Allport believed that the most important traits were those motivational traits related to our ____________________.

4. __________ suggests that our behavior is influenced by a combination of characteristics of the person (traits) and the situation.

a. Situationism **c.** Trait theory
b. Learning theory **d.** Person × situation interactionism theory

Correct Answers
1. b (p. 418), **2.** a (p. 418), **3.** values (p. 418), **4.** d (p. 420).

PERSONALITY ASSESSMENT: TAKING A MEASURE OF THE PERSON

Psychologists who work in business, schools, prisons, and clinics are frequently called on to make important decisions about people. Which employee should be promoted to sales manager? Should this person receive a parole from prison? What should be done to help this person out of a state of depression? Such questions can be answered with confidence only when the psychologist knows what the person is like—that is, how the person typically behaves in ways that distinguish him or her from other individuals. In other words, the psychologist must know a great deal about the person's personality.

You could probably describe the personality of your best friend, your sister or brother, or your parent fairly well. You have seen them in a variety of situations and know how they typically behave. But psychologists usually do not have the luxury of getting to know their clients over long periods of time. They must come up with a picture of their client's personality in short order. To do this, a number of ways of quickly assessing personality have been developed. These include interviews, structured observations of behavior, psychoanalytically inspired projective tests, and personality tests.

Interviews and Observational Methods

interview
A subjective method of personality assessment that involves questioning techniques designed to reveal the personality of the client.

The most widely used method of personality assessment is the **interview.** Although few psychologists use it by itself, nearly every psychologist interviews the client by asking questions designed to reveal his or her personality. These interviews can range from the highly structured and formal to the very unstructured.

Interviews are an essential part of getting to know the client, but they have serious limitations. For one thing, they are inherently subjective; different psychologists may evaluate the same behavior of the client during the interview in different ways. Second, interviews are artificial situations that bring into question the validity of the information obtained from them. Interviews are stressful events that may bring out atypical behavior. A person may feel very anxious when interviewing for a job but might ordinarily be a calm person when at work. In this way, interviews can be misleading. As a result, they are often supplemented by other methods to ensure a more complete and accurate view of the person's personality.

observational method
A method of personality assessment that involves watching a person's actual behavior in a natural or simulated situation.

One alternative to interviewing is *observing* the person's actual behavior in a natural or simulated situation. **Observational methods** are particularly popular in business. For example, psychologists who consult with businesses on employee promotion often observe the employees being considered for promotion in situations that simulate actual managerial situations. Several employees might be given the problem of dividing up a limited budget for an employee health plan and then be observed as they negotiate a solution to the simulated problem.

To make observational methods more objective, a variety of observational *rating scales* have been developed. In these scales, the observer responds to specific items in describing the behavior observed. For example, the rating scale might include the item "Was friendly" and ask the observer to circle one of the following responses: "strongly agree," "agree," "disagree," or "strongly disagree." Most rating scales provide a comprehensive assessment of the person by using many such items. A commonly used type of rating scale for children takes advantage of the fact that teachers have learned a great deal about the children in their classrooms by observing them in the normal course of teaching. School psychologists who are assessing the personality of children frequently ask teachers to fill out rating scales on their students.

Projective Personality Tests

projective test
A test that uses ambiguous stimuli designed to reveal the contents of the client's unconscious mind.

Another widely used method of personality assessment is the **projective test.** These tests are based on the belief of psychoanalysts that it's the unconscious mind that contains the important roots of personality. But since the ego works fervently to keep the contents of the unconscious mind out of awareness, a way must be found to slip past the censor of the ego. Psychoanalysts believe that the motives and conflicts of the unconscious mind can be revealed by projective tests.

Projective tests ask the individual to interpret ambiguous stimuli so that the contents of the unconscious mind can be "projected" into the interpretation, much like a slide projector projects an image on a blank screen. For example, the *Thematic Apperception Test (TAT)* (Murray, 1938, 1951) asks the individual to make up a story about ambiguous pictures like the one in figure 11.3. What do you see in this picture? Is it an old woman happily remembering her youth? Is it a picture of the evil side of a young woman who is plotting the murder of her father? Psychoanalysts believe that because the stimuli are ambiguous, the ego is not able to fully censor the unconscious thoughts and motives that are projected into the story made up about the picture.

Even more ambiguous stimuli are used in the *Rorschach inkblot test* (Rorschach, 1953). The test consists of 10 symmetrical inkblots like the ones in figure 11.4. The individuals

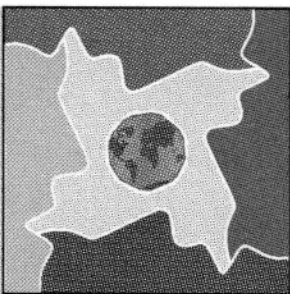

HUMAN DIVERSITY

Personality and Culture

Your introduction to psychology is occurring at an exciting time in the history of the field. Many psychologists are beginning to accept the notion that sociocultural factors such as ethnicity, race, gender, sexual preference, and physical challenges are important in understanding human personality. These factors have been neglected for most of the history of the science of psychology. Even today, not all psychologists accept this view. As Betancourt and Lopez (1993) note, "There seems to be a widespread assumption that the study of culture or ethnicity contributes little to the understanding of basic psychological processes or to the practice of psychology in the United States" (p. 629).

Personality theory provides a good example of an area of psychology that can benefit from an understanding of sociocultural factors. Many psychologists believe that a personality theory for a group of people must be rooted in the cultural context of that group. Too often, theories of personality have been developed by white psychologists based only on white Americans, and then applied to other ethnic and racial groups. But consider as an example the dramatically different experiences of persons of European and African heritage in the United States. The ancestors of most African Americans came to the United States in slavery, but no European entered America as enslaved. Moreover, African Americans still live in a racist society that treats them with anger, suspicion, and disdain. Similarly, Native Americans were once considered to be savages who could be killed without remorse to allow Europeans to settle their land, and today many Americans would prefer that they be "invisible" citizens who stay on their reservations. The prejudice experienced by Americans of Latin American descent can also be intense, especially given the recent pressures to prevent immigration from Mexico and other Latin countries.

We must understand the personalities of African Americans and other ethnic minorities in the context of racism and economic barriers. If not, we run the risk of labeling some characteristics of ethnic minorities as inferior when they reflect an attempt to adapt to racism, chronic lack of employment, and lack of educational opportunities. The focus of criticism should be on racism, sexism, and other forms of discrimination, not on the victims of prejudice and poverty.

Imagine how different you would be if you were raised in a culture that varies from yours in religion, family structure, and political system. Are you a member of an ethnic group that the majority culture views with anger and prejudice? If so, how has this influenced the development of your personality? If you are a member of the majority white culture, how would you be different if you had grown up African American, Native American, or the member of another ethnic minority group?

A number of psychology organizations have increased their focus on sociocultural factors. Most of these organizations welcome student members if you have a special interest in these topics. In some cases, they will help you locate a psychologist who can serve as mentor to students who are entering psychology as a profession. Mentoring can be particularly helpful for students who are members of groups that have been underrepresented among psychologists in the past.

Asian-American Psychological Association, Dr. Ann Kemmerer, Counseling and Educational Psychology Dept., Slippery Rock University, 119 Strain Behavioral Science Building, Slippery Rock, PA 16057-1326, (412) 738-2208, FAX (412) 738-2098.

Association of Black Psychologists, Inc. P.O. Box 55999, Washington, DC 20040-5999, (202) 722-0808.

Association of Black Social Workers, 1969 Madison Ave., New York, NY, (212) 348-0035.

National Black Child Development Institute, 1023 15th St. N.W., Suite 600, Washington, DC 20005, (202) 387-1281.

National Hispanic Psychologists Association, Texas Dept. of Mental Health and Mental Retardation, Austin State Hospital, 4110 Guadeloupe, Austin, TX 78751-4296, (512) 452-0381, Ext. 4802.

Society of Indian Psychologists, National Center for American Indian and Alaska Native Mental Health Research, University of Colorado Health Science Center, 4200 East 9th Ave., Campus Box C24-917, Denver, CO 80262, (303) 372-0000.

World Federation for Mental Health, 1021 Prince St., Alexandria, VA 22314-2971, (703) 684-7722.

FIGURE 11.3

The Thematic Apperception Test uses pictures like this to evaluate personality. The person is asked to make up a story based on such ambiguous pictures to allow the contents of the unconscious mind to be projected into the story.

tell what the inkblots look like and what parts of the inkblot they are focusing on. Do you see a vagina surrounded by a menacing spider? Are you projecting a fear of sex? Complex scoring systems are often used with the Rorschach inkblots (Exner, 1986), but many users interpret the responses subjectively.

Objective Personality Tests

A more recent development in personality assessment is the objective personality test. These tests have been widely used since World War II in an attempt to move away from the subjectivity of interviews and projective tests. The objective personality test consists of a number of written questions about the person. For example, the *Minnesota Multiphasic Personality Inventory* (MMPI) (now available in a revised form called the MMPI-2) consists of 566 true/false questions like the following.

1. I get along well with others.
2. Sometimes I hear voices telling me to do bad things.
3. At times I am full of energy.
4. I am afraid of losing my mind.
5. Everyone hates me.

The MMPI-2 is an objective test in the sense that no attempt is made to subjectively understand what the person meant by the answer to each question. Rather, the person's answers are compared with the answers of other individuals with known personality characteristics who have taken the test.

The items on the MMPI-2 are divided into 10 "scales," each designed to measure a different aspect of personality. The items were selected for each scale on the basis of the responses of individuals known to have that characteristic in extreme form. For example, one scale is designed to measure the extent to which a person is prone to experience depression. The scale was developed by administering a large number of questions to a group of people who were seeking treatment for depression and a group of individuals who were not depressed. The items that were selected for the depression scale were those that the depressed people consistently answered in one way, and others answered in the *opposite* way. For example, the depressed group would tend to answer "true" to a question like "Life often doesn't seem worth living," while the other group would tend to answer "false."

This method of test construction allows for the objective interpretation of scores. A person's score on the depression scale is simply determined by the number of questions answered in the same way as the depressed group, not a selective interpretation of the person's answers. Many other objective personality tests have been developed in the same or similar ways.

Evaluation of Personality Tests

It's obviously helpful for psychologists to be able to assess the personalities of the individuals with whom they are working. Not all psychologists agree, however, that personality tests are accurate enough to use for that purpose. A great deal of research has been done (but often with disappointing results) to determine whether personality tests are good at measuring what they are supposed to measure.

Research on the Rorschach, TAT, and other projective techniques suggests that these tests generally are not successful in distinguishing between individuals with and without psychological problems; they are even less successful in predicting behavior (Mischel, 1968). The objective personality tests fare somewhat better but still leave much to be desired. In spite of the fact that they were developed using groups with different personality characteristics, many studies have shown that the tests are unable to distinguish between groups that differ on these same characteristics (Mischel, 1968). Even in the most successful demonstrations, the tests are not always accurate. For example, chronic marijuana users can be distinguished from nonusers with 80 percent accuracy using objective personality tests (Hogan, Mankin, Conway, & Fox, 1970). Even so, the test is inaccurate 20 percent of the time.

One of the more serious problems with personality tests is that everyone is so prone to *believe* their findings—from the employer who asked you to take it to you yourself. There is something almost magical about personality tests that makes it seem as if they have a special power to see the real us, particularly when we are not sure who the "real" us is.

FIGURE 11.4
In the Rorschach inkblot test, the individual is asked to explain what he or she sees in ambiguous stimuli such as these.

Several studies have demonstrated the power of personality tests to be believable, even when the results are a complete hoax. In one such study (Stagner, 1958), 68 personnel managers—who work with psychological tests in their jobs—were given a published personality test. Later, each person was given a description of her or his personality. Supposedly, the description was based on the results of the test, but the managers were all actually given exactly the same made-up personality description. As in other similar studies, an astounding 50 percent of the managers thought that the fake personality descriptions were "amazingly accurate" portrayals of their actual personalities. Forty percent more thought that the descriptions were "rather good." Only 10 percent thought that the descriptions were inaccurate.

"It looks as if someone spilled ink on a piece of paper and then folded it in half."

Parts of the fake personality descriptions that the managers thought were particularly accurate descriptions of themselves were as follows.

> You have a tendency to be critical of yourself.
>
> You prefer a certain amount of change and variety and become dissatisfied when hemmed in by restrictions and limitations.
>
> You pride yourself as an independent thinker and do not accept others' statements without satisfactory proof.
>
> At times you are extroverted, affable, sociable, while at other times you are introverted, wary, reserved.

The success of this deception was due in part to the fact that the descriptions were vague and referred to the kinds of things that *most* people believe about themselves. Indeed, the descriptions were taken from popular astrology charts. Still, we should keep these findings in mind when interpreting the results of valid personality tests.

Thus, we should be cautious in interpreting the results of personality tests. Some psychologists even argue that we should not use personality tests at all. Advocates of personality testing point out, however, that understanding the personalities of the people with whom we are working is so important that we must try to assess personality using all available information. They point out that those studies that have shown only mediocre accuracy in personality tests have used the test scores alone. They have not allowed the psychologist to use other information about the person to reach an overall evaluation. It's only in this way, they argue, that personality tests have validity.

Review

Because psychologists usually do not have an opportunity to assess each client's personality by getting to know the person over a long period of time, they have had to develop methods of quickly learning about a person's personality. The most widely used method of personality assessment is the interview in which questions are asked that probe the nature of the individual's personality. Personality is often assessed by directly observing the individual in natural or simulated settings or by having people such as teachers or employers who have observed the person's behavior over a long period of time fill out checklists

Thinking Critically About Psychology

1. How do personality tests such as the MMPI-2 differ from the tests that appear in popular magazines?

2. Could someone else really understand your personality based on your answers to a list of questions? Why or why not?

Review—continued

describing the pattern of behavior that they have observed. Psychoanalytically oriented psychologists often rely on projective tests to learn about the unconscious roots of personality. These tests ask the person to respond to ambiguous stimuli in the hope that the person will project important features of his or her unconscious mind into the interpretation of the stimuli. Psychologists who prefer less subjective methods of personality assessment often use objective tests. These utilize items that were objectively selected for the test by comparing the answers of groups of individuals who do or do not possess the personality characteristics in question. In general, objective personality tests have been shown to be somewhat effective in distinguishing among groups with various personality traits, but some psychologists question whether even these tests are accurate enough to use in making decisions that affect people's lives.

Check Your Learning

To be sure that you have learned the key points from the preceding section, cover the answers below and try to answer each question. If you give an incorrect answer to any question, return to the page given next to the correct answer to see why your answer was not correct.

1. A(n) ____________________ is the most widely used method of personality assessment that involves a person questioning techniques designed to reveal the personality of the client.

a. observational method
b. interview
c. objective personality test
d. essay test

2. A(n) ____________________ like the TAT uses ambiguous stimuli designed to reveal the contents of the client's unconscious mind.

a. objective test
b. interview
c. subjective test
d. projective test

3. The items on the ____________________, an objective test, are divided into 10 "scales," each designed to measure a different aspect of personality.

a. Minnesota Multiphasic Personality Inventory
b. Rorschach inkblot test
c. Thematic Apperception Test
d. Beck Depression Inventory

4. Personality tests alone are consistently good predictors of humans personalities.

a. True
b. False

Correct Answers

1. b (p. 422), **2.** d (p. 422), **3.** a (p. 424), **4.** b (p. 425).

APPLICATION OF PSYCHOLOGY

SITUATIONAL INFLUENCES ON PERSONALITY IN EVERYDAY LIFE

The school of thought referred to in this textbook as *situationism* suggests that it's impossible to describe people solely in terms of traits because situations influence behavior so strongly. Take the trait of helpfulness. Are you a helpful person? Do you know people who you would describe as being very helpful or not at all helpful? Most of us think of helpfulness as a characteristic that some people have and some people do not have—that is, we think of it as a trait. Like other traits, we generally think of helpfulness as something that comes from within our personality rather than something that is determined by the situations we are in. But let's see if that commonsense understanding of helpfulness stands up under experimental scrutiny.

Most of us think of helpfulness as a fixed personality trait—either you tend to be helpful or not. But research suggests that our willingness to help can vary in different situations.

One classic study (Isen & Levin, 1972) that sheds light on the effects of even subtle aspects of situations on traits went like this: A male experimenter went to a pay telephone in a covered shopping mall and attempted to make a call. He acted as if there was no answer, hung up, and left. Sometimes he left the dime in the coin return and sometimes he took it. A female experimenter was window-shopping nearby, waiting for the next person to use the phone. The person could be male or female but was a research participant in the experiment only if he or she was alone and not carrying anything.

As the person—who had no idea that he or she was a participant in a psychology experiment—left the telephone booth, the female experimenter walked in front of her or his path and dropped a folder full of papers. Was the research participant helpful? Did the person stop and help the experimenter pick up her scattered papers? More to the point of this experiment, would a subtle situational event such as finding a coin in the telephone influence a person's tendency to be helpful?

Figure 11.5 shows the surprising results of this study. One hundred percent of the female research participants and 75 percent of the male participants who had found a coin were helpful, but almost none of the people who had not found a coin stopped to help pick up papers. Now what do you think about helpfulness: Is it a trait

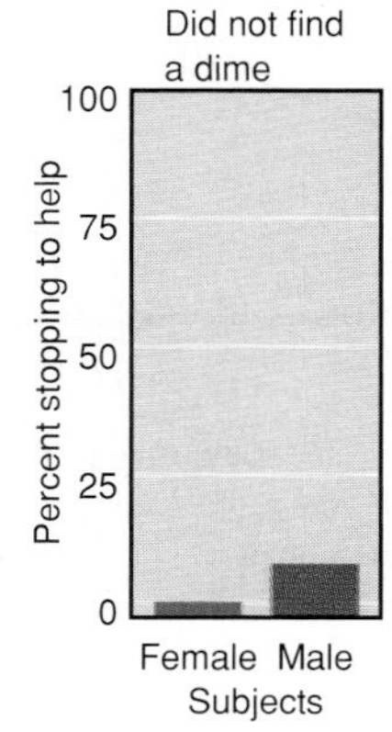

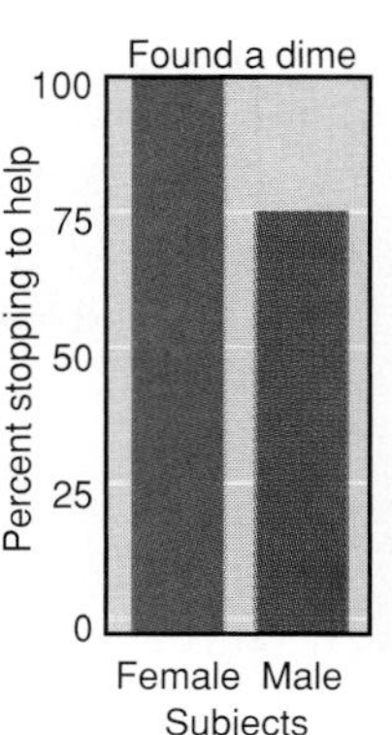

FIGURE 11.5

The percentage of subjects who stopped to help a person pick up scattered papers after finding or not finding a dime in a pay telephone coin return.

Source: Data from A. M. Isen and P. F. Levin, "The Effect of Feeling Good on Helping: Cookies and Kindness," *Journal of Personality and Social Psychology,* 21:384–388, 1972.

within the person or simply behavior that is determined by the situation? Even the small windfall of finding a coin influenced helpfulness to an amazing extent. As stated in the text, few psychologists presently believe that it's sufficient to think of personality as being influenced only by situations—different people react to the same situations differently—but this experiment may help you understand why many psychologists feel that describing personality only in terms of fixed traits is inadequate as well. Both a description of characteristics of the person and how these personal characteristics interact with changing situations is needed for a full description of personality.

Psychologists at the University of Illinois at Chicago (Romer, Gruder, & Lizardo, 1986) have provided us with an excellent example of the interaction of situational and personal characteristics in determining helpfulness. Try to put yourself in the position of these college students: You have participated in an experiment in which you filled out personality tests and received course credit. A month later a different experimenter calls and says that she got your name from the class roster and asks for your help. She explains that she is a graduate student and must complete a research project by the end of the term. Would you help her by volunteering to be a participant in another experiment?

The experimenters were interested both in the personal characteristics of the persons who volunteer and in aspects of the situation (in this case, some of the students were offered more course credit and some were not). But of greater interest was the combined effect—the interaction—between personal and situational factors. On the basis of the personality tests that the students had previously filled out, the experimenters divided the students into three "types." *Altruistic* persons were ones who indicated in their test responses that they are typically helpful to others when there is no expectation of something good being done for them in return. The *Receptive-giving* persons were those who were typically helpful in response to some kind of reward. The third type, the *Selfish* persons were ones who were typically interested in receiving help from others but not in giving it.

Figure 11.6 shows the number of each personality type who volunteered to help the experimenter and the number who volunteered to help when they were or were not offered course credit in return. As was easily predicted, the selfish students were least likely to offer to help and were not influenced by the offer of a small amount of course credit. However, the other two groups showed a dramatic person × situation interaction. The receptive-giving students were much more likely to volunteer when offered course credit whereas the altruistic students reacted to the different situations in the *opposite* manner—they were more likely to volunteer when there was no payoff offered. These results strongly suggest that our behavior is influenced not only by situations and our personal characteristics, but also strongly by the joint effects of both of these factors.

What about happiness and general satisfaction with life? How much is that influenced by situational influences? Many survey studies have been done in recent years in almost 100 different countries that show that some situations have a powerful influence on happiness (Myers & Diener, 1995). People who live in countries with stable democracies and people who are in stable relationships are considerably more likely to be happy than people who are not. People who live in poverty are less happy than average, but above the poverty line, people with more money are only slightly more likely to be happy. Happily, people of different ages, genders, and race and ethnic groups are equally likely to be happy after income and other factors are taken into account.

For our last example, we'll go to the opposite end of the continuum of human behavior to violent aggression against others. Is aggressiveness influenced by situational influences? We often speak of regrettable acts of human violence as being committed in the "heat of the moment" or as being acts of "hotheads." Craig Anderson (1989) has reviewed a large number of studies that make it clear that there is an unintended wisdom about situational influences on aggression in those phrases: Violent acts that are committed in "heated" emotions are more common when the physical temperature of the climate is hot. Figure 11.7 shows the relationship between the month of the year and four types of physical aggression. The four graphs are dramatically similar in showing that aggression is more common during unusually hot months.

It is likely that most of the persons who committed these aggressive acts tended to behave in aggressive ways in

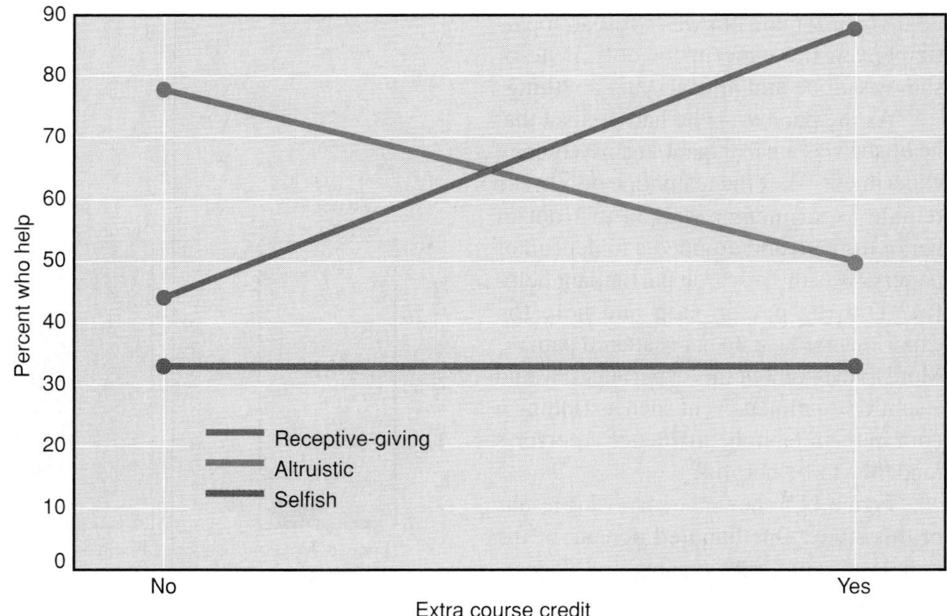

FIGURE 11.6

The percentage of students who agreed to volunteer for an extra experiment to help a graduate student. Students of different "personality types" were compared in situations in which extra course credit was or was not offered.

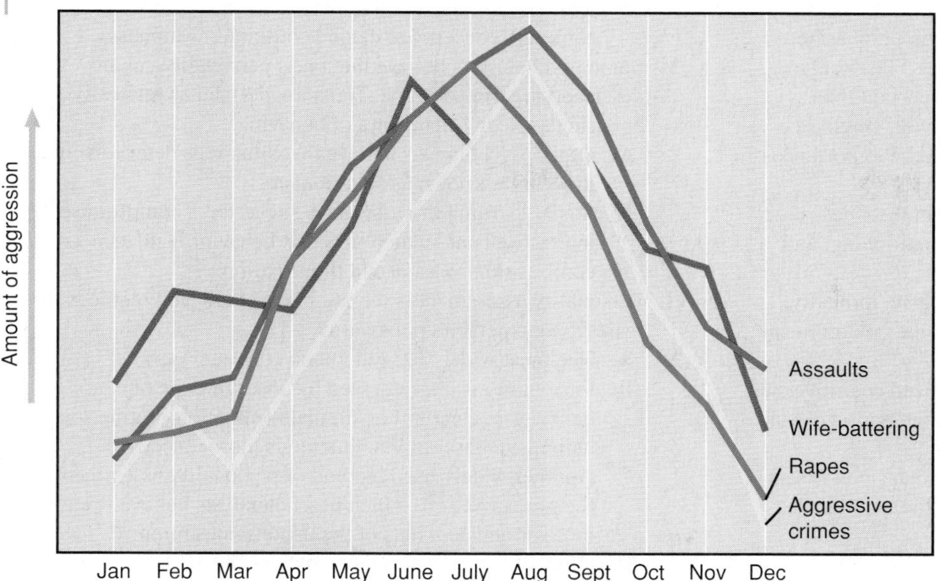

FIGURE 11.7

The results of four studies showing the strong relationship between the month of the year and four kinds of physical aggression. Note that violence is more common in the warmer months.

other situations, but even if that is the case, a simple aspect of the situation—temperature—clearly influenced the likelihood of aggression. Situational factors can have a marked impact on our behavior. Need more convincing? Think back to chapter 9 to the discussion of "falling in love on a swaying suspension bridge" (page 348). In that section, I described a study that showed that young males were more attracted to a female interviewer when they met her on a wobbly suspension bridge high above a gorge (probably because they attributed the arousal from the bridge to the young woman). Situations also play a role in whether or not you fall in love!

Why is this point important enough for me to devote this entire section to it? We often find ourselves in the position of predicting how other people will behave. In doing so, it's important to keep the powerful influence of situations in mind. For example, think about someone you know who is in high school now (a sibling, cousin, or neighbor). Now let me ask you to use your imagination for a moment. First, imagine that you have graduated and that you were offered a wonderful job, but you have to move across country tomorrow to start the new job. As a result of the new job, you finally are able to buy a really nice car, but it won't be ready until after you have left for the new job. Do you think the high school student is mature enough to drive your car across country alone for you? As you think about this question, you will find that it is important to keep in mind the high school student's traits, but also the unusual situation that she or he will be in. The same kind of reasoning should go into predicting how you will do in the new city and in the new job. You are usually a happy, outgoing person, but will you find yourself a little moody and shy in a new city where you know no one? Situations are important influences on us all.

Summary

Chapter 11 defines personality, explores three major perspectives on personality—psychoanalytic, social learning, and humanistic—describes traits, and discusses several approaches to personality assessment.

I. Personality is the sum total of all of the ways of acting, thinking, and feeling that are typical for that person and make that person unique.

II. Psychoanalytic theory was developed by Sigmund Freud in the late nineteenth century.

- **A.** Freud distinguished three levels of conscious awareness—the conscious mind, the preconscious mind, and the unconscious mind. In his view, the mind is composed of three parts—id, ego, and superego.
  - **1.** The id operates on the pleasure principle. It seeks to obtain immediate pleasure and avoid pain.
  - **2.** The ego operates on the reality principle. It seeks safe and realistic ways to satisfy the id.
  - **3.** The superego opposes the id by imposing moral restrictions and by striving for perfection.
- **B.** When the ego cannot find ways to satisfy the id, it seeks a substitute.
  - **1.** The substitution of a more acceptable goal is displacement, and displacement of a socially desirable goal is called sublimation.
  - **2.** Identification is the tendency to sublimate by modeling our actions on individuals who are successful in life.
- **C.** Freud's theory is developmental in that it distinguishes five stages in the development of personality: the oral stage, the anal stage, the phallic stage, the latency stage, and the genital stage. During the phallic stage, boys experience the Oedipus complex, and girls experience the Electra complex.
- **D.** Alfred Adler, Carl Jung, and Karen Horney broke away from Freud primarily over the issues of sexual motivation,

the presence of positive aspects of personality, and the importance of adequate social relationships.

  - **E.** Contemporary psychoanalysts generally de-emphasize unconscious sexual and aggressive motives. They believe that conscious ego functions are more important than unconscious id functions in guiding behavior, emphasize positive aspects of personality, and assert the importance of developing adequate social relationships.

III. To social learning theorists, the key concepts in the study of personality are classical conditioning, operant conditioning, and modeling.

  - **A.** Albert Bandura says that social learning is reciprocally determined by the actions of behavior on the environment, and vice versa.
  - **B.** Behavior is self-regulated by our internalized cognitive standards for self-reward and limited by our perception of our own self-efficacy.

IV. Humanistic theory is based on a belief that humans possess an inner-directedness that pushes them to grow. To the humanist, reality is subjective.

  - **A.** Self-concept is our subjective perception of who we are and what we are like. Carl Rogers distinguishes between the self (the person I think I am) and the ideal self (the person I wish I were).
  - **B.** Problems result when the ideal self is unrealistic or when feelings and information that are incongruent with a person's self-concept are denied conscious awareness.

V. Some psychologists believe that one's personality can be described in terms of traits. Traits are defined as relatively enduring and consistent ways of behaving.

  - **A.** Other psychologists believe that situations determine behavior. This is known as situationism.
  - **B.** Social learning theorists have suggested a compromise—interactionism—which says that behavior is influenced by a combination of traits and the situation.

VI. Personality assessment is the use of psychological methods to learn about a person's personality.

  - **A.** The most widely used method is the interview.
  - **B.** Personality is also assessed by observing the person's behavior in a natural or simulated situation. Rating scales help make observational methods more objective.
  - **C.** Another widely used method of personality assessment is the projective test, which psychoanalysts believe reveals the motives and conflicts of the unconscious mind.
  - **D.** Objective personality tests, such as the MMPI-2, consist of questions that measure different aspects of personality. Objective personality tests are generally better at assessing personality than projective techniques, but all personality tests are only partly accurate.

Suggested Readings

1. For in-depth discussions of the major theories of personality: Feshbach, S., & Weiner, B. (1991). *Personality* (3rd ed.). Lexington, MA: D. C. Heath; Liebert, R. M., & Spiegler, M. D. (1990). *Personality: Strategies and issues* (6th ed.). Chicago: Dorsey Press; and Hall, C. S., & Lindsey, G. (1978). *Theories of personality* (3rd ed.). New York: Wiley.
2. For a readable, detailed summary of Sigmund Freud's basic concepts: Hall, C. S. (1954). *A primer of Freudian psychology.* Cleveland: World Publishing.
3. For a summary of recent books that criticize the scientific basis of Freud's theory of personality: Crews, F. (1996). The verdict on Freud. *Psychological Science, 1,* 63–68.
4. A readable summary of Carl Jung's theory of personality is presented in: Hall, C. S., & Nordby, V. J. (1973). *A primer of Jungian psychology*. New York: Taplinger.
5. Interviews with leading humanists Carl Rogers, Abraham Maslow, and others are presented in: Frick, W. B. (1971). *Humanistic psychology.* Columbus, OH: Merrill.
6. An excellent statement of the social learning view of personality is presented by: Bandura, A. (1977). *Social learning theory.* Englewood Cliffs, NJ: Prentice-Hall.
7. No one presents Carl Rogers' views on successful and happy lives like Carl Rogers does: Rogers, C. R. (1980). *A way of being*. Boston, MA: Houghton Mifflin.

   For excellent sources on the importance of sociocultural factors in personality theory, see:
8. Jones, R. (Ed.). (1992). *Black psychology* (3rd ed.). Berkeley, CA: Cobb & Henry.
9. Markus, H. R., & Kitayama, S. (1991). Culture and the self: Implications for cognition, emotion and motivation. *American Psychologist, 93*, 2, 224–253.
10. Nobles, W. W. (1986). *African Psychology: Towards its reclamation, reascension and revitalization*. Oakland, CA: Black Family Institute.

PART 6

Health and Adjustment

CHAPTER

12

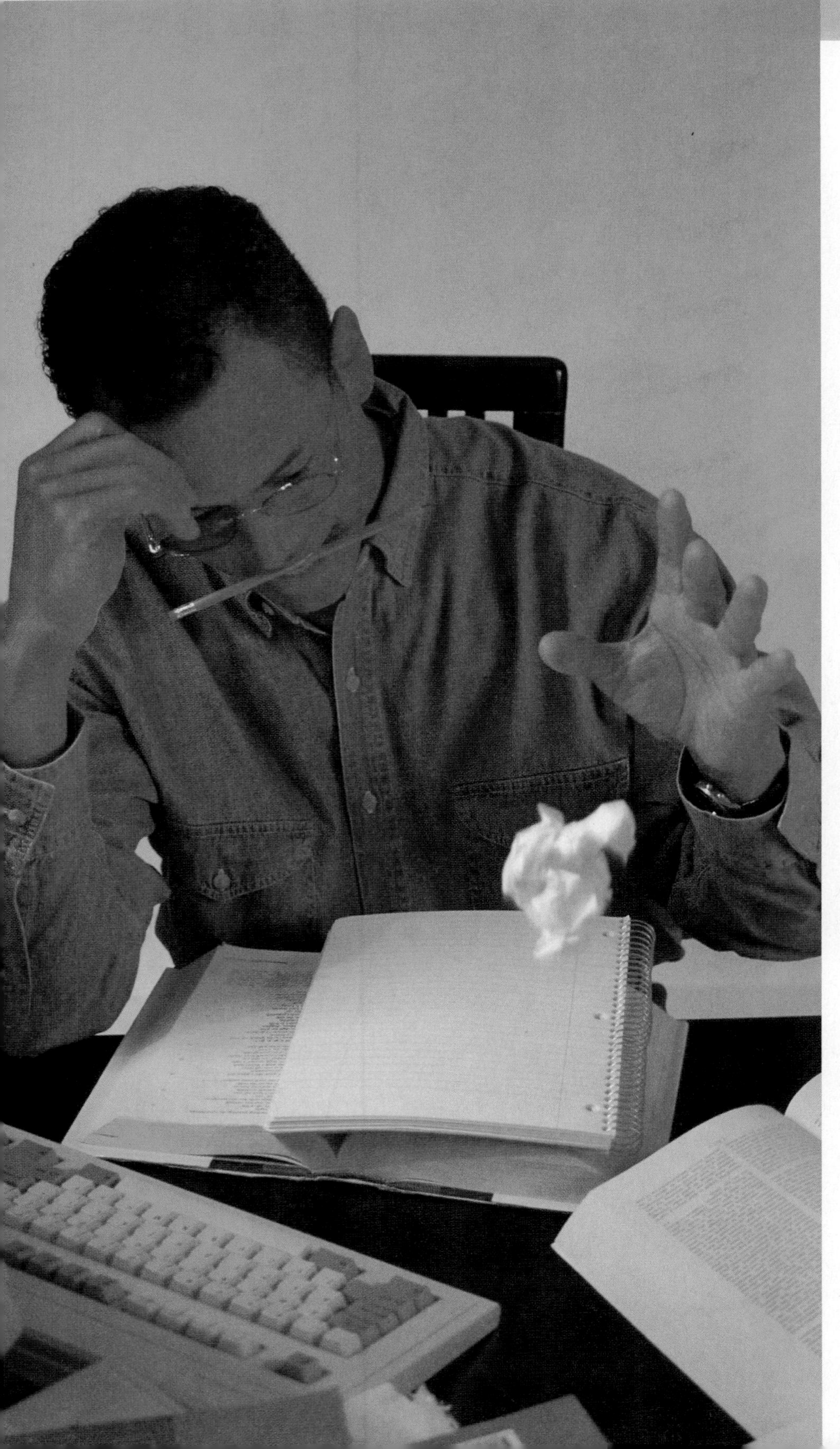

CHAPTER OUTLINE

Stress and Health

PROLOGUE

No one's life is free of stress. Regardless of how sensible, intelligent, or privileged you are, you will be challenged at times by frustrations, losses, changes, and conflicts. Stress comes from negative events, such as failing a college course, but stress is part of many positive events, too, such as starting a new job or having a baby. Stress is as inescapable as death and taxes.

A certain amount of stress is probably healthy—it energizes us and challenges us to grow. But stress is generally experienced as an uncomfortable, unhealthy force that most of us would be happier without. If you have experienced the death of a loved one or a divorce, you have firsthand knowledge of the emotions that such stress can bring. But don't forget that the psychological part of you exists in the biological part of you, and that what affects your "mind" also affects your body. Consider the following landmark studies.

Bengt Arnetz of Harvard University (Arnetz et al., 1987) conducted a study of the effects of psychological stress on the body's ability to fight disease. Arnetz studied a large group of Swedish women who had lost their jobs and had remained unemployed for 9 months. Compared with women with secure jobs, women who had lost their jobs had white blood cells that were less reactive to infections. Similarly, Janice Kiecolt-Glaser and colleagues (1987) of Ohio State University compared the immune system functioning of married and divorced women. The immune systems of recently divorced women functioned less well than married women, but with gradual improvements occurring over the first year after divorce. Within the group of married women, furthermore, immune functioning was poorest for those women with the unhappiest marriages. These findings may explain why disease and death rates are higher for recently divorced and unhappily married persons than for happily married persons (Kiecolt-Glaser et al., 1987).

In the few years since these remarkable studies were conducted, many other studies have confirmed their basic findings (summarized by Cohen, 1996, and Weisse, 1992). These studies offer strong evidence for the intimate relationship between our psychological selves and our physical health. It now seems clear that psychological stressors can diminish the body's ability to fight disease.

If stress is inevitable, and if too much stress is a threat to our psychological and physical well-being, then *coping* well with stress is of paramount importance. A healthy and happy person is someone who can enjoy the good times and cope with the bad. Sometimes we can cope with stress by removing it—by changing jobs or filing a complaint against a sexually harassing boss. But we cannot remove all the stress from our lives and will have to cope with some of it. Generally, we are better able to cope with the kinds of stress that we have had previous experience with and that we can control somewhat. Good social support also improves our ability to cope with stress. Simply disclosing our feelings to friends (or to a psychotherapist) has been shown to improve immune system functioning and reduce need for medical care (Pennebaker, Colder, & Sharp, 1990; Pennebaker, Kiecolt-Glaser, & Glaser, 1988). But there will be times when we cope ineffectively with stress. The trick, of course, is to cope as effectively as possible and not worry too much about the rest.

The link between psychology and health encompasses more than just stress and coping, however. Our patterns of *behavior* affect our health as well. Some behaviors, such as

KEY TERMS

smoking and overeating, create health risks, whereas others, such as exercising and relaxing, promote good health. The field of health psychology has emerged within psychology over the past 20 years to promote healthy behavior and reduce the impact of illness.

STRESS: CHALLENGES TO COPING

health psychology
The field of psychology that uses psychological principles to encourage healthy lifestyles and to minimize the impact of physical illness.

stress
Any event or circumstance that strains or exceeds an individual's ability to cope.

As we noted in chapter 1, one of the goals of psychology is to *influence* your psychological functioning in beneficial ways. The recently emerged specialty of **health psychology** seeks to improve the well-being of your body as well. In this section, we address perhaps the key factor that must be understood if psychology is to improve our health and happiness—stress. **Stress** can be thought of as any event that strains or exceeds an individual's ability to cope (Lazarus & Launier, 1978). The goal of this discussion of stress is to provide you with a new perspective on both your feelings and your health. Most of us are not used to thinking, "I'm feeling this way because it's a natural reaction to the stress I'm under." But, in many cases, stress is the cause for our most puzzling emotions and health problems.

The extent to which stress is related to some of our most serious medical conditions was greatly underestimated until recent research dramatically altered our perceptions of our own health. Leading causes of death and disability such as heart disease and stroke are almost certainly linked to stress and, as we have seen in the prologue to this chapter, immunity to infections is greatly affected by stress (Cohen & Williamson, 1991). It is even probable that the link between stress and immunity extends to susceptibility to cancer (O'Leary, 1990; Taylor, 1986). In an era in which effective treatments are available for a wide variety of infectious diseases, the major killers are stress-related diseases and cancer. This makes the interface with psychology one of the most important frontiers in medical research today.

Frustration results when we are unable to satisfy a motive.

Sources of Stress

We need to begin our discussion of stress by looking at its causes. Most sources of stress are obvious to us all—they rip and tear at our lives—but other sources of stress are quite surprising. Knowing what causes stress is the first step in understanding and coping with it. The major sources of stress include the following factors.

Frustration

When we are not able to satisfy a motive, **frustration** results. You see frustration in the face of a child who cannot reach the candy he's dropped or in the exasperation of the college senior who finds that she cannot register for the one class that she needs to graduate. When frustrations are serious, as in the case of the woman who has been denied a deserved and hoped for promotion, or when they are prolonged, as when individuals living in poverty cannot obtain proper food or medical care, they can be a major source of stress.

frustration
The result of being unable to satisfy a motive.

conflict
The state in which two or more motives cannot be satisfied because they interfere with one another.

approach-approach conflict
Conflict in which the individual must choose between two positive goals of approximately equal value.

Conflict

Conflict is closely related to the concept of frustration. **Conflict** occurs when two or more motives cannot be satisfied because they interfere with one another. Suppose you have been invited to spend a week skiing with friends, and then your car breaks down. You check your budget and find that you can afford to either fix your car *or* go skiing—that is a conflict. Psychologists use the terms *approach* and *avoidance* in discussing conflicts. In this sense we "approach" things that we want and "avoid" things that we do not want. There are four major kinds of conflicts involving approach and avoidance (Lewin, 1931; Miller, 1944):

1. *Approach-approach conflicts.* In **approach-approach conflicts,** the individual must choose between two positive goals of approximately equal value. Suppose that when you finish school you are fortunate enough to be offered two attractive jobs. Both seem to offer good working conditions, good prestige, and reasonable salary. If both jobs are so good, why do you feel so anxious? Why are

you having stomachaches and trouble sleeping? Even though both goals are positive—you would be happy with either job—the choice between these two goals can be very stressful. This is an example of a hidden source of stress. Because everything looks so positive, it's often difficult to see that you are in a serious conflict. The choice between two colleges, two roommates, or two ways of spending the summer can be similarly stressful.

2. *Avoidance-avoidance conflicts.* This type of conflict involves more obvious sources of stress. In **avoidance-avoidance conflicts,** the individual must choose between two or more negative outcomes. The person with a toothache must choose between the pain of the tooth and the pain of going to the dentist.
3. *Approach-avoidance conflicts.* **Approach-avoidance conflicts** arise when obtaining a positive goal necessitates a negative outcome as well. A student who is accepted to college in another state will be in a stressful conflict if she knows that it will mean being separated from her serious boyfriend, who works in his family's business in her hometown. Attending the college will have both positive and negative consequences, so she may experience considerable stress, especially as the time grows nearer for beginning school.

avoidance-avoidance conflict
Conflict in which the individual must choose between two negative outcomes of approximately equal value.

approach-avoidance conflict
Conflict in which achieving a positive goal will produce a negative outcome as well.

Notice that I said the student would especially experience stress *as the time grows nearer* for her to attend college. There is an important and interesting fact about approach-avoidance conflict behind that statement. As the positive and negative outcomes grow nearer (attending college and leaving the boyfriend, respectively), either in distance or time, the relative strength of the motives to approach and avoid them changes. This change has been described graphically in terms of the gradients of approach and avoidance. Notice in figure 12.1 that the strength of the motive to avoid the negative consequence of losing the boyfriend increases quickly (has a steep gradient) as distance (or time) from the goal decreases. The strength of the motive to approach the positive goal of attending college, on the other hand, increases slowly (has a gradual gradient). At any particular distance from the goal, the effective amount of motive to approach or avoid is the remainder when the motive to avoid is subtracted from the motive to approach.

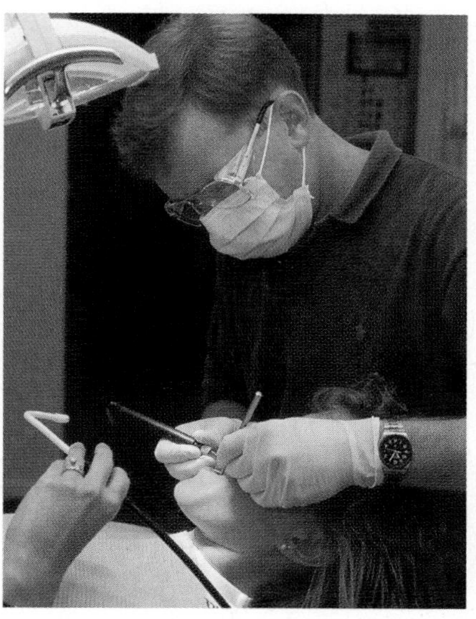

In an avoidance-avoidance conflict, the individual must choose between two or more negative outcomes, such as the pain of the tooth or the expected pain of going to the dentist.

At greater distances, there is a stronger motive to approach than avoid, so the net motive is to approach. At shorter distances, the motive to avoid is stronger than the motive to approach, so there is a net motive to avoid. Let's look at what this means in terms of our example.

The student who had been accepted to college began to experience a high level of stress about the time that the strength of the approach and avoidance motives were about equal. If the motives to approach and avoid were actually about equal in strength as diagrammed in figure 12.1, she might have even changed her mind and given up her admission to college as the time to attend

Avoidance gradient
Approach gradient
Strength of motive to approach or avoid
Strong
Weak
Far
Near
Distance from goal

FIGURE 12.1
Gradients of approach and avoidance in an approach-avoidance conflict.

came nearer and the net motive switched strongly in favor of avoidance. After turning down her admission, however, she would have again been at a great "distance" from college. She might again feel a motive to approach and wish she had not decided against going.

Have you ever found yourself in such a conflict? Did you find yourself going back and forth on a decision? If so, you have had a very common human experience. The actual outcome of such a conflict depends on many factors, particularly the relative strength of the two motives.

Researcher Seymour Epstein has vividly demonstrated the stressfulness of approach-avoidance conflicts in his studies of parachute jumpers (Epstein, 1982). Epstein views parachute jumping as an approach-avoidance conflict because the jump entails both dangerous risks and exhilarating thrills. In his research, inexperienced jumpers were rigged with devices to measure the amount of sympathetic autonomic arousal by monitoring changes in skin sweat. As shown in figure 12.2, the autonomic reaction of the jumpers mounted dramatically to a peak at the moment of the jump, then returned to normal levels immediately after they landed. While few of us face such obvious approach-avoidance conflicts, the more subtle conflicts in our lives affect us in similar ways.

multiple approach-avoidance conflict Conflict that requires the individual to choose between two alternatives, each of which contains both positive and negative consequences.

4. *Multiple approach-avoidance conflicts.* Sometimes the conflicts that we face are complex combinations of approach and avoidance conflicts. A **multiple approach-avoidance conflict** requires the individual to choose between alternatives that contain both positive and negative consequences. Imagine that you are a promising high school athlete and you have been offered athletic scholarships to two colleges. One is from a strong school that won its conference championship in basketball last season, but you strongly dislike the coach and several of the players on the team. The other is from a weaker school that has had an embarrassing record of performance in recent years, but you like the coach and players. What do you do? Do you go to the stronger college where there are people you do not like, or do you go to the weaker school where you like the people with whom you will be playing? This is a multiple approach-avoidance conflict because both choices involve both positive and negative outcomes.

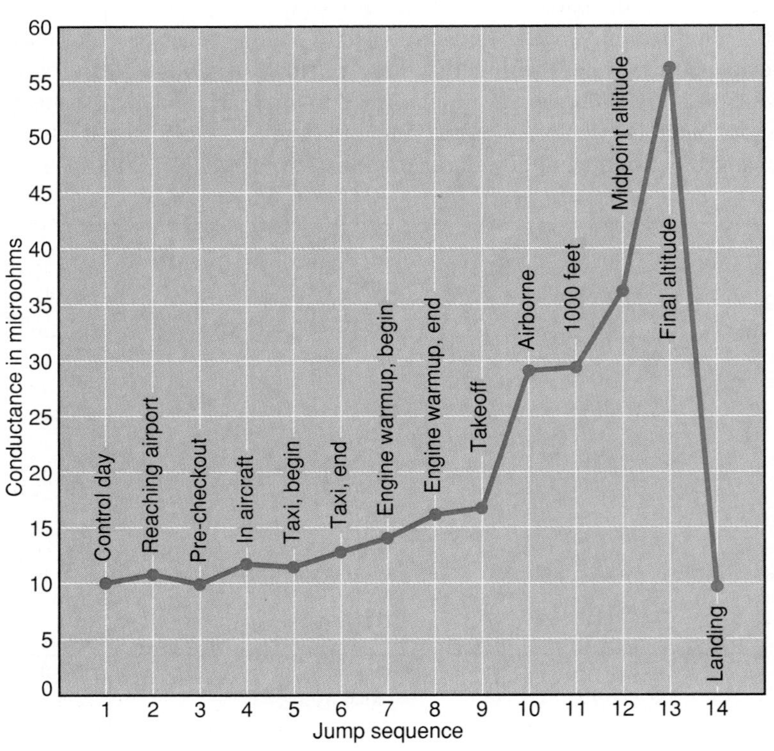

FIGURE 12.2

The amount of sympathetic autonomic arousal (as measured by changes in the electrical conductance of the skin caused by changes in skin sweat) in inexperienced parachutists at different "distances" from the approach-avoidance goal of jumping.

Source: Data from S. Epstein and W. D. Fenz, "Steepness of Approach and Avoidance Gradients in Humans as a Function of Experience: Theory and Experiment," *Journal of Experimental Psychology,* 70:1–12, 1965. Copyright 1965 by the American Psychological Association.

Pressure

Does the pressure of working for good grades ever get to you? If you have been employed, was it a high-pressure job? The term **pressure** is used to describe the stress that arises from threats of negative events. In school, there is always the possibility that you will not perform well and you will fail. Some jobs are loaded with possibilities for making a mess of things and getting fired. Some unhappy marriages are sources of pressure because one spouse always seems to displease the other, no matter how hard he or she tries to avoid it. The pressure of trying to avoid these negative events can sometimes be more stressful than the negative events themselves.

The term *pressure* is used to describe the stress that arises from threats, such as the possibility of poor performance on an exam.

pressure
Stress that arises from the threat of negative events.

life events
Psychologically significant events that occur in a person's life, such as divorce, childbirth, or change in employment.

Life Events

In recent years, a great deal of research has focused on the stressful nature of important **life events.** Major events and changes in our lives require adjustment and coping, whether they are negative changes such as divorce or positive changes such as marriage.

Negative life events are clearly a source of stress: Death of a family member, learning that one has a life-threatening illness, being assaulted, and the loss of a job are potent sources of stress. For example, Darrin Lehman and associates (1987) of the University of Michigan interviewed individuals who had lost a spouse or a child in a fatal automobile accident. Although the deaths had occurred 4 to 7 years earlier, the persons still experienced more depression than a control group who had not lost a loved one. Similarly, Sidney Zisook and Stephen Shuchter (1991) examined the stressful effects of the death of a spouse in a large sample of men and women. As shown in figure 12.3, widowed men and women were considerably more likely to exhibit serious depression during the first 13 months after the death of their spouse than were married men and women.

Natural disasters also can be potently stressful negative life events. Paul and Gerald Adams (1984) showed that the 1980 Mount Saint Helens volcanic eruption was extremely stressful to the residents of nearby Othello, Washington. Compared with the preceding year, the residents of Othello made 90 percent more emergency room visits, were diagnosed by the town's physicians and mental health workers as having 200 percent more stress-related physical illnesses and psychological disorders, and the town police responded to 45 percent more reports of family violence. Sadly, the number of deaths in Othello increased by 19 percent. Similar effects have been reported for persons who were in the direct path of hurricanes, earthquakes, and other life-threatening natural disasters (Escobar, Canino, Rubio-Stipec, & Bravo, 1992; Hanson, Kilpatrick, Freedy, & Saunders, 1995; Shaw et al., 1995).

Other studies have documented the stressful impact of witnessing violence, being physically or sexually assaulted, and other stresses of modern life (Breslau, Davis, Andreski, & Peterson, 1991; Kendall-Tackett, Williams, & Finkelhor, 1993). For example, Edna Foa and David Riggs (1995) of the Medical College of Pennsylvania interviewed every month for a year a group of women who were the victims of assault. They asked the women if they were experiencing high levels of irritability and anxiety, upsetting memories or dreams about

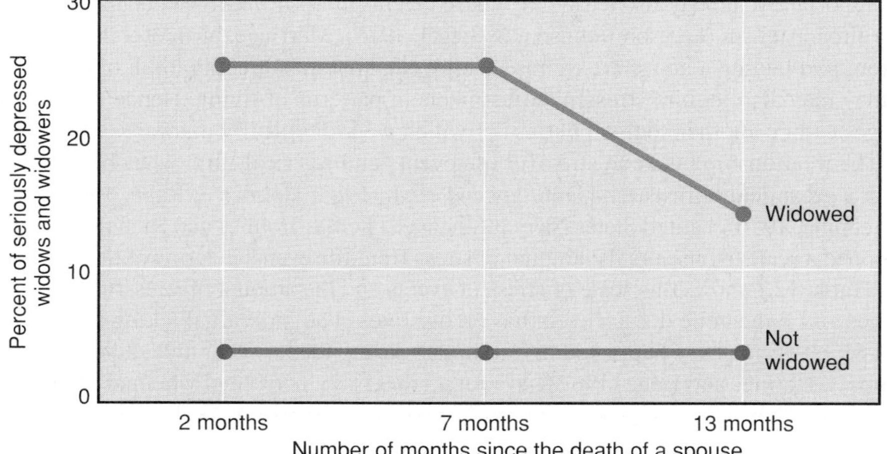

FIGURE 12.3
The death of a spouse is a severe stressor that leads to serious depression in some widowed men and women (Zisook & Schuchter, 1991).

FIGURE 12.4

The percentage of women who experience serious levels of stress symptoms following the traumatic stress of assault is very high one month after the assault but declines gradually over the first year. Many women still show serious levels of stress symptoms a year after being assaulted, particularly if the assault was sexual (Foa & Riggs, 1995).

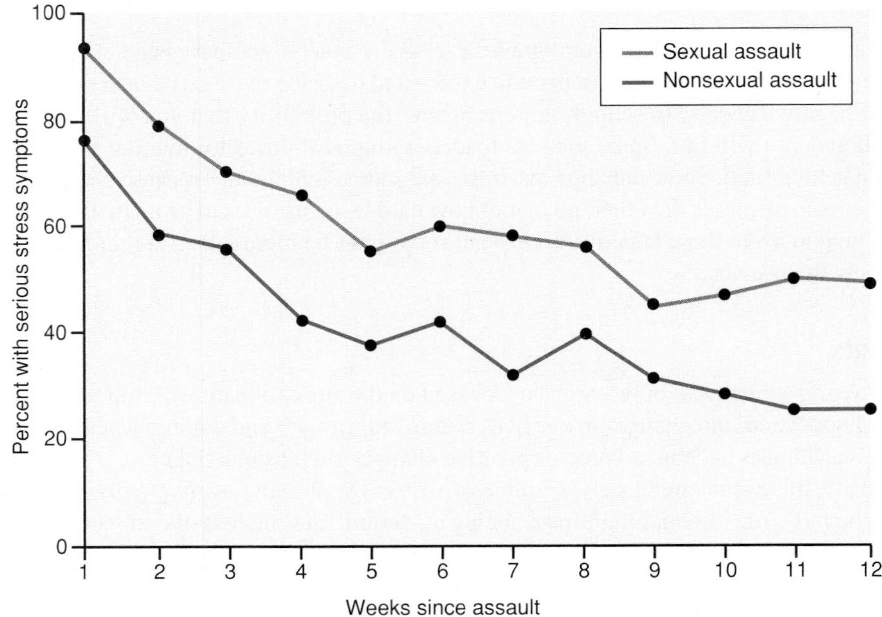

the assault, and distressing flashbacks in which they had the illusion of being assaulted again. As shown in figure 12.4, the great majority of women experienced high levels of such stress symptoms one month after the assault, with the percentage declining gradually over the course of the first year. Overall, it is clear that being a victim of sexual assault results in more severe stress reactions than other kinds of physical assault. Sadly, over 40 percent of the women in this study who had been sexually assaulted still experienced serious levels of posttraumatic stress symptoms a year after the sexual assault.

It is not surprising that major negative events such as earthquakes and the loss of a loved one are stressful, but Richard Lazarus (1982) of the University of California at Berkeley reminds us that the small *hassles* of daily life are also important sources of stress. Getting a speeding ticket, losing your sunglasses, having your friend arrive an hour late for dinner, and countless other microscopic irritants can grate abrasively on mind and body. Indeed, Lazarus (1984) asked a group of 100 educated, middle-class individuals to record their major life events, daily hassles, and daily positive events for a year and found that daily hassles were the best predictors of both health and psychological well-being. Although it is probable that daily hassles are an important source of stress, we must be cautious in estimating how potent they are. If we are not happy or not feeling well, it may well be that we would remember to write down more of the hassles of the day, or indeed, would be more likely to experience events like a slow drive home through traffic as a hassle. That is, hassles may be *both* a cause and a result of stress.

Importantly, there is also reason to believe that *positive life events* can be stressful under some circumstances (Sarason, Johnson, & Siegel, 1978). Marriage, birth of a child, job promotion, and buying a house are examples of events that most people think of as positive, but they may also require stressful adjustments in patterns of living. Hence, positive life changes can be another source of stress of which we are typically unaware.

The relationship between stressful life events and physical illness has been the subject of a great deal of research (Dohrenwend et al., 1982; Holmes & Rahe, 1967; Rabkin & Streuning, 1976). United States Navy physicians Thomas Holmes and Richard Rahe have developed a scale to measure the amount of stress from life events in terms of the life change units. Table 12.1 shows this scale of stress of events and the amount of stressful impact that Holmes and Rahe believe each event has on our lives. The individual taking the test indicates which events have happened to him or her during the last year and adds up the units of impact. Holmes and Rahe (1967) have found that Navy personnel who had experienced unusually high levels of life stress during the past year were more likely to develop a wide range of medical problems while on sea duty than individuals with lower life change units.

TABLE 12.1 The social readjustment rating scale

Life Event	Mean Value	Life Event	Mean Value
Death of Spouse	100	Son or daughter leaving home	29
Divorce	73	Trouble with in-laws	29
Marital separation	65	Outstanding personal achievement	28
Jail term	63	Spouse begins or stops work	26
Death of close family member	63	Begin or end school	26
Personal injury or illness	53	Change in living conditions	25
Marriage	50	Revision of personal habits	24
Fired at work	47	Trouble with boss	23
Marital reconciliation	45	Change in work hours or conditions	20
Retirement	45	Change in residence	20
Change in health of family member	44	Change in schools	20
Pregnancy	40	Change in recreation	19
Sex difficulties	39	Change in church activities	19
Gain of new family member	39	Change in social activities	18
Business readjustment	39	Mortgage or loan for lesser purchase (car, TV, etc.)	17
Change in financial state	38	Change in sleeping habits	16
Death of close friend	37	Change in number of family get-togethers	15
Change to different line of work	36	Change in eating habits	15
Change in number of arguments with spouse	35	Vacation	13
Mortgage or loan for major purchase (home, etc.)	31	Christmas	12
Foreclosure on mortgage or loan	30	Minor violations of the law	11
Change in responsibilities at work	29		

Adapted with permission from *Journal of Psychosomatic Research,* 11:213–218, Thomas H. Holmes and R. H. Rahe, "The Social Readjustment Scale," Pub. 1967, Elsevier Science Ltd., Pergamon Imprint, Oxford, England.

The scale of life change units developed by Holmes and Rahe (1967) has stimulated a great deal of useful research, but it is important to note that it was developed using men and may not apply equally well to women. If a similar scale were developed for women, would the stressful life changes be different, or would the order be different? A colleague of mine suggested that the death of a child, violent victimization, and serious conflicts with family members would be at the top. What do you think?

One moral of the story about life events: Space out your life changes when you can (Lloyd, Alexander, Rice, & Greenfield, 1980). Try not to graduate from college, move to a new city, take a new job, buy a new house, get married, and have a baby all in one year. If you do, don't be surprised if you are tense, moody, have stomachaches, and have more colds.

Environmental Conditions

There is growing evidence that aspects of the environment in which we live (temperature, air pollution, noise, humidity, etc.) can be sources of stress (Staples, 1996). For example, urban riots have occurred much more frequently on hot (mid-80s Fahrenheit) than cool days, although they have been rare on extremely hot days, perhaps because extreme heat leads to lethargic lack of energy (Baron & Ramsberger, 1978). Similarly, visits to the psychiatric emergency room of California's Sacramento Medical Center were found to be related to environmental conditions (Briere, Downes, & Spensley, 1983). Visits for all types of psychological problems were higher during periods of high air pollution and there were more emergency visits for depression during cloudy, humid days. These environmental sources of stress do not appear to be as potent as other stressors but apparently contribute to our overall stress levels.

Stress Reactions

Now that we have looked at the causes of stress, let's examine our reactions to it. When we are under stress, we feel it—we *react* to it. To fully benefit from the lessons that recent psychological and medical research has taught us about stress reactions, we must understand two important insights about stress.

1. First, we react to stress *as a whole*. That is, stress produces *both* psychological and physiological reactions—not one or the other, but both. If we remember from chapter 2 that several key aspects of the nervous system—the hypothalamus and the autonomic nervous system—control both psychological functioning (emotions and motives) *and* bodily functioning, including the endocrine glands, this concept is easier to understand. It is through these joint systems that stress affects both our physical and psychological selves.
2. Second, the reactions of the "mind and body" to stress are highly similar whether the stress is physical or psychological. Although each source of stress will evoke coping reactions that are specific to it, a *general* reaction to all types of stress also occurs, based largely on the interlinked responses of the hypothalamus, the sympathetic division of the autonomic nervous system, and the adrenal glands. This rather astonishing fact is a key to the modern field of health psychology, which we discuss later in the chapter.

The General Adaptation Syndrome

Let's look more closely at this general reaction to stress. Canadian medical researcher Hans Selye first gave us the insight more than 50 years ago that the body reacts in much the same general way to any threat, whether the threat is in the form of an infection, an injury, a tumor, or a psychological stress. Regardless of the source of the stress, the body mobilizes its defenses to ward off the threat in a pattern referred to by Selye as the **general adaptation syndrome (GAS).** Three stages can be distinguished in this syndrome (see fig. 12.5).

general adaptation syndrome (GAS)
According to Selye, the mobilization of the body to ward off threats, characterized by a three-stage pattern of the alarm reaction, the resistance stage, and the exhaustion stage.

1. *Alarm reaction.* The body's initial response to threat or other stress is to mobilize its stored resources. The sympathetic division of the autonomic nervous system increases heart rate and blood pressure, diverts blood away from digestion and into the skeletal muscles, increases perspiration, and in other ways prepares the body for a physical struggle. The endocrine glands pump epinephrine and other hormones into the bloodstream that aid the actions of the autonomic nervous system and increase levels of blood sugar. This is sometimes referred to as the *fight-or-flight* reaction, as it prepares the body to either fight with the source of stress or run away from it.

FIGURE 12.5

Changes in resistance to stress during the three stages of the general adaptation syndrome. Note that a second stress produces a more rapid dissipation of resistance.

Source: Data from H. Selye, *The Stress of Life.* Copyright © 1976 McGraw-Hill Book Company.

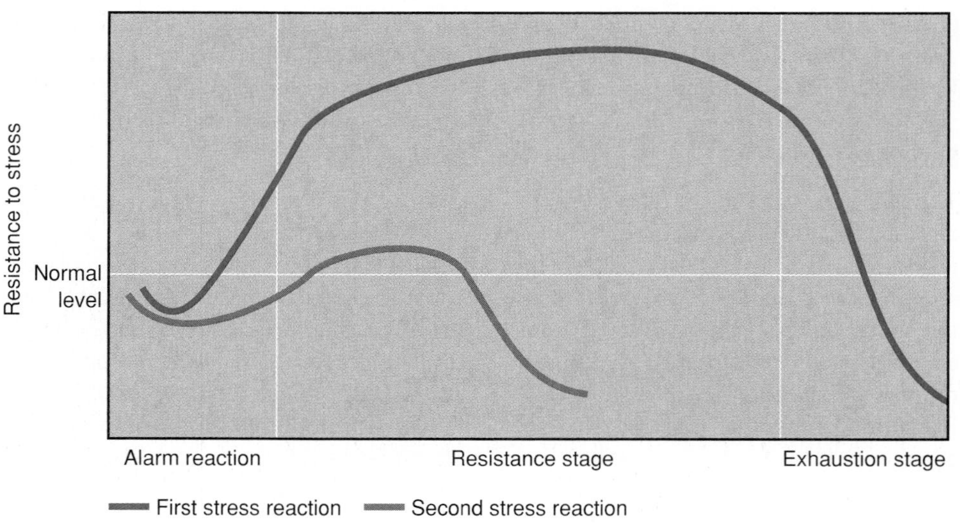

When the stress is intense or prolonged, these bodily changes give rise to conscious feelings of general muscle tension, stomachaches, headaches, and other feelings of "sickness." In the early stages of the general adaptation syndrome, it's often difficult to distinguish between the feelings associated with catching a cold, being under psychological stress, or even falling in love. Because anything that causes an alarm reaction produces essentially the same response from the body, the differences are often relatively subtle.

During the alarm reaction stage, the rapid mobilization of resources leaves the individual temporarily less resistant to the stress than originally. This state of affairs is quickly changed as the next stage is entered.

2. *Resistance stage.* During the second stage of the GAS, the body's resources have been fully mobilized, and resistance to the stress is high. This resistance is costly in terms of resources, however. If new stress (psychological or physical) is encountered, the body is less able to deal with it. In this way, psychological stress can leave the person more vulnerable to physical stress (disease), and vice versa. Moreover, if the stress continues, the individual's resources will eventually become depleted, leading to the third stage of the GAS.
3. *Exhaustion stage.* Finally, the individual's resources have become exhausted, and resistance to the stress is lowered. In cases of prolonged exposure to severe physical stress (such as intense cold), death can occur during the exhaustion stage. Psychological stress is rarely able to precipitate death, but it can severely disrupt bodily functioning (Selye, 1976).

Notice in figure 12.5 that if a second stressor is encountered when the individual has already entered the GAS, the progress toward exhaustion is much more rapid. Keep in mind two additional points as you think about the GAS. First, not all stressors overwhelm and exhaust the body; obviously we cope effectively with most stress. Second, emotional and other psychological reactions to stress follow roughly the same GAS pattern, sometimes resulting in "emotional exhaustion" when coping fails.

Healthy and Unhealthy Aspects of the GAS

As Selye (1976) helped us see, the general adaptation syndrome is the body's protective response to dangers. Without the GAS, we humans would be very frail creatures, indeed. Then the body's complex reaction to stress—the GAS—is a blessing, right? Unquestionably, but it is a very mixed blessing. The GAS can be our best defense at times, but our own worst enemy at other times.

The GAS does its best work during emergencies. Whether suddenly exposed to a deadly virus or being lost on a freezing ski trail, we need our bodies to respond with an alarm reaction to such emergencies. Our physical ability to endure such threats is enhanced by the GAS.

Even our ability to cope behaviorally is helped by the GAS at times. I once nearly stepped on a water moccasin, and my body responded with a full-blown GAS alarm reaction! My autonomic nervous system went into screaming sympathetic arousal and produced a multitude of changes in my body that prepared me to respond behaviorally to the snake. For purposes of simplicity let's look only at changes in my cardiac system during the moments that followed. As we know from our discussion of these topics in chapter 2, sympathetic arousal caused my adrenal glands to pump epinephrine, norepinephrine, and other stress hormones into my bloodstream. These, in turn, increased my blood pressure and caused my blood to create substances that make the blood clot faster. My heart beat faster, rushing oxygen to my muscles, and blood flow was diverted from my liver and digestive organs to the muscles in my legs and arms.

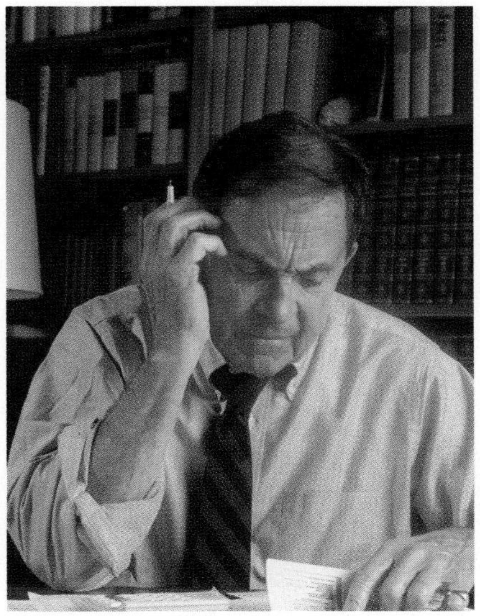
Modern-day stressors, such as preparing forms for tax deadlines, call for all of the bodily reactions of the general adaption syndrome. Although the GAS is a lifesaver in emergencies, it can be life-threatening if stress is prolonged.

Those physiological changes that we call the alarm phase of the GAS were very welcome indeed as I jumped, turned tail, and ran from the water moccasin. My legs were supplied with the necessary oxygen to run to the next county, and I didn't mind one bit that my lunch was never digested properly. Because blood flow to my liver was diminished during the GAS, it was not filtered as usual and my cholesterol levels probably rose, but I didn't mind that either. And if I had fallen and cut my knee, I would have been glad that hormones had prepared my blood to clot quickly.

Most of the stressors that we face in contemporary society, however, are not snakes or bears or avalanches. More often, they are the day-to-day stresses of school, work, and families; but remember that the body's reaction is much the same regardless of the source of stress. As a result, much of the GAS is not only unnecessary for some stressors; it is often dangerous. Take the example of preparing your income taxes—a dreaded stress, but not one requiring speedy legs or fast-clotting blood. Nonetheless, a group of accountants was given repeated blood tests for several months and found to have normal levels of blood clotting factors and cholesterol, until the time grew near for the April 15 deadline for filing tax returns; then their cholesterol and clotting factors shot up (Friedman & Rosenman, 1974).

Unfortunately, elevated levels of cholesterol and blood clotting factors are a potentially deadly combination because they cause the formation of the "clots" of cholesterol inside arteries called *plaque* that clog and harden blood vessels. When the affected blood vessels are those that supply the heart muscles with oxygen, a heart attack can result. Since the time of this original study, many other studies have been conducted that suggest that many kinds of stressful life events affect blood clotting, blood flow to the heart, and other aspects of the functioning of the heart that increase the risk of heart attack (Kamarck & Jennings, 1991). Thus, although the GAS is a lifesaver in the face of emergencies and disease, prolonged stress can paradoxically lead to changes in the cardiac system that can be quite dangerous to our health.

Stress, the GAS, and the Immune System

immune system
The complex bodily system of defenses to illness, such as white cells and natural killer cells of the blood.

As we have already seen in the prologue to this chapter, one negative aspect of the GAS is that stress causes decreases in the effectiveness of the body's natural disease-fighting system, the **immune system** (Cohen, 1996; Maier, Watkins, & Fleshner, 1994; Weisse, 1992). You will be unhappy to learn that even the stress of studying for important examinations causes temporary damage to the nuclei of important immune system cells (Glaser et al., 1990).

The negative effects of stress are most evident, however, in persons who are depressed (Schleifer, Keller, Bartlett, Eckholdt, & Delaney, 1996; Avissar et al., 1997; Weisse, 1992; Zorilla, McKay, Luborsky, & Schmidt, 1996). This is most likely to occur in individuals who are undergoing severe stress, such as divorce or loss of employment, but as we will see in chapter 13, it may occur in persons who are prone to develop depression for other reasons. A group of researchers at the University of California at San Diego have shown, for example, that the number of immune cells known as *natural killer cells* was significantly reduced in depressed persons compared with nondepressed persons (Irwin et al., 1990).

But let's think critically about this finding. The first assumption in reading about this study is that depression reduces the effectiveness of the immune system because the autonomic and endocrine systems that are disturbed during depression control the immune system. However, there are other possible explanations as well. People who are depressed are more likely to eat and sleep poorly and are more likely to drink excessively, smoke cigarettes, and not exercise—all of which are known to reduce the activity of the immune system. Maybe depression has no direct effect on the immune system at all but simply leads to behaviors that suppress immunity.

To test this possibility, Sheldon Cohen (Cohen, 1996) conducted an elegant experiment on the effects of negative life events on immunity to the common cold virus. Volunteers completed questionnaires that measured stressful life events and were interviewed about a variety of health practices. Then they were exposed to live cold virus and watched to see who developed a cold. Even after the effects of poor health practices (smoking, drinking, poor eating, poor exercising, and poor sleeping) were considered, life events were associated with less immunity to the cold virus. As shown in figure 12.6, more volunteers with above-average numbers of life events developed upper respiratory infections than volunteers with below-average numbers of life events.

Thus, there is strong evidence that stress and depression take a direct toll on our immune systems (Herbert & Cohen, 1993; Cohen, 1996). But the poor health practices listed above do, too. Multiple assaults on the immune system add up in their negative effects.

Clearly, then, stress and physical health are intimately related. Fortunately, something can be done about it. At the University of California at Los Angeles, researchers found that persons with medically treated cancer showed significant increases in immune system functioning as the result of a program that taught the patients to relax and cope with stress more effectively (Fawzi et al., 1990). Thus, it works both ways: Psychological factors such as stress can harm the functioning of the immune system, but psychological treatments such as stress management can restore immune system functioning in some cases.

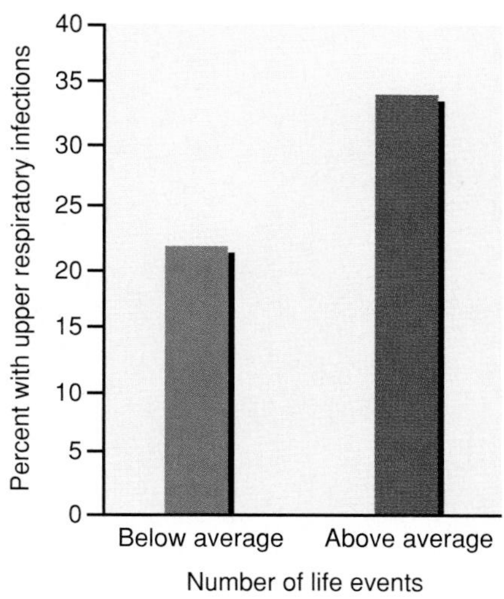

FIGURE 12.6

Volunteers with above-average numbers of stressful life events were more likely than volunteers with below-average numbers of life events to develop upper respiratory infections ("colds") after being experimentally exposed to live cold viruses.

Psychological Reactions to Stress

The physiological reactions to stress are also accompanied by psychological reactions. These changes primarily involve emotions, motivations, and cognitions. Under stress, we feel anxious, depressed, and irritable. We experience changes in our appetite for food and may gain or lose large amounts of weight. Our interest in sex often decreases, but it may increase. Cognitive changes occur as well: We have difficulty concentrating, lose our ability to think clearly, and find that our thoughts keep returning to the source of the stress. We will have more to say on this topic in the next chapter on abnormal behavior.

Review

A human life that was completely free of stress would be pretty dull, but excess stress can take a toll. Stress comes from a variety of sources in our lives. Frustration over not being able to satisfy a motive, conflicts arising from mutually incompatible motives, pressure, and unpleasant environmental conditions are all sources of stress. Similarly, life events, both negative ones like the loss of employment and positive ones like marriage, can be potent sources of stress. These sources of stress lead to stress reactions. People react to stress in both psychological and bodily ways. Stress brings anxiety, anger, and depression but also bodily changes such as increased appetite, headaches, and difficulty sleeping. Under some circumstances, stress even leads to high blood pressure, increased blood cholesterol, and decreases in the efficiency of the body's immune system. The body tends to react to all stressors, psychological and physical ones, in much the same way. This nonspecific response to stress has been called the general adaptation syndrome.

Thinking Critically About Psychology

1. Using your knowledge of the stages of the general adaptation syndrome, what advice would you give someone who is experiencing a traumatic divorce or breakup of a long-term relationship?

2. What are the major sources of stress in your life? Are they caused by things that you have much influence over?

Check Your Learning

To be sure that you have learned the key points from the preceding section, cover the answers below and try to answer each question. If you give an incorrect answer to any question, return to the page given next to the correct answer to see why your answer was not correct. Remember that these questions cover only some of the important information in this section; it is important that you make up your own questions to check your learning of other facts and concepts.

1. ____________________ can be thought of as any event that strains or exceeds an individual's ability to cope.

2. In ____________________, the individual must choose between two or more negative outcomes. For example, a person with a toothache must choose between the pain of the tooth and the pain of going to the dentist.

- **a.** approach-approach conflict
- **b.** avoidance-avoidance conflict
- **c.** approach-avoidance conflict
- **d.** simple conflict

3. A ____________________ is a psychologically significant event that occurs in a person's life; it can be positive, like marriage, or negative, like divorce.

- **a.** pressure
- **b.** repression
- **c.** life event
- **d.** milestone

Check Your Learning—continued

4. When the body encounters a stress, such as the threat of injury, it mobilizes its defenses in a pattern referred to by Selye as the ________________ .

   a. alarm reaction
   b. stress reaction
   c. generalized stress response
   d. general adaptation syndrome

Correct Answers

1. Stress (p. 434), **2.** b (p. 435), **3.** c (p. 437), **4.** d (p. 440).

FACTORS THAT INFLUENCE REACTIONS TO STRESS

More is involved in our reactions to stress than the stress itself. Much remains to be learned about these factors, but enough is currently known to outline some of the reasons for individual differences in reactions to stress. In addition to the sheer amount of stress, what determines how we will react to stress?

Prior Experience with the Stress

Stress reactions are generally less severe when the individual has had some prior experience with the stress event. For example, a soldier who is going into combat for the fourth time will usually be less stressed by it than a soldier facing combat for the first time. In a sense, prior exposure to a kind of stress often "inoculates" us to that stressor.

Developmental Factors

We saw in chapter 8 that people are often quite different psychologically at different ages and levels of development. Understandably, then, the impact of stress is frequently rather different at different ages as well. For example, younger widows and widowers (65 or younger) are more than twice as likely to still be depressed 13 months after the death of their spouse than older widows and widowers. Perhaps the stressfulness of the death of a spouse is less during a period in life when it is more common and when the surviving spouse expects to live less time without the lost spouse. Similarly, the effects of the stress of sexual abuse are more likely to leave the victimized children with serious anxiety when the victim is younger (61 percent of preschool children compared with 8 percent of adolescents) but leads to more suicidal thinking in older children (41 percent of adolescent victims compared with no preschool victims) (Kendall-Tackett, Williams, & Finkelhor, 1993). The effects of stress depend, in part, on the developmental level of the person who is stressed.

Predictability and Control

In general, stress events are less stressful when they are predictable than when they are not; and they are less stressful when the individual perceives that he or she can exert some degree of control over the stress. Let's look at several experiments that address the related issues of *predictability and control.*

Mild electric shocks are unpleasant stressful events that are often used in laboratory studies of stress. In one study, three groups of participants listened to a voice counting. At the count of 10, one group received an electric shock 95 percent of the time, a second group received a shock 50 percent of the time, and the third group received a shock only 5 percent of the time. A measure of sympathetic autonomic arousal (the amount of skin sweat) was taken during the counting. Which group do you think showed the strongest reaction? The shocks were least predictable for the group that received shocks only 5 percent of the time. Even though they received the fewest shocks, the high degree of uncertainty resulted in greater sympathetic autonomic arousal than for the other two groups (Epstein & Roupenian, 1970). However, when the stress continues over long periods of time, predictable stress appears to become more stressful than unpredictable stress (Abbott, Schoen, & Badia, 1984).

A second study focused on personal control over stress events. Two groups of participants participated in a difficult cognitive task in which errors were punished by electric shocks. One group could exercise some control over this stressful situation by taking breaks whenever they wished, but the other group could take breaks only when told to do so. The amount of increase in blood pressure was significantly greater for the group that had no personal control over the stress (Hokanson, DeGood, Forrest, & Brittain, 1963).

The effects of uncontrollable stress on health have also been shown in an experiment using laboratory rats as subjects. Three groups of rats were placed in similar Skinner boxes and electrodes were attached to their tails. One group never received any shocks and served as a standard of comparison to use in evaluating the health of the other two groups. The other two groups received occasional mild electric shocks to their tails. Group A was able to exert some control over the shocks because turning the wheel in the box would allow the rat to avoid upcoming shocks or turn off shocks that had already started. Rats in Group B had no control over the shocks. Turning the wheel in their box actually had nothing to do with the shocks; they simply received all the same shocks that their "partner" in Group A received. Again, the effects of lack of control were dramatic. The rats in Group B who had no control over the stressful shocks were significantly more likely to develop stomach ulcers and to lose weight than the rats in Group A who could exert some control (Weiss, 1972).

Furthermore, lack of control over stress has been shown to have a variety of highly important consequences for health. Rats receiving uncontrollable shocks show a suppression in the proliferation of the white blood cells, which play an important role in the body's immune response (Laudenslager, Ryan, Drugan, Hyson, & Maier, 1983), and exhibit less immunity to cancer cells (Visitainer, Volpicelli, & Seligman, 1982). Importantly, only animals that were exposed to *uncontrollable* stress showed these ill effects; controllable stress did not take a detectable toll on the body in these cases.

The results of these studies are extremely important in the lesson they provide for personal stress management. Stress events in our daily lives that are not predictable or controllable are all the more stressful. It is highly important therefore that we seek ways to exert control over our stressors or to leave situations that result in uncontrollable stress. For example, working under a supervisor who often lashes out at you in unpredictable and uncontrollable ways may need to be dealt with by talking to your supervisor, by asking for assistance from your supervisor's boss, or by finding another job.

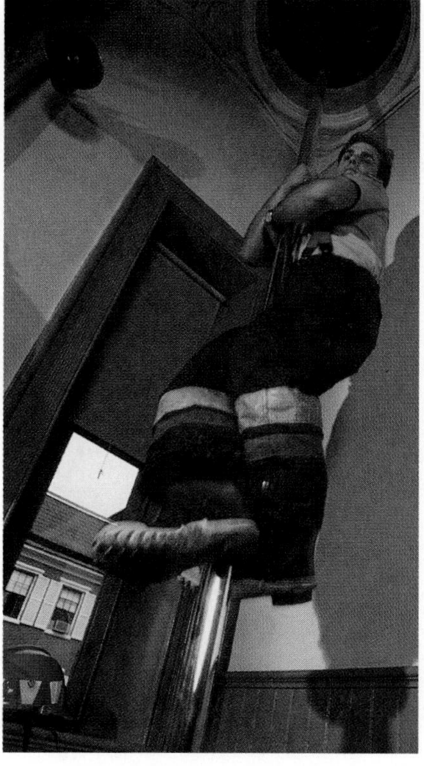

Unpredictable events over which we have little control, such as when the fire alarm will call this firefighter into action, can be unpleasantly stressful.

Social Support

The magnitude of reactions to stress is considerably less for individuals with good social support from close friends and family members than for individuals with inadequate social support. It's not yet completely clear how **social support** functions to buffer us against stress, but having someone to talk to, receive advice from, and be cheered and reassured by is an important factor determining our reactions to stress (Heller, Swindle, & Dusenbury, 1986; Kaniasty & Norris, 1995; Sutker, Uddo, Davis, & Ditta, 1995).

social support
The role played by friends and relatives in providing advice, assistance, and someone in whom to confide private feelings.

Individuals with good social support are less likely to react to negative life events with depression, anxiety, and health problems. For example, persons who learn that they are infected with the human immunodeficiency virus, the virus that causes AIDS, react with less anxiety, despair, and depression if they have good social support (Dew, Ragni, & Nimorwicz, 1990). Similarly, children who have been sexually abused are less likely to experience anxiety, depression, and other symptoms of stress if they have good social support from their mothers (Kendall-Tackett et al., 1993). Likewise, a large study of elderly adults showed that men who experienced the death of a family member (who was not their spouse) showed an increase in depression only if they did not have the social support of a wife or did not belong to a church or temple. Interestingly, a gender difference was found in this study. Elderly women were much less likely to become depressed than men after the death of a family member (other than a spouse), perhaps because women tend to have greater social support from friends than men do (Siegel & Kuykendall, 1990).

The social support of friends and family helps to buffer the effects of stress.

One aspect of social support that has been studied experimentally is the opportunity to "get it off your chest." The common belief in our culture that the simple act of telling someone else about your troubles is good for you probably is correct. A clever experiment conducted by James Pennebaker and Sandra Beall (1986) shows us the surprising extent to which this appears to be true. College student subjects participated in a study in which they spent 15 minutes on each of four consecutive nights writing to the experimenter about a traumatic event in their lives—both a description of the event itself and the feelings surrounding it. For purposes of comparison, another group of students wrote about unimportant topics assigned by the experimenter.

Writing about the traumatic events, such as the death of a family member, understandably caused the students to feel sad and to have brief elevations in blood pressure immediately after venting their feelings. However, over the next 6 months, the students who "got it off their chest" reported being ill less often and making fewer visits to the university health center. Apparently, it is good for your health to share your negative feelings with someone else. Therefore, having someone to confide in seems to be one of the important benefits of social support.

Under some circumstances, the best "social support" comes from a trained psychotherapist. We will have much more to say about this process in chapter 14, but it is important to note here that receiving psychotherapy is associated with improvements in physical as well as emotional health (Mumford, Schlesinger, & Glass, 1981).

Social support can also help us make stressful decisions and successfully follow through on those decisions. Yale University psychologist Irving Janis developed a program to help cigarette smokers stop smoking—and not resume smoking. Some clients were given "buddies" who were also in the program and were instructed to keep in close contact during the first crucial weeks (they met weekly and spoke daily on the telephone for 5 weeks). Ten years later, almost all of these high social support clients were still total nonsmokers. In contrast, clients who were not given buddies or who contacted their buddies infrequently were averaging over a pack of cigarettes a day. Similar positive effects of buddies were found in other programs to stop smoking (Mermelstein, Cohen, Lichtenstein, Baer, & Kamarck, 1986) and increase exercise and change eating habits (Janis, 1983; Janis & Hoffman, 1982). When we are under stress, a little help from our friends can bring out the best in us in many ways.

Person Variables in Reactions to Stress

We have seen that our reactions to stress are influenced by a number of factors: our prior experience with the stressor, the degree to which we can predict and control the stressor, and the availability of social support. But our personal characteristics—the so-called **person variables**—are also important in determining our responses to stress (Advisory Mental Health Council, 1996; Cui & Vaillant, 1996).

person variables
All characteristics of an individual that are relatively enduring, such as ways of thinking, beliefs, or physiological reactivity to stress.

As we saw in chapter 11, many personality theorists believe that the best way to understand behavior is to acknowledge that we are influenced by both the situations in which we find ourselves *and* some key characteristics we have as individuals. This view, referred to as *person x situation interactionism,* was described on p. 420. In terms of stress, it means that our reactions are partly determined by the situation (the stressor, our social support, etc.) and partly determined by some of our personal characteristics (how we think about the stressor, how "reactive" our bodies are to stress, etc.).

Cognitive Factors in Stress Reactions

An important reason that different people react differently to the same stressor is that we *think* about these events differently (Beck, 1976; Holroyd & Lazarus, 1982). Some individuals appear more likely than other persons to interpret events in more stress-provoking ways. For example, suppose you are a graduate student in clinical psychology and your supervisor suggests a better way to help a client. She says, "You're doing very well with this client, but a better way to help him with his fear of automobiles might be to . . ." and she proceeds to spell out her recommendations. Some individuals would be likely to interpret her statement as a combination of a nice compliment and a helpful bit of advice from a master therapist. Other individuals would interpret the same statement as a criticism of how they are doing as a student of therapy and expect to be dismissed from the program. As we have noted before, the interpretation of the event determines its stressfulness.

Another cognitive characteristic that helps to explain differences in reactions to stress is the different way people have of dealing with information about the stressful event. Several researchers have found evidence of two different styles of processing information about stressors (Roth & Cohen, 1986). **Sensitizers** actively seek out information and think about stressful events, whereas **repressors** avoid information about their stressors and do not think about them. For example, an unusual rash on the face would send some individuals to the dermatologist or the library for more information (sensitizers), whereas other individuals would not seek out information, would become upset if their attention were called to the rash by an interested friend, and would not even think about the rash (repressors). In essence, repressors try to deny, even to themselves, that the problem exists.

sensitizers
Persons who tend to seek out information and think about stressful events.

repressors
Persons who tend to avoid information and do not think about stressful events.

Far more is known about the differences between individuals who tend to repress or sensitize with regard to handling stress than about their differences on other personal characteristics. Repressors tend to cope effectively with stress in the short run but pay a price for their denial in terms of less effective long-term coping. For example, a study of men who were hospitalized for either heart attacks or coronary bypass operations showed that, during the initial hospital stay, individuals who were classified as repressors on the basis of a psychological test were released from intensive care earlier and had fewer signs of continued heart dysfunction than those classified as sensitizers. Over the course of the following year, however, the repressors followed their physician's prescriptions less well and were admitted for more days of further hospitalization (Levine et al., 1987).

As noted in the beginning of this section, however, the role of personal variables in determining reactions to stress depends in part on the situation. To a considerable degree, a person's tendency to repress or sensitize operates in this type of person x situation interaction in two ways. First, repression is a more adaptive coping style in situations where the individual has no control, such as coping with paralysis. In contrast, a woman can control the outcome of breast cancer to a great extent by seeking early medical treatment. The fact that repressors put off medical examinations when lumps are detected (Katz, Weiner, Gallagher, & Hellman, 1970) means that their repressive style is harmful in situations where control is possible. Second, a repressive style is not harmful when useful information about the stressor is not available, and a sensitizing style is not beneficial in the same situation. For example, surgery patients who were sensitizers experienced less distress when a great amount of information about the upcoming surgery was given to them, whereas repressors were less distressed when little information was provided (Miller & Mangan, 1983).

Type A Personality

A second person variable that appears to be extremely important in determining our reactions to stress has been termed the *Type A personality.* Some people simply react better to the stress of our pressured, competitive world than others. Have you ever watched a group of people play video games? For some people it is a pleasant diversion, whereas for others it is a matter of life-or-death competition! A group of health psychologists watched subjects play a video game and took measures of the activity of their cardiovascular system. Some subjects reacted to the game with large increases in heart rate. These same subjects also showed the largest increases in blood pressure and cholesterol (Jorgensen, Nash, Lasser, Hymowitz, & Langer, 1988). What is going on here? What kind of personality reacts even to trivial competitive stress with health-threatening sympathetic arousal?

Highly motivated achievers who compete in an aggressive, hostile manner may have Type A personality, which can lead to heart disease.

Type A personality
Pattern of behavior characterized most importantly by intense competitiveness, hostility, overwork, and a sense of time urgency.

Meyer Friedman and Ray Rosenman (1974) are physicians specializing in heart disease. They were observant enough to look beyond their medical tests to see that many of their heart disease patients, particularly younger men aged 30 to 60, were often of the "same type" behaviorally. They were hard-driving, impatient, hostile individuals who rarely slowed down to smell the roses. This pattern of behavior they identified as **Type A personality.** The following characteristics more specifically describe the Type A personality (Diamond, 1982; Friedman & Rosenman, 1974; Matthews, 1982):

1. Highly competitive, hard-driving, and ambitious in work, sports, and games.
2. Works hurriedly, always rushing, has a sense of "time urgency," and often does two things at once.
3. Workaholic, takes little time off for relaxation or vacation.
4. Speaks loudly or "explosively."
5. Perfectionistic and demanding.
6. Hostile, aggressive, and frequently angry with others.

If this description sounds like you, keep in mind that there is a little Type A behavior in most of us, and you should be concerned only if it's excessive.

Friedman and Rosenman followed up on their observation with a major study of the association of Type A behavior and coronary heart disease. Among 3,400 men between the ages of 30 and 59, the frequency of heart disease for Type A men was more than twice as high as normal (Friedman & Rosenman, 1974), and in another large-scale study, the risk for cardiac disease was twice as high in Type A men and women (Rosenman & Chesney, 1982). Other studies have generally found the same relationship between Type A behavior and heart disease, but one major study failed to find any relationship (Shekelle et al., 1985), suggesting that earlier findings of a doubling of heart disease in Type A individuals may be an overestimate (Matthews, 1988). Clearly, however, the Type A behavior pattern takes a toll on the cardiac system.

Interestingly, although Type A behavior is clearly related to the occurrence of heart attacks, the relationship to *deaths* from heart attacks is less clear. Apparently the emotionality of Type A behavior triggers heart attacks in many persons with relatively healthy hearts. If they survive the initial attack—as most do—the person with Type A behavior is no more likely to die of a subsequent heart attack than other persons. Indeed, Type A persons may be slightly more likely to survive after the initial heart attack (Matthews, 1988).

Of all the components of the Type A behavior pattern, the most important one appears to be a *particular kind of hostility.* Individuals who are hostile in the sense of reacting to frustration with verbal aggression (yelling, criticizing, insulting) or even physical aggression seem to be at risk for coronary heart disease, but individuals who are hostile in the sense of being chronically suspicious and resentful are not (Friedman & Booth-Kewley, 1987; Siegman, Dembroski, & Ringel, 1987; Weidner, Sexton, McLellarn, Connor, & Matarazzo, 1987).

Why is Type A behavior associated with increased risk of coronary heart disease? Type A behavior appears to be indirectly linked to heart disease through two major risk factors: high blood pressure and cholesterol (Matthews, 1982; Weidner et al., 1987). One theory suggests that this is because Type A individuals react physiologically more to stress than other individuals. Researchers at Duke University Medical Center (Williams et al., 1982) classified a group of undergraduate males as Type A or normal. Both groups were asked to subtract 13 from 7,683, then subtract 13 from the answer, and so on, with a prize being given to the person with the fastest subtraction rate. In this competitive situation, the Type A individuals showed greater increases in blood flow to the skeletal muscles and in the amount of epinephrine and norepinephrine in the blood. Because these changes are associated with the formation of cholesterol plaques, as we have already seen in discussing the GAS, the greater responsiveness of the Type A individuals may indirectly lead to hardening of the arteries of the heart. Similarly, Type A individuals also have been shown to respond to stress with greater increases in blood pressure—another key risk factor for coronary disease (Haynes, Feinleib, & Kannel, 1980; Matthews, 1982; Williams et al., 1982).

Review

The magnitude of the emotional, cognitive, and bodily toll that stress takes on us varies from individual to individual and from time to time for the same individual. The factors that seem to be related to the magnitude of stress reactions are prior experience with the stress, predictability and control over the stress, and social support.

The degree to which we react to stress also varies according to our personal characteristics. Different people react differently to stress partly because of cognitive factors. Some people actively seek out information about stress, whereas others avoid such information and block the event from their minds. These and other cognitive styles are important in determining stress reactions. In addition, some individuals seem to react calmly to the pressures of competitive life, but the so-called Type A personality finds competitive situations to be highly stressful. The hostility that often accompanies Type A behavior seems to be an important link to wear and tear on the body, particularly cardiovascular disease.

Thinking Critically About Psychology

1. Is there some negative aspect of your college life that could be eased by better social support?

2. How does our society's emphasis on monetary success and power influence the Type A personality?

Check Your Learning

To be sure that you have learned the key points from the preceding section, cover the answers below and try to answer each question. If you give an incorrect answer to any question, return to the page given next to the correct answer to see why your answer was not correct.

1. In general, recent stress events are ____________________ when they are predictable or controllable than when they are not.

a. more stressful
b. less stressful
c. not stressful at all
d. slightly stressful

2. Having ____________________, or someone to talk to, receive advice from, and be cheered and reassured by, is an important factor determining our reactions to stress.

3. ____________________ refers to all characteristics of an individual that are relatively enduring, such as ways of thinking, beliefs, or physiological reactivity to stress.

a. Identity
b. Person variables
c. Individuality
d. Superego

4. A person who exhibits a pattern of behavior characterized by intense competitiveness, hostility, overwork, and a sense of time urgency would be identified as ____________________.

a. abnormal
b. Type B personality
c. Type A personality
d. high strung

Correct Answers

1. b (p. 444), **2.** social support (p. 445), **3.** b (p. 446), **4.** c (p. 448).

COPING WITH STRESS

An issue of utmost importance to psychologists who work to promote both mental and physical health is that we obviously are not all equally effective at coping with stress. What are the best ways to cope?

Effective Coping

coping
Attempts by individuals to deal with the source of stress and/or control their reactions to it.

Effective methods of **coping** either remove the source of stress or control our reactions to it.

1. *Removing stress.* One effective way of dealing with stress is to remove the source of stress from our life. If an employee holds a job that is stressful, discussions could be held with the employer that might lead to a reduction in the pressures of the job, or the employee could simply resign. If the stress stems from an unhappy marriage, either marriage counseling could be sought or the marriage could be ended. In a variety of ways, coping with stress can take the form of locating its source and eliminating it. Unfortunately, this is not always possible. It's not always feasible or appropriate to quit a job or leave a marriage, and some sources of stress, such as the death of a spouse, just cannot be removed.
2. *Cognitive coping.* As we have discussed several times in the book already, our cognitions are intimately linked to our reactions to stressful events. One effective method of coping, then, can be changing how we think about—or interpret—the events that push and shove our lives. For example, I know a musician who had a successful first record, but his second album was a flop—the critics panned it and the public didn't buy it. At first, he saw this as a sign that the first record was a fluke and that he had no real talent. As a result, the failure of the second album was a huge stress. However, a veteran musician convinced him that having an unsuccessful second album is a common "sophomore slump" among musicians who go on to be very successful. This conversation changed his interpretation of his unsuccessful album and allowed him to view it as a challenge to do better next time. Finding an interpretation that is realistic and minimizes the stress of the events of our lives is a key part of coping with stress.

   Psychologist Shelley Taylor (1983, 1986) has been interested in the fact that some individuals cope more effectively with traumatic illness than others. Her studies of women who have undergone surgery for breast cancer provide potentially helpful information for women who face this stressful illness and may help us to understand better the general process of coping with stressful events. Because many women achieve a level of satisfaction with life after breast surgery that is as good as or better than before surgery, Taylor wondered if some ways of interpreting the stress of breast cancer tend to reduce the stressful impact of this illness. To begin answering this question, Taylor interviewed 78 women who were receiving treatment for breast cancer.

   The better-adjusted women were more likely to find positive meaning in the experience, such as learning to focus on what is important and to enjoy living to the fullest: "I have no time for game-playing any more. I want to get on with life" (Taylor, 1983, p. 1163). Better-adjusted women also were able to develop a sense of control over their illness. They had a greater belief than less well-adjusted women that improving diets, reducing stress, thinking positively, or prescribed medical therapies would prevent recurrences of their cancer. In addition, the better-adjusted women were able to improve their self-esteem in some way. This was frequently accomplished through some kind of comparison. An older woman might be glad that she had not lost the breast when she was younger. A woman with only a lump removed might compare herself favorably to those who lost the entire breast. Or a woman who lost both breasts might feel luckier than a friend who lost a leg to bone cancer.

   Are there lessons for all of us in Taylor's description of successful cognitive coping strategies? We must keep in mind the possibility that the cognitions of well-adjusted cancer patients may not be the *cause* of their good adjustment;

other factors may lead to more positive emotions and cognitions. But, until we learn more about ways to cope with traumatic stress, it seems unlikely that it would hurt to search for positive meaning, personal control, and favorable ways of comparing our situation with those of others.

3. *Managing stress reactions.* When the source of stress cannot realistically be removed or changed, another effective option is to manage the reaction to the stress. For example, an individual may decide to start a new business knowing full well that the first year or two will be hectic. She would be unwilling, then, to remove the source of the stress (the new business) but could learn to control the reactions to the stress. One strategy might be to schedule as much time as possible for relaxing activities, such as aerobic exercise, hobbies, or time with friends. Another would be to seek special training from a psychologist in controlling the bodily reactions to stress by learning to deeply relax the large body muscles (relaxation training is discussed more fully in a later section of this chapter).

   Happily, psychological counseling that encourages all three methods of effective coping has even been successful in changing the Type A behavior pattern. Some 20 studies have demonstrated marked improvement in the behavior pattern; more importantly, two of the studies followed the individuals for 3 years after treatment to determine whether there were actual improvements in cardiac health. It is encouraging that the treated patients showed a 50 percent reduction in heart attacks and deaths compared with Type A individuals who did not receive treatment (Nunes, Frank, & Kornfeld, 1987). We will look at some of the specific treatment procedures used to modify Type A behavior later in this chapter and at others in chapter 14.

Ineffective Coping

Unfortunately, many of our efforts to cope with stress are ineffective. They may provide temporary relief from the discomfort produced by stress but do little to provide a long-term solution and may even make matters worse. Three common, but ineffective, coping strategies are as follows.

An ineffective method of coping with stress from an unhappy marriage is to withdraw to the refuge of a bar.

1. *Withdrawal.* Sometimes we deal with stress by withdrawing from it. Many students encounter courses in college that are far more difficult than anything they had experienced in high school. Attempting to study difficult material can be highly stressful, and that stress can lead to a withdrawal from studying—by playing electronic games, talking on the telephone, partying, and the like. Similarly, a husband may ineffectively cope with the stress of an unhappy marriage by withdrawing to the refuge of a bar every day after work.

   Notice that it is not *what* you do, but *how* and *why* you do it, that makes a coping strategy effective or ineffective. Spending your time playing electronic video games actually may be an effective coping strategy *if* you only do it for reasonable periods of time to relax. It becomes withdrawal if you use it excessively as a way to avoid the necessity for more effective coping (studying).

   In this context, it is also important to recognize that there is a big difference between actually removing a source of stress and withdrawing from it. If you find that you have signed up for an extremely difficult course for which you are not prepared, dropping that class until you are ready to take it would be an effective way to *remove* the stress. However, simply not studying for the tests in that course because you have *withdrawn* to the refuge of long philosophical discussions with friends would obviously be an ineffective solution.

2. *Aggression.* As we discussed in chapter 9, a common reaction to frustration and other stressful situations is aggression. The woman who has tried unsuccessfully to create romantic interest in a man may suddenly become hostile toward him. The man who cannot get a screw to fit into a curtain rod may throw a temper tantrum and hurl the rod to the floor in disgust.

3. *Defense mechanisms.* According to Freud, one of the key functions of the ego is to "defend" the person from a buildup of uncomfortable tension. When

defense mechanisms According to Freud, the unrealistic strategies used by the ego to discharge tension.

something stressful occurs (such as frustration or embarrassment) or when conflict arises because the superego blocks an id desire, tension is created that must be discharged somehow. Freud believed that the ego possesses a small arsenal of **defense mechanisms** that are unconsciously used to discharge tension. When they are not overused, defense mechanisms can be a relatively harmless crutch to a healthy personality—all of us use them to some extent. Unfortunately, many individuals rely too heavily on defense mechanisms. The major defense mechanisms are as follows:

Displacement: When it's unsafe or inappropriate to express aggressive or sexual feelings toward the person who is creating stress (such as a boss who pressures you), that feeling can be directed toward someone safe (such as yelling at your friend when you are really angry with your boss).

Sublimation: Stressful conflicts over dangerous feelings or motives are reduced by converting the impulses into socially approved activities, such as schoolwork, literature, sports, and so on.

Projection: One's own dangerous or unacceptable desires or emotions are seen not as one's own, but as the desires or feelings of others. A person who has stressful conflicts about sex might perceive himself as having little sexual desire but views other people as being "obsessed" with sex.

Reaction formation: Conflicts over dangerous motives or feelings are avoided by unconsciously transforming them into the opposite desire. A married man with strong desires for extramarital sex might start a campaign to rid his city of massage parlors and prostitutes. A woman who wishes her hateful mother would die might devote herself to finding ways to protect her mother's health.

Regression: Stress may be reduced by returning to an earlier pattern of behavior, such as a business executive who has a stomping, screaming temper tantrum when his company suffers a major setback.

Rationalization: Stress is reduced by "explaining it away" in ways that sound logical and socially acceptable. A man who is rejected by his lover may decide that he is glad because she had so many faults or because he really did not want to give up the single life.

"You keep insisting that this isn't happening, Edwards, but in my opinion you're mistaken. I really believe myself to be firing you."

Repression: Potentially stressful, unacceptable desires are kept out of consciousness without the person being consciously aware that the repression is occurring.

Denial: Upsetting or threatening thoughts and emotions related to stressful events are not allowed into conscious awareness. For example, a person who finds that she has high blood pressure during a routine medical checkup may never again think about that upsetting fact, even though her physician has urged her to change her habits of diet and exercise.

Intellectualization: The emotional nature of stressful events is lessened at times by reducing it to cold, intellectual logic. For example, the person who learns that he has lost a large sum of money in an overly risky investment may think about it in a detached way as a temporary debit in a successful lifelong program of investment, rather than as a painful financial mistake that should be avoided in the future through more careful planning.

Defense mechanisms can be effective in the short run in helping us feel better, but they inhibit long-term solutions to stress if they *distort reality* to a great extent. For example, suppose that a woman copes reasonably well with the stress of failing a course in college by deciding that her instructor graded her test papers unfairly because she asks too many questions in class. If her instructor is actually fair and competent, she would be distorting reality by using the defense mechanism of rationalization. A simple change in study habits or test-taking strategies might make a big difference in her grades, but she will never see the need for change if she distorts reality through rationalization. The other defense mechanisms can be harmful in similar reality-distorting ways.

Review

Although some of us are exposed to more stress than others, we all face stressful events that require some form of coping. The most common sources of stress are frustration, the many forms of conflicts, pressure, and positive and negative life events. At times, we cope effectively with stress either by finding ways to remove the source of stress or by managing the stress reaction. At other times, however, we cope ineffectively through withdrawal, aggression, and defense mechanisms.

Thinking Critically About Psychology

1. What would you say are the main differences between effective and ineffective coping?

2. What kinds of help would you suggest to someone interested in finding more effective methods for coping with stress?

Check Your Learning

To be sure that you have learned the key points from the preceding section, cover the answers below and try to answer each question. If you give an incorrect answer to any question, return to the page given next to the correct answer to see why your answer was not correct.

1. The term ________________ refers to attempts to deal with the source of the stress or control our reactions to it, or both.

a. endurance **c.** restructuring
b. strategize **d.** coping

2. Doing reasonable amounts of aerobic exercise to relax would be considered an effective coping strategy.

a. True **b.** False

3. Spending most of your time playing electronic video games as a way to avoid the stress of studying would be considered to be ________________ .

a. cognitive coping **c.** withdrawal
b. stress management **d.** removal

4. According to Freud, ________________ are unrealistic strategies used by the ego to discharge tension, such as repression and sublimation.

a. cognitive coping strategies **c.** rationalizations
b. withdrawal **d.** defense mechanisms

Correct Answers
1. d (p. 450), **2.** a (p. 451), **3.** c (p. 451), **4.** d (p. 452).

CHANGING HEALTH-RELATED BEHAVIOR PATTERNS

A major goal of health psychology is to *prevent* health problems by helping individuals modify behaviors that create health risks through strategies such as learning to relax, not smoking or abusing other substances, exercising and eating properly, and the like (Winett, 1995). One of the most frequently used strategies is teaching individuals how to relax.

Learning to Relax

Is it easy for you to relax—really relax in a way that results in decreased sympathetic arousal? Relaxation is very difficult for a great many people. **Progressive relaxation training** teaches individuals to deeply relax their large body muscles. Although the method was first developed by a physician in the 1930s (Jacobsen, 1938), the use of a simplified version has been popularized in recent years primarily by psychologists (Rimm & Masters, 1979).

progressive relaxation training
A method of learning to deeply relax the muscles of the body.

In progressive relaxation training, the individual is first taught to sense the difference between tense and relaxed muscles. Stop reading for a few seconds and tense the muscles in your right hand and arm as tightly as you can. Focus your attention on the tension, carefully noticing how it feels. Then release the tension, letting your hand and arm relax limply. Notice how your relaxed muscles feel. Now try tensing the muscles in your neck while leaving the muscles in your shoulders relaxed. Now relax your neck. Can you do it? Many people cannot at first, but progressive relaxation training would teach you how.

The therapist slowly takes the individual through all of the muscle groups so that he or she becomes aware of how tension and relaxation feel. Over many sessions of practice, the individual becomes more able to achieve a very deep state of relaxation. As a result, progressive relaxation training has been found to be effective in the treatment of insomnia (sleep problems), tension headaches, migraine headaches, ulcers, general anxiety, and high blood pressure (Jenkins, 1988; Rimm & Masters, 1979).

A team of researchers at the Virginia Polytechnic State Institute and State University (Longo, Clum, & Yeager, 1988) has even shown that relaxation training reduced the recurrence of severe genital herpes infections. This finding again shows the intimate relationship between our psychological functioning and the immune system.

Eating Right, Exercising, and Doing Just What the Doctor Ordered

Health psychologists are very much involved in encouraging a variety of other patterns of behavior that promote good health (Davidson & Davidson, 1982). Marked reductions in heart attacks for vulnerable individuals result from weight reduction in overweight individuals, decreased salt intake for some individuals with high blood pressure, and moderate levels of regular exercise (Farquhar, 1979; Jenkins, 1988). It is not easy to change one's pattern of eating and exercising; bad habits are difficult to break. Therefore, psychologists are often involved in the design and implementation of programs to change and maintain changes in eating and exercising.

Improved Eating Habits

It is increasingly clear that diet plays an important role in our health. Eating excessive amounts of fatty red meats, eggs, and high-fat dairy products, for example, can lead to high levels of blood cholesterol in many individuals and contribute to hardening of the arteries and increased risk for heart attack and stroke. On the other hand, reducing blood cholesterol through diet and medication has been shown in a variety of studies to reduce the incidence and severity of coronary heart disease (Jeffrey, 1988; Taylor, 1986). Similarly, reducing the amount of salt that is ingested and controlling one's weight can have very beneficial effects on high blood pressure and coronary heart disease, and diet has been linked to some forms of cancer (Jeffrey, 1988; Taylor, 1986). In addition, many of us use enormous quantities of consciousness-altering drugs, usually without even being aware that we are taking "drugs." Our coffee contains the stimulant caffeine, cigarettes contain the stimulant nicotine, and alcohol is a powerful depressant drug. Millions of individuals who would never consider using "drugs" use, abuse, or are addicted to these drugs. Unfortunately, serious health risks are associated with the use of each of these substances.

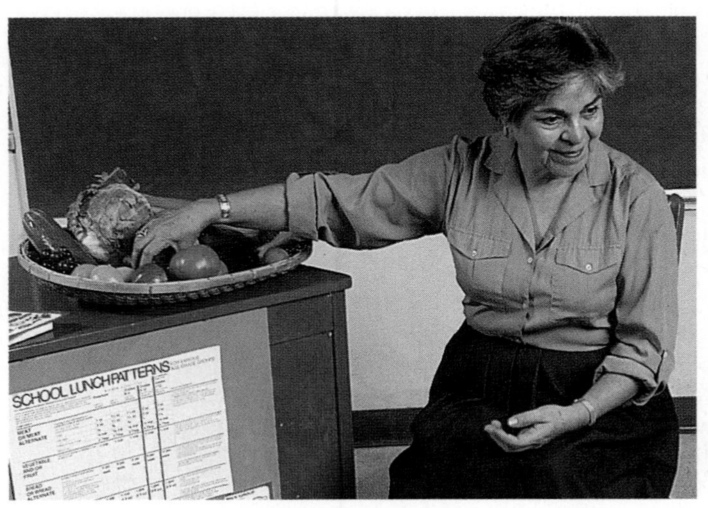

Part of the reason that so much of our dietary behavior is unhealthy is lack of knowledge. Education can produce changes in our eating patterns.

Why, then, do most Americans still eat so poorly? Why don't we view a breakfast of eggs, bacon, biscuits, butter, and three cups of coffee as being as dangerous as eating asbestos for some people?

Part of the reason that so much of our dietary behavior is unhealthy is lack of knowledge—most of us are not aware of the importance of good diet. Psychologists have only recently become involved in the search for effective ways to change unhealthy dietary behavior for the same reason. Few of us knew until recently just how important diet is to health. But, even armed with the facts, psychologists have sometimes found that convincing people to change their diets is not always easy. One large-scale study in Houston (Foreyt, Scott, Mitchell, & Gotto, 1979) found that although booklets on diet, classes on nutrition, and group discussions all led to better eating and lower levels of blood cholesterol for a short period of time, few participants stuck with their improved diets for long. Similarly, a Minnesota study of a successful weight reduction program conducted in an industrial worksite found that only 21 percent stayed at their new lower weight a year later; the rest had regained their lost weight (Forster, Jeffrey, & Snell, 1988). In addition, a study of 1,000 patients with high blood pressure who were taught the importance of restricting salt intake found that only 20 percent of the patients were following the advice 3 1/2 years later (Evers, Bass, Donner, & McWhinney, 1987). Apparently, it will be difficult for us to learn to eat less of the foods that our parents served us—especially when fatty, salty, and sweet calories taste so good.

However, a more successful program blitzed the citizens of three California communities with ads advocating lower fat diets through television, radio, newspapers, bus displays, billboards, and direct mailings in addition to one-on-one counseling in behavioral self-management skills (Meyer, Nash, McAlister, Maccoby & Farquhar, 1980). And, an in-school program in Los Angeles found that teaching children who are at risk for chronic health problems the importance of low-fat diets produced significant changes in eating behavior (Marcus, Wheeler, Cullen, & Crane, 1987). Apparently it is difficult to change unhealthy eating behavior, but it is not impossible (Jeffrey, 1988).

Regular Aerobic Exercise

We all know that exercise is good for our health. But most of us would be surprised to see the large amount of evidence that links regular moderate aerobic exercise to good health (Jenkins, 1988). By moderate aerobic exercise, I mean at least 30 minutes of continuous exercise that raises the heart rate to 70 to 85 percent of maximum capacity at least four times each week (Taylor, 1986). Unless the individual has a preexisting medical problem that prohibits exercise, regular aerobic exercise has been shown to reduce high blood pressure, blood cholesterol levels, and the risk of coronary heart disease (Leon, 1983; Roy & Steptoe, 1991). Then why is it that so few of us exercise regularly? You know from my confessions in chapter 9 that my history of exercise is an irregular one. I have worked out three times this week, but last week I was "too busy" to exercise at all. Why do I—a person who values good health and decries hypocrisy—often fail to practice what I preach? The unfortunate fact is that I am not the exception, but the rule. It has been estimated that only 21 percent of adults in the United States engage in regular aerobic exercise (White, Powell, Hogelin, Gentry, & Forman, 1987).

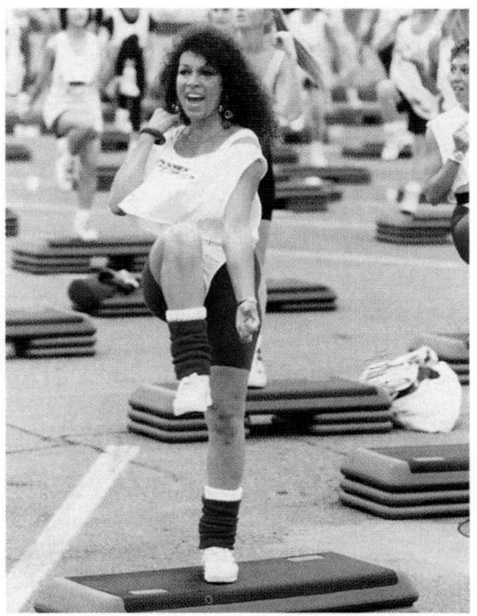

A routine of moderate exercise helps to promote good health.

Part of the answer seems to be a lack of information. The number of Americans who exercise regularly increased by 50 percent between 1975 and 1980 (American Running and Fitness Association, 1981), probably mostly because of publicity concerning the health benefits. But the number of us who know about the health benefits of exercise and still don't exercise regularly is very high. The real problem is *adherence*. Far more of us begin exercise programs than stick with them. On the average, only half the individuals who begin a regular program of exercise are still at it only 6 months later (Dishman, 1982).

What, then, can a person do to help keep his or her commitment to a program of regular exercise? Psychologists are still actively working on this problem, but so far, it seems that social support from a friend who exercises with you, setting clear personal goals and providing reinforcement to yourself, and avoiding excessively strenuous exercise all help long-term adherence (Taylor, 1986). A clearer belief that regular exercise really will benefit *you* also seems to help, as individuals who believe that they should take charge of their own health and those who know they are at risk for coronary heart disease for other reasons are more likely to exercise regularly (Dishman, 1982). We all need to find a reason and a way to keep exercising.

Medical Compliance

Psychologists have also found themselves called on by physicians to help solve a surprisingly difficult and widespread problem in health care delivery. Patients with chronic health problems, such as high blood pressure and diabetes, frequently do not take their prescribed medication. This is extremely unfortunate because proper use of medication can

HUMAN DIVERSITY

Psychology and Women's Health

Judith Rodin and Jeanette Ickovics (1990) have provided an excellent summary of what psychologists know about the health and health care of women and have called for new research efforts in this area.

Health Concerns of Women

A number of health issues are unique to women. Breast, ovarian, and cervical cancer, hysterectomy (surgical removal of the uterus), and menstrual dysfunction are concerns only of women, and osteoporosis (thinning of the bones), eating disorders, lupus, and rheumatoid arthritis are far more common in women than men. In addition, two-thirds of all surgery in the United States is performed on women, mostly because of the high rates of cesarean deliveries and hysterectomies (Travis, 1988).

Women also have unique health concerns because they are often prescribed the hormone estrogen. Estrogen is contained in birth control pills and is prescribed for women who have reached menopause to replace the natural supply that has diminished. Birth control pills and estrogen replacement may increase the risk for some forms of cancer. In addition, although estrogen replacement appears to decrease the rate of heart disease, birth control pills may increase the risk for heart disease under some circumstances (Rodin & Ickovics, 1990).

In spite of these clear differences in the health concerns of women, women have been excluded from health research to a great extent in the past. This means that much of what has been learned in medical research may not apply to women. The National Institutes of Health have mandated a policy that women can no longer be excluded from research unless there is a strong reason, but researchers continue to come up with reasons for excluding women from their studies that are considered acceptable. This is clearly an area requiring greater change in the near future.

Changes in High-Risk Behavior

The second reason that a focus on women's health is needed is that women are behaving more like men in terms of health behavior in recent years. This century has seen marked increases in women in risky behaviors that greatly increase the chance of illness, such as cigarette smoking and excessive alcohol use. As a result, the death rates for men and women are growing more similar, particularly because of a large increase in the rates of cigarette-related lung cancer.

Different Equation Between Health Behaviors and Illnesses

Third, the equation relating health-related behaviors and illness is somewhat different for women and men. For example, behaviors that create health risks for both women and men, such as cigarette smoking, moderate to excessive alcohol consumption, obesity, and high-fat diets are particularly dangerous for women who take birth control pills. Women need to be made aware of interactions among their risk factors that do not affect men.

Another way in which the health behavior equation is different for women can be seen in the example of AIDS. Men can and do acquire the HIV virus that leads to AIDS—HIV—from intercourse with women, but it is more common for women to acquire the virus through either vaginal or anal intercourse. While only 2 percent of men with AIDS acquired HIV through heterosexual intercourse, 31 percent of women with AIDS acquired HIV in this way. Thus, the risks for contracting HIV (and AIDS) from essentially the same behaviors are quite different for women and men (Rodin & Ickovics, 1990).

A third way in which the health behavior equation is different for women concerns the effects of employment. Women who are employed tend to be healthier than women who are not, but women who are employed in demeaning, low-paying, and pressured jobs have much poorer health. Interestingly, women who have satisfying jobs, are married, and have children are the healthiest of all, in spite of the pressures involved in handling all of these roles (Waldron, 1991).

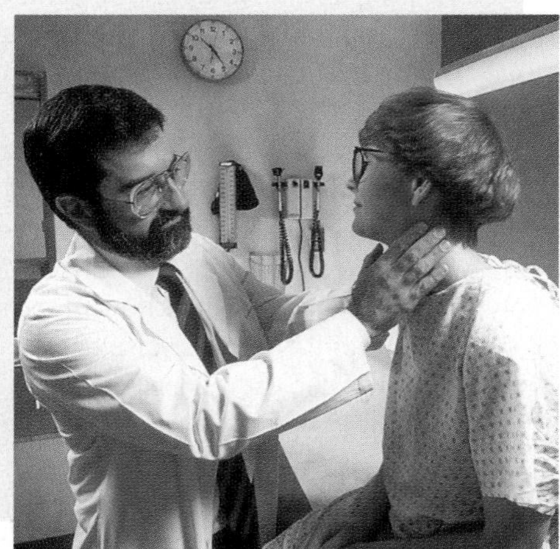

Women have different health concerns than men, but the medical profession is still dominated by men who are not properly trained to meet the needs of women.

greatly reduce the risk of stroke and heart attack associated with high blood pressure and reduce the risk of blindness, amputation of limbs, and other complications of diabetes. Reasons for failing to follow prescribed treatments include not understanding the physician's instructions, not wanting to experience the side effects of some medications, and simple denial of the need to continue treatment. Some health psychologists, therefore, devote a substantial amount of their time to implementing programs to help patients comply most effectively with their doctor's orders (Brownlee-Dufek et al., 1987).

SUMMING UP: HOW BENEFICIAL COULD HEALTH PSYCHOLOGY BE?

You have read a great deal in this chapter about the relationship between psychology and health. As a result, I hope that you have a better understanding of the ways in which stress, coping, and health-related behaviors can affect your physical well-being. But just how important is all this information about health psychology? You've heard me explain since chapters 1 and 2 that the mind and the body are intricately and profoundly interrelated, but how much impact could psychological factors *really* have on physical health? *A lot.* Let me try to convince you.

To understand the potential benefits of psychology to health, we need to look at what medicine has already accomplished during this century. In 1900 the leading causes of death in the United States were infectious diseases, such as tuberculosis (Levy & Moskowitz, 1982). Since that time advances in antibiotics and other aspects of medical care have made deaths due to these causes rare.

Now the major unconquered killers, in order of their frequency as causes of death, are heart disease, cancer, and accidents (Jenkins, 1988; Levy & Moskowitz, 1982). Medical research has accomplished about all that it can in the area of bacterial infections. The next breakthroughs in medicine that save large numbers of lives will probably be more effective treatments for heart diseases, improved treatments for cancer, and treatments or vaccines for AIDS.

But notice two things: First, these expected medical breakthroughs have not happened yet and may possibly never happen; and second, the number one and two killers of Americans today—heart disease and cancer—are disorders in which stress and lifestyle (eating, drinking, smoking, exercising, etc.) play a major role. And as we just noted, although it is completely preventable, AIDS is a major cause of death. Health psychology may very well take the lead in the fight against these diseases. To take but one example: Since cigarette smoking is the leading cause of lung cancer and a prime factor in heart disease, is it more reasonable to expect medicine to cure these diseases or for us to seek more effective ways of helping smokers stop smoking and preventing nonsmokers from ever starting?

So the possibilities of health psychology having a major impact on our health are quite good. Even if we accept the premise that the major causes of death in the United States are related to stress and lifestyle, however, we need to know how *much* impact psychological factors can have on our health. Until we have an answer to that question, we cannot estimate the potential benefits of health psychology. A complete answer is impossible at this time, but a very impressive tentative answer can be given by looking at an extremely important study of health-related behavior.

Nearly 7,000 adults living in Alameda County, California, answered questions concerning their health, including the following questionnaire, which you can take yourself. How many of these positive health practices do you engage in?

1. Moderate or no use of alcohol.
2. Sleeping 7 to 8 hours nightly.
3. Never or rarely eating between meals.
4. Being at or near your ideal weight for your height.
5. Regular physical exercise.
6. Never smoking cigarettes.
7. Eating breakfast almost every day.

Two studies of the health of these individuals 5 1/2 and 9 1/2 years later (Belloc, 1973; Breslow & Enstrom, 1980) revealed a dramatic relationship between health practices and

FIGURE 12.7

The number of positive health practices was found to be dramatically related to the percentage of deaths over 5 1/2 years in the Alameda County study.

Source: Data from N. B. Belloc, "Relationship of Health Practices to Mortality," *Preventive Medicine* 2:67–81, 1973. Copyright © 1973 Academic Press, Orlando, FL.

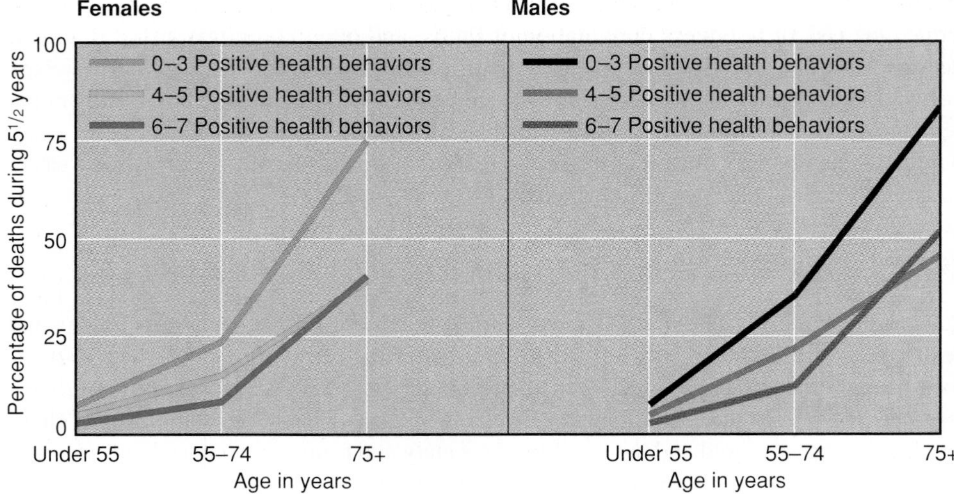

mortality. As shown in figure 12.7, those individuals who engaged in 0 to 3 positive health practices were considerably more likely to have died in the first 5 1/2 years of the study than individuals who engaged in 6 to 7 positive health practices, particularly in middle age and beyond. After 9 1/2 years, the death rate of the group engaged in 0 to 3 positive health practices was, astoundingly, *twice* as high as for the group engaging in 6 to 7 positive health practices.

These findings provide strong encouragement for the idea that changes in lifestyle could produce dramatic improvements in health and longevity. Before we use this information to evaluate the potential of health psychology, consider the following. This research showed that people who engage in more positive health practices live markedly longer, but to date health psychology has shown only modest success in helping individuals who engage in few positive health behaviors to engage in more. On the other hand, this study looked only at the relationship of a few psychological factors that appear to be related to health, and in particular, did not measure stress. In this sense, then, even the dramatic findings of the Alameda County study may underestimate the potential benefits of health psychology (Winett, 1995).

Psychology and the Cost of Health Care

One of the most pressing problems of personal economics facing all of us today is the surging cost of health care. The cost of routine health care and hospitalization has risen dramatically over the past decades. Even for those with adequate health insurance or who are members of a health maintenance organization (HMO), the increased costs are a drain through increased premiums and membership fees. For this reason, a great deal of effort has gone into the search for ways to reduce health care expenses. In particular, insurance companies and HMOs—which provide for an individual's health care needs for a flat annual fee—have been active in trying to find ways to reduce health care costs.

Surprisingly, psychology offers two of the best solutions to this problem. First, as we have seen in this chapter, health psychology has the ability to *prevent* serious health problems and to reduce recurrences of problems such as heart attacks. The savings in preventing health problems over treating them once they have developed are dramatic. Second, more traditional forms of services provided by clinical psychologists can also play a major role in the reduction of health care costs.

Physicians have long known that 50 to 75 percent of the patients that they see either have pains and other symptoms without any known physical cause or have genuine physical problems, such as ulcers, that are caused by stress, alcohol abuse, and other psychological factors. HMO members with such problems visit physicians twice as often as other members (Turkington, 1987). A number of studies have been conducted to see whether referring these patients actually results in a reduction in the use of medical services. These studies show that providing psychological services greatly reduces the overall cost of medical care and further benefits employers, who often pay part of the cost of insurance or HMOs, by reducing the number of days missed from work due to illness (Gabbard et al., 1997; Turkington, 1987).

Review

Psychological methods have been successfully used in the prevention and treatment of medical problems. Methods have been developed to help people drink less alcohol, exercise regularly, stop smoking, lose excess weight, and make other behavioral changes that reduce the risk of heart attack and other serious diseases. Progressive relaxation training and other treatment techniques have also been successful in treating problems such as high blood pressure, headaches, epilepsy, and diabetes. The more that we are willing to apply the advances in understanding of illness from the field of health psychology to our lives, the more we will be able to prevent unnecessary disease and control the cost of health care.

Thinking Critically About Psychology

1. Do the members of your family exercise enough? If not, do you think there is any way that you could convince them to change?

2. Why do you think that eating breakfast every day is a sign of good health? Could there be an explanation that has nothing to do with nutrition?

Check Your Learning

To be sure that you have learned the key points from the preceding section, cover the answers below and try to answer each question. If you give an incorrect answer to any question, return to the page given next to the correct answer to see why your answer was not correct.

1. ________________ refers to a method of learning to deeply relax the muscles of your body.

a. Psychoanalysis
b. Cognitive therapy
c. Aerobics
d. Progressive relaxation training

2. A surprisingly difficult and widespread problem in health care delivery is the lack of ________________ .

a. pharmacies
b. drugs
c. transportation
d. medical compliance

3. ________________ is a disease that greatly impairs the ability of the body's immune system to fight bacteria, viruses, and cancer.

a. AIDS
b. Tuberculosis
c. Chicken pox
d. Heart disease

4. Changes in lifestyle could produce dramatic improvements in health and longevity in the United States.

a. True
b. False

Correct Answers

1. d (p. 453), **2.** d (p. 455), **3.** a (p. 460), **4.** a (p. 458).

APPLICATION OF PSYCHOLOGY

PREVENTION AND TREATMENT OF AIDS

Six years ago, the brother of one of my colleagues died of **acquired immune deficiency syndrome,** or AIDS. This tragedy brought the spectre of AIDS very much closer to home for me, as he was a decent and talented man who died unnecessarily in his twenties.

As we are all well aware, our planet is in the midst of a truly horrible fatal epidemic of AIDS. This disease, which is caused by the *human immune deficiency virus (HIV),* has already killed tens of thousands of men, women, and children. But we are only beginning to see the full scope of the epidemic. This is because the disease progresses slowly from HIV infection to full-blown AIDS in an average of 8 to 10 years in adults. To date, therefore, we have seen only the "tip of the iceberg" of fatalities that will result from AIDS.

Each of the thousands of blocks in this huge quilt memorializes someone who has died of AIDS.

Obviously, an epidemic of this magnitude demands our attention, but why bring up a medical disease in a psychology textbook? The answer is that, like most other physical diseases, there are important *psychological* aspects to the transmission and treatment of AIDS. It is extremely important that you, as an educated person, understand this point. To explain the role of psychological factors in AIDS, we look first at the physical nature of the disease.

AIDS is a disease that greatly impairs the ability of the body's immune system to fight bacteria, viruses, and cancer. HIV has many effects on the immune system, but most importantly the virus results in mass destruction of the immune cells known as *lymphocytes* and, indirectly, leaves the important *B-cells* of the immune system useless. HIV disables the B-cells by invading the nucleus of another type of immune cell known as *T-4 Helper cells.* The T-4 Helper cells help the B-cells identify hostile bacteria and viruses and signal the B-cells to destroy them. Unfortunately, HIV either destroys the T-4 cells or deactivates them, making the B-cells useless and leaving the body vulnerable to disease. The person with AIDS does not actually die from the AIDS, but from the other diseases such as pneumonia and cancer that flourish because of the weakened immune system.

AIDS is the direct result of patterns of behavior that bring persons into contact with the AIDS virus. During the 1990s, an additional 2 million persons are expected to be infected with HIV (WHO, 1990). What are the patterns of *high-risk behaviors* that will result in these new infections? If we know what the high-risk behaviors are, it may be possible for us all to help *prevent* AIDS by reducing high-risk behaviors.

HIV is spread through bodily fluids—especially blood and semen, but also by saliva and other fluids. The most common means of transmission is all forms of sexual intercourse—vaginal (contact of penis and vagina), oral (contact of penis and mouth), and anal (contact of penis and anus). Although anal intercourse is believed to create an especially high risk of transmission, vaginal intercourse is actually a greater source of transmission because it is practiced more widely (Ironson & Schneiderman, 1991). Although AIDS was first spread among homosexual men in the United States and is still far more common among them, the spread of HIV by sexual acts is not limited in any way to homosexuals. Engaging in any form of intercourse with an HIV-infected partner of either the same or the opposite sex is equally likely to result in the spread of AIDS. Indeed, sometime during the 1990s, transmission of HIV through heterosexual contact is expected to become more common than through homosexual contact.

The next most frequent modes of transmission are intravenous drug use and transmission from an infected mother to her infant during birth, with infection from blood transfusions and other means being much less common (Ironson & Schneiderman, 1991). Persons who use drugs that are injected are at high risk for acquiring HIV through the blood if they share a needle with someone infected with HIV, but also because such drugs suppress the functioning of the immune system themselves (O'Leary, 1990).

AIDS is much more common in some cultures than others. Worldwide, AIDS is less common in Asian and Arabic countries, but there are exceptions to this rule, such as the high rate of AIDS among prostitutes in Bangkok and some other cities with high levels of international tourism.

In the United States, AIDS is found in all ethnic groups, but this tragic burden is not equally distributed. For example, among heterosexuals in the United States, 74 percent of the male AIDS cases and 71 percent of the female cases are of African or Latin descent (Ironson & Schneiderman, 1991).

Prevention of AIDS Through Behavior Change

It is estimated that at least one-third of the projected new cases of HIV infection in the 1990s can be prevented through programs designed to change high-risk behaviors (WHO, 1990). What behaviors would need to be changed? First, persons have virtually no chance of acquiring AIDS if (a) they are not sexually active or are involved in a completely monogamous sexual relationship (with a single partner who is not infected with HIV and who is not involved in a sexual relationship with anyone else), and (b) they do not use intravenous drugs. In that sense, AIDS is not a difficult disease to avoid. Moreover, the risk of AIDS is also greatly decreased just by having fewer sex partners, engaging in such "safe sex" practices as the use of condoms, and not having sex with persons who may have been exposed to HIV.

As simple as it sounds, however, it is very difficult to convince people to change their behavior—especially their sexual behavior. College students currently have low rates of HIV infection, but because they have been slow to adopt safe sex practices, they are placing themselves at risk. Needle drug users continue to share needles because it is difficult to obtain new needles, and, almost unbelievably, some women who know they have HIV infection allow themselves to become pregnant in spite of the high risk of transmission to their own infants (Ironson & Schneiderman, 1991). What can health psychologists do to help prevent these situations?

Jeffrey Kelly and his colleagues at the University of Mississippi (1989) have given us a good example of the ways in which psychologists can help. Kelly's research group recently published the results of a promising approach to decreasing the rate of high-risk sexual behaviors among homosexual men. Describing this study will involve the discussion of sexual practices that some of you may not wish to read about. But discussing these matters openly may save human lives.

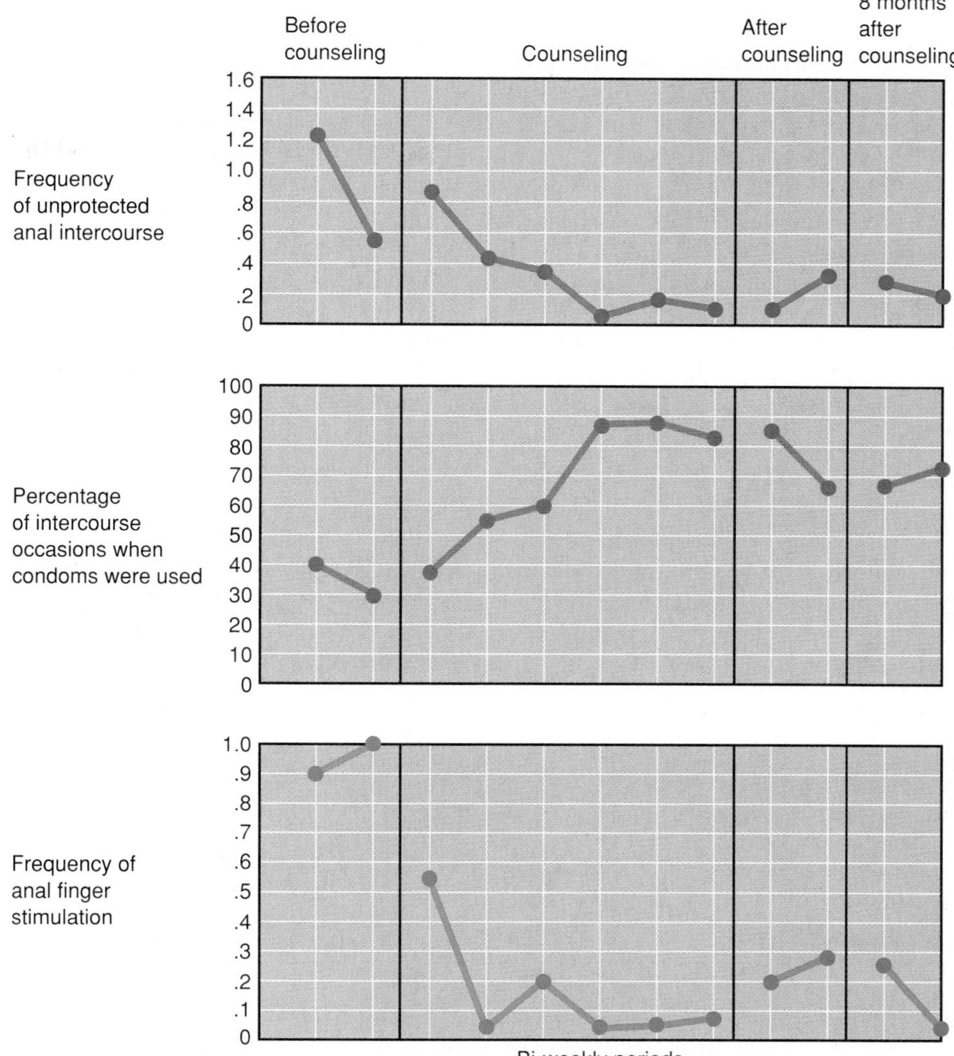

FIGURE 12.8

The results of a counseling program designed to reduce the frequency of sexual behaviors that increase the risk of infection with AIDS.

Source: Data from J. A. Kelley, et al., "Behavioral Intervention to Reduce AIDS Risk Activities," in *Journal of Consulting and Clinical Psychology*, 57:60–67, 1989. Copyright 1989 by the American Psychological Association.

As described earlier, certain sexual practices are believed to especially increase the risk of spreading the virus, whether practiced by homosexual or heterosexual persons. These include, but are not limited to, anal intercourse without the use of a condom for protection and stimulating the anus of the partner by finger or mouth. Decreasing these and other high-risk sexual practices, therefore, would decrease the spread of AIDS.

Kelly's research group recruited a group of 51 gay men who did not have the AIDS virus. As shown in figure 12.8, the men engaged in a high rate of anal intercourse and anal finger stimulation and did not consistently use condoms prior to the start of counseling.

The men attended 12 weekly group counseling sessions led by clinical psychologists. These sessions provided information on AIDS that explained why high-risk behaviors should be avoided, discussed factors that led to abandoning precautions in the past (being in a depressed mood, excessive drinking, etc.), and suggested ways to better cope with these factors in the future. The sessions helped the men learn to assertively insist that their partners follow safe sex practices and counseled the men on establishing lasting monogamous relationships.

The counseling sessions led to a steady decrease in the frequency of both forms of unprotected anal sex and increase in the use of condoms. Eight months after the counseling sessions ended, the changes in sexual behavior were still evident. Thus, the counseling approach and other similar methods (Coates, 1990) offer real hope in the fight against AIDS. Unfortunately, not enough psychologists are trained in such counseling methods and there is too little available funding for all types of preventive programs.

Psychological Factors in the Treatment of AIDS

AIDS is currently a disease with no cure. Medical treatments have been developed that slow the progress of the HIV infection, but they cannot cure AIDS. Still, slowing the progress of the infection is an extremely worthwhile goal, both because every day of human life is precious and because it may prolong life until a medical cure is found.

A great deal of research is currently under way to find ways in which psychological interventions might be useful in slowing the progression of HIV infection. As has been made clear throughout this chapter, it is well known that stress and other psychological variables affect the immune system. Therefore, it may be possible to develop psychological interventions that help strengthen the immune system and slow the progression of AIDS by changing health-related behavior and managing stress (Antoni et al., 1990). Some promising progress has been made in this area. For example, an intensive program of regular aerobic exercise has been shown to buffer the detrimental effects of stressful events on several key aspects of immune functioning that are important in AIDS (Antoni et al., 1990). Unfortunately, the beneficial effects of aerobic exercise are only modest, and it is not known if they would actually slow the progress of the HIV infection itself. Research is still in the beginning stages, but stress-management training may also be helpful in slowing the progress of the HIV infection (Antoni et al., 1990). Much remains to be learned in these areas, but fortunately some of psychology's brightest minds have turned to this problem.

Summary

I. Health psychology attempts to prevent health problems by helping individuals cope with stress and change health related behavior.

II. There are many sources of stress in our lives, some obvious and some hidden.

- **A.** Frustration is the result of failure to satisfy a motive.
- **B.** Conflict is the result of two or more incompatible motives. The four major types of conflicts are:
  - **1.** Approach-approach conflicts
  - **2.** Avoidance-avoidance conflicts
  - **3.** Approach-avoidance conflicts
  - **4.** Double approach-avoidance conflicts
- **C.** Pressure is the stress that arises from the threat of negative events.
- **D.** Both positive and negative life events can lead to stressful changes and the need for readjustment.
- **E.** Environmental conditions such as heat, cold, and pollution can be stressful.

III. We react to stress in relatively predictable ways.

- **A.** Reactions to stress involve both psychological and physiological reactions.
- **B.** Some important general aspects of stress reactions are the same regardless of the source of stress.
  - **1.** The fact that the body reacts to stress with an alarm reaction, a phase of resistance to the stress, and a stage of exhaustion if coping is not successful has been termed the general adaptation syndrome.
  - **2.** Common psychological reactions to stress are anxiety, depression, decreased ability to think, concentrate, and make decisions, and changes in motives such as increased hunger and decreased interest in sex.

IV. We do not just react passively to stress; we actively attempt to cope with it.

- **A.** Effective coping strategies involve either removal of the source of the stress or managing the degree of the stress reactions.
- **B.** Ineffective coping strategies do not help in the long run, either because they create more stress (such as aggression) or because they distort reality (defense mechanisms).

V. Stress requires greater control under some circumstances than others.

- **A.** Sources of stress are more stressful when we have no prior experience with them.
- **B.** Sources of stress are more stressful when they are unpredictable and when we have no control over them.
- **C.** Stress creates more severe reactions when we have little social support.
- **D.** Some stressors are easier to deal with when we are younger and some are easier when we are older.

VI. Characteristics of the person also influence the magnitude of stress reactions in a "person x situation interaction"; these characteristics include:

- **A.** Differences in cognitive appraisal of potential stress events and the degree to which an individual "sensitizes" (seeks information about the stress) or "represses" (avoids seeking information or thinking about the stress).

B. The Type A behavior pattern, including hostile reaction to competitive pressure, is a risk factor for heart disease.

VII. Several aspects of our behavior are related to our health.

A. Learning to relax deeply can reduce health risks.

B. Abuse of substances like alcohol and caffeine and the use of tobacco products are behaviors that create serious health risks.

C. Health psychologists also seek to reduce health risks by helping individuals exercise properly, control their weight, and follow medical treatments properly.

D. Because AIDS is usually acquired from high-risk behaviors, and because psychological factors are intimately related to immune system functioning, the science of psychology is playing a key role in the fight against the AIDS epidemic.

Suggested Readings

1. A sophisticated but readable discussion of stress by the father of the concept: Selye, H. (1976). *The stress of life*. New York: Knopf.
2. Overviews of the field of health psychology: Winett, R. A. (1995). A framework for health promotion and disease prevention programs. *American Psychologist, 50*, 341–350. Wilson, D. K., Rodrigue, J. R., & Taylor, W. C. (1997). *Health-promoting and health-compromising behaviors among minority adolescents.* Washington, DC: American Psychological Association.
3. For more on the important topic of social support: Heller, K. (Ed.), Special series: Disaggregating the process of social support. *Journal of Consulting and Clinical Psychology, 54*, 415–470.
4. An excellent description of effective methods of treating victims of rape: Calhoun, K. C., & Atkeson, B. M. (1989). *Treatment of rape victims*. NY: Pergamon Press.
5. An excellent, readable discussion of Type A personality: Wright, L. (1988). The Type A behavior problem and coronary artery disease. *American Psychologist, 43*, 2–14.
6. For a strong discussion of the stressful impact on women's mental health of filling multiple roles: McBride, A. B. (1990). Mental health effects of women's multiple roles. *American Psychologist, 45*, 381–384.

CHAPTER 13

CHAPTER OUTLINE

Abnormal Behavior

PROLOGUE

Does making a speech make you nervous? How about meeting people? If these situations make you nervous, you're not alone; anxiety is quite common in these and other social situations where other people are scrutinizing you. But, for some people, the level of anxiety is so intense that it disrupts their ability to function in important social situations. Let's consider the experience of a woman whom we will call Carol. Carol is an intelligent and attractive woman who is successful in her professional career. She went to a university psychological clinic specializing in anxiety disorders to learn more about her intense anxiety in social situations.

The psychologists observed Carol in three different anxiety-provoking social situations. In the first situation, a stranger played the role of a man on a first date with Carol at a restaurant. In the second scene, a woman pretended to be a new neighbor of Carol's. In the third situation, Carol delivered a brief impromptu speech to two psychologists. During these three tests, Carol wore sensors that monitored her heart rate and blood pressure, and immediately after each test she was asked to choose statements that accurately reflected her thoughts and feelings about her performance during the tests, what she thought that other people thought about her, and her ability to cope.

Carol acted very nervously in each situation. She rarely made eye contact, spoke very little, and frequently shifted her posture. Her blood pressure and her heart rate rose dramatically, particularly during the speech, but was almost as high during the first date. She felt subjectively nervous in all situations and thought that she behaved in ways that no one would like.

Carol's anxiety was intense enough that it caused serious problems in her life. It led her to turn down dates and other social invitations, and even led her to change her major to avoid taking a course in which she would have to give speeches. Because her anxiety was serious enough to cause a problem, she was considered to have a social phobia by the psychologists—one of the forms of abnormal behavior that we will study in this chapter.

Does it surprise you to learn that something as understandable as exaggerated social anxiety would be considered to be "abnormal" by psychologists and psychiatrists? Actually, most forms of abnormal behavior aren't very different from what we would consider to be normal. Abnormal behavior is simply a pattern acting, thinking, or feeling that is harmful in some way to the individual or to others. That may involve behavior that is quite unusual, but it also encompasses behavior that seems like only an exaggeration of normal behavior.

Abnormal behavior takes many forms. Excessive anxiety and depression are the most common types of abnormal behavior. Other types include alterations of perception and sudden changes in personality and identity. Other psychological disorders involve false beliefs and hallucinations that result in the individual's being "out of touch with reality." Other forms involve symptoms of health problems that have no known physical cause.

What causes abnormal behavior? Many answers have been given to this question throughout history. The earliest answer was that evil spirits caused it, but other views are more common today. Some theorists believe that abnormal behavior results from disturbances of the brain; others believe that it has psychological causes, such as excessive stress or learning faulty cognitions about ourselves or others. Currently, there is a movement toward explanations for abnormal behavior that combine both biological and psychological factors.

KEY TERMS

ABNORMAL BEHAVIOR

abnormal behavior
Actions, thoughts, and feelings that are harmful to the person or to others.

The term *abnormal* is one of the most elusive terms in psychology. It's not a difficult term to define in words, but it's often difficult to apply to specific individuals because the definition involves so much *subjectivity*. **Abnormal behavior** is defined as those actions, thoughts, and feelings that are harmful to the person or to others. In the United States, approximately 15 percent of all persons exhibit actions, thoughts, or feelings that are considered harmful enough to be labeled abnormal (Regnier et al., 1988).

This harm may take many forms, ranging from personal discomfort (as in feeling depressed) to physical damage (as in assaulting another person). Notice that abnormality is defined only in terms of harm. It's not enough that a pattern of behavior is *unusual* (statistically uncommon for that group of people) to be considered abnormal. Extreme intelligence and total honesty are unusual, but they would hardly be considered abnormal. On the other hand, some patterns of behavior that are not uncommon are clearly harmful. For example, the intense prejudice against Jews that was so prevalent during the days of Hitler's Germany was common, but abnormal. Many psychologists think that cigarette smoking, which is common in our culture today, should be considered abnormal because of the health problems that it causes.

This definition of abnormality requires subjective judgments in two ways. First, even though abnormality is defined in terms of harm rather than unusualness, it must be decided whether an individual's problems are *severe enough* to be considered "harmful." For example, almost everyone suffers some discomfort at times from shyness. How shy does a person have to be to be considered abnormally shy? Shier than 90 percent of other people? More than 95 percent of others? Clearly, psychologists must make largely arbitrary decisions about it in different ways.

Second, subjectivity is also a problem in defining what is *harmful*. That decision reflects the values of the person making the determination, and values differ greatly from one culture to another. For example, the Zuñi Indians of the southwestern United States believed it was good to be able to have hallucinations without taking drugs, for it meant that the gods were blessing you with visits. Nearly all psychologists in the United States would consider hallucinations harmful, but differences of opinion exist on other issues, such as the normality or abnormality of homosexuality or cigarette smoking in our culture. There is probably no complete solution to the problem of subjectivity. The best we can do is to be aware of the problem and try to minimize the role played by our personal values in making subjective judgments about the behavior of others.

continuity hypothesis
The view that abnormal behavior is just a more severe form of normal psychological problems.

discontinuity hypothesis
The view that abnormal behavior is fundamentally different from normal psychological problems.

The concept of abnormal behavior is difficult to use not only because of its inherent subjectivity but also because psychologists have not been able to agree on how abnormal behavior differs from normal behavior. The **continuity hypothesis** of abnormal behavior states that abnormal behavior is just a more severe form of normal psychological problems. This hypothesis is held by many humanists and social learning theorists. The **discontinuity hypothesis,** on the other hand, suggests that abnormal behavior is entirely different from normal psychological problems. Advocates of the continuity hypothesis argue that terms like *insanity* and *mental illness* should not be used because they imply that the individuals have *sick minds* that separate them from the rest of society. Advocates of the discontinuity hypothesis believe that only such strong terms can accurately portray the true nature of abnormal behavior.

Historical Views of Abnormal Behavior

Before we discuss contemporary views of the causes of abnormal behavior, it's instructive to look back through history at beliefs about its cause. This historical perspective will make the important point that our ideas about the causes of abnormal behavior determine what we do to help those who experience it.

Supernatural Theories

The oldest writings about behavior, including those of Plato, the Bible, and the tablets of Babylonian King Hammurabi (1750 B.C.), indicate that, in our earliest belief, abnormal behavior was thought to be caused by evil spirits. Although some people disagreed with this notion during every period in history, the idea that people with psychological problems are possessed by evil spirits was the most influential view during the entire 3,500-year period of history stretching from Hammurabi to shortly before the American Revolution.

During most of the time that the supernatural theory held sway, the consequences for those with psychological problems were not too severe. Treatment mostly took the form of prayer, with the most unpleasant treatment being purgatives—foul liquids that were supposed to help the person vomit out the evil spirit. During the Middle Ages (500–1500), however, these supernatural beliefs were translated into far more harmful forms of "treatment."

In medieval Europe, the Catholic Church published an official document called the *Malleus Maleficarum,* or the *Witches' Hammer.* It gave detailed descriptions of the methods of treatment, or *exorcism,* for those people acting in abnormal ways that "revealed" possession by the devil. Treatment began with a stiff regimen of prayer, fasting, and drinking foul concoctions that caused vomiting, but for those whose behavior did not improve, the *Malleus* recommended stronger methods. People who could not stop acting in deviant ways after exorcism were considered to be witches or warlocks (male witches). It was believed that the only way to save their souls was to destroy their bodies to drive out Satan. As a result, half a million so-called "witches," mostly women, were put to death in Europe alone (Loftus, 1993). Even as late as 1692, 20 individuals were put to death as witches in Salem, Massachusetts. Nineteen were hanged for "witchcraft" while the twentieth victim died as a result of heavy rocks being placed on him in an effort to force him to confess (Phillips, 1933).

Peculiar behavior was once explained as demon possession. Here St. Catherine exorcises a demon from a woman.

Fortunately, much has changed in our conceptions of abnormal behavior during the past 500 years. But have we completely abandoned the supernatural beliefs of the Dark Ages? Consider the following news report from the May 8, 1978, issue of *Time* magazine:

> When Anneliese Michel died at the age of 23 in Klingenberg, West Germany, in the summer of 1976, she was little more than a skeleton, weighing a mere 68 lbs. Yet shortly before she died, her parents said Anneliese performed an astonishing 500 deep knee-bends in one day. The source of her power, her parents believed, was nothing less than the devil himself. Anneliese's release from evil spirits came only with death, after she starved herself during a nightmarish ten-month series of Roman Catholic exorcism rituals. Two weeks ago, a court in Aschaffenburg found two priests and Anneliese's parents, wealthy mill-owner Josef Michel, 60, and his wife Anna, 57, guilty of negligent homicide in her death. The four, who last week appealed their conviction, drew six-month suspended prison sentences.
>
> Anneliese's parents had agreed to the exorcism with the local bishop's approval after doctors failed to rid her of epileptic-like convulsions. The prosecution took no issue with the rite of exorcism, which Fathers Wilhelm Renz and Ernst Alt conducted according to a Catholic ritual promulgated in 1614. But prosecutor Karl Stenger argued that calling a doctor to examine the girl "would not have compromised the defendants' religious convictions." Churchmen seemed to agree. Munich's Joseph Cardinal Katzinger said that the 1614 ritual "must be thoroughly revised," and the German Bishops' Conference ruled last week that no more exorcisms would be permitted unless a doctor was called in.

Anneliese Michel

Biological Theories

An ancient voice that argued against the supernatural theory of abnormal behavior was the fifth century B.C. Greek physician Hippocrates. He believed that biological disorders of the body caused abnormal behavior. According to Hippocrates's view, the body contains four important fluids, or *humors:* blood, phlegm, black bile, and yellow bile. If these fluids get out of balance, abnormal behavior is the result. An excess of black bile, for example, leads to depression; an excess of yellow bile causes irritability.

Hippocrates's theory was inaccurate, of course, and so he was not able to punch much of a hole in the supernatural approach. But he set the stage for later developments by suggesting that abnormal behavior might have *natural* rather than supernatural causes. During the 2,000 years after Hippocrates, a number of scientists who had been influenced by Hippocrates's idea searched in vain for a biological cause of abnormal behavior. Finally, in the 1800s medical researchers such as German physician Richard von Krafft-Ebing made discoveries that led to a resurgence of biological theory and the eventual birth of psychiatry as a discipline.

Krafft-Ebing was working with a now rare form of severe psychological disturbance called *paresis.* He and a number of independent researchers discovered that paresis was

Richard von Krafft-Ebing (1840–1902)

actually an advanced stage of the venereal disease *syphilis*. Syphilis is a bacterial infection that begins with a sore, or chancre, on the genitals or on another point of entry, that is later followed by a copper-colored skin rash. The untreated disease then goes through a long "invisible" period that eventually leads to the destruction of important bodily organs. If the bacteria destroy brain cells, paresis is the result. Because of the long period of time between the original infection and the later paresis, it was not known that the two conditions were related until Krafft-Ebing demonstrated through inoculation tests that all individuals with paresis also had syphilis.

The discovery that paresis had a biological cause sent shock waves through the medical community. Soon physicians—who up to this time had little to do with people with abnormal behavior—were placed in charge of mental institutions, and the medical specialty of psychiatry was formed. There were high expectations that the biological causes for all the other forms of abnormal behavior would soon be discovered. But although the discovery of penicillin and its use in the treatment of syphilis almost totally eradicated paresis, few other biological causes of abnormal behavior were discovered. In recent years, however, major advances in the treatment of some severe forms of abnormal behavior have been made possible by the development of effective drug therapies.

Psychological Theories

Hippocrates was not the only ancient Greek suggesting a *natural* explanation for abnormal behavior. Pythagoras, who also gave us geometry, was very active in the treatment of psychological problems. He held the then-radical belief that psychological problems are caused by *psychological* factors such as stress. He placed individuals with problems in "temples" where they received rest, exercise, a good diet, an understanding person to talk to, and practical advice on how to straighten out their lives. Records from his temples suggest that Pythagoras's methods were highly successful. Unfortunately, the psychological ideas of Pythagoras were not able to compete with those of the supernaturalists until modern times.

Although there were many important advocates of psychological theory, it was not until Sigmund Freud published his influential views that psychological theory was able to compete with the supernatural and biological approaches. Although Freud's model of unconscious conflicts was quite different from the ideas of Pythagoras, Freud was the champion of the view that psychological problems had psychological causes until recent times.

Contemporary Views of Abnormal Behavior

Today, abnormal behavior is believed to be a natural phenomenon with natural causes. As research evidence has accumulated, it has become increasingly clear that both biological and psychological factors are involved in the origins of many psychological disorders. Some disorders are solely biological in origin (such as those caused by brain injuries), and some are solely psychological in origin (such as acute grief reactions to the death of a loved one in normal individuals). But many other disorders appear to involve both kinds of causes. Inherited predispositions to certain kinds of problems, abnormal amounts of specific neurotransmitter substances in the brain, and tendencies to react autonomically to stress in an abnormal way are some of the biological factors believed to be partially responsible for a variety of psychological disorders. The psychological factors involved in these same disorders include stress, abnormal social learning histories, ineffective coping strategies, and inadequate social support. Apparently, biological and psychological factors work together to determine whether a person will experience psychological problems. For example, individuals whose autonomic nervous systems tend to react excessively to stress will have problems only if their lives are filled with considerable stress and if they have poor social support. If present trends continue, we will probably see a fusion of the biological and psychological approaches into a single, naturalistic viewpoint.

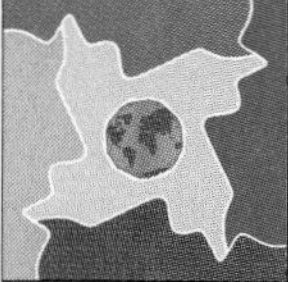

HUMAN DIVERSITY

Ethnicity and Psychological Diagnosis

When we meet someone, our gender, age, race, and ethnicity are factors that influence their opinion of us. But when a person goes to a psychologist or psychiatrist because of a problem, do these sociocultural factors influence the diagnosis of an expert? Unfortunately, a number of studies provide evidence that ethnicity, race, age, and gender can all have an impact on how clinical staff evaluate the problems of their clients. Jenkins-Hall and Sacco (1991) assert that "studies suggest that therapy is not a culture-free activity and that cultural variables enter into treatment in ways that parallel their operation in society" (pp. 322–323). For example, two African-American and two white female actors portrayed clients in videotaped interviews. White male and female counselors with at least 3 years of experience each viewed one of the videotapes and rated the psychological well-being of the person depicted in the taped interview. Did the ethnicity of the actor playing the role of the client bias the evaluation of the counselor? Sadly, the African-American women who portrayed a depressed person were rated as more disturbed than white women who portrayed a depressed person, even though they said exactly the same things on videotape and were matched on attractiveness, educational background, employment experience, and age.

Other researchers have arrived at similar conclusions. Bagley and Binitie (1970) found that psychiatrists in England were more likely to give Irish males a diagnosis of alcoholism regardless of the symptoms that they described. The authors felt that stereotypes about the drinking problems of Irish men led the psychiatrists to misinterpret the symptoms that were described to them. Similarly, Loring and Powell (1988) discovered that when mental health professionals read a description of 10 problems of hypothetical people of different races and genders, the sex and race of the client influenced the diagnosis even though the description of problems was the same for everyone.

One recent study found no ethnic bias in diagnosis, however. Littlewood (1992) distributed a description of a hypothetical client to 339 mental health professionals in London, varying only the description of the patient as "born locally" or "born to Jamaican parents." There were no differences between the diagnosis for the two ethnic groups. Hopefully, this means that some mental health professionals are becoming aware of the role that prejudice can play in psychological diagnosis; however, we should not be confident of the findings of a single study. Prejudice is a powerful force in the lives of all humans, and psychologists and psychiatrists are only human after all. A great deal needs to be done at all levels of the education of mental health professionals to reduce the dangerous effects of ethnic prejudice in diagnosis (Fairchild, 1984; Garretson, 1993; Stricker et al., 1990; Whitten, 1993a).

Have you even been misunderstood by others because of your gender, ethnicity, race, or age? If you were a psychologist treating a person who was different from you in some way, do you think you could keep your stereotypes about others from influencing your evaluation of that person? What do you think could be done to reduce the impact of cultural stereotypes in mental health settings?

The Concept of Insanity

Now that we have closely examined the term *abnormal behavior,* let's turn to the concept of **insanity.** What does it mean to be insane? Actually *insanity* is not a psychological or psychiatric term but a legal term. And to make matters more complex, insanity has not one but three different legal meanings, depending on whether it's used as a criminal defense, in a hearing on competency to stand trial, or in a hearing on involuntary commitment to a mental institution.

insanity
A legal definition concerning a person's inability to tell right from wrong, ability to understand the trial proceedings, or whether the person is a direct danger to self or others.

1. *Not guilty by reason of insanity.* In some states, individuals cannot be convicted of a crime if they were legally "insane" at the time the crime was committed. There are many definitions of the term *insane* in this context, but perhaps the most influential formula was proposed by the American Law Institute and adopted by many state and federal courts in the 1970s. It states, "A person is not responsible for criminal conduct if at the time of such conduct, as a result of mental disease or defect, he lacks substantial capacity either to appreciate the wrongfulness of his conduct or to conform his conduct to the requirements of the law." This definition means that people committing crimes are considered "not

John Hinckley Jr. was found not guilty (by reason of insanity) of his attempted assassination of President Reagan.

guilty by reason of insanity" if they had little ability to tell right from wrong or had little ability to control their actions at the time of the crime because of serious psychological problems. Generally, juries will consider only severely psychotic or severely mentally retarded persons to be insane according to this rule, and since individuals with these problems rarely commit crimes, it's rarely a successful defense.

The controversial nature of this use of the term *insanity* in the courtroom was made clear in the public reaction to the trial of John W. Hinckley Jr. in 1982. Hinckley admitted to having shot Ronald Reagan and others in an unsuccessful attempt to assassinate the President. The jurors found Hinckley not guilty because they believed that he was insane. As a result, Hinckley received no prison sentence for his actions but was committed to St. Elizabeth's Psychiatric Hospital in Washington, D.C. If he convinces his doctors that he is sane at some point in the future, he could be released at any time. Public dissatisfaction with this verdict was intense and was partly responsible for changes in the law concerning the insanity defense. Juries in a number of states can now find defendants "guilty but mentally ill." In this case the person receives a prison sentence but is also given psychiatric treatment.

2. *Competence to stand trial.* The term *insanity* is also used in hearings to determine whether the individuals are competent to stand trial. In this sense, the question of insanity is whether the people are able to understand the proceedings of the trial sufficiently to aid in their own defense. Again, it's primarily severely psychotic and mentally retarded individuals who are considered incompetent according to this definition.
3. *Involuntary commitment.* A third meaning of the term *insanity* arises in hearings on the involuntary commitment of individuals to mental institutions. It's legal in most states to commit people to an institution against their will if a court finds them to be insane. The courts generally interpret this as meaning that the individuals are a direct danger—usually meaning a physical danger—to themselves or to others. Behaving in strange ways is not enough to justify involuntary commitment. There must be an element of danger.

Thinking Critically About Psychology

1. Could biological and psychological theories of abnormal behavior both be correct?

2. Do you think smoking cigarettes should be considered to be abnormal? How might psychologists who hold either the continuity hypothesis or discontinuity hypothesis differ on this question?

Review

Actions, thoughts, and feelings that are harmful to the individual or to others are considered to be abnormal. This definition is a difficult one to implement because of the subjectivity involved. How severe must an individual's problem be before he or she is considered harmful? And by whose cultural standards should harmfulness be defined? Moreover, psychologists have not been able to agree on how abnormal behavior differs from normal psychological problems. Is abnormal behavior just a more severe version of normal problems, or is it fundamentally different? Advocates of the continuity hypothesis take the former view, whereas advocates of the discontinuity hypothesis take the latter view.

Differences in perspectives among contemporary psychologists seem minor, however, when compared with differing views of abnormal behavior that have been taken throughout history. Abnormal behavior has been thought to result from supernatural causes or from biological abnormalities, as well as from psychological causes. The supernatural theory is of little importance in today's psychology, but both biological and psychological factors are currently thought to be involved in the origins of abnormal behavior.

In legal terms, persons are considered to be insane if they lack the capacity to deal with the demands of life in significant ways, either to avoid danger to themselves or others, to understand the difference between right and wrong and to behave accordingly, or to safeguard themselves or others. Legal decisions concerning insanity are made in the context of trials (Is a person not guilty by reason of insanity? Is a person competent to stand trial?) and in hearings concerning involuntary commitment to mental institutions.

Check Your Learning

To be sure that you have learned the key points from the preceding section, cover the answers below and try to answer each question. If you give an incorrect answer to any question, return to the page given next to the correct answer to see why your answer was not correct. Remember that these questions cover only some of the important information in this section; it is important that you make up your own questions to check your learning of other facts and concepts.

1. ________________ is defined as those actions, thoughts, and feelings that are harmful to the person or to others.
2. The discovery that paresis developed from syphilis gave support to the ________________ theories of abnormal behavior.
   - **a.** supernatural
   - **b.** biological
   - **c.** psychological
   - **d.** cognitive
3. The writings by Sigmund Freud gave the ________________ theories enough credibility to compete with the other popular theories of the time.
   - **a.** supernatural
   - **b.** biological
   - **c.** psychological
   - **d.** cognitive
4. Research supports the view that both biological factors and psychological factors are involved in the origins of many psychological disorders.
   - **a.** True
   - **b.** False

Correct Answers
1. Abnormal behavior (p. 466), **2.** b (p. 468), **3.** c (p. 468), **4.** a (p. 468).

ANXIETY DISORDERS

Every life is a mixture of positive and negative emotions for everyone. But many people experience excessive levels of the kinds of negative emotions that we identify as being *nervous, tense, worried, scared,* and *anxious.* These terms all refer to anxiety. Ten to 15 million Americans experience such uncomfortable and disruptive levels of anxiety that they are said to have **anxiety disorders.** Anxiety disorders take a variety of different forms as described in the following sections.

anxiety disorders
Psychological disorders that involve excessive levels of negative emotions, such as nervousness, tension, worry, fright, and anxiety.

Phobias

A **phobia** is an intense, unrealistic fear. In this case, the anxiety is focused so intensely on some object or situation that the individual is acutely uncomfortable around it and will often go to great pains to avoid it. There are three types of phobias: (a) *specific phobia,* (b) *social phobia,* and (c) *agoraphobia.*

phobia
An intense, irrational fear.

Specific phobia is the most specific and least disruptive of the phobias. Examples include intense fear of heights, dogs, blood, hypodermic injections, and closed spaces (Ost, 1992). Individuals with specific phobias generally have no other psychological problems, and their lives are disrupted only if the phobia creates a direct problem in daily living. For example, a fear of elevators would be highly disruptive for a person who works in a skyscraper, but it probably would not be for a vegetable farmer.

specific phobia
A phobic fear of one relatively specific thing.

Other forms of phobia, by their very nature, always cause serious problems for the individual. **Social phobia** involves extreme fears of social interactions, particularly those with strangers and those in which the person might be evaluated negatively, such as a job interview or a first date. Because this kind of phobia severely limits social interactions, it disrupts the individual's life.

social phobia
A phobic fear of social interactions, particularly those with strangers and those in which the person might be viewed negatively.

Agoraphobia is the most damaging of all of the phobias. Literally meaning "fear of open spaces," agoraphobia involves an intense fear of leaving one's home or other familiar

agoraphobia
(ag´´o-rah-fō´bē-ah) An intense fear of leaving one's home or other familiar places.

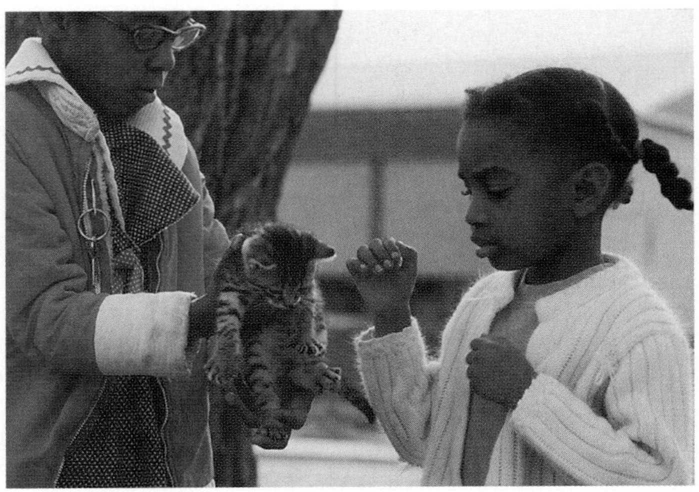

This child's fear may be a conditioned response resulting from the association of cats and unpleasant experiences.

places. In extreme cases, the agoraphobic individual is totally bound to his or her home, finding a trip to the mailbox an almost intolerable experience. Other agoraphobic individuals are able to travel freely in their neighborhood but cannot venture beyond it.

A 30-year-old German man recounts his experience with agoraphobia in the following passage.

> The brief trips to Bonn filled me with a surging sense of the impossible and the far . . . a feeling, especially as to distance, that could convert a half mile, or even five blocks from home, in terms of subjective need and cowardice, into an infinity of remoteness. . . . I start a little walk down the street about a hundred feet from the house, I am compelled to rush back, in horror of being so far away . . . a hundred feet away . . . from home and security. I have never walked or ridden, alone or with others, as a normal man, since that day. . . .
>
> At times this emotional effect remains merely a diffuse state of terror, an intensity running the whole scale from vague anxiety to intense feeling of impending death; . . . I am in terror of the seizure of terror; and I fear seizure at a given distance; there are then perfectly rational subterrors lest I may panic and make a public spectacle of myself, or I am in front of an automobile, or actually collapse from nervous exhaustion as soon as I get a certain distance from home—a distance varying back and forth from yards to miles—for the past 15 years I am overwhelmed with the feeling of insecurity, or terror that I can't get back. (Leonard, 1928, pp. 238, 278, 302, 319)

Generalized and Panic Anxiety Disorders

generalized anxiety disorder
An uneasy sense of general tension and apprehension that makes the individual highly uncomfortable because of its prolonged presence.

panic anxiety disorder
A pattern of anxiety in which long periods of calm are broken by an intensely uncomfortable attack of anxiety.

Whereas phobias are linked to specific stimulus situations, the other anxiety disorders involve a kind of anxiety that is independent of environmental triggers. Individuals with **generalized anxiety disorder** experience a vague, uneasy sense of tension and apprehension, sometimes referred to as *free-floating anxiety.* Generalized anxiety makes the individual highly uncomfortable, not because it's an intense kind of anxiety—it's generally relatively mild—but because of its relentless, almost unending presence. The person with generalized anxiety disorder does experience periods of calm, but they are often few and far between.

The individual with **panic anxiety disorder** experiences a pattern of anxiety that is almost the exact opposite of generalized anxiety. There may be long periods without anxiety, but that calm is suddenly broken without warning and without obvious cause. The individual is seized by a sharp, intensely uncomfortable attack of anxiety. Respiration increases and suddenly rapid heartbeats can be felt pounding with such intensity that the individual often feels that he or she is having a heart attack, or at the very least is going crazy.

Recent research has suggested that persons with panic disorders are extremely sensitive to small fluctuations in the performance of their hearts (Ehlers & Breuer, 1992) and the level of carbon dioxide in their blood (Rapee, Brown, Antony, & Barlow, 1992). Furthermore, they interpret these minor normal fluctuations in "catastrophic" ways. That is, their attacks of anxiety are exaggerated reactions to normal bodily stimuli that most persons ignore.

A relatively small percentage of the population (less than 3 percent) experience panic attacks that are frequent and severe enough to be said to have panic disorder, but a surprisingly high percentage of adults experience occasional attacks of panic. In one survey study of 2,375 college students, 12 percent had experienced at least one panic attack at some time during their lifetime (Telch, Lucas, & Nelson, 1989). It is important to know that such uncomfortable events are relatively common and that they should not be a source of serious concern unless they are severe or frequent enough to disrupt the individual's functioning or well-being.

The fact that panic attacks involve a sudden and intense increase in sympathetic autonomic arousal was demonstrated by British psychiatrist Michael Lader (Lader & Matthews, 1970). While he was studying the autonomic activity of a woman who was prone to panic attacks, she spontaneously experienced an attack in his laboratory. Figure 13.1 graphically shows the sudden changes in three measures of autonomic arousal that took place during the panic attack.

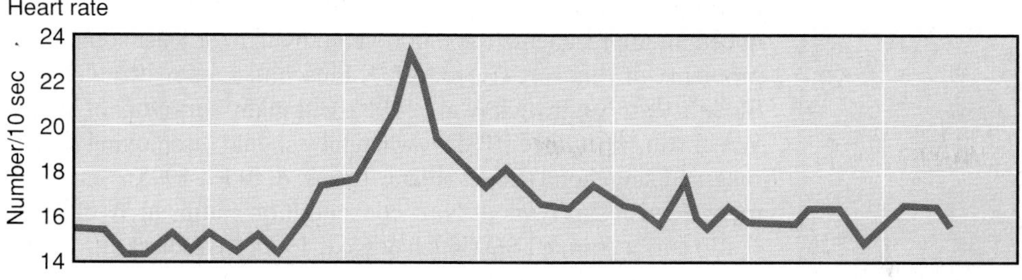

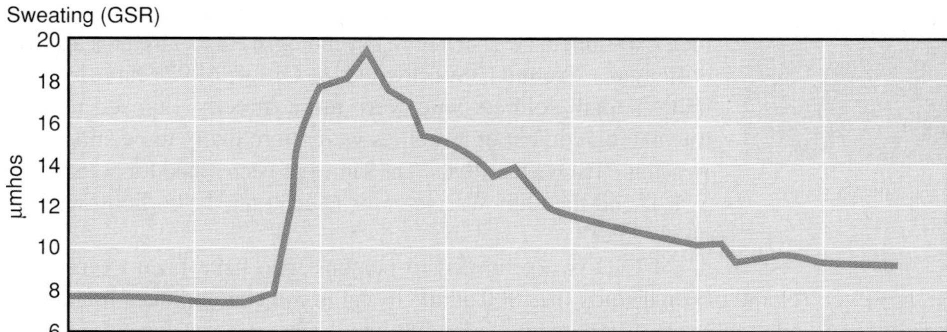

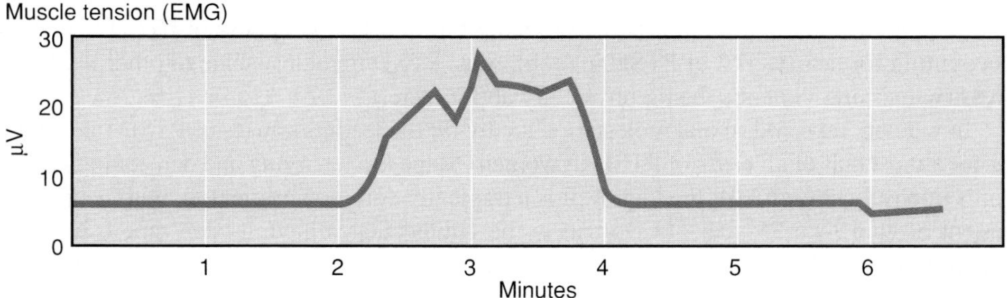

FIGURE 13.1

Changes in three measures of sympathetic autonomic arousal that occurred when an individual experienced a panic attack while being studied in a laboratory.

Source: Data from M. Lader and A. Matthews, "Changes in Autonomic Arousal in a Woman Undergoing a Spontaneous Panic Attack," *Journal of Psychosomatic Research,* 14:377–382. Copyright 1970, Pergamon Press, Ltd.

The case of Richard Benson further illustrates the experience of panic anxiety disorder.

Richard Benson, age 38, applied to a psychiatrist for therapy because he was suffering from severe and overwhelming anxiety which sometimes escalated to a panic attack. He had been treated for this problem in a private psychiatric hospital, but several weeks after his release, the severe anxiety symptoms recurred and he decided to seek outpatient therapy. During the times when he was experiencing intense anxiety, it often seemed as if he were having a heart seizure. He experienced chest pains and heart palpitations, numbness, shortness of breath, and he felt a strong need to breathe in air. He reported that in the midst of the anxiety attack, he developed a feeling of tightness over his eyes and he could only see objects directly in front of him (tunnel vision). He further stated that he feared that he would not be able to swallow.

Mr. Benson indicated that he had been anxious most of his life, but it was only since his promotion at work six months ago that the feelings of anxiety became a severe problem. The intensity of the anxiety symptoms was frightening to him and on two occasions his wife had rushed him to a local hospital because he was in a state of panic, sure that his heart was going to stop beating and he would die. (Leon, 1977, p. 113)

Posttraumatic Stress Disorder

Operation Desert Storm ended almost five years ago. The last American soldiers returned from Vietnam more than 20 years ago, and from World War II more than 50 years ago. Yet tens of thousands of former servicemen and women continue to "fight" those wars in their minds. They cannot leave the stress of the war behind: Extremely upsetting recollections of their combat experiences involuntarily intrude upon their awareness; horrible combat dreams rob them of sleep; they feel guilt that they survived while others did not; and they feel a pervasive tenseness and sense of unrest. Their agony has been given the unwieldy name of **posttraumatic stress disorder (PTSD).** In simple terms, they are still suffering reactions years after the

posttraumatic stress disorder
The condition caused by extremely stressful experiences in which the person later experiences anxiety and irritability; has upsetting memories, dreams, and realistic flashbacks of the experience; and tries to avoid anything that reminds him or her of the experience.

Researchers estimate that half a million Vietnam War veterans suffered some symptoms of posttraumatic stress disorder.

traumatic stress of combat. The Vietnam War appears to have produced an unprecedented 500,000 veterans with at least some mild problems of this sort (Egendorf, Kaduschin, Laufer, Rothbart, & Sloan, 1981; Southwick et al., 1995). But many survivors of World War II still experience PTSD—when they should be enjoying peaceful grandparenthood (Lee, Vaillant, Torrey, & Elder, 1995). Similarly, many Jewish survivors of Nazi concentration camps in World War II still suffer from PTSD (Kuch & Cox, 1992; Yehuda et al., 1995).

It is tragically easy to see the causes of posttraumatic stress disorder in war veterans because soldiers can be compared in terms of their exposure to combat stress. Psychologist Rachel Yehuda and her colleagues (Yehuda, Southwick, & Giller, 1992) have shown that Vietnam soldiers who were more directly exposed to life-threatening combat or atrocities were more likely to be still experiencing PTSD in the 1990s. The same has been found for both World War II and the Gulf War veterans (Lee et al., 1995; Southwick et al., 1995).

PTSD is not limited to persons who have been exposed to war, however. A large national study of 8,000 adults living in the United States found that 5 percent of all adult males and 10 percent of all adult females have experienced PTSD for at least a month during their lifetimes (Kessler, Sonnega, Bromet, Hughes, & Nelson, 1995). Although combat-related stress is the most common single cause of PTSD in males (accounting for nearly 30% of PTSD in men), most PTSD in males is due to other kinds of stress (witnessing violence, being physically abused, etc.).

In women, rape and sexual molestation are by far the leading causes of PTSD (accounting for almost half of all cases of PTSD in women). Rape is a terrifying and demeaning crime that is intensely stressful for the victim. It is a tragically common crime, too, with nearly 10 percent of all 15- to 55-year-old women in the United States having been raped. Among women who have been raped, 75 percent reported that they experienced PTSD for at least 6 months (Kessler et al., 1995). More distressingly, Burgess and Holstrom (1974) found that 6 to 10 years after the assault, approximately 25 percent of rape victims felt that they had not fully recovered. Psychologist Dean Kilpatrick's (1985) research group compared victims of rape with victims of aggravated assault and other crimes. They found substantially more mental health problems among the victims of rape. Tragically, nearly one rape victim in five had attempted suicide. It is abundantly clear that rape is one of the most stressful affronts to human dignity that a woman can experience. It is also clear that, without treatment, the pain of the assault can last indefinitely in some victims of rape. Finding ways to reduce the frequency of rape, facilitate the apprehension and prosecution of rapists, and minimize the effects of rape on its victims must be a priority for everyone. Fortunately, treatment can be effective with the victims of rape (Calhoun & Atkeson, 1989). In the next chapter we will learn more about treatments for PTSD.

Obsessive-Compulsive Disorders

obsessive-compulsive disorders Disorders that involve obsessions (anxiety-provoking thoughts that will not go away) and/or compulsions (irresistible urges to engage in specific irrational behaviors).

Also classified with anxiety disorders are the **obsessive-compulsive disorders.** Obsessions and compulsions are two separate problems, but they often occur together in the same individuals. *Obsessions* are anxiety-provoking thoughts that will not go away. They seem uncontrollable and even alien, as if they do not belong to the individual's mind. Thoughts such as a recurrent fear of losing control and killing someone or about having an incestuous sexual relationship can cause extreme anxiety.

Compulsions are irresistible urges to engage in behaviors such as repeatedly touching a spot on one's shoulder, washing one's hands, or checking the locks on doors. If the individual tries to stop engaging in the behavior, he or she experiences an urgent anxiety until the behavior is resumed. Obsessions and compulsions are often found in the same person, like the person who compulsively washes his hands because he is obsessed with thoughts about germs. About 70 percent of all people with obsessive-compulsive disorder have both obsessions and compulsions, 25 percent have only obsessions, and 5 percent have only compulsions (Wilner, Reich, Robins, Fishman, & van Doren, 1976). Recent evidence from several studies that employed modern brain-imaging techniques suggests that portions of the limbic system (see p. 68) function improperly in individuals with obsessive-compulsive disorder (Baxter et al., 1987).

SOMATOFORM DISORDERS

Somatoform disorders are conditions in which the individual experiences the symptoms of physical health problems that have psychological rather than physical causes. *Soma* is the Latin word for body, hence somatoform disorders are thought to be disorders in which psychological problems "take the form" of bodily problems. Although these symptoms of health problems are not physically caused, they are very real and uncomfortable to the individual. In other words, they are not faked. There are four types of somatoform disorders: *somatization disorder, hypochondriasis, conversion disorder,* and *somatoform pain disorder.* Because of similarities among them, these four disorders are discussed in pairs.

somatoform disorders
(sō´´mah´to-form) Disorders in which the individual experiences the symptoms of physical health problems that have psychological rather than physical causes.

Somatization Disorders and Hypochondriasis

Somatization disorders are intensely and chronically uncomfortable conditions that indirectly create a high risk of medical complications. They are far more common in women than in men (Golding, Smith, & Kashner, 1991). They take the form of chronic and recurrent aches, pains, fever, tiredness, and other symptoms of somatic (bodily) illness. In addition, individuals with these disorders frequently experience memory difficulties, problems with walking, numbness, blackout spells, nausea, menstrual problems, and a lack of pleasure from sex. These complaints are often expressed in dramatic ways that increase the probability of sympathy and special treatment from others.

Individuals with somatization problems also typically experience other psychological difficulties as well, particularly anxiety and depression. They frequently have problems with their jobs, schoolwork, or in meeting household responsibilities. The most dangerous aspect of somatization disorders, however, concerns the measures the affected individuals take to find relief from their discomfort. They frequently become addicted to alcohol or tranquilizers and often take medications prescribed by many different physicians whom they are seeing simultaneously (without telling the other physicians), thus increasing the risk of dangerous chemical interactions among the drugs. Worse still, because of their frequent complaints to physicians, they are often eventually the recipients of unnecessary surgery, especially unnecessary hysterectomies (removal of the uterus in women).

Hypochondriasis can be thought of as a milder form of somatization disorder with some special features of its own. The hypochondriac experiences somatic symptoms, but they are not as pervasive or as intense as in somatization disorders. Hypochondriacs also do not experience most of the serious side effects, such as depression, drug addiction, and unnecessary operations. Their lives, however, are dominated by their concerns about their health. They show a preoccupation with health, overreact with concern to minor coughs and pains, and go to unreasonable lengths to avoid germs, cancer-causing agents, and the like.

somatization disorders
(sō´´mah-ti-zā´shun) Intensely and chronically uncomfortable psychological conditions that involve numerous symptoms of somatic (bodily) illnesses without physical cause.

hypochondriasis
(hī´pō-kon-drī´ah-sis) A mild form of somatization disorder characterized by excessive concern about one's health.

"He was a dreadful hypochondriac."

Conversion Disorders and Pain Disorders

Conversion disorders are the most dramatic of the somatoform disorders. The name comes from the Freudian theory that anxiety has been "converted" into serious somatic symptoms in this condition rather than being directly experienced as anxiety. Individuals with this problem experience functional blindness, deafness, paralysis, fainting, seizures, inability to speak, or other serious impairments in the absence of any physical cause. In addition, these individuals appear to be generally ineffective and dependent upon others. These symptoms understandably impair the individuals' lives, particularly their ability to work. Conversion disorders can usually be distinguished from medical problems without great difficulty. In most cases, the symptoms are not medically possible. For example, in conversion disorders the areas of paralysis and loss of sensation are not shaped in the way they would be if there were actual nerve damage (see fig. 13.2). Similarly, people with conversion paralysis of the legs can be observed to move their legs normally when sleeping.

conversion disorders
Somatoform disorders in which individuals experience serious somatic symptoms such as functional blindness, deafness, and paralysis.

FIGURE 13.2

Because of the pattern in which the sensory nerves serve the skin surface, it would be medically possible to experience anesthesia within any of the lines shown on the hand on the right. Typical conversion anesthesias do not conform to these patterns, however.

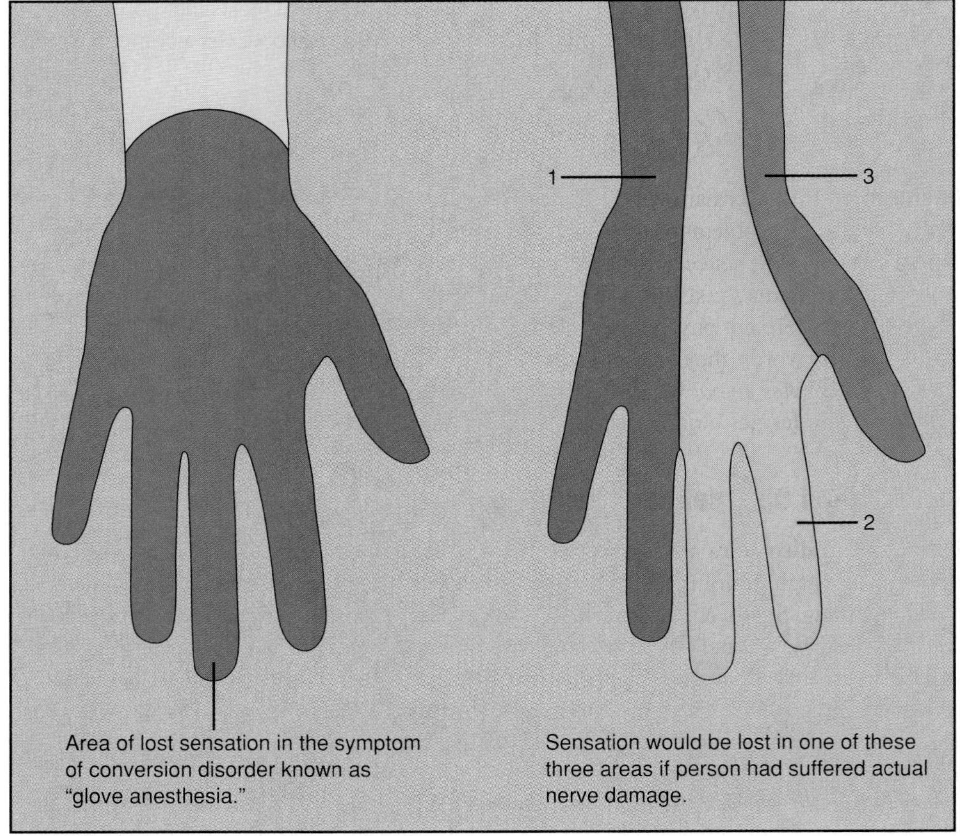
1
3
2
Area of lost sensation in the symptom of conversion disorder known as "glove anesthesia."
Sensation would be lost in one of these three areas if person had suffered actual nerve damage.

Perhaps the most interesting characteristic of conversion disorders is known as *la belle indifference,* "beautiful indifference." Individuals with conversion disorders often are *not upset* by their condition. The individual with conversion disorder who wakes up paralyzed one morning may show some emotional response, but not nearly to the extent as a person who is physically paralyzed, for example, in an automobile accident. Some psychologists believe that the conversion symptoms are welcome, in a sense, as they serve to get these people out of responsibilities or to force others to take care of them.

Consider the following case:

> A 22-year-old man . . . was referred with complaints of night blindness and failing vision. His visual acuity had deteriorated rapidly and he was found to have tubular fields of vision and a gross abnormality of dark adaptation. . . .
>
> The onset of his symptoms seemed closely related to his difficulties with a girlfriend who lived some miles away from his home. In order to visit her he would have to drive at night which was made impossible by his night blindness. Soon after the relationship was broken and the girl became engaged to another man the symptoms cleared up. Visual acuity improved . . . and the visual fields showed only slight contraction. (Behrman & Levy, 1970, p. 193)

Conversion disorders usually begin during acute stress and generally provide some kind of benefit (i.e., reinforcement) to the individual. In the case of the 22-year-old man just described, the benefit was in not having to admit that he did not want to visit his girlfriend.

pain disorders

(sō-ma´to-form) Somatoform disorders in which the individual experiences a relatively specific and chronic pain that has a psychological rather than physical cause.

Pain disorders are very similar to conversion disorders except that the primary symptom is *pain* that has no physical cause. Sometimes somatoform pain can be distinguished from physically caused pain because it does not follow nerve pathways. But in the case of low back pain, joint pains, and chest pains, a diagnosis of somatoform pain disorder can be made only after all possible physical causes have been carefully ruled out. Like conversion disorders, somatoform pain usually occurs at times of high stress and is generally beneficial to the individual in some way, as in getting the person out of a dull job and onto disability payments.

DISSOCIATIVE DISORDERS

Dissociative disorders cover a broad category of loosely related rare conditions involving sudden alterations in cognition. The various types of dissociative disorders are characterized by a change in memory, perception, or "identity." There are four kinds of dissociative disorders: *amnesia, fugue, depersonalization,* and *multiple personality.*

dissociative disorders
(dis-sō´´sē-a-tiv) A category of conditions involving sudden cognitive changes, such as a change in memory, perception, or identity.

Dissociative Amnesia and Fugue

As described in chapter 6, amnesia is a loss of memory that can have either a physical or psychological cause. **Dissociative amnesia** is psychologically caused; it most often occurs after a period of intense stress and involves loss of memory for all or part of the stressful experience itself, such as loss of memory for an automobile accident in which the individual was responsible for the death of another person. Individuals who suffer amnesia as a result of stress generally have no other psychological problems and typically recover their memories in time.

dissociative amnesia
A dissociative disorder that involves a loss of memory and that has a psychological rather than a physical cause.

Dissociative fugue states resemble amnesia in that there is a loss of memory, but the loss is so complete that the individual cannot remember his or her identity or previous life. The fugue episode is also typified by a period of semiconscious "wandering" that may take the individual around the corner or across the continent. In many instances, the individual takes on a new personality during the fugue episode, usually one that is more sociable, more fun-loving, and less conventional than the previous one. Generally these changes are transient. Consider the following case:

dissociative fugue
(fūg) A period of "wandering" that involves a loss of memory and a change in identity.

> When Mrs. Y. was brought to the hospital by her husband, she was dazed, confused, and weeping. Apparently aware of her surroundings and able to answer brief questions in filling out the admitting form, she could not, at the time, discuss any of her problems with the admitting physician. Her husband reported that she had left their home two weeks previously while he was at work. All the efforts of her husband and the police to trace her had failed until approximately 24 hours prior to her admission to the hospital when Mr. Y. received a report that a woman of her description had been arrested in a nearby city. When he arrived and identified her, she did not at first recognize him, did not know her own name, and could not remember what had happened to her or anything about her past. The police informed Mr. Y. that she had been arrested for "resorting" after a motel owner had called the police to complain that several different men had visited the motel room she had rented three days before in the company of a sailor. Mrs. Y. seemed unable to remember any of these alleged events. Gradually she came to recognize her husband as he talked anxiously with her whereupon she began to weep and requested to be brought home. . . .
>
> Mrs. Y. was very fatigued, and for the next three days she slept a great deal of the time. . . . On the fourth day she became much more alert, joked with the other patients, watched TV, and joined in a card game. Her doctor attempted to interview her and she seemed eager to cooperate, but soon after entering the room she burst into tears and fled back to her bed. Her condition continued to improve, and two days later she was able to talk at length with her doctor about her marriage and her childhood, but remained amnesic about the events immediately preceding her hospitalization.
>
> Only much later in treatment did the patient have any recollection at all of what had occurred during the previous two weeks and even then her memories were spotty. (Goldstein & Palmer, 1963, pp. 71–72)

Depersonalization

The term **depersonalization** refers to experiences in which the individual feels that he or she has become distorted or "unreal," or that distortions have occurred in one's surroundings. The individual might feel that his hands have become enlarged, numb, or out of control. Or she might feel that she has become a robot—even though she knows she is a real person—or that her room is not real or that her parents are not real people. The individual generally knows that these feelings are not accurate, although they have an eerie reality to them. One of the more common experiences of depersonalization is the sense of leaving one's body and being able to look back at it from the ceiling.

depersonalization
(de-per´´sun-al-i-zā´shun) The perceptual experience of one's body or surroundings becoming distorted or unreal in some way.

As was mentioned when we discussed depersonalization as an altered state of consciousness in chapter 4, experiences of depersonalization are rather common, especially in young adults. Unless they are accompanied by other problems or become recurrent to the point of being uncomfortable, these depersonalized experiences are not considered abnormal. Generally, they are nothing more than an unsettling experience that makes one question one's sanity for a few days.

Dissociative Identity Disorder (Multiple Personality)

dissociative identity disorder
A dissociative disorder in which the individual shifts abruptly and repeatedly from one "personality" to another.

Individuals who exhibit **dissociative identity disorder** (formerly known as *multiple personality*) shift abruptly and repeatedly from one "personality" to another as if more than one person were inhabiting the same body. Generally, the two or more personalities are quite different from one another. The original one is typically conventional, moralistic, and unhappy, while the other personalities tend to be quite the opposite. At least one other personality is usually sensual, uninhibited, and rebellious. In most cases, the individual is not aware of the other personalities when they are "in" their original personality, but the other personalities know about their rival personalities and are often antagonistic toward the original one.

Chris Sizemore, the real "Eve," and one of her paintings. She exhibited a total of 22 personalities, including her final, permanent identity.

In 1977 Chris Sizemore published an autobiography revealing that she was the case of dissociative identity disorder made famous in the 1950s movie, *The Three Faces of Eve*. Initially, she experienced two distinctly different personalities, referred to in the movie as Eve White and Eve Black. Eve White was depressed, anxious, conventional, and inhibited, whereas Eve Black was seductive, uninhibited, and wild. In her autobiography, Chris Sizemore reveals that she eventually went through 22 separate personalities but that in recent years she feels she has a single well-adjusted personality. A similar pattern was reported for the case of "Sybil," a woman who developed 16 personalities during the course of 42 years (Schreiber, 1973).

Dissociative identity disorder is quite rare, but it has been described in detail enough times now that most clinical psychologists agree that such a syndrome exists (Boon & Draijer, 1992; Modestin, 1992; Rosenzweig, 1988). Indeed, there is now evidence on the cause of dissociative identity disorder. It it possible that it is an extreme reaction to childhood sexual abuse (Modestin, 1992).

Thinking Critically About Psychology

1. How would a social learning theorist account for a phobic fear of dogs? How might a psychoanalyst account for the same phobia?

2. Our media system seems to highlight cases of dissociative identity disorder, even though they are very rare. What role do you think the media plays in our society's understanding of abnormal behavior?

Review

Anxiety disorders are common problems characterized by anxiety that may be experienced as low and relatively constant levels of generalized anxiety, as sharp and intense attacks of anxiety, as focalized phobias of various sorts, or as linked to obsessive thoughts or compulsive actions.

In somatoform disorders, the individual experiences the symptoms of medical conditions that have psychological rather than physical causes. In some types of somatoform disorders the symptoms are dramatic and clear-cut, such as blindness, paralysis, or chronic pain. In other cases, the individual experiences multiple aches, pains, and maladies or is just excessively concerned with health.

Dissociative disorders are uncommon psychological problems involving sudden alterations in cognition. These may take the form of memory losses, changes of identity, or feelings of unreality. In rare cases, the alteration of identity is so dramatic that the individual appears to possess more than a single personality.

Check Your Learning

To be sure that you have learned the key points from the preceding section, cover the answers below and try to answer each question. If you give an incorrect answer to any question, return to the page given next to the correct answer to see why your answer was not correct.

1. Psychological disorders that involve excessive levels of nervousness, tension, worry, fright, and anxiety are termed ________________ disorders.

   a. panic **c.** behavior
   b. somatoform **d.** anxiety

2. Individuals with ________________ experience a vague, uneasy sense of tension and apprehension, sometimes referred to as free-floating anxiety, that makes the individual uncomfortable because of its prolonged presence.

   a. panic disorder **c.** generalized anxiety disorder
   b. dissociative identity disorder **d.** agoraphobia

3. ________________ are conditions in which the individual experiences the symptoms of physical health problems that have psychological rather than physical causes.

   a. Anxiety disorders **c.** Somatoform disorders
   b. Dissociative disorders **d.** Social phobias

4. ________________ disorders refer to a category of conditions involving sudden cognitive changes, such as a change in memory, perception, or identity.

   a. Panic **c.** Obsessive-compulsive
   b. Conversion **d.** Dissociative

Correct Answers
1. d (p. 471), 2. c (p. 472), 3. c (p. 475), 4. d (p. 477).

mood disorders
Psychological disorders involving depression and/or abnormal elation.

major depression
An affective disorder characterized by episodes of deep unhappiness, loss of interest in life, and other symptoms.

MOOD DISORDERS

There are two primary forms of **mood disorders,** depression and mania. Depression can occur alone (a condition known as *major depression*), but mania seems to always alternate with periods of depression (*bipolar affective disorder*). Both conditions produce great misery for the individual.

Major Depression

The individual experiencing **major depression** is deeply unhappy and finds little pleasure in life. But major depression is more than merely intense sadness. The person with major depression believes that the future is bleak, holds a negative opinion of self and others, and often sees no reason to live. This state is accompanied by at least some of the following: increased or decreased sleep, increased or decreased appetite, loss of interest in sex, loss of energy or excessive energy, difficulties concentrating and making decisions, and sometimes suicidal thinking or actual attempts. Half of all individuals who experience an episode of major depression will recover, but 12 percent still will not have recovered after 5 years (Keller et al., 1992). Many individuals who experience depression will experience it only once, but others will be depressed many times during their lifetime if not properly treated. In these cases, the depression comes in episodes that last from several days to many months, followed by periods of normal moods.

Major depression is quite common, affecting 10 million or more Americans. Worldwide, as many as 100 million persons experience major depression (Gotlib, 1992). As shown in

FIGURE 13.3

The probability that an individual will develop major depression for the first time during a given year of life changes over the life span.

Source: Data from P. M. Lewinsohn, et al., "Age at First Onset for Nonbipolar Depression," *Journal of Abnormal Psychology,* 95:378–383, 1986. Copyright 1986 by the American Psychological Association.

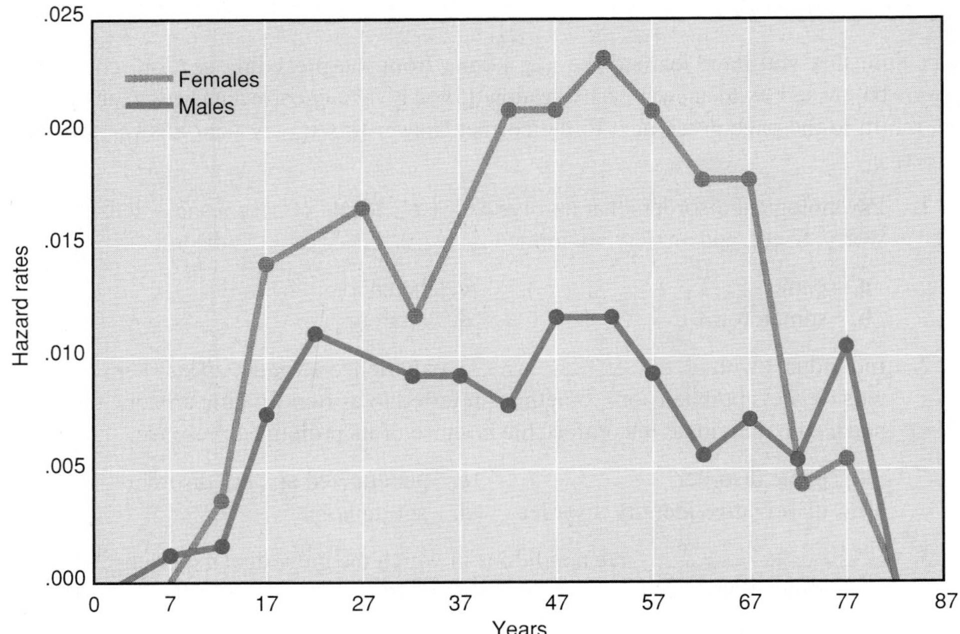

figure 13.3, the probability that an individual will develop major depression for the first time is very low until puberty, rises until a peak is reached between 45 and 55 years of age, then declines again in old age. Overall, the risk for major depression is twice as high for women than men, particularly during middle age (Lewinsohn, Duncan, Stanton, & Hautzinger, 1986; Strickland, 1992). The risk is clearly elevated in persons experiencing high levels of stress (Lewinsohn, Hoberman, & Rosenbaum, 1988; Shrout et al., 1989).

Major depression, despite its name, is often relatively mild. People with mild depression are very uncomfortable, but they often can cope with the demands of daily living. Severe major depression is less common, but far more disabling. This is often accompanied by bizarre beliefs and perceptions that represent a psychotic distortion of reality. The following excerpt describes a case of severe (psychotic) depression that required the individual to be hospitalized during treatment because of his suicidal tendencies and distortions of reality (e.g., he believed that his stomach was rotting away).

> E. D., aged 60, was admitted to the hospital because he was depressed, ate insufficiently, and believed that his stomach was "rotting away." At 51 the patient suffered from a depression and was obliged to resign his position. This depression continued for about 9 months, after which he apparently fully recovered. He resumed his work but after 2 years suffered from a second depression. Again he recovered after several months and returned to a similar position and held it until 2 months before his admission. At this time he began to worry lest he was not doing his work well, talked much of his lack of fitness for his duties, and finally resigned. He spent Thanksgiving Day at his son's in a neighboring city, but while there he was sure that the water pipes in his own house would freeze during his absence and that he and his family would be "turned out into the street." A few days later he was found standing by a pond, evidently contemplating suicide. He soon began to remain in bed and sometimes wrapped his head in the bed clothing to shut out the external world. He declared that he was "rotting away inside" and that if he ate, the food would kill him. He urged the family not to touch the glasses or towels he used lest they become contaminated. (Kolb, 1977, p. 455)
>
> From L. C. Kolb, *Modern Clinical Psychiatry,* 9th ed. Copyright © 1977 W.B. Saunders Co., Philadelphia, PA. Reprinted by permission.

Cognitive Factors in Depression

As discussed in chapters 9 and 11, Aaron T. Beck, and others believe that our *cognitions* are an important factor in emotional problems. For example, Beck has suggested that negative views of one's self, the world in which we live, and the future lead some persons to experience life in such negative terms that they develop depression. Much evidence is consistent with this view, particularly Beck's theory that negative views of one's self are a critical component of depression. Recent studies (Brown, Hammen, Craske, & Wickens, 1995; Scott & O'Hara, 1993; Strauman, 1992) showed that people who believe that they fall very short of being the person they would like to be are more likely to experience depression. One reason that depressed persons often fall short of their ideal is that their beliefs are often *perfectionistic*. Paul Hewitt and Gordon Flett (1993) found that people who believe that they should be perfect in their work are likely to develop depression if they fail at work. Similarly, people who hold out perfectionistic expectations for themselves in social relationships are often depressed if their personal relationships are not going well. In contrast, people who do not expect perfection of themselves do not become depressed when things do not go well. These findings support the basic premise of the cognitive view: It is not bad things happening to us that are upsetting; it is our *interpretation* of them that makes all the difference (Gotlib, 1992).

Other studies have suggested that having a positive opinion of yourself makes depression less likely following stressful life events (Hammen, Marks, Mayol, & deMayo, 1985; Holahan & Moos, 1987; Lewinsohn et al., 1988; Robinson, Garber, & Hilsman, 1995; Zuroff & Mongrain, 1987). Studies have also shown that a cognitive style of repressive coping (described in chapter 12) increases the risk of depression under stress (Folkman & Lazarus, 1986; Holahan & Moos, 1987). In addition, individuals who believe that they can be happy only when they are in a close relationship are understandably more likely to respond to the loss of a relationship with depression than individuals who did not hold this dependent belief (Hammen, Elliott, Gitlin, & Jamison, 1989; Hammen et al., 1985; Zuroff & Mongrain, 1987).

It seems clear that our beliefs about ourselves and our relationships with others make us more or less vulnerable to depression when buffeted by life's inevitable stress. However, the relationship between cognition and depression is a two-way street. When persons become depressed, their cognitions change. They become more pessimistic, more critical of themselves, more likely to blame themselves for everything bad that happens, and so on. When the depression lifts, fortunately, these cognitions return to a more positive state (Dohr, Rush, & Bernstein, 1989). Thus, although negative cognitions appear to predispose us to depression, we never think more negatively than when we are depressed.

Interestingly, the research of Peter Lewinsohn and his associates (1980), suggests that at least some aspects of the "distorted" cognitions that are characteristic of depressed individuals are not distortions at all. Lewinsohn asked individuals who were experiencing major depression to participate in a group discussion for approximately 20 minutes. During this time, they were rated by a group of judges on their friendliness, assertiveness, warmth, and other social qualities. After the group discussion, each participant also rated himself or herself on the same dimensions. Another group of people who were not depressed went through exactly the same procedure.

When asked to rate their participation after a group discussion, people with major depression give more accurate ratings than do people who aren't depressed. It seems some positive "distortion" of our self-perception can be healthy.

As would have been predicted by Beck, the depressed group rated their social skills as being less adequate than did the nondepressed participants. Is this evidence that depressed individuals distort their view of themselves? Actually, it turns out that the self-ratings of the depressed group were *quite accurate* when compared with the ratings of the judges. It was the normal participants whose view of themselves was distorted! The nondepressed persons rated themselves as being significantly more socially skilled than the judges did. Furthermore, when the depressed individuals were given treatment and became less depressed, their self-perceptions became more like the normal group: They, too, began to rate themselves in unrealistically positive terms. Perhaps having this kind of "distorted" perception of ourselves is a good thing. Maybe we would all be depressed if we saw ourselves in the realistic terms in which others see us!

Postpartum Depression

Psychiatrists have long used the term *postpartum depression* (Marce, 1858) to refer to episodes of major depression in women that begin around the time of the birth of a child (*post* = after; *partum* = birth). Perhaps because childbirth is expected to be a time of joy in our society, and because caring for an infant is demanding under the best of circumstances, women with depression following childbirth are of particular concern to all of us.

But is depression more common after the birth of a child? Is there any such thing as postpartum depression? An excellent recent study by a group of researchers at the University of Iowa (O'Hara, Zekoski, Philipps, & Wright, 1990) sheds important light on this topic. These psychologists followed a group of 182 pregnant women from the second trimester of pregnancy (the fourth through the sixth months) until nine weeks after the birth of their children. In addition, a similar control group of women who were not pregnant were followed for the same period of time.

Both groups of women completed tests measuring their level of depression. The childbearing women had higher depression scores than the nonchildbearing women, but three important points should be noted. First, most women in the childbearing group experienced no increase in depression. Second, the increased average scores on the depression inventory of the childbearing group remained well within the normal range. In fact, the symptoms of depression most frequently reported by women who had just given birth were sleep and appetite disturbances that probably were related to childbirth and not to depression. Thus, these may not have been true symptoms of depression at all.

Third, although about 10 percent of the women in the childbearing group did develop full episodes of serious depression, this proportion was no higher than in the nonchildbearing group. This key finding was replicated in an independent study by Susan Campbell and Jeffrey Cohn (1991) and other studies suggesting that the postpartum period is not a time of increased depression for women. That is, the 10 percent of women who are depressed around the time of the birth of a child are probably depressed for reasons that are unrelated to the birth. More study is needed before definite conclusions are reached, but "postpartum depression" may be no more than another myth about the moods of women.

Bipolar Affective Disorder

bipolar affective disorder
(bī-pō´lar) A condition in which the individual experiences periods of mania that alternate irregularly with periods of severe depression.

mania
(mā´nē-ah) A disturbance of mood in which the individual experiences a euphoria characterized by unrealistic optimism and heightened sensory pleasures.

In the condition known as **bipolar affective disorder,** periods of mania alternate irregularly with periods of severe depression. **Mania** is a disturbance of mood that can be quite enjoyable to the individual in the short run but is usually damaging both to the person and to others in the long run. During the manic episode, the individual experiences a remarkable "high"—an intense euphoria in which sensory pleasures are heightened, one's self-esteem is very high, thoughts race, little sleep is needed, and unrealistic optimism prevails. Grandiose and financially damaging schemes and buying sprees are common during these periods, as are quitting jobs, divorce, and sexual promiscuity. Psychotic distortions of reality are also common during manic periods. When well-meaning friends and family members try to control the manic individual, they are often rebuffed in sharp anger. Although an intensely pleasurable state, mania can be quite harmful to the person's finances and personal relationships. This harm can be clearly seen in the case of "Mrs. M."

> At 17 she suffered from a depression . . . for several months, although she was not hospitalized. At 33, shortly before the birth of her first child, the patient was greatly depressed. For a period of four days she appeared in a coma. About a month after the birth of the baby she "became excited" and was entered as a patient in an institution for neurotic and mildly psychotic patients. As she began to improve, she was sent to a shore hotel for a brief vacation. The patient remained at the hotel for one night and on the following day signed a year's lease on an apartment, bought furniture, and became heavily involved in debt. Shortly thereafter Mrs. M. became depressed and returned to the hospital. . . . After several months she recovered and, except for relatively mild fluctuations of mood, remained well for approximately 2 years.
>
> She then became overactive and exuberant in spirits and visited her friends, to whom she outlined her plans for reestablishing different forms of lucrative business. She purchased many clothes, bought furniture, pawned her rings, and wrote checks without funds. She was returned to a hospital. Gradually her manic symptoms subsided, and after four months she

was discharged. For a period thereafter she was mildly depressed. In a little less than a year Mrs. M. again became overactive, played her radio until late in the night, smoked excessively, and took out insurance on a car that she had not yet bought. Contrary to her usual habits, she swore frequently and loudly . . . and instituted divorce proceedings. On the day prior to her second admission to the hospital, she purchased 57 hats. (Kolb, 1977, pp. 455–456)

Mania may occur only once but often returns in multiple episodes. When mania is recurrent, it alternates irregularly with episodes of severe depression. This alternating disorder was formerly known as *manic-depressive psychosis* and is now known as bipolar affective disorder. Bipolar affective disorders are relatively uncommon problems; only 15 percent of individuals with affective disorders show this alternating pattern of intense highs and lows. Fortunately, bipolar affective disorder generally can be treated somewhat effectively with medication.

SCHIZOPHRENIA AND DELUSIONAL DISORDER

Psychologist: "Why do you think people believe in God?"

Patient: Uh, let's, I don't know why, let's see, balloon travel. He holds it up for you, the balloon. He don't let you fall out, your little legs sticking out down through the clouds. He's down to the smokestack, looking through the smoke trying to get the balloon gassed up you know. Way they're flying on top that way, legs sticking out, I don't know, looking down on the ground, heck, that'd make you so dizzy you just stay and sleep you know, hold down and sleep there. The balloon's His home you know up there. I used to sleep outdoors, you know, sleep outdoors instead of going home. He's had a home but His not tell where it's at you know. (Chapman & Chapman, 1973, p. 3)

The person giving this confused and confusing answer has a serious problem known as **schizophrenia.** Schizophrenia is an uncommon disorder that affects slightly less than 1 percent of the general population. However, it's a dramatic form of abnormality that, unless successfully treated, often renders normal patterns of living impossible.

schizophrenia
(skiz´´o-fren´-ē-ah) A psychological disorder involving cognitive disturbance (delusions and hallucinations), disorganization, and reduced enjoyment and interests.

Schizophrenia is characterized by three types of serious problems (Andreasen, Arndt, Alliger, Miller, & Flaum, 1995; Arndt, Andreasen, Flaum, Miller, & Nopoulos, 1995):

1. *Delusions and hallucinations.* The central feature of schizophrenia is distortions of cognition that put the individual "out of touch with reality." Persons with schizophrenia often hold strange false beliefs (**delusions**) and have distorted and bizarre false perceptual experiences (**hallucinations**). We will discuss these distortions of cognition in greater detail in discussing the subtypes of schizophrenia.
2. *Disorganized thinking, emotions, and behavior.* As is clear in the preceding example, persons with schizophrenia often think in fragmented and disorganized ways. Their emotions and behavior are similarly disorganized and illogical at times. A person with schizophrenia might laugh when told sad news, or shift rapidly from happiness to sadness and back again for no apparent reason. As a result, most of us find it very difficult to have conversations with persons with schizophrenia.
3. *Reduced enjoyment and interests.* Persons with schizophrenia often show what is called "blunted affect." They find less pleasure in life than most persons and have fewer interests and goals that are important to them. Although their emotions change in unpredictable ways, both their positive and negative emotions lack normal intensity. In many ways, they just do not care about things as much as other people. Often, this includes not being as interested in having close friendships as is typical.

delusion
A false belief that distorts reality.

hallucination
A false perceptual experience that distorts reality.

Long-term studies of persons with schizophrenia show that their reduced enjoyment and interests is usually chronic and does not improve, but their delusions, hallucinations, and disorganization may improve for a while between episodes of worsened symptoms (Arndt et

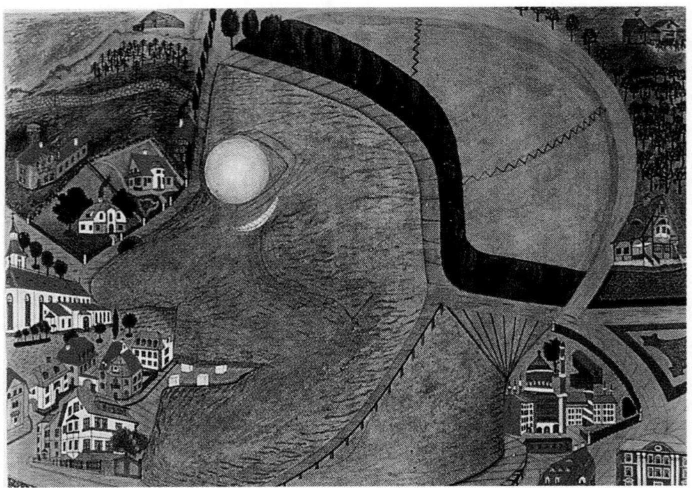

German psychiatrist Hans Prinzhorn is responsible for the most extensive collection of artwork by mental patients available. This painting from the collection, by August Neter, illustrates the hallucinations and the paranoid fantasies from which many schizophrenic patients suffer. In reviewing a showing of artworks by schizophrenic patients, such as the painting shown here, poet John Ashby wrote: "The lure of the work is strong, but so is the terror of the unanswerable riddles it proposes."

al., 1995; Breier, Schreiber, Dyer, & Pickar, 1991; Loebel et al., 1992). Schizophrenia is a broad class of psychotic disorders that is broken down into three major subtypes in the 1993 edition of the *American Psychiatric Association's Diagnostic and Statistical Manual of Mental Disorders (DSM-IV): paranoid, disorganized,* and *catatonic schizophrenia.* A fourth category, *undifferentiated schizophrenia,* is used to classify individuals who do not fit into the other three categories.

Paranoid Schizophrenia

A person with **paranoid schizophrenia** holds *false beliefs,* or *delusions,* that seriously distort reality. Most often, these are beliefs in the exceptional importance of oneself, so-called *delusions of grandeur*—such as being Jesus Christ, a CIA agent, the inventor of a cure for war. These are often accompanied by delusions that, because one is so important, others are "out to get me" in attempts to thwart the individual's important mission. These are known as *delusions of persecution,* or *paranoic.*

If I were schizophrenic and believed that I were an agent of the CIA who alone had the ability to save the president from assassination by terrorists, I might also believe that my students were terrorists also who were trying to confuse and poison me. Think for a moment how bizarre I would seem to others who learned of my paranoid delusions. Think, too, about the terrifying, bewildering existence I would live if I believed those things. It would be small wonder that my emotions would seem unpredictable and strange and that I would withdraw from social contact.

Unfortunately, the cognitive disturbances of the paranoid schizophrenic do not stop with delusions. Many individuals with this disorder also experience false perceptual experiences, or *hallucinations.* Their perceptions are either strangely distorted or they may even hear, see, or feel things that are not there. These bizarre experiences further add to the terrifying, perplexing unreality of the paranoid schizophrenic's existence.

paranoid schizophrenia
(par´-ah noid) A subtype of schizophrenia in which the individual holds delusions of persecution and grandeur that seriously distort reality.

disorganized schizophrenia
A subtype of schizophrenia characterized by shallow silliness, extreme social withdrawal, and fragmented delusions and hallucinations.

catatonic schizophrenia
(kat´´ah-ton´ik) A subtype of schizophrenia in which the individual spends long periods in an inactive, statuelike state.

Disorganized Schizophrenia

Disorganized schizophrenia resembles paranoid schizophrenia in that delusions and hallucinations are present, but the cognitive processes of the disorganized schizophrenic, as the name implies, are so disorganized and fragmented that the delusions and hallucinations have little recognizable meaning. The central features of this type of schizophrenia are extreme withdrawal from normal human contact and a shallow "silliness" of emotion. The disorganized schizophrenic acts in childlike ways, reacts inappropriately to both happy and sad events, and generally presents a highly bizarre picture to others.

Catatonic Schizophrenia

Catatonic schizophrenia is quite different in appearance from other forms of schizophrenia. While catatonics sometimes experience delusions and hallucinations, their most obvious abnormalities are in social interaction, posture, and body movement. There are long periods of catatonic stupor, an inactive statuelike state in which the individuals seem locked into a posture. Catatonic schizophrenics are often said to exhibit "waxy flexibility" during these stupors—they will passively let themselves be placed into any posture and will maintain it. Often the individual ceases to talk, appears not to hear what is spoken to him or her, and may no longer eat without being fed.

Frequently, however, the stupor is abruptly broken by periods of agitation. The person may pace and fidget nervously or may angrily attack others. Both of these patterns may alternate with periods of relative normality.

Catatonic individuals sometimes exhibit a state of catatonic stupor during which they may maintain a single posture for several hours.

Delusional Disorder

Delusional disorder is a rare disorder that is characterized by paranoid delusions of grandeur and persecution. It's not a form of schizophrenia, however, and can be distinguished from paranoid schizophrenia because the delusions in delusional disorder are less illogical and are not accompanied by hallucinations. The paranoid schizophrenic might think that he is Napoleon and that he is currently working as a disc jockey for the CIA. The person with delusional disorder, on the other hand, might believe that she can see a truth that no one else has seen and that it's essential that she lead Americans away from reliance on machines. The delusions are more subtle and more believable.

Often it's the believability of these delusions that makes them so dangerous. The Reverend Jim Jones is a frightening case in point. Jones was a minister who had an impressive record of working for the poor when he came to believe that he was a prophet of God, perhaps even a new Messiah. He convinced a large number of people of the truth of his delusion and founded a new religious sect. When he began to feel that his sect was being persecuted by the government, he took his followers to the South American country of Guyana and founded the People's Temple Jonestown Settlement. There, he ruled as an absolute master over his flock, at one point decreeing that only he was fit to have sex with and impregnate the women of Jonestown. When a task force from the United States flew to Jonestown to investigate rumors of human rights violations, his followers killed members of that group. Realizing that trouble was ahead and believing that he had the wisdom of God, Jones ordered all of his followers to commit suicide by drinking a poison that was always on hand for just such a situation. Believing that they were told to take their lives by the new Messiah, hundreds of men, women, and children drank the poison and died.

The man who took the name David Koresh and created a religious community in Waco, Texas, also exhibited qualities that suggested that he may have had delusional disorder. His alleged religious delusions, physical abuse of the children living in his compound, and the collection of a massive and illegal arsenal of weapons may have set the stage for the confrontation that tragically killed many of his followers. Individuals with delusional disorder are not always dangerous, but they can be when they act on their delusions.

Aftermath of the mass suicide at Jonestown. How do cultlike groups recruit new devotees?

Cult leader David Koresh's refusal to surrender a stockpile of illegal weapons eventually led to the death of Koresh and many of his followers.

PERSONALITY DISORDERS

To this point, we have been talking about psychological problems that develop in individuals who were once considered to be normal. To oversimplify the case, schizophrenia and the other disorders that we have considered are "breakdowns" in relatively normal personalities. In contrast, the **personality disorders** discussed in this section are believed to result from personalities that developed improperly in the first place.

A number of different personality disorders differ widely from one another but share several common characteristics: (a) all personality disorders begin early in life; (b) they are disturbing to the person or to others; and (c) they are very difficult to treat. We will first look at two very different personality disorders to provide examples of this type of problem, then provide a brief description of the other personality disorders.

delusional disorder
A nonschizophrenic disorder characterized by delusions of grandeur and persecution that are more logical than those of paranoid schizophrenics in their absence of hallucinations.

personality disorders
Psychological disorders that are believed to result from personalities that developed improperly during childhood.

Schizoid Personality Disorder

The suffix *-oid* means "like," hence *schizoid personality disorder* is like schizophrenia, particularly in that blunted emotions and social withdrawal are exhibited. Unlike true schizophrenia, however, this condition is not characterized by serious cognitive disturbances.

schizoid personality disorder
(skiz´oid) A personality disorder characterized by blunted emotions, lack of interest in social relationships, and withdrawal into a solitary existence.

Individuals with **schizoid personality disorder** have little or no desire to have friends and indeed are not interested in even casual social contact. They are classic "loners." Usually, they are very shy as children but are not abnormally withdrawn until later childhood or adolescence. Gradually, they seem to lose interest in friends, family, and social activities, and retreat more and more into a solitary existence.

They display little emotion and appear cold and aloof. Later in life, people with schizoid personality disorder often lose interest in personal appearance, hygiene, and other polite social conventions. Often they do not work and may even fall into homelessness or work as a street-walking prostitute.

Antisocial Personality Disorder

antisocial personality disorder
A personality disorder characterized by smooth social skills and a lack of guilt about violating social rules and laws and taking advantage of others.

Individuals with **antisocial personality disorder** have a personality disorder quite different from the schizoid group. They frequently violate social rules and laws, take advantage of others, and feel little guilt about it. These individuals often have smooth social skills: They are sweet-talking con artists who are very likable at first. But they experience great difficulties in maintaining close personal relationships. They enter into marriages and other intimate relationships easily, but they tend to break up quickly.

People with antisocial personality disorder frequently violate social laws and rules, while feeling little guilt about it. The disorder begins in childhood, when the person usually was a bully.

Antisocial personalities have a low tolerance for frustration. They act on impulse, lose their temper quickly, and lie easily and skillfully. They are often hardened criminals. In childhood, antisocial personalities are very difficult children. They are often bullies who fight, lie, cheat, steal, and are truant from school. They blame others for their misdeeds, feel picked on by their parents and teachers, and never seem to learn from their mistakes.

Individuals with antisocial personality disorder rarely feel anxious or guilty—they are calm, cool characters. They are highly uncomfortable, however, when they are kept from excitement. They have an abnormal need for stimulation, novelty, and thrills. Because they often turn to alcohol and drugs for excitement, they frequently become addicts. The primary harmfulness of the antisocial personality disorder is in the damage that is done to others. They often leave a trail of victims—victims of their lies, their crimes, their violent outbursts, and their broken intimate relationships.

The following case of antisocial personality disorder illustrates these problems well:

> Donald's misbehavior as a child took many forms including lying, cheating, petty theft, and the bullying of smaller children. As he grew older he became more and more interested in sex, gambling, and alcohol. When he was 14 he made crude sexual advances toward a younger girl, and when she threatened to tell her parents he locked her in a shed. It was about 16 hours before she was found. Donald at first denied knowledge of the incident, later stating that she had seduced him and that the door must have locked itself. He expressed no concern for the anguish experienced by the girl and her parents, nor did he give any indication that he felt morally culpable for what he had done.
>
> When he was 17, Donald left the boarding school, forged his father's name to a large check, and spent about a year traveling around the world. He apparently lived well, using a combination of charm, physical attractiveness, and false pretenses to finance his way. During subsequent years he held a succession of jobs, never staying at any one for more than a few months. Throughout this period he was charged with a variety of crimes, including theft, drunkenness in a public place, assault, and many traffic violations. In most cases he was either fined or given a light sentence.
>
> His sexual experiences were frequent, casual, and callous. When he was 22 he married a 41-year-old woman whom he had met in a bar. Several other marriages followed, all bigamous. In each case the pattern was the same: he would marry someone on impulse, let her support him for several months, and then leave. . . . (Lahey & Ciminero, 1980, pp. 326–327)

Other Personality Disorders

The following are brief descriptions of the other eight types of personality disorders listed in DSM-IV. Be careful not to diagnose yourself or your friends while reading this list. The pattern must be extreme and consistent to qualify for a diagnosis.

1. *Schizotypal personality disorder.* Few friendships, suspiciousness, strange ideas, such as belief that his or her mind can be read by others and that messages are being received in strange ways.
2. *Paranoid personality disorder.* High degree of suspiciousness and mistrust of others, extreme irritability and sensitivity, coldness and lack of tender feelings.
3. *Histrionic personality disorder.* Self-centered, frequently seeking to be the center of attention, manipulating others through exaggerated expression of emotions and difficulties, superficially charming but lacking genuine concern for others, frequent angry outbursts.
4. *Narcissistic personality disorder.* Unrealistic sense of self-importance, preoccupied with fantasies of future success, requires constant attention and praise, reacts very negatively to criticism or is indifferent to criticism, exploits others, feels entitled to special consideration, lack of genuine concern for others.
5. *Borderline personality disorder.* Impulsive and unpredictable, unstable personal relationships, angry, almost constantly needs to be with others, lack of clear identity, feelings of emptiness.
6. *Avoidant personality disorder.* Extreme shyness or social withdrawal in spite of a desire for friendships, extremely sensitive to rejection, very low self-esteem.
7. *Dependent personality disorder.* A pattern in which the person is passively dependent on others for support and decisions, has low self-esteem, and puts needs of others before self.
8. *Obsessive-compulsive personality disorder.* Perfectionistic, dominating, poor ability to express affection, excessive devotion to work, indecisive when faced with major decisions.

Review

Major depression involves one or more episodes of this negative mood state. These episodes range from mild to severe, with severe episodes sometimes being accompanied by bizarre perceptions and beliefs that distort reality. In bipolar affective disorder, the episodes of depression alternate irregularly with periods of the mood disturbance known as mania. Although this is an intensely pleasurable state, it's harmful in that it can lead to financial difficulties, can destroy personal relationships, and can often be accompanied by reality-distorting perceptions and beliefs.

Schizophrenia is a broad range of psychotic disorders characterized by disturbances of cognition that grossly distort reality, by distortions of emotions, and by withdrawal from social relationships. There are three major subtypes of schizophrenia. Paranoid schizophrenia is characterized by delusions of grandeur and persecution, often accompanied by hallucinations. Disorganized schizophrenia resembles paranoid schizophrenia but is typified by even more fragmented cognition and by shallow, silly emotions. Catatonic schizophrenia is quite different from the other types, being marked by stupors in which the individual may maintain postures for long periods of time. Biological factors—genetics, cortical deterioration, and abnormal prenatal development—are believed to be important in the origins of schizophrenia, but stress may be the immediate cause that triggers episodes. Delusional disorder is characterized by delusions that are less bizarre and more believable than in paranoid schizophrenia. Because they are more believable, persons with delusional disorders often convince many others that they have divine powers or are important religious figures, often with tragic results.

While other kinds of psychological disorders are thought to result from the "breakdown" of a normal personality, personality disorders are thought to result from faulty personality development during childhood. These disorders begin early in life, are disturbing to the individual or to others, and are difficult to treat. For example, individuals with schizoid personality

Thinking Critically About Psychology

1. What are some possible explanations for the higher incidence of major depression in women?
2. The various forms of schizophrenia are quite different. What do they all have in common?
3. Why do you think personality disorders are generally difficult to treat?

Review—continued

disorder are very shy children who increasingly lose interest in social relationships as they grow older. Eventually, they lose interest in proper dress and social conditions, display little emotion, and rarely hold regular jobs. Antisocial personality disorders are characterized by rule-violating behavior as a child that develops into a disregard for the customs of society as adults. Such individuals are often dishonest con artists who are smooth and likable at first but who have great difficulties maintaining normal relationships. They also have an abnormal need for stimulation, are prone to violence, and do not seem to learn from punishment.

Check Your Learning

To be sure that you have learned the key points from the preceding section, cover the answers below and try to answer each question. If you give an incorrect answer to any question, return to the page given next to the correct answer to see why your answer was not correct.

1. The individual experiencing ________________ is deeply unhappy, finds little pleasure in life, and experiences other symptoms such as sleeping and eating problems and loss of energy.

- **a.** bipolar affective disorder
- **b.** major depression
- **c.** delusional disorder
- **d.** somatoform pain disorders

2. In the condition known as ________________ periods of mania alternate irregularly with periods of severe depression.

- **a.** major depression
- **b.** mania disorder
- **c.** unipolar depression
- **d.** bipolar affective disorder

3. The three major areas of abnormality in schizophrenia are: **(a)** ____________, **(b)** ________________, and **(c)** ________________.

4. Strange and false perceptual experiences are termed

- **a.** delusions.
- **b.** paranoia.
- **c.** hallucinations.
- **d.** social withdrawal.

5. The type of schizophrenia characterized by stupor and "waxy flexibility" is called

- **a.** catatonic.
- **b.** paranoid.
- **c.** disorganized.
- **d.** stuporous.

6. ________________ personality disorder is similar to schizophrenia, particularly in that blunted emotions and social withdrawal are exhibited, but unlike true schizophrenia, this condition is not characterized by serious cognitive disturbances.

- **a.** Antisocial
- **b.** Schizoid
- **c.** Dependent
- **d.** Histrionic

Correct Answers

1. b (p. 479), **2.** d (p. 482), **3.** delusions and hallucinations; disorganized thinking; emotions and affect; and reduced enjoyment and interests (p. 483), **4.** c (p. 483), **5.** a (p. 484), **6.** b (p. 486).

APPLICATION OF PSYCHOLOGY

ABNORMAL PSYCHOLOGY AND CIVIL LIBERTIES

The goal of clinical psychology, psychiatry, and the other mental health professions is to help persons with mental disorders. In most cases, this means offering services to persons who come to the office or hospital and request professional services. In other cases, mental health professionals play more of an activist role. I am never more proud to be a psychologist than when I see members of my profession attempting to prevent abnormal behavior in the community, offering services to the indigent, and attempting to bring a scientific perspective to debates about important social issues. No mental health profession does enough in these areas, but these efforts are often significant.

In some cases, these outreach efforts are relatively uncomplicated matters. If enough psychologists and psychiatrists volunteer their time, and if funding can be obtained from public or private sources to rent space and pay the heating bill, it is a simple matter to set up a free clinic in an area where homeless persons live. As long as the persons who receive services voluntarily seek them, there is no conflict with the laws that protect civil liberties. In other cases, the attempt to provide assistance raises difficult legal and ethical issues.

In this section we will discuss two burning social issues to which psychology and psychiatry have recently turned their attention: homelessness and physician-assisted suicide. We will see that psychological concepts lie at the heart of these complicated issues. We will also see that important questions concerning civil liberties must be resolved before psychology will be able to play an effective role.

Abnormal Psychology and Homelessness

It has become commonplace in large cities in the United States to see homeless people sleeping on heating vents next to their bag of belongings. Who are these unfortunate persons? How have they fallen between the cracks in the world's most affluent society?

Although opinions vary, the primary factors associated with the recent increases in homelessness are prolonged periods of high unemployment, government policies that have greatly reduced the amount of low-cost housing available to the poor, old-fashioned prejudice against ethnic minorities, and changes in vagrancy laws that, in many cases, give people the legal right to be homeless (to sleep on the street, to panhandle, etc.). Another reason for the increase in homeless persons is the inability of psychiatric hospitals and mental health centers to provide adequate services due to massive cuts in funding.

Many homeless persons—but certainly not all—have serious psychological disorders. As funding for mental health service programs is cut, the number of the homeless rises. A study of homeless individuals in inner-city Los Angeles (Koegel, Burnam, & Farr, 1988) found 62.2 percent to have a serious chronic mental disorder and/or alcohol or drug dependence. In the same city, very high rates of symptoms of schizophrenia were found among homeless adolescents (Mundy, Robertson, Robertson, & Greenblatt, 1990). A similar study in New York (Susser, Struening, & Conover, 1989) found serious mental and substance abuse disorders in 71 percent of homeless men.

We can see the role played by mental disorders in the true stories of Karen and Kevin, two homeless persons in New York City (Brosnahan & Giffen, 1993). In the words of 38-year-old Karen, "I was one of those people you see on street corners screaming at imaginery people, completely out of my mind." She was homeless for 13 years, periodically being treated in mental hospitals. But she was lucky and found her way into a program that provided consistent medication and therapy and found her affordable housing. As a result, Karen has been employed almost continuously for the past three years and has regained custody of her 14-year-old son.

Contrast her story to that of Kevin McKiever, the homeless man who was charged in 1991 with murdering a former Radio City Rockette with a knife. He had gone to Bellevue Psychiatric Hospital a few weeks before the stabbing seeking treatment, but he was turned away because the hospital had no openings in its underfunded community-care program. Another recent article reported that between 1975 and 1991, 52 persons were pushed in front of subway trains in New York by strangers, mostly by psychotic homeless persons (Martell & Dietz, 1992). Would these truly terrifying tragedies have happened if mental health services for the homeless were better funded and more effective?

Many homeless people need and want psychiatric or psychological help. However, some mental health professionals argue that the right of homeless people to refuse treatment must be respected as well.

Even if adequate funding were to be made available, however, it would not be a simple matter to provide services to all the homeless with mental disorders. Not all persons with mental disorders want treatment, especially those with substance abuse disorders and psychotic conditions. This fact has spurred tremendous debate in the mental health professions. Well-meaning professionals on both sides of this issue cannot agree on the best course of action. Some favor strong outreach programs that will search for mentally disordered homeless persons and provide them with mental hospitalization and medication, whether they want it or not. Some even favor "conservatorships," in which private individuals or public agencies are given the legal right to control the finances, medication, and hospitalization of persons with mental disorders who are judged to be incompetent to make their own decisions (Lamb & Weinberger, 1992). Other mental health professionals, however, argue that we must protect the civil rights of the homeless and provide treatment only to those who seek it voluntarily (Mossman & Perlin, 1992). Meanwhile the public is just as deeply divided on this social issue that is, in equal measures, sad and frightening.

Physician-Assisted Suicide

Another emotionally laden issue is physician-assisted suicide. Like homelessness, this matter involves a complex interplay of civil rights and concepts from abnormal psychology.

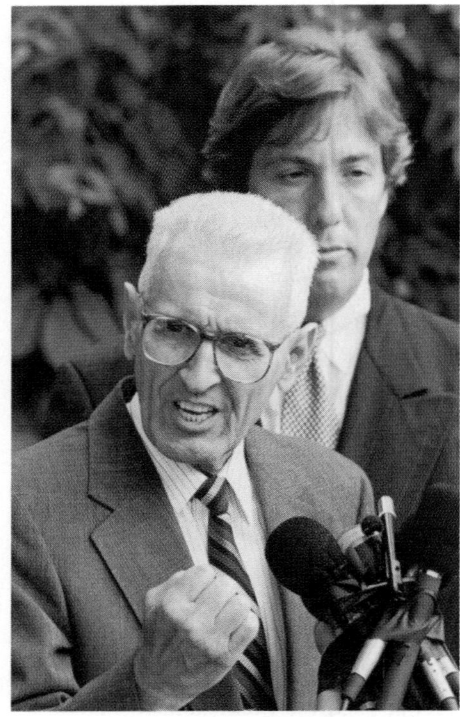

Much of the controversy concerning physician-assisted suicide was created by the actions of the "suicide doctor," Dr. Jack Kevorkian.

Much of the publicity surrounding this issue has come from the outspoken efforts of Dr. Jack Kevorkian to convince lawmakers that it should be legal for physicians to assist terminally ill patients in committing suicide painlessly, as by taking an overdose of sleeping pills or inhaling carbon monoxide. Dr. Kevorkian, who is a retired pathologist in Michigan, has helped many patients commit suicide. For example, he told the story of assisting the suicide of a 30-year-old man with a terminal and progressive disease commonly known as Lou Gehrig's disease. Dr. Kevorkian said that his patient wished to die because he had completely lost all motor control and knew that he would probably die by choking on his own saliva.

Dr. Kevorkian and other advocates of the right to commit suicide painlessly have argued forcefully that they are only attempting to prevent needless suffering and preserve human dignity. Recently, however, psychiatrists Herbert Hendin and Gerald Klerman (1993) and Harvey Chochinov (Chochinov et al., 1995) have written moving and cogent articles pointing out what they believe to be the dangers involved in legalized physician-assisted suicide. They noted that studies have consistently shown that 95 percent of persons who commit suicide have mental disorders at the time of the suicide, usually depression. This is particularly true of elderly persons who take their lives during the kind of depressive episodes that are highly treatable. They state that persons who are prevented from committing suicide during an episode of depression are almost invariably grateful to be alive when they recover from the depression.

In the case of persons with terminal illnesses who seek assistance from a physician in committing suicide, Hendin and Klerman (1993) offer these sobering observations. Learning that one has a terminal illness is an extremely stressful event, but autopsy studies have shown that more elderly people commit suicide because they *mistakenly* thought they had a fatal illness than actually had such an illness. Furthermore, the first reaction of many persons who learn that they actually have a terminal illness is depression and anxiety, but most recover from this phase and live meaningful lives until the end. Should patients with terminal illnesses be allowed to commit suicide during the initial depressed phase, when most of them would have later chosen to live? Should elderly patients who are depressed because they mistakenly believe that their relatives wish they were gone be provided with psychotherapy or assistance in suicide?

Hendin and Klerman (1993) also provided chilling evidence that suicide pacts between spouses or lovers, which are often romanticized in the press, often involve pressured decisions for one of the partners. Detailed studies of such cases reveal that suicide pacts often involve a man who wishes to die who coerces his wife into joining him to prove her love. They even report evidence from the videotaped suicide note and writings of a woman who committed suicide, perhaps partly over guilt that she had helped her 92-year-old father and 78-year-old mother commit suicide, even though she suspected that her mother had been pressured and was not ready to die. Ironically, the woman was the cofounder of the Hemlock Society, a society that advocates the right to commit suicide. Cases of double suicides must be the cause of particular concern.

Hendin and Klerman (1993) argue strongly that if physician-assisted suicide is legalized, physicians without training in psychiatry will make decisions regarding the patient's wish to die without understanding the role that depression and other mental disorders can play in suicidal wishes. Furthermore, such laws might encourage unscrupulous physicians and nonphysicians to offer assistance in suicide without regard for the best interest of the person.

What are your thoughts about these serious and complicated issues?

Summary

Chapter 13 introduces us to the wide range of abnormal thoughts, feelings, and actions that humans experience.

I. Abnormal behavior includes those actions, thoughts, and feelings that are harmful to the person and/or others.
  - **A.** Our ideas about the causes of abnormal behavior determine what we do to help those who experience it.
  - **B.** Abnormal behavior is viewed today as a natural, rather than a supernatural, phenomenon.

II. Anxiety disorders are characterized by excessive anxiety.
  - **A.** Intense, unrealistic fears are called phobias.
  - **B.** Generalized anxiety disorder is characterized by free-floating anxiety.
  - **C.** Panic anxiety disorder involves attacks of intense anxiety.
  - **D.** Obsessions are anxiety-provoking thoughts that will not go away; compulsions are urges to repeatedly engage in a behavior.

III. Somatoform disorders are conditions in which an individual experiences symptoms of health problems that are psychological rather than physical in origin.
  - **A.** Somatization disorders are a type of somatoform disorder that involves multiple symptoms of illness that indirectly create a high risk of medical complications; hypochondriasis is characterized by excessive concern with health.
  - **B.** Conversion disorders are a type of somatoform disorder that involves serious specific somatic symptoms in the absence of any physical cause. Pain disorders involve pain without physical cause.

IV. In the various types of dissociative disorders, there is a change in memory, perception, or identity.
  - **A.** Dissociative amnesia and fugue states involve memory loss that has psychological rather than physical causes.
  - **B.** In depersonalization, individuals feel that they or their surroundings have become distorted or unreal.
  - **C.** Individuals who exhibit dissociative identity disorder act as if they possess more than one personality in the same body.

V. Mood disorders are disturbances of positive or negative moods.
  - **A.** The individual experiencing major depression is deeply unhappy and lethargic and shows other characteristic symptoms.
  - **B.** In the condition known as bipolar affective disorder, periods of mania alternate irregularly with periods of severe depression.

VI. Schizophrenia involves three major areas of abnormality: (a) delusions and hallucinations, (b) disorganized thinking, emotions, and behavior, and (c) reduced enjoyment and interests.
  - **A.** The paranoid schizophrenic holds false beliefs or delusions—usually of grandeur and persecution—that seriously distort reality.
  - **B.** Disorganized schizophrenia is characterized by extreme withdrawal from normal human contact, fragmented delusions and hallucinations, and a shallow "silliness" of emotion.
  - **C.** Catatonic schizophrenia is marked by stupors in which the individual may maintain postures for long periods of time.

VII. Personality disorders are thought to result from personalities that developed improperly during childhood rather than from breakdowns under stress.
  - **A.** Schizoid personality disorders are characterized by a loss of interest in proper dress and social contact, a lack of emotion, and an inability to hold regular jobs.
  - **B.** The antisocial personality frequently violates social rules and laws, is often violent, takes advantage of others, and feels little guilt about it.

Suggested Readings

1. An overview of the psychology of psychological disorders: Davison, G. C., & Neale, J. M. (1996). *Abnormal psychology: An experimental clinical approach.* (7th ed.). New York: John Wiley.
2. For more on abnormal psychology and individual rights: Winick B. J. (1996). *The right to refuse mental health treatment.* Washington, DC: American Psychological Association.
3. A moving personal account of the experience of schizophrenia is found in the classic book: Sechehaye, M. (1951). *Reality lost and regained: Autobiography of a schizophrenic girl.* New York: Grune & Stratton.
4. For a cognitive view of dissociative identity disorder: Spanos, N. P. (1997). *Multiple identities and false memories.* Washington, DC: American Psychological Association.

CHAPTER

14

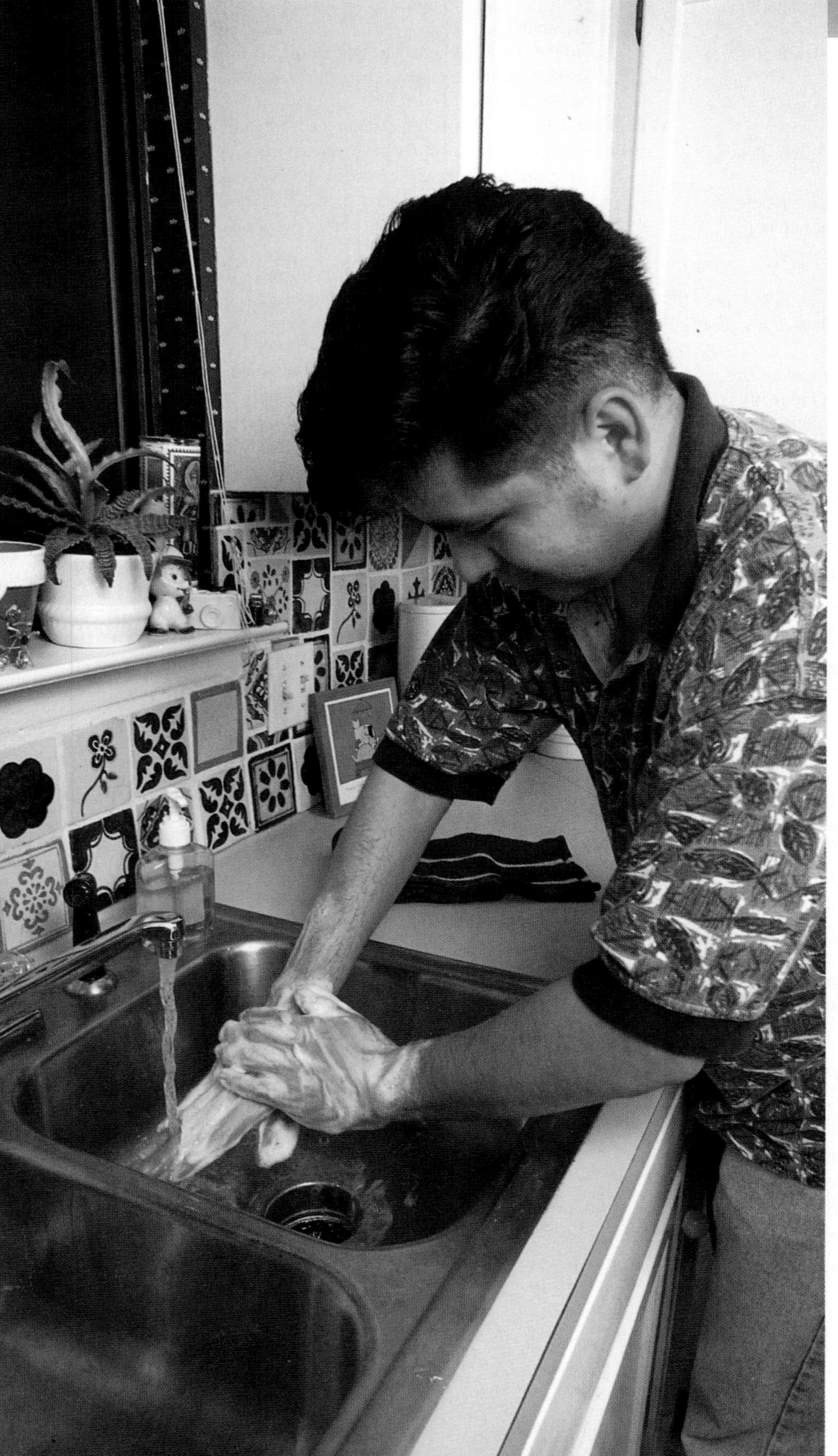

CHAPTER OUTLINE

Therapies

PROLOGUE

David had always been a neat and orderly person. During his first session with the therapist, he described with a half-hearted smile an incident in which he slipped and fell in mud on the way to his elementary school and returned home sobbing. But David's cleanliness caused only minor problems until his daughter was diagnosed with pinworms. David became intensely anxious when he heard the doctor describe how pinworms are spread through their eggs and recommend that the clothes of everyone in the family be boiled to prevent contagion.

David immediately went home and boiled the family's clothes and sheets. After he finished, he washed his hands. But as soon as he did, he thought that there might still be pinworm eggs on them and he washed them again. Soon David began worrying about germs, dirt, and feces that might be on his hands. Within days, he was washing his hands 200 times a day!

David's worse times were at night: He would lie in bed after washing his hands and try to resist the urge to get up and wash them again, only to fail over and over. When his wife became worried about his sanity, and his hands began to crack and bleed because of the constant washing, he decided to contact a therapist (based on Prochaska, 1984, pp. 268–271).

David had developed a form of abnormal behavior called obsessive-compulsive disorder. We will see in this chapter that, fortunately, several forms of treatment are effective for this and other psychological problems. One remedy for obsessive-compulsive disorder that often helps is medication, but a simple form of psychological therapy is also effective. In this therapy, the person agrees to be prevented from washing and to endure the anxiety that being unable to wash produces. In time, the anxiety drops to normal levels if the individual does not give in to the urge to wash (Baxter, Schwartz, Bergman, & Szuba, 1992).

Psychotherapy is a process of people helping people. In psychotherapy, a trained professional seeks to help a person with a psychological problem by using methods based on psychological theories of the nature of the problem. These therapy methods include everyday activities such as asking questions, making suggestions, and demonstrating alternative ways of behaving, but psychotherapy differs from commonsense attempts to help because of the theories that determine what is asked and what is suggested. Several different forms of psychotherapy are based on the theories of personality that we studied in chapter 11.

Psychoanalysts feel that abnormal behavior is the result of unconscious conflicts among the id, ego, and superego. These conflicts remain hidden from consciousness because the ego and superego see them as dangerous and block them out. The process of psychoanalysis, then, is a process of relaxing the censorship exerted by the conscious mind and bringing unconscious conflicts into awareness where they can be intelligently resolved. Because the contents of the unconscious are revealed only in disguised, symbolic ways, however, the psychoanalyst must help the individual interpret glimpses of the hidden side of the mind.

Humanistic psychologists also believe that the goal of psychotherapy is to help the person achieve greater self-awareness, but in ways that differ from those of psychoanalysts. Humanists believe that feelings that conflict with a person's self-concept are often denied conscious awareness. The humanistic psychotherapist seeks to help the person allow this information into his or her consciousness and thus achieve fuller self-awareness.

KEY TERMS

Behavior therapy is an approach to psychotherapy that is associated with the social learning view of personality. Because psychological problems are believed to be the result of unfortunate learning experiences, the behavior therapist plays the role of a teacher helping the person *unlearn* abnormal ways of behavior. Cognitive therapy is a newer approach to therapy that is also based on social learning theory. Cognitive therapists believe that we have learned illogical ways of thinking that cause abnormal behavior. They attempt to change these faulty cognitions primarily by pointing out their irrationality.

Help for abnormal behavior is not delivered only in one-to-one psychotherapy, however. It's sometimes provided in the form of group or family therapy, and often takes the form of medication and other kinds of medical treatment.

DEFINITION OF PSYCHOTHERAPY

People with the serious kinds of psychological problems described in chapter 13 generally need professional help. Many different forms of help are available for psychological disorders from psychologists, psychiatrists, clinical social workers, and counselors. In this chapter, the major forms of therapy are described and related to differing theories of personality (chapter 11) and differing views of abnormal behavior (chapter 13).

psychotherapy
(sī-kō-ther´ah-pē) A form of therapy in which a trained professional uses methods based on psychological theories to help a person with psychological problems.

In general terms, **psychotherapy** can be defined as a specialized process in which a trained professional uses psychological methods to help a person with psychological problems. The term *psychological methods* can refer to almost any kind of human interaction (such as talking or demonstrating) that is based on a psychological theory of the problem, but it does *not* include medical treatment methods such as medications or surgery.

Different forms of psychotherapy associated with psychoanalytic, humanistic, and social learning theories of personality involve very different psychological methods. The approach to psychotherapy associated with social learning theory, known as behavior therapy, views the process of helping as a form of teaching. The therapist helps the person learn not to engage in harmful behaviors and to learn adaptive behaviors to take their place. The approaches to psychotherapy associated with psychoanalytic and humanistic views of personality see their goal as providing insight, that is, bringing feelings (or conflicts of information) of which the person is unaware into conscious awareness. Although the methods of psychoanalysis and humanistic therapy differ greatly, they both view the therapist not as a teacher but as a catalyst, an agent who makes change possible but does not actually cause or enter into the change. Therapies that strive for increased awareness view the person with problems as the agent of his or her own improvement.

personal growth therapy
Psychotherapy for normal individuals who want to enhance their personal adjustment, improve interpersonal relationships, learn to react better to stress, and so on.

Defining psychotherapy as a psychological process of helping people with psychological problems is correct but is limited in an important way. Many individuals legitimately enter into psychotherapy to improve their daily lives rather than to rid themselves of abnormal behavior. Individuals often seek therapy because they feel that they simply are not getting full enjoyment from their careers or are not approaching intimate personal relationships in appropriate ways. Psychotherapy is also often used to enhance sexual and marital relationships, to learn to manage normal reactions to stress better, and so on. This use of psychotherapy is often called **personal growth therapy.**

ETHICAL STANDARDS FOR PSYCHOTHERAPY

The relationship between client and psychotherapist is a unique one. The patient divulges large amounts of personal information in an emotion-laden setting and places her or his future in the hands of the psychotherapist. Because this places the therapist in a position of power relative to the client, it's essential that the highest ethical standards be followed in the practice of psychotherapy. The following discussion of ethical principles is based on the policies prepared by the American Psychological Association (1990, 1993) and the Association for Advancement of Behavior Therapy (1978).

Psychotherapy is considered to be ethical only under the following circumstances:

1. The goals of treatment must be carefully considered with the client. These goals should be in the best interest of the client and society and they must be fully understood by the client. For example, we will look later in this chapter at

methods of therapy for people with severe shyness. If you had that problem and went to a therapist, the first step should be a discussion of the goals of therapy. You may simply wish to learn to live with your shyness, while your therapist may wish to help you to be less shy. Therapy would not be ethical unless the goals were carefully discussed and agreed upon in advance.

2. The choices for alternative treatment methods should be carefully considered. In this chapter we will look at a wide variety of treatments for psychological problems. A choice must be made among them before beginning therapy. Sometimes the choice can be made on the basis of published research that shows that one procedure is the best one available for the problem. In other cases, there will be two or more effective treatments that differ in the degree of discomfort, treatment time and cost, and potential side effects. The range of choices should be discussed with the client before therapy starts. The difficulty is that different therapists do not always agree on which methods are most effective, so the consumer may have to do some investigating before choosing a therapist. For example, after reading this chapter, you may know whether you would prefer a therapist who takes a psychoanalytic, cognitive, behavioral, or other approach.
3. The therapist must only treat problems that she or he is qualified to treat. No therapist is trained to use all forms of therapy or to handle all types of problems (adults, children, marital problems, etc.). Therefore, the therapist must refer cases that fall outside his or her expertise to qualified therapists.
4. The effectiveness of treatment must be evaluated in some way. The best way of doing this is to use meaningful measures of the problem and progress in treating it. Some therapists, however, feel that their subjective impressions that take many factors into consideration are the best measures of progress.
5. The rules and laws regarding the confidentiality of all information obtained about the client during treatment must be fully explained to the client. Under most circumstances it is unethical and illegal for the therapist to reveal any information about you (even the fact that a person is a client in therapy) to anyone without the written permission of the client. However, there are exceptions to that rule. First, sometimes other psychologists in a practice will cover for the therapist in emergencies and will need to learn about the client. Second, if the therapist is still in training and being supervised by a licensed therapist, it is essential that the client be told of that fact and the name of the supervisor. Third, in some circumstances regarding court matters, the courts can require the therapist to reveal confidential information. Fourth, if the therapist learns that the client is in immediate danger of harming himself or herself or of harming anyone else, the therapist is obligated to report that information to the proper authorities.

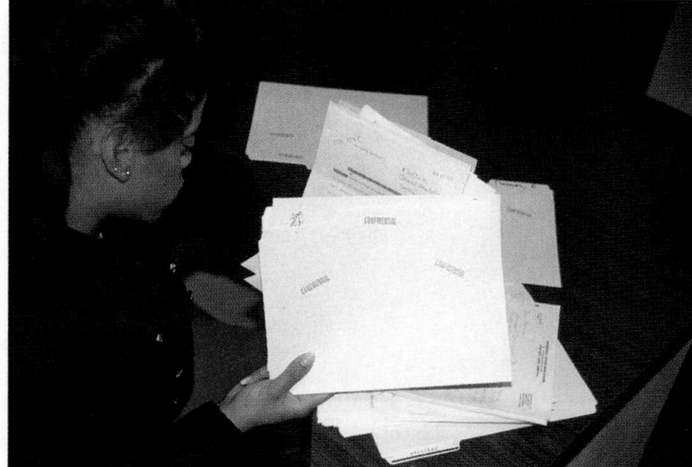

Psychotherapists must respect the rules and laws regarding the confidentiality of information about their clients.

6. The therapist must not use the power of the intense relationship with the client to exploit the client in sexual or other ways. Sexual or romantic intimacies with clients have long been strictly forbidden, but in contrast to novels and movies in which therapists and current or former clients fall in love and marry, ethical regulations even forbid romantic or sexual relationships with former clients under virtually all circumstances. Sexual harassment of clients is similarly strictly forbidden.
7. The therapist must treat human beings with dignity and understand and respect differences based on gender, ethnicity, sexual orientation, and other sociocultural factors. To the greatest extent possible, therapists must understand and respect human differences and not try to sway clients to their own beliefs and ways. For

example, this means that a traditional male therapist must not try to influence a woman who identifies with the feminist philosophy to adopt a more subservient feminine role. Similarly, a therapist who believes that homosexuality is immoral must not attempt to convince a homosexual who is comfortable with her or his sexual orientation to change. If the therapist cannot respect the beliefs and ways of the client, the therapist must refer that person to another therapist.

PSYCHOANALYSIS

psychoanalysis
(sī´kō-ah-nal´i-sis) A method of psychotherapy developed by Freud based on his belief that the root of all psychological problems is unconscious conflicts between the id, the ego, and the superego.

Psychoanalysis is the approach to psychotherapy founded by Sigmund Freud. It's based on Freud's belief that the root of all psychological problems is unconscious conflicts among the id, ego, and superego. Conflicts inevitably exist among these three competing forces, but they can cause problems if they get out of hand. If too much of the energy of the superego and ego is devoted to holding the selfish desires of the id in check, or if these prohibitions are weak and the id threatens to break free, psychological disturbances result. According to Freud, these conflicts must be brought into consciousness if they are to be solved.

A patient and therapist in a session of psychoanalysis.

Bringing unconscious conflicts into consciousness is not an easy matter, though. Recall from chapter 11 that the id is completely unconscious. Even the sexual and aggressive motives that we consciously experience have been transformed by the ego into safe and socially acceptable versions of the id's true desires. According to Freud, the ego operates as if the raw, selfish desires of the id are too dangerous to allow into consciousness, so it works diligently to dam up the id in the recesses of our unconscious mind. Special therapy methods must be used, therefore, to allow information about unconscious id conflicts to slip past the censorship of the ego.

It's generally possible to bring information out of the unconscious only when the ego's guard is temporarily relaxed, and even then, the id is able to reveal itself only in disguised symbolic forms. Thus, the job of the psychoanalyst is to (a) create conditions in which the censorship of the ego is relaxed and (b) to interpret the disguised symbolic revelations of the unconscious mind to the patient.

Techniques of Psychoanalytic Psychotherapy

Most contemporary psychoanalysts do not practice an orthodox version of psychoanalysis, but rather practice versions based on the revisions of Jung, Adler, Horney, and more contemporary psychoanalysts. Still, many of the specific techniques of therapy used by Freud are still in use today. These include free association, dream interpretation, interpretation of resistance, and interpretation of transference.

Free Association

free association
A tool used by Freud in which the patient is encouraged to talk about whatever comes to mind, allowing the contents of the unconscious mind to slip past the censorship of the ego.

Freud's primary tool of therapy was the method of **free association.** In this method, the individual talks in a loose and undirected way about whatever comes to mind. No thought or feeling is to be withheld, no matter how illogical, trivial, unpleasant, or silly it might seem. Freud hoped that this technique would lead to a "turning off" of the intellectual control of the ego and allow for glimpses of the unconscious. Occasionally, as the mind wanders, the id slips out. To make this more likely to happen, Freud had his patients lie on a couch facing the ceiling. He sat out of sight behind them so they would feel that they were talking to themselves rather than revealing forbidden information to another.

Incidentally, contemporary research suggests that Freud's choice of a reclining position for his patients may have had an important effect on his approach to psychotherapy. After working with many patients, Freud came to believe that he must help the patient achieve insight primarily about events that happened in childhood. Interestingly, Pope (1978) found that when individuals are asked to let their "mind wander" aloud, reclining people speak significantly more about the past than people who are sitting. Freud's choice of a reclining posture for his patients may have led them to focus on the past and led him to think of the past as being of prime importance in therapy.

The "glimpses of the unconscious" revealed during free association have hidden, symbolic meaning that must be translated or interpreted to the patient by the psychoanalyst. For example, the patient might mention during the course of free association that he wanted to go hunting with his father, but that he never asked him to go hunting because he was afraid that his father was too old and might get hurt. To the psychoanalyst, this statement might be about phallic symbols (guns) and the son's unresolved Oedipus conflict (see chapter 11, p. 405) that has left him with an unacceptable desire to shoot his father. When properly interpreted to the patient, Freud believed that this information about the unconscious would help the person consciously solve his or her problems.

In traditional psychoanalysis, the therapist sits out of the patient's sight. Freud had his patients lie on a couch while he sat in a chair to the left.

Dream Interpretation

Dream interpretation was used by Freud in much the same manner as free association. As we mentioned in chapter 4, the obvious or manifest content of dreams is believed by psychoanalysts to symbolically mask the true or latent content of dreams. By asking patients to recall dreams, Freud believed he had obtained another "window" on the unconscious.

dream interpretation
A method developed by Freud in which the symbols of the manifest content of dreams that are recalled by the patient are interpreted to reveal their latent content.

For example, a recurrent dream of an adolescent boy in which he was drifting through a slimy swamp on a raft, reaching down repeatedly into the dirty water, and pulling up shoes might have no meaning at all to the adolescent. The psychoanalyst might translate it to mean that the boy was experiencing conflicts over his heterosexual desires. Shoes are commonly taken to symbolize vaginas in psychoanalytic thinking, and the dirty, forbidding water from which he was attempting to possess these vaginas might represent his guilt feelings about sex.

Interpretation of Resistance

Freud also placed heavy emphasis on the interpretation of what he called resistance in therapy. **Resistance** is any form of opposition of the patient to the process of psychoanalysis. Resistance can occur in two ways. It might take vague forms, such as missing appointments with the therapist or questioning the value of psychoanalysis. Or it might be a specific resistance to the interpretations of the therapist. In either case, resistance meant to Freud that he had located a conflict in the patient that was so laden with anxiety that the patient wanted to avoid talking about it. This avoidance of the topic made Freud all the more interested in pursuing it.

resistance
Any form of patient opposition to the process of psychoanalysis.

Angrily telling a psychoanalyst that he or she is wrong for suggesting that you ever wanted to have casual sex with a person you did not love may convince your therapist that this is something that you actually want to do but that you consider morally unacceptable. To give you better insight into your own motives, your psychoanalyst might interpret this resistance to you. The analyst would believe that if you erroneously continue to think you do not want casual sex, you will not be able to understand and deal with the anxiety that you experience. If, on the other hand, you become aware that you do want casual sex, but that you feel that it would be immoral to do so, you can make more rational, informed choices about your behavior.

Interpretation of Transference

The relationship that forms between patient and therapist can also be a source of information about the unconscious to the psychoanalyst. Because the patient comes to the therapist in need of help, reveals a great deal of private information, and receives acceptance and support, it's not surprising that a rather intense relationship often develops. This relationship is not like the one you have with your dentist, but more like a close parent-child relationship.

Because of the intensity of the relationship in therapy, psychoanalysts believe that the kind of relationship the patient has with the therapist reveals a great deal about the way the

"Mr. Prentice is *not* your father. Alex Binster is *not* your brother. The anxiety you feel is *not* genuine. Dr. Froelich will return from vacation September 15th. Hang on."

transference
(trans-fer´ens) The phenomenon in psychoanalysis in which the patient comes to feel and act toward the therapist in ways that resemble how he or she feels and acts toward other significant adults.

patient relates to his or her parents and other significant authority figures. Psychoanalysts call this phenomenon **transference.** When patients repeatedly ask for reassurance that they will not be dropped as clients, or argue about fees, or make sexual advances, they are believed to be transferring to the therapist feelings that they have for other significant adults in their lives. That is, they are feeling and acting toward the therapist in the same basic ways that they feel and act toward their parents, employers, and so on. When interpreted to the patients, psychoanalysts believe that transference can serve as another valuable source of insight.

Catharsis

catharsis
The release of emotional energy related to unconscious conflicts.

In addition to the interpretation of symbolic revelations of unconscious conflicts, psychoanalysis allows the patient to release some of the emotion that is pent up with unconscious conflicts. All forms of psychotherapy can be very emotional experiences that at times involve talking about highly upsetting topics. Letting these emotions out—a process psychoanalysts call **catharsis**—provides a temporary relief from discomfort. Catharsis is not a technique of psychoanalysis; rather, it is one of its benefits.

This relief does not solve problems in and of itself, but it does make the patient feel better. Catharsis may also facilitate the process of psychoanalysis, however, because a patient who feels better will generally be better able to make intelligent decisions about discoveries from the unconscious.

Excerpt from Psychoanalytic Psychotherapy

In the following excerpt from a session of psychoanalytic psychotherapy, the therapist attempts to get the client to reinterpret his anxiety:

Client: We had a salesmen's meeting, and a large group of us were cramped together in a small room and they turned out the lights to show some slides, and I got so jumpy and anxious I couldn't stand it.

Therapist: So what happened?

C: I just couldn't stand it. I was sweating and shaking, so I got up and left, and I know I'll be called on the carpet for walking out.

T: You became so anxious and upset that you couldn't stand being in the room even though you knew that walking out would get you into trouble.

C: Yeah. . . . What could have bothered me so much to make me do a dumb thing like that?

T: You know, we've talked about other times in your life when you've become upset in close quarters with other men, once when you were in the army and again in your dormitory at college.

C: That's right, and it was the same kind of thing again.

T: And if I'm correct, this has never happened to you in a group of men and women together, no matter how closely you've been cramped together.

C: Uh. . . . Yes, that's right.

T: So it appears that something especially about being physically close to other men, and especially in the dark, makes you anxious, as if you're afraid bad things might happen in that kind of situation.

C: (Pause): I think you're right about that . . . and I know I'm not physically afraid of other men. Do you think I might get worried about something homosexual taking place?

Review

Psychoanalysis is the method of psychotherapy based on Freud's theory of personality. The therapist attempts to help the patient by bringing unconscious conflicts into consciousness so they can be intelligently resolved. Because the ego works to block from consciousness the contents of the unconscious mind (including conflicts among the id, ego, and superego), the psychoanalyst must create conditions to relax the censorship of the ego. Even when the unconscious mind reveals itself at these times, however, it does so in disguised, symbolic ways. This means that a second function of the psychoanalyst is to interpret the disguised information revealed during psychoanalysis to the patient. The specific method most commonly used by the psychoanalyst to relax the ego's censorship is free association. Comments made by the patient during these wandering, unguided conversations are believed to symbolically reveal hidden conflicts. In addition, the psychoanalyst interprets information from dreams, resistance to the process of therapy, and the way the patient acts toward the psychoanalyst (transference) to reveal further the unconscious mind to the patient. Finally, psychoanalysis is believed to provide temporary relief by allowing the patient to vent some of the emotion tied up in unconscious conflicts (catharsis).

Thinking Critically About Psychology

1. Give a brief personality description of the type of patients who you believe would benefit most from psychoanalysis. Would you include women? How about members of ethnic groups different from Freud's?

2. What would you consider to be the strengths of psychoanalysis? What might be its weaknesses?

Check Your Learning

To be sure that you have learned the key points from the preceding section, cover the answers below and try to answer each question. If you give an incorrect answer to any question, return to the page given next to the correct answer to see why your answer was not correct. Remember that these questions cover only some of the important information in this section; it is important that you make up your own questions to check your learning of other facts and concepts.

1. In general terms, ________________ can be defined as a specialized process in which a trained professional uses psychological methods to help a person with psychological problems.

2. ________________ is based on Freud's belief that the root of all psychological problems is unconscious conflicts among the id, ego, and superego that must be brought into conscious awareness.

   a. Behavior therapy
   b. Client-centered therapy
   c. Psychoanalysis
   d. Cognitive therapy

3. Freud's primary tool of therapy was the method of ________________ in which the individual talks in a loose and undirected way about whatever comes to mind.

   a. free association
   b. transference
   c. dream interpretation
   d. resistance

4. ________________ describes the release of emotional energy related to unconscious conflicts.

   a. Emotional cleansing
   b. Catharsis
   c. Liberation
   d. Outletting

Correct Answers

1. psychotherapy (p. 494), **2.** c (p. 496), **3.** a (p. 496), **4.** b (p. 498).

HUMANISTIC PSYCHOTHERAPY

The humanistic and psychoanalytic schools of thought both believe that the primary goal of therapy is to bring forth feelings of which the individual is unaware into conscious awareness. Recall from chapter 11 that Carl Rogers gives us an alternative way of thinking about feelings and information of which we are not consciously aware. Unlike Freud, Rogers does not believe that we are born with an unconscious mind. Rather, we deny awareness to information and feelings that differ too much from our concepts of self and ideal self (by not symbolizing them).

Using the same example that we used to illustrate Freud's concept of the unconscious, suppose you were a person who wanted casual sex. If your ideal self (the one you think you should ideally be) were the kind of person who would never have casual sex, you might deny conscious awareness to that desire. The desire for casual sex did not arise from an unconscious id according to Rogers, but the end result is the same: When a feeling is denied awareness, it can create anxiety until it's brought into the open. That is, it creates trouble until the individual achieves full awareness of his or her feelings. Because humanists view full self-awareness as necessary for the complete realization of our inner-directed potential, they speak of the process of therapy in terms of "growth in awareness" rather than in insight.

The methods used by humanistic therapists differ considerably from those used in psychoanalytic psychotherapy. A description of methods of humanistic therapy is complicated by the fact that a number of different approaches are grouped together under the name of humanism. We can get a perspective on these therapies, however, by looking at the methods of two leaders of the humanistic psychotherapy movement, Carl Rogers and Fritz Perls.

Client-Centered Psychotherapy

client-centered psychotherapy
Carl Rogers's approach to humanistic psychotherapy in which the therapist creates an atmosphere that encourages clients to discover feelings of which they are unaware.

reflection
(re-flek´shun) A technique in humanistic psychotherapy in which the therapist reflects the emotions of the client to help clients clarify their feelings.

Rogers refers to his humanistic approach as **client-centered psychotherapy** (he prefers the term *client* to the more medically oriented term *patient*) because the client, not the therapist, is at the center of the process of psychotherapy (Rogers, 1951). The emphasis is on the ability of clients to help themselves rather than on the ability of the therapist to help the clients. The job of the therapist in client-centered therapy is not to employ specific therapy techniques or to interpret the client's behavior, but to create an atmosphere that is so emotionally safe for the clients that they will feel free to express to the therapist (and to themselves) the feelings they have denied awareness. Growth in awareness comes not from interpretations, but from the client's feeling safe enough to explore hidden emotions in the therapy sessions. Rogers believes that the creation of this safe atmosphere requires three elements from the therapist. The therapist must be (a) warm, (b) must genuinely be able to like the clients and unconditionally accept everything they think, feel, or do without criticism, and (c) must have empathy, an accurate understanding and sharing of the emotions of the client. Importantly, a number of studies have shown that warmth of the therapist is an important determinant of the effectiveness of psychotherapy, even when the method of psychotherapy is not client-centered therapy (Rounsaville et al., 1987).

Carl Rogers (top right) facilitating the discussion during a group therapy session.

The closest thing to a specific "technique" in client-centered therapy is the process of **reflection.** The therapist helps the clients clarify the feelings expressed in their statements by reflecting back the emotions of the client. Sometimes the therapists ask questions, but other than reflections, client-centered therapists say relatively little in therapy. In particular, they strictly avoid giving advice to clients. They feel that clients can easily learn to solve their own problems after they have gained awareness, but that they will remain dependent on the therapist if the therapist solves their problems for them.

Excerpt from Client-Centered Psychotherapy

The following is an excerpt from a conversation between humanistic psychologist Carl Rogers and a client, a depressed young man. Notice the complete, nonjudgmental acceptance of the client's feelings.

Rogers: Everything's lousy, huh? You feel lousy? (Silence of 39 seconds)

Rogers: Want to come in Friday at 12 at the usual time?

Client: [Yawns and mutters something unintelligible.] (Silence of 48 seconds)

Rogers: Just kind of feel sunk way down deep in these lousy, lousy feelings, hm? Is that something like it?

Client: No.

Rogers: No? (Silence of 20 seconds)

Client: No. I just ain't no good to nobody, never was, and never will be.

Rogers: Feeling that now, hm? That you're just no good to yourself, no good to anybody. Just that you're completely worthless, huh? Those really are lousy feelings. Just feel that you're no good at all, hm?

[From a session three days later]

Client: I just want to run away and die.

Rogers: M-hm, m-hm, m-hm. It isn't even that you want to get away from here to something. You just want to leave here and go away and die in a corner, hm? (Silence of 30 seconds)

Rogers: I guess as I let that soak in I really do sense how, how deep that feeling sounds, that you—I guess the image that comes to my mind is sort of a—wounded animal that wants to crawl away and die. It sounds as though that's kind of the way you feel that you just want to get away from here and vanish. Perish. Not exist. (Silence of 1 minute)

Client: [almost inaudibly] All day yesterday and all morning I wished I were dead. I even prayed last night that I could die.

Rogers: I think I caught all of that, that for a couple of days now you've just wished you could be dead and you've even prayed for that, I guess that. One way this strikes me is that to live is such an awful thing to you, you just wish you could die, and not live. (Silence of 1 minute, 12 seconds)

Rogers: So that you've been just wishing and wishing that you were not living. You wish that life would pass away from you. (Silence of 30 seconds)

Client: I wish it more'n anything else I've ever wished around here.

Rogers: M-hm, m-hm, m-hm. I guess you've wished for lots of things but boy! It seems as though this wish to not live is deeper and stronger than anything you ever wished before. (Silence of 1 minute, 36 seconds)

Gestalt Psychotherapy

Fritz Perls (1893–1970)

Humanistic psychologist Fredrick (Fritz) Perls named his approach to humanistic psychotherapy Gestalt therapy (Perls, Hefferline, & Goodman, 1951). The term *gestalt* was chosen to emphasize a point first made by the Gestalt psychologists (whom we initially encountered in chapter 1). Writing in the early 1900s, this group pointed out that sensations have no meaning unless they are organized into "whole" perceptions. In an analogous way, Fritz Perls wanted to help his clients perceive themselves in a whole way by admitting conflicting information into awareness.

The goal of **Gestalt therapy** is essentially the same as that of client-centered therapy, namely, creating a therapeutic experience that will help the client achieve greater self-awareness. But the kinds of therapeutic experiences created by Gestalt and client-centered psychotherapists are as different as night and day.

Gestalt therapy
A humanistic therapy in which the therapist takes an active role (questioning and challenging the client) to help the client become more aware of his or her feelings.

Gestalt psychologists are actively involved in the conversations of therapy sessions. In particular, they challenge their client's statements when they think the statements do not reflect their client's true feelings, and they point out revealing inconsistencies in the present. For example, if a client claimed to never feel anxious about her performance on the job, she might get a reply like, "Oh, come now Mary, everyone gets anxious about job performance sometime. And what do you think it means that you start nervously tapping your fingers and squirming in your seat every time I bring up the subject? I think your denials of anxiousness cover up your true feelings."

The emotional atmosphere of Gestalt therapy is also quite different from client-centered therapy. Although Gestalt therapists show concern for their clients, they often deal with them in a confrontational, challenging manner. They are far from warm and accepting in their pushing, prodding, and questioning. Perls refers to this confrontation as a "safe emergency": While it's upsetting to the clients, it occurs in the safe environment of therapy. He feels that the safe emergency of confrontation with the therapist is necessary to shake loose feelings that have been denied awareness.

Thinking Critically About Psychology

1. How can client-centered therapy and Gestalt therapy both be consistent with the views of humanistic therapy when they are so different?

2. What would you describe as the key difference between humanistic psychotherapy and psychoanalysis? How significant is this difference?

Review

Humanistic psychotherapy strives to help clients achieve fuller self-awareness. Humanists believe that information about individuals that differs too much from their concept of self—both the self they think they are and the self they think they should be—will be denied awareness. This lack of awareness is harmful both because it keeps the individual from having an accurate view of self to use in making decisions and because the unsymbolized information threatens the person's inaccurate self-image and creates anxiety. Different approaches to humanistic psychotherapy use different methods to bring unsymbolized information into the open and give the person self-awareness. Client-centered psychotherapists create a safe emotional environment in therapy that they believe will allow clients to grow in self-awareness. This is accomplished through the therapist's warmth, empathy, and unconditional acceptance. In addition, the therapist uses the technique of reflection; the humanistic therapist repeats the message that she hears in the client's statements to help the client clarify what he is feeling. Gestalt therapists take a very different approach to humanistic therapy. They actively confront clients about inconsistencies in their statements, as well as between their statements and nonverbal behavior, that they feel reveal conflicting information and feelings. By pointing out these inconsistencies, they hope to help the clients achieve greater self-awareness.

Check Your Learning

To be sure that you have learned the key points from the preceding section, cover the answers below and try to answer each question. If you give an incorrect answer to any question, return to the page given next to the correct answer to see why your answer was not correct.

1. Humanists view full *self-awareness* as necessary for the complete realization of our inner-directed potential.

a. True **b.** False

2. Rogers refers to his humanistic approach to psychotherapy as ______________ because the emphasis is on the ability of the clients to help themselves rather than on the ability of therapists to help clients.

3. The process of ___________ describes a technique used in client-centered psychotherapy in which the therapist restates the emotions of the client to help clients clarify their feelings.

a. mimicking **c.** repetition
b. reflection **d.** recapitulation

Check Your Learning—continued

4. A humanistic therapy in which the therapist takes an active role (questioning and challenging) to help the client become more aware of her or his feelings is referred to as __________ therapy.

   a. client-centered **c.** Gestalt
   b. confrontational **d.** trial

Correct Answers

1. a (p. 500), 2. client-centered (p. 500), 3. b (p. 500), 4. c (p. 501).

BEHAVIOR THERAPY

Behavior therapy is the approach to psychotherapy that is associated with the social learning theory of personality. Recall from chapter 11 that abnormal behavior is viewed by social learning theorists as *learned* behavior. Rather than the product of unconscious conflicts, abnormal behavior simply is learned from inappropriate experiences of classical conditioning, operant conditioning, and modeling. In other words, individuals are abnormal because their environment taught them to be. For example, a young man who was frightened by social encounters might be reinforced for social withdrawal by the reduction in anxiety (negative reinforcement) that it produced. If so, social learning theorists would predict that this individual would learn to withdraw more and more.

behavior therapy
Psychotherapy based on social learning theory in which the therapist helps the client unlearn abnormal ways of behaving and learn more adaptive ways to take their place.

Because of this view of the origins of abnormal behavior, it's natural that behavior therapists would see the process of learning as central to the process of therapy as well. As mentioned earlier in the chapter, the behavior therapist plays the role of a teacher, a person who helps the client *unlearn* abnormal ways of behaving and *learn* more adaptive ways to take their place. The behavior therapist would attempt to help the socially withdrawn young man we just talked about to unlearn his fear of social interaction, and then teach him appropriate ways of interacting socially.

A number of different therapy methods have been derived from the basic principles of learning for use in behavior therapy. We survey a few of the major techniques used to reduce abnormal fears, teach new skills, and break abnormal habits. As you read about each of them, notice the innovative ways in which they teach adaptive behavior.

Fear Reduction Methods

Several behavior therapy methods are used to treat the abnormal fears that we call phobias. In different ways, each attempts to extinguish the fear response to the phobic stimulus and replace it with relaxation. The most widely used methods are systematic desensitization, graded exposure, and flooding.

Systematic Desensitization and Graded Exposure

Developed by psychiatrist Joseph Wolpe (1958), **systematic desensitization** is a complex procedure that involves two steps—progressive relaxation training and graded exposure. The first step in systematic desensitization is **progressive relaxation training,** a method of deeply relaxing the muscles of the body. The purpose is to put the client into a deep state of relaxation that can be conditioned to the phobic stimulus in place of the fear response.

Once the client has mastered deep muscle relaxation, the **graded exposure** part of the systematic desensitization procedure is begun. The therapist and the client rank all aspects of the phobic stimulus from least feared to most feared. For example, a medical student who is phobic of blood might react with a slight amount of fear to watching a patient's finger being pricked but with intense fear to watching open-heart surgery. A number of such fear-provoking stimuli are arranged in a graded list of phobic stimuli. The client is placed in a state of deep relaxation and asked to vividly imagine the weakest phobic stimulus on the hierarchy (in our

systematic desensitization
A behavior therapy method in which the client is taught not to fear phobic stimuli by learning to stay relaxed in the presence of successively more threatening stimuli.

progressive relaxation training
A method of learning to deeply relax the muscles of the body.

graded exposure
A behavior therapy technique in which a person with a phobia is first exposed to a stimulus that is mildly fear provoking. Once the client has mastered his or her anxiety in that situation, he or she is exposed to a graded series of more fearful situations.

example of the medical student, the weakest stimulus is watching a finger being pricked). If imagining that scene causes any fear at all, the individual is asked to raise a finger as a signal and stop imagining the scene. If the client can imagine the scene without fear, however, the therapist asks her to imagine the next scene. If that is too fear provoking, the client returns to the first scene for a while and later attempts to imagine the more intense scene without fear. When this can be done, she moves up the hierarchy. Over a number of sessions, the client is often able to imagine even the most feared scene without disturbing her relaxed state.

Often the graded exposure procedure is conducted in real-life settings without putting the client in a state of deep relaxation (called "in vivo graded exposure"). Typically the therapist accompanies the patient through a series of increasingly more fearful situations, beginning with mildly fearful ones. For a person with an intense specific phobia of heights, the therapist might accompany the client as he or she first walks to the edge of a second-story balcony. After the client has mastered that first situation and feels calm, he or she would walk to the railing of a third-story balcony, then a fourth-story balcony, and so on, until he or she can be in high places with little anxiety. A substantial literature attests to the effectiveness of these behavior therapies for fears (Barlow & Lehman, 1996; Barlow, 1996). Recently, modern technology has made graded exposure more convenient for both clients and therapists by safely exposing the client to a graded series of highly realistic frightening situations in the therapist's office using computer-generated "virtual reality" techniques (Rothbaum et al., 1995).

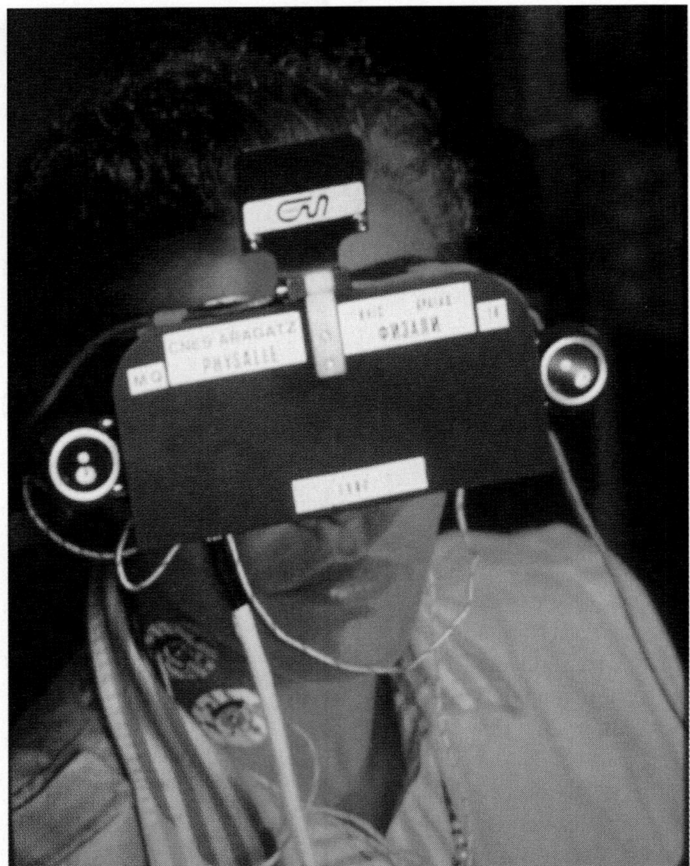

The technology of virtual reality can be used in graded exposure techniques to give the client the experience of being in a graded series of fearful situations in the therapist's office.

Flooding

An alternative to systematic desensitization and graded exposure is flooding. This procedure takes less time to implement, but it involves considerably more discomfort for the client. Whereas systematic desensitization can be completed with the client's experiencing no more than a slight degree of fear, **flooding** requires the client to be "flooded" with high levels of the fear for prolonged periods of time. The procedure is sometimes conducted in a single session that lasts from 2 to 8 hours. The session is not terminated until the fear response is extinguished and the phobic stimulus is no longer capable of eliciting the fear response.

flooding
A method of behavior therapy in which the client is confronted with high levels of phobic stimulus until the fear response is extinguished.

Flooding is often conducted by having the client imagine the phobic stimulus, but the most effective fear reduction method of all is *in vivo flooding,* flooding that is conducted in the presence of the actual phobic stimulus. For example, if the client is afraid of crowds, the therapist would take him or her to shopping malls, for rides on crowded buses, for walks on crowded sidewalks, and so on until the fear response had been exhausted in a wide variety of crowded situations.

For example, flooding is often used in the treatment of posttraumatic stress disorder (PTSD) (Keane & Kaloupek, 1982). Flooding is an unpleasant procedure that can be used only with clients who are highly motivated to find a solution to their problems. One such individual was a 36-year-old veteran of combat in Vietnam who came to a medical center seeking help for his many problems. He was chronically anxious, slept very little, had intense paniclike attacks of anxiety two to three times a week, and had catastrophic nightmares and daytime "flashbacks" in which he vividly relived traumatic war events in his imagination. In addition, he had been attempting unsuccessfully to drown his problems in a quart of gin each day for the past 5 years.

The veteran's psychologist began treatment by asking him to imagine a particularly upsetting scene in which a buddy was accidentally shot and killed in the mess hall while a gun was being cleaned. The therapist helped him to remember the situation in vivid detail to make the image as realistic and as upsetting as possible—the location, the weather, the terrain, and his companions. The veteran was then asked to recall how he was feeling just before the shooting, and he was urged to continue imaging the scene in vivid detail until he was emotionally exhausted. After 20 such daily sessions, dramatic improvements had occurred. The veteran was sleeping normally, had virtually no more flashback recollections or nightmares, and was no longer feeling anxious.

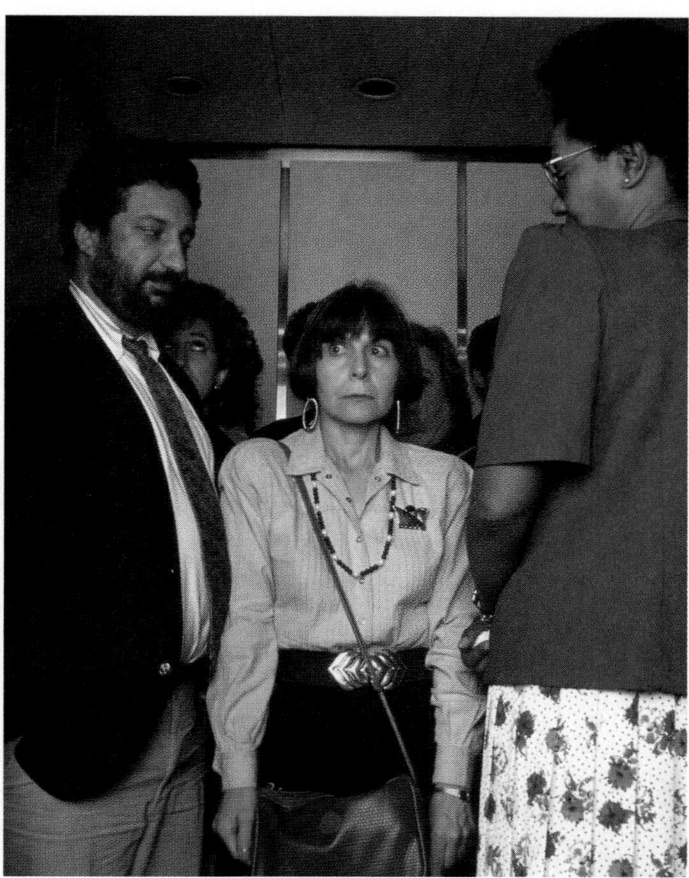

A person with a fear of elevators might be treated by asking him or her to ride in elevators all day—perhaps for several days in a row—until the anxiety was reduced. This would be an example of the behavior therapy technique of flooding.

Social Skills Training

A major emphasis of behavior therapy is on the teaching of adaptive skills using methods derived from operant conditioning. People with severe anxiety disorders, affective disorders, and schizophrenia frequently have difficulties interacting with other people. They tend to appear shy, awkward, "odd," and have difficulties expressing their feelings. Most of us experience similar difficulties in interacting with others in some situations (such as first dates and job interviews), but for some people this is a pervasive experience coloring nearly all of their social encounters that requires a form of therapy.

In **social skills training** *shaping* and *positive reinforcement* are used to teach persons with these social deficiencies to speak more often in social situations, to speak in a voice that is loud enough to be heard, to make appropriate eye contact, and to make fewer odd comments. This is usually accomplished by **role playing,** whereby the therapist and clients act as if they are people in problematic social situations. For example, if the client has great difficulties on job interviews and will soon be seeking a job, the therapist might role-play hypothetical job interviews. The therapist might first take the role of the client and model appropriate social behavior. Then, the client would play the role of herself in the next hypothetical job interview. The therapist would then provide positive reinforcement in the form of praise for the good aspects of the client's social behavior and suggest ways of improving the inappropriate aspects. Over a number of role-play sessions, enough improvement is usually obtained to allow the client to try role-played job interviews with other people and eventually to take a crack at the real thing.

social skills training
The use of techniques of operant conditioning to teach social skills to persons who lack them.

role playing
A therapeutic technique in which the therapist and client act as if they are people in problematic situations.

Let's focus for a moment on a study that evaluated the effectiveness of social skills training. Robin Cappe and Lynne Alden (1986) of the University of British Columbia evaluated a combination of social skills training and systematic desensitization for persons with *social phobias* (see p. 471). Their age ranged from 20 to 50 years, with all of them having been shy most of their lives. Most were not married and had either never dated or had not dated in years due to their shyness. Several had dropped out of college and others held jobs that were below their capabilities due to their social anxiety.

The subjects were divided into two groups that received different therapies. The first group was given a modified version of *systematic desensitization* (see p. 503). Each person was first trained in progressive relaxation. When this was mastered, each individual constructed a list of social situations that were arranged in order from the least anxiety provoking (e.g., "saying good morning to a waitress in a restaurant") to the most anxiety provoking (e.g., "asking a person for a date"). The person then practiced these social situations with the therapist, beginning with the least anxiety-provoking scenes and working up to the most difficult ones until they could perform these role-play scenes with little or no anxiety.

The second group received not only systematic desensitization but also a form of *social skills training* (see beginning of this section) in which they were taught social skills to make them better conversationalists.

The third group did not receive any treatment during the same period in which the first two treatments were evaluated. Rather, this group, known as the *wait list control group,* was given the better of the other two treatments *after* the experiment was over. This group was used to rule out the unlikely possibility that simply meeting with the therapist about their

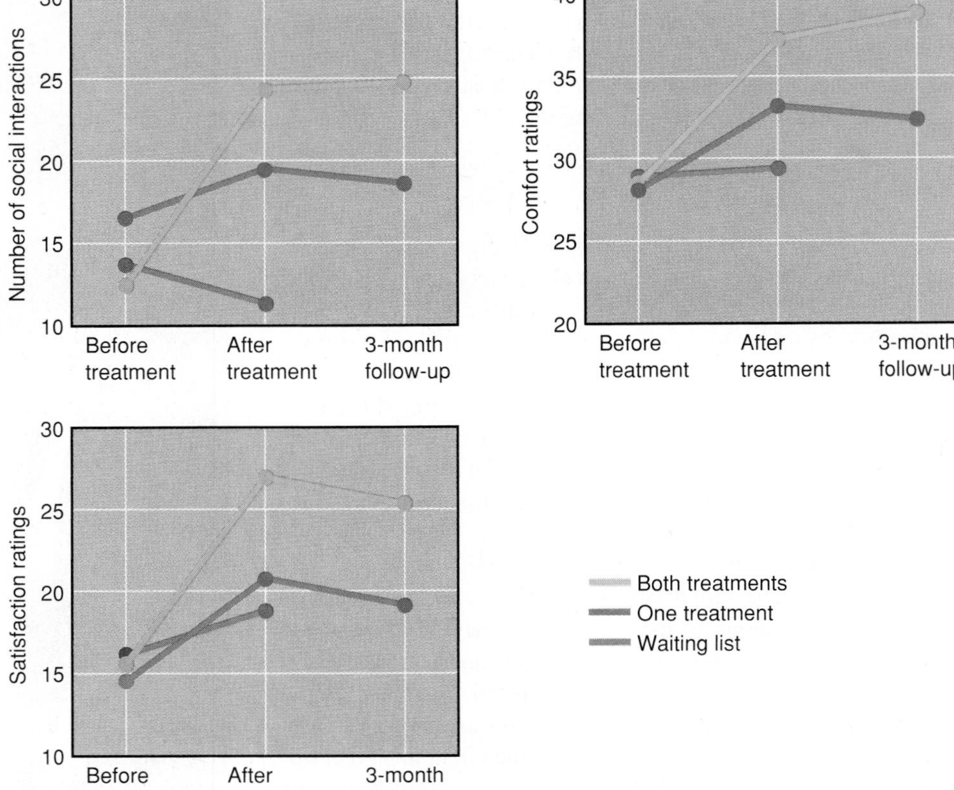

FIGURE 14.1

The degree of improvement in three groups of extremely shy individuals. One group received only systematic desensitization; another group received both systematic desensitization and social skills training; and a third group waited to begin treatment until the other two groups were completed.

Source: Data from R. F. Cappe and L. E. Alden, "A Comparison of Treatment Strategies for Clients Functionally Impaired by Extreme Shyness and Social Avoidance," *Journal of Consulting and Clinical Psychology,* 54:796–801. Copyright 1986 by the American Psychological Association.

shyness would be enough to make it go away. In doing so, the researchers could be more confident that it was their treatment that actually made the individuals get better.

The results of the study are shown in figure 14.1. Both treatments resulted in significant improvement in the frequency of social interactions in which the persons engaged, the comfort level (lack of anxiety) that they experienced during social interactions, and the degree of satisfaction that they derived from these social interactions. Furthermore, the group that received both systematic desensitization and social skills training improved the most on all three measures.

Assertiveness Training

Particular attention has been paid by behavior therapists to the widespread social skill problem of unassertiveness. Many people—both "normal" individuals and people with problems—have a difficult time expressing their true feelings, asking questions, disagreeing, and standing up for their rights. Sometimes these individuals continuously hold their feelings in and let others take advantage of them, partly because other people do not know what they want. In most cases, however, unassertive people keep their feelings inside until they become so angry that they pour them out in an aggressive tantrum.

assertiveness training

A method of behavior therapy that teaches individuals assertive rather than passive or aggressive ways of dealing with problematic situations.

Assertiveness training is used to develop assertive rather than aggressive ways of expressing feelings to others. This is usually done by role-playing as in other forms of social skills training. For example, the client might initially take the role of a friend who asks the therapist for a loan of 50 dollars even though he knows that the therapist is short on money and that he has owed the therapist 60 dollars for the past 3 months. The therapist would model an assertive way of handling the request ("I wish I could help you, but I don't have enough money to do it, and I really don't think it would be a good idea for me to lend you more money until you're able to pay me back what you already owe me"). Then they would reverse roles and let the client try to handle a similarly difficult situation. After considerable practice with the therapist, the client should possess enough skills and feel comfortable enough to handle real-life situations in an assertive way.

Aversive Conditioning

Aversive conditioning is a highly controversial behavior therapy technique that involves the use of unpleasant, negative (aversive) stimuli to eliminate abnormal habits such as alcoholism and deviant sexual practices. For example, alcoholics who wish to stop drinking sometimes undergo treatment in which alcoholic beverages are mixed with substances that cause nausea and vomiting. Thus, through classical conditioning, the taste of alcohol is associated with the aversive nauseous state. Similar aversive methods have been used with abnormal sexual practices. Men who engage in behaviors such as breaking into women's apartments, stealing underwear, and then masturbating with it are given painful electric shocks while they imagine engaging in these behaviors (Marks & Gelder, 1967).

aversive conditioning
(ah-ver´siv) A method of behavior therapy that involves the use of unpleasant negative stimuli to eliminate abnormal habits such as alcoholism and abnormal sexual practices.

Although behavior therapists are careful to use aversive conditioning only with clients who volunteer after a full discussion of what's involved, these painful methods understandably evoke skeptical, even negative reactions from the public. Aversive conditioning methods appear to give frightening power to behavior therapists to control behavior through pain. Fortunately, except for a few problems such as substance abuse and sexual molestation of children (Adams & Chiodo, 1984; Cannon, Baker, Gino, & Nathan, 1986), methods not involving aversive stimuli are often more effective (Kendall & Norton-Ford, 1982). As a result, aversive methods are not widely used today.

Excerpt from Behavior Therapy

In the following excerpt from a session of behavior therapy, the therapist is persuading the client to practice behaving in more effective ways in a role-playing session in the therapist's office so that the therapist can shape and reinforce the more effective behavior. The statements in brackets are comments of the therapist that were not stated during the therapy session.

Client: The basic problem is that I have the tendency to let people step all over me. I don't know why, but I just have difficulty in speaking my mind.

Therapist: [My immediate tendency here is to reflect and clarify what the client said, adding a behavioral twist. In paraphrasing what she has already said, I can cast it within a behavioral framework by introducing such terms as *situation, respond,* and *learn.*] So you find yourself in a number of different situations where you don't respond the way you would really like to. And if I understand correctly, you would like to learn how to behave differently.

Client: Yes. But you know, I have tried to handle certain situations differently, but I just don't seem to be able to do so.

Therapist: [Not a complete acceptance of my conceptualization, seemingly because she has tried to behave differently in the past and nothing has happened. What I should do, then, is somehow provide some explanation of why previous attempts may have failed, and use this to draw a contrast with a potentially more effective treatment strategy that we'll be using in our sessions.] It's almost as if there is a big gap between the way you react and the way you would like to react.

Client: It seems that way, and I don't know how to overcome it.

Therapist: Well, maybe you've tried to do too much too fast in the past, and consequently weren't very successful. Maybe a good way to look at the situation is to imagine yourself at the bottom of a staircase, wanting to get to the top. It's probably too much to ask to get there in one gigantic leap. Perhaps a better way to go about changing your reaction in these situations is to take it one step at a time.

Client: That would seem to make sense, but I'm not sure if I see how that could be done.

Therapist: Well, there are probably certain situations in which it would be less difficult for you to assert yourself such as telling your boss that he forgot to pay you for the past four weeks.

Client: (Laughing.) I guess in that situation, I would say something. Although I must admit, I would feel uneasy about it.

Therapist: But not as uneasy as if you went in and asked him for a raise.

Client: No. Certainly not.

Therapist: So, the first situation would be low on the staircase, whereas the second would be higher up. If you can learn to handle easier situations, then the more difficult ones would present less of a problem. And the only way you can really learn to change your reactions is through practice.

Client: In other words, I really have to go out and actually force myself to speak up more, but taking it a little bit at a time?

Therapist: [This seems like an appropriate time to introduce the function of behavior rehearsal. I won't say anything about the specific procedure yet, but instead will talk about it in general terms and maybe increase its appeal by explaining that any failures will not really "count." If the client goes along with the general description of the treatment strategy, she should be more likely to accept the details as I spell them out.] Exactly. And as a way of helping you carry it off in the real-life situation, I think it would be helpful if we reviewed some of these situations and your reactions to them beforehand. In a sense, going through a dry run. It's safer to run through some of these situations here, in that it really doesn't "count" if you don't handle them exactly as you would like to. Also, it can provide you an excellent opportunity to practice different ways of reacting to these situations, until you finally hit on one which you think would be best.

Client: That seems to make sense.

Therapist: In fact, we could arrange things so that you can actually rehearse exactly what you would say, and how you would say it.

Client: That sounds like a good idea.

Excerpt reprinted by permission of the authors from *Clinical Behavior Therapy* by M. R. Goldfried and G. C. Davison, copyright 1976 Holt, Rinehart & Winston, Inc.

Thinking Critically About Psychology

1. How could both social skills training and flooding be effective in treating problems, such as the fear of meeting new people? What do they have in common?

2. If you needed it, do you think you would prefer flooding or systematic desensitization to overcome a fear of heights?

Review

The approach to psychotherapy associated with the social learning theory of personality is known as behavior therapy. Abnormal behavior is viewed as learned behavior. It's simply behavior that results from inappropriate learning experiences. The role of the behavior therapist is to serve as a teacher who helps the client unlearn abnormal behavior and learn adaptive ways of behaving to take its place. In systematic desensitization, for example, the behavior therapist teaches clients no longer to fear phobic stimuli by first teaching them to relax deeply and then exposing them to graduated versions of the phobic stimulus in their imagination until the full stimulus does not disturb the state of relaxation. In this way, relaxation becomes the response to the formerly phobic stimulus instead of fear. Flooding provides an alternative to systematic desensitization in which the individual is "flooded" with a prolonged dose of the phobic stimulus until the fear response is extinguished. Other behavior therapy methods use principles of operant conditioning to teach specific skills and aversive conditioning methods to break abnormal habits in individuals who volunteer for treatment.

Check Your Learning

To be sure that you have learned the key points from the preceding section, cover the answers below and try to answer each question. If you give an incorrect answer to any question, return to the page given next to the correct answer to see why your answer was not correct.

1. A __________ plays the role of teacher, a person who helps the client unlearn abnormal ways of behaving and learn more adaptive ways to take their place.

a. psychoanalyst
b. behavior therapist
c. humanistic therapist
d. group therapist

2. __________ is a behavior therapy method in which the client is taught not to fear phobic stimuli by learning to relax deeply in the presence of successively more threatening stimuli.

a. Progressive relaxation training
b. Meditation
c. Reflection
d. Systematic desensitization

3. In __________________ people with social deficiencies are taught social skills through operant conditioning.

Correct Answers

1. b (p. 503), **2.** d (p. 503), **3.** social skills training (p. 505).

COGNITIVE THERAPY

Cognitive therapy is an important new approach to therapy that rests on the assumption that faulty cognitions—maladaptive beliefs, expectations, and ways of thinking—are the cause of abnormal behavior. Cognitive therapy originated in the cognitive emphasis of contemporary social learning theorists (Bandura, 1977) and contemporary psychoanalysts (Kelly, 1955). Because a great deal of carefully designed research has supported the effectiveness of cognitive therapy for many psychological disorders, it has quickly become one of the most widely used therapy approaches.

cognitive therapy
An approach to therapy that teaches individuals new cognitions—adaptive beliefs, expectations, and ways of thinking—to eliminate abnormal emotions and behavior.

Relationship Between Cognition and Behavior

Early in the development of behavior therapy, it was assumed that cognitions were relatively unimportant in the origins and treatment of abnormal behavior. For example, if a client came to a behavior therapist because she was unassertive, the conversations with the therapist might reveal that she believed (a cognition) that her friends would stop liking her if she expressed her true feelings to them. The behavior therapist would feel that it would be unnecessary to change this faulty belief directly, however. The behavior therapist would assume that if the client were taught assertive ways of expressing feelings, then she would see for herself that her friends still liked her and, therefore, change her faulty cognition herself. The cognitive therapy movement on the other hand, suggests that behavior therapists can be more effective if they directly teach both more adaptive behavior and cognition.

Moreover, cognitive therapists believe that problems do not always stem from inappropriate overt actions. For example, some socially anxious people behave in appropriate, even charming ways in social situations, but they still experience anxiety because they inaccurately think of themselves as dull, awkward, and unlikable. Trying to modify their already appropriate overt actions would be fruitless in such cases. Instead, it's necessary to modify their maladaptive cognitions.

Aaron T. Beck

Albert Ellis

Maladaptive Cognitions

Psychologist Albert Ellis (1962) and psychiatrist Aaron T. Beck (Beck, 1976; Beck, Rush, Shaw, & Emery, 1979) have described a number of patterns of cognition that they believe contribute greatly to abnormal behavior and emotions.

To better understand the cognitive therapy approach, we should look more closely at one of the most widely used versions, Aaron Beck's cognitive therapy program for depression. Beck believes that depression is caused primarily by the following erroneous patterns of thinking (do not be upset if you see some of your own ways of thinking here—we all think in these erroneous ways to some extent):

1. *Selective abstraction.* Let's say you ask the woman with whom you have had a committed relationship for three years if she has kissed another man since she started dating you. She answers, "Never, not once. I've never even flirted with another man. I'm not blind and I can still tell that a guy is cute, but I'm not romantically interested in anybody but you." Most persons would be reassured by the message of commitment in that statement, but would you go into a raging fit because she said she notices that some other men are attractive or not? If so, that would be selective abstraction—basing your thinking on a small detail taken out of context and given an incorrect meaning.
2. *Overgeneralization.* This is the process of reaching a general conclusion based on a few specific bits of evidence. The young scientist who gets a harsh rejection of the first article she submits to a scientific journal would be overgeneralizing if she concluded that no journal will ever publish her research.
3. *Arbitrary inference.* This is the logical error of reaching a conclusion based on little or no logical evidence—as the name says, the conclusion is arbitrary. For example, if you received an invitation to have lunch with your boss, would you conclude that the boss was going to gently break the news to you that you will be fired? Some people reason in this arbitrary way, concluding that everything means something bad.
4. *Magnification/minimization.* When the guy sitting next to you says that your ears have an interesting point at the top, do you magnify this statement and blow it out of proportion? ("No wonder everybody hates me—I have grotesque Mr. Spock ears!") Or, if you receive a heartfelt compliment from a friend, do you minimize it to nothing? ("Lynne just says nice things to me because she feels sorry for me.") These examples illustrate the process of magnification/minimization.
5. *Personalization.* Suppose you drove to the beach with your friends and it rained all weekend. Would you become gloomy and really mean it when you complained to your friends, "Nothing ever works out for me—every time I try to have fun it turns into a nightmare!" Some people would falsely conclude that it rained just because they were at the beach. Personalization is the erroneous pattern of reasoning in which external events are seen as being related to you when there is no logical reason for doing so.
6. *Absolutistic thinking.* The person who did not have good enough grades to get into medical school, but who has made an excellent living as a highly respected hospital administrator tells a former classmate at his 25-year high school reunion, "Ever since college, my life has been a total failure." Although it might be realistic to say that he failed in an important arena, he certainly has not been a total failure. His absolutistic thinking in all-or-nothing terms—either everything is absolutely wonderful, or everything is absolutely terrible—is erroneous and maladaptive.

It should come as no surprise that people who think in such maladaptive ways are miserable because of it. In cognitive therapy, the therapist uses a variety of techniques of persuasion to help the client change her or his faulty patterns of thinking.

Excerpt from Cognitive Therapy

In the following excerpt from a session of cognitive therapy, see how the therapist uses a series of probing questions to get the client to contradict her own absolutistic thinking and arbitrary inference.

Therapist: Why do you want to end your life?

Patient: Without Raymond, I am nothing . . . I can't be happy without Raymond. . . . But I can't save our marriage.

T: What has your marriage been like?

P: It has been miserable from the very beginning . . . Raymond has always been unfaithful . . . I have hardly seen him in the past five years.

T: You say that you can't be happy without Raymond. . . . Have you found yourself happy when you are with Raymond?

P: No, we fight all the time and I feel worse.

T: Then why do you feel that Raymond is essential for your living?

P: I guess it's because without Raymond I am nothing.

T: Would you please repeat that?

P: Without Raymond I am nothing.

T: What do you think of that idea?

P: . . . Well, now that I think about it, I guess it's not completely true.

T: You said you are "nothing" without Raymond. Before you met Raymond, did you feel you were "nothing"?

P: No, I felt I was somebody.

T: Are you saying then that it's possible to be something without Raymond?

P: I guess that's true. I *can* be something without Raymond.

T: If you were somebody before you knew Raymond, why do you need him to be somebody now?

P: (puzzled) Hmmm . . .

T: You seemed to imply that you couldn't go on living without Raymond.

P: Well, I just don't think that I can find anybody else like him.

T: Did you have male friends before you knew Raymond?

P: I was pretty popular then.

T: If I understand you correctly then, you were able to fall in love before with other men and other men have fallen in love with you.

P: Uh huh.

T: Why do you think you will be unpopular without Raymond now?

P: Because I will not be able to attract any other man.

T: Have any men shown an interest in you since you have been married?

P: A lot of men have made passes at me but I ignore them.

T: If you were free of the marriage, do you think that men might be interested in you—knowing that you were available?

P: I guess that maybe they would be.

T: Is it possible that you might find a man who would be more constant than Raymond?

P: I don't know, . . . I guess it's possible.

T: Do you think there are other men as good as Raymond around?

P: I guess there are men who are better than Raymond because Raymond doesn't love me.

From A. T. Beck, et al., *Cognitive Theory of Depression*. Copyright 1979 The Guilford Press, New York, NY. Reprinted by permission of the authors.

Cognitive therapy has been shown to be quite effective with a variety of anxiety disorders (Borkovec & Costello, 1993; Barlow, 1996; Bruce, Spiegel, Gregg, & Nuzzarello, 1995; Chambless & Gillis, 1993; Clum, Clum, & Surls, 1993), the eating disorder bulimia (Garner et al., 1993; Thackwray, Smith, Bodfish, & Meyers, 1993), and major depression (Clarkin, Pilkonis, & Magruder, 1996; Simons, Gordon, Thase, & Monroe, 1995). Indeed in many studies, cognitive therapy has been found to be more effective than more traditional psychodynamic or humanistic therapies. Comparisons with psychiatric medication have yielded slightly more complicated findings. In the case of depression, there is evidence that cognitive therapy is equally effective as psychiatric antidepressant medications in the treatment of people experiencing depressive episodes (Hollon, Shelton, & Davis, 1993). But cognitive therapy has been shown to be more than twice as effective as medication in preventing *future* episodes of depression (Evans et al., 1992; Hollon et al., 1993). For the eating disorder bulimia, cognitive therapy combined with medication appears to be superior to either single treatment alone (Agras et al., 1992).

Thinking Critically About Psychology

1. We have seen that cognitive therapy is effective in treating several kinds of disorders. Can you think of other human ailments for which cognitive therapy might be effective?

2. Reexamine each of Aaron Beck's list of erroneous thinking patterns associated with depression. Can you think of examples for each based on your own experience?

Review

Cognitive therapy is a therapeutic approach that has grown out of both contemporary psychoanalytic theories of personality and social learning theory; but it has become subsumed by, and has contributed to the expansion of, behavior therapy. While behavior therapists originally believed that the irrational beliefs and ways of thinking (cognitions) that generally accompany abnormal behavior and emotions would simply change when the behavior and emotions changed, cognitive therapists have emphasized the necessity of sometimes changing cognitions first. They believe that behavior and emotional problems will improve when maladaptive cognitions are changed. Consequently, cognitive therapists conduct psychotherapy in an attempt to change cognitions by demonstrating their irrationality to clients.

Check Your Learning

To be sure that you have learned the key points from the preceding section, cover the answers below and try to answer each question. If you give an incorrect answer to any question, return to the page given next to the correct answer to see why your answer was not correct.

1. __________ is an important approach to therapy that rests on the assumption that faulty cognitions—maladaptive beliefs, expectations, and ways of thinking—are the cause of abnormal behavior.

a. Cognitive therapy
b. Psychoanalysis
c. Anticipation therapy
d. Reflection

2. __________ refers to the cognitive distortion of basing your thinking on a small detail taken out of context and given an incorrect meaning.

a. Selective abstraction
b. Overgeneralization
c. Personalization
d. Absolutistic thinking

3. If a person loses her job because the company laid off a thousand workers and then gets depressed because "I knew they thought I was awful at my job," she would be engaging in

a. selective abstraction.
b. overgeneralization.
c. personalization.
d. absolutistic thinking.

Check Your Learning—continued

4. In the excerpt from cognitive therapy in the preceding section, the suicidal client says, "Without Raymond, I am nothing. . . ." This person is engaging in

   a. selective abstraction.
   b. overgeneralization.
   c. personalization.
   d. absolutistic thinking.

Correct Answers

1. a (p. 509), 2. a (p. 510), 3. c (p. 510), 4. d (p. 511).

OTHER APPROACHES AND MODELS OF THERAPY

We now look at an approach to psychotherapy that focuses on the unique difficulties faced by women in society and their needs in psychotherapy. Therapy is not always conducted on an individual basis, however. Some methods of therapy are carried out with groups or entire families, and some programs are designed to prevent rather than treat problems. Moreover, some treatments for psychological problems use medical rather than psychological methods. In this section, we will survey these alternative approaches to the solution of human problems.

Feminist Psychotherapy

feminist psychotherapy
An approach to psychotherapy that encourages women to confront issues created by living in a sexist society as part of their psychotherapy.

Over the past 25 years, an approach to understanding the psychological problems of women and providing treatment for them has evolved from the philosophical foundation of feminism. Some see **feminist psychotherapy** as a radical approach to therapy; others see the principles that underlie the feminist approach to psychotherapy as eminently reasonable ideas that should have always been a part of psychotherapy for women. You may see these ideas as radical if you believe that women are placed on a pedestal in society and given an easier, more privileged place in life than men. On the other hand, you will find feminist psychotherapy to be reasonable and long overdue if you believe that women are treated as second-class citizens in many ways (personally, politically, and economically), and that even placing them on the pedestal of femininity contributes to their second-class citizenship by treating them more like Barbie dolls than people.

Over the past 25 years, feminist psychotherapy has evolved as an approach to understanding and treating the psychological problems of women.

The fundamental concepts of feminist psychotherapy are the following (based on Worrell, 1980):

1. Feminist psychotherapy advocates an equal relationship between the client and therapist. The therapist avoids treating the client as someone who must be told what is best for her and encourages the client to trust her own ability to make good decisions. This therapy is designed to counteract the sexist view of women as needing guidance from their fathers and husbands. Sometimes this is aided by conducting therapy with groups of similar women to afford them the opportunity to make constructive suggestions to one another and minimize the role of the therapist.
2. Women clients are encouraged to see the ways in which society has limited their development and has pushed them into dependent roles. To counter these forces, women are encouraged to view themselves as powerful

human beings who can effectively use their power in the personal, economic, and political spheres of life.

3. Another goal of feminist psychotherapy is to encourage women to become aware of the anger that they feel over living as second-class citizens in a sexist society and to find constructive ways of expressing that anger.
4. Feminist psychotherapy helps women define themselves in ways that are independent of their roles as wife, mother, and daughter. It also seeks to assist women in dealing with the natural anxiety that they may experience about leaving or redefining these expected traditional roles.
5. Women are encouraged to consider their own needs to be as valid and as worthy of taking care of as those of others. The goal is to help women increase their sense of worth and self-esteem.
6. Finally, women are encouraged to develop skills that are not traditionally encouraged in women. These include assertiveness, career skills, and the skills to deal effectively with traditional persons who oppose such changes.

It is important to understand that feminist psychotherapy isn't just for women! Its guiding principles of equality, independence, and assertiveness are healthy for everyone. As a result, it is increasingly integrated into all forms of psychotherapy rather than being considered as a separate approach to therapy.

Group Therapy

group therapy
Psychotherapy conducted in groups, typically of four to eight clients at a time.

Psychotherapy is usually conducted on a one-to-one basis, but sometimes it's carried out with groups of clients in **group therapy.** One or two therapists typically work with four to eight clients at a time. Group therapy is believed to offer therapeutic experiences that cannot be obtained in individual therapy (Yalom, 1975). Some of these advantages are (a) encouragement from other group members, (b) learning that a person is not alone in his or her problems, (c) learning from the advice offered by others, and (d) learning new ways to interact with others. In addition, providing therapy in a group can sometimes make more efficient use of the therapist's time.

The format of group therapy differs widely depending on the approach taken by the therapist (psychoanalytic, humanistic, or behavioral), but all provide an opportunity for the client to interact with other clients and to learn from these interactions with the help of the therapist. Each approach to psychotherapy has adapted its own methods for use in groups. Psychoanalysts play the role of interpreter in group therapy just as they do in individual therapy. They avoid becoming part of the interactions of the group members except to offer interpretations of what these interactions reveal. Humanists use group interactions to help clients develop more accurate self-perceptions through the actions and reactions of other group members toward them. Behavior therapists use groups to facilitate the teaching of adaptive behavior. For example, groups of individuals with problems in social interactions are given instructions in how to relate more effectively, are allowed to practice interacting with one another, and then are given feedback and reinforcement from the therapist and other group members.

An advantage of group therapy is the opportunity for clients to learn from interacting with other members of the group.

Psychotherapists from all of these orientations generally believe that interaction with other group members offers special therapeutic advantages to some clients. Individuals with complex problems that require the full attention of the therapist, or who do not wish to discuss their personal problems in front of others, however, will benefit more from individual psychotherapy.

Family Therapy

Another important variation of psychotherapy in which the therapist works with groups of individuals is **family therapy.** In this case, the group is the family composed of parents, children, and any other family members living in the home. Although family therapy is conducted by therapists who take psychoanalytic, humanistic, and behavioral approaches, the approach that we most often associate with family therapy is the systems approach of Jay Haley (1976) and Salvador Minuchin (1974).

family therapy
An approach to psychotherapy that emphasizes an understanding of the roles of each of the members of the family system, usually conducted with all members of the family present.

The family systems view takes the position that it's not possible to understand adequately the psychological problems of an individual without knowing the role of that individual in the family system. This is thought to be true for two reasons. First, the problem of the individual is often caused by problems within the family. For example, a depressed mother or aggressive child may be reacting to the unhappy, conflict-laden relationship of the mother and father. Although the mother or child may be brought to the clinic identified as "the problem," and no mention is initially made of the marital problems, neither the depression nor the aggression can be helped until the marriage problems are resolved.

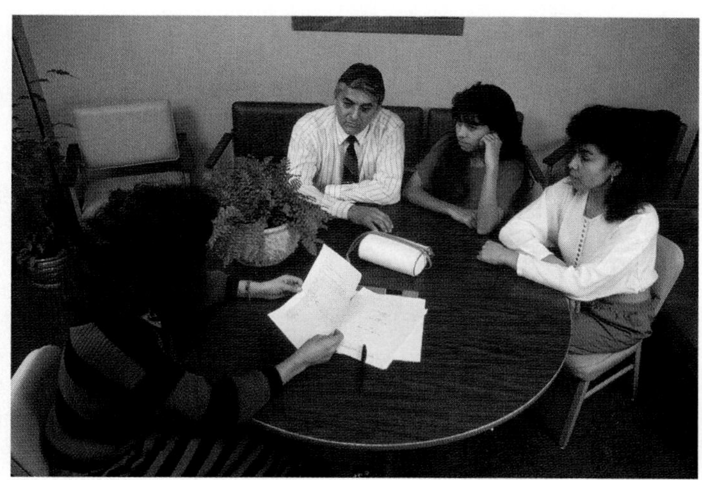

Family therapy emphasizes an understanding of the roles of each of the members of the family system.

The second reason that Haley and Minuchin give for needing to understand the operation of the entire family system in order to understand the problems of an individual family member is that the individual's problems may serve a *function* in the family system. For example, the teenage girl who refuses to eat until she has reached a dangerously low weight may be doing so (consciously or unconsciously) to focus concern on her and keep her parents from divorcing. Similarly, parents who blame all of the family's problems on the supposedly wild behavior of their son may be using him as a scapegoat to shift attention away from the fact that they are both unemployed alcoholics. Without working with all of the members of the family system, these factors in the origins of the problems of the individual would have been difficult, if not impossible, to uncover.

The family therapist attempts to solve the problems of all of the family members by improving the functioning of the family system as a whole. The therapist attempts to reach this goal in four primary ways. The family therapist works (a) to give the family members insights into the workings of family systems in general and to correct any dysfunctions in their family, (b) to increase the amount of warmth and intimacy among family members, (c) to improve communication among family members, and (d) to help family members establish a reasonable set of rules for the regulation of the family. In this way, it's hoped that the family will become a system that provides each member with an accurate view of self, a positive opinion of self, and a sense of belonging.

Medical Therapies

In addition to psychotherapy, medical therapies are commonly used in the treatment of abnormal behavior. **Medical therapies** are generally designed to correct a physical condition that is believed to be the cause of the psychological disorder. There are three general types of medical therapy: drug therapy in which medication is used, electroconvulsive therapy in which seizures are electrically induced in the brain, and psychosurgery in which brain tissue is surgically destroyed.

medical therapies
Those therapies—including drug therapy, electroconvulsive therapy, and psychosurgery—generally designed to correct a physical condition that is believed to be the cause of a psychological disorder.

Drug Therapy

By far, the most widely used medical treatment is **drug therapy** in which medications are used to treat abnormal behavior. The idea that chemicals can be used to treat abnormal behavior dates back at least to the special diets used by Pythagoras around 490 B.C. But the widespread use of effective psychiatric drugs has come about only in the last 35 years. The era of modern drug therapy began in 1954 with the introduction of the phenothiazine drugs, such as Thorazine for the treatment of schizophrenia. Thorazine gave physicians a tool that

drug therapy
A medical therapy that uses medications to treat abnormal behavior.

TABLE 14.1 The Most Commonly Used Psychiatric Drugs

Physicians have a variety of medications at their disposal for use in the treatment of temporary stress reactions and psychological disorders. Some examples of these medications and their benefits are given here. Note that some of these medications have several uses and may be prescribed by a physician for reasons other than psychological problems.

Trade Name	Generic Name	For Relief of
Tofranil	imipramine	Depression
Elavil	amitriptyline	Depression
Prozac	fluoxetine	Depression
Xanax	alprazolam	Anxiety
Valium	diazepam	Anxiety
Mellaril	thioridazine	Psychotic symptoms
Stelazine	trifluoperazine	Psychotic symptoms
Haldol	haloperidol	Psychotic symptoms
Navane	thiothixene	Psychotic symptoms
Eskalith	lithium	Bipolar affective disorder

for the first time in history substantially improved the lives of schizophrenic persons. So effective is this drug that it's given partial credit for reversing the growth in the number of patients in mental institutions during the 1960s. Other drugs were also introduced during the 1960s to help in the treatment of depression (antidepressants) and anxiety (tranquilizers).

Today the use of these drugs is widespread. Some examples of the most commonly used psychiatric drugs are given in table 14.1. In spite of the effectiveness and general acceptance of drugs, they are not without shortcomings. Prolonged use of antipsychotic medications, for example, can result in impairment of walking and other serious side effects. Other drugs can be highly addictive.

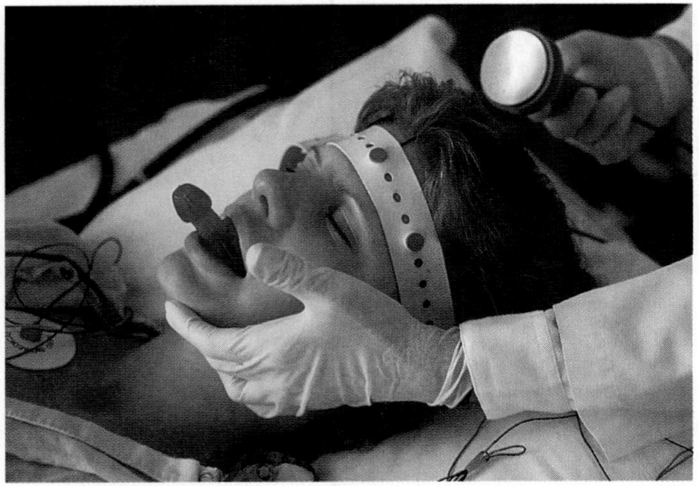

Although electroconvulsive therapy, which was introduced in the 1930s, continues to be used with some severely depressed individuals, it's not endorsed universally by the mental health profession.

Electroconvulsive Therapy

The idea that people can be "shocked" out of their psychological problems has been around in one form or another for nearly 2,400 years. Hippocrates recommended the use of the herb hellebore to induce seizures that supposedly restored balance to the body's four humors. Several different kinds of "shock" treatment were popular in mental institutions during the 1800s: patients were thrown in tubs full of eels, spun in giant centrifuges, and nearly drowned by dropping them into lakes through trapdoors in bridges known as "surprise baths" (Altschule, 1965).

Other forms of shock therapy have also been used, particularly ones in which seizures are intentionally induced. In the 1930s it was noticed that people with epilepsy rarely developed schizophrenia. Several psychiatrists experimented with chemicals that caused seizures to see if they would cure schizophrenia, but camphor, insulin, and other chemicals were found to be of little use with schizophrenics. Italian physicians first used the method of passing an electric current through two metal plates held to the sides of the head to induce convulsive brain seizures. This method, known as **electroconvulsive therapy (ECT),** continues in widespread use today. Although ineffective with most disorders, it's believed by most psychiatrists to be useful with severely depressed individuals. ECT is believed to alter the same neurotransmitters as those affected by antidepressants, but to this day no one knows for sure how ECT works.

electroconvulsive therapy (ECT) (e-lek´´tro-con-vul´siv) A medical therapy that uses electrical current to induce controlled convulsive seizures that alleviate some types of mental disorders.

Although ECT has been used successfully for 50 years, the procedure is surrounded by considerable controversy. In large part, this controversy is a holdover from the primitive methods that were used when the procedure was first introduced. The shocks were given without anesthesia and the seizures were so violent that broken bones were not uncommon. Today, the use of anesthesia and muscle relaxants makes ECT a far less unpleasant experience, but temporary or permanent memory loss and confusion are still relatively common side effects (Campbell, 1961). The use of ECT is also controversial because even after extended use, little adequate research has been conducted to evaluate its effectiveness. The few well-designed studies that have been carried out, however, suggest that it's at least somewhat effective in treating depression (Barton, 1977).

Psychosurgery

Undoubtedly the most controversial medical treatment for abnormal behavior is **psychosurgery,** a therapy in which the brain is operated on to try to alleviate the behavior. As with the other medical therapies, there is a historical precedent for the idea that people with psychological disorders can be helped by operating on their brains. In fact, the precedent for psychosurgery is perhaps the oldest of all. Archaeologists have found Stone Age skulls in which holes called *trephines* had been "surgically" cut with crude stone knives. These trephining operations—signs of healing indicate that some of these poor souls actually survived the procedure—were apparently performed in an attempt to treat abnormal behavior.

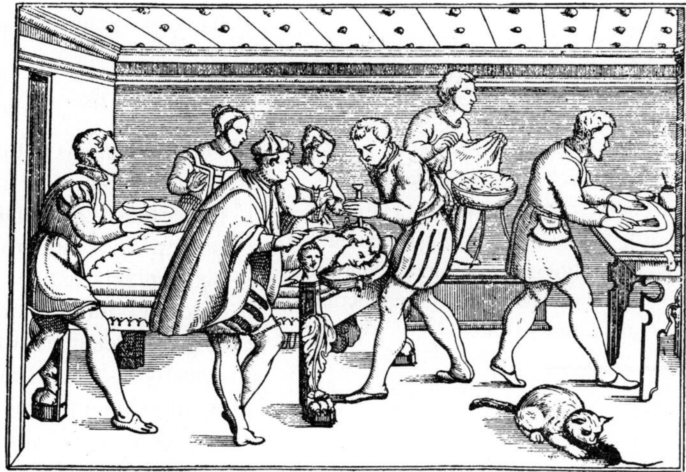

Trephining operations were apparently performed in the Middle Ages to treat abnormal behavior.

Surgical operations on the brain to treat psychological disorders came into vogue in the 1940s and 1950s. In the most common version, the prefrontal lobotomy, a double-edged, butter knife–shaped instrument is inserted through holes drilled in the temple region of the skull. Neural fibers are cut that connect the frontal region of the cerebral cortex with the hypothalamus. The theory is that the operation will prevent disturbing thoughts and perceptions from reaching the hypothalamus and related brain structures where they would be translated into emotional outbursts. Lobotomies are not successful in most cases, however, and loss of intellectual functioning and seizures are common side effects (Barahal, 1958). Because of their ineffectiveness and because of the success of drug therapies with schizophrenics, the use of lobotomies and other forms of psychosurgery has declined considerably (Swayze, 1995). However, as late as 1973 some 500 prefrontal lobotomies were being performed in the United States each year (Holden, 1973).

psychosurgery
(sī´´kō-ser´jer-ē) A medical therapy that involves operating on the brain in an attempt to alleviate some types of mental disorders.

More recently, the development of more precise methods of operating on the brain with needle-thin electrical instruments has revived interest in psychosurgery (Martuza, Chiocca, Jenike, Giriunas, & Ballantine, 1990). These instruments are used to operate directly on the parts of the brain associated with emotional control. For example, a type of precise psychosurgery called **cingulotomy** is sometimes performed on persons with severe obsessive-compulsive disorder who have not responded to repeated attempts to treat the disorder with behavior therapy and medication. In cingulotomy, the part of the limbic system called the *cingulate cortex* (chapter 2, p. 56) is partially destroyed by electrical probes. A team of researchers at Harvard Medical School (Baer et al., 1995) have evaluated 18 individuals with obsessive-compulsive disorder two years after their cingulotomies to see whether they had been helpful. They found significant improvement in about one-fourth of the patients, but most cases did not benefit from the surgery. Such operations are performed infrequently and are used only as a last resort. Even in such cases, psychosurgery is still a hotly debated procedure.

cingulotomy
A type of psychosurgery for severe and otherwise untreatable obsessive-compulsive disorder that involves surgical destruction of part of the cingulate cortex.

Community Psychology and Prevention

A movement within psychology that has achieved considerable prominence in the 1970s and 1980s is the community psychology movement. Community psychologists resemble clinical psychologists and psychiatrists in that their goal is to reduce human suffering through the application of principles of psychology. But community psychologists work with large groups of people rather than individual clients, and they seek to prevent psychological problems rather than solve existing ones. Community psychology seeks to identify the aspects of a community contributing to psychological disorders and eradicate them before they harm people.

For example, many community psychologists believe racial prejudice creates severe stress that contributes to psychological problems in members of minority groups. They attempt, therefore, to create programs that will reduce racial prejudice. Notable, and somewhat successful, projects to reduce racial prejudice have been conducted in the U.S. Armed Forces and in some school systems. Similar programs are being conducted in industries to reduce sexual prejudice that makes work adjustment stressful for women in jobs that were traditionally held by men. Other programs identify children with early signs of psychological problems and provide preventive treatment in the schools. Courses for parents are offered in many areas designed to reduce the incidence of inappropriate child rearing that contributes to juvenile delinquency. And the nationwide Head Start programs provide help to disadvantaged preschool children to prevent later school adjustment problems. As with other community-based programs, these preventive efforts are sadly underfunded in most areas.

Thinking Critically About Psychology

1. Which type of psychotherapy makes the most sense to you? Why?

2. If you were seeking treatment for a psychological problem, would you be more likely to try group therapy or individual psychotherapy? Why?

Review

One-to-one psychotherapy is not the only approach taken to solve psychological problems. For one thing, each method of psychotherapy is sometimes practiced with groups of clients rather than individual clients. Group therapy is practiced primarily because the presence of other people with problems offers advantages to some clients. Other clients provide encouragement, give advice, show the client that he or she is not alone in having problems, and provide opportunities for learning new ways of interacting with others. Group therapy also often makes efficient use of the therapist's time. Individuals with complex problems, or who have sensitive problems that they do not want to discuss in front of others, may be better served by individual psychotherapy, however. In recent years, group therapy has become popular among normal individuals as a form of personal growth therapy. Entire families are also often worked with as a group by therapists who believe that the faulty operation of some family systems can cause psychological problems. Family therapy seeks to reestablish proper functioning in these families.

In addition to psychological treatments for psychological problems, physicians often use biological methods. The most widely used medical treatments are drugs. Drugs introduced since the 1950s have been partially responsible for the progress in treating psychological problems, which has resulted in a decrease in the number of institutionalized mental patients in the United States. Electroconvulsive therapy—in which an electric current produces controlled brain seizures—is sometimes used in the treatment of severe depression. The controversial method of psychosurgery in which parts of the brain are destroyed to prevent excessive emotional reactions is no longer widely used in the United States; but newer, more precise methods are still used in some cases as a last resort.

Check Your Learning

To be sure that you have learned the key points from the preceding section, cover the answers below and try to answer each question. If you give an incorrect answer to any question, return to the page given next to the correct answer to see why your answer was not correct.

1. ________________, or psychotherapy conducted in groups, is believed to offer therapeutic experiences that cannot be obtained in individual therapy, such as learning from the advice offered by others.

2. ________________ emphasizes an understanding of the roles of each of the members of a family system with the hope that the family will become a system that provides each member with an accurate view of self, a positive opinion of self, and a sense of belonging.

3. ________________, such as drug treatment or psychosurgery, is generally designed to correct a physical condition that is believed to be the cause of the psychological disorder.

Correct Answers

1. Group therapy (p. 514), **2.** Family therapy (p. 515), **3.** Medical therapy (p. 515).

APPLICATION OF PSYCHOLOGY

WHAT TO DO IF YOU THINK YOU NEED HELP

All of us face difficult and painful times in our lives. Sometimes we choose to struggle through these stressful periods on our own; sometimes we ask for the support and advice of friends; and at times, we may seek professional help. If you, or someone close to you, are among the many millions of Americans who will use professional mental health services this year, consider these thoughts.

First, you must face the issue of *stigma*—the implication that seeking professional help means that you are not a normal or even fully competent person. If you believe that myth, then it will be very difficult indeed for you to lift the telephone and make the first appointment. You should know, however, that mental health professionals do *not* believe there is something fundamentally wrong with people who ask for help. They know that a large portion of their clients are completely normal people who are simply asking for assistance in the tricky business of avoiding—or crawling out of—life's pitfalls. So do not be afraid to ask for help if you think you need it.

There are many ways to find help with psychological problems if you feel that you need it.

Once you have decided to seek help, where do you look for it? As we first mentioned in chapter 1, there are many different mental health professions that operate through a number of different kinds of mental health facilities. The trick is in deciding which kind of professional or facility would be best for you. For college students, this decision is often an easy one: Most colleges and universities have a student counseling or mental health center that provides high-quality services at little or no cost. The professionals who work in these centers are experienced in meeting the mental health needs of students.

In addition, most psychology departments in larger universities operate their own psychology clinics that provide services both to students and to people in the general community. And most cities also have a community mental health center that provides a wide range of services. Both university psychology clinics and community mental health centers often charge fees that are based on your ability to pay. These centers often operate 24 hours a day, providing suicide prevention telephone lines that are listed under such titles as "help line" or "crisis line" or that can be reached through the telephone operator.

Services are also provided by professionals in private practice. Like a physician or attorney, these individuals provide services for a fee. Psychiatrists, psychologists, and other professionals in private practice are listed in the telephone book under titles such as "Physicians—Psychiatrists" and "Psychologists." You might want to turn back to chapter 1, page 20 to familiarize yourself with the differences between these and other mental health professions. In most states, only licensed individuals can list their names in the telephone directory as a psychiatrist, psychologist, psychotherapist, counselor, or marriage counselor. In some states, however, some of these titles (except for psychologist and psychiatrist) are not regulated by law. This means that anyone—qualified or not—can set up a private practice in many states under one of these titles. You should be careful, therefore, to ask for a referral to one of these professionals from a qualified physician or psychologist if you choose their services.

Referrals are the best guide to choosing the services of a licensed psychologist or psychiatrist. Like other professions, some are better than others—or are better in dealing with certain kinds of cases—and the advice of someone who knows both you and the professionals in the community could be very helpful. If you do not have access to someone to refer you, it would be wise to ask the psychologist or psychiatrist about "board certification." It's legal in most states for a physician to practice psychiatry without ever having had specific training in that field, but a board-certified psychiatrist has met the criteria of a national board for competence in psychiatry. In psychology, board certification means something different. Only a small proportion of experienced psychologists take and pass a special examination of their skills. They are awarded a diploma by the American Board of Professional Psychology, which is designated in their listing in the telephone directory as "Diplomate in Clinical (or Counseling) Psychology, ABPP." Board-certified psychiatrists and psychologists are not necessarily more competent than those who are not, but it's another way of reducing the uncertainty in choosing a therapist.

Which Is the Most Effective Form of Psychotherapy?

We have seen that there are many different approaches to psychotherapy—which one is the most effective? This seems like a simple question that psychologists should be able to answer, but it is actually quite complicated. Hundreds of experiments have been conducted, but there is still no conclusive answer available. Psychologists Mary Smith and Gene Glass (1977) provided tentative answers by using an interesting statistical technique that uses data from many different studies. They identified 375 studies in which improvement in patients receiving some form of psychotherapy was compared with a group of patients with similar problems who were not given treatment until after the study was completed. The results of these studies ordinarily could not be directly compared because researchers used patients with different kinds of problems and they evaluated improvement using different criteria. Some studies used therapist's ratings of improvement, some used scores on personality tests, some used direct observations of specific aspects of the patient's abnormal behavior, and so on. Regardless of what criteria was used, however, Smith and Glass calculated a measure of the *magnitude of treatment effect* by comparing the amount of improvement in the treated patients with that of the untreated ones.

Although the specific statistics involved are complicated, an effect size of .00 would indicate that treated patients improved no more than untreated patients, whereas an effect size of 1.00 would indicate that treated patients improved more than approximately 85 percent of the untreated ones.

Table 14.2 shows the average magnitude of effect for the types of psychotherapy described in this chapter, and for *eclectic* psychotherapy in which the therapist blends methods from two or more kinds of therapy.

Note that all of the forms of psychotherapy were effective on the average: All produced average effect sizes that were greater than .00. But note also that there were differences among the kinds of therapy. The behavioral methods, cognitive methods, client-centered therapy, and the revised psychoanalytic methods based on the approach of Alfred Adler were more effective than orthodox psychoanalysis, Gestalt therapy, and eclectic psychotherapy. Strictly speaking, this cannot be taken to mean that one form of psychotherapy is superior to another, since the different psychotherapies did not use the same criteria for improvement or the same kinds of patients. Furthermore, it may be that one form of psychotherapy works best for one kind of problem and another works best for other problems. Still, it's encouraging to note that all of the psychotherapies were at least slightly more effective than no treatment and that the ones that had the largest effects also are the ones that used the most rigorous criteria for improvement, a conclusion that has often been confirmed by others (Borkovec & Mathews, 1988; Clum & Bowers, 1990).

TABLE 14.2 Average Magnitude of Treatment Effects for Different Methods of Psychotherapy

Methods of Psychotherapy	Average Effect Size
Psychoanalytic	
Orthodox psychoanalysis	.50
Psychoanalytic (Adlerian)	.71
Behavior Therapy	
Systematic desensitization	.91
Operant skills training	.76
Cognitive	.77
Humanistic	
Client-centered	.63
Eclectic Psychotherapy	.48

Source: Data from M. L. Smith and G. V. Glass, "Meta-Analysis of Psychotherapy Outcome Studies," *American Psychologist,* 32:752–760. Copyright 1977 by the American Psychological Association.

As discussed in the text, research on the effectiveness of psychotherapy has focused in more recent years on identifying the most effective form of therapy for specific disorders. With this narrower focus, greater success has been achieved. For example, George Clum, Gretchen Clum, and Rebecca Surls (1993) of Virginia Polytechnic Institute and State University calculated effect sizes for different forms of medical and psychological therapy for panic disorder. As can be seen in table 14.3, the effect size for tranquilizers was quite small, but most other treatments had quite large effect sizes.

Ethnic and Gender Issues in Seeking a Psychotherapist

Does your ethnicity matter in seeking psychological help? Sadly, it does. The United States has one of the most advanced mental health systems in the world, but it cannot be said to fully meet the needs of all of our citizens. As a professional who deals with persons in need of psychological help, I often see the frustration and tragedy of persons who cannot receive assistance due to lack of money or other barriers. Recently, much has been written about inequities in the receipt of psychological services in the United States. For example, a large-scale survey conducted in Los Angeles showed that, among persons with mental disorders, only *half* as many Hispanics with psychological disorders were receiving outpatient mental health treatment as non-Hispanic whites (Hough et al., 1987). In contrast, other researchers have raised concern about the fact that African Americans are more likely than whites to be committed to psychiatric hospitals, often involuntarily, when they have a mental disorder (Lindsey & Paul, 1989; Snowden & Cheung, 1990). Thus, much remains to be done to ensure that we have not only an effective mental health system, but a fair one as well.

How about gender? Are men and women provided psychological services in the same way? Nancy Felipe Russo (1990) has pointed out probable inequities in mental health services provided to women. Although national surveys have shown that women are more likely than men to exhibit the most common forms of mental disorder (anxiety and depressive disorders), fewer women receive mental health services than men. It appears that our society is more willing to provide services for the disorders that are more common in males (substance abuse, antisocial personality disorder, and schizophrenia) than the difficulties that are more likely for women. One factor that

TABLE 14.3 Comparison of Average Magnitude of Treatment Effects for Various Alternative Treatments of Panic Disorder

Treatment Method	Average Effect Size
Antidepressants	.82
Tranquilizers	.29
Behavior Therapy	1.36
Cognitive Therapy	1.41

a person should always consider in selecting a therapist is her or his attitudes toward your ethnicity, gender, and sexual orientation.

For additional information on selecting a therapist, and for information concerning organizations such as Alcoholics Anonymous that provide help for individuals with specific kinds of problems, you may wish to contact one of the following organizations:

Mental Health Association
1800 North Kent Street
Arlington, VA 22209

American Psychological Association
750 First Street, N.E.
Washington, DC 20002-4242

American Psychiatric Association
1700 Eighteenth Street, N.W.
Washington, DC 20009

Suicide Prevention Center
1041 South Menlo Avenue
Los Angeles, CA 90006

Summary

Chapter 14 outlines the major forms of therapy through which individuals are helped with psychological problems.

I. Psychotherapy is the use of methods such as talking, demonstrating, and reinforcing that are based on a theory of psychological disorders to solve human problems.
  - **A.** Freud is the founder of the form of psychotherapy known as psychoanalysis, which helps the patient bring unconscious conflict into consciousness. The principal techniques of psychoanalysis are:
    1. Free association is used to relax the censorship of the ego.
    2. Dream interpretation allows the therapist to obtain another "window" on the unconscious.
    3. Resistance is any form of opposition of the patient to the process of psychoanalysis.
    4. Transference occurs when there is a relatively intense relationship between patient and therapist during therapy; this can be interpreted to give insights to the patient.
  - **B.** Catharsis is the release of some of the emotion that is pent up with unconscious conflicts in psychoanalysis.

II. Humanistic psychotherapies strive to help the person achieve full self-awareness so that the person's inner-directed tendency to growth can be realized. Client-centered psychotherapy and Gestalt therapy are two major types of humanistic psychotherapy.
  - **A.** Client-centered psychotherapy helps the client explore unsymbolized feelings and information by providing a safe emotional climate.
  - **B.** Gestalt therapy helps the individual achieve greater self-awareness by using directive techniques, such as pointing out inconsistencies in behavior.

III. Behavior therapists use a form of psychotherapy in which they help the client unlearn abnormal behavior and learn adaptive ways of thinking, feeling, and acting.
  - **A.** Systematic desensitization and flooding are widely used methods of fear reduction.
  - **B.** Social skills training and developmental skills training are examples of teaching new adaptive skills using methods derived from operant conditioning.
  - **C.** Aversive conditioning uses unpleasant negative stimuli to eliminate abnormal habits.
  - **D.** Cognitive therapy rests on the assumption that faulty cognitions cause abnormal emotions and actions.

IV. Some methods of therapy are carried out with groups or entire families, and some are designed to enhance personal growth rather than treat problems.
  - **A.** Group therapy makes efficient use of therapists' time, and the presence of other people with problems offers advantages to some clients.
  - **B.** Family therapy seeks to reestablish proper functioning within families.
  - **C.** Medical therapies are designed to correct a physical condition believed to be the cause of a psychological disorder.

Suggested Readings

1. Descriptions of the major methods of psychotherapy are presented in: Nietzel, M. T., & Bernstein, D. A. (1987). *Introduction to clinical psychology* (2nd ed.). Englewood Cliffs, NJ: Prentice-Hall; Phares, E. J. (1988). *Clinical psychology: Concepts, methods, and profession* (3rd ed.). Chicago: Dorsey Press.
2. Group psychotherapy is discussed in depth in: Yalom, I. D. (1975). *The theory and practice of group psychotherapy* (2nd ed.). New York: Basic Books.
3. A major comparison of the effectiveness of different forms of psychotherapy is presented in: Smith, M. L., & Glass, G. V. (1977). Meta-analysis of psychotherapy outcome studies. *American Psychologist, 32,* 752–760.
4. Four helpful booklets on depression are available from the Superintendent of Documents, Government Printing Office, Washington, D.C. 20402-9325:

   Depressive illness: Treatments bring new hope (017-024-01370-6).

   Bipolar disorder (017-024-01368-4).

   Plain talk about . . . depression (017-024-01382-0).

   What do you do when a friend is depressed? (017-024-01376-5).

PART

7

The Social Context

CHAPTER

15

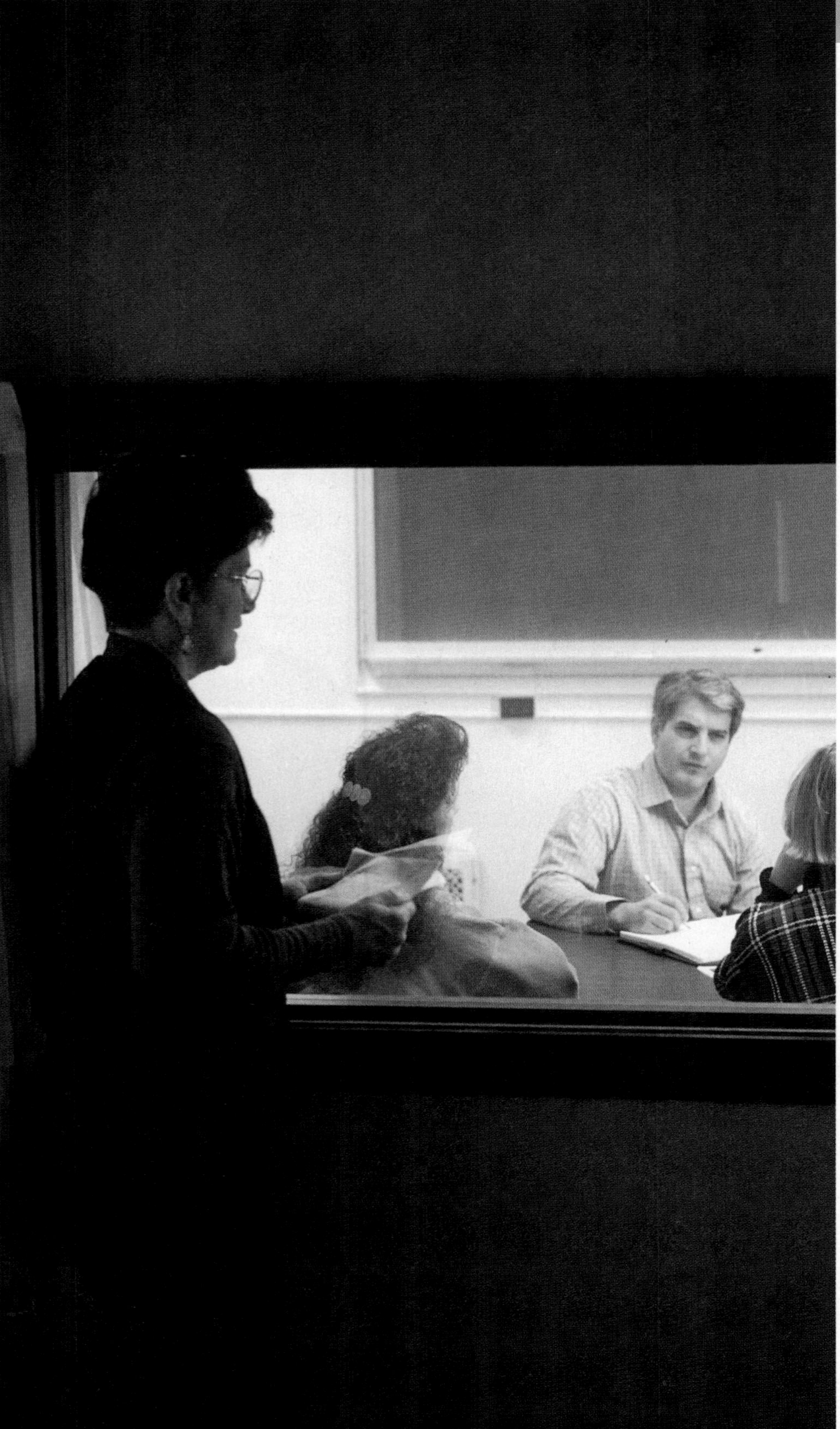

CHAPTER OUTLINE

Social Psychology

PROLOGUE

Human beings are social animals: We enjoy people, need people, and are profoundly influenced by them. Indeed, we often behave a bit like sheep in a flock. We are likely to dress and act like other people even when we are not asked to conform, and we are often influenced by persuasive arguments—even illogical ones.

Social psychologists focus on attitudes because they play a key role in our social interactions; they are a large part of what determines our behavior toward others. Most of our attitudes are learned from others and can be changed through persuasion. But other people are not the only cause of attitude change. Surprisingly, when circumstances cause our behavior to be inconsistent with our attitudes, our attitudes will often change to become consistent again with our behavior.

For most of us, our most important interactions are with the people we like and love. We like to walk with them, talk with them, and snuggle with them. Who do you like and why? Other things being equal, we are attracted to people who are similar to us (or whose opposite characteristics are good for us), who are reasonably competent (but not perfect), who are physically attractive, and who like us, too. Once mutual attraction leads to a relationship, our likelihood of staying in that relationship is determined by (a) how well our expectations of what the person is like are met and (b) how fairly balanced the relationship is.

The process of liking or disliking others is based on a complex combination of the positive and negative qualities that we see in them. Some of our reasons for liking a person have little to do with the other person at all, however. Let's look at one extraneous factor that influences the process of liking by looking at a well-known experiment (Curtis & Miller, 1987). You walk to the psychology department to take part in a study. You are introduced to another student whom you have never met and spend 5 minutes in a "get to know one another" conversation. Then you are separated and taken to separate cubicles. The experimenter talks with the other student for a while, then comes to your cubicle. She tells you that the study is about the ways in which people get to know one another. She also tells you that the other student has been misled into thinking that you are not a very likable person (by showing the other student a bogus "personality test" that made you look bad). To prove it, the experimenter shows you what the other student's initial ratings of you are, and they are not very positive!

The experimenter explains that she wants to know how the other student will act toward you after being given this initial negative opinion. You and the other research participant are brought together for a 10-minute conversation. Then you and the other student rate each other on likability, warmth, and a number of other similar dimensions.

What you don't find out until later is that half of the students who participated in the study were told that the other person was given positive information about them and half were given negative information. Actually, the experimenters didn't give either positive or negative information to the other students. The social psychologists who conducted this study wanted to know if we act differently toward people that we *think* like or dislike us. The experimenters observed the students through a one-way mirror and rated their behavior. You and the other research

KEY TERMS

social psychology 526
fundamental attribution error 526
attribution 526
situational attribution 526
dispositional attribution 526
deindividuation 527
diffusion of responsibility 529
social loafing 529
social facilitation 529
social impairment 530
polarization 530
groupthink 531
conformity 531
obedience 533
attitudes 536
persuasion 537
sleeper effects 538
cognitive dissonance 541
prejudice 542
stereotype 542
attribution theory 543
person perception 546
primacy effect 547
equity theory 553

participants who thought the other students did not like them were rated as less warm, less open, and disagreed more often. Not surprisingly, the other person rated you and the other individuals in your group as much less likable at the end of the study, too. The other person that you *thought* did not like you actually *didn't* like you very much in the end. Human relationships are maddeningly—and fascinatingly—complex.

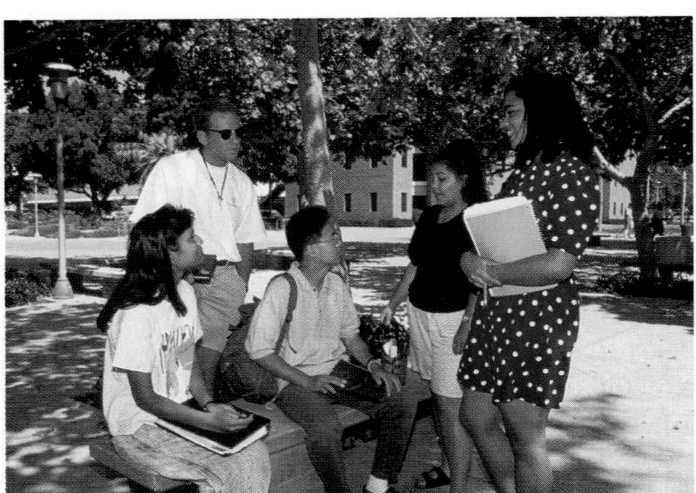

Social psychology is the branch of psychology that studies individuals as they interact with others.

DEFINITION OF SOCIAL PSYCHOLOGY

Social psychology is a branch of psychology that studies individuals as they interact with others. Up to this point, we have studied people as individuals removed from the social context in which they live. But it has been clear all along that people live with other people. Their most important learning comes from others, their most important motives are social motives, and so on.

People are almost always with others. It's part of human nature to be social. Social psychologist Elliot Aronson (1995) reminds us that this insight is among the oldest in psychology. In 328 B.C. Aristotle wrote, "Man is by nature a social animal. . . . Anyone who either cannot lead the common life or is so self-sufficient as not to need to, and therefore does not partake of society, is either a beast or a god." People need, like, and are profoundly influenced by people. Social psychologists study these attractions, needs, and influences.

We have looked at human beings in isolation, and we have examined the psychology of the individual out of the context of the social situations in which they live. To fully understand people, however, we must see how they are influenced by their social context.

SOCIAL INFLUENCE AND THE ATTRIBUTION PROCESS

A first step in appreciating the power of social influence is to understand how we think about the behavior of other people. We have a strong tendency to evaluate other people both in terms of *what* they do and *why* we think they do it. Moreover, when we judge the reasons that people behave as they do, we typically *underestimate* the effects of the social situation and *overestimate* the importance of their personal characteristics (Aronson, 1995; Ross, 1977). If you meet a man at a party who is acting sullen and depressed, you are more likely to assume that he is an unhappy person in general than to assume that he is usually happy, but something has happened recently to make him feel lousy.

In contrast, it is easier for us to see the influence of social situations on our *own* behavior. For example, a few years ago I was invited to a large party hosted by an association of African-American woman attorneys in Los Angeles. Although I usually do not think of myself as shy, I found myself quite shy in the company of these women, nearly all of whom seemed more intelligent, self-secure, and stylish than I. It was easy for me to see the effect of this social situation on my own behavior, but if I had seen another male behaving shyly at the same party, I probably would have just assumed he was an inherently shy person without thinking about it.

Social psychologist Fritz Heider (1958) has termed this the **fundamental attribution error,** meaning our tendency to underestimate the impact of situations on others, while more easily seeing its impact on ourselves. In simple terms, **attribution** is the process of making judgments about what causes people to behave the way they do. The most important aspect of the attribution process is deciding whether a person is behaving in a particular way because of some external cause (**situational attribution**) or because of an internal motive or trait (**dispositional attribution**). Unless we can see that the behavior *consistently* occurs in that situation, and other people behave in the same way in the same situation, we tend to attribute other people's behavior to dispositional causes (Kelley, 1973). Because we often lack information on the extent to which another person's behavior is consistently influenced by situations, we make dispositional attributions too often.

social psychology
The branch of psychology that studies individuals as they interact with others.

fundamental attribution error
The tendency to underestimate the impact of situations on others while overestimating the impact on oneself.

attribution
The process of trying to explain why things happen; that is, attribute them to some cause.

situational attribution
An explanation for behavior that is based on an external cause.

dispositional attribution
(dis´´po-zish´un-al) An explanation for behavior that is based on a personal characteristic of the individual.

The *self-serving bias* is closely related to the fundamental attribution error. We have a tendency to take credit for our successes by attributing them to our own talents (dispositional attribution), but we attribute our failures to difficult circumstances (situational attribution). If you get an A on a test, it's because you're smart. If you get an F on a test, on the other hand, it's because the test was unfair. Although the self-serving bias protects our self-esteem, it can cause problems for us when we fail to acknowledge the real reasons for our failures and learn from our mistakes.

Hopefully, this discussion of the effect of social situations on the behavior of individuals will help you see how powerful they can be. But unless you work to overcome the fundamental attribution error and the self-serving bias, it will be difficult to apply this information to your everyday life. Even when we know that social situations can have a profound impact on our behavior, it is difficult to see that impact on the behavior of others.

Groups and Social Influences

Let's begin our study of social influence with a look at the effects of being a member of a group. Although some of what you will learn will make you embarrassed to be a member of the human race, we can understand the power of social influence only by looking at both its negative and positive faces.

Lynch Mobs and Deindividuation

Near the turn of the century, an African-American man named William Carr was arrested and charged with killing the cow of a white family in southern Louisiana. A mob of solid citizens took him from the sheriff, who did not resist them, and hanged him without a trial. During the era in which this hanging took place, an average of two African Americans were lynched each week in the United States. These lynchings say much about racial prejudice—a topic that we turn to later in the chapter—but they also say a great deal about the effects of groups on the behavior of individuals. The members of lynch mobs were almost never men who had murdered before when alone or who would murder alone afterward. Something about being in a group transformed men who were incapable of murder into a mob that was very capable of murder.

People who feel unidentifiable, or deindividuated, because they are in a large group are more likely to behave aggressively or in other unacceptable ways.

In some situations, being in a group can make a person feel anonymous and unidentifiable. This feeling can lead to a process known as **deindividuation** (Zimbardo, 1969). In this state, people are less aware of their own behavior and less concerned with what others think of their behavior. The result can be an increased likelihood of performing actions that you typically wouldn't do. Think about your own behavior at a crowded ball game or at a large rock concert. You might have screamed vulgar insults at the opposing team or pledged your undying love to the lead singer. The weakened restraints that result from deindividuation can have more serious effects as well. When people are unidentifiable, they are more aggressive (Zimbardo, 1969). Similarly, an analysis of lynchings occurring over a 47-year period found that the worst atrocities occurred in larger groups, where, presumably, people felt more anonymous (Mullen, 1986).

deindividuation
State in which people in a group can feel anonymous and unidentifiable and therefore feel less concerned with what others think of their behavior.

Uninvolved Bystanders

Let's look at another negative outcome of being in groups. I vividly remember reading about the death of Kitty Genovese some years ago. I was more than a little disappointed in the human race when I read that she had been beaten and stabbed to death in a residential area of New York City over the course of 30 minutes while 38 of her neighbors came to their windows and watched. Incredibly, no one came out to help her; no one even called the police.

How could such a thing have happened? Did Kitty just happen to live in a neighborhood of uncaring cowards? Social psychologists don't think that is the answer. For example, Bibb Latané, John Darley, and Judith Rodin carried out a series of experiments in an attempt to understand the lack of action by bystanders like these. In one experiment (Latané & Rodin, 1969), a female experimenter asked college students to fill out a questionnaire, and while they worked, she went behind a curtain where she staged a fake accident. The students heard her climbing and then falling from a chair. She moaned as if in great pain and begged for someone to help her get her foot out from under a heavy object. When students were alone in the other part of the room, 70 percent came to help her. But when they were paired with one other student who did not respond to the woman's pleas, only 7 percent tried to help!

In a similar experiment (Darley & Latané, 1968), college students "overheard" a staged epileptic seizure through an intercom. Eighty-five percent of the students tried to find help for the seizure victim when they thought they alone had heard it, but when they thought that others were also listening, only 30 percent sought help. Social psychologists do not think that bystanders who fail to help in an emergency are lacking in some personal quality; rather, they are influenced by being in a group. Many studies have shown that the larger the group, the less likely any particular person is to offer to help a person in distress (Latané & Nida, 1981).

To understand why people fail to help in such situations, we must understand that the decision to help or not help is complex. Latané and Darley (1970) propose that the decision to help can be best understood as a *decision tree* with many steps (see figure 15.1). First, a person must *notice* that something is out of the ordinary. A drowning victim who is screaming for help might not be noticed because everyone else at the beach is screaming and yelling in fun. If the victim is noticed, though, the person still might not help unless the situation is *interpreted* as an emergency. The bystander might think that the drowning victim is yelling and thrashing in the water for fun. A man slumped over in the street could just be drunk and not have had a heart attack. If the situation is not interpreted as an emergency, the victim will not receive help from that bystander.

FIGURE 15.1
Latané & Darley's decision model of helping (1970).

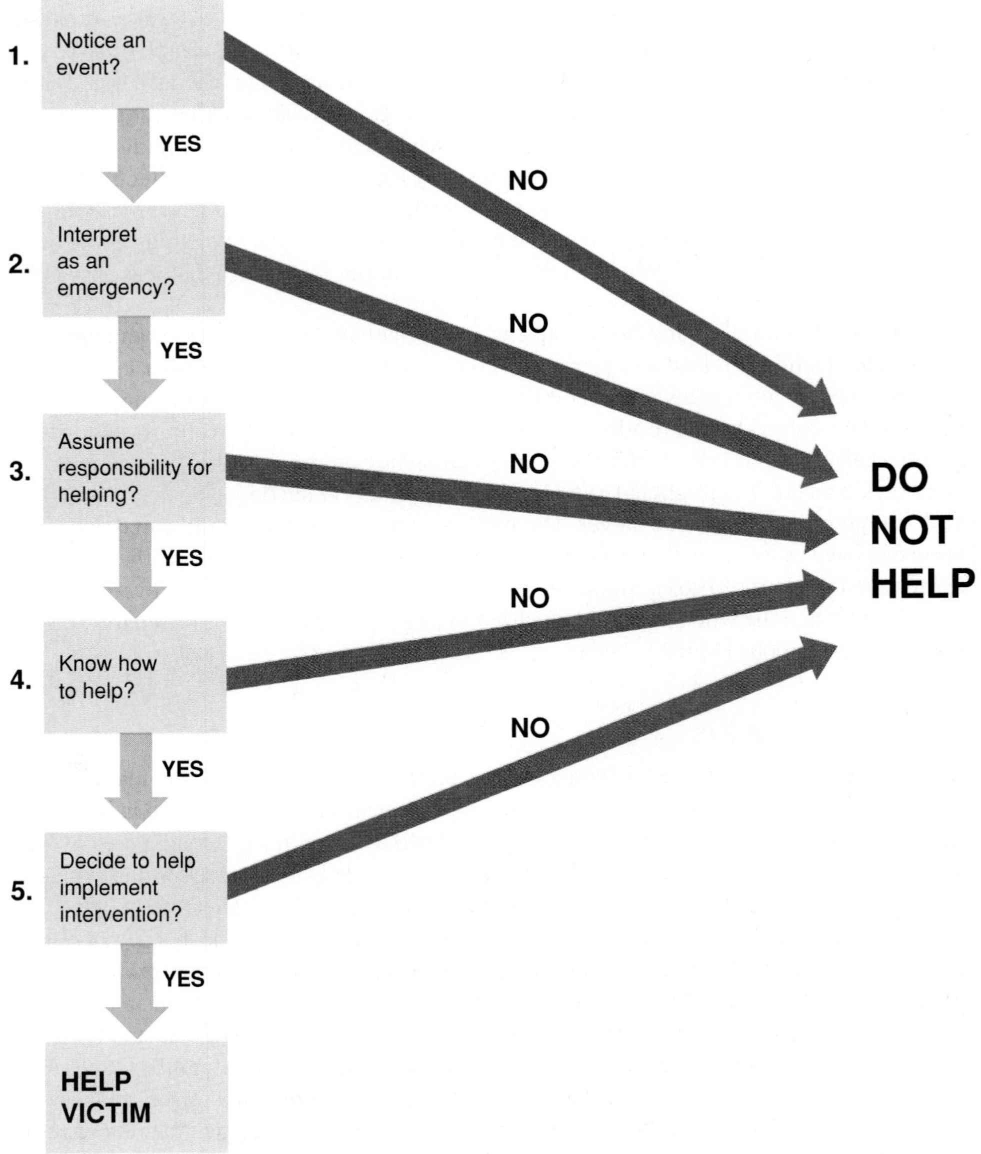

Once the event is interpreted as an emergency, the bystander must decide whether she or he should *assume responsibility* for helping. If a lifeguard is present, or if others are around to help, a bystander might not assume the responsibility for helping. Even if the bystander assumes responsibility for helping, the bystander might not help if he or she does *not know how to help*. Finally, the bystander still might *decide not to help* for some reason. For example, you might notice a commotion in the water, interpret that situation as one in which a person is drowning, assume responsibility to help the victim, and know how to swim out and rescue the person, but if you are afraid that the person is so heavy that you would be drowned trying to help, you still might decide not to help. As you can see, the decision to help is only the last step in a complex process.

What social factors influence the decision tree? Latané and Darley have suggested that being in the presence of other people primarily affects the second and third stage of the decision process—interpreting the event as an emergency and assuming responsibility for helping. When we notice an event and try to interpret it, we look to others for information. If nobody else is making an effort to help, then it's less likely that we will help, because it looks as if there is no reason to help: "No one looks worried, so there must not be a problem." As mentioned, in the Latané and Rodin "woman in distress" experiment, 70 percent of the individuals who were alone went to find help for the person who had fallen, but that number was reduced to 7 percent when they were paired with another person (actually a confederate of the experimenter) who made no effort at all to offer help. In other bystander experiments in which the confederate tried to find a way to help, the research participants were more likely to help, too.

The second stage that the presence of other bystanders is most likely to affect is assuming responsibility for helping. Groups create a **diffusion of responsibility.** If everyone in the group is responsible for a lynching, then no one person is individually responsible: "I didn't do it; we all just got worked up and did it." In emergencies, a person who is alone is clearly responsible for helping the person in need; but in a group of bystanders, the reasoning is that I do not need to help because someone else will.

diffusion of responsibility
The effect of being in a group that apparently reduces the sense of personal responsibility of each group member to act appropriately.

Working and Solving Problems in Groups

We humans often gather together to perform work in groups. We sometimes study together, raise barns together, and hold meetings to discuss solutions to problems in our colleges, businesses, and cities. Is this a good thing? Does working together in groups bring out the best in us? Sometimes yes, and sometimes no.

Working as part of a group can affect how hard we work and how well we get the job done.

Let's first look at group efforts—all of the members are trying to reach the same goal together. Suppose you convince your instructor to use the next class period to have a tug-of-war among members of your class. Do you think that you would pull harder on the rope if you were tugging alone against one classmate, or if you were part of a team of four persons tugging against four classmates? As the number of people involved in a tug-of-war increases, the average amount of force exerted by each person *declines* (Kravitz & Martin, 1986). The diminished effort of each individual in a group of tug-of-war is partly the result of lack of coordination among members of the group—some rest while others pull, resulting in less average effort. But even persons who are blindfolded and led to believe that others are pulling with them exert less effort than when they think they are pulling alone (Ingham, Levinger, Graves, & Peckham, 1974). Similarly, if you are asked to clap as loudly as you can, you will make more noise if you think your clap is being measured individually than if you think the loudness of a group of clappers is being measured together (Latané, Williams, & Harkins, 1979). Social psychologist Bibb Latané of Florida Atlantic University calls this phenomenon **social loafing.**

social loafing
The tendency of members of groups to work less hard when group performance is measured than when individual performance is measured.

Sometimes groups can influence our *individual* performance even when we are not working on a group project; just working in the *presence* of other people can affect our behavior. Sometimes being in a group improves our performance on individual projects. When this is the case, **social facilitation** is said to occur (Levine, Resnick, & Higgins, 1993). In one of the earliest experiments in social psychology, Triplett (1898) found that teenagers wound fishing

social facilitation
An effect in which working in a group improves one's performance on individual projects.

reels faster in the presence of other teenagers doing the same thing than when they were alone. Sometimes, however, working in the presence of others impairs our individual performance, causing what is termed **social impairment.** When do other people help or hurt our performance? It depends on how difficult and *unfamiliar* the task is. For example, Markus (1978) asked research participants to dress in preparation for a later phase in an experiment. This task of dressing was either easy, putting on everyday shoes and socks, or difficult, involving dressing in strange, unfamiliar clothes. Participants performed this dressing task either alone, with a confederate who observed them, or with a confederate who was busy repairing equipment on the other side of the room. When individuals performed the easy dressing task, they dressed faster when there was another person present in the room, compared with when they dressed alone. When the research participants had to perform the difficult dressing task, they dressed more slowly in the presence of others than they did when they were alone.

social impairment
An effect in which working in a group impairs individual performance.

Why does the presence of other people improve performance on easy tasks and impair performance on difficult ones? Nearly all theorists agree with Zajonc (1965) that the presence of other people is arousing. If you will recall the discussion of *optimal levels of arousal* in chapter 9 (p. 336), easy tasks are easier to do when people are aroused, but difficult tasks are more difficult when people are aroused. The same is true for social facilitation and social impairment. High levels of arousal, such as that produced by performing in front of an audience, may promote social facilitation for easy or skilled tasks and social impairment for difficult or unfamiliar tasks. Professional athletes, musicians, and other performers often do their best work in the presence of an audience, because they are performing skills that have been practiced over and over again. In contrast, amateur performers who lack practice and skill are likely to perform more poorly when an audience is present.

What about more intellectual tasks such as problem solving? Is it better or worse to work together in groups when trying to solve problems? Suppose a friend asks you for advice about the following dilemma:

> "I want to go to graduate school in filmmaking, but to get in I have to make an impressive grade in undergraduate scriptwriting. I could take the course from a famous instructor who is respected by the graduate school, but the famous instructor is so hard that hardly anyone gets an A or B. Or I could take the course from an easier, less famous instructor that the graduate school might not be impressed by. What should I do?"

What would you recommend? Would you tell your friend to go for broke and take the course from the famous-but-tough instructor, even though the chances of getting a good grade are very low? Studies have shown that most of us do *not* recommend such risky options *when we are alone with the person asking for advice.* However, when *groups* of persons discuss such dilemmas they are much more likely to take extreme positions and recommend risky options (Stoner, 1961). The discussion of issues in groups often leads to the **polarization** of thinking by pushing our opinions toward one extreme "pole" of the issue or the other.

polarization
The tendency for group discussion to make beliefs and attitudes more extreme.

For example, suppose you are a person with mildly prejudiced views about other ethnic groups. You are with a group of people and someone makes a *very* prejudicial remark about an ethnic group. You may find yourself taking a more extreme position against prejudice than you typically would—and meaning what you say. You have been pushed toward the nonprejudiced pole of the argument, and your statements have probably driven the other fellow to an even more prejudiced position. A classic study of polarization of attitudes occurring in group discussions found exactly these results during a discussion of ethnic attitudes among high school students (Myers & Bishop, 1970).

These studies looked at the kind of everyday decisions made by regular people like you and me. What about really important decision making by groups of experts? In those high-powered, sophisticated groups, experts wouldn't fall victim to the biases of group decision making—or would they?

Psychologist Irving Janis (1982) has studied the factors involved in group problem solving by knowledgeable and sophisticated decision makers. He proposed that some of the most significant and disastrous decisions made in history—such as President Kennedy's ill-fated decision to send Cuban freedom fighters to sure defeat in the Bay of Pigs invasion of Castro's Cuba or NASA's fatal decision in 1986 to launch the space shuttle Challenger, despite warnings from engineers about defective O-rings (Kruglanski, 1986)—were the result of faulty group decision making. Janis calls the faulty decision-making processes that occur in these

"All those in favor say 'Aye.' "
"Aye." "Aye." "Aye."
"Aye." "Aye."

Drawing by H. Martin; © 1979 The New Yorker Magazine.

groups **groupthink.** Groupthink is more likely to occur in tightly knit, cohesive groups. The members of cohesive groups prefer to agree with one another and discourage dissent. For that reason contradictory evidence and opinions often are not presented, leaving the group with a false sense of the correctness of their decision. It is easy to see how unsound decisions could be made under these conditions. To guard against groupthink, at least one member of the group should take the role of the "devil's advocate," regularly challenging the group's thinking.

groupthink
The faulty decision-making processes that may occur in groups.

Conformity, Social Roles, and Obedience

I hope that you are beginning to have a new appreciation for the powerful influence of social situations on the behavior of the individual. Clearly, social situations influence us every day in important ways. But there is still a great deal more to the story of social influence. Next, we consider our tendency to conform to the expectations of our peer groups and our cultures, the influence of socially prescribed roles and norms on our behavior, and our tendency to obediently follow the instructions of authority figures.

Conformity

When we are members of a group, we tend to behave like others in the group—we tend to conform. **Conformity** is yielding to group pressure to act like everyone else even when no direct request has been made. A most informative and now classic study of conformity was conducted by Solomon Asch (1956). He asked college students to serve as research participants in an experiment that he said concerned visual perception. Each student participated in a group with other "research participants" all of whom were actually confederates of the experimenter. The group was shown four straight lines, depicted in figure 15.2. The task was to tell which of the three lines on the right side of the figure was the same length as line *A*.

conformity
Yielding to group pressure even when no direct request to comply has been made.

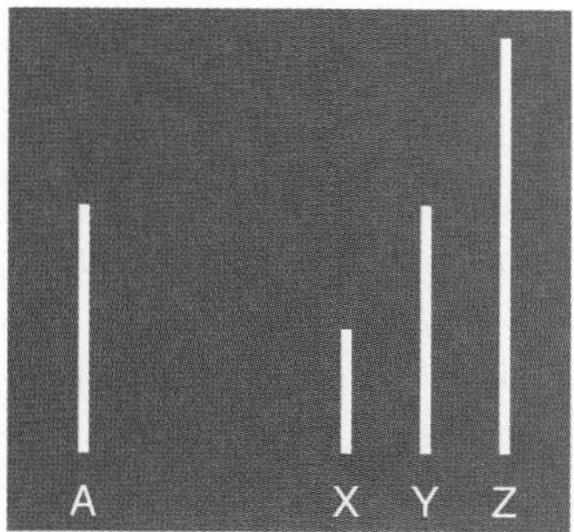

FIGURE 15.2
Stimuli like those used in Asch's study of conformity.

The task was intentionally made easy, with line *Y* being the obvious correct choice. But the real participant was the last one in line as each student was asked to state his or her choice out loud. One by one, the confederates playing the part of real research participants chose line *X*. The distress of the real participant was immediately apparent. He seemed to be asking, "Am I crazy or are they?" But in an amazing 74 percent of the cases, the participants conformed to the pressure of the group and gave the wrong answer at least part of the time.

How "deep" was this conformity? Did the research participants know that they were just going along with the group's opinion, or did the group actually change their judgment? People may conform for two reasons: to gain rewards and avoid punishments (such as social approval or disapproval) or to gain information. In the Asch situation, people seemed to conform for the former reason, to seek approval and avoid disapproval. How do we know? When the same line-judging experiment was conducted in a slightly different way that allowed the research participants to make their judgments privately, almost no conformity to the erroneous judgments of other individuals occurred. Apparently, we are able to make up our minds privately even in the face of pressure from others, but often go along with the crowd in terms of outward behavior.

Sometimes, however, we conform to the behavior of others at a much deeper level. This happens when the "correct" judgment is less clear than in Asch's line-judging experiment. Sherif (1936) conducted a study that took advantage of a perceptual phenomena called the *autokinetic effect*. When a person is placed in a completely darkened room with no reference points, a fixed point of light on a wall will appear to move. Because the movement of light is not real, and the distance that it seems to move differs from person to person, this is an extremely ambiguous situation (as compared with Asch's line-judging task, which was very clear-cut). Sherif placed individuals in a room with confederates and asked them to estimate the distance that a fixed light had moved. The confederates gave either extremely low or extremely high estimates of movement, and the research participants tended to agree with the confederates. In this ambiguous situation, however, they still tended to agree with the confederates even when they could report their estimates of the movement of the light in private. When the appropriate response in a situation is not clear, we look to others for information and will not only go along with them, but may actually change our judgments.

In terms of outward behavior, we tend to conform to group norms.

Several factors have been found to increase the likelihood of conformity to the group:

1. *Size of the group.* Up to a point, the more people there are in a group, the more likely we are to go along. When the group gets too large, however, conformity drops off.
2. *Unanimous groups.* Conformity is highest when we face a group that all feels the same way about a topic—the group is unanimous. But, conformity is greatly reduced when even one person in the group feels as we do.
3. *Culture and conformity.* A recent article by British psychologists Rod Bond and Peter Smith (1996) shows us that culture is an important factor that influences conformity. The experiment showing conformity in the judgment of the length of lines originally conducted by Solomon Asch in 1956 has now been conducted 133 times in 17 different cultures. Conformity occurs in all cultures, but persons from cultures that place an emphasis on the welfare of the individual—as in the United States—are less conforming on the Asch task than persons from cultures that emphasize the welfare of society as a whole, rather than the individual.
4. *Gender and conformity?* What about gender? According to our stereotypes, males are more independent and less likely to conform than females. Research conducted before the mid-1950s suggested that females were more likely to conform than males at that time. More recent research, however, has shown that this is no longer the case (Eagly, 1978; Eagly & Johnson, 1990). Maybe our stereotypes will eventually catch up with the changing realities of gender.

Social Roles and Social Norms

social roles
Culturally determined guidelines that tell people what behavior is expected of them.

social norms
Guidelines provided by every culture for judging acceptable and unacceptable behavior.

When people work together in groups, the efforts of each individual need to be coordinated with those of others to avoid chaos. In response to this need, every culture has evolved many **social roles** and **social norms** to give guidelines as to what is expected of us (Levine et al., 1993). Just like actors in a play who have scripts for their roles, social roles tell us how we are expected to behave. In this course, you play the role of the student and the nice person who tells you interesting things about psychology plays the role of the instructor. Each social role gives the person a different set of expectations for appropriate behavior. You are not surprised when the person in the role of instructor stands in the front of the classroom and lectures, but you would be surprised if the student sitting next to you stood up and delivered a 45-minute lecture on the importance of Pavlov's studies of salivating dogs to our understanding of romantic love.

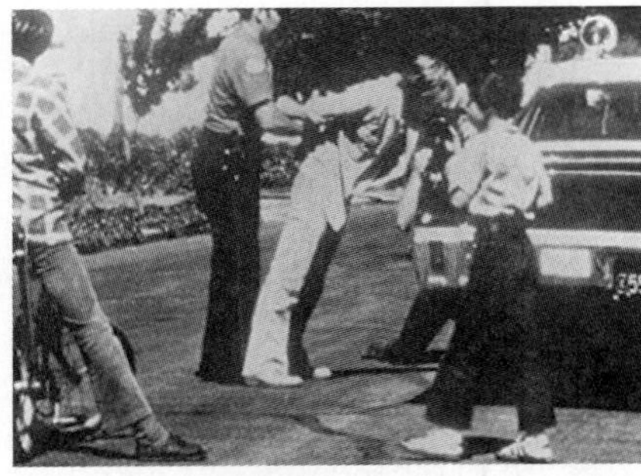

In Zimbardo's prison experiment, volunteers assigned to the social roles of guard and prisoner dramatically conformed to those roles.

Social roles have a powerful impact on the behavior of individuals. When we are placed in a new role, our behavior often changes to fit the role. In a dramatic example of the power of social roles in influencing behavior, social psychologist Philip Zimbardo of Stanford University looked at the social roles that exist in prisons. Zimbardo was interested in these particular roles because he felt that they lead to the mistreatment of convicts in a way that worsens their behavior. This is Zimbardo's description of what was learned.

> We carefully screened over 70 volunteers who answered an ad in a Palo Alto city newspaper and ended up with about two dozen young men who were selected to be part of this study. Half were arbitrarily designated as prisoners by a flip of a coin, the others as guards. These were the roles they were to play in our simulated prison. The guards were made aware of the potential seriousness and danger of the situation and their own vulnerability. They made up their own formal rules for maintaining law, order, and respect, and were generally free to improvise new ones during their eight-hour, three-man shifts. The prisoners were unexpectedly picked up at their homes by a city policeman in a squad car, searched, handcuffed, fingerprinted, booked at the Palo Alto station house, and taken blindfolded to our jail. There they were stripped, deloused, put into a uniform, given a number, and put into a cell with two other prisoners where they expected to live for the next two weeks. The pay was good . . . and their motivation was to make money. . . . At the end of only six days we had to close down our mock prison because what we saw was frightening. It was no longer apparent to most of the subjects (or to us) where reality ended and their roles began. The majority had indeed become prisoners or guards, no longer able to clearly differentiate between role playing and self. There were dramatic changes in virtually every aspect of their behavior, thinking, and feeling. In less than a week the experience of imprisonment undid (temporarily) a lifetime

of learning; human values were suspended, self-concepts were challenged, and the ugliest, most base, pathological side of human nature surfaced. We were horrified because we saw some boys (guards) treat others as if they were despicable animals, taking pleasure in cruelty, while other boys (prisoners) became servile, dehumanized robots who thought only of escape, of their own individual survival, and of their mounting hatred for the guards. We had to release three prisoners in the first four days because they had such acute situational traumatic reactions as hysterical crying, confusion in thinking, and severe depression. Others begged to be paroled, and all but three were willing to forfeit all the money they had earned if they could be paroled.

Excerpt from Philip G. Zimbardo, "The Pathology of Imprisonment" in *Society*, April 1972, vol. 9, no. 6, p. 4. Used with permission of Transaction Publishers, Rutgers–The State University of New Jersey.

It is clear that social roles can influence our behavior. What is not always clear is that we play numerous roles in our lives, and that each role influences us whether we are aware of it or not. I play the roles of man, spouse, father, middle-aged person, person of Irish ancestry, heterosexual, brother, son, and psychology professor to name only the most obvious ones. Each role is a source of social influence on my behavior whether I like it or not. I can work hard at not being the typical male or the typical father, but these roles inevitably influence me. How about you? What roles do you play and how do they make you different from me?

In addition to conforming to our social roles, we also behave according to spoken and unspoken rules known as *social norms*. The social norms of our culture tell us how we should behave in particular situations. We avoid making eye contact with other people in an elevator and cover our mouths when we cough because these are widely held social norms for Americans. Most people conform to the social norms of their culture most of the time.

The influence of roles and norms is not all bad. I have emphasized the extent to which social roles can be harmful because I want to alert you to the fact that they can detract from your individuality, but it is important to recognize that social roles and norms play an essential positive function in society. Without social roles and norms, you would not know what to expect of your psychology instructor, to take but one example. Being a student would be much more difficult if you did not know that the person who plays the role of the instructor will give lectures on which you are supposed to take notes, and that she or he will give tests and will give you a grade at the end of the term. Understanding the roles of others—and those of ourselves—greatly facilitates our ability to work together in society for the common good. But they are potent sources of influence that must be understood.

Obedience: Direct Influence by Authority Figures

One of the most fascinating, and often frightening, lines of inquiry in social psychology has been research on **obedience,** doing what we are told to do by people in authority. This research was prompted in part by the behavior of soldiers in World War II, and other wars, who committed unthinkable atrocities when ordered to do so. What kind of person would help abuse and murder 6 million Jews during the Holocaust? What kind of person would not refuse to obey such an order? The disturbing answer from research is that most of us are that kind of person.

obedience
Doing what one is told to do by people in authority.

Stanley Milgram (1963, 1965) conducted a series of studies that cast a glaring light on the subject of obedience. To get the full impact of his findings, try to imagine that you are a research participant in one of his experiments. You have volunteered for a study of memory. When you arrive at the appointed time, you and another person, a middle-aged man, meet a somewhat stern, authoritarian experimenter wearing a white lab coat. The experimenter chooses you to be the "teacher" in the experiment and the other participant to be the "learner." The learner will have to memorize a list of word pairs, but you have to test him and operate the equipment. The "equipment" is a console labeled "SHOCK GENERATOR" with a bank of switches that are marked from 15 to 450 volts.

You help strap the learner into something that looks like an electric chair and you attach electrodes to him that are connected to the shock generator in the other room. The learner asks whether the experiment could be dangerous to his heart condition, but the experimenter assures him that while the shocks could be extremely painful, they should cause no physical harm. You return to the next room, take your seat at the console, and are told how you should use the shocks to "help" the learner memorize the list.

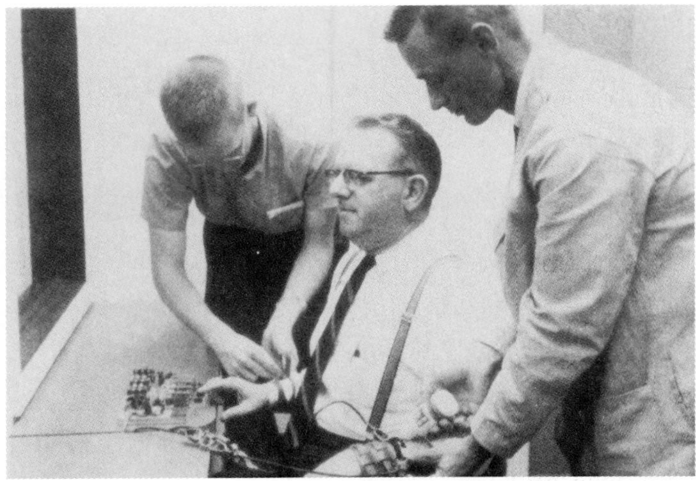

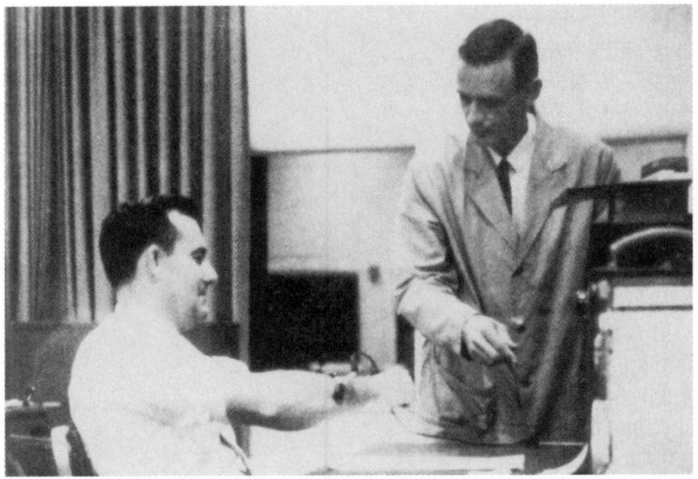

In Milgram's classic obedience experiments, the "learner" was strapped to a chair while participants were instructed to use what they believed was an electronic shock generator to shock him after errors in learning.

You are to listen to him attempt to recite the list over the intercom and shock him by throwing one of the switches after each error. You are to begin with the weakest shock and increase the intensity each time he makes a mistake. You are even given a 45-volt shock so you can see what it feels like (it's unpleasant) and the experiment begins. The learner recalls the list fairly accurately, but makes a few mistakes, and you shock him as you have been instructed to do.

What you do not know is that the learner is not really getting shocked. He is a confederate of the experimenter who is acting a role. He is not even talking over the intercom; you are hearing a tape recording instead. But the important thing is that you *believe* that a man with a heart condition is strapped into an electric chair in the next room and that you are giving him shocks every time he makes a mistake.

The learner groans after an intensity of 75 volts has been reached. At 150 volts, he says that his heart is bothering him and asks to be let out of the experiment. The experimenter denies the request and tells you to give him the shock when he makes a mistake. When the learner has been given the 180-volt shock, the learner screams that he cannot stand the pain, and as you are told to turn the shock apparatus to 300 volts—the level marked "Danger: Extreme Shock"—he refuses to recite the list of word pairs any more. When you look toward the experimenter expecting him to stop the proceedings, he firmly tells you to administer the next shock.

What would you do? Would you give the extremely dangerous shock even though the learner was begging you to stop? Or would you refuse to continue? Milgram asked a panel of psychiatrists how many research participants they thought would continue giving shocks at this point, and they predicted that less than 5 percent would continue. What percentage would you predict? Milgram found that an incredible 65 percent not only gave the next shock but also continued participating until they had given the highest shock (450 volts).

Milgram's findings were astonishing, even to other social psychologists who understood the power of social situations. Could his results have been a fluke? Did Milgram just happen to recruit a group of sadistic individuals? To find out, Milgram repeated his study and found the same results with men and women from many different walks of life: students, blue-collar workers, white-collar workers, and professionals. He conducted his study in laboratories at prestigious Yale University and in an office space in downtown Bridgeport, Connecticut. This study has been replicated in other countries as well. The results of these studies are a painful reminder of the power of social situations and a warning of the ease with which misguided authorities can use ordinary people like you and me to obediently carry out their wishes.

It is somewhat comforting that later studies found that individuals were less likely to obey the instruction to give the high-voltage shocks when their victim was in the same room with them, acting distressed by the shocks. In addition, when the prestige of the experimenter was reduced, the percentage of obedient persons fell to about 50 percent. When the experimenter gave instructions by telephone rather than in person, the percentage fell to about 25 percent. Furthermore, when the research participant was in the presence of two other participants who refused to give the high-intensity shocks, only 10 percent obeyed the experimenter's instructions to the end. Obedience is also reduced when individuals are led to feel more personal responsibility for their actions and when it is obvious that authorities have self-serving goals. These latter facts are somewhat encouraging, but they do not lessen the impact of Milgram's findings: The power of social situations over human behavior can be terrifying and must be guarded against.

A final comment is in order about Milgram's study of obedience. Although this study was of great value in exploring an important aspect of human nature in the laboratory, this study would not be considered ethical by today's standards (Baumrind, 1964). The experimenter would not be allowed to command the research participant to continue against her or his will—participants may leave an experiment at any time without penalty.

The Positive Side of Groups

Has this discussion of social loafing, polarization, and groupthink convinced you that people should never work together on anything? Or that the only way to remain a good person is to live in a cave as a hermit? It shouldn't at all. Think of the benefits that being in groups give us. There are many things that a single person working alone could not accomplish. Although it is true that people pull harder alone than when pulling in a group, four people working together could pull hard enough to pull a heavy boat ashore that a single person could never pull. Group discussion of issues can lead to faulty decision making, but it can also allow one person to point out the logical flaws in a solution offered by another person. In Milgram's obedience study, you saw how individuals who were in the presence of others who refused to obey the experimenter's instructions were more likely to disobey the authority figure as well.

Groups also can be therapeutic—think of support groups and group therapies—and can provide emotional support and comfort. Recall that you learned in chapter 12 that the effects of stress can be reduced considerably by strong social support (p. 445). Therefore, we must be aware of the negative effects of groups on our behaviors not so that we will avoid groups but so that we can make the best advantage of being in them.

Review

Because we are social animals, we are almost always in the company of others. This is a fundamentally important observation because people can be fully understood only if our social nature is understood. Other people influence our behavior and we must understand that process of influence. We all need to be more aware of the power of social situations in influencing behavior. Unfortunately, we have a strong tendency to ignore the influence of the social situations on other people and overemphasize the role played by their internal attributes. Ironically, ignoring the power of social situations only makes us more vulnerable to their influence.

The very fact of being with others can influence behavior; people often behave differently when they are in groups from the way they do when alone. Mobs commit crimes that the individuals alone would not commit, and groups of bystanders fail to help people in distress even though most members of that group would have done so if alone.

Groups influence individual behavior through our strong tendency to conform with the group even when not asked to do so. We may conform in terms of outward behavior and, in some instances, may change our inner judgments and attitudes as well. Groups also influence us through the expectations for our behavior that are inherent in social roles and social norms. Frighteningly, we are likely to be persuaded to obey even inappropriate requests from a prestigious authority figure, especially when we face the authority figure alone. When working in groups, individual effort declines under some circumstances and group problem solving can become distorted.

Despite these negative effects, groups can accomplish what an individual could never do when working alone, individual performance improves under some conditions, and the impact of stress can be softened by social support. The effects of our tendency to band together in groups can be positive, especially if we are aware of the potentially negative effects of groups on individual behavior.

Thinking Critically About Psychology

1. Can you think of a situation in your life in which you blamed a person's behavior on his or her personality even though the social situation might have strongly influenced the person's behavior?

2. What do you think is the significance of Stanley Milgram's studies? What does it say about individual responsibility to behave ethically in a society?

Check Your Learning

To be sure that you have learned the key points from the preceding section, cover the answers below and try to answer each question. If you give an incorrect answer to any question, return to the page given next to the correct answer to see why your answer was not correct. Remember that these questions cover only some of the important information in this section; it is important that you make up your own questions to check your learning of other facts and concepts.

1. Social psychology is the branch of psychology that studies ____________________ .

2. People often incorrectly believe that __________ in influencing the behavior of others.

   a. personality is more important than the situation
   b. the situation is more important than personality

3. People may behave as they do in lynch mobs and at ball games because of a process called __________________ .

4. In a situation where the solution is not obvious, we are most likely to conform

   a. publicly in terms of outward behaviors.
   b. privately in terms of judgments and attitudes.
   c. neither a nor b.
   d. both a and b.

5. When workers exert less effort in a group than they would when working alone, the result is called

   a. social loafing.
   b. group polarization.
   c. groupthink.
   d. social facilitation.

Correct Answers

1. individuals as they interact with others (p. 526), **2.** a (p. 526), **3.** deindividuation (p. 527), **4.** d (p. 531), **5.** a (p. 529).

ATTITUDES, PERSUASION, AND SOCIAL INFLUENCE

Attitudes are a pivotal concept in social psychology. They are of special interest because other people attempt to influence our attitudes through persuasion, and our attitudes are often reflected in our behavior toward others. If I give a speech to parents that changes their attitudes toward discipline practices (such as, it's more important to praise children for their good behavior than to punish them for their bad behavior), they may tend to change the way they actually rear their children, too. As we will see shortly, attitudes and social behavior are not perfectly correlated by any means. But there is enough relationship between the two to make attitudes a favorite topic of study of social psychologists, especially attitudes related to important aspects of social behavior such as prejudice based on a person's gender, ethnicity, age, sexual preference, or other factors.

attitudes
Beliefs that predispose one to act and feel in certain ways.

Social psychologists define **attitudes** as beliefs that predispose us to act and feel in certain ways. Note that this definition has three components: (a) *beliefs,* such as the belief that door-to-door salespeople are generally dishonest; (b) *feelings,* such as a strong dislike for door-to-door salespeople; and (c) *dispositions to behave,* such as a readiness to be rude to them when they come to the door. Where do our attitudes come from, and what causes them to change?

Origins of Attitudes

The origins of most of our attitudes are fairly obvious: We learn them directly from our experiences, and we learn them from others (Olson & Zanna, 1993). Some of our attitudes are learned from firsthand experience. Children who are bitten by dogs often carry negative attitudes toward dogs for the rest of their lives, especially toward the kind of dog that bit them. In contrast, the sweet crunch of chocolate chip cookies generally leads to a favorable attitude toward them. In other words, some attitudes appear to be *classically conditioned.* If a stimulus (dogs or cookies) is paired with a positive or negative experience, the attitude will be similarly positive or negative.

Attitudes are also commonly learned from others. Parents who model positive attitudes toward their Hispanic neighbors are likely to have children who have positive attitudes toward Hispanics. Children whose best friends think baseball is awful may pick up this attitude through modeling. Similarly, children who are reinforced by their parents and friends for prejudicial attitudes are likely to have these attitudes strengthened. In sum, other people instill attitudes in us through their modeling and reinforcement.

Persuasion and Attitude Change

Attitudes are not chiseled in granite; they can change after they have been formed. Indeed, the earliest known writings on social psychology were about changing people's attitudes through **persuasion.** Aristotle's *Rhetoric* was an essay on factors that make for persuasive arguments when orators debate. You probably do not listen to many orators debate, but you are on the receiving end of other kinds of persuasive communications nearly every day. Commercials on the radio and television and advertisements in newspapers and magazines are designed to change your attitude about the sponsor's products. Political speeches and billboards are intended to persuade you how to vote. Your friend who wants to borrow your car tries to persuade you. And when you ask your professor to let you take an exam early, you try to persuade him or her. Persuasion is a natural and necessary part of our interactions with other members of society. But because of the potentially important consequences of persuasive communications (your friend might actually talk you into lending her your car!), it's important to know something about their nature. The persuasiveness of a communication is not determined merely by the logical quality of the argument. Logic may, in fact, be one of the *least important* factors. That's a scary thought, because we would like to believe that we live in a world where logic and truth win out. But if you know what makes an argument persuasive, you can at least be on your guard. Notice that the qualities of persuasive communication fall into three general categories: characteristics of the *speaker,* of the *communication* itself, and of the *people who hear it.*

persuasion
The process of changing another person's attitudes through arguments and other related means.

Characteristics of the Speaker

Several characteristics of the speaker are important in determining how persuasive a communication will be.

1. *Credibility.* If you listened to a speech on the value of arithmetic, do you think you would be more persuaded if the speech were given by a noted engineer or a dishwasher? Elliot Aronson and Burton Golden (1962) conducted exactly this experiment and found that the engineer swayed opinions considerably more than the dishwasher, even though they gave exactly the same speech. In fact, the same person gave the same speech each time, just the introduction identifying his job differed. Many other studies have reached the same conclusion (Aronson, 1995). Our perception of the credibility of the speaker has a great deal to do with the persuasiveness of the communication.

   But credibility should not be confused in the previous example with being highly educated, intelligent, high in status, or even nice. The key is whether the speaker is a credible source of information *about the specific argument being presented.* Elaine Walster and her colleagues performed a clever experiment that forcefully makes this point (Walster, Aronson, & Abrahams, 1966). Individuals were given newspaper clippings of interviews with either a mobster or a politician. Half of the research participants read clippings that argued for more lenient treatment of criminals by the courts, and half read arguments for stricter treatment. When the mobster argued for more lenient treatment, he was completely ineffective and, in fact, slightly swayed attitudes in the opposite direction. When the mobster argued for *stricter* treatment, however, he was as persuasive as the politician. Apparently, the reasoning was that if a criminal (who knows about crime and would not personally benefit from stricter enforcement) thinks we need stricter enforcement of the laws, then it must be so.

sleeper effects
According to Hovland, the potential for low-credibility speakers to influence opinion after a period of time.

In general, the more credible the speaker, the more persuasive the message. But Carl Hovland has qualified this conclusion with the identification of what he called **sleeper effects** (Hovland & Weiss, 1951). Although attempts at persuasion by speakers who are low in credibility are ineffective at first, their messages tend to become more persuasive over time. This is because people tend to forget what speaker presented what message. If you forget that a low credibility speaker presented a certain message, then later on that message will not seem so unbelievable.

Attractive, popular, or famous speakers tend to be more persuasive than unattractive speakers. But their persuasiveness seems to be limited to relatively unimportant issues.

2. *Attractiveness.* Other things being equal, a speaker who is attractive, popular, famous, and likable will be more effective in changing our opinions than an unattractive speaker. That is why Cindy Crawford and Bo Jackson are paid enormous sums to endorse products in commercials and I am not. Fortunately, the persuasiveness of attractive speakers seems to be limited to relatively unimportant issues—but that includes almost everything that advertisers want us to buy (Aronson, 1995; Chaiken & Eagly, 1983).

3. *Intent.* Speakers are generally less persuasive if they obviously intend to change your opinion, particularly if the speaker has something to gain by changing your opinion (Aronson, 1992). If a real estate agent tells you that a lot he wants you to buy is going to rise dramatically in value, you might not believe him. On the other hand, if you overhear two realtors at a cocktail party say the same thing, the message would probably be more persuasive because no one is trying to convince you or make a commission from the sale. That is the rationale behind the "hidden camera" testimonials that are included in some television commercials. Since the people supposedly do not know they are on camera, they do not seem to be trying to sell us anything.

Characteristics of the Message

In addition to the qualities of the speaker, the characteristics of the message are also important determinants of persuasiveness.

1. *Fear appeals.* Are messages that arouse fear more persuasive than unemotional ones? Adolf Hitler appealed strongly to the fears and frustrations of the German people in the speeches he gave to rally support behind his Nazi party. Were the emotions he aroused part of the reason for his success? The American Cancer Society uses scare tactics in some of their ads to convince people to stop smoking. Are they going about it in the right way?

   Considerable evidence suggests that communications that arouse fear—such as graphic pictures of rotten teeth and gums in messages urging proper dental care—are more effective than the same messages without the fear-provoking images. Fear can enhance the persuasiveness of a communication, but only under certain circumstances (Mewborn & Rogers, 1979; Rogers, 1975). Listeners will respond favorably to a fear-inducing persuasive communication only if (a) the emotional appeal is a relatively strong one (but not too strong), (b) the listeners think that the fearful outcome (such as rotten teeth or lung cancer) is likely to happen to them, and (c) the message offers an effective way of avoiding the fearful outcome (such as an easy way to stop smoking). If all of these elements are present, emotional appeals can be highly persuasive.

2. *Two-sided arguments.* There are two sides to most arguments. If, for example, we use more coal in generating electric power, we will reduce our dependence on foreign oil and may be able to keep utility costs from rising as rapidly as in the past. That is good. But if we burn more coal, we will also increase pollution of the atmosphere, damage a great deal of land and water in the process of strip mining, and lose lives during the mining process. That is obviously bad. If you were trying to convince Congress to support the use of greater amounts of coal, would it be more effective to tell them just the good side of the argument, or both sides?

   There is no simple answer to this question. In part, it depends on how favorable the audience is to your position before you start talking. If the audience is leaning in your favor or has information only about your position, your message will be more persuasive if you just tell them about the benefits of burning coal. Telling them about the negative side to the argument may just lose you some supporters. But if your audience is initially unfavorable to your position or is knowledgeable about both sides of the issue, it's generally better to give them both sides of the argument. That will make you seem more credible and less biased (Baron & Byrne, 1982). So the next time somebody does an admirable job of presenting both sides of an issue, you may be dealing with a strong believer in honesty and the democratic process, but you may just be listening to a shrewd operator who is trying to change your mind.

3. *Message framing.* If you will recall from chapter 7 on cognition (p. 250), the way in which problems are presented to us in words—or *framed*—strongly influences how we solve those problems. Humans are so influenced by the wording of problems that we often reach very different solutions to exactly the same problem if it is framed differently. New research suggests that the same appears to be true of persuasive communications—framing the same message in different ways can sometimes make all the difference.

   An excellent and inherently important example has been provided by psychologists Beth Meyerowitz and Shelly Chaiken (1987). They compared the persuasiveness of two messages designed to encourage college-age women to conduct breast self-examinations. Two groups of women read a three-page pamphlet on breast cancer and self-examinations. Their pamphlets were identical except for several statements. One group read statements framed to emphasize the *gains* of breast self-examination:

   > By doing breast self-examination now, you can learn what your normal healthy breasts feel like so that you will be better prepared to notice any small, abnormal changes that might occur as you get older. Research shows that women who do breast self-examination have an increased chance of finding a tumor in the early, more treatable stage of the disease (p. 504).

   The other group read statements framed to emphasize the *loss* involved in not conducting breast self-examination:

   > By not doing breast self-examination you will not learn what your normal, healthy breasts feel like so that you will be ill-prepared to notice any small, abnormal changes that might occur as you get older. Research shows that women who do not do breast self-examination have a decreased chance of finding a tumor in the early, more treatable stage of the disease (p. 504).

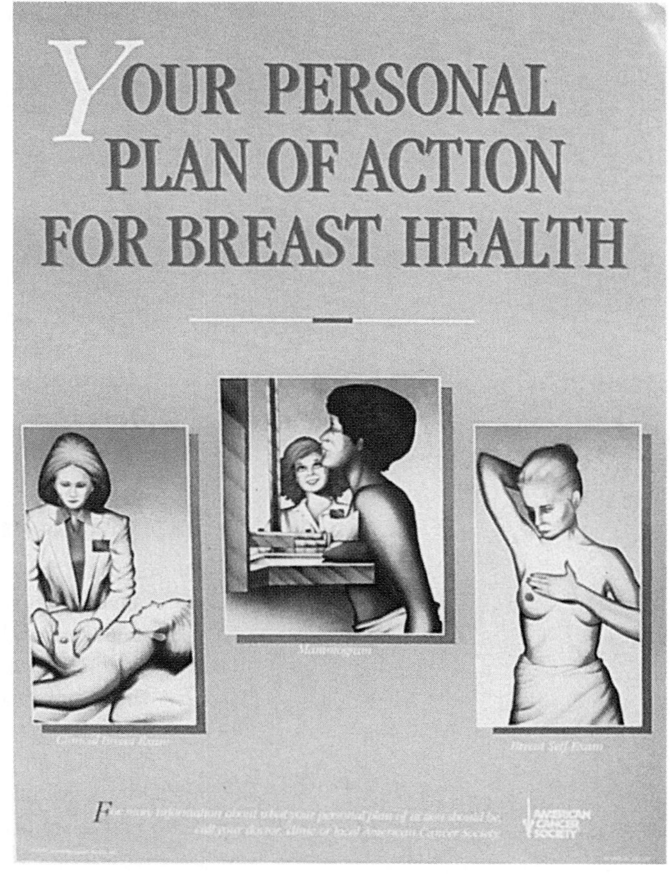

Do messages persuade women to conduct breast self-examination? It depends on how the message is framed.

Four months later, the women were interviewed to determine if the messages had had any positive effects. The results showed that the second message, framed in terms of potential loss, was more effective than the first version. Women reading the loss-framed message had much more positive attitudes toward breast self-examination and were almost twice as likely to have practiced it. Women reading the pamphlet framed in terms of potential gains were no more likely to engage in breast self-examination than a group that had not read either pamphlet.

Interestingly, the two pamphlets did not arouse different amounts of fear, so we cannot conclude that this is just another example of the greater effects of fear-arousing communications. Too little research has been done at this point on message framing to consider it to be a general principle of persuasive communication, but it is a promising new area of research. It also helps us make the point that effective persuasion is not just the result of *what* you say, but *how* you say it.

Characteristics of the Listeners

In addition to qualities of the speaker and the message, certain characteristics of the listeners help determine how persuasive an argument will be.

1. *Intelligence.* Less intelligent people are generally easier to persuade. The exception is when the message is complex and difficult to understand; under this condition, more intelligent listeners are easier to persuade (Rhodes & Wood, 1992).
2. *Need for social approval.* Some people have a greater need for social approval (a need to be approved of or liked by others) than other people do. People with a high need for social approval are generally easier to persuade than people who are low in this need (Baron & Byrne, 1982).
3. *Self-esteem.* Individuals whose self-esteem is moderate (have opinions of themselves that are about as positive as most people's) are generally easier to convince than people with either high self-esteem or low self-esteem (Rhodes & Wood, 1992; Zellner, 1970). Persons with high self-esteem are generally very confident of their opinions and difficult to influence. Persons with low self-esteem, in contrast, tend not to pay attention to the communication enough to be swayed. For example, a person with a very low opinion of himself might hear a speech on financing public schools and become lost in his own thoughts about his own poor educational performance (Rhodes & Wood, 1992).
4. *Audience size.* People are generally easier to persuade when they are listening to the message in a group rather than alone. And bigger crowds lead to greater persuasion than smaller ones (Newton & Mann, 1980).
5. *Gender.* Early studies on persuasion suggested that females were more persuadable than men. However, these studies were biased, using messages that were of greater interest to men. Later studies controlling for this interest variable show that there are no differences in persuadability between men and women (Eagly, 1978).

Techniques of Persuasion

Some people are better at persuasion than other people are. This is partly because they have the characteristics of persuasive speakers, and partly because they understand the characteristics of the message and the audience just described—they know how to pitch the most persuasive argument to their audience. But persuasive people—from politicians to salespeople—also often know and use some simple *techniques of persuasion.* As you read, try to recall if these techniques have been used on you by salespeople.

A classic technique of persuasion is the *foot-in-the-door technique.* The person first makes a small, reasonable request. After you agree to that request, however, he or she follows up with a larger request. If someone called you at home and said that she was a researcher at another university who would like to come over and inspect your home apartment, would you agree to let her in? Most people would be reluctant to agree, but people who first agree to answer a few questions over the telephone are more likely to allow researchers to inspect their homes. Agreeing to one small request makes us more likely to agree to a second larger request.

The *low-ball technique* is similar to the foot-in-the-door. First, you are offered a very reasonable deal. When you accept it, the deal is changed—for the worse. This is a favorite of some auto salespeople. First, they get you to commit to a particular car for a fair price. While you're dreaming of driving this wonderful car, you get the bad news that the salesperson forgot to figure in the delivery charge and the undercoating. Now the car costs more than you thought—do you still buy it? This technique of persuasion works more often than not—most people don't walk away from the deal (Burger, 1986).

Behavior and Attitude Change: Cognitive Dissonance Theory

As we have seen, persuasion is an important source of attitude change, but the discrepancy that often exists between our attitudes and behavior is another key cause of changed attitudes. Even though attitudes are partially defined in terms of a disposition to behave, there is sometimes a great difference between our attitudes and our behavior. For example, during the Vietnam War, many men who held attitudes that were strongly opposed to the war obeyed their draft orders and became a part of the war. Similarly, opinion pollsters know that not everyone who has a favorable attitude toward a product will actually buy it.

An interesting point is that when behavior and attitudes are inconsistent, the attitudes often change to match the behavior *rather than the other way around.* Leon Festinger (1957) proposed the theory of **cognitive dissonance** to explain the tendency of attitudes to sometimes shift to be consistent with behavior. This theory, which has sparked some of the greatest controversy and most interesting research in social psychology, states that inconsistencies between attitudes and behavior are uncomfortable. This discomfort motivates people to do what they can to reduce the discomfort, or *dissonance.*

cognitive dissonance
(dis´so-nans) The discomfort that results from inconsistencies between attitudes and behavior.

For example, if you smoke cigarettes (behavior), and you know that cigarette smoking is the leading cause of lung cancer and other horrible diseases (attitude), your behavior and attitude would be inconsistent, which would produce dissonance. Dissonance theory predicts that either your attitude or your behavior will change to reduce the dissonance (see figure 15.3). You could change the behavior and quit smoking, but that is often very difficult for smokers. Unfortunately, human beings usually reduce dissonance in the easiest way possible. In this case, it might be easier to change your attitude toward smoking. How many smokers do you know who say that the research linking cancer and smoking is faulty, or who say, "So what if smoking causes cancer, I'll die of something anyway?" These are irrational and self-defeating arguments, but they are sadly effective ways of reducing dissonance.

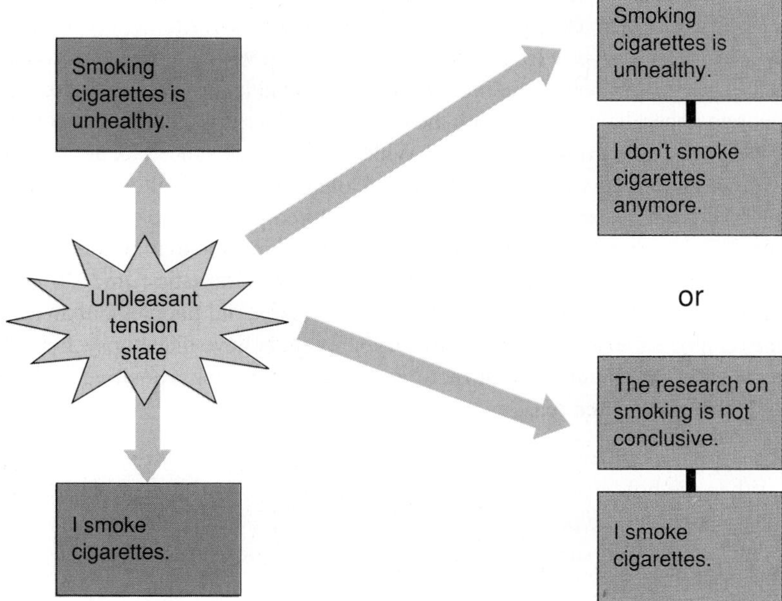

FIGURE 15.3
Cognitive dissonance: If attitudes and behavior are inconsistent, dissonance is aroused. To reduce this unpleasant state, either attitudes or behaviors change to be consistent with one another.

Festinger and other social psychologists have tested the theory of cognitive dissonance in a large number of experiments. One of the best known (Festinger & Carlsmith, 1959) involved asking research participants to perform a boring spool-stacking and peg-turning task for an hour. Afterward, the participants were each asked to tell the next person that the task was an interesting one. Half of the individuals were offered $20 to say that the task was interesting, and half were offered $1. A third group of individuals stacked spools but were not asked to say anything to the next research participant. Later, all of the participants were asked how interesting they really thought the task was.

Which group do you think reported the most favorable attitude toward the task? Perhaps surprisingly—but just as predicted by cognitive dissonance theory—the most positive attitudes were expressed by the group offered only $1. The group offered $20 was not placed in a state of dissonance: "the task was really boring, but I'll lie to the next person to get the $20." The group offered $1 was placed in a state of dissonance, however; there was no good explanation for their stating an opinion about the task that was inconsistent with their attitude, so their attitudes improved to be more consistent with their behavior.

Cognitive dissonance is relevant to more than just our attitudes about stacking spools (Cooper & Mackie, 1983). For example, university students who supported Ronald Reagan in the 1980 presidential election were the research participants in this experiment. They were asked to write an essay favoring an issue that Ronald Reagan opposed (federally sponsored health care) or an essay supporting the candidacy of Reagan's democratic opponent, Jimmy Carter. Half of the students were given very little choice about writing the essays. This group could be expected to experience little cognitive dissonance ("I wrote an essay that was contrary to what I believe, but I had to do it"). The other group of students was given much more choice as to whether or not the students would write the essay. These students were likely to experience considerable cognitive dissonance, since they wrote an essay favoring something that they opposed even though they did not have to do so. As Festinger would have predicted, attitudes toward Jimmy Carter and federally sponsored health care changed very little in the low-cognitive dissonance group (the individuals given little choice about writing the essays), but changed significantly more in the high-cognitive dissonance group (the ones given more choice). When the behavior of writing the essays created cognitive dissonance, attitudes changed to be more consistent with the behavior.

It's a little scary, isn't it? You probably thought your attitudes were always thoughtfully arrived at and based on reality. If Festinger is right, they may sometimes reflect nothing more than an escape from cognitive dissonance.

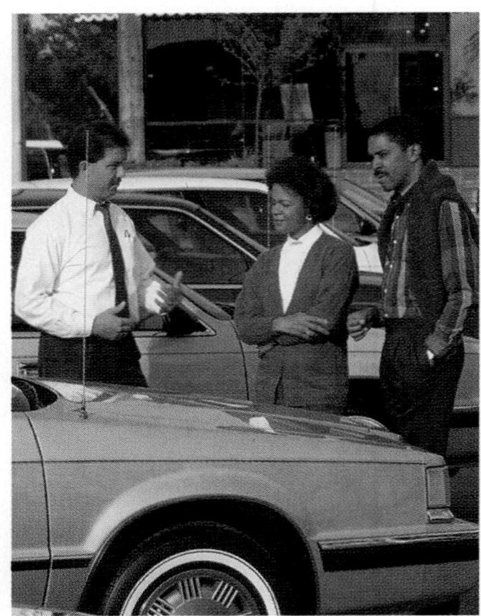

Stereotyping people, such as the "typical" salesperson, detracts from our ability to treat members of a group as individuals and leads to faulty attributions.

Prejudice and Stereotypes

Of all the attitudes that we hold about other people, the kind that is most worthy of improved understanding is prejudice. **Prejudice** is a harmful attitude based on inaccurate generalizations about a group of people based on their skin color, religion, sex, age, or any other noticeable difference. In some way, however, the difference is believed by the prejudiced person to imply something negative about the entire group ("They're all lazy, or hysterical, or pushy").

The inaccurate generalization on which the prejudice is based is called a **stereotype.** We all hold stereotypes of other groups of people. What does a "rock star" look and act like? If you were producing a movie, would you cast Bob Dole or Barbara Walters in the role of a rock star? You wouldn't because neither of them fits the stereotyped image of rock stars. What are Russians like? Do you have a stereotyped view of them? Think about it for a second. Would you cast Goldie Hawn as a Russian army officer in a serious dramatic film? Do you hold stereotypes of women, men, Cambodians, African Americans, old people, Cubans?

Stereotypes can be either negative or positive (you might believe that all psychology textbook authors are charming, witty, and attractive), but all stereotypes, positive or negative, are inherently harmful for three reasons.

prejudice
A harmful attitude based on inaccurate generalizations about a group of people.

stereotype
An inaccurate generalization upon which a prejudice is based.

1. *Stereotypes take away our ability to treat each member of a group as an individual.* When we hold a stereotyped view of a group, we tend to treat each member of that group as if the person has the exact characteristics of the stereotype, whether or not he or she really has those characteristics. Even when the

stereotype is partially based on fact, many members of the group will differ from the stereotype in significant ways. Take the view that many of us have of the Chinese: One aspect of the stereotype is that they are highly intelligent. Although it's true that *on the average* Chinese do score slightly higher than whites on some specific measures of intelligence, not all Chinese are highly intelligent. If a teacher's expectations for a Chinese child of below-average intelligence were based on this stereotype, the child might be criticized for not living up to his or her supposed high intelligence when the child was, in fact, performing up to his or her ability. Stereotyped beliefs that an ethnic group is low in intelligence can have even more serious consequences in limiting the educational and occupational opportunities of members of that group.

2. *Stereotypes lead to narrow expectations for behavior.* Our stereotypes lead us to expect the members of the stereotyped group to behave in certain ways. For example, we expect women to be gentle, nurturing, caring, and cooperative, but we expect men to be competitive, ambitious, aggressive, and strong. Individuals of either sex who do not conform to these expectations are viewed as abnormal and are often the objects of anger or ridicule. Thus, stereotypes can be a limiting force for persons who do not conform to the narrow expectations for their group (gender, ethnicity, age, etc.).

3. *Stereotypes lead to faulty attributions.* As we saw earlier, **attribution theory** is based on the idea that humans tend to try to explain why things happen, that is, attribute them to some cause. One of the things that we are most fond of doing is explaining behavior, both others and our own. One of our friends has just invited herself over for dinner for the third time this month—why? Is she broke? Is she a moocher? Does she just like our company? According to attribution theory, we tend to attribute all behavior to some cause.

   Our stereotypes influence the attributions that we make about other people's behavior. As Elliot Aronson (1992) points out, if a prejudiced white man sees an overturned trash can and garbage strewn around the yard of a white family, he is apt to attribute the mess to a stray dog looking for food. But if he sees the same thing in the yard of an African-American family, he would more likely attribute it to their supposed lazy, slovenly ways.

   These faulty attributions have the effect of deepening and strengthening our prejudices as we keep "seeing" evidence that "supports" our stereotypes and rejecting evidence that is contrary to them. For more on the harmful effects of stereotypes, see Application of Psychology: Gender Stereotypes–Gender Discrimination in the Workplace at the end of this chapter.

attribution theory
(ah-tri-bu´shun) The theory that people tend to look for explanations for their own behavior and that of others.

Causes of Stereotypes and Prejudice

If we are to have any hope of reducing prejudice, it is essential to understand the causes of these harmful attitudes. Social psychologists have proposed four different explanations for why prejudice arises:

1. *Realistic conflict.* The *realistic conflict theory* suggests that people who are competing for scarce resources, such as jobs, food, and territory, come to view others in increasingly negative ways (White, 1977). Although this theory may explain many instances of prejudice, prejudice often exists when there is no conflict over resources.

2. *Us versus them.* Another source of prejudice is the tendency people have to divide the world into two groups—*us versus them* (Turner et al., 1987). Our group becomes the "in-group," and those who are excluded become the "out-group." In a classic study, Sherif and others (1967) randomly divided middle-class 11- and 12-year-old boys of the same race into two groups: the Rattlers and the Eagles. After a series of activities designed to promote in-group solidarity and between-group competition, the rival groups began to engage in fighting

and name calling—they developed prejudices about one another even though the groups had been created randomly. Fortunately, the experimenters were able to restore goodwill among the boys by involving them in tasks requiring cooperation.

3. *Social learning.* Like any other kind of attitude, it is clear that prejudice can be learned from others. When we observe the stereotypes and prejudices expressed by parents, friends, teachers, and the media, we are likely to adopt the same prejudices.

Combating Prejudice

Prejudice is harmful to the human race. But is there anything that can be done about it? There are some effective antidotes:

1. *Recognize prejudice.* Most people believe that they are not prejudiced. We tend to view any negative attitudes we hold as true and justifiable. The first and most important step in reducing prejudice is to become aware of our own prejudices and their harmful consequences (Aronson, 1995).
2. *Control automatic responses.* It is not easy to rid yourself of prejudices that took a lifetime to acquire, even if you sincerely want to. Often the difference between a person who acts in an overtly prejudiced way and a person who does not is simply making the effort to control automatic reactions, however (Devine, 1996). Imagine that a student in one of your classes asks you if she could borrow your notes from the last class. She says that she missed the class because she was sick. If she were a member of an ethnic group that your parents always said was lazy, you might immediately think, "I'll bet she was just too lazy to come to class." People who are genuinely trying to reject prejudice, however, control those immediate prejudice reactions and deal with others on their own merits—not on the basis of automatic prejudice.
3. *Increase contact among prejudiced groups.* Prejudice can sometimes be reduced by increasing direct contact with people from other groups (Stephan, 1987). As most people who attended multiethnic schools can tell you, however, simple direct contact with other ethnic groups is not enough to reduce prejudice. For the direct contact to work, it must occur under certain conditions.

Although prejudice can sometimes be reduced through increasing contact among ethnic groups, simple direct contact, such as attending a multiethnic school, is not enough.

First, the two groups must be approximately *equal in status.* For example, if two groups of accountants from two different ethnic groups spend time together, their prejudice may decrease, but if accountants from one ethnic group spend time with unskilled laborers from another ethnic group, there is little likelihood that the prejudice will diminish. Similarly, the environment in which the two groups interact should be one that encourages group equality. The interactions that occur between managers of one race and employees of another race will not decrease prejudice.

Second, prejudice between groups will decline only if the group members *view each other as typical of their respective groups*—not as exceptions to the rule. There will be no improvement in relations if the members of one group think "This person is pretty darn smart—not like the others."

Third, when two groups who are prejudiced against one another interact, their prejudice will decrease if they are engaged in *cooperative rather than competitive tasks.* If a city were trying to decrease prejudice among teenagers of two different ethnic groups by bringing them together in a basketball league, they should mix the ethnic groups on the same teams, not put them on opposing teams. Cooperation builds respect, competition maintains prejudice.

Finally, *the contact should be informal* so that one-on-one interactions can occur. Formal interactions among employees of different ethnic groups are not as beneficial as the time spent together on breaks or after work.

Review

Attitudes are a focus of research for social psychologists because they play a key role in the interactions among people: People influence our attitudes, and those attitudes, in turn, are reflected to some extent in the way that we interact with others. They are defined in terms of three components: beliefs, feelings, and dispositions to behave. Attitudes appear to be learned, sometimes through direct experience with the object of our attitude and sometimes from others.

Attitudes are subject to change after they have been formed. One common form of attitude change is through direct persuasion by others. Nearly every day someone tries to persuade us to change our attitudes or behavior. The effectiveness of these attempts to influence depends on qualities of the speaker, the message, and the listener. Speakers are more influential when they appear credible, are attractive, and do not appear to be trying to influence us for their own personal gain. We are most likely to be influenced by fear-inducing messages if the fear appeal is strong, if the listener thinks the fearful outcome is likely, and if reasonable ways of avoiding the fearful outcome are presented. Messages that present some information favoring both sides of the argument are more persuasive to listeners who are knowledgeable about both sides of an issue and are initially opposed to the message. The way that a message is framed can affect persuasion. And listeners tend to be more easily persuaded when they are less intelligent, have a high need for social approval, are somewhat low in self-esteem, and are in large groups. Gender is not related to persuadability, however.

Discrepancies between our behavior and attitudes provide another potent source of attitudes. Sometimes there is a big difference between the attitudes that we express and the way we behave. Under some circumstances, changes in behavior that create a discrepancy between behavior and attitudes will be followed by a change in attitudes that makes the attitudes consistent with behavior again. This is most likely to occur when there is no obvious external cause of the change in behavior. Cognitive dissonance theory explains this change in attitude by stating that the discrepancy between behavior and attitudes creates an uncomfortable state. This discomfort is reduced when the attitudes change to fit the behavior.

Prejudice is a negative attitude based on inaccurate generalizations about a group of people. These inaccurate generalizations, called stereotypes, are inherently harmful because they make it difficult to evaluate members of that group on an individual basis and lead to faulty generalizations about their behavior. At times prejudice can be reduced if people become aware of their prejudices, control automatic prejudicial reactions, and interact more with members of groups against whom they are prejudiced under positive conditions. Increased interaction will decrease prejudice only when the interactions are among persons of equal status, those involved in the interactions view each other as typical of their respective groups, the interactions are cooperative rather than competitive, and the interactions are informal.

Thinking Critically About Psychology

1. If you were trying to convince others to donate money to your favorite cause, how would you use the information contained in this section?

2. Design a program that might reduce racial prejudice in your old high school.

Check Your Learning

To be sure that you have learned the key points from the preceding section, cover the answers below and try to answer each question. If you give an incorrect answer to any question, return to the page given next to the correct answer to see why your answer was not correct.

1. Attitudes consist of three components: ________________ , ________________ , and ____________________ .

2. Which of the following speakers would be the least persuasive?

   a. a speaker who intends to persuade you, and you know it
   b. a credible speaker
   c. an attractive speaker
   d. all of the above

Check Your Learning—continued

3. Two-sided arguments are most persuasive when
   - **a.** the audience knows only one side of the argument.
   - **b.** the audience knows both sides of the argument.
   - **c.** the audience leans against your side of the argument.
   - **d.** both b and c.

4. Prejudices are harmful attitudes based on inaccurate generalizations known as
   - **a.** attributions.
   - **b.** stereotypes.
   - **c.** negativities.
   - **d.** all of the above.

Correct Answers

1. beliefs, feelings, dispositions to behave (p. 536), **2.** a (p. 538), **3.** d (p. 539), **4.** b (p. 542).

INTERPERSONAL ATTRACTION: FRIENDSHIP AND LOVE

Who are your friends? Why do you suppose you became friends with them rather than with other people you know? Are you in love with someone, or have you ever been in love? What attracted you to him or her and made you experience such intense feelings? Friendship and love are powerful social phenomena that touch all of our lives in one way or another. As such, they have been of special interest to social psychologists. In this section we look at variables that influence our perception of others, the role played by attribution processes in person perception, the qualities of others that make them attractive to us, and the factors involved in maintaining personal relationships.

Person Perception

person perception
The process of forming impressions of others.

The first step toward understanding why we are attracted to one person rather than another is to understand something about the process of **person perception.** What factors are important in the way we perceive others? We seem to go through a complex process of "cognitive algebra" to reach an average of all the many factors that enter into our perceptions of others—with some factors contributing more to the average than others (Fiske, 1993; Kaplan, 1975). We sum up a person as if we assign a weight to each person's positive and negative characteristics in accordance with how important that characteristic is to us, and then we add them all together to arrive at a total perception of the person. But as the following sections show, the process of person perception is complicated further by the ways we gather and use information about others.

Negative Information: The Bad Outweighs the Good

Other things being equal, we tend to assign higher weights to negative than to positive information (Hamilton & Zanna, 1972). Put yourself in this situation: You are a person who values warmth, physical attractiveness, and honesty in others. You meet a person in class whom you find extremely warm and attractive; you have an enjoyable conversation with him after class, but during the course of the conversation he asks you to help him think of a lie to tell his girlfriend explaining where he has been. Your opinion of him will probably become quite negative if honesty is really important to you. The fact that he is being dishonest with his girlfriend will overshadow his positive characteristics. Most of us will pass up a delicious-looking cake if we know it contains even a small amount of rat poison.

Primacy Effects: The Importance of First Impressions

Our first impressions are usually very important in the person perception process. When you pause for a moment and think about this, it's quite disturbing. A factor that is irrelevant to the nature of the person we are perceiving—the order in which we learn information about that person—can greatly influence our perception of that person. All of us have our good days and bad days, and it's a shame that the perception that others form of us is influenced so much by whether they form their first impression of us on a good or a bad day.

The first information that we are exposed to about a person tends to be given greater weight than later information (Asch, 1946; Belmore, 1987; Hovland, 1957). This is called the **primacy effect.** If you were introduced to Barbara right after you heard her deliver a polished and interesting talk to your sales group on the importance of ethics in business, your impression would probably be quite positive. Later, if you ran into her in a bar sitting alone, looking forlorn, disheveled, and half-drunk, you would be seeing a very different side of Barbara. But since your initial impression of her was favorable, there would be a strong tendency for you to ignore or "explain away" this new information ("Something awful must have happened to Barbara to make her act this way").

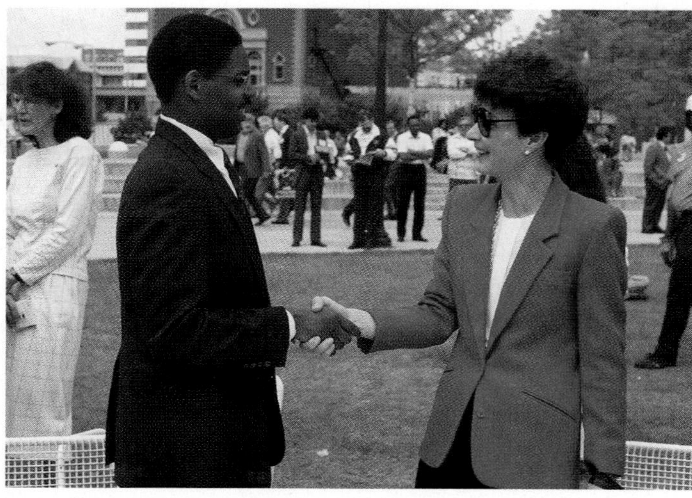

First impressions are often given greater weight than later information in the person perception process.

Suppose, however, that seeing Barbara in the bar was your *first* exposure to her. In that case, your first impression of her would be negative and would tend to dominate your perception of her even after you were exposed to more positive information about her later. If your second meeting with her was hearing her lecture on business ethics, you would tend to discount the positive impression she was giving in that encounter ("She's holding herself together pretty well today—I bet most people here don't know she's really a drunken slob").

primacy effect
The tendency for first impressions to heavily influence opinions about other people.

First impressions (primacy effects) are not always of overriding importance, however. Their impact is greatly reduced under three conditions.

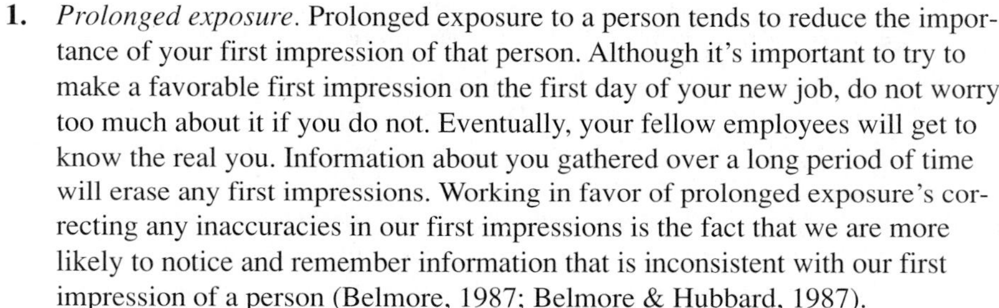

1. *Prolonged exposure.* Prolonged exposure to a person tends to reduce the importance of your first impression of that person. Although it's important to try to make a favorable first impression on the first day of your new job, do not worry too much about it if you do not. Eventually, your fellow employees will get to know the real you. Information about you gathered over a long period of time will erase any first impressions. Working in favor of prolonged exposure's correcting any inaccuracies in our first impressions is the fact that we are more likely to notice and remember information that is inconsistent with our first impression of a person (Belmore, 1987; Belmore & Hubbard, 1987).
2. *Passage of time.* Like anything else, first impressions tend to be forgotten over time. If a substantial period of time passes between first and subsequent impressions, the more recent impression will be of greater importance. So if you flubbed your first attempt to favorably impress that gorgeous person, wait awhile and try again later.
3. *Knowledge of primacy effects.* When people are warned to avoid being influenced by first impressions, the primacy effect can be reduced (Hovland, 1957). Personnel managers and others to whom accurate person perception is important are educated to the dangers of primacy effects and are often able to eliminate them from their perceptions.

Emotions and Person Perception

Another important factor in person perception that can be irrelevant to the nature of the person about whom we are forming an impression is our emotions. The emotional state that we are in when we meet a person has a great deal to do with our liking that person. Positive emotional states lead to greater attraction to others than negative emotions do. William Griffith and Russell Veitch (1971) had a radio news broadcast turned on as individuals waited for an experiment in interpersonal attraction to begin. The broadcast was actually taped beforehand so that half of the participants heard a depressing broadcast and half heard happy news. Afterward, the participants hearing the sad news did not like the strangers they had met in the experiment as well as the persons who had heard the good news. These findings were confirmed in a well-designed study by Joseph Forgas and Gordon Bower (1987), who also found that we are better able to remember positive information about another person when we met him or her in a good mood and better able to remember negative information when we meet another person in a bad mood. The effects of mood on person perception are likely, then, to be relatively enduring.

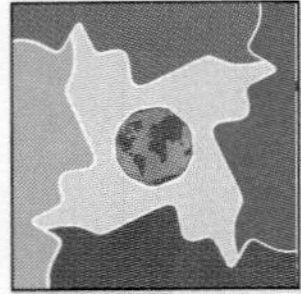

HUMAN DIVERSITY

Stereotypes About College Students with Physical Challenges

Most Americans are "able-bodied" persons with no serious limitations on their ability to see, hear, speak, or move about. Many of us, however, are challenged by physical conditions that make these everyday activities more difficult or impossible. Like any group that is *different* from most of the people in society, persons with physical challenges are the subject of stereotypes, prejudices, limitations, and stigma. These factors can profoundly influence their lives.

An important study by Catherine Fichten and her colleagues at Dawson College found that able-bodied students' perceptions of peers with disabilities are quite different from these students' perceptions of themselves (Fichten, Robillard, Judd, & Amsel, 1989). Three groups of students participated in the study: wheelchair users, students with a visual impairment, and able-bodied students. They completed several questionnaires that measured self-concept, dating behavior, and anxiety in social situations. First they completed these questionnaires about themselves, and then completed the same measures in the way that they thought the other groups would respond.

Fichten and her colleagues found that able-bodied students and students with physical challenges viewed each other in stereotyped ways. For example, the able-bodied students believed that the students with physical challenges were more anxious about dating and dated less frequently than able-bodied students. In addition, the able-bodied students viewed the students who had physical challenges as nervous, unaggressive, insecure, dependent, and unhappy. The stereotyping was not all negative, however. Able-bodied students also viewed students with physical challenges as quiet, honest, softhearted, nonegotistical, and undemanding. The students with physical challenges held stereotypes about able-bodied students, too. They viewed the able-bodied students as demanding, argumentative, overconfident, phony, and complaining.

In most instances, however, the stereotyped perceptions were based on myths. For example, Fichten and her colleagues found no differences in either the number of dates or anxiety about dating reported by students with physical challenges and able-bodied students, even though the able-bodied students thought that students with physical challenges would be less satisfied with their dating. Similarly, although able-bodied students believed that the self-esteem scores of students with physical challenges were lower than their own, there were no actual differences in the self-esteem of able-bodied students, students who were visually impaired, or students who used wheelchairs. It is striking that even the students with physical challenges themselves sometimes believed the same myths about students with other physical challenges. Both able-bodied students and students with physical challenges attributed more "handicapped" stereotypes to students with physical challenges than to able-bodied students in the Fichten study.

The Americans with Disabilities Act of 1990 brought the needs of persons with physical challenges into the consciousness of people in the United States. It was designed to enable persons with physical challenges to gain access to public facilities and to the workplace. As is the case with other Civil Rights legislation, societal changes require more than just the passage of laws, however. If the stereotypes are to be reduced, able-bodied persons and persons with physical challenges must learn more about each other through extended contact under conditions of equal status. Hopefully, however, the laws that guarantee the rights of persons with physical challenges to education, employment, and recreation will create conditions under which persons with and without physical challenges can get to know each other as individuals. In time, such interactions may improve the degree to which people with disabilities will be able to participate fully in society without stereotypes and discrimination.

If you are not physically challenged yourself, what kinds of exposure have you had to persons who are? As you walk around your campus and your community today, notice how you react when you see a person with physical challenges. Do you react in the same way as to able-bodied persons? Can you see the influence of stereotypes in these reactions? How could you make it easier for persons with physical challenges at your school to interact with able-bodied students on an equal basis?

It is important to note that use of the term "physical disability" has been discouraged in recent years to emphasize the fact that the physical condition often does not disable the person in any absolute sense. Many persons prefer the more neutral term of "physically challenged." But some persons reject the newer term "physically challenged" as well, stating that they alone should decide whether or not their physical condition is "challenging" (Bregante, Martinez, & O'Toole, 1993).

Attribution Processes in Person Perception

The process of attribution that we first encountered at the opening of this chapter and again in the discussion of prejudice is also very much involved in the perception of other people. We try to understand the behavior of people (other people and ourselves) by attributing the behavior to various causes. The kinds of attributions that we make for the behavior of others have a great deal to do with the perceptions we form of them.

The attribution process is a step toward our ultimate goal in person perception. We want to know what other people are *really* like. We know how they behave, but what is the person behind the behavior like? We want to know about their motives, values, and traits. We make those judgments through the process of attribution. For example, Sharon's boss asks her to stay late for a dinner meeting with him. Why did he do that? Does he have an important assignment that he wants to discuss with her? Is she being considered for a promotion? Or is this leading to sexual harassment? The attribution that Sharon makes will strongly influence her perception of her boss.

Recall from earlier in this chapter that the attribution process is *biased,* however. Most importantly, we are biased toward making the *fundamental attribution error*—we tend to underestimate the impact of social situations on others, but not on ourselves (Heider, 1958). This means that we tend to form judgments about people based on their behavior in the situation in which we meet them, assuming that they are always the same. In fact, however, that "insensitive brute" might actually be a gentle and caring soul in most situations.

General Determinants of Interpersonal Attraction

Through the complicated process of person perception, a unique impression of each person is formed. But although person perception is a highly personal process, some *general* factors influence whether one person will be attracted to another. These include proximity, similar and complementary characteristics, competence, physical attractiveness, and mutual liking.

Proximity

An important, but not very romantic, cause of attraction is proximity, or geographical closeness. It's difficult to fall in love with someone you hardly ever spend time with. Physical closeness and the resulting interpersonal contact is essential to the development of attraction. You are more friendly with people who live next door to you than with people who live farther away. Why does this happen? Physical proximity increases interactions, and repeated exposure to people tends to increase liking (Zajonc, 1968). Perhaps you can remember a song you didn't like at first, but learned to like after hearing it played on the radio many times—it's the same with people.

Similar and Complementary Characteristics

In terms of interpersonal attraction, do "birds of a feather flock together" or do "opposites attract"? Are you more likely to be attracted to someone as a friend or lover who is similar to you in many ways or quite different from you? The answer is *both,* in different ways.

Jennifer probably values people who have an interest in exercise, nutrition, and philosophy because she is also interested in those things. It's enjoyable to have a friend to jog with, who pats you on the back for the healthy way you eat, and shares long, delicious philosophical discussions with you. In general, similarity is highly important in attractiveness. We tend to be most attracted to those people who have similar values, interests, and attitudes (Caspi & Herbener, 1990; Feingold, 1988).

Opposites can also attract, however, when the opposite characteristic *complements* or advantageously "fits" with one of our own characteristics. Jennifer might also be attracted to the fellow at the party tonight in part because he has an outgoing personality while she is more reserved. She may feel that she is a good listener who gets along better with talkative people than ones who are quiet like herself. And she may feel that when she is with an outgoing person at social gatherings he makes it easier for her to interact with other couples than a quiet man does. Similarly, a dominant person might prefer a submissive person, and a person who likes to nurture and "take care of" others might prefer someone who likes to be taken care of (Winch, 1958).

Another condition under which opposites attract is when people who are different from you *like* you (Aronson, 1995). It's more flattering and attractive to be liked by someone who holds opposite values and opinions than someone who holds similar ones (Jones, Bell, & Aronson, 1971). But take note that opposites usually do not attract; instead opposites usually repel in personal relationships. A person who intensely advocates liberal causes probably would not like a person who vocally supports conservative causes. And a highly religious person probably would not find a disdain for religion attractive in another person.

Competence

We tend to be more attracted to competent than to incompetent people. Intelligence, strength, social skill, education, and athletic prowess are generally thought of as attractive qualities. But people who are seen as *too* competent may suffer a loss in attractiveness, perhaps because it makes us uncomfortable to compare ourselves unfavorably with them. Elliot Aronson and associates conducted a clever experiment that demonstrates that it's best to be a *little* less than perfect (Aronson, Willerman, & Floyd, 1966). Participants listened to one of four audiotapes of people who were supposedly trying out to be members of their university's College Bowl quiz team. Two of the people scored over 90 percent correct on difficult questions and were portrayed as being honor students, athletes, and active in student activities. The other two answered 30 percent of the questions and were portrayed as average, unathletic students. Near the end of the tape one of the superior students and one of the average students blundered—each spilled a cup of coffee on himself. Who from this group do you think the participants rated as most attractive? The two superior students were rated higher than the two average students, but the superior student who committed the blunder was rated as most attractive of all. Apparently, the slightly clumsy pratfall made him more endearing to others. However, the blunder did not have the same positive effect for the average student: The average student who blundered was rated least attractive of all.

Physical attractiveness seems to be the most important factor in the early stages of attraction between people.

Physical Attractiveness

Other things equal, people tend to be more attracted to physically beautiful people. In the absence of other information, we tend to like beautiful people more and think of them as nicer, better adjusted, more sexual, and more intelligent (Dion, 1980; Eagly, Ashmore, Makhijani, & Longo, 1991; Feingold, 1992b). Not only is physical attractiveness important, it seems to be the *most* important factor in the early stages of attraction.

Elaine Walster and colleagues randomly paired male and female college students for blind dates. They rated each student's physical attractiveness and gave them tests to measure attitudes, intelligence, and personality characteristics. After the blind dates, the students were asked how much they liked each other and whether they intended to go out on other dates with one another. The overwhelmingly important variable in determining attraction was physical attractiveness—more so than intelligence, personality, and attitudes. The couples who were most likely to like each other well enough to continue dating were the ones in which both the male and female rated each other as attractive (Walster, Aronson, Abrahams, & Rottman, 1966).

One of the key ways that physical attractiveness influences interpersonal attraction was demonstrated in an ingenious experiment (Snyder, Tauke, & Berscheid, 1977). Male and female college students played somewhat different roles in the study. Males were asked to participate in a study of how people get acquainted. They were asked to speak to a woman over a telephone (to rule out nonverbal communication), but each male was given written information describing the woman he was speaking to and a photograph of her.

The females in the study were paired randomly with the males on the other end of the telephone, but the information sheets and pictures had nothing to do with them. All of the information sheets seen by the males were the same, but half of the males saw a picture of a very attractive woman and half saw a picture of a much less attractive woman. After they had talked with her on the telephone, the men who thought they were talking to a beautiful woman rated her as being more sociable, poised, and humorous than did the men who thought they were talking to an unattractive woman. As in previous studies, greater physical attractiveness led to greater likability. But that's not the only interesting finding of this study.

When observers rated tape recordings of the males' conversations, they found that males who *thought* they were talking to a beautiful woman spoke to her in a more sociable way (e.g., warm, outgoing, interesting) and were rated as enjoying themselves more in the conversation. Thus, perceiving the woman as beautiful led the men to be more charming to her.

The females' recorded conversations were even more interesting. The women knew nothing about the pictures that the men were seeing, but when the man thought that the woman was beautiful, the women spoke in a more charming, confident manner and were rated as seeming to like the man more. Apparently, thinking the woman was beautiful led the man to treat her in a way that *induced her to act in a more likable way.* If Alan thinks he will like Eileen because she is pretty, he will probably speak to her in ways that will bring out her most likable side. It's a lovely self-fulfilling prophecy, *if* you happen to be physically attractive.

But don't despair; there may be some hope for the rest of us yet! While we might all prefer to be dating Mel Gibson or Michelle Pfeiffer, people tend actually to choose dates and mates who closely match themselves in degree of physical attractiveness (Berscheid, Dion, Walster, & Walster, 1971). What is more, physical beauty is a highly subjective quality. So, even if you do not think your next-door neighbor is much to look at, chances are that someone else will soon come along who thinks he or she is just beautiful.

Perhaps the nicest thing about physical attractiveness and liking, though, is that the relationship goes both ways. Not only is it true that we tend to like people better when we think they are beautiful, but as we get to like people better, we begin to think they are more beautiful (Langlois & Stephan, 1981). So to a certain extent, love *is* blind and beauty *is* in the eye of the beholder—and nothing could be nicer.

Mutual Liking

Let's end this discussion of factors involved in interpersonal attractiveness on an upbeat note. Liking often leads to liking in return. If Vicki likes Neal, she has made herself more attractive to Neal simply by liking him. Neal, if he is like most everyone else, will be more attracted to people who like him than to people who do not like him. Liking someone will not turn you into an irresistible beauty, but it will help.

One reason why this seems to be so is that liking someone actually makes you seem more *physically* attractive, especially if a little lust is thrown in. You have heard people say that a person is more beautiful when in love, and it's true. Your eyes are more attractive. The pupils are more dilated (opened) when you look at someone you find sexually attractive, and others find large pupils more attractive sexually (Hess, 1975). And your posture and movements are more attractive and seductive. In subtle ways, you are more physically alluring when you are attracted to another person.

Another reason that liking tends to lead to liking is that you are nicer to the people that you like, and being nicer makes you more attractive to them. A number of studies show, for example, that we tend to like people more when they praise us or when they have done favors for us. Favors and praise feel nice and we like the giver better for having given them to us. So, send him flowers or give her a compact disc—it might just tip the balance of love in your favor. As you might expect, there are limits on the impact of praise and favors. If they are excessive, and especially if the other person thinks you are insincere and have selfish motives for giving them, praise and gifts will not lead to increased liking and may even lessen the liking (Aronson, 1995).

Gender Differences in Interpersonal Attraction

It's a commonly held belief in our culture that men are not very interested in romantic love but, rather, enter into long-term relationships for the sex and the domestic help (cooking, cleaning, and mending). Women, in contrast, are viewed in our society as approaching relationships in a more emotional, romantic way. The results of surveys conducted during the 1960s, however, suggested that this popular stereotype not only is incorrect but has reality reversed. Men rated falling in love as being a more important reason for beginning a relationship than did women. Women saw other qualities of the relationship such as respect and support as being more important. In one survey, two-thirds of male unmarried college students said they would not marry unless they felt romantic love for their prospective wife, while less than one-fourth of college women felt that romantic love was a prerequisite for marriage (Hill, Rubin, & Peplau, 1976; Kephart, 1967).

However, more recent surveys suggest that things have changed in the United States concerning gender differences in valuing romantic love (Simpson, Campbell, & Berscheid, 1986). Today, the great majority of both women and men feel that being in love is necessary for marriage. Perhaps as women have come to feel less dependent on marriage for financial support, they have felt able to enter into marriage only when they are in love with their future partner.

This does not mean that men and women fall in love for all the same reasons, however. Alan Feingold (1990, 1992a) of Yale University has recently summarized the results of many studies on gender differences in romantic attraction. The evidence is clear that women place more emphasis on their romantic partner's intelligence, character, education, occupational status, ambition, and income than do men. These qualities are not unimportant to men, but they are comparatively more important to women. In contrast, there are no gender differences in how much sense of humor and a pleasant personality are valued in romantic relationships, but men place greater emphasis on physical attractiveness than do women (ah, men, when will we learn?). Again, it is not that physical attractiveness does not play a role in romantic attraction for women (it does), but women place considerably less emphasis on physical attractiveness than do men. Interestingly, these same results have been found in different generations in the United States and across a number of different cultures (Feingold, 1992a).

It is important to keep in mind, however, that there are large differences among the members of both genders. Perhaps the most striking thing about the cognitive algebra of person perception is that different people often seem to be using different equations! Whether a characteristic is considered positive or negative and how much weight it will carry in person perception differ markedly from individual to individual. Jennifer may feel that an interest in sports, nutrition, and philosophy, and an outgoing personality are all highly positive characteristics. Angela may feel that these same characteristics are not very important one way or another. And Lydia might find them all to be highly negative characteristics. If Jennifer, Angela, and Lydia were to meet a man with these characteristics at a party tonight, they would each form a very different perception of him. It's like that for everyone. Because different people evaluate the same characteristics in different ways, some people are going to love you, some are going to dislike you, and the rest will find you so-so.

Maintaining Relationships

We have talked about some of the factors that determine whether you will be attracted to another person. But how about the factors that are involved in maintaining relationships? Assuming that one of the people that you are attracted to becomes your friend, lover, or spouse, what things determine whether you and your partner will stay in the relationship? So many relationships that begin in joy end in a long cry. Why? Two of the major factors are the difference between what you expect to find in a relationship and what you actually find, and the degree to which the relationship is fairly balanced or equitable.

Expectations vs. Reality in Relationships

When you begin a relationship with someone you do not know very well, part of what you fall in love with is what you *expect* the person to be like. Some of these expectations may be based on good evidence. One of his friends has told you that he is an especially nice and fair person, so it's reasonable to expect him to be fair and nice to you. You know that he is in the same profession as you, so you can expect to be able to share your workday experiences easily with him. Other expectations are based on less evidence. He has behaved in a strong, self-assured way so far, so you assume that he will always be this way even though the biggest challenge you have seen him handle is the waiter's mistake of bringing tomato soup instead of minestrone. You *know* that he is a wonderful lover even though he has only just kissed you goodnight once. He dresses like an outdoorsman, so you expect him to love backpacking as much as you do. And he is well educated, so you feel sure he will share your love of serious literature.

Relationships that last tend to be based on realistic expectations and on the perception of equity in the relationship.

The point is that, even when your expectations are fairly well grounded, some of them will turn out to be incorrect. He will not be exactly like you expect him to be before the relationship begins. This is one primary reason why relationships end. If the other person turns out to be significantly different from the person you expected, you may be unwilling to stay in the relationship. This disappointment may not lead directly to an end of the relationship; it may affect the relationship indirectly. Disappointment can lead you to be an unenthusiastic or irritable partner, which can lead to discord and an unhappy ending of the relationship (Graziano & Musser, 1982).

Even when you know a person well before beginning a serious relationship, differences between expectations and reality can be a problem. One common source of unfulfilled expectations is the predictable shift from **passionate love** to **companionate love** (Hatfield, 1988). When two people first fall in love, they often feel intense passions that are a heady and magnificent mixture of romantic, sexual, and other feelings. Even in the most healthy and enduring relationships, however, passionate love gradually becomes companionate love—a less intense but wonderful blend of friendship, intimacy, commitment, and security. Although romantic and sexual emotions often continue to be an important part of companionate love, these feelings are almost inevitably much less intense.

passionate love
The mixture of romantic, sexual, and other feelings of love.

companionate love
The blend of friendship, intimacy, commitment, and security that generally develops after passionate love.

If one or both of the partners does not expect passionate love to change, or if the change takes place before expected, the reality of passionate love blending into companionate love can be difficult. On the other hand, if both partners truly want a long-term relationship (many people only stay in relationships as long as the passionate love remains, then leave feeling unfulfilled or hurt), and if the disappointment that often surrounds the lessening of romantic love is handled with compassion on both sides, the transition usually can be managed.

Finally, expectations about a love relationship can fail to match its reality because partners change over time. Sometimes, the outdoor person becomes a happy couch potato, and the party animal becomes a health-conscious jogging vegetarian. If children arrive, and if promotions are received (or not received), these and other changes can alter the reality of the relationship as well. If these changes in one's partner are not welcome, the reality of the changed relationship can be upsetting. Sometimes, however, a change in a partner can make a good relationship even better.

Equity in Relationships

Relationships are more likely to endure when the good things that we give to our partner are about equal to what our partner gives us. These good "things" that partners give to one another are many and varied. They include compliments, back rubs, help with homework, a day off without the kids, flowers, jokes, making love, a willingness to listen about a bad day, interesting meals, kisses, pats on the bottom, and interesting conversations. They also include things like physical attractiveness (a nice-looking person is enjoyable to look at), honesty, faithfulness, and integrity.

The commonsense idea that enduring relationships are ones in which the partners give and receive in equal proportion has been formalized and improved by social psychologists (Adams, 1965; Walster & Walster, 1978) under the name of **equity theory.** Equity theory states that partners will be comfortable in their relationship only when the ratio between their perceived contributions and benefits are equal. Equity theory is often summarized by the following equation:

equity theory
The theory that partners will be comfortable in their relationship only when the ratio between their perceived contributions and benefits is equal.

$$\frac{\text{Perceived benefits of person X}}{\text{Perceived contributions of person X}} = \frac{\text{Perceived benefits of person Y}}{\text{Perceived contributions of Person Y}}$$

These benefits and contributions cannot be easily translated into numerical terms, but suppose for a moment that person X perceives that she "gives" 10 things to the relationship, while person Y perceives that he only gives 5 things. Would this be an equitable relationship? It would be if person X perceived 10 benefits from the relationship while person Y perceived 5 benefits because the equation would be in balance.

$$\frac{10}{10} = \frac{5}{5}$$

There are two important points to notice in the equity theory equation: First, the benefits that the two people receive from one another do not have to be equal, but the *ratio* between their benefits and contributions must be equal. A person who both gives and receives a lot can be in an equitable relationship with a person who gives and receives much less.

Second, notice that the equation is written in terms of *perceived* benefits and contributions. The only person who can judge how much he or she is giving and receiving is the person himself or herself. An outside observer might see a relationship as being highly inequitable when the partners themselves are very happy with it. Tender lovemaking might be highly important to one person, but much less important than good cooking to someone else. Unfortunately, people tend to believe that the amount of "good things" that we ourselves should fairly receive is higher than the amount that we think that others should fairly receive (Messick & Sentis, 1979). If we are not careful to compensate for this natural perceptual distortion, it can lead us to perceive an inequity in our relationships when there is none at all.

If either member of a relationship perceives the relationship to be inequitable, that partner will either take steps to restore equity or will leave the relationship. Interestingly, we become uncomfortable in relationships either when we feel that we receive *too little* compared with what we give, *or* when we receive *too much* compared with what we give. In either case, we will be motivated to restore equity by giving more or less, or by asking (or in some other way inducing) the other person to give more or less.

Thinking Critically About Psychology

1. To what extent has it been true that "first impressions are lasting impressions" in your life?

2. What are the most important relationships in your life? Have you learned anything in this chapter that could help you enhance and prolong them?

Review

What determines which people we will like or love? Our perceptions of others can be thought of as being based on a complex cognitive algebra in which we reach a weighted average of all of the positive and negative characteristics we see in others. Person perception is complicated by several factors, however: Different people evaluate the same characteristics in a person in different ways, and our emotional state influences person perception; negative information about a person carries more weight than positive information; and first impressions usually are more important than later impressions.

Attribution plays an important role in our perceptions of others. We want to know what a person's enduring traits and motives are. We attribute the behavior of others to external causes (situational attributions) when it consistently occurs in only one kind of situation and they consistently react in the same way. Otherwise, we tend to attribute the behavior of others to their supposed traits and motives (dispositional attributions). We also tend to attribute our own behavior to dispositional causes, but mostly our desirable behavior. We tend to attribute our undesirable behavior to situational causes, although females are less likely to do this than males.

Although person perception is a highly complex and personal process, some general factors determine whether one person will be attracted to another. Other things being equal, you are more likely to be attracted to a person who has characteristics similar to yours or who has opposite characteristics that complement your own. Other factors in attractiveness include the other person's being competent (but not excessively competent), looking physically attractive, and liking and being nice to you.

Once two people are attracted to each other, a number of other factors are involved in whether the relationship will endure. We enter into relationships partly because of our

Review—continued

expectations as to what the other person will be like. Since those expectations are generally based on partial information, they are sometimes not met and the relationship fails. Relationships generally fail, too, when they are not equitable. In happy relationships, each person perceives a balance between what each person puts into the relationship and what each person gets out of it.

Check Your Learning

To be sure that you have learned the key points from the preceding section, cover the answers below and try to answer each question. If you give an incorrect answer to any question, return to the page given next to the correct answer to see why your answer was not correct.

1. The process of forming impressions of others is known as

a. person perception.
b. the primacy effect.
c. attribution theory.
d. the fundamental attribution error.

2. The impact of the primacy effect can be reduced under three conditions: ________________ , ________________ , and ________________ .

3. The fundamental attribution error refers to our tendency to give greater weight to __________ causes of behavior in others and to neglect __________ causes.

a. positive; negative
b. negative; positive
c. dispositional; situational
d. situational; dispositional

Correct Answers

1. a (p. 546), **2.** prolonged exposure, passage of time, knowledge of primacy effects (p. 547), **3.** c (p. 549).

APPLICATION OF PSYCHOLOGY

GENDER STEREOTYPES—GENDER DISCRIMINATION IN THE WORKPLACE

In 1982 Ann Hopkins was a successful consultant working for Price Waterhouse, one of the nation's "big eight" accounting firms, and she was up for possible promotion to a partnership in the firm. She had brought in $25 million dollars in business and had billed for more hours than the other 87 accountants who had been proposed for partner that year, all of whom were males. She had the praise of her clients and recommendations of supporters within the company who described her as hardworking, demanding, exacting, independent, self-confident, outspoken, assertive, and courageous. The decision regarding her partnership was postponed for a year, and the following year she was told that she would not be considered further for partnership.

Ms. Hopkins's detractors at Price Waterhouse portrayed her as being overbearing, arrogant, self-centered, and abrasive. In more specific terms, those who voted against her criticized her for being "macho" and suggested that she needed a "course at charm school." Indeed, one partner who favored her promotion suggested that her chances would improve if she would "walk more femininely, talk more femininely, dress more femininely, wear make-up, have her hair styled, and wear jewelry" (*Hopkins v. Price Waterhouse*, 1985, p. 1117).

In 1984 Ann Hopkins sued Price Waterhouse for violation of her civil rights under Title VII of the 1964 Civil Rights Act, which prohibits sex discrimination. Her former firm countered that she had not been denied a partnership because of her gender, but because she had problems in interpersonal skills. Nevertheless, she won her suit in federal court, and the decision was confirmed in both the Federal Court of Appeals and the U.S. Supreme Court. Federal Judge Gerhard Gesell stated in his 1990 opinion, "The firm of Price Waterhouse refused to make Ann Hopkins a partner. Gender-based stereotyping played a role in this decision" (*Hopkins v. Price Waterhouse,* 1990, p. 1).

the help of psychological research as evidence, A Hopkins successfully sued her employer for ge r discrimination.

Psychologist Susan T. Fiske testified on behalf of Ann Hopkins in this case, and because it was the first sex discrimination case in which psychological evidence on gender stereotyping had been introduced as evidence, the American Psychological Association filed a "friend of the court" brief that summarized what is known about gender discrimination. A full description of the court case and the brief have been published and make fascinating reading for anyone interested in the application of social psychology to real-world problems (Fiske, Bersoff, Borgida, Deaux, & Heilman, 1991).

If you recall from this chapter (p. 542), stereotypes are harmful because they lead us to treat all members in the groups as the same, lead to narrow expectations for the behavior of members of the group, and lead to inaccurate attributions. The courts found that these aspects of gender stereotyping led to discrimination in the partnership decision of Ann Hopkins.

The evidence presented by Susan Fiske as an expert witness pointed to these three sources of gender-based job discrimination. First, in studies that simulated hiring and promotion decisions in the workplace, job performances tended to be influenced by the stereotyped beliefs that we hold about the two genders. Males were viewed as more confident, influential, and deserving of respect than females, *even when the behavior of the females was exactly the same as the males* (Fiske et al., 1991). People see what they expect to see based on gender stereotypes in the workplace. Although the differences are not large, they are real. Gender stereotypes are especially potent in making hiring decisions when the gender of the job applicant is more obvious than her or his actual qualifications (Fiske et al., 1991).

Psychologist Susan T. Fiske testified as an expert on gender discrimination issues in the U.S. Supreme Court Case involving Ann Hopkins and Price Waterhouse Accounting Firm.

Second, the narrow expectations for appropriate behavior that gender stereotypes encourage can play a role in discrimination in the workplace. In other job simulation studies, women in leadership roles were given lower marks than males if their leadership was carried out in ways that fit the stereotype for males—directive or authoritarian leadership. In addition, the ratings of women were lower when they were in roles that are more typically held by men than women. Violating the expectations for your gender can be dangerous in the workplace. Again, the effect of gender stereotypes is not large in this context, but large enough to matter (Eagly, Makhijani, & Klonsky, 1992).

Third, a number of studies have shown that faulty attributions based on gender stereotypes operate in the workplace. The supervisors of male employees tend to attribute their successes to competence and ability, but they are more likely to attribute the successes of females to good luck, to their physical attractiveness, or, at best, to hard work (Fiske et al., 1991).

Dr. Fiske also presented evidence that the kind of gender discrimination that was alleged in Ms. Hopkins's suit was more likely to occur when the number of women is few, the criteria for evaluation are ambiguous, and the amount of factual information on the employee is small. The attorney for Ann Hopkins was able to argue successfully that all three of these conditions were true for Ann Hopkins.

The courts found that these negative aspects of gender stereotyping played at least some part in Ann Hopkins being denied a partnership. The evidence suggested to the court that her detractors gave her low marks because her behavior violated the expectations for women, and that these same traits would not have been grounds for denying a partnership to a male. The decision of the Supreme Court put it this way:

> An employer who objects to aggressiveness in women but whose positions require this trait places women in an intolerable Catch-22: out of a job if they behave aggressively and out of a job if they don't. Title VII [of the Civil Rights Act] lifts women out of this bind. (*Price Waterhouse v. Hopkins,* 1989, pp. 1790–1791) It takes no special training to discern sex stereotyping in a description of an aggressive female employee as requiring "a course at charm school." Nor . . . does it require expertise in psychology to know that, if an employee's flawed "interpersonal skills" can be corrected by a soft-hued suit or a new shade of lipstick, perhaps it is the employee's sex and not her interpersonal skills that has drawn the criticism. (p. 1793)

The decision of the court and its affirmation by the Supreme Court should be encouraging for everyone, men and women alike, as everyone benefits when the best employees are hired and promoted. Perhaps the most encouraging aspect of the decision was that it held Price Waterhouse firm accountable for its failure to prevent gender discrimination from playing a role in Ann Hopkins's partnership decision. The courts concluded that the firm should have had a clearly stated and vigorously enforced partnership policy that prohibited discrimination on the basis of gender (its policy prohibited discrimination on the basis of age or health but did not mention gender or ethnicity). The firm should have investigated the criticisms against Ann Hopkins to see if they were based on gender bias, and the firm should have encouraged interactions within the firm that would decrease gender stereotyping, such as having men and women work together on mutually beneficial projects. These three points would be a good starting point for any firm that wishes to discourage discrimination on the basis of gender, ethnicity, age, disability, sexual orientation, or any other characteristic. And the *Hopkins v. Price Waterhouse* decision is a warning that firms will be held accountable if they fail to deal with discrimination based on gender and other stereotypes in the workplace.

Summary

Chapter 15 defines social psychology and explores the influence people have on other people, the nature of attitudes and persuasion, and interpersonal attraction.

I. Social psychology is the branch of psychology that studies individuals as they interact with others.
  - **A.** People are often unaware of the power of social situations in influencing the behavior of other people and overemphasize a person's internal attributes when explaining behavior. This bias is termed the fundamental attribution error.
  - **B.** Because of the self-serving bias, people tend to attribute success to their personal characteristics and failure to their situations.

II. Behavior is often influenced powerfully by its social context.
  - **A.** Deindividuation may be responsible for some behavior in mob situations.
  - **B.** The failure to help when in a group is a complex process. The presence of others affects the interpretation of an event as an emergency and creates a diffusion of responsibility.
  - **C.** Individual effort may decline when people work in groups, group problem solving may lead to bad decisions when opinions become polarized, and even groups of sophisticated decision makers may be susceptible to the effects of "groupthink."
  - **D.** Conformity is yielding to group pressure even when no direct request to comply has been made. Conformity can be seen in behavior only or can be seen in changes in beliefs.
  - **E.** Social roles and social norms are important ways in which social factors can influence the behavior of individuals.
  - **F.** Research by Stanley Milgram indicates that authority figures can command substantial obedience from individuals.
    1. Obedience is greatest when we are instructed to do something by a person who is high in status and who is physically present.
    2. Obedience is less likely to occur when we are in the presence of other disobedient individuals.
  - **G.** It is important to remember that groups can sometimes accomplish what no single person can and that social support can soften the impact of stress.

III. Attitudes are beliefs that predispose us to act and feel in certain ways.
  - **A.** Attitudes are learned from direct experience and from others.
  - **B.** Attitude change through persuasion is determined by the characteristics of the speaker, the communication itself, and the people who hear it.
    1. Three characteristics of the speaker are important: credibility, attractiveness, and intent.
    2. Characteristics of the message that are important determinants of persuasiveness are fear appeals, the number of arguments in the message, and message framing.
    3. Characteristics of the listener that help determine how persuasive an argument will be include their intelligence, their need for social approval, their self-esteem, and the size of the audience.
    4. Techniques of persuasion such as the "foot-in-the-door," and "low-balling" are often used by persuasive individuals.
  - **C.** Attitudes sometimes change to become more consistent with our behavior, according to Leon Festinger's cognitive dissonance theory.
  - **D.** Prejudice is a harmful attitude based on inaccurate generalizations about a group of people. These generalizations are called stereotypes.
  - **E.** Stereotypes are harmful because they take away our ability to treat each member of a group as an individual and because they lead to faulty attributions.

IV. Friendship and love are social phenomena based on the process of person perception.
  - **A.** The process of person perception can be said to involve a "complex algebra" in which we combine and evaluate information about others to form an impression.
    1. Negative information is generally weighted more than positive information in person perception.
    2. First impressions (the primacy effect) generally influence person perception more than information learned later. The primacy effect is lessened under three conditions:
       - **a.** The person has prolonged exposure to the individual about whom the first impression was formed.
       - **b.** Time has passed since the first impression was formed, even if there has been no further exposure.
       - **c.** The person who formed the first impression understands the primacy effects and tries to minimize it.
    3. Person perception is influenced by the emotional state of the perceiver.
    4. The attribution process is involved in the perception of others. One aspect of the attribution process is deciding whether a person's behavior is caused by the situation (a situational attribution) or by a trait of the person (a dispositional attribution).
  - **B.** Although many factors ensure that each individual's perception of another individual will be unique, some general factors partly determine to whom we will be attracted.
    1. In general, we tend to be attracted to persons who:
       - **a.** Have characteristics that are similar or complementary to our own,
       - **b.** Are competent, but not perfect,
       - **c.** Are physically attractive, and
       - **d.** Also like us.
    2. Women are more likely to be attracted to a person's intelligence, character, education, occupational status, ambition, and income than are men.
    3. Men are more likely to be attracted by physical attractiveness than are women.
    4. Within each gender, however, different people perceive the same individual differently because of differences in the weight assigned to the same characteristics and even the perception of them as positive or negative.
  - **C.** Two major factors in determining if a relationship will last are the difference between what you expect to find in a relationship and what you actually find, and the degree to which the relationship is fairly balanced or equitable. The most enduring love relationships are able to make the transition from primarily passionate love to primarily companionate love.

Suggested Readings

1. A wonderfully readable, yet scholarly overview of social psychology: Aronson, E. (1995). *The social animal* (5th ed.). San Francisco: W. H. Freeman.
2. The role of cognitive factors in social interactions is described in: Wyer, R. S., & Carlston, D. W. (1980). *Social cognition, inference, and attribution.* Hillsdale, NJ: Lawrence Erlbaum.
3. Attitude change is discussed in scholarly but understandable terms in: Zimbardo, P. G., & Leippe, M. R. (1991). *The psychology of attitude change and social influence* (3rd ed.). Boston: McGraw-Hill.
4. To learn more about the psychology of persuasion: Cialdini, R. (1996). *Influence: Science and practice.* New York: Talman.

C H A P T E R

16

CHAPTER OUTLINE

Psychology Applied to Business and Other Professions

PROLOGUE

Since the early 1970s the number of women and minorities in business management positions has risen dramatically. This increase has resulted in part from the realization that good managers are good for business, regardless of their gender or race. Initially, however, the influx of women and minorities into higher-level business positions was stimulated by *affirmative action* laws. These laws require that equally qualified women and minorities be given preference in hiring to remedy past discrimination against them. These regulations have been successful in providing qualified women and minorities greater access to jobs that would have been denied to them previously. Equal opportunity programs also have provided more successful role models to younger women and minorities, encouraging a wider selection of career choices for these groups.

Equal opportunity hiring programs are hotly debated on many grounds, however. For example, psychologist Madeline Heilman of New York University (Heilman, Simon, & Repper, 1987) has used the tools of psychological research to raise an important concern: Has the first group of women paid a price to be the role models for future generations of women? In one study, female undergraduates were asked to take a leadership role in a simulated management experiment. All of the research participants first took a test that they were told measured their "communication skills." Some of the women were told that they were given the leadership role on the basis of their high score on the test of communication skills. Other women, however, were told that they were given the leadership role because "there just haven't been enough female subjects signing up"—in other words, because of their gender rather than their qualifications.

After the task, the women who believed that they had been selected for the leadership role on the basis of their gender thought that they hadn't been good leaders, took less credit for successful outcomes of the group, and were less interested in being a leader in the future. The women who believed that they had been selected on the basis of merit, however, did not undervalue themselves as leaders (Heilman et al., 1987).

Other studies similarly have shown that the performance of women managers is valued less highly by coworkers when it is believed that they obtained their position on the basis of gender rather than qualifications (Heilman & Herlihy, 1984; Jacobsen & Koch, 1977). We should not assume that all women managers and their fellow employees believe that they were chosen on the basis of their gender, however. The qualifications of most successful women are clear to everyone, including to themselves. Still, some of the first wave of women managers who were less sure of why they were hired may have paid a personal price for equality.

Psychology is both a scientific and an applied field. The job of many psychologists is to apply the principles and methods of psychology to the solution of human problems. Most applied psychologists work in clinical psychology, and, partly as a result, we are better able to treat psychological problems today than ever before. But clinical psychology is only one of the ways in which psychology has been successfully applied to human concerns.

Psychologists working in business seek to increase the satisfaction we derive from our jobs and to improve our productivity in those jobs. They do so by using their knowledge of psychological assessment to find the right person for the right job, by using knowledge of social relationships to improve methods of managing workers, and by designing the physical characteristics

KEY TERMS

of the job to fit the psychological characteristics of people. Psychologists have long been involved in the courtroom practice of law as expert witnesses on questions of insanity, but in recent years they have also studied the behavior of the people involved in the trial process—jurors, witnesses, attorneys, and others. Psychologists working in the field of education have used their knowledge of learning and cognition to develop improved ways of educating children. And we have already seen that psychologists working in the field of health psychology attempt to influence people to live healthier lives. Whenever a profession involves the welfare of *people*—and what profession doesn't—psychology has the potential to help that profession meet its goals better.

APPLIED FIELDS OF PSYCHOLOGY

Now that you have reached the last chapter of this text, take a moment to think back to chapter 1. We noted on page 5 that the four goals of psychology are to *describe, predict, understand,* and *influence* behavior and mental processes. This chapter focuses on the last of these goals—the use of psychological principles to influence and improve the lives of human beings. In other words, it is about the *application* of psychology to the solution of human concerns. Most of our attention until now has been on the basic principles of psychology—facts and concepts about perception, learning, memory, problem solving, emotion, and many other topics. But we have already covered a great deal of information about the applications of psychology. Within each chapter, many examples of new concepts were illustrated by describing applications of those ideas. Moreover, the chapters on abnormal behavior and therapies covered the heart of the applied fields of clinical and counseling psychology, and the chapter on stress and health gave us a description of the field of health psychology.

We turn now to other important applications of psychology—to the worlds of business, architecture, law, and education. Fewer psychologists are employed in these applied settings than in clinical, counseling, and health psychology, but they are significant and growing fields of application.

PSYCHOLOGY AND WORK: EMPLOYEES AND MANAGERS ARE PEOPLE

When you think of the word *work,* do the words *happiness* and *quality of life* come to mind? They should, because work is linked to the quality of our lives in important ways. The standard of living that we enjoy in terms of material goods and services is the product of business. Your car, clothes, haircut, compact disc, and newspaper would not exist without the multifaceted business sector. Moreover, our quality of life is also linked to the satisfaction that comes from our work. Most men and women spend a major part of their lives working for pay. Our sense of well-being depends in part on whether our jobs are boring and demeaning or meaningful and rewarding.

industrial-organizational psychologist
A psychologist who studies organizations and seeks ways to improve the functioning and human benefits of business.

Psychologists who work with business are known as **industrial-organizational (I/O) psychologists.** They attempt to improve the human benefits of work in a number of ways. For example, they seek ways to help businesses and government organizations produce more goods and services, to increase job satisfaction by changing methods of management and training, and to find "the right person for the right job" by improving methods of employee selection. To be sure, psychological principles are sometimes used to improve profits rather than human lives—such as by developing advertisements that are more persuasive than informative—but such abuses are the exception rather than the rule for professional psychologists in business today.

Personnel departments are where industrial-organizational psychologists can be found most frequently, since employee selection and training is the primary responsibility of these departments. Some large companies employ one or more psychologists to work in personnel. Other companies use the services of industrial-organizational psychologists who work for independent consulting firms. They teach both personnel and general managers to put the principles of psychology to work in helping people contribute more effectively and happily to the goals of the business.

Other industrial-organizational psychologists work for consumers rather than businesses. They are employed by government or public-interest groups performing such jobs as helping consumers make more informed choices in their purchases.

Employee Selection and Evaluation

Recall from chapters 1 and 7 that around the turn of the century France's Alfred Binet gave us the first practical way of measuring intelligence. Since Binet's time numerous useful ways of measuring intelligence and other psychological attributes have been used in educational, clinical, and business settings. In business, the most significant uses of psychological measurements have been in selecting and hiring new employees and in evaluating the performance of current employees. The measures most commonly used in employee decisions include interviews, evaluations of biographical data (called biodata), paper-and-pencil tests, performance tests, job performance ratings, and the evaluation of simulated job performance in assessment centers (Saal & Knight, 1988). Employee selection and evaluation is an essential part of business; finding the right person for the right job not only improves employee morale and productivity, but decreases employee turnover and absenteeism as well.

Psychologists have learned that applicants with average qualifications rate higher if they are interviewed after two poorly qualified candidates than if they are interviewed after two highly qualified candidates.

Interviews

interviews
A subjective method of personality assessment that involves questioning techniques designed to reveal the personality of the client.

Interviews are the heart of the process of evaluating job applicants and play a significant role in the assessment of current employees for possible promotion. Interviews are more or less structured conversations in which the employee or job applicant is questioned about her or his training, experience, and future goals. The suitability of the individual for the job is evaluated partly in terms of factual answers to questions, but also in terms of the individual's personality, spoken language, potential for leadership, and other personal factors.

The role of the industrial-organizational psychologist is to educate personnel specialists and other managers about the biases inherent in interviews. We discussed several biases in person perception that influence interviews, such as the importance of primacy effects, or "first impressions," when we discussed the general process of person perception in chapter 15. Industrial-organizational psychologists have discovered a great many other factors that interfere with our ability to form objective impressions of people during interviews. For example, the *order* in which job applicants are interviewed sometimes influences our opinion of the applicants. If an applicant of average qualifications is interviewed after poorly qualified applicants, his or her ratings will be much higher than if interviewed after highly qualified applicants. The contrast with previously interviewed applicants makes applicants with average qualifications look better or worse than they really are. Fortunately, ratings of highly qualified and poorly qualified applicants are not influenced by previously interviewed applicants. Their ratings are essentially the same regardless of the quality of the applicants who were interviewed just before them (Wexley, Yukl, Kovacs, & Sanders, 1977).

Other biasing factors such as physical attractiveness, gender, and ethnicity also influence judgments based on interviews. For example, 30 employment interviewers who recruit on college campuses were shown 12 hypothetical resumes of college students and asked to rate them for a beginning managerial position in a department store (Dipboye, Fromkin, & Wilback, 1975). Four of the resumes described individuals with high scholastic achievement, four described average scholastic achievement, and four described low scholastic achievement. In each of these three groups (high, average, or low scholastic achievement), the pictures attached to the resumes were of an attractive male, an attractive female, an unattractive male, or an unattractive female.

As figure 16.1 shows, although scholastic achievement was the most important factor in determining ratings of the hypothetical applicants, attractive applicants were consistently rated higher than unattractive applicants within each level of achievement! Other studies have shown that this bias toward physical attractiveness even results in higher earning capacity after being hired. One study that used a five-point scale for rating attractiveness found that both male and female employees were earning over $2,000 per year more for every point higher on the attractiveness scale (Frieze, Olson, & Russell, 1991).

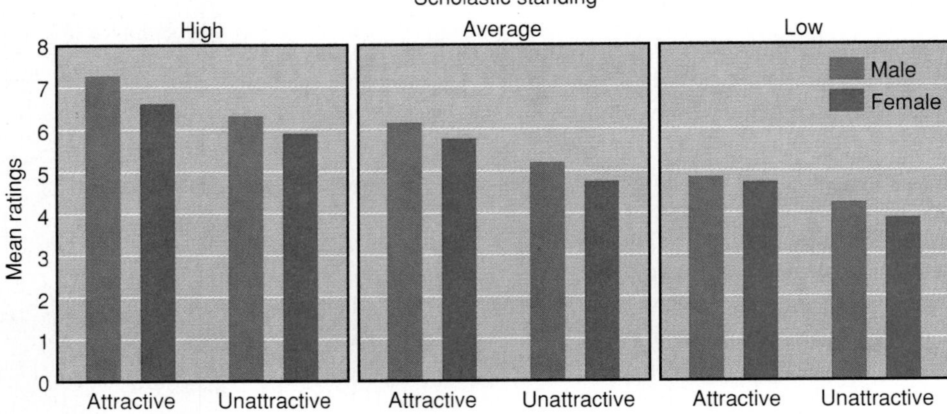

FIGURE 16.1

Ratings by personnel recruiters from businesses of 12 hypothetical job applicants (six male and six female) who were portrayed as high, medium, or low in academic achievement, and attractive or unattractive.

Source: Data from R. L. Dipboye, et al., "The Importance of Applicant Sex, Attractiveness, and Scholastic Standing in Evaluation of Job Application Resumes," *Journal of Applied Psychology,* 60:39–43, 1975. Copyright 1975 by the American Psychological Association.

Also note in figure 16.1 that males were rated higher than females in every category! Gender discrimination continues to play an important role in hiring practices in the United States and most other countries. What do you think the results would have been if some of the photos of applicants showed obvious symbols of their ethnic identity? Would men in turbans or women wrapped in saris have been rated lower?

Employment interviewers can be trained to reduce somewhat the effects of irrelevant prejudicial factors such as gender, ethnicity, and physical attractiveness in job interviews (Wexley, Sanders, & Yukl, 1973). One method for reducing bias is the use of a structured interview, in which the same questions are given to all employees for a position (Campion et al., 1988). Structured interviews have been found to be more reliable than standard interviews in selecting successful candidates for a wide variety of positions (Wiesner & Cronshaw, 1988). However, biases in employee selection will not go away easily.

Biodata

biodata
The biographical information used by potential employers to evaluate a job candidate.

The biographical data, or **biodata,** that we give our potential employers on employment applications sometimes play an important role in determining whether or not we are hired. Examples of biodata are previous job history, hobbies, education, and special skills. Such biodata are sometimes used in the employment selection process in sophisticated ways that are based on careful research. To use a purely hypothetical example, suppose a life insurance company did a study of the biodata of their most and least successful sales agents and found that most of their successful agents are active in sports, attended community colleges, and know how to type, but very few of their unsuccessful agents have these same characteristics. That information might lead the company to give preference in hiring new agents to individuals who have those specific biodata. You can readily see why I had to use a hypothetical example: Companies generally will not reveal the actual biodata they use, so that applicants cannot fake their biographical histories.

Although biodata are a reasonably good way to select employees, they are used by less than 1 percent of all U.S. businesses (Schmidt & Ones, 1992). Biodata can be used in employee selection only by large companies who employ their own psychologist and who hire large numbers of employees to perform the same kind of job. This is the case because large amounts of biographical data must be amassed on the characteristics of successful and unsuccessful employees in a specific job before biodata can be used meaningfully.

Paper-and-Pencil Tests

Paper-and-pencil tests are another important part of the evaluation of employees and job applications (Schmidt & Ones, 1992). Employers need a wide variety of tests to evaluate different characteristics of employees for different jobs. Both general tests, such as those measuring intelligence and personality, and specific measurements of skills and abilities are used. For example, spelling and reading tests are often given to applicants for secretarial and clerical jobs. Applicants who are more skilled in these areas can generally be expected to perform better on jobs like typing and proofreading.

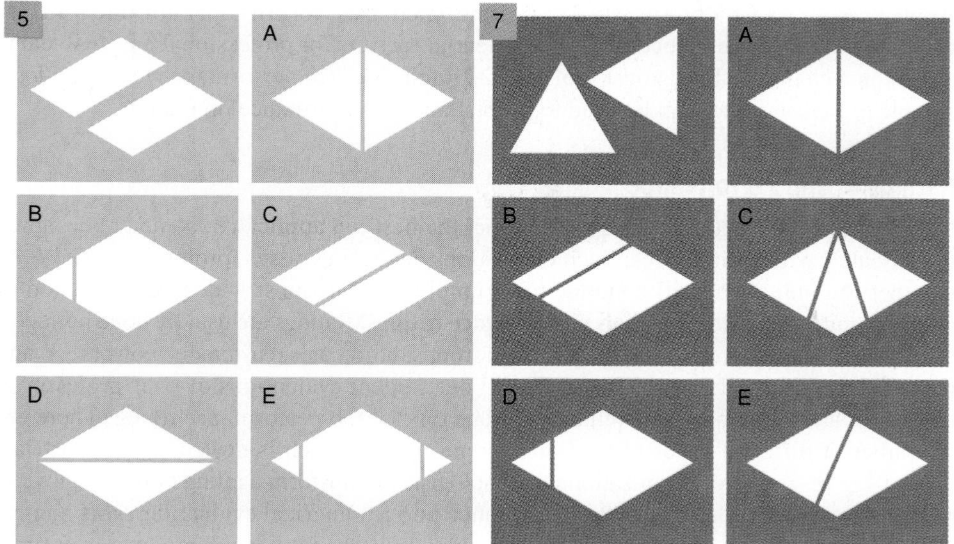

FIGURE 16.2

Sample items from a test designed to measure an individual's ability to visualize spatial relationships.

A
B
Example X
Which person has the heavier load? (If equal, mark C.)
Example Y
Which weighs more? (If equal, mark C.)
A
B

FIGURE 16.3

Sample items from a paper-and-pencil test designed to measure an individual's mechanical comprehension.

Applicants for mechanical and engineering jobs are often given tests like those pictured in figures 16.2 and 16.3. These tests tap a person's abilities to mentally visualize spatial relationships and to understand mechanical concepts. And applicants for sales positions are frequently given tests of sales aptitude. These tests describe problematic situations that often arise in sales work and require the applicant to choose the best course of action from a number of options. These are only a few of the variety of pencil-and-paper tests used today.

Performance Tests

Tests that measure actual manual performance are often used in selecting employees such as assembly-line workers or equipment repair specialists. **Performance tests** are based on the assumption that the only valid way to find out if applicants can work with their hands is to evaluate them while they are actually working. The Purdue Pegboard is an example of this kind of performance test (see fig. 16.4). In this test, pins, collars, and washers are fitted together in ways specified by the tester to evaluate the applicant's manual speed and accuracy. Other types of performance tests more closely resemble the job to be performed.

performance tests
Employee selection tests that resemble the actual manual performance required on a job.

Applicants for typist jobs are asked to type in timed tests; forklift operators are asked to drive forklifts in a prescribed path; and potential recruits for professional baseball teams are given a chance to bat against professional pitchers. Each performance test provides a sample of behavior that can be used to predict actual performance on the job.

Ratings of Job Performance

job performance ratings
Ratings of the actual performance of employees in their jobs by supervisors.

Not all evaluation methods are used to select the best job applicants; some are designed to evaluate current employees. Such evaluations determine raises, promotions, and even whether the individual will continue to be employed. The most widely used method of assessing current employees is **job performance ratings.** Ratings are usually done by supervisors, but information may also be obtained from subordinates, customers, coworkers, and the employee himself or herself. If you fill out student evaluations of your professor at the end of a term, you are participating in one type of job performance rating. There are a number of different types of performance ratings, but each is designed by industrial-organizational psychologists to transform a rating of the employee's actual job performance into a numerical evaluation. This numerical information is used to track an employee's progress over time, or to compare the performances of a group of employees.

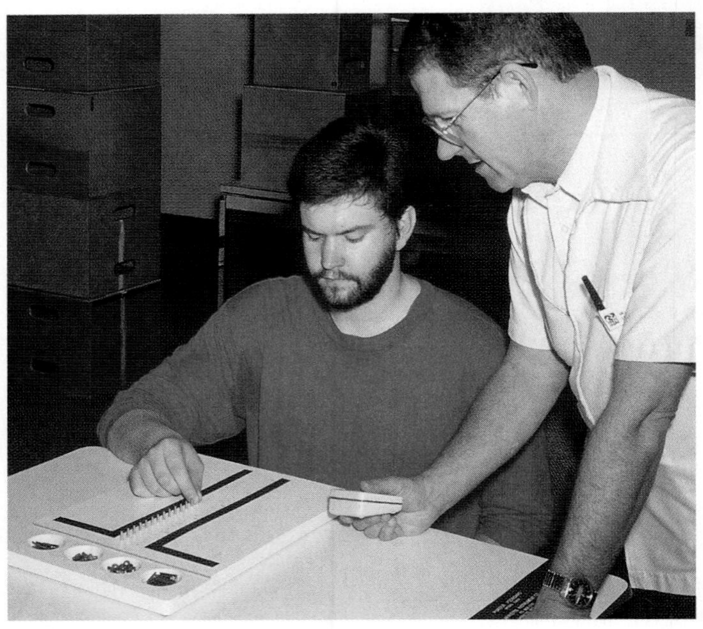

FIGURE 16.4
An example of a performance test that might be used to select employees for a job assembling small machine parts.

In job performance ratings, the employee is rated on a number of different dimensions of job performance. The evaluator checks the statement that best describes the employee from most to least desirable. Three job dimensions from a hypothetical multiple-step rating scale are shown in figure 16.5. The statements are each assigned a value (5, 4, 3, 2, 1) so the ratings can be summed across all of the dimensions to obtain an overall evaluation of the employee.

Checklists provide numerical evaluations of job performance in a somewhat different way. Evaluators are asked to read a series of statements such as the following:

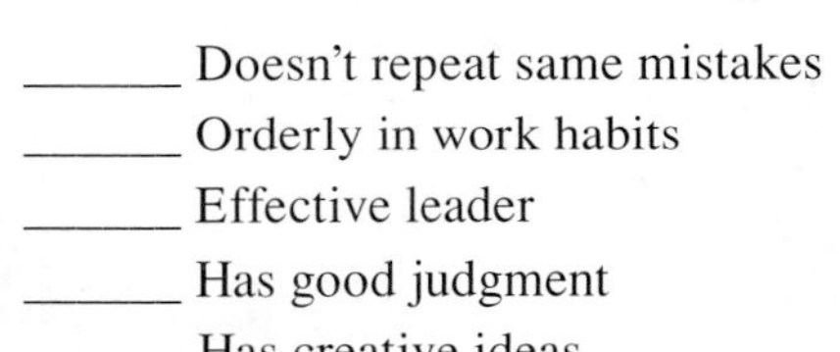
______ Doesn't repeat same mistakes
______ Orderly in work habits
______ Effective leader
______ Has good judgment
______ Has creative ideas

The evaluator checks those items that are characteristic of the employee. Each characteristic is assigned a numerical value according to how important it is for the job, with the sum of these values giving the overall evaluation of the employee. Many varieties of job performance ratings are used to assess different types of employees when numerical evaluations are needed.

Performance evaluations, like interviews, are less than perfect. In both methods, evaluators may be influenced by the same principles of person perception we discussed in chapter 15. However, supervisors can be trained to identify potential biases, to attend to job-relevant behaviors, and to use rating scales effectively (Hedge & Kavanagh, 1988).

Assessment Centers

assessment centers
Program for the evaluation of employees that uses simulated management tasks as its primary method of evaluation.

Decisions on the hiring or promotion of managers in large companies are often based in part on evaluations made in **assessment centers.** Assessment centers are usually staffed by a team of upper managers and outside psychological consultants. Several candidates for the same position are brought together in the assessment center so they can be intensively evaluated outside of the usual work environment. This technique was developed during World War II to evaluate candidates for undercover spy assignments and has continued to be a popular method of management selection (Bray, Campbell, & Grant, 1974).

Assessment centers use traditional methods of evaluating the candidates for promotion, such as interviews and tests, but the distinctive feature of the approach is the evalu-

Dependability				
Unsatisfactory	Below average	Average	Above average	Outstanding
Requires constant supervision to ensure that directions are followed	Requires considerable supervision; does not always follow directions	Requires average to normal supervision	Can usually be depended upon to complete assignments	Needs virtually no supervision; completely reliable

Quantity of work				
Unsatisfactory	Below average	Average	Above average	Outstanding
Consistently below job requirements	Frequently below job requirements	Meets job requirements	Frequently exceeds job requirements	Consistently exceeds job requirements

Job knowledge				
Unsatisfactory	Below average	Average	Above average	Outstanding
Unsatisfactory	Below average	Average	Knows job well	Thorough knowledge

FIGURE 16.5

Examples of items from a multiple-step rating scale like those used to evaluate employee performance. The rater marks one category for each item.

ation of candidates while they are carrying out a **simulated management task** (Thornton & Cleveland, 1990). A frequently used simulation is the **in-basket exercise.** The candidate is given a problem that might show up in the "in basket" of the new management position. Candidates would be asked to indicate the actions they would take, such as calling a meeting, obtaining additional information, and communicating a decision. Ratings of the candidate's performance in these simulation exercises would be used in the hiring or promotion decision.

simulated management task
A contrived task requiring managerial skills that is given to candidates for management positions to evaluate their potential as managers.

in-basket exercise
A type of management simulation task in which the individual attempts to solve a problem that is typical of the ones that appear in a manager's "in-basket."

Validity of Job Selection Measures

One major purpose of the measures described (biodata, performance tests, etc.) is to increase the productivity of industry and government by selecting the best employees for each job. But just how good are these methods in improving employee selection? To use a term introduced in our discussion of intelligence tests in chapter 7, how *valid* are these measures?

An excellent summary of the extensive research on this topic has been provided by Michigan State University psychologists John and Rhonda Hunter (1984). Their summary indicates marked differences in the validity of the several measures, with paper-and-pencil tests of intellectual ability generally being the best predictors of later job performance and success in job-training programs. The use of intellectual ability tests considerably improves the selection of employees (Ree & Earles, 1992). For example, Hunter (1979) calculated that if the city of Philadelphia, Pennsylvania, stopped using an intellectual ability test for the selection of police officers, it would lose $170 million over a 10-year period. These dollar losses would result from the increased cost of training officer candidates who could not pass the course or had to be fired later, needing more officers to complete the same amount of work, and the like.

Hunter and Hunter (1984) also found that performance tests, assessment centers, and biodata were valid measures but were less useful than intellectual ability tests in selecting employees for most jobs. For example, Hunter (1981) indicated that the federal government's use of intellectual ability tests in its hiring of approximately 460,000 new employees each year saves the government $15.6 billion compared with hiring at random. In contrast, the use of biodata—the second most valid method—would save the federal government only $10.5 billion, a loss of $5.1 billion. Finally, of the methods that we discussed, interviews have been found to be the least valid method of selecting more productive employees. But projective personality tests and handwriting analyses have been found not to be valid at all for employee selection (Reilly & Chao, 1982).

Why is intellectual ability important to job performance? Frank Schmidt and John Hunter (1992) have proposed a model of how intellectual ability and other factors leads to superior job performance. It will sound familiar as it is consistent with Earl Hunt's (1995) views on intelligence that we discussed in chapter 7. In this model, knowledge of the job is the most important factor in job performance. Job knowledge, in turn, is the result of both the employee's job experience and intellectual ability (see fig. 16.6). Schmidt and Hunter (1992) have found that employees steadily gain job knowledge over the first 5 years; then the benefits of on-the-job experience level off. Intellectual ability mostly influences how quickly the employee gains this job knowledge when he or she starts the job. Higher intellectual ability does improve job performance somewhat after it has been learned (by leading to better solutions to complex problems that arise on the job), but the main reason that more intelligent employees perform better is that they learn the job more quickly. Therefore, the benefits of high intelligence are most obvious in the first 5 years on the job when job knowledge is still being learned. After 5 years on the job, that advantage of higher intelligence is small, because experience tends to equalize the job knowledge of employees.

Intellectual ability tests are the most valid selection measures for a wide range of jobs, but they are less useful for some jobs than others (Schmidt & Hunter, 1992). Intellectual ability tests are very useful in selecting employees for more complex jobs (sales, managerial, etc.) but less useful when the job is less complex (vehicle operator, semiskilled factory worker, etc.). For these jobs, performance tests of job knowledge are more useful than intellectual ability tests.

Schmidt and Hunter (1992) have also found that one of the "big five" personality traits that we discussed in chapter 11 (p. 419) is important in predicting job success in many occupations. Employees who are more conscientious learn job knowledge more quickly and perform their jobs better. In part, this is because employees who are low in conscientiousness are more likely to miss work and develop conflicts with supervisors and other employees. Thus, intelligence is not the only psychological dimension that is associated with good job performance.

Fair Selection of Minority Employees

The use of intellectual ability tests to select employees raises a number of important questions about the hiring of ethnic minority applicants. Because African Americans and Hispanics, on the average, still score somewhat lower on intellectual ability tests than whites, the use of such tests in employee selection means that a smaller proportion of applicants from these ethnic groups would be selected on the basis of the test (Schmidt & Ones, 1992). For example, if an intellectual ability test is used that selects 50 percent of the white applicants, it would select an average of only 16 percent of African-American applicants (Hunter & Hunter, 1984). Not only does this raise social and ethical questions of fairness, but it also raises legal issues. In some circumstances, this use of intellectual ability tests would be considered illegal (Schmidt & Ones, 1992).

What is the cause and the proper cure for this dilemma? Hunter and Hunter (1984) offer an informed opinion, but it is not one with which everyone will agree. Indeed, it and all conceivable alternatives are sure to generate considerable controversy. To make sense of Hunter and Hunter's proposal, we need to think back to chapter 7 again. Some psychologists have argued that some ethnic minority groups score lower than whites on intellectual ability tests because the tests reflect information and skills that are emphasized in the white culture and, hence, are *biased* against people from minority groups (e.g., Williams, 1972). Hunter and Hunter argue, however, that intellectual ability tests are just as valid in predicting job performance for minorities as they are for whites. For example, although the average scores of African-American and white groups of applicants are different, a given score on the test predicts exactly the same level of performance for African Americans as for whites. Therefore, Hunter and Hunter suggest that differences in intellectual ability scores reflect the disadvantages and prejudice faced by minorities in our society more than "cultural bias" in the tests.

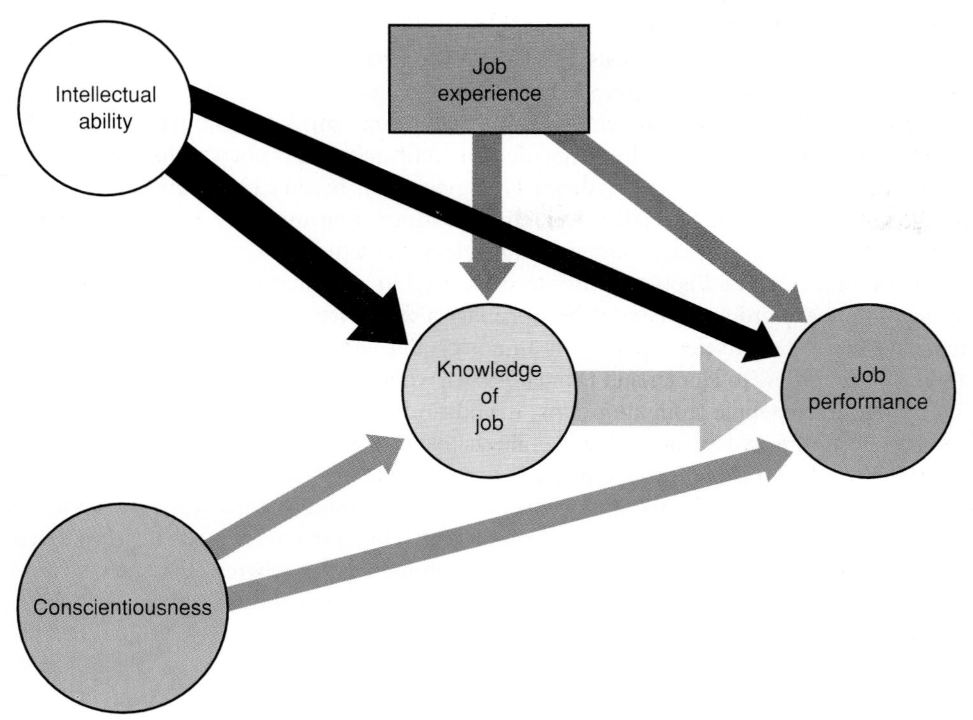

FIGURE 16.6

Employees who know the skills and information needed to perform a job well tend to perform their jobs better. Employees with higher intellectual ability perform their jobs better mostly because they learn job knowledge faster. Similarly, more experienced employees perform better mostly because they have greater job knowledge. Employees who are higher on the personality trait of conscientiousness also tend to learn job knowledge better. To a smaller extent, all three factors (high intelligence, experience, and conscientiousness) also contribute to better job performance in ways that are unrelated to the learning of job knowledge.

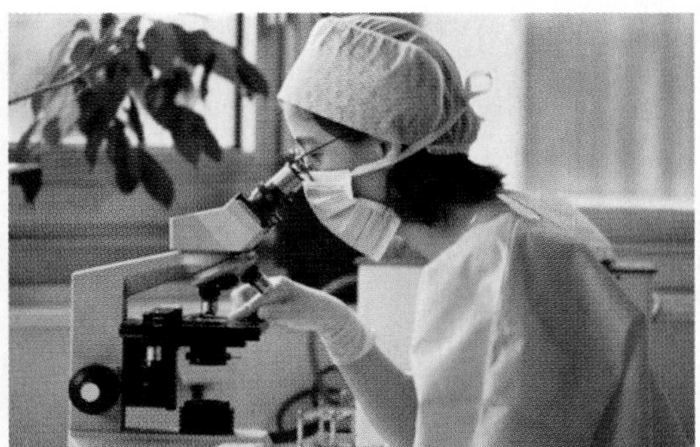

But, if intellectual ability tests are indeed valid for minorities, and their lower scores reflect disadvantages and prejudices, what do we do about the inequities in hiring produced by the use of such tests? Hunter and Hunter (1984) argue that if we as a society take the position that hiring equal proportions of minority groups will help eliminate some of the economic disadvantages faced by minorities, then the question is not whether to use intellectual ability tests, but how to use them. Their position is based partly on the fact that not using these tests would hurt all job applicants—including minority applicants—since they would have to be replaced by less valid selection methods.

How, then, can intellectual ability tests be used in a manner that will ensure the fair hiring of minority groups? There are two primary alternatives. One is to lower the required score on the test and select qualifying minority and white applicants at random. This approach, according to Hunter and Hunter (1984), would result in the employment of many poorly qualified people from all groups; in addition, it would not ensure that a fair number of minorities would be hired. Another alternative is to set quotas for each minority group and then hire the most qualified applicants in each group. Hunter and Hunter suggest that this method would achieve the goal of balance among ethnic groups while hiring fewer unqualified individuals. They estimate that if the federal government used the first method, it would cost $13.1 billion to achieve ethnic balance, whereas the latter method would cost $780 million (one-seventeenth as much). The quota approach, however, is sure to generate ethical and legal controversy for some time to come.

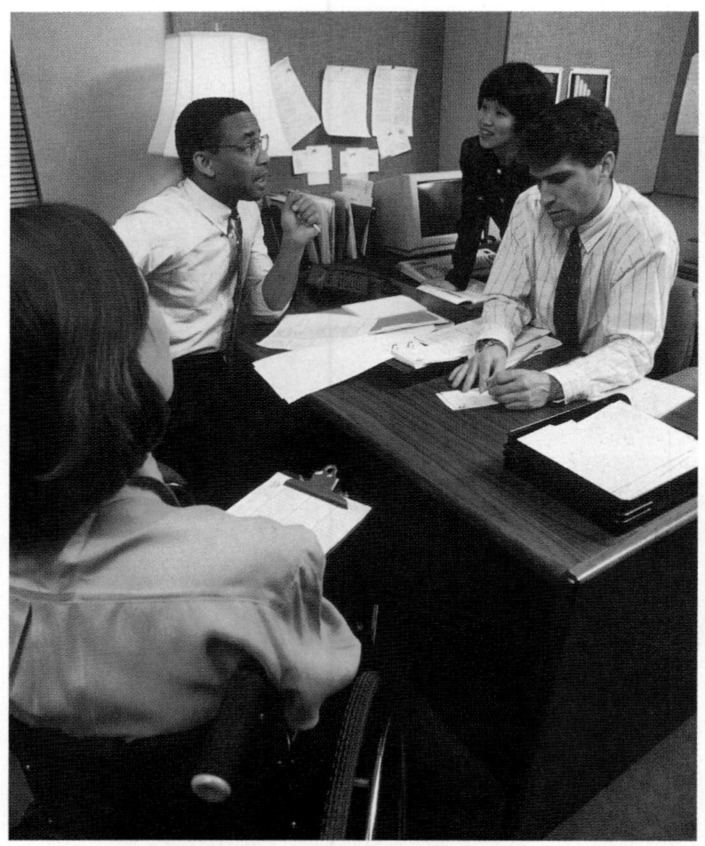

Job satisfaction is not directly related to productivity. But it's good for both the business and the employees because it reduces employee turnover and absenteeism.

Job Satisfaction and Productivity

Psychologists working in business have two inherently important goals: to improve the satisfaction of employees and to improve their productivity. The goals of improving job satisfaction and productivity can be met in two principal ways. As we have just discussed, one is to use methods of employee selection to match the right person with the right job. The other way is to improve working conditions, particularly the ways in which employees are managed and supervised. We first look at the relationship between job satisfaction and productivity; then we examine the ways in which supervisory style and managerial, organizational, and physical conditions are related to these goals.

Are happy workers productive workers? That has been the assumption of industrial-organizational psychologists for many years, but research suggests that it may not always be the case (Iaffaldano & Muchinsky, 1985). Job satisfaction is not *directly* related to how well employees perform in most instances, probably because productivity is influenced by so many different factors (McCormick & Ilgen, 1980). For example, one worker may be highly productive because she is *unsatisfied* with her job as a clerk and hopes her high level of productivity will get her selected for the management trainee program. Another worker may love his job but may be unproductive because he likes his coworkers and does not want to anger them by producing more than they do.

But although job satisfaction is not directly related to *individual* productivity, recent evidence shows that it has a much stronger effect on performance of the organization as a whole (Ostroff, 1992). High job satisfaction improves the performance of organizations in the following ways:

1. Reducing employee turnover—the rate at which employees quit and seek new jobs;
2. Reducing absenteeism—the frequency with which employees fail to show up for work;
3. Improving relations between labor and management;
4. Improving the ability of organizations to recruit good employees;

5. Improving the reputation that employees give to an organization by what they say about it in the community (Anastasi, 1987).

Drawing by Anthony; © 1988 The New Yorker Magazine, Inc.

Management Strategies to Improve Job Satisfaction and Productivity

Thus, although productivity and job satisfaction are not directly linked, keeping employees satisfied with their jobs is indirectly good for the employer in the ways just listed. This is a happy state of affairs because it gives employers a strong economic reason for improving the job satisfaction of their workers. Fortunately, there is another strong economic incentive for adopting management policies that enhance job satisfaction: Although they are not directly related, many of the management practices that lead to higher job satisfaction also improve productivity.

Three major strategies are used to improve both job satisfaction and productivity:

1. *Improving management supervisory style.* The most effective managers and supervisors are *considerate* (warm, friendly, and concerned in dealing with employees) and *communicative* (can clearly tell employees what is expected of them and how they will be evaluated on their performance). In addition, the most effective supervisors are also often high in **structuring** (spending a great deal of time organizing and directing the work of their employees). However, being high in structuring is an advantage only when the supervisor is also highly considerate. It may even be a disadvantage when less considerate supervisors closely structure their employees' activities (Anastasi, 1987).

structuring
Activities of managers that organize and direct the work of employees.

2. *Improving managerial organization.* In recent years, a great deal of attention has been paid to how the efforts of management are organized. Do messages always come down from top management, or are employees involved in decision making to some extent? Are employees told specifically how to work, or are they given specific production goals but allowed freedom in the ways they meet those goals? Does it make any difference? Two strategies of managerial organization that appear to make a significant difference in promoting job satisfaction and productivity are *participative management* and *management by objectives.*

   In the **participative management** method, employees at every level of the organization are actively involved in decision making (Hollander & Offermann, 1990; Turnage, 1990). For instance, when a dressmaking plant must change over to making a new line of clothes, the sewing machine operators would work out the most efficient ways to do this in discussions with their supervisors. The supervisors would link this decision-making process to higher management by participating in decision-making conferences with their supervisors, who would then participate in decisions with the next level of management, and so on up to the top. In a classic example of the benefits of participative management, employees of the Weldon Pajama Factory showed an almost 50 percent increase in productivity and earning when such a system was introduced (Likert, 1967). Interestingly, recent research suggests that female managers are more likely than male managers to adopt the effective participative management strategy (Eagly & Johnson, 1990).

participative management
The practice of involving employees at all levels in management decisions.

   Another effective strategy of managerial organization is **management by objectives** (Locke & Latham, 1990). In this approach, employees are given a specific goal to accomplish—anything from producing 1,000 dishes per month, to reducing air pollution from the factory by 80 percent, to reducing corporate taxes by 20 percent—but they are given considerable freedom in *how* they meet those objectives. This method benefits the company because it ensures that management focuses on what is really important to the company (its objectives). But management by objectives also gives employees a greater sense of

management by objectives
The strategy of giving employees specific goals but giving them considerable freedom in deciding how to reach those goals.

independence and an easier way to tell whether they are doing a good job of meeting their goals. It is an especially good management strategy when employees believe that the goals are reasonable and appropriate (Locke & Latham, 1990). Management by objectives is often used along with a participative management strategy, allowing employees at all levels to participate in setting and reviewing goals. Increasingly, too, meeting and exceeding the goals is often tied to bonuses, thus giving the employee positive reinforcement for greater productivity in the form of greater monetary income (McCormick & Ilgen, 1980).

3. *Improving physical conditions.* Considerable research has been done by industrial-organizational psychologists on the influence of physical conditions (such as lighting, noise, and temperature) on productivity and job satisfaction. For example, psychologists have found that working in 95-degree temperatures produces significant increases in perceptual and decision-making errors after 4 to 5 hours on the job (Fine & Kobrick, 1978). Considerable attention has also been paid to the design of machines that fit well with the psychological characteristics of the human beings who will be operating them.

A good working environment improves productivity and job satisfaction.

Management Strategies to Minimize "Social Loafing"

Recall from the last chapter on social psychology that when people work together on a joint project, some people usually work less hard than they would if they were working on an individual project—termed *social loafing* (Latané et al., 1979). Since organizations often need their employees to work together as a group—on group projects ranging from building automobiles to writing governmental regulations—it is important to understand what encourages social loafing and what minimizes it. University of Florida psychologist James Shepard (1995) has recently summarized research on this topic. According to Shepard, social loafing is the result of low motivation to work on the group project. Low motivation, in turn, results from individuals perceiving their contributions to be either unrewarded, unnecessary, or too costly to the individual.

Social loafing can be minimized, therefore, by reducing its three causes:

1. If the individual believes that his or her contribution to the group effort will not be recognized or rewarded even if the group goal is met, the solution is to provide clear incentives to each individual's contribution to the group effort. This incentive could be anything from a good performance evaluation to bonuses that are tied *not to the effort of the group as a whole,* but to the effort of the individual.
2. If the individual mistakenly believes that the group goal will be achieved just as well regardless of how much he or she contributes as an individual, the solution would be to show each individual that his or her contribution is indispensable. This can be accomplished by dividing up the task so that each individual contributes something that is both unique and important.
3. Sometimes individuals feel that their contributions to the group effort will cost more than they are worth. For example, a young salesperson might feel that time spent working on a new group retirement plan could be better devoted to earning commissions from sales. Paradoxically, some hard workers start to loaf on group tasks if they think that *other* members of the group are exploiting them by loafing. These causes of social loafing can be combated by making the task easier (e.g., by getting a consultant to write the first draft of the new retirement plan) or by discouraging social loafing in every member of the group so that no one will feel exploited by others.

Interestingly, studies of social loafing in different cultures have found that social loafing is universal—it apparently happens in all cultures to some extent (Shepard, 1995). Group effort seems to be motivated by different factors in different cultures, however. The Japanese tend to motivate contributions to group work by mutually monitoring the performance of group members and responding positively to good effort and shaming poor effort. Americans, on the other hand, comment less on each other's performance and rely more on each individual's sense of duty to the group. As a result, Japanese workers are more likely than American workers to withdraw from groups where social loafing is going on if it is permitted (Shepard, 1995).

Leadership

The success of any organization also depends on the quality of its leadership. Leadership is the influence of one group member on the others as they work toward shared goals. Psychologists have studied the *traits* of successful leaders. Traits such as drive, honesty, leadership motivation, intelligence, and creativity contribute to a person's leadership potential (Kirkpatrick & Locke, 1991). Not surprisingly, the trait of *flexibility* also seems to be important for successful leadership (Mumford et al., 1993). Effective leaders understand that leadership styles must be adapted to each individual situation.

Some leaders seem especially capable of inspiring their followers to reach a common goal. Whether the goal is positive, as in the case of Martin Luther King, or negative, as in the case of Adolf Hitler, these leaders share the traits of charisma, clear vision, inspiration, and personalized attention to their followers (Bass, 1985; Bass & Aviolo, 1990).

Leadership Among Women and Minorities

Women appear to approach organizational leadership in ways that are different yet effective. Eagly and Johnson (1990) analyzed more than 150 studies of gender and leadership and concluded that women are as task-oriented as men. However, women tend to be more democratic—interacting more with their subordinates, sharing information and power, and developing extensive networks (Helgesen, 1990). In spite of their effectiveness, women tend to be undervalued in leadership positions, especially when their leadership style appear "masculine" or they are in a traditionally "masculine" occupation (Eagly et al., 1992).

Minorities may experience difficulty obtaining leadership positions because of subtle racism in the workplace. Irons and Moore (1985) found that African Americans in the banking industry were not "networked" and lacked the mentoring necessary for moving up in the organization.

Women and minorities continue to experience the "glass ceiling" in American organizations. They can rise to a certain level of leadership, but the top positions elude them (Morrison & Von Glinow, 1990).

Human Factors Engineering

We live in a technological society where more and more of our work is done by machines. But machines must be operated by people, so increasingly the work of people has become the operation of machines. For this reason, one branch of industrial-organizational psychology, known as **human factors engineering,** has as its goal the design of machines that can be more easily and efficiently operated by human beings.

human factors engineering
The branch of industrial-organizational psychology interested in the design of machines to be operated by human beings.

For example, airplane pilots must operate a number of different manual controls while their eyes are occupied looking at radar, reading gauges, and watching where the plane is going. The job of the human factors engineer is to design manual controls in a way that will make them easier and safer to use. In this case, the controls would probably be designed in a way that makes use of the pilot's sense of touch, because controls do not have to be seen to be perceived. Controls of different shapes can be easily distinguished by touch and are particularly easy to use if their shape is related to their function, as shown in figure 16.7. Human factors research has also found that controls are more easily operated when they are located next to the dial that they influence rather than in separate clusters (see fig. 16.8) and when the direction of turning a control matches the direction of the corresponding dial (see fig. 16.9).

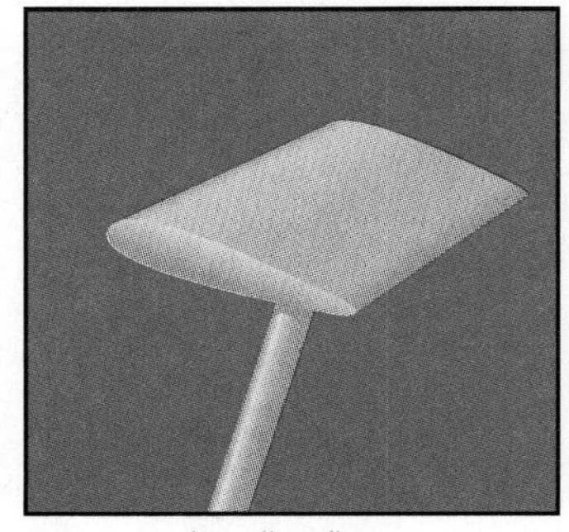
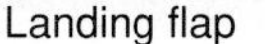
Landing flap

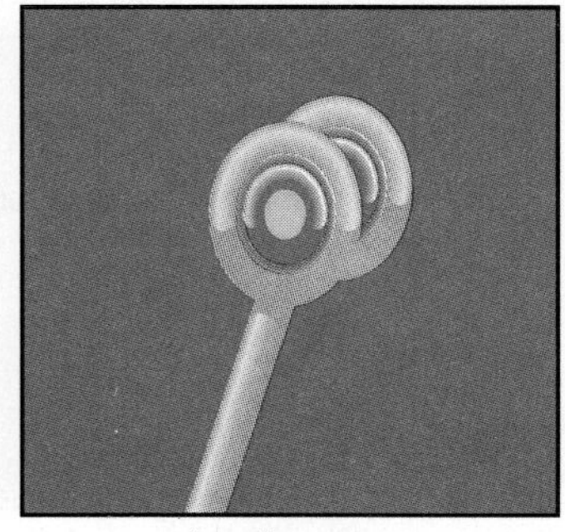
Landing gear

FIGURE 16.7
An example of controls that are designed to be easily distinguished by touch and related in form to their function.

Taking a different approach to improving the interface between people and machines, human factors engineers have found that short rest periods greatly improve efficiency in many tasks. For example, workers who need to detect infrequent visual signals, such as an air traffic controller would have to do, have been found to maintain nearly perfect accuracy over an hour and a half when they take a 10-minute break every 30 minutes. When the workers do not take breaks, however, their accuracy in detecting the signals falls below 75 percent after being on the job for more than 30 minutes (Bergum & Lehr, 1962).

Human factors engineering was in the spotlight in the 1980s after serious accidents at nuclear power plants at Three Mile Island and Chernobyl released large amounts of radioactivity. Although the causes of these accidents were complex, investigations suggested that the plant operators were asked to deal with too much information that was presented in confusing ways. The design of the operating system and its computer displays of information overloaded the cognitive capacities of the operators and fatal mistakes were made (Wickens, 1992). Human factors engineers have been working to simplify computer displays of information in many work settings (Howell, 1993).

In recent years, the scope of human factors engineering has expanded tremendously. For example, some research suggests that persons with some personality profiles are better at handling stressful jobs than others. Persons who are high on the personality trait of *extraversion* that we read about in chapter 11 (p. 419) tend to react less to stress on the job than persons who are lower in this trait (more *introverted*) (Howell, 1993). To take another example, should you go to work if you have a cold or the flu? Recent research suggests that there are some serious safety reasons for not performing some jobs when you have certain minor illnesses. A British research group (Smith, Tyrell, Coyle, & Willman, 1987) conducted a study for which I am pleased not to have been a subject. Volunteers performed complex tasks requiring either excellent eye-hand coordination (such as flying an airplane or operating machinery) or vigilant signal detection (such as required by an air traffic controller whose job it is to detect signals on a radar screen indicating the presence of aircraft). They performed these tasks both when sick and well. The subjects were actually *given* these minor illnesses by exposing them to either a flu virus or a common cold virus. When sick with the flu, signal detection was impaired, but not eye-hand coordination. So it might be okay to fly an airplane with the flu, unless you think it's important to detect other airplanes in your path (and if you don't, I'll take the train). Volunteers given a common cold, in contrast, showed impairment of eye-hand coordination, but not signal detection. So, assuming they can tell the difference between having the flu and a common cold, it seems safe for air traffic controllers to work with a cold.

Human factors engineers have also turned their attention to consumer safety issues in recent years. For example, some kinds of automobile safety belts pose a danger to children and smaller adults because the shoulder strap is close to the neck. In response to this concern, human factors engineers have developed a new type of shoulder harness that can be easily and effectively adjusted to fit the height of the passenger using only one hand (Tillman & Tillman, 1991). Such efforts by human factors engineers make the marriage between people and machines happier, safer, and more efficient.

Acceptable arrangement

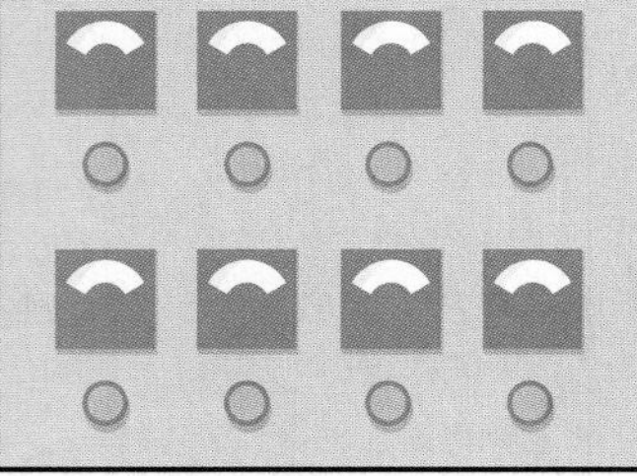

Preferred arrangement

FIGURE 16.8

Examples of controls and dials arranged to fit the cognitive characteristics of human operators.

FIGURE 16.9

Examples of controls designed to operate in a way that is compatible with the direction of operation of the corresponding dial.

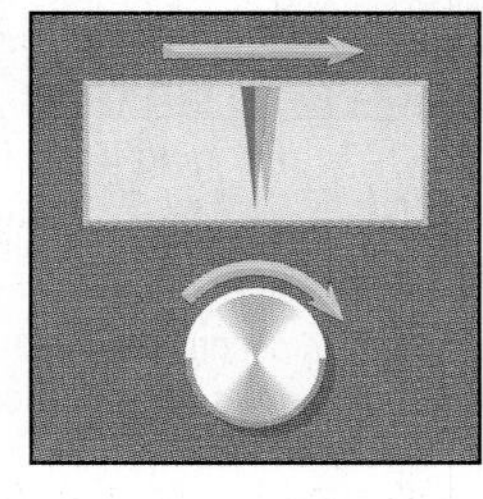

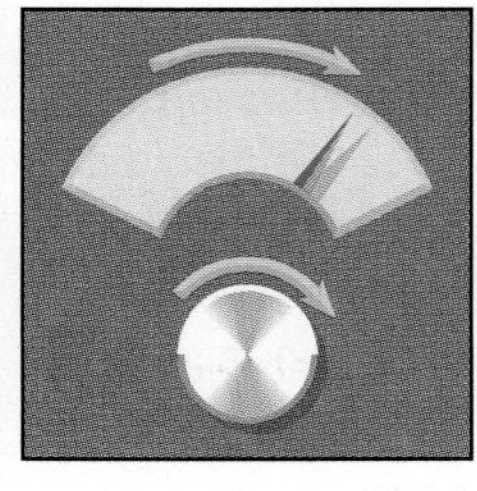

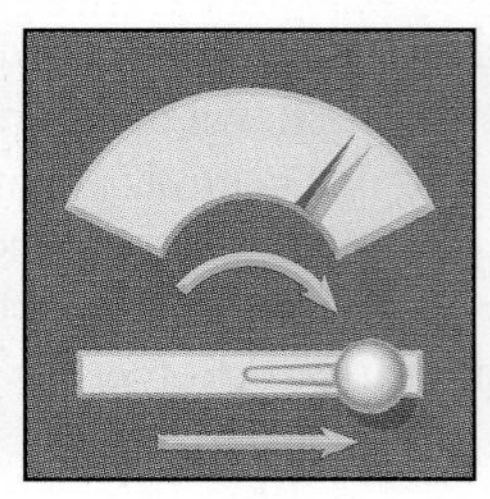

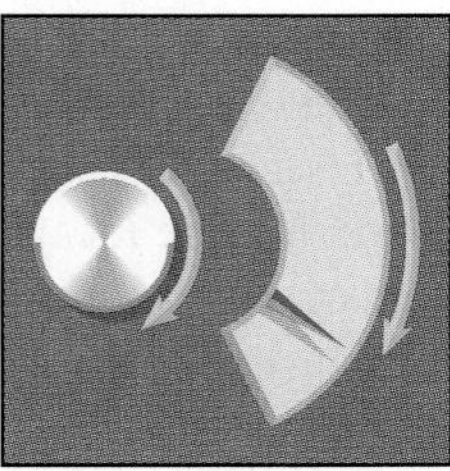

Health Psychology in the Workplace

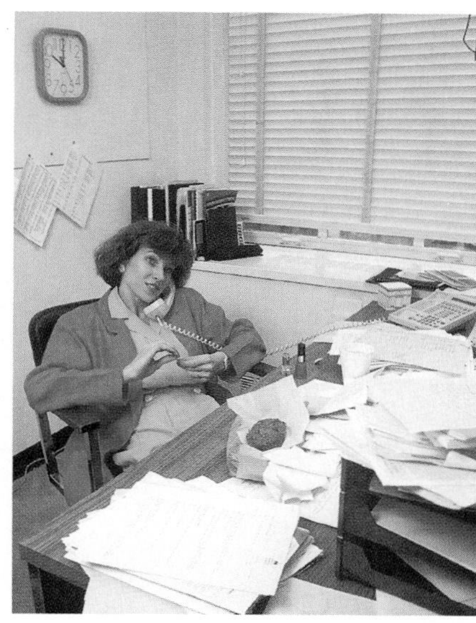
The risk of cardiovascular disease is twice as high for people with sedentary habits as for those who exercise regularly.

We first discussed the field of *health psychology* in chapter 12. We learned about the growing awareness among both medical professionals and the general public that stress and unhealthy patterns of behavior (such as overwork, poor diet, and lack of exercise) are extremely important threats to good health. There is an increasing understanding in the business world, too, that good health among employees is good business (Ilgen, 1990). Healthy employees are more productive, miss fewer days of work, make fewer claims for health benefits, and are less likely to die or become disabled during their most valuable and productive years. When Lee Iacocca (1984) took over as chair of the Chrysler Corporation, he was shocked to find that Chrysler paid more each year for employee health benefits than for the steel and rubber to make automobiles. And those costs did not reflect the indirect costs of absenteeism, poor performance, and the loss of valuable employees to early death that are associated with bad health. The cost of poor health to business is enormous.

Fortunately, many American businesses have concluded that programs to improve employee health are good for everyone—and profitable as well. Consider, for example, programs to increase the cardiovascular fitness of employees. The Centers for Disease Control have determined that the risk of cardiovascular disease is *twice* as high for sedentary persons as for persons who exercise regularly—making it a risk factor as important as high blood pressure, high serum cholesterol, and smoking (Powell, Thompson, Caspersen, & Kendrick, 1987). Thus, some 50,000 businesses in the United States have instituted some type of program to increase the fitness of their employees.

Suppose you are offered two jobs after graduation with identical work requirements, salaries, and opportunities for advancement—but one gives you the option of a free membership in the health club of your choice or a locker in the company gym (and time during the day to take an exercise break). The same company prohibits smoking in the workplace and has fruit juice rather than soft drinks in the vending machines. Assuming you are health conscious, which job would you take?

If you took the job with the company that makes exercise easy, would you be working for a company that made a profitable decision in this case? Yes, indeed. First, your company would tend to attract healthier employees who were excited about the opportunity to exercise and who would incur fewer health-related costs. Second, the company would likely save money by *keeping* its employees healthy through exercise. For example, the Johnson & Johnson Corporation studied the costs of such a health plan for 11,000 of its employees and found that it saved the company almost a quarter of a million dollars per year in direct health care claims (Bly, Jones, & Richardson, 1986). In these and other ways psychologists are beginning to show business that a healthy work environment yields not only employee well-being, but healthy profits, too.

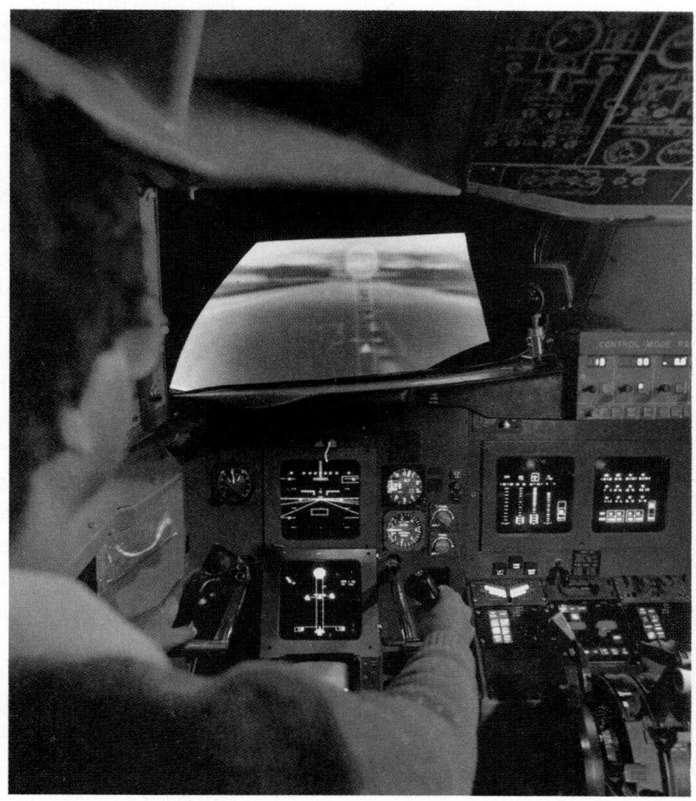
Computerized flight simulators allow new pilots to "fly" aircraft in the safety of the training laboratory until they develop the skill for real flying.

Other Applications of Psychology to the Workplace

We have sampled a few of the ways in which psychology has been applied to business, but there are many others. Psychological principles and methods have been used in developing methods of *training* new employees and in developing the potential of current employees through continued education (Tannenbaum & Yukl, 1992). When a new person is hired by IBM to repair computers, she or he must first be trained to do it. When a salesperson is promoted to a sales management position by Prudential, he or she must be taught how to manage sales. When a new management trainee is hired by McDonald's, she or he must be trained in purchasing, hiring, safely storing foods, and so on. When the number of employees who need training is multiplied by the number of jobs they must learn, it's easy to see why the efficiency of business depends in part on the efficiency of their training programs.

In many areas of the workplace, computers have come to play an increasingly large role in training. Computer-assisted instruction can be used to teach basic information, from insurance underwriting to telephone repair, in ways that are more efficient for both the employer and the employee. It is in the area of *computer simulation,* however, that computers offer their greatest advantages in training. It is neither ethical nor feasible to teach sailors to operate multimillion dollar submarines or jet aircraft by allowing them to "learn from their mistakes." One error during the training process could result in loss of life and the destruction of enormously expensive vehicles. In response to this need, extremely realistic computerized simulators have been developed that allow new pilots to "fly" aircraft in the safety of the training laboratory until they develop the skills to handle the real thing. Similar computer simulations have been developed for physicians to practice medical diagnosis and for investment managers to test their decision-making skills in the stock market.

Psychologists have also contributed to the advertising and marketing end of business. Advertising is almost as old as civilization itself. Excavation of the ruins of the ancient city of Pompeii, for example, found announcements of the availability of products and services painted on the walls of buildings (Anastasi, 1979). And psychologists have been trying to find ways to improve the effectiveness of advertising almost as long as there has been a field of psychology. The first book on the psychology of advertising was published by Walter Scott in 1908.

Psychologists have found that a number of perceptual factors such as size, color, repetition, and spatial position influence the effectiveness of advertisements. For example, half-page magazine ads are noticed by readers only half as often as full-page ads, and full-color ads are read by 50 percent more readers than are black-and-white ads (Anastasi, 1979).

Attempts to improve advertising effectiveness often involve emotional appeals. Recall from chapter 15 that fear appeals are sometimes effective in making communications more persuasive. Advertisers of mouthwash, toothpaste, hair dye, and the like would have us believe that if we do not use their products we will be coldly rejected by the people we care about. Manufacturers of boots, bathing suits, perfumes, and sports cars similarly imply in their ads that if we would only buy their goods we will be adored by others for our sexiness.

Psychologists in industry also work to determine the preferences of consumers. Others conduct research to determine the best ways to convey information about the contents of foods and drugs to consumers. Still others concentrate on reducing prejudice and other barriers to equal opportunities for minority groups in business. The roles for psychologists in business are as varied as the business sector of society.

Review

The quality of our lives is linked to business in terms of both our enjoyment of the goods and services that business produces and the satisfaction that we derive from our jobs. Industrial-organizational psychologists help business improve its productivity, improve worker safety and health, and help workers obtain more meaning and enjoyment from their jobs. Psychologists most frequently work through personnel departments because they have responsibility for selecting and training employees. They work to improve employee selection (matching the right person to the right job) by consulting with personnel managers on psychological factors that limit the usefulness of interviews, by interpreting biographical data, and by constructing methods of numerically evaluating applicants (and current employees) using tests, job simulations, and performance ratings.

Although job satisfaction and productivity are not perfectly correlated, industrial-organizational psychologists attempt to improve both through essentially the same methods. These methods principally involve helping managers improve managerial style (how they relate to their employees), the organizational structure of management (such as through participative management or management by objectives), and the physical and health conditions of work. Through these and many other methods, psychologists are able to contribute to both worker satisfaction and productivity.

Thinking Critically About Psychology

1. If interviews are the least valid method for selecting employees, why do they continue to be such a popular technique?

2. What questions might you ask a potential employer about working conditions to determine your likelihood of achieving a high level of job satisfaction?

Check Your Learning

To be sure that you have learned the key points from the preceding section, cover the answers below and try to answer each question. If you give an incorrect answer to any question, return to the page given next to the correct answer to see why your answer was not correct. Remember that these questions cover only some of the important information in this section; it is important that you make up your own questions to check your learning of other facts and concepts.

1. A(n) __________ is a psychologist who seeks ways to improve the functioning and human benefits of business.

- **a.** developmental psychologist
- **b.** industrial-organizational psychologist
- **c.** clinical psychologist
- **d.** Gestalt psychologist

2. __________ refer to the types of biographical information used by potential employers to evaluate a job candidate.

- **a.** Data
- **b.** Person variables
- **c.** Biodata
- **d.** Personality characteristics

3. __________ are the most valid selection measures for most complex jobs.

- **a.** Projective tests
- **b.** Performance tests
- **c.** Biodata
- **d.** Intellectual ability tests

4. __________, or spending a great deal of time organizing and directing the work of employees, is most effective when the supervisor is also considerate of others.

- **a.** Structuring
- **b.** Authoritative direction
- **c.** Decentralizing
- **d.** Categorizing

5. __________ refers to the branch of industrial-organizational psychology interested in the design of machines to be operated by human beings.

- **a.** Mechanical engineering
- **b.** Architectural engineering
- **c.** Graphic design
- **d.** Human factors engineering

Correct Answers
1. b (p. 562), 2. c (p. 564), 3. d (p. 568), 4. a (p. 571), 5. d (p. 573).

ENVIRONMENTAL PSYCHOLOGY

Architects and interior designers strive to create environments where people can live and work more happily, healthfully, and productively (Stokols, 1995). In recent years, **environmental psychologists** have become actively involved in the study of psychological reactions to different aspects of the physical environment. Most findings to date have been interesting, but perhaps not surprising. For example, people perceive others in less positive ways and are less interested in socializing in drab, ugly rooms than in attractive rooms (Maslow & Mintz, 1956; Russell & Mehrabian, 1978). Adding touches like potted plants and an aquarium to professors' offices makes students feel more welcome (Campbell, 1978). And people are less positive toward others in hot rooms than in comfortable rooms (Griffith & Veitch, 1971). Other findings have been less expected and have contributed more to architecture and interior design.

environmental psychologist
A psychologist who studies the effects of the physical environment on behavior and mental processes.

Office and Workspace Design

A great deal of effort has gone into the design of workspaces to make them enjoyable and safe for employees and to promote productive performance. For example, a popular trend today is to design office space in the so-called *office landscape* format. In this format, offices

Psychologists have helped architects design workspaces that are conducive to both job satisfaction and productivity. Do these workers have enough private space?

are laid out in large open spaces and separated from one another only by low movable partitions, desks, and file cabinets. This creates a space that can be flexibly rearranged, is inexpensive to construct, and is attractive in appearance. Contrary to expectation, however, studies of the psychological effects of office landscapes have not painted a positive picture. One study was conducted after a number of workers moved from a building with traditional separate offices into a new building that was equally divided into traditional offices and an office landscape area. After 6 months, workers who moved into the office landscape area were considerably less satisfied with their surroundings. They reported that they interacted more with each other, but they cooperated less. In addition, they found the new office area less private and noisier, and reportedly accomplished less work (Hundert & Greenfield, 1969).

Greg Oldham and Yitzhak Fried (1987) have also examined characteristics of favorable and unfavorable work environments. Studying clerical employees from different departments in the same large university, they found that the physical nature of the environment explained much of the differences between the departments in terms of employee turnover and satisfaction. Workers were most likely to be dissatisfied and to resign from their jobs when the office was poorly lighted, few enclosures provided privacy to the workers, employees were seated close together, and many employees occupied the same office. Clerical workers like well-lighted private space.

Architectural Design of Living Units

Psychologists have increasingly played a role in the design of living units. Perhaps because psychologists tend to work in universities, college dormitories have been a frequent subject of such research. Traditional plans for college dormitories call for a single long corridor into which a number of small rooms open. Typically, the residents of these rooms share a single common lounge and bathroom that are also located off the corridor. In contrast to this traditional single corridor design is the suite design. In this concept, three or four rooms are clustered around a small lounge and bathroom shared only by the residents of that one suite. Proponents of the suite design concept suggest that although the same number of people can be housed per square foot in this design (see fig. 16. 10), it's a far more "human" approach to dense housing. In this case, psychological studies have rather strongly supported the suite design concept. Residents of single corridor dorms spend less time in the dorms, express greater desire to avoid interaction with other residents, and feel that they have less control over what happens in their dormitory than residents of suite design dorms (Baum & Valins, 1977).

Even more impressive is the finding that the effects of living in a single corridor dorm extend outside of the dorm setting. Freshmen living in both types of dorms were brought to a laboratory where they were asked to wait with other students in a waiting room. Residents of single corridor dorms initiated fewer conversations, sat at greater physical distance from the other students, and spent less time looking at the faces of other students. Apparently, their unsatisfactory living environment led them to be somewhat less sociable even outside of the dormitory (Baum, Harpin, & Valins, 1975). If you live in a single corridor dorm, you should not be concerned about lasting damage to your social life, but it may have some minor effect on your current behavior.

Duncan Case (1981) has also provided evidence that the architecture of college dormitories influences friendship patterns over long periods of time. According to Case, the key element in dormitories is "shared required paths"—shared elevators, drinking fountains, and the like. College students who lived in dormitories were studied. During their sophomore year, over 80 percent of these students shared a room with someone with whom they had shared a required path during their freshman year. Even during their senior year, 50 percent of the roommates had met through shared required paths during their freshman year. Since the students reported that their best friend was one of their roommates 73 percent of the time, it is clear that friendships are dictated in part by architecture.

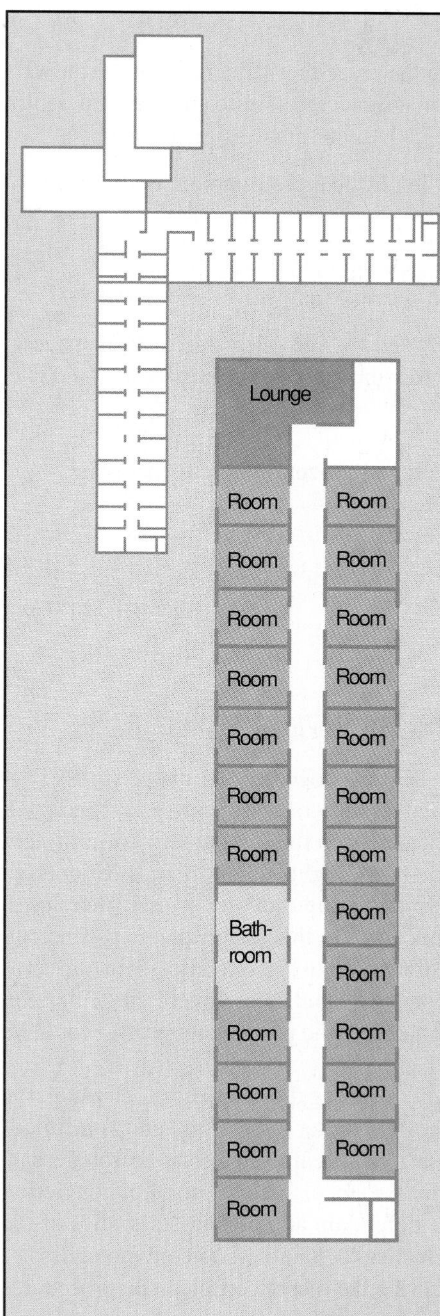

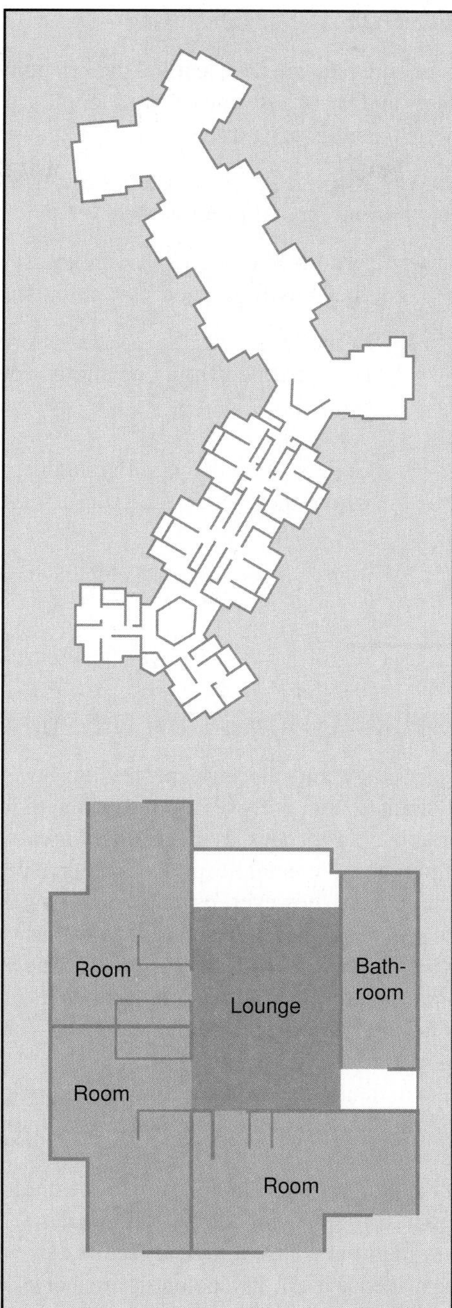

FIGURE 16.10

Examples of the single corridor and suite design floor plans for college dormitories.

Review

Environmental psychologists conduct research on the psychological impact of our physical environment. They have found that some aspects of the interior design of rooms, such as the drabness of colors or the presence of plants, influences the mood of the persons in those rooms and their interest in socializing. Similarly, the temperature of the room and other physical characteristics also influence emotions and social behavior. Friendship patterns have been found to be affected by the architecture of living units, as individuals who share "required paths" are more likely to develop friendships in a dormitory than those who do not. By studying environments such as these and the environments of workspaces, environmental psychologists can offer information to architects and interior designers that helps them design spaces with optimal psychological impact.

Thinking Critically About Psychology

1. Does the physical environment of your home, apartment, or dormitory make it easy or difficult to meet your neighbors? In what ways?

2. Is your college campus conducive to both learning and social interaction? Why or why not?

Check Your Learning

To be sure that you have learned the key points from the preceding section, cover the answers below and try to answer each question. If you give an incorrect answer to any question, return to the page given next to the correct answer to see why your answer was not correct.

1. A(n) __________ studies the effects of the physical environment on behavior and mental processes.

   a. developmental psychologist **c.** clinical psychologist
   b. environmental psychologist **d.** psychoanalyst

2. In the ______________ format, offices are laid out in large open spaces and separated from one another only by low movable partitions, desks, and file cabinets.

3. College students who live in dormitories tend to meet other students with whom they have ______________ .

Correct Answers

1. b (p. 577), **2.** office landscape (p. 577), **3.** shared required paths (p. 578).

PSYCHOLOGY AND LAW: THE BEHAVIOR OF JURIES AND WITNESSES

Psychology and the legal profession have been working together for many years. Psychologists frequently testify regarding an individual's sanity or competency to stand trial. Moreover, attorneys are necessarily involved in hearings on the involuntary commitment of patients to mental hospitals and in the protection of the rights of psychiatric patients. In recent years, however, psychologists have begun to apply their methods and principles to the *practice* of law in the courtroom. When you think about it, this application of psychology to the practice of law is not surprising. The administration of justice is a process that involves *people*—attorneys, defendants, witnesses, and judges. Any understanding of the profession of law that ignores the human element—the psychology of the people involved—would be an incomplete understanding.

To date, the most extensive psychological study of the legal process has focused on the criminal trial. The findings suggest that, unless they are better understood and controlled, psychological factors in the trial process pose a serious threat to our constitutional guarantee of a fair trial. In addition to the quality of the evidence, the likelihood of conviction depends in part on personal characteristics of the defendant and on characteristics of the jury members. Psychological factors can even influence the quality and convincingness of the evidence itself. Psychologists are increasingly serving the role of consultant on procedures such as jury selection and the presentation of evidence.

Characteristics of Defendants

Although we would like to believe that all of us would be treated equally in court, it is not always the case. Your chance of being acquitted in a criminal trial in the United States is better if you are physically attractive, wealthy, and white. Poor people are more likely to be convicted than affluent ones when charged with similar assault and larceny charges (Haney, 1980). Physically attractive defendants are less likely to be convicted than unattractive ones, unless the attractiveness seemed to play a part in the crime (as in a swindle) (Nemeth, 1981). And racially prejudiced jury members are more likely to convict African Americans than whites (Haney, 1980).

The same characteristics of the defendants also play a role in the harshness of the sentence. In first-degree murder cases, blue-collar workers are more likely to be sentenced to death than white-collar workers. And from 1930 to 1979, 2,066 African Americans were executed compared with 1,751 whites even though there are four times as many whites in the United States as African Americans (Haney, 1980). These findings suggest that justice is not equal for different kinds of defendants, probably because of the prejudices held by jury members about different groups of people. Since characteristics such as income, attractiveness, and race have nothing to do with one's guilt or innocence, these person perception variables make it difficult for all people to receive equal protection under the law.

Characteristics of Jury Members

Certain types of jury members are more likely to vote for conviction and recommend harsher sentences than other types. Jurors who are more conviction-prone and punitive in sentencing are those who are white, older, better educated, higher in social status, more conservative, and believe more strongly that authority and law should be respected (Nemeth, 1981). There is mixed evidence as to whether men are more likely to vote for conviction than women, but there is clear-cut evidence of gender differences in cases of rape. Women are more likely to convict and to be harsher in sentencing than male jurors, while males are more likely to believe that the female victim encouraged the rapist (Nemeth, 1981). Overall, juries tend to be "kinder to their own kind." Affluent, educated, white jurors tend to be harsher in their treatment of less affluent, less educated, minority defendants.

There is also evidence that jurors who believe in the death penalty are more likely to convict than those who do not. Prior to 1968, individuals who had strong objections to the death penalty were routinely barred from serving on juries in cases involving a possible death penalty. In a landmark ruling in 1968, however, an appeals judge commuted a death penalty to life imprisonment in the case of *Witherspoon v. Illinois* on the grounds that the jury was composed only of persons who favored the death penalty and was not, therefore, a fair and "representative" jury. In making this ruling, the judge cited a Gallup poll conducted at that time that found that only about 55 percent of the people surveyed favored the death penalty. The judge ruled that prospective jurors could be excluded only when they were so opposed to the death penalty that they would vote against it regardless of the evidence.

Was this a good decision? Was the judge correct in assuming that a jury composed only of individuals who favor the death penalty—a "death-qualified" jury—might not give the defendant a fair trial? Actually, a number of studies support the decision of the judge (Nemeth, 1981). For example, a study was conducted on the relationship between attitudes toward the death penalty and the tendency to convict in a sample of 207 industrial workers. They were initially asked to fill out a number of questionnaires including the following:

Capital Punishment Attitude Questionnaire

Directions. Assume you are on a jury to determine the sentence for a defendant who has already been convicted of a very serious crime. If the law gives you a *choice* of death or life imprisonment, or some other penalty: (check *one* only)

1. I could not vote for the death penalty regardless of the facts and circumstances of the case.
2. There are some kinds of cases in which I know I could not vote for the death penalty even if the law allowed me to, but others in which I would be willing to consider voting for it.
3. I would consider all of the penalties provided by the law and the facts and circumstances of the particular case.
4. I would usually vote for the death penalty in a case where the law allows me to.
5. I would always vote for the death penalty in a case where the law allows me to.

From G. L. Jurow, "New Data on the Effects of a 'Death-Qualified' Jury on the Guilt Determination Process," *Harvard Law Review* 84:59. ©1971 Harvard Law Review Association. Used by permission.

As these workers did, try to imagine that you have been selected to serve on the jury in a murder trial in a state that imposes the death penalty. Which alternative would you choose? All of the participants were shown two videotapes of mock murder trials that contained all of the standard elements of procedure and evidence. The first concerned a

TABLE 16.1 Number of Jurors in a Simulated Trial Who Voted to Convict or Acquit, Divided According to Their Willingness to Impose the Death Penalty

Willingness to Impose Death Penalty if Serving as a Juror	Number Voting to	
	Convict	Acquit
Low (1 and 2)	19	40
Medium (3)	59	73
High (4 and 5)	14	2

From G. L. Jurow, "New Data on the Effects of a 'Death-Qualified' Jury on the Guilt Determination Process," *Harvard Law Review* 84:59.

robbery of a liquor store in which the proprietor of the store was killed in the process. The second case was of a man charged with robbing, raping, and killing a college student in her apartment. After each videotaped trial the "jurors" voted to convict or acquit the defendant.

The jurors in this experiment were divided into three groups on the basis of their responses to the questionnaire concerning capital punishment. Jurors scoring low in willingness to impose the death penalty (who checked items 1 or 2) were far more likely to vote for acquittal than conviction in the first trial (see table 16.1). Conversely, jurors who were high in willingness to impose the death penalty (who checked items 4 or 5) were much more likely to vote for conviction. The same pattern was shown in the voting after the second trial, although not as strongly.

Thus, this and other studies finding similar differences do suggest that juries composed only of jurors who are in favor of the death penalty (who are also more likely to be conservative, high status, authoritarian males) are biased in favor of conviction of defendants (Nemeth, 1981). This means that the current practice of excluding only those jurors who are most strongly opposed to the death penalty or of using separate juries for the trial and the sentencing may make good psychological sense.

Psychological Factors in Presenting Evidence

"Your Honor, the jury finds the defendant weakly developed as a central character, overshadowed by the principal witnesses, unconvincingly portrayed as a victim of society, and guilty as charged."

Drawing by Cheney; © 1988 The New Yorker Magazine, Inc.

It's somewhat reassuring to learn that several studies have suggested that although characteristics of the defendants and jurors are important in determining conviction or acquittal, the evidence is several times more important (Nemeth, 1981). Unfortunately, facts are not the only important aspect of courtroom evidence; psychological factors are involved here as well.

Criminal trials are "adversarial proceedings." The attorneys for the prosecution and defense each attempt to convince the jury of the guilt or innocence of the defendant as if they were competing in a debate. Since both attorneys cannot talk at the same time, they obviously must make their presentations one at a time. Unfortunately, the *order* in which evidence is presented appears to make a difference in the outcome of the trial. One study investigated the effect of order of presentation in a simulated trial in which law students played the roles of attorneys for the defense and prosecution and undergraduate students served as jurors. The simulated case concerned a man who was charged with murder but claimed he had acted in self-defense. Half of the time, the prosecutor went first, and half of the time the defense attorney went first. The results showed that the attorney who went second held a decided advantage (Thibaut & Walker, 1975). This is not good news if you are falsely accused of a crime, since tradition has it that the prosecutor is allowed to make the last statement to the jury.

Recall from chapter 15 that information you encounter first when getting to know a stranger ("first impressions") is stronger in determining your overall impression of that person *unless* a relatively long time elapses between the first and subsequent information. That last qualification may help to explain the findings about the order of presentation of courtroom evidence. It may be that because courtroom arguments are lengthy and complex, recently presented information is more easily remembered and potent. This interpretation is strengthened by the finding that the advantage of presenting in the second position is increased further if an attorney states the most convincing points at the very end of the second presentation rather than at the beginning (Thibaut & Walker, 1975).

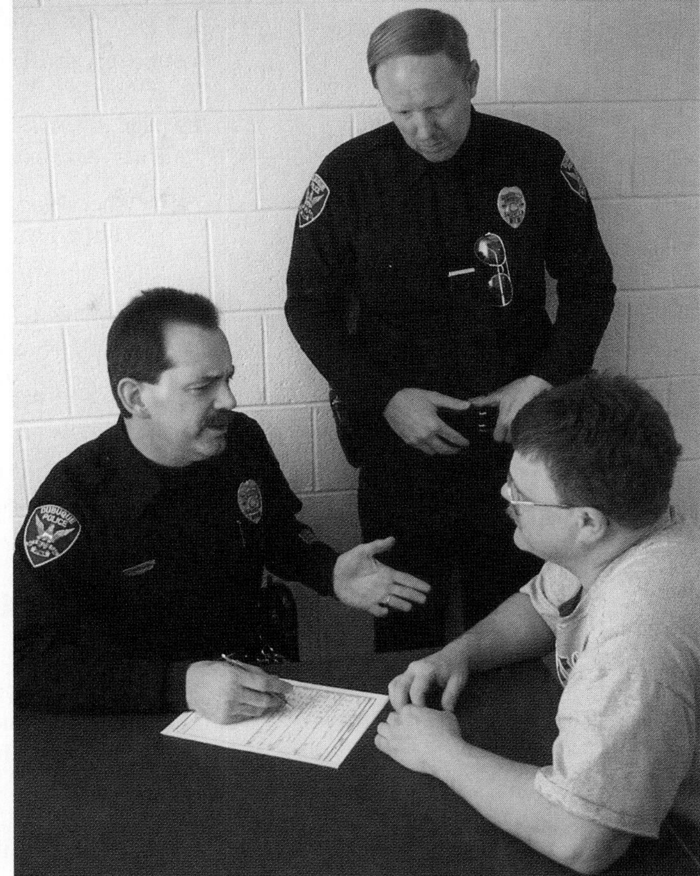

Police interrogations use many psychological pressures to obtain information.

Interrogating Criminal Suspects

Social psychologist Craig Haney (1980) has analyzed the standard American method of police interrogation to examine its psychological aspects. Police use a number of psychological techniques to increase the probability of a confession. Imagine that you have been taken to a barren interrogating room. You are alone with the interrogators—the room does not even have a telephone—giving you a feeling of being completely cut off from the outside world. The interrogator often stands very close to you, violating your personal space, and giving you a feeling of powerlessness.

The interrogator begins the questioning by pointing out your apparent guilt. But the crime is discussed in such a way as to make it seem so understandable—almost morally justifiable—that you feel that the interrogator would not shame you if you confessed. If the crime is not a big deal, why not just admit to doing it? But the interrogator soon grows impatient with you for not admitting to the crime and storms out of the room. A second officer in the room steps over, though, and asks you to excuse the behavior of the first interrogator—it's been a long and frustrating day. This second officer is very sympathetic to your situation and emphasizes how much easier the court would be on you if you confessed. This officer really seems to feel genuine concern for you. Just then, the first interrogator enters the room again and asks you for a confession. You see anger beginning to build, and you blurt out a confession just to avoid the angry outburst. This kind of scene is repeated many times a day in police stations across the country, although not always with favorable results. Many suspects are as accustomed to the routine of interrogation as are the police (Haney, 1980).

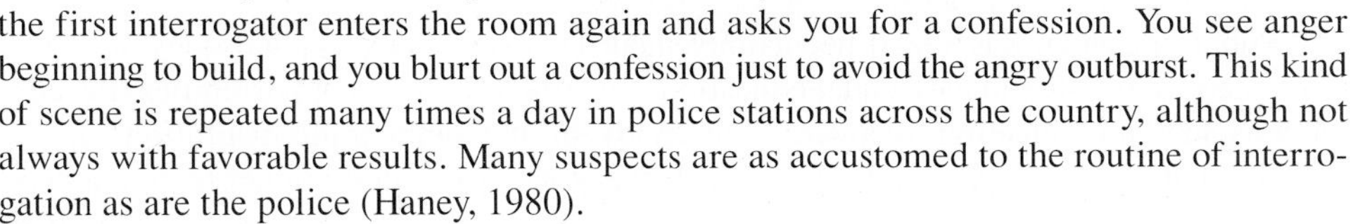

Review

Criminal trials are conducted by people, so it's not surprising to learn that psychological factors play a role. What may be more surprising—and disturbing—is to see how strong a role they can play. Having different types of people involved in the trial process is likely to produce different outcomes. Poor, uneducated, minority defendants are more likely to be convicted and receive harsher sentences. Jurors who are white, older, higher in social status, more conservative, and more authoritarian than average, as well as those who believe in capital punishment, are more likely to vote for conviction and impose harsh punishments. The quality of the evidence presented in criminal trials is more important in determining the jury's decision than the psychological characteristics of the defendant and jurors, but psychological factors are also involved in courtroom evidence. Even the order in which evidence is presented can influence the outcome of a trial. Obviously, these factors must be understood and controlled as much as possible if the judicial system is to be fair for all concerned.

Thinking Critically About Psychology

1. In what ways might a psychologist be able to assist a defendant in preparing for a criminal trial? What are the ethical issues involved in giving such assistance?

2. Based on the information presented, can someone get a "fair" trial? Why or why not?

Check Your Learning

To be sure that you have learned the key points from the preceding section, cover the answers below and try to answer each question. If you give an incorrect answer to any question, return to the page given next to the correct answer to see why your answer was not correct.

Answer each question with True or False.

1. Other things being equal, you have a greater chance of being acquitted in a criminal trial by a white, middle-class jury if you are physically attractive, high in social status, and white.
2. Jurors who believe in the death penalty are less likely to vote for the conviction of a defendant.
3. The attorney who speaks last in a trial has an advantage in persuading the jury.

Correct Answers

1. True (p. 580), **2.** False (p. 581), **3.** True (p. 582).

PSYCHOLOGY AND EDUCATION: BETTER TEACHING AND TESTING

educational psychology
The field in which principles of learning, cognition, and other aspects of psychology are applied to improve education.

Like industrial-organizational psychology, **educational psychology** is almost as old as the discipline of psychology itself. Binet's development of a useful intelligence test for schoolchildren laid the foundation for educational testing. Others, like Edward Lee Thorndike of Columbia University, conducted research during the early 1900s on factors that influence school learning and memory. But while educational psychology is an old field, its current excitement stems from relatively new developments. These innovations show particular promise in improving the education of children with special educational needs. Psychologists serve education as professors who help train teachers in the psychology of education, as consultants on the development of testing programs, and as specialists employed by school systems (**school psychologists**) to consult with teachers and to test children who may need special educational programs.

school psychologist
A psychologist who aids schools by testing children to determine eligibility for placement in special education programs and who consults with teachers and parents.

Public education was established to implement Thomas Jefferson's philosophy that every American citizen should have equal educational as well as political opportunities. Because citizens need an education to govern themselves through democratic institutions, it was decided that education should be available to every American child rather than as a privilege of the rich. The most important recent innovations in educational psychology have been ones that help more children benefit fully from their time in school: the mastery learning approach, effective methods of educating economically disadvantaged children, the development of more meaningful tests of achievement, and the integration of children with psychological and physical challenges into the normal classroom environment, known as mainstreaming.

Mastery Learning and Intelligent Tutoring Systems

If you were a teacher, would you try to teach a child to add and subtract before she had learned to count? Would you teach trigonometry to a child before he had mastered the basics of plane geometry? It does not make much sense to try to teach a child a new skill before she or he has learned the basic skills that are the foundation for further learning. Yet it happens every day in American education—children are pushed from one subject to another before they are ready to progress. Why? The reason is that in many schools, education is conducted according to group schedules. A certain amount of time is allotted for the group to learn to count, and then the group moves on to addition. Students take plane geometry in the fall semester and then trigonometry in the spring. If an individual child is not ready to progress, he or she must usually move on with the group anyway.

mastery learning
The concept that children should never progress from one learning task to another until they have mastered the more basic one.

Educational psychologist Benjamin Bloom has been an outspoken critic of this approach and has proposed the **mastery learning** concept to take its place (Bloom, 1974). Quite simply, Bloom insists that children should never progress from one learning task to another until they have fully mastered the first one. If this rule is followed, Bloom suggests that learning will be far more effective in the long run. For example, a group of high school students who were enrolled in a course on automobile mechanics took part in an evaluation of the mastery learning approach. The course was divided into eight units that built upon one another in succession. Half of the students progressed through the units as a group according to a prearranged schedule. The other students—the mastery learning group—moved at their own pace and did not begin the next unit until they had passed a test on the previous unit. At the end of the course, the mastery learning group had learned far more in the same amount of time (Wentling, 1973).

Bloom suggests that the mastery learning approach is particularly effective for slow-learning children, but it does not penalize brighter children. In the traditional approach of group scheduling, the top fifth of American students learns three times as much as the bottom fifth by the time they graduate from high school. When students use a mastery learning approach, however, the learning of the bottom fifth improves so much as to cut this difference in half (Bloom, 1974).

More recently, the availability of inexpensive computers that can be used in the classroom has made possible an improvement on the mastery learning approach called **intelligent tutoring systems** (or ITS) (Snow & Swanson, 1992). In the ITS approach a computer is programmed to serve as an individualized tutor to the student. In the case of arithmetic, the computer would tell the student about a new rule of, say, subtraction (visually on the screen and orally through headphones) and then ask the student to solve some problems based on the new rule. As in mastery learning, the computer would not allow the student to progress to the next rule until the current one was mastered. But ITS can also respond to any errors that the student makes and adapt the instruction accordingly. Let's say the student is learning to "borrow" when subtracting two-digit numbers and makes a mistake. The computer might see that the mistake was based on a misunderstanding of the rule for borrowing and would then repeat the rule—possibly in simpler language. On the other hand, the computer might detect that the mistake was based on forgetting how to subtract single-digit numbers and go back to a brief review of that material. Not only does ITS make it easier for teachers to work with children who are at different levels of mastery in the same classroom, but it also allows individual remediation of any "gaps" in the learning process. The only bad news about ITS is that it is only being used in a handful of schools.

intelligent tutoring systems
Approach to learning in which computers provide tutoring to students.

The availability of inexpensive classroom computers lets intelligent tutoring systems tailor lessons to each student's level of mastery.

Project Follow Through: Educating Economically Disadvantaged Children

One of the harshest realities of American life is that millions of people live in extreme poverty despite the overall affluence of the nation. Who are the poor? Where do they come from? Sadly, most of the people living in poverty today are the children of the last generation of poor people and will be the parents of the next generation of the poor. Poverty tends to run in families.

A key element in the development of a lifestyle of poverty is educational failure. People who do not learn enough in school to be employable have little chance of rising above poverty. The cycle of educational failure in economically disadvantaged children is an all too familiar story. Each year in school, children from disadvantaged families learn about two-thirds of what the average child learns. This means that they fall farther behind their classmates each successive year in a dangerous downward spiral that often ends in dropping out of school (Becker & Carnine, 1980).

In the mid-1960s a massive experiment was conceived by the U.S. Office of Education to test new ways of educating economically disadvantaged children. Nine groups of researchers were given funds to design and implement what they thought would be ideal educational programs, and independent research organizations were contracted to evaluate their effectiveness. This massive educational experiment—involving tens of thousands of children across the country—was named **Project Follow Through.** This program followed children through the crucial years of kindergarten through third grade, in contrast to the earlier attempts to help disadvantaged children that had stopped at the kindergarten level.

Project Follow Through
A federally sponsored program designed to help educate economically disadvantaged children.

The nine Follow Through projects differed considerably in educational philosophy, and most were clearly unsuccessful in improving educational progress. The most successful of the projects was consistently able, however, to bring disadvantaged children to the national average or above. This project, designed by Wesley Becker and Siegfried Engelmann of the University of Oregon and known as the Direct Instruction Project, made simple but powerful use of what is now known about the psychology of education. Becker and Engelmann designed a curriculum based on a knowledge of the cognitive skills needed in reading and other subjects. They also designed a teaching method based on the principles of learning—particularly positive reinforcement—and used practice methods designed to enhance memory for what had been learned. The success of this program is an impressive testimony to the value of the accumulated knowledge of educational psychology.

Person X Situation Interaction in the Classroom

We learned in chapter 11 that our traits and the situations we find ourselves in work together to influence our behavior—the *person X situation interaction.* This concept is highly important in understanding and evaluating efforts to improve teaching and the school environment. For example, one of the recurrent debates among American educators concerns how structured the classroom should be. Should the classroom be open and unfettered by walls with relatively relaxed rules concerning student behavior, or are small rooms and firm rules best? The answer to this question, in part, is that different students tend to react better to different school environments. The school achievement of children in structured classrooms is generally better than in unstructured classrooms, but a child's tendency to be anxious interacts with this characteristic of the environment. As shown in figure 16.11, anxious children perform slightly better than less anxious children in structured classrooms, but the performance of anxious children takes a nosedive in unstructured classrooms (Grimes & Allinsmith, 1961). In evaluating new educational approaches, we must remember to take into account the person X situation interaction.

Criterion-Referenced Testing

criterion-referenced testing Testing designed to determine whether a child can meet the minimum standards of a specific educational objective.

The renewed interest in finding better ways to prepare students to lead successful adult lives has also led to the development of a new approach in evaluating how much students have learned in school. In traditional approaches to educational testing, children are compared with one another. For example, a traditional test of computational skills in arithmetic would require children to work a large number of problems. A child who correctly solved the same number of problems as the average for children in her or his grade would be considered to be "on grade level." The goal of **criterion-referenced testing,** however, is not to compare children but to determine whether a given child can meet the minimum criteria for a specific educational objective. These objectives are usually practical in nature. For example, one criterion-referenced test asks children to fill in a personal information blank like the ones required by most employment applications. The issue in this kind of testing is not how well a child can fill in the blank compared with other children, but simply whether the child can *do* it appropriately. This is a skill well worth teaching to students, since adults who cannot fill out employment forms stand little chance of being hired. Sadly, one study showed that only 61 percent of American 17-year-olds could fill out an employment application form without errors (Mellon, 1975).

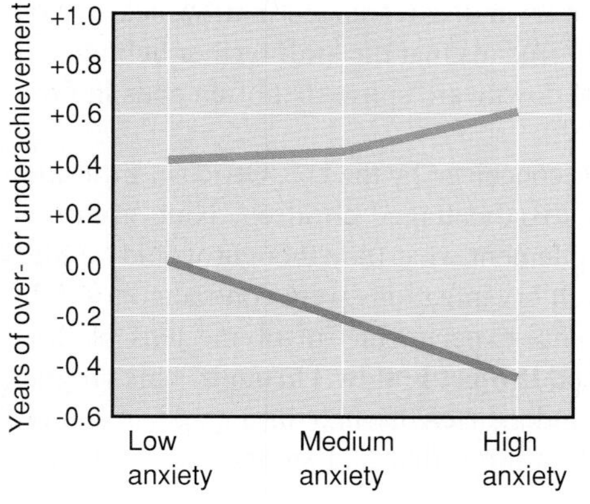

FIGURE 16.11

In unstructured classrooms, the academic achievement of anxious children is much poorer than that of less anxious children. But, in structured classrooms, children's anxiety does little damage to their school performance. In evaluating different approaches to education, we must remember to consider the person X situation interaction.

Source: J. W. Grimes and W. Allinsmith, "Compulsivity, Anxiety, and School Achievement" in *Merrill-Palmer Quarterly,* 7:247–271, © 1961 Wayne State University Press, Detroit, MI.

Criterion-referenced testing provides the kind of information that teachers need to improve education. If the items accurately reflect the goals of education, then criterion-referenced test scores can provide feedback to teachers on how well they are teaching. If Mary cannot fill out a personal information blank, then the teacher knows that Mary needs more instruction on that skill. If most of the students in a school cannot fill them out, then the school administration knows that a better teaching method must be implemented. Thus, criterion-referenced tests play an important role in evaluating and improving teaching methods.

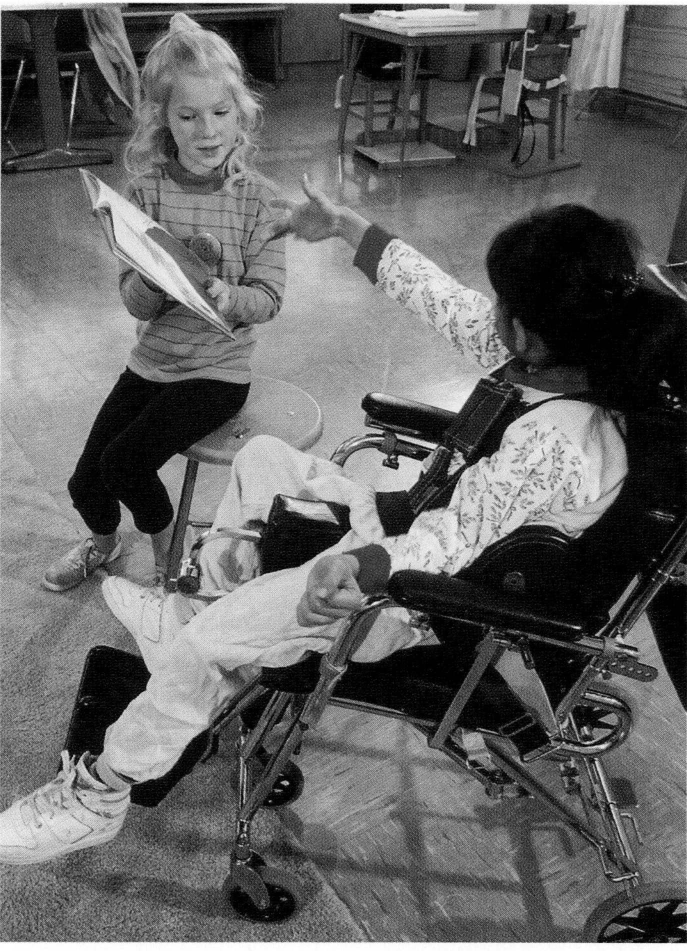

Mainstreaming provides children with special needs a public education in the least restrictive environment. Public Law 94-142 helped get many such children into regular classrooms.

Mainstreaming: Education for Persons with Special Needs

During the 1970s, enormous strides were made in the legal standing of children with challenging conditions such as mental retardation, emotional problems, and physical challenges. Federal legislation—now famous as *Public Law 94–142*—established that *every* child has a *right* to a public education, regardless of his or her special needs. This means that many more children with severe challenges are being served by public schools than ever before.

Furthermore, Public Law 94–142 states that the child is entitled to receive her or his education in the *least restrictive environment*. This legal phrase means that children must receive educational and psychological assistance in circumstances that are as similar as possible to the normal day-to-day environment of nonhandicapped children. Thus, it's no longer legal to isolate children with special needs in separate schools *if* it's possible to educate them in regular schools and allow them to interact with other children. Whenever possible, in fact, children with special needs must be kept in the regular classroom for as large a part of the school day as possible and removed for special assistance only when necessary. This practice is known as **mainstreaming,** because it keeps such children within the mainstream of normal social and educational development.

In addition to protecting the legal rights of people with special needs, Public Law 94–142 offers some important benefits to all concerned. First, it gives students with special needs an opportunity to learn how to fit into the world of youngsters without disabilities. Equally important, it gives children without special needs a chance to learn firsthand that children with special needs are fully human and well worth having as friends (Augustine, Gruber, & Hanson, 1990).

mainstreaming
The practice of integrating children with special needs into regular classrooms.

Review

Educational psychologists have long sought to improve ways of teaching and testing schoolchildren, but the recent excitement in educational psychology stems from new concepts and methods of teaching and testing that promise to help more children benefit fully from the opportunities offered by the educational system. The mastery learning approach provides a way to both enhance learning and decrease the gap between the most and least successful learners; the Project Follow Through experiment has identified effective methods for educating disadvantaged children; and the shift toward criterion-referenced testing provides us with a more meaningful way of evaluating success in teaching necessary skills and knowledge to children. In a different way, the mainstreaming approach assures children with special needs of their rightful place in the educational system.

Thinking Critically About Psychology

1. How could the mastery learning approach provide a greater degree of equality of opportunity to all people?

2. This textbook was designed to increase your ease of learning. What could be done to make it better?

Check Your Learning

To be sure that you have learned the key points from the preceding section, cover the answers below and try to answer each question. If you give an incorrect answer to any question, return to the page given next to the correct answer to see why your answer was not correct.

1. __________ psychology is the field in which principles of learning, cognition, and other aspects of psychology are applied to improve teaching and learning.

a. Developmental
b. School
c. Environmental
d. Educational

2. __________ is the concept that children should never progress from one learning task to another until they have mastered the more basic one.

a. Stage theory
b. Mastery learning
c. Step learning
d. Progression theory

3. __________ testing is designed to determine whether a child can meet the minimum standards of a specific educational objective.

a. Intelligence
b. Aptitude
c. Criterion-referenced
d. Personality

4. The practice of integrating children with special needs into regular classrooms is called __________ .

a. integration
b. assimilation
c. combining
d. mainstreaming

Correct Answers
1. d (p. 584), **2.** b (p. 584), **3.** c (p. 586), **4.** d (p. 587).

APPLICATION OF PSYCHOLOGY

PREVENTION OF ENVIRONMENTAL DESTRUCTION

A "New Environmental Psychology" has evolved over the past two decades in response to increasing concern over the deteriorating global environment. It is no secret that the life-support system we call earth is in serious jeopardy. Three broad categories of assaults on our environment can be identified: (a) overpopulation, (b) resource depletion, and (c) pollution. Although scientists, politicians, and others disagree about the severity and the urgency of these environmental problems, there can be no doubt that most environmental problems have a basis in human behavior. *This means that we must change human behavior to solve environmental problems.* Therefore, the efforts of psychologists to find ways of changing the environmentally destructive behaviors that lead to global warming, food and water shortages, ozone depletion, acid rain, and overpopulation may well be the most significant work in the history of psychology.

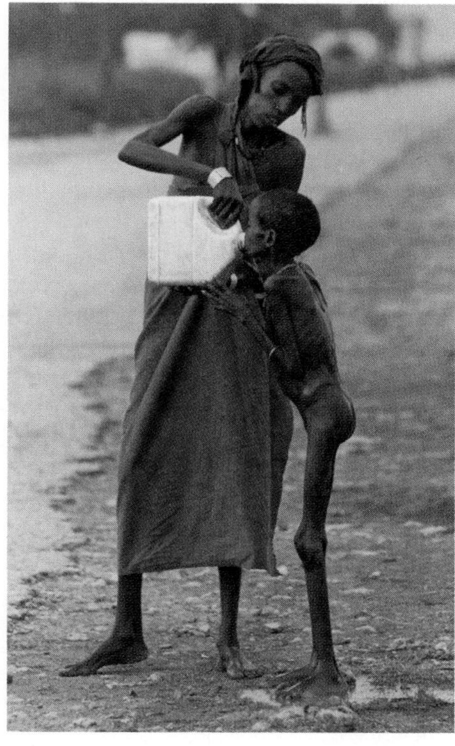

Mismanagement of the earth's resources can have tragic effects for both the environment and the people of the world. Approximately one-fifth of the world's population lives in extreme poverty that puts them at risk for death and disease. Every day, more than 40,000 infants and children die of starvation or nutrition-related problems.

Overpopulation, Resource Depletion, and Pollution: Three Assaults on the Earth's Environment

In this section, we will describe the main threats to the environment that result from human behavior. In the next section, we will look at the attempts of psychologists to change these environmentally destructive behaviors.

Overpopulation

It took about 3 million years to reach a population of 1 billion people on the planet. Now, with the addition of approximately 97 million people to the planet every year, another billion of us are added almost every decade. The current population of 5.2 billion will double in about 47 years, putting the world's population at 10 to 12 billion near the middle of the twenty-first century. At the current rate, we are adding close to 184 additional mouths to feed every minute! There is no question that the human behavior of reproducing at these high rates is a major threat to the environment.

Of the 5.2 billion people currently on earth, approximately 1 billion of them live in absolute poverty that puts them at high risk of death or serious health problems due to malnutrition and disease. Each day an average of 40,000 infants and children die as a result of starvation and nutrition-related illness. Many of these people live in developing or "third world" countries, where the difference between average incomes of industrialized and developing countries is greater now than it was in 1977. Not surprisingly, people show little concern for preserving the environment when daily survival of self and family is in jeopardy. As a result, people in many developing countries are forced into behaviors that are harmful to the environment. Examples include exhausting natural resources for export to industrial nations (such as the ongoing destruction of the hardwood forests of Indonesia and South America), degrading the soil through poor farming techniques, and polluting water supplies through poor agricultural, industrial, and sanitation practices. In developing nations throughout the world, these problems are multiplied as the increasing populations become concentrated in large cities. Although it is still possible to find experts who deny it, the earth's carrying capacity for human beings is quickly reaching its limit (many would say that it has already been surpassed).

Resource Depletion

A second major environmental problem involves the rate at which humankind is depleting the earth's natural resources. Some of those resources are necessary to our lifestyles—for example, we must have oil and coal (fossil fuels) to maintain our electrified and automobile-driven way of life. But other resources are essential to our very survival (clean air, clean water, topsoil that can be farmed, etc.). It is the rare American who is not generally aware of the shrinking supply of usable fossil fuels. We consume millions of barrels of oil each day, a thirst that has already resulted in the depletion of half of what is estimated to be our total oil supply. America has about 200 years worth of coal left, but its

Our electrified and automobile-driven way of life is fast depleting the earth's irreplaceable resources.

use creates other problems (e.g., air pollution and global warming) that will make this alternative unfeasible.

Water and soil are resources that are already in short supply throughout much of the world. In our own country, primarily in the southwest, demands have surpassed the region's ability to provide adequate amounts of fresh water. Amazingly, the Colorado River, the great provider of water for the southwest, no longer reaches its former final destination to the Pacific Ocean—it is completely exhausted by humanity along the way. Still, the competition among western states for water is already fierce. In developing nations, only about half the people have access to safe drinking water today, and the problem will only grow worse in the future. As population continues to increase, more and more water will be needed for agricultural, industrial, and personal uses. It is essential that ways be found to preserve and protect the earth's limited water resources. In addition, the amount of land that is available for agriculture is diminishing. Each year erosion, urban sprawl, and other factors create a net loss of tillable land for growing crops.

Similar stories could be told about the loss of other resources such as precious metals, the oceans' supply of fish, forests, the rapid extinction of plants and animal species, and numerous other gifts that are supplied by earth's life support system. They all point to a pattern of excessive consumption that is surpassing the earth's ability to sustain itself.

Pollution

The third major insult to the environment comes from pollution of earth's air, land, and water. We have all heard about the problems of acid rain, smog and high ozone levels, toxic waste, and polluted rivers, lakes, and saltwater bays. We have also heard about the threats of *global warming* and the *greenhouse effect,* which refer to the very real possibility that average temperatures may be increasing because of pollutants (primarily excessive carbon dioxide and methane) trapping the earth's heat and not letting it escape into space. Although scientists disagree about the extent of this threat, most experts predict that even a relatively small overall warming could have devastating effects on the earth's ability to sustain its current population. The great American "breadbasket" in the Midwest, for example, could become much less suitable for agriculture. The climate most appropriate for farming would move north to Canada, which would allow that country to become the new "breadbasket," were it not for that fact that it generally lacks the topsoil necessary for the task.

Pollution of our fresh water resources is another problem that must be addressed soon. Not only are some of our aquifers (underground water supplies) shrinking, but our waters are being polluted by numerous sources such as industrial and mining wastes, agricultural pesticides and fertilizers, and acid rain. Even now, it is estimated that more than 25 million people die in third world countries each year as a result of polluted water. As with other environmental problems, the extent of humankind's polluting behaviors is surpassing the earth's ability to sustain and renew itself.

Psychological Approaches to Environmental Problems

Although technological innovations such as antipollution devices on automobiles help reduce some of these threats to our environmental quality, it is clear that behavior changes ultimately offer the primary hope for preserving our global life-support system. Staying below the earth's human carrying capacity will require control of populations and our propensity to consume resources. It is in the arena of human behavior change that psychologists have a critical contribution to make.

Psychology's involvement in environmental concerns comes primarily from two quite different perspectives. The behavioral approach attempts to alter specific target behaviors through the principles of learning (especially modeling, positive reinforcement, and punishment). The humanistic approach, on the other hand, emphasizes the importance of promoting changes in cognitions and values regarding the environment, which then hopefully affect environmentally relevant behaviors in beneficial ways.

Reminders to engage in pro-environmental behavior can help improve people's habits, but rewards for appropriate behavior have a stronger effect.

The Behavioral Approach

The behavioral approach focuses on changing specific behaviors by using the principles of learning. Recently, psychologists Bill Dwyer, Frank Leeming, and their colleagues (1993) summarized the studies conducted during the 1980s that attempted to alter environmentally relevant behavior. During that time period, 54 studies were published on environmental topics such as conserving home energy, bicycle riding, carpooling, use of public transportation, reducing litter, and recycling.

An example of a behavioral approach to the new environmental psychology is an experiment by Cope and Geller (1984). This experiment investigated the effectiveness of both verbal prompts and tangible rewards in promoting the use of automobile litter bags to reduce littering. The investigators first observed the percentage of cars that had a litter bag when coming through the drive-in window of a fast-food restaurant. Subsequently, they tested the effects both of asking people to take and use a litter bag and of rewarding with a free soft drink those who had a litter bag in their automobile. Both techniques resulted in an increase in the percentage of cars observed to have a litter bag in use.

Another example of the behavioral approach is an experiment by Van Houwelingen and Van Raaij (1989) testing a technique to reduce consumption of natural gas. Meters showing rate of gas consumption and its cost were installed in 50 homes so that occupants could see immediately when gas consumption increased or decreased. Over the full year that the meters were in place, households receiving this feedback showed a reduction in gas consumption of about 10 percent compared with 50 control households that did not have meters. However, the old wasteful pattern of consumption resumed when the meters were removed. In general, studies of behavioral interventions show that prompts and reminders to engage in proenvironmental behaviors are less effective than positive reinforcement and punishment, but that positive and negative consequences for environmentally sensitive behaviors are effective only as long as they are given.

The Humanistic Approach

Compared with the behavioral approach, the tradition of humanistic psychology focuses more on individual beliefs and attitudes. This approach is based on the assumption that changes in behavior will result from changes in awareness and attitudes brought about by providing people with new information and experiences.

One example of the humanistic approach is research to determine how people who are highly *eco*centric (focused on the needs of our ecology) differ from people who are *ego*centric (focused on their own selfish needs). Based upon extensive studies of people who believe in environmental preservation and conduct their lives accordingly, Richard Borden (1986) identified eight common characteristics:

1. They had witnessed a sense of unfulfillment in others who are economically successful.
2. They had an introspective childhood that involved significant early (and often private) experiences with nature.
3. They were influenced by role models with some natural history or ecological interests.
4. They had an intense emotional experience with the death (and sometimes the birth) of animals.
5. They lost a "magical" play-place in the out-of-doors (e.g., the cutting down of a favorite tree, development of a woodland, pollution of a stream or beach, etc.).
6. They experienced romantic fantasies derived from specific books, films, or television programs.
7. They had early outdoor experiences such as backpacking, camping, bird watching, hunting, and fishing.
8. They experienced dreams or daydreams of being a victim of a nuclear catastrophe.

The hope of this line of research is that it may be possible to encourage experiences that will lead to the development of increased concern for the environment. For example, Ramsey and Hungerford (1989) conducted an evaluation of a school-based program of environmental education. Four classes of seventh-grade students received an 18-week unit focusing on identifying and dealing with environmental problems. Four other classes received only the standard science curriculum during this period. Tests showed that the students who had received the exposure to environmental education had greater knowledge of both environmental problems and possible ways to solve these problems. More importantly, these students also reported engaging in a greater number of behaviors to preserve and protect the environment.

Environmental Psychology in the Future

As population, pollution, and resource depletion pressures continue to threaten the earth's ability to sustain human life, it will become increasingly important to find ways of controlling the excessive consumption behaviors that are at the root of the problem. We are already witnessing examples of stringent controls placed on humans in an attempt to preserve the earth's carrying capacity. In the arena of population control, the approach undertaken by China in its one-child-per-family effort involves a combination of prompts, rewards (such as occupational, educational, and housing benefits), and penalties (including withdrawal of economic opportunities and even systematic harassment of women pregnant with their second child until they agree to an abortion). Ultimately governments will resort to such penalties because they are inexpensive and very effective. Part of the mission for psychology, therefore, will be to develop other, less aversive strategies that are effective in promoting environmentally conscious behavior. These solutions will undoubtedly represent a combination of behavioral and humanistic strategies that promote behavior change from the "outside in," as well as from the "inside out." Psychologists will play a major role in devising these strategies.

Summary

Chapter 16 describes the influence of psychology on four areas: business, architecture, law, and education. The objective is to show that psychology is an applied, as well as a scientific, field.

I. Psychologists who work for businesses are known as industrial-organizational psychologists. They are found most frequently in personnel departments.
   - **A.** Interviews help managers assess current employees for possible promotion. The role of the psychologist is to educate managers about the nature and limitations of interviews.
   - **B.** Biographical data, biodata, are used to help employers in large companies select large numbers of employees who will perform the same kind of job.
   - **C.** Paper-and-pencil tests include intellectual ability and personality tests. Tests used to measure specific skills and abilities are also frequently used.
   - **D.** Performance tests measure actual manual performance that can be used to predict behavior on the job.
   - **E.** Several methods exist for assessing performance of currently employed workers.
     1. Worker performance is evaluated using job performance ratings, such as multiple-step rating scales and checklists.
     2. Assessment centers are frequently used to evaluate applicants or currently employed candidates for management positions in companies.
   - **F.** The most valid method of evaluating job applicants for complex jobs is paper-and-pencil intellectual ability tests, whereas performance tasks appear to be more valid when the job is less complex.
   - **G.** The goals of psychologists working in business are to improve the satisfaction of employees and to improve their productivity. They can accomplish the goals by:
     1. Improving supervisory style.
     2. Improving managerial organization.
     3. Improving physical conditions.
   - **H.** Employee health programs can also improve job satisfaction while reducing both the direct costs of health benefits and the indirect costs due to poor health and premature death of valuable employees.

II. The field of environmental psychology uses the methods of experimental psychology to evaluate human reactions to architectural spaces.

III. In recent years, psychologists have begun to apply their methods to the practice of the law in the courtroom.
   - **A.** They have found that the characteristics of defendants affect the likelihood of conviction and the harshness of the sentence.
   - **B.** They have also found that certain types of jury members are more likely than other types to vote for conviction and to recommend harsher sentences.
   - **C.** Psychological factors are involved in the effectiveness of courtroom evidence. Eyewitness testimony is the most convincing evidence, but eyewitnesses can and do make mistakes.
   - **D.** The order in which evidence is presented appears to affect the outcome of the trial.

IV. Psychologists serve the field of education as professors who help train teachers, as consultants on testing programs, and as school psychologists employed by school systems.
   - **A.** One development is mastery learning, based on Benjamin Bloom's belief that children should never progress from one learning task to another until they have fully mastered the previous one.
   - **B.** Another development is Project Follow Through, a federally funded experiment to test new ways of educating economically disadvantaged children.
   - **C.** Another new approach is criterion-referenced testing, a form of testing designed to determine if a given child can meet the minimum criteria for a specific educational objective.
   - **D.** Public Law 94–142, the mainstreaming law, established that every child has a right to public education, regardless of his or her disability. The law states that the education must take place in the least restrictive environment.

Suggested Readings

1. An excellent overview of industrial-organizational psychology: Saal, F. E., & Knight, P. A. (1988). *Industrial/organizational psychology: Science and practice*. Pacific Grove, CA: Brooks/Cole.
2. For a fascinating commentary on human engineering and other applications of psychology: Norman, D. A. (1990). *The design of everyday things*. New York: Doubleday; Norman, D. A. (1993). *Things that make us smart: Defending human attributes in the age of the machine*. New York: Addison-Wesley.
3. Extremely well-written summaries of the teaching methods that educational psychologists have found make important differences in how much children learn: Brophy, J. (1986). Teacher influences on student achievement. *American Psychologist, 41*, 1069–1077; Brophy, J. (1996). *Teaching problem students*. New York: Guilford; Dweck, C. (1986). Motivational processes affecting learning. *American Psychologist, 41,* 1040–1048.
4. For more on the psychology of juries: Saks, M. J. (1977). *Jury verdicts*. Lexington, MA: Lexington Books; Bull, R. H., & Carson, D. (1995). *Handbook of psychology in legal contexts*. Orlando: Wiley.
5. A nice summary of the past and future of environmental psychology is provided by Stokols, D. (1995). The paradox of environmental psychology. *American Psychologist, 50,* 821–837.
6. For a very readable discussion of reducing "social loafing" in work settings: Shepard, J. A. (1995). Remedying motivation and productivity losses in collective settings. *Current Directions in Psychological Science, 4,* 131–139.

APPENDIX

Measurement, Research Design, and Statistics

RICHARD E. MAYER University of California, Santa Barbara

The purpose of this appendix is to help you understand some of the basic statistical concepts and research methods used in psychology. Even if you never conduct a psychological study, you need to learn about statistics and research methods in psychology for two reasons. First, the ability to read and evaluate research that is presented in this textbook or discussed in class helps you to avoid being intimidated by the research data of "experts"; it helps you to assess the soundness of an experiment; and it helps you to interpret the results. Second, a basic understanding of psychological statistics and research methods is rapidly becoming a "survival skill" for every educated member of our society. You need to avoid being fooled by "scientific" surveys, government reports, advertiser's evidence, and the like. You need to be able to recognize the difference between a useful study and one that is seriously flawed. Thus, this appendix is designed to help you as a student and as an educated citizen.

For example, suppose you came across the following article in your local newspaper:

> **TV Viewing Linked to School Failure**
>
> *Garden City*—Researchers at State University have found that students who watch in excess of 3 hours of television per day get lower grades than other students. The study was based on a survey of students at Garden Valley School. The average student watched approximately 2 hours of TV per day. Efforts to discourage TV watching have been announced by the school's principal, Mr. George Elliot. "We must get our kids to stop watching TV," Mr. Elliot stated.

As you read this summary of a research study, you should ask yourself such questions as *Is this a sound study?* and *How should I interpret the results?* After reading this appendix you will be better able to answer questions like these concerning research studies that you read about.

DESCRIPTIVE STATISTICS

One of the basic uses for statistics in psychological studies is to *describe behavior* in an understandable way. This is called *descriptive statistics.* Two common examples of descriptive statistics are as follows:

Describing behavior concerning one variable. For example, a study may report that the "average" student watches 2 hours of TV per day.

Describing the relation between two variables. For example, a study may report that students who watch more television tend to score lower on tests of school achievement than those who watch less.

As you can see, descriptive statistics summarize the data for a group of subjects. Figure A.1 lists the two uses of statistics that are discussed in the remainder of this part of the appendix.

FIGURE A.1
Some uses of statistics.

Use	Situation	Example	Typical statistics
Describing one variable	There is one score for each subject.	Each of 20 students in Mrs. Perkins's class tells how many hours he or she watched TV yesterday.	Frequency distribution Mean, median, or mode Standard deviation, variance, or range
Describing the relation between two variables	There are two scores for each subject—one score on variable X and one score on variable Y.	Each of 20 students in Mrs. Perkins's class tells how many hours he or she watched TV yesterday, and each student gets a score on the school achievement test.	Correlation

In the Garden Valley study, the researchers obtained data on only a small number of schoolchildren from just one school; however, the researchers want to generalize their data to all schoolchildren in the United States. Thus, it is important for you to understand the distinction between a *parameter* and a *statistic* as they are used here.

Parameter. Parameters are numbers that describe the behavior of an *entire population.* A population consists of all possible subjects or objects or cases, such as all schoolchildren in the United States. For example, if we asked every schoolchild in the United States how many hours he or she watched TV each day, then we could develop parameters such as the average number of hours of TV viewing.

Statistic. Statistics are numbers that describe the behavior of only a *sample* drawn out of a larger population. A sample is a portion of an entire population, such as some of the schoolchildren at one school.

Sample statistics—such as the average number of hours of TV watching of some students at Garden Valley School—are rarely identical to population parameters, such as the average number of hours of TV viewing of all U.S. schoolchildren.

Another distinction that you need to understand is the difference between a *variable* and a *score.*

Variable. A variable is a measurable characteristic or behavior, such as age, sex, weight, height, or shoe size. In the Garden Valley study, one variable is the number of hours of TV viewing per day.

Score. A score is the value a given person has for a given variable, such as Joe's age being 27 years or his shoe size being 8 1/2. In the Garden Valley study, Mary watched 3 hours of TV per day, so her score is 3 on the variable "hours of TV viewing per day."

The data for a study consists of all the scores obtained for each variable that is used.

Describing Behavior Concerning One Variable

Problem

One of the major uses of statistics in psychology is to describe the behavior of a group on one variable. For example, the Garden Valley study attempted to describe the TV-viewing behavior of schoolchildren. Let's suppose that we go to Garden Valley School and ask 20 students from Mrs. Perkins's class to tell us how many hours they watched TV yesterday. Suppose that we get one answer from each student, as listed in the left panel of figure A.2.

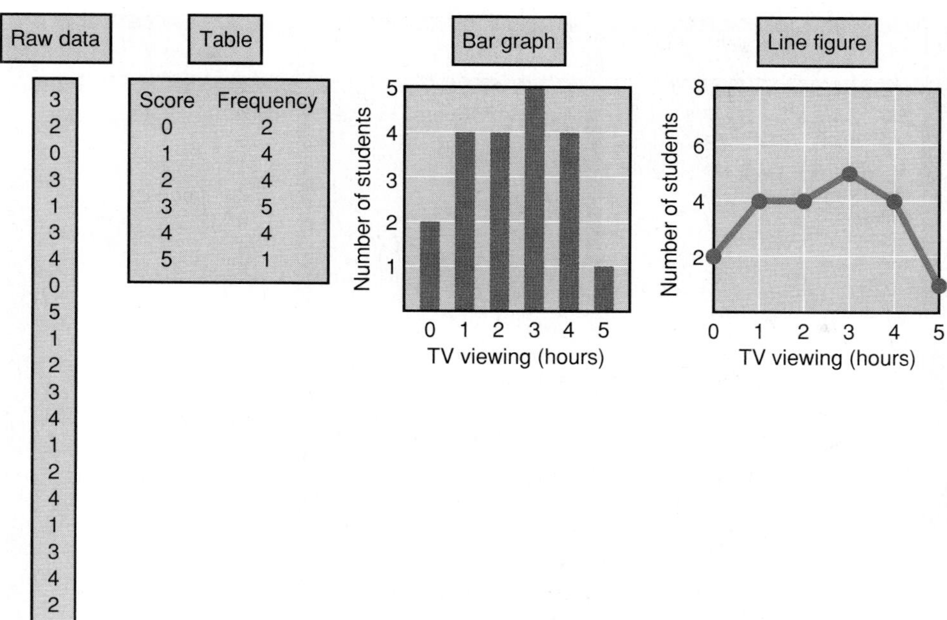

FIGURE A.2
Frequency distributions for some TV-viewing data.

Frequency Distribution

What are the TV-viewing habits of school students? One way to provide data for this question is simply to list the number of hours that each of 20 students reported watching TV. However, since it's hard to make much sense out of a long list of numbers, researchers often organize their data into a *frequency distribution.* A frequency distribution is a table or graph that shows the relationship between score (such as number of hours of TV watching) and frequency (such as the number or percentage of students who gave each score).

Figure A.2 shows some frequency distributions for the TV-viewing data using the formats of a table, bar graph, and line figure. In the table, the first column gives the possible scores (0, 1, 2, 3, 4, or 5) for hours of TV viewing per day, and the second column gives the frequency of each score (that is, how many of the 20 students fell into that category). In the bar graph and line figure, the X-axis gives the possible scores and the Y-axis gives the frequency.

Although the frequency distribution helps you organize data, you may want to summarize the description even further. You could summarize the frequency distribution by giving two numbers—a measure of *central tendency* and a measure of *dispersion.* A measure of central tendency tells where the middle of the distribution is, such as, how many hours, on the average, do school students watch TV? A measure of dispersion tells you how spread out the scores are, such as, how different are the school students in the number of hours they view TV? These are discussed in the next two subsections.

Central Tendency

How many hours per day does the "average student" watch TV? There are three major measurers of central tendency: mean, median, and mode.

The *mean* is the arithmetic average of all the scores. To compute the mean, you simply add all the scores and divide the sum by the number of scores. The formula for finding the mean is $\overline{X} = \Sigma X/n$, where $\overline{X}$ is the mean, ΣX is the sum or total of the scores, and n is the number of scores. The left portion of figure A.3 shows that the sum of the scores is 48, the number of scores is 20, and the mean is 2.4 hours. One problem with using mean as a measure of central tendency is that it's sensitive to extreme scores. For example, if the only student who reported watching 5 hours per day changed his answer to 24 hours, the mean would increase from 2.4 to 3.35.

The *median* is the score that divides the distribution in the middle, so that half of the frequency is greater than the median and half is less than the median. To determine the median, list the scores in ascending (or descending) order, and count down until you

FIGURE A.3

Measures of central tendency for some TV-viewing data.

Mean

$\Sigma X = 3 + 2 + 0 + 3 + 1 + 3 + 4 + 0 + 5 + 1 + 2 + 3 + 4 + 1 + 2 + 4 + 1 + 3 + 4 + 2 = 48$

$n = 20$

$$\bar{x} = \frac{\Sigma X}{n} = \frac{48}{20} = 2.4$$

Median

Ranking		Scores in order
1st		0
2nd		0
3rd		1
4th		1
5th		1
6th		1
7th		2
8th		2
9th	Middle of	2
10th	rankings	2
11th		3
12th		3
13th		3
14th		3
15th		3
16th		4
17th		4
18th		4
19th		4
20th		5

Median = point midway between 2 and 3 (i.e., 2.5)

Mode

Score		Frequency
0		2
1	Most	4
2	frequent	4
3		5
4		4
5		1

Mode = 3

reach the score in the middle. An example is given in the middle panel of figure A.3. As you can see, the median is not as sensitive to extreme scores. If the student who watched 5 hours was replaced by a student who watched 24 hours, the median would remain the same!

The *mode* is the score that occurs most often. For example, the mode in figure A.3 is 3 because 5 people watch TV for 3 hours while fewer than 5 watch TV for each other score. There can be ties among modes; for example, the scores 3, 1, 2, 1, 3, 0, 4, 1, 3, 5 have two modes—1 and 3. This called a *bimodal distribution* because there are two modes. If there is a tie among several scores, such as 1, 1, 2, 2, 3, 3, 4, 4, 0, 0, then there can be several modes—such as 5 modes in the preceding example. This is called a *multimodal distribution.* Although the mode is not often used in research studies, in some cases it may be preferred. For example, the designer of apartments will find it is *more useful* to know that the "modal" family unit is either 1 or 4 than to know that the mean family is 2.5. The builder who includes studio apartments for single adults is likely to rent the available space faster than the builder who believes that only two-bedroom apartments are needed for all those families with 2.5 people.

Dispersion

How different are the scores from one another? There are two major measures of dispersion: standard deviation and range.

The *standard deviation* is a sort of average difference between each score and the mean. It's a statistic that indicates how widely or narrowly scores are spread around the mean on the average. To compute the standard deviation, subtract the mean score from each score, square each of these differences, divide by the number of scores, and then take the square root. The formula for standard deviation is

$$s = \sqrt{\frac{\Sigma(X - \bar{X})^2}{n}}$$

where s is the standard deviation, $\Sigma(X - \bar{X})^2$ is the sum of the square of the differences, and n is the number of scores. The left panel of figure A.4 shows how to compute the standard deviation for TV-viewing scores.

Standard deviation

Raw data	Deviation $(X-\bar{X})$	Square of deviation $(X-\bar{X})^2$
3	.6	.36
2	−.4	.16
0	−2.4	5.76
3	.6	.36
1	−1.4	1.96
3	.6	.36
4	1.6	2.56
0	−2.4	5.76
5	2.6	6.76
1	−1.4	1.96
2	−.4	.16
3	.6	.36
4	1.6	2.56
1	−1.4	1.96
2	−.4	.16
4	1.6	2.56
1	−1.4	1.96
3	.6	.36
4	1.6	2.56
2	−.4	.16

$$\Sigma(X-\bar{X})^2 = 38.80$$

$$S = \sqrt{\frac{\Sigma(X-\bar{X})^2}{n}} = \sqrt{\frac{38.8}{20}} = 1.39$$

Range

0 Lowest
0
1
1
1
1
2
2
2
2
3
3
3
3
3
4
4
4
4
5 Highest

Range = (highest − lowest) + 1
Range = 5 − 0 + 1 = 6

FIGURE A.4

Measures of dispersion for some TV-viewing data.

The *range* is the distance between the highest score and the lowest score. To compute the range, simply subtract the lowest score from the highest and add 1. The right panel of figure A.4 shows that if the lowest score is 0 and the highest score is 5, then the range is 6; that is, the distance between 0 and 5 is 6 units. The range is rarely used as a measure of dispersion because it's so sensitive to extreme scores. For example, if the student who watched 5 hours of TV was replaced by a student who watched 24 hours, the range would jump to 25.

Normal Curve

The scores for any frequency distribution can be plotted on a graph, as in the right-hand panel of figure A.2, and they can take a multitude of shapes. A sort of ideal frequency distribution is the normal curve. It has fascinated scientists and statisticians because many different characteristics in nature tend to be normally distributed—such as adult height, weight, intelligence, and so on. This does not mean they all have the same mean and standard deviation; rather, they all have the same general *shape* of frequency distribution. An example of a normal curve is given in figure A.5.

The normal curve is a frequency distribution that has the following characteristics:

Symmetrical. The right side is a mirror image of the left side.

Bell shaped. The most common scores are near the mean, with scores becoming less common as you move away from the mean in either direction.

68-95-99 density. The area on the normal curve that is within one standard deviation above the mean and one standard deviation below the mean contains 68.26-percent of the cases; within two standard deviations there are 95.42 percent of the cases; and within three standard deviations there are 99.74 percent of the cases.

To make sure that you understand the shape of the normal curve, let's try some examples. Look at the percentages of cases in each area of the normal curve in figure A.5. Suppose

FIGURE A.5
The normal curve.

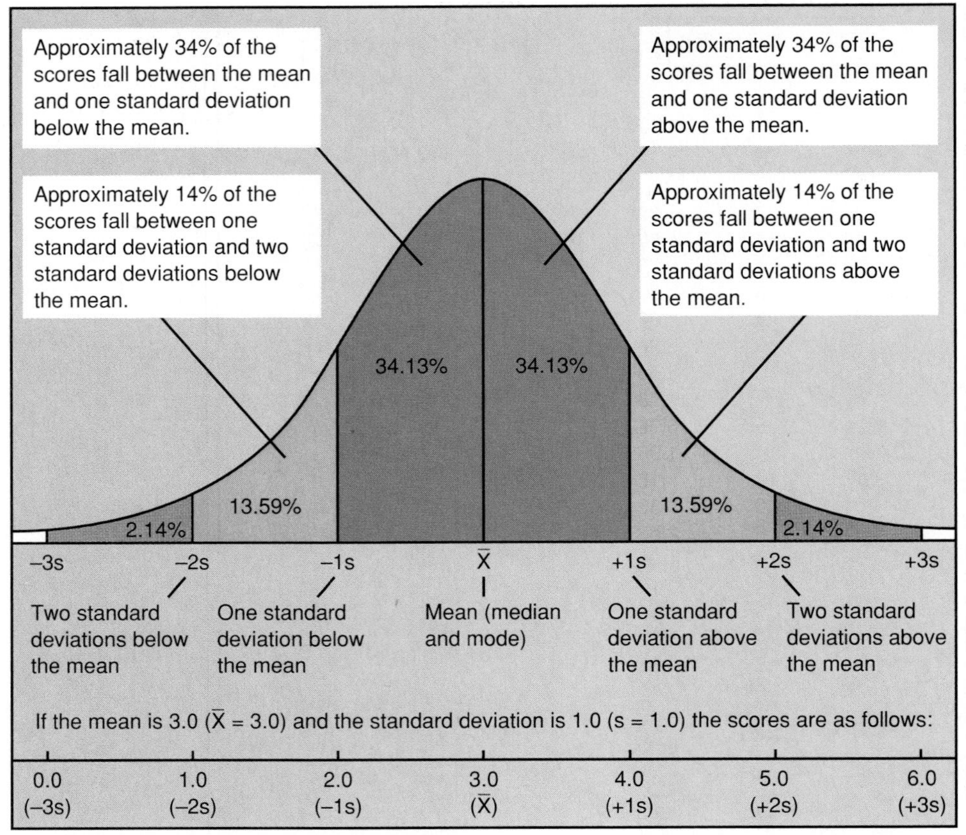

Approximately 34% of the scores fall between the mean and one standard deviation below the mean.
Approximately 34% of the scores fall between the mean and one standard deviation above the mean.
Approximately 14% of the scores fall between one standard deviation and two standard deviations below the mean.
Approximately 14% of the scores fall between one standard deviation and two standard deviations above the mean.
34.13%
34.13%
13.59%
13.59%
2.14%
2.14%
–3s
–2s
–1s
X̄
+1s
+2s
+3s
Two standard deviations below the mean
One standard deviation below the mean
Mean (median and mode)
One standard deviation above the mean
Two standard deviations above the mean
If the mean is 3.0 (X̄ = 3.0) and the standard deviation is 1.0 (s = 1.0) the scores are as follows:
0.0 (–3s)
1.0 (–2s)
2.0 (–1s)
3.0 (X̄)
4.0 (+1s)
5.0 (+2s)
6.0 (+3s)

that Susan scores one standard deviation above the mean on a test. If the scores are normally distributed, she performed better than __________ percent of the class. Try another one: Tom scored one standard deviation below the mean, so he did better than __________ percent of the class. Finally, try this one: Mary scored better than 98 percent of the other students, so she scored __________ standard deviations (*above/below*) the mean. Look at figure A.6 for the answers.

Flaws in Research Design

When presented with a problem such as the one described at the beginning of this section, you should ask yourself, "What is wrong with the way that the researcher collected data?" A researcher can present you with perfectly calculated statistics and still not be of much help. Your first step in dealing with descriptive data should be to understand any flaws in the research design—that is, in how the data were collected. Some of the more common flaws are described below:

Unrepresentative sample. The people or behavior in the study may not be representative or typical of the larger population. For example, in the TV-viewing study, perhaps the two or three most heavy TV viewers are not included because they are at home watching TV, or perhaps two or three students who watch a lot of TV refused to participate in the study. Mrs. Perkins's class might consist of all "college prep" students who have little time for TV. There might have been some excellent special shows on the night the data were collected, so the students watched more TV than usual.

Experimenter bias. The expectations of the experimenter may influence the data. For example, the experimenter who expects that students watch a lot of TV may inadvertently make errors in posting the data, such as reading 1 hour as 7 hours.

Response bias. The research participants' responses might be influenced by their general question-answering style. For example, most people prefer to answer yes rather than no, and most people prefer to give socially desirable answers. Thus,

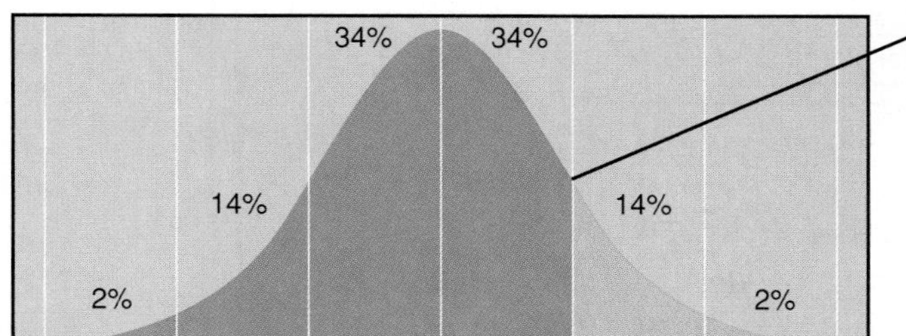
34%
34%
14%
14%
2%
2%
Susan scored one standard deviation above the mean.
Susan performed better than 84% of the class.
−3s
−2s
−1s
X̄
+1s
+2s
+3s

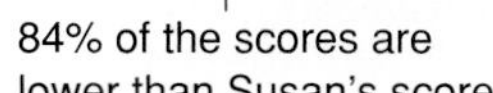
84% of the scores are lower than Susan's score.

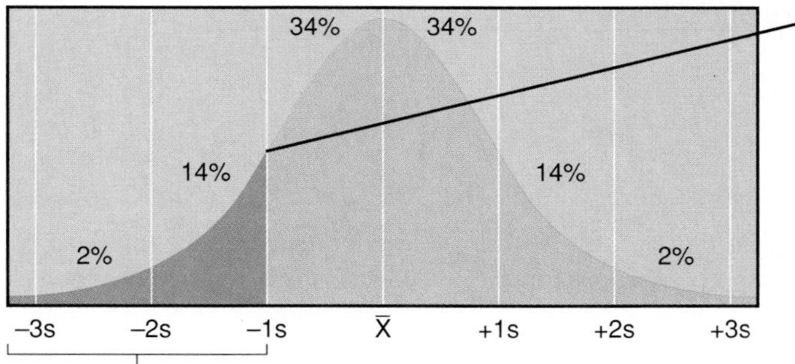
34%
34%
14%
14%
2%
2%
Tom scored one standard deviation below the mean.
Tom performed better than 16% of the class.
−3s
−2s
−1s
X̄
+1s
+2s
+3s
16% of the scores are lower than Tom's score.

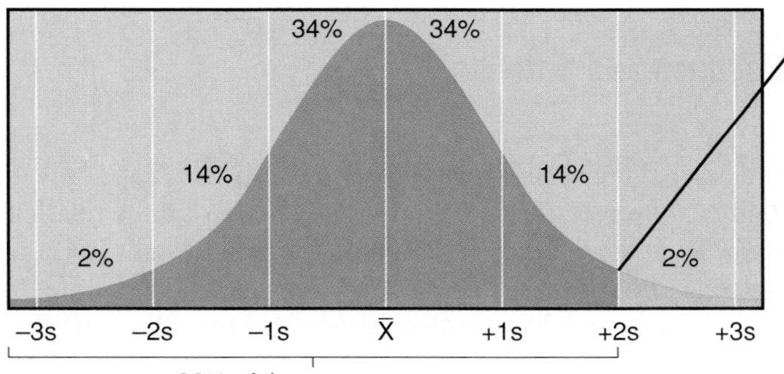
34%
34%
14%
14%
2%
2%
Mary scored two standard deviations above the mean.
Mary performed better than 98% of the class.
−3s
−2s
−1s
X̄
+1s
+2s
+3s
98% of the scores are lower than Mary's score.

FIGURE A.6

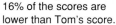

Three normal curves.

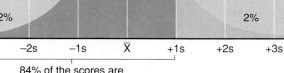

students may underestimate their actual TV-viewing time if they think that watching TV is "bad."

Situational bias. Extraneous factors in the research situation may influence the person's response. For example, the participant might try to give data that are consistent with what he or she thinks the experimenter wants. If the experimenter begins by saying, "Wow, I am happy to see that kids in your class watch a lot of TV," and then asks "How many hours did you watch TV yesterday?" participants may be more likely to give higher estimates. This type of situational bias is sometimes called *demand characteristics;* in other words, individuals are sensitive to what is demanded by the situation. Other examples of situational bias include the possibility that students will give different answers depending on who the experimenter is, how the question is phrased, whether peers or others are present when the survey is given, and so on.

Invalid scores. The scores used in the study may not accurately measure the research participants' behavior. For example, students may not be able to remember how many hours they watched TV the previous day, or a test may not adequately measure school achievement.

Nonstandard conditions. The scores may be obtained under different conditions for different participants. For example, some students may be asked "face-to-face" by the teacher to tell how many hours they watched TV, while others may be asked to

Raw scores

	TV-viewing score (X)	Achievement score (Y)
Student 1	2	25
Student 2	0	40
Student 3	1	40
Student 4	3	30
Student 5	5	5
Student 6	4	15
Student 7	3	20
Student 8	1	35
Student 9	2	30
Student 10	4	10

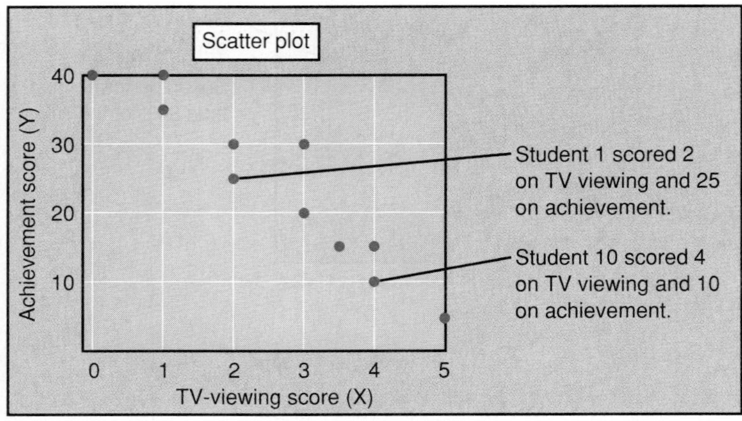

FIGURE A.7

Correlation between TV-viewing and achievement scores for 10 students.

fill out an anonymous questionnaire. If all students are not tested under standard conditions, then there may be differences in their scores that are due to extraneous factors.

Once you are satisfied that you have explored any potential flaws in the research methodology, you are ready to go on and investigate the statistics.

Describing the Relation Between Two Variables

Problem

So far you have learned how to describe scores on one variable using statistics such as mean and standard deviation. Sometimes, however, your goal might be to describe the relation between two variables. For example, in the Garden Valley study, you might want to know whether there is any relation between the number of hours of TV viewing and the score on a school achievement test. Let's suppose we go to Garden Valley School and ask 10 students from Mrs. Perkins's class to tell us how many hours they watched TV yesterday and that we get test scores for each student's performance on a school achievement test. Thus, we will have two scores for each of 10 students, as listed in the left panel of figure A.7.

Scatter Plot

What is the relation between TV viewing and school achievement? One way to provide data on this question is to draw a scatter plot of the scores. A scatter plot is a graph consisting of two axes—such as hours of TV viewing on the X-axis and achievement score on the Y-axis—with one dot corresponding to each score on the two variables. An example for the Garden Valley study is shown in the right panel of figure A.7. As you can see, there seems to be a pattern in which a score on one axis is negatively, or inversely, related to a score on the other; in other words, the higher your TV-watching score, the lower your achievement score.

Figure A.8 shows five scatter plots, ranging from a strong positive relation between the variables to no relation to a strong negative relation. Although scatter plots provide a general description of the relation between two variables, you may want to summarize the data even further. You could mathematically summarize your scatter plot by giving a measure of correlation.

Correlation

The *correlation coefficient* is a number between –1 and +1 that indicates the degree of relation between two variables. A strong positive correlation (such as $r = +.8$) indicates that TV viewing is strongly related to school achievement, with more TV viewing corre-

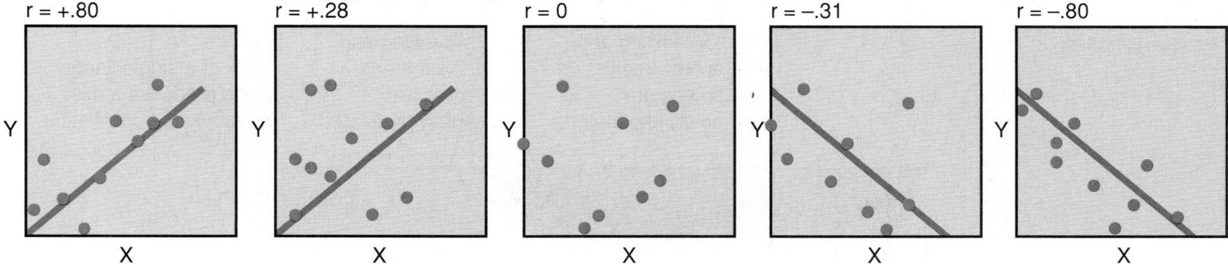

FIGURE A.8

Five scatter plots.

Subject	TV-viewing score (X)	Deviation $(X - \bar{X})$	Squared deviation $(X - \bar{X})^2$	Achievement score (Y)	Deviation $(Y - \bar{Y})$	Squared deviation $(Y - \bar{Y})^2$	Cross product $(X - \bar{X})\cdot(Y - \bar{Y})$
1	2	−.5	.25	25	0	0	0
2	0	−2.5	6.25	40	15	225	−37.5
3	1	−1.5	2.25	40	15	225	−22.5
4	3	.5	.25	30	5	25	2.5
5	5	2.5	6.25	5	−20	400	−50
6	4	1.5	2.25	15	−10	100	−15
7	3	.5	.25	20	−5	25	−2.5
8	1	−1.5	2.25	35	10	100	−15
9	2	−.5	.25	30	5	25	−2.5
10	4	1.5	2.25	10	−15	225	−22.5
	$\bar{X} = 2.5$		$\Sigma(X - \bar{X})^2 = 22.50$	$\bar{X} = 25$		$\Sigma(Y - \bar{Y})^2 = 1350$	$\Sigma[(X - \bar{X})\cdot(Y - \bar{Y})] = -165$

$$r = \frac{\Sigma xy}{\sqrt{\Sigma x^2 \cdot \Sigma y^2}} = \frac{\Sigma[(X - \bar{X}) \cdot (Y - \bar{Y})]}{\sqrt{\Sigma(X - \bar{X})^2 \cdot \Sigma(Y - \bar{Y})^2}} = \frac{-165}{\sqrt{(22.50)(1350)}} = -.95$$

FIGURE A.9

How to compute a correlation coefficient.

sponding to lower achievement. A strong negative correlation (such as r = –.8) indicates that TV viewing is strongly related to school achievement, with more TV viewing corresponding to lower achievement. A neutral correlation (coefficients close to r = .0) indicates that no relation exists between the two variables.

Figure A.8 shows the correlation coefficients for five scatter plots. You can think of correlation in the following way. First, draw a scatter plot. Then, draw a straight line through the scatter plot so that the distance between each dot and the line is minimized. The closer the dots are to the line, the stronger the relationship between the two variables—in either a positive correlation or a negative correlation. If the dots are spread across the whole graph, as in the middle panel of figure A.8, no correlation exists between the variables.

The formula for computing the correlation coefficient is

$$r = \frac{\Sigma xy}{\sqrt{\Sigma x^2 \cdot \Sigma y^2}}$$

where x is the difference between each X variable minus the mean; y is the difference between each Y variable and the mean; Σxy is the sum of the cross products (each x score multiplied by its corresponding y score); Σx^2 is the sum of the squares of the x scores; and Σy^2 is the sum of the squares of the y scores. Figure A.9 shows how to compute the value of r (that is, the correlation coefficient) for the Garden Valley data.

FIGURE A.10
A curvilinear relation between two variables.

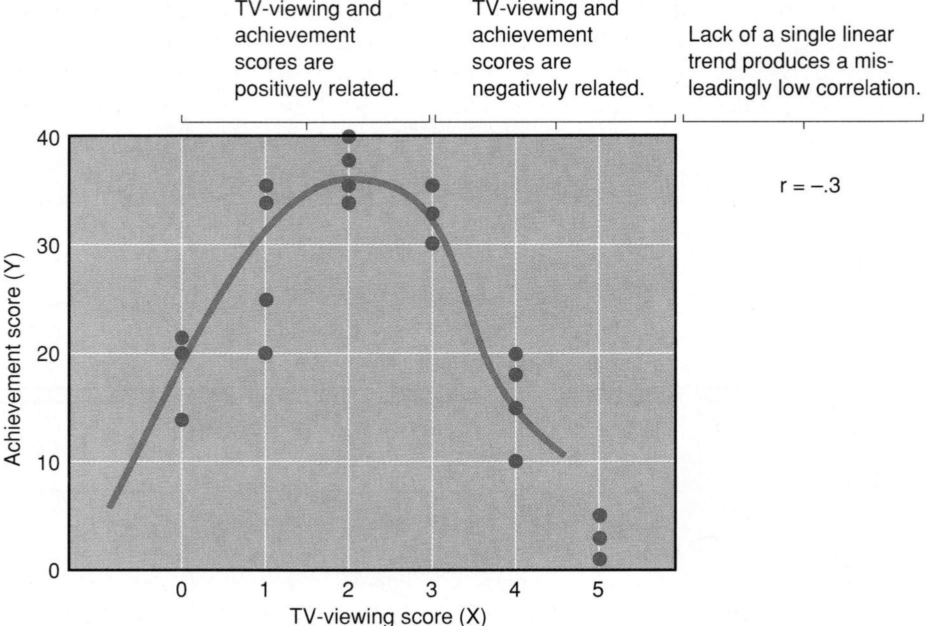
For 0 to 3 hours, TV-viewing and achievement scores are positively related.
For 3 to 5 hours, TV-viewing and achievement scores are negatively related.
Lack of a single linear trend produces a misleadingly low correlation.
r = –.3
Achievement score (Y)
40
30
20
10
0
0
1
2
3
4
5
TV-viewing score (X)

Misinterpretations

Correlation coefficients are useful ways of summarizing the relation between variables, but they can lead to errors in interpretation. Whenever you are presented with a correlation coefficient, you should ask yourself, "How should I interpret this correlation?" Some of the most common errors in interpretation follow:

Failure to recognize curvilinear trends. If you obtain a low correlation, this may be because no relation exists between the two variables or it may be due to other factors. A correlation coefficient looks only for a straight-line relation between two variables; more of one variable is related to more (or less) of another variable. But some relationships between variables change as scores change, producing a curvilinear line that will not be reflected in the coefficient of correlation. Hence, a strong curvilinear relation may exist without producing a strong correlation. An example is shown in figure A.10. In this case, TV viewing up to 3 hours seems to be related positively with school achievement; thereafter, increased viewing is negatively related with school achievement.

Use of restricted range. A low correlation may also be due to using only a small range of scores along one of the variables. This is because there must be both high and low scores on each variable to see what is related to these scores. For example, if you do a separate correlation for heavy viewers (that is, 3 or more hours) and a separate correlation for light viewers (that is, 0 to 2 hours), the correlation coefficients may be lowered because you included only high scores the first time and only low scores the second time. Since accurate correlations depend on the use of scores distributed across the entire range of both variables, restricting the range of one of the variables will artificially lower the correlation coefficient. Similarly, when conducting experiments using college students to see what is correlated with IQ, the experimenter may find low correlation coefficients since college students have mostly high IQs.

Inferring causation. If you obtain a high correlation (either negative or positive), you may want to make an inference concerning which variable *caused* the values of the other. For example, if TV viewing and school achievement are strongly negatively correlated, you might want to conclude that TV viewing causes poor school achievement. However, such a conclusion is not justified based on correlation coefficients.

Correlation does not mean causation. It does not indicate that one variable caused the other. Although it's possible that TV viewing causes poor school achievement, it's just as logical to argue that lower school achievement causes increased TV viewing. (Students who do poorly in school are "turned off" to school, so they turn on the TV.) A third possibility is that both TV viewing and low school achievement are caused by a third variable not included in the study, such as family stability or student health.

INFERENTIAL STATISTICS

Thus far you have learned how behavior can be described using statistics. In many cases, however, description of behavior is just the first step. The second basic use of statistics is to draw conclusions regarding hypotheses based on data. This is called *inferential statistics* because it involves making inferences about causes of behavior that can apply to the entire population from which the sample was taken.

Problem

In the Garden Valley study, you might want to know whether TV viewing causes poor school performance. To test this idea, we could ask 20 students from Mrs. Perkins's class to volunteer for a study of TV viewing and school achievement. We can divide our 20 students into two groups: those who are asked to watch 2 hours or less ("light group") and those who are asked to watch 3 hours or more ("heavy group"). This will provide us with two sets of achievement scores that can be analyzed with statistical tests. Figure A.11 shows the score on a school achievement test 2 weeks later for each of the students in the light group and each of the students in the heavy group.

Research Design

In the preceding example, we have conducted a formal experiment. To understand the nature of formal experiments, let's review the following ideas that were introduced in chapter 1:

Independent variable. The independent variable is what the experimenter tries to manipulate or to control the value of in the groups (or conditions or treatments). In the Garden Valley study, the independent variable is the degree of TV viewing, and the two groups (or conditions or treatments) are heavy versus light.

Dependent variable. The dependent variable is the measurement that is taken as a result of the manipulations, that is, the score that each research participant gives as an outcome. In the Garden Valley study, the dependent variable is the score on the achievement test.

Hypothesis. The hypothesis is a prediction concerning the specific results of the study, in terms of the independent and dependent variables. For example, in the Garden Valley study, the hypothesis might be that heavy and light groups will not differ on school achievement scores.

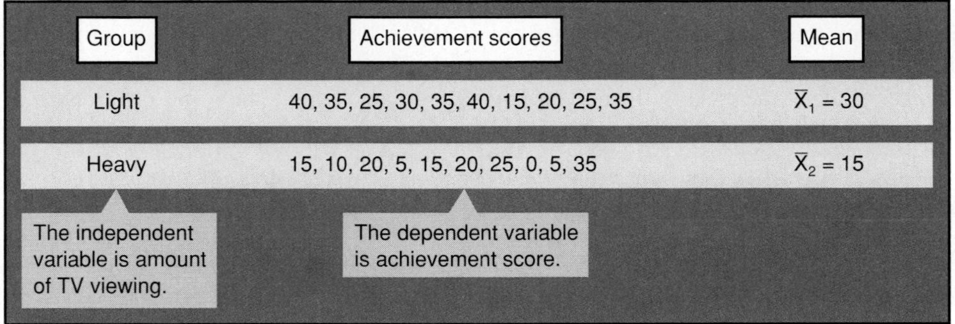

Group	Achievement scores	Mean
Light	40, 35, 25, 30, 35, 40, 15, 20, 25, 35	$\bar{X}_1 = 30$
Heavy	15, 10, 20, 5, 15, 20, 25, 0, 5, 35	$\bar{X}_2 = 15$

The independent variable is amount of TV viewing.
The dependent variable is achievement score.

FIGURE A.11
Achievement scores for 10 heavy and 10 light TV viewers.

For any formal experiment that is limited to two variables, you should be able to identify the independent variable, the dependent variable, and the hypothesis.

Flaws in Research Design

As you think about the experiment suggested earlier, you should be asking yourself, "Is there anything wrong in the way that the researcher is testing the hypothesis?" One of the most common flaws is *lack of control*. Control refers to the idea that the two groups should be identical in every way *except* for the one thing that is being manipulated in the independent variable. Lack of control refers to the existence of differences between the characteristics or treatments of the two groups other than the independent variable. For example, we may find that the heavy group consists of all boys while the light group consists of all girls, or that the average age of the heavy group is lower than the average age of the light group. Then, we do not know whether differences in school achievement between the groups are due to TV viewing or to other factors, such as age or sex. Similarly, the experimenter may create more favorable testing conditions for the light group as compared with the heavy group. You must be careful to make sure that the experimenter does not overlook the *real* independent variable in an experiment; that is, the variable that causes the differences between the groups might not be the experimenter's independent variable. When another variable is the cause of the difference—such as age or sex or testing conditions—this variable is called a *confounding variable*.

In addition, each of the types of bias discussed for descriptive statistics can affect the outcome of formal experiments as well.

Tests for Significance

Researchers will calculate the mean achievement score for each of the two groups and compare the results. In the Garden Valley study, the mean achievement score for the heavy TV viewers is 15 while the mean achievement score for the light TV viewers is 30. This does not necessarily mean that heavy TV viewers have lower scores than light viewers. Although it looks like the heavy group scores lower than the light group, in this experiment the difference could be due to chance. For example, if you rolled a die six times with your left hand, you might get 1, 2, 4, 3, 4, 1 for a mean of 2.5; then, if you rolled the same die six times with your right hand, you might get 4, 6, 2, 5, 4, 3 for a mean of 4.0. This does not mean that your right hand is a better die roller than your left. The difference between 2.5 versus 4.0 is due to chance; in this case, if you had rolled the die 1,000 times with your left hand and then 1,000 times with your right, you probably would have gotten both means to average very near 3.5. Thus, in formal experiments it's possible to obtain a difference between the groups that is just due to chance. A statistical test can be performed to determine whether a difference between two means is *statistically significant*—in other words, a difference that is probably not due to chance.

A test of significance is used when each research participant has one score, and the researcher wants to determine whether the mean for one group is different from the mean for another group. The test will reveal whether the difference between the means is probably due to chance or to an actual difference between the groups. The researcher will report the results and include a *p-value,* which represents the level of significance. A p-value of .01 means that the difference in mean scores would be expected to occur by chance only 1 time out of every 100 trials, and a p-value of .05 means that the difference would be expected on the basis of chance 5 times out of 100. Usually, if a p-value is less than .05, then the differences obtained are tentatively accepted as genuine ones—that is, not due to chance. Such is the case with the Garden Valley data, which show the differences to exceed the .05 level of significance.

Misinterpretations

As with any statistical test, there are many ways to misinterpret the results. The following are some common mistakes.

Multiple tests. If the researcher obtains a significant result, this does not automatically guarantee that the difference is not due to chance. For example, let's suppose that we gave 20 different ability and achievement tests to our heavy and light groups, and then looked for differences between the groups on each test. If we use a p-value of .05, this means that 5 percent of the time (or 1 out of 20) we would expect to find a significant difference that is due to chance. With 20 such tests, we could expect one of them to show a significant result just by chance. Thus, when an experimenter performs many statistical tests, you should be leery of the one or two tests that come out to be significant. To be on the safe side, you might like to see a replication—that is, a repeat of the same experiment with different participants.

Low sample size. If the researcher fails to obtain significant results, this does not guarantee that there is really no difference between the groups. When very low sample sizes are used (such as, below 15 per group), one or two extreme scores can throw off the results. In general, small sample sizes require a larger difference between the means for the difference to be statistically significant. Thus, before you decide for sure that the difference is not significant, you should allow for a fair test—with several replications and adequate sample size.

GLOSSARY

A

abnormal behavior: Actions, thoughts, and feelings that are harmful to the person or to others. (p. 466)

absolute threshold: The smallest magnitude of a stimulus that can be detected half the time. (p. 91)

achievement motivation (n Ach): The psychological need in humans for success in competitive situations. (p. 337)

acquired immune deficiency syndrome (AIDS): A viral disease spread by blood and other bodily fluids that eventually destroys the body's immune system. (p. 391)

action potential: A brief electrical signal that travels the length of the axon. (p. 44)

adolescence: The period from the onset of puberty until the beginning of adulthood. (p. 304)

adolescent egocentrism: The quality of thinking that leads some adolescents to believe that they are the focus of attention in social situations, to believe that their problems are unique, to be unusually hypocritical and to be "pseudostupid." (p. 306)

adolescent growth spurt: The rapid increase in weight and height that occurs around the onset of puberty. (p. 305)

adrenal glands (ah-drē´nal): Two glands on the kidneys that secrete epinephrine and norepinephrine and that are involved in emotional arousal. (p. 67)

afferent neurons (af´er-ent): Neurons that transmit messages from sense organs to the central nervous system. (p. 47)

agoraphobia (ag´´o-rah-fō´bē-ah): An intense fear of leaving one's home or other familiar places. (p. 471)

alcoholism: Addiction to alcohol. (p. 167)

algorithms (al´go-rith´m): A systematic pattern of reasoning that guarantees finding a correct solution to a problem. (p. 252)

all-or-none principle: The law that states that once an action potential is produced, its shape and size are always the same. (p. 44)

Alzheimer's disease: Deterioration in memory and other cognitive and emotional processes due to the accumulation of protein deposits and neural tangles in the brain. (p. 80)

amphetamine psychosis (sī-kō´sis): A prolonged reaction to the excessive use of stimulants, characterized by disordered thinking, confused and rapidly changing emotions, and intense suspiciousness. (p. 160)

amphetamines (am-fet´ah-mīnz): Powerful stimulants that produce a conscious sense of increased energy and a euphoric high. (p. 160)

amygdala (ah-mig´dah-lah): Part of the limbic system that plays a role in emotional arousal. (p. 55)

anal expulsive personality: A personality type based on anal fixation in which the person is cruel, pushy, messy, and disorderly. (p. 405)

anal retentive personality: A personality type based on anal fixation in which the person is stingy, obstinate, stubborn, and compulsive. (p. 405)

anal stage: According to Freud, the second psychosexual stage (from 1 to 3 years), in which gratification is focused on the anus. (p. 405)

androgynous: Having both feminine and masculine characteristics. (p. 362)

angiotensin (an´´jē-ō-ten´sin): A substance in the blood that signals the hypothalamus that the body needs water. (p. 334)

animism (an´i-mizm): The egocentric belief of preoperational children that inanimate objects are alive like children are. (p. 301)

anterograde amnesia (an´ter-ō-grād): Disorder of memory characterized by an inability to store and/or retrieve new information in long-term memory. (p. 233)

antidiuretic hormone (ADH) (an´´tī-dī´´ū-ret´ik): A hormone produced by the pituitary that causes the kidneys to conserve water in the body by reabsorbing it from the urine. (p. 333)

antisocial personality disorder: A personality disorder characterized by smooth social skills and a lack of guilt about violating social rules and laws and taking advantage of others. (p. 486)

anxiety disorders: Psychological disorders that involve excessive levels of negative emotions, such as nervousness, tension, worry, fright, and anxiety. (p. 471)

aphasia (ah-fa´zē-ah): An impairment of the ability to understand or use language. (p. 57)

applied psychologist: A psychologist who uses knowledge of psychology to solve and prevent human problems. (p. 19)

approach-approach conflict: Conflict in which the individual must choose between two positive goals of approximately equal value. (p. 434)

approach-avoidance conflict: Conflict in which achieving a positive goal will produce a negative outcome as well. (p. 435)

artificial intelligence: Computers that are programmed to solve problems like human brains. (p. 252)

assertiveness training: A method of behavior therapy that teaches individuals assertive rather than passive or aggressive ways of dealing with problematic situations. (p. 506)

assessment centers: Program for the evaluation of employees that uses simulated management tasks as its primary method of evaluation. (p. 566)

association areas: Areas within each lobe of the cerebral cortex believed to play general rather than specific roles. (p. 59)

astral projection (as´tral): Depersonalization that includes the illusion that the mind has left the body. (p. 156)

attachment: The psychological bond between infants and caregivers. (p. 300)

attitudes: Beliefs that predispose one to act and feel in certain ways. (p. 536)

attribution: The process of trying to explain why things happen; that is, attribute them to some cause. (p. 526)

attribution theory (ah-tri-bu´shun): The theory that people tend to look for explanations for their own behavior and for that of others. (p. 543)

atypical sexual behavior: Sexual practice that differs considerably from the norm. (p. 382)

audition (aw-dish´un): The sense of hearing. (p. 103)

autonomic nervous system (aw´´to-nom´ik): The division of the peripheral nervous system that control the involuntary actions of internal body organs, such as heartbeat and breathing, and is important in the experience of emotion. (p. 49)

aversive conditioning (ah-ver´siv): A method of behavior therapy that involves the use of unpleasant negative stimuli to eliminate abnormal habits such as alcoholism and abnormal sexual practices. (p. 507)

avoidance-avoidance conflict: Conflict in which the individual must choose between two negative outcomes of approximately equal value. (p. 435)

avoidance conditioning: Operant conditioning in which the behavior is reinforced because it prevents something negative from happening (a form of negative reinforcement). (p. 187)

axons (ak´sonz): Neuron endings that transmit messages to other neurons. (p. 43)

B

basilar membrane (bas´i-lar): One of the membranes that separates the two tubes of the cochlea and upon which the organ of Corti rests. (p. 105)

basket cells: Sensory receptor cells at the bases of hairs that detect pressure. (p. 109)

behavior: Directly observable and measurable human actions. (p. 5)

behavior therapy: Psychotherapy based on social learning theory in which the therapist helps the client unlearn abnormal ways of behaving and learn more adaptive ways to take their place. (p. 503)

behaviorism (be-hāv´yor-izm): The school of psychology that emphasizes the process of learning and the measurement of overt behavior. (p. 12)

binocular cues (bin-ok´ū-lar): Visual cues that require both eyes to allow us to perceive distance. (p. 121)

biodata: The biographical information used by potential employers to evaluate a job candidate. (p. 564)

bipolar affective disorder (bī-pō´lar): A condition in which the individual experiences periods of mania that alternate irregularly with periods of severe depression. (p. 482)

blind spot: The spot where the optic nerve attaches to the retina, containing no rods or cones. (p. 96)

bone conduction hearing: Sounds transmitted through the bones of the head directly to the cochlear fluid. (p. 105)

brain: The complex mass of neural cells and related cells encased in the skull. (p. 42)

Broca's area: An area of the frontal lobe of the left cerebral hemisphere that plays a role in the ability to speak language. (p. 57)

C

Cannon-Bard theory of emotion: The theory that conscious emotional experiences and physiological reactions and behavior are relatively independent events. (p. 346)

castration anxiety (kas-trā´shun): According to Freud, the fear of a young boy that his father will punish his sexual desire for his mother by removing his genitals. (p. 406)

catatonic schizophrenia (kat´´ah-ton´ik skiz´´o-fre´nē-ah): A subtype of schizophrenia in which the individual spends long periods in an inactive, statuelike state. (p. 484)

catharsis (kah-thar´sis): The release of emotional energy related to unconscious conflicts. (p. 352, 498)

cell body: The central part of the neuron that includes the nucleus. (p. 43)

cell membrane: The covering of a neuron or other cell. (p. 44)

central nervous system: The brain and the nerve fibers that make up the spinal cord. (p. 47)

cerebellum (ser´´e-bel´um): Two rounded lumps behind the medulla responsible for maintaining muscle tone and muscular coordination. (p. 53)

cerebral cortex (ser´e-bral): The largest structure in the forebrain, controlling conscious experience and intelligence, and involved with the somatic nervous system. (p. 56)

cerebral hemispheres: The two main parts of the cerebral cortex. (p. 60)

cervix: The neck of the uterus that is connected to the vagina. (p. 373)

child molestation: Sexual behavior between an adult and a child without force or direct threat of force. (p. 385)

child rape: Sexual behavior with a child achieved by force or direct threat of force. (p. 385)

chromosome (krō´mo-sōm): The strip in the cell nucleus that contains genes. (p. 70)

chunks: Units of memory. (p. 215)

ciliary muscle (sil´e-er´´e): The muscle in the eyes that controls the shape of the lens. (p. 95)

cingulate cortex: Part of the limbic system that processes cognitive information in emotion. (p. 56)

cingulotomy: A type of psychosurgery for severe and otherwise untreatable obsessive-compulsive disorder that involves surgical destruction of part of the cingulate cortex. (p. 517)

circadian rhythm: A cycle of waking and sleeping that regulates our pattern of sleep. (p. 149)

classical conditioning: A form of learning in which a previously neutral stimulus (CS) is paired with an unconditioned stimulus (UCS) to elicit a conditioned response (CR) that is identical to or very similar to the unconditioned response (UCR). (p. 179)

client-centered psychotherapy: Carl Rogers' approach to humanistic psychotherapy in which the therapist creates an atmosphere that encourages clients to discover feelings of which they are unaware. (p. 500)

climacteric (kli-mak´ter-ik): The period between about ages 45 and 60 in which there is a loss of capacity to sexually reproduce in women and a decline in the reproductive capacity of men. (p. 314)

clinical method: The method of studying people while they are receiving psychological help from a psychologist. (p. 24)

clitoris: The structure at the upper part of the vagina that is most sensitive to sexual stimulation in females. (p. 373)

cochlea (cok´lē-ah): A curved structure of the inner ear that is filled with fluid. (p. 105)

coefficient of correlation: The numerical expression of the strength of a relationship between two variables. (p. 25)

cognition (kog-nish´un): The intellectual processes through which information is obtained, transformed, stored, retrieved, and otherwise used. (p. 9, 244)

cognitive dissonance (kog´ni-tiv dis´so-nans): The discomfort that results from inconsistencies between attitudes and behavior. (p. 541)

cognitive map: An inferred mental awareness of the structure of a physical space or related elements. (p. 197)

cognitive theory of emotion: The theory that the cognitive interpretation of events in the outside world and stimuli from our own bodies is the key factor in emotions. (p. 346)

cognitive therapy: An approach to therapy that teaches individuals new cognitions—adaptive beliefs, expectations, and ways of thinking—to eliminate abnormal emotions and behavior. (p. 509)

collective unconscious: According to Jung, the content of the unconscious mind with which all humans are born. (p. 407)

companionate love: The blend of friendship, intimacy, commitment, and security that generally develops after passionate love. (p. 553)

computerized tomography (CT): An imaging technique utilizing X rays to provide two-dimensional images of brain structure. (p. 63)

concepts: Categories of things, events, or qualities that are linked together by some common feature or features in spite of their differences. (p. 245)

concrete operational stage: In Piaget's theory, the period of cognitive development from ages 7 to 11. (p. 303)

conditioned response (CR): A response that is similar or identical to the unconditioned response that comes to be elicited by a conditioned stimulus. (p. 177)

conditioned stimulus (CS): A stimulus that comes to elicit responses as a result of being paired with an unconditioned stimulus. (p. 177)

conditions of worth: The standards used by others or ourselves in judging our worth. (p. 414)

cones: The 6 million receptor cells located mostly in the center of the retina that transduce light waves into neural impulses, thereby coding information about light, dark, and color. (p. 95)

conflict: The state in which two or more motives cannot be satisfied because they interfere with one another. (p. 434)

conformity: Yielding to group pressure even when no direct request to comply has been made. (p. 531)

conjunctive concepts (kon´´junk-tiv´): Concepts defined by the simultaneous presence of two or more common characteristics. (p. 245)

conscience: According to Freud, the moral inhibitions of the superego. (p. 404)

conscious mind: That portion of the mind of which one is presently aware. (p. 402)

consciousness (kon´shus-nes): A state of awareness. (p. 138)

conservation: The concept understood by concrete operational children that quantity (number, mass, etc.) does not change just because shape or other superficial features have changed. (p. 303)

continuity hypothesis: The view that abnormal behavior is just a more severe form of normal psychological problems. (p. 466)

control group: The group in simple experiments that receives none of the independent variable and is used for comparisons with the treatment group. (p. 27)

convergent thinking: Thinking that is logical, conventional, and that focuses on a problem. (p. 254)

conversion disorders: Somatoform disorders in which individuals experience serious somatic symptoms such as functional blindness, deafness, and paralysis. (p. 475)

cooperative play: Play that involves cooperation between two or more children. (p. 302)

coping: Attempts by individuals to deal with the source of stress and/or control their reactions to it. (p. 450)

cornea (kor´nē-ah): The protective coating on the surface of the eye through which light passes. (p. 95)

corpus callosum (kor´pus kah-lō´sum): The link between the cerebral hemispheres. (p. 60)

correlational method (kor´´e-lā´shun-al): A research method that measures the strength of the relation between variables. (p. 24)

cortisol: A hormone produced by the adrenal glands. (p. 67)

counterconditioning: The process of eliminating a classically conditioned response by pairing the conditioned stimulus (CS) with an unconditioned stimulus (UCS) for a response that is stronger than the conditioned response (CR) and that cannot occur at the same time as the CR. (p. 179)

creativity: The ability to make human products and ideas (such as symphonies or solutions to social problems) that are both novel and valued by others. (p. 254)

cretinism (krē´tin-izm): A type of mental retardation in children caused by a deficiency of thyroxin. (p. 68)

criterion-referenced testing: Testing designed to determine if a child can meet the minimum standards of a specific educational objective. (p. 586)

critical period: A biologically determined period in the life of some animals during which certain forms of learning can take place most easily. (p. 288)

criticism trap: An increase in the frequency of a negative behavior that often follows the use of criticism, reinforcing the behavior it is intended to punish. (p. 189)

crystallized intelligence: The ability to use previously learned skills to solve familiar problems. (p. 266)

cultural relativity: The perspective that promotes thinking of different cultures in relative terms rather than judgmental terms. (p. 17)

culture: The patterns of behavior, beliefs, and values shared by a group of people. (p. 16)

cupula (ku´pu-lah): A gelatinlike structure containing a tuft of hairlike sensory receptor cells in the semicircular canals. (p. 109)

D

dark adaptation: Increased sensitivity of the eye in semidarkness following an abrupt reduction in overall illumination. (p. 98)

day residue: Content in dreams that is similar to events in the person's waking life. (p. 146)

daydreams: Relatively focused thinking about fantasies. (p. 139)

decay theory: The theory that forgetting occurs as the memory trace fades over time. (p. 225)

decenter (dē-sen´ter): To think about more than one characteristic of a thing at a time; a capacity of concrete operational children. (p. 303)

decibel (db) (des´i-bel): Measurement of the intensity of perceived sound. (p. 104)

declarative memory: Semantic and episodic memory. (p. 218)

deep structure: The underlying structure of a statement that holds its meaning. (p. 257)

defense mechanisms: According to Freud, the unrealistic strategies used by the ego to discharge tension. (p. 452)

deindividuation: State in which people in a group can feel anonymous and unidentifiable and therefore feel less concerned with what others think of their behavior. (p. 527)

delay of reinforcement: The passage of time between the response and the positive reinforcement that leads to reduced efficiency of learning. (p. 183)

delusion: A false belief that distorts reality. (p. 483)

delusional disorder: A nonschizophrenic disorder characterized by delusions of grandeur and persecution that are more logical than those of paranoid schizophrenics in their absence of hallucinations. (p. 485)

dendrites (den´drits): Small extensions on the cell body that receive messages from other neurons. (p. 43)

denial: The defense mechanism in which threatening information is blocked from conscious awareness. (p. 452)

deoxyribonucleic acid (DNA) (dē-ok´´sē-rī´´bō-nu-klā´ik): The complex molecule containing the genetic code. (p. 70)

dependent variable: The variable whose quantitative value depends on the effects of the independent variable. (p. 26)

depersonalization (dē-per´´sun-al-i-zā´shun): The perceptual experience of one's body or surroundings becoming distorted or unreal in some way. (p. 156, 477)

depolarization: The process during which positively charged ions flow into the axon, making it less negatively charged inside. (p. 44)

depressants: Drugs that reduce the activity of the central nervous system, leading to a sense of relaxation, drowsiness, and lowered inhibitions. (p. 162)

depression: Disorder characterized by extreme sadness, lack of energy, disturbance in sleep and/or appetite, negative self-evaluation, and a pervasive sense of hopelessness and helplessness. (p. 207)

development: The more-or-less predictable changes in behavior associated with increasing age. (p. 286)

developmental psychology: Field of psychology that focuses on the development across the life span. (p. 286)

deviation IQ: Intelligence quotient based on the degree of deviation from average of the person's score on an intelligence test. (p. 269)

difference threshold: The smallest difference between two stimuli that can be detected half the time. (p. 91)

diffusion of responsibility: The effect of being in a group that apparently reduces the sense of personal responsibility of each group member to act appropriately. (p. 529)

directed consciousness: Focused and orderly awareness. (p. 138)

discontinuity hypothesis: The view that abnormal behavior is fundamentally different from normal psychological problems. (p. 466)

disinhibition (dis´´in-hi-bish´un): A temporary increase in the strength of an extinguished response caused by an unrelated stimulus event. (p. 195)

disjunctive concept (dis´´junk-tiv´): Concepts defined by the presence of one of two common characteristics or both. (p. 245)

disorganized schizophrenia: A subtype of schizophrenia characterized by shallow silliness, extreme social withdrawal, and fragmented delusions and hallucinations. (p. 484)

displacement (dis-plās´ment): A defense mechanism in which the individual directs aggressive or sexual feelings away from the primary object to someone or something safe. (p. 404)

dispositional attribution (dis´´po-zish´un-al): An explanation for behavior that is based on a personal characteristic of the individual. (p. 526)

dissociative amnesia: A dissociative disorder that involves a loss of memory and that has a psychological rather than a physical cause. (p. 477)

dissociative disorders (dis-sō´´sē-a-tiv): A category of conditions involving sudden abnormal cognitive changes, such as a change in memory, perception, or identity. (p. 477)

dissociative fugue (fūg): A period of "wandering" that involves a loss of memory and a change in identity. (p. 477)

dissociative identity disorder: A dissociative disorder in which the individual shifts abruptly and repeatedly from one "personality" to another. (p. 478)

divergent thinking: Thinking that is loosely organized, only partially directed, and unconventional. (p. 254)

divided consciousness: The splitting off of two conscious activities that occur simultaneously. (p. 139)

dizygotic twins (dī´´zī-got´ik): Twins formed from the fertilization of two ova by two sperm. (p. 72)

dominant gene: The gene that produces a trait in the individual even when paired with a recessive gene. (p. 71)

Down syndrome: An abnormality caused by the presence of an additional 21st chromosome. (p. 72)

dream interpretation: A method developed by Freud in which the symbols in the manifest content of dreams that are recalled by the patient are interpreted to reveal their latent content. (p. 497)

drug therapy: A medical therapy that uses chemicals to treat abnormal behavior. (p. 515)

dyspareunia (dis´´pah-roo´nē-ah): A sexual dysfunction in which the individual experiences pain during intercourse. (p. 388)

E

eardrum: Thin membrane that sound waves cause to vibrate; the first structure of the middle ear. (p. 104)

early experiences: Experiences occurring very early in development, believed by some to have lasting effects. (p. 288)

educational psychology: The field in which principles of learning, cognition, and other aspects of psychology are applied to improve education. (p. 584)

efferent neurons (ef´er-ent): Neurons that transmit messages from the central nervous system to organs and muscles. (p. 47)

ego (ē´go): According to Freud, that part of the mind that uses the reality principle to satisfy the id. (p. 403)

ego ideal: According to Freud, the standard of perfect conduct of the superego. (p. 404)

egocentric (e´´gō-sen´trik): The self-oriented quality in the thinking of preoperational children. (p. 301)

elaboration (e-lab´´o-rā´shun): The process of creating associations between a new memory and existing memories. (p. 224)

Electra complex (e-lek´trah): According to Freud, the transfer of a young girl's sexual desires from her mother to her father after she discovers she has no penis. (p. 406)

electroconvulsive therapy (ECT) (e-lek´´trō-con-vul´siv): A medical therapy that uses electrical current to induce controlled convulsive seizures that alleviate some types of mental disorders. (p. 516)

electroencephalogram (EEG) (e-lek´´trō-en-sef´ah-lo-gram): A recording of the electrical activity of the brain obtained through electrodes placed on the scalp. (p. 52, 142)

electromagnetic radiation (e-lek´´trō-mag-net´ik): A form of energy including electricity, radio waves, and X rays, of which visible light is a part. (p. 94)

emotions: Positive or negative feelings generally in reaction to stimuli that are accompanied by physiological arousal and related behavior. (p. 328)

encode (en´cōd): To represent information in some form in the memory system. (p. 212)

endocrine system (en´dō-krin): The system of glands that secretes hormones. (p. 66)

engram (en´gram): The as yet unidentified memory trace in the brain that is the biological basis of memory. (p. 232)

environmental psychologist: A psychologist who studies the effects of the physical environment on behavior and mental processes. (p. 577)

epididymis: Structure that holds sperm cells until ejaculation. (p. 374)

epinephrine (ep´´i-nef´rin): A hormone produced by the adrenal glands. (p. 67)

episodic memory (ep´i-sod-ik): Memory for specific experiences that can be defined in terms of time and space. (p. 218)

equity theory: The theory that partners will be comfortable in their relationship only when the ratio between their perceived contributions and benefits is equal. (p. 553)

erectile dysfunction: Condition in which the penis does not become erect enough for intercourse under sexually arousing circumstances. (p. 388)

escape conditioning: Operant conditioning in which the behavior is reinforced because it causes a negative event to cease (a form of negative reinforcement). (p. 187)

estrogen (es´tro-jen): A female sex hormone. (p. 68)

ethnic group: A group of persons who are descendants from a common group of ancestors. (p. 16)

ethnic identity: Each person's sense of belonging to a particular ethnic group. (p. 16)

everyday intelligence: The intellectual abilities needed to deal with everyday problems, rather than perform well in school. (p. 272)

excitement phase: The first stage of the sexual response cycle during which the penis becomes erect and the vagina lubricates. (p. 375)

exhibitionism (ek´´si-bish´u-nizm´´): The practice of obtaining sexual pleasure by exposing one's genitals to others. (p. 384)

experimental group: The group in an experiment that receives some value of the independent variable. (p. 27)

expert systems: Problem-solving computer programs for specific applications, such as diagnosis and treatment of medical disorders. (p. 253)

external auditory canal: The tube connecting the pinna to the middle ear. (p. 104)

extinction (eks-ting´shun): The process of unlearning a learned response because of the removal of the original source of learning. (p. 194)

extrinsic motivation (eks-trin´sik): Human motives stimulated by external rewards. (p. 341)

extroversion (eks´´tro-ver´zhun): According to Jung, the tendency of some individuals to be friendly and open to the world. (p. 407)

F

fallopian tubes: Tube through which ova (eggs) reach the uterus. (p. 373)

family therapy: An approach to psychotherapy that emphasizes an understanding of the roles of each of the members of the family system, usually conducted with all members of the family present. (p. 515)

feelings of inferiority: According to Adler, the feelings that result from children being less powerful than adults that must be overcome during the development of the healthy personality. (p. 408)

female sexual arousal disorder: Condition in which sexual arousal does not occur in appropriate circumstances in a female. (p. 388)

feminist psychotherapy: An approach to psychotherapy that encourages women to confront issues created by living in a sexist society as part of their psychotherapy. (p. 513)

fertilization (fer´ti-li-zā-shun): The uniting of sperm and ovum, which produces a zygote. (p. 70)

fetishism (fet´ish-izm): The practice of obtaining sexual arousal primarily or exclusively from specific objects. (p. 383)

fixed interval schedule: A reinforcement schedule in which the reinforcer is given following the first response occurring after a predetermined period of time. (p. 185)

fixed ratio schedule: A reinforcement schedule in which the reinforcer is given only after a specified number of responses. (p. 184)

flooding: A method of behavior therapy in which the client is confronted with high levels of the phobic stimulus until the fear response is extinguished. (p. 504)

flowing consciousness: Drifting, unfocused awareness. (p. 138)

fluid intelligence: The ability to learn or invent new strategies to deal with new problems. (p. 266)

forebrain: The parts of the brain, including the thalamus, hypothalamus, and cerebral cortex, that cover the hindbrain and midbrain and fill much of the skull. (p. 53)

formal experiment: Research method that allows the researcher to manipulate the independent variable to study its effect on the dependent variable. (p. 25)

formal operational stage: In Piaget's theory, the period of intellectual development usually reached by about age 11 and characterized by the ability to use abstract concepts. (p. 305)

fovea (fō´vē-ah): The central spot of the retina containing the greatest concentration of cones. (p. 95)

free association: A tool used by Freud in which the patient is encouraged to talk about whatever comes to mind, allowing the contents of the unconscious mind to slip past the censorship of the ego. (p. 496)

free nerve endings: Sensory receptor cells in the skin that detect pressure, temperature, and pain. (p. 109)

frequency of cycles: Rate of vibration of sound waves; determines pitch. (p. 103)

Freud's instinct theory: The theory that aggression is caused by an inborn aggressive instinct. (p. 352)

frontal lobes: Part of the cerebral cortex in the front of the skull involved in planning, organization, voluntary motor movements, and speaking. (p. 56)

frustration: The result of being unable to satisfy a motive. (p. 434)

frustration-aggression theory: The theory that aggression is a natural reaction to frustration. (p. 9, 352)

functionalism (funk´shun-al-izm): The nineteenth-century school of psychology that emphasized the useful functions of consciousness. (p. 9)

fundamental attribution error: The tendency to underestimate the impact of situations on others while overestimating the impact on oneself. (p. 526)

G

g: A broad general factor of intelligence, a concept endorsed by some investigators of intelligence. (p. 263)

gamete (gam´ēt): A sex cell, which contains 23 chromosomes instead of the normal 46. (p. 70)

ganglia (gang´glē-ah): Clusters of cell bodies of neurons outside of the central nervous system. (p. 50)

gender: The psychological experience of being male or female. (p. 362)

gender identity: One's view of oneself as male or female. (p. 16, 362)

gender role: The behaviors consistent with being male or female in a given culture. (p. 362)

gene (jēn): The hereditary unit made up of deoxyribonucleic acid. (p. 70)

general adaptation syndrome (GAS): According to Selye, the mobilization of the body to ward off threats, characterized by a three-stage pattern of the alarm reaction, the resistance stage, and the exhaustion stage. (p. 440)

generalized anxiety disorder: An uneasy sense of general tension and apprehension that makes the individual highly uncomfortable because of its prolonged presence. (p. 472)

generative property of language (jen´e-ra´´tiv): The ability to create an infinite set of utterances using a finite set of elements and rules. (p. 257)

genital stage (jen´i-tal): According to Freud, the psychosexual stage (from 11 years through adulthood) in which sexual and romantic interest is directed toward one's peers. (p. 406)

gestalt (ges-tawlt´): An organized or unified whole. (p. 8)

Gestalt psychology: The school of thought based on the belief that human consciousness cannot be broken down into meaningful components. (p. 8)

Gestalt therapy: A humanistic therapy in which the therapist takes an active role (questioning and challenging the client) to help the client become more aware of his or her feelings. (p. 501)

glands: Structures in the body that secrete substances. (p. 66)

glucagon (gloo´kah-gon): A hormone produced by the islets of Langerhans that causes the liver to release sugar into the bloodstream. (p. 68, 331)

gonads (gō´nadz): The glands that produce sex cells and hormones important in sexual arousal and that contribute to the development of secondary sex characteristics. (p. 68)

graded exposure: A behavior therapy technique in which a person is first exposed to a stimulus that is mildly fear provoking. Then the client is exposed, once he or she has mastered anxiety in the first situation, to a graded series of more fearful situations. (p. 503)

group therapy: Psychotherapy conducted in groups, typically of four to eight clients at a time. (p. 514)

groupthink: The faulty decision-making processes that may occur in groups. (p. 531)

gustation (gus-tā´shun): The sense of taste. (p. 116)

H

hallucination: A false perceptual experience that distorts reality. (p. 483)

hallucinogens (hah-lū´si´´no-jenz): Drugs that alter perceptual experiences. (p. 163)

hammer, anvil, and stirrup: Three linked bones of the middle ear that help pass sound waves to the inner ear. (p. 105)

health psychology: The field of psychology that uses psychological principles to encourage healthy lifestyles and to minimize the impact of physical illness. (p. 434)

hertz (Hz): Measurement of the frequency of sound waves in cycles per second. (p. 103)

heterosexuals: Persons who are romantically and sexually attracted to those of the different sex. (p. 368)

heuristics (hu-ris´tik): Patterns of reasoning that increase the probability of finding a correct solution to a problem. (p. 252)

hindbrain: The lowest part of the brain, located at the base of the skull. (p. 53)

hippocampus (hip´´o-kam´pus): Part of the limbic system that plays a role in emotional arousal and memory. (p. 56, 233)

homeostatic mechanisms (hō´´mē-ō-stat´ik): Internal bodily mechanism that senses biological imbalances and stimulates actions to restore the proper balance. (p. 329)

homosexuals: Persons who are romantically and sexually attracted to those of the same sex, as distinguished from heterosexuals. (p. 368)

hormones (hor´mōnz): Chemical substances, produced by endocrine glands, that influence internal organs. (p. 66)

human factors engineering: The branch of industrial-organizational psychology interested in the design of machines to be operated by human beings. (p. 573)

humanistic psychology: The psychological view that human beings possess an innate tendency to improve and determine their lives by the decisions they make. (p. 13)

hyperphagia (hī´´per-fā´jē-ah): Excessive overeating that results from the destruction of the satiety center of the hypothalamus. (p. 330)

hypnagogic state (hip´´nah-goj´ik): A relaxed state of dreamlike awareness between wakefulness and sleep. (p. 142)

hypnosis (hip-nō´sis): An altered state of consciousness in which the individual is highly relaxed and susceptible to suggestions. (p. 154)

hypochondriasis (hī´´pō-kon-drī´ah-sis): A mild form of somatization disorder characterized by excessive concern about one's health. (p. 475)

hypothalamus (hī´´po-thal´ah-mus): The small part of the forebrain involved with motives, emotions, and the functions of the autonomic nervous system. (p. 55, 330)

I

id: According to Freud, the inborn part of the unconscious mind that uses the primary process to satisfy its needs and that acts according to the pleasure principle. (p. 403)

ideal self: According to humanists, the person one wishes he or she were. (p. 414)

identification: The tendency to base one's identity and actions on individuals who are successful in gaining satisfaction from life. (p. 405)

immune system: The complex bodily system of defenses to illness, such as white cells and natural killer cells of the blood. (p. 442)

imprinting (im´print-ing): A form of early learning that occurs in some animals during a critical period. (p. 288)

in-basket exercise: A type of management simulation task in which the individual attempts to solve a problem that is typical of the ones that appear in a manager's "in basket." (p. 567)

incentives: An external cue that activates motivation. (p. 332)

incest (in´sest): Sexual relations between relatives. (p. 385)

independent variable: The variable whose quantitative value can be independently controlled by the researcher. (p. 26)

industrial-organizational psychologist: A psychologist who studies organizations and seeks ways to improve the functioning and human benefits of business. (p. 562)

inhalants (in-hā´lants): Toxic substances that produce a sense of intoxication when inhaled. (p. 163)

inhibited female orgasm: A female sexual dysfunction in which the individual is unable to experience orgasm. (p. 388)

inhibited sexual desire: Condition in which a person desires sex rarely or not at all. (p. 387)

inner-directedness: A force that humanists believe all people possess that internally leads them to grow and improve. (p. 413)

insanity: A legal definition concerning a person's inability to tell right from wrong, ability to understand legal proceedings, or whether the person is a direct danger to self or others. (p. 469)

insight (in´sīt): A form of cognitive change that involves recognition of previously unseen relationships. (p. 199)

insomnia: Disorder in which the person sleeps less than desired. (p. 149)

insulin (in´su-lin): A hormone produced by the islets of Langerhans that reduces the amount of sugar in the bloodstream. (p. 68, 331)

intellectualization: The process of thinking about stressful events in overly intellectual ways that do not accurately reflect the emotional nature of the event. (p. 452)

intelligence (in-tel´i-jens): The cognitive ability of an individual to learn from experience, to reason well, and to cope with the demands of daily living. (p. 262)

intelligence quotient (IQ): A numerical measure of intelligence derived from the results of an intelligence test. (p. 267)

intelligent tutoring systems: Approach to learning in which computers provide tutoring to students. (p. 585)

intensity: Density of vibrating air molecules; determines the loudness of sound. (p. 104)

interference theory: The theory that forgetting occurs because similar memories interfere with the storage or retrieval of information. (p. 226)

interneurons: Neurons that are not sensory or motor neurons. (p. 47)

interview: A subjective method of personality assessment that involves questioning techniques designed to reveal the personality of the client. (p. 422, 563)

intrinsic motivation (in-trin´sik): Human motives stimulated by the inherent nature of the activity or its natural consequences. (p. 341)

introspection (in´´tro-spek´shun): The process of looking inward at one's own consciousness. (p. 7)

introversion (in-tro-ver´zhun): According to Jung, the tendency of some individuals to be shy and to focus their attention on themselves. (p. 407)

ions (ī´ons): Electrically charged particles. (p. 44)

iris (ī´ris): The colored part of the eye behind the cornea that regulates the amount of light that enters. (p. 95)

islets of Langerhans (i´lets *of* lahng´er-hanz): Endocrine cells in the pancreas that regulate the level of sugar in the blood. (p. 68)

J

James-Lange theory of emotion: The theory that conscious emotional experiences are caused by feedback to the cerebral cortex from physiological reactions and behavior. (p. 344)

job performance ratings: Ratings of the actual performance of employees in their jobs by supervisors. (p. 566)

K

kinesthetic receptors (kin´´es-thet´ik): Receptors in the muscles, joints, and skin that provide information about movement, posture, and orientation. (p. 108)

Korsakoff's syndrome (Kor-sak´ofs): A disorder involving both anterograde and retrograde amnesia caused by excessive use of alcohol. (p. 234)

L

labia majora: The larger outer lips of the vulva. (p. 373)

labia minora: The smaller inner lips of the vulva. (p. 373)

language: A symbolic code used in communication. (p. 256)

latency stage: According to Freud, the fourth psychosexual stage (from about 6 to 11 years) during which sexual energy is sublimated and converted into socially valued activities. (p. 406)

latent content of dreams: According to Freud, the true meaning of dreams that is found in the symbols in their manifest content. (p. 147)

lateral hypothalamus: A portion of the hypothalamus involved in feeling hungry and starting to eat (the feeding center). (p. 330)

learned helplessness: A pattern of learned behavior characterized by a lack of effort to avoid negative events; caused by previous exposure to unavoidable negative events. (p. 207)

learned taste aversion (ah-ver´shun): Negative reaction to a particular taste that has been associated with nausea or other illness. (p. 203)

learning: Any relatively permanent change in behavior brought about through experience. (p. 174)

learning set: Improvement in the rate of learning to solve new problems through practice solving similar problems. (p. 199)

lens: Transparent portion of the eye that focuses light on the retina. (p. 95)

levels of processing model: An alternative to the stage theory of memory stating that the distinction between short-term and long-term memory is a matter of degree rather than different kinds of memory and is based on how incoming information is processed. (p. 223)

life events: Psychologically significant events that occur in a person's life, such as divorce, childbirth, or change in employment. (p. 437)

light adaptation: Regaining sensitivity of the eye to bright light following an abrupt increase in overall illumination. (p. 98)

limbic system: Complex brain system composed of the amygdala, hippocampus, septal area, and the cingulate gyrus that works with the hypothalamus in emotional arousal. (p. 55)

linguistic relativity hypothesis: The idea that the structure of a language may influence the way individuals think. (p. 258)

long-term memory (LTM): The third stage of memory, involving the storage of information that is kept for long periods of time. (p. 215)

M

magnetic resonance imaging (MRI): A safe imaging technique utilizing magnetic resonance used to obtain detailed views of brain structure and function. (p. 52)

mainstreaming: The practice of integrating handicapped children into regular classrooms. (p. 587)

major depression: An affective disorder characterized by episodes of deep unhappiness, loss of interest in life, and other symptoms. (p. 479)

male sexual arousal disorder: Condition in which sexual arousal does not occur in appropriate circumstances in a male. (p. 388)

management by objectives: The strategy of giving employees specific goals but giving them considerable freedom in deciding how to reach those goals. (p. 571)

mania (mā´nē-ah): A disturbance of mood in which the individual experiences a euphoria characterized by unrealistic optimism and heightened sensory pleasures. (p. 482)

manifest content of dreams: According to Freud, the obvious, but superficial, meaning of dreams. (p. 147)

mantra (man´trah): A word or sound containing religious meaning used during meditation. (p. 154)

Maslow's hierarchy of motives: The concept that more basic needs must be met before higher level motives become active. (p. 341)

mastery learning: The concept that children should never progress from one learning task to another until they have mastered the more basic one. (p. 584)

maturation (mach´´u-rā´shun): Systematic physical growth of the body, including the nervous system. (p. 286)

medical therapies: Those therapies—including drug therapy, electroconvulsive therapy, and psychosurgery—generally designed to correct a physical condition that is believed to be the cause of a psychological disorder. (p. 515)

meditation (med´´i-tā´shun): Several methods of focusing concentration away from thoughts and feelings and generating a sense of relaxation. (p. 153)

medulla (me-dul´ah): The swelling at the top of the spinal cord responsible for controlling breathing and a variety of reflexes. (p. 53)

menarche (me-nar´kē): The first menstrual period. (p. 305)

menopause (men´o-pawz): The cessation of menstruation and the capacity to reproduce in women. (p. 314)

mental processes: Private psychological activities that include thinking, perceiving, and feeling. (p. 5)

mental set: A habitual way of approaching or perceiving a problem. (p. 251)

metabolism (me-tab´o-lizm): The process through which the body burns energy. (p. 68)

midbrain: The small area at the top of the hindbrain that serves primarily as a reflex center for orienting the eyes and ears. (p. 53)

modeling: Learning based on observation of the behavior of another. (p. 201)

monocular cues (mon-ok´u-lar): Seven visual cues that can be seen with one eye that allow us to perceive distance. (p. 121)

monozygotic twins (mon´´ō-zī-got´ik): Twins formed from a single ovum; they are identical in appearance because they have the same genetic structure. (p. 72)

mons: Fleshy mound that sits at the top of the vulva. (p. 373)

mood disorders: Psychological disorders involving depression and/or abnormal elation. (p. 479)

morpheme (mor´fēm): The smallest unit of meaning in a language. (p. 257)

motivated forgetting: Forgetting that is believed to be based on the upsetting or threatening nature of the information that is forgotten. (p. 230)

motivation: Internal state or condition that activates and gives direction to our thoughts, feelings, and actions. (p. 328)

motive for affiliation: The need to be with other people and to have personal relationships. (p. 337)

motives: Internal states or conditions that activate behavior and give it direction. (p. 12)

multiple approach-avoidance conflict: Conflict that requires the individual to choose between two alternatives that each contain both positive and negative consequences. (p. 436)

myelin sheath (mī´e-lin): The protective fatty covering wrapped around part of the neuron. (p. 45)

myoclonia (mi´´o-klō´nē-ah): An abrupt movement that sometimes occurs during the hypnagogic state in which the sleeper often experiences a sense of falling. (p. 142)

N

narcolepsy: Sleep disorder in which the person suddenly falls asleep during activities usually performed when fully awake. (p. 149)

narcotics: Powerful and highly addictive depressants. (p. 163)

naturalistic observation: A research method based on recording behavior as it occurs in natural life settings. (p. 24)

negative reinforcement: Reinforcement that comes about from the removal or avoidance of a negative event as the consequence of behavior. (p. 187)

neonatal period (ne´´ō-nā´tal): The first 2 weeks of life following birth. (p. 298)

nerve: A bundle of long neurons outside the brain and spinal cord. (p. 43)

neural pruning: The pruning in which unnecessary neural connections are actively destroyed, or "pruned," between the ages of 5 and the early teens. (p. 273)

neuron (nu´ron): An individual nerve cell. (p. 42)

neurotransmitters (nu´´rō-tranz´-mit-erz): Chemical substances produced by axons that transmit messages across the synapse. (p. 45)

nightmare: A dream that occurs during REM sleep whose content is exceptionally frightening, sad, angry, or in some other way uncomfortable. (p. 148)

night terror: An upsetting nocturnal experience that occurs most often in preschool-age children during deep non-REM sleep. (p. 148)

nodes of Ranvier (rahn´-vē-ā): Gaps in the myelin sheath covering the nerves. (p. 45)

norepinephrine (nor´´ep-i-nef´rin): A hormone produced by the adrenal glands. (p. 67)

normal distribution: The symmetrical pattern of scores on a scale in which a majority of the scores are clustered near the center and a minority are at either extreme. (p. 269)

norms: Standards (created by the scores of a large group of individuals) used as the basis of comparison for scores on a test. (p. 270)

novel stimulation: New or changed experiences. (p. 335)

O

obedience: Doing what one is told to do by people in authority. (p. 533)

objectivity: Lack of subjectivity in a test question so that the same score is produced regardless of who does the scoring. (p. 270)

object permanence: The understanding that objects continue to exist when they are not in view. (p. 299)

observational method: A method of personality assessment that involves watching a person's actual behavior in a natural or simulated situation. (p. 422)

obsessive-compulsive disorders: Disorders that involve obsessions (anxiety-provoking thoughts that will not go away) and/or compulsions (irresistible urges to engage in specific irrational behaviors). (p. 474)

occipital lobes (ok-sip´i-tal): The part of the cerebral cortex located at the base of the back of the head that plays an essential role in the processing of sensory information from the eyes. (p. 59)

Oedipus complex (ed´i-pus): According to Freud, the unconscious wish of all male children to kill their fathers and sexually possess their mothers. (p. 405)

olfaction (ol-fak´shun): The sense of smell. (p. 116)

olfactory epithelium (ōl-fak´to-rē ep´´i-thē´lē-um): The sheet of receptor cells at the top of the nasal cavity. (p. 117)

operant conditioning (op´e-rant): Learning in which the consequences of behavior lead to changes in the probability of its occurrence. (p. 181)

opiates (ō´pē-ats): Narcotic drugs derived from the opium poppy. (p. 163)

opponent-process theory of color vision: The theory of color vision contending that the eye has two kinds of cones that respond to light in either the red-green or yellow-blue ranges of wavelength. (p. 100)

opponent-process theory of motivation: Solomon's theory of the learning of new motives based on changes over time in contrasting feelings. (p. 339)

optic chiasm: Area in the occipital lobes of the left visual hemisphere where the optic nerves cross. (p. 96)

optic nerve: The nerve that carries neural messages about vision to the brain. (p. 96)

optimal level of arousal: The apparent human need for a comfortable level of stimulation, achieved by acting in ways that increase or decrease it. (p. 336)

oral aggressive personality: A personality type in which the person seeks pleasure by being verbally hostile to others. (p. 405)

oral receptive personality: A personality type in which the person seeks pleasure through overeating, smoking, and other oral means. (p. 405)

oral stage: According to Freud, the first psychosexual stage (from birth to 1 year), in which id gratification is focused on the mouth. (p. 405)

organ of Corti (kor´tē): Sensory receptor in the cochlea that transduces sound waves into coded neural impulses. (p. 105)

orgasm: The reflexive phase of the sexual response cycle accompanied by peak levels of arousal and pleasure, and usually by ejaculation in males. (p. 376)

oval window: The membrane of the inner ear that vibrates, creating sound waves in the fluid of the cochlea. (p. 105)

ovaries (o´vah-rēz): Female endocrine glands that secrete sex-related hormones and produce ova, or eggs. (p. 68, 373)

P

pain disorders: Somatoform disorders in which the individual experiences a relatively specific and chronic pain that has a psychological rather than physical cause. (p. 476)

pancreas (pan´krē-as): The organ near the stomach that contains the islets of Langerhans. (p. 68)

panic anxiety disorder: A pattern of anxiety in which long periods of calm are broken by an intensely uncomfortable attack of anxiety. (p. 472)

papillae (pah-pil´ē): Clusters of taste buds on the tongue. (p. 116)

parallel play: Playing near but not with another child. (p. 302)

paranoid schizophrenia (par´ah-noid): A subtype of schizophrenia in which the individual holds delusions of persecution and grandeur that seriously distort reality. (p. 484)

parasympathetic division (par´´ah-sim´´pah-thet´ik): The division of the autonomic nervous system that generally "calms" internal organs. (p. 49)

parathormone (par´´ah-thor´mōn): A hormone that regulates ion levels in neurons and controls excitability of the nervous system. (p. 68)

parathyroid glands (par´´ah-thī´roid): Four glands embedded in the thyroid that produce parathormone. (p. 68)

paraventricular nucleus: A part of the hypothalamus that plays a role in the motive of hunger by regulating the level of blood sugar. (p. 331)

parietal lobes (pah-rī´e-tal): The part of the cerebral cortex located behind the frontal lobes at the top of the skull containing the body sense area. (p. 58)

participative management: The practice of involving employees at all levels in management decisions. (p. 571)

passionate love: The mixture of romantic, sexual, and other feelings of love. (p. 553)

peak experience: An intensely moving experience in which the individual feels a sense of unity with the world. (p. 415)

pedophilia (pe´´do-fil´ē-ah): The practice of obtaining pleasure from sexual contact with children. (p. 385)

penis: The tubular structure that becomes erect during sexual arousal and through which sperm is ejaculated. (p. 374)

penis envy: According to Freud, the desire of a girl to possess a penis. (p. 406)

perception (per-sep´-shun): The process of organizing and interpreting information received from the outside world. (p. 90)

perceptual constancy: The tendency for perceptions of objects to remain relatively unchanged in spite of changes in raw sensations. (p. 120)

performance tests: Employee selection test that resembles the actual manual performance required in a job. (p. 565)

peripheral nervous system (pe-rif´er-al): The network of nerves that branch from the brain and spinal cord to all parts of the body. (p. 47)

person perception: The process of forming impressions of others. (p. 546)

person × situation interactionism (in´´ter-ak´shun-izm): The view that behavior is influenced by a combination of the characteristics of both the person and the situation. (p. 420)

person variables: All characteristics of an individual that are relatively enduring, such as ways of thinking, beliefs, or physiological reactivity to stress. (p. 446)

personal growth therapy: Psychotherapy for normal individuals who want to enhance their personal adjustment, improve interpersonal relationships, learn to react better to stress, and so on. (p. 494)

personality: The sum total of the typical ways of acting, thinking, and feeling that makes each person unique. (p. 400)

personality disorders: Psychological disorders that are believed to result from personalities that developed improperly during childhood. (p. 485)

personal unconscious: According to Jung, the motives, conflicts, and information that are repressed by a person because they are threatening to that individual. (p. 407)

persuasion: The process of changing another person's attitudes through arguments and other related means. (p. 537)

phallic stage (fal´ik): According to Freud, the third psychosexual stage (from 3 to 6 years), in which gratification is focused on the genitals. (p. 405)

phi phenomenon (fī fe-nom´e-non): The perception of apparent movement between two stationary stimuli. (p. 8)

phobia: An intense, irrational fear. (p. 471)

phoneme (fō´nēm): The smallest unit of sound in a language. (p. 257)

pineal gland (pīn´ē-al): The endocrine gland that is largely responsible for the regulation of biological rhythms. (p. 69)

pinna (pin´nah): The external part of the ear. (p. 104)

pitch: The experience of sound vibrations sensed as high or low. (p. 104)

pituitary gland (pi-tu´i-tār´´ē): The body's master gland, located near the bottom of the brain, whose hormones help regulate the activity of the other glands in the endocrine system. (p. 66, 333)

plateau phase: High levels of sexual arousal and pleasure that are maintained for variable periods of time. (p. 375)

pleasure principle: According to Freud, the attempt of the id to seek immediate pleasure and avoid pain regardless of how harmful it might be to others. (p. 403)

polarization: The tendency for group discussion to make beliefs and attitudes more extreme. (p. 530)

polarized state (pō´lar-īz´d): The resting state of a neuron, when mostly negative ions are inside and mostly positive ions are outside the cell membrane. (p. 44)

pons (ponz): Part of the hindbrain that is involved in balance, hearing, and some parasympathetic functions. (p. 53)

positive reinforcement (rē´´in-fors´ment): Any consequence of behavior that leads to an increase in the probability of its occurrence. (p. 182)

positron emission tomography (PET): A brain-imaging technique that produces an X-ray-like image. (p. 52)

posttraumatic stress disorder: The condition caused by extremely stressful experiences in which the person later experiences anxiety and irritability; has upsetting memories, dreams, and realistic flashbacks of the experience; and tries to avoid anything that reminds him or her of the experience. (p. 473)

preconscious mind: That portion of the mind containing information that is not presently conscious but can be easily brought into consciousness. (p. 402)

prejudice: A harmful attitude based on inaccurate generalizations about a group of people. (p. 542)

premature ejaculation: A male sexual dysfunction in which the individual reaches orgasm and ejaculates sperm too early. (p. 389)

preoperational stage: In Piaget's theory, the period of cognitive development from ages 2 to 7. (p. 301)

pressure: Stress that arises from the threat of negative events. (p. 437)

primacy effect: The tendency for first impressions to heavily influence opinions about other people. (p. 547)

primary motives: Human motives for things that are necessary for survival, such as food, water, and warmth. (p. 329)

primary process thinking: According to Freud, the attempt by the id to satisfy its needs by forming a wish-fulfilling mental image of the desired object. (p. 403)

primary reinforcement: Reinforcement from innate positive reinforcers that do not have to be acquired through learning. (p. 183)

primary sex characteristics: Ovulation and menstruation in females and production of sperm in males. (p. 305)

proactive interference (prō-ak´tiv in´´ter-fēr´ens): Interference created by memories from prior learning. (p. 227)

problem solving: The cognitive process through which information is used to reach a goal that is blocked by some obstacle. (p. 250)

procedural memory: Memory for motor movements and skills. (p. 217)

progressive relaxation training: A method of learning to deeply relax the muscles of the body. (p. 453, 503)

Project Follow Through: A federally sponsored program designed to help educate economically disadvantaged children. (p. 585)

projection (pro-jek´shun): According to Freud, a defense mechanism in which unacceptable id desires are viewed as the desires of others and not as one's own. (p. 452)

projective test: A test that uses ambiguous stimuli designed to reveal the contents of the client's unconscious mind. (p. 422)

prostate gland: One of the structures that produces fluid for semen. (p. 374)

psychoanalysis (sī´´kō-ah-nal´i-sis): A method of psychotherapy developed by Freud based on his belief that the root of all psychological problems is unconscious conflicts between the id, the ego, and the superego. (p. 12, 496)

psychoanalytic theory: Freud's theory that the origin of personality lies in the balance between the id, the ego, and the superego. (p. 401)

psychological motives: Motives related to the individual's happiness and well-being, but not to survival. (p. 335)

psychology: The science of behavior and mental processes. (p. 5)

psychophysics (sī´´kō-fiz´iks): A specialty area of psychology that studies sensory limits, sensory adaptation, and related topics. (p. 91)

psychosexual stages: In the personality theory of Sigmund Freud, developmental periods during which the sexual energy of the id finds different sources of satisfaction. (p. 405)

psychosurgery (sī´´ko-ser´jer-ē): A medical therapy that involves operating on the brain in an attempt to alleviate some types of mental disorders. (p. 517)

psychotherapy (sī-kō-ther´ah-pē): A form of therapy in which a trained professional uses methods based on psychological theories to help a person with psychological problems. (p. 494)

psychotropic drugs (si´´ko-trōp´pik): The class of drugs that alters conscious experience. (p. 157)

puberty (pu´ber-tē): The point in development at which the individual is first physically capable of sexual reproduction. (p. 304)

punishment: A negative consequence of a behavior that leads to a decrease in the frequency of the behavior. (p. 188)

pupil (pu´pil): The opening of the iris. (p. 95)

Q

quantitative measures (kwon´ti-ta-tiv): Capable of being measured in numerical terms. (p. 26)

R

rape: The act of forcing sexual activity on an unwilling person. (p. 384)

rape trauma syndrome: Effects of rape on the emotions, behavior, and well-being of many victims long after the rape occurred. (p. 384)

ratio IQ: Intelligence quotient based on the ratio between the person's mental age and chronological age. (p. 268)

rationalization (rash´´un-al-i-zā´shun): According to Freud, a defense mechanism in which stress is reduced by "explaining" events in ways that reduce their stressful qualities. (p. 452)

reaction formation: According to Freud, a defense mechanism in which unacceptable id desires are avoided by transforming them into the opposite desires. (p. 452)

reality principle: According to Freud, the attempt by the ego to find safe, realistic ways of meeting the needs of the id. (p. 403)

recall method: A measure of memory based on the ability to retrieve information from long-term memory with few cues. (p. 220)

receptor sites: Sites on the dendrite that are sensitive to the neurotransmitter substance. (p. 45)

recessive gene: The gene that produces a trait in the individual only when the same recessive gene has been inherited from both parents. (p. 71)

reciprocal determination (re-sip´´ro-kal): Bandura's observation that the individual's behavior and the social learning environment continually influence one another. (p. 411)

recognition method: A measure of memory based on the ability to select correct information from among the options provided. (p. 220)

reconstruction theory: The theory that forgetting is due to changes in the structure of a memory that make it inaccurate when retrieved. (p. 227)

reflection (re-flek-shun): A technique in humanistic psychotherapy in which the therapist reflects the emotions of the client in order to help clients clarify their feelings. (p. 500)

refractory period: The period of time following orgasm during which males are incapable of sexual arousal. (p. 376)

regression: According to Freud, a defense mechanism in which tension is reduced by returning to an earlier pattern of behavior. (p. 452)

rehearsal: Mental repetition of information for retention in short-term memory. (p. 213)

relearning method: A measure of memory based on the length of time it takes to relearn forgotten material. (p. 221)

reliability: A test's ability to produce similar scores if the test is administered on different occasions or by different examiners. (p. 270)

REM sleep: Rapid-eye-movement sleep, characterized by movement of the eyes under the lids; often accompanies dreams. (p. 143)

repression: Sigmund Freud's theory that unpleasant information is often pushed into unconsciousness without our being aware of it. (p. 230, 402)

repressors: Persons who tend to avoid information and do not think about stressful events. (p. 447)

resistance: Any form of patient opposition to the process of psychoanalysis. (p. 497)

resolution phase: The stage in the sexual response cycle following orgasm when arousal and pleasure diminish. (p. 376)

response prevention: The prevention of avoidance responses to ensure that the individual sees that the negative consequence will not occur to speed up the extinction of avoidance responses. (p. 194)

retarded ejaculation: Condition in which a male does not ejaculate despite adequate sexual stimulation. (p. 389)

reticular formation (re-tik´u-lar): The system of neural structures spanning parts of the hindbrain, midbrain, and forebrain that plays a role in cortical arousal and attention. (p. 336)

retina (ret´i-nah): The area at the back of the eye on which images are formed and that contains the rods and cones. (p. 95)

retroactive interference (ret´´rō-ak´tiv): Interference created by memories from later learning. (p. 227)

retrograde amnesia (ret´ro-grād): Disorder of memory characterized by an inability to retrieve old long-term memories, generally for a specific period of time extending back from the beginning of the disorder. (p. 234)

reversibility (re-ver´si-bil-i-tē): The concept understood by concrete operational children that logical propositions can be reversed (if 2 + 3 = 5, then 5 – 3 = 2). (p. 303)

rods: The 125 million cells located outside the center of the retina that transduce light waves into neural impulses, thereby coding information about light and dark. (p. 95)

role playing: A therapeutic technique in which the therapist and client act as if they are people in problematic situations. (p. 505)

rooting reflex: An automatic response in which an infant turns its head toward stimulation on the cheek. (p. 298)

round window: The membrane that relieves pressure from the vibrating waves in the cochlear fluid. (p. 105)

S

saccule and utricle (sak´ul *and* u´tre-k´l): Fluid-filled sacs of the vestibular organ that inform the brain about the body's orientation. (p. 108)

schizoid personality disorder (skiz´oid): A personality disorder characterized by blunted emotions, lack of interest in social relationships, and withdrawal into a solitary existence. (p. 486)

schizophrenia (skiz´´o-fren´ē-ah): A severe psychological disorder characterized by strange, false beliefs and distorted perceptions. (p. 74, 483)

school psychologist: A psychologist who aids schools by testing children to determine eligibility for placement in special education programs and who consults with teachers and parents. (p. 584)

science: Approach to knowledge based on systematic observation. (p. 5)

scientific methods: Methods of gathering information based on systematic observation. (p. 22)

scrotum: The loose skin sac that encloses the testes. (p. 374)

secondary reinforcement: Reinforcement from learned positive reinforcers. (p. 183)

secondary sex characteristics: Development of the breasts and hips in females; growth of the testes, broadening of the shoulders, lowered voice, and growth of the penis and facial hair in males; and growth of pubic and other body hair in both sexes. (p. 305)

sedatives: Depressants that in mild doses produce a state of calm relaxation. (p. 162)

self: According to humanists, the person one thinks he or she is. (p. 414)

self-actualization: According to Maslow, the seldomly reached full result of the innerdirected drive of humans to grow, improve, and use their potential to the fullest. (p. 341, 414)

self-concept: Our subjective perceptions of who we are and what we are like. (p. 413)

self-efficacy: According to Bandura, the perception of being capable of achieving one's goals. (p. 411)

self-regulation: According to Bandura, the process of cognitively reinforcing and punishing our own behavior, depending on whether or not it meets our personal standards. (p. 412)

semantic content (se-man´tik): The meaning in symbols, such as language. (p. 257)

semantic memory: Memory of meaning without reference to the time and place of learning. (p. 218)

semen: The fluid that contains sperm cells. (p. 374)

semicircular canals (sem´´e-ser´ku-lar): Three nearly circular tubes in the vestibular organ that inform the brain about tilts of the head and body. (p. 108)

seminal vesicle: One of the structures that produces fluid for semen. (p. 374)

semipermeable (sem´´e-per´mē-ah-b´l): A surface that allows some, but not all, particles to pass through. (p. 44)

sensation (sen-sā´shun): The process of receiving, translating, and transmitting messages from the outside world to the brain. (p. 90)

sense organs: Organs that receive stimuli. (p. 90)

sensitizers: Persons who tend to seek out information and think about stressful events. (p. 447)

sensorimotor stage: In Piaget's theory, the period of cognitive development from birth to 2 years. (p. 299)

sensory adaptation: Weakened magnitude of a sensation resulting from prolonged presentation of the stimulus. (p. 91)

sensory receptor cells: Cells in sense organs that translate messages into neural impulses that are sent to the brain. (p. 90)

sensory register: The first stage of memory, in which an exact image of each sensory experience is held until it can be processed. (p. 212)

separation anxiety: The distress experienced by infants and children when they are separated from their caregivers. (p. 300)

septal area: Part of the limbic system that processes cognitive information in emotion. (p. 56)

serial position effect: The finding that immediate recall of items listed in a fixed order is often better for items at the beginning and end of the list than for those in the middle. (p. 222)

sex: The distinction between male and female based on biological characteristics. (p. 362)

sexual aversion disorder: Condition in which a person fearfully avoids sexual behavior. (p. 387)

sexual dysfunction: An inability to engage successfully or comfortably in normal sexual activities. (p. 387)

sexual harassment: Unwanted sexual advances, comments, or any other form of coercive sexual behavior by others. (p. 385)

sexual masochism (mas´o-kizm): A condition in which receiving pain is sexually exciting. (p. 383)

sexual orientation: The tendency to prefer romantic and sexual partners of the same or different sex. (p. 362)

sexual sadism (sād´izm): The practice of obtaining sexual pleasure by inflicting pain on others. (p. 383)

sexually transmitted diseases (STDs): Physical diseases, such as syphilis and AIDS that are often transmitted through sexual contact. (p. 390)

shaping: A strategy of positively reinforcing behaviors that are successively more similar to desired behaviors. (p. 185)

short-term memory (STM): The second stage of memory, in which five to nine bits of information can be stored for brief periods of time. (p. 213)

simulated management task: A contrived task requiring managerial skills that is given to candidates for management positions to evaluate their potential as managers. (p. 567)

situational attribution: An explanation for behavior that is based on an external cause. (p. 526)

situationism (sit´´ū-ā´shun-izm): The view that behavior is not consistent, but is strongly influenced by different situations. (p. 420)

Skinner box: A cage for animals equipped with a response lever and a food tray dispenser used in research on operant conditioning. (p. 186)

sleep apnea: Sudden interruption of breathing during sleep. (p. 149)

sleep disorders: Any of a variety of disturbances of sleep. (p. 149)

sleep-inhibiting system: An area of the brain that inhibits sleep. (p. 147)

sleep-promoting systems: Two areas of the brain that promote sleep. (p. 147)

sleeper effects: According to Hovland, the potential for low-credibility speakers to influence opinion after a period of time. (p. 538)

sleeptalking: Talking during any phase of the sleep cycle. (p. 149)

sleepwalking: Walking and carrying on complicated activities during the deepest part of non-REM sleep. (p. 148)

social facilitation: An effect in which working in a group improves one's performance on individual projects. (p. 529)

social impairment: An effect in which working in a group impairs individual performance. (p. 530)

social learning theory: The viewpoint that the most important parts of our behavior are learned from other persons in society—family, friends, and culture. (p. 12, 410)

social loafing: The tendency of members of groups to work less hard when group performance is measured than when individual performance is measured. (p. 529)

social norms: Guidelines provided by every culture for judging acceptable and unacceptable behavior. (p. 532)

social phobia: A phobic fear of social interactions, particularly those with strangers and those in which the person might be viewed negatively. (p. 471)

social psychology: The branch of psychology that studies individuals as they interact with others. (p. 526)

social roles: Culturally determined guidelines that tell people what behavior is expected of them. (p. 532)

social skills training: The use of techniques of operant conditioning to teach social skills to persons who lack them. (p. 505)

social support: The role played by friends and relatives in providing advice, assistance, and someone in whom to confide private feelings. (p. 445)

sociocultural perspective: The theory of psychology that states that it is necessary to understand one's culture, ethnic identity, and other sociocultural factors to fully understand a position. (p. 16)

solitary play: Playing alone. (p. 302)

somatic nervous system (sō-mat´ik): Division of the peripheral nervous system that carries messages from the sense organs, muscles, joints, and skin to the central nervous system, and from the central nervous system to the skeletal muscles. (p. 48)

somatization disorders (sō´´mah-ti-zā´shun): Intensely and chronically uncomfortable psychological conditions that involve numerous symptoms of somatic (bodily) illnesses without physical cause. (p. 475)

somatoform disorders (sō´´mah´to-form): Disorders in which the individual experiences the symptoms of physical health problems that have psychological rather than physical causes. (p. 475)

somatosensory area: The strip of parietal cortex running parallel to the motor area of the frontal lobes. (p. 58)

sound waves: Vibratory changes in the air that carry sound. (p. 103)

specialized end bulbs: Sensory receptor cells that detect pressure and skin pleasure. (p. 109)

specific phobia: A phobic fear of one relatively specific thing. (p. 471)

spinal cord: The nerve fibers in the spinal column. (p. 42)

spontaneous recovery: A temporary increase in the strength of a conditioned response that is likely to occur during extinction after the passage of time. (p. 195)

stage: One of several time periods in development that is qualitatively distinct from the periods that come before and after. (p. 292)

stage theory of memory: A model of memory based on the idea that we store information in three separate but linked memories. (p. 212)

standardization: Administering a test in the same way to all individuals. (p. 270)

stereochemical theory: The theory that different odor receptors can be stimulated only by molecules of a specific size and shape that fit them like a "key" in a lock. (p. 117)

stereotype: An inaccurate generalization upon which a prejudice is based. (p. 542)

stimulants: Drugs that increase the activity of the central nervous system, providing a sense of energy and well-being. (p. 160)

stimulus (stim´ū-lus): Any aspect of the outside world that directly influences our behavior or conscious experience. (p. 90)

stimulus discrimination: The tendency for responses to occur more often in the presence of one stimulus than others. (p. 191)

stimulus generalization: The tendency for similar stimuli to elicit the same response. (p. 191)

stimulus incorporation: Stimuli that occur during sleep that are incorporated into dreams either directly or in altered form. (p. 146)

stress: Any event or circumstance that strains or exceeds an individual's ability to cope. (p. 434)

stroke: A rupture of a blood vessel in the brain that results in the destruction of a part of the brain. (p. 57)

structuralism (struk´tūr-al-izm): The nineteenth-century school of psychology that sought to determine the structure of the mind through controlled introspection. (p. 8)

structuring: Activities of managers that organize and direct the work of employees. (p. 571)

subjective reality: Each person's unique perception of reality that, according to humanists, plays a key role in organizing our personalities. (p. 413)

sublimation (sub´´li-mā´shun): According to Freud, a form of displacement in which a socially desirable goal is substituted for a socially harmful goal; the best form of displacement for society as a whole. (p. 405)

superego: According to Freud, that part of the mind that opposes the desires of the id by enforcing moral restrictions and by striving to attain a goal of perfection. (p. 404)

superstitious behavior: Behavior that is reinforced when the reinforcing stimulus accidentally follows the response. (p. 206)

surface structure: The superficial spoken or written structure of a statement. (p. 257)

survey method: A research method that utilizes interviews and questionnaires with individuals in the community. (p. 23)

symbolization: In Rogers' theory, the process of representing experience, thoughts, or feelings in mental symbols of which we are consciously aware. (p. 414)

sympathetic division (sim´´pah-thet´ik): The division of the autonomic nervous system that generally activates internal organs during emotional arousal or when physical demands are placed on the body. (p. 49)

synapse (sin aps´): The space between the axon of one neuron and the dendrite of another. (p. 45)

synaptic facilitation: Process by which neural activity causes structural changes in the synapses. (p. 232)

synaptic gap: The small space between two neurons at a synapse. (p. 45)

synaptic knob (si-nap´tik): The knoblike top of the axon. (p. 45)

synaptic vesicles: Tiny vessels containing stored quantities of the neurotransmitter substance held in the synaptic knobs of the axon. (p. 45)

syntax (sin´taks): The grammatical rules of a language. (p. 257)

syphilis: A sexually transmitted disease caused by the spirochete bacteria. (p. 390)

systematic desensitization: A behavior therapy method in which the client is taught not to fear phobic stimuli by learning to relax in the presence of successively more threatening stimuli. (p. 503)

T

tactile discs (tak´til): Sensory receptor cells that detect pressure. (p. 109)

taste cells: The sensory receptor cells for gustation located in the taste buds. (p. 116)

telegraphic speech: The abbreviated speech of 2-year-olds. (p. 300)

temporal lobes: The part of the cerebral cortex extending back from the area of the temples beneath the frontal and parietal lobes containing areas involved in the sense of hearing and understanding language. (p. 58)

testes (tes´tēz): Male endocrine glands that secrete sex-related hormones and produce sperm cells. (p. 68, 374)

testosterone (tes-tos´ter-ōn): A male sex hormone. (p. 68)

thalamus (thal´ah-mus): That part of the forebrain that primarily routes sensory messages to appropriate parts of the brain. (p. 53)

theory: Tentative explanation of facts and relationships in sciences. (p. 5)

thyroid gland (thī´roid): The gland below the voice box that regulates metabolism. (p. 68).

thyroxin (thi-rok´sin): A hormone produced by the thyroid that is necessary for proper mental development in children and helps determine weight and level of activity in adults. (p. 68)

timbre (tim´ber, tam´br): The characteristic quality of a sound as determined by the complexity of the sound wave. (p. 104)

traits: Relatively enduring and consistent ways of thinking, acting, and feeling that are believed by some theorists to be the basic units of personality. (p. 418)

transcendental state: An altered state of consciousness, sometimes achieved during meditation, that is said to transcend normal human experience. (p. 154)

transduction (trans-duk´shun): The translation of energy from one form to another. (p. 90)

transductive reasoning (trans-duk´tiv): Errors in understanding cause-and-effect relationships that are commonly made by preoperational children. (p. 302)

transference (trans-fer´ens): The phenomenon in psychoanalysis in which the patient comes to feel and act toward the therapist in ways that resemble how he or she feels and acts toward other significant adults. (p. 498)

transsexualism (trans-seks´u-ah-lizm): A condition in which an individual feels trapped in the body of the wrong sex. (p. 382)

transvestism (trans-ves´tizm): The practice of obtaining sexual pleasure by dressing in the clothes of the opposite sex. (p. 382)

trial and error: The random application of one possible solution after another. (p. 252)

triarchic theory of intelligence (trī-ar´kik): Sternberg's theory distinguishing three aspects of intelligence: learning new information, solving specific problems, and solving problems in general. (p. 265)

trichromatic theory (trī´´krō-mat´ik): The theory of color vision contending that the eye has three different kinds of cones, each of which responds to light of one range of wavelength. (p. 99)

Type A personality: Pattern of behavior characterized most importantly by intense competitiveness, hostility, overwork, and a sense of time urgency. (p. 448)

U

unconditioned response (UCR): An unlearned, inborn reaction to an unconditioned stimulus. (p. 177)

unconditioned stimulus (UCS): A stimulus that can elicit a response without any learning. (p. 177)

unconscious mind: The part of the mind of which we can never be directly aware; the storehouse of primitive instinctual motives and of memories and emotions that have been repressed. (p. 12, 140, 402)

uterus: The muscular structure that carries the fetus during pregnancy. (p. 373)

V

vaginismus (vaj´´i-niz´mus): A female sexual dysfunction in which the individual experiences involuntary contractions of the vaginal walls, making the vagina too narrow to allow the penis to enter comfortably. (p. 388)

validity: The extent to which a test measures what it's supposed to measure. (p. 270)

variable: A factor whose numerical value can change. (p. 24)

variable interval schedule: A reinforcement schedule in which the reinforcer is given following the first response occurring after a variable amount of time. (p. 185)

variable ratio schedule: A reinforcement schedule in which the reinforcer is given after a varying number of responses have been made. (p. 184)

vas deferens: Structure that carries sperm from the epididymis toward the outside of the body during ejaculation. (p. 374)

ventromedial hypothalamus: A part of the hypothalamus involved in inhibiting eating when sufficient food has been consumed (the satiety center). (p. 330)

vestibular organ (ves-tib´ū-lar): The sensory structures in the inner ear that provide the brain with information about movement. (p. 108)

vicarious punishment (vī-kar´ē-us): Observed punishment of the behavior of a model that also decreases the probability of the same behavior in the observer. (p. 202)

vicarious reinforcement: Observed reinforcement of the behavior of a model that also increases the probability of the same behavior in the observer. (p. 202)

visual acuity (vizh´u-al ah-ku´i-tē): Clearness and sharpness of vision. (p. 95)

voyeurism (voi´yer-izm): The practice of obtaining sexual pleasure by watching members of the opposite sex undressing or engaging in sexual activities. (p. 383)

vulva: The external genital structures of the female. (p. 373)

W

wavelength: Frequency of light waves; determines the color we see. (p. 94)

Weber's law: A law stating that the amount of change in a stimulus needed to detect a difference is in direct proportion to the intensity of the original stimulus. (p. 93)

Wernicke's aphasia: A form of aphasia in which persons can speak normally but cannot make sense out of language spoken to them by others. (p. 59)

Wernicke's area: The language area of the cortex that plays an essential role in understanding spoken language. (p. 59)

Y

Yerkes-Dodson law: A law stating that effective performance is more likely if the level of arousal is suitable for the activity. (p. 336)

Z

zygote (zī´gōt): The stable cell resulting from fertilization; it has 46 chromosomes—23 from the sperm and 23 from the ovum. (p. 70)

REFERENCES

Abbey, A. (1982). Sex differences in attributions for friendly behavior: Do males misperceive females' friendliness? *Journal of Personality and Social Psychology, 42,* 830–838.

Abbey, A., & Melby, C. (1986). The effects of nonverbal cues on gender differences in perceptions of sexual intent. *Sex Roles, 15,* 283–298.

Abbott, B. B., Schoen, L. S., & Badia, P. (1984). Predictable and unpredictable shock: Behavioral measures of aversion and physiological measures of stress. *Psychological Bulletin, 96,* 45–71.

Abel, G., Barlow, D., Blanchard, E., & Guild, D. (1977). Components of rapists' arousal. *Archives of General Psychiatry, 34,* 895–908.

Abhold, J. (1992). Unpublished doctoral dissertation, University of Arkansas, cited in Loftus, E. F. (1993). The reality of repressed memories. *American Psychologist, 48,* 518–537.

Ackerman, D. (1991). *A natural history of the senses.* New York: Vintage Books.

Adams, H. E., & Chiodo, J. (1984). Sexual deviations. In H. E. Adams & P. B. Sutker (Eds.), *Comprehensive handbook of psychopathology.* New York: Plenum.

Adams, J. (1965). Inequity in social exchange. In L. Berkowitz (Ed.), *Advances in experimental social psychology* (Vol. 2). New York: Academic Press.

Adams, P. R., & Adams, G. R. (1984). Mount Saint Helens' ashfall: Evidence for a disaster stress reaction. *American Psychologist, 39,* 252–260.

Adelson, J. (1979, February). Adolescence and the generalization gap. *Psychology Today,* pp. 33–38.

Ader, R. (Ed.). (1981). *Psychoneuroimmunology.* New York: Academic Press.

Ader, R., & Cohen, N. (1981). Conditioned immunopharmacologic responses. In R. Ader (Ed.), *Psychoneuroimmunology.* New York: Academic Press.

Ader, R., & Cohen, N. (1993). Psychoneuroimmunology: Conditioning and stress. *Annual Review of Psychology, 44,* 53–85.

Agras, W. S., Rossiter, E. M. et al. (1992). Pharmacologic and cognitive-behavioral treatment for bulimia nervosa: A controlled comparison. *American Journal of Psychiatry, 149,* 82–87.

Ainsworth, M. D. S. (1979). Infant-mother attachment. *American Psychologist, 34,* 932–937.

Aizawa, M. (1994). Molecular interfacing for protein molecular devices and neurodevices. *IEEE Engineering in Medicine and Biology Magazine, 13(1),* 94.

Allen, J. J., Iacono, W. G., Laravuso, J. J., & Dunn, L. A. (1995). An event-related potential investigation of posthypnotic recognition amnesia. *Journal of Abnormal Psychology, 104,* 421–430.

Allen, K. E., Hart, R. M., Buell, J. S., Harris, F. R., & Wolf, M. M. (1964). Effects of social reinforcement on isolate behavior of a nursery school child. *Child Development, 35,* 511–518.

Allport, G. W. (1937). *Personality: A psychological interpretation.* New York: Holt, Rinehart & Winston.

Allport, G. W. (1961). *Pattern and growth in personality.* New York: Holt, Rinehart & Winston.

Allport, G. W., & Odbert, H. S. (1936). Trait names: A psycholexical study. *Psychological Monographs, 47* (no. 211), 1–171.

Altschule, M. D. (1965). *Roots of modern psychiatry* (2nd ed.). New York: Grune & Stratton.

American Psychiatric Association. (1987). *Diagnostic and statistical manual of mental disorders* (3rd ed. Revised). Washington, DC: Author.

American Psychological Association. (1982). *Ethical principles in the conduct of research with human participants.* Washington, DC: Author.

American Psychological Association. (1993). *Behavior research with animals.* Washington, DC: Author.

American Psychological Association. (1990). Ethical principles of psychologists. *American Psychologist, 45,* 390–395.

American Psychological Association. (1993). Guidelines for providers of psychological services to ethnic, linguistic, and culturally diverse populations. *American Psychologist, 48,* 45–48.

American Running and Physical Fitness Association. (1981). *Statistical report.* Washington, DC.

Amoore, J. E., Johnston, J. W., & Rubin, M. (1964, February). The stereochemical theory of odor. *Scientific American.*

Anastasi, A. (1970). *Fields of applied psychology* (2nd ed.). New York: McGraw-Hill.

Anastasi, A. (1987). *Psychological testing.* (6th ed.). New York: Macmillan.

Ancoli-Israel, S., Kripke, D. F., & Mason, W. (1987). Characteristics of obstructive and central sleep apnea in the elderly: An interim report. *Biological Psychiatry, 22,* 741–750.

Andersen, K. (1983). Crashing on cocaine. *Time,* April 13.

Anderson, C. A. (1989). Temperature and aggression: Ubiquitous effects of heat on occurrence of human violence. *Psychological Bulletin, 106,* 74–96.

Anderson, K. E., Lytton, H., & Romney, D. M. (1986). Mother's interactions with normal and conduct-disordered boys: Who affects whom? *Developmental Psychology, 22,* 604–609.

Anderson, N. H. (1968). Application of a linear-serial model to personality-impression task using serial presentation. *Journal of Personality and Social Psychology, 10,* 354–362.

Andreasen, N. C., Arndt, S., Alliger, R., Miller, D., & Flaum, M. (1995). Symptoms of schizophrenia: Methods, meanings, and mechanisms. *Archives of General Psychiatry, 52,* 341–351.

Andreasen, N. C., Ehrhardt, J. C., Swayze, V. W., Alliger, R. J., Yuh, W. T. C.,

Cohen, G., & Ziebell, S. (1990). Magnetic resonance imaging of the brain in schizophrenia: The pathophysiologic significance of structural abnormalities. *Archives of General Psychiatry, 47,* 35–44.

Angoff, W. H. (1988). The nature-nurture debate, aptitudes, and group differences. *American Psychologist, 43,* 713–720.

Annon, J. (1984). Simple behavioral treatment of sexual problems. In J. M. Swanson & K. Forrect (Eds.), *Men's reproductive health.* New York: Springer.

Antoni, M. H., et al. (1990). Psychoneuro-immunology and HIV-1. *Journal of Consulting and Clinical Psychology, 58,* 38–49.

Aral, S. O., & Holmes, K. K. (1991). Sexually transmitted diseases in the AIDS era. *Scientific American, 264,* 62–70.

Ardrey, R. (1966). *The territorial imperative.* New York: Atheneum.

Arndt, S., Andreasen, N. C., Flaum, M., Miller, D., & Nopoulos, P. (1995). A longitudinal study of symptom dimensions in schizophrenia: Prediction and patterns of change. *Archives of General Psychiatry, 52,* 352–360.

Arnett, J. (1995). The young and the reckless: Adolescent reckless behavior. *Current Directions in Psychological Science, 4,* 67–76.

Arnetz, B., et al. (1987). Immune function in unemployed women. *Psychosomatic Medicine, 49,* 3–18.

Arnold, M. B. (1960). *Emotion and personality* (2 vols.). New York: Columbia University Press.

Aronson, E. (1990). Applying social psychology to desegregation and energy conservation. *Personality and Social Psychology Bulletin, 16,* 118–132.

Aronson, E. (1995). *The social animal* (6th ed.). San Francisco: W. H. Freeman.

Aronson, E., & Golden, B. (1962). The effect of relevant and irrelevant aspects of communicator credibility on opinion change. *Journal of Personality, 30,* 135–146.

Aronson, E., Willerman, B., & Floyd, J. (1966). The effect of a pratfall on increasing interpersonal attractiveness. *Psychonomic Science, 4,* 227–228.

Arvidson, K., & Friberg, U. (1980). Human taste: Response and taste bud number in fungiform papillae. *Science, 209,* 807–808.

Asch, S. (1946). Forming impressions of personality. *Journal of Abnormal and Social Psychology, 41,* 258–290.

Asch, S. (1956). Studies of independence and conformity. A minority of one against a unanimous majority. *Psychological Monographs, 70* (9, Whole No. 416).

Aschoff, J. (1981). *Handbook of behavioral neurobiology: Vol. 4. Biological rhythms.* New York: Plenum.

Association for Advancement of Behavior Therapy. (1978). *Ethical issues for human services* (pamphlet). New York: AABT.

Astin, A. W., Korn, W. S., & Berz, E. R. (1991). *The American freshman: National norms for 1990.* Los Angeles: American Council on Education.

Atkeson, B. M., Calhoun, K. S., Resick, P. A., & Ellis, E. M. (1982). Victims of rape. Repeated assessment of depressive symptoms. *Journal of Consulting and Clinical Psychology, 50,* 96–102.

Atkeson, B. M., Forehand, R. L., & Rickard, K. M. (1982). The effects of divorce on children. In B. B. Lahey & A. E. Kazdin (Eds.), *Advances in clinical child psychology* (Vol. 5). New York: Plenum.

Atkinson, J. W. (1964). *An introduction to motivation.* New York: Van Nostrand Reinhold.

Atkinson, R. C., & Shiffrin, R. M. (1968). Human memory: A proposed system and its control processes. In K. W. Spence & J. T. Spence (Eds.), *The psychology of learning and motivation* (Vol. 2). New York: Academic Press.

Augustine, D. K., Gruber, K. D., & Hanson, L. R. (1990). Cooperation works. *Educational Leadership, 47,* 4–11.

Ausubel, D. P. (1960). The use of advance organizers in the learning and retention of meaningful verbal material. *Journal of Educational Psychology, 51,* 267–272.

Avissar, S., Nechamkin, Y., Roitman, G., & Schreiber, G. (1997). Reduced G protein functions and immunoreactive levels in mononuclear leukocytes of patients with depression. *Archives of General Psychiatry, 154,* 211–217.

Ayllon, T., & Haughton, E. (1964). Modification of the symptomatic verbal behaviour of mental patients. *Behaviour Research and Therapy, 2,* 87–97.

Baddeley, A. (1992). Working memory. *Science, 255,* 556–559.

Baer, L., Rauch, S. L., Ballantine, T., Martuza, R., Cosgrove, R., Cassem, E., Giriunas, I., Manzo, P. A., Domino, C., & Jenike, M. A. (1995). Cingulotomy for intractable obsessive-compulsive disorder. *Archives of General Psychiatry, 52,* 384–392.

Bagley, C., & Binitie, A. (1970). Alcoholism and schizophrenia in Irishmen in London. *British Journal of Psychiatry, 17,* 292–304.

Bahrick, H. P. (1984). Semantic memory content in permastore: 50 years of memory for Spanish learned in school. *Journal of Experimental Psychology: General, 113,* 1–29.

Bahrick, H. P., Bahrick, L. E., Bahrick, A. S., & Bahrick, P. E. (1993). Maintenance of foreign language vocabulary and the spacing effect. *Psychological Science, 4,* 316–321.

Bahrick, H. P., Bahrick, P. O., & Wittlinger, R. P. (1975). Fifty years of memory for names and faces: A cross-sectional approach. *Journal of Experimental Psychology, 104,* 54–75.

Bailey, M. J., & Pillard, R. C. (1991). A genetic study of male sexual orientation. *Archives of General Psychiatry, 48,* 1089–1096.

Baker, H. (1969). Transsexualism—problems in treatment. *American Journal of Psychiatry, 125,* 118–124.

Baltes, P. B., & Staudinger, U. M. (1993). The search for a psychology of wisdom. *Current Directions in Psychological Science, 2,* 75–80.

Bandura, A. (1969). *Principles of behavior modification.* New York: Holt, Rinehart & Winston.

Bandura, A. (1973). *Aggression: A social learning analysis.* Englewood Cliffs, NJ: Prentice-Hall.

Bandura, A. (1977). *Social learning theory.* Englewood Cliffs, NJ: Prentice-Hall.

Bandura, A. (1982). Self-efficacy mechanism in human agency. *American Psychologist, 37,* 122–147.

Bandura, A. (1989). Human agency in social cognitive theory. *American Psychologist, 44,* 1175–1184.

Bandura, A., Blanchard, E. B., & Ritter, B. (1969). The relative efficacy of desensitization and modeling approaches for inducing behavioral, affective, and attitudinal changes. *Journal of Personality and Social Psychology, 13,* 173–199.

Bandura, A., Ross, D., & Ross, S. A. (1963). Imitation of film-mediated aggressive models. *Journal of Abnormal and Social Psychology, 66,* 3–11.

Banks, M., & Salapatek, P. (1981). Infant pattern vision: A new approach based on the contrast sensitivity function. *Journal of Experimental Child Psychology, 31,* 1–45.

Barahal, H. S. (1958). 1000 prefrontal lobotomies. Five- to ten-year follow-up study. *Psychiatric Quarterly, 32,* 653–678.

Barber, T. X. (1969). *Hypnosis: A scientific approach.* New York: Van Nostrand Reinhold.

Barber, T. X., & Wilson, S. C. (1977). Hypnosis, suggestions, and altered states of consciousness. Experimental evaluation of the new cognitive behavioral theory and the traditional trance-state theory of hypnosis. In W. E. Edmundson (Ed.), *Conceptual and investigative approaches to hypnosis and hypnotic phenomena.* New York: New York Academy of Sciences.

Bard, P. (1934). Emotion I: The neurohumoral basis of emotional reactions. In C. Murchison (Ed.), *Handbook of general experimental psychology.* Worcester, MA: Clark University Press.

Barlow, D. H. (1996). Health care policy, psychotherapy research, and the future of psychotherapy. *American Psychologist, 51,* 1050–1058.

Barlow, D. H., & Lehman, C. L. (1996). Advances in the psychosocial treatment of anxiety disorders: Implications for national health care. *Archives of General Psychiatry, 53,* 727–735.

Barnes, K. E. (1971). Preschool play norms. A replication. *Developmental Psychology, 5,* 99–103.

Baron, J. B., & Sternberg, R. J. (Eds.). (1987). *Teaching thinking skills.* San Francisco: W. H. Freeman.

Baron, R., & Byrne, D. (1982). *Exploring social psychology* (2nd ed.). Boston: Allyn & Bacon.

Baron, R. A., & Ramsberger, V. M. (1978). Ambient temperature and the occurrence of collective violence: The "long hot summer" revisited. *Journal of Personality and Social Psychology, 36,* 351–360.

Barr, C. E., Mednick, S. A., & Munk-Jorgensen, P. (1990). Exposure to influenza epidemics during gestation and adult schizophrenia. *Archives of General Psychiatry, 47,* 869–874.

Bartlett, F. C. (1932). *Remembering: A study in experimental and social psychology.* New York: Cambridge University Press.

Barton, J. L. (1977). ECT in depression: The evidence of controlled studies. *Biological Psychiatry, 12,* 687–695.

Bartoshuk, L. (1988). Taste. In R. C. Atkinson, R. J. Herrnstein, G. Lindzey, & R. D. Luce (Eds.), *Stevens' handbook of experimental psychology: Vol. 1. Perception and motivation.* New York: Wiley-Interscience.

Bashore, T. R., & Rapp, P. E. (1993). Are there alternatives to traditional polygraph procedures? *Psychological Bulletin, 113,* 3–22.

Batshaw, M. L., & Perret, Y. M. (1981). *Children with handicaps: A medical primer.* Baltimore: Paul H. Brooks.

Baum, A., Harpin, R. E., & Valins, S. (1975). The role of group phenomena in the experience of crowding. *Environment and Behavior, 7,* 185–198.

Baum, A., & Valins, S. (1977). *Architecture and social behavior: Psychological studies of social density.* Hillsdale, NJ: Erlbaum.

Baumrind, D. (1964). Some thoughts on ethics of research: After reading Milgram's "Behavioral study of obedience." *American Psychologist, 19,* 421–423.

Baumrind, D. (1972). An exploratory study of socialization effects on Black children: Some Black-White comparisons. *Child Development, 43,* 261–267.

Baumrind, D. (1983). Rejoinder to Lewis's reinterpretation of parental firm control effects: Are authoritative families really harmonious? *Psychological Bulletin, 94,* 132–142.

Baumrind, D. (1991). Parenting styles and adolescent development. In J. Brooks-Gunn, R. Lerner, & A. Peterson (Eds.), *The encyclopedia of adolescence.* New York: Garland.

Baxter, L. R., Phelps, M. E., Maziotta, J. C., Guze, B. H., Schwartz, J. M., & Selin, C. E. (1987). Local cerebral glucose metabolic rates in obsessive-compulsive disorder. *Archives of General Psychiatry, 44,* 211–218.

Baxter, L. R., Schwartz, J. M., Bergman, K. S., & Szuba, M. P. (1992). Caudate glucose metabolic rate changes with both drug and behavior therapy for obsessive-compulsive disorder. *Archives of General Psychiatry, 49,* 681–689.

Bayley, N. (1965). Research in child development: A longitudinal perspective. *Merrill-Palmer Quarterly, 11,* 8–35.

Beatty, J. (1995). *Principles of behavioral neuroscience.* Dubuque, IA: Brown & Benchmark Publishers.

Beck, A. T. (1976). *Cognitive therapy and the emotional disorders.* New York: International Universities Press.

Beck, A. T., Rush, A. J., Shaw, B. F., & Emery, G. (1979). *Cognitive therapy of depression.* New York: Guilford Press.

Beck, A. T., Sokol, L., Clark, D. A., Berchick, R., & Wright, F. (1992). A crossover study of focused cognitive therapy for panic disorder. *American Journal of Psychiatry, 149,* 778–783.

Beck, J. G. (1995). Hypoactive sexual desire disorder: An overview. *Journal of Consulting and Clinical Psychology, 63,* 919–927.

Becker, W. C., & Carnine, D. (1980). Direct instruction: An effective approach to educational intervention with the disadvantaged and low performers. In B. B. Lahey & A. E. Kazdin (Eds.), *Advances in clinical child psychology* (Vol. 3). New York: Plenum.

Becker, W. C., Engelmann, S., & Thomas, D. R. (1975). *Teaching: A course in applied psychology.* Chicago Science Research Associates.

Behrman, J., & Levy, R. (1970). Neurophysiological studies on patients with hysterical disturbances of vision. *Journal of Psychosomatic Research, 14,* 187–194.

Beiman, I., Graham, L., & Ciminero, A. R. (1978). Self-control progressive relaxation training as an alternative nonpharmacological treatment for essential hypertension: Therapeutic effects in the natural environment. *Behaviour Research and Therapy, 16,* 371–375.

Beiman, I., Majestic, H., Johnson, S. A., Puente, A., & Graham, L. (1976). *Transcendental meditation versus behavior therapy: A controlled investigation.* Paper presented to the Association for the Advancement of Behavior Therapy.

Bell, N. J., & Carver, W. (1980). A reevaluation of gender label effects: Expectant mothers' responses to infants. *Child Development, 51,* 925–927.

Bell, R. Q. (1968). A reinterpretation of the direction of effects in studies of socialization. *Psychological Review, 75,* 81–95.

Belloc, N. B. (1973). Relationship of health practices to mortality. *Preventive Medicine, 2,* 67–81.

Belmore, S. M. (1987). Determinants of attention during impression formation. *Journal of Experimental Psychology: Learning, Memory, and Cognition, 13,* 480–489.

Belmore, S. M., & Hubbard, M. L. (1987). The role of advance expectancies in person memory. *Journal of Personality and Social Psychology, 53,* 61–70.

Belzer, E. G. (1981). Orgasmic expulsions of women: A review and heuristic inquiry. *Journal of Sex Research, 17,* 1–12.

Bem, S. (1974). The measurement of psychological androgyny. *Journal of Consulting and Clinical Psychology, 42,* 155–162.

Bem, S. (1981). Gender schema theory: A cognitive account of sex typing. *Psychological Review, 88,* 354–364.

Bem, D. J., & Allen, A. (1974). On predicting some of the people some of the time: The search for cross-situational consistencies in behavior. *Psychological Review, 81,* 506–520.

Benbow, C. P. (1990). Gender differences: Searching for facts. *American Psychologist, 45,* 988.

Benedict, R. F. (1934). *Patterns of culture.* Boston: Houghton Mifflin.

Benedict, R. (1935). *Sex and temperament in three primitive societies.* New York: Morrow.

Bennett, W., & Gurin, J. (1982, March). Do diets really work? *Science, 82.*

Benson, H. (1975). *The relaxation response.* New York: Morrow.

Bentall, R. P. (1990). The illusion of reality: A review and integration of research on hallucinations. *Psychological Bulletin, 107,* 82–95.

Benton, D., & Sargent, J. (1992). Breakfast, blood glucose and memory. *Biological Psychology, 33,* 207–210.

Berger, K. S. (1986). *The developing person through childhood and adolescence* (2nd ed.). New York: Worth.

Bergum, B. O., & Lehr, D. J. (1962). Vigilance performance as a function of interpolated rest. *Journal of Applied Psychology, 46,* 425–427.

Berkowitz, L. (1983). Aversively stimulated aggression. *American Psychologist, 38,* 1135–1160.

Berkowitz, L. (1984). Some thoughts on anti- and prosocial influence of media events: A cognitive-neoassociation analysis. *Psychological Bulletin, 95,* 410–427.

Berkowitz, L. (1989). Frustration-aggression hypothesis: Examination and reformulation. *Psychological Bulletin, 106,* 59–73.

Berkowitz, L. (1993). *Aggression: Its causes, consequences, and control.* New York: McGraw-Hill.

Berlin, B., & Kay, P. (1969). *Basic color terms: Their universality and evolution.* Berkeley: University of California Press.

Berman, K. F., Illowsky, B. P., & Weinberger, D. R. (1988). Physiological dysfunction of dorsolateral prefrontal cortex in schizophrenia: Further evidence for regional and behavioral specificity. *Archives of General Psychiatry, 45,* 616–622.

Bermant, G. (1976). Sexual behavior: Hard times with the Coolidge effect. In M. H. Siegel & H. P. Ziegler (Eds.), *Psychological research: The inside story.* New York: Harper & Row.

Bernstein, B. (1970). A sociolinguistic approach to socialization. With some reference to educability. In F. Williams (Ed.), *Language and poverty.* Chicago: Markham.

Bernstein, I. L. (1978). Learned taste aversions in children receiving chemotherapy. *Science, 200,* 1302–1309.

Bernstein, I. L. (1985). Learned food aversions in the progression of cancer and its treatment. In N. S. Braverman & P. Bernstein (Eds.), *Experimental assessments and clinical applications of conditioned food aversions. Annals of the New York Academy of Sciences, 443.*

Bernstein, I. L., Webster, M. M., & Bernstein, P. (1982). Food aversions in children receiving chemotherapy for cancer. *Cancer, 50,* 2961–2963.

Berry, J. W., & Bennett, J. A. (1992). Cree conceptions of cognitive competence. *International Journal of Psychology, 27,* 1, 73–88.

Berscheid, E., Dion, K. K., Walster, E., & Walster, G. W. (1971). Physical attractiveness and dating choice: A test of the matching hypothesis. *Journal of Experimental Social Psychology, 7,* 173–189.

Betancourt, H., & Lopez, S. R. (1993). The study of culture, ethnicity, and race in American psychology. *American Psychologist, 48,* 6, 629.

Bigelow, H. J. (1850). Dr. Harlow's case of recovery from the passage of an iron bar through the head. *American Journal of Medical Science, 20,* 13–22.

Birch, H. C. (1945). The relation of previous experience to insightful problem solving. *Journal of Comparative Psychology, 38,* 367–383.

Birren, J. E., Butler, R. N., Greenhouse, S. W., Sokoloff, L., & Yarrow, M. R. (Eds.). (1963). *Human aging: A biological and behavioral study.* Washington, DC: U.S. Government Printing Office.

Bitterman, M. E., & Marcuse, F. L. (1945). Autonomic response in posthypnotic amnesia. *Journal of Experimental Psychology, 35,* 248–252.

Bjorklund, D. F., & Green, B. L. (1992). The adaptive nature of cognitive immaturity. *American Psychologist, 47,* 46–54.

Bland, R. C., Newman, S. C., & Orn, H. (1986). Recurrent and nonrecurrent depressions: A family study. *Archives of General Psychiatry, 11,* 1085–1089.

Bliss, T. V. P., & Lomo, T. (1973). Long-lasting potentiation of synaptic transmission in the dentate area of the anaesthetized rabbit following stimulation of the perforant path. *Journal of Physiology* (London), *232,* 331–356.

Blonder, L. X., Bowers, D., & Heilman, K. M. (1991). The role of the right hemisphere in emotional communication. *Brain, 114,* 1115–1127.

Bloom, B. S. (1974). Time and learning. *American Psychologist, 29,* 681–688.

Blumenthal, J. A., Sanders, W., Williams, R., Needels, T. L., & Wallace, A. G. (1982). Psychological changes accompany aerobic exercise in healthy middle-aged adults. *Psychosomatic Medicine, 44,* 529–536.

Bly, J., Jones, R., & Richardson, T. (1986). Impact of worksite health promotion on healthcare costs and utilization: Evaluation of Johnson and Johnson's Life for Life program. *Journal of the American Medical Association, 256,* 3235–3240.

Bock, M. (1986). The influence of emotional meaning on the recall of words processed for form or self-reference. *Psychological Research, 48,* 107–112.

Bock, M., & Klinger, E. (1986). Interaction of emotion and cognition in word recall. *Psychological Research, 48,* 99–100.

Bolm-Andorff, U., Schwämmle, J., Ehlenz, K., Koop, H., & Kaffarnik, H. (1986). Hormonal and cardiovascular variations during a public lecture. *European Journal of Applied Physiology, 54,* 669–674.

Bond, R., & Smith, P. B. (1996). Culture and conformity: A meta-analysis of studies using Asch's (1952b, 1956) line judgment task. *Psychological Bulletin, 119,* 111–137.

Bondareff, W., Raval, J., Woo, B., Hauser, D. L., & Colletti, P. M. (1990). Magnetic resonance imaging and the severity of dementia in older adults. *Archives of General Psychiatry, 47,* 47–51.

Boon, S., & Draijer, N. (1992). Multiple personality in the Netherlands: A clinical investigation of 71 patients. *American Journal of Psychiatry, 150,* 489–494.

Borden, R. J. (1986). Ecology and identity. In J. F. G. Grosser & F. Schmeidler (Eds.), *Proceedings of ecosystems and new energetics* (pp. 25–41). Academia Cosmologica Nova, Munich, Germany: Man and Space.

Borke, H. (1975). Piaget's mountains revisited: Changes in egocentric landscape. *Developmental Psychology, 11,* 240–243.

Borkovec, T. D., & Costello, E. (1993). Efficacy of applied relaxation and cognitive-behavioral therapy in the treatment of generalized anxiety disorder. *Journal of Consulting and Clinical Psychology, 61,* 611–619.

Borkovec, T. D., & Mathews, A. M. (1988). Treatment of nonphobic anxiety disorders: A comparison of nondirective, cognitive, and coping desensitization therapy. *Journal of Consulting and Clinical Psychology, 56,* 877–884.

Bosse, J. J., Croghan, L. M., Greenstein, M. B., Katz, N. W., Oliver, J. M., Powell, D. A., & Smith, W. R. (1975). Frequency of depression in the freshman year as measured in a random sample by a retrospective version of the Beck Depression Inventory. *Journal of Consulting and Clinical Psychology, 43,* 746–747.

Bouchard, T. J., Jr. (1984). Twins reared together and apart: What they tell us about human diversity. In S. W. Fox (Ed.), *Individuality and determinism: Chemical and biological bases* (pp. 147–184). New York: Plenum.

Bouchard, T. J., & McGue, M. (1981). Familial studies of intelligence: A review. *Science, 212,* 1055–1059.

Bourne, L. E. (1966). *Human conceptual behavior.* Boston: Allyn & Bacon.

Bourne, L. E., Ekstrand, B. R., & Dominowski, D. (1971). *The psychology of thinking.* Englewood Cliffs, NJ: Prentice-Hall.

Bourque, L. B., & Back, K. W. (1977). Life graphs and life events. *Journal of Gerontology, 32,* 669–674.

Bousfield, W. A. (1953). The occurrence of clustering in recall of randomly arranged associates. *Journal of General Psychology, 49,* 229–240.

Bousfield, W. A., & Sedgwick, C. H. (1944). An analysis of sequences of restricted associative responses. *Journal of General Psychology, 30,* 149–165.

Bower, G. H. (1973). Educational applications of mnemonic devices. In K. O. Doyle (Ed.), *Interaction: Readings in human psychology.* Boston: D. C. Heath.

Bower, G. H. (1981). Mood and memory. *American Psychologist, 36,* 129–148.

Bower, G. H., & Clark, M. C. (1969). Narrative stories as mediators for serial learning. *Psychonomic Science, 14,* 181–182.

Bower, G. H., & Mayer, J. D. (1985). Failure to replicate mood-dependent retrieval. *Bulletin of the Psychonomic Society, 23,* 39–42.

Bower, T. G. R. (1971). The object in the world of the infant. *Scientific American, 220,* 30–38.

Bower, T. G. R. (1974). *Development in infancy.* San Francisco: W. H. Freeman.

Bowers, K. S. (1973). Situationism in psychology: An analysis and a critique. *Psychological Review, 80,* 307–336.

Bowers, K. S. (1976). *Hypnosis for the seriously curious.* Monterey, CA: Brooks/Cole.

Bracha, H. S., Torrey, E. F., Gottesman, I. I., Bigelow, L. B., & Cunniff, C. (1992). Second-trimester markers of fetal size in schizophrenia: A study of monozygotic twins. *American Journal of Psychiatry, 149,* 1355–1361.

Bradley-Johnson, S., McCarthy, R., & Jamie, M. (1984). Token reinforcement during WISC-R administration. *Applied Research on Mental Retardation, 5,* 43–52.

Bransford, J. D., & Franks, J. J. (1971). The abstraction of linguistic ideas. *Cognitive Psychology, 2,* 331–350.

Braverman, L. B. (1989). Beyond the myth of motherhood. In M. McGoldrick, C. M. Anderson, & F. Walsh (Eds.), *Women and families.* New York: Free Press.

Bray, D. W., Campbell, R. J., & Grant, D. L. (1974). *Formative years in business: A long term AT&T study of managerial lives.* New York: Wiley.

Brecher, E. M., & Brecher, J. (1976). Sex is good for your health. *Playboy,* June, 125ff.

Bregante, J. L., Martinez, K., & O'Toole, C. J. (1993). New bridges: building community between disabled and nondisabled women. Presentation at the Fifth International Interdisciplinary Conference on Women.

Breggin, P. R. (1973). Psychosurgery. *Journal of the American Medical Association, 226,* 1121.

Breier, A., Schreiber, J. L., Dyer, J., & Pickar, D. (1991). National Institute of Mental Health longitudinal study of chronic schizophrenia: Prognosis and predictors of outcome. *Archives of General Psychiatry, 48,* 239–246.

Breland, K., & Breland, M. (1961). The misbehavior of organisms. *American Psychologist, 16,* 681–684.

Breslau, N., Davis, G. C., Andreski, P., & Peterson, E. (1991). Traumatic events and posttraumatic stress disorder in an urban population of young adults. *Archives of General Psychiatry, 48,* 216–222.

Breslow, L., & Enstrom, J. E. (1980). Persistence of health habits and their relationship to mortality. *Preventive Medicine, 9,* 469–483.

Breuer, J., & Freud, S. (1895). *Studies in hysteria.* New York: Basic Books.

Briere, J., Downes, A., & Spensley, J. (1983). Summer in the city: Urban weather conditions and psychiatric emergency-room visits. *Journal of Abnormal Psychology, 92,* 77–80.

Briggs, G. C., Freeman, R. K., & Yaffe, S. J. (1986). *Drugs in pregnancy and lactation.* Baltimore: Williams & Wilkins.

Brooks, C. M. (1988). The history of thought concerning the hypothalamus and its functions. *Brain Research Bulletin, 20,* 657–667.

Brosnahan, M., & Giffen, D. (1993). Out of hospitals, left on the streets. *New York Times,* No. 49, 416, 7–11.

Brown, E. L., & Deffenbacher, K. (1979). *Perception and the senses.* New York: Oxford University Press.

Brown, G. P., Hammen, C. L., Craske, M. G., & Wickens, T. D. (1995). Dimensions of dysfunctional attitudes as vulnerabilities to depressive symptoms. *Journal of Abnormal Psychology, 104,* 431–435.

Brown, R., Galanter, E., Hess, E. H., & Mandler, G. (Eds.). (1962). *New directions in psychology.* New York: Holt, Rinehart & Winston.

Brown, R., & Kulik, J. (1977). Flashbulb memories. *Cognition, 5,* 73–99.

Brown, R. W., & McNeil, D. (1966). The "tip of the tongue" phenomenon. *Journal of Verbal Learning and Verbal Behavior, 5,* 325–337.

Brownell, K. D. (1991). Dieting and the search for the perfect body: Where physiology and culture collide. *Behavior Therapy, 22,* 1–12.

Brownell, K. D., & Rodin, J. (1994). The dieting maelstrom: Is it possible and advisable to lose weight? *American Psychologist, 49,* 781–791.

Brownlee-Dufek, M., Peterson, L., Simonds, J. F., Goldstein, D., Kilo, C., & Hoette, S. (1987). The role of health beliefs in the regimen adherence and metabolic control of adolescents and adults with diabetes mellitus. *Journal of Consulting and Clinical Psychology, 55,* 139–144.

Bruce, T. J., Spiegel, D. A., Gregg, S. F., & Nuzzarello, A. (1995). Predictors of alprazolam discontinuation with and without cognitive behavior therapy in panic disorder. *American Journal of Psychiatry, 152,* 1156–1160.

Bruner, J. S. (Ed.). (1974). *The growth of competence.* New York: Academic Press.

Bruner, J. S., & Goodman, C. C. (1947). Value and need as organizing factors in perception. *Journal of Abnormal and Social Psychology, 42,* 33–44.

Buchanan, C. M., Eccles, J. S., & Becker, J. B. (1992). Are adolescents victims of raging hormones: Evidence for activational effects of hormones on moods and behavior during adolescence. *Psychological Bulletin, 111,* 62–107.

Buchsbaum, M. (1983). The mind readers. *Psychology Today, 17(7),* 58–62 (p. 60).

Buchsbaum, M. S., Someya, T., et al. (1996). PET and MRI of the thalamus in never-medicated patients with schizophrenia. *American Journal of Psychiatry, 153,* 191–199.

Buckhout, R. (1974). Eyewitness testimony. *Scientific American, 231,* 23–33.

Buenker, J. D., & Ratner, L. (1992). *Multiculturalism in the United States: A comparative guide to acculturation and ethnicity.* Westport, CT: Greenwood.

Burger, J. M. (1986). Temporal effects on attributions: Actor and observer differences. *Social Cognition, 4,* 377–387.

Burgess, A. W., & Holstrom, K. L. (1974). Rape trauma syndrome. *American Journal of Psychiatry, 131,* 981–986.

Burish, T. G., & Carey, M. P. (1986). Conditioned aversive responses in cancer chemotherapy patients. Theoretical and developmental analysis. *Journal of Consulting and Clinical Psychology, 54,* 593–600.

Burling, T. A., Marotta, J., et al. (1989). Computerized smoking cessation program for the worksite: Treatment outcome and feasibility. *Journal of Consulting and Clinical Psychology, 57,* 619–622.

Burn, S. M., & Oskamp, S. (1986). Increasing community recycling with persuasive communication and public commitment. *Journal of Applied Social Psychology, 16,* 29–41.

Buss, A. (1989). Personality as traits. *American Psychologist, 44,* 1378–1388.

Bussey, K., & Bandura, A. (1992). Self-regulatory mechanisms governing gender development. *Child Development, 63,* 1236–1250.

Butcher, H. J. (1968). *Human intelligence: Its nature and assessment.* New York: Harper Torchbooks.

Butler, R. A. (1953). Discrimination learning by rhesus monkey by visual-exploration motivation. *Journal of Comparative and Physiological Psychology, 46,* 95–98.

Buys, C. J. (1978). Humans would do better without groups. *Personality and Social Psychology Bulletin, 4,* 123–125.

Byrne, D. (1971). *The attraction paradigm.* New York: Academic Press.

Cadoret, R. J., Troughton, E., O'Gorman, T. W., & Heywood, E. (1986). An adoption study of genetic and environmental factors in drug abuse. *Archives of General Psychiatry, 12,* 1131–1136.

Cain, W. S. (1988). Olfaction. In R. C. Atkinson, R. J. Herrnstein, G. Lindzey, & R. D. Luce (Eds.), *Stevens' handbook of experimental psychology: Vol. 1. Perception and motivation.* New York: Wiley-Interscience.

Calabrese, J. R., Kling, M. A., & Gold, P. W. (1987). Alterations in immunocompetence during stress, bereavement, and depression: Focus on neuroendocrine regulators. *American Journal of Psychiatry, 144,* 1123–1134.

Calahan, D. (1970). *Problem drinkers.* San Francisco: Jossey-Bass.

Calahan, D., & Room, R. (1974). *Problem drinking among American men.* New Brunswick, NJ: Rutgers Center of Alcohol Studies.

Calhoun, K. S., & Atkeson, B. M. (1989). *Treatment of rape victims.* New York: Pergamon Press.

Calhoun, K. S., Atkeson, B. M., & Resick, P. A. (1982). *A longitudinal examination of fear reactions in victims of rape.* Unpublished manuscript, University of Georgia.

Calkins, M. W. (1893). Statistics of dreams. *American Journal of Psychology, 5,* 311–343.

Campbell, D. E. (1961). The psychological effects of cerebral electroshock. In H. J. Eysenck (Ed.), *Handbook of abnormal psychology.* New York: Basic Books.

Campbell, D. E. (1978). *Interior office design and visitor response.* Paper presented to the American Psychological Association, Toronto.

Campbell, S. B., & Cohn, J. F. (1991). Prevalence and correlates of postpartum depression in first-time mothers. *Journal of Abnormal Psychology, 100,* 594–599.

Campion, M. A., Pursell, E. D., & Brown, B. K. (1988). Structured interviewing: Raising the psychometric properties of the employment interview. *Personnel Psychology, 41,* 25–42.

Campos, J. J., Bertenthal, B. I., & Kermonian, R. (1992). Early experience and emotional development: The emergence of wariness of heights. *Psychological Science, 3,* 61–64.

Cannon, D. S., Baker, T. B., Gino, A., & Nathan, P. E. (1986). Alcohol-aversion therapy: Relation between strength of aversion and abstinence. *Journal of Consulting and Clinical Psychology, 54,* 582–830.

Cannon, T. D., Mednick, S. A., Parnas, J., Schulsinger, F., Praestholm, J., & Vestergaard, A. (1993). Developmental brain abnormalities in the offspring of schizophrenic mothers: I. Contributions of genetic and perinatal factors. *Archives of General Psychiatry, 50,* 551–564.

Cannon, W. B. (1927). The James-Lange theory of emotions: A critical examination and an alternative theory. *American Journal of Psychology, 39,* 106–124.

Cannon, W. B., & Washburn, A. L. (1912). An explanation of hunger. *American Journal of Physiology, 29,* 441–454.

Cappe, R. F., & Alden, L. E. (1986). A comparison of treatment strategies for clients functionally impaired by extreme shyness and social avoidance. *Journal of Consulting and Clinical Psychology, 54,* 796–801.

Caprara, G. V., D'Imperio, G., Gentilomo, A., Mammucari, A., Renzi, P., & Travaglia, G. (1987). The intrusive commercial: Influence of aggressive TV commercials on aggression. *European Journal of Social Psychology, 17,* 23–31.

Carey, S. (1977). The child as a word learner. In M. Halle, J. Bresnan, & G. A. Miller (Eds.), *Linguistic theory and psychological reality.* Cambridge, MA: MIT Press.

Carmichael, L., Hogan, H. P., & Walter, A. A. (1932). An experimental study of the effect of language on the reproduction of visually perceived form. *Journal of Experimental Psychology, 15,* 73–86.

Carroll, C. R. (1989). *Drugs in modern society* (2nd ed.). Dubuque, IA: Wm. C. Brown Publishers.

Case, F. D. (1981). Dormitory architecture influences: Patterns of student social relations over time. *Environment and Behavior, 13,* 23–41.

Caspi, A., & Herbener, E. S. (1990). Continuity and change: Assortative marriage and the consistency of personality in adulthood. *Journal of Personality and Social Psychology, 58,* 250–258.

Castelluci, V., & Kandel, E. R. (1976). Presynaptic facilitation as a mechanism for behavioral sensitization in *Aplysia. Science, 194,* 1176–1178.

Cattell, R. B. (1950). *Personality: A systematic, theoretical, and factual style.* New York: McGraw-Hill.

Cattell, R. B. (1966). *The scientific analysis of personality.* Chicago: Aldine.

Cattell, R. B. (1982). *The inheritance of personality and ability.* New York: Academic Press.

Cattell, R. B., Saunders, D. R., & Stice, G. F. (1950). *The 16 personality factor questionnaire.* Champaign, IL: Institute for Personality and Ability Testing.

Centers for Disease Control. (January, 1993). *HIV/AIDS Surveillance.* Atlanta, GA: Author.

Chaiken, S., & Eagley, A. H. (1983). Communication modality as a determinant of persuasion: The role of communicator salience. *Journal of Personality and Social Psychology, 45,* 241–256.

Chambless, D. L., & Gillis, M. M. (1993). Cognitive therapy of anxiety disorders. *Journal of Consulting and Clinical Psychology, 61,* 248–260.

Chapman, L. J., & Chapman, J. P. (1973). *Disordered thought in schizophrenia.* New York: Appleton-Century-Crofts.

Chapman, S. F., Krantz, D. H., & Silver, R. (1992). Mathematics anxiety and science careers among able college women. *Psychological Science, 3,* 292–295.

Chase, W. G., & Simon, H. A. (1973). The mind's eye in chess. In W. G. Chase (Ed.), *Visual information processing.* New York: Academic Press.

Chochinov, H. M., Wilson, K. G., Enns, M., Mowchun, N., Lander, S., Levitt, M., & Clinch, J. J. (1995). Desire for death in the terminally ill. *American Journal of Psychiatry, 152,* 8.

Chodorow, N. J. (1989). Family structure and feminine personality. In *Feminism and psychoanalytic theory.* New Haven: Yale University Press.

Chomsky, N. (1957). *Syntactic structures.* The Hague: Mouton.

Christensen, A., & Arkowitz, H. (1974). Preliminary report on practice dating and feedback on treatment for college dating problems. *Journal of Counseling Psychology, 21,* 92–95.

Chruschel, T. L. (1982). General pharmacology and toxicology of alcohol. In F. Hoffmeister & G. Stille (Eds.), *Psychotropic agents. Part III: Alcohol and Psychotomimetics* (Vol. 55). New York: Springer-Verlag.

Church, R. M. (1969). Response suppression. In B. A. Campbell & R. M. Church (Eds.), *Punishment and aversive behavior.* New York: Appleton-Century-Crofts.

Cialdini, R. B. (1988). *Influence: Science and practice* (2nd ed.). Glenview, IL: Scott, Foresman.

Cialdini, R. B., Vincent, J. E., Lewis, S. K., Catalan, J., Wheeler, D., & Darby, B. L. (1975). Reciprocal concession procedure for inducing compliance: The door-in-the-face technique. *Journal of Personality and Social Psychology, 31,* 206–215.

Clark, K. B., & Clark, M. P. (1939). The development of self and the emergence of racial identification in Negro preschool children. *Journal of Social Psychology, 10,* 591–599.

Clarke, A. M., & Clarke, A. B. D. (Eds.). (1976). *Early experience: Myth and science.* New York: Appleton-Century-Crofts.

Clarkin, J. F., Pilkonis, P. A., & Magruder, K. M. (1996). Psychotherapy of depression: Implications for reform of the health care system. *Archives of General Psychiatry, 53,* 717–723.

Clemens, S. (1959). *The autobiography of Mark Twain* (C. Neider, Ed.). New York: Harper & Row.

Clum, G. A., & Bowers, T. G. (1990). Behavior therapy better than placebo treatments: Fact or artifact? *Psychological Bulletin, 107,* 110–113.

Clum, G. A., Clum, G. A., & Surls, R. (1993). A meta-analysis of treatments for panic disorder. *Journal of Consulting and Clinical Psychology, 61,* 317–326.

Coates, T. J. (1990). Strategies for modifying sexual behavior for primary and secondary prevention of HIV disease. *Journal of Consulting and Clinical Psychology, 58,* 57–69.

Coates, T. J., McKusick, L., Kuno, R., & Stites, D. P. (1989). Stress reduction training changed number of sexual partners but not immune function in men with HIV. *American Journal of Public Health, 79,* 885–887.

Cofer, C. N. (1972). *Motivation and emotion.* Glenview, IL: Scott, Foresman.

Cohen, L. B. (1979). Our developing knowledge of infant perception and cognition. *American Psychologist, 34,* 894–899.

Cohen, S. (1996). Psychological stress, immunity, and upper respiratory infections. *Current Directions in Psychological Science, 5,* 86–90.

Cohen, S., Tyrrell, D. A., & Smith, A. P. (1993). Negative life events, perceived stress, negative effect, and susceptibility to the common cold. *Journal of Personality and Social Psychology, 64,* 131–140.

Cohen, S., & Williamson, G. (1991). Stress and infectious disease in humans. *Psychological Bulletin, 109,* 5–24.

Colby, C. Z., Lanzetta, J. T., & Kleck, R. E. (1977). Effects of the expression of pain on autonomic and pain tolerance responses to subject controlled pain. *Psychophysiology, 14,* 537–540.

Coleman, J. (1980). *Contemporary psychology and effective behavior.* Glenview, IL: Scott, Foresman.

Coleman, J., Butcher, J., & Carson, R. (1990). *Abnormal psychology and modern life*. (7th ed.). Glenview, IL: Scott, Foresman.

Collins, A. M., & Loftus, E. F. (1975). A spreading activation theory of semantic processing. *Psychological Review, 82,* 407–428.

Condry, J. C., Simon, M. L., & Bronfenbrenner, U. (1968). *Characteristics of peer- and adult-oriented children.* Unpublished manuscript, Cornell University.

Cook, E. W., Hodes, R. L., & Lang, P. (1986). Preparedness and phobia: Effects of stimulus content on human visceral learning. *Journal of Abnormal Psychology, 95,* 195–207.

Cook, M., & Mineka, S. (1990). Selective association in the observational learning of fear in monkeys. *Journal of Abnormal Psychology, 98,* 448–459.

Cooper, J., & Mackie, D. (1983). Cognitive dissonance in an intergroup context. *Journal of Personality and Social Psychology, 44,* 536–544.

Cooper, J. R., Bloom, F. E., & Roth, R. H. (1986). *The biochemical basis of neuropharmacology* (5th ed.). New York: Oxford University Press.

Cooper, R. M., & Zubek, J. P. (1958). Effects of enriched and restricted early environments on the learning ability of bright and dull rats. *Canadian Journal of Psychology, 12,* 159–164.

Cope, J. G., & Geller, E. S. (1984). Community-based interventions to increase the use of automobile litterbags. *Journal of Resource Management and Technology, 13,* 127–132.

Coren, S., & Girgus, J. S. (1978). *Seeing is deceiving: The psychology of visual illusions.* Hillsdale, NJ: Erlbaum.

Cornelius, S. W., & Caspi, A. (1987). Everyday problem solving in adulthood and old age. *Psychology and Aging, 2,* 144–153.

Costa, P. T., & McCrae, R. R. (1976). Age differences in personality structure: A cluster analytic approach. *Journal of Gerontology, 31,* 564–570.

Costa, P. T., & McCrae, R. R. (1978). Objective personality assessment. In M. Storandt, I. C. Siegler, & M. F. Elias (Eds.), *The clinical psychology of aging.* New York: Plenum.

Costanzo, P. R., & Shaw, M. E. (1966). Conformity as a function of age level. *Child Development, 36,* 967–975.

Cowan, N. (1987). Auditory sensory storage in relation to the growth of sensation and acoustic information extraction. *Journal of Experimental Psychology, 13,* 204–215.

Cowan, N. (1988). Evolving conceptions of memory storage, selective attention, and their mutual constraints within the human information-processing system. *Psychological Bulletin, 104,* 163–191.

Craik, F. I. M., & Lockhart, R. S. (1972). Levels of processing. A framework for memory research. *Journal of Verbal Learning and Verbal Behavior, 11,* 671–684.

Craik, F. I. M., & McDowd, J. M. (1987). Age differences in recognition and recall. *Journal of Experimental Psychology: Learning, Memory, and Cognition, 13,* 474–479.

Crasilneck, H. B., & Hall, J. A. (1985). *Clinical hypnosis: Principles and applications* (2nd ed.). Orlando: Grune & Stratton.

Crutchfield, R. A. (1955). Conformity and character. *American Psychologist, 10,* 191–198.

Cui, X., & Vaillant, G. E. (1996). Antecedents and consequences of negative life events in adulthood: A longitudinal study. *American Journal of Psychiatry, 153,* 1.

Curtis, R. C., & Miller, K. (1987). Believing another person likes or dislikes you: Behaviors making the beliefs come true. *Journal of Personality and Social Psychology, 51,* 284–290.

Dakof, G. A., & Taylor, S. E. (1990). Victims' perception of social support: What is helpful from whom? *Journal of Personality and Social Psychology, 58,* 80–89.

Dale, N., & Kandel, E. R. (1990). Facilitatory and inhibitory transmitters modulate spontaneous transmitter release at cultured Aplysia sensorimotor synapses. *Journal of Physiology, 421,* 203–222.

Darley, J., & Latané, B. (1968). Bystander intervention in emergencies. Diffusion of responsibility. *Journal of Personality and Social Psychology, 8,* 377–383.

Darling, N., & Steinberg, L. (1993). Parenting style as context: An integrative model. *Psychological Bulletin, 113,* 487–496.

Dash, P. K., Hochner, B., & Kandel, E. R. (1990). Injection of the cAMP-responsive element into the nucleus of Aplysia sensory neurons blocks long-term facilitation. *Nature, 345,* 718–721.

Davidson, P. O., & Davidson, S. M. (Eds.). (1982). *Behavioral medicine: Changing health life-styles.* New York: Brunner/Mazel.

Davidson, R. J. (1992). Emotion and affective style: Hemispheric substrates. *Psychological Science,* 39–43.

Davidson, R. J., Ekman, P., Saron, C. D., Senulis, J. A., & Friesen, W. V. (1990). Approach-withdrawal and cerebral asymmetry: Emotional expression and brain physiology. *Journal of Personality and Social Psychology, 58,* 330–341.

Davidson, R. J., & Fox, N. A. (1989). Frontal brain asymmetry predicts infants' response to maternal separation. *Journal of Abnormal Psychology, 98,* 127–131.

Davis, H. P., & Squire, L. R. (1984). Protein synthesis and memory: A review. *Psychological Bulletin, 96,* 518–559.

Deaux, K., & Emswiller, R. T. (1974). Explanation of successful performance on sex-linked tasks: What is skill for the male is luck for the female. *Journal of Personality and Social Psychology, 29,* 80–85.

DeBono, K. G. (1992). Pleasant scents and persuasion: An information processing approach. *Journal of Applied Social Psychology, 22,* 910–919.

Deese, J., & Deese, E. K. (1979). *How to study* (3rd ed.). New York: McGraw-Hill.

Deikman, A. J. (1980). De-Automization and the mystic experience. In J. R. Tisdale (Ed.), *Growing edges in the psychology of religion* (pp. 201–217). Chicago: Nelson-Hall.

Delgado, J. M. R. (1969). *Physical control of the mind: Toward a psycho-civilized society.* New York: Harper & Row.

Dember, W. N. (1964). Birth order and the need for affiliation. *Journal of Abnormal and Social Psychology, 68,* 555–557.

Dember, W. N. (1965). The new look in motivation. *American Scientist, 53,* 409–427.

Dennis, W., & Dennis, M. (1941). The effect of cradling practices on the onset of walking in Hopi children. *Journal of Genetic Psychology, 23,* 143–189.

Devine, P. G. (1996, January/February). Breaking the prejudice habit. *Psychological Science Agenda,* 10–11.

Devlin, M. J., Walsh, B. T., Kral, J. G., Heysfield, S. B., Pi-Sunyer, F. X., & Dantzic, S. (1990). Metabolic abnormalities in bulimia nervosa.

Archives of General Psychiatry, 47, 144–148.

Dew, M. A., Ragni, M. V., & Nimorwicz, P. (1990). Infection with human immunodeficiency virus and vulnerability to psychological distress. *Archives of General Psychiatry, 47,* 437–445.

Dewsbury, D. A. (1990). Early interactions between animal psychologists and animal activists and the founding of the APA Committee on Precautions in Animal Experimentation. *American Psychologist, 45,* 315–327.

Diamond, E. L. (1982). The role of anger and hostility in essential hypertension and coronary heart disease. *Psychological Bulletin, 92,* 410–433.

Dindia, K., & Allen, M. (1992). Sex differences in self-disclosure: A meta-analysis. *Psychological Bulletin, 112,* 106–124.

Diokno, A. C., & Hollander, J. B. (1991). Diagnosis of erectile dysfunction. In J. F. Leyson (Ed.), *Sexual rehabilitation of the spinal cord patient.* Clifton, NJ: Humana Press.

Dion, K. K. (1980). Physical attractiveness, sex roles, and heterosexual attraction. In M. Cook (Ed.), *The bases of human sexual attraction.* New York: Academic Press.

Dipboye, R. L., Fromkin, H. L., & Wilback, K. (1975). The importance of applicant sex, attractiveness, and scholastic standing in evaluation of job application resumes. *Journal of Applied Psychology, 60,* 39–43.

Dishman, R. K. (1982). Compliance/adherence in health-related exercise. *Health Psychology, 1,* 237–267.

Dobson, V., Teller, D. Y., Lee, C. P., & Wade, B. (1978). A behavioral method for efficient screening of visual acuity in young infants. *Investigative Ophthalmology and Visual Science, 17,* 1142–1150.

Dodd, D. H., & White, R. M. (1980). *Cognition, mental structures and processes.* Boston: Allyn & Bacon.

Dohr, K. B., Rush, A. J., & Bernstein, I. H. (1989). Cognitive biases and depression. *Journal of Abnormal Psychology, 98,* 263–267.

Dohrenwend, B., Pearlin, L., Clayton, P., Hamburg, B., Dohrenwend, B., Riley, M., & Rose, R. (1982). Report on stress and life events. In G. R. Elliott & C. Eisdorfer (Eds.), *Stress and human health: Analysis and implications on research.* New York: Springer-Verlag.

Doleys, D. M. (1977). Behavioral treatments for nocturnal enuresis in children: A review of the recent literature. *Psychological Bulletin, 84,* 30–54.

Dollard, J., Doob, L. W., Miller, N. E., Mowrer, O. H., & Sears, R. R. (1939). *Frustration and aggression.* New Haven: Yale University Press.

Dolnick, E. (1993). Deafness as culture. *Atlantic Monthly, 272,* 37–53.

Doyle, J., & Paludi, M. (1991). *Sex and Gender* (2nd ed.). Dubuque, IA: Wm. C. Brown.

Dravnieks, A. (1983). Odor character profiling. *Journal of the Air Pollution Control Association, 33,* 752–755.

Drucker-Colin, R. R., & Spanis, C. W. (1976). Is there a sleep transmitter? *Progress in Neurobiology, 6,* 1–22.

Duncker, K. (1945). On problem solving. *Psychological Monographs, 58* (No. 5).

Durbin, D. L., Darling, N., Steinberg, L., & Brown, B. B. (1993). Parenting style and peer group membership among European-American adolescents. *Journal of Research on Adolescence, 3,* 87–100.

Dutton, D. G., & Aron, A. P. (1974). Some evidence for heightened sexual attraction under conditions of high anxiety. *Journal of Personality and Social Psychology, 30,* 510–517.

Dwyer, W. O., Leeming, F. C., Cobern, M. K., Porter, B. E., & Jackson, J. M. (1993). Critical review of behavioral interventions to preserve the environment: Research since 1980. *Environment and Behavior, 25,* 275–321.

Dyck, D. G., Greenberg, A. H., & Osachuk, T. A. (1986). Tolerance to drug-induced (Poly I:C) natural killer cell activation: Congruence with a Pavlovian conditioning model. *Journal of Experimental Psychology: Animal Behavior Processes, 12,* 25–31.

Dywan, J., & Bowers, K. (1983). The use of hypnosis to enhance recall. *Science, 222,* 184–185.

Eagly, A. H. (1978). Sex differences in influenceability. *Psychological Bulletin, 85,* 86–116.

Eagly, A. H. (1995). The science and politics of comparing women and men. *American Psychologist, 50,* 145–158.

Eagly, A. H., Ashmore, R. D., Makhijani, M. G., & Longo, L. C. (1991). What is beautiful is good, but . . .: A meta-analytical review of research on the physical attractiveness stereotype. *Psychological Bulletin, 110,* 109–128.

Eagly, A. H., & Carli, L. (1981). Sex of researchers and sex-typed communications as determinants of sex differences in influence ability: A meta-analysis of social influence studies. *Psychological Bulletin, 90,* 1–20.

Eagly, A. H., & Johnson, B. T. (1990). Gender and leadership style. *Psychological Bulletin, 108,* 233–256.

Eagly, A. H., Makhijani, M. G., & Klonsky, B. G. (1992). Gender and the evaluation of leaders: A meta-analysis. *Psychological Bulletin, 111,* 3–22.

Ebbinghaus, H. (1885). *Uber das Gedachnis.* Leipzig: Duncker & Humboldt.

Ebert, P. D., & Hyde, J. S. (1976). Selection for agonistic behavior in wild female *Mus musculus. Behavior Genetics, 6,* 291–304.

Eckert, E. D., Bouchard, T. J., Bohlen, J., & Heston, L. L. (1986). Homosexuality in monozygotic twins reared apart. *British Journal of Psychiatry, 148,* 421–425.

Egan, K. J., Carr, J. E., Hunt, D. D., & Adamson, R. (1988). Endogenous opiate system and systematic desensitization. *Journal of Consulting and Clinical Psychology, 56,* 287–291.

Egendorf, A., Kaduschin, C., Laufer, R. S., Rothbart, G., & Sloan, L. (1981). *Legacies of Vietnam: Comparative adjustment of veterans and their peers.* (Publication No. V101 134P-630). Washington, DC: U.S. Government Printing Office.

Ehlers, A., & Breuer, P. (1992). Increased cardiac awareness in panic disorder. *Journal of Abnormal Psychology, 101,* 371–382.

Eibl-Eibesfeldt, I. (1973). The expressive behavior of the deaf and blind-born. In M. von Cranach & I. Vine (Eds.), *Social communication and movement.* New York: Academic Press.

Ekman, P. (1992). Facial expressions of emotion: New findings, new questions. *Psychological Science, 3,* 34–38.

Ekman, P., Levenson, R. W., & Friesen, W. V. (1983). Autonomic nervous system activity distinguishes among emotions. *Science, 221,* 1208–1210.

Ekman, P., & Oster, H. (1979). Facial expressions of emotions. In M. R. Rosenzweig & L. W. Porter (Eds.), *Annual Review of Psychology* (Vol. 30). Palo Alto, CA: Annual Reviews.

Elkind, D. (1967). *Children and adolescents: Interpretive essays on Jean Piaget.* New York: Oxford University Press.

Elkind, D. (1981). Understanding the young adolescent. In L. D. Steinberg (Ed.), *The life cycle: Readings in human development.* New York: Columbia University Press.

Elkind, D., & Bowen, R. (1979). Imaginary audience behavior in children and adolescents. *Developmental Psychology, 15,* 38–44.

Elliott, D., Huizinga, D., & Menard, S. (1989). *Multiple problem youth: Delinquency, substance use, and mental health problems.* New York: Springer-Verlag.

Ellis, A. (1962). *Reason and emotion in psychotherapy.* New York: Lyle Stuart.

Ellis, H. C. (1987). Recent developments in human memory. In V. Mokosky (Ed.), *The G. Stanley Hall Series.* Washington, DC: American Psychological Association.

Ellis, H. C., & Hunt, R. R. (1989). *Fundamentals of human memory and cognition* (4th ed.). Dubuque, IA: Wm. C. Brown Publishers.

Ellis, H. C., & Hunt, R. R. (1993). *Fundamentals of cognitive psychology.* Madison, WI: Brown & Benchmark.

Ellis, L. (1989). *Theories of rape: Inquiries into causes of sexual aggression.* New York: Hemisphere.

Emery, V. O., & Oxmans, T. E. (1992). Update on the dementia spectrum of depression. *American Journal of Psychiatry, 149,* 305–317.

Emmons, R. A., & Diener, E. (1986). Situation selection as a moderator of response consistency and stability. *Journal of Personality and Social Psychology, 51,* 1013–1019.

Eppley, K. R., Abrams, A. I., & Spear, J. (1989). Differential effects of relaxation techniques on trait anxiety: A meta-analysis. *Journal of Clinical Psychology, 45,* 957–973.

Epstein, S. (1982). Conflict and stress. In L. Goldberger & S. Breznitz (Eds.), *Handbook of stress.* New York: The Free Press.

Epstein, S., & Fenz, W. D. (1965). Steepness of approach and avoidance gradients in humans as a function of experience: Theory and experience. *Journal of Experimental Psychology, 70,* 1–12.

Epstein, S., & Roupenian, A. (1970). Heart rate and skin conductance during experimentally induced anxiety. *Journal of Personality and Social Psychology, 16,* 20–28.

Ericsson, K. A., Krampe, R. T., & Teschmer, R. C. (1993). The role of deliberate practice in the acquisition of expert performance. *Psychological Review, 100,* 383–406.

Erikson, E. (1963). *Childhood and society.* New York: Norton.

Erlenmeyer-Kimling, L., & Jarvik, L. F. (1963). Genetics and intelligence: A review. *Science, 142,* 1477–1479.

Eron, L. D., & Huesmann, L. R. (1984). Television violence and aggressive behavior. In B. B. Lahey & A. E. Kazdin (Eds.), *Advances in clinical child psychology* (Vol. 7). New York: Plenum.

Escobar, J. I., Canino, G., Rubio-Stipec, M., & Bravo, M. (1992). Somatic symptoms after a natural disaster: A prospective study. *American Journal of Psychiatry, 149,* 965–967.

Evans, M. D., et al. (1992). Differential relapse following cognitive therapy and pharmacotherapy for depression. *Archives of General Psychiatry, 49,* 802–808.

Evers, S. E., Bass, M., Donner, A., & McWhinney, I. R. (1987). Lack of impact on salt restriction advice on hypertensive patients. *Preventive Medicine, 16,* 213–220.

Exner, J. (1986). *The Rorschach: A comprehensive system: Vol. 2. Current research and advanced interpretation.* New York: Wiley.

Eysenck, M. W., Mogg, K., May, J., Richards, A., & Mathews, A. (1991). Bias in interpretation of ambiguous sentences related to threat in anxiety. *Journal of Abnormal Psychology, 100,* 144–150.

Ezell, C. (1994). The long and short of short- and long-term memory. *Journal of NIH Research, 6,* 56–61.

Ezell, C. (1995). Fat times for obesity research: Tons of new information, but how does it all fit together? *Journal of NIH Research, 7,* 39–43.

Fagot, B. I. (1974). Sex differences in toddlers' behavior and parental reaction. *Developmental Psychology, 10,* 554–558.

Fairchild, H. (1984). Teaching Black psychology. *Western Journal of Black Studies, 8,* 55–60.

Fairweather, G. W., Sanders, D. H., Cressler, D. L., & Maynard, M. (1969). *Community life for the mentally ill.* Chicago: Aldine.

Fallon, A. E., & Rozin, P. (1985). Sex differences in perceptions of desirable body shape. *Journal of Abnormal Psychology, 94,* 102–105.

Fantz, R. L. (1961). The origin of form perception. *Scientific American, 204,* 66–72.

Fantz, R. L. (1966). *Perceptual development in children.* New York: International Universities Press.

Farber, S. (1982). Genetic diversity and differing reactions to stress. In L. Goldberger & S. Breznitz (Eds.), *Handbook of stress.* New York: The Free Press.

Farmer, A. E., McGuffin, P., & Gottesman, I. I. (1987). Twin concordance for DSM-III schizophrenia: Scrutinizing the validity of the definition. *Archives of General Psychiatry, 44,* 634–641.

Farquhar, J. W. (1979). *The American way of life need not be hazardous to your health.* New York: Norton.

Farrell, M. P., & Rosenberg, S. D. (1981). *Men at midlife.* Boston: Auburn House.

Faust, M. S. (1960). Developmental maturity as a determinant of prestige in adolescent girls. *Child Development, 31,* 173–184.

Faust, M. S. (1977). Somatic development of adolescent girls. *Monographs of the Society for Research in Child Development, 42* (No. 169), 1.

Fawzi, F. I., et al. (1990). A structured psychiatric intervention for cancer patients: 2. Changes over time in immunological measures. *Archives of General Psychiatry, 47,* 729–736.

Federal Bureau of Investigation. (1990). *Crime in the United States.* Washington, DC: Author.

Feifel, H. (1990). Psychology and death: meaningful rediscovery. *American Psychologist, 45,* 537–543.

Feingold, A. (1988). Matching for attractiveness in romantic partner and same-sex friends: A meta-analysis and theoretical critique. *Psychological Bulletin, 104,* 226–235.

Feingold, A. (1990). Gender differences in effects of physical attractiveness on romantic attraction: A comparison across five research paradigms. *Journal of Personality and Social Psychology, 59,* 981–993.

Feingold, A. (1992a). Gender differences in mate selection processes: A test of the parental investment model. *Psychological Bulletin, 112,* 125–139.

Feingold, A. (1992b). Good-looking people are not what we think. *Psychological Bulletin, 111,* 304–341.

Feingold, A. (1994). Gender differences in personality: A meta-analysis. *Psychological Bulletin, 116,* 429–456.

Fenz, W. D., & Epstein, S. (1962). Theory and experiment on the measurement of approach-avoidance conflict. *Journal of Abnormal and Social Psychology, 64,* 97–112.

Fenz, W. D., & Epstein, S. (1967). Gradients of psychological arousal of experienced and novice parachutists as a function of an approaching jump. *Psychosomatic Medicine, 29,* 33–51.

Ferster, C. B., & Skinner, B. F. (1957). *Schedules of reinforcement.* New York: Appleton-Century-Crofts.

Festinger, L., Schachter, S., & Back, K. (1950). *Social pressures in informal groups: A study of a housing community.* New York: Harper.

Festinger, L. A. (1957). *A theory of cognitive dissonance.* Evanston, IL: Harper & Row, Peterson.

Festinger, L. A., & Carlsmith, L. M. (1959). Cognitive consequences of forced compliance. *Journal of Abnormal and Social Psychology, 58,* 203–210.

Fichten, C. S., Robillard, K., Judd, D., & Amsel, R. (1989). College students with physical disabilities: Myths and realities. *Rehabilitation Psychology, 34,* 243–257.

Field, T. M., Woodson, R., Greenberg, R., & Cohen, D. (1982). Discrimination and imitation of facial expressions by neonates. *Science, 218,* 179–181.

Fine, B. J., & Kobrick, J. L. (1978). Effects of altitude and heat on complex cognitive tasks. *Human Factors, 20,* 115–122.

Finkelhor, D. (1990). Early and long-term effects of child sexual abuse: An update. *Professional Psychology: Research and Practice, 21,* 325–330.

Finkelhor, D., & Browne, A. (1985). The traumatic impact of child sexual abuse. *American Journal of Orthopsychiatry, 55,* 530–541.

Fishbach, G. D. (1992). Mind and brain. *Scientific American, 267* (September), 48–57.

Fisher, E. B., Delamater, A. M., Bertelson, A. D., & Kirkley, B. G. (1982). Psychological factors in diabetes and its treatment. *Journal of Consulting and Clinical Psychology, 50,* 993–1003.

Fisher, R. P., & Geiselman, R. E. (1988). Enhancing eyewitness memory with the cognitive interview. In M. M. Gruneberg, P. E. Morris, & R. N. Sykes (Eds.), *Practical aspects of memory: Current research and issues: Vol. 1. Memory in everyday life* (pp. 34–39). Chichester, England: Wiley.

Fiske, S. T. (1993). Social cognition and social perception. *Annual Review of Psychology, 44,* 155–194.

Fiske, S. T., Bersoff, D. N., Borgida, E., Deaux, K., & Heilman, M. E. (1991). Social science research on trial: Use of sex stereotyping research in *Price Waterhouse v. Hopkins. American Psychologist, 46,* 1049–1060.

Flor, H., Elbert, T., Knecht, S., Wienbruch, C., Pantev, C., Birbaumer, N., Larbig, W., & Taub, E. (1995). Phantom-limb pain as a perceptual correlate of cortical reorganization following arm amputation. *Nature, 375,* 482–490.

Foa, E. B., & Riggs, D. S. (1995). Posttraumatic stress disorder following assault: Theoretical considerations and empirical findings. *Current Directions in Psychological Science, 4,* 61–65.

Folkman, S., & Lazarus, R. S. (1986). Stress processes and depressive symptomatology. *Journal of Abnormal Psychology, 95,* 107–113.

Folkman, S., Lazarus, R. S., Pimley, S., & Nowacek, J. (1987). Age differences in stress and coping processes. *Psychology and Aging, 2,* 171–184.

Ford, J. M., & Roth, W. T. (1977). Do cognitive abilities decline with age? *Geriatrics, 32,* 59–62.

Fordyce, W. E. (1978). Learning processes in pain. In R. A. Sternbach (Ed.), *The psychology of pain.* New York: Raven Press.

Foreyt, J. P., Scott, L. W., Mitchell, R. E., & Gotto, A. M. (1979). Plasma lipid changes in the normal population following behavioral treatment. *Journal of Consulting and Clinical Psychology, 47,* 440–452.

Forgas, J. P., & Bower, G. H. (1987). Mood effects on person-perception judgments. *Journal of Personality and Social Psychology, 53,* 53–60.

Forster, J. L., Jeffrey, R. W., & Snell, M. K. (1988). One-year follow-up study to a worksite weight control program. *Preventive Medicine, 17,* 129–133.

Foulkes, D. (1989, December). Understanding our dreams. *Natural Science,* pp. 296–301.

Foulkes, D., & Schmidt, M. (1983). Temporal sequence and unit composition in dream reports from different stages of sleep. *Sleep, 6,* 265–280.

Foulkes, W. D. (1962). Dream reports from different stages of sleep. *Journal of Abnormal and Social Psychology, 65,* 14–25.

Fowles, D. C. (1992). Schizophrenia: Diathesis-stress revisited. *Annual Review of Psychology, 43,* 303–336.

Fox, S. I. (1984). *Laboratory guide to human physiology: Concepts and clinical applications* (3rd ed.). Dubuque, IA: Wm. C. Brown Publishers.

Foxx, R., & Rubinoff, A. (1981). A behavioral treatment of caffeinism. *Journal of Applied Behavior Analysis, 14,* 21–30.

Foxx, R. M., & Brown, R. A. (1979). Nicotine fading and self-monitoring for cigarette abstinence or controlled smoking. *Journal of Applied Behavior Analysis, 12,* 111–125.

Foy, D. W., Sipprelle, R. C., Rueger, D. B., & Carroll, E. M. (1984). Etiology of posttraumatic stress disorder in Vietnam veterans: Analysis of premilitary, military, and combat exposure experience. *Journal of Consulting and Clinical Psychology, 52,* 79–87.

Frankel, F. H. (1995, August 31). Discovering new memories in psychotherapy—Childhood revisited, fantasy, or both? *New England Journal of Medicine,* 591–594.

Frederiksen, N. (1986). Toward a broader conception of human intelligence. *American Psychologist, 41,* 445–452.

Freedman, J. L. (1984). Effect of television violence on aggressiveness. *Psychological Bulletin, 96,* 227–246.

Freedman, J. L., & Fraser, S. C. (1966). Compliance without pressure: The foot-in-the-door technique. *Journal of Personality and Social Psychology, 4,* 195–202.

Freeman, L. (1972). *The story of Anna O.* New York: Walker Publishing.

French, E. G. (1956). Motivation as a variable in work-partner selection. *Journal of Abnormal and Social Psychology, 53,* 96–99.

Freud, S. (1905). *Three essays on the theory of sexuality.* London: Hogarth Press.

Friedman, H. S., & Booth-Kewley, S. (1987). The "disease-prone" personality: A meta-analytic view of the construct. *American Psychologist, 42,* 539–555.

Friedman, H. S., Tucker, J. S., Schwartz, J. E., Tomlinson-Keasey, C., Martin, L. R., Wingard, D. L., & Criqui, M. H. (1995). Psychosocial and behavioral predictors of longevity: The aging and death of the "termites." *American Psychologist, 50,* 69–78.

Friedman, M., & Rosenman, R. H. (1974). *Type A behavior and your heart.* New York: Knopf.

Friedman, R. C., & Downey, J. (1993). Neurobiology and sexual orientation. *Journal of Neuropsychiatry and Clinical Neurosciences, 5,* 131–153.

Frieze, I. H., Olson, J. E., & Russell, J. (1991). *Journal of Applied Social Psychology, 21,* 1039–1057.

Frijda, N. (1988). The laws of emotion. *American Psychologist, 43,* 349–357.

Fry, A. F., & Hale, S. (1996). Processing speed, working memory, and fluid intelligence: Evidence for a developmental cascade. *Psychological Science, 7,* 237–241.

Furomoto, L. (1992). Joining separate spheres—Christine Ladd-Franklin, Woman-scientist (1847–1930). *American Psychologist, 47,* 174–182.

Furomoto, L., & Scarborough, E. (1986). Placing women in the history of psychology: The first women psychologists. *American Psychologist, 41,* 35–42.

Furth, H. G. (1966). *Thinking without language: Psychological implications of deafness.* New York: The Free Press.

Fuster, J. M. (1995). *Memory in the cerebral cortex.* Cambridge, MA: MIT Press.

Gabbard, G. O., Lazar, S. G., Hornberger, J., & Spiegel, D. (1997). The economic impact of psychotherapy: A review. *American Journal of Psychiatry, 154,* 147–155.

Gaertner, S. L.; Rust, M. C.; Dovidio, J. F.; and Bachman, B. A. (1994). The contact hypothesis: The role of a common ingroup identity on reducing intergroup bias. *Small Group Research, 25*(2), 224–249.

Galambos, N. L. (1992). Parent-adolescent relations. *Current Directions in Psychological Science, 1,* 146–149.

Galanter, E. (1962). *New directions in psychology.* New York: Holt, Rinehart & Winston.

Gallup, G., & Proctor, W. (1982). *Adventures in immortality.* New York: McGraw-Hill.

Galotti, K. (1990). Approaches to studying formal and everyday reasoning. *Psychological Bulletin, 105,* 331–351.

Garcia, J., Hankins, W. G., & Rusiniak, K. W. (1974). Behavioral regulation of the *milieu interne* in man and rat. *Science, 185,* 824–831.

Garcia, L. T. (1982). Sex-role orientation and stereotypes about male-female sexuality. *Sex Roles, 8,* 863–876.

Gardner, B. T., & Gardner, R. A. (1971). Two-way communication with an infant chimpanzee. In A. M. Schrier & F. Stollnitz (Eds.), *Behavior of nonhuman primates* (Vol. 4). New York: Academic Press.

Gardner, H. (1983). *Frames of mind: The theory of multiple intelligence.* New York: Basic Books.

Garner, D. M., Garfinkel, P. E., Schwartz, D., & Thompson, M. (1980). Cultural expectations of thinness in women. *Psychological Reports, 47,* 483–491.

Garner, D. M., Rockert, W., Davis, R., Garner, M. V., Olmsted, M. P., & Eagle, M. (1993). Comparison of cognitive-behavioral and supportive-expressive therapy for bulimia nervosa. *American Journal of Psychiatry, 150,* 37–46.

Garretson, D. (1993). Psychological misdiagnosis of African Americans. *Journal of Multicultural Counseling and Development, 21,* 119–126.

Garro, L. C. (1990). Culture, pain and cancer. *Journal of Palliative Care, 6,* 34–44.

Gates, A. I. (1917). Recitation as a factor in memorizing. *Archives of Psychology of New York,* No. 40.

Gazzaniga, M. S. (1967). The split brain in man. *Scientific American, 217,* 24–29.

Gazzaniga, M. S. (1983). Right hemisphere language following brain bisection: A 20-year perspective. *American Psychologist, 38,* 525–537.

Gebhardt, D. L., & Crump, C. L. (1990). Employee fitness and wellness programs in the workplace. *American Psychologist, 45,* 262–272.

Geen, R. G., & Quanty, M. B. (1977). The catharsis of aggression: An evaluation of a hypothesis. In L. Berkowitz (Ed.), *Advances in experimental social psychology* (Vol. 10). New York: Academic Press.

Geer, J., Heiman, J., & Leitenberg, H. (1984). *Human sexuality.* Englewood Cliffs, NJ: Prentice-Hall.

Gelles, R. J. (1977). *Violence towards children in the United States.* Paper presented to the Annual Meeting of the American Association for the Advancement of Science.

Gelles, R. J., & Strauss, M. A. (1977). Determinants of violence in the family: Toward a theoretical integration. In W. R. Barr, R. Hill, F. I. Nye, & I. L. Reiss (Eds.), *Contemporary theories about the family.* New York: The Free Press.

Gentile, D. A. (1993). Just what are sex and gender, anyway? A call for a new terminological standard. *Psychological Science, 4,* 120–126.

Gerson, E. S., & Rieder, R. O. (1992, September). Major disorders of mind and brain. *Scientific American, 267,* 126–133.

Gibson, E., & Walk, R. (1960). The "visual cliff." *Scientific American, 202,* 64–71.

Gildea, W. (1993, August 29). Seeing pride in his accomplishments. *Washington Post,* D, 7, 2.

Gilligan, C. (1982). *In a different voice.* Cambridge, MA: Harvard University Press.

Glanzer, M., & Cunitz, A. R. (1966). Two storage mechanisms in free recall. *Journal of Verbal Learning and Verbal Behavior, 5,* 351–360.

Glaser, R., & Chi, M. T. H. (1988). Overview. In M. T. H. Chi, R. Glaser, & M. J. Farr (Eds.), *The nature of expertise.* Hillsdale, NJ: Erlbaum.

Glaser, R., et al. (1990). Psychological stress-induced modulation of interleukin 2 receptor gene expression and interleukin 2 production in peripheral blood leukocytes. *Archives of General Psychiatry, 47,* 707–712.

Goldberg, L. R. (1993). The structure of phenotypic personality traits. *American Psychologist, 48,* 26–34.

Goldfried, M., & Davison, G. (1976). *Clinical behavior therapy.* New York: Holt, Rinehart & Winston.

Golding, J. M., Smith, R., & Kashner, T. M. (1991). Does somatization disorder occur in men? *Archives of General Psychiatry, 48,* 231–235.

Goldman-Rakic, P. S. (1992). Working memory and the mind. *Scientific American, 267,* 111–117.

Goldsmith, H. H., & Alansky, J. A. (1987). Maternal and infant temperamental predictors of attachment: A meta-analytic review. *Journal of Consulting and Clinical Psychology, 55,* 805–816.

Goldsmith, L. (1988). Treatment of sexual dysfunction. In E. Weinstein & E. Rosen (Eds.), *Sexuality counseling: Issues and implications.* Monterey, CA: Brooks/Cole.

Goldstein, M. J., & Palmer, J. O. (1963). *The experience of anxiety.* New York: Oxford University Press.

Goleman, D. (1976, March). Why the brain blocks daytime dreams. *Psychology Today,* pp. 69–70.

Goleman, D. (1980, February). 1,528 little geniuses and how they grew. *Psychology Today,* pp. 28–143.

Goodwin, D. W., Schulsinger, J., Hermansen, L., Guze, S. B., & Winokur, G. (1973). Alcohol problems in adoptees raised apart from alcoholic biological parents. *Archives of General Psychiatry, 28,* 238–243.

Goodwin, F. W., Schulsinger, J., Moller, N., Hermansen, L., Winokur, G., & Guze, S. B. (1974). Drinking problems in adopted and non-adopted sons of alcoholics. *Archives of General Psychiatry, 31,* 164–169.

Gotlib, I. (1992). Interpersonal and cognitive aspects of depression. *Current Directions in Psychological Science, 1,* 149–154.

Gould, R. L. (1978). *Transformations: Growth and change in adult life.* New York: Simon & Schuster.

Grady, C. L., McIntosh, A. R., Horwitz, B., Maisog, J. Ma., Ungerleider, L. G., Mentis, M. J., Pietrini, P., Schapiro, M. B., & Haxby, J. V. (1995). Age-related reductions in human recognition memory due to impaired encoding. *Science, 269,* 218–220.

Graf, P., Squire, L. R., & Mandler, G. (1984). The information that amnesic patients do not forget. *Journal of Experimental Psychology, Learning, Memory, and Cognition, 10,* 164–178.

Gray, P. (1993). What is love? *Time,* February 15, 47–51.

Graziano, W. G., & Musser, L. M. (1982). The going and parting of the ways. In S. Duck (Ed.), *Personal relationships 4: Dissolving personal relationships.* London: Academic Press.

Greden, J. F. (1974). Anxiety or caffeinism: A diagnostic dilemma. *American Journal of Psychiatry, 131,* 1089–1092.

Griffith, W., & Veitch, R. (1971). Influences of population density on interpersonal affective behavior. *Journal of Personality and Social Psychology, 17,* 92–98.

Grilo, C. M., Shiffman, S., & Wing, R. R. (1989). Relapse crises and coping among dieters. *Journal of Consulting and Clinical Psychology, 57,* 488–495.

Grimes, J. W., & Allinsmith, W. (1961). Compulsivity, anxiety, and school achievement. *Merrill-Palmer Quarterly, 7,* 247–269.

Grossman, S. P. (1960). Eating and drinking elicited by direct adrenergic and cholinergic stimulation of hypothalamus. *Science, 132,* 301–302.

Groth, N. (1979). *Men who rape: The psychology of the offender.* New York: Plenum.

Groves, P., & Schlesinger, K. (1979). *Biological psychology.* Dubuque, IA: Wm. C. Brown Publishers.

Groves, P. M., & Rebec, G. V. (1988). *Introduction to biological psychology.* (3rd ed.). Dubuque, IA: Wm. C. Brown Publishers.

Guilford, J. P. (1950). Creativity. *American Psychologist, 5,* 444–454.

Guilford, J. P. (1967). *The nature of human intelligence.* New York: McGraw-Hill.

Guilford, J. P. (1982). Cognitive psychology's ambiguities: Some suggested remedies. *Psychologist Review, 89,* 48–59.

Guisinger, S., & Blatt, S. J. (1994). Individuality and relatedness: Evolution of a fundamental dialectic. *American Psychologist, 49,* 104–111.

Gunnar, M. R., Malone, S., & Fisch, R. O. (1988). The psychobiology of stress and coping in the human neonate: Studies of adrenocortical activity in response to stress in the first week of life. In T. Field, P. McCabe, & N. Schneiderman (Eds.), *Stress and coping.* Hillsdale, NJ: Lawrence Erlbaum.

Gustavson, C. R., Garcia, J., Hankins, W. G., & Rusiniak, K. W. (1974). Coyote predation control by aversive conditioning. *Science, 184,* 581–584.

Guthrie, R. (1976). *Even the rat was white: A historical view of psychology.* New York: Harper & Row.

Gutmann, D. (1977). The cross-cultural perspective. In J. E. Birren & K. W. Shaie (Eds.), *Handbook of the psychology of aging.* New York: Van Nostrand.

Haan, N. (1976). ". . . Change and sameness . . ." reconsidered. *International Journal of Aging and Human Development, 7,* 59–65.

Haber, R. N., & Haber, R. B. (1964). Eidetic imagery: I. Frequency. *Perceptual and Motor Skills, 19,* 131–138.

Hafer, J. C., & Richmond, E. D. (1988). What hearing parents should learn about deaf culture. *Perspectives for Teachers of the Hearing Impaired, 7,* 2–5.

Haier, R. J., Siegel, B. V., & MacLachlan, A. (1992). Regional glucose metabolic changes after learning a complex visuospatial/motor task: A positron emission tomography study. *Brain Research, 570,* 134–143.

Haier, R. J., Siegel, B. V., & Tang, C. (1992). Intelligence and changes in regional cerebral glucose metabolic rate following learning. *Intelligence, 16,* 415–426.

Haimov, I., & Lavie, P. (1996). Melatonin—A soporific hormone. *Current Directions in Psychological Science, 5,* 106–111.

Haley, J. (1976). *Problem-solving therapy.* San Francisco: Jossey-Bass.

Halikas, J. A., & Rimmer, J. D. (1974). Predictors of multiple drug abuse. *Archives of General Psychiatry, 31,* 414–418.

Hall, C. S. (1951). What people dream about. *Scientific American, 184,* 60–63.

Hall, C. S., & Lindzey, G. (1978). *Theories of personality* (3rd ed.). New York: Wiley.

Hall, G. S. (1904). *Adolescence.* New York: Appleton.

Halpern, D. (1992). *Sex differences in cognitive abilities* (2nd ed.). Hillsdale, NJ: Erlbaum.

Hamer, D. H., Hu, S., Magnuson, V. L., Hu, N., & Pattatucci, A. J. (1993). A linkage between DNA markers on the X chromosome and male sexual orientation. *Science, 261,* 321–327.

Hamilton, D. L., & Zanna, M. P. (1972). Differential weighting of favorable and unfavorable attributes in impressions of personality. *Journal of Experimental Research in Personality, 6,* 204–212.

Hamilton, G. V. (1978). Obedience and responsibility: A jury simulation. *Journal of Personality and Social Psychology, 36,* 126–146.

Hammen, C., Elliott, A., Gitlin, M., & Jamison, K. R. (1989). Sociotropy/autonomy and vulnerability to specific life events in patients with unipolar depression and bipolar disorders. *Journal of Abnormal Psychology, 98,* 154–160.

Hammen, C., Marks, T., Mayol, A., & deMayo, R. (1985). Depressive self-schema, life stress, and vulnerability to depression. *Journal of Abnormal Psychology, 94,* 308–319.

Hanawalt, H. F., & Demarest, I. H. (1939). The effect of verbal suggestion in the recall period upon the reproduction of visually perceived forms. *Journal of Experimental Psychology, 25,* 159–174.

Haney, C. (1980). Social psychology and the criminal law. In P. W. Middlebrook (Ed.), *Social psychology and modern life* (2nd ed.). New York: Knopf.

Hanson, D. R., Gottesman, I. I., & Heston, L. L. (1976). Some possible childhood indicators of adult schizophrenia. *British Journal of Psychiatry, 129,* 142–154.

Hanson, R. F., Kilpatrick, D. G., Freedy, J. R., & Saunders, B. E. (1995). Los Angeles County after the 1992 civil disturbances: Degree of exposure and impact on mental health. *Journal of Consulting and Clinical Psychology, 63,* 987–996.

Harlow, H. F. (1949). The formation of learning sets. *Psychological Review, 56,* 51–56.

Harlow, H. F., & Harlow, M. K. (1965). The affectional systems. In A. M. Schrier, H. F. Harlow, & F. Stollnitz (Eds.), *Behavior of nonhuman primates* (Vol. 2). London: Academic Press.

Harlow, H. F., Harlow, M. K., & Meyer, D. R. (1950). Learning motivated by a manipulation drive. *Journal of Experimental Psychology, 40,* 228–234.

Harlow, H. F., & Novak, M. A. (1973). Psychopathological perspectives. *Perspectives in Biology and Medicine, 16,* 461–478.

Harlow, H. F., & Suomi, S. J. (1970). Nature of love—simplified. *American Psychologist, 25,* 161–168.

Harlow, S. D., Goldberg, E. L., & Comstock, G. W. (1991). A longitudinal study of the prevalence of depressive symptomatology in elderly widowed and married women. *Archives of General Psychiatry, 48,* 1065–1068.

Harmon, T. M., Hyan, M. T., & Tyre, T. E. (1990). Improved obstetric outcomes using hypnotic analgesia and skill mastery combined with childbirth education. *Journal of Consulting and Clinical Psychology, 58,* 525–530.

Harris, T. G. (1973, July). As far as heroin is concerned, the worst is over. *Psychology Today,* pp. 68–79.

Hartley, D., Roback, H. R., & Abromowitz, S. F. (1976). Deterioration effects in encounter groups. *American Psychologist, 31,* 247–255.

Hartmann, E., Russ, D., Oldfield, M., Sivian, I., & Cooper, S. (1987). Who has nightmares? The personality of the lifelong nightmare sufferer. *Archives of General Psychiatry, 44,* 49–56.

Hatfield, E. (1988). Passionate and companionate love. In R. J. Sternberg & M. L. Barnes (Eds.), *The psychology of love.* New Haven: Yale University Press.

Hawton, K., & Osborn, M. (1984). Suicide and attempted suicide in children and adolescents. In B. B. Lahey & A. E. Kazdin (Eds.), *Advances in clinical child psychology* (Vol. 7, pp. 57–108). New York: Plenum.

Hayduck, L. A. (1983). Personal space: Where we now stand. *Psychological Bulletin, 94,* 293–335.

Hayes, J. R. (1978). *Cognitive psychology: Thinking and creating.* Homewood, IL: Dorsey Press.

Hayes, K. J., & Hayes, C. (1951). Intellectual development of a home-raised chimpanzee. *Proceedings of the American Philosophical Society, 95,* 105–109.

Hayflick, L. (1965). The limited *in vitro* lifetime of human diploid cell strains. *Experimental Cell Research, 37,* 614–636.

Hayflick, L. (1986). The cell biology of human aging. *Scientific American, 242,* 58–65.

Haynes, S. G., Feinleib, M., & Kannel, W. B. (1980). The relationship of psychosocial factors to coronary heart disease in the Framingham Study. Part III: Eight-year incidence of CHD. *American Journal of Epidemiology, 3,* 37–58.

Hebb, D. O. (1949). *Organization of behavior.* New York: Wiley.

Hedge, J. W., & Kavanagh, M. J. (1988). Improving the accuracy of performance evaluations: Comparison of three methods of performance appraiser training. *Journal of Applied Psychology, 73,* 68–73.

Hedges, L. V., & Nowell, A. (1995). Sex differences in mental test scores, variability, and numbers of high-scoring individuals. *Science, 269,* 41–45.

Heider, E. R., & Oliver, D. C. (1972). The structure of color space in naming and memory for two languages. *Cognitive Psychology, 3,* 337–354.

Heider, F. (1958). *The psychology of interpersonal relations.* New York: Wiley.

Heien, D. M., & Pittman, D. J. (1993). The external costs of alcohol abuse. *Journal of Studies on Alcohol, 54,* 302–307.

Heilman, M. E., & Herlihy, J. M. (1984). Affirmative action, negative reaction? Some moderating conditions. *Organizational Behavior and Human Performance, 33,* 204–213.

Heilman, M. E., Simon, M. C., & Repper, D. P. (1987). Intentionally favored, unintentionally harmed? Impact of sex-based preferential selection on self-perceptions and self-evaluations. *Journal of Applied Psychology, 72,* 62–68.

Heiman, J. R., & LoPiccolo, J. (1983). Clinical outcome of sex therapy: Effects of daily versus weekly treatment. *Archives of General Psychiatry, 40,* 443–449.

Held, R., & Hein, A. (1963). Movement-produced stimulation in the development of visually guided behavior. *Journal of Comparative and Physiological Psychology, 56,* 23–44.

Helgesen, S. (1990). *The female advantage: Women's ways of leadership.* New York: Doubleday Currency.

Heller, K., Swindle, R. W., & Dusenbury, L. (1986). Components of social support processes. *Journal of Consulting and Clinical Psychology, 54,* 466–470.

Helson, R., & Moane, G. (1987). Personality change in women from college to midlife. *Journal of Personality and Social Psychology, 53,* 176–186.

Hennekens, C. H., Rosner, B., & Cole, D. S. (1978). Daily alcohol consumption and fatal coronary heart disease. *American Journal of Epidemiology, 107,* 196–200.

Henriques, J. B., & Davidson, R. J. (1990). Regional brain asymmetries discriminate between previously depressed and healthy control subjects. *Journal of Abnormal Psychology, 99,* 22–31.

Herbert, T. B., & Cohen, S. (1993). Depression and immunity: A meta-analytic review. *Psychological Bulletin, 113,* 472–486.

Herek, G. M. (1990). Gay people and government security clearance. *American Psychologist, 45,* 1035–1042.

Herek, G. M. (1993). Sexual orientation and military service: A social science perspective. *American Psychologist, 48,* 538–549.

Heron, W. (1957). The pathology of boredom. *Scientific American, 196,* 52–69.

Herrnstein, R. (1971). IQ. *The Atlantic Monthly, 228,* 43–64.

Herrnstein, R. J., & Murray, C. (1994). *The bell curve: Intelligence and class structure in American life.* New York: The Free Press.

Hervey, G. P. (1959). The effects of lesions in the hypothalamus in parabiotic rats. *Journal of Physiology, 145,* 336–352.

Hess, E. H. (1975, November). The role of pupil size in communication. *Scientific American,* 110–119.

Heston, L. L. (1966). Psychiatric disorder in foster home-reared children of schizophrenic mothers. *British Journal of Psychiatry, 112,* 819–825.

Hetherington, M. (1979). Divorce: A children's perspective. *American Psychologist, 34,* 851–858.

Hewitt, P. L., & Flett, G. L. (1993). Dimensions of perfectionism, daily stress, and depression: A test of the specific vulnerability hypothesis. *Journal of Abnormal Psychology, 102,* 58–65.

Hilgard, E. R. (1975). Hypnosis. *Annual Review of Psychology, 26,* 19–44.

Hilgard, E. R. (1978). Hypnosis and pain. In R. A. Sternbach (Ed.), *The psychology of pain.* New York: Raven Press.

Hilgard, E. R. (1980). Consciousness in contemporary psychology. In M. R. Rosenzweig & L. W. Porter (Eds.), *Annual review of psychology* (Vol. 31). Palo Alto, CA: Annual Reviews.

Hilgard, E. R., & Hilgard, J. R. (1975). *Hypnosis in the relief of pain.* Los Altos, CA: William Kaufmann.

Hill, C., Rubin, Z., & Peplau, L. (1976). Breakups before marriage: The end of 103 affairs. *Journal of Social Issues, 32,* 147–168.

Hill, E. M., Nocks, E. S., & Gardner, L. (1987). Physical attractiveness: Manipulation by physique and status displays. *Ethology and Sociobiology, 8,* 143–154.

Hirst, W. (1982). The amnesic syndrome: Descriptions and explanations. *Psychological Bulletin, 91,* 435–460.

Hobson, J. A. (1989). *Sleep.* New York: Scientific American Library.

Hochberg, J. (1988). Visual perception. In R. C. Atkison, R. J. Herrnstein, G. Lindzey, & R. D. Luce (Eds.), *Stevens' handbook of experimental psychology: Vol. 1. Perception and motivation.* New York: Wiley-Interscience.

Hoffman, C., Lau, L., & Johnson, D. R. (1986). The linguistic relativity of person cognition: An English-Chinese comparison. *Journal of Personality and Social Psychology, 51,* 1097–1105.

Hoffman, L. W. (1989). Effects of maternal employment in the two-parent family. *American Psychologist, 44,* 283–292.

Hogan, R., Mankin, D., Conway, J., & Fox, S. (1970). Personality correlates of undergraduate marijuana use. *Journal of Consulting and Clinical Psychology, 35,* 58–63.

Hokanson, J. E., DeGood, D. E., Forrest, M. S., & Brittain, T. M. (1963). Availability of avoidance behaviors for modulating vascular-stress responses. *Journal of Personality and Social Psychology, 67,* 60–68.

Holahan, C. J., & Moos, R. H. (1987). Risk, resistance, and psychological distress: A longitudinal analysis with adults and children. *Journal of Abnormal Psychology, 96,* 3–13.

Holden, C. (1973). Psychosurgery: Legitimate therapy or laundered lobotomy? *Science, 179,* 1109–1112.

Hole, J. W. (1990). *Human anatomy and physiology* (5th ed.). Dubuque, IA: Wm. C. Brown Publishers.

Holinger, P. C., & Offer, D. (1993). *Adolescent suicide.* New York: Guilford Press.

Hollander, E. P., & Offermann, L. R. (1990). Power and leadership in organizations: Relations in transition. *American Psychologist, 45,* 179–189.

Hollon, S. D., Shelton, R. C., & Davis, D. D. (1993). Cognitive therapy for depression: Conceptual issues and clinical efficacy. *Journal of Consulting and Clinical Psychology, 61,* 270–275.

Holmes, D. S. (1984). Meditation and somatic arousal: A review of experimental evidence. *American Psychologist, 39,* 1–10.

Holmes, T. H., & Rahe, R. H. (1967). The social readjustment rating scale. *Journal of Psychosomatic Research, 11,* 213–218.

Holroyd, K. A., & Lazarus, R. S. (1982). Stress, coping, and somatic adaptation. In L. Goldberger & S. Breznitz (Eds.), *Handbook of stress.* New York: The Free Press.

Honeck, R. P. (1973). Interpretive vs. structural effects on semantic memory. *Journal of Verbal Learning and Verbal Behavior, 12,* 448–455.

Hopkin, K. (1995). Sugar 'n spice vs. puppy-dog tails: Sex differences in the brain. *Journal of NIH Research, 7,* 39–43.

Hopkins, J., Marcus, M., & Campbell, S. B. (1984). Postpartum depression: A critical review. *Psychological Bulletin, 95,* 498–515.

Horgan, J. (1993). Eugenics revisited. *Scientific American, 208,* June, 122–131.

Horne, J. (1988). *Why we sleep: The functions of sleep in humans and other mammals.* New York: Oxford University Press.

Horner, M. S. (1969, March). Fail: Bright women. *Psychology Today,* pp. 36–38.

Horney, K. (1937). *The neurotic personality of our time.* New York: Norton.

Hosken, F. P. (1979). *The Hosken report: Genital and sexual mutilation of females* (2nd ed.). Lexington, MA: Women's International Network News.

Hotelling, K. (1991). Sexual harassment: A problem shielded by silence. *Journal of Consulting and Clinical Psychology, 69,* 487–501.

Hough, R. L., et al. (1987). Utilization of health and mental health services by Los Angeles Mexican-Americans and non-Hispanic whites. *Archives of General Psychiatry, 44,* 702–709.

House, W. C. (1974). Actual and perceived differences in male and female expectancies and minimal goal levels as a function of competition. *Journal of Personality, 42,* 493–509.

Houston, J. P. (1985). *Motivation.* New York: Macmillan.

Hovland, C. I. (Ed.). (1957). *The order of presentation in persuasion.* New Haven: Yale University Press.

Hovland, C. I., & Weiss, W. (1951). The influence of source credibility on communication effectiveness. *The Public Opinion Quarterly, 15,* 635–650.

Howard, A., Pion, G. M., Gottfredson, G. D., Flattau, P. E., Oskamp, S., Pfafflin, S. M., Bray, D. W., & Burnstein, A. G. (1986). The changing face of American Psychology. *American Psychologist, 41,* 1311–1327.

Howell, W. C. (1993). Engineering psychology in a changing world. *Annual Review of Psychology, 44,* 231–263.

Hubel, D. H. (1979). The brain. *Scientific American, 241,* 44–53.

Huesman, L. R., Gruder, C. L., & Dorst, G. A. (1987). A process model of posthypnotic amnesia. *Cognitive Psychology, 19,* 33–62.

Hugdahl, K., & Karker, A. C. (1981). Biological versus experiential factors in phobic conditioning. *Behaviour Research and Therapy, 16,* 315–321.

Hughes, J., & Sandler, B. (1987). *Friends raping friends: Could it happen to you?* Washington: Project on the Status and Education of Women, Association of American Colleges.

Hughes, J. R., Oliveto, A. H., Helzer, J., Higgins, S. R., & Bickel, W. K. (1992). Should caffeine abuse, dependence, or withdrawal be added to DSM-IV and ICD-10? *American Journal of Psychiatry, 149,* 33–40.

Hultsch, D. F., & Deutsch, F. (1981). *Adult development and aging: A life-span perspective.* New York: McGraw-Hill.

Hundert, A. J., & Greenfield, N. (1969). *Physical space and organizational behavior: A study of an office landscape.* Paper presented to the American Psychological Association, Los Angeles.

Hunt, E. (1995). The role of intelligence in modern society. *American Scientist, 83,* 356–368.

Hunt, M. (1975). *Sexual behavior in the 1970s.* New York: Dell.

Hunter, J. E. (1979). *An analysis of the validity, test fairness, and utility for the Philadelphia Police Officers Selection Examination prepared by Educational Testing Service.* Report to the Philadelphia Federal District Court, Alvarez v. City of Philadelphia.

Hunter, J. E. (1981). *The economic benefits of personnel selection using ability tests: A state-of-the-art review including a detailed analysis of the dollar benefit of U.S. Employment Office placements and a critique of the low-cutoff method of test use.* Washington, DC: U.S. Employment Service, U.S. Department of Labor.

Hunter, J. E., & Hunter, R. F. (1984). Validity and utility of alternative predictors of job performance. *Psychological Bulletin, 96,* 72–98.

Hyde, J. S. (1981). How large are cognitive gender differences? A meta-analysis using omega-squared and d. *American Psychologist, 36,* 892–901.

Hyde, J. S. (1985). *Half the human experience: The psychology of women.* Lexington, MA: D. C. Heath.

Hyde, J. S., Fennema, E., & Lamon, S. J. (1990). Gender differences in mathematics performance: A meta-analysis. *Psychological Bulletin, 107,* 139–155.

Hyde, J. S., & Linn, M. C. (1988). *The psychology of gender: Advances through meta-analysis.* Baltimore: Johns Hopkins Press.

Hyde, J. S., & Plant, E. A. (1995). Magnitude of psychological gender differences: Another side to the story. *American Psychologist, 50,* 159–161.

Iacocca, L. (1984). *Iacocca: An autobiography.* New York: Bantam Books.

Iaffaldano, M. T., & Muchinsky, P. M. (1985). Job satisfaction and job performance. A meta-analysis. *Psychological Bulletin, 97,* 251–273.

Ilgen, D. R. (1990). Health issues at work: Opportunities for industrial/organizational psychologists. *American Psychologist, 45,* 273–283.

Ingham, A. G., Levinger, B., Graves, J., & Peckham, V. (1974). The Ringelmann effect: Studies of group size and group performance. *Journal of Experimental Social Psychology, 10,* 371–384.

Inhelder, B., & Piaget, J. (1958). *The growth of logical thinking from childhood to adolescence.* New York: Basic Books.

Irons, E. D., & Moore, G. W. (1985). *Black managers: The case of the banking industry.* New York: Praeger.

Ironson, G., & Schneiderman, N. (1991). Psychoimmunology and HIV-1: Scope of the problem. In N. Schneiderman et al. (Ed.), *Psychoimmunology and HIV-1.* Geneva: World Health Organization.

Irwin, M., Daniels, M., Bloom, E. T., Smith, T. L., & Weiner, H. (1987). Life events, depressive symptoms, and immune function. *American Journal of Psychiatry, 144,* 437–441.

Irwin, M., et al. (1990). Major depression disorder, alcoholism, and reduced natural killer cell cytotoxicity. *Archives of General Psychiatry, 47,* 713–719.

Isen, A. M., & Levin, P. F. (1972). The effect of feeling good on helping: Cookies and kindness. *Journal of Personality and Social Psychology, 21,* 384–388.

Iverson, L. L. (1979). The chemistry of the brain. *Scientific American, 241,* 134–149.

Izard, C. E. (1972). *Patterns of emotions: A new analysis of anxiety and depression.* New York: Academic Press.

Izard, C. E. (1977). *Human emotions.* New York: Plenum.

Izard, C. E. (1978). Emotions as motivations: An evolutionary-developmental perspective. In H. E. Howe & R. A. Dienstbeier (Eds.), *Nebraska Symposium on Motivation* (Vol. 26). Lincoln: University of Nebraska Press.

Izard, C. E. (1991). *The psychology of emotions.* New York: Plenum Press.

Jacobs, B. L. (1976, March). Serotonin: The crucial substance that turns dreams on and off. *Psychology Today,* pp. 70–71.

Jacobsen, M. B., & Koch, W. (1977). Women as leaders: Performance evaluation as a function of the method of leader selection. *Organizational Behavior and Human Performance, 20,* 149–157.

Jacobson, E. (1938). *Progressive relaxation.* Chicago: University of Chicago Press.

James, W. (1890). *The principles of psychology.* New York: Holt, Rinehart & Winston.

Janis, I. L. (1982). *Groupthink: Psychological studies of policy decisions and fiascoes.* Boston: Houghton-Mifflin.

Janis, I. L. (1983). The role of social support in adherence to stressful decisions. *American Psychologist, 38,* 143–160.

Janis, I. L., & Hoffman, D. (1982). Effective partnerships in a clinic for smokers. In I. L. Janis (Ed.), *Counseling on personal decisions: Theory and research on short-term helping relationships.* New Haven: Yale University Press.

Jeffrey, R. W. (1988). Risk behaviors and health: Contrasting individual and population perspectives. *American Psychologist, 44,* 1194–1202.

Jenkins, C. D. (1988). Dietary risk factors and their modification in cardiovascular disease. *Journal of Consulting and Clinical Psychology, 56,* 350–357.

Jenkins, R. W. (1988). Epidemiology of cardiovascular diseases. *Journal of Consulting and Clinical Psychology, 56,* 324–332.

Jenkins-Hall, K., & Sacco, W. P. (1991). Effect of client race and depression on evaluations by White therapists. *Journal of Social and Clinical Psychology, 10,* 3, 322–333.

Jensen, A. R. (1973). *Educability and group differences.* New York: Harper & Row.

Jensen, A. R. (1980). *Bias in mental testing.* New York: The Free Press.

Jernigan, T. L., Archibald, S. L., Berhow, M. T., Sowell, E. R., Foster, D. S., & Hesselink, J. R. (1991). Cerebral structure on MRI, Part I: Localization of age-related changes. *Biological Psychiatry, 29,* 55–67.

Jessor, S. L., & Jessor, R. (1975). Transition from virginity to nonvirginity among youth: A social-psychological study over time. *Developmental Psychology, 11,* 473–484.

Johnson, M. K., Bransford, J. P., & Solomon, S. (1973). Memory for tacit implications of sentences. *Journal of Experimental Psychology, 98,* 203–205.

Jones, E., Bell, L., & Aronson, E. (1971). The reciprocation of attraction from similar and dissimilar others: A study in person perception and evaluation. In C. McClintock (Ed.), *Experimental social psychology.* New York: Holt, Rinehart & Winston.

Jones, G. V. (1983). Identifying basic categories. *Psychological Bulletin, 94,* 423–428.

Jones, L. V. (1984). White-black achievement differences: The narrowing gap. *American Psychologist, 39,* 1207–1213.

Jones, M. C. (1924). A laboratory study of fear: The case of Peter. *Pedagogical Seminary, 31,* 308–315.

Jones, M. C. (1965). Psychological correlates of somatic development. *Child Development, 36,* 899–911.

Jones, M. C., & Bayley, N. (1950). Physical maturing among boys as related to behavior. *Journal of Educational Psychology, 41,* 129–148.

Jones, M. C., & Mussen, P. H. (1958). Self-conceptions, motivations, and interpersonal attitudes of early- and late-maturing girls. *Child Development, 29,* 491–501.

Jones, R. (1977). *The other generation: The new power of older people.* Englewood Cliffs, NJ: Prentice-Hall.

Jorgensen, R. S., Nash, J. K., Lasser, N. L., Hymowitz, N., & Langer, A. W. (1988). Heart rate acceleration and its relationship to total serum cholesterol, triglycerides, and blood pressure. *Psychophysiology, 25,* 39–44.

Julian, J. (1973). *Social problems.* Englewood Cliffs, NJ: Prentice-Hall.

Jung, J. (1978). *Understanding human motivation: A cognitive approach.* New York: Macmillan.

Jurow, G. L. (1971). New data on the effects of a "death-qualified" jury on the guilt determination process. *Harvard Law Review, 84,* 567–611.

Kagan, J. (1978). *The growth of the child.* New York: Norton.

Kagan, J. (1984). *The nature of the child.* New York: Basic Books.

Kagan, J., & Moss, H. A. (1962). *Birth to maturity: A study in psychological development.* New York: Wiley.

Kahneman, D., & Tversky, A. (1982). The psychology of preferences. *Scientific American, 246,* 160–173.

Kail, R. (1984). *The development of memory in children.* San Francisco: W. H. Freeman.

Kalichman, S. C. (1989). Sex roles and sex differences in adult spatial performance. *Journal of Genetic Psychology, 150,* 93–100.

Kalichman, S. C. (1990). Affective and personality characteristics of replicated MMPI profile subgroups of incarcerated adult rapists. *Archives of Sexual Behavior, 19,* 443–459.

Kalichman, S. C., & Hunter, T. (1992). Disclosure of celebrity HIV infection: Effects on public attitudes. *American Journal of Public Health, 82,* 1374–1376.

Kalichman, S. C., Hunter, T. L., & Kelly, J. A. (1992). Perceptions of AIDS susceptibility among minority and nonminority women at risk for HIV infection. *Journal of Consulting and Clinical Psychology, 60,* 725–732.

Kalish, R. A., & Reynolds, D. K. (1976). *Death and ethnicity: A psychocultural study.* Los Angeles: University of Southern California Press.

Kallmann, W. D., & Gilmore, J. D. (1981). Vascular disorders. In S. M. Turner, K. S. Calhoun, & H. E. Adams (Eds.), *Handbook of clinical behavior therapy.* New York: Wiley.

Kamarck, T., & Jennings, J. R. (1991). Biobehavioral factors in sudden cardiac death. *Psychological Bulletin, 109,* 42–75.

Kamin, L. J. (1974). *The science and politics of IQ.* Potomac, MD: Lawrence Erlbaum.

Kandel, E. R., & Hawkins, R. D. (1992). The biological basis of learning and individuality. *Scientific American, 267,* 79–86.

Kandel, E. R., & Schwartz, J. H. (1982). Molecular biology of learning: Modulation of transmitter release. *Science, 218,* 433–443.

Kandel, E. R., & Schwartz, J. H. (Eds.). (1985). *Principles of neuroscience* (2nd ed.). New York: Elsevier.

Kandel, E. R., Schwartz, J. H., & Jessel, T. M. (1995). *Essentials of neural science and behavior.* East Norwalk, CT: Appleton & Lange.

Kanfer, F. H., & Phillips, J. S. (1970). *Learning foundations of behavior therapy.* New York: Wiley.

Kaniasty, K., & Norris, F. H. (1995). Mobilization and deterioration of social support following natural disasters. *Current Directions in Psychological Science, 4,* 94–98.

Kaplan, H. S. (1983). *The evaluation of sexual disorders.* New York: Brunner/Mazel.

Kaplan, M. F. (1975). Information integration in social judgment: Interaction of judge and informational components. In M. F. Kaplan & S. Schwartz (Eds.), *Human judgment and decision processes.* New York: Academic Press.

Kasper, S., Rogers, S. L. B., Yancey, A., Shulz, P. M., Skwerer, R. G., & Rosenthal, N. E. (1989). Phototherapy in individuals with and without subsyndromal seasonal affective disorder. *Archives of General Psychiatry, 46,* 837–844.

Kasper, S., Wehr, T. A., Bartko, J. J., Gaist, P. A., & Rosenthal, N. E. (1989). Epidemiological findings of seasonal changes in mood and behavior. *Archives of General Psychiatry, 46,* 823–833.

Kassin, S. M., Ellsworth, P. C., & Kassin, S. M. (1989). The "general acceptance" of psychological research on eyewitness testimony: A survey of experts. *American Psychologist, 44,* 1089–1098.

Katz, J., Weiner, H., Gallagher, T., & Hellman, L. (1970). Stress, distress, and ego defenses. *Archives of General Psychiatry, 23,* 131–142.

Kaye, K. (1967). Infant sucking behavior and its modification. In L. P. Lipsitt & C. C. Spiker (Eds.), *Advances in child development and behavior* (Vol. 3). New York: Academic Press.

Keane, T. M., & Kaloupek, D. G. (1982). Imaginal flooding in the treatment of posttraumatic stress disorder. *Journal of Consulting and Clinical Psychology, 50,* 138–140.

Kearins, J. (1986). Visual spatial memory in aboriginal and White Australian children. *Australian Journal of Psychology, 38,* 3, 203–214.

Keenan, K. (in press). Social and developmental influences on young girls' behavioral and emotional problems. *Psychological Bulletin.*

Kehoe, P., & Bass, E. M. (1986). Conditioned aversions and their memories in 5-day-old rats during suckling. *Journal of Experimental Psychology: Animal Behavior Processes, 12,* 40–47.

Keller, M. B., Lavori, P. W., Mueller, T. I., Endicott, J., Coryell, W., Hirschfeld, R. M. A., & Shea, T. (1992). Time to recovery, chronicity, and levels of psychopathology in major depression: A five-year prospective follow-up of 431 subjects. *Archives of General Psychiatry, 49,* 809–816.

Kelley, H. H. (1973). The processes of causal attribution. *American Psychologist, 28,* 107–128.

Kellogg, W. N., & Kellogg, L. A. (1933). *The ape and the child.* New York: McGraw-Hill.

Kelly, G. A. (1955). *The psychology of personal constructs.* New York: Norton.

Kelly, J. A., St. Lawrence, J. S., Hood, H. V., & Brasfield, T. L. (1989). Behavioral intervention to reduce AIDS risk activities. *Journal of Consulting and Clinical Psychology, 57,* 60–67.

Kelsoe, J. R., Cadet, J. L., Pickar, D., & Weinberger, D. R. (1988). Quantitative neuroanatomy in schizophrenia: A controlled magnetic resonance imaging study. *Archives of General Psychiatry, 45,* 533–541.

Kendall, P. C., & Norton-Ford, J. D. (1982). *Clinical psychology: Scientific and professional dimensions.* New York: Wiley.

Kendall-Tackett, K. A., Williams, L. M., & Finkelhor, D. (1993). Impact of sexual abuse on children: A review and synthesis of recent empirical studies. *Psychological Bulletin, 113,* 164–180.

Kendler, K. S., Heath, A. C., Martin, N. G., & Eaves, L. J. (1992). Symptoms of anxiety and symptoms of depression: Same genes, different environments? *Archives of General Psychiatry, 44,* 451–457.

Kendler, K. S., Neale, M. C., Kessler, R. C., Heath, A. C., & Eaves, L. J. (1992). The genetic epidemiology of phobias in women: The interrelationship of agoraphobia, social phobia, situational phobia, and simple phobia. *Archives of General Psychiatry, 49,* 273–281.

Kephart, W. (1967). Some correlates of romantic love. *Journal of Marriage and the Family, 29,* 470–474.

Kessler, R. C., McGonagle, Z. S., Nelson, C. B., Hughes, M., Eshelman, S., Wittchen, H. U., & Kendler, K. S. (1993). Lifetime and 12-month prevalence of DSM-III-R psychiatric disorders in the United States: Results from the National Comorbidity Survey. *Archives of General Psychiatry, 51,* 8–19.

Kessler, R. C., Sonnega, A., Bromet, E., Hughes, M., & Nelson, C. B. (1995). Posttraumatic stress disorder in the national comorbidity survey. *Archives of General Psychiatry, 52,* 1048–1060.

Kiecolt-Glaser, J. K., Fisher, L. D., Orgrocki, P., Stout, J. C., Speicher, C. E., & Glaser, R. (1987). Marital quality, marital disruption, and immune function. *Psychosomatic Medicine, 49,* 13–30.

Kilmann, P., & Sotile, W. (1976). The marathon encounter group: A review of the outcome literature. *Psychological Bulletin, 83,* 827–850.

Kilpatrick, D. G., Best, C. L., Veronen, L. J., Amick, A. E., Villeponteaux, L. A., & Ruff, G. A. (1985). Mental health correlates of criminal victimization: A random community survey. *Journal of Consulting and Clinical Psychology, 53,* 866–873.

Kilpatrick, D., Resick, P., & Veronen, S. (1981). Long-term effects of rape on the victim. *Journal of Social Issues, 37,* 105–122.

Kimball, M. M. (1989). A new perspective on women's math achievement. *Psychological Bulletin, 105,* 198–214.

Kimmel, E. B. (1992). Women's contributions to psychology. *Contemporary Psychology, 37,* 201–202.

Kinsbourne, M. (1981, May). Sad hemisphere, happy hemisphere. *Psychology Today,* p. 92.

Kinsbourne, M. (1988). *Cerebral dysfunction in depression.* Washington, DC: American Psychiatric Association Press.

Kinsey, A. C., Pomeroy, W. B., & Martin, C. E. (1948). *Sexual behavior in the human male.* Philadelphia: W. B. Saunders.

Kinsey, A. C., Pomeroy, W. B., & Martin, C. E. (1953). *Sexual behavior in the human female.* Philadelphia: W. B. Saunders.

Kirsch, I., & Lynn, S. J. (1995). The altered state of hypnosis: Changes in the theoretical landscape. *American Psychologist, 50,* 846–858.

Kitayama, S., & Markus, H. R. (1992). Construal of the self as cultural frame: Implications for the internationalizing psychology. Paper presented to the symposium on internationalizing higher education, Ann Arbor, University of Michigan.

Klatzky, R. L. (1980). *Human memory: Structures and processes.* San Francisco: W. H. Freeman.

Kleitman, N. (1960). The nature of dreaming. In G. E. W. Wolstenholme & M. O'Connor (Eds.), *Ciba Foundation symposium on the nature of sleep.* Boston: Little, Brown.

Koegel, P., Burnam, A., & Farr, R. K. (1988). The prevalence of specific psychiatric disorders among homeless individuals in the inner city of Los Angeles. *Archives of General Psychiatry, 45,* 1085–1092.

Kohlberg, L. (1964). The development of moral character. In M. L. Hoffman & L. W. Hoffman (Eds.), *Review of child development research* (Vol. I). New York: Russell Sage Foundation, p. 400.

Kohlberg, L. (1966). A cognitive-developmental analysis of children's sex-role concepts and attitudes. In E. E. Maccoby (Ed.), *The development of sex differences.* Stanford, CA: Stanford University Press.

Kohlberg, L. (1969). Stage and sequence: The cognitive-developmental approach to socialization. In D. A. Goslin (Ed.), *Handbook of socialization theory and research.* Chicago: Rand McNally.

Köhler, W. (1969). *The task of gestalt psychology.* Princeton, NJ: Princeton University Press.

Kohn, A. (1987). Shattered innocence. *Psychology Today, 21,* 54–58.

Kolb, L. C. (1977). *Modern clinical psychiatry* (9th ed.). Philadelphia: W. B. Saunders.

Korman, A. K. (1974). *The psychology of motivation.* Englewood Cliffs, NJ: Prentice-Hall.

Koss, M. P. (1990). The women's mental health research agenda: Violence against women. *American Psychologist, 45,* 374–380.

Koss, M. P., Gidycz, C. A., & Wisniewski, N. (1987). The scope of rape: Incidence and prevalence of sexual aggression and victimization in a national sample of higher education students. *Journal of Consulting and Clinical Psychology, 55,* 162–170.

Koss, M., Leonard, K., Beezley, D., & Oros, C. (1985). Nonstranger sexual aggression: A discriminant analysis of the psychological characteristics of undetected offenders. *Sex Roles, 12,* 981–992.

Koss, M., & Oros, C. (1982). Sexual experiences survey: A research instrument investigating sexual aggression and victimization. *Journal of Consulting and Clinical Psychology, 50,* 455–457.

Krasner, L. (1988). Mary Cover Jones: A legend in her own time. *The Behavior Therapist, 11,* 101–102.

Krause, N. (1987). Chronic financial strain, social support, and depressive symptoms among older adults. *Psychology and Aging, 2,* 185–192.

Kravitz, D. A., & Martin, B. (1986). Ringelmann rediscovered: The original article. *Journal of Personality and Social Psychology, 50,* 936–941.

Kreps, J., & Spengler, J. (1973). Future options for more free time. In F. Best (Ed.), *The future of work.* Englewood Cliffs, NJ: Prentice-Hall.

Kroger, W. S., & Douce, R. G. (1979). Hypnosis in criminal investigation. *International Journal of Clinical and Experimental Hypnosis, 27,* 358–384.

Krueger, R. W. C. F. (1929). The effect of overlearning on retention. *Journal of Experimental Psychology, 12,* 71–78.

Kruglanski, A. W. (1986, August). Freeze-think and the Challenger. *Psychology Today,* pp. 48–49.

Kübler-Ross, E. (1969). *On death and dying.* New York: Macmillan.

Kübler-Ross, E. (1974). *Questions and answers on death and dying.* Englewood Cliffs, NJ: Prentice-Hall.

Kuch, K., & Cox, B. J. (1992). Symptoms of PTSD in 124 survivors of the holocaust. *American Journal of Psychiatry, 149,* 337–340.

Kunugi, H., Nanko, S., et al. (1995). Schizophrenia following in utero exposure to the 1957 influenza epidemics in Japan. *American Journal of Psychiatry, 152,* 450–452.

Labov, W. (1970). The logic of nonstandard English. In F. Williams (Ed.), *Language and poverty: Perspectives on a theme.* Chicago: Markham.

LaCroix, A. Z., Mead, L. A., Liang, K., Thomas, C. B., & Pearson, T. P. (1986). Coffee consumption and the incidence of coronary heart disease. *New England Journal of Medicine, 315,* 977–982.

Lader, M. H., & Mathews, A. (1970). Physiological changes during spontaneous panic attacks. *Journal of Psychosomatic Research, 14,* 377–382.

Lahey, B. B. (1973). Minority group languages. In B. B. Lahey (Ed.), *The modification of language behavior.* Springfield: Charles C. Thomas.

Lahey, B. B., & Ciminero, A. R. (1980). *Maladaptive behavior.* Glenview, IL: Scott, Foresman.

Lahey, B. B., Hartdagen, S. E., Frick, P. J., McBurnett, K., Connor, R., & Hyrd, G. W. (1988). Conduct disorder: Parsing the confounded relation to parental divorce and antisocial personality. *Journal of Abnormal Psychology, 97,* 334–337.

Lamb, H. R., & Weinberger, L. E. (1992). Conservatorship for gravely disabled psychiatric patients: A four-year follow-up study. *American Journal of Psychiatry, 149,* 909–913.

Lang, P. J. (1995). The emotion probe: Studies of motivation and attention. *American Psychologist, 5,* 372–385.

Lange, C. G. (1922). *The emotions.* Baltimore, MD: Williams & Williams.

Langlois, J. H., & Stephan, C. W. (1981). Beauty and the beast: The role of physical attractiveness in the development of peer relations and social behavior. In S. S. Brehm, S. M. Kassin, & F. X. Gibbons (Eds.), *Developmental social psychology.* New York: Oxford University Press.

Lapierre, A., Schneiderman, N., Antoni, M. H., & Fletcher, M. A. (1990). Aerobic exercise training and the psychoimmunology of AIDS. In A. Baum & L. Temoshok (Eds.), *Psychological aspects of AIDS.* Hillsdale, NJ: Erlbaum.

Larsen, R. J., & Kasimatis, M. (1990). Individual differences in entrainment of mood to the weekly calendar. *Journal of Personality and Social Psychology, 58,* 164–171.

Latané, B., & Darley, J. (1970). *The unresponsive bystander: Why doesn't he help?* New York: Appleton-Century-Crofts.

Latané, B., & Nida, S. (1981). Ten years of research on group size and helping. *Psychological Bulletin, 89,* 308–324.

Latané, B., & Rodin, J. (1969). A lady in distress: Inhibiting effects of friends and strangers on bystander intervention. *Journal of Experimental Social Psychology, 5,* 189–202.

Latané, B., Williams, K., & Harkins, S. (1979). Too many hands make light the work: The causes and consequences of social loafing. *Journal of Personality and Social Psychology, 37,* 822–832.

Laudenslager, M. L., Ryan, S. M., Drugan, R. C., Hyson, R. L., & Maier, S. F. (1983). Coping and immuno-suppression: Inescapable but not escapable shock suppresses lymphocyte proliferation. *Science, 221,* 568–570.

Lauer, C., Rieman, D., Lund, D., & Berger, M. (1987). Shortened REM latency: A consequence of psychological strain? *Psychophysiology, 24,* 263–271.

Lazarus, R. S. (1982). Thoughts on the relations between emotion and cognition. *American Psychologist, 37,* 1019–1024.

Lazarus, R. S. (1984). On the primacy of cognition. *American Psychologist, 39,* 117–123.

Lazarus, R. S. (1991). *Emotion and adaptation.* New York: Oxford University Press.

Lazarus, R. S., & Launier, R. (1978). Stress-related transactions between person and environment. In L. A. Pervin & M. Lewis (Eds.), *Perspectives in interactional psychology.* New York: Plenum.

Lee, K. A., Vaillant, G. E., Torrey, W. C., & Elder, G. H. (1995). A 50-year prospective study of the psychological sequelae of World War II combat. *American Journal of Psychiatry, 152,* 4.

Lehman, D. R., Wortman, C. B., & Williams, A. F. (1987). Long-term effects of losing a spouse or child in a motor vehicle crash. *Journal of Personality and Social Psychology, 52,* 218–231.

Lenneberg, E. H. (1967). *Biological foundations of language.* New York: Wiley.

Lennison, D. J. (1987). A conception of adult development. *American Psychologist, 41,* 3–13.

Leon, A. S. (1983). Exercise and coronary heart disease. *Hospital Medicine, 19,* 38–59.

Leon, G. R. (1977). *Case histories of deviant behavior: An interactional perspective* (2nd ed.). Boston: Holbrook Press.

Leonard, W. E. (1928). *The locomotive god.* London: Chapman & Hall.

Lepper, M. R., Greene, D., & Nisbett, R. E. (1973). Undermining children's intrinsic interest with extrinsic reward: A test of the "overjustification" hypothesis. *Journal of Personality and Social Psychology, 28,* 129–137.

LeVay, S. (1991). A difference in hypothalamic structure between heterosexual and homosexual men. *Science, 253,* 1034–1037.

Leventhal, H., & Tomarken, A. J. (1986). Emotion: today's problem. *Annual Review of Psychology, 37,* 565–610.

Levine, C., Kohlberg, L., & Hewer, A. (1985). The current formulation of Kohlberg's theory in response to critics. *Human Development, 28,* 94–100.

Levine, J. D., Gordon, N. C., & Fields, H. C. (1979). The role of endorphin in placebo analgesia. In J. J. Bonica, J. G. Liebeskind, & D. Albe-Fressard (Eds.),

Advances in pain research and therapy (Vol. 3). New York: Raven Press.

Levine, J., et al. (1987). The role of denial in recovery from coronary heart disease. *Psychosomatic Medicine, 49,* 109–117.

Levine, J. M., Resnick, L. B., & Higgins, E. T. (1993). Social foundations of cognition. *Annual Review of Psychology, 44,* 585–612.

Levinson, D. J. (1978). *The seasons of a man's life.* New York: Knopf.

Levinson, D. J. (1986). A conception of adult development. *American Psychologist, 41,* 3–13.

Levy, J. (1985). Right brain, left brain: Fact and fiction. *Psychology Today,* May, 38–44.

Levy, R., & Moskowitz, J. (1982). Cardiovascular research: Decades of progress, a decade of promise. *Science, 217,* 121–128.

Lewin, K. (1931). Environmental forces in child behavior and development. In C. Murchison (Ed.), *A handbook of child psychology.* Worcester, MA: Clark University Press.

Lewinsohn, P. M., Duncan, E. M., Stanton, A. K., & Hautzinger, M. (1986). Age at first onset for nonbipolar depression. *Journal of Abnormal Psychology, 95,* 378–383.

Lewinsohn, P. M., Hoberman, H. M., & Rosenbaum, M. (1988). A prospective study of risk factors for major depression. *Journal of Abnormal Psychology, 97,* 251–264.

Lewinsohn, P. M., Mischel, W., Chaplin, W., & Barton, R. (1980). Social competence and depression: The role of illusory self-perceptions. *Journal of Abnormal Psychology, 89,* 203–212.

Lewis, M., & Rosenblum, L. A. (Eds.). (1978). *The development of affect.* New York: Plenum.

Lewontin, R. (1982). *Human diversity.* New York: Scientific American Library.

Lezak, M. D. (1976). *Neuropsychological assessment.* New York: Oxford University Press.

Liebert, R. M., Neale, J. M., & Davidson, E. S. (1983). *The early window: The effects of television on children and youth.* New York: Pergamon Press.

Likert, R. (1967). *The human organization: Its management and value.* New York: McGraw-Hill.

Lindsey, K. P., & Paul, G. L. (1989). Involuntary commitment to public mental institutions: Issues involving the overrepresentation of blacks as assessment of relevant functioning. *Psychological Bulletin, 106,* 171–183.

Linn, M. C., & Peterson, A. C. (1986). A meta-analysis of gender differences in spatial ability: Implications for mathematics and science achievement. In J. S. Hyde & M. C. Linn (Eds.), *The psychology of gender: Advances through meta-analysis.* Baltimore: Johns Hopkins University Press.

Linton, M. (1979, July). I remember it well. *Psychology Today,* pp. 89–98.

Linville, P. W., Fischer, O. W., & Salovey, P. (1989). Perceived distributions of the characteristics of in-group and out-group members: Empirical evidence and a computer simulation. *Journal of Personality and Social Psychology, 57,* 165–188.

Lissner, L., et al. (1991). Variability of body weight and health outcomes in the Framingham population. *New England Journal of Medicine, 324,* 1839–1844.

Littlewood, R. (1992). Psychiatric diagnosis and racial bias: Empirical and interpretative approaches. *Social Science and Medicine, 34* (2), 141–149.

Lloyd, C., Alexander, A. A., Rice, D. G., & Greenfield, N. S. (1980). Life change and academic performance. *Journal of Human Stress, 6,* 15–25.

Locke, E. A., & Latham, G. P. (1990). *A theory of goal setting and task performance.* Englewood Cliffs, NJ: Prentice-Hall.

Locke, E. A., Latham, G. P., & Erez, M. (1988). The determinants of goal commitment. *Academy of Management Review, 13,* 23–39.

Loebel, A. D., Lieberman, J. A., Alvir, J. M. J., Mayerhoff, D. I., Geisler, S. H., & Szymanski, S. R. (1992). Duration of psychosis and outcome in first-episode schizophrenia. *American Journal of Psychiatry, 149,* 1183–1188.

Loehlin, J. C. (1985). Fitting heredity-environment models jointly to twin and adoption data from the California Psychological Inventory. *Behavior Genetics, 15,* 199–221.

Loehlin, J. C., Lindzey, G., & Spuhler, J. N. (1975). *Race differences in intelligence.* San Francisco: Freeman.

Loftus, E. F. (1992). When a lie becomes memory's truth: Memory distortion after exposure to misinformation. *Current Directions in Psychological Science, 1,* 121–123.

Loftus, E. F. (1993). The reality of repressed memories. *American Psychologist, 48,* 518–537.

Loftus, E. F., & Loftus, G. R. (1980). On the performance of stored information in the human brain. *American Psychologist, 35,* 409–420.

Loftus, E. F., & Palmer, J. C. (1974). Reconstruction of automobile destruction: An example of the interaction between language and memory. *Journal of Verbal Learning and Verbal Behavior, 13,* 585–589.

Loftus, E. F., Polonsky, S., & Fullilove, M. T. (1993). Memories of childhood sexual abuse: Remembering and repressing. Unpublished manuscript and Columbia University cited in Loftus, E. F. (1993). The reality of repressed memories. *American Psychologist, 48,* 518–537.

London, E. D., Broussolle, E. P. M., et al. (1990). Morphine-induced metabolic changes in the human brain: Studies with positron emission tomography and [fluorine 18] fluorodeoxyglucose. *Archives of General Psychiatry, 47,* 73–81.

Long, I. (1976). Human sexuality and aging. *Social Casework, 57,* 237–244.

Longo, D. J., Clum, G. A., & Yeager, N. J. (1988). Psychosocial treatment for recurrent genital herpes. *Journal of Consulting and Clinical Psychology, 56,* 61–66.

LoPiccolo, J. (1985). Diagnosis and treatment of male sexual dysfunction. *Journal of Sex and Marital Therapy, 11,* 215–232.

LoPiccolo, J., & Friedman, J. M. (1988). Blood-spectrum treatment of low sexual desire: Integration of cognitive, behavioral, and systematic therapy. In S. R. Leiblum & R. C. Rosen (Eds.), *Sexual desire disorders.* New York: Guilford.

Lore, R. K., & Schultz, L. A. (1993). Control of human aggression: A comparative perspective. *American Psychologist, 48,* 16–25.

Lorenz, K. (1937). The companion in the bird's world. *Auk, 54,* 245–273.

Lorenz, K. (1967). *On aggression.* New York: Bantam.

Loring, M., & Powell, B. (1988). Gender, race, and DSM-III: A study of the objectivity of psychiatric diagnostic behavior. *Journal of Health and Social Behavior, 29* (1), 1–22.

Lou, A. C., Henriksen, L., & Bruhn, P. (1984, August). Focal cerebral hypoperfusion in children with dysphasia and/or attention deficit disorder. *Archives of Neurology, 41,* 825–829.

Lowenthal, M. F., Thurnher, M., & Chiriboga, D. (1975). *Four stages of life: A comparative study of women and men facing transitions.* San Francisco: Jossey-Bass.

Luchins, K. S. (1942). Mechanization in problem solving: The effects of "Einstellung." *Psychometric Monographs, 54* (No. 6).

Luepnitz, R. R., Randolph, D. L., & Gutsch, K. U. (1982). Race and socioeconomic status as confounding variables in the accurate diagnosis of alcoholism. *Journal of Clinical Psychology, 33,* 3, 665–669.

Lykken, D. T. (1979). The detection of deception. *Psychological Bulletin, 86,* 47–53.

Maas, H. S., & Kuypers, J. A. (1974). *From thirty to seventy.* San Francisco: Jossey-Bass.

Maccoby, E. (1987). The varied meanings of "masculine" and "feminine." In J. M. Reinisch, L. A. Rosenblum, & S. A. Saunders (Eds.), *Masculinity/ Femininity: Basic perspectives.* New York: Oxford University Press.

Maccoby, E. E., & Jacklin, C. N. (1974). *The psychology of sex differences.* Stanford: Stanford University Press.

Macklin, E. J. (1974). Cohabitation in college: going very steady. *Psychology Today, 8,* 53–59.

Maddox, G. L. (1964). Disengagement theory: A critical evaluation. *The Gerontologist, 4,* 80–83.

Mader, S. S. (1985). *Inquiry into life* (4th ed.). Dubuque, IA: Wm. C. Brown Publishers.

Madigan, S., & O'Hara, R. (1992). Short-term memory at the turn of the century: Mary Whiton Calkins's memory research. *American Psychologist, 47,* 170–174.

Maier, N. R. F. (1931). Reasoning in humans: II. The solution of a problem and its appearance in consciousness. *Journal of Comparative and Physiological Psychology, 12,* 181–194.

Maier, S. F., & Keith, J. R. (1987). Shock signals and the development of stress-induced analgesia. *Journal of Experimental Psychology: Animal Behavior Processes, 13,* 226–238.

Maier, S. F., Watkins, L. R., & Fleshner, M. (1994). Psychoneuroimmunology: The interface between behavior, brain, and immunity. *American Psychologist, 49,* 1004–1017.

Mandel, D. R., Jusczyk, P. W., & Pisoni, D. B. (1995). Infants' recognition of the sound patterns of their own names. *Psychological Science, 6,* 314–317.

Mann, J., Tarantola, D., & Netter, T. (1992). *A global report: AIDS in the world.* Cambridge, MA: Harvard University Press.

Marce, L. V. (1858). *Treatise on the madness of pregnant women, recently delivered women, and nursing women.* Paris: J. B. Baillere et Fils.

Marcus, A. C., Wheeler, R. C., Cullen, J. W., & Crane, L. A. (1987). Quasi-experimental evaluation of the Los Angeles Know Your Body program: Knowledge, beliefs, and self-reported behaviors. *Preventive Medicine, 16,* 803–815.

Mark, V. H. (1974). The continuing polemic of psychosurgery. *Journal of the American Medical Association, 227,* 943.

Mark, V. H., & Ervin, E. P. (1970). *Violence and the brain.* New York: Harper & Row.

Marks, I. M. (1969). *Fears and phobias.* New York: Academic Press.

Marks, I. M., & Gelder, M. (1967). Transvestism and fetishism: Clinical and psychological changes during faradic aversion. *British Journal of Psychiatry, 119,* 711–730.

Markus, H. (1978). The effect of mere presence on social facilitation: An unobtrusive test. *Journal of Experimental Social Psychology, 14,* 389–397.

Marlatt, G. A., & Rose, F. (1980). Addictive disorders. In A. E. Kazdin, A. S. Bellack, & M. Hersen (Eds.), *New perspectives in abnormal psychology* (pp. 298–324). New York: Oxford University Press.

Marquis, D. P. (1941). Learning in the neonate. *Journal of Experimental Psychology, 29,* 22–40.

Martell, D. A., & Dietz, P. E. (1992). Mentally disordered offenders who push or attempt to push victims onto subway tracks in New York City. *Archives of General Psychology, 49,* 472–475.

Martin, R. J., White, B. D., & Hulsey, M. G. (1991). The regulation of body weight. *American Scientist, 79,* 528–541.

Martuza, R. L., Chiocca, E. A., Jenike, M. A., Giriunas, I. E., & Ballantine, H. T. (1990). Stereotactic radio-frequency thermal cingulotomy for obsessive compulsive disorder. *Journal of Neuropsychiatry, 2,* 331–336.

Maslow, A. (1967). A theory of metamotivation: The biological rooting of the value-life. *Journal of Humanistic Psychology, 7,* 93–127.

Maslow, A. (1970). *Motivation and personality* (2nd ed.). New York: Harper & Row.

Maslow, A. H., & Mintz, N. L. (1956). Effects of aesthetic surroundings: I. Initial effects of three aesthetic conditions upon perceiving "energy" and "well-being" in faces. *Journal of Psychology, 41,* 247–254.

Masters, W. H., & Johnson, V. E. (1966). *Human sexual response.* Boston: Little, Brown.

Masters, W. H., & Johnson, V. E. (1970). *Human sexual inadequacy.* Boston: Little, Brown.

Masters, W. H., & Johnson, V. E. (1982). *Human sexuality.* Boston: Little, Brown.

Matefy, R. E., & Kroll, R. G. (1974). An initial investigation of psychedelic drug flashback phenomena. *Journal of Consulting and Clinical Psychology, 42,* 854–860.

Matlin, M. (1938). *Cognition.* New York: Holt, Rinehart & Winston.

Matlin, M. W. (1988). *Sensation and perception* (2nd ed.). Boston: Allyn and Bacon.

Matthews, A., & MacLeod, C. (1986). Discrimination of threat cues without awareness in anxiety states. *Journal of Abnormal Psychology, 95,* 131–138.

Matthews, D. B., Best, P. J., White, A. M., Vandergriff, L., & Simpson, P. E. (1996). Ethanol impairs spatial cognitive processing: New behavioral and electrophysiological findings. *Current Directions in Psychological Science, 5,* 111–115.

Matthews, E. L. (1982). Psychological perspectives on the Type A behavior pattern. *Psychological Bulletin, 91,* 293–323.

Matthews, K. A. (1988). Coronary heart disease and Type A behaviors: Update and alternative to the Booth-Kewley and Friedman (1987) quantitative review. *Psychological Bulletin, 104,* 373–380.

Matthews, K. E., & Canon, L. K. (1975). Environmental noise level as a determinant of helping behavior. *Journal of Personality and Social Psychology, 32,* 571–577.

Maugh, T. H. (1973). LSD and the drug culture: New evidence of hazard. *Science, 179,* 1221–1222.

Maupin, H. E., & Fisher, R. J. (1989). The effects of superior female performance and sex-role orientation on gender conformity. *Canadian Journal of Behavioral Science, 21,* 55–69.

Mavromatis, A. (1987). *Hypnogogia.* London: Routledge.

Maylor, E. A., Rabbitt, P. M. A., & Kingstone, A. (1987). Effects of alcohol on word categorization and recognition memory. *British Journal of Psychology, 78,* 233–239.

McBroom, W. H. (1987). Longitudinal change in sex role orientations: Differences between men and women. *Sex Roles, 16,* 439–445.

McCall, R. B. (1979). *Infants.* Cambridge, MA: Harvard University Press.

McCarley, R. W., Faux, S. F., et al. (1989). CT abnormalities in schizophrenia. *Archives of General Psychiatry, 46,* 698–708.

McClelland, D. C., & Atkinson, J. W. (1948). The projective expression of needs: I. The effect of different intensities of the hunger drive on perception. *Journal of Psychology, 25,* 205–222.

McClelland, D. C., Atkinson, J. W., Clark, R. W., & Lowell, E. L. (1953). *The achievement motive.* New York: Appleton-Century-Crofts.

McClelland, D. C., & Winter, D. G. (1969). *Motivating economic achievement.* New York: The Free Press.

McCloskey, M., Wible, C. G., & Cohen, N. J. (1988). Is there a special flashbulb-memory mechanism? *Journal of Experimental Psychology: General, 117,* 171–181.

McConaghy, M. J. (1979). Gender permanence and the genital basis of gender: stages in the development of constancy of gender identity. *Child Development, 50,* 1223–1226.

McConnell, J. F., & Malin, D. H. (1973). Recent experiments in memory transfer. In H. P. Zippel (Ed.), *Memory and transfer of information.* New York: Plenum.

McCormick, E. J., & Ilgen, D. (1980). *Industrial psychology* (7th ed.). Englewood Cliffs, NJ: Prentice-Hall.

McCrae, R. R., Arenberg, D., & Costa, P. T. (1987). Declines in divergent thinking with age: Cross-sequential analyses. *Psychology and Aging, 2,* 130–137.

McCrae, R. R., & Costa, P. T. Jr. (1994). The stability of personality: Observations and evaluations. *Current Directions in Psychological Science, 3,* 173–175.

McGaugh, J. L. (1983). Preserving the presence of the past. Hormonal influences on memory storage. *American Psychologist, 38,* 161–174.

McGaugh, J. L. (1990). Significance and remembrance: The role of neuromodulatory systems. *Psychological Science, 1,* 15–25.

McGaugh, J. L., & Dawson, R. G. (1971). Modification of memory storage processes. In W. K. Honig and P. H. R. James (Eds.), *Animal memory.* New York: Academic Press.

McGraw, M. B. (1940). Neural maturation as exemplified in achievement of bladder control. *Journal of Pediatrics, 16,* 580–590.

McGue, M., Pickens, R. W., & Svikis, D. S. (1992). Sex and age effects on the inheritance of alcohol problems: A twin study. *Journal of Abnormal Psychology, 101,* 3–17.

McKinlay, S. M., & Jeffreys, M. (1974). The menopausal syndrome. *British Journal of Preventive and Social Medicine, 28,* 108.

McRae, R. R., & Costa, P. T. (1987). Validation of the five-factor model of personality across instruments and observers. *Journal of Personality and Social Psychology, 52,* 81–90.

McRae, R. R., & Costa, P. T. (1994). Stability of personality: Observations and evaluations. *Current Directions in Psychological Science, 3,* 173–175. **... this is the same as 53**

McWilliams, S. A., & Tuttle, R. J. (1973). Long-term psychological effects of LSD. *Psychological Bulletin, 79,* 341–351.

Mead, M. (1935). *Sex and temperament in three primitive societies.* New York: Morrow.

Meador, B. D., & Rogers, C. R. (1979). *Current psychotherapies* (2nd ed.). Itasca, IL: F. E. Peacock.

Meck, W. H., Smith, R. A., & Williams, C. L. (1989). Organizational changes in cholinergic activity and enhanced visuospatial memory as a function of choline administered prenatally or postnatally or both. *Behavioral Neuroscience, 103,* 1234–1241.

Mednick, S. A., Machon, R. A., Huttunen, M. O., & Bonett, D. (1988). Adult schizophrenia following prenatal exposure to an influenza epidemic. *Archives of General Psychiatry, 45,* 189–192.

Meichenbaum, D. H. (1966). Sequential strategies in two cases of hysteria. *Behaviour Research and Therapy, 4,* 89–94.

Mellon, J. C. (1975). *National assessment and the teaching of English.* Urbana, IL: National Council of Teachers of English.

Melzack, R. (1973). *The puzzle of pain.* New York: Basic Books.

Melzack, R. (1992). Phantom limbs. *Scientific American,* April, 120–126.

Melzack, R., & Dennis, S. G. (1978). Neurophysiological foundations of pain. In R. A. Sternbach (Ed.), *The psychology of pain.* New York: Raven Press.

Melzack, R., & Wall, P. D. (1983). *The challenge of pain.* New York: Basic Books.

Mercklebach, H., van den Hout, M., Jansen, A., & van der Molen, G. M. (1988). Many stimuli are frightening, but some are more frightening: The contributions of preparedness, dangerousness, and unpredictability to making a stimulus fearful. *Journal of Psychopathology and Behavioral Assessment, 10,* 355–366.

Mermelstein, R., Cohen, S., Lichtenstein, E., Baer, J. S., & Kamarck, T. (1986). Social support and smoking cessation and maintenance. *Journal of Consulting and Clinical Psychology, 54,* 447–453.

Messick, D. M., & Sentis, K. P. (1979). Fairness and preference. *Journal of Experimental Social Psychology, 15,* 418–434.

Mewborn, C. R., & Rogers, R. W. (1979). Effects of threatening and reassuring components of fear appeals on physiological and verbal measures of emotion and attitudes. *Journal of Experimental Social Psychology, 15,* 242–253.

Meyer, A. J., Nash, J. D., McAlister, A. L., Maccoby, N., & Farquhar, J. W. (1980). Skills training in a cardiovascular health education campaign. *Journal of Consulting and Clinical Psychology, 48,* 129–142.

Meyer, D. E., & Schvaneveldt, R. W. (1971). Facilitation in recognizing pairs of words: Evidence of a dependence between retrieval operations. *Journal of Experimental Psychology, 90,* 227–234.

Meyer, M. E. (1979). *Foundations of contemporary psychology.* New York: Oxford University Press.

Meyerowitz, B. E., & Chaiken, S. (1987). The effect of message framing on breast self-examination attitudes, intentions, and behavior. *Journal of Personality and Social Psychology, 52,* 500–510.

Michael, R. T., Gagnon, J. H., Laumann, E. O., & Kolata, G. (1994). *Sex in America: A definitive survey.* Boston: Little, Brown.

Middlebrook, P. N. (1980). *Social psychology and modern life* (2nd ed.). New York: Knopf.

Middlemist, R., Knowles, E., & Matter, C. (1976). Personal space invasions in the lavatory. *Journal of Personality and Social Psychology, 33,* 541–546.

Milgram, S. (1963). Behavioral study of obedience. *Journal of Abnormal and Social Psychology, 67,* 371–378.

Milgram, S. (1965). Some conditions of obedience and disobedience to authority. *Human Relations, 18,* 57–76.

Miller, D. T., & Ross, M. (1975). Self-serving biases in attribution of causality: Fact or fiction? *Psychological Bulletin, 82,* 313–325.

Miller, G. A. (1956). The magic number seven, plus or minus two. Some limits on our ability to process information. *Psychological Review, 63,* 81–97.

Miller, M. E., & Bowers, K. S. (1993). Hypnotic analgesia: Dissociated experience or dissociated control? *Journal of Abnormal Psychology, 102,* 29–38.

Miller, N. E. (1944). Experimental studies of conflict, in J. McV. Hunt (Ed.), *Personality and the behavior disorders* (Vol. 1). New York: Ronald Press.

Miller, N. E. (1978). Biofeedback and visceral learning. *Annual Review of Psychology, 29,* 373–392.

Miller, N. E. (1980). Effects of learning on physical symptoms produced by psychological stress. In H. Selye (Ed.), *Selye's guide to stress research.* New York: Van Nostrand Reinhold.

Miller, S., & Mangan, C. E. (1983). Interacting effects of information and coping style in adapting to gynecological stress: When should the doctor tell all? *Journal of Personality and Social Psychology, 45,* 223–236.

Milner, B. (1974). Hemispheric specialization: Scope and limits. In F. O. Schmitt & F. G. Worden (Eds.), *The neurosciences: Third study program* (pp. 75–89). Cambridge, MA: MIT Press.

Milner, B., Corkin, S., & Teuber, H. L. (1968). Further analysis of the hippocampal amnesic syndrome: 14-year follow-up study of H. M. *Neuropsychologia, 6,* 215–234.

Mineka, B., Davidson, M., Cook, M., & Keir, R. (1984). Observational conditioning of snake fears in rhesus monkeys. *Journal of Abnormal Psychology, 93,* 355–372.

Mineka, S., & Sutton, S. K. (1992). Cognitive biases and the emotional disorders. *Psychological Science, 3,* 65–69.

Minuchin, S. (1974). *Families and family therapy.* Cambridge, MA: Harvard University Press.

Mischel, W. (1968). *Personality and assessment.* New York: Wiley.

Mischel, W. (1981). *Introduction to personality* (3rd ed.). New York: Holt, Rinehart & Winston.

Mischel, W. (1984). Convergences and challenges in the search for consistency. *American Psychologist, 39,* 351–364.

Mischel, W., & Shoda, Y. (1995). A cognitive-affective system theory of personality: Reconceptualizing situations, dispositions, dynamics, and invariance in personality structure. *Psychological Review, 102,* 246–268.

Mitchell, J. E., Pyle, R. L., Eckert, E. D., Hatsukami, D., Pomeroy, C., & Zimmerman, R. (1990). A comparison study of antidepressants and structured intensive group psychotherapy in the treatment of bulimia nervosa. *Archives of General Psychiatry, 47,* 149–160.

Modestin, J. (1992). Multiple personality disorder in Switzerland. *American Journal of Psychiatry, 149,* 88–92.

Modigliani, V., & Hedges, D. G. (1987). Distributed rehearsals and the primacy effect in single-trail free recall. *Journal of Experimental Psychology: Learning, Memory, and Cognition, 13,* 426–436.

Mogil, J. S., Sternberg, W. F., Kest, B., Marek, P., & Liebeskind, J. C. (1993). Sex differences in the antagonism of swim-stress induced analgesia: Effects of gonadectomy and estrogen replacement. *Pain, 53,* 17.

Mohr, J. W., Turner, R. E., & Jerry, M. B. (1964). *Pedophilia and exhibitionism.* Toronto: University of Toronto Press.

Mohs, R. C., Breitner, J. C. S., Silverman, J. M., and Davis, K. L. (1987). Alzheimer's disease: Morbid risk among first-degree relatives. *Archives of General Psychiatry, 44,* 405–408.

Money, J. (1955). Linguistic resources and psychodynamic theory. *British Journal of Medical Psychology, 20,* 264–266.

Money, J. (1987a). Sin, sickness, or status: Homosexual gender identity and psychoneuroendocrinology. *American Psychologist, 42,* 384–389.

Money, J. (1987b). Propaedeutics of diecious G-I/R: Theoretical foundations for understanding dimorphic gender-identity/role. In J. M. Reinisch, L. A. Rosenblum, & S. A. Sanders (Eds.), *Masculinity/Femininity: Basic perspectives.* New York: Oxford University Press.

Money, J. (1988). *Gay, straight, and in-between.* New York: Oxford Press.

Monroe, L. J., Rechtschaffen, A., Foulkes, D., & Jensen, J. (1965). Discriminability of REM and NREM reports. *Journal of Personality and Social Psychology, 2,* 456–460.

Moody, R. (1976). *Life after life.* Covington, GA: Mockingbird Books.

Mook, D. G. (1986). *Motivation: The organization of action.* New York: W. W. Norton.

Moore-Ede, M. C., Sulzman, F. M., & Fuller, C. A. (1982). *The clocks that time us.* Cambridge: Harvard University Press.

Morell, P., & Norton, W. T. (1980, May). Myelin. *Scientific American,* pp. 88–118.

Morgan, S. W., & Mausner, B. (1973). Behavioral and fantasized indicators of avoidance of success in men and women. *Journal of Personality, 41,* 457–470.

Morris, N. (1986). A working memory, 1974–1984. A review of a decade of research. *Current Psychological Research and Reviews, 5,* 281–295.

Morris, W. N., & Miller, R. S. (1975). The effects of consensus-breaking and consensus-preempting partners on reduction of conformity. *Journal of Personality and Social Psychology, 11,* 215–223.

Morrison, A. M., & Von Glinow, M. A. (1990). Women and minorities in management. *American Psychologist, 45,* 200–208.

Moscovitch, M., & Olds, J. (1982). Asymmetries in emotional facial expressions and their possible relation to hemisphere specialization. *Neuropsychologia, 20,* 71–81.

Mosher, F. A., & Hornsby, J. R. (1966). On asking questions. In J. Bruner (Ed.), *Studies in cognitive growth.* New York: Wiley.

Moss, H. A., & Susman, E. J. (1980). Longitudinal study of personality development. In O. G. Brim & J. Kagan (Eds.), *Constancy and change in human development.* Cambridge, MA: Harvard University Press.

Mossman, D., & Perlin, M. L. (1992). Psychiatry and the homeless: A reply to Dr. Lamb. *American Journal of Psychiatry, 149,* 951–957.

Mowrer, O. H., & Mowrer, W. M. (1938). Enuresis: A method for its study and treatment. *American Journal of Orthopsychiatry, 8,* 436–459.

Muehlenhard, C., & Hollabaugh, L. (1988). Do women sometimes say no when they mean yes? The prevalence and correlates of women's token resistance to sex. *Journal of Personality and Social Psychology, 54,* 872–879.

Mullen, B. (1986). Atrocity as a function of lynch mob composition: A self-attention perspective. *Personality and Social Psychology Bulletin, 12,* 187–197.

Muller, E. E., & Nistico, G. (1989). *Brain messengers and the pituitary.* Orlando: Academic Press.

Mullis, I. V. S., Dossey, J. A., Foertsch, M. A., Jones, L. R., & Gentile, C. A. (1991). *Trends in academic progress* (Report No. 21–T–01). Washington, DC: U.S. Government Printing Office.

Mumford, E., Schlesinger, H. J., & Glass, G. V. (1981). Reducing medical cost through mental health treatment: Research problems and recommendations. In A. Broskowski, E. Marks, & S. H. Budman (Eds.), *Linking health and mental health.* Beverly Hills, CA: Sage.

Mundy, P., Robertson, M., Robertson, J., & Greenblatt, M. (1990). The prevalence of psychotic symptoms in homeless adolescents. *Journal of the American Academy of Child and Adolescent Psychiatry, 29,* 724–731.

Munjack, D. J., & Staples, F. R. (1977). Psychological characteristics of women with sexual inhibition (frigidity) in sex clinics. *Journal of Nervous and Mental Diseases, 163,* 117–129.

Murchison, C. (Ed.). (1929). *Foundations of experimental psychology.* Worcester, MA: Clark University Press.

Murray, H. (1938). *Exploration in personality.* New York: Oxford University Press.

Murray, H. (1951). Uses of the T. A. T. *American Journal of Psychiatry, 107,* 577–581.

Murray, H. A. (1943). *Thematic apperception test.* Boston: Harvard University Press.

Myers, D. G., & Bishop, G. D. (1970). Discussion effects on racial attitudes. *Science, 169,* 778–779.

Myers, D. G., & Diener, E. (1995). Who is happy? *Psychological Science, 6,* 10–18.

Myers, D. H., & Grant, G. A. (1972). A study of depersonalization in students. *British Journal of Psychiatry, 121,* 59–65.

Nachman, M. (1962). Taste preference for sodium salts in adrenolectomized rats. *Journal of Comparative and Physiological Psychology, 55,* 1124–1129.

Nachman, M. (1963). Learned aversion to the taste of lithium chloride and generalization to other salts. *Journal of Comparative and Physiological Psychology, 56,* 343–349.

Nadelson, C. C. (1990). Consequences of rape: Clinical and treatment aspects. *Psychotherapy and Psychosomatics, 51,* 187–192.

Nash, M. (1987). What, if anything, is regressed about hypnotic age regression? A review of the empirical literature. *Psychological Bulletin, 102,* 42–52.

Nash, M. R., Drake, S. D., Wiley, S., Khalsa, S., & Lynn, S. J. (1986). The accuracy of recall by hypnotically age-regressed subjects. *Journal of Abnormal Psychology, 95,* 298–300.

Nash, S. C. (1975). The relationship among sex-role stereotyping, sex-role performance, and sex differences in spatial visualization. *Sex Roles, 1,* 15–32.

National Advisory Mental Health Council. (1995a). *Basic behavioral research for mental health: A national investment.* Rockville, MD: National Institute of Mental Health.

National Advisory Mental Health Council. (1995b). Basic behavioral science research for mental health: A national investment (emotion and motivation). *American Psychologist, 50,* 838–845.

National Advisory Mental Health Council. (1996). Basic behavioral science research for mental health: Vulnerability and resilience. *American Psychologist, 51,* 22–28.

National Center for Health Statistics. (1984). Births, marriages, divorces, and deaths. United States. *Monthly Vital Statistics Report* (Vol. 32, No. 12), DHHS Pub. No. PHS–84–1120.

National Gay and Lesbian Task Force. (1988). *The national anti-gay lesbian victimization report.* New York: Author.

National Institute on Alcohol Abuse and Alcoholism. (1987). *Report.* Washington, DC: U.S. Government Printing Office.

National Victim Center. (1992). *Rape in America: A report to the nation.* Fort Worth, TX: Author.

Neale, J. M., & Oltmanns, T. F. (1980). *Schizophrenia.* New York: Wiley.

Nebes, R. D. (1989). Semantic memory in Alzheimer's disease. *Psychological Bulletin, 106,* 377–394.

Nelson, L. P., & Nelson, V. (1973). *Religion and death anxiety.* Paper presented at the Society for the Scientific Study of Religion. San Francisco.

Nemeth, C. J. (1981). Jury trials. Psychology and law. In L. Berkowitz (Ed.), *Advances in experimental social psychology* (Vol. 14). New York: Academic Press.

Neugarten, B. L. (1964). *Personality in middle and late life.* New York: Atherton Press.

Neugarten, B. L. (1968). The awareness of middle age. In B. L. Neugarten (Ed.), *Middle age and aging.* Chicago: University of Chicago Press.

Neugarten, B. L., & Hagestad, G. O. (1976). Age and the life course. In R. H. Binstock & E. Shanas (Eds.), *Handbook of aging and the social sciences.* New York: Van Nostrand Reinhold.

Newton, J. W., & Mann, L. (1980). Crowd size as a factor in the persuasion process: A study of religious crusade meetings. *Journal of Personality and Social Psychology, 39,* 874–883.

Nisbett, R. E. (1993). Violence and U.S. regional culture. *American Psychologist, 48,* 441–449.

Nogrady, H., McConkey, K. M., & Perry, C. (1985). Enhancing visual memory: Trying hypnosis, trying imagination, and trying again. *Journal of Abnormal Psychology, 94,* 195–204.

Nolen-Hoeksema, S. (1987). Sex differences in unipolar depression: Evidence and theory. *Psychological Bulletin, 101,* 259–282.

Nopoulos, P., Torres, I., Flaum, M., Andreasen, N. C., Ehrhardt, J. C., & Yuh, W. T. C. (1995). Brain morphology in first-episode schizophrenia. *American Journal of Psychiatry, 152,* 1721–1723.

Norton, A. J. (1974). The family life cycle updated: Components and uses. In R. F. Winch & G. B. Spanier (Eds.), *Selected studies in marriage and the family.* New York: Holt, Rinehart & Winston.

Nuckolas, K., Cassel, J., & Kaplan, B. H. (1972). Psychological assets, life crisis, and the prognosis of pregnancy. *American Journal of Epidemiology, 95,* 431–444.

Nunes, E. V., Frank, K. A., & Kornfeld, D. S. (1987). Psychologic treatment for the Type A behavior pattern and for coronary heart disease: A meta-analysis of the literature. *Psychosomatic Medicine, 48,* 159–166.

Nydegger, C. N. (1973, November). *Late and early fathers.* Paper presented to Annual Meeting of American Gerontological Society, Miami Beach.

Offer, D. (1969). *The psychological world of the teenager: A study of normal adolescent boys.* New York: Basic Books.

Offer, D., & Offer, J. (1975). *From teenage to young manhood.* New York: Basic Books.

Offer, D., Ostrov, E., & Howard, K. I. (1981). *The adolescent: A psychological self-portrait.* New York: Basic Books.

Offer, D., & Schonert-Reichl, K. A. (1992). Debunking the myths of adolescence: Findings from recent research. *Journal of the American Academy of Child and Adolescent Psychiatry, 31,* 1003–1014.

O'Hara, M. W. (1980). *A prospective study of postpartum depression: A test of cognitive and behavioral theories.* Unpublished doctoral dissertation, University of Pittsburgh.

O'Hara, M. W., Zekowski, E. M., Phillips, L. H., & Wright, E. J. (1990). Controlled prospective study of postpartum mood disorders: Comparison of childbearing and nonchildbearing mothers. *Journal of Abnormal Psychology, 99,* 3–15.

Ohman, A., Erixon, G., & Löfberg, I. (1975). Phobias and preparedness: Phobic versus neutral pictures as conditioned stimuli for human autonomic responses. *Journal of Abnormal Psychology, 84,* 41–45.

Olasov, B., & Jackson, J. (1987). Effects of expectancies on women's reports of moods during the menstrual cycle. *Psychosomatic Medicine, 49,* 65–74.

Oldham, G. R., & Fried, Y. (1987). Employee reactions to workplace characteristics. *Journal of Applied Psychology, 72,* 75–80.

Olds, J., & Milner, P. (1954). Positive reinforcement produced by electrical stimulation of septal area and other regions of rat brain. *Journal of Comparative and Physiological Psychology, 47,* 419–427.

O'Leary, A. (1990). Stress, emotion, and human immune function. *Psychology Bulletin, 108,* 363–382.

O'Leary, A., Temoshok, L., Jenkins, S. R., & Sweet, D. M. (1989). Autonomic reactivity and immune function in men with AIDS. *Psychophysiology, 26,* 47.

O'Leary, D. D. M. (1992). Development of connectional diversity and specificity in the mammalian brain by the pruning of collateral projections. *Current Opinion in Neurobiology, 2,* 70–77.

Olsen, K. M. (1969). *Social class and age-group differences in the timing of family status changes: A study of age norms in American society.* Unpublished doctoral dissertation, University of Chicago.

Olson, J. M., & Zanna, M. P. (1993). Attitudes and attitude change. *Annual Review of Psychology, 44,* 117–154.

Orme-Johnson, D. (1987). Medical care utilization and the transcendental meditation program. *Psychosomatic Medicine, 49,* 493–507.

Osherson, D. N., & Markman, E. (1974). Language and the ability to evaluate contradictions and tautologies. *Cognition, 3,* 213–226.

Ost, L. G. (1992). Blood and injection phobia: Background and cognitive, physiological, and behavioral variables. *Journal of Abnormal Psychology, 101,* 68–74.

Ostroff, C. (1992). The relationship between satisfaction, attitudes and performance: An organizational level analysis. *Journal of Applied Psychology, 77,* 963–974.

Pahnke, W. N. (1980). Drugs and mysticism. In J. R. Tisdale (Ed.), *Growing edges in the psychology of religion* (pp. 183–200). Chicago: Nelson-Hall.

Parker, G. B., Barrett, E. A., & Hickie, I. B. (1992). From nurture to network: Examining links between perceptions of parenting received in childhood and social bonds in adulthood. *American Journal of Psychiatry, 149,* 877–885.

Parkes, C. M. (1972). *Bereavement: Studies of grief in adult life.* New York: International Universities Press.

Parry, H. J., Balter, M. B., Mellinger, G. D., Cisin, I. H., & Manheimer, D. I. (1973). National patterns of psychotherapeutic drug use. *Archives of General Psychiatry, 28,* 769–783.

Patterson, F. (1977). The gestures of a gorilla: Language acquisition in another primate species. In J. Hambrug, J. Goodall, & L. McCown (Eds.), *Perspectives in human evolution* (Vol. 4). Menlo Park, CA: W. A. Benjamin.

Pauly, I. (1968). The current status of the change of sex operation. *Journal of Nervous and Mental Disorders, 147,* 460–471.

Paykel, E. S., Emms, E. M., Fletcher, J., & Rassaby, E. S. (1980). Life events and social support in puerperal depression. *British Journal of Psychiatry, 136,* 339–346.

Pearlson, G. D., Jeffrey, P. J., Harris, G. J., Ross, C. A., Fischman, M. W., & Camargo, E. E. (1993). Correlation of acute cocaine-induced changes in local cerebral bloodflow with subjective effects. *American Journal of Psychiatry, 150,* 495–497.

Pearlson, G. D., Kim, et al. (1989). Ventricle-brain ratio, computed tomographic density, and brain area in 50 schizophrenics. *Archives of General Psychiatry, 46,* 690–697.

Peele, T. L. (1961). *Neuroanatomical basis for clinical neurology* (2nd ed.). New York: McGraw-Hill.

Pennebaker, J. W., & Beall, J. K. (1986). Confronting a traumatic event: Toward an understanding of inhibition and disease. *Journal of Abnormal Psychology, 95,* 274–281.

Pennebaker, J. W., Colder, M., & Sharp, L. K. (1990). Accelerating the coping process. *Journal of Personality and Social Psychology, 58,* 528–537.

Pennebaker, J. W., Kiecolt-Glaser, J. K., & Glaser, R. (1988). Disclosure of traumas and immune function: Health implications for psychotherapy. *Journal of Consulting and Clinical Psychology, 56,* 239–245.

Perkins, D. N. (1987). Knowledge as design: Teaching critical thinking through content. In J. B. Baron & R. J. Sternberg (Eds.), *Teaching thinking skills.* San Francisco: W. H. Freeman.

Perls, F. S., Hefferline, R. F., & Goodman, P. (1951). *Gestalt therapy.* New York: Julian Press.

Perry, J. D., & Simpson, M. E. (1987). Violent crimes in a city: Environmental determinants. *Environment and Behavior, 19,* 77–90.

Perry, J. D., & Whipple, B. (1981). Pelvic muscle strength of female ejaculators: Evidence in support of a new theory of orgasm. *Journal of Sex Research, 17,* 22–39.

Petersen, A. C. (1979, January). Can puberty come any faster? *Psychology Today,* pp. 45–56.

Petersen, R. C., & Stillman, R. C. (1978). *Phencyclidine (PCP) abuse: An appraisal* (National Institute on Drug Abuse Monograph No. 21). Washington, DC: U.S. Government Printing Office.

Peterson, L. R., & Peterson, M. J. (1959). Short-term retention of individual items. *Journal of Experimental Psychology, 58,* 193–198.

Petito, J. M., Folds, J. D., Ozer, H., Quade, D., & Evans, D. L. (1992). Abnormal diurnal variation in circulating natural killer cell phenotypes and cytotoxic activity in major depression. *American Journal of Psychiatry, 149,* 694–696.

Petri, H. L. (1986). *Motivation: Theory and research* (3rd ed.). Belmont, CA: Wadsworth.

Petty, R. E., & Cacioppo, J. T. (1981). *Attitudes and persuasion: Classic and contemporary approaches.* Dubuque, IA: Wm. C. Brown.

Petty, R. E., & Cacioppo, J. T. (1986). The elaboration likelihood model of persuasion. In L. Berkowitz (Ed.), *Advances in experimental social psychology* (Vol. 19). New York: Academic Press.

Pfefferbaum, A., Zipursky, R. B., Lim, K. O., Zatz, L. M., Stahl, S. M., & Jernigan, T. L. (1988). Computed tomographic evidence for generalized sulcal and ventricular enlargement in schizophrenia. *Archives of General Psychiatry, 45,* 633–640.

Phifer, J. F., & Murrell, S. A. (1986). Etiologic factors in the onset of depressive symptoms of older adults. *Journal of Abnormal Psychology, 95,* 282–291.

Phillips, D. P., & Feldman, K. A. (1973). A dip in deaths before ceremonial occasions: Some new relationships between social integration and mortality. *American Sociological Review, 38,* 678–696.

Phillips, J. D. (1933). *Salem in the seventeenth century.* Cambridge, MA: Riverside Press.

Phinney, J. (1996). When we talk about American ethnic groups, what do we mean? *American Psychologist, 51,* 918–927.

Piaget, J. (1972). Intellectual development from adolescence to adulthood. *Human Development, 15,* 1–12.

Piaget, J., & Inhelder, B. (1963). *The child's conception of space.* London: Routledge and Paul.

Pincomb, G. A., Lovallo, W. R., Passey, R. B., Brackett, D. J., & Wilson, M. F. (1987). Caffeine enhances the physiological response to occupational stress in medical students. *Health Psychology, 6,* 101–112.

Pines, M. (1980, December). The sinister hand. *Science, 80,* 26–27.

Pines, M. (1981, September/October). Genie. *Dallas Morning News.*

Pines, M. (1983, September). The human difference. *Psychology Today,* p. 52.

Piorkowski, G. (1983). Survivor guilt in the university setting. *Personnel and Guidance Journal, 61,* 620–622.

Plomin, R. (1989). Environment and genes: Determinants of behavior. *American Psychologist, 44,* 105–111.

Plomin, R. (1995). Molecular genetics and psychology. *Current Directions in Psychological Science, 4,* 114–117.

Plutchik, R. (1980). *Emotion: A psychoevolutionary synthesis.* New York: Plenum.

Pope, K. S. (1978). The flow of consciousness. In K. S. Pope & J. L. Singer (Eds.), *The stream of consciousness: Scientific investigations into the flow of human experience.* New York: Plenum.

Pope, K. S. (1996). Memory, abuse, and science: Questioning claims about the false memory syndrome epidemic. *American Psychologist, 51,* 957–974.

Pope, K. S., & Singer, J. L. (1980). The waking stream of consciousness. In J. M. Davidson & R. J. Davidson (Eds.), *The psychobiology of consciousness* (pp. 169–191). New York: Plenum.

Pope, K. S., & Singer, J. L. (Eds.). (1978). *The stream of consciousness.* New York: Plenum.

Posner, M. I. (1973). *Cognition: An introduction.* Glenview, IL: Scott, Foresman.

Powell, K. E., Thompson, P. D., Caspersen, C. J., & Kendrick, J. S. (1987). Physical activity and incidence of coronary heart disease. *American Review of Public Health, 8,* 253–287.

Prentice, W. C. H. (1954). Visual recognition of verbally labeled figures. *American Journal of Psychology, 67,* 315–320.

Price, D. D. (1988). *Psychological and neural mechanisms of pain.* New York: Raven Press.

Price, D. D., & Barber, J. (1987). An analysis of factors that contribute to the efficiency of hypnotic analgesia. *Journal of Abnormal Psychology, 96,* 46–51.

Prinzmetal, W. (1995). Visual feature integration in a world of objects. *Current Directions in Psychological Science, 4,* 90–94.

Prochaska, J. O. (1984). *Systems of psychotherapy: A transtheoretical analysis* (2nd ed.). Pacific Grove, CA: Brooks/Cole.

Pugh, E. N. (1988). Vision: Physics and retinal physiology. In R. C. Atkinson, R. J. Herrnstein, G. Lindzey, & R. D. Luce (Eds.), *Stevens' handbook of experimental psychology: Vol. 1. Perception and Motivation.* New York: Wiley-Interscience.

Puig-Antich, J., Dahl, R., Ryan, N., Novacenko, D., Goetz, D., Goetz, R., Twomey, J., & Klepper, T. (1989). Cortisol secretion in prepubertal children with major depressive disorder. *Archives of General Psychiatry, 46,* 801–812.

Quay, H. C. (1959). The effect of verbal reinforcement on the recall of early memories. *Journal of Abnormal and Social Psychology, 59,* 254–257.

Raaheim, K., & Kaufmann, G. (1972). Level of activity and success in solving an unfamiliar task. *Psychological Reports, 30,* 271–274.

Raaijmakers, J. G. W., & Shiffrin, R. M. (1992). Models for recall and recognition. *Annual Review of Psychology, 43,* 205–234.

Rabkin, J. G., & Streuning, E. L. (1976). Life events, stress, and illness. *Science, 194,* 1013–1019.

Rachman, S. (1966). Sexual fetishism: An experimental analogue. *Psychological Record, 16,* 293–296.

Ramsey, J., & Hungerford, H. R. (1989). The effects of issue investigation and action training on environmental behavior in seventh grade students. *Journal of Environmental Education, 20,* 29–34.

Ranken, H. B. (1963). Language and thinking: Positive and negative effects of naming. *Science, 141,* 48–50.

Rapee, R. M., Brown, T. A., Antony, M. M., & Barlow, D. H. (1992). Response to hyperventilation and inhalation of 5.5% carbon dioxide enriched air across the DSM-III-R anxiety disorders. *Journal of Abnormal Psychology, 101,* 538–552.

Rapp, P. R., & Amaral, D. G. (1992). Individual differences in the cognitive and neurobiological consequences of normal aging. *Trends in Neuroscience, 15,* 340–344.

Raugh, M. R., & Atkinson, R. C. (1975). A mnemonic method for learning a second-language vocabulary. *Journal of Educational Psychology, 67,* 1–16.

Ray, O. S. (1974). *Drugs, society, and human behavior* (2nd ed.). St. Louis: C. V. Mosby.

Rechtschaffen, A., & Buchignami, C. (1983). Visual dimensions and correlates of dream images. *Sleep Research, 12,* 189.

Redd, W. H., Jacobsen, P. B., Die-Trill, M., Dermatis, H., McEvoy, M., & Holland, J. C. (1987). Cognitive/attentional distraction in the control of conditioned nausea in pediatric cancer patients receiving chemotherapy. *Journal of Consulting and Clinical Psychology, 55,* 391–395.

Ree, M. J., & Earles, J. A. (1992). Intelligence is the best predictor of job performance. *Current Directions in Psychological Science, 1,* 86–89.

Reed, C. F. (1984). Terrestrial passage theory of the moon illusion. *Journal of Experimental Psychology: General, 113,* 489–516.

Reeves, A., & Plumb, F. (1969). Hyperphagia, rage, and dementia accompanying a ventromedial hypothalamic neoplasm. *Archives of Neurology, 20,* 616–624.

Regier, D. A., et al. (1988). One-month prevalence of mental disorders in the United States: Based on five epidemiological catchment area sites. *Archives of General Psychiatry, 45,* 977–986.

Reilly, R. R., & Chao, G. T. (1982). Validity and fairness of some alternative employee selection procedures. *Personnel Psychology, 35,* 1–62.

Reisenzein, R. (1983). The Schachter-Singer theory of emotion: Two decades later. *Psychological Bulletin, 94,* 239–264.

Reiss, L. L. (1980). *Family systems in America* (3rd ed.). New York: Holt, Rinehart & Winston.

Rescorla, R. A. (1967). Pavlovian conditioning and its proper control procedures. *Psychological Review, 74,* 71–80.

Rescorla, R. A. (1988). Pavlovian conditioning: It's not what you think it is. *American Psychologist, 43,* 151–160.

Resick, P. A., Calhoun, K. S., Atkeson, B. M., & Ellis, E. M. (1981). Social adjustment in victims of sexual assault. *Journal of Consulting and Clinical Psychology, 49,* 705–712.

Reynolds, A. G., & Flagg, P. W. (1983). *Cognitive Psychology* (2nd ed.). Boston: Little, Brown.

Rhodes, N., & Wood, W. (1992). Self-esteem and intelligence affect influenceability: The mediating role of message reception. *Psychological Bulletin, 111,* 156–171.

Rice, J., et al. (1987). The familial transmission of bipolar illness. *Archives of General Psychiatry, 44,* 441–445.

Riegel, K. F., & Riegel, R. M. (1972). Development, drop, and death. *Development Psychology, 6,* 306–319.

Rimm, D. C., & Masters, J. (1979). *Behavior therapy* (2nd ed.). New York: Academic Press.

Roberts, P., & Newton, P. M. (1987). Levinsonian studies of women's adult development. *Psychology and Aging, 2,* 154–163.

Robins, M. B., & Jensen, G. G. (1978). Multiple orgasm in males. *Journal of Sex Research, 13,* 21–26.

Robinson, N. S., Garber, J., & Hilsman, R. (1995). Cognitions and stress: Direct and moderating effects on depressive versus externalizing symptoms during the junior high school transition. *Journal of Abnormal Psychology, 104,* 3.

Robinson, R. G., & Starkstein, S. E. (1990). Current research in affective disorders following stroke. *Journal of Neuropsychiatry and Clinical Neurosciences, 2,* 1–14.

Rock, I., & Kaufman, L. (1972). The moon illusion. In R. Held & W. Richards (Eds.), *Perception: Mechanisms and models.* San Francisco: W. H. Freeman.

Rodin, J. (1985). Insulin levels, hunger, and food intake: An example of feedback loops in body weight regulation. *Health Psychology, 4,* 1–18.

Rodin, J., Bartoshuk, L., Peterson, C., & Schank, D. (1990). Bulimia and taste: Possible interactions. *Journal of Abnormal Psychology, 99,* 32–39.

Rodin, J., & Ickovics, R. (1990). Women's health: Review and research agenda as we approach the 21st century. *American Psychologist, 45,* 1018–1034.

Roe, A. (1946). The personality of artists. *Educational Psychology Measurement, 6,* 401–408.

Roe, A. (1953). *The making of a scientist.* New York: Dodd, Mead.

Roediger, H. L., & McDermott, K. B. (1995). Creating false memories: Remembering words not presented in lists. *Journal of Experimental Psychology: Learning, Memory, and Cognition, 21,* 803–814.

Roffwarg, H. P., Muzio, J. N., & Dement, W. C. (1966). Ontogenetic development of the human sleep-dream cycle. *Science, 152,* 604–619.

Rogers, C. R. (1951). *Client-centered therapy: Its current practice, implications, and theory.* Boston: Houghton Mifflin.

Rogers, D. (Ed.). (1980). *Issues in life-span human development.* Monterey, CA: Brooks/Cole.

Rogers, R. W. (1975). A protection motivation theory of fear appeals and attitude change. *Journal of Psychology, 91,* 93–114.

Rollins, B. C., & Feldman, H. (1970). Marital satisfaction over the family life cycle. *Journal of Marriage and the Family, 32,* 20–28.

Rolls, E. T., Burton, M. J., & Mora, F. (1976). Hypothalamic neuronal responses associated with the sight of food. *Brain Research, 111,* 53–66.

Roman, P. (1987). *Personal communication.* Center for Research on Deviance, University of Georgia.

Romer, D., Gruder, C. L., & Lizardo, T. (1986). A person-situation approach to altruistic behavior. *Journal of Personality and Social Psychology, 51,* 1001–1012.

Rorschach, H. (1953). *Psychodiagnostics* (5th ed.). New York: Grune & Stratton.

Rosch, E. (1973). Natural categories. *Cognitive Psychology, 4,* 328–350.

Rosch, E. (1975). Cognitive representations of semantic categories. *Journal of Experimental Psychology: General, 104,* 192–233.

Rosch, E. H., Mervis, C. B., Gray, W. B., Johnson, D. M., & Boyes-Braem, P. (1976). Basic objects in natural categories. *Cognitive Psychology, 8,* 382–439.

Rosen, R. C., & Leiblum, S. R. (1995). Treatment of sexual disorders in the 1990s: An integrated approach. *Journal of Consulting and Clinical Psychology, 63,* 877–890.

Rosenman, R. H., & Chesney, M. A. (1982). Stress, Type A behavior, and coronary disease. In L. Goldberger & S. Breznitz (Eds.), *Handbook of stress.* New York: The Free Press.

Rosenzweig, M. R. (1984). *Cognition.* New York: Holt, Rinehart & Winston.

Rosenzweig, S. (1988). The identity and idiodynamics of the multiple personality "Sally Beauchamp": A confirmatory supplement. *American Psychologist, 43,* 45–48.

Ross, L. (1977). The intuitive psychologist and his shortcomings: Distortions in the attribution process. In L. Berkowitz (Ed.), *Advances in experimental social psychology* (Vol. 10, pp. 173–220). New York: Academic Press.

Ross, R. T. (1986). Pavlovian second-order conditioned analgesia. *Journal of Experimental Psychology: Animal Behavior Processes, 12,* 32–39.

Rossi, A. S. (1980). Aging and parenthood in the middle years. In P. B. Balter & O. G. Brim (Eds.), *Life-span development and behavior* (Vol. 3). New York: Academic Press.

Roth, S., & Cohen, L. J. (1986). Approach, avoidance, and coping with stress. *American Psychologist, 41,* 813–819.

Rothbaum, B. O., Hodges, L. F., Kooper, R., Opdyke, D., Williford, J. S., & North, M. (1995). Effectiveness of computer-generated (virtual reality) graded exposure in the treatment of acrophobia. *American Journal of Psychiatry, 152,* 626–628.

Rounsaville, B. J., Chevron, E. S., Prusoff, B. A., Elkin, I., Imber, S., Sotsky, S., & Watkins, J. (1987). The relation between specific and general dimensions of the psychotherapy process in interpersonal psychotherapy of depression. *Journal of Consulting and Clinical Psychology, 55,* 379–384.

Rowland, K. F. (1977). Environmental events predicting death for the elderly. *Psychological Bulletin, 84,* 349–372.

Roy, M., & Steptoe, A. (1991). The inhibition of cardiovascular responses to mental stress following aerobic exercise. *Psychophysiology, 28,* 689–700.

Rozin, P. (1996). Towards a psychology of food and eating: From motivation to model to marker, morality, meaning, and metaphor. *Current Directions in Psychological Science, 5,* 18–24.

Rubenstein, E. A. (1983). Television and behavior: Research conclusions of the 1982 NIMH report and their policy implications. *American Psychologist, 38,* 820–825.

Ruble, D. N., & Ruble, T. L. (1980). Sex stereotypes. In A. G. Miller (Ed.), *In the eye of the beholder: Contemporary issues in stereotyping.* New York: Holt, Rinehart & Winston.

Ruderman, A. J., & Besbeas, M. (1992). Psychological characteristics of dieters and bulimics. *Journal of Abnormal Psychology, 101,* 383–390.

Rumbaugh, D. M., & Gill, T. V. (1976). The mastery of language-type skills by the chimpanzee (*Pan*). In S. Harnad, H. Steklis, & J. Lancaster (Eds.), *Origins and evolution of language and speech.* New York: New York Academy of Sciences.

Rumelhart, D. E., & McClelland, J. L. (Eds.). (1986). *Parallel distributed processing: Explorations in the microstructure of cognition, Vol. 1: Foundations.* Cambridge, MA: MIT Press.

Russell, J. A., & Mehrabian, A. (1978). Approach-avoidance and affiliation as functions of the emotion-eliciting equality of an environment. *Environment and Behavior, 10,* 355–387.

Russell, M. A. H. (1971). Cigarette smoking: natural history of a dependence disorder. *British Journal of Medical Psychology, 44,* 1–16.

Russo, N. F. (1990). Overview: Forging research priorities for women's mental health. *American Psychologist, 45,* 368–373.

Rutherford, S. D. (1988). The culture of American deaf people. *Sign Language Studies, 59,* 129–147.

Saal, F. E., & Knight, P. A. (1988). *Industrial/organizational psychology: Science and practice.* Pacific Grove, CA: Brooks/Cole.

Sachar, E. J. (1985). Disorders of thought: The schizophrenic syndromes. In E. R. Kandel & J. H. Schwartz (Eds.), *Principles of neuroscience* (2nd ed.). New York: Elsevier.

Sachs, J. D. S. (1967). Recognition memory for syntactic and semantic aspects of connected discourse. *Perception and Psychophysics, 2,* 437–442.

Sagan, C. (1979). *Broca's brain.* New York: Random House.

Saks, M. J. (1992). Obedience versus disobedience to legitimate versus illegitimate authorities issuing good versus evil directions. *Psychological Science, 3,* 221–223.

Salapatek, P. (1977). Stimulus determinants of attention in infants. In B. Wolman (Ed.), *International encyclopedia of psychiatry, psychology, psychoanalysis, and neurology* (Vol. 10). New York: Aesculapis Publishers.

Santrock, J. W. (1987). *Adolescence: An introduction* (2nd ed.). Dubuque, IA: Wm. C. Brown Publishers.

Santrock, J. W. (1994). *Child development* (6th ed.). Dubuque, IA: Brown & Benchmark.

Santrock, J. W. (1995). *Children* (4th ed.). Dubuque, IA: Brown & Benchmark.

Sarason, I. G., Johnson, J. H., & Siegel, J. M. (1978). Assessing the impact of life change: Development of the life experiences survey. *Journal of Consulting and Clinical Psychology, 46,* 932–946.

Sargent, C. (1984). Between death and shame: Dimensions of pain in Bariba culture. *Social Science and Medicine, 19,* 1299–1304.

Saxe, L., Doughterty, D., & Cross, T. (1985). The validity of polygraph testing: Scientific analysis and public controversy. *American Psychologist, 40,* 355–366.

Scarr, S., & Eisenberg, M. (1993). Child care research: Issues, perspectives, and results. *Annual Review of Psychology, 44,* 613–644.

Scarr, S., Philips, D., & McCartney, K. (1990). Facts, fantasies, and the future of childcare in the United States. *Psychological Science, 1,* 26–35.

Scarr, S., & Salapatek, P. (1970). Patterns of fear development during infancy. *Merrill-Palmer Quarterly, 16,* 53–90.

Scarr, S., Webber, P. L., Weinberg, R. A., & Witting, M. A. (1981). Personality resemblance among adolescents and their parents in biologically related and adoptive families. *Journal of Personality and Social Psychology, 40,* 885–898.

Schachter, S. (1959). *The psychology of affiliation. Experimental studies of sources of gregariousness.* Stanford, CA: Stanford University Press.

Schachter, S. (1971). Some extraordinary facts about obese rats and humans. *American Psychologist, 26,* 129–144.

Schachter, S., & Singer, J. E. (1962). Cognitive, social and physiological determinants of emotional state. *Psychological Review, 69,* 379–399.

Schacter, J. (1989). Why we need a program for the control of *Chlamydia trachomatis. New England Journal of Medicine, 320,* 802–803.

Schaffer, H. R. (1971). *The growth of sociability.* London: Penguin.

Schaie, K. W., & Labouvie-Vief, G. (1973). Generational and cohort-specific differences in adult cognitive behavior: A 14-year cross-sequential study. *Developmental Psychology, 9,* 151–166.

Schaie, K. W., & Parham, I. A. (1977). Cohort-sequential analysis of adult intellectual development. *Developmental Psychology, 13,* 649–653.

Schiff, M., & Lewontin, R. (1986). *Education and class: The irrelevance of IQ genetic studies.* Oxford, England: Clarendon.

Schiffman, H. R. (1976). *Sensation and perception. An integrated approach.* New York: Wiley.

Schleifer, S. J., Keller, S. E., Bartlett, J. A., Eckholdt, H. M., & Delaney, B. R. (1996). Immunity in young adults with major depressive disorder. *American Journal of Psychiatry, 153,* 4.

Schmidt, F. L., & Hunter, J. E. (1992). Development of a causal model of processes determining job performance. *Current Directions in Psychological Science, 1,* 89–92.

Schmidt, F. L., & Hunter, J. E. (1993). Tacit knowledge, practical intelligence, general mental ability, and job knowledge. *Current Directions in Psychological Science, 2,* 8–9.

Schmidt, F. L., & Ones, D. S. (1992). Personnel selection. *Annual Review of Psychology, 43,* 627–670.

Schreiber, F. R. (1973). *Sybil.* New York: Henry Regnery.

Schulz, R., & Ewen, R. B. (1988). *Adult development and aging: Myths and emerging realities.* New York: Macmillan.

Schwartz, N., & Clare, G. L. (1983). Mood misattribution, and judgments of well-being informative and directive functions of affective states. *Journal of Personality and Social Psychology, 45,* 513–523.

Scott, L., & O'Hara, M. W. (1993). Self-discrepancies in clinically anxious and depressed university students. *Journal of Abnormal Psychology, 102,* 282–287.

Scott, W. D. (1908). *Psychology of advertising.* Boston: Small, Maynard.

Scoville, W. B., & Milner, B. (1957). Loss of recent memory after bilateral hippocampal lesions. *Journal of Neurology, Neurosurgery, and Psychiatry, 20,* 11–21.

Sechehaye, M. (1951). *Reality lost and regained: Autobiography of a schizophrenic girl* (G. Rubin-Rabson, Trans.). New York: Grune & Stratton.

Segall, M. H., Campbell, D. T., & Herskovits, M. J. (1963). Cultural differences in the perception of geometric illusions. *Science, 139,* 769–771.

Seligman, M. E. P. (1975). *Helplessness: On depression, development, and death.* San Francisco: W. H. Freeman.

Seligman, M. E. P., et al. (1988). Explanatory style change during cognitive therapy for depression. *Journal of Abnormal Psychology, 97,* 13–18.

Selye, H. (1976). *The stress of life.* New York: Knopf.

Serbin, L. A. (1980). Sex role socialization: A field in transition. In B. B. Lahey & A. E. Kazdin (Eds.), *Advances in clinical child psychology* (Vol. 3). New York: Plenum.

Shapiro, C. M., Boortz, R., Mitchell, D., Bartel, P., & Jooste, P. (1982). Slow-wave sleep: A recovery period after exercise. *Science, 214,* 1253–1254.

Shaver, P., Schwartz, D., Kirson, D., & O'Connor, C. (1987). Emotion knowledge. *Journal of Personality and Social Psychology, 52,* 1061–1086.

Shaw, J. A., Applegate, B., Tanner, S., Perez, D., Rothe, E., Campo-Bowen, A. E., & Lahey, B. B. (1995). Psychological effects of Hurricane Andrew on an elementary school population. *Journal of the American Academy of Child and Adolescent Psychiatry, 34,* 9.

Shaywitz, B. A., Shaywitz, S. E., et al. (1995). Sex differences in the functional organization of the brain for language. *Nature, 373,* 607–609.

Sheffield, F. D., Wulff, J. J., & Backer, R. (1951). Reward value of copulation without sex drive reduction. *Journal of Comparative and Physiological Psychology, 44,* 3–8.

Shekelle, R. B., et al. (1985). The MRFIT behavior pattern study: II. Type A behavior and the incidence of coronary heart disease. *American Journal of Epidemiology, 122,* 559–570.

Shepard, J. A. (1995). Remedying motivation and productivity losses in collective settings. *Current Directions in Psychological Science, 4,* 131–139.

Shepherd, M., Cooper, B., Brown, A. C., & Kalton, G. W. (1966). *Psychiatric illness in general practice.* London: Oxford University Press.

Sheppard, W. C., & Willoughby, R. H. (1975). *Child behavior.* Chicago: Rand McNally.

Sherif, M. (1936). *The psychology of social norms.* New York: Harper Bros.

Sherif, M., Harvey, O. J., White, B. J., Hood, W. R., & Sherif, C. W. (1961). *Intergroup conflict and cooperation: The Robbers Cave experiment.* University of Oklahoma, Institute of Group Relations.

Shimamura, A. P., Berry, J. M., Mangels, J. A., Rusting, C. L., & Jurica, P. J. (1995). Memory and cognitive abilities in university professors: Evidence for successful aging. *Psychological Science, 6,* 271–277.

Shneidman, E. (1989). The Indian summer of life: A preliminary study of septuagenarians. *American Psychologist, 44,* 684–694.

Shortliffe, E. H., Axline, S. G., Buchanan, B. G., Merigan, T. C., & Cohen, N. S. (1973). An artificial intelligence program to advise physicians regarding antimicrobial therapy. *Computers and Biomedical Research, 6,* 544–560.

Shotland, R. L. (1985). When bystanders just stand by. *Psychology Today,* June, 50–55.

Shrout, P. E., Link, B. G., Dohrenwend, B. P., Skodol, A. E., Stueve, A., & Mirotznik, J. (1989). Characterizing life events as risk factors for depression: The role of fateful loss events. *Journal of Abnormal Psychology, 96,* 460–467.

Siegel, J. M., & Kuykendall, D. H. (1990). Loss, widowhood, and psychological distress among the elderly. *Journal of Consulting and Clinical Psychology, 58,* 519–524.

Siegman, A. W., Dembroski, T. M., & Ringel, N. (1987). Components of hostility and the severity of coronary heart disease. *Psychosomatic Medicine, 49,* 127–137.

Signorella, M., & Jamison, W. (1986). Masculinity, femininity, androgyny, and cognitive performance: A meta-analysis. *Psychological Bulletin, 100,* 207–228.

Silverstein, L. B. (1991). Transforming the debate about child care and maternal employment. *American Psychologist, 46,* 1025–1032.

Silverton, L., Mednick, S. A., Schulsinger, F., Parnas, J., & Harrington, M. E. (1988). Genetic risk for schizophrenia, birthweight, and cerebral ventricular enlargement. *Journal of Abnormal Psychology, 97,* 496–498.

Simons, A. D., Gordon, J. S., Thase, M. E., & Monroe, S. M. (1995). Toward an integration of psychologic, social, and biological factors in depression: Effects on outcome and course of cognitive therapy. *Journal of Consulting and Clinical Psychology, 63,* 369–377.

Simpson, J. A., Campbell, B., & Berscheid, E. (1986). The association between romantic love and marriage: Kephart (1967) twice revisited. *Personality and Social Psychology Bulletin, 12,* 363–372.

Singer, J. A., & Saloveg, P. (1988). Mood and memory: Evaluating the network theory of affect. *Clinical Psychology Review, 8,* 211–251.

Skeels, A. M. (1966). Adult status of children with contrasting early life experiences. *Monographs for the Society for Research in Child Development, 31,* 1–65.

Skinner, B. F. (1953). *Science and human behavior.* New York: Macmillan.

Skolnik, A. (1966). Stability and interrelations of thematic test imagery over 20 years. *Child Development, 37,* 389–396.

Slobin, D. I. (1979). *Psycholinguistics.* Glenview, IL: Scott, Foresman.

Smart, R. G., & Fejer, D. (1972). Drug use among adolescents and their parents: Closing the generation gap in mood modification. *Journal of Abnormal Psychology, 79,* 153–160.

Smith, A. P., Tyrell, D. A. J., Coyle, K., & Willman, J. S. (1987). Selective effects of minor illnesses on human performance. *British Journal of Psychology, 78,* 183–188.

Smith, D. E., King, M. B., & Hoebel, B. C. (1970). Lateral hypothalamic control of killing: Evidence for a cholinoceptive mechanism. *Science, 167,* 900–901.

Smith, E. M., Brown, H. O., Toman, J. E. P., & Goodman, L. S. (1947). The lack of cerebral effects of *d*-tubocurarine. *Anesthesiology, 8,* 1–14.

Smith, M. L., & Glass, G. V. (1977). Meta-analysis of psychotherapy outcome studies. *American Psychologist, 32,* 752–760.

Smith, V. L., & Ellsworth, P. C. (1987). The social psychology of eyewitness accuracy: Misleading questions and communicator expertise. *Journal of Applied Psychology, 72,* 294–300.

Snow, R. E., & Swanson, J. (1992). Instructional psychology: Aptitude, adaptation, and assessment. *Annual Review of Psychology, 43,* 583–626.

Snowden, L. R., & Cheung, F. K. (1990). Use of inpatient mental health services by members of ethnic minority groups. *American Psychologist, 45,* 347–355.

Snyder, D. M. (1982). An explanation of mood and learning. *Perceptual and Motor Skills, 55,* 727–733.

Snyder, M., Tauke, E. D., & Berscheid, E. (1977). Social perception and interpersonal behavior: On the self-fulfilling nature of social stereotypes. *Journal of Personality and Social Psychology, 35,* 656–666.

Snyder, S. H. (1974). *Madness and the brain.* New York: McGraw-Hill.

Sokolov, E. N. (1977). Brain functions: Neuronal mechanisms of learning and memory. *Annual Review of Psychology, 28,* 85–112.

Solomon, R. L. (1980). The opponent-process theory of acquired motivation. *American Psychologist, 35,* 691–712.

Sorenson, R. C. (1973). *Adolescent sexuality in contemporary America.* New York: World.

Souetre, E., et al. (1989). Circadian rhythms in depression and recovery: Evidence for blunted amplitude as the main chronobiological abnormality. *Psychiatry Research, 28,* 263–278.

Southwick, S. M., Morgan, C. A. III, Darnell, A., Bremner, D., Nicolaou, A. L., Nagy, L. M., & Charney, D. S. (1995). Trauma-related symptoms in veterans of Operation Desert Storm: A 2-year follow-up. *American Journal of Psychiatry, 152,* 8.

Spanos, N. P. (1996). *Multiple identities and false memories: A sociocognitive perspective.* Washington, DC: American Psychological Association Press.

Spearman, C. E., & Wynn-Jones, L. (1950). *Human ability.* London: Macmillan.

Speisman, J. C., Lazarus, R. S., Mordokoff, A. M., & Davison, L. (1964). Experimental reduction of stress based on ego-defense theory. *Journal of Abnormal and Social Psychology, 68,* 367–380.

Spence, J. T., & Helmreich, R. L. (1978). *Masculinity and femininity: Their psychological dimensions, correlates, and antecedents.* Austin: University of Texas Press.

Sperling, G. (1960). The information available in brief visual presentations. *Psychological Monographs, 74,* 1–29.

Squire, L. R. (1987). *Memory and the brain.* New York: Oxford University Press.

Squire, L. R., Knowlton, B., & Musen, G. (1993). The structure and organization of memory. *Annual Review of Psychology, 44,* 453–495.

Squire, L. R., Slater, P. C., & Chase, P. M. (1975). Retrograde amnesia: Temporal gradient in very long term memory following electro-convulsive therapy. *Science, 187,* 77–79.

Sroufe, L. A. (1978). The ontogenesis of emotion. In J. Osofoslay (Ed.), *Handbook of infancy.* New York: Wiley.

Stagner, R. (1958). The gullibility of personnel managers. *Personnel Psychology, 11,* 347–352.

Staples, S. L. (1996). Human response to environmental noise: Psychological research and public policy. *American Psychologist, 51,* 143–150.

Stapp, J., Tucker, A. M., & VandenBos, G. R. (1985). Census of psychological personnel, 1983. *American Psychologists, 12,* 1317–1351.

Stark, E. (1984). To sleep, perchance to dream. *Psychology Today,* October 16.

Starkstein, S. E., & Robinson, R. G. (1988). Lateralized emotional response following stroke. In M. Kinsbourne (Ed.), *Cerebral dysfunction in depression.* Washington, DC: American Psychiatric Association Press.

Starkstein, S. E., Robinson, R. G., & Price, T. R. (1988). Comparison of patients with and without poststroke major depression matched for size and the location of lesion. *Archives of General Psychiatry, 45,* 247–252.

Staub, E. (1996). Cultural-societal roots of violence: The examples of genocidal violence and of contemporary youth violence in the United States. *American Psychologist, 51,* 117–132.

Steele, C. M., & Josephs, R. A. (1990). Alcohol myopia: Its prized and dangerous effects. *American Psychologist, 45,* 921–933.

Steen, S., Oppliger, R., & Brownell, K. D. (1988). Metabolic effects of repeated weight loss and regain in adolescent wrestlers. *Journal of the American Medical Association, 260,* 47–50.

Steinberg, J. (1995). The graying of the senses. *Journal of NIMH Research, 7,* 32–33.

Steinmetz, S. K., & Strauss, M. A. (Eds.). (1974). *Violence in the family.* New York: Harper & Row.

Steketee, G., & Cleere, L. (1990). Obsessive-compulsive disorders. In A. S. Bellack, M. Hersen, & A. E. Kazdin (Eds.), *International handbook of behavior modification and therapy* (2nd ed., pp. 307–332). New York: Plenum.

Stephan, W., Berscheid, E., & Walster, E. (1971). Sexual arousal and heterosexual perception. *Journal of Personality and Social Psychology, 20,* 93–101.

Stephan, W. G. (1987). The contact hypothesis in intergroup relations. In C. Hendrick (Ed.), Group processes and intergroup relations. *Review of Personality and Social Psychology, 9,* 41–67.

Stern, R. M., & Koch, K. L. (1996). Motion sickness and differential susceptibility. *Current Directions in Psychological Science, 4,* 115–120.

Sternbach, R. A. (Ed.). (1978). *The psychology of pain.* New York: Raven Press.

Sternberg, R. J. (1979). The nature of mental abilities. *American Psychologist, 34,* 214–230.

Sternberg, R. J. (1981). Testing and cognitive psychology. *American Psychologist, 36,* 1181–1189.

Sternberg, R. J. (1985a). *Beyond IQ: A triarchic theory of intelligence.* New York: Cambridge University Press.

Sternberg, R. J. (1985b). Human intelligence: The model is the message. *Science, 230,* 1111–1118.

Sternberg, R. J. (1995). For whom the bell curve tolls: A review of *The Bell Curve. Psychological Science, 6,* 257–261.

Sternberg, R. J., & Gardner, M. K. (1982). A componential interpretation of the general factor in human intelligence. In J. J. Eysenck (Ed.), *A model for intelligence.* Berlin: Springer.

Sternberg, R. J., & Lubart, T. I. (1992). Buy low and sell high: An investment approach to creativity. *Current Directions in Psychological Science, 1,* 1–5.

Sternberg, R. J., & Lubart, T. I. (1993). Creative giftedness: A multivariate investment approach. *Gifted Child Quarterly, 37,* 7–15.

Sternberg, R. J., & Wagner, R. K. (1993). The egocentric view of intelligence and job performance is wrong. *Current Directions in Psychological Science, 2,* 1–5.

Sternberg, S. (1969). Memory scanning: Mental processes revealed by reaction time experiments. *Acta Psychologica, 30,* 276–315.

Stevens, C. F. (1979). The neuron. *Scientific American, 241,* 54–65.

Stokols, D. (1995). The paradox of environmental psychology. *American Psychologist, 50,* 821–837.

Stoner, J. A. F. (1961). *A comparison of individual and group decisions involving risk.* Unpublished master's thesis, Massachusetts Institute of Technology, Cambridge.

Strauch, I., & Meier, B. (1996). *In search of dreams: Experimental dream research.* Albany, NY: State University of New York Press.

Strauman, T. J. (1992). Self-guides, autobiographical memory, and anxiety and dysphoria: Toward a cognitive model of vulnerability to emotional distress. *Journal of Abnormal Psychology, 101,* 87–95.

Strayer, D. L., Wickens, C. D., & Braune, R. (1987). Adult age differences in speed and capacity of information processing: 2. An electrophysiological approach. *Psychology and Aging, 2,* 99–110.

Stricker, G., Davis-Russell, E., Bourg, E., Duran, E., Hammond, W. R., McHolland, J., Polite, K., & Vaughn, B. (1990). Toward ethnic diversification in psychology education and training. Washington, DC: American Psychological Association.

Strickland, B. R. (1992). Women and depression. *Current Directions in Psychological Science, 1,* 132–135.

Strongman, K. T. (1987). *The psychology of emotion* (3rd ed.). New York: Wiley.

Sturgis, E. T., Tollison, C. D., & Adams, H. E. (1978). Modification of combined migraine-muscle contraction headaches using BVP and EMG feedback. *Journal of Applied Behavior Analysis, 11,* 215–223.

Subotnik, R., Kassan, L., Summers, E., & Wasser, A. (1993). *Genius revisited: High IQ children grown up.* Norwood, NJ: Ablex.

Suedfeld, P., & Piedrahita, L. E. (1984). Intimations of mortality: Integrative simplification as a precursor of death. *Journal of Personality and Social Psychology, 47,* 848–852.

Suomi, S. (1988). *Genetic and environmental influences on social-emotional development in rhesus monkeys.* Presentation to the Fourth Annual Colloquium of the Center of Family Research, Athens, GA, University of Georgia.

Surwit, R. S., & Feinglos, M. N. (1983). The effects of relaxation on glucose tolerance in noninsulin-dependent diabetes care. *Diabetes Care, 6,* 176–179.

Surwit, R. S., Feinglos, M. N., & Scovern, A. W. (1983). Diabetes and behavior: A paradigm for health psychology. *American Psychologist, 38,* 255–262.

Susser, E., Neugebauer, R., et al. (1996). Schizophrenia after prenatal famine: Further evidence. *Archives of General Psychiatry, 53,* 25–31.

Susser, E., Struening, E. L., & Conner, S. (1989). Psychiatric problems in homeless men. *Archives of General Psychiatry, 46,* 845–850.

Susser, E. S., & Lin, S. P. (1992). Schizophrenia after prenatal exposure to the Dutch hunger winter of 1944–45. *Archives of General Psychiatry, 49,* 983–988.

Sutker, P. B., Uddo, M., Davis, J. M., & Ditta, S. R. (1995). War zone stress, personal resources, and PTSD in Persian Gulf war returnees. *Journal of Abnormal Psychology, 104,* 444–452.

Swaab, D. F., & Hofman, M. A. (1990). An enlarged superchiasmatic nucleus in homosexual men. *Brain Research, 537,* 141.

Swayze, V. W. (1995). Frontal leukotomy and related psychosurgical procedures in the era before antipsychotics (1935–1954): A historical overview. *American Journal of Psychiatry, 152,* 505–515.

Tannenbaum, S. I., & Yukl, G. (1992). Training and development in work organizations. *Annual Review of Psychology, 43,* 399–441.

Tanner, J. M. (1970). Physical growth. In P. H. Mussen (Ed.), *Carmichael's manual of child psychology* (Vol. 1). New York: Wiley.

Tanner, J. M., Whitehouse, R. H., & Takaishi, M. (1966). Standard from birth to maturity for height, weight, height velocity, and weight velocity. *Archives of Diseases in Childhood, 41.*

Tarpy, R. M., & Mayer, R. E. (1978). *Foundations of learning and memory.* Glenview, IL: Scott, Foresman.

Tart, C. T. (1975). *States of consciousness.* New York: Dutton.

Tavris, C., & Wade, C. (1984). *The longest war: Sex differences in perspective* (2nd ed.). San Diego: Harcourt Brace Jovanovich.

Taylor, M. L., & Hall, J. A. (1982). Psychological androgyny: Theories, methods, and conclusions. *Psychological Bulletin, 92,* 347–366.

Taylor, S. E. (1983). Adjustment to threatening events: A theory of cognitive adaptation. *American Psychologist, 38,* 1161–1173.

Taylor, S. E. (1986). *Health psychology.* New York: Random House.

Telch, M. J., Lucas, J. A., & Nelson, P. (1989). Nonclinical panic in college students: An investigation of prevalence and symptomology. *Journal of Abnormal Psychology, 98,* 300–306.

Terman, L. M. (1925). Mental and physical traits of a thousand gifted children. In M. Terman (Ed.), *Genetic studies of genius.* Stanford: Stanford University Press.

Terrace, H. S. (1980). *Nim.* New York: Knopf.

Thackwray, D. E., Smith, M. C., Bodfish, J. W., & Meyers, A. W. (1993). A comparison of behavioral and cognitive-behavioral interventions for bulimia nervosa. *Journal of Consulting and Clinical Psychology, 61,* 639–645.

Thal, L. J. (1989). Pharmacological treatment of memory disorders. In F. Boller and J. Grafman (Eds.), *Handbook of neuropsychology,* Vol. 3 (pp. 247–267). New York: Elsevier.

Thayer, R. E. (1987). Energy, tiredness, and tension effects of a sugar snack versus moderate exercise. *Journal of Personality and Social Psychology, 52,* 119–125.

Thibaut, J., & Walker, L. (1975). *Procedural justice: A psychological analysis.* Hillsdale, NJ: Erlbaum.

Thomas, M. H., & Drabman, R. S. (1975). Toleration of real-life aggression as a function of exposure to televised violence and age of subject. *Merrill-Palmer Quarterly, 21,* 227–232.

Thompson, J. K., Jarvie, G. J., Lahey, B. B., & Cureton, K. J. (1982). Exercise and obesity: Etiology, physiology, and intervention. *Psychological Bulletin, 91,* 55–79.

Thorndike, E. L. (1911). *Animal intelligence: Experimental studies.* New York: Macmillan.

Thornhill, N. W., & Thornhill, R. (1990). An evolutionary analysis of psychological pain following rape. *Ethology and Sociobiology, 11,* 155–193.

Thornton, G. C., & Cleveland, J. N. (1990). Developing managerial talent through simulation. *American Psychologist, 45,* 190–199.

Thurstone, L. L. (1938). Primary mental abilities. *Psychometric Monographs,* No. 1.

Tillman, P., & Tillman, B. (1991). *Human factors essentials.* New York: McGraw-Hill.

Todd, J. T., & Akerstrom, R. A. (1987). Perception of three-dimensional form from patterns of optical texture. *Journal of Experimental Psychology: Human Perception and Performance, 13,* 242–255.

Tollison, C. D., & Adams, H. E. (1979). *Sexual disorders: Treatments, theory, research.* New York: Gardner Press.

Tolman, E. C., & Honzik, C. H. (1930). Introduction and removal of reward, and maze performance in rats. *University of California Publications in Psychology, 4,* 257–276.

Tolman, E. C., Ritchie, B. F., & Kalish, D. (1946). Studies in spatial learning. I: Orientation and the shortcut. *Journal of Experimental Psychology, 36,* 13–25.

Torgersen, S. (1986). Genetic factors in moderately severe and mild affective disorders. *Archives of General Psychiatry, 43,* 222–226.

Travis, C. B. (1988). *Women and health psychology: Biomedical issues.* Hillsdale, NJ: Erlbaum.

Triandis, H. (1991). Training for diversity. Paper presented to the annual meeting of the American Psychological Association, San Francisco.

Triplett, N. (1898). The dynamogenic factors in peacemaking and competition. *American Journal of Psychology, 9,* 507–533.

Tulving, E. (1972). Episodic and semantic memory. In E. Tulving & W. Donaldson (Eds.), *Organization and memory.* New York: Academic Press.

Tulving, E. (1985). How many memory systems are there? *American Psychologist, 40,* 385–398.

Tulving, E. (1987). Multiple memory systems and consciousness. *Human Neurobiology, 6,* 67–80.

Tupes, E. C., & Christal, R. E. (1958). Stability of personality trait rating factors obtained under diverse conditions (USAF WADC Technical Note No. 59–61). Lackland Air Force Base, TX: U.S. Air Force.

Turkat, I. D., & Calhoun, J. F. (1980). The problem-solving flow chart. *The Behavior Therapist, 3,* 21.

Turkington, C. (1987). Help for the worried well. *Psychology Today,* August, 44–48.

Turnage, J. J. (1990). The challenge of new workplace technology for psychology. *American Psychologist, 45,* 171–178.

Turnbull, C. (1962). *The forest people.* New York: Simon & Schuster.

Turner, J. C., Hogg, M. A., Oakes, P. J., Richer, S. D., & Wetherell, M. S. (1987). *Rediscovering the social group: A self-categorization theory.* Oxford, England: Blackwell.

Turner, J. H. (1970). Entrepreneurial environments and the emergence of achievement motivation in adolescent males. *Sociometry, 33,* 147–165.

Turner, S. M., Beidel, D. C., & Larkin, K. T. (1986). Situational determinants of social anxiety in clinic and nonclinic samples: Physiological and cognitive correlates. *Journal of Consulting and Clinical Psychology, 54,* 523–527.

Tversky, A., & Kahneman, D. (1973). Judgment under uncertainty: Heuristics and biases. *Science, 185,* 1124–1131.

Tversky, A., & Kahneman, D. (1983). Extensional versus intuitive reasoning: The conjunction fallacy in probability judgment. *Psychological Review, 90,* 293–315.

Tyler, L. E. (1965). *The psychology of human differences.* New York: Appleton-Century-Crofts.

Uhr, S., Stahl, S. M., & Berger, P. A. (1984). Unmasking schizophrenia. *VA Practitioner, 1,* 42–53.

Van De Graaff, K. (1984). *Human anatomy.* Dubuque, IA: Wm. C. Brown Publishers.

Van Houwelingen, J. H., & Van Raaij, W. F. (1989). The effect of goal-setting and daily electronic feedback on in-home energy use. *Journal of Consumer Research, 16,* 98–105.

Varca, P. E., Shaffer, G. S., & Saunders, V. (1984). *A longitudinal investigation of sports participation and life satisfaction.* Unpublished manuscript, University of Georgia.

Vega, Suzanne. Men in a War, 1990. AGF Music Ltd./Waifersongs Ltd. (ASCAP).

Veleber, D. M., & Templer, D. I. (1984). Effects of caffeine on anxiety and depression. *Journal of Abnormal Psychology, 93,* 120–122.

Velten, E. (1968). A laboratory task for induction of mood states. *Behaviour Research and Therapy, 6,* 473–482.

Ventura, J., Neuchterlein, K. H., Lukoff, D., & Hardesty, J. P. (1989). A prospective study of stressful life events and schizophrenic relapse. *Journal of Abnormal Psychology, 98,* 407–411.

Visitainer, M. A., Volpicelli, J. R., & Seligman, M. E. P. (1982). Tumor rejection in rats after inescapable or escapable shock. *Science, 216,* 437–439.

von Frisch, K. (1953). *The dancing bees: An account of the life and senses of the honeybee.* New York: Harcourt, Brace, & World.

Voyer, D., Voyer, S., & Bryden, M. P. (1995). Magnitude of sex differences in spatial abilities: A meta-analysis and consideration of critical variables. *Psychological Bulletin, 117,* 250–270.

Wald, G. (1950, August). Eye and camera. *Scientific American,* pp. 1–11.

Waldron, I. (1991). Gender and health-related behavior. In D. S. Goodman (Ed.), *Health behavior: Emerging research perspectives.* New York: Plenum.

Walker, L. (1986). Cognitive processes in moral development. In G. L. Sapp (Ed.), *Handbook of moral development: Models processes, techniques, and research.* Birmingham: Religious Education Press.

Wallace, B., & Fisher, L. E. (1983). *Consciousness and behavior.* Boston: Allyn & Bacon.

Wallace, R. K., & Benson, H. (1972). The physiology of meditation. *Scientific American, 226,* 85–90.

Wallas, G. (1926). *The art of thought.* New York: Harcourt Brace.

Walsh, B. T., Kissileff, H. R., Cassidy, S. M., & Dantzic, S. (1989). Eating behavior of women with bulimia. *Archives of General Psychiatry, 46,* 54–60.

Walster, E., Aronson, V., & Abrahams, D. (1966). On increasing the persuasiveness of a low prestige communicator. *Journal of Experimental Social Psychology, 2,* 325–343.

Walster, E., Aronson, V., Abrahams, D., & Rottman, L. (1966). Importance of physical attractiveness in dating behavior. *Journal of Personality and Social Psychology, 5,* 508–516.

Walster, E. W., & Walster, G. W. (1978). *Equity: Theory and research.* Boston: Allyn & Bacon.

Ward, W. C., Frederiksen, N., & Carlson, S. B. (1980). Construct validity of free-response and machine scorable tests. *Journal of Educational Measurement, 17,* 11–29.

Warga, C. (1987, August). Pain's gatekeeper. *Psychology Today,* pp. 51–56.

Warrington, E. K., & Weiskrantz, L. (1968). A study of learning and retention in amnesic patients. *Neuropsychologia, 6,* 283–292.

Warrington, E. K., & Weiskrantz, L. (1978). Further analysis of the prior learning effect in amnesic patients. *Neuropsychologia, 16,* 169–177.

Watson, J. B. (1925). *Behaviorism.* Chicago: University of Chicago Press.

Watson, J. B., & Rayner, R. (1920). Conditioned emotional reactions. *Journal of Experimental Psychology, 3,* 1–4.

Watson, R. I. (1971). *The great psychologists* (4th ed.). Philadelphia: J. B. Lippincott.

Webb, S. B., & Collette, J. (1975). Urban ecological and household correlates of stress-alleviative drug use. *American Behavioral Scientist, 18,* 750–769.

Webb, W. B. (1968). *Sleep: An experimental approach.* New York: Macmillan.

Webb, W. B. (1975). *Sleep, the gentle tyrant.* Englewood Cliffs, NJ: Prentice-Hall.

Webb, W. B. (1982). Sleep and biological rhythms. In W. B. Webb (Ed.), *Biological rhythms, sleep, and performance,* pp. 87–110. New York: Wiley.

Webb, W. B., & Bonnet, M. H. (1979). Sleep and dreams. In M. E. Meyer (Ed.), *Foundations of contemporary psychology.* New York: Oxford University Press.

Wechsler, D. (1955). *Manual for the Wechsler Adult Intelligence Scale.* New York: Psychological Corporation.

Weddington, W. W., et al. (1990). Changes in mood, craving, and sleep during short-term abstinence reported by male cocaine addicts. *Archives of General Psychiatry, 47,* 861–868.

Weidner, G., Sexton, G., McLellarn, R. M., Connor, S. L., & Matarazzo, J. D. (1987). The role of Type A behavior and hostility in an elevation of plasma lipids in adult women and men. *Psychosomatic Medicine, 49,* 136–145.

Weinberger, D. R., Berman, K. F., & Illowsky, B. P. (1988). Physiological dysfunction of the dorsolateral prefrontal cortex in schizophrenia III: A new cohort and evidence for a monoaminergic mechanism. *Archives of General Psychiatry, 45,* 609–615.

Weiner, I. B. (1975). *Principles of psychotherapy.* New York: Wiley.

Weiss, R. L. (1975). *Marital separation.* New York: Basic Books.

Weiss, T. M. (1972). Psychological factors in stress and disease. *Scientific American, 126,* 226–240.

Weisse, C. S. (1992). Depression and immunocompetence: A review of the literature. *Psychological Bulletin, 111,* 475–489.

Wells, G. L. (1993). What do we know about eyewitness identification? *American Psychologist, 48,* 553–571.

Wender, P. H., Kety, S. S., Rosenthal, D., Schulsinger, F., Ortmann, J., & Lunde, I. (1986). Psychiatric disorders in the biological and adoptive families of adopted individuals with affective disorders. *Archives of General Psychiatry, 43,* 923–929.

Wentling, T. (1973). Mastery versus nonmastery instruction with varying test item feedback treatments. *Journal of Educational Psychology, 65,* 50–58.

Wexley, K. N., Sanders, R. E., & Yukl, G. A. (1973). Training interviewers to eliminate contrast effects in employment interviews. *Journal of Applied Psychology, 57,* 233–236.

Wexley, K. N., Yukl, G. A., Kovacs, S. Z., & Sanders, R. E. (1977). Importance of contrast effects in employment interviews. *Journal of Applied Psychology, 56,* 43–48.

White, C. C., Powell, K. E., Hogelin, G. C., Gentry, E. M., & Forman, M. R. (1987). The behavioral risk factor surveys: IV. The descriptive epidemiology of exercise. *Preventive Medicine, 3,* 304–310.

White, R. K. (1977). Misperception in the Arab-Israeli conflict. *Journal of Social Issues, 25,* 41–78.

Whitehurst, R. N. (1977). Youth views marriage: Awareness of present and future potentials. In R. W. Libby & R. N. Whitehurst (Eds.), *Marriage and alternatives: Exploring intimate relationships.* Glenview, IL: Scott, Foresman.

Whitten, L. (1992). Survival guilt and survival conflict in African-American college students. In M. Lang & C. Ford (Eds.), *Strategies for retaining minority students in higher education.* Springfield, IL: Charles C. Thomas.

Whitten, L. (1993a). Infusing Black psychology into the introductory psychology course. *Teaching of Psychology, 20* (1), 13–21.

Whitten, L. (1993b). Survival conflict, coping style and perception of the college classroom: Factors in the academic success of African-American college students in three colleges in the New York/New Jersey metropolitan area. *Afro-Americans in New York Life and History, 17,* 41–55.

Whorf, B. L. (1956). Science and linguistics. In J. B. Carroll (Ed.), *Language, thought and reality: Selected writings of Benjamin Lee Whorf.* Cambridge, MA: MIT Press.

Wickens, C. D. (1992). *Engineering psychology and human performance.* New York: Harper Collins.

Wickens, D. D., Born, D. G., & Allen, C. K. (1963). Proactive inhibition item similarity in short-term memory. *Journal of Verbal Learning and Verbal Behavior, 2,* 440–445.

Wiesner, W. H., & Cronshaw, S. F. (1988). A meta-analytic investigation of the impact of interview format and degree of structure on the validity of the employment interview. *Journal of Occupational Psychology, 61,* 275–290.

Wiggins, J. S., & Pincus, A. L. (1992). Personality: Structure and assessment. *Annual Review of Psychology, 43,* 473–504.

Wilder, D. A. (1977). Perception of groups, size of opposite, and social influence. *Journal of Experimental Social Psychology, 13,* 253–268.

Wilkinson, R., Allison, S., Feeney, M., & Kaminska, Z. (1989). Alertness of night nurses: Two shift systems compared. *Ergonomics, 32,* 281–292.

Williams, G. V., & Goldman-Rakic, P. S. (1995). Modulation of memory fields by dopamine D1 receptors in prefrontal cortex. *Nature, 376,* 572–575.

Williams, R. B., Lane, J. D., Kunn, C. M., Melosh, W., White, A. D., & Schanberg, S. M. (1982). Type A behavior and elevated physiological and neuroendocrine responses to cognitive tasks. *Science, 218,* 483–485.

Williams, R. L. (1972). Abuses and misuses in testing black children. *Journal of Black Psychology, 4,* 77–92.

Wilner, A., Reich, T., Robins, I., Fishman, R., & van Doren, T. (1976). Obsessive-compulsive neurosis. *Comprehensive Psychiatry, 17,* 527–529.

Wilson, J. R., Kuehn, R. E., & Beach, F. A. (1963). Modification in the sexual behavior of male rats produced by changing the stimulus female. *Journal of Comparative and Physiological Psychology, 56,* 636–644.

Winch, R. F. (1958). *Mate-selection.* New York: Harper & Row.

Windle, C., Bass, R. D., & Taube, C. A. (1974). PR aside: Initial results from NIMH's service program evaluation studies. *American Journal of Community Psychology, 2,* 311–327.

Winett, R. A. (1995). A framework for health promotion and disease prevention programs. *American Psychologist, 50,* 341–350.

Witelson, S. F. (1991). Neural sexual mosaicism: Sexual differentiation of the human temporo-parietal region for sexual asymmetry. *Psychoneuro-endocrinology, 16,* 131.

Witters, P. J., & Witters, W. L. (1983). *Drugs and society: A biological perspective.* New York: Van Nostrand Reinhold.

Wolpe, J. (1958). *Psychotherapy by reciprocal inhibition.* Stanford, CA: Stanford University Press.

Wood, J. M., Bootzin, R. R., Rosenhan, D., Nolen-Hoeksema, S., & Jourdon, F. (1992). Effects of the 1989 San Francisco earthquake on frequency and content of nightmares. *Journal of Abnormal Psychology, 101,* 219–224.

Wood, W., Wong, F. Y., & Chachere, J. G. (1991). Effects of media violence on viewers' aggression in unconstrained social interaction. *Psychological Bulletin, 109,* 371–383.

World Health Organization. (1990). *Current and future directions of the HIV/AIDS pandemic.* Geneva: World Health Organization.

Worrell, J. (1980). New directions in counseling women. *Personnel and Guidance Journal, 58,* 477–484.

Wyatt, R. J. (1996). Neurodevelopment abnormalities and schizophrenia: A family affair. *American Journal of Psychiatry, 53,* 11–15.

Wyler, S. (1985, December). Food fantasies of the rich and famous. *Food and Wine,* pp. 34–42.

Yalom, I. D. (1975). *The theory and practice of group psychotherapy* (2nd ed.). New York: Basic Books.

Yankelovich, D. (1974). *The new morality: A profile of American youth in the seventies.* New York: McGraw-Hill.

Yehuda, R., Kahana, B., Schmeidler, J., Southwick, S. M., Wilson, S., & Giller, E. L. (1995). Impact of cumulative lifetime trauma and recent stress on current posttraumatic stress disorder symptoms in holocaust survivors. *American Journal of Psychiatry, 152,* 12.

Yehuda, R., Southwick, S. M., & Giller, E. L. (1992). Exposure to atrocities and severity of chronic posttraumatic stress disorder in Vietnam veterans. *American Journal of Psychiatry, 149,* 333–336.

Yuille, J. C., & Tollestrup, D. A. (1990). Some effects of alcohol on eyewitness memory. *Journal of Applied Psychology, 75,* 268–273.

Zajonc, R. B. (1965). Social facilitation. *Science, 149,* 269–274.

Zajonc, R. B. (1968). Attitudinal effects of mere exposure. *Journal of Personality and Social Psychology Monograph Supplement, 9,* 1–27.

Zajonc, R. B. (1980). Feeling and thinking: Preferences need no inferences. *American Psychologist, 35,* 151–175.

Zajonc, R. B. (1984). On the primacy of affect. *American Psychologist, 39,* 117–123.

Zamble, E., Mitchell, J. B., & Findlay, H. (1986). Pavlovian conditioning of sexual arousal: Parametric and background manipulations. *Journal of Experimental Psychology: Animal Behavior Processes, 12,* 403–411.

Zaragoza, M. S., & Mitchell, K. J. (1996). Repeated exposure to suggestion and the creation of false memories. *Psychological Science, 1,* 294–300.

Zeki, S. (1992). The visual image in mind and brain. *Scientific American,* September, 69–76.

Zellner, M. (1970). Self-esteem, reception, and influenceability. *Journal of Personality and Social Psychology, 15,* 87–93.

Zilbergeld, B. (1978). *Male sexuality: A guide to sexual fulfillment.* Boston: Little, Brown.**Zimbardo, P.** (1969). The human choice: Individuation, reason, and order versus deindividuation, impulse, and chaos. In W. Arnold and D. Levine (Eds.), *Nebraska Symposium on Motivation, 17,* 237–307.

Zimbardo, P. G. (1972). The pathology of imprisonment. *Society, 9* (6), 4.

Zinbarg, R. E., Barlow, D. H., Brown, T. A., & Hertz, R. M. (1992). Cognitive-behavioral approaches to the nature and treatment of anxiety disorders. *Annual Review of Psychology, 43,* 235–267.

Zisook, S., & Shuchter, S. R. (1991). Depression through the first year after the death of a spouse. *American Journal of Psychiatry, 148,* 1346–1352.

Zorrilla, E. P., McKay, J. R., Luborsky, L., & Schmidt, K. (1996). Relation of stressors and depressive symptoms to clinical progression of viral illness. *American Journal of Psychiatry, 153,* 5.

Zubek, J. P. (1973). Review of effects of prolonged deprivation. In J. E. Rasmussen (Ed.), *Man in isolation and confinement.* Chicago: Aldine.

Zuckerman, M. (1995). Good and bad humors: Biochemical bases of personality and its disorders. *Psychological Science, 6,* 325–332.

Zumpe, D., & Michael, R. P. (1987). Relation between the dominance rank of female rhesus monkeys and their access to males. *American Journal of Primatology, 13,* 155–169.

Zuroff, D. C., & Mongrain, M. (1987). Dependency and self-criticism: Vulnerability factors for depressive affective states. *Journal of Abnormal Psychology, 96,* 14–22.

CREDITS

Section Openers

© Christian Pierre/Superstock

Chapter 1

Opener: © David Frazier Photolibrary; p. **4**: The Bettmann Archive; p. **5** (top): © Tony Freeman/PhotoEdit; p. **5** (bottom): © Rhoda Sidney/The Image Works, Inc.; p. **7** (top): National Library of Medicine; p. **7** (bottom): Dictionary of American Portraits, Dover Publications, Inc.; p. **9** (top): Archives of the History of American Psychology; p. **9** (bottom): National Library of Medicine; p. **10** (top): The Bettmann Archive; p. **10** (bottom): Archives of the History of American Psychology; p. **11**: The Bettmann Archive; p. **12** (top): Archives of the History of American Psychology; p. **12** (bottom): © Christopher Johnson/Stock Boston; p. **13** (top) The Bettmann Archive; p. **13** (bottom): Carl Rogers Memorial Library; p. **15**: © Walter Bibikow/The Image Bank; p. **14**: Rare Books and Print Department/Francis A. Countway Medical Library/Harvard Medical School; p. **16**: © Steve Leonard/Tony Stone Images; p. **18** (top): The University of Texas Institute of Texan Cultures; p. **18** (middle): Courtesy of Kenneth Clark; p. **18** (bottom): The Institute of Texan Cultures, San Antonio, Texas; p. **24**: © Penelope Breese/Gamma Liaison; 1.7A: © Catherine Ursillo/Photo Researchers, Inc.; p. **28**: © Martin Rogers/Tony Stone Images; p. **31** (top): © David Frazier Photolibrary; p. **31** (middle): © Robert Brenner/PhotoEdit; p. **31** (bottom): © David Frazier Photolibrary; p. **32** (top): © Dan Bosler/Tony Stone Images; p. **32**(middle): © SuperStock, Inc.; p. **32** (bottom): © Lou Jones/The Image Bank; p. **33** (top): © David Frazier Photolibrary; p. **33** (middle): © Val Corbett/Tony Stone Images; p. **33** (bottom): Benelux Press, b.v./Leo de Wys, Inc.; p. **34**: © HMS Images/The Image Bank; p. **36** (bottom): © Bill Losh/FPG International Corp.; p. **36** (top): © Labat/Jerrican/Photo Researchers, Inc.

Chapter 2

Opener: © Scott Camazine/Photo Researchers, Inc.; p. **42**: UPI/Bettmann Newsphotos; p. **43**: © Manfred Kage/Peter Arnold, Inc.; 2.8: Courtesy of Dr. Monte S. Buchsbaum; 2.9 A-K: Courtesy of Edythe D. London, Ph.D., National Institute on Drug Abuse; 2.10: Courtesy of David N. Levin, MD, PhD, University of Chicago; 2.14: Courtesy of Dr. Nancy Andreasen, University of Iowa Hospitals and Clinics. Mental Health Clinical Research Center, Iowa City; 2.16: National Library of Medicine; 2.18: © Dr. M. Raichle/Peter Arnold, Inc.; p. **63** (top): © Stock Montage; p. **63** (bottom): © Musee du Louvre, Paris/Giraudon/SuperStock, Inc.; p. **70**: UPI/Bettmann Newsphotos; p. **71** (top right): © Science Photo Library/Photo Researchers, Inc.; 2.23: © Science Photo Library/Photo Researchers, Inc.; p. **71** (bottom): © Manfred Kage/Peter Arnold, Inc.; p. **72**: © SuperStock, Inc.; 2.25: Courtesy of Drs. E.F. Torrey and D.R. Weinberger, NIMH Neruoscience Center, Washington, D.C.; 2.26A-B: Courtesy of Dr. Nancy Andreason, University of Iowa Hospitals and Clinics. Mental Health Clinical Research Center, Iowa City; 2.27A-B: Courtesy of Dr. Monte S. Buchsbaum; Mt. Sinai School of Medicine, New York, NY.; p. **81** (top): © Science Photo Library/Photo Researchers, Inc.; 2.29: © Richard Anderson, M.D., Ph.D.

Chapter 3

Opener: © Bob Daemmrich/The Image Works; p. **91**: © David R. Frazier Photolibrary; p. **99**: © The McGraw-Hill Companies, Inc./Bob Coyle, photographer; p. **107**: © Stephen Dalton/Photo Researchers, Inc.; p. **109** (top): © Chad Slattery/Tony Stone Images; p. **109** B: Photo of Salisbury Hand at the MIT AI lab courtesy of David Lampe, MIT; p. **111**: AP/Wide World Photos; p. **113**: © PhotoDisc, Inc.; p. **114**: © TROPIX/ M & V Birley; 3.23: Kaiser Porcelain Ltd. England; p. **121** © The McGraw-Hill Companies, Inc./Bob Coyle, photographer; 3.29A: © Digital Stock; 3.29B: © E. Van Hoorick/SuperStock, Inc.; 3.29C: © L. Prosor/SuperStock, Inc.; 3.29D: © Frank Pedrick/The Image Works; 3.29E: © Michael Okoniewski/The Image Works; 3.31A: The Bettmann Archive; 3.31B: The Bettmann Archive; 3.36: © Arthur Sirdofsky; p. 127B: © R. Joedecke/The Image Bank; 3.42: Erich Lessing/Art Resource, NY; 3.43: The Royal Collection © 1994 Her Majesty Queen Elizabeth II; 3.44: © 1997 Succession H Matisse, Paris/Artists Rights Society (ARS), New York; 3.45: The Baltimore Museum of Art: The Cone Collection, formed by Dr. Claribel Cone and Miss Etta Cone of Baltimore, Maryland BMA 1950.258. © 1997 Succession H. Matisse, Paris/Artists Rights Society (ARS), New York; 3.46: The Carnegie Museum of Art, Acquired through the generosity of the Sarah Mellon Scaife family, 71.23. © 1997 Succession H. Matisse, Paris/Artists Rights Society (ARS), New York

Chapter 4

Opener: Images © 1997 PhotoDisc, Inc.; p. **138**: © David Young-Wolff/PhotoEdit; p. **143**: © Renee Lynn/Photo Researchers, Inc.; p. **144**: © Kevin Beebe/Custom Medical Stock Photo; p. **146**: Reuters/Bettmann Newsphotos; p. **149**: Science Photo Library/Photo Researchers, Inc.; p. **154**: © Lori Adamski Peek/Tony Stone Images; p. **155** Science Photo Library/Photo Researchers, Inc.; p. **160**: © Dr. Robert B. Innis; p. **161** (top): © Mulvehill/The Image Works; p. **161** (bottom left): © Mark C. Burnett/PhotoEdit; p. **161** (bottom right): © James Prince/Photo Researchers, Inc; p. **164**: © Mark Richards/PhotoEdit; p. **166**: © Rhoda Sidney/The Image Works, Inc.; p. **167**: © Henryk Kaiser/Leo de Wys, Inc.; **168** (right) © Michael Newman/PhotoEdit; **168** (left): © Michael Newman/PhotoEdit

Chapter 5

Opener: © Culver Pictures; p. **174**: © PhotoDisc, Inc.; p. **175**: The Bettmann Archive; p. **179**: Courtesy of Professor Benjamin Harris, University of Wisconsin-Parkside; p. **184** (top): © Myrleen Ferguson/PhotoEdit; p. **184** (bottom): AP/Wide World Photos; p. **185**: © Terje Rakke/The Image Bank; p. **186**: © Dan Bosler/Tony Stone Images; p. **187**: © David Young-Wolff/PhotoEdit; p. **191**: © Tony Freeman/PhotoEdit; p. **196**: © Explorer/Photo Researchers, Inc.; p. **199**: © Richard Zigmond/Peter Marler; p. **201** (top): © Michael Siluk; p. **201** (bottom): Courtesy of Dr. Albert Bandura; p. **202**: Courtesy of Dr. Albert Bandura; p. **206**: © Jerry Wachter/Photo Researchers, Inc.; p. **207**: © Marv Lyons/The Image Bank

Chapter 6

Opener: © Joseph Schuvler/Stock Boston; p. **212**: © Eunice Harris/Photo Researchers, Inc.; p. **213**: © Richard Hutchings/Photo Researchers, Inc.; p. **214**: © Steve Dunwell/The Image Bank; p. **216**: © Jim Sulley/The Image Works; p. **219**: © David Frazier Photolibrary; p. **221**: © David Austen/Tony Stone Images; p. **222**: © Elizabeth Crews/The Image Works; p. **223**: © David de Lossy/The Image Bank; p. **226**: © Michael Siluk; p. **230**: © Ellis Herwig/Stock Boston; p. **232**: © Dr. Eric Kandel/Peter Arnold, Inc.; 6.10: © NYT Pictures; p. **238**: UPI/Bettmann; p. **239** (left): © David Young-Wolff/PhotoEdit; p. **239** (right): © Science Photo Library/Photo Researchers, Inc.

Chapter 7

Opener: © Jean Higgins/Unicorn Stock Photos; p. **244**: © Bob Krist/Leo de Wys, Inc.; p. **246**: © James L. Shaffer; p. **247**: © Bobbie Kingsley/Photo Researchers, Inc.; 7.6: © The McGraw-Hill Companies, Inc./Bob Coyle, photographer; 7.7: © The McGraw-Hill Companies, Inc./Bob Coyle, photographer; p. **252** (top): © SuperStock, Inc.; p. **253**: © Bruce Ayers/Tony Stone Images; p. **254**: © Mary Wolf/Tony Stone Images; p. **255**: © Daniel Bosler/Tony Stone Images; p. **257**: © Deborah Davis/PhotoEdit; p. **259** (left): © SuperStock, Inc.; p. **259** (right): © Lynn McLaren/The Picture Cube; p. **261**: © Dr. R. Allen Gardner; p. **263**: The Bettmann Archive; p. **264** (left): © Rick Rusing/Leo de Wys, Inc.; p. **264** (right): © David Madison/Tony Stone Images; p. **265**: © Thelma Shumsky/The Image Works, Inc.; p. **268**: © Jerome E. Brisson/SportsLight Photography; p. **267**: The Bettmann Archive; p. **272**: © Brent Jones/Leo de Wys, Inc.; p. **273**: © Michael Siluk; p. **274**: © SPL/Custom Medical Stock Photo; p. **275**: © Will & Deni McIntyre/Photo Researchers, Inc.

Chapter 8

Opener: © SuperStock, Inc.; p. **286**: © Dan Bosler/Tony Stone Images; p. **287**: © Maragaret Miller/Photo Researchers, Inc.; p. **288**: Raika Po'ndorf/Austria © Sybille Kalas; p. **289** (top left): Archives of the History of American Psychology; p. **289** (top right): Harlow Primate Laboratory, University of Wisconsin; p. **289** (middle): Harlow Primate Laboratory, University of Wisconsin; p. **290**: © Robert Daemmrich/Tony Stone Images; p. **289** (bottom): © Dennis O'Clair/Tony Stone Images; p. **292**: © Yves DeBraine/Black Star; p. 293: Harvard University Office of News and Public Affairs; p. **294**: © Lillian Kemp Photography; p. **295**: The Bettmann Archive; p. **298**: © Petit Format/Photo Researchers, Inc.; p. **299**: Courtesy of Dr. Tiffany Field; 8.2: © Enrico Ferorelli; p. **300** (top): © Michael Siluk; p. **300** (bottom): © Doug Goodman/Monkmeyer Press; p. **302** (top): © Blair Seitz/Photo Researchers, Inc.; p. **302** (bottom): © SuperStock, Inc.; p. **303** (top): © David Young Wolff/PhotoEdit; p. **303** (bottom): © Tony Freeman/PhotoEdit; p. **305**: © David R. Frazier Photolibrary; p. **306**: © Robert E Daemmrich/Tony Stone Images; p. **307**: © David R. Frazier Photolibrary; p. **308**: © Mary Kate Denny/PhotoEdit; p. **311**: © Daniel Bosler/Tony Stone Images; 8.4A: © Brad Martin/The Image Bank; 8.4B: © Kay Chernush/The Image Bank; 8.4C: © Tony Freeman/PhotoEdit; 8.4D: © CLEO/PhotoEdit; 8.4E: © Nancy Brown/The Image Bank; 8.4F: © David R. Frazier Photolibrary; 8.4G: © David R. Frazier Photolibrary; 8.4H: © David Young-Wolff/PhotoEdit; p. **313**: © Michael Newman/PhotoEdit; p. **314**: © Lori Adamski Peek/Tony Stone Images; p. **316**: The Bettmann Archive; p. **317**: © Oliver Benn/Tony Stone Images; p. **319** (bottom): © Tony Freeman/PhotoEdit; p. **319** (top): © Lawrence Migdale/Tony Stone Images; p. **320**: © Robert Brenner/PhotoEdit; p. **321**: © Michael Newman/PhotoEdit

Chapter 9

Opener: ESBIN/Anderson/Omni-Photo Communications; p. **328**: © SuperStock, Inc.; 9.3: Courtesy Dr. Philip Teitelbaum; p. **332**: © The Photo Works/Photo Researchers, Inc.; p. **333** (top): © Steve Leonard/Tony Stone Images; p. **333** (bottom) : © Michael Newman/PhotoEdit; p. **335**: Harlow Primate Laboratory, University of Wisconsin; 9.5: University of Wisconsin Primate Laboratory, © Harry F. Harlow; p. **336** (bottom): © SuperStock, Inc.; p. **337**: © Stephen Wikes/The Image Bank; p. **338**: © Elena Rooraid/PhotoEdit; p. **339**: © David R. Frazier Photolibrary; 9.10 (love): © Richard Hutchings/PhotoEdit; 9.10 (joy): © Marc Romanelli; 9.10 (anger): © Tony Latham/Tony Stone Images; 9.10 (fear): © Robert Brenner/PhotoEdit; 9.10 (sadness): © HMS Images/The Image Bank; 9.10 (surprise): © Richard Hutchings/PhotoEdit; p. **348** (top): © Thomas Kitchin; p. **348** (bottom): © Thomas Kitchin; p. **349**: © Paul Conkin/Uniphoto Picture Agency; p. **350**: © Robert Brenner/PhotoEdit; p. **351**: © Bill Bachman/PhotoEdit; p. **353**: © Ulli Seer/Tony Stone Images; p. **356** (bottom): © Tony Freeman/PhotoEdit; p. **356** (top): © Michael Newman/PhotoEdit; p. **358** (bottom): © Gary Conner/PhotoEdit; p. **358** (top): © EX Rouchon Explorer/Photo Researchers, Inc.

Chapter 10

Opener: © Stock Montage; p. **363** (left): © Blumebild/FPG International Corp.; p. **363** (right): © Aaron Haupt/David R. Frazier Photolibrary; 10.2: © Shaywitz,et.al., 1995/NMR Research/Yale Medical School; p. **367** (left): © Tony Freeman/PhotoEdit; p. **367** (right): © Erika Stone/Photo Researchers, Inc.; p. **369** (left): © Bill Bachmann/The Image Works; p. **369** (right): © Thelma Shumsky/The Image Works; p. **370**: © Judy G. Rolfe/Uniphoto Picture Agency; p. **373**: UPI/Bettmann; p. **379**: © Jan Halaska/Photo Researchers, Inc.; p. **383** (top): AP/Wide World Photos; p. **383** (bottom): The Bettmann Archive; p. **385**: The Bettmann Archive; p. **387**: © Will & Deni McIntyre/Photo Researchers, Inc.; p. **390**: © Robert Brenner/PhotoEdit; p. **391**: © Science Photo Library/Photo Researchers, Inc.; p. **394**: © Royce Bair/Uniphoto Picture Agency

Chapter 11

Opener: © Arni Katz/Unicorn Stock Photos; p. **400**: AP/Wide World Photos; p. **401**: © Sigmund Freud Copyrights/Mary Evans Picture Library; p. **404**: © Uniphoto Picture Agency; p. **405**: © James Levin/FPG International Corp.; p. **407** (top): The Bettmann Archive; p. **407** (middle): © Chuck Savage/Uniphoto Picture Agency; p. **407** (bottom): © Marc Romanelli/The Image Bank; p. **408** (top): © Stock Montage; p. **408** (bottom): The Bettmann Archive; p. **410**: Courtesy of Albert Bandura; p. **414**: Carl Rogers Memorial Library; p. **415** (top): The Bettmann Archive; p. **415** (bottom left): © Stock Montage; p. **415** (bottom middle): The Bettmann Archive; p. **415** (bottom right): © Stock Montage; p. **418**: © Archives of the History of American Psychology; 11.3: Reprinted by permission of the publishers from Henry A. Murray, THEMATIC APPERCEPTION TEST, Cambridge, Mass.: Harvard University Press, Copyright © 1943 by the President and Fellows of Harvard College, © 1971 by Henry A. Murray.; p. **423**: © Mercury Archives/The Image Bank; 11.5B: © Michelle Bridwell/PhotoEdit; p. 427 (top): © Arthur Tilley/FPG International Corp.

Chapter 12

Opener: © Esbin-Anderson/The Image Works; p. **434**: © Jonathan Nourok/PhotoEdit; p. **435**: © Craig Newbauer/Peter Arnold, Inc.; p. **437**: © T. Rosenthal/SuperStock, Inc.; p. **441**: © Uniphoto Picture Agency; p. **445**: © Blair Seitz/Photo Researchers, Inc.; p. **446**: © Ulrike Welsch/Photo Researchers, Inc.; p. **447**: UPI/Bettmann; p. **451**: © Michael Siluk; p. **454**: © Don Klumpp/The Image Bank;

p. **455**: © David Young-Wolff/PhotoEdit; p. **456**: © Jay Freis/The Image Bank; p. **460**: Reuters/Bettmann

Chapter 13

Opener: © Young-Wolff/PhotoEdit; p. **467** (top): © Giraudon/Art Resource, NY; p. **467** (bottom): Neue Revue Magazine, Hamburg, West Germany; p. **468**: The Bettmann Archive; p. **469**: © Michael Newman/PhotoEdit; p. **470**: AP/Wide World Photos; p. **472**: © Willie Hill, Jr./The Image Works, Inc.; p. **474**: UPI/Bettmann; p. **478**: © Gerald Martineau/The Washington Post; p. **479**: © David De Lossy/The Image Bank; p. **481**: © Rick Brady/Uniphoto Picture Agency; p. **484** (top): August Natterer, Inv. Nr. 184, "Hexenkopf," date unknown, mixed media, 259 x 342 mm, Prinzhorn - Collection of the Psychiatric Clinic, University of Heidelberg, Jugeborg Klinger.; p. **484** (bottom): © Grunnitus/Monkmeyer; p. **485** (top): UPI/Bettmann; p. **485** (bottom): Reuters/Bettmann; p. **486**: © Catherine Ursillo; p. **489**: UPI/Bettmann; p. **490**: Reuters/Bettmann

Chapter 14

Opener: © Michelle Bridwell/PhotoEdit; p. **495**: © James L. Shaffer; p. **496**: © Will & Deni McIntyre/Photo Researchers, Inc.; p. **497**: Freud Museum, London; p. **500**: Michael Rougier/Life Magazine © Time Warner; Inc.; p. **501**: © Paul B. Herbert/Eslan Institute; p. **504**: © Gontier/jerrican/Photo Researchers, Inc.; p. **505**: © John Griffin/The Image Works; p. **510** (top): Courtesy Aaron Beck; p. **510** (bottom): Institute for Rational-Emotive Therapy; p. **513**: © Zigy Kaluzny/Tony Stone Images; p. **514**: © Ken Whitmore/Tony Stone Images; p. **515**: © Bob Daemmrich/Uniphoto Picture Agency; p. **516**: © Will & Deni McIntyre/Photo Researchers, Inc.; p. **517**: © Stock Montage; p. **519**: © Ken Reid/FPG International Corp.

Chapter 15

Opener: © James L. Shaffer; p. **526**: © Michael Newman/PhotoEdit; p. **527**: © Jake Rajs/The Image Bank; p. **529**: © David Young-Wolff/PhotoEdit; p. **531**: © Uniphoto Picture Agency; p. **532**: © P.G. Zimbardo, Inc.; p. **534**: © 1965 by Stanley Milgram. From the film "OBEDIENCE" distributed by the Pennsylvania State University, PCR; p. **538**: AFP/Corbis-Bettmann; p. **539**: American Cancer Society; p. **542**: © Bill Bachmann/Leo de Wys, Inc.; p. **544**: © David Young-Wolff/PhotoEdit; p. **547**: © Margaret Finefrock/Unicorn Stock Photos; p. **548**: © David W. Hamilton/The Image Bank; p. **550**: © ESBIN/Anderson/Omni-Photo; p. **553**: © Ron Chapple/FPG International Corp.; p. **556** (bottom): © Cynthia Johnson/Time Magazine; p. **556** (top): Courtesy of Susan T. Fiske

Chapter 16

Opener: © SuperStock, Inc.; p. **563**: © Mike Malyszko/FPG International Corp.; 16.4: © James L. Shaffer; 16.6: Designer: © David R. Frazier Photolibrary/Photo Researchers, Inc.; Lab: © SuperStock, Inc.; Machinist: © James L. Shaffer; Baker: © John Coletti/Stock Boston; Construction: © A. Ramey/Stock Boston; p. **570**: © SuperStock, Inc.; p. **572**: © John Coletti/Stock Boston; p. **575** (top): © Rhoda Sidney/PhotoEdit; p. **575** (bottom): NASA; p. **578**: © Chuck Keeler/Tony Stone Images; p. **583**: © James L. Shaffer; p. **585**: © Bob Daemmrich/The Image Works, Inc.; p. **587**: © Bob Daemmrich/The Image Works, Inc.; p. **589** (top): Reuters/Bettmann; p. **589** (bottom): © Steve Allen/The Image Bank; p. **590**: © Frank Cezus/Tony Stone Images

NAME INDEX

C

D

E

F

M

N

O

T

U

V

W

Y

Z

SUBJECT INDEX

C

D

E

F

G

H

I

J

P